# Vietnam

## Robert Storey
## Daniel Robinson

**Vietnam**

**4th edition**

**Published by**
  **Lonely Planet Publications**
  Head Office:   PO Box 617, Hawthorn, Vic 3122, Australia
  Branches:      155 Filbert St, Suite 251, Oakland, CA 94607, USA
                 10 Barley Mow Passage, Chiswick, London W4 4PH, UK
                 71 bis rue du Cardinal Lemoine, 75005 Paris, France

**Printed by**
  SNP Printing Pte Ltd, Singapore

**Photographs by**

| | | |
|---|---|---|
| Greg Alford | Mark Kirby | Helen Savory |
| Glenn Beanland | Brendan McCarthy | Deborah Soden |
| Sara Jane Cleland | Emma Miller | Robert Storey |
| Juliet Coombe | Bernard Napthine | Deanna Swaney |
| Lisa Croker | Karen O'Connor | Genevieve Webb |
| Mick Elmore | Peter Robinson | Phil Weymouth |
| Mason Florence | Simon Rowe | Tony Wheeler |

Front cover: Vietnamese duck farmer. Guido Alberto Rossi (The Image Bank)

**First Published**
  February 1991

**This Edition**
  September 1997

National Library of Australia Cataloguing in Publication Data

  Storey, Robert.
  Vietnam.

  4th ed.
  Includes index.
  ISBN 0 86442 515 5.

  1. Vietnam - Guidebooks. I. Title.

915.970444

text & maps © Lonely Planet 1997
photos © photographers as indicated 1997

## Robert Storey

After graduating from the University of Nevada with a worthless liberal arts degree, Robert pursued a distinguished career as a slot machine repairman in a Las Vegas casino. He later worked for the government bureaucracy, though he is not quite sure what his job was. Seeking the meaning of life, Robert became a backpacker and drifted around Asia before he finally reached nirvana in Taiwan. He is the author or co-author of numerous Lonely Planet Guides, including *Taiwan, China* and *Korea*. He hopes to soon release his first novel, *The Road*.

## Daniel Robinson

Daniel, researcher and writer of the 1st edition's Vietnam and Cambodia sections, grew up in the USA and Israel. He has travelled extensively in the Middle East and Asia. Daniel holds a BA in Near Eastern Studies from Princeton University. He has contributed to Lonely Planet's shoestring series and is also co-author of our guide to *France*.

## From the Authors

For this edition, special thanks to Dale Wahren (Australia), Carla Erculiani (Switzerland), Laurent Cauchy (France), Richard Flasher (USA) and Gary Tobis (USA).

## From the Publisher

This 4th edition of *Vietnam* was produced in LP's Melbourne office. It was edited by Linda Suttie, with assistance from Peter Cruttenden and Kristin Odijk. Glenn Beanland was responsible for mapping, design and layout. Janet Watson, Sally Gerdan and Anthony Phelan assisted with mapping, and illustrations were done by Trudi Canavan and Ann Jeffree. David Kemp and Adam McCrow designed the cover. Peter Cruttenden and Sharon Benson compiled the index.

## Thanks

Many thanks to the following travellers who used the last edition and wrote to us with helpful hints, useful advice and interesting anecdotes:

Warwick Abrahams, John Abrahamsen, Garry Adams, Mary Aldred, Gaynor Allen, Sallie Aprahamian, Andrew Aungthwin, Eric Baber, Bruce Baldock, Ben Bangs, Kevin Barrows, Mandy Barton, Bhaskar Baruah, Paul Baumgartner, Gladys Beatty, Max Beeson, Jon & Suzanne Benjamin, P Berenguer, Catherine Berryman, Melissa Beswick, Harry Biddulph, Emma Birch, Michael K Birmmeyer, Melissa Blanch, Adrian Bloch, Miranda Blum, Markus Bohnert, B Bolton, Chantal de Bondt, Marc Bontemps, Chris Boomaars, Dennis Borg, Elizabeth Bowdrtch, Susan Boyd, Hartger van Brakel, Lynda Britz, Paul Brown, Joseph Bruckner, Rachel Brun, Robin Buckley, Thom Burns, Warren Calhoun, Dick & Nanci Calvert, Samantha Cameron, Adam Camilleri, Anne Cappodanno, Partick Carter, Lainie Chandler, Leung Chi Tak, Phillip Chilton, Lawrence Chin, Vilma R Cirimele, Marie Coloccia, Chris Conley, Daniel Cook, Jim Cooper, Stanley Corbett, Ray Corness, Siobhan Coshery, Tony Coulson, S Courtmanche, Brian & Pat Croft, Peter Cromie, J Crowther, Julie Cunningham, Q & I Cutler

Steve Daley, Trish Daley, Dave Dallimore, Hans & Mirjam Damen, Ian Davison, Michael Davison, Alex Derom, John Devison, U Diehr, A Dietrich, Nan Dodds, Annie Dore, A Duflos, Christian Dupuis, Robin Dutt-Gupta, Frank Dutton, D Eargle, Delwyn Eason, Ann Eaton, Richard Edgell, Ellen Edmonds-Wilson, David Ellard, Steven Emmet, M J Enderby, Mia Erkkila, M

Evers, Jim Fairhall, Moira Farrelly, Dean Fergie, T Fletcher, Enid Flint, Julie Foreman, Kent Foster, Clare Freedman, Wayne P Frey, Bill Fridl, Claire & Peter Frost, Walter Frost, Mark Gadbois, Allen & Shari Gaerber, Hilary Gallagher, James Garber, Ann Gates, Barbara Gibbs, Steve Golden, Jill Goldstein, Dan Goldthorp, David Goode, Albert Gordon, Nigel & Michelle Gough, Dean Gould, N Gray, D Gwilym-Williams

R Haggar, Shawn Hainsworth, Rachael Hall, Eammon Hamilton, Steve Hammerton, Allan Hansell, Natasha Hanson, Inger Hansson, Valerie Harridge, Lucy Hayter, Andrew Heafield, P Healy, Ashley Heath, Gary Hedges, Fran Hegarty, Mary Helme, Scott Hemphill, Elisabeth Heraud, David Hill, Tim Hill, Tanya Hines, Judith & Colin Holbrook, Bevan Holland, Niels Hollum, Mrs Gaylene Holt, Debbie Hooglond, Maura Horkan, I Hoskins, Bruce Houldsworth, Martin Howard, Philip Howard, Merilyn Howorth, Adrian Huber, C Huber, Darril Hudson, Doug & Cathy Hull, Lee Hunt, Stephen Iremonger, Alice Iversen, Jerry Jackson, Aage Jacobsen, Kenneth & Britt Jademo, E Jahnichen, Bill & Lee Jane Mastipieu, Jock Janice, H Javelle, Ian Jenkins, Zena Jenkins, Henrik Thorlund Jensen, Paul Jewell, Ann Johns, Steve Johnson, John Jones, Peter D Jones, Kate Judd , Richard Juterbock, Chern Siang Jye, Jeffrey Kadet, Bernhard Kasparek, S Katsanis , Louis B Katz, Gina Kaye, V Keks, Colette Kelly, K Kemmis-Betty, Charlie Kime, Susan Klock, David Kneser, Steve Knode, Ingo Koeker, Steven Kram, Laszlo Kuster, Heidi Kuttler

John Lam-Po-Tang, Sylvio Lamarche, Miles Lampson, Ian Laurenson, Linda Layfield, Tranvan Le, Tim Lee, Justin Leibowitz, Tym Lenderking, Murray S Levin, Steven Li, Inge Light, Cathy Lincoln, Stuart Lindsay, Amanda Lister, H Locke, Rebecca Loveless, Alex J Low, Peter Lyden, Mary MacNeill, Stuart Malcolm, Marian Manders, Nigel Marsh, Judy Marshall, Steven Mathieson, Mr & Mrs Matropieri, Shisho Matsushima, Mr & Mrs McBride, Kevin McCourt, Craig McGrath, Tom McLaren, Anthony Merritt, Chad Miller, Jon Miller, Ron Miller, J Mindel, Michael Minen, Rachel Moilliet, Kai Monkkonen, Pablo Ruiz Monroy, Shiela & Tom Mooney, David Morgan, Lin Morgan, Paul Morris, Rachel Morris, Lene Mortensen, Anne Mosher, Annie Murphy, J Murphy, Alastair Murray, Paul Murray, Teena Myscowsky, Craig Napier, Andrew Neale, Kerryn Newton, Trung Nguyen, Lisa Nicholson, B & C Nickel, Steven Nightingale, Ashok Nikapota, Jane Norris, Shane Nunan, Omer Nurie

Jenna Oakley, Quinn Okamoto, Alex Olah, David Olive, B Oliver, S Oliver, John Page, Yudi Palkova, Kerryn Palmer, A Parienty, Janine Parker, Clem Parry, David Parry, Mel Parsonage, Steve Partridge, Mike Pattison, Becky Payne, John & Diane Peake, Gary & Linda Pedersen, Klaus Rydahl Pedersen, S Pegrum, Josep Penella, Joseph Pereira, Chris Peres, Tomas Persson, Kelli Peterson, I Pfalzgraf , Mark Pickens, Sophie Pith, Clive Porter, Andreas Poulakidas, William de Prado, Julian Pringle, Mark Proctor, David Pryke, R Rabenstein, Daniel Radack, Petra Raddatz, John Rainy, Bruce Ramsey, Jarmo Rautiola, Chad Raymond, Mady Reichliung, T Renken, Adrian Rice, Clifford Rich, S Rispin, Louise Roberts, Paul Robertson, Suzie Robin, Paul Robinson, Bill Rose, Helen Rose, Sabine & Helmut

Rosel, Dan Rosenberg, Matthew Ross, Neal Ross, Kevin Ryan, V Ryan, Ann Ryckaert, Erik de Ryk, Marianne Rynefeldt-Skog

A Salomaa, Jevan Sayer, Gunther Schafer, Anthony Schlesinger, Martin Schmidt, K Schoenban, Ivan Scholte, Ernst Schonmann, Sara Schroter, Peter & Florence Shaw, Saverio Silva, U Simonsen, Edward Simpson, Ken Sloane, Margaret Smyth, M Snall, Jack Sneed, Patrick Sodergren, Richard Southern, A Spiers, Fiona Stephens, J Stijnman, Hans van der Stock, Lucy Stockoe, Pieter Swart, John W Swartz

Kevin Taggart, A Tanenbaum, Lillian Tangen, D Tapp, Tansy Tazewell, Bob Tennent, David Teoh, Anette Terlutter, Renee Melchert Thorpe, Neil Todd, Margaret Traeger, Hanh Tran, Jakki Trenbath, Philippa & Henrik Tribler, W Tross, Peter Tse, Marc Turuow, JP Umber, Noam Urbach, Z Urquhart, L Visseren, Brandon R Vogt, Lisa Wachtell, B & J Walker, Stuart Walker, Ian Wallach, Mark Wallem, Ian Waters, David Watkins, Mike Watson, Nicholas Wellington, Julie Westrupp, Annie White, Charles Wilding-White, Bev Williams, Martin Williams, Silke Wirtz, Tom Witt, Judy & Chris Woods, Penny Wright, Michael Wycks, Sue Youngman, Elizabeth Yuan, Blaz Zabukovec, Ben Zabulis, Robert Zafran, Rudy Zaugg, Val Zogopoulos, LA Zook

## Warning & Request

Things change – prices go up, schedules change, good places go bad and bad places go bankrupt – nothing stays the same. So, if you find things better or worse, recently opened or long since closed, please tell us and help make the next edition even more accurate and useful.

We value all of the feedback we receive from travellers. Julie Young coordinates a small team who read and acknowledge every letter, postcard and email, and ensure that every morsel of information finds its way to the appropriate authors, editors and publishers.

Everyone who writes to us will find their name in the next edition of the appropriate guide and will also receive a free subscription to our quarterly newsletter, *Planet Talk*. The very best contributions will be rewarded with a free Lonely Planet guide.

Excerpts from your correspondence may appear in new editions of this guide; in our newsletter, *Planet Talk*; or in updates on our Web site – so please let us know if you don't want your letter published or your name acknowledged.

# Contents

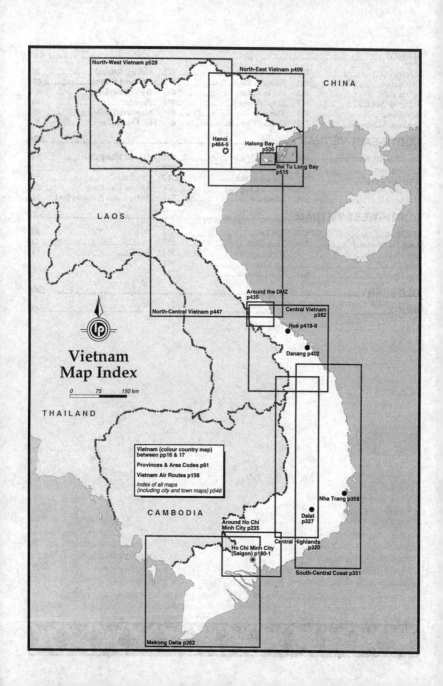

# Vietnam Map Index

North-West Vietnam p528

North-East Vietnam p499

CHINA

Hanoi p464-5

Halong Bay p506

Bai Tu Long Bay p515

LAOS

Around the DMZ p435

North-Central Vietnam p447

Central Vietnam p382

Hué p418-9

Danang p402

0    75    150 km

THAILAND

Vietnam (colour country map) between pp16 & 17

Provinces & Area Codes p91

Vietnam Air Routes p158

Index of all maps (including city and town maps) p546

CAMBODIA

Nha Trang p358

Dalat p327

Around Ho Chi Minh City p235

Central Highlands p320

Ho Chi Minh City (Saigon) p180-1

South-Central Coast p351

Mekong Delta p262

# Map Legend

## BOUNDARIES

............... International Boundary
............... Regional Boundary

## ROUTES

............... Freeway
............... Highway
............... Major Road
............... Unsealed Road or Track
............... City Road
............... City Street
............... Railway
............... Underground Railway
............... Tram
............... Walking Track
............... Walking Tour
............... Ferry Route
............... Cable Car or Chairlift

## AREA FEATURES

............... Parks
............... Built-Up Area
............... Pedestrian Mall
............... Market
............... Christian Cemetery
............... Non-Christian Cemetery
............... Reef
............... Beach or Desert
............... Rocks

## HYDROGRAPHIC FEATURES

............... Coastline
............... River, Creek
............... Rapids, Waterfalls
............... Lake, Intermittent Lake
............... Canal
............... Swamp

## SYMBOLS

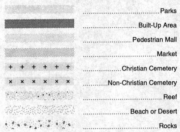

| | | |
|---|---|---|
| ❁ CAPITAL | | National Capital |
| ◉ Capital | | Regional Capital |
| CITY | | Major City |
| ● City | | City |
| ● Town | | Town |
| ● Village | | Village |

| | | |
|---|---|---|
| ■ | ▼ | Place to Stay, Place to Eat |
| ♆ | ❸ | Pub or Bar, Bank |
| ✉ | ☎ | Post Office, Telephone |
| ❶ | ⚑ | Tourist Information, Golf Course |
| ● | ℗ | Transport, Parking |
| 🏛 | ⛺ | Museum, Youth Hostel |
| ⚏ | ⚘ | Caravan Park, Camping Ground |
| ✚ | ✚ | Church, Cathedral |
| ☾ | ✡ | Mosque, Synagogue |
| 🛕 | 🏛 | Temple, Villa |
| ✚ | ★ | Hospital, Police Station |

| | | |
|---|---|---|
| ◔ | ◗ | Embassy, Petrol Station |
| ✈ | ✝ | Airport, Airfield |
| 🛏 | ✿ | Swimming Pool, Gardens |
| ❖ | 🐘 | Shopping Centre, Zoo |
| ⚘ | π | Winery or Vineyard, Picnic Site |
| ← | A25 | One Way Street, Route Number |
| ✕ | ⚑ | Battlefield, Monument |
| 🏰 | ◘ | Castle, Tomb |
| ⌒ | ⌂ | Cave, Hut or Chalet |
| ▲ | ✺ | Mountain or Hill, Lookout |
| 🗼 | ⚓ | Lighthouse, Shipwreck |
| )( | ◎ | Pass, Spring |
| 🐬 | ⚑ | Beach, Surf Beach |
| | ∴ | Archaeological Site or Ruins |
| | | Ancient or City Wall |
| | | Cliff or Escarpment, Tunnel |
| | | Railway Station |

Note: not all symbols displayed above appear in this book

# Introduction

Vietnam, a country made famous by a war, has a unique and rich civilisation, spectacular scenery and highly cultured, friendly people. While no doubt the war continues to weigh heavily on the consciousness of all who can remember the fighting, the Vietnam of today is a country at peace.

After the fall of South Vietnam to the Communist North Vietnamese forces in 1975, Vietnam was virtually isolated from the world. But towards the end of the 1980s, the Cold War thawed and the Hanoi government succeeded in reducing Vietnam's international isolation, in part by opening the country's doors to foreign visitors. Not long thereafter, the dramatic collapse of the Eastern Bloc and the ending of the Cambodian civil war greatly reduced tensions in Indochina.

At the same time, a change of presidential administration in the USA resulted in a perceptible shift in US policy towards Vietnam. The reasons for this are for the most part political and economic, but the results have given travellers the first opportunity in over a generation to visit a Vietnam at peace with itself and its neighbours.

Most visitors to Vietnam are overwhelmed by the sublime beauty of the country's natural setting. The Red River Delta in the north, the Mekong Delta in the south and almost the entire coastal strip are a patchwork of brilliant green rice paddies tended by peasant women in conical hats. Vietnam's 3451km of coastline includes countless kilometres of unspoiled beaches and a number of stunning lagoons; some sections are shaded by coconut palms and casuarinas, others bounded by seemingly endless expanses of sand dunes or the rugged spurs of the Truong Son Mountains.

Between the two deltas, the coastal paddies lining the South China Sea give way to soaring mountains – the slopes of some are cloaked with the richest of rainforests. Slightly farther from the littoral are the refreshingly cool plateaus of the Central Highlands, which are dotted with waterfalls. The area is home to dozens of distinct ethnolinguistic groups (hill tribes), more than almost any other country in Asia.

Visitors to Vietnam have their senses thrilled by all the sights, sounds, tastes and smells of a society born of over a century of contact between an ancient civilisation and the ways of the west. There's nothing quite like grabbing a delicious lunch of local delicacies at a food stall deep inside a marketplace, surrounded by tropical fruit vendors and legions of curious youngsters. Or sitting by a waterfall in the Central Highlands, sipping soda water with lemon juice and watching newly wed couples on their honeymoon tiptoe up to the stream-bank in their 'Sunday finest'. Or being invited by a Buddhist monk to attend prayers at his pagoda conducted, according to ancient Mahayana rites, with chanting, drums and gongs.

Of the 30 or so countries I have been to, Vietnam is easily the most beautiful. I saw more shades of green then I knew existed. Rice fields manually tended from dawn to dusk were always in view as were forest-covered mountains. I also frequently caught glimpses of pristine deserted beaches from the train window as we made our way along the coast ...

**David Fisher**

Fiercely protective of their independence and sovereignty for 2000 years, the Vietnamese are also graciously welcoming of foreigners who come as their guests rather than as conquerors. No matter what side they or their parents were on during the war, the Vietnamese are, almost without exception, extremely friendly to western visitors (including Americans) and supportive of more contact with the outside world. People who visit Vietnam during the first years of the country's renewed interaction with the west will play an important role in conveying to the Vietnamese the potentialities of such contact. And now that 'capitalism' is no longer a four-letter word, private Vietnamese businesses have mushroomed, adding an atmosphere of hustle and bustle to Saigon, Hanoi and other cities whose resurgent dynamism is reviving the Vietnamese economy.

The astonishing pace of economic development in East Asia has made many of these countries considerably more expensive, more polluted and less enchanting than they used to be. Rice paddies have given way to industrial estates belching out black smoke; bicycles have been replaced by tour buses; and thatched huts have been bulldozed to make way for five-star hotels and office towers.

Vietnam has not yet reached that level of development and a visit to this country is almost like a journey back through time. Red tape kept foreign tourists and investors out for nearly two decades, but visiting has become considerably easier in the past couple of years and the tourist flood-gates have opened wide. Already, the short period of economic liberalisation and openness to outsiders have brought dramatic changes. Vietnam offers a rare opportunity to see a country of traditional charm and beauty taking the first hesitant steps into the modern world.

# Facts about the Country

## HISTORY

Visitors to Vietnam will notice that, invariably, the major streets of every city and town bear the same two dozen or so names. These are the names of Vietnam's greatest national heroes who, over the last 2000 years, have led the country in its repeated expulsions of foreign invaders and whose exploits have inspired subsequent generations of patriots.

## Prehistory

The origins of the Vietnamese people are shrouded in legend. Recent archaeological finds indicate that the earliest human habitation of northern Vietnam goes back about 500,000 years. Mesolithic and Neolithic cultures existed in northern Vietnam 10,000 years ago; these groups may have engaged in primitive agriculture as early as 7000 BC. The sophisticated Bronze Age Dong Son culture emerged around the 3rd century BC.

From the 1st to the 6th centuries AD, the south of what is now Vietnam was part of the Indianised kingdom of Funan, which produced notably refined art and architecture. The Funanese constructed an elaborate system of canals which were used for both transportation and the irrigation of wet rice agriculture. The principal port city of Funan was Oc-Eo in what is now Kien Giang Province. Archaeological excavations have yielded evidence of contact between Funan and China, Indonesia, India, Persia and even the Mediterranean. One of the most extraordinary artefacts found at Oc-Eo was a gold Roman medallion dated 152 AD and bearing the likeness of Antoninus Pius. In the mid-6th century, Funan was attacked by the pre-Angkorian kingdom of Chenla, which gradually absorbed the territory of Funan into its own.

The Hindu kingdom of Champa appeared around present-day Danang in the late 2nd century. Like Funan, it became Indianised (eg the Chams adopted Hinduism, employed Sanskrit as a sacred language and borrowed a great deal from Indian art) by lively commercial relations with India and through the immigration of Indian literati and priests. By the 8th century, Champa had expanded southward to include what is now Nha Trang and Phan Rang. Champa was a semi-piratic country that lived in part from conducting raids along the entire Indochinese coast; as a result, it was in a constant state of war with the Vietnamese to the north and the Khmers to the west. Brilliant examples of Cham sculpture can be seen in the Cham Museum in Danang.

## Chinese Rule (circa 200 BC to 938 AD)

When the Chinese conquered the Red River Delta in the 2nd century BC, they found a feudally organised society based on hunting, fishing and slash-and-burn agriculture; these proto-Vietnamese also carried on trade with other peoples in the area. Over the next few centuries, significant numbers of Chinese settlers, officials and scholars moved to the Red River Delta, taking over large tracts of land. The Chinese tried to impose a centralised state system on the Vietnamese and to forcibly Sinicise their culture, but local rulers made use of the benefits of Chinese civilisation to tenaciously resist these efforts.

The most famous act of resistance against the Chinese during this period was the rebellion of the Trung Sisters (Hai Ba Trung). In 40 AD, the Chinese executed a high-ranking feudal lord. His widow and her sister, the Trung Sisters, rallied tribal chieftains, raised an army and led a revolt that compelled the Chinese governor to flee. The sisters then had themselves proclaimed queens of the newly independent Vietnamese entity. In 43 AD, however, the Chinese counterattacked and defeated the Vietnamese; rather than surrender, the Trung Sisters threw themselves into the Hat Giang River.

The early Vietnamese learned a great deal from the Chinese, including the use of the metal plough and domesticated beasts of burden and the construction of dikes and irrigation works. These innovations made possible the establishment of a culture based on rice growing, which remains the basis of the Vietnamese way of life to this day. As food became more plentiful, the population grew, forcing the Vietnamese to seek new lands on which to grow rice.

During this era, Vietnam was a key port of call on the sea route between China and India. The Vietnamese were introduced to Confucianism and Taoism by Chinese scholars who came to Vietnam as administrators and refugees. Indians sailing eastward brought Theravada (Hinayana) Buddhism to the Red River Delta while, simultaneously, Chinese travellers introduced Mahayana Buddhism. Buddhist monks carried with them the scientific and medical knowledge of the civilisations of India and China; as a result, Vietnamese Buddhists soon counted among their own great doctors, botanists and scholars.

There were major rebellions against Chinese rule – which was characterised by tyranny, forced labour and insatiable demands for tribute – in the 3rd and 6th centuries, but all (along with numerous minor revolts) were crushed. In 679, the Chinese named the country Annam, which means the Pacified South. Ever since this era, the collective memory of those early attempts to throw off the Chinese yoke has played an important role in shaping Vietnamese identity.

## Independence from China (10th Century)

In the aftermath of the collapse of the Tang Dynasty in China in the early 10th century, the Vietnamese revolted against Chinese rule. In 938 AD, Ngo Quyen vanquished the Chinese armies at a battle on the Bach Dang River to end 1000 years of Chinese rule. Ngo Quyen established an independent Vietnamese state, but it was not until 968 that Dinh Bo Linh ended the anarchy that followed

Ngo Quyen's death and, following the custom of the times, reached an agreement with China: in return for recognition of their de facto independence, the Vietnamese accepted Chinese sovereignty and agreed to pay triennial tribute.

The dynasty founded by Dinh Bo Linh survived only until 980, when Le Dai Hanh overthrew it, beginning what is known as the Early Le Dynasty (980-1009).

The dynasties of independent Vietnam were:

| | |
|---|---|
| Ngo Dynasty | 939-65 |
| Dinh Dynasty | 968-80 |
| Early Le Dynasty | 980-1009 |
| Ly Dynasty | 1010-1225 |
| Tran Dynasty | 1225-1400 |
| Ho Dynasty | 1400-07 |
| Post-Tran Dynasty | 1407-13 |
| Chinese Rule | 1414-27 |
| Later Le Dynasty (nominally until 1788) | 1428-1524 |
| Mac Dynasty | 1527-92 |
| Trinh Lords of the North | 1539-1787 |
| Nguyen Lords of the South | 1558-1778 |
| Tay Son Dynasty | 1788-1802 |
| Nguyen Dynasty | 1802-1945 |

## Ly Dynasty (1010-1225)

From the 11th to the 13th centuries, the independence of the Vietnamese Kingdom (Dai Viet) was consolidated under the emperors of the Ly Dynasty, founded by Ly Thai To. They reorganised the administrative system, founded the nation's first university (the Temple of Literature in Hanoi), promoted agriculture and built the first embankments for flood control along the Red River. Confucian scholars fell out of official favour because of their close cultural links to China; at the same time, the early Ly monarchs, whose dynasty had come to power with Buddhist support, promoted Buddhism.

The Confucian philosophy of government and society, emphasising educational attainment, ritual performance and government authority, reasserted itself with the graduation of the first class from the Temple of Literature in 1075. Following years of study which emphasised classical education, these scholars went into government service, becoming what the west came to call mandarins. The outlines of the Vietnamese mandarinal system of government – according to which the state was run by a scholar class recruited in civil service examinations – date from this era.

During the Ly Dynasty, the Chinese, Khmers and Chams repeatedly attacked Vietnam, but were repelled, most notably under the renowned strategist and tactician Ly Thuong Kiet (1030-1105), a military mandarin of royal blood who is still revered as a national hero.

Vietnamese conquests of Cham territory, which greatly increased the acreage under rice cultivation, were accompanied by an aggressive policy of colonisation that reproduced social structures dominant in the north in the newly settled territories. This process did not make allowances for the potential technological and cultural contributions of the Chams (and indeed destroyed Cham civilisation), but it did result in a chain of homogeneous villages that eventually stretched from the Chinese border to the Gulf of Thailand.

## Tran Dynasty (1225-1400)

After years of civil strife, the Tran Dynasty overthrew the Ly Dynasty. The Tran increased the land under cultivation to feed the growing population and improved the dikes on the Red River.

After the dreaded Mongol warrior Kublai Khan completed his conquest of China in the mid-13th century, he demanded the right to cross Vietnamese territory on his way to attack Champa. The Vietnamese refused this demand, but the Mongols – 500,000 of them – came anyway. The outnumbered Vietnamese under Tran Hung Dao attacked the invaders and forced them back to China, but the Mongols returned, this time with 300,000 men. Tran Hung Dao then lured them deep into Vietnamese territory; at high tide he attacked the Mongol fleet as it sailed on the Bach Dang River, ordering a tactical retreat of his forces to lure the Mongols into staying and fighting. The battle continued for many hours until low tide when a sudden Vietnamese counteroffensive forced the Mongol boats back, impaling them on steel-tipped bamboo stakes set in the river bed the night before. The entire fleet was captured or sunk.

When the Tran Dynasty was overthrown in 1400 by Ho Qui Ly, both the Tran loyalists and the Chams (who had sacked Hanoi in 1371) encouraged Chinese intervention. The Chinese readily complied with the request and took control of Vietnam in 1407, imposing a regime characterised by heavy taxation and slave labour; Chinese culture and ways of doing things were forced on the population. The Chinese also took the national archives (and some of the country's intellectuals as well) to China, an irreparable loss to Vietnamese civilisation. Of this period, the great poet Nguyen Trai (1380-1442) would write:

Were the water of the Eastern Sea to be exhausted, the stain of their ignominy could not be washed away; all the bamboo of the Southern Mountains would not suffice to provide the paper for recording all their crimes.

## Later Le Dynasty (1428-1524)

Le Loi was born into a large and prosperous family in the village of Lam Son in Thanh Hoa Province and earned a reputation for using his wealth to aid the poor. The ruling Chinese invited him to join the mandarinate, but he refused. In 1418, Le Loi began to organise what came to be known as the Lam Son Uprising, travelling around the countryside to rally the people against the Chinese. Despite several defeats, he persisted in his efforts, earning the respect of the peasantry by ensuring that even when facing starvation his guerrilla troops did not pillage the land. After his victory in 1428, Le Loi declared himself Emperor Ly Thai To, thus beginning the Later Le Dynasty. To this day, Le Loi is revered as one of Vietnam's greatest national heroes.

After Le Loi's victory over the Chinese, Nguyen Trai, a scholar and Le Loi's companion in arms, wrote his famous *Great Proclamation (Binh Ngo Dai Cao)*, extraordinary for the compelling voice it gave to Vietnam's fierce spirit of independence:

Our people long ago established Vietnam as an independent nation with its own civilisation. We have our own mountains and our own rivers, our own customs and traditions, and these are different from those of the foreign country to the north … We have sometimes been weak and sometime powerful, but at no time have we suffered from a lack of heroes.

The Later Le Dynasty ruled until 1524 and, nominally, up to 1788. Le Loi and his successors instituted a vast programme of agrarian reform and land redistribution. They also launched a campaign to take over Cham lands to the south. In the 15th century Laos was forced to recognise Vietnamese suzerainty.

Under the Le Dynasty, an attempt was made to break free of the cultural and intellectual domination of Chinese civilisation. In the realms of law, religion and literature, indigenous traditions were brought to the fore. The Vietnamese language gained favour among scholars – who had previously disdained it, preferring Chinese – and a number of outstanding works of literature were produced. Legal reforms gave women almost-equal rights in the domestic sphere, but two groups were excluded from full civil rights: slaves (many of them prisoners of war) and, oddly, actors. In the culture of the elite, however, Chinese language and traditions continued to hold sway and neo-Confucianism remained dominant in the areas of social and political morality.

### Trinh & Nguyen Lords
Throughout the 17th and 18th centuries, Vietnam was divided between the Trinh Lords, who ruled in the north under the titular kingship of the Later Le monarchs, and the Nguyen Lords, who controlled the south and also nominally recognised the Later Le Dynasty. The Trinh Lords repeatedly failed in attempts to take over areas under Nguyen control, in part because the

Portuguese weaponry used by the Nguyen was far superior to the Dutch armaments supplied to the Trinh. During this period the Nguyen extended Vietnamese control into the Khmer territories of the Mekong Delta, populating the area with Vietnamese settlers. Cambodia was forced to accept Vietnamese suzerainty in the mid-17th century.

Buddhism enjoyed the patronage and support of both the Trinh and the Nguyen, and pagodas were built all over the country. But by this time Vietnamese Buddhism was no longer doctrinally pure, having become intermingled with animism, ancestor worship and popularised Taoism.

### Early Contact with the West
According to Chinese records, the first Vietnamese contact with Europeans took place in 166 AD when travellers from the Rome of Marcus Aurelius arrived in the Red River Delta.

The first Portuguese sailors landed in Danang in 1516; they were followed by Dominican missionaries 11 years later. During the next few decades the Portuguese began to trade with Vietnam, setting up a commercial colony alongside those of the Japanese and Chinese at Faifo (present-day Hoi An near Danang).

Franciscan missionaries from the Philippines settled in central Vietnam in 1580, followed in 1615 by the Jesuits who had just been expelled from Japan. In 1637, the Dutch were authorised to set up trading posts in the north and one of the Le kings even took a Dutch woman as one of his six wives. The first English attempt to break into the Vietnamese market ended with the murder of an agent of the East India Company in Hanoi in 1613.

One of the most illustrious of the early missionaries was the brilliant French Jesuit Alexandre de Rhodes (1591-1660). He is most recognised for his work in devising quoc ngu, the Latin-based phonetic alphabet in which Vietnamese is written to this day. Over the course of his long career, de Rhodes flitted back and forth between Hanoi,

JULIET COOMBE

MASON FLORENCE

MASON FLORENCE

### Vietnam in focus

Top: The giant rock formations of Hoa Lu in north-central Vietnam.

Middle: Rice - Vietnam's staple food and major export.

Bottom: The Po Klong Garai Cham Towers at Phan Rang.

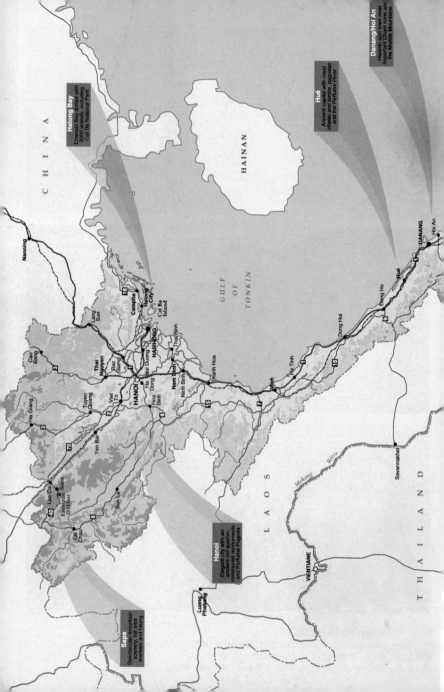

CHINA

Nanning

Halong Bay
Emerald Bay with
3000 islands, including
Cat Ba National Park

HAINAN

GULF
OF
TONKIN

Lang Son

Campha

Halong
City

Cat Ba
Island

Cao
Bang

Ha Giang

Thai
Nguyen

Bac
Giang

HAIPHONG

Thai Binh

Tuyen
Quang

Viet
Tri

HANOI

Ha
Dong

Hai Duong

Nam Dinh

Ninh Binh

Hoa
Binh

Lao Cai

Sapa

Fansipan
(3143m)

Lai
Chau

Yen Bai

Son La

Red River

Black River

Ma River

Thanh Hoa

Vinh

Ha Tinh

Dong Hoi

Dong Ha

Huế

DANANG

Hoi An

Huế
Ancient capital with royal
citadel, tombs, pagodas
and the Perfume River

Danang/Hoi An
Historic port town near
important Cham ruins and
the Marble Mountains

LAOS

Mekong River

Savannakhet

THAILAND

VIENTIANE

Luang
Phabang

Hanoi
Elegant city with an
ancient old quarter,
communist monuments
and Perfume Pagoda

Sapa
Spectacular mountain
scenery, hill tribe
markets and hiking

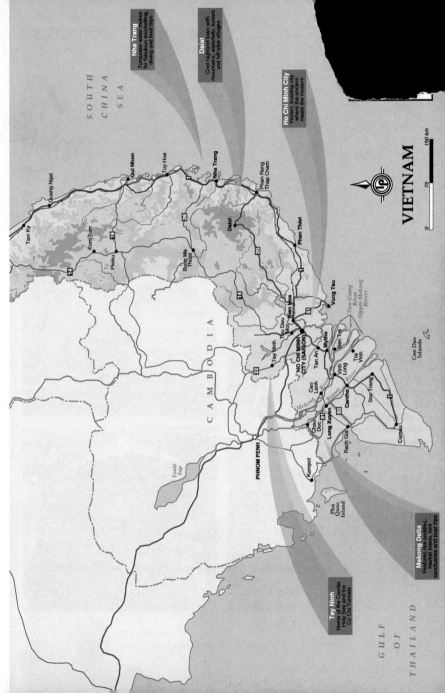

**Nha Trang**
Turquoise water makes for fabulous snorkelling, diving and boat trips

**Dalat**
Cool highland town with mountains, forests, waterfalls, and hill tribe villages

**Ho Chi Minh City**
Vibrant, bustling city where the ancient meets the modern

**VIETNAM**

0    75    150 km

*SOUTH CHINA SEA*

Tam Ky
Quang Ngai
Kom Tum
Qui Nhon
Tuy Hoa
Pleiku
Buon Ma Thuot
Nha Trang
Phan Rang Thap Cham
Dalat
Phan Thiet
Vung Tau
Bien Hoa

*C A M B O D I A*

PHNOM PENH
Tay Ninh
Tru Dau
Moc Bai
**HO CHI MINH CITY (SAIGON)**
Tan An
Mytho
Ben Tre
Cao Lanh
Vinh Long
Tra Vinh
Chau Doc
Canctho
Long Xuyen
Soc Trang
Rach Gia
Camau

Kampot

*Mekong River*
*Bassac River*
*Tien Giang River (Upper Mekong River)*

Con Dao Islands

Phu Quoc Island

*Tonlé Sap*

*GULF OF THAILAND*

**Tay Ninh**
Home of the Caodai Holy See and the Cu Chi Tunnels

**Mekong Delta**
Features rice paddies, market towns, bird sanctuaries and boat trips

**People of Vietnam**

Macau, Rome and Paris, seeking support and funding for his missionary activities and battling both Portuguese colonial opposition and the intractable Vatican bureaucracy. In 1645, he was sentenced to death for illegally entering Vietnam to proselytise, but was expelled instead; two of the priests with him were beheaded.

By the late 17th century most of the European merchants were gone; trade with Vietnam had not proved particularly profitable. But the missionaries remained and the Catholic Church eventually had a greater impact on Vietnam than on any country in Asia except the Philippines, which was ruled by the Spanish for 400 years. The Vietnamese – especially in the north – proved highly receptive to Catholicism, but mass conversions were hindered by the Catholic stand against polygamy and by the opposition of the Vatican to ancestor worship. The Catholic emphasis on individual salvation undermined the established Confucian order and wary officials of the mandarinate often restricted the activities of missionaries and persecuted their followers. But despite this friction, the imperial court retained a contingent of Jesuit scholars, astronomers, mathematicians and physicians.

The European missionaries did not hesitate to use secular means to help them achieve their goal – the conversion to Catholicism of all of Asia. Towards this end, French missionaries, who had supplanted the Portuguese by the 18th century, actively campaigned for a greater French political and military role in Vietnam.

## Tay Son Rebellion (1771-1802)

In 1765, a rebellion against misgovernment broke out in the town of Tay Son near Qui Nhon. It was led by three brothers from a wealthy merchant family: Nguyen Nhac, Nguyen Hue and Nguyen Lu. By 1773, the Tay Son Rebels (as they came to be known) controlled the whole of central Vietnam and in 1783 they captured Saigon and the rest of the south, killing the reigning prince and his family (as well as 10,000 Chinese residents

of Cholon). Nguyen Lu became king of the south and Nguyen Nhac became king of central Vietnam.

Prince Nguyen Anh, the only survivor of the defeated Nguyen clan, fled to Thailand and requested military assistance from the Thais. He also met the French Jesuit missionary Pigneau de Behaine (the Bishop of Adran), whom he eventually authorised to act as his intermediary in seeking assistance from the French. As a sign of good faith, Nguyen Anh sent his four-year-old son Canh with Pigneau de Behaine to France. The exotic entourage created quite a sensation when it arrived at Versailles in 1787 and Louis XVI authorised a military expedition. Louis XVI later changed his mind, but the bishop managed to convince French merchants in India to buy him two ships, weapons and supplies. With a force of 400 French deserters he had recruited, de Behaine set sail from Pondicherry, India, in June 1789.

Meanwhile, the Tay Son overthrew the Trinh Lords in the north and proclaimed allegiance to the Later Le Dynasty. The weak Le emperor, however, proved unable to retain his control of the country, but rather than calling on the Tay Son, he asked the Chinese for help. Taking advantage of the unstable situation, the Chinese sent 200,000 troops to Vietnam under the pretext of helping the emperor. In 1788, with popular sentiment on his side, one of the Tay Son brothers, Nguyen Hue, proclaimed himself Emperor Quang Trung and set out with his army to expel the Chinese. In 1789, Nguyen Hue's forces overwhelmingly defeated the Chinese army at Dong Da (near Hanoi) in one of the most celebrated military achievements in Vietnamese history.

In the south, Nguyen Anh, whose forces were trained by Pigneau de Behaine's young French adventurers, gradually pushed back the Tay Son. In 1802, Nguyen Anh proclaimed himself Emperor Gia Long, thus beginning the Nguyen Dynasty. When he captured Hanoi, his victory was complete and, for the first time in two centuries, Vietnam was united. Hué became the new national capital.

## Nguyen Dynasty (1802-1945)

Emperors of the Nguyen Dynasty:

| | |
|---|---|
| Gia Long | 1802-19 |
| Minh Mang | 1820-40 |
| Thieu Tri | 1841-47 |
| Tu Duc | 1848-83 |
| Duc Duc | 1883 |
| Hiep Hoa | 1883 |
| Kien Phuc | 1883-84 |
| Ham Nghi | 1884-85 |
| Dong Khanh | 1885-89 |
| Thanh Thai | 1889-1907 |
| Duy Tan | 1907-16 |
| Khai Dinh | 1916-25 |
| Bao Dai | 1925-45 |

The turbulent past of the Thien Mu Pagoda, built by Emperor Thieu Tri in 1844, has included its destruction and reconstruction on five different occasions, plus a role as a rallying point during anti-government demonstrations in the 60s and 80s.

Emperor Gia Long (reigned 1802-19) initiated what historian David Marr has called 'a policy of massive reassertion of Confucian values and institutions' in order to consolidate the dynasty's shaky position by appealing to the conservative tendencies of the elite, who had felt threatened by the atmosphere of reform stirred up by the Tay Son Rebels.

Gia Long also began a large-scale programme of public works (dikes, canals, roads, ports, bridges and land reclamation) to rehabilitate the country, which had been devastated by almost three decades of warfare. The Mandarin Road linking the national capital, Hué, to both Hanoi and Saigon was constructed during this period, as was a string of star-shaped citadels – built according to the principles of the French military architect Vauban – in provincial capitals. All these projects imposed a heavy burden on the population in the forms of taxation, military conscription and *corvée* (forced labour).

Gia Long's son, Emperor Minh Mang (reigned 1820-40), worked to consolidate the state and establish a strong central government. Because of his background as a Confucian scholar, he emphasised the importance of traditional Confucian education, which consisted of the memorisation and orthodox interpretation of the Confucian classics and texts of ancient Chinese history. As a result, education and spheres of activity dependent on it stagnated.

Minh Mang was profoundly hostile to Catholicism, which he saw as a threat to the Confucian state, and he extended this antipathy to all western influences. Seven missionaries and an unknown number of Vietnamese Catholics were executed in the 1830s, inflaming passions among French Catholics, who demanded that their government intervene in Vietnam.

Serious uprisings broke out in both the north and the south during this period, growing progressively more serious in the 1840s and 1850s. To make matters worse, the civil unrest in the deltas was accompanied by smallpox epidemics, tribal uprisings, drought, locusts and – most serious of all – repeated breaches in the Red River dikes, the result of government neglect.

The early Nguyen emperors continued the expansionist policies followed by preceding dynasties, pushing into Cambodia and westward into the mountains along a wide front. They seized huge areas of Lao territory and clashed with Thailand over control of the lands of the weak Khmer Empire.

The first half of the 19th century was marked by a great deal of literary activity. It was during this period that Nguyen Du (1765-1820), a poet, scholar, mandarin and diplomat, wrote one of Vietnam's literary masterpieces, *The Tale of Kieu (Kim Van Kieu)*.

Minh Mang was succeeded by Emperor Thieu Tri (reigned 1841-47), who expelled most of the foreign missionaries. He was followed by Emperor Tu Duc (reigned 1848-83), who continued to rule according to conservative Confucian precepts and in imitation of Qing practices in China. Both responded to rural unrest with repression.

### French Rule (1859-1954)

Ever since Pigneau de Behaine's patronage of Nguyen Anh in the late 18th century and his son Canh's appearance at Versailles had 1787, certain segments of French society had retained an active interest in Indochina. But it was not until the Revolution of 1848 and the advent of the Second Empire that there arose a coalition of interests – Catholic, commercial, patriotic, strategic and idealistic (fans of the *mission civilisatrice*) – with sufficient influence to initiate large-scale, long-term colonial efforts. However, for the next four decades the French colonial venture in Indochina was carried out haphazardly and without any preconceived plan. In fact, it was repeatedly on the verge of being discontinued altogether and at times only the insubordinate and reckless actions of a few adventurers kept it going.

France's military activity in Vietnam began in 1847, when the French Navy attacked Danang harbour in response to Thieu Tri's actions against Catholic missionaries. In 1858, a joint military force of 14 ships from France and the Spanish colony of the Philippines stormed Danang after the killing of several missionaries. As disease began to take a heavy toll and the expected support from Catholic Vietnamese failed to materialise, the force left a small garrison in Danang and followed the monsoon winds southward, seizing Saigon in early 1859. Huge quantities of Vietnamese cannon, firearms, swords, saltpetre, sulphur, shot and copper coins were seized; a fire set in rice storage granaries is said to have smouldered for three years.

The French victory in the 1861 Battle of Ky Hoa (Chi Hoa) marked the beginning of the end of formal, organised Vietnamese military action against the French in the south and the rise of popular guerrilla resistance led by the local scholar-gentry, who had refused en masse to collaborate with the French administration. This resistance took the form of ambushing French river-craft, denying food supplies to French bases and assassinating collaborators.

In 1862, Emperor Tu Duc signed a treaty that gave the French the three eastern provinces of Cochinchina. In addition, missionaries were promised the freedom to proselytise everywhere in the country, several ports were opened to French and Spanish commerce, and Tu Duc undertook to pay a large indemnity. To raise the necessary cash he authorised the sale of opium in the north and sold the monopoly to the Chinese. Additionally, he debased the meritocratic mandarinate by putting low-ranking mandarinal posts up for sale.

The French offensive of 1867 broke the morale of the resistance, causing the scholar-gentry who had not been killed to flee the delta. Cochinchina became a French colony and the peasantry assumed a position of non-violent resignation. At the same time, voices among the more educated classes of Vietnamese began to advocate cooperation with, and subordination to, the French in the interest of technical and economic development.

During this era, the Vietnamese might have been able to reduce the impact of the arrival of the European maritime powers and to retain their independence, but this would have required a degree of imagination and dynamism lacking in Hué. Indeed, until the mid-19th century, the imperial court at Hué, which was dominated by extreme Confucian conservatism, behaved almost as if Europe did not exist, though events such as the Opium War of 1839 in China should have served as a warning. In addition, resistance to colonialism was severely handicapped by an almost total lack of political and economic intelligence about France and the French.

The next major French action came in the years 1872 to 1874, when Jean Dupuis, a merchant seeking to supply salt and weapons to a Yunnanese general by sailing up the Red River, seized the Hanoi Citadel. Captain Francis Garnier, ostensibly dispatched to reign in Dupuis, instead took over where Dupuis left off. After capturing Hanoi, Garnier's gunboats proceeded to sail around the Red River Delta demanding tribute from provincial fortresses, an activity that ended only when Garnier was killed by the Black Flags (Co Den), a semi-autonomous army of Chinese, Vietnamese and hill tribe troops who fought mostly for booty but resisted the French in part because of a strong antipathy toward westerners.

These events threw the north into chaos: the Black Flags continued their piratic activities; local bands were organised to take vengeance on the Vietnamese – especially Catholics – who had helped the French; Chinese militias in the pay of both the French and the Nguyen emperors sprung up; Le Dynasty pretenders began asserting their claims; and the hill tribes revolted. As central government authority collapsed and all established order broke down, Tu Duc went so far as to petition for help from the Chinese and to ask for support from the British and even the Americans.

In 1882, a French force under Captain Henri Rivière seized Hanoi, but further conquests were stubbornly resisted by both Chinese regulars and the Black Flags, especially the latter. The following year, Black Flags units ambushed Rivière at Cau Giay, killing him and 32 other Frenchmen, and

triumphantly paraded his severed head from hamlet to hamlet.

Meanwhile, only a few weeks after the death of Tu Duc in 1883, the French attacked Hué and imposed a Treaty of Protectorate on the imperial court. There then began a tragi-comic struggle for royal succession notable for its palace coups, mysteriously dead emperors and heavy-handed French diplomacy. Emperors Duc Duc and Hiep Hoa were succeeded by Kien Phuc (reigned 1883-84), who was followed by 14-year-old Emperor Ham Nghi (reigned 1884-85). By the time Ham Nghi and his advisers decided to relocate the court to the mountains and to lead resistance activities from there, the French had rounded up enough mandarin collaborators to give his French-picked successor, Emperor Dong Khanh (reigned 1885-89), sufficient legitimacy to survive.

Ham Nghi held out against the French until 1888 when he was betrayed, captured by the French and exiled to Algeria. Although the Indochinese Union (consisting of Cochinchina, Annam, Tonkin, Cambodia, Laos and the port of Qinzhouwan in China), proclaimed by the French in 1887, effectively ended the existence of an independent Vietnamese state, active resistance to colonialism continued in various parts of the country for the duration of French rule. The establishment of the Indochinese Union ended Vietnamese expansionism and the Vietnamese were forced to give back lands taken from Cambodia and Laos.

Continuing in the tradition of centuries of Vietnamese dynasties, the French colonial authorities carried out ambitious public works, constructing the Saigon-Hanoi railway, as well as ports, extensive irrigation and drainage systems, improved dikes, various public services and research institutes. To fund these activities, the government heavily taxed the peasants, devastating the traditional rural economy. The colonial administration also ran alcohol, salt and opium monopolies for the purpose of raising revenues. In Saigon, they produced a quick-burning type of opium which helped increase addiction and thus revenues.

And since colonialism was supposed to be a profitable proposition, French capital was invested for quick returns in anthracite coal, tin, tungsten and zinc mines, as well as in tea, coffee and rubber plantations – all of which became notorious for the abysmal wages they paid and the subhuman treatment to which their Vietnamese workers were subjected. Out of the 45,000 indentured workers at one Michelin rubber plantation, 12,000 died of disease and malnutrition between 1917 and 1944.

As land, like capital, became concentrated in the hands of a tiny percentage of the population (in Cochinchina, 2.5% of the population came to own 45% of the land), a sub-proletariat of landless and uprooted peasants was formed. In the countryside these people were reduced to sharecropping, paying up to 60% of their crop in rents. Whereas the majority of Vietnamese peasants had owned their land before the arrival of the French, by the 1930s about 70% of them were landless. Because French policies impoverished the people of Indochina, the area never became an important market for French industry.

## Vietnamese Anti-colonialism

Throughout the colonial period, the vast majority of Vietnamese retained a strong desire to have their national independence restored. Seething nationalist aspirations often broke out into open defiance of the French, which took forms ranging from the publishing of patriotic periodicals and books to an attempt to poison the French garrison in Hanoi.

The imperial court in Hué, though corrupt, was a centre of nationalist feeling, a fact most evident in the game of musical thrones orchestrated by the French. Upon his death the subservient Dong Khanh was replaced by 10-year-old Emperor Thanh Thai (reigned 1889-1907), whose rule the French ended when he was discovered to have been plotting against them. He was deported to the Indian Ocean island of Réunion, where he remained until 1947.

His son and successor, Emperor Duy Tan

(reigned 1907-16), was only in his teens in 1916 when he and the poet Tran Cao Van planned a general uprising in Hué that was discovered the day before it was scheduled to begin; Tran Cao Van was beheaded and Duy Tan was exiled to Réunion. Duy Tan was succeeded by the docile Emperor Khai Dinh (reigned 1916-25). On his death he was followed by his son, Emperor Bao Dai (reigned 1925-45), who at the time of his accession was 12 years old and at school in France.

Some Vietnamese nationalists (such as the scholar and patriot Phan Boi Chau, who rejected French rule but not western ideas and technology) looked to Japan and China for support and political inspiration, especially after Japan's victory in the Russo-Japanese war of 1905 showed all of Asia that western powers could be defeated. Sun Yatsen's 1911 revolution in China was also closely followed in Vietnamese nationalist circles.

The Viet Nam Quoc Dan Dang (VNQDD), a largely middle-class, nationalist party modelled after the Chinese Kuomintang, was founded in 1927 by nationalist leaders. One of them, Nguyen Thai Hoc, was guillotined along with 12 comrades in the savage French retribution for the abortive 1930 Yen Bai uprising.

Another source of nationalist agitation was among those Vietnamese who had spent time in France, where they were not hampered by the restrictions on political activity in force in the colonies. In addition, over 100,000 Vietnamese were sent to Europe as soldiers during WWI.

Ultimately, the most successful anti-colonialists proved to be the Communists, who were uniquely able to relate to the frustrations and aspirations of the population – especially the peasants – and to effectively channel and organise their demands for more equitable land distribution.

The institutional history of Vietnamese Communism – which in many ways is the political biography of Ho Chi Minh – is rather complicated. In brief, the first Marxist grouping in Indochina was the Vietnam

Revolutionary Youth League (Viet Nam Cach Menh Thanh Nien Dong Chi Hoi), founded by Ho Chi Minh in Canton, China, in 1925. The Revolutionary Youth League was succeeded in February 1930 by the Vietnamese Communist Party (Dang Cong San Viet Nam), a union of three groups effected by Ho which was renamed the Indochinese Communist Party (Dang Cong San Dong Duong) in October 1930. In 1941, Ho Chi Minh formed the League for the Independence of Vietnam (Viet Nam Doc Lap Dong Minh Hoi), better known as the Viet Minh, which resisted the Japanese occupation (and thus received Chinese and American aid) and carried out extensive political organising during WWII. Despite its broad nationalist programme and claims to the contrary, the Viet Minh was, from its inception, dominated by Ho's Communists.

Communist successes in the late 1920s included major strikes by urban workers. During the Nghe Tinh Uprising (1930-31), revolutionary committees (or soviets) took control of parts of Nghe An and Ha Tinh provinces (thus all the streets named 'Xo Viet Nghe Tinh'), but after an unprecedented wave of terror the French managed to re-establish control. A 1940 uprising in the south was also brutally suppressed, seriously damaging the Party's infrastructure. French prisons, filled with arrested cadres, were turned by the captives into revolutionary 'universities' in which Marxist-Leninist theory was taught.

## WWII

When France fell to Nazi Germany in 1940, the Indochinese government of Vichy-appointed Admiral Jean Decoux concluded an agreement to accept the presence of Japanese troops in Vietnam. For their own convenience the Japanese, who sought to exploit the area's strategic location and its natural resources, left the French administration in charge of the day-to-day running of the country. The only group that did anything significant to resist the Japanese occupation was the Communist-dominated Viet Minh, which from 1944 received funding and arms

from the US Office of Strategic Services (OSS), the predecessor of the CIA. This affiliation offered the Viet Minh the hope of eventual US recognition of their demands for independence; it also proved useful to Ho in that it implied that he had the support of the Americans.

In March 1945, as a Viet Minh offensive was getting under way and Decoux's government was plotting to resist the Japanese – something they hadn't tried in the preceding 4½ years – the Japanese overthrew Decoux, imprisoning both his troops and his administrators. Decoux's administration was replaced with a puppet regime – nominally independent within Japan's Greater East-Asian Co-Prosperity Sphere – led by Emperor Bao Dai, who abrogated the 1883 treaty that made Annam and Tonkin French protectorates. During the same period, Japanese rice requisitions and the Japanese policy of forcing farmers to plant industrial crops, in combination with floods and breaches in the dikes, caused a horrific famine in which two million of northern Vietnam's 10 million people starved to death.

By the spring of 1945 the Viet Minh controlled large parts of the country, especially in the north. In mid-August – after the atomic bombing of Japan – Ho Chi Minh formed the National Liberation Committee and called for a general uprising, later known as the August Revolution (Cach Mang Thang Tam), to take advantage of the power vacuum. Almost immediately, the Viet Minh assumed complete control of the north. In central Vietnam, Emperor Bao Dai abdicated in favour of the new government (which later appointed him its 'Supreme Adviser', whatever that means). In the south, the Viet Minh soon held power in a shaky coalition with non-Communist groups. On 2 September 1945, Ho Chi Minh – with American OSS agents at his side and borrowing liberally from the stirring prose of the American Declaration of Independence – declared the Democratic Republic of Vietnam independent at a rally in Hanoi's Ba Dinh Square. During this period, Ho wrote no fewer than eight letters to US president Harry Truman and the State Department asking for US aid, but did not receive replies.

A minor item on the agenda of the Potsdam Conference of 1945 was the procedure for disarming the Japanese occupation forces in Vietnam. It was decided that the Chinese Kuomintang (Nationalist Party) would accept the Japanese surrender north of the 16th parallel and the British would do the same south of that line.

When the British arrived in Saigon, chaos reigned with enraged French settlers beginning to take matters into their own hands and competing Vietnamese groups on the verge of civil war. With only 1800 British, Indian and Ghurka troops at his disposal, British General Gracey ordered the defeated Japanese troops (!) to help him restore order. He also released and armed 1400 imprisoned French paratroopers, who immediately went on a rampage around the city, overthrowing the Committee of the South government, breaking into Vietnamese homes and shops and indiscriminately clubbing men, women and children. The Viet Minh and allied groups responded by calling a general strike and by beginning a guerrilla campaign against the French. On 24 September, French General Jacques Philippe Leclerc arrived in Saigon, declaring, 'We have come to reclaim our inheritance'.

Meanwhile, in Hué, the imperial library was demolished (priceless documents were being used in the marketplace to wrap fish). In the north 180,000 Chinese Kuomintang troops were fleeing the Chinese Communists and pillaging their way southward towards Hanoi. Ho tried to placate them, but as the months of Chinese occupation dragged on, he decided to accept a temporary return of the French in order to get rid of the anti-Communist Kuomintang, who, in addition to everything else, were supporting the Viet Minh's nationalist rivals. Most of the Kuomintang soldiers were packed off to Taiwan. The French were to stay for five years in return for recognising Vietnam as a free state within the French Union.

The British wanted out, the French wanted in, Ho Chi Minh wanted the Chinese to go and the Americans under President Truman were not as actively opposed to colonialism as they had been under President Franklin Roosevelt. So the French managed to regain control of Vietnam, at least in name. But when the French shelled Haiphong in November 1946 after an obscure customs dispute, killing hundreds of civilians, the patience of the Viet Minh ended. A few weeks later fighting broke out in Hanoi, marking the start of the Franco-Viet Minh War. Ho and his forces fled to the mountains, where they would remain for eight years.

## Franco-Viet Minh War (1946-54)
In the face of Vietnamese determination that their country regain its independence, the French proved unable to reassert their control. Despite massive American aid and the existence of significant indigenous anti-Communist elements – who in 1949 rallied to support Bao Dai's 'Associated State' within the French Union – it was an unwinnable war. As Ho said to the French at the time: 'You can kill 10 of my men for every one I kill of yours, but even at those odds, you will lose and I will win'.

After eight years of fighting, the Viet Minh controlled much of Vietnam and neighbouring Laos. On 7 May 1954, after a 57-day siege, over 10,000 starving French troops surrendered to the Viet Minh at Dien Bien Phu – a catastrophic defeat that shattered the remaining public support for the war in France. The next day, the Geneva Conference opened to negotiate an end to the conflict; 2½ months later, the Geneva Accords were signed. The Geneva Accords provided for an exchange of prisoners, the temporary division of Vietnam into two zones at the Ben Hai River (near the 17th parallel), the free passage of people across the 17th parallel for a period of 300 days and the holding of nationwide elections on 20 July 1956. In the course of the Franco-Viet Minh War, more than 35,000 men were killed and 48,000 wounded on the French side, but Vietnamese casualties were much greater.

## South Vietnam

After the signing of the Geneva Accords, the South was ruled by a government led by Ngo Dinh Diem (pronounced 'zee-EM'), a fiercely anti-Communist Catholic whose brother had been killed by the Viet Minh in 1945. His power base was significantly strengthened by some 900,000 refugees – many of them Catholics – who fled the Communist North during the 300-day free-passage period.

In 1955 Diem, convinced that if elections were held Ho Chi Minh would win, refused – with US encouragement – to implement the Geneva Accords; instead, he held a referendum on his continued rule. Diem claimed to have won 98.2% of the vote in an election that was by all accounts rigged (in Saigon, he received a third more votes that there were registered voters!). After Diem declared himself president of the Republic of Vietnam, the new regime was recognised by France, the USA, Great Britain, Australia, New Zealand, Italy, Japan, Thailand and South Korea.

During the first few years of his rule, Diem consolidated power fairly effectively, defeating the Binh Xuyen crime syndicate and the private armies of the Hoa Hao and Caodai religious sects. During a 1957 official visit to the USA, President Dwight Eisenhower called Diem the 'miracle man' of Asia. But as time went on he became increasingly tyrannical in dealing with dissent. Running the government became a family affair (Diem's much-hated sister-in-law became Vietnam's powerful 'first lady' while his father-in-law was appointed US ambassador).

Such blatant nepotism was offensive enough, but worse still, Diem's land-reform programme ended up reversing land redistribution effected by the Viet Minh in the 40s. The favouritism he showed to Catholics alienated many Buddhists. In the early 1960s, the South was rocked by anti-Diem unrest led by university students and Buddhist clergy, including several self-immolations by monks that shocked the world. When Diem used French contacts to explore negotiations with Hanoi, the USA threw its support behind a military coup; in November 1963, he was overthrown and killed. Diem was succeeded by a succession of military rulers who continued his repressive policies.

## North Vietnam

The Geneva Accords allowed the leadership of the Democratic Republic of Vietnam to return to Hanoi and to assert control of all territory north of the 17th parallel. The new government immediately set out to eliminate elements of the population that threatened its power. A radical land-reform programme was implemented, providing about half a hectare of land to some 1.5 million peasants. Tens of thousands of 'landlords', some with only tiny holdings – and many of whom had been denounced to 'security committees' by envious neighbours – were arrested. Hasty 'trials' resulted in 10,000 to 15,000 executions and the imprisonment of 50,000 to 100,000 people. In 1956, the Party, faced with serious rural unrest caused by the programme, recognised that the People's Agricultural Reform Tribunals had gotten out of hand and began a 'Campaign for the Rectification of Errors'.

On 12 December 1955 – shortly after Diem had declared the South a republic – the USA closed its consulate in Hanoi.

## The North-South War

Although there were Communist-led guerrilla attacks on Diem's government during the mid-1950s, the real campaign to 'liberate' the South began in 1959 when Hanoi, responding to the demands of Southern cadres that they be allowed to resist the Diem regime, changed from a strategy of 'political struggle' to one of 'armed struggle'. Shortly thereafter, the Ho Chi Minh Trail, which had been in existence for several years, was expanded. In April 1960, universal military conscription was implemented in the North. Eight months later, Hanoi announced the formation of the National Liberation Front (NLF), whose platform called for a neutralisation of Vietnam, the withdrawal of all foreign troops and gradual reunification of the north and south. In the South, the NLF came to be known derogatorily as the 'Viet Cong' or just the 'VC'; both are abbreviations for Viet Nam Cong San, which means 'Vietnamese Communist' (today, the words 'Viet Cong' and 'VC' are no longer considered pejorative). American soldiers nicknamed the Viet Cong 'Charlie'.

When the NLF campaign got under way, the military situation of the Diem government rapidly deteriorated. To turn things around, the Strategic Hamlets Programme (Ap Chien Luoc) was begun in 1962. Following tactics employed successfully by the British in Malaya during the 50s, peasants were forcibly moved into fortified 'strategic hamlets' in order to deny the Viet Cong bases of support. The programme was widely criticised for incompetence and brutality, and many of the strategic hamlets were infiltrated by the VC and fell under their control. The Strategic Hamlets Programme was finally abandoned with the death of President Diem, but after the war ended the VC admitted that the programme had caused them very serious concern and that they had expended a major effort sabotaging it.

And for the South it was no longer just a battle with the VC. In 1964, Hanoi began infiltrating regular North Vietnamese Army (NVA) units into the south. By early 1965, the Saigon government was in desperate straits; desertions from the Army of the Republic of Vietnam (ARVN), whose command was notorious for corruption and incompetence, had reached 2000 per month. It was losing 500 men and a district capital each week, yet since 1954 only one senior South Vietnamese army officer had been wounded. The army was getting ready to evacuate Hué and Danang, and the Central Highlands seemed about to fall. The South Vietnamese general staff even prepared a plan to move its headquarters from Saigon to the Vung Tau peninsula, which was easy to defend and was only minutes from ships that could spirit them out of the country. It was at this point that the USA committed its first combat troops.

## Enter the Americans

The first Americans to set foot in Vietnam were the crew of the clipper ship *Franklin* under the command of Captain John White of Salem, Massachusetts, which docked at Saigon in 1820. Edmund Roberts, a New Englander selected by President Andrew Jackson, led the first official American mission to Vietnam in 1832. In 1845, the USS *Constitution* under Captain 'Mad Jack' Percival sent an armed party ashore at Hué to rescue a French bishop who was under sentence of death, taking several Vietnamese officials hostage. When this failed to convince Emperor Thieu Tri to free the bishop, Percival's men opened fire on a crowd of civilians. In the 1870s, Emperor Tu Duc sent a respected scholar, Bui Vien, to Washington in an attempt to garner international support to counter the French. Bui Vien met President Ulysses S Grant, but lacking the proper documents of accreditation was sent back to Vietnam empty-handed.

The theory was rapidly gaining acceptance in the west that there was a worldwide Communist movement intent on overthrowing one government after another by waging various 'wars of liberation' (the 'Domino Theory', as it came to be known). The Domino Theory gained considerable support after the start of the Korean War in 1950, and the Americans saw France's colonial war in Indochina as an important part of the worldwide struggle to stop Communist expansion. By 1954, US military aid to the French war effort topped two billion dollars (and that's 1950s dollars). In 1950, 35 US soldiers arrived in Vietnam as part of the US Military Assistance Advisory Group (MAAG), ostensibly to instruct troops receiving US weapons how to use them; there would be American soldiers on Vietnamese soil for the next 25 years.

The People's Republic of China established diplomatic relations with the Democratic Republic of Vietnam in 1950; shortly thereafter, the Soviet Union did the same. Only then did Washington recognise Bao Dai's French-backed government. The circumstances of this event are instructive:

though Ho's government had been around since 1945, the USSR didn't get around to recognising it until the Communist Chinese did so, and the US State Department – which at the time was reverberating with recriminations over who was to blame for 'losing China' to Communism – recognised Bao Dai's government as a reaction to these events. From that point on, US policy in Indochina largely became a knee-jerk reaction against whatever the Communists did.

When the last French troops left Vietnam in April 1956, the MAAG, now numbering several hundred men, assumed responsibility for training the South Vietnamese military; the transition couldn't have been neater. The first American troops to die in Vietnam were killed at Bien Hoa in 1959 at a time when about 700 US military personnel were in the country.

As the military position of the South Vietnamese government continued to deteriorate, the Kennedy administration (1961-63) sent more and more military advisers to Vietnam. By the end of 1963, there were 16,300 US military personnel in the country.

Vietnam became a central issue in the USA's 1964 presidential election. The candidate for the Republican Party, Senator Barry Goldwater of Arizona, took the more aggressive stance – he warned that if elected he would tell Ho Chi Minh to stop the war 'or there won't be enough left of North Vietnam to grow rice on it'. Many Americans, with bitter memories of how Chinese troops came to the aid of North Korea during the Korean War, feared the same would happen again if the US invaded North Vietnam. The thought of a possible nuclear confrontation with Russia could not be ruled out either. With such horrors in mind, voters overwhelming supported Lyndon Baines Johnson.

Ironically, it was 'peace candidate' Johnson who rapidly escalated the USA's involvement in the war. A major turning-point in American strategy was precipitated by the August 1964 Tonkin Gulf Incidents in which two American destroyers, the *Maddox* and the *Turner Joy*, claimed to have come

under 'unprovoked' attack while sailing off the North Vietnamese coast. Subsequent research indicates that the first attack took place while the *Maddox* was in North Vietnamese territorial waters assisting a secret South Vietnamese commando raid and that the second attack simply never took place.

But on President Lyndon Johnson's orders, carrier-based jets flew 64 sorties against the North, the first of thousands of such missions that would hit every single road and rail bridge in the country, as well as 4000 of North Vietnam's 5788 villages. Two American aircraft were lost and the pilot of one, Lieutenant Everett Alvarez, became the first American prisoner of war (POW) of the conflict; he would remain in captivity for eight years.

A few days later, an indignant (and misled) Congress almost unanimously (two senators dissented) passed the Tonkin Gulf Resolution, which gave the president the power to 'take all necessary measures' to 'repel any armed attack against the forces of the United States and to prevent further aggression'. Only later was it established that the Johnson administration had in fact drafted the resolution before the 'attacks' had actually taken place. Until its repeal in 1970, the resolution was treated by US presidents as a blank cheque to do whatever they chose in Vietnam without congressional oversight.

As the military situation of the Saigon government reached a new nadir, the first US combat troops splashed ashore at Danang in March 1965, ostensibly to defend Danang air base. But once you had 'American boys' fighting and dying, you had to do everything necessary to protect and support them, including sending over more American boys. By December 1965, 184,300 American military personnel were in Vietnam, and American dead numbered 636. Twelve months later, the totals were 385,300 US troops in Vietnam and 6644 dead. By December 1967, 485,600 US soldiers were in the country and 16,021 had died. In 1967, with South Vietnamese and 'Free World Forces' counted in, there were 1.3 million men – one for every

15 people in South Vietnam – under arms for the Saigon government.

By 1966, the failed Strategic Hamlets Programme of earlier years was replaced with a policy of 'pacification', 'search and destroy' and 'free-fire zones'. Pacification meant building a pro-government civilian infrastructure of teachers, health-care workers and officials in each village, as well as soldiers to guard them and keep the VC away from the villagers. To protect the villages from VC raids, mobile 'search and destroy' units of soldiers moved around the country (often by helicopter) to hunt bands of VC guerrillas. In some cases, villagers were evacuated so the Americans could use heavy weapons like bombs, napalm, artillery and tanks in areas that were declared 'free-fire zones'. A relatively little publicised strategy was dubbed 'Operation Phoenix', a controversial programme run by the CIA aimed at eliminating VC cadres by assassination, capture or defection.

These strategies were only partially successful – US forces could control the countryside by day while the VC usually controlled it by night. The VC proved adept at infiltrating 'pacified' villages. Although lacking heavy weapons like tanks and aircraft, VC guerrillas still continued to inflict heavy casualties on US and ARVN troops in ambushes and by using mines and booby traps. Although free-fire zones were supposed to prevent civilian casualties, plenty of villagers were nevertheless shelled, bombed, strafed and napalmed to death – their surviving relatives often joined the Viet Cong.

## The Turning Point

In January 1968, North Vietnamese troops launched a major attack at Khe Sanh. This battle, the single largest of the war, was in part a massive diversion for what was to come only a week later: the Tet Offensive.

The Tet Offensive of early 1968 marked a crucial turning point in the war. On the evening of 31 January, as the country celebrated the New Year, the Viet Cong launched a stunning offensive in over 100 cities and

towns, including Saigon. As the TV cameras rolled, a VC commando team took over the courtyard of the downtown-Saigon US embassy building.

The American forces had long been wanting to engage the VC in an open battle rather than a guerrilla war where the enemy couldn't be seen. The Tet Offensive provided the opportunity. Though taken by complete surprise (a major failure of US military intelligence), the South Vietnamese and Americans quickly counterattacked with massive firepower, bombing and shelling heavily populated cities as they had the open jungle. The effect was devastating on the VC, but also on the civilian population. In Ben Tre, an American officer bitterly explained that 'we had to destroy the town in order to save it'.

The Tet Offensive killed about 1000 American soldiers and 2000 ARVN troops, but Viet Cong losses were more than 10 times higher at approximately 32,000 deaths. In addition, some 500 Americans and 10,000 North Vietnamese troops died at the battle of Khe Sanh a week before the Tet Offensive began. According to American estimates, 165,000 civilians also died in the three weeks following the start of the Tet Offensive; two million more became refugees.

The VC only held the cities for three or four days (with the exception of Hué, which they held for 25 days). The surviving VC then retreated to the jungles. The VC had hoped that their offensive would lead to a popular uprising against the Americans and that ARVN forces would desert or switch sides – this did not happen. General William Westmoreland, commander of US forces in Vietnam, insisted that the uprising had been a failure and a decisive military blow to the Communists (and he was right – by their own admission, the VC never recovered from their high casualties). Westmoreland then asked for an additional 206,000 troops – he didn't get them and was replaced in July by General Creighton W Abrams.

Perhaps the VC lost the battle, but they were far from losing the war. After years of hearing that they were winning, many

Americans – having watched the killing and chaos in Saigon on their nightly TV newscasts – stopped believing what they were being told by their government. While US generals were proclaiming a great victory, public tolerance of the war and its casualties reached the breaking point. For the VC, the Tet Offensive proved to be a big success after all – it made the cost of fighting the war (both in dollars and in lives) unbearable for the Americans.

Anti-war demonstrations rocked US campuses and spilled out into the streets. Seeing his political popularity plummet in the polls, President Johnson decided not to stand for re-election.

Richard Nixon was elected president of the USA, in part because of a promise that he had a 'secret plan' to end the war. Many suspected that his secret plan would be a military invasion of North Vietnam, but it didn't turn out that way. The plan, later to be labelled the 'Nixon Doctrine', was unveiled in July 1969 and called on Asian nations to be more 'self-reliant' in defence matters and not expect the USA to become embroiled in future civil wars. Nixon's strategy called for 'Vietnamisation' – making the South Vietnamese military fight the war without American troops.

Nixon Doctrine or not, the first half of 1969 saw still greater escalation. In April, the number of US soldiers in Vietnam reached an all-time high of 543,400. By the end of 1969, US troop levels were down to 475,200; 40,024 Americans had been killed in action, as had 110,176 ARVN troops. While the fighting raged, Nixon's chief negotiator, Henry Kissinger, pursued talks in Paris with his North Vietnamese counterpart Le Duc Tho.

In 1969, the USA began secretly bombing Cambodia. The following year, American ground forces were sent into Cambodia to extricate ARVN units whose fighting ability was still unable to match the enemy's. This new escalation infuriated previously quiescent elements of the American public, leading to bitter anti-war protests. The TV screens of America were almost daily filled with scenes of demonstrations, student strikes and even deadly acts of self-immolation. A peace demonstration at Kent State University in Ohio resulted in four protesters being shot dead by National Guard troops.

The rise of organisations like 'Vietnam Veterans Against the War' demonstrated that it wasn't just 'cowardly students fearing military conscription' who wanted the USA out of Vietnam. It was clear that the war was ripping the USA apart. Nor were the protests just confined to the USA – huge anti-American demonstrations in Western Europe were shaking the NATO alliance. There was even a Vietnamese peace movement – at great risk to themselves, idealistic young students in Saigon protested against the US presence in their country.

In 1971, excerpts from a scandalous top secret study of US involvement in Indochina were published in the New York Times after a legal battle which went to the US Supreme Court. The study, known as the 'Pentagon Papers', was commissioned by the US Defense Department and detailed how the military and former presidents had systematically lied to Congress and the American public. The Pentagon Papers infuriated the US public and caused anti-war sentiment to reach new heights. The New York Times obtained the study from one of its authors, Dr Daniel Ellsberg, who had turned against the war. Ellsberg was subsequently prosecuted for espionage, theft and conspiracy. A judge dismissed the charges after Nixon's notorious 'White House Plumbers' (so called because they were supposed to stop 'leaks') burgled the office of Ellsberg's psychiatrist to obtain evidence.

In the spring of 1972, the North Vietnamese launched an offensive across the 17th parallel; the USA responded with increased bombing of the North and mined seven North Vietnamese harbours. The 'Christmas Bombing' of Hanoi and Haiphong at the end of 1972 was meant to wrest concessions from North Vietnam at the negotiating table. Finally, Henry Kissinger and Le Duc Tho reached agreement. The Paris Agreements, signed by the USA, North Vietnam, South

Vietnam and the Viet Cong on 27 January 1973, provided for a cease-fire, the establishment of a National Council of Reconciliation and Concord, the total withdrawal of US combat forces and the release of 590 American POWs. The agreement made no mention of approximately 200,000 North Vietnamese troops then in South Vietnam.

Richard Nixon was re-elected president in November 1972, shortly before the Paris peace agreements were signed. By 1973, he became hopelessly mired in the 'Watergate Scandal' resulting from illegal activities regarding his re-election campaign. The Pentagon Papers and Watergate contributed to such a high level of public distrust of the military and presidents that the US Congress passed a resolution prohibiting any further US military involvement in Indochina after 15 August 1973. Nixon resigned in disgrace in 1974 and was succeeded by Gerald Ford.

In total, 3.14 million Americans (including 7200 women) served in the US armed forces in Vietnam during the war. Officially, 58,183 Americans (including eight women) were killed in action or are listed as missing-in-action. The US losses were nearly double that of the Korean War. Pentagon figures indicate that by 1972, 3689 fixed-wing aircraft and 4857 helicopters had been lost and 15 million tonnes of ammunition had been expended. The direct cost of the war was officially put at US$165 billion, though its true cost to the economy was at least twice that. By comparison, the Korean War had cost America US$18 billion.

By the end of 1973, 223,748 South Vietnamese soldiers had been killed in action; North Vietnamese and Viet Cong fatalities have been estimated at one million. Approximately four million civilians – 10% of the population of Vietnam – were killed or injured during the war, many in the North due to the American bombing. Over 2200 Americans and 300,000 Vietnamese are still listed as missing-in-action.

As far as anyone knows, the Soviet Union and China – who supplied all the weapons to North Vietnam and the Viet Cong – did not suffer a single casualty.

## Other Foreign Involvement

Australia, New Zealand, South Korea, Thailand and the Philippines sent military personnel to South Vietnam as part of what the Americans called the 'Free World Military Forces', whose purpose was to internationalise the American war effort and thus confer upon it legitimacy. The Korean (who numbered nearly 50,000), Thai and Filipino forces were heavily subsidised by the Americans.

Australia's participation in the Vietnamese conflict constituted the most significant commitment of Australian military forces overseas since the 1940s. At its peak strength, the Australian forces in Vietnam – which included army, navy and air force units – numbered 8300, two-thirds larger than the size of the Australian contingent in the Korean War. Overall, 46,852 Australian military personnel served in Vietnam, including 17,424 draftees; Australian casualties totalled 496 killed and 2398 wounded.

Most of New Zealand's contingent, which numbered 548 at its high point in 1968, operated as an integral part of the Australian Task Force, which was stationed near Baria (just north of Vung Tau).

The Australian foreign affairs establishment decided to commit Australian troops to America's cause in order to encourage US military involvement in South-East Asia. This, they argued, would further Australia's defence interests by having the Americans play an active role in an area of great importance to Australia's long-term security. The first Australian troops in Vietnam were 30 guerrilla warfare specialists, with experience in Malaya and Borneo, sent to Vietnam in May 1962. Australia announced the commitment of combat units in April 1965, only a few weeks after the first American combat troops arrived in Danang. The last Australian combat troops withdrew in December 1971; the last advisers returned home a year later. The Australian and New Zealand forces preferred to operate independently of US units, in part because they felt that the Americans took unnecessary risks and were willing to sustain unacceptably high numbers of casualties.

Royal Thai army troops were stationed in Vietnam from 1967 to 1973; Thailand also allowed the US Air Force to base B-52s and fighter aircraft on its territory. The Philippines sent units for non-combat 'civic action' work. South Korea's soldiers, who operated in the South between 1965 and 1971, were noted for both their exceptional fighting ability and extreme brutality.

Taiwan's brief role was one of the most under-reported facts of the war because it was such an embarrassment. At that time, the USA still recognised Taiwan's ruling Kuomintang as the legitimate government of all China. Ever since 1949, when the Kuomintang troops were defeated by the Communists, Taiwan's president Chiang Kaishek had been promising to 'retake the mainland'. When US president Johnson asked Taiwan to supply around 20,000 troops, Chiang was happy to comply, and some troops were immediately dispatched to Saigon. Chiang then rapidly tried to increase the number to 200,000! It soon became apparent that Chiang was planning to use Vietnam as a stepping stone to invade mainland China and draw the USA into his personal war against the Chinese Communists. The USA wanted no part of this and asked Chiang to withdraw his troops from South Vietnam – it was promptly done and the whole incident was hushed up.

It's not generally known that Spain's General Franco – whose regime was regarded by the USA as a bulwark against Communism – supplied about 50 military personnel to the war effort. However, their role was noncombatant.

### Fall of the South (1975)

Except for a small contingent of technicians and CIA agents, all US military personnel were out of Vietnam by 1973. The bombing of North Vietnam had ceased and the American POWs were released, but the guerrilla war was still on – the only difference was that the fighting had been thoroughly 'Vietnamised'. However, foreign powers continued to bankroll the war. America supplied the South Vietnamese military with weapons, ammunition and fuel while the USSR and China did the same for the North.

Although the USA had ended its combat role, anti-war organisations such as the Indochina Resource Center continued to lobby the US government to cut off all financial and military assistance to South Vietnam. They nearly succeeded – the US Senate came within two votes of doing just that. While the anti-war lobby failed to cut off all funding, they did succeed in having it greatly reduced. In 1975, America gave South Vietnam US$700 million in aid, less than half of what military experts estimated was needed. The South Vietnamese suddenly found that they were running desperately low on stocks of ammunition and fuel.

The North Vietnamese were quick to assess the situation. They continued a major military buildup and in January 1975 launched a massive conventional ground attack across the 17th parallel using tanks and heavy artillery. The invasion – a blatant violation of the Paris agreements – panicked the South Vietnamese army and government, which in the past had always depended on the Americans. In March, the NVA quickly occupied a strategic section of the Central Highlands at Buon Ma Thuot. In the absence of US military support or advice, President Nguyen Van Thieu personally decided on a strategy of tactical withdrawal to more defensible positions. This proved to be a spectacular military blunder. Rather than stand and fight as expected, South Vietnamese troops were ordered to retreat from Central Highland bases at Pleiku and Kon Tum. The totally unplanned withdrawal was a disaster. Retreating ARVN soldiers were intercepted and attacked by the well-disciplined North Vietnamese troops. The withdrawal became a rout as panicked ARVN soldiers deserted en masse in order to try to save their families.

Whole brigades of ARVN soldiers disintegrated and fled southward, joining the hundreds of thousands of civilians clogging National Highway 1. City after city – Buon

Ma Thuot, Quang Tri, Hué, Danang, Qui Nhon, Tuy Hoa, Nha Trang – were simply abandoned by the defenders with hardly a shot fired. So quickly did the ARVN troops flee that the North Vietnamese army could barely keep up with them. The US Congress, fed up with the war and its drain on the treasury, refused to send emergency aid that President Nixon (who had resigned the previous year because of Watergate) had promised would be forthcoming in the event of such an invasion.

President Nguyen Van Thieu, in power since 1967, resigned on 21 April 1975 and fled the country, allegedly taking with him millions of dollars in ill-gotten wealth. He moved to Britain, rather than the USA, and bitterly blamed the Americans for 'abandoning' his regime.

President Thieu was replaced by Vice President Tran Van Huong, who quit a week later, turning the presidency over to General Duong Van Minh, who surrendered on the morning of 30 April 1975 in Saigon's Independence Palace (now Reunification Palace) after only 43 hours in office.

The last Americans were evacuated to US ships stationed offshore, transported by helicopter from the US embassy roof just a few hours before South Vietnam surrendered. Thus brought to an end more than a decade of US military involvement. Throughout the entire episode, the USA had never declared war on North Vietnam.

The Americans weren't the only ones who left. As the South collapsed, 135,000 Vietnamese also fled the country; in the next five years, at least 545,000 of their compatriots would do the same. Those who left by sea would become known to the world as 'boat people'.

## Since Reunification

On the first day of their victory, the Communists changed Saigon's name to Ho Chi Minh City. That proved to be only the first change of many.

The sudden success of the 1975 North Vietnamese offensive surprised the North almost as much as it did the South. As a result, Hanoi had not prepared specific plans to deal with integrating the two parts of the country, whose social and economic systems could hardly have been more different.

The North was faced with the legacy of a cruel and protracted war that had literally fractured the country; there was understandable bitterness (if not hatred) on both sides, and a mind-boggling array of problems. War damage extended from unmarked minefields to war-focussed, dysfunctional economies, from vast acreages of chemically poisoned countryside to millions of people who had been affected physically or mentally. The country was diplomatically isolated and its old allies were no longer willing or able to provide significant aid. Peace may have arrived, but in many ways the war was far from over.

Until the formal reunification of Vietnam in July 1976, the South was nominally ruled by a Provisional Revolutionary Government. Because the Communist Party did not really trust the Southern urban intelligentsia – even those of its members who had supported the Viet Cong – large numbers of Northern cadres were sent southward to manage the transition. This created resentment among Southerners who had worked against the Thieu government and then, after its overthrow, found themselves frozen out of positions of responsibility (even today, most of the officials and police in Saigon are from the North).

After months of debates, those in Hanoi who wanted to implement a rapid transition to socialism (including the collectivisation of agriculture) in the South gained the upper hand. Great efforts were made to deal with the South's social problems: millions of illiterates and unemployed, several hundred thousand prostitutes and drug addicts, and tens of thousands of people who made their living by criminal activities. Many of these people were encouraged to move to the newly collectivised farms in the countryside. This may have had some beneficial effects, but the results of the transition to socialism were mostly disastrous to the South's economy.

## Disorderly Departure

The Orderly Departure Programme (ODP), carried out under the auspices of the United Nations High Commission for Refugees (UNHCR), was designed to allow orderly resettlement in the west (mostly in the USA) of Vietnamese political refugees who otherwise might have tried to flee the country by land or sea. After years of stalling by Hanoi, the programme finally began functioning properly at the end of the 1980s and thousands of Vietnamese and their families were flown via Bangkok to the Philippines, where they underwent six months of English instruction before proceeding to the USA.

The ODP failed to stem the flow of refugees from the north. After the Vietnam-China border opened in 1990, many refugees simply took the train to China, from where they only had to take a short boat ride across the Pearl River to Hong Kong to be declared 'boat people'. As the refugee camps in Hong Kong swelled to the bursting point, the public's patience ran out. 'Refugee fatigue' became the new buzzword in Hong Kong and the public demanded that something be done.

China's government also insisted that something be done. With Hong Kong's return to China in 1997 (after 156 years as a British colony), the last thing the Chinese wanted was to inherit Vietnamese refugees.

Since all but a handful of the arrivals were declared to be economic migrants rather than political refugees, the Hong Kong government experimented with forcible repatriations in 1990. This prompted a vehement protest from the USA and the UNHCR. The Hong Kong government backed off temporarily, but held negotiations with Vietnam and reached an agreement in October 1991 on a programme of combined voluntary and forced repatriation. Under the agreement, those willing to return would not be penalised by Vietnam and would receive a resettlement allowance of US$30 per month for several months to be paid by the UNHCR. Vietnam also had to agree to give refugees back their citizenship (the previous policy was to strip all refugees of their citizenship, thus rendering them stateless).

The voluntary repatriations didn't go quite as planned; some of the volunteers were back in Hong Kong a few months later seeking another resettlement allowance. In such cases, forcible repatriation swiftly followed. The programme produced results – by the end of 1992 practically no new Vietnamese refugees arrived in Hong Kong.

Nevertheless, solving the refugee problem was not so easy as simply herding the refugees onto aircraft and flying them to Vietnam. Among the thousands of legitimate refugees was a small hardcore faction of misfits with a criminal past. The Vietnamese government didn't want them back. Hong Kong certainly didn't want them either, nor would any western countries roll out the welcome mat. And so the worst of the refugees were stuck in the camps behind razor wire, preying on each other and staging occasionally violent protests over their grim situation. Major riots broke out in the camps in 1995 and 1996, and some of the refugees escaped. They may still be hiding in Hong Kong, possibly surviving by illegal means such as theft, smuggling, drug dealing and prostitution.

However, the refugee problem may be the least of Hong Kong's problems. China's critics note with some irony that the illegal Vietnamese refugees might be the only ones willing to stay in Hong Kong after 1997. Many Hong Kongers themselves have already fled and many of those who remain have obtained second passports. If China does anything to hurt the economy of its newly acquired colony, Hong Kong may face a 'refugee crisis' of a different sort. ∎

---

Reunification was accompanied by large-scale political repression. Despite repeated promises to the contrary, hundreds of thousands of people who had ties to the previous regime had their property and homes confiscated and were subsequently rounded up and imprisoned without trial in forced-labour camps euphemistically known as 're-education camps'. Tens of thousands of business people, intellectuals, artists, journalists, writers, trade-union leaders, Buddhist monks, Catholic priests and Protestant clergy – some of whom had opposed both Thieu and the war – were detained under horrendous conditions.

Some were able to buy themselves out, but most of the wealthy people simply had their bank accounts and property confiscated. While the majority of the detainees were released within a few years, some (declared to be 'obstinate and counterrevolutionary elements') were to spend the next decade or more in the camps. The purge and terrible economic conditions prompted hundreds of thousands of Southerners to flee their homeland by sea and overland through Cambodia.

The purge affected not only former opponents of the Communists, but also their families. Even today, the children of former 'counterrevolutionaries' can be discriminated against. One way this is done is to deny a *ho khau*, a sort of residence permit needed for attending school, seeking employment, owning farmland, a home or a business and so on.

Relations with China to the north and its Khmer Rouge allies to the west were rapidly deteriorating and war-weary Vietnam seemed beset by enemies.

An anti-capitalist campaign was launched in March 1978, during which private property and businesses were seized. Most of the victims were ethnic-Chinese – hundreds of thousands soon became refugees, and relations with China soured further. Meanwhile, repeated attacks on Vietnamese border villages by the Khmer Rouge forced Vietnam to respond. Vietnamese forces entered Cambodia at the end of 1978. They succeeded in driving the Khmer Rouge from power in early 1979 and set up a pro-Hanoi regime in Phnom Penh.

China viewed the attack on their Khmer Rouge allies as a serious provocation. In February 1979, Chinese forces invaded Vietnam and fought a brief, 17-day war before withdrawing.

Khmer Rouge forces, with support from China and Thailand, continued a costly guerrilla war against the Vietnamese on Cambodian soil for the next decade. Vietnam pulled its forces out of Cambodia in September 1989. The Cambodian civil war was officially settled in 1992 and United Nations peace-keeping forces were called in to monitor the peace agreement. Although Khmer Rouge units continue to violate the terms of the peace plan, Vietnam is no longer involved in the conflict. For the first time since WWII began, Vietnam is finally at peace.

## Opening the Door

The recent liberalisation of foreign investment laws and the relaxation of visa regulations for tourists seem to be part of a general Vietnamese opening-up to the world.

Sweden, the first western country to establish diplomatic relations with Hanoi, did so in 1969; since that time, most western nations have followed suit.

The Soviet Union began its first cautious opening to the west in 1984 with the appointment of Mikhail Gorbachev as Secretary General of the Communist Party. Vietnam followed suit in 1986 by choosing reform-minded Nguyen Van Linh as General Secretary of the Vietnamese Communist Party. However, the dramatic changes in Eastern Europe and the USSR were not viewed with favour in Hanoi. The Vietnamese Communist Party denounced the participation of non-Communists in Eastern Bloc governments, calling the democratic revolutions 'a counterattack from imperialist circles' against socialism.

General Secretary Linh declared at the end of 1989 that 'we resolutely reject pluralism, a multiparty system and opposition parties'. But in February 1990, the government called for more openness and criticism. The response came swiftly, with an outpouring of news articles, editorials and letters from the public condemning corruption, inept leadership and the high living standards of senior officials while most people lived in extreme poverty. Taken aback by the harsh criticism, official control over literature, the arts and the media were tightened once again in a campaign against 'deviant ideological viewpoints'. An effort was made to blame public dissatisfaction on foreign imperialists. Interior Minister Mai Chi Tho wrote in the army's newspaper:

Through modern communications means and newspapers, letters and video tapes brought to Vietnam, they have conducted virulent attacks against Marxism-Leninism and the Party's leadership, blaming all socio-economic difficulties on the Communist Party in order to demand political pluralism, a multiparty system and bourgeois-type democracy.

At age 75, ailing Party Secretary General Nguyen Van Linh was replaced in June 1991 by Prime Minister Do Muoi. Regarded as a conservative, Muoi nevertheless vowed to continue the economic reforms started by Linh. At the same time, a major shake-up of the ruling Politburo and Central Committee of the Communist Party saw many members forcibly retired and replaced by younger, more liberal-minded leaders. The sudden collapse of the USSR just two months later caused the government to reiterate its stand that political pluralism would not be tolerated, but at the same time economic reforms were speeded up.

Secretary General Do Muoi and Prime Minister Vo Van Kiet visited Beijing in November 1991 to heal Vietnam's 12-year rift with China. The visit was reciprocated in December 1992 when Chinese prime minister Li Peng visited Hanoi. Although it was all smiles and warm handshakes in front of the cameras, relations between Vietnam and China still remain tense. On the other hand, trade across the China-Vietnam border (both legal and otherwise) is booming.

Vietnam has also seen considerable easing of tensions with its old nemesis, the USA. In early 1994, the USA lifted its economic embargo, which had been in place against the old North Vietnam since the 1960s. With the embargo removed, Vietnam is now able to obtain loans from the International Monetary Fund (IMF), import high-tech goods and do business directly with American companies.

Full diplomatic relations with the USA have been restored. The USA has established an embassy in Hanoi and Vietnam has an embassy in Washington, DC.

## GEOGRAPHY

Vietnam stretches over 1600km along the eastern coast of the Indochinese Peninsula (from 8°34' N to 23°22' N). The country's land area is 329,566 sq km, including water, or 326,797 sq km of land surface. This makes it slightly larger than Italy and a bit smaller than Japan. Vietnam has 3451km of coastline and land borders of 1555km with Laos, 1281km with China and 982km with Cambodia.

Vietnamese often describe their country as resembling a bamboo pole supporting a basket of rice on each end. The country is S-shaped, broad in the north and south and very narrow in the centre, where at one point it is only 50km wide.

The country's two main cultivated areas

are the Red River Delta (15,000 sq km) in the north and the Mekong Delta (60,000 sq km) in the south. Silt carried by the Red River and its tributaries, which are confined to their paths by 3000km of dikes, has raised the level of the river beds above that of the surrounding plains. Breaches in the levees result in disastrous flooding.

Three-quarters of the country consists of mountains and hills, the highest of which is 3143m-high Fansipan (also spelled Phan Si Pan) in the Hoang Lien Mountains in the far north-west. The Truong Son Mountains (Annamite Cordillera), which form the Central Highlands, run almost the full length of the country along Vietnam's borders with Laos and Cambodia.

The largest metropolis is Ho Chi Minh City (usually still called Saigon), followed by Hanoi, Haiphong and Danang.

## GEOLOGY

There are several notable geological features found in Vietnam, but the most striking by far are the karst formations. Karst consists of irregular limestone in which erosion has produced fissures, caves, sinkholes and underground rivers. The northern part of Vietnam has a spectacular assemblage of these formations, notably around Halong Bay, Bai Tu Long Bay and Tam Coc. At Halong and Bai Tu Long bays, an enormous limestone plateau has gradually sunk into the ocean – the old mountain tops stick out of the sea looking like vertical fingers pointing towards the sky. At Tam Coc, the karst formations are similar except that it is all still above sea level. In the south there is a less impressive collection of these formations around the Ha Tien area in the Mekong Delta. The Marble Mountains near Danang in central Vietnam are yet another example.

Not all of Vietnam's mountains consist of limestone. The coastal ranges near Nha Trang and at Hai Van Pass (Danang), for example, are composed of granite. The giant granite boulders littering the hillsides can be quite an impressive sight.

The western part of the Central Highlands (near Buon Me Thuot and Pleiku) is known for its red volcanic soil, which is extremely fertile. However, the highlands are just that – high above sea level, but mostly flat land and not too scenic.

The Mekong River has produced one of the world's great deltas, composed of fine silt which has washed downstream for millions of years. The silt is fertile and supports lush tropical vegetation. The Mekong Delta continues to grow at a rate of about 100m per year, though global warming (and a consequent rise in world sea levels) could submerge it.

## CLIMATE

There are no good or bad seasons for visiting Vietnam. When one region is wet or cold or steamy hot, there is always somewhere else that is sunny and pleasantly warm.

Vietnam has a remarkably diverse climate because of its wide range of latitudes and altitudes. Although the entire country lies in the tropics and subtropics, local conditions vary from frosty winters in the far northern hills to the year-round, sub-equatorial warmth of the Mekong Delta. Because about one-third of Vietnam is more than 500m above sea level, much of the country enjoys a subtropical or – above 2000m – even a temperate climate.

Vietnam lies in the East Asian monsoon zone. Its weather is determined by two monsoons, which set the rhythm of rural life. The winter monsoon comes from the north-east between October and March and brings wet chilly winters to all areas north of Nha Trang, but dry and warm temperatures to the south. From April or May to October, the south-western monsoon blows, its winds laden with moisture picked up while crossing the Indian Ocean and the Gulf of Thailand. The south-western monsoon brings warm, humid weather to the whole country except those areas sheltered by mountains (such as the central coastal lowlands and the Red River Delta).

Between July and November, violent and unpredictable typhoons often develop over the ocean east of Vietnam, hitting central and northern Vietnam with devastating results.

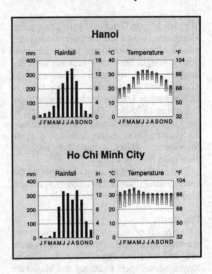

Most of Vietnam receives about 2000mm of rain annually, though parts of the Central Highlands get approximately 3300mm of precipitation per annum.

### The South

The south, where the climate is sub-equatorial, has two main seasons: the wet and the dry. The wet season lasts from May to November (June to August are the wettest months). During this time, there are heavy but short-lived downpours almost daily, usually in the afternoon. The dry season runs from December to April. Late February through May is hot and very humid, but things cool down slightly when the summer rainy season begins.

In Saigon, the average annual temperature is 27°C. In April, daily highs are usually in the low 30s. In January, the daily lows average 21°C. Average humidity is 80% and annual rainfall averages 1979mm. The coldest temperature ever recorded in Saigon is 14°C.

### Central Vietnam

The coastal lowlands are denied significant rainfall from the south-western monsoon

(April or May to October) by the Truong Son Mountains, which are very wet during this period. Much of the coastal strip's precipitation is brought between December and February by the north-eastern monsoon. Nha Trang's dry season lasts from June to October while Dalat's dry season goes from December to March. Dalat, like the rest of the Central Highlands, is much cooler than the Mekong Delta and the coastal strip. From November to March, Dalat's daily highs are usually in the low to mid-20s.

The cold and wet winter weather of the north-central coastal lowlands is accompanied by fog and fine drizzle.

## The North

Areas north of the 18th parallel have two seasons: winter and summer. Winter is quite cool and wet, and usually lasts from about November to April. February and March are marked by a persistent drizzling rain the Vietnamese call 'rain dust' *(crachin)*. The hot summers run from May to October. The north is subject to occasional devastating typhoons during the summer months.

## ECOLOGY & ENVIRONMENT

Vietnam's environment is not in the worst of shape, but there are troubling signs. Because Vietnam is a poor, densely populated agricultural country, humans often compete head-on with native plants and animals for the same resources.

Deforestation is perhaps the most serious problem. Originally, almost the whole of Vietnam was covered with dense forests. Since the arrival of the first human beings many millennia ago, Vietnam has been progressively denuded of forest cover. While 44% of the original forest cover was extant in 1943, by 1976 only 29% remained, by 1983 only 24% was left and in 1995 it was down to 20%.

Each hectare of land denuded of vegetation contributes to the flooding of areas downstream from water catchment areas, irreversible soil erosion (upland soils are especially fragile), the silting up of rivers, streams, lakes and reservoirs, loss of wildlife habitat and unpredictable climatic changes.

For many years, Vietnam has had an active reafforestation programme in which Ho Chi Minh himself is said to have taken a keen interest. However, only 36% of the 8720 sq km of land on which trees were planted between 1955 and 1979 was still forested at the end of the period. Currently, about 1600 sq km are planted with some 500 million trees each year. The Ministry of Education has made the planting and taking care of trees by pupils part of the curriculum. However, even at this rate, reafforestation is not keeping up with forest losses. In 1992, Vietnam announced the banning of unprocessed timber exports.

Vietnam has some interesting wildlife, but it is rapidly disappearing. The cause is mostly destruction of wildlife habitat, though hunting, poaching and pollution all take their toll.

Vietnam has so far suffered little industrial pollution largely because there are not many industries to do the polluting. However, the nation's rapid economic and population growth indicate environmental trouble ahead. The dramatic increase in noisy, smoke-spewing motorbikes over the past few years should be taken as a sign of abominations to come.

## FLORA & FAUNA
### Flora

Despite widespread deforestation, Vietnam's vegetation is what you'd expect to find in a tropical country – abundant and varied.

The remaining forests of Vietnam are estimated to still contain 12,000 plant species, only 7000 of which have been identified and 2300 of which are known to be useful to humans for food, medicines, animal fodder, wood products and other purposes.

Some have found it suspicious that Australian aid in the field of forestry has been accompanied by the sudden appearance of large tracts of young eucalyptus trees in the Vietnamese countryside. Are we witnessing a form of ecological imperialism?

## Fauna

Because Vietnam includes a wide range of habitats – ranging from equatorial lowlands to high, temperate plateaux and even alpine peaks – the country's wild fauna is enormously diverse. Vietnam is home to 273 species of mammals, 773 species of birds, 180 species of reptiles, 80 species of amphibians, hundreds of species of fish and thousands of kinds of invertebrates. Larger animals of special importance in conservation efforts include the elephant, rhinoceros, tiger, leopard, black bear, honey bear, snub-nosed monkey, douc langur (remarkable for its variegated colours), concolour gibbon, macaque, rhesus monkey, serow (a kind of mountain goat), flying squirrel, kouprey (a blackish-brown forest ox), banteng (a kind of wild ox), deer, peacock, pheasant, crocodile, python, cobra and turtle.

**Wildlife Books** Useful books about Vietnam's wildlife are few and far between, and some of the better ones produced in the Vietnamese language are no longer in print. *A Guide to the Birds of Thailand* (Philip Round & Boonsong Lakagul, Saha Kam Bhaet Company, 1991) covers the majority if not all of Vietnam's birds. It's particularly relevant to the bird species in the southern and central regions of Vietnam. Slightly out-of-date and difficult to use is *A Field Guide to the Birds of South-East Asia* (Ben King, Martin Woodcock & Edward Dickinson, Collins, 1975), but it gives thorough coverage to Vietnam. These two books are not available in Vietnam, but you should be able to find them in Bangkok (try Asia Books).

## Endangered Species

Tragically, Vietnam's wildlife is in a precipitous decline as forest habitats are destroyed and waterways become polluted. In addition, uncontrolled illegal hunting – many people in remote areas have access to weapons left over from the war – has exterminated the local populations of various animals, in some cases eliminating entire species from the country. Officially, the government has recognised 54 species of mammals and 60 species of birds as endangered. The tapir and Sumatran rhinoceros are already extinct in Vietnam, and there are thought to be fewer than 20 koupreys and 20 to 30 Javan rhinoceroses left in the country.

It is encouraging that some wildlife seems to be returning to reafforested areas. For example, birds, fish and crustaceans have reappeared in replanted mangrove swamps. But unless the government takes immediate remedial measures – including banning the sale and export of tiger skins and ivory – hundreds of species of mammals, birds and plants will become extinct within the next decade. Unfortunately, the impact of tourism could speed up the destruction of native species, as one traveller noted:

The locals sell colourful live coral dredged up from the sea floor, which of course goes white and dead in a few hours anyway. Coral reefs are becoming scarce enough without tourists depleting them further. If you want to take home souvenirs, try to find something else besides coral and rare seashells.

Vietnam seems to be the last place in the world where zoologists are discovering previously unknown species of large mammals. None had been found for nearly 50 years until 1992, when a large ox was discovered at Vu Quang in northern Vietnam by John MacKinnon, who was working for the World Wildlife Fund (now renamed World Wide Fund for Nature). This ox was only the fourth large land mammal to be discovered in the 20th century. In 1994, a hitherto-unknown species of muntjac deer was discovered near the same site. It is believed that both animals occur in border areas with Laos and Cambodia, from Nghe An to Dak Lak. However, travellers are advised not to try to see these rare animals in the wild, as they may put them in even greater peril – many local people believe that tourists want to buy skins and skulls. In general, travellers to Vietnam should not buy products made from wildlife.

Continued habitat destruction and poaching means that many now-rare species are headed for the extinction list. Captive breeding programmes may be the only hope for some species.

# Flora & Fauna of Vietnam

Vietnam is a land of high rainfall and diverse landscapes, and consequently supports rich natural vegetation communities. In its original state the land was once virtually covered in forest, from vast mangrove swamps fringing the coast to dense rainforest in mountainous regions. The forests have been progressively pushed back over millennia: first by gradual clearing for the cultivation of rice and other crops, and then by a rapidly expanding population and the ravages of the American War.

Much has been said about the human and economic devastation wrought by the war, but it was also notable as the most intensive attempt to destroy a country's natural environment in history – 'ecocide'. In an effort to destroy natural cover for Viet Cong troops, American forces sprayed 72 million litres of herbicides, known as Agents Orange, White and Blue (after the colour of the canisters in which they were stored), over 16% of South Vietnam's land area.

Although the scars of war can still be seen and much of the damage is irreversible, reafforestation programs have been implemented and today the landscape is showing signs of recovery. Natural forests at higher elevations, such as in the north-west, feature wild rhododendrons, dwarf bamboo and many varieties of orchids; the central coast is drier and features stands of pines; and the river deltas support mangrove forests, which are valuable nurseries for fish and crustaceans and provide feeding sites for many bird species. Scientists are only beginning to catalogue the country's flora and fauna, and few doubt that biological treasures await discovery in remote regions.

Vietnam's fauna is diverse and exciting, and includes rarely seen large mammals, several varieties of monkeys and hundreds of bird species. More than 270 species of mammals have been recorded. Areas in which large animals were thought to have been wiped out by war and poaching are proving to be 'hot spots' of biodiversity and abundance. The once-extensive forests are still home to spectacular examples, such as the tiger, the Asian elephant, the clouded leopard and the sun bear, although their numbers are dwindling under pressure from hunting and habitat destruction. Visitors are far more likely to encounter one or more species of monkeys, such as macaques or rhesus monkeys, and tree squirrels.

Early in the 1990s a small population of the world's rarest rhinoceros, the Javan rhino, was discovered in the Nam Cat Tien National Park, south-west of Dalat. In 1992 Vietnam became the focus of international scientific interest when a new species of mammal was discovered at the Vu Quang reserve. Dubbed the Vu Quang ox, it is a small, boldly marked, forest-dwelling herbivore that resembles a small antelope, although genetically it appears to be akin to the ox.

*Box: The douc langur (or leaf monkey) is notable for its complex digestive system, which has adapted to cope with a diet based largely upon leaves. It has short, grey fur with red and white markings and is endangered in Vietnam.*

*Right: Two new species of mammals have been discovered in the more remote reaches of northern Vietnam since 1992. Pictured is a new species of barking deer, spotted near Vu Quang in 1994.*

*The sun bear is the smallest member of the bear family and is found across the South-East Asian mainland. Sometimes called the honey bear, the sun bear is a shy, mainly nocturnal omnivore, notable for the yellow/orange blaze on its chest. It is endangered in Vietnam.*

The discovery of a hitherto-unknown animal so late in the 20th century in a country with such a high population is in itself extraordinary, but when in 1994 a second mammal new to science was discovered in the same area the full conservation value of this remote, forested region started to dawn on scientists. The second discovery was a species of barking deer that rejoices under the scientific name of *Megamantiacus vuquangensis*. The scientific and conservation interest of these recent discoveries has not been lost on authorities, and the Vietnam government recently expanded the reserve from 16,000 to 60,000 hectares and banned logging in the park.

Vietnam is home to two species of crocodile – the dangerous estuarine crocodile and the Siamese crocodile. Two members of the python family are present (reticulated and Indian) and poisonous snakes include the king cobra, krait and various vipers. A visitor is highly unlikely to encounter either snakes or crocodiles.

Birdwatchers prepared to visit one or more of the national parks will be well rewarded by a trip to Vietnam – more than 770 species have been recorded. Rare and little-known birds previously thought extinct are turning up and more no doubt await, particularly in the extensive forests of the Lao border region. For example, Edwards' pheasant, a species previously thought to be extinct in the wild, was recently rediscovered; other rare and endangered species that have been located by scientific expeditions have included the white-winged wood duck and the white-shouldered ibis.

Even a casual visitor will notice a few birds: swallows and swifts flying over fields and along watercourses; flocks of finches at roadsides and in paddies; and bulbuls and mynas in gardens and patches of forest. Enthusiasts walk the forest trails of Tam Dao Hill Station and Cuc Phuong National Park near Hanoi in search of gems such as pittas, laughing thrushes and various species of pheasants and partridges. The latter is also home to the rare Tonkin leaf monkey. Two good birding locations near Ho Chi Minh City are Dalat and Nam Cat Tien National Park. The range of birds at these two sites is quite different from those in the north, and two or three days in either would be a pleasant diversion for any nature lover. Mammals at Nam Cat Tien include crested and white-cheeked gibbons, the hog badger and the tiger.

Vietnam is on the East Asian Flyway and is an important stopover for migratory waders en route from their breeding grounds in Siberia to their winter quarters in Australia. A coastal reserve has been established at the mouth of the Red River for the protection of these birds, including rare species such as the spoon-billed sandpiper, Nordmann's greenshank and the black-faced spoonbill.

The government is showing enthusiasm for ecological protection and Vietnam today has a surprising amount to offer the visitor interested in wildlife. A total of 87 reserves cover about 3.3% of Vietnam's land area. Recent moves forward in conservation have included the protection of an area straddling the Lao border which includes the provinces of Nghe An, Ha Tinh and Quang Binh in Vietnam and Bolikhamsai and Khammuan in Laos as a refuge for the region's biodiversity. This region includes two of the world's most endangered monkeys, the douc langur and the Ha Tinh langur, and is potentially home to other rare or even undiscovered forms.

**David Andrew**

## National Parks

Vietnam has several national parks, the main ones being Cat Ba, Ba Be Lakes and Cuc Phuong national parks in the north; Bach Ma National Park in the centre; and Nam Cat Tien and Yok Don national parks in the south.

Cat Ba National Park is a beautiful island, and during the summer months attracts a steady stream of foreign travellers willing to make the boat journey. Ba Be Lake National Park features spectacular waterfalls and is accessible by rented jeep or motorbike from Hanoi. Cuc Phuong National Park is less visited and has suffered more ecological damage from logging and burning, but it is now protected. Bach Ma National Park near Hué is not developed and seldom visited, but has good potential. Nam Cat Tien National Park, in the Central Highlands of the south, is difficult to reach and sees few visitors. Also in the Central Highlands is Yok Don National Park, which has little scenery but is home to local minority tribes. The government also plans to create an underwater national park off the coast near Nha Trang.

In an attempt to prevent an ecological and hydrological catastrophe, the government has plans to set aside tens of thousands of sq km of forest land and to create 87 national parks and nature reserves. Thirty-seven reserves (including the national parks) have already received government approval. Ecologists hope that because tropical eco-systems have a high species diversity but low densities of individual species, reserve areas will be large enough to contain viable populations of each species. However, there are development interests which are not amenable to increasing the size of Vietnam's national parks and forest reserves – as in the west, even the best-laid plans sometimes go awry.

Another problem is poaching, and this is one threat that travellers should take seriously. Poachers often carry guns, both for their illegal hunting activities and to drive away any potential witnesses or law enforcement authorities. They are also not above supplementing their income with armed robberies. Especially in areas near the Cambo-dian and Lao borders, there is a fairly high chance of getting shot at if you go strolling in the jungle. The government discourages foreigners from visiting these remote nature reserves near the border, while scientists seeking permission to visit are usually obliged to take along a few AK-47-toting soldiers for protection. Of course, this doesn't apply to those parts of national parks which see a reasonable amount of tourist traffic.

I met the director of Bach Ma National Park. He expressed his desire to see more visitors to the park, used terms like 'eco-tourism' and explained that overseas interest in Vietnam's national parks programme was vital in order to raise the government's commitment. There are serious pressures from logging, poaching, agriculture etc, which require national and provincial government assistance in overcoming. This will only happen if the park's tourist potential is seen as something worth protecting.

**Tim Weisselberg**

## GOVERNMENT & POLITICS

When it comes to both government and politics, Vietnam has a lot of it.

The Socialist Republic of Vietnam (SRV; Cong Hoa Xa Hoi Chu Nghia Viet Nam) came into existence in July 1976 as a unitary state comprising the Democratic Republic of Vietnam (DRV; North Vietnam) and the defeated Republic of Vietnam (RVN; South Vietnam). From April 1975 until the declaration of the SRV, the South had been ruled – at least in name – by a Provisional Revolutionary Government.

Officially, the government espouses a Marxist-Leninist political philosophy. Its political institutions have borrowed a great deal from the Soviet and Chinese models, in particular the ability to create mountains of red tape.

The Orwellian national slogan, which appears at the top of every official document, is *Doc Lap, Tu Do, Hanh Phuc*, which means 'Independence, Freedom, Happiness'. It's based on one of Ho Chi Minh's sayings.

Vietnam's political system is dominated by the two-million-member Communist Party (Dang Cong San Viet Nam), whose influence is felt at every level of the country's social and political life.

The leadership of the Party has been collective in style and structure ever since its founding by Ho Chi Minh in 1930. The Party's decentralised structure, though originally necessitated by the difficulty of communications between Party headquarters and its branches, has allowed local leaders considerable leeway for initiative. Unfortunately, this has also allowed the development of localised corruption, which Hanoi has had a difficult time controlling.

The official media has described a number of cases. In Thanh Hoa Province, local Party chief Ha Trong Hoa turned his police force into a band of Mafia-style gangsters and ruled for years before Hanoi finally stepped in and ousted him. Pham Chi Tin, the son of a high-ranking Communist Party official, was arrested by the military in 1994 after his gang (the Nha Trang police force) terrorised local residents for years – Hanoi took action after he kidnapped a tourist from Hong Kong to extort money from the victim's family. There was a similar crackdown in Vung Tau recently.

Relatively speaking, the policies of the Vietnamese Communist Party have been characterised by a flexible and non-doctrinaire approach.

The most powerful institution in the Party is the Political Bureau (Politburo), which has about a dozen members. It oversees the Party's day-to-day functioning and has the power to issue directives to the government. The Politburo is formally elected by the Central Committee, whose 125 or so full members and about 50 alternate members meet only once or twice a year.

Party Congresses, at which major policy changes are ratified after a long process of behind-the-scenes discussions and consultations, were held in 1935, 1951, 1960, 1976, 1982, 1986, 1991 and 1996. The last few Party Congresses have reflected intense intra-Party disagreements over the path Vietnamese Communism should take, with changing coalitions of conservatives and dogmatists squaring off against more prag-matic elements. The position of Party Chairman has been left vacant since Ho Chi Minh's death.

The unicameral National Assembly (Quoc Hoi) is Vietnam's highest legislative authority. Its 500 or so deputies, whose terms last five years, each represent 100,000 voters. The National Assembly's role is to rubber-stamp – usually unanimously – Politburo decisions and Party-initiated legislation during its biannual sessions, which last about a week.

The Council of State functions as the country's collective presidency. Its members, who currently number 15, are elected by the National Assembly. The Council of State carries out the duties of the National Assembly when the latter is not in session. The Council of Ministers is also elected by the National Assembly. It functions as does a western-style cabinet.

During the 1980s and early 1990s thousands of Party members were expelled, in part to reduce corruption (seen by a fed-up public as endemic) and in part to make room for more young people and workers. As in China, Vietnam has been ruled by a gerontocracy. Few high-ranking officials ever retire – they just fade away. At the Eighth Party Congress in 1996, the three highest ranking members of the Party were re-elected to five-year terms – General Secretary Do Muoi, age 79; President Le Duc Anh, age 75; and Prime Minister Vo Van Kiet, the youngster at 73.

Despite official rhetoric about the equality of women, females are under-represented in the Party, especially at the highest levels (there have been no female members of the Politburo since 1945).

Candidates to the National Assembly and local People's Committees are elected to office. The voting age is 18. Everyone of voting age is required to vote, though proxy-voting is allowed (and is very common). This permits the government to boast that elections produce 100% voter participation, thus conferring legitimacy on the process. Only Party-approved candidates are permitted to run and opposition parties are prohibited.

Some independents have appeared on the slate, but they must also have the government's approval to run.

The military does not seem to have any direct political role, even though virtually all of Vietnam's high-ranking politicians and officials came from the military.

The government seems to have a hard time deciding how to carve the political turkey. After reunification, the provincial structure of the south was completely reorganised. Then on 1 July 1989, several provinces that were joined after 1975 were split apart. Since then there have been even more splits; the last one was in 1996 when eight new provinces were created. Even the Vietnamese have difficulty keeping up with the redrawing of political boundaries.

## ECONOMY

Vietnam is one of the poorest countries in Asia with an estimated per capita income of less than US$300 per year and US$1.4 billion in hard currency debts (owed mainly to Russia, the IMF and Japan). Unable to repay these loans, Vietnam has been unofficially bankrupt since the 1980s.

An agreement reached in 1996 reduced Vietnam debt by 50%, with the remainder to be paid off gradually. The country's improving economy increases the possibility that Vietnam will meet its obligations to lenders. Vietnam has hopes of issuing new bonds overseas in the remainder of this century.

Despite its hard-working, educated workforce, the country's economy is beset by low wages, poor infrastructure, a trade deficit, unemployment, under-employment and, until recently, erratic runaway inflation (700% in 1986, 30% in 1989, 50% in 1991 and 3% in 1996). The economy was hurt by wartime infrastructure damage (not a single bridge in the North survived American airraids, while in the South many bridges were blown up by the VC), but by the government's own admission the present economic fiasco is the result of ideologically driven policies followed after reunification, plus corruption and the burden of heavy military spending.

Just how the average Vietnamese manages to survive economically is a mystery. Salaries in Ho Chi Minh City are in the neighbourhood of US$50 to US$90 per month, but elsewhere they're about half that. You simply can't survive on such wages unless you can grow your own food and build your own house (possible in the countryside, but not in Saigon or Hanoi). So people scrounge on the side, finding some odd job they can do. In the case of women, many are forced to resort to part-time prostitution, while government officials and police often turn to corruption.

Although Vietnam and Russia are still officially as close as lips and teeth, Vietnamese from all parts of the country seem to harbour an unreserved hostility towards the few remaining Russian experts in their country. This bitterness is an outgrowth of the widespread belief that Soviet economic policies are to blame for Vietnam's economy going straight down the toilet after reunification. The once ubiquitous posters of those two white guys, Marx and Lenin, served to underline the foreign origin of much of the Party's unpopular ideology, including collectivisation and centralised planning. Perhaps not surprisingly, the posters disappeared almost overnight when the Soviet Union also disappeared in 1991.

### Economic Reforms

Vietnam might well have collapsed had it not been for Soviet aid and recent capitalist-style reforms. Vietnam's efforts to restructure the economy really got under way with the Sixth Party Congress held in December 1986. At that time, Nguyen Van Linh (a proponent of reform) was appointed General Secretary of the Communist Party.

Immediately upon the legalisation of limited private enterprise, family businesses began popping up all over the country. But it is in the south, with its experience with capitalism, where the entrepreneurial skills and managerial dynamism needed to effect the reforms are to be found. With 'new thinking' in Hanoi now remaking the economic life of the whole country in the mould of the pre-reunification south, people have been remarking that, in the end, the South won the war.

Directly as a result of the reforms, Vietnam moved from being a rice importer in the mid-1980s to become the world's third-largest rice exporter in 1991 (after Thailand and the USA).

Vietnam's economy started growing in the late 1980s, reversing the trend of the previous decade when the country experienced precipitous negative economic growth. But official growth figures don't tell the whole story; there is a significant 'black economy' not recorded in the government's statistics. Indeed, the amount of smuggling going on across the Cambodian-Vietnamese border (much of it done by the army and police) easily exceeds official trade between those two countries. Another fact the government doesn't like to admit is that the urban economy is improving much faster than that of rural areas, widening the already-signifi-cant gap in standards of living. The Vietnamese government fears what China is already experiencing – a mass exodus of rural residents into the already overcrowded cities.

Before 1991, Vietnam's major trading partners were the USSR and other members of COMECON (Council for Mutual Economic Assistance – the Eastern Bloc's equivalent to the European Union). Most of the trade with COMECON was on a barter basis; Vietnam traded its crude oil, wood and sugar cane for refined oil, machinery and weapons. Because the value of Vietnam's agricultural products was not nearly enough to pay for the expensive war toys, the USSR had to subsidise the Vietnamese economy, leaving Vietnam with an enormous rouble-denominated debt.

The disintegration of COMECON and the USSR in 1991 could have brought complete economic collapse to Vietnam. Almost miraculously, this was avoided because Vietnam moved quickly to establish hard

Most of Vietnam's rice production is achieved without modern agricultural machinery, but economic reforms, combined with the strong work ethic of the Vietnamese, has resulted in Vietnam's moving from an importer of rice during the 80s to the world's third largest exporter of rice in the 90s.

currency trade relations with China, Hong Kong, Japan, Singapore, South Korea, Taiwan, Thailand and western nations. This explains why Vietnamese officials have suddenly become so anxious to do business with the west. Many other former Eastern Bloc countries have not fared as well as Vietnam – their economies collapsed along with the USSR.

The transition from an isolated socialist barter economy to a free market, hard currency trading economy is not complete and has not been easy. Many of Vietnam's manufactured goods (bicycles, shoes, even toothpaste) are of such poor quality that they are practically unsaleable, especially in the face of competition from foreign goods. One of the first effects of free (or free-ish) trade with capitalist countries was to wipe out many state-run enterprises, leading to job lay-offs and increased unemployment. Even Vietnam's sugar-cane growers were hurt – shoddy equipment at state-run sugar refineries produced such a low-quality product that imported refined sugar replaced the domestic product for a while.

The Vietnamese government has responded with a number of 'temporary import bans' (protectionism). Such bans theoretically give a boost to struggling domestic industries, but also lead to increased smuggling. But, slowly, the country is regaining its ability to compete in foreign markets; low wages and the strong Vietnamese work ethic (when given incentives) bodes well for Vietnam's export industries.

The more liberal rules have had a dramatic effect on foreign joint-venture operations – foreign investors have been tripping over themselves to get into the country. Some of the most successful joint ventures to date have involved hotels, though some of these 'investments' are clear cases of real-estate speculation (foreigners cannot buy land directly, but businesses can with a Vietnamese partner). The leading foreign investors are the Koreans, Singaporeans and Taiwanese, though many of their investments are little more than disguised land speculation.

Unfortunately, political meddling hasn't stopped completely. The bureaucracy is plagued by middle-level functionaries whose jobs are essentially worthless (or counterproductive) and should be eliminated. Such bureaucrats view the reforms as a serious threat and would like to see them fail. Despite recent successes, the reformers still do not have the upper hand.

The Vietnamese bureaucracy, official incompetence, corruption and the ever-changing rules and regulations continue to irritate foreign investors. On paper, intellectual property rights are protected, but enforcement is lax – patents, copyrights and trademarks are openly pirated. Tax rates and government fees are frequently revised without warning. Some municipalities have forced foreign companies to hire employees from state employment agencies, with the only employees available being the 'spoiled brats' of cadres.

## Economic Backlash

Recalcitrant bureaucrats or not, the reforms have already gained enough momentum that it's hard to imagine reversing them – putting the toothpaste back in the tube might well be impossible. However, there has been a conservative backlash against the reforms. Rather than shrinking, the state sector has been expanding. Various government regulations make it difficult or impossible for private businesses to function except in a joint-venture with a state-owned company. Such joint-ventures often come to grief and many foreign investors are starting to become disillusioned with Vietnam. In 1996, the number of foreign investment projects actually dropped by 17% from the previous year's figures.

One of the most visible signs of the anti-market backlash was the 'social evils' campaign launched with much fanfare in late 1995. Borrowing phrases from China's goofy 'spiritual campaign' of the 1980s, the government declared that evil ideas from the west were 'polluting' Vietnamese society. The pollution would have to be 'cleaned up'. Aside from obvious foreign pollution such as prostitution, drugs and karaoke, one of the major evils identified was the use of English in advertising. Vietnamese police were ordered to destroy English signs – foreign companies like Coca-Cola and Sony watched in disbelief as their multi-million-dollar advertising campaigns were annihilated by enthusiastic vigilantes.

Meanwhile, socially evil foreign video tapes, music tapes and magazines were burned in public bonfires. Vietnam's official *Moi* newspaper said, 'thanks to education and propaganda, people voluntarily gave up 27,302 video tapes'.

After foreign investors threatened to pull out of the country, the Vietnamese authorities relaxed the rules somewhat. However, the Vietnamese press still rants periodically about social evils and, even now, every business must have a sign in Vietnamese larger than the English sign.

Tourists were also affected by the social evils campaign. During the first half of 1996, the authorities refused all visa extensions. Then during the month of June, 1996 (during the Eighth Party Congress), all tourist visas were refused. This brought about the near collapse of the tourist industry, forcing the government to beat a retreat and ease up on the restrictions. The industry didn't start to recover until nearly the end of the year, but overall 1996 tourist-related revenues declined by an estimated 30%.

Privatisation of large state industries has not yet begun but is being considered. Likely candidates would be Vietnam Airlines, the banking industry and telecommunications. Whether or not the generation of socialist leaders can bring themselves to put the state's prime assets on the auction block remains to be seen. At the present time, Vietnam has no stock market – establishing one would be a prerequisite to any privatisation moves. In 1995, the government promised to open a capital market by year's end, but in the end it just didn't happen and seems to have been postponed indefinitely.

On a more positive note, Vietnam has seen economic growth rates of around 8 to 9% annually in the past few years. Vietnam joined ASEAN (Association of South-East Asian Nations) in 1995, a step which observers say should greatly benefit Vietnam's economy and spur further reforms.

Hanoi is intent on limiting Vietnam's restructuring *(doi moi)* to the economic sphere, keeping ideas such as pluralism and democracy from undermining the present power structure. Whether it is possible to have economic liberalisation without a concurrent liberalisation in the political sphere remains to be seen. Vietnam's role model at the moment is China, where economic liberalisation coupled with harsh political controls seems to be at least partially successful in reviving the economy. The role model of the former Soviet Union – where political liberalisation preceded economic restructuring – is pointed to as an example of the wrong way to reform.

## Malthus vs. Marx

Thomas Robert Malthus (1766-1834) was a political economist and the first to publish the theory that population growth would lead to mass poverty. The 'Malthusian Theory' had many critics, including the Pope. Another critic was Karl Marx (1818-83). Marx believed that more people meant more production and he accused Malthus of being a apologist for the capitalists.

Not surprisingly, when the Vietnamese government adopted Marxism as an economic model, birth control was viewed as a capitalist plot to make Third World countries weak. In this regard, the Vietnamese were encouraged by their Soviet mentors – in the USSR, family planning was prohibited and 'hero mothers' were given rewards for having over 10 children. But when the USSR collapsed in 1991, the Vietnamese were forced to critically review their economic and social policies. The threat posed by runaway population growth was finally recognised and a family planning programme was instituted. Couples are now encouraged to have no more than two children. ∎

## POPULATION & PEOPLE

In 1996, Vietnam's population reached 75 million, making it the 12th most populous country in the world. Eighty-four percent of the population is ethnic-Vietnamese, 2% ethnic-Chinese and the rest Khmers, Chams and members of some 60 ethno-linguistic groups.

Vietnam has an overall population density of 225 persons per sq km, one of the world's highest for an agricultural country. Much of the Red River Delta has a population density of 1000 people per sq km or more. Overall life expectancy is 66 years and infant mortality is 48 per 1000. The current rate of population growth is 2.1% per year and, until recently, ideology prevented effective family planning.

Unfortunately, the 15 years or so during which Vietnam encouraged large families will be a burden for quite some time to come. The country's population will likely double in the next century before zero population growth can be achieved. The task of reducing population growth in Vietnam is daunting. As elsewhere in the Third World, low education and low incomes tend to encourage large families. Unable to afford modern birth control techniques, most Vietnamese couples still rely on condoms, abortion or self-induced miscarriage to avoid unwanted births.

The Vietnamese government takes a carrot and stick approach to family planning. For couples who limit their family size to two children or less, there are promises of benefits in education, housing, health care and employment (though lack of funding means these promises are often not kept). The stick comes for those who exceed the two-child limit. To begin with, the government can deny the third child household registration (needed to obtain an ID card, admission to school and access to various crucial permits). If the parents have a government job, they can be fired. In general, these inducements have succeeded in urban areas – a two-child family is now the norm in Hanoi and Saigon. However, family planning campaigns have had only a minor impact on birth rates in rural areas.

### Ethnic-Vietnamese

The Vietnamese people (called 'Annamites' by the French) developed as a distinct ethnic group between 200 BC and 200 AD through the fusion of a people of Indonesian stock with Viet and Tai immigrants from the north and Chinese who arrived, along with Chinese rule, as of the 2nd century AD. Vietnamese civilisation was profoundly influenced by China and, via Champa and the Khmers, India, but the fact that the Vietnamese were never absorbed by China indicates that a strong local culture existed prior to the 1000 years of Chinese rule, which ended in 938 AD.

The Vietnamese have lived for thousands of years by growing rice and, as a result, have historically preferred to live in lowland areas suitable for rice growing. Over the past two millennia, they have slowly pushed southward along the narrow coastal strip, defeating the Chams in the 15th century and taking over the Mekong Delta from the Khmers in the 18th century. The Vietnamese have tended to view highland areas (and their inhabitants) with suspicion.

Vietnamese who have emigrated abroad are known as Overseas Vietnamese (Viet Kieu). They are intensely disliked by the locals, who accuse them of being cowards, arrogant, pampered, privileged and so on. These negative judgments are likely coloured by jealousy. In the 1980s, returning Viet Kieu were often followed by the police and everyone they spoke to was questioned and harassed by the authorities. This has all changed. Indeed, official policy is now to welcome the Viet Kieu and encourage them to resettle in Vietnam. Many Viet Kieu are cynical about this. 'They don't want us back, just our money, professional skills and connections' is a comment you'll likely to hear in Overseas Vietnamese communities. The fact that the police still often shake down the Viet Kieu for money is not encouraging. The Vietnamese press frequently writes about the importance to the economy of receiving money transfers from relatives abroad.

# Ethnic Minorities in Vietnam

# Ethnic Minorities in Vietnam

While the ethnic-Vietnamese and Chinese live mainly in urban centres and coastal areas, the remaining people, an estimated 10% of Vietnam's total population, are found primarily in the high country. While several of these groupings, such as the Tay, Tai, Muong and Nung, number in the vicinity of a million people, others, like the Romam and O-du, are feared to have dwindled to as few as 100. Undoubtedly the most colourful of the hill tribes reside in the north-west, in the plush mountain territory along the Lao and Chinese borders, while many of the tribes in the Central Highlands and the south can be difficult to distinguish, at least by dress alone, from ordinary Vietnamese.

The French called them *montagnards* (meaning 'highlanders' or 'mountain people') and still use this term when speaking in French or English. The Vietnamese generally refer to them as *moi*, a derogatory term meaning 'savages', which unfortunately reflects all-too-common popular attitudes. The present government, however, prefers to use the term 'national minorities'. Some have lived in Vietnam for thousands of years, while others migrated into the region during the past few centuries. The areas inhabited by each group are often delimited by altitude, with later arrivals settling at higher elevations.

Historically, the highland areas were allowed to remain virtually independent as long as their leaders recognised Vietnamese sovereignty and paid tribute and taxes. The 1980 Constitution abolished two vast autonomous regions established for the ethnic minorities in the northern mountains in 1959. During wartime in the 1960s and early 70s, both the Communists and the USA actively recruited fighters among the Montagnards of the Central Highlands, and in fact it was only quite recently that special restrictions were lifted on American tourists wanting to visit hill tribe areas around Dalat (just in case somehow the CIA happens to be still conducting business?).

Most of the individual ethnic groups share basic, similar traits in their daily lives and are often most easily identified by differences in language, physical features and traditional dress. They have a rural, agricultural lifestyle and show similarities in village architecture and traditional rituals and have a long history of intertribal warfare. Many of the tribes are semi-nomadic, cultivating crops such as 'dry' rice using slash-and-burn methods, which have taken a heavy toll on the environment.

Because such practices destroy the ever-dwindling forests, the government has been trying to encourage them to adopt more settled agriculture, often at lower altitudes, with wet (paddy) rice and cash crops such as tea, coffee and cinnamon. Still, despite the allure of benefits like subsidised irrigation, better education and health care, a long history of nonconformist attitudes, coupled with a general distrust of the lowland ethnic-Vietnamese majority, keeps many away from the lowlands.

As is the case in other parts of Asia, the rich, inherent culture of so many of Vietnam's ethnic minorities has slowly given way to a variety of outside influences. Many tribes have been so assimilated into mainstream Vietnamese society that very few even dress in traditional garb. Most of those who do are found in the remote villages of the far north, and even there it is still often only the women who do so, while the men more typically have switched over to Vietnamese or western-style clothes. While factors such as the introduction of electricity, modern medicine and education do create advantages, unfortunately such evolution has brought about the abandonment of many age-old traditions.

A more recent, and perhaps equally threatening, outside influence is the effect of tourism. With growing numbers of people travelling to see the different ethnic minorities, further exposure to lowlanders and a developing trend toward commercialism will likely worsen the situation. In some areas, such as Sapa, adorable children who used to just stare, laugh or run away at the sight of a foreigner have begun to warm up, often expecting handouts of money or candy.

*Title Page: Hmong mother and child, Sapa, north-west Vietnam (photograph by Juliet Coombe)*

MASON FLORENCE

MARK KIRBY

EMMA MILLER

*Top: A Bahnar woman enjoys a pipe at Pleiku in the central highlands.*

*Middle: Hmong girls in Sapa in northern Vietnam.*

*Bottom: A Hmong boy with a traditional woven carrying basket.*

Top: A Dzao boy and his sibling at Sapa in northern Vietnam.

Bottom: Two Hmong girls with a fishing basket outside Sapa.

MASON FLORENCE

MASON FLORENCE

*Top: An elderly woman from the Koho tribe in the Dalat area, central Vietnam.*

*Bottom: A woman of the Ma group with her grandson in a village near Dalat.*

EMMA MILLER

JULIET COOMBE

*Top: Women of the Dzao tribe display the common dress style at the market in Sapa.*

*Middle: Weaving is a skill and the means of making money for many of Vietnam's Montagnard groups.*

*Bottom: The markets of northern Vietnam provide an opportunity to see local ethnic groups engaging in day to day activities.*

BERNARD NAPTHINE

Photographing hill tribe people demands patience and the utmost respect for local customs. The beauty and colour of the people and surrounding scenery provides ample opportunity, but it is important to remember that you are just visiting and that not only might your actions be interpreted as rude or offensive, but you also pave the way for future visitors. That is not to say that taking pictures is bad, but just keep in mind the various effects a camera can have. The popular weekend market in Sapa is a good example of where a crowd of camera-toting tourists can appear somewhat overwhelming to the local folk. While the entrepreneurial Hmong here, for example, do not generally mind being photographed (though buying some handicraft will help facilitate this), other groups in the area such as the Red Dzao tend to be far more camera-shy and have had their fair share of 'must get this shot' photographers literally chasing them through the market!

Vietnam's minorities have substantial autonomy and, though the official national language is Vietnamese, all minority children still learn their local dialect. Taxes are supposed to be paid, but Hanoi is far away and it seems that as long as they don't interfere with political agendas, they can live as they please. Police officers and members of the army in minority areas are often members of local tribal groups and the National Assembly in Hanoi is represented by a good number of ethnic minorities. While there may be no official discrimination system, the hill tribes, however, still remain at the bottom of the educational and economic ladder. Despite improvements in rural schooling, many minorities marry young, have children and die early. Those who live closer to urban centres and the coast fare better.

The task of neatly classifying the different highland groups is not an easy one. Ethnologists typically classify the Montagnards by linguistic distinction and commonly refer to three main groups (which further splinter into vast and complex sub-groupings). The Austro-Asian family includes the Viet-Muong, Mon-Khmer, Tay-Tai and Meo-Dzao language groups; the Austronesian family speaks Malayo-Polynesian languages; and the Sino-Tibetan family encompasses the Chinese and Tibeto-Burmese language groups. Furthermore, within a single spoken language, there are often myriad varying dialectical variations.

Following is a close-up of some dominant hill tribe groups. Ethnic minority groups with members numbering upwards of 500,000 include the Tay (Tho), Tai (Thai), Hmong (Meo or Miao), Muong (Mol) and Nung. Other large tribes (over 250,000) include the Jarai (Gia Rai) and Ede (Rhade), while groups like the Bahnar (Ba-na), and Sedang (Xo-dang) have more than 100,000 members.

# Tay

With a million-plus population, the Tay people are the largest of the hill tribes and are found throughout the north of Vietnam. They traditionally live in stilt wooden houses, though a long history of proximity to the ethnic-Vietnamese has seen a gradual change to more typical Vietnamese brick and earthen housing. The Tay are known for their abilities in cultivating wet rice in addition to crops such as tobacco, fruit, herbs and spices. Religiously they adhere closely to Vietnamese beliefs in Buddhism, Confucianism and Taoism, but also worship genies and local spirits. In the 16th century, the Tay developed their own written script and Tay literature and arts have gained substantial renown.

# Tai

Theories vary on their actual relation to the Thais of Siam (Thailand), as do the reference to colours in the sub-groupings such as the Red, Black and White Tai. Some contend that the colours coincide with those of the women's skirts, while others believe the names come from the nearby Black and Red Rivers. Villages typically have 40 to 50 bamboo-stilt households. Tai women don close-fitting black skirts, blouses with silver clasps and colourful robes and kerchiefs and are also known for creating beautiful embroidery. The Tai, using a script developed in the 5th century, have produced literature ranging from poetry and love stories to folk tales and song, and are renowned for their celebrations of music and dance. Like the Tay, the Tai originated in southern China and reside mainly in the north-west. They settled along fertile riverbeds, which serve as the source of irrigation for fields of rice, corn, cotton, beans and so on.

# Hmong

Since initially migrating from China in the 19th century, the Hmong have grown to one of the largest, and most underprivileged, of the ethnic groups in Vietnam. Their spoken tongue resembles Mandarin Chinese, and the people fall into various sub-classifications, including the Black, White, Red, Green and Flower Hmong, each bearing subtle variations on traditional dress. The Hmong reside at high altitudes and cultivate dry rice, vegetables and fruit, in addition to medicinal plants (including opium), and also raise pigs, cows, chickens and horses. Well known for their skills in weaving, the Hmong dye cloth in a deep indigo-blue which practically gives off a metallic shine. Hmong women typically wear large silver necklaces and clusters of several bracelets and earrings. The Hmong are found elsewhere in other parts of South-East Asia and many also fled Vietnam to western countries as refugees (and are said to have a considerably more difficult time adjusting than the ethnic-Vietnamese due to being undereducated and coming from very large families).

# Muong

Found predominantly in Hoa Binh Province, the male-dominated Muong live in small stilt-house hamlets called *quel*, which are grouped into larger village units called *muong*. Each muong is overseen by an hereditary noble family (*lang*) who rules the communal land and collects the benefits of labour and tax through the use of it by locals. Though their origins lie close to the ethnic-Vietnamese and they are nowadays difficult to distinguish, the Muong have a rich culture and are more similar to the Tai. They are known for producing notable folk literature, poems and songs, much of which has been translated into Vietnamese. They too cultivate rice in water paddies, though in the past sticky rice, like that found in Laos and north-east Thailand, was part of their staple diet.

# Nung

Close to a million Nung are known to inhabit areas in Cao Bang and Lang Son Provinces. Concentrated into small villages, Nung homes are typically divided into two sections, one to serve as living quarters and the other for work and worship. Their astute gardening skills are known to reap a wide variety of healthy crops like vegetables, fruit, spices and bamboo. In addition to weaving, the Nung are known for their handicrafts such as bamboo furniture, basketry, silverwork and paper making. Spiritually and socially, the Nung are similar to the Tay, from their deep ancestral worship to traditional festivities. Both were also heavily exploited by foreign militaries (French and American). Nung brides traditionally command high dowries from prospective grooms and tradition dictates inheritance from father to son, a sign of strong Chinese influences. In most Nung villages medicine men still exist and are called upon to help get rid of evil spirits and cure the ill.

# Jarai

The Jarai people are the most populous minority in the Central Highlands, with the greatest concentration around Pleiku in Kon Tum Province. Villages are often named for a nearby river, stream or tribal chief and in the centre of each can be found a large stilt house *nha-rong*, which acts as a kind of community centre. Jarai women typically propose marriage to men through a matchmaker, who delivers the prospective groom a copper bracelet. Animistic beliefs and rituals still abound and the Jarai pay respect to their ancestors and nature through a host of genies (*yang*). Popular spirits include the King of Fire (Po Teo Pui) and the King of Water (Po Teo La), whom they summon to bring forth rain. Perhaps more than any of Vietnam's other hill

*The Montagnards of the Dalat region regularly sell hand-woven garments, bags and other items on the stairs above the market on Nguyen Thi Minh Khai St.*

tribes, the Jarai are renowned for their indigenous musical instruments, from stringed 'gongs' to bamboo tubes, which act as wind flutes and percussion.

# Ede

The polytheist Ede, another Central Highlands group, are found mostly in Dak Lak Province, living communally in beamless, boat-shaped longhouses built on stilts. These homes, which frequently accommodate large extended families, allot about a third of the living space for communal use, with the rest partitioned into smaller quarters to give privacy to married couples. Like the Jarai, the families of Ede girls make proposals of marriage to men, and once wed the couple resides with the wife's family and children bear the mother's family name. Inheritance is also reserved solely for women, in particular the youngest daughter of the family.

# Bahnar

Long ago the Bahnar are believed to have migrated up to the Central Highlands from the coast. They are animists and worship trees such as the banyan and ficus. The Bahnar keep their own traditional calendar, which calls for 10 months of cultivation, the remaining two months set aside for social and personal duties such as marriage, weaving, buying and selling of food and wares, ceremonies and festivals. Traditionally, when babies reached one month of age, a ceremony was held in which, after their ears were blown into, the ear lobes were pierced, thus making the child officially a member of the village. Those who died without such holes were believed to be taken to a land of monkeys by a black-eared goddess called Duydai.

# Sedang

Native to the Central Highlands, the Sedang have relations stretching as far as Cambodia. Like many of their neighbours, the Sedang have been adversely affected by centuries of war and outside invasion. They do not carry family names, and there is said to be complete equality between the sexes. The children of one's siblings are also given the same treatment as one's own, creating a strong fraternal tradition. Although most Sedang spiritual and cultural ceremonies relate to agriculture, they still practice unique customs such as grave-abandonment and sharing of property with the deceased, and childbirth is conducted at the forest's edge.

**Mason Florence**

*This Montagnard woman from the Central Highlands comes from one of the 60 distinct 'minority' groups found in Vietnam. Economically and educationally, the Montagnards are among the poorest in Vietnam and exist mostly on the fringes of mainstream society.*

## Ethnic-Chinese

The ethnic-Chinese (Hoa) constitute the largest single minority group in Vietnam. Today, most of them live in the south, especially in and around Saigon's sister-city of Cholon. Although the families of most of Vietnam's ethnic-Chinese have lived in Vietnam for generations, they have historically tried to maintain their separate Chinese identities, languages, school systems and even citizenship. The Chinese have organised themselves into communities, known as 'congregations' *(bang)*, according to their ancestors' province of origin and dialect. Important congregations include Fujian (Phuoc Kien in Vietnamese), Cantonese (Quang Dong in Vietnamese or Guangdong in Chinese), Hainan (Hai Nam), Chaozhou (Tieu Chau) and Hakka (Nuoc Hue in Vietnamese or Kejia in Mandarin Chinese).

During the 1950s, President Diem tried without much success to forcibly assimilate South Vietnam's ethnic-Chinese population. In the North, too, the ethnic-Chinese have resisted Vietnamisation.

The Chinese are well known for their entrepreneurial abilities – before the fall of South Vietnam in 1975, ethnic-Chinese controlled nearly half of the country's economic activity. Historical antipathies between China and Vietnam and the prominence of ethnic-Chinese in commerce have generated a great deal of animosity towards them. In March 1978, the Vietnamese Communists launched a campaign against 'bourgeois elements' (considered a euphemism for the ethnic-Chinese) which turned into open racial persecution. The campaign influenced China's decision to attack Vietnam in 1979 and caused about one-third of Vietnam's ethnic-Chinese to flee to China and the west. Vietnamese officials now admit that the anti-Chinese and anti-capitalist campaign was a tragic mistake which cost the country heavily.

## Other Minorities

Vietnam has one of the most diverse and complex ethno-linguistic mixes in all of Asia. Many of the country's 54 distinct ethnic groups have not-so-distant relations scattered throughout neighbouring Laos, southern China and Cambodia, as well as Thailand and Myanmar. Most of the country's ethnic minorities, believed to number between six and eight million, reside in the Central Highlands and the mountainous regions of the north-west, with a spattering along the coastal plains in the south.

See the previous special section 'Ethnic Minorities in Vietnam'.

**Chams** Vietnam's 60,000 Chams are the remnant of the once-vigorous Indianised kingdom of Champa, which flourished from the 2nd to the 15th centuries and was destroyed as the Vietnamese expanded southward. Most of them live along the coast between Nha Trang and Phan Thiet and in the Mekong Delta province of An Giang.

Today, the Chams are best known for the many brick sanctuaries (known as 'Cham towers') they constructed all over the southern half of the country. The Cham language is of the Malayo-Polynesian (Austronesian) group. It can be written either in a traditional script of Indian origin or in a Latin-based script created by the French. Most of the Chams, who were profoundly influenced by both Hinduism and Buddhism, are now Muslims. There is a superb collection of Cham statues at the Cham Museum in Danang.

**Khmers** The Khmers (ethnic-Cambodians) numbers are estimated at about 700,000 and are concentrated in the south-western Mekong Delta. They practise Hinayana (Theravada) Buddhism.

**Indians** Almost all of South Vietnam's population of Indians, most of whose roots were in southern India, left in 1975. The remaining community in Saigon worships at the Mariamman Hindu temple and the Central Mosque.

**Westerners** Vietnam has a handful of ethnic 'westerners', most of whom are in fact racially mixed American-Vietnamese, French-Vietnamese or French-Chinese.

## EDUCATION

Compared with other Third World countries, Vietnam's population is very well educated. Vietnam's literacy rate is estimated at 82%, although official figures put it even higher (95%). Before the colonial period, the majority of the population possessed some degree of literacy, but by 1939 only 15% of school-age children were receiving any kind of instruction and 80% of the population was illiterate.

During the late 19th century, one of the few things that French colonial officials and Vietnamese nationalists agreed on was that the traditional Confucian educational system, on which the mandarinal civil service was based, was in desperate need of reform. Mandarinal examinations were held in Tonkin until WWI and in Annam until the war's end.

Many of Indochina's independence leaders were educated in elite French-language secondary schools such as the Lycée Albert Sarraut in Hanoi and the Lycée Chasseloup Laubat in Saigon.

Although the children of foreign residents can theoretically attend Vietnamese schools, the majority of expat children go to special private academies. These are expensive, but if you're working for a foreign company then it's possible that they will pay the bill.

In Hanoi, most expats send their kids to the Amsterdam School (☎ 832-7379; fax 832-7535) on Giang Vo St. Instruction is offered in several languages, not just Dutch as the name implies. The other possibility is the Rainbow Montessori School (☎ 826-6194), 18B Ngo Van So St.

There are more options in Saigon. The line-up of expat schools includes:

Ecole Française Colette
    124 Cach Mang Thang Tam St, District 3 (fax 829-1675)
International Grammar School
    236 Nam Ky Khoi Nghia St, District 3 (☎ 822-3337; fax 823-0000)
Saigon Kids
    72/7C Tran Quoc Toan St, District 3 (☎ 829-1324; fax 822-8439)
Saigon Village Kindergarten
    17 To Hien Thanh St, District 10 (☎ 865-0287; fax 865-7247)

## ARTS
### Film

One of Vietnam's first cinematographic efforts was a newsreel of Ho Chi Minh's 1945 proclamation of independence. After Dien Bien Phu, parts of the battle were restaged for the benefit of movie cameras.

Prior to reunification the South Vietnamese movie industry concentrated on producing sensational, low-budget flicks. Until recently, most North Vietnamese filmmaking efforts have been dedicated to 'the mobilisation of the masses for economic reconstruction, the building of socialism and the struggle for national reunification'. Predictable themes include 'workers devoted to socialist industrialisation', 'old mothers who continuously risk their lives to help the people's army' and 'children who are ready to face any danger'.

The relaxation of ideological censorship of the arts has proceeded in fits and starts, but in the last few years the gradual increase in artistic freedoms has affected filmmaking, as well as other genres. But paranoia about the changes sweeping Eastern Europe has caused a return to greater government control of the arts.

## Music

Though heavily influenced by the Chinese and, in the south, the Indianised Cham and Khmer musical traditions, Vietnamese music has a high degree of originality in style and instrumentation. The traditional system of writing down music and the five note (pentatonic) scale are of Chinese origin. Vietnamese choral music is unique in that the melody must correspond to the tones; it cannot be rising during a word that has a falling tone.

There are three broad categories of Vietnamese music:

- Folk, which includes children's songs, love songs, work songs, festival songs, lullabies, lamentations and funeral songs. It is usually sung without instrumental accompaniment.
- Classical (or 'learned music'), which is rather rigid and formal. It was performed at the imperial court and for the entertainment of the mandarin elite. A traditional orchestra consists of 40 musicians. There are two main types of classical chamber music: *hat a dao* (from the north) and *ca Hue* (from central Vietnam).
- Theatre, which includes singing, dancing and instrumentation.

Each of Vietnam's ethno-linguistic minorities has its own musical traditions which often include colourful costumes and instruments such as reed flutes, lithophones (similar to xylophones), bamboo whistles, gongs and stringed instruments made from gourds. At present, there are music conser-

vatories teaching both traditional Vietnamese and western classical music in Hanoi, Hué and Saigon.

Strange as it seems, most of the world's Vietnamese pop music is originally recorded in California by Overseas Vietnamese. One reason that Vietnam itself produces so few home-grown singers is that all music tapes are instantly pirated, thus depriving the singing stars of the revenue they would need to survive. As a result, only Overseas Vietnamese are economically secure enough to pursue a career in music.

## Dance
### Traditional Dance

Not surprisingly, ethnic minorities have their own dancing traditions, which differ sharply from the Vietnamese majority. While in most hill tribes the majority of the dancers are women, a few hill tribe groups allow only the men to dance. A great deal of anthropological research has been carried out in recent years in order to preserve and revive minority traditions.

## Theatre & Puppetry

Vietnamese theatre integrates music, singing, recitation, declamation, dance and mime into a single artistic whole. There are five basic forms:

- Classical theatre is known as *hat tuong* in the north and *hat boi* ('songs with show dress') in the south. It is based on Chinese opera and was probably brought to Vietnam by the 13th century Mongol invaders chased out by Tran Hung Dao. Hat tuong is very formalistic, employing gestures and scenery similar to Chinese theatre. The accompanying orchestra, which is dominated by the drum, usually has six musicians. Often, the audience also has a drum so it too can comment on the on-stage action.

Hat tuong has a limited cast of typical characters who establish their identities using combinations of make-up and dress that the audience can readily recognise. For instance, red face-paint represents courage, loyalty and faithfulness. Traitors and cruel people have white faces. Lowlanders are given green faces; highlanders have black ones. Horizontal eyebrows represent honesty, erect eyebrows symbolise cruelty and lowered eyebrows belong to characters with a cowardly nature. A male character can express emotions (pensiveness, worry, angers etc) by fingering his beard in various ways.

- Popular theatre *(hat cheo)* often engages in social protest through the medium of satire. The singing and declamation are in everyday language and include many proverbs and sayings. Many of the melodies are of peasant origin.
- Modern theatre *(cai luong)* originated in the south in the early 20th century and shows strong western influences.
- Spoken drama *(kich noi* or *kich)*, whose roots are western, appeared in the 1920s. It's popular among students and intellectuals.
- Conventional puppetry *(roi can)* and that uniquely Vietnamese art form, water puppetry *(roi nuoc)*, draw their plots from the same legendary and historical sources as other forms of traditional theatre. It is thought that water puppetry developed when determined puppeteers in the Red River Delta managed to carry on with the show despite flooding.

These days, the various forms of Vietnamese theatre are performed by dozens of state-funded troupes and companies around the country. Water puppetry can be seen at the Saigon Zoo, in Hanoi and at Thay Pagoda near Hanoi.

### Literature

Vietnamese literature can be divided into three types:

- Traditional oral literature *(truyen khau)*, which was begun long before recorded history and includes legends, folk songs and proverbs.
- Sino-Vietnamese literature *(Han Viet)*, which was written in Chinese characters *(chu nho)*. It dates from 939 AD, when the first independent Vietnamese kingdom was established. Sino-Vietnamese literature was dominated by Confucian and Buddhist texts and was governed by strict rules of metre and verse.
- Modern Vietnamese literature *(quoc am)* includes anything recorded in *nom* characters or the Romanised *quoc ngu* script. The earliest extant text written in nom is the late 13th century *Van Te Ca Sau (Ode to an Alligator)*. Literature written in quoc ngu has played an important role in Vietnamese nationalism.

### Architecture

The Vietnamese have not been great builders like their neighbours the Khmers, who erected the monuments of Angkor in Cambodia, and the Chams, whose graceful brick towers, constructed using sophisticated masonry technology, adorn many parts of the southern half of the country. For more information on Cham architecture, see Po Klong Garai under Phan Rang/Thap Cham in the South-Central Coast chapter, Po Nagar in the section on Nha Trang (in the same chapter) and My Son in the Danang chapter.

Most of what the Vietnamese have built has been made of wood and other materials that proved highly vulnerable in the tropical climate. Because almost all of the stone structures erected by the Vietnamese have been destroyed in countless feudal wars and invasions, very little pre-modern Vietnamese architecture is extant.

Plenty of pagodas and temples founded hundreds of years ago are still functioning, but their physical plan has usually been rebuilt many times with little concern for making the upgraded structure an exact copy of the original. As a result, modern elements have been casually introduced into pagoda architecture, with neon haloes for statues of the Buddha only the most glaring example of this.

Because of the Vietnamese custom of ancestor worship, many graves from previous centuries are still extant. These include temples erected in memory of high-ranking mandarins, members of the royal family and emperors.

Memorials for Vietnamese who died in the wars against the French, Americans and Chinese are usually marked by cement obelisks inscribed with the words *To quoc ghi cong* (The country will remember their exploits). Many of the tombstones were erected over empty graves; most Viet Minh and Viet Cong dead were buried where they fell.

### Sculpture

Vietnamese sculpture has traditionally centred on religious themes and functioned as an adjunct to architecture, especially that of pagodas, temples and tombs. Many inscribed stelae (carved stone slabs or columns), erected hundreds of years ago to commemorate the founding of a pagoda or important national events, can still be seen (eg at Thien Mu Pagoda in Hué and the Temple of Literature in Hanoi).

The Cham civilisation produced spectacular carved sandstone figures for its Hindu and Buddhist sanctuaries. Cham sculpture was profoundly influenced by Indian art but over the centuries also incorporated Indonesian and Vietnamese elements. The largest single collection of Cham sculpture in the world is at the Cham Museum in Danang.

## Lacquerware

The art of making lacquerware was brought to Vietnam from China in the mid-15th century. Before that time, the Vietnamese used lacquer solely for practical purposes (such as making things watertight). During the 1930s, the Fine Arts School in Hanoi employed several Japanese teachers who introduced new styles and production methods. Their influence can still be seen in the noticeably Japanese elements in some Vietnamese lacquerware, especially that made in the north. Although a 1985 government publication declares that 'at present, lacquer painting deals boldly with realistic and revolutionary themes and forges unceasingly ahead', most of the lacquerware for sale is inlaid with mother-of-pearl and seems of traditional design.

Lacquer is a resin extracted from the *son* tree *(cay son)*. It is creamy white in raw form but is made black *(son then)* or brown *(canh dan,* 'cockroach wing') by mixing it with resin in an iron container for 40 hours. After the object to be lacquered (traditionally made of teak) has been treated with a fixative, 10 coats of lacquer are applied. Each coat must be dried for a week and then thoroughly sanded with pumice and cuttlebone before the next layer can be applied. A specially refined lacquer is used for the 11th and final coat, which is sanded with a fine coal powder and lime wash before the object is decorated. Designs may be added by engraving in low relief, by painting or by inlaying mother-of-pearl, egg shell, silver or even gold.

## Ceramics

The production of ceramics *(gom)* has a long history in Vietnam. In ancient times, ceramic objects were made by coating a wicker mould with clay and baking it. Later, ceramics production became very refined, and each dynastic period is known for its particular techniques and motifs.

## Painting

**Traditional** Painting done on frame-mounted silk dates from the 13th century. Silk painting was at one time the preserve of scholar-calligraphers, who also painted scenes from nature. Before the advent of photography, realistic portraits for use in ancestor worship were produced. Some of these – usually of former head monks – can still be seen in Buddhist pagodas.

**Modern** During this century, Vietnamese painting has been influenced by western trends. Much of the recent work done in Vietnam has had political rather than aesthetic or artistic motives. According to an official account, the fighting of the French and Americans provided painters with 'rich human material: People's Army combatants facing the jets, peasant and factory women in the militia who handled guns as well as they did their production work, young volunteers who repaired roads in record time … old mothers offering tea to anti-aircraft gunners …' There's lots of this stuff at the Fine Arts Museum in Hanoi.

The recent economic liberalisation has convinced many young artists to abandon the revolutionary themes and concentrate on producing commercially saleable paintings. Some have gone back to the traditional silk paintings, while others are experimenting with new subjects. There is a noticeable tendency now to produce nude paintings, which might indicate either an attempt to appeal to western tastes or an expression of long-suppressed kinky desires.

The cheaper stuff (US$10 to US$50) gets spun off to hotel gift shops and street markets. Supposedly, the higher standard works are put on display in one of two government-run art galleries: the Vietnamese Art Association, 511 Tran Hung Dao St, Hanoi; and the Ho Chi Minh City Association of Fine Arts (☎ 823-0025), 218 Nguyen Thi Minh Khai St, District 1. Typical prices are in the US$30 to US$50 range, though the artists may ask 10 times that. It's important to know that there are quite a few forgeries around – just because you spot a painting by a 'famous Vietnamese artist' does not mean that it's an original, though it may still be an attractive work of art.

## SOCIETY & CONDUCT
### Traditional Culture
**Face** Having 'big face' is synonymous with prestige, and prestige is important in the Orient. All families, even poor ones, are expected to have big wedding parties and throw around money like water, in order to gain face. This is often ruinously expensive, but the fact that the wedding results in bankruptcy for the young couple is far less important than losing face.

**Beauty Concepts** The Vietnamese consider pale skin to be beautiful. On sunny days trendy Vietnamese women can often be seen strolling under the shade of an umbrella in order to keep from tanning. As in 19th century Europe, peasants get tanned and those who can afford it do not. Women who work in the fields will go to great lengths to preserve their pale skin by wearing long-sleeved shirts, gloves, a conical hat and wrapping their face in a towel. To tell a Vietnamese woman that she has white skin is a great compliment; telling her that she has a 'lovely suntan' would be an insult.

**Women in Society** Like in most parts of Asia, Vietnamese women are given plenty of hard work to do, but little authority at the decision-making level. Vietnamese women proved to be highly successful as guerrillas and brought plenty of grief to US soldiers. After the war, their contribution received plenty of lip-service, but all important government posts were given to men. In the countryside, you'll see women doing such jobs as farm labour, crushing rocks at construction sites and carrying baskets weighing 60kg. It's doubtful that most western men are capable of such strenuous activity.

Vietnam's recent two child per family policy does seem to be benefiting women, and more women are delaying marriage in order to get an education. University students are about 50% female, but it doesn't seem that their skills are put to much use after graduation.

One of the sadder ironies of Vietnam's recent opening to the capitalist west has been the influx of pimps posing as 'talent scouts'. Promises of lucrative jobs in developed countries are being dangled in front of naive Vietnamese women who only discover upon arrival abroad that the job is prostitution. With no money to return home, they usually have little choice but to submit. Japanese gangsters have been particularly active in this form of job recruitment.

**Geomancy** Geomancy is the art (or science if you prefer) of manipulating or judging the environment. The Vietnamese call it *phong thuy*, meaning 'wind water', but many westerners know it by its Chinese name, *fengshui*.

If you want to build a house or find a suitable site for a grave then you call in a geomancer. The orientation of houses, communal meeting halls *(dinh)*, tombs and pagodas is determined by geomancers, which is why cemeteries have tombstones turned every which way. The location of an ancestor's grave is an especially serious matter – if the grave is in the wrong spot or facing the wrong way, then there is no telling what trouble the spirits might cause. Ditto for the location of the family altar (which every Vietnamese family has).

Businesses that are failing may call in a geomancer. Sometimes the solution is to move the door or a window. If this doesn't do the trick, it might be necessary to move an ancestor's grave. Distraught spirits may have to be placated with payments of cash (donated to a temple), especially if one wishes to erect a building or other structure which blocks the spirits' view. The date on which you begin construction of the new building is also a crucial matter.

The concept of geomancy is believed to have originated with the Chinese. Although the Communists (both Chinese and Vietnamese) have disparaged geomancy as superstition, it still has influence on people's behaviour.

**Staring Squads** This problem – if it can be called that – is only likely to affect you in rural areas. People in hip places like Saigon and Hanoi no longer take much notice of foreigners.

If you are in the hinterlands and doing something especially interesting (such as just standing there), many curious people – especially children – may gather round you to watch. They will sometimes follow you around and even try to accompany you into the toilet!

If you keep a diary or take notes, just about everyone will stick their nose into your notebook. The fact that they can't read your handwriting is no deterrent. Some people might even lift the notebook out of your hands just to get a better look. On the other hand, some people get paranoid if you take notes – it's perhaps not the best thing to do in front of the police.

**No Knock** Since privacy is not a big deal in Vietnam, don't expect many people to knock on your door before entering. What happens is you're sitting starkers in your hotel room, but the maid unlocks the door and walks in unannounced. If you'd rather not do nude modelling, check to see if there's a bolt on the door which cannot be opened from the outside with a key. Failing that, prop a chair up against the door. Otherwise, just grin and bare it.

**Ong Tay & Ba Tay** The main reason children shout *Ong Tay!* (Mr Westerner) and *Ba Tay!* (Mrs Westerner) at Caucasians has something to do with people's motivations for tapping on aquarium fish tanks and catching the attention of primates at the zoo: they want to be recognised by an exotic being and to provoke some kind of reaction.

Often, children will unabashedly come up to you and pull the hair on your arms or legs (they want to test if it's real) or dare each other to touch your skin. Some travellers have been pinched or kicked without provocation, but this is rare.

In the recent past, you often heard the term *Lien Xo!* (Soviet Union) shouted at westerners, all of whom were assumed to be Russians. This may have been partly to annoy the Russians residing in Vietnam, whose unpopularity was legendary. However, Russian tourists and technical advisers are far less common now than they used to be – few of them can afford a holiday in Vietnam any more and their technical skills are considered inferior to those available from the west. Therefore, Lien Xo is going out of fashion as an attention-getting phrase.

In the markets, vendors may try to woo you by calling you *Dong Chi!* (Comrade) on the assumption that you will find this a kindred term of endearment.

If you are cycling, you may also hear people say *Tay di xe dap* at you, which simply means 'Westerner travelling by bicycle'. While it may seem a strange form of address in the land of bicycles, it's perhaps understandable in a place where foreigners have in the past only been seen travelling first in Citroëns, then in jeeps, then in black Volgas and now in white Toyotas. But another explanation is that though the Vietnamese virtually all ride bicycles, they would never look back at one if they had the means to travel by motorbike or car. They simply do not believe that anyone, let alone a rich foreigner, would choose to travel by bicycle – there is obviously something wrong with such a person.

## Dos & Don'ts

**Greetings** The traditional Vietnamese form of greeting is to press your hands together in front of your body and to bow slightly. These days, the western custom of shaking hands has taken over, but the traditional greeting is still sometimes used by Buddhist monks and nuns, to whom it is proper to respond in kind.

**Name Cards** Name cards are very popular in Vietnam and, like elsewhere in east Asia, exchanging business cards is an important part of even the smallest transaction or business contact. Get some printed before you arrive in Vietnam and hand them out like confetti. In Bangkok and Hong Kong, machines using the latest laser-printing technology can make inexpensive custom-designed business cards in 20 minutes. You need to put your occupation on your name card; if you don't have one, try 'backpacker'.

**Deadly Chopsticks** Leaving a pair of chopsticks sticking vertically in a rice bowl looks very similar to the incense sticks which are burned for the dead. This is a powerful death sign and is not appreciated anywhere in the Orient.

**Mean Feet** Like the Chinese and Japanese, Vietnamese are obsessed with clean floors and it's usual to remove shoes when entering somebody's home. If you are entering a 'shoes off' home, your host will provide a pair of slippers. Shoes must be removed inside most Buddhist temples, but this is not universal so watch what others do. If a bunch of shoes are piled up near the doorway, you should pay heed.

It's rude to point the bottoms of your feet towards other people except maybe with close friends. When sitting on the floor, you should fold your legs into the lotus position so as to not be pointing your soles at others. And most importantly, never point your feet towards anything sacred such as figures of Buddhas.

In formal situations, when sitting on a chair do not sit with your legs crossed.

**Keep Your Hat in Hand** As a form of respect to the elderly or other people regarded with respect (monks etc), take off your hat and bow your head politely when addressing them.

**Pity the Unmarried** Telling the Vietnamese that you are single or divorced and enjoying a life without children will disturb them greatly. Not having a family is regarded as bad luck and

such people are to be pitied, not envied. Almost every Vietnamese will ask if you are married and have children. If you are young and single, simply say you are 'not yet married' and that will be accepted. If you are not so young (over 30) and unmarried, it's better to lie. Divorce is scandalous and you'd be better off claiming that your former spouse died.

**Show Some Respect** In face-conscious Asia, foreigners should pay double attention to showing respect (it's not a bad idea even at home). One expat in Vietnam had this to say on the matter:

The main reason I write is to plead with you to clearly (in boldface if necessary) and strongly implore your readers to show a little respect for the locals. Fighting over and gloating about ripping off a cyclo driver for US$0.10 is a small 'victory' and shameful thing to do. These people obviously need the money. If nothing else, travellers should at least be cordial and respectful – smile, it works wonders here. What I've seen recently here where I work has made me realise that imperialism is not yet dead. Because of the power of money, some foreigners act like they're inherently superior. The imperialist of old came with a gun and a uniform, the imperialist today comes with a camera.

**Steve McNicholas**

Vernon Weitzel of the Australian National University sends these 10 tips for successfully dealing with Vietnamese officials, businesspeople etc:

- Always smile and be pleasant.
- Don't run around complaining about everything.
- If you want to criticise someone, do it in a joking manner to avoid confrontation.
- Expect delays – build them into your schedule.
- Never show anger – ever! Getting visibly upset is not only rude – it will cause you to lose face.
- Don't be competitive. Treating your interaction as a cooperative enterprise works much better.
- Don't act as though you deserve service from anyone. If you do, it's likely that you will be delayed.
- Don't be too inquisitive about personal matters.
- Sitting and sipping tea and the exchange of gifts (sharing cigarettes, for instance) are an important prelude to any business interaction.
- The mentality of officialdom is very Confucian. Expect astounding amounts of red tape.

## Lunar Calendar

The Vietnamese lunar calendar closely resembles the Chinese one. Year 1 of the Vietnamese lunar calendar corresponds to 2637 BC and each lunar month has 29 or 30 days, resulting in years with 355 days. Approximately every third year is a leap year; an extra month is added between the third and fourth months to keep the lunar year in sync with the solar year. If this weren't done, you'd end up having the seasons gradually rotate around the lunar year, playing havoc with all elements of life linked to the agricultural seasons. To find out the Gregorian (solar) date corresponding to a lunar date, check any Vietnamese or Chinese calendar.

Instead of dividing time into centuries, the Vietnamese calendar uses units of 60 years called *hoi*. Each hoi consists of six 10-year cycles *(can)* and five 12-year cycles *(ky)*. The name of each year in the cycle consists of the *can* name followed by the *ky* name, a system which never produces the same combination twice.

The 10 heavenly stems of the *can* cycle are as follows:

| | |
|---|---|
| giap | water in nature |
| at | water in the home |
| binh | lighted fire |
| dinh | latent fire |
| mau | wood |
| ky | wood prepared to burn |
| canh | metal |
| tan | wrought metal |
| nham | virgin land |
| quy | cultivated land |

The 12 zodiacal stems of the *ky* are as follows:

| | |
|---|---|
| ty | rat |
| suu | cow |
| dan | tiger |
| mau | rabbit |
| thin | dragon |
| ty | snake |
| ngo | horse |
| mui | goat |
| than | monkey |
| dau | rooster |
| tuat | dog |
| hoi | pig |

## RELIGION

Four great philosophies and religions have shaped the spiritual life of the Vietnamese people: Confucianism, Taoism, Buddhism

### Vietnamese Zodiac

If you want to know your sign in the Vietnamese zodiac, look up your year of birth in the following chart (future years are included so you can know what's coming). However, it's a little more complicated than this because Vietnamese astrology goes by the lunar calendar. The Vietnamese Lunar New Year usually falls in late January or early February, so the first month will be included in the year before.

| Rat | 1924 | 1936 | 1948 | 1960 | 1972 | 1984 | 1996 |
|---|---|---|---|---|---|---|---|
| Ox/Cow | 1925 | 1937 | 1949 | 1961 | 1973 | 1985 | 1997 |
| Tiger | 1926 | 1938 | 1950 | 1962 | 1974 | 1986 | 1998 |
| Rabbit | 1927 | 1939 | 1951 | 1963 | 1975 | 1987 | 1999 |
| Dragon | 1928 | 1940 | 1952 | 1964 | 1976 | 1988 | 2000 |
| Snake | 1929 | 1941 | 1953 | 1965 | 1977 | 1989 | 2001 |
| Horse | 1930 | 1942 | 1954 | 1966 | 1978 | 1990 | 2002 |
| Goat | 1931 | 1943 | 1955 | 1967 | 1979 | 1991 | 2003 |
| Monkey | 1932 | 1944 | 1956 | 1968 | 1980 | 1992 | 2004 |
| Rooster | 1933 | 1945 | 1957 | 1969 | 1981 | 1993 | 2005 |
| Dog | 1934 | 1946 | 1958 | 1970 | 1982 | 1994 | 2006 |
| Pig | 1935 | 1947 | 1959 | 1971 | 1983 | 1995 | 2007 |

and Christianity. Over the centuries, Confucianism, Taoism and Buddhism have fused with popular Chinese beliefs and ancient Vietnamese animism to form what is known collectively as the Triple Religion, or Tam Giao. Confucianism, more a system of social and political morality than a religion, took on many religious aspects. Taoism, which began as an esoteric philosophy for scholars, mixed with Buddhism among the peasants, and many Taoist elements became an intrinsic part of popular religion. If asked their religion the Vietnamese are likely to say that they are Buddhist, but when it comes to family or civic duties they are likely to follow Confucianism while turning to Taoist conceptions in understanding the nature of the cosmos.

## Mahayana Buddhism

Mahayana Buddhism (Dai Thua or Bac Tong, which means From the North – ie China – also known as the Greater Wheel school, Greater Vehicle school and Northern Buddhism) is the predominant religion in Vietnam. The largest Mahayana sect in the country is Zen (Dhyana; in Vietnamese, Thien), also known as the school of meditation. Dao Trang (the Pure Land school), the second-largest Mahayana sect in Vietnam, is practised mainly in the south.

Mahayana Buddhism differs from Theravada Buddhism in several important ways. Whereas the Theravada Buddhist strives to become a perfected saint (arhat) ready for nirvana, the Mahayanist ideal is that of the Bodhisattva, one who strives to perfect himself or herself in the necessary virtues (generosity, morality, patience, vigour, concentration and wisdom), but even after attaining perfection chooses to remain in the world in order to save others.

Mahayanists consider Gautama Buddha to be only one of the innumerable manifestations of the one ultimate Buddha. These countless Buddhas and Bodhisattvas, who are as numberless as the universes to which they minister, gave rise in popular Vietnamese religion – with its innumerable Taoist divinities and spirits – to a pantheon of

deities and helpers whose aid can be sought through invocations and offerings.

Mahayana Buddhist pagodas in Vietnam usually include a number of elements. In front of the pagoda is a white statue of a standing Quan The Am Bo Tat (Avalokiteçvara Bodhisattva in Hindi, Guanyin in Chinese, Goddess of Mercy in English). A variation of the Goddess of Mercy shows her with multiple arms and sometimes multiple eyes and ears, permitting her to touch, see and hear all. This version of the Goddess of Mercy is called Chuan De (Qianshou Guanyin in Chinese).

Inside the main sanctuary are representations of the three Buddhas: A Di Da (pronounced 'AH-zee-dah'; Amitabha), the Buddha of the Past; Thich Ca Mau Ni (Sakyamuni, or Siddhartha Gautama), the historical Buddha; and Di Lac (pronounced 'zee-lock'; Maitreya), the Buddha of the Future. Nearby are often statues of the eight Kim Cang (Genies of the Cardinal Directions), the La Han (arhats) and various Bo Tat (Bodhisattvas) such as Van Thu (Manjusri), Quan The Am Bo Tat

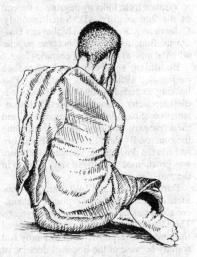

Mahayana Buddhism, also known as the Greater Wheel school, is the predominant religion in Vietnam.

(Avalokiteçvara) and Dia Tang (Ksitigartha). Sometimes, an altar is set aside for Taoist divinities such as Ngoc Hoang (the Jade Emperor) and Thien Hau (the Goddess of the Sea, or Queen of Heaven). Thien Hau is known as Tin Hau in Hong Kong and Matsu in Taiwan. Every pagoda has an altar for funerary tablets commemorating deceased Buddhist monks (who are often buried in stupas near the pagoda) and lay people.

The function of the Vietnamese Buddhist monk *(bonze)* is to minister to the spiritual and superstitious needs of the peasantry, but it is largely up to him whether he invokes the lore of Taoism or the philosophy of Buddhism. A monk may live reclusively on a remote hilltop or he may manage a pagoda on a busy city street. And he may choose to fulfil any number of functions: telling fortunes, making and selling talismans *(fu)*, advising where a house should be constructed, reciting incantations at funerals or even performing acupuncture.

**History** Theravada Buddhism was brought to Vietnam from India by pilgrims at the end of the 2nd century AD. Simultaneously, Chinese monks introduced Mahayana Buddhism. Buddhism did not become popular with the masses until many centuries later.

Buddhism received royal patronage during the 10th to 13th centuries. This backing included recognition of the Buddhist hierarchy, financial support for the construction of pagodas and other projects, and the active participation of the clergy in ruling the country. By the 11th century, Buddhism had filtered down to the villages. Buddhism was proclaimed the official state religion in the mid-12th century.

During the 13th and 14th centuries, Confucian scholars gradually replaced Vietnamese monks as advisers to the Tran Dynasty. The Confucians accused the Buddhists of shirking their responsibilities to family and country because of the Buddhist doctrine of withdrawal from worldly matters. The Chinese invasion of 1414 reinvigorated Confucianism while at the same time result-

ing in the destruction of many Buddhist pagodas and manuscripts. The Nguyen Lords (1558-1778), who ruled the southern part of the country, reversed this trend.

A revival of Vietnamese Buddhism began throughout the country in the 1920s, and Buddhist organisations were created in various parts of the country. In the 1950s and 60s, attempts were made to unite the various streams of Buddhism in Vietnam. During the early 1960s, South Vietnamese Buddhist monks and lay people played an active role in opposing the regime of Ngo Dinh Diem.

Over the centuries, the Buddhist ideals and beliefs held by the educated elite touched only superficially the rural masses (90% of the population), whose traditions were transmitted orally and put to the test by daily observance. The common people were far less concerned with the philosophy of good government than they were with seeking aid from supernatural beings for problems of the here and now.

Gradually, the various Mahayana Buddhas and Bodhisattvas became mixed up with mysticism, animism, polytheism and Hindu tantrism, as well as the multiple divinities and ranks of deities of the Taoist pantheon. The Triple Religion flourished despite clerical attempts to maintain some semblance of Buddhist orthodoxy and doctrinal purity. Although most of the population has only a vague notion of Buddhist doctrines, they invite monks to participate in such life-cycle ceremonies as funerals. And Buddhist pagodas have come to be seen by many Vietnamese as a physical and spiritual refuge from an uncertain world.

After 1975, many monks, including some who actively opposed the South Vietnamese government and the war, were rounded up and sent to re-education camps. Temples were closed and the training of young monks was prohibited. In the last few years, most of these restrictions have been lifted and a religious revival of sorts is taking place.

### Theravada Buddhism
Theravada Buddhism (Tieu Thua or Nam Tong, which means From the South) is also

known as Hinayana, the Lesser Wheel school, the Lesser Vehicle school and Southern Buddhism; it came to Vietnam directly from India. It is practised mainly in the Mekong Delta region, mostly by ethnic-Khmers. The most important Theravada sect in Vietnam is the disciplinary school, Luat Tong.

Basically, the Theravada school of Buddhism is an earlier and, according to its followers, less corrupted form of Buddhism than the Mahayana schools found in most of East Asia and the Himalayan region. The Theravada school is called the Southern school because it took the southern route from India, its place of origin, through South-East Asia (it came directly from India to Vietnam), while the Northern school proceeded north into Nepal, Tibet, China, Korea, Mongolia, Vietnam and Japan. Because the Southern school tried to preserve or limit the Buddhist doctrines to only those canons codified in the early Buddhist era, the Northern school gave Theravada Buddhism the name Hinayana, or Lesser Vehicle. They considered themselves Great Vehicle because they built upon the earlier teachings, 'expanding' the doctrine in such a way so as to respond more to the needs of lay people.

## Confucianism

While it is more a religious philosophy than an organised religion, Confucianism (Nho Giao or Khong Giao) has been an important force in shaping Vietnam's social system and the everyday lives and beliefs of its people.

Confucius (in Vietnamese: Khong Tu) was born in China around 550 BC. He saw people as social beings formed by society yet capable of shaping their society. He believed that the individual exists in and for society and drew up a code of ethics to guide the individual in social interaction. This code laid down a person's specific obligations to family, society and the state. Central to Confucianism is an emphasis on duty and hierarchy.

According to Confucian philosophy, which was brought to Vietnam by the Chinese during their 1000-year rule (111 BC to 938 AD), the emperor alone, governing under the mandate of heaven, can intercede on behalf of the nation with the powers of heaven and earth. Only virtue, as acquired through education, gave one the right (the mandate of heaven) to wield political power. From this it followed that an absence of virtue would result in the withdrawal of this mandate, sanctioning rebellion against an unjust ruler. Natural disasters or defeat on the battlefield were often interpreted as a sign that the mandate of heaven had been withdrawn.

Confucian philosophy was in some senses democratic: because virtue could be acquired only through learning, education rather than birth made a person virtuous. Therefore, education had to be widespread. Until the beginning of this century, Confucian philosophy and texts formed the basis of Vietnam's educational system. Generation after generation of young people – in the villages as well as the cities – were taught their duties to family (including ancestor worship) and community and that each person had to know their place in the social hierarchy and behave accordingly.

A system of government-run civil service examinations selected from among the country's best students those who would join the non-hereditary ruling class, the mandarins. As a result, education was prized not only as the path to virtue, but as a means to social and political advancement. This system helped create the respect for intellectual and literary accomplishment for which the Vietnamese are famous to this day.

The political institutions based on Confucianism finally degenerated and became discredited, as they did elsewhere in the Chinese-influenced world. Over the centuries, the philosophy became conservative and backward-looking. This reactionary trend became dominant in Vietnam in the 15th century, suiting despotic rulers who emphasised the divine right of kings rather than their responsibilities under the doctrine of the mandate of heaven.

## Taoism

Taoism (Lao Giao or Dao Giao) originated in China and is based on the philosophy of Laotse (Thai Thuong Lao Quan). Laotse (literally The Old One) lived in the 6th century BC. Little is known about Laotse and there is some question as to whether or not he really existed. He is believed to have been the custodian of the imperial archives for the Chinese government and Confucius is supposed to have consulted him.

It is doubtful that Laotse ever intended his philosophy to become a religion. Chang Ling has been credited with formally establishing the religion in 143 BC. Taoism later split into two divisions, the Cult of the Immortals and The Way of the Heavenly Teacher.

Understanding Taoism is not easy. The philosophy emphasises contemplation and simplicity of life. Its ideal is returning to the Tao (the Way – the essence of which all things are made). Only a small elite in China and Vietnam has ever been able to grasp Taoist philosophy, which is based on various correspondences (eg the human body, the microcosmic replica of the macrocosm) and complementary contradictions (am & duong, the Vietnamese equivalents of Yin & Yang). As a result, there are very few pure Taoist pagodas in Vietnam, yet much of Taoist ritualism has been absorbed into Chinese and Vietnamese Buddhism. You are most likely to notice the Taoist influence on temples in the form of the dragons and demons which decorate the temple rooftops.

According to the Taoist cosmology, Ngoc Hoang, the Emperor of Jade (in Chinese: Yu Huang), whose abode is in heaven, rules over a world of divinities, genies, spirits and demons in which the forces of nature are incarnated as supernatural beings and great historical personages have become gods. It is this aspect of Taoism that has become assimilated into the daily lives of most Vietnamese as a collection of superstitions and mystical and animistic beliefs. Much of the sorcery and magic that are now part of popular Vietnamese religion have their origins in Taoism.

## Ancestor Worship

Vietnamese ancestor worship, which is the ritual expression of filial piety (hieu), dates from long before the arrival of Confucianism or Buddhism. Some people consider it to be a religion unto itself.

The cult of the ancestors is based on the belief that the soul lives on after death and becomes the protector of its descendants. Because of the influence the spirits of one's ancestors exert on the living, it is considered not only shameful for them to be upset or restless, but downright dangerous. A soul with no descendants is doomed to eternal wandering because it will not receive homage.

Traditionally, the Vietnamese venerate and honour the spirits of their ancestors regularly, especially on the anniversary of the ancestor's death, when sacrifices are offered to both the god of the household and the spirit of the ancestors. To request intercession for success in business or on behalf of a sick child, sacrifices and prayers are offered to the ancestral spirits. The ancestors are informed on occasions of family joy or sorrow, such as weddings, success in an examination or death. Important elements in the cult of the ancestor are the family altar, a plot of land whose income is set aside for the support of the ancestors, and the designation of a direct male descendent of the deceased to assume the obligation to carry on the cult.

Many pagodas have altars on which memorial tablets and photographs of the deceased are displayed. One may look at the young faces in the photographs and ponder the tragedy of so many people having had their lives cut short. Some visitors wonder if they died as a result of the wars. The real explanation is less tragic: most of the dead had passed on decades after the photos were taken, but rather than use a picture of an aged, infirm parent, survivors chose a more flattering (though slightly outdated) picture of the deceased in their prime.

## Caodaism

Caodaism is an indigenous Vietnamese sect that seeks to create the ideal religion by fusing the secular and religious philosophies of both east and west. It was founded in the early 1920s based on messages revealed in seances to Ngo Minh Chieu, the group's founder. The sect's colourful headquarters is in Tay Ninh, 96km north-west of Saigon. There are currently about two million followers of Caodaism in Vietnam. For more information about Caodaism, see Tay Ninh in the Around Ho Chi Minh City chapter.

## Hoa Hao Buddhist Sect

The Hoa Hao Buddhist sect (Phat Giao Hoa Hao) was founded in the Mekong Delta in 1939 by Huynh Phu So, a young man who had studied with the most famous of the region's occultists. After he was miraculously cured of sickliness, So began preaching a reformed Buddhism based on the common people and embodied in personal faith rather than elaborate rituals. His philosophy emphasised simplicity in worship and denied the necessity for intermediaries between human beings and the Supreme Being.

In 1940 the French, who called Huynh Phu So the 'mad monk', tried to silence him. When arresting him failed, they committed him to an insane asylum, where he soon converted the Vietnamese psychiatrist assigned to his case. During WWII, the Hoa Hao Sect continued to grow and to build up a militia with weapons supplied by the Japanese. In 1947, after clashes between Hoa Hao forces and the Viet Minh, Huynh Phu So was assassinated by the Viet Minh, who thereby earned the animosity of what had by then become a powerful political and military force in the Mekong Delta, especially around Chau Doc. The military power of the Hoa Hao was broken in 1956 when one of its guerrilla commanders was captured by the Diem government and publicly guillotined. Subsequently, elements of the Hoa Hao army joined the Viet Cong.

There presently are thought to be approximately 1½ million followers of the Hoa Hao sect.

## Catholicism

Catholicism was introduced into Vietnam in the 16th century by missionaries from Portugal, Spain and France. Particularly active during the 16th and 17th centuries were the French Jesuits and Portuguese Dominicans. Pope Alexander VII assigned the first bishops to Vietnam in 1659 and the first Vietnamese priests were ordained nine years later. According to some estimates, there were 800,000 Catholics in Vietnam by 1685. Over the next three centuries, Catholicism was discouraged and at times outlawed. The first known edict forbidding missionary activity was promulgated in 1533. Foreign missionaries and their followers were severely persecuted during the 17th and 18th centuries.

When the French began their efforts to turn Vietnam into a part of their empire, the treatment of Catholics was one of their most important pretexts for intervention. Under French rule the Catholic church was given preferential status and Catholicism flourished. Though it incorporated certain limited aspects of Vietnamese culture, Catholicism (unlike Buddhism, for instance) succeeded in retaining its doctrinal purity.

Today, Vietnam has the highest percentage of Catholics (8 to 10% of the population) in Asia outside the Philippines. Many of the 900,000 refugees who fled North Vietnam to the South in 1954 were Catholics, as was the then South Vietnamese president Ngo Dinh Diem. Since 1954 in the North and 1975 in the South, Catholics have faced severe restrictions on their religious activities, including strict limits on the ordination of priests and religious education. As in the former Soviet Union, all churches were viewed as being a capitalist institution and a rival centre of power which could subvert the government.

Since around 1990, the government has taken a more liberal line. There is no question that the Catholic religion is now making a comeback, though the old churches have become quite dilapidated and there is a shortage of trained clergy. Also, a lack of funds prevents many churches from doing necessary restoration work, but donations from both locals and Overseas Vietnamese is gradually solving this problem.

## Protestantism

Protestantism was introduced to Vietnam in 1911. The majority of Vietnam's Protestants, who number about 200,000, are Montagnards living in the Central Highlands. The Protestants have been doubly unfortunate in that they were persecuted first by former South Vietnamese president Ngo Dinh Diem (who was a Catholic) and later by the Communists.

Until 1975, the most active Protestant group in South Vietnam was the Christian & Missionary Alliance, whose work went mostly unhindered after Diem's assassination in 1963. After reunification, many Protestant clergymen – especially those trained by American missionaries – were imprisoned. But since 1990, the government has mostly ignored the Protestant church.

## Islam

Muslims – mostly ethnic-Khmers and Chams – constitute about 0.5% of Vietnam's population. There were small communities of Malaysian, Indonesian and south Indian Muslims in Saigon until 1975, when almost all of them fled. Today, Saigon's 5000 Muslims (including a handful of south Indians) congregate in about a dozen mosques, including the large Central Mosque in the city centre.

Arab traders reached China in the 7th century and may have stopped in Vietnam on the way, but the earliest evidence of an Islamic presence in Vietnam is a 10th century pillar inscribed in Arabic which was found near the coastal town of Phan Rang. It appears that Islam spread among Cham refugees who fled to Cambodia after the destruction of their kingdom in 1471, but that these converts had little success in propagating Islam among their fellow Chams still in Vietnam.

The Vietnamese Chams consider themselves Muslims despite the fact that they have only a vague notion of Islamic theology and laws. Their communities have very few copies of the Koran and even their religious dignitaries can hardly read Arabic. Though Muslims the world over pray five times a day, the Chams pray only on Fridays and celebrate Ramadan (a month of dawn to dusk fasting) for only three days. Their worship services consist of the recitation of a few Arabic verses from the Koran in a corrupted form. Instead of performing ritual ablutions, they make motions as if they were drawing water from a well. Circumcision is symbolically performed on boys at age 15; the ceremony consists of a religious leader making the gestures of circumcision with a wooden knife. The Chams of Vietnam do not make the pilgrimage to Mecca and though they do not eat pork, they do drink alcohol. In addition, their Islam-based religious rituals exist side-by-side with animism and the worship of Hindu deities. The Chams have even taken the Arabic words of common Koranic expressions and made them into the names of deities.

Cham religious leaders wear a white robe and an elaborate turban with gold, red or brown tassels. Their ranks are indicated by the length of the tassels.

## Hinduism

Champa was profoundly influenced by Hinduism and many of the Cham towers, built as Hindu sanctuaries, contain lingas (phallic symbols of Shiva) that are still worshipped by ethnic-Vietnamese and ethnic-Chinese alike. After the fall of Champa in the 15th century, most Chams who remained in Vietnam became Muslims, but continued to practise various Brahmanic (high-cast Hindu) rituals and customs.

## LANGUAGE

The Vietnamese language *(Kinh)* is a fusion of Mon-Khmer, Tai and Chinese elements. From the monotonic Mon-Khmer languages, Vietnamese derived a significant percentage of its basic words. From the Tai languages, it adopted certain grammatical elements and tonality. Chinese gave Vietnamese most of its philosophical, literary, technical and governmental vocabulary, as well as its traditional writing system.

From around 1980 to about 1987, anyone caught studying English was liable to get arrested. This was part of a general crackdown against people wanting to flee to the west. That attitude has changed and today the study of English is being pursued with a passion. The most widely spoken foreign languages in Vietnam are Chinese (Cantonese and Mandarin), English and French, more or less in that order. People in their 50s and older (who grew up during the colonial period) are much more likely to understand some French than southerners of the following generation, for whom English was indispensable for professional and commercial contacts with the Americans. Some southern Vietnamese men – former combat interpreters – speak a quaint form of English peppered with all sorts of charming southern-American expressions like 'y'all come back' and 'it ain't worth didley-squat', pronounced with a perceptible drawl. Apparently, they worked with Americans from the Deep South, carefully studied their pronunciation and diligently learned every nuance.

Many of the Vietnamese who speak English – especially former South Vietnamese soldiers and officials – learned it while working with the Americans during the war. After reunification, almost all of them spent periods of time ranging from a few months to 15 years in 're-education camps'. Many such former South Vietnamese soldiers and officials will be delighted to renew contact with Americans, with whose compatriots they spent so much time, often in very difficult circumstances, half-a-lifetime ago. Former long-term prisoners often have friends and acquaintances all over the country (you meet an awful lot of people in 10 or more years), constituting an 'old-boys' network' of sorts.

These days, almost everyone has a desire to learn English. If you're looking to make contacts with English students, the best place is at the basic food-stalls in university areas. But at times you might find yourself looking to avoid such contacts, as one foreigner commented:

At a sightseeing spot I was awaited by a group studying English in evening classes. They go in their spare time to tourist areas hoping to get a chance to talk with foreigners. Sometimes it gets a bit tiresome to cope with enthusiastic students having a very limited vocabulary, but I believe it is a must to be polite and never to be arrogant or rude. I observed that foreigners are often disrespectful towards Vietnamese, and that really annoyed me. Often the locals told me that foreigners are reluctant, evasive and also insulting when approached by Vietnamese students. I tried to explain to my counterparts that some travellers might be afraid when approached and surrounded by a group of strangers. I explained to them the paranoia caused by crime in the west, which they found surprising – they simply weren't aware of the problems of western societies. When I told them openly of the negative aspects of my country, they immediately opened up to me too, telling off-the-record facts. Silly small talk is not what they are interested in, only the language barrier reduces conversations to that level. Better be prepared for questions about capitalistic societies: economics, law, the parliamentary system and so on.

Spoken Chinese (both Cantonese and Mandarin dialects) is making a definite comeback after years of being repressed. The large number of free-spending tourists and investors from Taiwan and Hong Kong provides the chief motivation for studying Chinese. In addition, cross-border trade with mainland China has been increasing rapidly and those who can speak Chinese are well positioned to profit from it.

After reunification, the teaching of Russian was stressed all over the country. With the collapse of the USSR in 1991, all interest in studying Russian has ground to a screeching halt. Most Vietnamese who bothered to learn the language have either forgotten it or are in the process of forgetting.

## Writing

For centuries, the Vietnamese language was written in standard Chinese characters (chu nho). Around the 13th century, the Vietnamese devised their own system of writing (chu nom or just nom), which was derived by combining Chinese characters or using them for their phonetic significance only. Both writing systems were used simultaneously until the 20th century – official business and scholarship was conducted in chu nho, while chu nom was used for popular literature.

The Latin-based *quoc ngu* script, in wide use since WWI, was developed in the 17th century by Alexandre de Rhodes, a brilliant French Jesuit scholar who first preached in Vietnamese only six months after arriving in the country in 1627. By replacing nom characters with quoc ngu, Rhodes facilitated the propagation of the gospel to a wide audience. The use of quoc ngu served to undermine the position of mandarin officials, whose power was based on traditional scholarship written in chu nho and chu nom and largely inaccessible to the masses.

The Vietnamese treat every syllable as an independent word, so 'Saigon' gets spelled 'Sai Gon' and 'Vietnam' is written as 'Viet Nam'. Foreigners aren't too comfortable with this system – we prefer to read 'London' rather than 'Lon Don'. This leads to the notion that Vietnamese is a 'monosyllabic language', where every syllable represents an independent word. This idea appears to be a hangover from the Chinese writing system, where every syllable was represented by an independent character and each character was treated as a meaningful word. In reality, Vietnamese appears to be polysyllabic, like English. However, writing systems do influence people's perceptions of their own language, so Vietnamese themselves will insist that their language is monosyllabic – it's a debate probably not worth pursuing.

## Pronunciation & Tones

Most of the names of the letters of the quoc ngu alphabet are pronounced like the letters of the French alphabet. Dictionaries are alphabetised as in English except that each vowel/tone combination is treated as a different letter. The consonants of the Romanised Vietnamese alphabet are pronounced more or less as they are in English with a few exceptions, and Vietnamese makes no use of the Roman letters 'f', 'j', 'w' and 'z'.

**c**      like a 'k' but with no aspiration.
**d**      with a crossbar; like a hard 'd'.

**d**      without a crossbar; like a 'z' in the north and a 'y' in the south.
**gi-**   like a 'z' in the north and a 'y' in the south.
**kh-**   like '-ch' in the German buch.
**ng-**   like the '-nga-' in 'long ago'.
**nh-**   like the Spanish 'ñ' (as in mañana).
**ph-**   like an 'f'.
**r**      like a 'z' in the north and an 'r' in the south.
**s**      like an 's' in the north and 'sh' in the south.
**tr-**    like 'ch-' in the north and 'tr-' in the south.
**th-**    like a strongly aspirated 't'.
**x**      like an 's'.
**-ch**   like a 'k'.
**-ng**   like '-ng' in 'long' but with the lips closed.
**-nh**   like '-ng' in 'sing'.

The hardest part of studying Vietnamese for westerners is learning to differentiate between the tones. There are six tones in spoken Vietnamese. Thus, every syllable in Vietnamese can be pronounced six different ways. Depending on the tones, the word *ma* can be read to mean phantom, but, mother, rice seedling, tomb or horse. *Ga* can mean railway station or chicken as well several other things.

The six tones of spoken Vietnamese are indicated with five diacritical marks in written form (the first tone is left unmarked). These should not be confused with the four other diacritical marks used to indicate special consonants (such as the 'd' with a cross through it).

## Grammar

Vietnamese grammar is fairly straightforward, with a wide variety of possible sentence structures. The numbers and genders of nouns are generally not explicit, nor are the tenses and moods of verbs. Instead, tool words (such as *cua*, which means 'belong to') and classifiers are used to show a word's relationship to its neighbours. Verbs are turned into nouns by adding *su*.

Questions are asked in the negative, as with *n'est-ce pas?* in French. When the

Vietnamese ask 'Is it OK?' they say 'It is OK, is it not?' The answer 'no' means 'Not OK it is not,' which is the double-negative form of 'Yes, it is OK'. The answer 'yes', on the other hand, means 'Yes, it is not OK' or as we would say in English 'No, it is not OK'. The result is that when negative questions ('It's not OK, is it?') are posed to Vietnamese, great confusion often results.

## Proper Names

Most Vietnamese names consist of a family name, a middle name and a given name, in that order. Thus, if Henry David Thoreau had been Vietnamese, he would have been named Thoreau David Henry. He would have been addressed as Mr Henry – people are called by their given name, but to do so without the title Mr, Mrs or Miss is considered as expressing either great intimacy or arrogance of the sort a superior would use with his or her inferior.

In Vietnamese, Mr is *Ong* if the man is of your grandparents' generation, *Bac* if he is of your parents' age, *Chu* if he is younger than your parents and *Anh* if he is in his teens or early 20s. Mrs is *Ba* if the woman is of your grandparents' age and *Bac* if she is of your parents' generation or younger. Miss is *Chi* or *Em* unless the woman is very young, in which case *Co* might be more appropriate. Other titles of respect are Buddhist monk *(Thay)*, Buddhist nun *(Ba)*, Catholic priest *(Cha)* and Catholic nun *(Co)*.

There are 300 or so family names in use in Vietnam, the most common of which is Nguyen (pronounced something like 'nwyen'). About half of all Vietnamese have the surname Nguyen! When women marry, they usually (but not always) take their husband's family name. The middle name may be purely ornamental, may indicate the sex of its bearer or may be used by all the male members of a given family. A person's given name is carefully chosen so that it forms a harmonious and meaningful ensemble with his or her family and middle names and with the names of other family members.

To get you started, here are some useful survival words and phrases:

## Pronouns

I
   *tôi*
you (to an older man)
   *(các) ông*
you (to an older woman)
   *(các) bà*
you (to a man your own age)
   *(các) anh*
you (to a woman your own age)
   *(các) chi*
you (to a woman, formal)
   *(các) cô*
you (to a younger person)
   *(các) em*
he
   *cậu ấy/anh ấy* (north)
   *cậu đó/anh đó* (south)
she
   *chị ấy/cô ấy* (north)
   *chị đó/anh đó* (south)
we
   *chúng tôi*
they
   *họ*
you (pl)
   *quí vị*

## Useful Words & Phrases

| | |
|---|---|
| come | *đến* |
| give | *cho* |
| fast | *nhanh* (north) |
| | *mau* (south) |
| slow | *chậm* |
| man | *nam* |
| woman | *nữ* |
| understand | *hiểu* |
| I don't understand. | *Tôi không hiểu.* |
| I need... | *Tôi cần...* |
| change money | *đổi tiền* |

## Greetings & Civilities

| | |
|---|---|
| Hello. | *Xin chào.* |
| How are you? | *Có khoẻ không?* |
| Fine, thank you. | *Khoẻ, cám ơn.* |
| Good night. | *Chúc ngủ ngon.* |
| Excuse me. | *Xin lỗi.* |
| (often used before questions) | |
| Thank you. | *Cám ơn.* |

| Thank you very much. | *Cám ơn rất nhiều.* |
|---|---|
| Yes. | *Vâng.* (north) |
| | *Dạ.* (south) |
| No. | *Không.* |

## Small Talk

| What is your name? | *Tên là gì?* |
|---|---|
| My name is... | *Tên tôi là...* |
| I like... | *Tôi thích...* |
| I don't like... | *Tôi không thích...* |
| I want... | *Tôi muốn...* |
| I don't want... | *Tôi không muốn...* |

## Getting Around

What time does the first bus depart?
  *Chuyến xe buýt sớm nhất chạy lúc mấy giờ?*
What time does the last bus depart?
  *Chuyến xe buýt cuối cùng sẽ chạy lúc mấy giờ?*
How many km is it to...
  *Cách xa bao nhiêu ki-lô-mét...*
How many hours does the journey take?
  *Chuyến đi sẽ mất bao lâu?*
Go.
  *Đi.*
I want to go to...
  *Tôi muốn đi...*
What time does it arrive?
  *Mấy giờ đến?*
What time does it depart?
  *Xe chạy lúc mấy giờ?*
hire an automobile
  *thuê xe hơi* (north)
  *muớn xe hơi* (south)

| bus | *xe buýt* |
|---|---|
| bus station | *bến xe* |
| cyclo (pedicab) | *xe xích lô* |
| map | *bản đồ* |
| railway station | *ga xe lửa* |
| receipt | *biên lai* |
| sleeping berth | *giường ngủ* |
| timetable | *thời biểu* |
| train | *xe lửa* |

## Around Town

| office | *văn phòng* |
|---|---|
| post office | *bưu điện* |
| restaurant | *nhà hàng* |
| telephone | *điện thoại* |
| tourism | *du lịch* |

## Accommodation

Where is there a (cheap) hotel?
  *Ở đâu có khách sạn (rẻ tiền)?*
How much does a room cost?
  *Giá một phòng là bao nhiêu?*
I would like a cheap room.
  *Tôi thích một phòng loại rẻ.*
I need to leave at (5) o'clock tomorrow morning.
  *Tôi phải đi lúc (năm) giờ sáng mai.*

| hotel | *khách sạn* |
|---|---|
| guesthouse | *nhà khách* |
| air-conditioning | *máy lạnh* |
| bathroom | *phòng tắm* |
| blanket | *mền* |
| fan | *quạt máy* |
| hot water | *nước nóng* |
| laundry | *giặt ủi* |
| mosquito net | *mùng* |
| reception | *tiếp tân* |
| room | *phòng* |
| room key | *chìa khóa phòng* |
| 1st-class room | *phòng loại 1* |
| 2nd-class room | *phòng loại 2* |
| sheet | *ra trãi giường* |
| toilet | *nhà vệ sinh* |
| toilet paper | *giấy vệ sinh* |
| towel | *khăn tắm* |

## Geographical Terms & Directions

| street | *đường/phố* |
|---|---|
| boulevard | *đại lộ* |
| bridge | *cầu* |
| highway | *xa lộ* |
| island | *đảo* |
| mountain | *núi* |
| National Highway 1 | *Quốc Lộ 1* |
| river | *sông* |
| square (in a city) | *công viên* |

| east | *đông* |
|---|---|
| north | *bắc* |
| south | *nam* |
| west | *tây* |

## Shopping

Don't have...
*Không có...*
How much is this?
*Cái này giá bao nhiêu?*
I want to pay in dong.
*Tôi muốn trả bằng tiền Việt Nam.*

| | |
|---|---|
| buy | *mua* |
| sell | *bán* |
| cheap | *rẻ tiền* |
| expensive | *đắt tiền* (north) |
| | *mắc tiền* (south) |
| really expensive | *rất đắt* (north) |
| | *mắc qua* (south) |
| market | *chợ* |
| mosquito coils | *hương đốt chống muỗi* (north) |
| | *nhang chống muỗi* (south) |
| insect repellent | *thuốc chống muỗi* |
| sanitary pads | *băng vệ sinh* |

## Times & Dates

| | |
|---|---|
| evening | *chiều* |
| now | *bây giờ* |
| today | *hôm nay* |
| tomorrow | *ngày mai* |
| Monday | *Thứ hai* |
| Tuesday | *Thứ ba* |
| Wednesday | *Thứ tư* |
| Thursday | *Thứ năm* |
| Friday | *Thứ sáu* |
| Saturday | *Thứ bảy* |
| Sunday | *Chủ nhật* |

## Numbers

| | |
|---|---|
| 1 | *một* |
| 2 | *hai* |
| 3 | *ba* |
| 4 | *bốn* |
| 5 | *năm* |
| 6 | *sáu* |
| 7 | *bảy* |
| 8 | *tám* |
| 9 | *chín* |
| 10 | *mười* |

| | |
|---|---|
| 11 | *mười một* |
| 19 | *mười chín* |
| 20 | *hai mươi* |
| 21 | *hai mươi mốt* |
| 30 | *ba mươi* |
| 90 | *chín mươi* |
| 100 | *một trăm* |
| 200 | *hai trăm* |
| 900 | *chín trăm* |
| 1000 | *một ngàn* |
| 10,000 | *mười ngàn* |
| 1 million | *một triệu* |
| first | *thứ nhất* |
| second | *thứ hai* |

## Health

I'm sick.
*Tôi bị ốm.* (north)
*Tôi bị đau.* (south)
Please take me to the hospital.
*Làm ơn đưa tôi bệnh viện.*
Please call a doctor.
*Làm ơn gọi bác sĩ.*

| | |
|---|---|
| dentist | *nha sĩ* |
| doctor | *bác sĩ* |
| hospital | *bệnh viện* |
| pharmacy | *nhà thuốc tây* |
| backache | *đau lưng* |
| diarrhoea | *tiêu chảy* (north) |
| | *ỉa chảy* (south) |
| dizziness | *chóng mặt* |
| fever | *cảm/cúm* |
| headache | *nhức đầu* |
| malaria | *sốt rét* |
| stomachache | *đau bụng* |
| toothache | *nhức răng* |
| vomiting | *ói/mửa* |

## Emergencies

| | |
|---|---|
| Help! | *Cứu tôi với!* |
| Thief! | *Cướp, cắp!* |
| Pickpocket! | *Móc túi!* |
| police | *công an* |
| Immigration Police Office | *phòng quản lý người nước ngoài* |

# Facts for the Visitor

## PLANNING
### When to Go
There are no good or bad seasons for visiting Vietnam. When one region is wet, cold or steaming hot, there is always somewhere else that is sunny and pleasantly warm.

Visitors should take into account that around Tet, the colourful Vietnamese New Year celebration which falls in late January or early February, flights into, out of and around the country are likely to be booked solid and accommodation can be almost impossible to find. The New Year festival is more than just a one day event – it goes on for at least a week. For at least a week before and two weeks after Tet you are likely to encounter some difficulties in booking hotels and flights; this applies also to the whole of eastern Asia.

### Maps
**Within Vietnam** Excellent maps of Saigon, Hanoi, Danang, Hué and a few other major cities are issued in slightly different forms every few years. Unfortunately, maps of smaller towns and cities are practically non-existent. Most Vietnamese have never seen a map of the town they live in.

Almost every bookstore in Vietnam can sell you a map of the entire country. However, these maps are lacking in detail and are often several years out of date.

Maps of individual provinces can sometimes be bought in the provincial capitals, but it's hit or miss.

Highly detailed topographic maps are a boon to hikers and cyclists, but these are not easy to find. The Vietnamese government treats them like military secrets – ridiculous in this age of satellite photos. The best of these maps were produced by the Americans during the war, but these are rather out of date – towns have changed names and new roads have been built. The Vietnamese government has produced new ones, but you need special permission to buy them.

However, you can sometimes find a few of these on sale from street vendors in Hanoi and Saigon.

If you can obtain the necessary special permission, the place which sells these topographic maps (for US$3 each) is Gecase Company (☎ 845-2670; fax 842-4216) at 28 Nguyen Van Troi St, Phu Nhuan District, Ho Chi Minh City. It's very close to Vinh Nghiem Pagoda.

**Outside Vietnam** Lonely Planet produces the *Vietnam travel atlas*. Nelles has a large fold-up map of Vietnam, Cambodia and Laos. There are also the excellent 'operational navigation charts' produced in the USA for air navigation purposes. These are designed to be used in conjunction with a geopositioning device which receives a signal from satellites and plots your exact position. While it will probably be some time before you'll be able to fly your own ultralight across Vietnam, the maps are of limited use to back-country explorers. They are in Romanised form and very detailed, but provincial boundaries are not shown.

### What to Bring
Bring as little as possible. Many travellers try to bring everything bar the kitchen sink. Keep in mind that you can and will buy things in Vietnam (especially clothing), so don't burden yourself with a lot of unnecessary junk.

Nevertheless, there are things you will want to bring from home. But the first thing to consider is what kind of bag you will use to carry all your goods.

Backpacks are the easiest type of bag to carry and a frameless or internal-frame pack is the easiest to manage on buses and trains. Packs that close with a zipper can usually be secured with a padlock. Of course, any pack can be slit open with a razor blade, but a padlock will usually prevent pilfering by hotel staff and baggage handlers at airports.

A cable lock (or loop cable with lock) can be used to secure the backpack on buses and trains (pack snatchers are a serious problem).

A daypack can be handy. Leave your main luggage at the hotel or left-luggage room in the train stations. A beltpack is OK for maps, extra film and other miscellanea, but don't use it for valuables such as your travellers cheques and passport, as it's an easy target for pickpockets.

If you don't want to use a backpack, a shoulder bag is much easier to carry than a suitcase. Some cleverly designed shoulder bags can also double as backpacks by rearranging a few straps. Forget suitcases.

Inside? Lightweight and compact are two words that should be etched in your mind when you're deciding what to bring. Dark coloured clothing is preferred because it doesn't show the dirt – white clothes will force you to do laundry daily. You will, no doubt, be buying clothes along the way – you can find some real bargains in Vietnam and neighbouring countries. However, don't believe sizes – 'large' in Asia is often equivalent to 'medium' in the west.

Nylon sports shoes are best – comfortable, washable and lightweight. Sandals are appropriate footwear in the tropical heat – even Ho Chi Minh wore them during his public appearances. Rubber thongs are somewhat less appropriate for formal occasions, but are nevertheless commonly worn in the south. In the north, many people will laugh at foreigners wearing rubber thongs (even if the laughers are wearing thongs themselves).

A Swiss army knife (even if not made in Switzerland) comes in handy, but you don't need one with 27 separate functions. Basically, you need one small sharp blade, a can opener and a bottle opener – a built-in magnifying glass or backscratcher isn't necessary.

The secret of successful packing is plastic bags or nylon 'stuff bags' – they keep things not only separate and clean, but also dry.

The following is a checklist of things you might consider packing. You can delete whatever you like from this list (though unlike on a computer, there will be no warning like 'Are you sure?'). If you do forget to bring some 'essential' item, most likely it can be bought in Vietnam, at least in Saigon and Hanoi.

Passport, visa, documents (vaccination certificate, diplomas, marriage licence photocopy, student ID card), money, moneybelt, air ticket, address book, namecards, visa photos (about 10), calculator (for currency conversions), Swiss army knife, camera and accessories, extra camera battery, colour slide film, video camera and blank tapes, radio, Walkman and rechargeable batteries, battery recharger (220V), reading material, padlock, cable lock (to secure luggage on trains), sunglasses, contact lens solution, alarm clock, leakproof water bottle, torch (flashlight) with batteries and bulbs, comb, compass, daypack, long pants, short pants, long shirt, T-shirt, nylon jacket, sweater (only in winter), raincover for backpack, umbrella or rain poncho, razor, razor blades, shaving cream, sewing kit, spoon, sunhat, sunscreen (UV lotion), toilet paper, tampons, toothbrush, toothpaste, dental floss, deodorant, shampoo, laundry detergent, underwear, socks, thongs, nail clipper, tweezers, mosquito repellent, insecticide, moist towelettes, vitamins, laxative, anti-diarrhoea drugs, condoms, contraceptives, special medications you use and medical kit (see the Health section).

If you'll be doing any cycling, bring all necessary safety equipment (helmet, reflectors, mirrors etc), as well as an inner tube repair kit.

A final thought: airlines do lose bags from time to time – you have a much better chance of it not being yours if it is tagged with your name and address *inside* the bag as well as outside. Other tags can always fall off or be removed.

Clothing is very cheap and abundant in Vietnam, so don't be concerned about bringing everything from abroad. The only problem might be in finding large western sizes.

To the relief of backpackers, Vietnamese are less formal in dress than in many neighbouring countries (they can't afford the tailored suits and dresses yet). If you see a man walking around wearing a tie, he's more likely to be a Chinese businessman than a local.

Wearing short pants is generally considered rude in most parts of Vietnam and this particularly applies to women. Until very recently, Vietnamese women never wore shorts in public, even when labouring in the rice paddies under the sweltering sun. But times are changing, especially in go-go Saigon, where western trends are copied first before spreading around the country. Since about 1994, young women have started wearing shorts in Saigon and then in Hanoi, a fashion no doubt copied from western tourists. At first the shorts were fairly conservative, but lately the styles have grown more bold. As for the Vietnamese men, short shorts are not on, but the baggy Bermuda type have started to gain popularity. However, you are only likely to see people wearing shorts in major cities that see a lot of tourist traffic. Elsewhere, it is still regarded as indecent and that particularly applies to hill tribe areas such as the Central Highlands and far north.

For women, two-piece swimsuits are considered OK, but skimpy bikinis are pushing the limits. At hotel swimming pools frequented by foreigners, bikinis are now acceptable though the locals may do a bit of staring. However, public beaches tend to be more conservative.

As for public nudity, it's just not acceptable anywhere in the country, not even beaches or hot springs resorts. It will be some years – if ever – before Vietnam can compete with the French Riviera or the Australian Sunshine Coast in this regard.

Definitely not recommended are the hill-climbing boots with 25 eyelets on each side. These may be great for mountain climbing, but you will regret them at every private home, temple and even mini-hotel where shoes should be removed. The often hot weather and need to take shoes off frequently would argue for wearing slip-off thongs or sandals. Just make sure that you buy a comfortable pair that you can walk in and won't fall off when you ride on a motorbike. One innovative type of sandal which you can easily purchase in Bangkok (but not yet in Vietnam) is fastened to your feet with Velcro straps – secure, but easy to remove.

If you have particularly large feet, finding shoes to fit you could be difficult in Vietnam. For the average western tourist, this will probably not be a problem.

## HIGHLIGHTS

Vietnam offers tremendous variety and can suit many different tastes – it's difficult to say just what places should be on the top of your list. Beach lovers will almost certainly want to check out Nha Trang and – for the more adventurous – Phu Quoc Island. Dalat – with its park-like setting, waterfalls, ethnic minorities and cool mountain climate – is considered the jewel of the Central Highlands. The splendid rock formations, sea cliffs and grottoes of Halong Bay could easily rate as one of the wonders of the world. Nearby Cat Ba Island also gets rave reviews from all who make the effort to get there. Similar scenery (but without the water) can be seen at the Perfume Pagoda and Tam Coc. Sapa and nearby Bac Ha offer a glimpse of minority lifestyles near the mountains along the Chinese border. Other opportunities to visit minority villages and do some hiking exist at Mai Chau. The rugged overland trip to Dien Bien Phu passes through one of Vietnam's most wild and remote areas, home to numerous ethnic minorities. The Mekong Delta is more varied than most people imagine – popular scenic spots include Cantho, Soc Trang and Chau Doc.

History and architecture buffs will be attracted to Hué and Hoi An. For those fascinated by the American war effort and all its implications, what better place to pursue the topic than the old Demilitarised Zone (DMZ)?

And if you've had enough of seeing what Vietnam's landscape looks like, perhaps you'd like to see what's under it? There are few better places to do this than at Phong Nha Cave.

Finally, one should not forget the cities. Freewheeling Saigon, with its dilapidated colonial elegance, outstanding food and bustling nightlife, is a laboratory for Vietnam's economic reforms. Hanoi, with its monuments, parks, lakes and tree-lined boulevards, is the beguiling seat of power in a country trying to figure out which direction to head.

## SUGGESTED ITINERARIES
### One Week
Fly into Saigon, do a day trip to the Cu Chi tunnels, a three day tour of the Mekong Delta and a day trip to Vung Tau. Use the rest of the time for sightseeing, eating, shopping and carousing in Saigon.

### Two Weeks
Do all of the foregoing, plus a trip to Dalat and Nha Trang. If time permits, you could head for Hoi An and then fly back to Saigon from Danang.

### One Month
This is enough time to take in most of the major sights. Do everything mentioned previously, then from Hoi An or Danang press on to Hué. Many people do a DMZ tour out of Hué and after that head overland (or fly) to Hanoi. The Hanoi area offers many interesting side trips including the Perfume Pagoda, Halong Bay, Cat Ba Island, Tam Coc, Mai Chau, Bac Ha and Sapa. You can exit Vietnam by air from Hanoi or continue overland to China. It's entirely possible to do the trip in reverse, starting from the north and going south.

### Two Months
This will allow you to see everything in detail. Aside from what has already been mentioned, explore the Mekong Delta more thoroughly and make a side trip to lovely Phu Quoc Island. Visit the giant sand dunes at Phan Thiet before heading up to Nha Trang. A trip to the western part of the Central Highlands should include a visit to Kon Tum. Don't forget Phong Nha Cave to the north of the DMZ. In the far north, you can get to such backwaters as Dien Bien Phu, Cao Bang, Ba Be Lakes and Bai Tu Long Bay.

## TOURIST OFFICES
Vietnam's tourist offices are not like those found in capitalist countries. If you were to visit a government-run tourist office in Australia, western Europe, Japan or decidedly free-market Hong Kong, you'd get lots of free colourful, glossy brochures and maps and helpful advice on transport, places to stay, where to book tours and so on. Such tourist offices make no profit – indeed, they are big money losers, though they may be supported by a tax on travel agencies or hotels which benefit from the tourist office's services.

Vietnam's tourist offices operate on a different philosophy. They are government-owned enterprises whose primary interests are booking tours and earning a profit. In fact, these 'tourist offices' are little more than travel agencies, but they are among the most profitable hard-currency cash cows the Vietnamese government has. Don't come here looking for freebies; even the colourful brochures and maps – when they have them – are for sale.

Vietnam Tourism (Tong Cong Ty Du Lich Viet Nam) and Saigon Tourist (Cong Ty Du Lich Thanh Pho Ho Chi Minh) are the oldest examples of this genre. However, nowadays every province has at least one such organisation, while big cities like Saigon and Hanoi may have dozens of competing government-run 'tourist offices', with each one earning a tidy profit. Many private companies have formed joint ventures with the state-run organisations, thus further diluting any real distinction between these 'tourist offices' and private travel agencies.

## VISAS & DOCUMENTS
### Visas
Without a doubt, bureaucratic visa hassles considerably reduce the number of tourists who visit Vietnam. However, arranging the necessary paperwork for a Vietnamese visa has become fairly straightforward – the problem is just that it tends to be expensive and unnecessarily time-consuming. Furthermore, Vietnamese visas come with numerous restrictions, as mentioned below.

A significant restriction (but not the only one) is that your visa must specify exactly where you will enter the country and where you will exit. Vietnam might just be the only country in the world to slap on this restriction. This limits your flexibility, but it is possible to change the exit point after you've arrived in Vietnam. This must be arranged at the immigration police (located in each provincial capital) or at the Foreign Affairs Ministry in Hanoi. The cost for this rubber stamp is US$25. Making this simple change can take from one to three days – if you want it fast then you may be charged extra for 'express service'.

In most cases you are better off getting your visa from a travel agent rather than from the Vietnamese embassy directly. This is because all visas issued by embassies will be stamped directly into your passport, while travel agencies will get it on a separate piece of paper *if you ask*. In most cases, having it on a separate paper will prove safer. The reason is that within Vietnam itself you will often be required to leave your visa with the hotel reception desk (they need it to register your presence with the police), with a travel agency (to get a local travel permit) or with bureaucratic ministries of every sort. In Vietnam, it seems that everyone wants your passport or visa to do something or other. With so many hands shuttling your visa from one place to another, this valuable piece of paper could get lost. Replacing a lost visa will be a hassle, but still *much* easier than replacing your entire passport.

The travel agency doing your visa needs a photocopy of your passport and two or three photos (the actual number differs in various countries). Do not leave your passport with the travel agency or it's likely the visa will be stamped into it despite any instructions to the contrary.

Bangkok has always been the most convenient place to get Vietnamese visas. Even travel agents in neighbouring countries send the paperwork by courier to Bangkok for processing because it's so much cheaper than dealing with the local Vietnamese embassy (the one in Beijing is notorious). In Bangkok, single-entry tourist visas cost US$40 at budget travel agencies. Many travel agencies offer package deals with a visa and round-trip air ticket included (Bangkok-Saigon, returning Hanoi-Bangkok). The place to look for competitive prices is Khao San Rd in Bangkok.

**Tourist Visas** Processing a visa application takes five working days in Bangkok (two days for an express visa), five days in Malaysia, five to 10 days in Hong Kong and 10 working days in Taiwan. No one has yet to offer a satisfactory explanation of why it should take so much longer in some countries than in others.

Tourist visas are valid for only a single 30-day stay. To make matters worse, the visa specifies the exact date of arrival and departure. Thus, you must solidify your travel plans well in advance. You cannot arrive even one day earlier than your visa specifies. And if you change your plans and postpone your trip by two weeks, then you'll only have 16 days remaining on your visa instead of 30 days.

Theoretically, you can enter Vietnam with a sponsor's letter and get your visa stamped into your passport on arrival for US$110. In practice, this is more trouble than it's worth. Aside from being expensive, this 'visa on arrival' process is not easy to arrange and is usually only done for group tours. Only a few travel agencies are authorised to do the sponsor's letter, so for most travellers this just isn't an option. If you do use this procedure, note that you must have the right cash (US dollars in the exact amount) because there is no place to change money before you pass through immigration.

You might think that once you've obtained your visa and landed in Vietnam that all is well. Unfortunately, you still have to pass Vietnamese immigration and the people in charge of this have complete authority to decide on how long you can stay. While most people get through OK, the immigration staff may arbitrarily give you a shorter stay than what your visa calls for. Thus, your 30-day visa might be validated for only one week, or a three-month visa for just one month. No matter what it says on the front side of your visa, immediately after it's been stamped by the immigration officer, look on the back side and see how many days they've given you. If you've only been given a week, sometimes you can get it changed right at the airport or border checkpoint – otherwise you will be forced to visit the immigration police and apply for an extension. It's been our experience that your physical appearance will play a part in the reception you receive from immigration – if you wear shorts or scruffy clothing, look dirty or unshaven etc, then you can expect problems. You don't need to get all dressed up, but try to look 'respectable'.

Always have some photos with you because immigration police have been known to inexplicably give travellers more forms to fill out and attached photos are required. Of course, there is a photographer right there at the airport to serve you – for a substantial fee.

**Business Visas** There are several advantages in having a business visa: such visas are usually valid for three months, can be issued for multiple-entry journeys and will look more impressive when you have to deal with bureaucratic authorities. Also, you are permitted to work if you have a business visa, though doing so will make you subject to taxes and other bureaucratic regulations which change from week to week.

Getting a business visa has now become fairly easy. The travel agencies which do tourist visas can also do business visas. The main drawback is cost – a business visa costs about four times what you'd pay for a tourist visa. Trying to obtain the visa yourself through a Vietnamese embassy will probably be more trouble than it's worth – you'd better let a travel agent handle it. However, remember the preceding warning – immigration officials may validate your visa for only one month upon arrival even though a business visa is good for three months.

There is another category of business visa which remains valid for six months. To get these, you must apply in Vietnam. If approved, you must then go abroad (most travellers go to Phnom Penh or Vientiane) to pick up the visa from a Vietnamese embassy.

**Student Visas** A student visa is something you usually arrange after arrival. It's acceptable to enter Vietnam on a tourist visa, enrol in a Vietnamese language course and then apply at the immigration police for a change in status. Of course, you do have to pay tuition and are expected to attend class. A minimum of 10 hours of study per week is needed to qualify for student status.

**Resident Visas** Only a few foreigners can qualify for a resident visa. Probably the easiest way to do this is to marry a local, though anyone contemplating doing this had best be prepared for mountains of paperwork. Spouses of Vietnamese nationals gain a few other advantages besides a resident visa – for example, they can own 50% of the couple's property (including real estate).

Residency visas currently cost US$170 for six months, plus US$170 for each extension.

**Visa Extensions** If you've got the dollars, they've got the rubber stamp. In Saigon and Hanoi, visa extensions cost US$35. At least in those two cities, you should go to a travel agency to get this taken care of. Fronting up at the immigration police yourself usually doesn't work. The procedure takes one or two days and one photo is needed. You can apply for your extension even several weeks before it's necessary. Official policy is that you are permitted one visa extension only for a maximum of 30 days.

Be alert for sudden unannounced changes to these regulations. In the early 1990s, two visa extensions (60 days) were permitted, then suddenly in 1995 *no* visa extensions were permitted, but in 1996 one visa extension (30 days) was being allowed. Sudden and arbitrary changes to the regulations are standard procedure in Vietnam – try not to get caught short.

Usually the extension goes smoothly if you work through a reliable agent who has good connections. The less you personally get involved with the bureaucracy, the better off you are.

In theory, you should be able to extend your visa in any provincial capital. In practice, it goes smoothest in certain cities catering to mass tourism. Hué and Vung Tau have a reputation for being good about visa extensions.

I got my visa extension in Vinh, which only cost US$2, but in Saigon I was later told that this was invalid. The police cancelled my first extension, forced me to buy a second one, plus I had to pay a US$10 fine for overstaying 13 days. I also lost three days dealing with the bureaucracy.

**Gerhard Heinzel**

The official word is that even if you do get your visa extension in some obscure backwater (such as Vinh), the airport immigration police will accept this and allow you to depart with no problems.

**Re-entry Visas** If you wish to visit Cambodia, Laos or any other country, it is possible to do this and then re-enter Vietnam using your original single-entry Vietnamese visa. However, you must apply for a re-entry visa before departing Vietnam. If you do not have a re-entry visa, then you will have to go through the whole expensive and time-consuming procedure of applying for a new Vietnamese visa. Re-entry visas are easy enough to arrange in Hanoi or Saigon, but you will almost certainly have to ask a travel agent to do the paperwork for you. Travel agents charge about US$25 for this service and can complete the procedure in one or two days. Although travellers can theoretically secure the re-entry visa without going through a travel agent, Vietnamese bureaucrats usually thwart such individual efforts.

Remember that your re-entry visa also must show the point where you intend to re-enter Vietnam. So if you fly from Vietnam to Cambodia and want to re-enter overland, your re-entry visa must indicate this. However, this can be amended by the Vietnamese embassy in Cambodia if you didn't get it right the first time.

If you already have a valid multiple-entry visa for Vietnam, you do not need a re-entry visa.

**Photocopies**
The first thing you should do with both your passport and Vietnamese visa is photocopy them. The main reason for doing this is that in Vietnam you are almost certain to encounter various people who want to take your valuable documents away from you. This is particularly true of hotel clerks – they say they need your passport to register you with the police, though in many cases the only motive is to make sure you pay your hotel bill and don't steal the towels. Some hotels will accept photocopies, but most will not. Once you've handed over your passport and/or visa, this leaves you with no documentation at all. At least photocopies give you something to show to the authorities (the police, the railway ticket office, Vietnam Airlines etc) while the hotel holds you original documents. And if worse comes to worse, photocopies are helpful if you need to replace the documents that the hotel or police manage to lose.

If police stop you on the street and ask to see your passport, give them the photocopy rather than the original, explaining that the hotel has your original. Trusting the police with your documents always puts you in a very vulnerable position.

**Travel Permits**
Formerly, foreigners had to have internal travel permits *(giay phep di lai)* to go anywhere outside the city in which they arrived. From 1975 to 1988, even citizens of Vietnam needed these permits to travel around their own country (to prevent them from fleeing). The central government changed the rules in 1993 so you no longer need an internal travel permit. There have been reports of some con artists, though, who will insist you still need one and will happily sell you a fake 'internal travel permit'.

Although internal travel permits have been abolished, uncertainty still prevails in small towns and villages. Unfortunately, the police in many places seem to make up their own rules as they go along, no matter what the Interior Ministry in Hanoi says. What this means is that some provincial governments are chasing foreign dollars by charging for local 'travel permits' which consist of a photocopied piece of paper with a policeman's signature on it. The bottom line is that you may have to inquire locally to see if a permit is required.

The main purpose of the permits is to extract cash from foreigners. Some local provincial governments are demanding that you secure a permit on arrival to visit the surrounding area, pay a fee for this permit, hire a local guide and rent another car from the local government even if you've already arrived in an official government rental car!

Places where permits are currently required include Lat Village (in Dalat), minority villages around Buon Ma Thuot and Pleiku, Hon Khoai Island and the remote villages in the mountains of the north-west. Additional information about obtaining these permits is provided in the relevant chapters.

However, don't be absolutely sure that the information in this book is correct because the policies change. We are pleased to report that this tendency to require travel permits is diminishing. There seems to have been some strong pressure applied by Hanoi to stop this nonsense. The authorities would be much wiser to simply charge admission fees rather than involving tourists with the police.

### Travel Insurance

Although you may have medical insurance in your own country, it is probably not valid in Vietnam. A travel insurance policy is a very good idea – to protect you against cancellation penalties on advance purchase flights, against medical costs through illness or injury, against theft or loss of possessions and against the cost of additional air tickets if you get really sick and have to fly home.

If you undergo medical treatment, be sure to collect all receipts and copies of your medical report, in English if possible, for your insurance company. If you get robbed, you'll need a police report (good luck) if you want to collect from your insurance company.

Many student travel organisations offer insurance policies. Some of these are very cheap, but offer very minimal coverage. Read the small print carefully since it's easy to be caught out by exclusions.

### Driving Licence

If you plan to be driving abroad, get an International Driver's Licence from your local automobile association or motor vehicle department. In many countries, these are valid for only one year, so there's no sense getting one far in advance of departure. However, some countries will issue International Driver's Licences valid for several years – it depends on where you live. Make sure that your licence states that it is valid for motorcycles if you plan to ride one.

### Health Certificate

Useful (though not essential) is an International Health Certificate to record any vaccinations you've had. These can also be issued in Vietnam.

### Student & Youth Cards

Full-time students coming from the USA, Australia and Europe can often get some good discounts on international (not domestic) air tickets with the help of an International Student Identity Card (ISIC). To get this card, inquire at your campus. There is no place in Vietnam to issue these cards, nor are the cards of any use within the country.

Student Travel Australia (STA) issues STA Youth Cards to persons aged 13 to 26 years.

### Other Documents

If you're travelling with your spouse, a photocopy of your marriage licence just might come in handy should you become involved with the law, hospitals or other bureaucratic authorities.

If you're planning on working or studying in Vietnam, it could be helpful to have copies of transcripts, diplomas, letters of reference and other professional qualifications.

A collection of small photos for visas (about 10 should be sufficient) will be useful if you're planning on visiting several countries, but will also come in handy if you apply for visa extensions or other documents. Of course, these can be obtained in Vietnam and elsewhere. Visa photos must have a neutral background.

A passport is essential. If yours is within a few months of expiry, get a new one now – many countries will not issue a visa if your passport has less than six months of validity remaining. Be sure that your passport has at least a few blank pages for visas and entry and exit stamps. It could be very inconvenient to run out of blank pages when you are too far away from an embassy to get a new passport issued or extra pages added.

Losing your passport is very bad news indeed. Getting a new one takes time and money. It's wise to have a driver's licence, student card, ID card or some such thing with your photo on it – some embassies want this picture ID before issuing a replacement passport. Having an old expired passport is also very useful for this purpose.

It certainly helps to have a separate record of your passport number and issue date and a photocopy of the passport or birth certificate. While you're compiling that info, add the serial number of your travellers cheques, details of travel insurance and US$300 or so as emergency cash, and keep all that material separate from your passport and money (better hotels have a safe for valuables – that might be a good place to keep this stuff).

If you are a national of a country without diplomatic relations with Vietnam and you lose your passport while in the country, the situation is still not hopeless. If the immigration police are unable to locate the passport, you will be issued documents allowing you to leave the country. You may be allowed to stay in Vietnam until your visa (the validity of which is on record with the police) expires.

## EMBASSIES
### Vietnamese Embassies
Vietnamese embassies and consulates abroad include:

Australia
    6 Timbarra Crescent, O'Malley, Canberra, ACT 2603 (☎ (02) 6286-6059; fax 6286-4534)
Belgium
    Avenue de la Floride 130, 1180 Brussels (☎ (02) 374-9133; fax 374-9376)
Cambodia
    Son Ngoc Minh area (opposite 749 Achar Mean Blvd), Phnom Penh (☎ (23) 425-481)
Canada
    25B Davidson Drive, Gloucester, Ottawa, Ontario K1J6L7 (☎ (613) 744-4963; fax 744-1709)
China
    32 Guanghua Lu, Jianguomen Wai, Beijing (☎ (010) 532-1125; fax 532-5720)
    Guangzhou Consulate: (☎ (020) 776-9555; fax 767-9000)
    CITS in Nanning does Vietnam visas
France
    62-66 Rue Boileau, Paris 16 (☎ 01 44 14 64 00)
Germany
    Konstantinstrasse 37, 5300 Bonn 2 (☎ (228) 357-0201)
Indonesia
    Jalan Teuku Umar 25, Jakarta (☎ (021) 325-347; fax 314-9615)
Italy
    Piazza Barberini 12, 00187 Rome (☎ (06) 482-5286; fax 488-5007)
Japan
    50-11 Moto Yoyogi-Cho, Shibuya-ku, Tokyo 151 (☎ 3446-3311; fax 3466-3312)
Laos
    1 Thap Luang Rd, Vientiane (☎ (21) 5578)
Malaysia
    4 Pesiaran Stonor, Kuala Lumpur (☎ (03) 248-4036; fax 248-3270)
Myanmar (Burma)
    40 Komin Kochin Rd, Yangon (☎ (1) 50361)
Philippines
    54 Victor Cruz, Malate, Metro Manila (☎ (2) 500-364, 508-101)
Russia
    Bolshaya Pirogovskaya ul 13, Moscow (☎ (095) 245-0925)
Sweden
    Örby Slottsväg 26, 125 36 Älvsjö, Stockholm (☎ (8) 861-218; fax 899-5713)
Thailand
    83/1 Wireless Rd, Bangkok (☎ (2) 251-7201, 251-5836)
UK
    12-14 Victoria Rd, London W8 5RD (☎ (0171) 937-1912; fax 937-6108)
USA
    1233 20th St NW, Washington, DC 20036 (☎ (202) 861-0737; fax 861-0917)

## Foreign Embassies in Vietnam

With the exception of visas for Laos and Cambodia, Hanoi's embassies and Saigon's consulates do very little visa business. However, you may have several good reasons to visit your own country's embassy. Some embassies (by no means all) maintain a library where you can read newspapers from home. If you're staying a long time in Vietnam you should register your passport at your embassy (which makes it much easier to issue a new one if yours is lost or stolen). Embassies can help you obtain a ballot for absentee voting or provide forms for filing income tax returns. Embassies advise business people and will sometimes intervene in trade disputes.

Nevertheless, don't expect too much. Your embassy will not get involved if you have a fight with a taxi driver over the correct fare to the airport. Even when you really need help, many embassies will leave you twisting in the wind. You certainly won't find many embassies willing to lend you money or provide you with a ticket home if you get into trouble. Nor can your embassy get you out of prison if you've broken the law (though they can intervene to make sure that you're being treated fairly). And finally, remember that the people who work at your embassy are busy – please don't bother them with trivial matters.

The following list contains the addresses of foreign embassies in Hanoi and consulates in Ho Chi Minh City:

**Australia**
66 Ly Thuong Kiet St, Hanoi (☎ 825-2763, 826-1904; fax 825-9268)
Consulate: The Landmark, 5B Ton Duc Thang St, District 1, Ho Chi Minh City (☎ 829-6035, 829-9387; fax 829-6031)

**Belgium**
48 Nguyen Thai Hoc St, Hanoi (☎ 823-5005, 823-5006; fax 845-7165)
Consulate: 236 Dien Bien Phu St, District 3, Ho Chi Minh City (☎ 829-4526; fax 829-4527)

**Cambodia**
71 Tran Hung Dao St, Hanoi (☎ 825-3788, 825-3789; fax 826-5225)
Consulate: 41 Phung Khac Khoan St, District 1, Ho Chi Minh City (☎ 829-2751; fax 829-2744)

**Canada**
31 Hung Vuong St, Hanoi (☎ 823-5500; fax 823-5333)
Consulate: 203 Dong Khoi St, Suite 102, Ho Chi Minh City (☎ 824-2000, ext 1209; fax 829-4528)

**China**
46 Hoang Dieu St, Hanoi (☎ 845-3736; fax 823-2826)
Consulate: 39 Nguyen Thi Minh Khai St, Ho Chi Minh City (☎ 829-2457, 829-5009)

**Denmark**
19 Dien Bien Phu St, Hanoi (☎ 823-1888; fax 823-1999)
Consulate: 20 Phung Khac Khoan St, District 1, Ho Chi Minh City (☎ 822-8289, 822-8290; fax 822-4888)

**France**
57 Tran Hung Dao St, Hanoi (☎ 825-2719; fax 826-4236)
Consulate: 27 Pasteur St, District 3, Ho Chi Minh City (☎ 829-7231; fax 829-1675)

**Germany**
29 Tran Phu St, Hanoi (☎ 845-3836; fax 845-3838)
Consulate: 126 Nguyen Dinh Chieu St, District 3, Ho Chi Minh City (☎ 829-1967, 822-4385; fax 823-1919)

**India**
25 Lang Ha St, Hanoi (☎ 856-0463; fax 856-0462)
Consulate: 49 Tran Quoc Thao St, District 3, Ho Chi Minh City (☎ 823-1539; fax 829-9493)

**Indonesia**
50 Ngo Quyen St, Hanoi (☎ 825-7969; fax 825-9274)
Consulate: 18 Phung Khac Khoan St, District 1, Ho Chi Minh City (☎ 822-3799; fax 829-9493)

**Israel**
68 Nguyen Thai Hoc St, Hanoi (☎ 843-0514; fax 826-6920)

**Italy**
9 Le Phung Hieu St, Hanoi (☎ 825-6246; fax 826-7602)
Consulate: 3rd floor, 4 Dong Khoi St, District 1, Ho Chi Minh City (☎ 829-8721; fax 829-8723)

**Japan**
61 Truong Chinh St, Hanoi (☎ 869-2600; fax 869-2595)
Consulate: 13-17 Nguyen Hue St, District 1, Ho Chi Minh City (☎ 822-5314; fax 822-5316)

**Korea (South)**
29 Nguyen Dinh Chieu St, Hanoi (☎ 822-6677; fax 822-6328)
Consulate: 107 Nguyen Du St, District 1, Ho Chi Minh City (☎ 822-5757; fax 822-5750)

**Laos**
40 Quang Trung St, Hanoi (☎ 825-4576; fax 822-8414)

Malaysia
  Block A3, Van Phuc Diplomatic Quarter, Hanoi
  (☎ 845-3371; fax 823-2166)
  Consulate: 53 Nguyen Dinh Chieu St, District 3,
  Ho Chi Minh City (☎ 829-9023; fax 829-9027)
Myanmar (Burma)
  Block A3, Van Phuc Diplomatic Quarter, Hanoi
  (☎ 845-3396; fax 845-2404)
Netherlands
  Block D1, Van Phuc Diplomatic Quarter, Hanoi
  (☎ 843-0605; fax 843-1013)
New Zealand
  32 Hang Bai St, Hanoi (☎ 824-1481; fax 824-
  1480)
  Consulate: Level 5, Yoco Building, 41 Nguyen
  Thi Minh Khai St, District 1, Ho Chi Minh City
  (☎ 822-6907; fax 822-6905)
Philippines
  27B Tran Hung Dao St, Hanoi (☎ 825-7873; fax
  826-5760)
Russia
  58 Tran Phu St, Hanoi (☎ 845-4632; fax 845-
  6177)
Singapore
  41-43 Tran Phu St, Hanoi (☎ 823-3966; fax 823-
  3992)
  Consulate: 5 Phung Khac Khoan St, District 1,
  Ho Chi Minh City (☎ 822-5173; fax 825-1600)
Sweden
  2 358 St, Van Phuc Diplomatic Quarter, Hanoi
  (☎ 845-4824; fax 823-2195)
Switzerland
  77B Kiem Ma St, Hanoi (☎ 823-2019; fax 823-
  2045)
  Consulate: 270A Bach Dang St, Binh Thanh
  District, Ho Chi Minh City (☎ 844-2568; fax
  844-7601)
Taiwan
  Taiwan Economic & Cultural Office (not an
  embassy), 2B Van Phuc Diplomatic Quarter,
  Hanoi (☎ 823-4402)
  Trade Office: Taipei Economic & Cultural
  Office, 68 Tran Quoc Thao St, District 3, Ho Chi
  Minh City. Visa section, Ho Chi Minh City
  (☎ 829-9348); Commercial section, Ho Chi
  Minh City (☎ 829-9349).
Thailand
  63-65 Hoang Dieu St, Hanoi (☎ 843-5092; fax
  823-5088)
  Consulate: 77 Tran Quoc Thao St, District 3, Ho
  Chi Minh City (☎ 822-2637; fax 829-1002)
UK
  16 Ly Thuong Kiet St, Hanoi (☎ 825-2510, 825-
  2349; fax 826-5762)
  Consulate: 261 Dien Bien Phu St, District 3, Ho
  Chi Minh City (☎ 829-8433, 820-0127; fax 822-
  5740)
USA
  7 Lang Ha St, Hanoi (☎ 843-1500; fax 843-1510)

## CUSTOMS

If you enter Vietnam by air, customs inspection is usually fast and cursory. Unless the x-ray machine indicates that your backpack is filled with guns or heroin, you should be through the whole procedure in minutes.

However, if you enter overland, expect a rigorous search. Your bags may be completely emptied. It's easy to get the impression that Vietnam really doesn't want any visitors who don't arrive by air.

You are permitted to bring in duty-free 200 cigarettes, 50 cigars or 250g of tobacco; 2L of liquor; gifts worth up to US$50; and a reasonable quantity of luggage and personal effects. Items which you cannot bring in include opium, weapons, explosives and 'cultural materials unsuitable to Vietnamese society'.

During the height of the 'social evils' campaign in 1996, a letter was circulated to customs officials stipulating fines of 20 million dong (US$1820) for import/export of anything relating negatively to Vietnam. That included this book, the popular CD ROM *Vietnam: A Portrait* and all cassette tapes or CDs containing music produced by Overseas Vietnamese. Fortunately, the rule was seldom enforced and the social evils furore seems to have died down now, but it's best to keep such items out of sight anyway.

Tourists can bring an unlimited amount of foreign currency into Vietnam, but they are required to declare it on their customs form upon arrival. Theoretically, when you leave the country you should have exchange receipts for all the foreign currency you have spent, but in practice the authorities really don't care.

When entering Vietnam, visitors must also declare all precious metals (especially gold), jewellery, cameras and electronic devices in their possession. Customs is liable to tax you on gold bars, jewellery and diamonds – if you don't need this stuff, then don't bring it. Theoretically, declaring your goods means that when you leave, you will have no hassles taking these items out with you. It also means that you could be asked to show these items so that customs officials know you didn't sell them on the black market, though in practice you will seldom be troubled unless you bring in an unreasonable amount of goods or something of great value.

The import and export of Vietnamese currency and live animals is forbidden.

## MONEY
### Costs
Vietnam is one of the best travel bargains in East Asia, although accommodation costs more than it should (see the Accommodation section of this chapter for details).

The cost of travelling in Vietnam depends on your tastes and susceptibility to luxuries. Ascetics can get by on US$10 a day and for US$20 to US$25 a backpacker can live very well. Transport is likely to be the biggest expense if you rent a car, which many travellers wind up doing. If you choose to travel by bus or train, you can save a considerable sum.

Foreigners are frequently overcharged, particularly when it comes to buying souvenirs and occasionally in restaurants. Rapacious bus and taxi drivers will often ask several times the Vietnamese price too. However, don't assume that everyone is

trying to rip you off – despite severe poverty, many Vietnamese will only ask the local price for many goods and services.

### Carrying Money
Vietnam has its share of pickpockets. Rather than lose your precious cash and travellers cheques (not to mention your passport), large amounts of money and other valuables should be kept far from sticky fingers. Various devices which can usually thwart pickpockets include pockets sewn on the inside of your trousers, Velcro tabs to seal pocket openings, a moneybelt under your clothes or a pouch under your shirt. A vest (waistcoat) worn under your outer jacket will do very nicely only in those rare parts of Vietnam that get cold – this isn't a good option during summer or in the south where it's just too hot to wear an extra layer.

A secret stash (maybe inside your backpack frame?) is a good idea for those special emergencies.

### Currency
The currency of Vietnam is the dong (abbreviated by a 'd' following the amount). Banknotes in denominations of 200d, 500d, 1000d, 2000d, 5000d, 10,000d, 20,000d and

### Money for Nothing
The dong has certainly had a rocky history. In days of French Indochina, it was known as the piastre. The partitioning of Vietnam in 1954 created separate versions of the dong for North and South Vietnam. In 1975, US$1 was equal to 450 dong in South Vietnam. In 1976, the Communist Provisional Revolutionary Government (PRG) cancelled the South Vietnamese dong and issued its own PRG dong. The swap rate between the two dong was not set at 1:1, but rather at 500:1 in favour of the PRG dong. Furthermore, southerners were only permitted to exchange a maximum of 200 dong per family. This sudden demonetarisation of southern Vietnam instantly turned much of the affluent population into paupers and caused the swift collapse of the economy. Those with the foresight to have kept their wealth hidden in gold or jewellery escaped some of the hardships.

In 1977, both the North Vietnamese dong and the PRG dong were done away with and swapped for a reunification dong. In the north the swap was 1:1, but in the south the ratio was 1:1.2. In this case the southerners got a slightly better deal than the northerners, though it was small compensation for the 500:1 loss of the previous year.

The last great attempt at currency swapping was in 1985. Realising that inflation was rapidly eroding the value of the dong, the government decided to solve the problem by reissuing a new dong at a swap ratio of 10:1 in favour of the new dong. This time each family was allowed only 2000 dong of the new banknotes, though on special application more was allotted. Rather than controlling price increases as the government had hoped, the currency reissue ignited yet another new round of hyper-inflation. These days, the old 20d notes are literally not worth the paper they're printed on. ∎

50,000d are presently in circulation. It can be difficult to get change for the 50,000d notes in small backwaters, so keep a stack of small bills handy.

Now that Ho Chi Minh has been canonised (against his wishes) you'll find his picture on *every* banknote. There are no coins currently in use in Vietnam, though the dong used to be subdivided into 10 hao and 100 xu. All dong-denominated prices in this book are from a time when US$1 was worth 11,160d.

In the recent past, many upmarket hotels and restaurants demanded payment in US dollars and would not accept Vietnamese currency. In 1994, the Vietnamese government banned this practice – all businesses in Vietnam officially must now accept payment in dong only. In reality, many places still quote prices in dollars and will 'exchange' on the spot.

Even though US dollars are now prohibited for use as an unofficial currency, many prices (hotel rooms, air tickets etc) are still quoted in US dollars. We also prefer to quote prices in US dollars in this book. There are two reasons for this. One is that the Vietnamese themselves often quote prices in dollars. The second reason is that dong prices are unwieldy. For example, a night at a mid-range hotel can easily cost over 300,000d and buying a domestic air ticket from Hanoi to Saigon costs 1.9 million dong!

It's advisable to bring a small pocket calculator with you for converting currency, unless of course you are the sort of person who can nonchalantly multiply US$33.50 times 11,160 (and add 12.5% tax) in your head.

The Americans introduced western banking practices to South Vietnam – personal cheques were commonly used for large purchases, at least in Saigon. When the North took over, cheques, credit cards, South Vietnamese banknotes and South Vietnamese bank accounts became instantly worthless. As the Vietnamese dismantled the banking system, telegraphic transfers into Vietnam became practically impossible, though later a company called Cosevina was

set up to allow Overseas Vietnamese to send money to their relatives.

That was then and this is now. Vietnam is now trying to rejoin the world's banking system. Capitalist-style monetary instruments like travellers cheques, credit cards, telegraphic transfers and even letters of credit are all experiencing a revival. Domestic personal cheques have still not been re-introduced, but that should be coming soon.

Gold is also used extensively, especially for major transactions such as the sale of homes or cars. If you ask someone how much they paid for their house, they will probably tell you how many taels of gold.

It's a good idea to check that the dollars and travellers cheques you bring to Vietnam do not have anything scribbled on them or look too tattered, lest they be summarily rejected by uptight clerks. Ironically, some travellers have had problems changing dollars that looked 'too new' because the bank clerks often suspected that these were counterfeit!

Although you can at least theoretically convert French francs, German marks, pounds sterling, Japanese yen and other major currencies, the reality is that US dollars are still much preferred. Be sure to bring enough US dollars cash or travellers cheques for your whole visit and to keep it safe, preferably in a moneybelt. Try not to keep the whole lot in one place (if the moneybelt goes then everything goes with it). Unless you borrow from a foreigner or get someone to wire money to you (which is only possible in Saigon and Hanoi), losing your cash could put you in a really bad situation.

## Currency Exchange

The dong has certainly experienced its ups and downs. Past attempts by the government to solve the country's debt problems with the printing press led to devastating inflation and frequent devaluations. In 1991, the dong lost close to half its value. In 1992, the dong gained 35% against the US dollar, making it one of the best currency investments of the year! The surge in the dong's value was due to both shutting down the printing presses and the turnaround in Vietnam's chronic trade deficit – in 1992, the country experienced what is believed to be its first trade surplus since reunification.

| Country | Unit | | Dong |
|---|---|---|---|
| Australia | A$1 | = | 9095d |
| Canada | C$1 | = | 8527d |
| China | Y1 | = | 1404d |
| France | FFr1 | = | 2046d |
| Germany | DM1 | = | 6899d |
| Hong Kong | HK$1 | = | 1505d |
| Japan | ¥100 | = | 10,228d |
| New Zealand | NZ$1 | = | 8096d |
| Singapore | S$1 | = | 8145d |
| Taiwan | NT$1 | = | 419d |
| Thailand | B1 | = | 462d |
| UK | £1 | = | 19,271d |
| USA | US$1 | = | 11,650d |

### Changing Money

Beware of counterfeit cash, especially the 20,000d and 50,000d notes. These fakes are imported from China. There shouldn't be any problem if you've changed money in a bank, but out on the free market it's a different story.

Vietcombank is another name for the state-owned Bank for Foreign Trade of Vietnam (Ngan Hang Ngoai Thuong Viet Nam). Some other banks can change foreign currency and travellers cheques, but Vietcombank is the best organised for this activity. Banking hours are normally from 8 am to 3 pm on weekdays, 8 am to noon on Saturdays and closed on Sundays and holidays. Most banks also close for 1½ hours during lunch.

Travellers cheques can be exchanged only at authorised foreign exchange banks. The problem is that not every city (indeed, not every province) has a foreign exchange bank. Outrageously, there are no banks at the border crossings with Cambodia and Laos, nor is there one at Lao Cai and Dong Dang (both major border crossings with China). The only way to change money at these places is on the black market. Furthermore, the branches of Vietcombank at the airports in Saigon and Hanoi function only during

banking hours – they are closed when half the flights arrive and depart! Therefore, it's imperative that you do not rely entirely on travellers cheques – you may well be forced to deal with the black market upon arrival! You should keep a reasonable stash of US dollars cash in a variety of denominations for these transactions.

If you've arrived in Vietnam with only travellers cheques, you can stock up on US dollars cash at foreign exchange banks. These banks charge a 2% commission to change US dollar travellers cheques for US dollars cash (other banks charge more). Vietcombank charges no commission if you exchange travellers cheques for dong (but again, other banks do).

If your travellers cheques are denominated in other currencies besides US dollars, you may find them difficult to exchange. If you insist, the banks may exchange non-US dollar cheques for dong, but charge a hefty commission (perhaps 10%) to protect themselves from any possible exchange rate fluctuations – often they do not know the latest exchange rate for anything but US dollars.

Foreign exchange banks observe all major public holidays. If you arrive during the Lunar New Year, the banks may be closed for three or four days in a row. Try not to get caught short.

You can reconvert reasonable amounts of dong back to dollars on departure without an official receipt, though just how one defines 'reasonable' is open to question. Most visitors have had no problem, but having an official receipt should settle any arguments if they arise. You cannot legally take the dong out with you.

The relatively low value of Vietnamese banknotes means that almost any currency exchange will leave you with hundreds of banknotes to count. Notes are usually presented in brick-sized piles bound with rubber bands; even so, counting them is a slow, but necessary, process. Changing US$100 will net you over 1.1 million dong – a large brick of 5000d notes which will not fit in a moneybelt. You'll have to give some thought about just where you are going to keep these bricks as you cart them around the country.

Visa, MasterCard and JCB cards are now acceptable in all major cities and various touristy spots (Dalat, Halong Bay etc). However, you will usually be charged a 3% commission every time you use a credit card to purchase something or pay a hotel bill. Getting a cash advance from Visa, MasterCard and JCB is possible at Vietcombank in most cities. There is a 4% commission for doing this at banks, but hotels charge 5%.

There are a few banks in Saigon which have installed automatic teller machines which accept foreign ATM cards. Look for machines marked GlobalAccess, Cirrus, Interlink, Plus, Star, Accel, The Exchange or Explore. Payment is in dong and a commission is automatically deducted from the total.

At the time of writing, banks had announced that they would soon introduce debit cards in Saigon. No details are yet available. Presumably, you'll be able to purchase the cards at banks and other authorised outlets, and withdraw cash from ATMs or pay for goods at authorised stores. It will probably be a while before the system catches on, but it could be worth checking out if you'll be in Saigon for a while.

Foreigners who spend much time in Vietnam working, doing business or just hanging around, can open bank accounts at Vietcombank. The accounts can be denominated in Vietnamese dong or US dollars. Both demand-deposit and time-deposit accounts are available and interest is paid. Vietcombank can arrange letters of credit for those doing import and export business in Vietnam. It is even possible to borrow money from Vietcombank.

## Black Market

The black market is Vietnam's unofficial banking system. How to find it? Well, it's almost everywhere. Perhaps the term 'black market' is really too strong since it implies some cloak and dagger operation. It's in fact very open. Private individuals (taxi drivers etc) and some shops (jewellery stores, travel agencies) will swap cash US dollars for dong and vice versa. While supposedly illegal, enforcement is virtually nonexistent. But it's important to realise that black market exchange rates are *worse* than the official exchange rates. In other words, you don't gain anything by using the black market other than the convenience of changing money when and where you like. Typically you lose from 1% to 5% on black market transactions. In some backwaters (like Sapa) you can even change travellers cheques on the black market, but you'll have to pay an extortionate 10% commission.

If people approach you on the street with offers to change money at rates better than the official bank rate, then you can rest assured that you are being set up for a rip-off. Don't even think about trying it. Remember, if an offer is too good to be true, that's because it is.

## Tipping & Bargaining

Tipping according to a percentage of the bill is not expected in Vietnam, but it is enormously appreciated. For someone making US$50 per month, a US$1 tip is about half a day's wages. Upmarket hotels tend to slap a 10% to 15% service charge on top of the government's 12.5% room tax – this service charge might be considered a mandatory tip, though it's doubtful that much of it goes to the employees. In general, it's not a bad idea to tip the chambermaids who clean your room if you stay a couple of days in the same hotel – US$0.50 to US$1 should be enough. If you hire drivers and guides, also consider tipping them if they worked hard – after all, the time they spend on the road with you means time away from home and family. Ditto if you take a day tour with a group – the guides and drivers are paid next to nothing.

Men you deal with will also greatly appreciate small gifts such as a pack of cigarettes (women almost never smoke), but make sure it's a foreign brand of cigarettes. People will be insulted if you give Vietnamese cigarettes. The 555 brand (said to be Ho Chi Minh's favourite) is popular, as are most US brands. If you run out in Vietnam, don't worry – every street corner seems to have a little stand selling foreign cigarettes, sometimes for less than you paid duty-free!

It is considered proper to make a small donation at the end of a visit to a pagoda, especially if the monk has shown you around; most pagodas have contribution boxes for this purpose.

Many foreigners just assume that every Vietnamese is out to rip them off. That just isn't true – you needn't bargain for everything. But there are times when bargaining is essential. In touristy areas, postcard vendors have a reputation for charging about five times the going rate. Most cyclo and motorbike drivers also try to grossly overcharge foreigners – try to find out the correct rate in advance and then bargain accordingly. Remember, in the Orient, 'face' is important. Bargaining should be good-natured – smile, don't scream and argue. Many westerners seem to take bargaining too seriously and get all offended if they don't get the goods for less than half the original asking price. In some cases you will be able to get a 50% discount, at other times only 10%, but by no means should you get angry during the bargaining process. And once the money is accepted, the deal is done – if you harbour hard feelings because you later find out that someone else got it cheaper, the only one you are hurting is yourself.

## Taxes

On all goods you pay, the marked or stated price includes any relevant taxes. Only in some hotels and restaurants is there an additional 12.5% tax or service charge and this should be made clear to you from the beginning (ask if not sure).

If you're working in Vietnam, the issue of paying taxes is totally flaky. Normal income taxes are typically 40% to 50% depending on how much you earn. In reality, few Vietnamese report all their income. As a foreign resident, you can theoretically be taxed on your 'worldwide income', which includes money not earned in Vietnam! Needless to say, most expats 'forget' to report their foreign-earned income.

The Vietnamese government is said to be looking at ways to crack down on tax evasion. If the tax collectors really get their act together, it will be a disaster for the economy.

## POST & COMMUNICATIONS
### Postal Rates

Domestic rates are sinfully cheap. A domestic letter costs US$0.04 to mail.

International postal rates are similar to what you pay in European countries. While these rates might not seem expensive to you, the tariffs are so out of line with most salaries that locals literally cannot afford to send letters to their friends and relatives abroad. If you would like to correspond with Vietnamese whom you meet during your visit, try leaving them enough stamps to cover postage for several letters, explaining that the stamps were extras you didn't use and would be of no value to you at home. Or else buy a bunch of Vietnamese stamps to take home with you and when you write to Vietnamese friends include a few stamps for their replies.

### Sending Mail

Post offices all over the country usually keep long hours, about 6 am to 8 pm including weekends and public holidays (even Tet).

Items mailed from anywhere other than large towns and cities are likely to take over a month to arrive at their destinations. Air mail service from Saigon and Hanoi takes approximately ten days to most western countries provided it readily passes 'security' (is not considered subversive). The express mail service (EMS) available in Saigon and Hanoi can take as little as four days.

Foreigners sending parcels out of Vietnam sometimes have to deal with time-consuming inspections of the contents, but this is happening less frequently now. The most important thing is to keep the parcel small. If it's documents only, you should be OK. Sending out video tapes and the like can be problematic.

Express Mail Service (EMS) is available to most developed countries and a few less developed ones like Mozambique and

Ethiopia. It's perhaps twice as fast to use EMS than to use regular air mail, but the big advantage is that the letter or small parcel will be registered. There is also domestic EMS between Saigon and Hanoi promising next-day delivery, and the service exists to some smaller cities such as Danang and Nha Trang. The domestic EMS rates are very reasonable; US$0.35 for a letter weighing under 20g.

**Private Couriers** Private couriers can deliver both international and domestic small parcels or documents. For international service they charge approximately US$35 to US$60 (depending on destination) for the first 500g and about US$5 to US$17 for each additional 500g. For domestic service, the tariff is about US$20 for the first 500g and US$5 for each additional 500g.

DHL Worldwide Express operates from the Ho Chi Minh City post office (☎ 823-1525) and from their main office (☎ 844-6203; fax 844-5387) at 253 Hoang Van Thu Blvd, Tan Binh District, Ho Chi Minh City. In Hanoi, DHL (☎ 846-7020; fax 823-5698) can be found at 49 Nguyen Thai Hoc St, Ba Dinh District. Other phone numbers for collection include: Dong Nai (☎ 828094), Haiphong (☎ 842596), Nha Trang (☎ 822499), and Vung Tau (☎ 853932).

The main Federal Express Office (☎ 829-0747; fax 829-0477) is at 1 Nguyen Hau St, District 1, Ho Chi Minh City. Outside of Saigon you can call Federal Express at their toll-free number (☎ (018) 829-0747).

United Parcel Service (☎ 824-3597; fax 824-3596) has a representative at the post office, 2 Cong Xa Paris St, District 1, Ho Chi Minh City.

TNT Express Worldwide has its head office (☎ 844-6460, 844-6476, 844-6478; fax 844-6592) at 56 Truong Son St, Ward 2, Tan Binh District, Ho Chi Minh City.

Another alternative is Airborne Express (☎ 829-4310, 829-4315; fax 829-2961), with offices at two locations: the Ho Chi Minh City post office and the main office (☎ 829-2976) at 80C Nguyen Du St, District 1, Ho Chi Minh City.

**Freight Forwarders** Planning on shipping home Vietnamese furniture or moving an entire household? For this you need the services of an international mover.

In Vietnam, much of this business goes to Saigon Van (☎ 829-3502; fax 821-3003) at 76 Ngo Duc Ke St, District 1, Ho Chi Minh City. There is a smaller branch in Hanoi (mobile 090-404087; fax 824-0944) at 21 Ngo Van So St. This company is associated with the international Atlas Van Lines.

Another competitor in Hanoi is JVK International Movers (☎ 826-0334; fax 822-0143) at 5A Yet Kieu St.

### Receiving Mail

Every city, town, village and rural subdistrict in Vietnam has some sort of post office. All post offices are marked with the words 'Buu Dien'.

Mail delivery is mostly reliable and fast. However, reliability is greatly enhanced if your envelope or package contains nothing that somebody would want to steal. Normal letters and postcards should be fine. One of our correspondents in Saigon reports that his mail was opened and newspaper clippings about the Vietnamese economy were removed.

The poste restante windows work well at the post offices in both Hanoi and Saigon. Elsewhere, it's far less certain. Foreigners have to pay a US$0.04 service charge for each letter they pick up from poste restante.

Receiving even a small package from abroad can be a headache and large ones will be a migraine. If you're lucky, customs will clear the package and the clerks at the post office will simply let you take it. If you're unlucky, customs will demand an inspection at which you must be present. In that case, the post office will give you a written notice which you take to the customs office along with your passport. In Saigon, the customs office for incoming parcels is in the rear of the post office building. The procedure requires that you fill out numerous forms, pay some small fees (around US$1 in total), hand over your passport and hope that you eventually get it back along with the parcel.

Your package will be opened in front of you and inspected, but don't think that's all there is to it. Your parcel then gets packed up again and disappears into some other office along with your forms, passport and another fee. You take a seat in the waiting room, and after a few hours somebody hopefully will call your name. At that point, all your possessions should be returned to you, along with some more forms which you must get stamped before you can leave the building.

If you are particularly unlucky, customs may decide that you must pay import duty. If your parcel contains books, documents, video tapes, computer disks or other dangerous goods, it's possible that a further inspection will be required. This could take anywhere from a few days to a few weeks. Presumably, you will not have to spend the entire time in the waiting room while this is being done.

## Telephone

**Useful Phone Numbers** The following special phone numbers are available, but don't be surprised if the person answering only speaks Vietnamese:

| | |
|---|---|
| Ambulance | ☎ 15 |
| Directory Assistance | ☎ 16 |
| General Information | ☎ 108 |
| Fire Brigade | ☎ 14 |
| International Prefix | ☎ 00 |
| International Operator | ☎ 110 |
| Police | ☎ 13 |

**International Calls** Vietnam's international telecommunications charges are among the highest in the world, so unless you have some matter of earthshaking importance, it's better to wait until you reach Hong Kong, Bangkok or Singapore to call the loved ones at home. Otherwise, call them briefly and ask them to call you back.

If you're living in Vietnam you might be tempted to subscribe to a callback service, which would greatly reduce your phone bill. However, Vietnam is one of the few countries to make this illegal and there are draconian penalties if you get caught.

International and domestic long-distance calls can be booked at many hotels, but this is expensive.

It's somewhat less expensive to book long-distance phone calls from the post office. For operator-assisted calls, you will be charged for three minutes even if you only talk for one minute, plus the rate per minute will be higher. As in most countries, the cheapest way to make a long-distance call is to dial direct.

Foreigners are not permitted to make international reverse-charge calls. However, Vietnamese nationals can. Why? Because the DGPT (Directorate General of Posts & Telecommunications) earns less from a reverse-charge call than from calls paid for in Vietnam. However, since most Vietnamese cannot possibly afford to pay for an international call, they are permitted to call collect to their overseas relatives (the assumption being that those relatives will probably send them money).

This means that if your credit cards or travellers cheques are stolen, you will not be able to call collect to the issuing company to report the loss. At best this is a major nuisance – it could prove disastrous if you get robbed of all your cash and need to call abroad to get some help.

The cheapest and simplest way by far to make an international direct-dial (IDD) call is to buy a telephone card, known in Vietnam as a 'UniphoneKad'. They are on sale at the telephone company. UniphoneKads can only be used in special telephones which are mainly found in Saigon, usually in the lobbies of major hotels. The cards are issued in four denominations; 30,000d (US$2.72), 60,000d (US$5.45), 150,000d (US$10.90) and 300,000d (US$27.27). The 150,000d and 300,000d cards can be used to make both domestic and international calls, while the 30,000d and 60,000d cards will only work for domestic calls.

To make an IDD call, you must first dial the international prefix (00) followed by the country code, area code (if any) and the local number. Note that in many countries (Australia, for example), area codes start with a zero, but this zero must not be dialled when calling internationally. So to call Melbourne (area code 03) in Australia (country code 61) from Vietnam, you would dial 00-61-3-123-4567. Some useful country codes include:

Australia-61, Belgium-32, Canada-1, Denmark-45, France-33, Germany-49, Hong Kong-852, Italy-39, Japan-81, Korea (South)-82, Malaysia-60, Netherlands-31, New Zealand-64, Norway-47, Philippines-63, Singapore-65, Spain-34, Sweden-46, Switzerland-41, Taiwan-886, Thailand-66, UK-44, USA-1, Vietnam-84

From our own experience, we have found that international calls cost more than the advertised rate (perhaps there is some sort of hidden tax) – this applies even when you use a phone card. There is a 15% discount for calls placed between 11 pm and 7 am and on Sundays and public holidays.

Direct-dial calls to regional countries cost between US$3 and US$3.70 for the first minute and US$2.40 to US$2.70 per minute thereafter. Calls to Europe and North America cost US$4.10 for the first minute and US$3.10 thereafter. The most expensive calls are to the Middle East and Africa: US$4.50 for the first minute and US$3.50 for each additional minute. Calls are charged by six-second increments.

**Domestic Calls** Except for some short special numbers (like the fire brigade or directory assistance), all phone numbers in Hanoi and Ho Chi Minh City are seven digits long. Outside of those two cities, all phone numbers are six digits.

Local calls can usually be made from any hotel or restaurant phone and are usually free.

Area codes in Vietnam are assigned according to province. The current list is as follows:

Domestic long-distance calls are reasonably priced, but will be cheapest if you dial direct. You can save up to 20% by calling at night (10 pm to 5 am).

Any call between Hanoi and Saigon at the full daytime rate will cost US$0.45 per minute. An operator-assisted call costs

US$0.82 per minute and there is a three-minute minimum.

**Cellular Phones** As in other Third World countries, Vietnam is putting a lot of money into the cellular network simply because it's cheaper than laying thousands of kilometres of copper or fibre-optic cables. The day has not yet arrived where foreign tourists can visit Vietnam and simply make a cellular call using their own phones, which they've carried from home. However, that day is coming soon. In the meantime, resident foreigners can apply for one in Hanoi or Saigon. This is far more expensive than owning a pager, but you get what you pay for. Aside from offering the obvious advantages of portability and convenience, cellular phones bypass Vietnam's decrepit wiring system, which plagues conventional telephone calls with crackling static.

For expats, cellular phones also solve the problem posed by being forced to move from place to place every time the police decide you can't stay in the flat you just rented. At least if you have to move, the phone goes with you. If you can't afford a cellular phone, consider getting a pager (which is considerably cheaper).

There are two companies in Saigon offering cellular service. The older, established service is Call-Link (☎ 822-0288) at 5 Nguyen Hau St, District 1. The new kid on the block is MobiFone (☎ 835-1410) at 750 Dien Bien Phu St, District 10. In Hanoi, contact MobiFone (☎ 835-6696) at 44H Lang Ha St.

**Fax, Telex & Telegraph**
Most post offices and many tourist hotels in Vietnam offer domestic and international fax, telegraph and telex services. Hotels are likely to charge more than the post office.

If you happen to have your own portable computer with a built-in fax modem, it's tempting to attach it to any available phone line and send a fax. However, this is illegal – the Vietnamese government insists that all fax machines be registered and that includes computer fax modems.

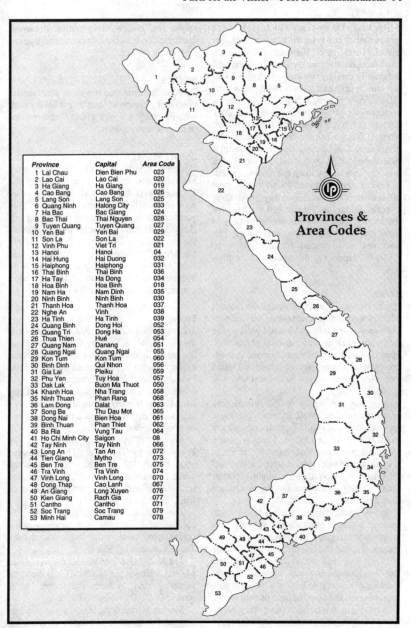

| Province | Capital | Area Code |
|---|---|---|
| 1 Lai Chau | Dien Bien Phu | 023 |
| 2 Lao Cai | Lao Cai | 020 |
| 3 Ha Giang | Ha Giang | 019 |
| 4 Cao Bang | Cao Bang | 026 |
| 5 Lang Son | Lang Son | 025 |
| 6 Quang Ninh | Halong City | 033 |
| 7 Ha Bac | Bac Giang | 024 |
| 8 Bac Thai | Thai Nguyen | 028 |
| 9 Tuyen Quang | Tuyen Quang | 027 |
| 10 Yen Bai | Yen Bai | 029 |
| 11 Son La | Son La | 022 |
| 12 Vinh Phu | Viet Tri | 021 |
| 13 Hanoi | Hanoi | 04 |
| 14 Hai Hung | Hai Duong | 032 |
| 15 Haiphong | Haiphong | 031 |
| 16 Thai Binh | Thai Binh | 036 |
| 17 Ha Tay | Ha Dong | 034 |
| 18 Hoa Binh | Hoa Binh | 018 |
| 19 Nam Ha | Nam Dinh | 035 |
| 20 Ninh Binh | Ninh Binh | 030 |
| 21 Thanh Hoa | Thanh Hoa | 037 |
| 22 Nghe An | Vinh | 038 |
| 23 Ha Tinh | Ha Tinh | 039 |
| 24 Quang Binh | Dong Hoi | 052 |
| 25 Quang Tri | Dong Ha | 053 |
| 26 Thua Thien | Hué | 054 |
| 27 Quang Nam | Danang | 051 |
| 28 Quang Ngai | Quang Ngai | 055 |
| 29 Kon Tum | Kon Tum | 060 |
| 30 Binh Dinh | Qui Nhon | 056 |
| 31 Gia Lai | Pleiku | 059 |
| 32 Phu Yen | Tuy Hoa | 057 |
| 33 Dak Lak | Buon Ma Thuot | 050 |
| 34 Khanh Hoa | Nha Trang | 058 |
| 35 Ninh Thuan | Phan Rang | 068 |
| 36 Lam Dong | Dalat | 063 |
| 37 Song Be | Thu Dau Mot | 065 |
| 38 Dong Nai | Bien Hoa | 061 |
| 39 Binh Thuan | Phan Thiet | 062 |
| 40 Ba Ria | Vung Tau | 064 |
| 41 Ho Chi Minh City | Saigon | 08 |
| 42 Tay Ninh | Tay Ninh | 066 |
| 43 Long An | Tan An | 072 |
| 44 Tien Giang | Mytho | 073 |
| 45 Ben Tre | Ben Tre | 075 |
| 46 Tra Vinh | Tra Vinh | 074 |
| 47 Vinh Long | Vinh Long | 070 |
| 48 Dong Thap | Cao Lanh | 067 |
| 49 An Giang | Long Xuyen | 076 |
| 50 Kien Giang | Rach Gia | 077 |
| 51 Cantho | Cantho | 071 |
| 52 Soc Trang | Soc Trang | 079 |
| 53 Minh Hai | Camau | 078 |

**Provinces &
Area Codes**

Telex is old technology which has become nearly extinct in the west due to fax machines and electronic mail. Vietnam still has telex machines, but they are dying off quickly and are mainly used by banks. Nevertheless, you can still easily send telexes from major post offices in Vietnam, though this service is useless if the person you need to reach does not have a telex number. Telex messages are charged by the minute with a one minute minimum. Considering the slow transmission speed of telex (about 50 words per minute), you'd best keep the message short.

The telegraph windows of major post offices are open 24 hours a day, seven days a week. Telegrams are charged by the word (including each word of the address) and there is a seven word minimum charge. The cost per word varies from US$0.30 to US$0.60 depending on country of destination.

### Email

If you have an already-established email address with a non-Vietnamese service provider, accessing it from Vietnam will require that you make an international phone call. Popular international email service providers such as CompuServe, America Online and Asia Online do *not* have local nodes in Vietnam.

Anybody can apply to the Vietnamese post office for an email account. The basic service costs only US$7 per month, plus a small per message charge. There is also a US$20 sign-up fee. Unfortunately, an email account is just that – you cannot use it to surf the Internet. Nevertheless, email is better than nothing and certainly much cheaper than a fax.

In Vietnam, there is such a thing as an Internet account, but it's a pale shadow of its western counterpart. The government is still paranoid about the Internet with all its loose political talk and pornography. Therefore, the 'Vietnamese Internet' consists of some politically correct Web sites which the government has downloaded onto its own server. To surf this near worthless thing, the government charges an outrageous US$500 application fee. Unless the situation improves dramatically, it's hard to recommend signing up for this service.

### BOOKS

To pass the time and preserve your sanity, you need to bring at least a few books with you. Purchasing books within Vietnam is hit or miss (mostly miss).

### Lonely Planet

Cyclists, hikers and other back-country explorers may want to score a copy of the *Vietnam travel atlas*. Our *Vietnamese phrasebook* is not only educational, it will also give you something to do during those long bus rides. And if you'd like some more details on the ins and outs of Saigon, there is the *Ho Chi Minh City guide*. Lonely Planet's *South-East Asia on a shoestring* has a chapter on Vietnam, but it's less detailed than the book you now hold in your hands.

### Travel

*Sparring with Charlie: Motorbiking down the Ho Chi Minh Trail* by Christopher Hunt is a recent light-hearted travelogue about the modern Vietnam. Take a peek at his Web site (www.well.com/user/cchunt).

*Vietnam: Opening Doors to the World* by Rick Graetz (Graetz Publications, 1989) is a full-colour coffee table book on Vietnam and its people today.

Another effort in this direction is *Ten Years After* by Tim Page. This impressive book boasts '12 months worth of photos taken 10 years after the war'. Tim Page also returned to Vietnam to write *Derailed in Uncle Ho's Victory Garden*.

The *Vietnam Insight Guide* by Apa Publications of Singapore is a more portable coffee table book with much information about Vietnamese culture.

The *Nelles Guide to Vietnam* is sort of like a small scale Insight Guide. This is the same company that produces the famed Nelles maps.

Murray Hiebert, the Hanoi correspondent for the *Far Eastern Economic Review*, has included a selection of his articles in his very interesting *Vietnam Notebook*.

*A Dragon Apparent* is about author Norman Lewis' fascinating journeys through Vietnam, Laos and Cambodia in 1950. This classic travelogue is now available as a reprint from Eland in London and Hippocrene in New York.

## History & Politics

*Vietnam: Politics, Economics and Society* by Melanie Beresford (Pinter Publishers, London & New York, 1988) gives a good overview of the aspects of post-reunification Vietnam mentioned in its title.

During the colonial period, French researchers wrote quite a number of works on Vietnam's cultural history and archaeology that remain unsurpassed. Several good ones on the Chams are *Les États Hinduisés d'Indochine et d'Indonésie* by Georges Coedes (Paris, 1928), *L'Art du Champa et Son Evolution* by Philippe Stern (Toulouse, 1942) and *Le Royaume du Champa* by Georges Maspero (Paris & Brussels, 1928). *Les Arts du Champa: Architecture et Sculpture* by Tran Ky Phuong, curator of the Cham Museum in Danang and Vietnam's foremost scholar of the Chams, was published in Paris in the early 1990s.

*The Birth of Vietnam* by Keith Weller Taylor (University of California Press, Berkeley, 1983) covers the country's early history.

*The Vietnamese Gulag* by Doan Van Toai (Simon & Schuster, New York, 1986) tells of one man's experiences in the post-reunification re-education camps.

For a very readable account of Vietnamese history from prehistoric times until the fall of Saigon, try Stanley Karnow's *Vietnam: A History* (Viking Press, New York, 1983), which was published as a companion volume to the American Public Broadcasting System series *Vietnam: A Television History*.

A number of biographies of Ho Chi Minh have been written, including *Ho Chi Minh: A Political Biography* by Jean Lacouture (Random House, New York, 1968) and *Ho* by David Halberstam (Random House, New York, 1971).

One of the most scholarly works on Caodaism is *Caodai Spiritism: A Study of Religion in Vietnamese Society* by Victor L Oliver (EJ Brill, Leiden, 1976).

An excellent reference work is *Vietnam's Famous Ancient Pagodas* (Viet Nam Danh Lam Co Tu), which is written in Vietnamese, English, French and Chinese. The publisher is the Social Sciences Publishing House and you should be able to find copies in Saigon and Hanoi.

**Franco-Viet Minh War** On this topic it's worth taking a look at Peter M Dunn's *The First Vietnam War* (C Hurst & Company, London, 1985); or two works by Bernard B Fall: *Street Without Joy: Indochina at War 1946-54* (Stackpole Company, Harrisburg, Pennsylvania, 1961) and *Hell in a Very Small Place: The Siege of Dien Bien Phu* (Lippincott, Philadelphia, 1967).

Graham Greene's 1954 novel *The Quiet American*, which is set during the last days of French rule, is probably the most famous western work of fiction on Vietnam. Much of the action takes place at Saigon's Continental Hotel and at the Caodai complex in Tay Ninh.

*The Lover* by Marguerite Duras is a fictional love story set in Saigon during the 1930s. The book has been made into a major motion picture.

**American War** What the Americans call the 'Vietnam War', the Vietnamese call the 'American War'. Whatever you call it, there are whole libraries of books on the topic.

The earliest days of US involvement in Indochina – when the OSS, predecessor of the CIA, was providing funding and weapons to Ho Chi Minh at the end of WWII – are recounted in *Why Vietnam?*, a riveting work by Archimedes L Patti (University of California Press, Berkeley, Los Angeles & London, 1980). Patti was the head of the OSS team in Vietnam and was at Ho Chi Minh's side when he declared Vietnam independent in 1945.

Three of the finest essays on the war are collected in *The Real War* by Jonathan Schell

(Pantheon Books, New York, 1987). An overview of the conflict is provided by George C Herring's *America's Longest War*, 2nd edition (Alfred A Knopf, New York, 1979 & 1986). *Fire in the Lake* by Francis Fitzgerald (Vintage Books, New York, 1972) is a superb history of American involvement in Vietnam; it received the Pulitzer Prize, the National Book Award and the Bancroft Prize for History.

A highly acclaimed biographical account of the US war effort is *A Bright Shining Lie: John Paul Vann & America in Vietnam* by Neil Sheehan (Random House, New York, 1988); it won both the Pulitzer Prize and the National Book Award.

Another fine biography is Tim Bowden's *One Crowded Hour* (Angus & Robertson, 1988), which is the life of Australian film journalist Neil Davis. He shot some of the most famous footage of the war, including that of the North Vietnamese tank crashing through the gate of the Presidential Palace in Saigon in 1975.

Ellen J Hammer's *A Death in November* (EP Dutton, New York, 1987) tells of the US role in Diem's overthrow in 1963.

*The Making of a Quagmire* by David Halberstam (Ballantine Books, New York) is one of the best accounts of America's effort in the war during the early 1960s.

Two accounts of the fall of South Vietnam are *The Fall of Saigon* by David Butler (Simon & Schuster, New York, 1985) and *55 Days: The Fall of South Vietnam* by Alan Dawson (Prentice Hall, Englewood Cliffs, New Jersey, 1977).

Perhaps the best book about the fall of South Vietnam is *Decent Interval* by Frank Snepp. Except for pirated editions sold in Vietnam itself, it's out of print and for a very interesting reason. The author was the CIA's chief strategy analyst in Vietnam, but he broke his contract with the CIA by publishing this book (CIA agents are prohibited from publishing anything about their work). The US government sued Snepp and all the royalties which he earned from book sales were confiscated. Copies of the book can still be found in some public libraries.

Highly recommended is *Brother Enemy* by Nayan Chanda (Asia Books, Macmillan, 1986). This is not actually a book about the war, but about its immediate aftermath. Chanda was a correspondent for the *Far Eastern Economic Review* and was in Saigon when it fell.

An oft-cited analysis of where US military strategy in Vietnam went wrong is *On Strategy* by Colonel Harry G Summers Jr (Presidio Press, Novato, California, 1982, and Dell Publishing, New York, 1984). *The Pentagon Papers* (paperback version by Bantam Books, Toronto, New York & London, 1971), a massive, top-secret history of the US role in Indochina, was commissioned by Defence Secretary Robert McNamara in 1967 and published amid a great furore by the *New York Times* in 1971.

*Valley of Decision* by John Prados and Ray W Stubbe is about the Siege of Khe Sanh, one of the largest battles of the war.

A story mostly neglected by writers is the painful experience of the fatherless Amerasian children left behind in Vietnam. The whole sordid tale is told in unforgettable detail by Thomas Bass in *Vietnamerica* (Soho Press).

**Australia** Australia's involvement in the American War is covered in *Australia's Vietnam* (Allen & Unwin, Sydney, London & Boston, 1983), a collection of essays edited by Peter King; *Australia's War in Vietnam* by Frank Frost (Allen & Unwin, Sydney, London & Boston, 1987); Gregory Pemberton's *All the Way: Australia's Road to Vietnam* (Allen & Unwin, Sydney & Boston, 1987); *Desperate Praise: The Australians in Vietnam* by John J Coe (Artlook Books, Perth, 1982); and *Vietnam: The Australian Experience* (Time-Life Books of Australia, Sydney, 1987).

**Soldiers' Experiences** Some of the better books about what it was like to be an American soldier in Vietnam include: *Born on the 4th of July* by Ron Kovic (Pocket Books, New York, 1976), which was made into a powerful movie; the journalist Michael

Herr's superb *Dispatches* (Avon Books, New York, 1978); *Chickenhawk* by Robert Mason (Viking Press, New York, 1983, and Penguin Books, Middlesex, UK, 1984), a stunning autobiographical account of the helicopter war; *A Rumor of War* by Philip Caputo (Ballantine Books, New York, 1977); and *Nam* by Mark Baker (Berkley Books, New York, 1981). *A Piece of My Heart* by Keith Walker (Ballantine Books, New York, 1985) tells the stories of American women who served in Vietnam.

Two oral histories are *Everything We Had* by Al Santoli (Ballantine Books, New York, 1981) and *Bloods: An Oral History of the Vietnam War by Black Veterans* by Wallace Terry (Ballantine Books, New York, 1984).

Some of the horror of the My Lai Massacre of 1968 comes through in Lieutenant General WR Peers' *My Lai Inquiry* (WW Norton & Company, New York & London, 1979).

Some of the horror of what American POWs endured comes through in *Chained Eagle* by Everett Alvarez Jr (Dell, 1989). Alvarez was a US pilot who spent 8½ years as a prisoner in North Vietnam.

*Brothers in Arms* by William Broyles Jr (Avon Books, New York, 1986) is the story of the 1984 visit to Vietnam by an American journalist who served as an infantry lieutenant during the war.

*Viet Cong Memoir* by Truong Nhu Tang (Harcourt Brace Jovanovich, San Diego, 1985) is the autobiography of a Viet Cong cadre who later became disenchanted with post-1975 Vietnam.

One of the finest books about the war written by a Vietnamese is *The Sorrow of War* by Bao Ninh. The author fought for North Vietnam, but his book is by no means a piece of anti-American propaganda. On the contrary, he's cynical about the entire war and its avowed goals and neither side comes out looking very good. The book won a literature prize in Vietnam in 1993 and English-language copies are available from bookstalls in Hanoi. However, Vietnamese-language editions of the book are banned in Vietnam!

## CD ROMS

The classic is *Passage to Vietnam*, a collection of beautiful photos and narrative. This CD was produced by Rick Smolan, who created the famed *Day in the Life* series.

Also noteworthy is *Vietnam in a Nutshell*, a CD ROM produced by Cymbidium Multimedia Productions.

Yet another popular one is *Vietnam: A Portrait*.

## ONLINE SERVICES

A peculiar irony is that most of the good online content about Vietnam originates in Vietnam's old nemesis, the USA. The reason has much to do with the fact that access to the Internet is essentially banned in Vietnam to all but government officials. A second factor is that not many Vietnamese can afford their own computers. The result is that Vietnamese online authors are mostly Overseas Vietnamese. Some of these people live in Vietnamese ethnic communities in Australia, Canada and France, but the majority reside in the USA. Web sites are published in both English and Vietnamese.

The Internet changes from day to day, so anything we can say about Web sites is likely to become dated fast. However, there are a few good sites that we've explored which are worth recommending – hopefully they will still be in existence by the time you read this.

Vietgate (www.saigon.com) offers links to Vietnamese activities and businesses in southern California. At www.realsaigon.com, you'll find Vietnamese music, poetry, gossip and news. *VietNet* is an online magazine with good articles, photos and information about multimedia CDs.

Using the foregoing Web sites, you should be able to find links to the *Democracy Newsletter*, Vietnamese photo collections, the Miss Vietnam Tet Pageant, the Vietnamese Professional Society and so on.

A general Web search on the words 'Vietnam', 'Saigon', 'Hanoi', 'Tet' etc should produce some interesting hits.

## FILMS

The book *When Heaven and Earth Changed*

*Places* by Le Ly Hayslip was been made into a fascinating movie, *Heaven and Earth*, by director Oliver Stone. *Born on the 4th of July* by Ron Kovic is another book which made the transition to blockbuster motion picture.

Almost all American-made movies about Vietnam are in fact about the war, but most were filmed in the Philippines. Some popular war movies include *Rambo, Full Metal Jacket, Platoon, The Deer Hunter, Good Morning Vietnam* and *Air America*. Perhaps the most memorable line about Vietnam was spoken by a captain in the movie *Apocalypse Now*: 'I love the smell of napalm in the morning'.

*The Lover* by Marguerite Duras is a French book set in Vietnam which has now been made into a movie. *Indochine*, starring Catherine Deneuve, is a French film about France's colonial experience in south-east Asia.

Two more-recent films set in Vietnam are Vietnamese director Tran Anh Hung's *The Scent of Green Papaya* and *Cyclo*.

## NEWSPAPERS & MAGAZINES

The *Vietnam News* is an English-language newspaper published daily. Despite the name, it contains little news about Vietnam – most of the stories are foreign news (including the sports section). If you're desperate for some news of the outside world, it will do in a pinch. It's also good for wrapping fish.

If you're looking to learn something about Vietnam, check out the English-language *Vietnam Investment Review*, a weekly newspaper. Subscription and advertising information is available in Ho Chi Minh City (☎ 839-8300; fax 839-8304) at 122 Nguyen Thi Minh Khai St, District 1; and in Hanoi (☎ 845-0537; fax 845-7937) at 175 Nguyen Thai Hoc St.

One of Vietnam's two best magazines is the *Vietnam Economic Times*, which is published monthly. For subscription information, contact the magazine in Hanoi (☎ 845-0537; fax 845-7937) at 175 Nguyen Thai Hoc St; or in Ho Chi Minh City (☎ 839-8300; fax 839-8304) at 63 Cao Thang St, District 3.

The other magazine to consider is *Vietnam Today*, published monthly by Communication Indochine Pty Ltd (☎ (65) 356-4326; fax 356-4327), c/o 17 Jalan Rajah No 06-19, Diamond Tower, Singapore 1232. This magazine has two representative offices in Vietnam: c/o 75/3 Su Van Hanh St, District 10, Ho Chi Minh City (☎ 862-5093; fax 862-5094); and c/o Ly Nam De St, Hoan Kiem District, Hanoi (☎ 843-4095; fax 823-5412).

It's been our unfortunate experience so far that when it comes to subscribing to Vietnamese magazines from abroad, the money tends to 'disappear' and no magazines arrive! This has happened to us twice with both the *Vietnam Economic Times* and the now-defunct *What's On in Saigon*, even when we hand-delivered the cash to the magazines' offices and obtained a receipt. We have not yet tried subscribing to the *Vietnam Investment Review* or *Vietnam Today* – the latter is based in Singapore and therefore is probably a safer bet.

Imported newspapers and magazines are readily available in Saigon and Hanoi, and occasionally in Danang. Elsewhere it's slim pickings.

## RADIO & TV
### Vietnamese Radio

The Voice of Vietnam broadcasts on short wave, AM and FM for about 18 hours a day. The broadcasts are mostly music, but there are also news bulletins in Vietnamese, English, French and Russian. Don't worry if you miss one bulletin – you can always catch the next one since it doesn't change throughout the day. The broadcast programmes are printed daily in the *Vietnam News*.

The first broadcast of the Voice of Vietnam took place in 1945. During the American War, the Voice of Vietnam broadcast a great deal of propaganda programming to the South, including special English programmes for American GIs. From 1968 to 1976, the Voice of Vietnam used the transmitters of Radio Havana-Cuba to deliver its message direct to the American people.

Vietnamese domestic national radio

# Vietnamese Food

HELEN SAVORY

Two typical Vietnamese specialities are *chia gio* and *pho*.

Chia gio are similar to the spring rolls served in Chinese restaurants. They're made from rice paper softened in water and stuffed with a mixture of pork mince, mushrooms, prawns, noodles and bean shoots; sometimes egg yolk is also added. The rolls are deep-fried and served hot with *nuoc mam* (fish sauce), fresh lettuce leaves, mint and other fragrant herbs. To eat chia gio, grab one with your chopsticks, roll it up in a lettuce leaf along with the herbs and dip the whole thing in the nuoc mam.

Pho is Vietnam's most famous dish. It's a broth flavoured with aniseed star, ginger and pepper. The broth is poured into bowls containing cooked rice noodles and beef, chicken or pork slices, either cooked or raw. It is served hot enough to cook any raw meat and is garnished with coriander leaves.

BERNARD NAPTHINE

GLENN BEANLAND

*Above Left: Fast food Vietnamese-style: the ever-present street vendors sell a range of simple, popular dishes.*

*Left: Pho can be eaten at any time, but it is a perennial breakfast favourite with the Vietnamese.*

# Ho Chi Minh

Ho Chi Minh is the best known of some 50 aliases assumed over the course of his long career by Nguyen Tat Thanh (1890-1969), founder of the Vietnamese Communist Party and president of the Democratic Republic of Vietnam from 1946 until his death. The son of a fiercely nationalistic scholar-official of humble means, he was educated in the Quoc Hoc Secondary School in Hué before working briefly as a teacher in Phan Thiet. In 1911, he signed on as a cook's apprentice on a French ship, sailing to North America, Africa and Europe. He remained in Europe, where, while working as a gardener, snow sweeper, waiter, photo retoucher and stoker, his political consciousness began to develop.

After living briefly in London, Ho Chi Minh moved to Paris, where he adopted the name Nguyen Ai Quoc (Nguyen the Patriot). During this period, he mastered a number of languages (including English, French, German and Mandarin Chinese) and began to write about and debate the issue of Indochinese independence. During the 1919 Versailles Peace Conference, he tried to present an independence plan for Vietnam to US president Woodrow Wilson. Ho was a founding member of the French Communist Party, which was established in 1920. In 1923, he was summoned to Moscow for training by the Communist International, which later sent him to Guangzhou (Canton), where he founded the Revolutionary Youth League of Vietnam, a precursor to the Indochinese Communist Party and the Vietnamese Communist Party.

After spending time in a Hong Kong jail in the early 30s and more time in the USSR and China, Ho Chi Minh returned to Vietnam in 1941 for the first time in 30 years. That same year – at the age of 51 – he helped found the Viet Minh Front, the goal of which was the independence of Vietnam from French colonial rule and Japanese occupation. In 1942, he was arrested and held for a year by the Nationalist Chinese. As Japan prepared to surrender in August 1945, Ho Chi Minh led the August Revolution, which took control of much of the country; and it was he who composed Vietnam's Declaration of Independence (modelled in part on the American Declaration of Independence) and read it publicly very near the site of his mausoleum.

The return of the French shortly thereafter forced Ho Chi Minh and the Viet Minh to flee Hanoi and take up armed resistance. Ho spent eight years conducting a guerrilla war until the Viet Minh's victory against the French at Dien Bien Phu in 1954. He led North Vietnam until his death in September 1969 – he never lived to see the North's victory over the South. Ho Chi Minh is affectionately referred to as 'Uncle Ho' (Bac Ho) by his admirers.

Uncle Ho may have been the father of his country, but he wasn't the father of any children, at least none that are known. Like his erstwhile nemesis, South Vietnamese president Ngo Dinh Diem, Ho Chi Minh never married.

*Despite never marrying and producing no children (that he acknowledged), Ho Chi Minh is regularly portrayed as a kindly father figure who evokes happiness and joy in children.*

BERNARD NAPTHINE

broadcasts news and music programmes from 7 am until 11 pm. In Saigon, frequencies to try include 610kHz and 820kHz in the AM band and 78.5MHz, 99.9MHz and 103.3MHz in the FM band.

Visitors interested in keeping up on events in the rest of the world – and in Vietnam itself – may want to bring along a small short-wave receiver. News, music and features programmes in a multitude of languages can easily be picked up, especially at night. Frequencies you might try for English-language broadcasts include:

### BBC World Service

Try the following frequencies (times vary):

5990kHz, 6080kHz, 7110kHz, 7135kHz, 7160kHz, 9600kHz, 9740kHz, 9605kHz, 11,920kHz, 15,280kHz and 17,760kHz

### Voice of America

5 am to 8 am: 6035kHz, 7215kHz, 9890kHz, 11,760kHz, 15,305kHz
8 to 10 am: 17,740kHz, 21,550kHz
5 to 6 pm: 11,720kHz, 15,425kHz
6 to 10 pm: 6110kHz, 9760kHz, 11,720kHz, 15,160kHz, 15,425kHz
10 pm to midnight: 6110kHz, 9760kHz

### Vietnamese TV

Vietnamese TV began broadcasting in 1970 and it's fair to say that the content hasn't

improved much since then. There are currently three channels in Hanoi and Saigon, and two channels elsewhere. Broadcast hours from Monday through Saturday are 9 to 11.30 am and 7 to 11 pm. On Sunday there is an extra broadcast from 3 to 4 pm. English-language news comes on in the evenings as the last broadcast at some time after 10 pm. Sometimes soccer or other sports come on at strange hours like 1.30 am.

### Satellite TV

Satellite TV is now widely available, which is a boon for foreign visitors. You're most likely to see it in the better hotels and upmarket pubs. Hong Kong's Star TV is the most popular station, along with CNN, the Sports Channel, ABN (Asia Business News) and Channel V (an MTV station). Depending on the satellite dish used, you can expect about 10 channels.

### VIDEO SYSTEMS

It's hard to know what Vietnam's official video standard is. That's because most new TVs and video tape players now sold in Vietnam are multi-standard. The three standards supported are PAL, NTSC and SECAM.

### PHOTOGRAPHY & VIDEO
### Film & Equipment

Colour print film is widely available, but

---

### Can't Stop the Music

If you think life in a remote Vietnamese village is tranquil, then you're in for a rude awakening. To be exact, the awakening comes at 5 am when the Voice of Vietnam comes blaring from some unseen loudspeaker. First you're treated to some militaristic marching music. Next comes the exercise routine, 'touch your toes, 1, 2, 3 ...' followed by the news and weather reports, some inspiring speeches by politicians, the latest statistics on cement production and then karaoke music. Most tourists probably wouldn't mind if it wasn't so damn *loud*. Adding to the cacophony are the bad acoustics – the loudspeakers seem designed to distort the sound and produce an echo.

Just how long the aural torment goes on depends on where you are. In most towns the bombardment lasts just one hour, but elsewhere the speakers groan, squeak and squawk from 5 am to 9 pm.

In most towns, the Vietnamese don't even notice the noise – they've learned to tune it out. However, the Saigonese made it clear long ago that they'd rather listen to their own radios – from 1975 to 1979, almost every loudspeaker in Ho Chi Minh City was sabotaged as fast as the authorities could replace them. Finally, the government threw in the towel. Many other communities have also dispensed with the speakers – tourist resorts like Dalat, Nha Trang and Sapa have recognised that it's bad for business. ■

check the expiration date printed on the box. Avoid buying film from outdoor souvenir stalls – the film may have been cooking in the sun for the past three months. Film prices are perfectly reasonable and you won't gain anything by bringing it from abroad.

Colour slide film can easily be bought in Hanoi and Saigon, but don't count on it elsewhere. In touristy resorts like Nha Trang and Halong Bay, look for slide film in hotel gift shops.

Black and white film is rapidly disappearing. It can still be found in speciality shops, but if you need the stuff then you'd best bring a supply from abroad.

Many tourists travel around Vietnam by van or minibus – note that the metal floors of these vehicles get very hot, but you might not notice if the vehicle is air-conditioned. Many travellers have roasted their film by placing it in their backpacks and setting the backpack on the floor of the vehicle.

Photo-processing shops have become ubiquitous in places where tourists congregate. Most of these shops are equipped with the latest Japanese one-hour, colour-printing equipment. Printing costs are reasonable and quality is good. Be sure to specify if you want glossy or matte finish on your prints.

Colour slide film can be developed quickly (three hours) in Hanoi and Saigon, but forget it outside of those two cities. Cost for processing is US$5 per roll, but most shops do not mount the slides unless you request it.

Plastic laminating is cheap. Just look for the signs saying 'Ep Plastic'. It's particularly advisable to laminate photos intended as presents to protect them from Vietnam's tropical climate. Unlaminated photos deteriorate and go mouldy.

Cameras are fairly expensive in Vietnam and the selection is limited – you'll do better to bring one from abroad. Happily, lithium batteries (needed by many of today's point-and-shoot cameras) are available in most cities, though not always in the hinterland.

## Photography

Some touristy sites charge a 'camera fee' of about US$0.50, or a 'video fee' of US$2 to US$5. If the staff refuses to issue a receipt for the camera fee, then you should refuse to pay – the 'fee' in that case is likely to go into their pocket.

Like their Japanese and Chinese counterparts, Vietnamese people have a near obsession with collecting hundreds (or thousands) of photos of themselves posing in front of something. The pose is always the same: a stiff, frontal shot, hands at the sides etc. The result is that all of their photos look nearly identical. The purpose of the photos seems to be to prove that they've been to a particular place. Since many Vietnamese cannot afford their own camera, virtually every site of tourist potential has a legion of photographers always ready to snap a few pictures. Some photographers will get the film processed and mail it to their customers, while others will shoot a roll and hand it over unprocessed. Most Vietnamese cannot understand why westerners shoot dozens of rolls of film without posing themselves in each and every frame. Furthermore, when westerners show off their best photographs, Vietnamese look at them and say the photos are 'boring' because there are seldom any people.

## Video

The authorities seem to be far more sensitive about video tape than film. Surprisingly, there is more of a problem when exiting the country than when entering (logically you would think the opposite). The great stumbling block seems to be what the authorities call 'cultural materials'. Video tapes are deemed to be 'cultural materials' which must be screened in advance by 'experts' from the Department of Culture.

## Restrictions

The Vietnamese police usually don't care what you photograph, but on occasion they get pernickety. Obviously, don't photograph something that is militarily sensitive (airports, seaports, military bases, border checkpoints etc). Photography from aircraft is now permitted, except for chartered aircraft.

Don't even think of trying to get a snapshot of Ho Chi Minh in his glass sarcophagus!

Perhaps it would be wise for you to memorise the following message, which appears on signs in various places: *'Cam Chup Hinh Va Quay Video'*, which means 'No Photography or Video Taping'.

## Photographing People

Vietnamese are not much different from westerners when it comes to having their photo taken. If anything, they are more easygoing about it. Payment is seldom demanded (and you should be careful about offering it, so as not to set a precedent). If you want to photograph some street vendor, you might offer first to buy something. Ditto for photographing cyclo drivers – hire the vehicle for a short spin and the driver may ham it up for the lens.

Of course, not everyone likes to be photographed. You should ask first and respect people's wishes. The 'I don't give a damn if I upset everyone' approach will make things tough for foreigners who come after you. A safe tactic is to use a long telephoto lens and photograph surreptitiously from far away.

Taking pictures inside pagodas and temples is usually all right, but as always it is better to ask permission from the monks.

One of the best things you can do for Vietnamese friends who don't own a camera is to take pictures of them or their families and send the photos to them after processing (or give them the roll of film and let them process it).

## Airport Security

The dreaded x-ray machines at the airports are no longer a problem – the old Soviet-made 'microwave ovens' could fry your film, but they've been replaced with modern 'film-safe' equipment imported from Germany. However, there is a hazard to your film if you attempt to film the airport security procedures (the film will most likely be ripped out of your camera).

## TIME

Vietnam, like Thailand, is seven hours ahead of GMT/UTC (Greenwich Mean Time/Universal Time Coordinated). Because it is so close to the equator, Vietnam does not have daylight saving time (summer time). Thus, when it's noon in Hanoi or Saigon it is 9 pm the previous day in Los Angeles, midnight in New York, 5 am in London, 1 pm in Perth and 3 pm in Sydney. When the above-listed cities are on daylight saving time, these times are one hour off.

## ELECTRICITY

Electric current in Vietnam is mostly 220V at 50Hz (cycles), but often you'll still find 110V (also at 50Hz). Unfortunately, looking at the shape of the outlet on the wall gives no clue as to what voltage is flowing through the wires. In the south, most outlets are US-style flat pins. Despite the American-inspired design, the voltage is still likely to be 220V. In the north, most outlets are the Russian-inspired round pins and also *usually* carrying 220V. If the voltage is not marked on the socket try finding a light bulb or appliance with the voltage written on it. All sockets are two-prong only – in no case will you find a third wire for ground (earth).

Much of the electrical wiring in Vietnam is improvised. Be especially careful in rural backwaters – exposed live wires are a fire hazard and offer opportunities to electrocute yourself.

In drought years, power failures increase sharply because hydroelectric power is used. The situation is getting worse due to the increase in air-conditioners and power-hungry factories. There are plans to build a new power station in the Mekong Delta to alleviate this situation, but no one is sure just when that will occur. The north had long had excess hydroelectric capacity, but consumerism has changed the picture and blackouts occasionally occur in summer when people start up the air-conditioners. A new power line opened in 1994 connecting the north and south has greatly alleviated wintertime electricity shortages, which formerly plagued Saigon.

In rural areas, power is usually supplied by diesel generators which frequently are shut down and restarted. This means you should keep your torch (flashlight) handy. More seriously, it also means that there are probably frequent surges in the current. Sensitive electronic equipment should be shielded with a surge suppressor or, better yet, run on rechargeable batteries.

## WEIGHTS & MEASURES

Vietnam uses the international metric system. For a metric conversion table, see the back of the book. In addition, there are two measurements for weight borrowed from the Chinese, the tael and the catty. A catty is 0.6kg (1.32lb). There are 16 taels to the catty, so one tael is 37.5g (1.32oz). Gold is always sold by the tael.

Some Vietnamese words for measurements are:

| | |
|---|---|
| gram | (same as English) |
| hectare | hec-ta |
| kg | (same as English) |
| km | cay so |
| litre | (same as English) |
| metre | met |
| metric tonne | ton |
| square metre | met vuong |
| tael | luong |
| catty | can |

## LAUNDRY

It is usually easy to find a hotel attendant who will get your laundry spotlessly clean for the equivalent of a US dollar or two. Budget hotels do not have clothes dryers – they rely on the sunshine. Therefore, allow at least a day and a half for washing and drying, especially in the wet season.

## HEALTH

The health section of this book is probably overkill, and after reading it you'll (almost) be qualified to set up your own medical practice. Remember that not all of the nasty diseases mentioned here are liable to afflict you. Still, you should read carefully – remember, it only takes one fatal disease to ruin your whole trip.

Vietnam's economy has improved in recent years, which has brought with it some significant improvements to the medical situation. People were frequently malnourished before and therefore highly prone to disease – this is not a huge problem any more. Also, immunisation programmes are helping to stop the spread of disease.

Rural areas can still be a problem. Though foreigners with cold, hard cash will receive the best treatment available, even bars of gold cannot buy you blood tests and x-rays when the local health clinic doesn't even have a thermometer or aspirins. If you become seriously ill while in rural parts of Vietnam, get to Saigon as quickly as you can. If you need any type of surgery or other extensive treatment, don't hesitate to fly to Bangkok, Hong Kong or some other reasonably developed country as soon as possible.

In the countryside, you will no doubt see Vietnamese covered with long bands of red welts on their necks and backs. This is not some kind of hideous skin disease, but rather a treatment. In traditional Vietnamese folk medicine, many illnesses are attributed to 'poisonous wind' (trung gio). The bad wind can be released by scraping the skin with spoons, coins etc, thus raising the welts. The results aren't pretty, but the locals say this treatment is good for what ails you. Try it at your own peril.

Another way to fight poisonous wind is a technique – borrowed from the Chinese – that employs suction cups made of bamboo placed on the patient's skin. A burning piece of alcohol-soaked cotton is briefly put inside the cup to drive out the air before it is applied. As the cup cools, a partial vacuum is produced, leaving a nasty-looking, but harmless, red circular mark on the skin.

The Traveller's Health Guide by Dr Anthony C Turner (Roger Lascelles, London) and Staying Healthy in Asia, Africa & Latin America (Moon Publications) are guides to staying healthy while travelling, or what to do if you fall ill.

You can buy plenty of dangerous drugs across the counter in Vietnam without a prescription, but you should exercise restraint – some drugs like steroids can make you feel

## Traditional Medicine

There are a number of traditional medical treatments practised in Vietnam. Herbal medicine, much of it imported from China, is widely available and sometimes surprisingly effective. As with western medicine, it's best not to experiment yourself but to see a doctor. Traditional medicine doctors, also mostly ethnic-Chinese, can be readily found wherever a large Chinese community exists, and that includes Saigon, Hanoi and Hoi An.

If you visit a traditional Chinese-Vietnamese doctor, you might be surprised by what he or she discovers about your body. For example, the doctor will almost certainly take your pulse and then may tell you that you have a slippery pulse or perhaps a thready pulse. Traditional doctors have identified more than 30 different kinds of pulses. A pulse could be empty, prison, leisurely, bowstring, irregular or even regularly irregular. The doctor may then examine your tongue to see if it is slippery, dry, pale, greasy, has a thick coating or maybe no coating at all. The doctor, having discovered that you have wet heat, as evidenced by a slippery pulse and a red greasy tongue, will prescribe the proper herbs for your condition.

One traditional treatment is called moxibustion. Various types of herbs, rolled into what looks like a ball of fluffy cotton, are held just near the skin and ignited. A slight variation of this method is to place the herb on a slice of ginger and then ignite it. The idea is to apply the maximum amount of heat possible without burning the patient. This heat treatment is supposed to be good for such diseases as arthritis.

Another technique employs suction cups made of bamboo placed on the patient's skin. A burning piece of alcohol-soaked cotton is briefly put inside the cup to drive out the air before it is applied. As the cup cools, a partial vacuum is produced, leaving a nasty-looking, but harmless, red circular mark on the skin. The mark goes away in a few days.

The horrible-looking red marks seen on the necks of Vietnamese (especially in the Mekong Delta region) are not from some disease. Rather, they are the result of the cure. The marks are made by pinching the skin or scraping it vigorously with a coin or spoon. This is supposed to bring blood to the surface – and indeed it does – producing nasty looking welts that eventually heal. This is a treatment for the common cold, fatigue, headaches and other ailments. Whether the cure hurts less than the disease is something one can only judge from experience.

Can you cure people by sticking needles into them? The adherents of acupuncture say you can and they have some solid evidence to back them up. For example, some major surgical operations have been performed using acupuncture as the only anaesthetic (this works best on the head). In this case, a small electric current (from batteries) is passed through the needles.

Getting stuck with needles might not sound pleasant, but if done properly it doesn't hurt. Knowing just where to insert the needle is crucial. Acupuncturists have identified more than 2000 insertion points, but only about 150 are commonly used. The exact mechanism by which acupuncture works is not fully understood. Practitioners talk of energy channels or meridians which connect the needle insertion point to the particular organ, gland or joint being treated. The acupuncture point is sometimes quite far from the area of the body being treated.

Non-sterile acupuncture needles pose a genuine health risk in this era of the AIDS epidemic. You'd be wise to purchase your own if you wish to try this treatment. ■

great and then kill you, especially if you have an infection. On any medicines you buy, take a look at expiration dates – drugs may not be of the same strength as in other countries or may have deteriorated due to age or poor storage conditions. Chinese shops often sell herbal medicines imported from China. If you need some special medication then take it with you.

The addresses and telephone numbers of the best medical facilities in Vietnam can be found under the Information section at the beginning of the chapters on Ho Chi Minh City and Hanoi. Those are the only two cities where you are likely to find health facilities that come close to meeting developed-country standards.

### Pre-departure Preparations

Your grandmother might have told you that 'an ounce of prevention is worth a pound of cure', though in these days of the metric system it's 'grams' and 'kilograms' respectively. No matter how you measure it, the advice is sound – you should practice preventative medicine. The best place to begin is with a trip to a doctor or public health clinic to update your vaccinations.

**Vaccinations** On the health form you fill out upon arrival in Vietnam, it's suggested (but not required) that you should be vaccinated for yellow fever and cholera, and have an international vaccination card to prove it. In theory, the authorities can require that you've had these vaccinations if you arrive in Vietnam within six days after leaving or transiting a yellow fever or cholera-infected area. But in most cases, you will not be required to prove anything. However, you'd be wise to get all useful vaccinations, required or not.

Various health authorities and other vaccination enthusiasts have recommended that travellers swallow or get jabbed with the following vaccines: meningitis, rabies, hepatitis A, hepatitis B, Japanese encephalitis, polio, typhoid, tetanus and diphtheria.

Plan ahead for getting your vaccinations: some of them require an initial shot followed by a booster, while some vaccinations should not be given together. If you are travelling with children, it's especially important to be sure that they've had all necessary vaccinations. The period of protection offered by vaccinations differs widely and some are contraindicated for pregnant women.

In some countries immunisations are available from airport or government health centres. Within Vietnam itself, vaccinations are difficult to come by and the few vaccines available are sometimes rendered ineffective because of age and mishandling.

You should have your vaccinations recorded in an International Health Certificate. This will serve as adequate proof of immunisation should you run into overzealous health authorities at the immigration queues.

Get your teeth checked and any necessary dental work done before you leave home. Always carry a spare pair of glasses or your prescription in case of loss or breakage.

**Medical Kit** You should assemble some sort of basic first-aid kit. You won't want it to be too large and cumbersome for travelling, especially since you can buy medicines easily at Vietnam's numerous pharmacies. With those caveats in mind, consider including the following:

Anti-malarial tablets; Band-Aids, gauze bandage, plaster (adhesive tape); a thermometer; tweezers; scissors; sunscreen; insect repellent; multi-vitamins; water sterilisation tablets; Chapstick; antibiotic ointment; an antiseptic agent (Detail or Betadine); any medication you're already taking; diarrhoea medication (Lomotil, Imodium or Berberin); rehydration salts for treatment of severe diarrhoea; paracetemol (Panadol), ibuprofen or aspirin for pain and fever; anti-fungal powder; contraceptives (including condoms); antihistamine (Benadryl, Hismanal etc), useful as a decongestant or for treating allergic reactions to insect stings; and a couple of syringes in case you need an injection.

Ideally, antibiotics should be administered only under medical supervision and should never be taken indiscriminately. Overuse of antibiotics can weaken your body's ability to deal with infections naturally and can reduce the drug's efficacy on a future occasion. Take only the recommended dose as prescribed. It's important that once you start a course of antibiotics you finish it, even if the illness seems to be cured earlier. If you stop taking the antibiotics after one or two days, a complete relapse is likely. If you think you are experiencing a reaction to any antibiotic (a sudden rash or increasing diarrhoea are warning signs), stop taking it immediately and consult a doctor.

### Basic Rules

**Everyday Health** Normal body temperature is 37°C or 98.6°F; more than 2°C (4°F) higher indicates a high fever. The normal adult pulse rate is 60 to 100 per minute (children 80 to 100, babies 100 to 140). As a general rule, the pulse increases about 20 beats per minute for each °C (2°F) rise in fever.

Respiration (breathing) rate is also an indicator of illness. Count the number of breaths per minute: between 12 and 20 is normal for adults and older children (up to 30 for younger children, 40 for babies). People with a high fever or serious respiratory illness breathe more quickly than normal. More than 40 shallow breaths a minute may indicate pneumonia.

**Food & Water** In Saigon and Hanoi, tap water is not too bad (it's chlorinated), but it's still recommended that you boil it before drinking. In other parts of Vietnam, the water varies from pretty safe to downright dangerous. Especially after a typhoon and the subsequent flooding, there is a problem with sewers overflowing into reservoirs, thus contaminating the tap water used for drinking and bathing. Outbreaks of cholera and typhoid occur most often after floods so you must be particularly careful at such times – do not even brush your teeth with unboiled water.

Reputable brands of bottled water (both imported and domestic) or soft drinks are generally fine. Unfortunately, in remote places bottles are sometimes refilled with tap water and resealed, and some travellers have suffered serious intestinal upsets (including dysentery) because of this. Take care with fruit juice, particularly if water may have been added. Milk should be treated with suspicion, as it is often unpasteurised. Boiled milk is fine if it is kept hygienically and yoghurt is usually OK.

Tea and coffee should both be safe since the water should have been boiled. You can also boil your own water if you carry an electric immersion coil and a large metal cup (plastic tends to melt). You can safely plug a 220V immersion coil into a 110V socket (not vice versa!), but the boiling time will be much longer. For emergency use, water purification tablets will help. Water is more effectively sterilised by iodine than by chlorine tablets, because iodine kills amoebic cysts. However, iodine is not safe for prolonged use and also tastes horrible. Bringing water to a boil is sufficient to kill most bacteria, but 20 minutes of boiling is required to kill amoebic cysts. Fortunately, amoebic cysts are relatively rare and you should not be overly concerned about these. If you have nothing to boil or purify your water, you have to consider the risks of drinking possibly contaminated water against the risks of dehydrating – the first is only possible, but the second is definite.

It's a good idea to carry a water bottle with you. You are dehydrating if you find you are urinating infrequently or if your urine turns a deep yellow or orange; you may also find yourself getting headaches. Dehydration is a real problem if you go hiking in Vietnam – if you can't find water along the way or can't carry enough with you, then you will soon learn just how hot this place really is!

While boiling will kill nasty microbes, freezing will not. Since most small eateries in Vietnam lack refrigeration equipment, factory-frozen ice is delivered daily. In Saigon and Hanoi, the ice comes from a factory which has to meet certain standards of hygiene (the water is at least chlorinated), while in rural areas the ice could be made from river (sewer?) water. Another problem is that even clean ice often makes its way to its destination in a filthy sack carried on the bare backs of delivery men. The filthy outer layer may melt off, but then again it may not, though any thoughtful restaurant will at least wash the ice before cracking it into pieces. If you do not want to risk a possibly serious gut infection, avoid ice in rural backwaters – admittedly easier said than done in a hot tropical country.

When it comes to food, use your best judgment. To be absolutely safe, everything should be thoroughly cooked – you can easily get diarrhoea or dysentery from salads and unpeeled fruit. Ice cream is usually OK if it is a reputable brand name, but beware of ice cream that has melted and been refrozen. Thoroughly cooked food is safest, but not if it has been left to cool or if it has been reheated. Take great care with shellfish or fish and avoid undercooked meat.

**Other Precautions** Sunglasses not only give you that fashionable 'Hollywood look', but will protect your eyes from the scorching Vietnamese sun.

Sunburn can be more than just uncomfortable. Among the undesirable effects of frying your hide are premature skin ageing and possible skin cancer in later years. Bring sunscreen (UV) lotion and wear something to cover your head.

If you're sweating profusely, you're going to lose a lot of salt and that can lead to fatigue and muscle cramps for some people. If necessary you can make it up by putting extra salt in your food (a teaspoon a day is plenty), but don't increase your salt intake unless you also increase your water intake. Soy sauce will also do the trick.

Take good care of all cuts and scratches. In this climate they take longer to heal and can easily get infected. Treat any cut with care; wash it out with sterilised water, preferably with an antiseptic (Betadine), keep it dry and keep an eye on it – they really can turn into tropical ulcers! It would be worth bringing an antibiotic cream with you. Cuts on your feet and ankles are particularly troublesome – a new pair of sandals can quickly give you a nasty abrasion which can be difficult to heal. Try not to scratch mosquito bites for the same reason.

The climate may be tropical, but you *can* catch a cold in Vietnam. One of the easiest ways is leaving a fan on at night when you go to sleep, and air-conditioners are even worse. You can also freeze by going up to mountainous areas without warm clothes. Antihistamines can give symptomatic relief, but the way to cure a cold is to rest, drink lots of liquids, keep warm (easy to do in Vietnam!) and wait it out.

## Environmental Hazards

**Prickly Heat & Fungus** You can sweat profusely in tropical Vietnam; the sweat can't evaporate fast when the air itself is already moist and, before long, you and your clothes are dripping in it. Prickly heat is a common problem for people from temperate climates. Small red blisters appear on the skin where your sweat glands have become swollen and blocked from the heavy workload. The problem is exacerbated because the sweat fails to evaporate. To prevent or cure it, wear clothes which are light and leave an air space between the material and the skin; don't wear synthetic clothing since it can't absorb the sweat; dry well after bathing; and use cala-

mine lotion or a zinc-oxide-based talcum powder. Anything that makes you sweat more – exercise, tea, coffee, alcohol – only makes the condition worse. You can also keep your skin dry with air-conditioning, electric fans or a trip to the cool mountains.

Fungal infections also occur more frequently in this sort of climate – travellers sometimes get patches of infection on the inside of the thigh. It itches like hell, but is easy to clear up with an anti-fungal cream or powder. Powder is preferred because it doesn't make a sticky mess of your clothing, but best of all is to use both cream and powder.

Fungal ear infections usually result from swimming or washing in unclean water – Aquaear drops, available over the counter in Australia, are a preventative to be used before you enter or wash in the water. Some travellers carry a broad-spectrum antibiotic like Septrim to cure fungal infections. This is not a bad idea, although antibiotics can lower your resistance to other infections.

Athlete's foot is also a fungal infection, usually occurring between the toes. Wearing open-toed sandals will often solve the problem without further treatment because this permits the sweat to evaporate. It also helps to clean between the toes with warm soapy water and an old toothbrush.

**Heat Exhaustion** Dehydration or salt deficiency can cause heat exhaustion. Take time to acclimatise to high temperatures, drink sufficient liquids and do not do anything too physically demanding.

Salt deficiency is characterised by fatigue, lethargy, headaches, giddiness and muscle cramps; salt tablets may help.

**Heat Stroke** This serious, occasionally fatal, condition can occur if the body's heat-regulating mechanism breaks down and the body temperature rises to dangerous levels. Long, continuous periods of exposure to high temperatures can leave you vulnerable to heat stroke.

The symptoms are feeling unwell, not sweating very much or at all and a high body temperature (39°C to 41°C or 102°F to 106°F). Where sweating has ceased, the skin becomes flushed and red. Severe, throbbing headaches and lack of coordination will also occur and the sufferer may be confused or aggressive. Eventually the victim will become delirious or convulse. Hospitalisation is essential, but in the interim get victims out of the sun, remove their clothing, cover them with a wet sheet or towel and then fan continually.

**Motion Sickness** Eating lightly before and during a trip will reduce the chances of motion sickness. If you are prone to motion sickness try to find a place that minimises disturbance – near the wing on aircraft, close to midship on boats, near the centre on buses. Fresh air usually helps; reading and cigarette smoke don't. Commercial motion-sickness preparations, which can cause drowsiness, have to be taken before the trip begins. Ginger (available in capsule form) and peppermint (including mint-flavoured sweets) are natural preventatives.

### Infectious Diseases

**Diarrhoea** Diarrhoea is often due simply to a change of diet. A lot depends on what you're used to eating and whether or not you've got an iron gut. If you do get diarrhoea, it will often go away by itself if you just switch to a light diet for a few days. On the other hand, diarrhoea can be a sign of a serious gut infection and should not be ignored for long.

Diarrhoea will cause you to dehydrate, which will make you feel much worse. The solution is not simply to drink water, since it will run right through you. You'll get much better results by mixing your water with oral rehydration salt, a combination of salts (both sodium chloride and potassium chloride) and glucose. Dissolve the powder in *cool* water (never hot!) and drink, but don't use it if the powder is wet. The quantity of water is specified on the packet. Rehydration salts are also useful for treating heat exhaustion caused by excessive sweating.

The usual treatment for simple diarrhoea

is Loperamide (eg Imodium, Loperin) or Lomotil tablets. Vietnam produces a local and very effective anti-diarrhoeal drug called Berberin, available from any pharmacy in the country. These drugs are prescription-only in the west, but are available over the counter in almost every Asian country. Anti-diarrhoeal drugs don't cure anything – the underlying disease is still there. The only thing these medicines do is to slow down the digestive system so that the cramps go away and you retain fluids and nutrition. Excessive use of anti-diarrhoeal drugs is not advised as they can cause dependency and other nasty side effects. As a general rule, you should take the minimum dose necessary to bring the diarrhoea under control, and stop taking the drugs as soon as the problem seems to be resolved.

Fruit juice, tea and coffee can aggravate diarrhoea – again, water with oral rehydration salts is the best drink. It will help tremendously if you eat a light, fibre-free diet. Yoghurt or boiled eggs with salt are basic staples for diarrhoea patients. Later you may be able to tolerate rice porridge or plain white rice. Keep away from vegetables, fruits and greasy foods for a while. If you suddenly decide to pig out on a peperoni pizza with hot sauce, you'll be back to square one. If the diarrhoea persists for a week or more, it's probably not simple travellers' diarrhoea – it could be dysentery and it might be wise to see a doctor.

**Dysentery** Many travellers claim to be suffering from 'dysentery' when all they've got is common, garden-variety diarrhoea. Dysentery causes diarrhoea, but it is worse – it's often accompanied by fever, blood and pus in the stool. The victim usually feels faint, totally lacking in energy, can barely eat and can hardly get out of bed. It's a real drag! Dysentery is classified into two categories, bacillary and amoebic.

Diarrhoea with blood or pus and fever is usually bacillary dysentery. It's quite common in Vietnam and many travellers fall prey to it. It's caused by bacteria infecting the gut. In most cases, bacillary dysentery will eventually clear up without treatment, but in some cases it's actually fatal, especially in children. Be sure to use water and rehydration salts (see previous section on Diarrhoea) to prevent dehydration. If the problem is severe, it should be treated with antibiotics.

A stool test is necessary to diagnose which kind of dysentery you have, so you should seek medical help urgently. In case of an emergency the recommended drugs for bacillary dysentery are norfloxacin (400mg twice daily for seven days) or ciprofloxacin (500mg twice daily for seven days).

An alternative is co-trimoxazole (Bactrim, Septrin, Resprim) 160-800mg twice daily for seven days. This should not be used by people with a sulpha allergy. Children can be treated with co-trimoxazole.

Antibiotics are heavy artillery, so don't start nuking yourself at the first sign of diarrhoea. With any diarrhoea, fluid replacement is the most important treatment, but persistent diarrhoea, or diarrhoea with fever or blood, will require antibiotics. The main problem is that antibiotics may upset the balance of intestinal flora. In some people this may actually *increase* the diarrhoea, so be careful! If the antibiotics seem to be making the diarrhoea worse, then stop taking them and consult a doctor. Women have an additional problem – antibiotics can cause yeast infections. Tetracycline is also contraindicated in women who are pregnant or breastfeeding.

Diarrhoea with blood or pus, but without fever, may be amoebic dysentery. This is a disease you should not neglect because it will not go away by itself. In addition, if you don't wipe out the amoebae while they are still in your intestine, they will eventually migrate to the liver and other organs, causing abscesses which could require surgery.

There are several ways to cure this disease. If you treat it promptly, the amoebae will still be restricted to the intestine.

The most sure-fire cure for amoebic dysentery is metronidazole (Flagyl), an anti-amoebic drug. It will wipe out amoebae no matter where they reside in the body, even in the liver and other organs. The dosage is 400-800mg three times daily for seven to 10 days. Before you Flagyl-ate yourself, keep away from alcohol – continue the sobriety for several days after you've stopped taking the drug. Flagyl and alcohol together can cause a very nauseating reaction, described by many as a feeling of 'imminent death'.

Children aged between eight and 12 years should have half the adult dose; the dosage for younger children is one third the adult dose.

Herbal medicine fanatics will be pleased to know that dried papaya seeds may actually cure amoebic dysentery, but only if it hasn't gone beyond the intestine. The dosage is one heaped tablespoon daily for eight days. If you're really worried about catching amoebic dysentery, papaya seeds can be used as a preventive measure – one heaped tablespoon weekly is usually effective.

Remember that the seeds must be thoroughly dried and that they taste awful. Just because something is 'natural' doesn't mean it's harmless – papaya seeds can cause miscarriage in pregnant women and they may have other unknown side effects. Treat papaya seeds as you would any other medicine – with caution.

**Giardia** This is another type of parasite which causes diarrhoea, bloating, nausea and weakness, but doesn't produce blood in the stool or cause fever. Giardia is very common throughout the world.

Although the symptoms are similar to amoebic dysentery, there are some important differences. On the positive side, giardia will not migrate to the liver and other organs – it stays in the intestine and therefore is much less likely to cause long-term health problems.

Treatment is with an anti-amoebic drug like metronidazole (Flagyl) or tinidazole (Fasigyn). Treatment is a 2gm dose of Fasigyn or 250mg of Flagyl three times daily for five to 10 days. Again, never drink alcohol while taking Flagyl. Without treatment, the symptoms may subside and you might feel fine for a while, but the illness will return again and again, making your life miserable.

It can sometimes be difficult to rid yourself of giardia, so you might need laboratory tests to be certain you're cured.

**Cholera** Cholera tends to travel in epidemics (often after floods) and outbreaks are generally widely reported, so you can often avoid such problem areas. This is a disease of insanitation, so if you've heard reports of cholera be especially careful about what you eat, drink and brush your teeth with.

Symptoms include a sudden onset of acute diarrhoea with 'rice water' stools, vomiting, muscular cramps and extreme weakness. You need medical help – but treat for dehydration, which can be extreme, and if there is an appreciable delay in getting to hospital then begin taking tetracycline. The adult dose is 250mg four times daily. It is not recommended for children or pregnant women.

**Meningococcal Meningitis** This very serious disease attacks the brain and can be fatal. It's not very common in Vietnam, but there are cases every year in the remote mountain areas of the north.

The disease is spread by close contact with people who carry it in their throats and noses, spread it through coughs and sneezes and may not be aware that they are carriers.

A scattered, blotchy rash; fever; severe headache; sensitivity to light; and neck stiffness (which prevents forward bending of the head) are the first symptoms. Death can occur within a few hours, so immediate treatment is important.

Treatment is large doses of penicillin given intravenously, or chloramphenicol injections.

**Tuberculosis (TB)** There is a world-wide resurgence of tuberculosis. It is a bacterial infection which is usually transmitted from person to person by coughing, but may be transmitted through consumption of unpasteurised milk. Milk that has been boiled is safe to drink, while the souring of milk to make yoghurt or cheese also kills the bacilli.

Typically, many months of contact with the infected person are required before the disease is passed on; the usual site of the disease is the lungs. Most infected people never develop symptoms. In those who do, especially infants, symptoms may arise within weeks of the infection occurring and may be severe. In most, however, the disease lies dormant for many years until, for some reason, the infected person becomes physically run down. Symptoms include fever, weight loss, night sweats and coughing. A skin test before and after travel, to determine whether exposure has occurred, may be considered. A vaccination is recommended for children if they will be in close contact with local people for three months or more.

**Typhoid** Typhoid fever is another gut infection that travels the faecal-oral route – ie contaminated water and food are responsible. Like cholera, epidemics can occur after floods because of sewage backing up into drinking water supplies.

Vaccination against typhoid is not totally effective and it is one of the most dangerous infections, so medical help must be sought.

In its early stages typhoid resembles many other illnesses: sufferers may feel like they have a bad cold or flu on the way, as early symptoms are a headache, a sore throat and a fever which rises a little each day until it is around 40°C or more. The victim's pulse is often slow relative to the degree of fever present and gets slower as the fever rises – unlike a normal fever where the pulse increases. There may also be vomiting, diarrhoea or constipation.

In the second week the high fever and slow pulse continue and a few pink spots may appear on the body; trembling, delirium, weakness, weight loss and dehydration are other symptoms. If there are no further complications, the fever and other symptoms will slowly dissipate during the third week. However you must get medical help before this because pneumonia (acute lung infection) or peritonitis (from burst appendix) are common complications, and also because typhoid is very infectious.

The fever should be treated by keeping the victim cool; dehydration also should be watched for. Ciprofloxin (750mg twice a day for 10 days) is good for adults, while Chloramphenicol is recommended in many countries. The adult dosage is two 250mg capsules four times a day. Children aged between eight and 12 years should have half the adult dose; younger children should have one third the adult dose.

**Polio** Polio is also a disease spread by insanitation and is found more frequently in hot climates. The disease is dangerous and easily transmitted. The effects on children can be especially devastating – they can be crippled for life. Fortunately, an excellent vaccination is available, but a booster every five to 10 years is recommended.

**Tetanus** Tetanus is due to a bacillus which usually enters the blood system through a cut, or as the result of a skin puncture by a rusty nail, wire etc. It is worth being vaccinated against tetanus since there is more risk of contracting the disease in warm climates where cuts take longer to heal. A tetanus booster shot should be given every five to 10 years.

**Malaria** The parasite that causes this disease is spread by the bite of the female Anopheles mosquito, though it *rarely* can get passed by blood transfusion. Malaria has a nasty habit of recurring in later years – even if you're cured at the time – and it can kill you.

In the 1950s, the World Health Organisation launched a two-pronged attack against malaria, spraying with the pesticide DDT and treating victims with the drug chloroquine. Meanwhile, research was begun to develop a malaria vaccine. Health authorities confidently predicted that by the year 2000, the malaria parasite would be extinct.

Unfortunately, mother nature has not cooperated. Rather than gracefully dropping dead, the mosquitoes developed resistance against DDT. The malaria parasite chipped in by developing resistance to chloroquine. And, to add insult to injury, DDT was found to cause environmental damage, while long-term use of chloroquine is now known to be harmful to human health. It's become obvious that malaria is a moving target – as soon as one strategy is developed to attack the disease, the mosquitoes and the parasite mutate.

To further complicate the picture, there are four different types of malaria, although 95% of all cases are one of two varieties. The more serious of these two types is *P falciparum* malaria, which is widespread in the southern part of Vietnam.

The illness develops 10 to 14 days after being bitten by the mosquito and symptoms consist of high fever with alternate shivering and sweating, intense headaches and, usually, nausea or vomiting. Without treatment the condition is fatal within two weeks in up to 25% of cases. It is this variety of malaria which is now showing widespread resistance to the most common anti-malarial drug, chloroquine. The problem is especially serious in the Mekong Delta.

*P vivax* malaria is the other main type (and the two rarer types are similar to *vivax*). *P vivax* malaria may be severe, but is not dangerous to life. However, if not adequately treated, the illness will continue to recur, causing chronic ill-health.

Malaria is a risk year-round in most parts of Vietnam below 1200m. The locals have some natural immunity to malaria resulting from exposure; foreigners from nontropical countries have no such resistance. While it is not yet possible to be inoculated against malaria, limited protection is simple – either a daily or weekly tablet (the latter is more common). The tablets kill the parasites in your bloodstream before they have a chance to multiply and cause illness.

If you're travelling with children or if you're pregnant, then the story with anti-malarial tablets is more complex. Basically, the problem is that some anti-malarials may stay in your system for up to a year after the last dose is taken and may cause birth defects. So if you get pregnant, or are planning to get pregnant within 12 months of taking anti-malarials, your unborn child could be endangered. With newer drugs there's not much information around on the effects of long-term use. It's also a fact that malaria *can* be passed from mother to child at birth.

A sensible precaution is to avoid being bitten in the first place. Most Vietnamese hotels are equipped with mosquito nets and you'd be wise to use them. In the evenings when mosquitoes are most active, cover bare skin, particularly the ankles. Use an insect repellent – any brand that contains the magic ingredient diethyl-toluamide ('deet') should work well. Autan and Off! are two such popular brands widely available in Asia. The liquid form of this stuff sometimes comes in a leaky bottle, making for a rather messy backpack – you can avoid this hassle if you buy it in stick form. As an emergency substitute, the 'green oil' (Vietnamese cure-all sold in pharmacies) works very well, but has to be applied regularly (about once every two hours) or it loses effectiveness. Mosquito coils work wonders, though the smoke thus produced irritates the lungs and eyes. There is also 'electric mosquito incense' – cardboard pads soaked in insecticide which are heated up by a very small machine. These work well, fit easily into a backpack and are widely available in Vietnam, but they aren't much use if the electricity goes off. Having an electric fan blowing on you while you sleep will keep the mossies away, but you might wind up with a cold instead. Finally, it's been found that large doses of vitamin B complex are excreted through the skin and seem to act as a mild mosquito repellent, but don't count on this alone.

Treating malaria is complicated and something you should not undertake yourself except in an emergency. Blood tests are needed to determine if you in fact have malaria rather than dengue fever (see next section) and the choice of drugs depends on how well you react to them (some people are allergic to quinine, for example). However, if you are far from hospitals and doctors, you may have no other choice than self-treatment, except to die. The most common drugs for treatment are Fansidar and quinine (often taken in combination), but note that these drugs are not candy – allergic reactions can occur and are sometimes fatal. And even if you think you've cured yourself, you still need to get to a hospital and have blood tests – otherwise there is the strong possibility of relapse.

For prevention, the most common anti-malarial drugs are mefloquine (Larium) and doxycycline (Doryx or Vibramycin), and new drugs are constantly under development. A lot of travellers are confused about what they should and should not be taking for malaria prevention – you should definitely consult a doctor before taking anything.

A brief rundown on common anti-malarial drugs follows (note that all dosages are for adults):

*Mefloquine* is marketed under the trade name *Larium*, but it's cheaper if you buy a generic prescription. This is one of the newest drugs and it's widely prescribed. It's both an effective prophylactic and cure, but is known to have serious side effects and not everyone can take it. The prophylactic dose is one 250mg tablet taken weekly. The curative dose is three tablets initially, followed by two tablets eight to 12 hours later and yet another two tablets eight to 12 hours after that.

*Doxycycline*, or trade names *Doryx* or *Vibramycin*, is a good preventative for the short-term (under one month) traveller. It's definitely not recommended for long-term use.

Doxycycline is a long-acting tetracycline (antibiotic). It is not recommended during pregnancy, breastfeeding or for children under age 10. Side effects include nausea, photosensitivity (severe sunburn) and vaginal yeast infections in women. It should not be taken with milk products.

The preventative dose is 100mg (one pill) daily. Treatment dose (with quinine) is 100mg two times daily for seven days. You should start taking doxycycline the day you enter the malarial area, and stop taking it the day you leave. Doxycycline is often taken in combination with chloroquine.

*Chloroquine* was previously the most commonly prescribed drug for malaria prevention, but it has gradually lost its effectiveness. It still works well against *P vivax* malaria, but as it's less than 50% effective against *P falciparum* it is not highly recommended. Chloroquine is safe in pregnancy. Long-term use (over five years) of chloroquine has caused permanent retinal damage to the eyes in some people. Other side effects which have been reported include nausea, dizziness, headache, blurred vision, confusion and itching, but such problems are rare.

Chloroquine tablets are available in at least two sizes – small (250mg) or large (500mg). Make sure you know which you have. The preventative dose is 500mg weekly (either two small tablets or one large). You have to start taking the tablets two weeks before entering the malarial zone and continue taking them for about four to six weeks after you've left it.

Chloroquine can be used as a treatment for *P vivax*. Treatment dose is 1000mg initially, then 500mg at six, 24 and 48 hours.

*Fansimef* is *Fansidar* with mefloquine added. Both are an effective treatment against *P falciparum* malaria, but Fansidar is a poor drug against *P vivax*. It may be offered in Vietnam as a preventative drug, but it is best used as a treatment rather than as a preventative. Also it is not recommended during pregnancy, especially the last trimester. It should not be taken at all if there is a history of sulpha allergy.

For treatment, three tablets are taken in a single dose. Fansidar is usually taken in combination with quinine.

*Quinine* is the venerable drug of choice for treating severe and resistant *P falciparum* malaria and cerebral malaria. It should *only* be used as a treatment, not as preventative. Side effects include ringing in the ears, headache, nausea, decreased hearing, tremor and allergic reactions (sometimes severe). There is some resistance to quinine and it is somewhat less effective against *P vivax* than chloroquine.

*Qing Haosu (Artemesinine)* is a herbal medicine from China which has generated much interest in medical circles. Qing haosu has been known since at least the 4th century AD when it was used to treat fevers, but only recently has its anti-malarial properties been established. It's important to note that just because this is a 'herbal medicine' it does not mean that it's harmless. Quinine – made from the bark of the cinchona tree – is also a herbal medicine, but it is certainly not harmless. At the time of writing, qing haosu was available only in China because studies have not yet been completed to determine the proper dosage and possible side effects. Testing in animals suggest it is toxic to the foetus and therefore not recommended in pregnancy.

**Dengue Fever** This is a mosquito-borne disease which resembles malaria, but is not fatal and doesn't recur once the illness has passed.

Dengue fever has two forms. The more dangerous form is dengue haemorrhagic fever. The World Health Organisation reports that this disease exists in over 100 countries and every year strikes 500,000 people, causing 24,000 deaths (90% of which are children). *Dengue Fever – A Fact Sheet for Municipal and Community Leaders* is on the World Wide Web, but requires an Acrobat reader. You can find it at www.who.ch/programmes/ctd/act/dengprev.htm.

A high fever, severe headache and pains in the joints are the usual symptoms – the aches are so bad that the disease is also called 'breakbone fever'. The fever usually lasts two to three days, then subsides, then comes back again and takes several weeks to pass. People who have had this disease say it feels like imminent death.

Despite the malaria-like symptoms, antimalarial drugs have no effect whatsoever on dengue fever. Only the symptoms can be treated, usually with complete bed rest, Panadol, codeine and an intravenous drip. There is no means of prevention other than to avoid getting bitten by mosquitoes, but once you've had dengue fever, you're immune for about a year. The patient should be kept under a mosquito net until after the fever passes – otherwise there is the risk of infecting others.

**Sexually Transmitted Diseases** South Vietnam was once famous for its legions of wartime prostitutes, but this supposedly came to an end in 1975. However, despite repeated declarations by the government that Communism has eliminated such vices, prostitution is staging a comeback. Many of the private mini-hotels and a number of government-owned hotels have massage services that can provide more than just relief from aching muscles. As the country reopened to the outside world, the situation quickly got out of hand – by 1992, beach resorts like Vung Tau and Nha Trang were becoming famous for 'sex tours'. Finally, the national government in Hanoi took notice and ordered a crackdown.

At the time of writing, the situation was very much a mixed bag. The police in some places, like Saigon, have closed down places which were obviously fronts for prostitution, but this has only had the effect of driving the business underground. Barbershops, for example, often double as brothels. In other places, the local People's Committee owns the brothels and are too busy shovelling money into their own pockets to pay much heed to moral guidelines from Hanoi.

It's no secret that prostitutes often contract sexually transmitted diseases (STDs) and pass these on to their customers. During the war, prostitutes often tried to cure themselves of STDs, but created penicillin-resistant strains of gonorrhoea and syphilis by under-medicating themselves with antibiotics. During the American War, American soldiers referred to these diseases as 'Vietnam Rose'.

Gonorrhoea and syphilis are the most common of these diseases. Sores, blisters or rashes around the genitals and discharges or pain when urinating are common symptoms. Symptoms may be less marked or not observed at all in women. Syphilis symptoms eventually disappear completely, but the disease continues and can cause severe problems in later years and, if untreated, can be fatal. There is no vaccine for gonorrhoea, but there is one for syphilis. Both diseases can be treated with antibiotics.

There are numerous other sexually transmitted diseases and effective treatment is available for most of them. However, there is neither a cure nor a vaccine for herpes and AIDS. Using condoms is the most effective preventative.

AIDS *(SIDA* in Vietnamese) has recently become a major source of concern. The first case of HIV infection (the virus which causes AIDS) detected in Vietnam was found in a 14-year-old girl when she applied for the Orderly Departure Programme in 1990 (her application was rejected). A spot check of Saigon prostitutes in 1992 found that 4% of them were carrying the HIV virus. Another random check in 1995 came to the alarming conclusion that 38% of the tested prostitutes were HIV positive! The accuracy of these figures is suspect, but there is clearly cause

for concern. There are now conspicuous billboards around Vietnam advocating the use of condoms.

AIDS can also be spread through infected blood transfusions; most developing countries cannot afford to screen blood for transfusions. It can also be spread by dirty needles – vaccinations, acupuncture, ear piercing and tattooing can potentially be as dangerous as intravenous drug abuse if the equipment is not clean.

**Hepatitis** Hepatitis is a general term for inflammation of the liver and it's a common disease worldwide. The symptoms are fever, chills, headache, fatigue, feelings of weakness and aches and pains, followed by loss of appetite, nausea, vomiting, abdominal pain, dark urine, light-coloured faeces and jaundiced (yellow) skin. The whites of the eyes also may turn yellow.

Hepatitis A is transmitted by contaminated food and drinking water. The disease poses a real threat to the traveller. You should seek medical advice, but there is not much you can do apart from resting, drinking lots of fluids, eating lightly and avoiding fatty foods. People who have had hepatitis should avoid alcohol for some time after the illness, as the liver needs time to recover. Protection against hepatitis A comes in two forms and is highly recommended. Havrix 1440 is a vaccination which provides long term immunity (possibly more than 10 years) after an initial injection and a booster at six to 12 months. Gamma globulin is not a vaccination but a ready-made antibody collected from blood donations. It should be given close to departure because, depending on the dose, it protects for only two to six months.

Hepatitis E is transmitted in the same way and it can be very serious in pregnant women.

There are almost 300 million chronic carriers of hepatitis B in the world. It is spread through contact with infected blood, blood products or body fluids, such as sexual contact, unsterilised needles and blood transfusions, or contact with blood via small breaks in the skin. Other risk situations include having a shave or tattoo or having your body pierced with contaminated equipment. The symptoms of type B may be more severe and may lead to long term problems. Travellers who should consider a hepatitis B vaccination include those visiting countries where there are known to be many carriers, where blood transfusions may not be adequately screened or where sexual contact is a possibility. It involves three injections, the quickest course being over three weeks with a booster at 12 months.

Hepatitis D is spread in the same way, but the risk is mainly in shared needles.

Hepatitis C can lead to chronic liver disease. The virus is spread by contact with blood usually via contaminated transfusions or shared needles. Avoiding these is the only means of prevention.

**Japanese Encephalitis** This illness was unheard of until the 1950s when US troops based in Okinawa (Japan) became infected. Later, cases starting showing up in Malaysia, Indonesia, Thailand and Vietnam. Although still rare, the disease is spreading and health authorities fear that the world may yet see an epidemic. Recently, there have been outbreaks in the Mekong Delta and occasionally in Saigon.

There is still much about Japanese encephalitis that is unknown. Estimates of the fatality rate range from 5% to 60%. What is certain is that if the disease infects the brain, the patient either dies or is left as a mental vegetable. Fortunately, not all cases reach the brain. Unfortunately, there is no treatment once you've been infected – all you can do is wait while the disease runs its course and hope for the best.

Mosquitoes transmit the bug that causes this illness. It's most likely to be a problem during the rainy season and you should take care in the late afternoons and evenings when mosquitoes are most active.

A very effective vaccine exists, but you are not very likely to find it outside of tropical countries. Bangkok would be a logical place to get the vaccination. You can also get vaccinated at the various foreigners' clinics

in Saigon and Hanoi. The big problem is the timing – you need three shots, each spread a week apart. You also should have a fourth jab after one year, and then every four years after that to maintain immunity.

The symptoms of Japanese encephalitis are sudden fever, chills and headache, followed by vomiting and delirium, a strong aversion to bright light, and sore joints and muscles. If it goes to the brain, convulsions, coma and death follow.

As with other mosquito-borne diseases, Japanese encephalitis can be prevented if you can avoid getting bitten by mosquitoes. See the section on malaria for some advice on how to do it.

**Rabies** Even if you're a devout dog lover, you aren't likely to go around petting the stray dogs you encounter in Vietnam. Third World dogs are not like the cute little fluffy creatures that play with children in the backyards of western suburbia – they are often half-starved and badly mistreated and have been known to take a bite out of tourism.

Fido is likely to be even less friendly if infected with rabies. Although your chances of getting it is small, rabies is a disease worth guarding against. A vaccine is available, but few people bother to get it. The vaccination requires three injections – once a week for three weeks – and is good for about two years. However, if you're bitten, the vaccine by itself is *not* sufficient to prevent rabies; you will still need two more vaccinations. If you haven't been vaccinated, a bite can be a major problem. Not only do you need the full set of vaccinations, which in Vietnam may be the sort which are now outmoded, you also need a human rabies immunoglobulin vaccine. As this is a blood product, getting a jab of this in Vietnam could present itself with a whole other series of risks.

The rabies virus infects the saliva of the animal and is usually transferred when the rabid animal bites you and the virus passes through the wound into your body. It's important to realise that not only dogs carry rabies – any mammal which bites (like a rat) can transmit the virus. Also, if you have a scratch, cut or other break in the skin you could catch rabies if an infected animal licks that break in the skin. If you are bitten or licked by a possibly rabid animal you should wash the wound thoroughly (but without scrubbing since this may push the infected saliva deeper into the your body) and then start on a series of injections which will prevent the disease from developing. Once it reaches the brain, rabies has a 100% fatality rate. New rabies vaccines have been developed which have fewer side effects than the older, animal-derived serums and vaccines.

The incubation period for rabies depends on where you're bitten. If on the head, face or neck then it's as little as 10 days, on the arms it's 40 days and on the legs 60 days. This allows plenty of time to be given the vaccine and for it to have a beneficial effect. Get yourself to a major centre, because with proper treatment administered quickly after being bitten, rabies will not develop.

**Eye Infections** Be careful about wiping your face with the reusable towels supplied by restaurants, as this is an easy way to transmit eye infections. When your hands are dirty from a dusty motorbike ride, try to keep them away from your eyes until you've had a chance to wash up.

There are several types of eye infections. The most common, but least serious, is conjunctivitis; the most serious, but fortunately rare in travellers, is trachoma. Mild conjunctivitis usually begins with pain in the eyes and headache in the morning, but goes away after you've been awake for a while. If the pain persists and your eyes burn, itch, get bloodshot and discharge pus, you should see a doctor.

While it's wise to get a medical opinion, you shouldn't panic. In many cases, burning and itching eyes are not the result of infection at all, but simply the effects of dust, petrol fumes and bright sunshine. Treating simple eye irritation with antibiotics is dangerous. After a day on a motorbike, using eyewash can help to rid your eyes of dust, but don't overdo it, since excessive use of eyewash and eye drops can also make your eyes burn.

If you don't have any commercial eyewash, just use water, but make sure it's clean.

There are a number of eyedrops sold across the counter in Vietnam and elsewhere for treating conjunctivitis. It's wise to use the mildest ones, which contain boric acid in a saline solution. Stronger eye drops containing steroids and antibiotics are available, but can seriously worsen an infection if misused. Trachoma must be treated as soon as possible with antibiotic eye ointments, but this is an area where qualified medical opinion should be sought.

Allergies can lead to simple conjunctivitis. Rather than use eyedrops, you might want to try a simple oral antihistamine such as Hismanal.

People prone to eye problems might want to supplement their diets with vitamin A tablets. Don't exceed the recommended dose, because excessive vitamin A is toxic.

**Intestinal Worms** Liver fluke infestation (Opisthorchiasis) is endemic in rural areas of north-west Vietnam. The worms can be present on unwashed vegetables or in undercooked meat and you can pick them up through your skin by walking in bare feet. Infestations may not show up for some time and, although they are generally not serious, if left untreated they can cause severe health problems. Consider having a stool test when you return home.

If you get roundworm, threadworm or hookworm, treatment is straightforward. Mebendazole (a generic name which is marketed under many different labels) is one of many worm treatments which are effective – you just take one pill which is good for three months. Children under six months old, nursing mothers and pregnant women should not take it without first consulting a doctor.

Ascaris, or roundworm, is the most common worm infestation that plagues foreigners. The eggs are usually ingested through vegetables that have been grown using human faeces as manure and have not been properly washed; the eggs hatch in the stomach and then the larvae burrow through the intestines, enter the bloodstream and make their way through the liver to the heart, from where they work their way up to the lungs and the windpipe. They are then coughed up, swallowed and deposited in the intestines, where they mature and grow up to from 20-35cm (8-14 inches) long. The most common symptom of adult roundworm infestation is abdominal discomfort increasing to acute pain due to intestinal blockage.

Threadworm eggs, when swallowed, hatch in the stomach. The worms enter the intestine, where they grow and mate; the mature female worms make their way through the bowel to the anus, where the depositing of their sticky eggs causes intense itching. One way to diagnose the presence of worms is to stretch a piece of adhesive tape over a flat stick, with the sticky area on the outside, and press it into the area around the anus. If there is an infestation you may be able to see worms and eggs on the tape – the mature worms look like little strands of cotton thread about 1.3 cm (half an inch) long.

Hookworms can be picked up by walking around in bare feet in soil littered with infected faeces. The eggs hatch in the soil and then the larvae enter the bloodstream by burrowing through the skin. Following much the same internal route as the roundworm, they reach the intestine and hook onto the lining. By feeding on the host's blood, hookworms can grow up to 1.3 cm (half an inch) long. The most common result of hookworm infestation is anaemia, although they can also do damage to the organs they come into contact with. The best prevention is to wear shoes unless on the beach. Even with shoes on, if you walk through muddy water there is a chance of getting it. Hookworms can also be absorbed by drinking infected water or eating uncooked and unwashed vegetables.

## Cuts, Bites & Stings

**Bedbugs & Lice** Bedbugs live in various places, but particularly in dirty mattresses and bedding, evidenced by spots of blood on bedclothes or on the wall. Bedbugs leave itchy bites in neat rows. Calamine lotion or Stingose spray may help.

If you don't mind spraying poison, insecticide is effective – a small amount sprayed around the periphery of the mattress serves as an effective barrier to those insects that live on the underside of the bed by day.

All lice cause itching and discomfort. They make themselves at home in your hair, in your clothing or in your pubic hair (crabs). You catch lice through direct contact with infected people or by sharing combs, clothing and the like. Powder or shampoo treatment will kill the lice and infected clothing should then be washed in very hot water.

**Snakes** Vietnam has several poisonous snakes, the most famous being the cobra. The small, green-coloured bamboo snake is highly venomous. Its habitat is not only bamboo trees but also grass fields, and it can swim across small bodies of water. All sea snakes are poisonous and are readily identified by their flat tails, but sea snakes have small mouths and cannot bite humans easily.

Fortunately, snakes tend to avoid contact with creatures larger than themselves, which is good news for humans. On the other hand, snakes eat rats and will sometimes pursue their rodent delicacies right into people's homes. However, most snake-bite victims are people who work in the fields and accidentally step on a snake. Be careful about walking through grass and underbrush. Wearing boots gives a little more protection than running shoes.

A snake's head can bite even after it's been cut off. The biting reflex remains active for perhaps 45 minutes after the head has been severed. Keep this in mind if you go to a snake restaurant and want to play with a fresh cobra head.

Should you be so unfortunate as to get bitten, try to remain calm (sounds easier than it really is) and not run around. The conventional wisdom is to rest and allow the poison to be absorbed slowly. Tying a rag or towel around the limb to apply pressure slows down the poison, but the use of tourniquets is not advisable because it can cut off circulation and cause gangrene. Cutting the skin and sucking out the poison has also been widely discredited. Immersion in cold water is also considered useless.

Treatment in a hospital with an antivenin would be ideal. However, getting the victim to a hospital is only half the battle – you will also need to identify the snake. In this particular case, it might be worthwhile to kill the snake and take its body along, but don't attempt that if it means getting bitten again. Try to transport the victim on a makeshift stretcher.

All this may sound discouraging, but the simple fact is that there is very little first-aid treatment you can give which will do much good. Fortunately, snakebite is rare and the vast majority of victims survive even without medical treatment.

**Wasps & Bees** Wasps, which are common in the tropics, are a more serious hazard than snakes because they are more aggressive and will chase humans when stirred up. They won't attack unless they feel threatened, but if they do attack, they usually do so en masse. This is not just uncomfortable, it can be fatal. If you're out hiking and see a wasp nest, the best advice is to move away quietly. A few brainless people like to see how skilful they are at throwing rocks at wasp nests – this is not recommended. Should you be attacked, the only sensible thing to do is run like hell.

It would take perhaps 100 wasp or bee stings to kill a normal adult, but a single sting can be fatal to someone who is allergic. In fact, death from wasp and bee stings is more common than death from snakebite. People who are allergic to wasp and bee stings are also allergic to bites by red ants. If you happen to have this sort of allergy, you'd be wise to throw an antihistamine such as epinephrine or Hismanal into your first-aid kit. Epinephrine is most effective when injected (though it can be taken in pill form), while Hismanal is preferred for long-term relief (just one pill per day). Both are prescription drugs in the west, but can be bought over the counter in many Asian countries.

**Women's Health**
**Gynaecological Problems** Poor diet, use of

antibiotics and the contraceptive pill can lead to vaginal infections when travelling in hot climates. Maintaining good personal hygiene and wearing loose-fitting clothes and cotton underwear will help to prevent infections.

Yeast infections, characterised by a rash, itch and discharge, can be treated with a vinegar or lemon-juice douche, or with yoghurt. Nystatin, miconazole or clotrimazole suppositories are the usual medical prescription. Trichomoniasis and gardnerella are more serious infections; symptoms are a smelly discharge and sometimes a burning sensation when urinating. Male sexual partners must also be treated and, if a vinegar-water douche is not effective, medical attention should be sought. Metronidazole (Flagyl) is the prescribed drug.

**Pregnancy** Most miscarriages occur during the first three months of pregnancy, so this is the most risky time to travel as far as your own health is concerned. Miscarriage is not uncommon and can occasionally lead to severe bleeding. The last three months should also be spent within reasonable distance of good medical care. A baby born as early as 24 weeks stands a chance of survival, but only in a good modern hospital. Pregnant women should avoid all unnecessary medication, but vaccinations and malarial prophylactics should still be taken where possible. Additional care should be taken to prevent illness and particular attention should be paid to diet and nutrition. Alcohol and nicotine, for example, should be avoided.

**TOILETS**
The issue of toilets and what to do with used toilet paper has caused some concern. As one traveller wrote:

We are still not sure about the toilet paper ... in two hotels they have been angry with us for flushing down the paper in the toilet. In other places it seems quite OK though.

In general, if you see a wastepaper basket next to the toilet, that is where you should throw the toilet paper. The problem is that in many hotels, the sewage system cannot handle toilet paper. This is especially true in old hotels where the antiquated plumbing system was designed in the pre-toilet paper era. Also, in rural areas there is no sewage treatment plant – the waste empties into an underground septic tank and toilet paper will really create a mess in there. For the sake of international relations, be considerate and throw the paper in the wastepaper basket.

Toilet paper is seldom provided in the toilets at bus and railway stations or in other public buildings, though hotels usually have it. You'd be wise to keep a stash of your own with you at all times while travelling around.

If you're wondering what poor Vietnamese do when they can't afford toilet paper (many actually cannot), the answer is simple: they use water and the left hand. There is often a bucket and water scoop next to the toilet for just such a purpose. Those who have been to other parts of south-east Asia should be well familiar with the procedure.

And while we're on this subject, another thing you need to be mentally prepared for is squat toilets. For the uninitiated, a squat toilet has no seat for you to sit on while reading the morning newspaper; it's a hole in the floor. The only way to flush it is to fill the conveniently placed bucket with water and pour it into the hole. While it takes some practice to get proficient at balancing yourself over a squat toilet, at least you don't need to worry if the toilet seat is clean. Furthermore, experts who study such things (scatologists?) claim that the squatting position is better for your digestive system.

Better hotels will have the more familiar western-style sit-down toilets, but squat toilets still exist in cheaper hotels and in public places like restaurants, bus stations etc.

The scarcity of public toilets seems to be a greater problem for women than for men. Vietnamese males can often be seen urinating in public, but this seems to be socially unacceptable for women. It is not very clear how Vietnamese women handle this situation.

## WOMEN TRAVELLERS

Like Thailand and other predominantly Buddhist countries, Vietnam is, in general, relatively free of serious hassles for female western travellers.

It's a different story for Asian women, particularly those who are young. An Asian woman accompanied by a western male will automatically be labelled a 'Vietnamese whore'. The fact that the couple could be married (or just friends) doesn't seem to occur to anyone, nor does it seem to register that the woman might not be Vietnamese at all. If she's Asian then she's Vietnamese, and if she's with a western male then she must be a prostitute. It will be difficult to convince many Vietnamese otherwise.

The problem is basically that many Vietnamese men believe that western men are out to 'steal their women'. Most Vietnamese women really don't care. Asian women travelling in Vietnam with a western male companion have reported frequent verbal abuse. The nasty words are all spoken entirely in Vietnamese, which means many women do not know what insults are being hurled at them. However, there will be no mistaking the hateful stares and obscene gestures. Occasionally, things get nasty – when greased with alcohol, Vietnamese men may throw rocks or any other object which is handy.

The Vietnamese government has made no attempt so far to educate the masses to stop this crude behaviour. For racially-mixed couples wanting to visit Vietnam, no easy solution exists. There's no need to be overly paranoid, but a few precautions are helpful. Of course, public intimacy (holding hands etc) is best avoided, but even just walking down the street together invites abuse. Four people travelling together are less likely to encounter trouble than just two, but this isn't guaranteed.

Dressing 'like a foreigner' is helpful – sewing some patches on your clothing with Japanese or Chinese characters can work wonders. One woman got good results by sewing a Korean flag onto her backpack. Vietnamese women usually have long, flowing hair – you don't have to cut yours, but tie it up or braid it.

In an actual confrontation, the woman should shout at the antagonist in any language *other* than Vietnamese – this might make the vigilante realise that he is confronting a foreigner rather than a 'Vietnamese whore'. If this revelation sinks in, he might suddenly apologise! The western male might be tempted to physically bash a Vietnamese man who is insulting his Asian wife or girlfriend, but this could lead to a brawl with serious consequences. Before you hit anyone, remember that some of the spectators could be the man's brothers and they may retaliate.

## DISABLED TRAVELLERS

Vietnam is not a particularly good place for disabled travellers, despite the fact that many Vietnamese are disabled with war injuries. Tactical problems include the crazy traffic, a lack of pedestrian footpaths, a lack of lifts in the buildings and ubiquitous squat toilets.

On the other hand, there are times when a 'disability' can be an asset. Given the level of noise, deaf travellers may enjoy Vietnam more than most foreign visitors.

## TRAVEL WITH CHILDREN

In general, foreign children have a good time in Vietnam mainly because almost everybody wants to play with them.

However, babies and unborn children present their own peculiar problems when travelling. Lonely Planet's *Travel with Children* by Maureen Wheeler gives a rundown on health precautions to be taken with kids and advice on travel during pregnancy.

## USEFUL ORGANISATIONS
### Chamber of Commerce

Vietcochamber, the Chamber of Commerce & Industry, is supposed to initiate and facilitate contacts between foreign business people and Vietnamese companies. They may also be able to help with receiving and extending business visas. Vietcochamber publishes a listing of government companies and how to contact them. They have offices in Saigon, Hanoi and Danang.

### Non-governmental Organisations

There are various non-governmental organisations (NGOs), including churches, humanitarian aid organisations and the like working in Vietnam. One organisation which helps the many amputees and war cripples in Vietnam is Vietnam Assistance for the Handicapped (☎ (703) 847-9582; fax 448-8207), PO Box 6554, McLean, VA 22106, USA.

## DANGERS & ANNOYANCES
### Culture Shock

The dangerous thing about Vietnam is your own psyche. As one traveller noted:

My first day on landing in Saigon was one of shock and horror. For he first couple of days I thought the whole idea of Vietnam was a terrible mistake. No matter how much reading and research you do prior to arriving, nothing prepares you for the sights, sounds and smells of this place. Three days after arriving I was OK, had settled down and was having a fantastic time.

**Craig McGrath**

This is not to say that nothing can go wrong. There are some things you should be concerned about, and those are listed below. Just remember that worrying about all the 'problems' you will encounter can do more to ruin your trip than the problems themselves.

### Theft

Vietnamese are convinced that their cities are very dangerous and full of criminals. Before reunification, street crime was rampant in the South, especially in Saigon. Motorbikeborne thieves (called 'cowboys' by the Americans) would speed down major thoroughfares, ripping pedestrians' watches off their wrists. Pickpocketing and confidence tricks were also common. After the fall of Saigon, a few bold criminals even swindled the newly arrived North Vietnamese troops. When a few such outlaws were summarily shot, street crime almost disappeared overnight.

Especially watch out for drive-by thieves on motorbikes – they specialise in snatching handbags and cameras from tourists riding in cyclos. Some have become proficient at grabbing valuables from the open window of a car and speeding away with the loot. Foreigners have occasionally reported having their eyeglasses and hats snatched too.

Pickpocketing – often involving kids, women with babies and newspaper vendors – is also a serious problem, especially in tourist areas of Saigon such as Dong Khoi and Pham Ngu Lao Sts.

The cute little children also wander right into cafes and restaurants where foreigners are eating, ostensibly to sell you a newspaper or postcards. In the process – and often with the help of another child accomplice – they can relieve you of your camera or handbag if you've set it down on an adjacent seat. If you must set things down while you're eating, at least take the precaution of fastening these items to your seat with a strap or chain. Remember, any luggage that you leave unattended for even a moment may grow legs and vanish.

There are also 'taxi girls' (often transvestites) who approach western men, give them a big hug and ask if they'd like 'a good time'. Then they suddenly change their mind and depart – along with a wristwatch and wallet.

We have had recent reports of people getting drugged and then robbed on long-distance public buses. The way it usually works is that a friendly fellow passenger offers you a free Coke, which in reality turns out to be a chloral hydrate cocktail. You wake up hours later to find your valuables and new-found 'friend' gone. If you're unlucky, you don't wake up at all because an overdose of chloral hydrate can easily be fatal.

Even assuming that you are too wise to accept gifts from strangers, there is at least one other way you can be drugged. One traveller we know well claims that his fellow passenger leaned across him to open a window, while an accomplice took advantage of the diversion to drop some drugs into his water bottle. The lesson seems to be that you should keep your water bottle where no one can easily get their hands on it.

Despite all this, you should not be overly paranoid. Although crime certainly exists and you need to be aware of it, theft in Vietnam does not seem to be any worse than elsewhere in the Third World (including 'Third World' cities in the west). Don't assume that everyone's a thief – most Vietnamese are very poor, but reasonably honest.

And finally, there is the problem of your fellow travellers. It's a disgusting reality that some backpackers subsidise their journey by ripping off whomever they can, including other backpackers. This is most likely to happen if you stay in a dormitory, though in this regard Vietnam is relatively safe since dormitories are rare. Perhaps most disturbing of all are attempts by foreigners to rip off the Vietnamese. There have been reports of backpackers slipping out of restaurants without paying their bills, cheating their guides out of promised pay etc. We know one fellow who deliberately short-changed his driver US$40 because the car's air-conditioner broke down on the last day of the trip. This is pretty sick.

To avoid theft, probably the best advice one can follow is to not bring anything valuable that you don't need. Expensive watches, jewellery and electronic gadgets invite theft and do you really need these things while travelling?

## Violence

Unlike in some western cities, recreational homicide is not a popular sport in Vietnam. The country is virtually free of terrorists harbouring a political agenda. In general, violence against foreigners is extremely rare and is not something you should waste much time worrying about. Vietnamese thieves prefer to pick your pocket or grab your bag and then run away – knives, guns, sticks and other weapons are almost never used.

However, there have been a few rare incidents involving guns, particularly on remote rural roads. One gang terrorised motorists in the Danang area for two years, stopping vehicles and robbing the passengers at gunpoint. After committing over 60 robberies, the gang was caught in mid-1994 and the thieves were sentenced to death. Another gang in the Mekong Delta robbed tourist boats at gunpoint before they were finally caught.

You do see a lot of street arguments between Vietnamese. Usually this takes the form of two young macho types threatening and pushing each other while their respective girlfriends try to separate them. The whole point of the threats and chest-thumping exercise is to save face and there is seldom any bloodshed. The cause of these arguments usually has something to do with money, often the result of a minor motor vehicle accident and who should pay for the broken headlight or squashed chicken. Such macho posturing is likely to exclude foreigners.

## Scams

Stories abound of friendly Vietnamese guides who take tourists to pricey restaurants and then arrange under-the-table commissions for themselves.

One western travel agent offering tours to Vietnam (who prefers to remain nameless) had this to say:

I've been burned too many countless times to be surprised by anything. The scams they think of! I remember the guide who I employed on my first tour – all he had to do was be mediocre and everyone would have been happy. For some reason, the people on my tours believed things more when told by a native, so I would brief him everyday on the background of the sites, people and historical aspects of the day's route. Unfortunately, he spent so much energy scheming elaborate cons that he paid little attention to being a guide. He and others have even tried to get me to fleece my tourists in a scam partnership. But I do want to add that I've had at least some very honest guides. Unfortunately, there are so many con artists that you can't afford to let your guard down.

Nor is the problem of scams is limited to guides. There have been persistent reports in the tourist zones (especially Dong Khoi St and Nguyen Hue Blvd in Saigon) of single male travellers being approached in the evening by women claiming to be prostitutes. Those foreigners foolish enough to even talk to these 'prostitutes' for a couple of minutes may suddenly be approached by a very angry, screaming 'husband' of the woman claiming that the foreigner is trying to rape his wife. He makes a big scene, a crowd gathers and he demands US$100 or so in 'compensation'.

On the other hand, she doesn't have to be a prostitute. Another traveller wrote:

I heard about a scam in Saigon – yes that's right, yet another – where women go back to hotels with a western male. Once they are in the hotel room, the local police (are they really police?) knock on the door and demand a bribe to turn a blind eye to the use of a prostitute, even though the male may have thought he had just got lucky and there was no discussion of payment.

**Andrew H**

Beware of a motorbike rental scam which some travellers have encountered in Saigon. What happens is that you rent a bike and the owner supplies you with an excellent lock and suggests you use it. What he doesn't tell you is that he, too, has a key and that somebody will follow you and 'steal' the bike at the first opportunity. You then have to pay for a new bike or forfeit your passport, visa, deposit or whatever security you left. And the person who rented the bike to you still has it!

More common is when your motorbike won't start after you parked it in a 'safe' area with a guard. But yes, the guard knows somebody who can repair your bike. The repairman shows up and reinstalls the parts he removed earlier from your bike and now it works fine. That will be US$10 please.

Con artists are, of course, always seeking new tricks to separate naive tourists from their money. We can't warn you about every trick you might encounter, so perhaps the best advice we can give is to maintain a healthy suspicion and be prepared to argue when demands are made for your money.

## Beggar Fatigue

Just as you're about to dig into the scrumptious Vietnamese meal you've ordered, you feel someone gently tugging on your

## Almost Conned

I thought I knew every swindle in the book. As a Lonely Planet writer, experienced traveller and jaded cynic, I was certain that no one would be able to fool me with yet another con game. I've seen it all. 'Scams' were something that happened to other people.

But I was almost taken in. A long-time Vietnamese friend volunteered to travel with me on my most recent update of the Vietnam guidebook. He wanted to be my translator and guide. He didn't want money for his efforts. For him it would be an experience to see his own country, to learn English from me, to find out what life as a travel writer is like. He would even write some travel articles himself for the Vietnamese newspapers. He had a jeep we could use, so we could bring a couple of friends along. It would be good fun.

I smiled at my friend's naivety. The life of a travel writer is not what most people imagine (getting a suntan on the beach and writing about it later). Instead, it's a high-speed slog from one town to another, collecting information and drawing maps continuously. Always in the back of your mind is that ever-pressing deadline. I've had other friends accompany me before on these trips – most burn out after a few days and head for the beach. Travel writers wind up working solo – they don't call this Lonely Planet for nothing.

My friend was unfazed by these warnings. He was used to working hard and would accept whatever difficulties came with life on the road.

Seduced by the prospect of good companionship and a reliable jeep, I agreed. As it turned out, the trip was more difficult than expected. It was the wettest year on record in Vietnam. Were it not for the jeep, we probably couldn't have made it.

My Vietnamese friends were undaunted by the mud floods and breakneck travel pace. Indeed, they showed considerable enthusiasm for the task at hand. And well they should have – for unbeknownst to me they were asking hotel and restaurant owners for substantial sums of money to be considered for a mention in the new guidebook.

Fortunately I discovered their con game, but was amazed my 'friends' would attempt such a scam. It didn't work, but if I'd been a little less savvy it could have – they were superb actors! I have given good reviews only to businesses that deserved it and I certainly did not accept payment.

My advice to travellers – bring a healthy dose of scepticism with you when you travel to Vietnam.

**Robert Storey**

shirt-sleeve. You turn around to deal with this latest 'annoyance' only to find it's a bony, eight-year-old boy holding his three-year-old sister in his arms. The little girl has a distended stomach, her palm is stretched out to you and her hungry eyes fixed on your plate of steaming chicken, vegetables and rice.

This is the face of poverty. How do you deal with these situations? If you're like most of us, not very well. On occasion, we've given food to a small group of beggars and watched in horror as they fought over it.

Nevertheless, it's probably better to give food than to give money – little children are often forced by their parents to beg for money, but the cash is frequently used to support the parents' drinking and gambling habits rather than to feed the children or send them to school. Of course, that's if the kids have parents, which many of them don't.

So what can you do to help these street people, many of whom are malnourished, illiterate and have no future? Good question – we wish we knew. Give or refuse as you wish and spare a moment to think of just how lucky you are.

I will always remember the beam of delight that came over the face of a hard-bitten child beggar when I offered him a cake similar to the one I was eating.

**Gordon Balderston**

## Undetonated Explosives

Four armies expended untold energy and resources for over three decades mining, booby-trapping, rocketing, strafing, mortaring and bombarding wide areas of Vietnam. When the fighting stopped most of this ordnance remained exactly where it had landed or been laid; American estimates at the time placed the quantity of unexploded ordnance at 150,000 tonnes.

Since 1975, many thousands of Vietnamese have been maimed or killed by this left-over ordnance while clearing land for cultivation or ploughing their fields. While cities, cultivated areas and well-travelled rural roads and paths are safe for travel, straying away from these areas could land you in the middle of a minefield which, though known to the locals, may be completely unmarked. In April 1997, several children were killed by a bomb left over from the American War in a schoolyard in Nghe An Province.

*Never* touch any rockets, artillery shells, mortars, mines or other relics of the war you may come across. Such objects can remain lethal for decades. In Europe, people are still sometimes injured by ordnance left over from WWII and even WWI and every few years you read about city blocks in London or Rotterdam being evacuated after an old bomb is discovered in someone's backyard.

Especially dangerous are white phosphorus artillery shells (known to the Americans as 'Willy Peter') in which the active ingredient does not deteriorate as quickly as in explosives. Upon contact with the air the white phosphorus contained in the shells ignites and burns intensely; if any of it gets on your body it will eat all the way through your hand, leg or torso unless scooped out with a razor blade – imagine that. This stuff terrifies even scrap-metal scavengers.

And don't climb inside bomb craters – you never know what undetonated explosive device is at the bottom. Remember, one bomb can ruin your whole day.

## Cockroaches

While some travellers are amused by the antics of cockroaches, at least some people find them very disturbing. Vietnamese cockroaches are well fed and can grow to an amazingly large size. Cockroach-infested hotel rooms are the norm in Vietnam, especially at the budget end of the scale.

Cockroaches are actually relatively easy to deal with if you come prepared. One way is to launch a chemical blitzkrieg against these beasties with insecticide, though such nerve-gas attacks might pose a hazard to your own health.

Boric acid (a white powder) is deadly poison to cockroaches if they so much as inhale the dust. This chemical is also very poisonous to humans if taken internally, but is harmless externally (mixed with water, boric acid is often used as eyewash). When checking into a hotel room, sprinkling some boric acid powder under the bed (not in the bed!), in the corners, on the washroom floor and along other likely cockroach routes will have the desired effect. At first you might think there are more cockroaches than ever because the poison drives them out into the open, but after a few hours your room will be cockroach-free.

Boric acid can be purchased easily and cheaply in almost any pharmacy, both inside and outside Vietnam. Try to keep it in a reasonably sturdy container (not a plastic bag) – small plastic jars are useful for this purpose. Some hazards: it's dangerous to keep around children and some travellers report being harassed by customs because of boric acid's physical resemblance to cocaine!

## Rats

Even cockroach enthusiasts are generally reluctant to share a hotel room with rats. If you encounter rats in Vietnam, they are not likely to be the cute, fluffy white creatures forced to smoke cigarettes and drink Diet Coke in western medical experiments. Rather, they are the grey, decidedly less friendly variety.

Avoiding nocturnal visits by these creatures is fairly simple; don't keep any food in your hotel room. As one traveller noted:

Rats are more clever than you might think. In the evening we put some biscuits inside our car, thinking that no way could rats get inside the vehicle. But they did – they climbed up tyres, trekked to the top of the engine and then chewed a hole through the rubber heater hose to get inside the passenger compartment. All we found the next morning was the empty package which they had chewed open. We half expected to find a thank you note from the creatures!

**Pamela Hong**

## Sea Creatures

If you spend your time swimming, snorkelling and scuba diving, you should be aware of various creatures which live in the sea that can be hazardous. It's a well-established fact that most nasty sea creatures live in warm water, so the future south you are in Vietnam, the greater the risk of unpleasant encounters. The list of dangerous sea creatures found in Vietnam is extensive and could include sharks, jellyfish, stonefish, scorpion fish, sea snakes and stingrays, to name a few. However, there is little cause for alarm – most of these creatures either avoid humans or humans avoid them, so the actual number of people injured or killed by sea animals is fairly small. Nonetheless, exercising some common sense is strongly advised.

Shark attacks mostly occur in deeper water – keeping to shallow spots decreases your chance of trouble. Sharks are attracted by bright colours like red, yellow and orange, so wearing a dark swimsuit is a reasonable precaution. Blood attracts sharks, so if you cut your foot you should get out of the water immediately.

Jellyfish tend to travel in groups, so avoiding them is usually not too difficult if you look before you leap into the sea. Make local inquiries – many places experience a 'jellyfish season' (usually summer). Jellyfish generally get nastier the closer one gets to the equator and some species are potentially fatal, but stings from most jellyfish are simply rather painful. Dousing in vinegar will deactivate any stingers which have not 'fired'. Calamine lotion, antihistamines and analgesics may reduce the reaction and relieve the pain.

Stonefish, scorpion fish and stingrays tend to hang out in shallow water along the ocean floor and can be very difficult to see. Stepping on one can be bad news indeed. One way to protect yourself would be to wear shoes while wading in the sea, but most people won't do this. To treat a sting by a stonefish or scorpion fish, immerse the affected part in hot water (the hotter the better, but don't burn yourself!) and seek medical treatment.

All sea snakes are poisonous but are generally nonagressive. Furthermore, their small fangs are placed towards the rear of the mouth and they would have a difficult time biting a large creature such as a human.

## Noise

One thing that can be insidiously draining on your energy during a trip to Vietnam is noise. At night, there is often a competing cacophony from motorbikes, dance halls, cafes, video parlours, karaoke lounges, restaurants and so on; if your hotel is situated near any of the above (and it's unlikely to be in a totally noise-free zone), sleep may be difficult. In some places, even the small carts of ice cream and snack vendors have a booming, distorted portable cassette player attached.

The Vietnamese themselves seem to be immune to the noise. Indeed, a cafe that doesn't have an eardrum-splitting cacophony emanating from a loudspeaker will have difficulty attracting customers; that is to say, 'Vietnamese customers'. The foreigners will flee as soon as the sound system is turned on. Those who stay long enough to finish a meal or a cup of coffee will walk away with their heads literally pounding.

Fortunately, most of the noise subsides around 10 or 11 pm, as few clubs stay open much later than that. Unfortunately, though, the Vietnamese are very early risers; most people are up and about from around 5 am onwards. This not only means that traffic noise starts early, but that you're likely to be woken up by the crackle of cafe speakers, followed by very loud (and often atrocious) karaoke music. It's worth trying to get a hotel room at the back, so the effect of street noise is diminished. Other than that, perhaps you could consider bringing a set of earplugs.

## LEGAL MATTERS
### Civil Law

The French gave the Vietnamese the Napoleonic Code, much of which has not been repealed, although these laws may conflict with later statutes. From about 1960 to 1975, South Vietnam modified much of its commercial code to resemble that of the USA. Since reunification, Soviet-style laws have been applied to the whole country with devastating consequences for private property owners. The recent economic reforms have seen a flood of new property legislation, much of it the result of advice from the United Nations, International Monetary Fund and other international organisations. The rapid speed at which legislation is being enacted is a challenge for those who must interpret and enforce the law.

On paper, it all looks good. In practice, the rule of law barely exists in Vietnam. Local officials interpret the law anyway it suits them, often against the wishes of Hanoi. This poses serious problems for joint ventures – foreigners who have gone to court in Vietnam to settle civil disputes have generally fared badly. It's particularly difficult to sue a state-run company, even if that company committed obvious fraud. The government has a reputation for suddenly cancelling permits, revoking licences and basically tearing up written contracts. There is no independent judiciary.

Not surprisingly, most legal disputes are settled out of court. In general, you can accomplish more with a carton of cigarettes and a bottle of XO than you can with a lawyer.

### Drugs

During the American War, US troops were known to partake in large quantities of noxious weeds, hashish and stronger recreational chemicals. After 1975, the loss of American customers, plus the Communists' sophisticated police state apparatus and the country's extreme poverty, suppressed domestic demand for drugs. However, the recent influx of foreign tourists along with economic progress has revived the drug trade. Vietnam has a serious problem with heroin and the authorities are not amused.

You may well be approached with offers to buy marijuana and occasionally opium. Giving in to this temptation is risky at best. There are many plainclothes police in Vietnam – just because you don't see them

doesn't mean they aren't there. If arrested, you could be subjected to a long prison term and/or a large fine.

The drug export market has also been doing well and Vietnam's reputation is such that customs officials at your next destination might vigorously search your luggage. In short, drug use in Vietnam is still a perilous activity and taking home samples is even riskier.

### The Police

The problem of police corruption has been acknowledged in official newspapers. The problems that plague many Third World police forces – very low pay and low levels of education and training – certainly exist in Vietnam. If something does go wrong, or if something is stolen, the police often can't do much more than write a report for your insurance company. Unfortunately, even to get this limited help, some people have found it necessary to pay a 'tip' for this service. The tip can be anything from a pack of Marlboros to perhaps US$100.

The government has attempted to crack down hard on the worst abuses. In 1996, one policeman was imprisoned after he shot and killed a motorcyclist who refused to pay an on-the-spot 'fine' for a bogus traffic violation. Hanoi has warned all provincial governments that any police caught shaking down foreign tourists will be fired and arrested.

The crackdown has dented the enthusiasm of the police to confront foreigners directly with demands for bribes. However, it has not eliminated the problem altogether. Especially when riding a motorcycle (or even just riding as a passenger in a car), you may be stopped for no apparent reason and have a 'fine' imposed.

Fines are generally negotiable – the bidding may start at US$25, but can be reduced all the way down to US$5. Generally, if you insist on an official receipt, then the fine will be US$25. If you're willing to do without the receipt, then it's US$5. If you refuse to pay the fine, your vehicle could be impounded.

With all this having been said, there is really no need for excessive paranoia. The Vietnamese police are a nuisance and you may have to occasionally pay, but you will usually not have to pay a lot. To avoid getting upset, you have to do as the Vietnamese do – think of 'fines' as a 'tax'.

Foreigners who stay long-term in Vietnam and attempt to do business can expect periodic visits from the police collecting 'taxes' and 'donations'. Often they will direct their 'requests' towards the Vietnamese employees rather than confront a foreign manager directly. The issue is further complicated by the fact that most Vietnamese police (perhaps 75%) are in plainclothes – so are those 'police' really who they say they are? It's just one of those things that makes doing business in Vietnam so exciting. Good luck.

## BUSINESS HOURS

Vietnamese rise early (and consider sleeping in to be a sure indication of illness). Offices, museums and many shops open between 7 and 8 am (depending on the season – things open a tad earlier in the summer) and close between 4 and 5 pm. Lunch is taken very seriously and virtually everything shuts down for 1½ hours between noon and 1.30 pm. Government workers tend to take longer breaks, so figure on getting nothing done from 11.30 am to 2 pm.

Most government offices are open on Saturday until noon, while Sunday is a holiday. Most museums are closed on Mondays. Temples are usually open all day every day. Vietnamese tend to eat their meals by the clock regardless of whether or not they are hungry and disrupting someone's meal schedule is considered very rude. This means, for example, that you don't visit people during lunch (unless invited). It also means that if you hire somebody for the whole day (a cyclo driver, a guide etc) you must take a lunch break by noon and dinner by 5 pm. Delaying the lunch break until 1 pm will earn you a reputation as a sadistic employer.

Many small privately owned shops, restaurants and street stalls stay open seven days a week, often until late at night – they need the money.

## PUBLIC HOLIDAYS & SPECIAL EVENTS

Politics affects everything, including public holidays. As an indication of Vietnam's new openness, Christmas, New Year' Day, Tet (Lunar New Year) and Buddha's Birthday have been added as holidays after a 15-year lapse. The following are Vietnam's public holidays:

1 January
  *New Year's Day (Tet Duong Lich)*
1st to 7th days of the 1st moon (late January to mid-February)
  *Tet (Tet Nguyen Dan)*, the Vietnamese Lunar New Year
3 February
  *Anniversary of the Founding of the Vietnamese Communist Party (Thanh Lap Dang CSVN)* – The Vietnamese Communist Party was founded on this date in 1930.
30 April
  *Liberation Day (Saigon Giai Phong)* – The date on which Saigon surrendered is commemorated nationwide as Liberation Day. Many cities and provinces also commemorate the anniversary of the date in March or April of 1975 on which they were 'liberated' by the North Vietnamese Army.
1 May
  *International Workers' Day (Quoc Te Lao Dong)* – Also known as *May Day*, this falls back-to-back with Liberation Day giving everyone a two day holiday.
19 May
  *Ho Chi Minh's Birthday (Sinh Nhat Bac Ho)* – Ho Chi Minh is said to have been born on this date in 1890 near Vinh, Nghe An Province.
8th day of the 4th moon (usually June)
  *Buddha's Birthday (Dan Sinh)*
2 September
  *National Day (Quoc Khanh)* – This commemorates the proclamation in Hanoi of the Declaration of Independence of the Democratic Republic of Vietnam by Ho Chi Minh on 2 September 1945.
25 December
  *Christmas (Giang Sinh)*

Special prayers are held at Vietnamese and Chinese pagodas on days when the moon is either full or just the thinnest sliver. Many Buddhists eat only vegetarian food on these days, which, according to the Chinese lunar calendar, fall on the 14th and 15th days of the month and on the last (29th or 30th) day of the month just ending and the 1st day of the new month.

The following major religious festivals are listed by lunar date:

1st to 7th days of the 1st moon

*Tet* – The Vietnamese Lunar New Year is the most important festival of the year and falls in late January or early February. This public holiday is officially three days, but many people take off an entire week.

Tet is a time for family reunions, the payment of debts, the avoidance of arguments, special foods, new clothes, flowers and new beginnings. Great importance is attached to starting the year properly because it is believed that the first day and first week of the new year will determine one's fortunes for the rest of the year. Homes are decorated with sprigs of plum tree blossoms *(cay mai)*.

The first pre-Tet ceremony, Le Tao Quan, is designed to send the Spirit of the Hearth (Tao Quan) off to report to the Jade Emperor (Ngoc Hoang) in a positive frame of mind. A New Year's Tree (Cay Neu) is constructed to ward off evil spirits. Later, a sacrifice (Tat Nien) is offered to deceased family members. Finally, at midnight, the old year is ushered out and the new welcomed in with the ritual of *giao thua*, which is celebrated both in homes and in pagodas. Firecrackers were used until 1995 (when the government banned them) to commemorate the new year and welcome back the Spirit of the Hearth. Now only gongs and drums are used for this purpose. The first visitor of New Year's Day is considered very important and great care is taken to ensure that they be happy, wealthy and of high status. For this reason foreigners are likely to receive an invite!

A seasonal favourite is *banh chung*, which is sticky rice, yellow beans, pig fat and spices wrapped in leaves and boiled for half a day.

Visitors to Vietnam around Tet should take into account that flights into, out of and around the country are likely to be booked solid and accommodation impossible to find. Ditto for all of north-east Asia (China, Hong Kong, Macau, Taiwan and Korea).

5th day of the 3rd moon

*Holiday of the Dead (Thanh Minh)* – People pay solemn visits to graves of deceased relatives – specially tidied up a few days before – and make offerings of food, flowers, joss sticks and votive papers.

8th day of the 4th moon

*Buddha's Birth, Enlightenment and Death* – This day is celebrated at pagodas and temples, which, like many private homes, are festooned with lanterns. Processions are held in the evening. This has recently been redesignated a public holiday.

5th day of the 5th moon

*Summer Solstice Day (Doan Ngu)* – Offerings are made to spirits, ghosts and the God of Death to ward off epidemics. Human effigies are burned to satisfy the requirements of the God of Death for souls to staff his army.

15th day of the 7th moon

*Wandering Souls Day (Trung Nguyen)* – This is the second-largest festival of the year. Offerings of food and gifts are made in homes and pagodas for the wandering souls of the forgotten dead.

15th day of the 8th moon

*Mid-Autumn Festival (Trung Thu)* – This festival is celebrated with moon cakes of sticky rice filled with such things as lotus seeds, watermelon seeds, peanuts, the yolks of duck eggs, raisins and sugar. Colourful lanterns in the form of boats, unicorns, dragons, lobsters, carp, hares, toads etc are carried by children in an evening procession accompanied by drums and cymbals.

28th day of the 9th moon

*Confucius' Birthday*

## ACTIVITIES
### Exercise Clubs

The Vietnamese government emphasises gymnastics, which is a mandatory subject at all schools from the elementary level through university. Other sports popular with the locals include tennis, badminton, table tennis and handball.

Unless you happen to be working at a school with such facilities, your best bet is to try the exercise clubs at major hotels. Some hotels open their exercise facilities to non-guests on a fee basis. Depending on the particular hotel, you may be charged a fee for a single day's use or for a monthly membership.

### Gambling

After being banned by the Communists for 14 years, gambling, that most bourgeois capitalist activity, is staging a comeback. Horse racing is once again popular in Saigon. Vietnam's first casino since liberation opened in 1994 at Do Son Beach near Haiphong.

And in the back alleys of large cities, slot machines have popped up inside of karaoke clubs – these machines are now legal as 'entertainment devices'.

You can easily avoid the horse racing, casinos and slot machines if you don't want to play, but you'll have a hard time escaping the state lottery. Touts (mostly children) selling lottery tickets will approach you anytime, anywhere and they are usually *very* persistent. If the kids seem miserable, it's not hard to understand – they get to keep only 12% of the face value of each ticket sold; 1% goes to the wholesaler and the other 87% goes to the government.

While your chances of winning are minuscule, hitting the jackpot in the state lottery can make you a dong multi-millionaire. The smallest denomination lottery ticket is 1000d (less than US$0.10), while the largest prize is 25 million dong (somewhat less than US$2500).

The official state lottery has to compete against an illegal numbers game *(danh de)* reputed to offer better odds. Two of the most popular forms of illegal gambling are dominoes *(tu sat)* and cock fighting. Some of the ethnic-Chinese living in the Cholon district of Ho Chi Minh City are said to be keen mahjong players.

## Golf

Mark Twain once said that playing golf was 'a waste of a good walk' and apparently Ho Chi Minh agreed with him. When the French departed Vietnam, Ho Chi Minh's advisers declared golf to be a 'bourgeois practice'. In 1975, after the fall of South Vietnam, golf was banned and all courses were shut down and turned into farming cooperatives. However, times have changed – golf was rehabilitated in 1992 and now even government officials can be seen riding around in electric carts in hot pursuit of a little white ball.

Throughout the Far East, playing golf can win you considerable points in the 'face game' even if you never hit the ball. For maximum snob value, you need to join a country club and the fees for this are outrageously high. In Vietnam, golf memberships start at around US$20,000 or so – Japanese travellers comment that this is incredibly cheap.

Most clubs (not all) will allow you to simply pay a steep guest fee for attacking a golf ball with a No 5 iron. Chances are good that you'll have the course to yourself, since most of the members will be back at the club house drinking scotch. Nevertheless, some clubs will require that you at least be accompanied by a member before they permit you to play.

Places to pursue this activity include the environs of Ho Chi Minh City, Hanoi, Dalat and Vung Tau. See the relevant chapters for details.

## Hash House Harriers

This organisation was founded in Malaysia in the mid-1930s and has slowly spread around the world.

Hash House Harriers is a loosely strung international club that appeals mainly to young people, or the young at heart. Activities typically include a weekend afternoon easy jogging session followed by a dinner and beer party which can extend until the wee hours of the morning.

The Hash is very informal. There is no club headquarters and no stable contact telephone or address. Nonetheless, finding the Hash is easy. Some embassy or consulate employees know about it; otherwise look for announcements in the *Vietnam Economic Times*, *Vietnam Investment Review* and expat bars. See the Hanoi and Ho Chi Minh City chapters (Activities section) of this book for information about the Hash.

There is a mandatory US$5 donation which also gains you a free T-shirt and refreshments. All excess funds are donated to local charities.

## Water Sports

With 3451km of mostly tropical coastline, Vietnam would seem like Asia's answer to Queensland, Florida or the Spanish Riviera. Indeed, there are some excellent beaches, though not quite as many as you'd expect.

Part of the reason is that the southern part of the country (which has the best tropical climate and highest population) is dominated by the huge Mekong Delta. While this region is lush, green and lovely, it's also very muddy and the 'beaches' tend to be mangrove swamps. One of the few beach areas in the delta region is Hon Chong, which faces the Gulf of Thailand. Even better are the beaches at nearby Phu Quoc Island, also in the Gulf of Thailand.

The southernmost sandy beach on the east coast is Vung Tau, a very popular place close to Saigon, but plagued by polluted water. Mui Ne beach near Phan Thiet is considerably cleaner and more beautiful, though so far it offers few economical places to stay. Ca Na (not far from Phan Thiet) offers cheaper accommodation though the beach is small.

Without a doubt, Nha Trang has emerged as Vietnam's premier beach resort, in part because of its year-round pleasant weather, offshore islands and superb accommodation offerings. Heading north towards Danang are numerous other good beaches, mostly undeveloped, but the weather becomes more seasonal – May to July is the best time, while during the winter powerful rip tides make swimming dangerous.

Hué has truly awful winter weather and it just gets worse as you go north. But in the summer, the beaches are thick with sun-tanned Vietnamese (though few foreigners). The best-known northern beaches are at Cua Lo (near Vinh), Sam Son (near Thanh Hoa) and Do Son (near Haiphong).

Most Vietnamese people love the beach, but have a respectful fear of the sea – they like to wade up to their knees, but seldom dive in and go for a proper swim. Where you are most likely to see Vietnamese actually swimming is in rivers and public swimming pools. Surfing and windsurfing have only recently arrived on the scene, so far only in the Danang area. Such activities are sure to expand.

It is possible to hire snorkelling gear and scuba equipment at several beach resorts, particularly at Nha Trang. But some warnings are in order. Equipment is sometimes good, sometimes not. Half-empty tanks of air have been rented out. If a squall comes up, boat operators have occasionally been known to head for shore, leaving the hapless divers for lost! Of course, fatal diving accidents can and do occur in developed countries as well, but extra precautions should be taken in any poor country. Don't always assume that equipment and training is up to international standards.

## LANGUAGE COURSES

If you'd like to learn to speak Vietnamese, courses are now being offered in Saigon, Hanoi and elsewhere. To qualify for student visa status, you need to study at a bona fide university (as opposed to a private language centre or with a tutor). Universities require that you study at least 10 hours per week. Lessons usually last for two hours per day, for which you pay tuition of around US$5.

You should establish early on whether you want to study in northern or southern Vietnam, because the regional dialects are very different. Foreign students who learned Vietnamese in Hanoi and then moved to Saigon to find work (or vice versa) have often been dismayed to discover that they cannot communicate. But (get ready for this) the majority of the teachers at universities in the south have been imported from the north and will tell you that the northern dialect is the 'correct one'! So even if you study at a university in Saigon, you may find that you need to hire a local private tutor (cheap at any rate) to help rid you of a northern accent.

For information on specific language schools where you can study Vietnamese, see the Activities section in the chapters dealing with Hanoi and Ho Chi Minh City.

## WORK

From 1975 to about 1990, Vietnam's foreign workers were basically technical specialists and military advisers from Eastern Europe and the now-defunct Soviet Union. The declining fortunes of the Eastern Bloc has caused most of these advisers to be withdrawn.

Vietnam's opening to capitalist countries has suddenly created all sorts of work opportunities for westerners. However, don't come to Vietnam looking for big money. The most well paid westerners living in Vietnam are those working for official foreign organisations such as the United Nations and embassies, or else have been hired by private foreign companies attempting to set up joint-venture operations. People with certain high-technology skills may also find themselves much in demand and able to secure high pay and cushy benefits.

It's nice work if you can get it, but such plum jobs are thin on the ground. Foreigners who look like Rambo have occasionally been approached by Vietnamese talent scouts wanting to recruit them to work as extras in war movies. But for the vast majority of travellers, the most readily available work opportunities will be teaching a foreign language.

English is by far the most popular foreign language with Vietnamese students. About 10% of foreign language students in Vietnam also want to learn French. There are also many Vietnamese who want to learn Chinese, but many ethnic-Chinese live in Vietnam so there is little need to import foreign teachers. There is also some demand for teachers of Japanese, German, Spanish and Korean.

Government-run universities in Vietnam hire some foreign teachers. Pay is generally around US$2 per hour, but certain benefits like free housing and unlimited visa renewals are usually thrown in. Teaching at a university requires some commitment – you may have to sign a one year contract, for example.

There is also a budding free market in private language centres and home tutoring, and this is where most newly arrived foreigners seek work. Pay in the private sector is slightly better than what the government offers – figure on US$3 to US$4 per hour depending on where in Vietnam you teach. At private schools, free housing and other perks are usually not included. A business visa is required to be legally employed and

the school may not be in a good position to help you out with the authorities. One possible way around the visa hurdles is to sign up for Vietnamese language lessons at a university, but be aware that you may actually be expected to attend class and study.

Private tutoring pays even better – around US$5 per hour and more. In this case, you are in business for yourself. The authorities may or may not turn a blind eye to such activities.

Everyone who has become a foreign language teacher in Vietnam will have a different story to tell. There is no one way to do it. One experienced English teacher in Saigon gave this summation of his experience:

There are countless schools which are willing to hire you. Pay is around US$4 per hour in Saigon. They tell you a business visa is required for it to be legal, but some will let this slide. I don't advise signing a contract unless the school is *very* reputable (ie other foreigners are working there and happy). Agreements mean nothing here. Your salary might be lowered without your consent, you might get underpaid (count the money in that envelope carefully) and you might find upon arriving for class that the director has decided that the lesson you have prepared has been replaced by another. Flakiness abounds on all fronts. The classes are huge (up to 60). You might find yourself yelling into a microphone, competing with the roar of traffic noises a few metres away and with the teachers shouting into microphones in the adjoining classrooms. Other than a few token nods to the Asian tradition of respecting teachers, the students are often uncooperative in these huge classes, talking to each other while you're lecturing, arriving late, leaving early etc.

The answer, I find, is to teach privately. The students are much more motivated and respectful, especially if you keep the class size small. Still, there's the flakiness factor. Classes routinely cancel at the last minute with no reason given. Or a group of students might cancel out forever with no warning. Everything is subject to change at a moment's notice. Ask for payment two weeks in advance and things go much better, but they'll only agree if they know that you too are reliable and won't abscond. In other words, you have to work awhile to build up your reputation. You can make between US$5 and US$10 per hour depending on the number of students in your class and how affluent they are. I have a teaching certificate, but I hardly think it's mandatory – plenty of people find work without one.

The authorities must know what I've been doing all along, but they've never bothered me. I've been

# Kingdom of Champa

The kingdom of Champa flourished from the 2nd to the 15th centuries. It first appeared around present-day Danang and later spread south to what is now Nha Trang and Phan Rang. Champa became Indianised through commercial relations with India: the Chams adopted Hinduism, employed Sanskrit as a sacred language and borrowed from Indian art.

The Chams, who lacked enough land for agriculture along the mountainous coast, were semi-piratic and conducted attacks on passing trading ships. As a result, they were in a constant state of war with the Vietnamese to the north and the Khmers to the west. The Chams successfully threw off Khmer rule in the 12th century but were entirely absorbed by Vietnam in the 17th century.

The Chams are best known for the many brick sanctuaries (Cham towers) they constructed throughout the south. The greatest collection of Cham art is in the Cham Museum in Danang. The major Cham site is at My Son (near Danang), and other Cham ruins can be found in Nha Trang and Phan Rang-Thap Cham.

*The 13th century Po Klong Garai towers at Phan Rang-Thap Cham are among the most recognisable sights of southern Vietnam.*

MASON FLORENCE

# Nguyen Dynasty

Hué became the capital of Vietnam in 1802, when Nguyen Anh crowned himself Emperor Gia Long, thus founding the Nguyen Dynasty. Upon his accession, he began the construction of the Citadel, the Imperial Enclosure and the Forbidden Purple City. Gia Long instituted conservative Confucian values and began a large-scale programme of public works, including the construction of dikes, bridges, canals and the Mandarin Road linking Hué with both Saigon and Hanoi.

The early Nguyen emperors were hostile to Catholicism and western influences. In keeping with their expansionist policies, they took over large areas of Cambodia and Laos. French colonial interest in Vietnam began in earnest in the 1840s, when the French responded to actions against Catholic missionaries. Following military defeat in 1862, Emperor Tu Duc signed a treaty that gave the French the three eastern provinces of Cochinchina, which became a French colony.

Upon the death of Tu Duc, the French attacked Hué and imposed a Treaty of Protectorate on the imperial court. From that time, the Nguyen Dynasty emperors ruled in name only. Anti-colonial resistance continued in Vietnam. In 1945, following Japanese occupation during WWII, the Communist Viet Minh gained power and Emperor Bao Dai abdicated. The capital was moved to Hanoi.

*Built in 1844 by Emperor Thieu Tri, the seven-storey tower of the Thien Mu Pagoda has become the unofficial symbol of Hué.*

TONY WHEELER

working on a tourist visa and have been getting away with it. Other teachers I know have obtained business visas through local companies, whom they basically bribed to exercise their pull with the authorities and say these teachers work for them as 'consultants'. The main hassle is finding a place to live. Landlords will tell you they're licensed to house foreigners and then the cops will come by and kick you out a few days after you've moved in.

Finding teaching jobs is relatively easy in places like Saigon and Hanoi, and is sometimes possible in towns that have universities. Pay in the smaller towns tends to be lower and work opportunities considerably scarcer. Looking for employment is a matter of asking around – jobs are rarely advertised. The longer you stay, the easier it is to find work – travellers hoping to land a quick job and depart two months later will probably be disappointed.

US citizens might be able to find volunteer work with the US Peace Corps. Citizens of the UK might want to contact the British Consul to find out about similar opportunities. Organisations like the International Red Cross might also be able to advise you.

Some western journalists and photographers manage to make a living in Vietnam by selling their stories and pictures to western news organisations. If you're lucky enough to land a full-time job with Reuters, that's great. However, most journalists and photojournalists are forced to work freelance and pay can vary from decent to dismal.

## ACCOMMODATION

If there is one thing that budget travellers frequently complain about in Vietnam, it's the cost of the hotels. Most government-run hotels maintain a price differential – foreigners are charged more than Vietnamese (usually double). The theory is that foreigners are richer than local Vietnamese and therefore can afford to pay a premium. This doesn't explain though why some hotels give discounts to Overseas Vietnamese and 'other Asians'.

Another thing pushing up prices are taxes. There is a room tax of 12.5% imposed by the Vietnamese government, but local governments add many other tariffs including an income tax, profit tax, business licence tax, land tax and ill-defined 'adjustment fees'. Paying off the police is an additional 'adjustment fee', which has to be factored into the total tax bill. Land taxes and the like have to be paid even if the hotel has few guests, so places which are not busy have to charge high rates or else risk bankruptcy.

There are now regulations requiring hotels and guesthouses to maintain 'acceptable standards' before they can be approved to receive foreign guests (you'd never know it by some of the dumps around). So it is possible that you will front up to what seems like a perfectly serviceable hotel and be refused a room even if the place is empty. In that case, there is little point arguing. The hotel staff won't risk trouble with the police just to accommodate you, though they might refer you elsewhere.

Theoretically, these regulations are meant to protect foreign tourists from staying in dirty and dangerous places. In practice, the motive is often less honourable. In some places, foreigners are simply not allowed to stay in private hotels because these compete with the government-owned ones, even though the private hotels are often of a higher standard. Occasionally, this can create a real problem for you – if the approved hotels are all full and you can't stay in the unapproved ones, your only choice is to sleep in the street. The Vietnamese have a name for sleeping in the street – it's called staying in a 'thousand-star hotel'.

### Reservations

A 'reservation' means next to nothing unless you've paid for the room in advance. It's possible to arrange this through some travel agencies, but don't expect much on the budget end of the spectrum. However, there is seldom much need for reservations – you can almost always find a place to stay. An important exception is during the Tet holiday (and the 10-day period immediately following Tet) – at that time reservations are definitely recommended.

## Camping

Perhaps because so many millions of Vietnamese spent much of the war years living in tents (either as soldiers or refugees), camping is not the popular pastime it is in the west. Even in Dalat, where youth groups often come for outdoor holidays, very little proper equipment can be hired. And in many locations, the local government prohibits foreigners to camp anyway.

The biggest problem with camping is finding a remote spot where curious locals and the police won't create difficulties for you. Faced with a shortage of hotel rooms, the authorities on Phu Quoc Island have permitted foreign tourists to camp on the beach, though in designated sites only. Furthermore, some innovative private travel agencies in Saigon now offer organised camping trips for groups.

## Dormitories

While there are dormitories (nha tro) all around Vietnam (especially at railway and bus stations), most (but not all) of these are officially off limits to foreigners. In this case, the government's motives are not simply to charge you more money for accommodation – there is a significant chance of getting robbed while sleeping in a Vietnamese dormitory. Even though budget travellers like to complain about this policy, it's one case where the Vietnamese government is really trying to protect you.

The concept of a relatively upmarket dormitory just for foreigners is starting to catch on. Some of these 'dormitories' are actually rooms with two beds – you need to share the room with only one other person. You are most likely to find these in private mini-hotels in areas frequented by budget travellers (Saigon's Pham Ngu Lao St pioneered the concept). Expect to see more such places in the future.

## Hotels

Most large hotels (khach san) and guesthouses (nha khach or nha nghi) are government owned or else are joint ventures. There is also a rapidly increasing number of small private hotels, usually referred to as 'mini-hotels'.

There is some confusion over the terms 'singles', 'doubles, 'double occupancy' and 'twins', so let's set the record straight here. A 'single' is a room containing one bed, even if two persons sleep in it. If there are two beds in the room, that is a 'twin', even if only one person occupies the room. If two people stay in the same room, that is 'double occupancy' – in most cases, there is *no extra charge* for this. There is considerable confusion over the term 'doubles' – in some hotels this means twin beds, while in others it means double occupancy. More than a few travellers have paid extra for twin beds when what they really wanted was a single bed for two people. It's always a good idea to take a look at the room to make sure that you're getting what you wanted and are not paying extra for something you don't need.

Most hotels now have rooms with attached private bath, but not always. Ask first or take a look at the room to be sure. Some hotels have an attached bath, but the toilet is outside (a peculiar arrangement). If your hotel has no hot bath, you can try looking for a local *tam goi* (bath house) though these are becoming rare.

A few hotels might try to charge the foreigners price for your Vietnamese guide and/or driver as long as they know that you're paying the bill. This is not on – if they stay in a separate room, they should be charged like any local tourist. Don't accept this nonsense from anyone.

The Vietnamese seem to be absolutely obsessed with air-conditioning, which has become a big prestige item. For them, finding a hotel room with air-conditioning seems more important than having a room with an attached bath. If you travel with guides, don't be surprised if they ask for an air-con room (which costs three times as much as a room with a fan) and then complain the next morning that they couldn't sleep because the room was too cold.

Most hotels do not issue receipts when you pay, but it's a good idea to ask for one anyway (and save it) if you'll be staying for more than a few days. Confusion can arise over how many days you have paid for and how much you still owe. At least a few hotels are guilty of chaotic bookkeeping (sometimes deliberate), and one shift at the front desk might have no clue about what people from other shifts have and have not done.

It's important to realise that many hotels have both an upmarket new wing and a squalid old wing, with a wide variation of prices between the two buildings. Furthermore, many Vietnamese hotels offer a wide range of prices even in the same building! For example, one popular hotel in Saigon has room prices running from US$15 to US$75. Cheap rooms are almost always on the top floor because few hotels have lifts and most guests paying US$75 are not keen to walk up seven storeys or more. The situation is rather different from the west, where the most expensive rooms are usually on the top floor.

Even at the biggest and most expensive hotels, it is possible to negotiate discounts if you are staying long term. For definition's sake, 'long term' can mean three days or more. Booking through some foreign or domestic travel agencies can also net you a discount. For practical purposes, the rates quoted in this book are the short-term, walk-in rates.

The following are some of the more common hotel names and their translations:

| | |
|---|---|
| *Binh Minh* | Sunrise |
| *Bong Sen* | Lotus |
| *Cuu Long* | Nine Dragons |
| *Doc Lap* | Independence |
| *Ha Long* | Descending Dragon |
| *Hoa Binh* | Peace |
| *Huong Sen* | Lotus Fragrance |
| *Huu Nghi* | Friendship |
| *Thang Long* | Ascending Dragon |
| *Thong Nhat* | Reunification |
| *Tu Do* | Freedom |

**Hotel Security** Hotel security can be a problem. Even though there may be a guard on each floor, the guards usually have keys to your room. Supposedly, they are responsible if anything gets stolen, but reports from

travellers indicate that this often means nothing.

Many hotels post a small sign warning you not to leave cameras, passports and other valuables in your room. Many hotel rooms come equipped with a closet which can be locked – if so, use it and take the key with you. You would be very wise to bring a chain with a padlock – this can be used to lock the closet and you won't have to worry about the employees having keys. If your room or the hotel's front desk has a safe, you can also make use of it. A few hotels have a place where you can attach a padlock to the outside of the door rather than a lock built into the door itself. At such hotels you will be provided with a padlock, but you'd be wise to bring your own, which means that you'll have the only key (don't lose it!). A combination lock might be more convenient, but make sure it's one that is not easily broken (the cheap ones can be pried apart with a screwdriver).

**Police Registration** Back in the old days when the Soviets told the Vietnamese how to run their country, all hotel guests had to deposit their passports and/or visas with reception – the staff then had to take these valuable documents over to the police station and register the guests. And it was not uncommon for the police to then pay a visit to your hotel room and question you about why you were there, how long would you be staying, where did you come from and where were you going to next, and finally terminate the interview by requesting a 'tip'. Your documents would be returned only upon your departure and there was always the worry that they could be 'lost'.

The good news is that the national government no longer requires police registration of hotel guests. The bad news is that provincial governments make up their own rules and so little has changed. In Ho Chi Minh City, you *do not* need to leave your passport or visa with hotel reception, though most government-owned hotels want it anyway for 'security' (ie to make sure you don't run away without paying). In Cantho, the police want to see your passport and visa (both are required here) and they will not accept photocopies. The Danang police require that you deposit your original visa and green entry card (the form you fill out on arrival at the airport), but you needn't show your passport.

In other words, these regulations are as clear as mud. Each city you visit will have its own arbitrary rules and these rules can change at the drop of a hat. There is no question that most foreigners do not like to see their valuable documents passing through so many hands with the chance that something could get lost. We've had some tense moments ourselves – on one occasion we were extremely annoyed to find our passports lying on the front counter unattended – the staff had gone off to dinner and simply left our passports lying around where anybody could have walked off with them! And on two occasions the hotel staff returned the *wrong* passports to us! Other travellers we've met had their passports returned with the wrong visa. When you check out of a hotel, you must check your documents very carefully. If somebody checked out before you and took your documents by mistake, all you can do is pray that they'll discover the error and come back.

And what compensation will you receive if the hotel loses your passport, visa or entry card? The simple answer is: none at all.

### Homestays
It's possible to arrange to stay in the homes of local people, but – depending on the local government – the family might have to register with the police all foreign visitors to their homes, including relatives. The police can – and often do – arbitrarily deny such registration requests and will force you to stay in a hotel or guesthouse licensed to accept foreigners.

### Rental Accommodation
Renting a medium-sized house in Saigon costs about US$50 per month for a Vietnamese family. Foreigners cannot do this. The local authorities set the price which foreigners pay and 85% of the rent money goes to

the government. Many landlords are unwilling to rent to foreigners because they get so little financial reward and so much unwanted attention from the authorities. Even once you've moved into your new home, the authorities can revoke your right to reside there with no notice at all.

The result is that foreigners are forced to rent high-priced villas or expensive luxury flats. In 1996, the government issued Decree 56/CP, which governs the renting of houses to foreigners. The decree was supposed to 'streamline' rentals, but it in fact hits landlords with new taxes that will cause rents to sharply increase. Protests from important expats (like embassy people and foreign investors) has caused the government to delay implementation of the new regulations. No one is sure how the issue will be resolved, but it seems likely that renting a house in Vietnam is not going to get cheaper anytime soon.

The result is that many expats wind up living in mini-hotels. Big discounts can be negotiated for long-term stays. It's wise to first live in the hotel for at least one night before agreeing to anything. You'll want to be sure that the place really is clean and quiet and has functional plumbing before you hand over a month's rent.

### FOOD
One of the delights of visiting Vietnam is the amazing cuisine – there are said to be nearly 500 different traditional Vietnamese dishes – which is, in general, superbly prepared and very reasonably priced.

You'll never have to look very far for food in Vietnam – restaurants (nha hang) of one sort or another seem to be in every nook and cranny. Most serve exclusively Vietnamese food, though some cafes can rustle up something western. The Vietnamese are much better at producing their native food than the western stuff – Vietnamese pizza is particularly notorious. But western restaurants are increasing in number and the cooks are slowly learning how to accommodate western tastes.

Unless you eat in exclusive hotels or

aristocratic restaurants, food is very cheap. At the bottom of the barrel are street stalls where a bowl of noodles costs around US$0.50. Very casual restaurants with bamboo and cardboard walls have rice, meat and vegetable meals costing perhaps US$1. Most cafes and decent restaurants can fill your stomach for US$2 to US$5. However, in classy restaurants the bill can add up fast; be aware that the small dishes of snacks which appear on the table cost money if you indulge (and are charged per person!). Check out the bill very carefully – overcharging is not uncommon when more than one person orders food or when many items are listed on the bill.

Most Vietnamese restaurants do not have any prices on the menu at all. In this case, you must definitely ask the total price when you place your order. Vietnamese diners know this and will always ask, so don't be shy about speaking up. If you don't, be prepared for a shock when the bill finally comes.

Unlike the western practice of each person getting their own individual plate of food, eating in most Asian countries is a communal affair. That is, various dishes are put out on the table to be shared by a small group. People often stick their individual chopsticks into the communal plate of food, which is not very sanitary but probably won't kill you. Using a serving spoon or 'serving chopsticks' solves this problem, but is not a common practice. Having three or four people to eat with you assures that you get to sample several different types of dishes. Once you get past the initial culture shock, this style of eating is much fun and very sociable – many foreigners come to prefer it over western individualism. If you eat with a group of Vietnamese, you may find that some of your fellow diners pick out the best-looking pieces of food with their chopsticks and put it into your rice bowl. Some travellers find this disturbing, but you shouldn't – this is a way of honouring you as a distinguished guest.

The proper way to eat Vietnamese food is to take rice from the large shared dish and put it in your rice bowl. Using your chopsticks, take meat, fish or vegetables from the serving dishes and add them to your rice. Then, holding the rice bowl near your mouth, use your chopsticks to eat. Leaving the rice bowl on the table and conveying your food, precariously perched between chopsticks, all the way from the table to your mouth strikes Vietnamese as odd, though they will be more amused than offended.

Except for upmarket establishments, no Vietnamese restaurant would be complete without a couple of half-starved canines hanging around the tables begging for handouts. More disturbing to animal lovers is the fact that Fido can wind up on the menu too. However, most Vietnamese do not in fact eat dog – it's a speciality item. Dog meat is most popular in the north and eating it is believed to bring good fortune. However, there is a definite schedule for this – in Hanoi, dog is only eaten during the second half of the lunar month. In the south, the dog eating schedule is totally different. Warning – eating dog at the wrong time of month can bring bad luck. To find (or avoid) a restaurant serving dog meat, look for a sign saying *thit cho* or *thit cay*.

Unlike dog, eating snake meat does not bring good fortune. However, it is believed to have some medicinal properties and is widely touted as an aphrodisiac. The more poisonous the snake, the worthier its reputation (and thus a higher price is charged). Cobras are a favourite, though pythons have considerably more meat. To get the full health benefits, the Vietnamese recommend that you drink the snake's blood mixed with rice wine and eat the gall bladder raw. Connoisseur's of this cuisine also recommend that you put the snake's still-beating heart into a glass of rice wine and 'bottoms up'. Feasting on such delicacies is not cheap – catching and raising snakes is a little tricky and prices are appropriately high. If you're interested, the Mekong Delta is the best place to look for this type of cuisine. Be aware that eating undercooked snake meat is dangerous – you can catch a nasty parasite called pentastomid.

To get the bill (check), politely catch the attention of the waiter or waitress and write in the air as if with a pen on an imaginary piece of paper.

## Snacks

Vietnamese spring rolls are called *cha gio* (pronounced 'chow yau') in the south and *nem Sai Gon* or *nem ran* in the north. They are made of rice paper filled with minced pork, crab, vermicelli, *moc nhi* (a kind of edible fungus), onion, mushroom and eggs and then fried until the rice paper turns a crispy brown. *Nem rau* are vegetable spring rolls.

A variation on the theme is the larger spring rolls called *banh trang* in the south and *banh da* in the north. With these you put the ingredients together yourself and roll your own. The outer shell is a translucent rice crepe. It's excellent, but pass on the shrimp paste.

*Banh cuon* is a steamed rice pancake into which minced pork and moc nhi is rolled. It is served with a special sauce made from watered-down nuoc mam (fermented fish sauce), vinegar, sugar, pepper, cloves and garlic.

*Oc nhoi* is snail meat, pork, chopped green onion, nuoc mam and pepper rolled up in ginger leaves and cooked in snail shells.

*Gio* is lean pork seasoned and then pounded into paste before being packed into banana leaves and boiled.

*Cha* is pork paste fried in fat or broiled over hot coals. *Cha que* is cha prepared with cinnamon.

*Chao tom* is grilled sugar cane rolled in spiced shrimp paste (the shrimp paste is horrible).

*Dua chua* is bean sprout salad that tastes vaguely like Korean kimchi.

There are a number of western-style foods. Excellent French bread is available everywhere – it's best in the morning when it's warm and fresh. Imported French cheese spread can be bought from street stalls for around US$1.50 per box and sometimes salami is also available.

Vietnamese-made biscuits are not too good, though slowly improving. Biscuits imported from China are truly awful, except for one brand labelled 'Coconut Crackers'.

## Main Dishes

**Rice** The staple of Vietnamese cuisine is plain white rice *(com)* dressed up with a plethora of vegetables, meat, fish and spices.

On menus, dishes are usually listed according to their main ingredient. For instance, all the chicken dishes appear together, as do all the beef dishes and so on.

*Cha ca* is filleted fish slices broiled over charcoal. It is often served with noodles, green salad, roasted peanuts and a sauce made from nuoc mam, lemon and a special volatile oil.

*Ech tam bot ran* is frog meat soaked in a thin batter and fried in oil. It is usually served with a sauce made of watered-down nuoc mam, vinegar and pepper.

*Rau xao hon hop* is fried vegetables.

*Bo bay mon* are sugar-beef dishes.

*Com tay cam* is rice with mushrooms, chicken and finely sliced pork flavoured with ginger.

**Noodles** Vietnamese noodle dishes *(pho)* are eaten at all hours of the day, but are a special favourite for breakfast. Most westerners would prefer their noodles for lunch and fortunately you can get bread, cheese and eggs in the morning. Noodles are usually eaten as a soup rather than 'dry' like spaghetti.

*Lau* is fish and vegetable soup served in a bowl resembling a samovar with the top cut off. Live coals in the centre keep it hot.

*Mien luon* is vermicelli soup with eel seasoned with mushrooms, shallots, fried eggs and chicken.

*Bun thang* is rice noodles and shredded chicken with fried egg and prawns on top. It is served with broth made by boiling chicken, dried prawns and pig bones.

*Xup rau* is vegetable soup.

*Canh kho hoa* is a bitter soup said to be especially good for the health of people who have spent a lot of time in the sun.

The noodles served with Vietnamese soups are of three types: white rice noodles *(banh pho)*, clear noodles made from rice mixed with manioc powder *(mien)* and yellow, wheat noodles *(mi)*. Many noodle soups are available either with broth *(nuoc leo)* or without *(kho,* literally 'dry').

## Vegetarian Food

Because Buddhist monks of the Mahayana tradition are strict vegetarians (at least they are supposed to be), Vietnamese vegetarian cooking *(an chay)* has a long history and is an integral part of Vietnamese cuisine. Because it does not include many expensive ingredients, vegetarian food is unbelievably cheap.

On days when there is a full moon (the 15th day of the lunar month) or sliver moon (the last day), many Vietnamese and Chinese do not eat meat or even nuoc mam. On such days, some food stalls, especially in the marketplaces, serve vegetarian meals. To find out when the next sliver or full moon will be, consult any Vietnamese calendar.

## Desserts

Sweets *(do ngot)* and desserts *(do trang mieng)* you are likely to have an opportunity to sample include the following:

*Banh chung,* a traditional Tet favourite, is a square cake made from sticky rice and filled with beans, onion and pork and boiled in leaves for 10 hours.

*Banh deo* is a cake made of dried sticky rice flour mixed with a boiled sugar solution. It is filled with candied fruit, sesame seeds, fat etc.

*Banh dau xanh* is mung bean cake. Served with hot tea it 'melts on your tongue'.

*Mut* (candied fruit or vegetables) is made with carrot, coconut, kumquat, gourd, ginger root, lotus seeds, tomato etc.

*Banh bao* is a filled Chinese pastry that can most easily be described as looking like a woman's breast, complete with a reddish dot on top. Inside the sweet, doughy exterior is meat, onions and vegetables. *Banh bao* is often eaten dunked in soy sauce.

*Banh it nhan dau,* a traditional Vietnamese treat, is a gooey pastry made of pulverised sticky rice, beans and sugar. It is steamed (and sold) in a banana leaf folded into a triangular pyramid. You often see banh it nhan dau on sale at Mekong Delta ferry crossings. *Banh it nhan dua* is a variation made with coconut instead of beans.

Ice cream *(kem)* was introduced to Vietnam on a large scale by the Americans, who made ensuring a reliable supply of the stuff a top wartime priority. The US army hired two American companies, Foremost Dairy and Meadowgold Dairies, to build dozens of ice cream factories all around the country. Inevitably, local people developed a taste for their product. Even 15 years after bona fide Foremost products ceased to be available in the Socialist Republic, the company's orange-and-white logo was prominently on display in shops selling ice cream. Recently, however, the government has been making an effort to purge the country of these obsolete signs because it wants to encourage these companies to return. Foremost did in fact return to Vietnam in 1994 to set up a new dairy.

Ice cream served in a baby coconut *(kem dua* or *kem trai dua)* deliciously mixes ice cream, candied fruit and the jelly-like meat of young coconut.

Ice cream stalls usually sell little jars or plastic cups of sweetened frozen yoghurt *(yaourt).*

## Fruit

Fruit *(qua* or *trai)* is available in Vietnam all year round, but many of the country's most interesting specialities have short seasons. Vietnamese bananas will fool you – the green bananas sold in the marketplace are usually ripe enough to eat and, in fact, taste better than the yellow ones.

Avocado is often eaten in a glass with ice and sweetened with either sugar or condensed milk.

Cinnamon apple is also known in English as custard apple, sugar apple and sweetsop. It is ripe when very soft and the area around the stem turns blackish.

Mature coconuts are eaten only by children or as jam. For snacking, Vietnamese prefer the soft jelly-like meat and fresher milk of young coconuts.

Some useful survival terms for the food battleground include the following:

**Breakfast**

| pancake | *bánh xèo ngọt* |
| banana pancake | *bánh chuối* |
| pineapple pancake | *bánh dứa* (north) |
| | *bánh khóm* (south) |
| papaya pancake | *bánh đu đủ* |
| orange pancake | *bánh cam* |
| plain pancake | *bánh không nhân* |

| bread | *bánh mì* |
| omelette | *trứng rán* (north) |
| | *trứng chiên* (south) |
| fried eggs | *trứng ốp la* |
| butter | *bơ* |
| butter & jam | *bơ - mứt* |
| jam | *mứt* |
| cheese | *phomát* (north) |
| | *phomai* (south) |
| butter & cheese | *bơ - phomát* |
| butter & honey | *bơ - mật ong* |
| sandwich | *săn huýt* |

**Lunch & Dinner**

noodles & rice noodles
  *mì - hủ tíu*
beef noodle soup
  *mì bò/phở bò* (north)
  *hủ tíu bò* (south)
chicken noodle soup
  *mì gà/phở gà* (north)
  *hủ tíu gà* (south)
vegetarian noodle soup
  *mì rau/mì chay*
duck, bamboo-shoot noodle soup
  *bún măng*

potatoes
  *khoai tây*
french fries
  *khoai rán* (north)
  *khoai chiên* (south)
fried potato & tomato
  *khoai xào cà chua*
fried potato & butter
  *khoai chiên bơ*

fried dishes
  *các món xào*
fried noodles with chicken
  *mì xào ga/hủ tíu xào gà*

fried noodles with beef
  *mì xào bò/hủ tíu xào bò*
mixed fried noodles
  *mì xào thập cẩm*
mixed fries
  *xào tổng hợp*

chicken
  *gà*
roasted chicken
  *gà quay/gà rô-ti*
chicken salad
  *gà xé phay*
fried chicken in mushroom sauce
  *gà sốt nấm*
batter-fried chicken
  *gà tẩm bột rán/chiên*
fried chicken with lemon sauce
  *gà rán/chiên sốt chanh*
curried chicken
  *gà cà-ri*

pork
  *lợn/heo*
skewered grilled pork
  *chả lợn xiên nướng/chả heo nướng*
sweet & sour fried pork
  *lợn xào chua ngọt/heo xào chua ngọt*
roasted pork
  *thịt lợn quay* (north)
  *heo quay* (south)
grilled pork
  *hịt tlợn nướng xả/heo nướng xả*

beef
  *thịt bò*
beefsteak
  *bít tết*
skewered grilled beef
  *bò xiên nướng*
spicy beef
  *bò xào sả ớt*
fried beef with pineapple
  *bò xào dứa* (north)
  *khóm* (south)
fried beef with garlic
  *bò xào tỏi*
grilled beef with ginger
  *bò nướng gừng*

rare beef with vinegar
*bò nhúng giấm*

hot pot (hot & sour soup)
*lẩu*
beef hot pot
*lẩu bò*
eel hot pot
*lẩu lươn*
fish hot pot
*lẩu cá*
combination hot pot
*lẩu thập cẩm*

spring roll
*nem* (north)
*chả giò* (south)
meat spring rolls
*nem thịt* (north)
*chả giò* (south)
vegetarian spring rolls
*nem rau* (north)
*chả giò chay* (south)
sour spring rolls
*nem chua*

pigeon
*chim bồ câu*
roasted pigeon
*bồ câu quay*
fried pigeon in mushroom sauce
*bồ câu xào nấm sốt*

soup
*súp*
chicken soup
*súp gà*
eel soup
*súp lươn*
combination soup
*súp thập cẩm*
maize soup
*súp ngô* (north)
*súp bắp* (south)
vegetarian soup
*súp rau*

fish
*cá*
grilled fish with sugarcane
*chả cá bao mía*
fried fish in tomato sauce
*cá rán/chiên sốt cà*
sweet & sour fried fish
*cá sốt chua ngọt*
fried fish with lemon
*cá rán/chiên chanh*
fried fish with mushrooms
*cá xào hành nấm rơm*
steamed fish with ginger
*cá hấp gừng*
boiled fish
*cá luộc*
grilled fish
*cá nướng*
steamed fish in beer
*cá hấp bia*

shrimp/prawns
*tôm*
sweet & sour fried shrimp
*tôm xào chua ngọt*
fried shrimp with mushrooms
*tôm xào nấm*
grilled shrimp with sugarcane
*tôm bao mía* (north)
*chạo tôm* (south)
batter-fried shrimp
*tôm tẩm bột/tôm hỏa tiễn*
steamed shrimp in beer
*tôm hấp bia*

crab
*cua*
salted fried crab
*cua rang muối*
crab with chopped meat
*cua nhồi thịt*
steamed crab in beer
*cua hấp bia*

squid
*mực*
fried squid
*mực chiên*
fried squid with mushrooms
*mực xào nấm*

fried squid with pineapple
  *mực xào dứa* (north)
  *khóm* (south)
squid in sweet & sour sauce
  *mực xào chua ngọt*

eel
  *lươn*
fried eel with chopped meat
  *lươn cuốn thịt rán/chiên*
simmered eel
  *lươn om* (north)
  *lươn um* (south)
fried eel with mushrooms
  *lươn xào nấm*

snail
  *ốc*
spicy snail
  *ốc xào sả ớt*
fried snail with pineapple
  *ốc xào dứa, khóm*
fried snail with tofu & bananas
  *ốc xào đậu phu (đậu hu) chuối xanh*

vegetarian
  *các món chay*
I'm a vegetarian.
  *Tôi là người ăn lạt.* (north)
  *Tôi là người ăn chay.* (south)
fried noodle with vegetable
  *mì/hủ tíu xào rau*
vegetarian noodle soup
  *mì/hủ tíu nấu rau*
fried vegetable
  *rau xào*
boiled vegetable
  *rau luộc*

vegetables
  *rau*
fried vegetables
  *rau xào*
boiled vegetables
  *rau luộc*
sour vegetable
  *dưa góp* (north)
  *dưa chua* (south)
fried bean sprouts
  *giá xào*

vegetable soup (large bowl)
  *canh rau*
salad
  *rau sa lát*
fried vegetable with mushrooms
  *rau cải xào nấm*

tofu
  *đậu phu/đậu hu*
fried tofu with chopped meat
  *thịt nhồi đậu phụ/đậu hủ*
fried tofu with tomato sauce
  *đậu phụ/đậu hủ sốt cà*
fried tofu with vegetable
  *đậu phụ/đậu hủ xào*

rice
  *cơm*
steamed rice
  *cơm trắng*
mixed fried rice
  *cơm rang thập cẩm* (north)
  *cơm chiên* (south)
rice porridge
  *cháo*

specialities & exotica
  *đặc sản*
lobster
  *con tôm hùm*
frog
  *con ếch*
oyster
  *con sò*
bat
  *con dơi*
cobra
  *rắn hổ*
gecko
  *con tắc kè/kỳ nhông/kỳ đà*
goat
  *con de*
pangolin
  *con trúc/tê tê*
porcupine
  *con nhím*
python
  *con trăn*
small hornless deer
  *con nai tơ*

turtle
*con rùa*
venison
*thịt nai*
wild pig
*con heo rừng*

## Fruits

| | |
|---|---|
| fruit | *trái cây* |
| apple | *trái táo* (north) |
| | *bơm* (south) |
| apricot | *trái lê* |
| avocado | *trái bơ* |
| banana | *trái chuối* |
| coconut | *trái dừa* |
| custard apple | *trái măng cầu* |
| durian | *trái sầu riêng* |
| grapes | *trái nho* |
| green dragon fruit | *trái thanh long* |
| guava | *trái ổi* |
| jackfruit | *trái mít* |
| jujube (Chinese date) | *trái táo ta* |
| persimmon | *trái hồng xiêm* |
| lemon | *trái chanh* |
| longan | *trái nhãn* |
| lychee | *trái vải* |
| mandarin orange | *trái quýt* |
| mangosteen | *trái măng cụt* |
| orange | *trái cam* |
| papaya | *trái đu đủ* |
| peach | *trái đào* |
| pineapple | *trái khóm/trái dừa* |
| plum | *trái mận/trái mơ* |
| pomelo | *trái bưởi* |
| rambutan | *trái chôm chôm* |
| starfruit | *trái khế* |
| strawberry | *trái dâu* |
| tangerine | *trái quýt* |
| three-seed cherry | *trái sê-ri* |
| water apple | *trái roi đường* (north) |
| | *trái mận* (south) |
| watermelon | *trái dưa hấu* |
| | |
| other dishes | *các món khác* |
| fruit salad | *sa lát hoa quả* (north) |
| | *trái cây các loại* (south) |

| | |
|---|---|
| yoghurt | *sữa chua* (north) |
| | *da-ua* (south) |
| mixed fruit cocktail | *cóc-tai hoa quả* |

## Condiments

| | |
|---|---|
| pepper | *tiêu xay* |
| salt | *muối* |
| sugar | *đường* |
| ice | *đá* |
| hot pepper | *ớt trái* |
| fresh chillis | *ớt* |
| soy sauce | *xì dầu* (north) |
| | *nước tương* (south) |
| fish sauce | *nước mắm* |

### Nuke Mom

*Nuoc mam* (pronounced 'nuke mom') is a type of fermented fish sauce – instantly identifiable by its distinctive smell – without which no Vietnamese meal is complete. Though nuoc mam is to Vietnamese cuisine what soy sauce is to Japanese food, many hotel restaurants do not automatically serve it to foreigners, knowing that the odour may drive away their western customers. Nuoc mam actually isn't bad once you get used to it and some foreigners even go home with a few bottles in their luggage (God help you if the bottle leaks). The sauce is made by fermenting highly salted fish in large ceramic vats for four to 12 months.

The price of nuoc mam varies considerably according to the quality. Connoisseurs insist the high-grade rocket fuel has a much milder aroma than the cheaper variety. Most foreigners will find it hard to tell the difference though.

If nuoc mam isn't strong enough for you, try *mam tom*, a powerful shrimp paste which American soldiers sometimes called 'Viet Cong tear gas'. It's often served with dog meat – foreigners generally find it far more revolting to eat than the dog itself. ■

## DRINKS
### Nonalcoholic Drinks

**Coffee** Vietnamese coffee is fine stuff, but there is one qualifier – you'll need to dilute it with hot water. The Vietnamese prefer their coffee so strong and so sweet that it will turn your teeth inside out. Ditto for Ovaltine and

Milo, which are regarded as desserts rather than drinks. Those restaurants which are accustomed to foreigners will be prepared with thermos bottles of hot water so you can dilute your coffee (or Ovaltine etc) as you wish. However, restaurants which deal with a mostly Vietnamese clientele will likely be dumbfounded by your request for hot water. You'll also need to communicate the fact that you need a large glass – ultra-sweet coffee is traditionally served in a tiny shot glass, thus leaving you no room to add any water.

Instant coffee (ca phe tan or ca phe bot) made its debut in 1996 – a disaster! Many cafes just assume that westerners prefer instant coffee because it's 'modern' and comes from the west. You need to communicate the fact that you want fresh-brewed Vietnamese coffee, not imported instant powder. The word for fresh-brewed coffee is ca phe phin.

Rather than prepare coffee in a pot, the Vietnamese prefer to brew it right at the table, French style – a dripper with coffee grounds is over the cup and hot water poured in. If you prefer iced coffee, the same method is applied, but with a glass of ice under the dripper.

Both the drippers and packaged coffee are favourite items with tourists looking for things to buy and take home.

**Tea** Vietnamese tea in the south is cheap, but disappointing – the aroma is like perfume, but the taste resembles the glue found on postal envelopes. Guests are always served tea when visiting a Vietnamese home or business and it's impolite to refuse. Hold your nose and drink it up (or wait for an opportunity to dump it when your host isn't looking).

Tea grown in the north is much better, but much stronger – be prepared for a caffeine jolt. The northern tea is similar to Chinese green tea and is almost always sold in loose form rather than teabags. The Vietnamese never put milk or sugar into green tea and will think you loony if you do.

Imported Lipton tea (in teabag format) can be bought in major cities, but is still rare in the backwaters. The price is perfectly rea-sonable so there's no need to bring it from abroad. Most restaurants can dig up some lemon and sugar for your tea, although milk is not always available.

### Mineral Water

The selection of mineral water (nuoc suoi) has been expanding rapidly ever since the Vietnamese realised that foreigners were willing to pay good money for water sealed in plastic bottles.

High quality mineral water in plastic bottles is readily available for about US$1 for the large size. If you prefer your mineral water with fizzy bubbles, look for Vinh Hao carbonated water (available only in the south). It's normally mixed with ice, lemon and sugar (outstanding!) and when served this way is called so-da chanh.

**Coconut Milk** There is nothing more refreshing on a hot day than fresh coconut milk (nuoc dua). The Vietnamese believe that coconut milk, like hot milk in western culture, makes you tired. Athletes, for instance, never drink it before a competition.

The coconuts grown around the Ha Tien area in the Mekong Delta are a special variety with delicious coconut flesh, but no coconut milk.

**Soft Drinks** Tri Beco is a domestic soft-drink manufacturer producing strawberry, lychee and other fruity, flavoured carbonated drinks. It's not overly sweet, which means it does a better job at quenching your thirst than some of the sugary imported brands. Tri Beco Coca (cola) is a touch watery compared with the western stuff, but not bad. In the north you'll find Feti cola, which is also OK.

An excellent domestic soft drink with a pleasant fruit flavour is called nuoc khoang kim boi; one bottle costs US$0.20.

Pepsi beat Coca-Cola into the Vietnamese market – a major coup. However, Coke has hit back hard with a high-pitched sales campaign and seems to have the dominant market share now. Sprite and 7-Up are widely available. Diet drinks sweetened with the usual suspected carcinogens can sometimes be found in the supermarkets of large cities, but are expensive.

## Alcoholic Drinks

**Beer** Saigon Export (do they really export it?) and Saigon Lager are two local brands of beer costing about two-thirds the price of the imported brands in cans and half that of bottles. Other 100% Vietnamese brands include Castel, Huda, Halida and 333.

Nameless regional beers, though watery and often flat, are available in bottles for less than the name brands. One traveller described such 'no-label beers' as being a cross between light beer and iced tea.

Memorise the words *bia hoi*, which means 'draft beer'. There are signs advertising it everywhere and most cafes have it on the menu. The quality varies, but it is generally OK and very cheap (US$0.32 per litre!). Places that serve bia hoi usually also have good, cheap food.

There are a number of foreign brands which are brewed in Vietnam under licence. This includes BGI, Carlsberg, Heineken and Vinagen. There's an interesting story about BGI: 333 was made by a French company that got kicked out of the country after the revolution and their operation was nationalised. When they came back to Vietnam in 1994 they could not reclaim their trade name, so now they market an almost identical product under the BGI label and compete with their former (now Vietnamese) brewery.

**Wine** Vietnam produces over 50 varieties of wine *(ruou)*, many of them made from rice. The cheapest rice wines *(ruou de)* are used for cooking – drink them at your peril.

Another Vietnamese speciality is snake wine *(ruou ran)*. This is basically rice wine with a pickled snake floating in it. Drinking snake wine is said to have some tonic properties. This elixir is claimed to cure everything from night blindness to impotence.

A variation on the theme is to have the snake killed right at your table and the blood placed into a cup. You take some of the blood and pour it into a glass of rice wine. This cocktail is believed to work as an aphrodisiac.

**Champagne** The Vietnamese will have to work on their techniques for distilling champagne. The presently available stuff tastes like it was drained from an old rusty radiator.

**Hard Liquor** Alcoholic beverages *(ruou manh)* from China are very cheap, taste like paint thinner and smell like diesel fuel. Russian vodka is one of the few things the former USSR has left to export. Locally produced Hanoi Vodka is also available.

Some useful terms for ordering Vietnamese drinks include the following:

### Coffee

| | |
|---|---|
| coffee | *cà phê* |
| hot black coffee | *cà phê đen nóng* |
| coffee with hot milk | |
| | *nâu nóng* (north) |
| | *cà phê sữa nóng* (south) |
| iced black coffee | *cà phê đá* |
| iced coffee with milk | |
| | *nâu đá* (north) |
| | *cà phê sữa đá* (south) |

### Tea

| | |
|---|---|
| tea | |
| | *chè* (north) |
| | *trà* (south) |
| hot black tea | |
| | *chè đen nóng* (north) |
| | *trà nóng* (south) |
| tea with hot milk | |
| | *chè đen sữa* (north) |
| | *trà pha sữa* (south) |
| black tea with honey | |
| | *chè mật ong* (north) |
| | *trà pha mật* (south) |

### Chocolate Drinks

| | |
|---|---|
| chocolate - milk | *cacao - sữa* |
| hot chocolate | *cacao nóng* |
| iced chocolate | *cacao đá* |
| hot milk | *sữa nóng* |
| iced milk | *sữa đá* |

## Fruit Drinks

| | |
|---|---|
| fruit juice | *nước quả/nước trái cây* |
| hot lemon juice | *chanh nóng* |
| iced lemon juice | *chanh đá* |
| hot orange juice | *cam nóng* |
| iced orange juice | *cam đá* |
| pure orange juice | *cam vắt* |
| fruit shake | *sinh to/trái cây xay* |
| banana shake | *nước chuối xay* |
| milk banana shake | *nước chuối sữa xay* |
| papaya shake | *nước đu đủ xay* |
| pineapple shake | *nước dứa* (north) *khóm xay* (south) |
| orange-banana shake | *nước cam/chuối xay* |
| mixed fruit shake | *sinh tố tổng hợp/ nước thập cẩm xay* |
| mango shake | *nước xoài xay* |

## Mineral Water

| | |
|---|---|
| mineral water | *nước khoáng* (north) *nước suối* (south) |
| lemon mineral water | *khoáng chanh* (north) *suối chanh* (south) |
| big spring water | *nước suối chai lớn* |
| small spring water | *nước suối chai nhỏq* |

## Beer & Soft Drinks

| | |
|---|---|
| beer | *bia* |
| Chinese beer | *bia Trung Quốc* |
| Halida beer | *bia Halida* |
| 333 beer | *bia 333* |
| Tiger beer | *bia Tiger* |
| Tiger (large bottle) | *bia Tiger (chai to)* |
| Amstel beer | *bia Amstel* |
| Carlsberg beer | *bia Carlsberg* |
| San Miguel beer | *bia San Miguel* |
| Heineken beer | *bia Heineken* |
| BGI beer | *bia BGI* |
| | |
| tinned soft drinks | *thức uống đóng hộp* |
| Coke | *Coca Cola* |
| Pepsi | *Pepsi Cola* |
| 7 Up | *7 Up* |
| tinned orange juice | *cam hộp* |
| soda water & lemon | *soda chanh* |
| soda water, lemon & sugar | *soda chanh đường* |

## ENTERTAINMENT

### Cinemas

Movie theatres are common in nearly all major towns and cities. Many urban maps have cinemas (*rap* in Vietnamese) marked with a special symbol.

Films from the former Eastern Bloc have been replaced with western movies which are either subtitled or dubbed. Vietnam now produces its own kung fu movies rather than importing them from China, Hong Kong and Taiwan. Love stories also are popular, but Vietnamese censors take a dim view of nudity and sex – murder and mayhem are OK.

### Discos

After reunification, ballrooms and discos were denounced as imperialist dens of iniquity and were shut down by the authorities. Since 1990 they have reopened, though certain forms of dancing (like Brazil's erotic dance, the lambada) remained banned. Young people unable to afford a night on the town often create impromptu discos with tape players and pirated rock music cassettes from the west. There are now even modern dance classes at public schools.

### Karaoke

Most westerners find karaoke as appealing as roasted gecko with shrimp paste. Nonetheless, karaoke has taken over Asia and you'll have a hard time avoiding it.

For those unfamiliar with karaoke, it's simply a system where you are supposed to sing along with a video. The words to the song are flashed on the bottom of the screen (a number of languages are possible) and participants are supplied with a microphone. Really fancy karaoke bars have superb audio systems and big screen video, but no matter how good the equipment, it's not going to sound any better than the ability of the singer. And with a few exceptions, it sounds truly awful. The Vietnamese only enjoy karaoke if it's played at over 150 decibels.

A big warning – many karaoke places have hidden charges. The beers might only be US$1 apiece, but there can be a hefty charge for use of the microphone and video-tapes. For English tapes you may well be charged double the rate for a Vietnamese one. Get this all worked out in advance.

## Pubs

Vietnamese-style pubs tend to be karaoke lounges – you know you've been assimilated when you start enjoying these places. However, the increasing number of expats (especially in Saigon) has caused a boom in western-style pubs. Many of these are husband-wife joint ventures (usually a western husband and Vietnamese wife). Aside from the Tiger beer, many of these places are indistinguishable from their counterparts in London, Berlin, New York or Melbourne. Darts, Mexican food, rock music, oak furniture and CNN can make you forget just where you are. Right now, such businesses are in their infancy, but they are spreading.

## Video Parlours

Vietnam's opening to the outside world is creating massive headaches for the country's censors. Despite their best efforts, customs agents haven't been able to hold back the flood of video tapes which are smuggled into Vietnam. The pirating of video tapes has become big business and the tapes are sold or rented all over the country. Kung fu movies from Hong Kong and pornography from the west and Japan are much in demand. Ditto for the latest MTV tapes. Video movies about the American War are also enthusiastically sought after.

Obviously, most Vietnamese cannot afford video equipment, but that hardly matters. Budding entrepreneurs have set up instant mini-theatres consisting of a video cassette recorder (VCR), a few chairs and curtains to keep out nonpaying onlookers. The admission price is very low, in the order of US$0.25. Some of these video parlours provide food and beverage services.

## SPECTATOR SPORTS

Football (soccer) is number one with specta-tors. Tennis has considerable snob appeal –

trendy Vietnamese like to both watch and play. The Vietnamese are incredibly skilled at badminton. Other favourites include vol-leyball and table tennis.

## THINGS TO BUY

As a general principal, try to find a shop that 1) does not cater particularly to tourists and 2) puts price tags on all its items. In touristy areas, items sold with no visible price tags must be bargained for – expect the vendor to start the bidding at two to five times the real price.

One annoying habit that you'll just have to get used to is the tendency of many vendors to start shoving one item after another practically into your face and urging you to buy it. They don't give you much chance to look at the items you really want to buy. It's a self-defeating sales tactic, since many foreigners will get flustered and walk out of any shop that does this. Too bad that more Vietnamese vendors don't read this book.

### Antiques

A Vietnamese speciality is the 'instant antique' with a price tag of around US$2 for a teapot or ceramic dinner plate. Of course, it's OK to buy fake antiques as long you aren't paying genuine antique prices. How-ever, a problem occurs if you've bought an antique (or something which looks antique) and didn't get an official export certificate:

When I was in the airport in Hanoi, a customs officer eyed out two porcelain vases I had bought and told me that I should go to the Department of Culture in Hanoi to have them assessed or pay a fine of US$20. Of course, there was no representative of the Depart-ment of Culture at the airport to make such an evalu-ation, so getting them assessed would require me to miss my flight.

**Anna Crawford Pinnerup**

Just what happens to confiscated 'antiques' is a good question. Some say that the author-ities sell them back to the souvenir shops. You might call it 'recycling'.

## Handicrafts

Hot items on the tourist market include lacquerware, mother-of-pearl inlay, ceramics (check out the elephants), colourful embroidered items (hangings, tablecloths, pillow cases, pyjamas and robes), greeting cards with silk paintings on the front, woodblock prints, oil paintings, watercolours, blinds made of hanging bamboo beads (many travellers like the replica of the Mona Lisa), reed mats, carpets, jewellery and leatherwork.

## Clothing

Ao dais are a popular item, especially for women. Ready-made ao dais cost about US$10 to US$20, while custom-tailored sets are notably more. Prices vary by the store and material used. If you want to buy custom-made clothing for your friends, you'll need their measurements; neck diameter, breast, waist, hip and length (from waist to hem). As a general rule, you get best results when you're right there and get measured by the tailor or seamstress.

Women all over the country wear conical hats, in part to keep the sun off their faces (though they also function like umbrellas in the rain). If you hold a well-made conical hat up to the light, you'll be able to see that between the layers of straw material are fine paper cuts. The best quality conical hats are produced in the Hué area.

T-shirts are ever popular items with travellers. A printed shirt costs around US$2 while an embroidered design will cost maybe US$3.50. Size XXL is about equivalent to medium in the west – if you are really large, forget it unless you want to have your shirts individually tailored.

Sandals are a practical item to take home and cheap at around US$3.50. Finding large sizes to fit western feet can be a problem, though. Make sure they are very comfortable before you purchase them – some tend to be poorly made and will give you blisters.

## Stamps

Postage stamps already set in a collector's book are readily available either inside or near the post office in major cities or at some hotel gift shops and bookstores. You can even find stamps from the now-extinct South Vietnamese regime.

## Gems

Vietnam produces some good gems, but there are plenty of fakes and flawed gems around. This doesn't mean that you shouldn't buy something if you think it's beautiful, but don't think that you'll find a cut diamond or polished ruby for a fraction of what you'd pay at home. Some travellers have actually thought that they could buy gems in Vietnam and sell these at home for a profit. Such business requires considerable expertise and good connections in the mining industry.

## Music

Saigon and Hanoi both have an astounding collection of audio tapes for sale, most of which are pirated. The majority of Vietnamese hits were originally recorded by Overseas Vietnamese in California and bootlegged in Vietnam. There are also the latest Chinese music tapes from Hong Kong and Taiwan (mostly soft rock). Hard rock from the west is not as popular, but there is a small and devoted core of avant-garde types who like it.

CDs are not yet manufactured in Vietnam, though it seems like only a matter of time. Plenty are imported – about 80% are pirated copies from China and therefore very cheap. The official word is that this illegal practice will be 'cleaned up' by the authorities, but don't hold your breath waiting.

## Electronics

Electronic goods sold in Vietnam are actually not such a great bargain and you'd be better off purchasing these in duty-free ports such as Hong Kong and Singapore. However, the prices charged in Vietnam are really not all that bad, mainly due to the black market (smuggling), which also results in 'duty-free' goods.

Only those items imported legally by an authorised agent will include a warranty card valid in Vietnam. Unfortunately, Vietnamese electronics which are not black market are often 'grey market' – that is, imported legally, but by someone besides the authorised importer. This does not circumvent the need to pay import taxes, but it creates a tidy profit for the resellers because they avoid paying commissions to the authorised agent. However, as with smuggled goods, grey market items are usually sold without warranty, or at least no warranty which is valid in Vietnam. However, some electronic goods include an international warranty card, which presumably solves this problem.

### Eyeglasses
In major cities you'll find plenty of opticians willing to sell eyeglasses for as little as US$10. Although the price is hard to beat, the bottom-end glasses are just that. Ultra-cheap eyeglass frames made in Vietnam or imported from China are mostly rubbish – the frames easily rust and soon break. These same shops usually sell European-made frames for a much higher price, but the primitive equipment used for checking your prescription and grinding the lenses almost ensures that you'll be dissatisfied with the final product.

This having been said, there are a couple of places in Saigon and Hanoi where you can get quality eyeglasses. The price for the frames and lenses will be similar to what you'd pay in the west, but the labour charge for the eye examination and lens grinding

should be a bargain. See the Things to Buy sections in the Hồ Chi Minh City and Hanoi chapters for details.

### War Souvenirs
In places frequented by tourists, it's easy to buy what looks like equipment left over from the American War. However, almost all of these items are reproductions and your chances of finding anything original is slim. Enterprising back-alley tailors turn out US military uniforms, while metalcraft shops have learned how to make helmets, bayonets and dog tags.

The 'Zippo' lighters seem to be the hottest-selling item. You can pay extra to get one that's been beat up to look like a war relic, or just buy a new shiny one for less money.

One thing you should think twice about purchasing are weapons and ammunition *even if fake*. You may have several opportunities to buy old bullets and dud mortar shells, especially around the area of the old DMZ. Most of these items are either fake or deactivated, but you can occasionally find real bullets for sale with the gunpowder still inside. Real or not, it's illegal to carry ammunition on airlines and many countries will arrest you if any such goods are found in your luggage. Customs agents in Singapore are particularly strict and thorough, and travellers carrying souvenir ammunition and weapons have run into some serious problems here.

# Getting There & Away

## AIR

### Airports & Airlines

Saigon's Tan Son Nhat airport is Vietnam's busiest international air hub, while Hanoi's Noi Bai airport is a poor second. A scant few international flights also serve Danang.

Vietnam Airlines (Hang Khong Viet Nam) is the nation's state-owned flag carrier. The majority of flights into and out of Vietnam are joint operations between Vietnam Airlines and foreign companies. The air ticket you purchase might have the words 'Vietnam Airlines' printed on it, but you could find yourself flying on, for example, Cathay Pacific or Thai Airways International.

To give Vietnam Airlines some needed competition, Pacific Airlines (with Czech flight crews) started operations in 1992. Its international flight schedule is very limited – the airline only connects Vietnam to Taiwan and Macau. However, Pacific Airlines is slightly cheaper than Vietnam Airlines and boasts all new aircraft.

### Buying Tickets

When you're looking for bargain air fares, you have to go to a travel agent rather than directly to the airline which can sell fares only at the full list price. But watch out – many discount tickets have restrictions (the journey must be completed within 30 days, no flights during holidays and so on). It's important to ask the agent what restrictions, if any, apply to your ticket.

If you purchase a ticket and later want to make changes to your route or get a refund, you need to see the original travel agent. Airlines issue refunds only to the purchaser of a ticket – if you bought it from a travel agent, then that agent is the purchaser, not you. Many travellers do in fact change their route half way through their trip, so think carefully before buying a ticket which is not easily refunded.

The one way in which you can get a significant discount on fares to Vietnam is to buy a group ticket. In theory, this means that you will arrive and depart with a tour group. In practice, you may never see the group or the tour guides. However, these tickets cannot be altered once issued – there are no changes permitted to arrival and departure dates, nor can you refund the unused portion of such tickets. Since many travellers do wind up extending their stay in Vietnam, buying such a ticket could be a false way to economise.

APEX (Advance Purchase Excursion) tickets are a variation on the theme. These don't require you to pretend to be with a group, but you are locked into a fairly rigid schedule. Such tickets must be purchased two or three weeks ahead of departure, do not permit stopovers and may have minimum and maximum stays, as well as fixed departure and return dates. Unless you definitely must return at a certain time, it's best to purchase APEX tickets on a one-way basis only. There are stiff cancellation fees if you decide not to use your APEX ticket.

There are plenty of discount tickets which are valid for 12 months, allowing multiple stopovers with open dates. These tickets allow maximum flexibility. Unfortunately, few such tickets are available to Vietnam, but you can easily get such a ticket that will take you to Bangkok. And of course, getting from Bangkok to Vietnam should prove very easy and reasonably cheap.

Round-the-World (RTW) tickets are usually offered by an airline or combination of airlines, and let you take your time (six months to a year) moving from point to point on their routes for the price of one ticket. Sometimes this works out to be cheaper than buying all the tickets separately as you go along, but often it is actually more expensive. Overall, RTW tickets are not a bargain. The main restriction is that you have to keep moving in the same direction; a drawback is that because you are usually booking individual flights as you go, and can't switch carriers, you can get caught out by flight availability and have to spend either more or less time in a place than you want.

Some airlines offer student discounts on their tickets of up to 25% to student card holders. Besides having an International Student Identity Card (ISIC), an official-looking letter from the school is also required by some airlines. Many airlines also require you to be age 26 or younger to qualify for a discount. These discounts are generally available only on ordinary economy-class fares. You wouldn't get one, for instance, on an APEX or an RTW ticket since these are already discounted.

Frequent flier deals can earn you a free air ticket or other goodies if you accumulate enough mileage with one airline. First, you must apply to the airline for a frequent flier account number (some airlines will issue these on the spot or by telephone if you call their head office). Every time you buy an air ticket and/or check in for your flight, you must inform the clerk of your frequent flier account number or you won't get credit. Save your tickets and boarding passes, since it's not uncommon for the airlines to fail to give proper credit. You should receive monthly statements by post informing you how much mileage you've accumulated. Once you've accumulated sufficient mileage to qualify for freebies, you are supposed to receive vouchers by mail. Many airlines have 'black-out periods', or times when you cannot fly free of charge (Christmas and the Lunar New Year are good examples). The worst thing about frequent flier programs is that these tend to lock you into one airline, and that airline may not always have the cheapest fares or most convenient flight schedule.

One thing to avoid are 'back-to-front' tickets. These are best explained by example. If you are living in Vietnam (where tickets are relatively expensive) and you want to fly to Bangkok (where tickets are noticeably cheaper), you can pay by check or credit card and have a friend or travel agent in Bangkok mail the ticket to you. The problem is that the airlines have computers and will know that the ticket was issued in Bangkok rather than Vietnam and they will refuse to honour it. Consumer groups have filed lawsuits over this practice with mixed results, but in most countries the law protects the airlines, not consumers. In short, the ticket is only valid starting from the country where it was issued. The only exception is if you pay the full fare, thus foregoing any possible discounts that Bangkok travel agents can offer.

Courier flights can be a bargain if you're fortunate enough to find one. The way it works is that an air freight company takes over your entire checked baggage allowance. You are permitted to bring along a carry-on bag, but that's all. In return, you get a steeply discounted ticket. These arrangements usually have to be made a month or more in advance and are only available on certain routes. There aren't many of these going to Vietnam yet, but you could possibly get one to Bangkok or Hong Kong. Another consideration is that these tickets are sold for a fixed date and schedule changes can be difficult or impossible to make. Courier flights are occasionally advertised in the newspapers, or contact air freight companies listed in the phone book.

Well worth considering are 'open jaw' tickets. These allow you to fly into Hanoi and exit from Saigon (or vice versa). This can save you considerable backtracking.

The 20kg checked-luggage weight limit is strictly enforced. Each kilogram above the limit will cost you 1% of the 1st class air fare – on a flight from Vietnam to Europe this could be over US$20 per kilogram.

It is difficult to get reservations for flights to or from Vietnam around the Lunar New Year (Tet), which can fall around late January to mid-February. If you will be in Vietnam during this period (which is a favourite time for family visits by Overseas Vietnamese) make reservations well in advance or you may find yourself marooned in Bangkok on the way in or stranded in Saigon on the way out.

Be aware that Vietnam is not the only country to celebrate the Lunar New Year – it's also *the* major holiday in Singapore,

Hong Kong, Macau, China, Taiwan and Korea and is also celebrated by the sizeable Chinese minorities in Thailand and Malaysia. People from these countries hit the road at that time with the result that airlines, trains and hotels are booked solid all over the Orient. The chaos begins about a week before the Lunar New Year and lasts until two weeks after it.

Except at peak holiday times, it's not too difficult to get a flight out of the country, but it's wise to book your departure at least a few days in advance. At peak times everything might be chock-a-block and your only hope will be to upgrade to business or first class (and pay through the nose for it).

If you bought an air ticket with a definite departure date, it's essential to reconfirm after you've arrived in Vietnam or your seat will likely be given away to somebody else. Officially, you must reconfirm at least 72 hours before departure, unless of course you'll be staying in Vietnam for less than 72 hours.

Keep your checked baggage locked. Travellers have reported things being pilfered from their luggage on departure (the baggage handlers don't even leave a 'thank you' note). Fortunately, there has been a recent serious effort to crack down on pilfering.

### Travellers with Special Needs

Most international airlines can cater to special needs – travellers with disabilities, people with young children and even children travelling alone.

Special dietary preferences (vegetarian, kosher etc) can also be catered to with advance notice. However, the 'special meals' usually aren't very special – basically you get a salad and fruit plate.

Airlines usually carry babies up to two years of age at 10% of the relevant adult fare – a few may carry them free of charge. Reputable international airlines usually provide nappies (diapers), tissues, talcum powder and all the other paraphernalia needed to keep babies clean, dry and half-happy. For children between the ages of two and 12 the fare on international flights is

usually 50% of the regular fare or 67% of a discounted fare. These days most air fares are likely to be discounted.

### Australia

Australia is not a cheap place to fly out of, and air fares between Australia and Asia are absurdly expensive considering the distances flown. Air tickets purchased in Vietnam are actually cheaper than those bought in Australia. Ethnic-Vietnamese living in Australia are known to have the inside scoop on ticket discounts.

Among the cheapest regular tickets available in Australia are APEX (Advanced Purchase Excursion) tickets. The cost depends on your departure date from Australia. The year is divided into 'peak' (expensive), 'shoulder' (less expensive) and 'low' (relatively inexpensive) seasons; peak season is December to January, Easter and school holidays.

It's possible to get reductions on the cost of APEX and other fares by going to travel agents in Australia that specialise in discounting.

The weekend travel sections of papers like the *Age* (Melbourne) or the *Sydney Morning Herald* are good sources of travel information. Also look at *Escape*, a magazine published by STA Travel, the Australian-based travel organisation which has offices worldwide. STA Travel has offices all around Australia (check your phone directory).

Also well worth trying is the Flight Centre. It has numerous branches in Australia, including Melbourne (☎ (03) 9670-0477) at 386 Little Bourke St; Sydney (☎ (02) 9233-2296); and Brisbane (☎ (07) 3229-9958).

Qantas and Vietnam Airlines offer a joint service from Saigon to both Melbourne (9½ hours) and Sydney (eight hours). Rock-bottom excursion fares are US$600/1000 for one-way/return tickets.

### Cambodia

There are daily flights between Phnom Penh and Saigon (US$60 one way, US$120 return) on either Cambodia Airlines or Vietnam Airlines. There are also flights between Phnom Penh and Hanoi (US$220 one way, US$440 return). There is a US$5 airport tax to fly out of Cambodia. Visas for Cambodia are available upon arrival at Phnom Penh airport free of charge if you stay less than 15 days.

## Canada

Getting discount tickets in Canada is much the same as in the USA – go to the travel agents and shop around until you find a good deal.

CUTS is Canada's national student bureau and has offices in a number of Canadian cities, including Vancouver, Edmonton, Toronto and Ottawa – you don't necessarily have to be a student. There are a number of good agents in Vancouver for cheap tickets.

There are currently no direct flights between Canada and Vietnam. Most Canadian travellers transit at Hong Kong.

## China

China Southern Airlines and Vietnam Airlines fly the China-Vietnam route using fuel-guzzling, Soviet-built Tupolev 134 aircraft. The only direct flight between Saigon and China is to Guangzhou (Canton). All other flights are via Hanoi. The Guangzhou-Hanoi flight (US$140 one way) takes 1½ hours; Guangzhou-Saigon (US$240 one way) takes 2½ hours. Return air fares cost exactly double.

The Beijing-Hanoi flight on China Southern Airlines stops at Nanning (the capital of China's Guangxi Province) en route – you can board or exit the plane there. Unfortunately, this flight is a favourite of traders ('smugglers' as far as the authorities are concerned). This not only makes it difficult to get a ticket, but travellers arriving in Hanoi on this flight have reported vigorous baggage searches and numerous customs hassles. In the other direction, arrival in Nanning *might* be a little bit smoother, but don't count on it – Chinese customs agents are diligently on the lookout for drugs, so if you look like 'the type', expect a thorough going over.

## France

Vietnam Airlines cooperates with Air France. Flights between Paris and Saigon (usually via Dubai and sometimes Berlin) run three times weekly. One-way/return fares are US$830/1245. Paris-Hanoi fares are slightly cheaper at US$800/1200.

## Germany

Germany's Lufthansa and Vietnam Airlines offer a joint service between Berlin and Saigon. There are two flights weekly which go via Dubai and flying time is at least 14½ hours. Bottom-end one-way/return fares are US$830/1245.

## Hong Kong

After Bangkok, Hong Kong is the second most popular point for departures to Vietnam. Hong Kong-Saigon flights run daily and require 2½ hours flying time. Hanoi-Hong Kong flights are also daily and take 1¾ hours.

A travel agent in Hong Kong specialising in discount air tickets and customised tours to Vietnam is Phoenix Services (☎ 2722-7378; fax 2369-8884) in Room B, 6th floor, Milton Mansion, 96 Nathan Rd, Tsimshatsui, Kowloon.

Hong Kong's flag carrier, Cathay Pacific, and Vietnam Airlines offer a joint service between Hong Kong and Saigon (one way/return US$291/535). There are also direct Hong Kong-Hanoi flights (US$264/500). The most popular ticket is an 'open jaw' deal for US$535 – this allows you to fly from Hong Kong to Saigon and return from Hanoi to Hong Kong (or vice versa).

## Indonesia

Vietnam Airlines does not fly to Indonesia, but Garuda Airlines does. A Jakarta-Saigon ticket costs US$438 each way. Round-trip excursion fares (good for 30 days) cost from US$705.

## Japan

Arranging visas and air tickets in Japan is so outrageously expensive and time-consuming that you might consider taking a boat to Korea instead and doing it from there. This does not seem to have slowed down the number of Japanese travellers though – you'll see plenty of them in Saigon.

If you have no choice and must fly from Japan, Vietnam Airlines flies between Osaka and Saigon three times weekly. At present, there are no direct flights from Tokyo, though that is expected to change. Osaka-Saigon flights take approximately 5½ hours. Japanese travel agents charge high prices to process visa applications.

Tickets purchased in Vietnam are cheaper than those available in Japan. Low-end prices in Vietnam for Saigon-Osaka one way/return are US$500/800.

### Korea

Korean Air, Asiana and Vietnam Airlines all fly the Seoul-Saigon route – there's at least one flight going every day. There are also direct Seoul-Hanoi flights at least three times weekly. Flying time between Saigon and Seoul is 4¾ hours. The cheapest one-way/return fares are currently US$350/500.

A good travel agency for discount tickets is Joy Travel Service (☎ 776-9871; fax 756-5342), 10th floor, 24-2 Mukyo-dong, Chung-gu, Seoul, which is directly behind City Hall.

### Laos

Lao Aviation and Vietnam Airlines offer joint service between Vientiane and Hanoi (US$90/180 one way/return) or Vientiane and Saigon (US$250/500).

### Macau

Pacific Airlines flies between Macau and Saigon. Odd as it might seem, the same company also has a Danang-Macau direct flight.

### Malaysia

Malaysia Airlines and Vietnam Airlines have a joint service from Kuala Lumpur to Saigon (US$150/300 one way/return). Flying time for Kuala Lumpur-Saigon is 1¾ hours. There are also Kuala Lumpur-Hanoi flights costing US$340/680 for one-way/return tickets.

### The Netherlands

KLM flies Amsterdam-Saigon nonstop. Cheaper still is China Airlines (of Taiwan), which flies Amsterdam-Taipei and then Taipei to either Hanoi or Saigon. You can make a free, 15-day transit stop in Taipei if you wish. The China Airlines flight is actually a joint operation with Vietnam Airlines, so you may be flying on a Vietnam Airlines aircraft. The best prices you can hope to get on one-way/return tickets are currently US$690/1100.

### The Philippines

Philippine Airlines and Vietnam Airlines fly Manila-Saigon. Economy one-way/return tickets start at US$185/300. Flying time from Manila to Saigon is 2½ hours.

### Singapore

Singapore Airlines and Vietnam Airlines offer a daily joint service on the Saigon-Singapore route. Flight time between Singapore and Saigon is 1¾ hours. The one-way fare is US$213 and the return fare is US$400. Most flights from Singapore continue to Hanoi. The Singapore-Hanoi one-way fare is US$330.

### Taiwan

The large numbers of Taiwanese who visit Vietnam have made Taiwan a good embarkation point for Vietnam, with frequent flights now offered by four competing airlines. The flight time between Vietnam and Taiwan is around three hours. However, there are no diplomatic relations between Taiwan and Vietnam, so visa processing goes via Bangkok and takes 10 working days. For many travellers, this delay is unacceptably long.

Taiwan's China Airlines offers a joint service with Vietnam Airlines daily between Saigon and Taipei. There are also Hanoi-Taipei flights five times weekly. Direct Saigon-Kaohsiung flights run three times weekly. The cheapest return fares are 30-day excursion tickets, but most travellers go for a 90-day fare. At the bottom end, one-way/return fares are US$350/525.

Pacific Airlines offers the cheapest Saigon-Taipei fares for US$460 return. The same fare is available on the Saigon-Kaohsiung route.

EVA Air claims to be Taiwan's luxury airline, but it charges luxury prices. There are some discounts on long routes such as Los Angeles-Taipei-Saigon. For a Taipei-Saigon excursion return ticket, figure around US$560.

Travel agents in Taiwan advertise return fares as low as US$420, but these are group tickets which must be booked well in advance and no changes are permitted.

A long-running discount travel agent with a good reputation is Jenny Su Travel (☎ (02) 594-7733, 596-2263; fax 592-0068), 10th floor, 27 Chungshan N Rd, Section 3, Taipei.

### Thailand

Bangkok, only 80 minutes flying time from Saigon, has emerged as the main port of embarkation for air travel to Vietnam.

Thai Airways International (THAI), Air France and Vietnam Airlines offer Bangkok-Saigon service for US$150 one way; round-trip tickets cost exactly double.

There are daily flights from Bangkok to Saigon and some of the flights continue on to Danang. There are also direct Bangkok-Hanoi flights (US$176 one way).

Khao San Rd in Bangkok is the budget travellers' headquarters and the place to look for bargain ticket deals. There are many agencies here milking the backpacker market.

### The UK

There are no direct flights between the UK and Vietnam, but relatively cheap tickets are available on the London-Hong Kong run. From Hong Kong, it's easy enough to make onward arrangements to Vietnam by air or overland.

Air-ticket discounting is a long-running business in the UK and it's wide open. The various agents advertise their fares and there is nothing under-the-counter about it at all. However, do be careful about handing over large sums of cash to what might be fly-by-

night operators who promise to deliver your ticket 'next week'.

To find out what's going, there are a number of magazines in Britain which have good information about flights and agents. These include: *Trailfinder*, free from the Trailfinders Travel Centre in Earl's Court; and *Time Out*, a weekly entertainment guide widely available in the UK. Discount tickets are available almost exclusively in London.

### The USA

At the time of writing, no US air carriers were flying into Vietnam. However, this is expected to change shortly. Airlines to watch include Northwest and United.

China Airlines (of Taiwan) currently offers the cheapest fares on US-Vietnam flights, all of which transit in Taipei. Low-season San Francisco-Saigon one-way/return tickets cost US$464/837; New York-Saigon is US$573/1047.

Other possible, but slightly pricier, US-Vietnam tickets are available from EVA Air (also via Taipei), Cathay Pacific (via Hong Kong), THAI (via Bangkok) and Asiana (via Seoul).

It's not advisable to send money (even cheques) through the post unless the agent is very well established – some travellers have reported being ripped off by fly-by-night mail-order ticket agents. Nor is it wise to hand over the full amount to Shady Deal Travel Services unless they can give you the ticket straight away – most US travel agencies have computers that can spit out the ticket on the spot.

Council Travel is the largest student travel organisation and, though you don't have to be a student to use them, they do have specially discounted student tickets. Council Travel has an extensive network taking in all major US cities and is listed in the telephone book. There are also Student Travel Network offices, which are associated with STA.

One of the cheapest and most reliable travel agents on the west coast is Overseas Tours (☎ (800) 222-5292), 475 El Camino Real, Room 206, Millbrae, CA 94030. Another good agent is Bolder Adventures

(☎ (303) 443-6789; fax 443-7078; email bolder@southeastasia.com), also known as Asia Transpacific Journeys (☎ (800) 642-2742; www.SoutheastAsia.com), PO Box 1279, Boulder, CO 80306. We've personally used Gateway Travel (☎ (214) 960-2000, (800) 878-2828; fax 490-6367), 4201 Spring Valley Rd, Suite 104, Dallas, TX 75244. All three of these places seem to be trustworthy for mail-order tickets.

## Departure Tax

The departure tax for international flights is US$8, payable in either dong or US dollars. Children under age two are exempt.

## LAND

There are currently six places where foreigners may cross overland into Vietnam. At all these crossings there are no legal money-changing facilities on the Vietnamese side, so upon arrival in Vietnam the first thing you have to do is find the black market. Bring some US dollars cash (travellers cheques and Visa cards will prove useless). The black market is also interested in local currencies – Vietnamese dong, Chinese renminbi, Lao kip and Cambodian riel. On the Chinese side try to find a bank or legal moneychanger – the black marketeers in China have a well-deserved reputation for short-changing and outright theft.

Vietnamese police at the land border crossings are known to be particularly problematic. Upon entry, they may only give you a one-week stay rather than the one month indicated on your visa. Most travellers find that it's easier to exit Vietnam overland than to enter the country that way. Travellers at the border crossings are often asked for a US$1 (or more) immigration fee and a US$1 customs fee. This is illegal.

In the finest bureaucratic tradition, the Vietnamese require a special visa for entering overland. These visas cost more and take longer to issue than the normal tourist visas needed for entering Vietnam by air. Travellers who have tried to use a standard visa for entering Vietnam overland have in the past reportedly been able to bribe the border guards to get in. However, there has been a recent crackdown on this and it is no longer possible to bribe your way past the regulations.

> Don't mess around with the Vietnamese border guards. My experience resulted in spending the night in 'no-man's land' as my girlfriend's entry point was not correct. The situation got us deported back to China with a 48-hour temporary visa (at a cost of US$40!). My only advice is to make certain that your visa is stamped correctly with the appropriate entry and exit points. Also, drug checks are common – they completely empty your backpack.
>
> **Scott Hemphill**

## Cambodia

Land travel in Cambodia is not especially recommended due to attacks by Khmer Rouge and other armed bandits, but the situation fluctuates from being reasonably safe to exceedingly dicey. On the main highways, where you have a troop escort, it should be OK, but safest of all is to fly. Make inquiries before proceeding.

The only frontier crossing between Cambodia and Vietnam which is open to westerners is at Moc Bai, which connects Vietnam's Tay Ninh Province with Cambodia's Svay Rieng Province. Other border crossings are considered too risky.

Buses run every day between Phnom Penh and Saigon (via Moc Bai). The cost is US$12 or US$5 depending on whether you take the air-con coach or the old rattletrap. In Vietnam, you purchase tickets from the Phnom Penh Bus Garage at 155 Nguyen Hue St, Saigon, adjacent to the Rex Hotel. However, the bus departs at 5 am from 145 Nguyen Du St. One disadvantage of this bus is that you must wait for everybody to clear customs at the border, a procedure which can take hours.

There is a faster and cheaper way, though a bit more complicated. You can board one of the many bus tours heading for the Caodai Great Temple at Tay Ninh (as little as US$4). But instead of going to Tay Ninh, you get off sooner at Go Dau where the highway forks. There will be motorcycle taxis waiting here and for as little as US$0.50 you can get a ride to the border crossing at Moc Bai. At the border you must walk across and you will find air-con share taxis waiting on the Cambodia side to take you to Phnom Penh for US$5 per person.

There are also share taxis that run directly from Saigon to Moc Bai border crossing, some costing as little as US$20 for three people. In Saigon, Kim Cafe at 270-272 De Tham St, District 1, is one place to book these, but also check other travel agencies.

To do this overland crossing, you will need a Cambodian visa (which takes seven working days to process) and a re-entry visa for Vietnam if you plan to return. If you are entering or exiting Vietnam by this route, your Vietnamese visa (or re-entry visa) must indicate the Moc Bai crossing. If you forgot to do that in Saigon, amendments to Vietnamese re-entry visas also can be made at the Vietnamese Embassy in Phnom Penh.

### China

The Vietnam-China border crossing is open from 7 am to 4 pm (Vietnam time) or 8 am to 5 pm China time. Set your watch when you cross the border – the time in China is one hour later than in Vietnam. Neither country observes daylight savings time.

There are currently three border checkpoints where foreigners are permitted to cross between Vietnam and China. There is a possibility that more will open in the future.

**Friendship Pass** The busiest border crossing is at the Vietnamese town of Dong Dang, 164km from Hanoi. The closest Chinese town to the border is Pinxiang, but it's about 10km north of the actual border gate. The crossing point (Friendship Pass) is known as Huu Nghi Quan in Vietnamese or Youyi Guan in Chinese.

Dong Dang is an obscure town. The nearest city is Lang Son, 18km to the south. Buses and minibuses on the Hanoi-Lang Son route are frequent. The cheapest way to cover the 18km between Dong Dang and Lang Son is to hire a motorbike for US$1.50. There are also minibuses cruising the streets looking for passengers. Just make sure they take you to Huu Nghi Quan – there is another

checkpoint, but Huu Nghi Quan is the only one where foreigners can cross. There is a customs checkpoint between Lang Son and Dong Dang and sometimes there are long delays while officials thoroughly search the luggage of Vietnamese and Chinese travellers. For this reason, a motorbike might prove faster than a van since you won't have to wait for your fellow passengers to be searched. Note that this is only a problem when you're heading south towards Lang Son, not the other way.

On the Chinese side, it's a 20-minute drive from the border to Pinxiang by bus or share taxi – the cost for the latter is US$3. Pinxiang is connected by train to Nanning, the capital of China's Guangxi Province. Trains to Nanning depart Pinxiang at 8 am and 1.30 pm. More frequent are the buses (once every 30 minutes) which take four hours to make the journey and cost US$4.

There is a walk of 600m between the Vietnamese and Chinese border posts.

A word of caution – because train tickets to China are expensive in Hanoi, some travellers buy a ticket to Dong Dang, walk across the border and then buy a Chinese train ticket on the Chinese side. This isn't the best way because it's several kilometres from Dong Dang to Friendship Pass and you'll have to hire someone to take you by motorbike. If you're going by train, it's better to buy a ticket from Hanoi to Pinxiang, and then in Pinxiang get the ticket to Nanning or beyond.

Trains on the Hanoi-Dong Dang route run according to the following schedule:

| No. | Depart Dong Dang | Arrive Hanoi |
| --- | --- | --- |
| HD4 | 11.40 am | 8 pm |
| HD2 | 5.40 pm | 1.50 am |

| No. | Depart Hanoi | Arrive Dong Dang |
| --- | --- | --- |
| HD3 | 5 am | 1.30 pm |
| HD1 | 10 pm | 5.10 am |

There is a twice-weekly international train running between Beijing and Hanoi, which stops at Friendship Pass. You can board or exit the train at numerous stations in China. The entire Beijing-Hanoi run is 2951km and takes approximately 55 hours, including a three-hour delay (if you're lucky) at the border checkpoint. Schedules are subject to change, but at present train No 5 departs Beijing at 11.20 pm on Monday and Friday, arriving in Hanoi at 6.30 am on Thursday and Monday, respectively. Going the other way, train No 6 departs Hanoi at 11 pm on Tuesday and Friday, arriving in Beijing at 9.21 am on Friday and Monday, respectively. The complete schedule follows:

| Station | To Hanoi Train No 5 | To Beijing Train No 6 |
|---|---|---|
| Beijing | 11.20 pm | 9.21 am |
| Shijiazhuang | 2.54 am | 5.58 am |
| Zhengzhou | 7.53 am | 12.53 am |
| Xinyang | 11.50 am | 8.53 pm |
| Hankou (Wuhan) | 2.59 pm | 5.35 pm |
| Wuchang (Wuhan) | 3.34 pm | 4.56 pm |
| Yueyang | 6.47 pm | 1.46 pm |
| Changsha | 8.56 pm | 11.42 am |
| Hengyang | 11.49 pm | 8.46 am |
| Lengshuitan | 2.07 am | 6.26 am |
| Guilin North | 5.38 am | 2.31 am |
| Guilin | 5.59 am | 2.12 am |
| Liuzhou | 8.45 am | 11.07 pm |
| Nanning | 3.10 pm | 6.49 pm |
| Pinxiang | 10.04 pm | noon |
| Friendship Pass | 10.00 pm* | 8.00 am* |
| Dong Dang | 1.00 am* | 5.00 am* |
| Hanoi | 6.30 am* | 11.00 pm* |

* Vietnamese Time

**Lao Cai-Hekou** A 762km metre-gauge railway, inaugurated in 1910, links Hanoi with Kunming in China's Yunnan Province. The border town on the Vietnamese side is Lao Cai, 294km from Hanoi. On the Chinese side, the border town is called Hekou, 468km from Kunming.

At the time of writing, the Vietnamese and Chinese authorities were planning on starting a direct international train service between Hanoi and Kunming. However, the schedule was not yet determined. If you want to take this train, make inquiries in either Kunming or Hanoi. Most likely, this train will *not* run daily, but probably two or three times a week.

Of course, you needn't bother with the international trains. Domestic trains run

daily on both sides of the border. On the Chinese side, Kunming-Hekou takes about 17 hours. Trains depart and arrive at Kunming's north railway station according to the following schedule:

| No. | Depart Kunming | Arrive Hekou |
|---|---|---|
| 313 | 9.30 pm | 1.55 pm |

| No. | Depart Hekou | Arrive Kunming |
|---|---|---|
| 314 | 2.45 pm | 7.50 am |

On the Vietnamese side, trains run according to the following schedule:

| No. | Depart Lao Cai | Arrive Hanoi |
|---|---|---|
| LC4 | 9.40 am | 8.20 pm |
| LC2 | 6.00 pm | 4.25 am |

| No. | Depart Hanoi | Arrive Lao Cai |
|---|---|---|
| LC3 | 5.10 am | 3.35 pm |
| LC1 | 9.00 pm | 7.10 am |

**Mong Cai-Dongxing** Vietnam's third, but little-known, border crossing is at Mong Cai in the north-east corner of the country, just opposite the Chinese city of Dongxing. The two opposing border towns are not particularly attractive and westerners are a rare sight indeed. But if you're looking to escape the throngs of backpackers, this is one place to do it. There are no railway connections here, but buses on both sides of the border are functional. On the Vietnamese side there are frequent minibuses between Mong Cai and Hon Gai (Halong Bay). On the Chinese side there are buses from Dongxing to Qinzhou, Nanning (via Qinzhou) or Beihai.

**Laos**
As in Cambodia, you do need to take care when travelling through Laos. The road between Luang Prabang and Vientiane goes through one very dangerous spot (Kasi) plagued by Hmong bandits/guerrillas. Lots of people get killed there every year. Two French tourists were shot near Kasi (they survived) in 1995, and in 1996 a French travel agent was shot and killed. The whole area stretching east from Luang Prabang to Xieng Khuang is considered very dangerous.

By contrast, the border area with Vietnam is not considered dangerous. There are currently two points where you can cross the border – at Lao Bao and the Keo Nua Pass.

**Lao Bao** The obscure Vietnamese village of Lao Bao is on National Highway 9, 80km west of Dong Ha and 3km from Laos. Just across the border is the southern Lao province of Savannakhet, but there is no border town. There is an international bus running between Danang (Vietnam) and Savannakhet. In Vietnam, you can catch this bus in Danang, Dong Ha or Lao Bao. In Laos, the only place you are likely to board is Savannakhet. This bus is supposed to make its runs on Sunday, Tuesday and Thursday, but this schedule is hardly engraved in stone. Dong Ha to Savannakhet on this bus costs US$15 for foreigners. From the Vietnamese side, departure from Danang is at 4 am, from Dong Ha at 10 am and from Lao Bao at 2 pm. Arrival in Savannakhet is at 7 pm. Border guards (both Lao and Vietnamese) have been known to ask for bribes.

There are also local buses which just go to the border from either side. It's cheaper to go by local bus rather than to take the cross-border express, but more of a hassle. For one thing, there is a 1km walk between the Vietnamese and Lao border checkpoints. Furthermore, the bus from Dong Ha terminates at Lao Bao, which is 3km from the actual border checkpoint (though you can cover this 3km by motorbike). The bus from Dong Ha to Lao Bao costs US$1 to US$4 depending on whether it's 'deluxe' or 'standard'. These buses normally depart twice daily (early morning and noon), but departure times are approximate because the buses won't leave until completely full.

There is a restaurant on the Lao side of the border, 500m back from the border post. You might be able to sleep in the restaurant if you ask nicely, but there are no hotels here. To say that the facilities around the border are primitive is an understatement.

Visas for Laos can be obtained in Saigon, Hanoi or Danang. If you are departing or entering Vietnam via this route, your Vietnamese visa must indicate the Lao Bao border crossing. If you have a Vietnamese re-entry visa, it can be amended at the Vietnamese embassy in Vientiane or even at the Vietnamese consulate in Savannakhet.

On the Lao side, the highway crosses the Ho Chi Minh Trail. This is one of the few places where you can actually get a look at it, although there is not a whole lot to see.

**Keo Nua Pass** Vietnam's National Highway 8 crosses the border at 734m-high Keo Nua Pass. The border crossing is known as Cau Treo in Vietnamese.

On the Vietnamese side, the nearest city of any importance is Vinh, about 80km from the border and reached by National Highway 8. On the Lao side it's about 200km from the border to Tha Khaek, just opposite Kakhon Phanom in Thailand. There is at least one international bus daily, plus local buses that approach the border checkpoint from either side but do not cross.

## SEA

Among fed-up Vietnamese nationals, unauthorised departure by sea suddenly became very popular in 1975. Since about 1990, the numbers of people fleeing the country by boat was first reduced by the Orderly Departure Programme and later by the opening of the Chinese border (which provided a much safer and easier route). Nowadays, few Vietnamese flee the country because most Western nations are suffering from compassion fatigue and will not grant them refugee status.

For foreign tourists, there seem to be few options to arrive or depart legally by sea. There is endless talk of allowing luxury cruisers to dock at Vietnamese ports, and one such visit was permitted in 1996. However, that vessel was an official delegation carrying representatives from ASEAN countries and therefore had political blessings from Hanoi.

Major port facilities in Vietnam include Haiphong, Danang, Vung Tau and Saigon – all frequent ports of call for freighters, especially from Singapore, Taiwan and Thailand.

Yachts and fishing boats that have shown

up without authorisation in Vietnamese territorial waters have been seized and their crews imprisoned – sometimes for many months – until a satisfactory payment in hard currency gets delivered to the aggrieved authorities.

## ORGANISED TOURS

Package tours are sold by a variety of agencies in Bangkok and elsewhere, but nearly all these tours, which usually follow one of a dozen or so set itineraries, are run by the omnipresent government tourism authorities. In most cases, this means Vietnam Tourism and Saigon Tourist.

You really can fly to Vietnam and make all the arrangements after arrival and probably have more fun that way. In other words, the only thing you gain by booking before arrival is that you might save a little time. However, if your time is more precious than money, a pre-booked package tour could be right for you.

Tours booked outside Vietnam are not a total rip-off given what you get (visa, air tickets, tourist-class accommodation, food, transport, a guide etc), but then again they're not inexpensive: they range in price from about US$500 for a three-day Saigon 'shopping tour' to over US$2,000 for a week-long trip that includes flying all around the country. An Australian travel agency advertises a 19-day excursion for US$1300 *not* including air fare. Doing the same things on your own can cost as little as US$20 a day (not including air fare), but self-propelled travel is more work.

Almost any reputable travel agency can book you onto a standard mad-dash minibus tour around Vietnam. More noteworthy are the adventure tours arranged for people with a particular obsession. This can include speciality tours for cyclists, trekkers, birdwatchers, war veterans, 4WD enthusiasts and Vietnamese cuisine buffs. For the really well-to-do, tours of Vietnam can be arranged by chartered helicopter. The infamous sex tours from Japan have been cracked down upon, but legitimate massage and acupuncture tours are quite all right.

If you have a particular interest and want to get together a tour group, you might advertise on the Internet. Otherwise, consider the following speciality travel outfits:

### Australia
Orbitours
   3rd floor, 73 Walker St (PO Box 834), North Sydney, NSW 2059 (☎ (02) 9954-1399; fax 9954-1655)
Peregrine
   5/38 York St, Sydney, NSW 2000 (☎ (02) 9290-2770)

### North America
Green Tortoise Adventure Travel (☎ (800) 867-8647, (415) 956-7500), 494 Broadway, San Francisco, CA 94133, USA, offers economical trips to all sorts of unusual destinations from Vietnam to Antarctica. Its Web site is at www.greentortoise.com.

Wild Card Adventures (☎ (800) 590-3776; fax (360) 387-9816), 751 Maple Grove Rd, Camano Island, WA 98292, USA, is close to Seattle. It focuses exclusively on Vietnam travel and offers unusual destination options including remote hill tribe areas. Group size is limited to 10 persons.

Another adventurous organisation is Club Adventure (☎ (514) 286-9683; fax 289-9776), 1221 St Hubert, Suite 11, Montreal, Quebec, H2L 3Y8 Canada.

VeloAsia (☎ (415) 664-6779; email veloasia@aol.com), 1271 43rd Ave, San Francisco, CA 94122, USA, specialises in bicycle tours.

Offering trekking is Journeys (☎ (800) 255-8735; www.journeys-intl.com), 4011 Jackson, Ann Arbor, MI 48103.

The Global Spectrum (☎ (800) 419-4446; email mselva@attmail.com), 1901 Pennsylvania Ave NW, Suite 204, Washington, DC 20006, USA, runs cycling and hiking trips.

A very good Web site for locating Vietnam adventure tours is www.destinationvietnam.com/resource.htm.

Asia Transpacific Journeys (☎ (800) 642-2742; www.SoutheastAsia.com), PO Box 1279, Boulder, CO 80306, USA, offers trekking tours and can arrange cycling trips.

Don't confuse the preceding company with the similarly named Asian Pacific Adventures (☎ (800) 825-1680; (213) 935-3156), 826 South Sierra Bonita Ave, Los Angeles, CA 90036, USA. This place does bicycle trips in Vietnam.

# Getting Around

## AIR

Vietnam Airlines has a near monopoly on domestic flights, though upstart Pacific Airlines flies three routes. Vasco (Vietnam Air Services Company) has no regularly scheduled flights – this foreign joint venture runs only charters using small planes and helicopters.

The Vietnam Airlines booking offices in Saigon and Hanoi are the two busiest in the land. Just before public holidays, buying an air ticket literally requires strong-arm tactics – the Vietnamese are not big on queuing up and what you sometimes face is a struggling mass of elbows, hands and slithering bodies. You can avoid this hassle by purchasing from a less congested booking office. There are many travel agents around which sell domestic air tickets, so there's no need to go to the airline office at peak times. The travel agents do not charge any more than the airline – the airline pays a commission to them.

You do need your passport and/or visa to make a booking on all domestic flights, and you will also need to show these documents at the check-in counter and yet again at the security checkpoint. Vietnamese nationals need to show their ID cards.

Vietnam Airlines is gradually getting its act together and many (but not all) branch offices will accept travellers cheques and credit cards for purchasing tickets. The airline has retired most (but not all) of its ancient Soviet-built fleet and has purchased new western-made aircraft. All of the planes owned by Pacific Airlines are new Boeings and Airbuses.

Vasco flies small, fixed-wing aircraft and helicopters. All the pilots are westerners, but the government requires that a Vietnamese observer be on board. If you want to take aerial photos, the government requires that you bring along a Ministry of Defence photographer. The planes are Beechcraft King Air B200s and Jetstream 31s, which can hold 10 passengers. The choppers are of two

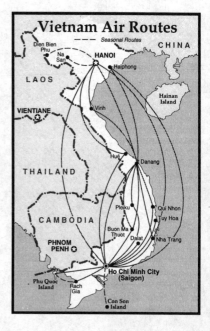

**Vietnam Air Routes**
— — — Seasonal Routes

types: the Eurocopter AS350 and AS355, both of which carry four passengers. Costs are US$1700 per hour for the B200; US$1800 for the Jetstream 31; US$1100 per hour for the Eurocopter AS350; and US$1250 for the AS355. There is an extra US$150 charge for offshore or night flights and a US$300 fee if you keep the aircraft overnight. The MOD photographer costs US$100 per hour, but at least film processing is included – the government will process the film first to make sure it doesn't reveal any military secrets and then will return all the acceptable film and prints to you. Aerial video is also permitted. Vasco has branches in Hanoi, Saigon and Vung Tau.

Flights between Hanoi and Saigon do not fly over Laos and Cambodia even though

## Domestic Airline Schedules
### Vietnam Airlines

| From | To | Frequency | Economy | 1st Class |
|------|-----|-----------|---------|-----------|
| Danang | Buon Ma Thuot | 5 Weekly | US$50 | - |
| Danang | Haiphong | 3 Weekly | US$91 | - |
| Danang | Nha Trang | 3 Weekly | US$50 | - |
| Danang | Pleiku | 1 Daily | US$50 | - |
| Danang | Qui Nhon | 3 Weekly | US$50 | - |
| Danang | Vinh | 3 Weekly | US$64 | - |
| Hanoi | Danang | 3 Daily | US$91 | US$109 |
| Hanoi | Dien Bien Phu | 4 Weekly | US$59 | - |
| Hanoi | Hué | 2 Daily | US$91 | US$109 |
| Hanoi | Na San (Son La) | 1 Weekly | US$50 | - |
| Hanoi | Nha Trang | 1 Daily | US$132 | - |
| Hanoi | Vinh | 3 Weekly | US$41 | - |
| Ho Chi Minh City | Buon Ma Thuot | 2 Daily | US$59 | - |
| Ho Chi Minh City | Dalat | 4 Weekly | US$41 | - |
| Ho Chi Minh City | Danang | 3 Daily | US$91 | US$109 |
| Ho Chi Minh City | Haiphong | 2 Daily | US$173 | US$223 |
| Ho Chi Minh City | Hanoi | 7 Daily | US$173 | US$223 |
| Ho Chi Minh City | Hué | 2 Daily | US$91 | US$109 |
| Ho Chi Minh City | Nha Trang | 2 Daily | US$59 | - |
| Ho Chi Minh City | Phu Quoc | 1 Daily | US$64 | - |
| Ho Chi Minh City | Pleiku | 1 Daily | US$64 | - |
| Ho Chi Minh City | Qui Nhon | 5 Weekly | US$64 | - |
| Ho Chi Minh City | Rach Gia | 5 Weekly | US$64 | - |
| Ho Chi Minh City | Tuy Hoa | 2 Weekly | US$64 | - |
| Phu Quoc | Rach Gia | Seasonal | US$41 | - |

### Pacific Airlines

| | | | | |
|------|-----|-----------|---------|-----------|
| Danang | Ho Chi Minh City | 2 Weekly | US$91 | - |
| Ho Chi Minh City | Hanoi | 1 Daily | US$173 | - |
| Ho Chi Minh City | Haiphong | 3 Weekly | US$173 | - |

### Vasco Airlines

| | | | | |
|------|-----|-----------|---------|-----------|
| Ho Chi Minh City | Con Son | 1 Daily | US$150 | - |

this route would be shorter. Regardless of any security concerns, the Vietnamese do not want to pay for flyover rights.

All aircraft return to their point of origin on the same day as their departure, so the Domestic Airline Schedules (above) covers all possible routes both coming and going.

The airlines charge you US$10 if you want to refund an unused domestic air ticket. If you bought the ticket from a travel agency, you also lose an additional 5% (the travel agent's commission).

### Departure Tax
The domestic departure tax is currently US$1.65, payable in dong only. Children under the age of two are exempt.

### BUS
Vietnam has an extensive network of dirt-cheap buses and other passenger vehicles which reaches virtually every corner of the country. However, few travellers use them, for reasons that will become obvious in the following paragraphs.

Road safety is not one of Vietnam's strong points. The Vietnamese intercity road network of two-lane highways is becoming more and more dangerous due to the rapid increase in the number of motor vehicles. High-speed, head-on collisions between buses, trucks and lesser vehicles has become a sickeningly familiar sight on National Highway 1. Vietnam does not have an emergency rescue system or even a proper ambulance network – if something happens to you out on the road, you could be many hours from even rudimentary medical treatment.

While Vietnam's bus network is incredibly cheap and reaches virtually every corner of the country, there are drawbacks. Poor roads, ancient buses, frequent breakdowns, chronic overcrowding, low average speeds and uncomfortable seats all combine for some unpredictable (and certainly memorable!) experiences.

If possible, try to travel during daylight hours only. Indeed, many drivers refuse to drive after dark in rural areas because the unlit highways often have huge potholes, occasional collapsed bridges and lots of bicycles and pedestrians (including dogs and chickens) who seem oblivious to the traffic. However, if you like living dangerously, there are some overnight buses.

Package-tour groups tend to travel on modern, Japanese-made buses with air-conditioning and cushy seats. However, public bus companies never use these because they're too expensive.

Public buses come in four flavours: Korean-made (almost new), Russian-made (circa 1970), American-made (circa 1965) and French-made (antique).

Most comfortable are the Korean-made (usually Hyundai) buses. Many are air-conditioned and the seats are reasonably comfortable. You'll find these almost exclusively on very long distance routes such as Saigon-Hanoi (a two-day, nonstop drive!). The bad news is that these buses are equipped with video tape players and evil karaoke machines. You can ignore the blood-splattered kung fu videos by closing your eyes (or wearing a blindfold), but you'll need to be deaf to sleep through the karaoke sessions.

The vast majority of Vietnam's buses are Russian-made and American-made. There is little difference between the two: most seem to have been designed for military use. The Vietnamese have modified the vehicles with fancy paint jobs – a nice touch. Considerably less nice is the fact that the bus companies have installed many additional seats – you can expect little legroom and much discomfort. You can purchase two tickets, which, theoretically, entitles you to two seats – but you might have to defend your turf when the bus gets packed to overflowing! Many buses are literally standing room only – if you drop dead, you'll never hit the floor. Luggage is stacked wherever it fits, which in many cases means that it gets tied onto the roof. The police frequently stop the buses to cite the drivers for overloading, though after a quick fix (US$5) the bus continues on its way. A bigger problem is mechanical breakdowns, which occur frequently.

The French-made buses are becoming rare, which is not surprising since they are about 50 years old. How the Vietnamese keep the old bangers running is anybody's guess. These museums-on-wheels sputter, creep and crawl along at around 30km/h – don't expect to get anywhere fast. As with the Russian and American buses, you can expect overloading, extreme discomfort and frequent breakdowns. After an eight-hour ride, one foreigner put it succinctly when she said, 'I feel like a million dong'.

It's fair to say that riding the buses will give you ample opportunity to have 'personal contact' with the Vietnamese people. If you're looking to meet locals, what better way than to have a few sitting on your lap! As one reader says:

I enjoyed the bus riding scene, the scenery and the conversations (gesturing) with people. Although I'd rate the conditions as terrible, the riding community suffered, slept and ate together.

Figuring out the bus system is anything but easy. Many cities have several bus stations and responsibilities are divided according to the location of the destination (whether it is north or south of the city) and the type of service being offered (local or long distance, express or nonexpress).

Most long-distance buses depart in the early morning. Often, a half dozen vehicles to the same destination will leave at the same time, usually around 5.30 am. The first thing they do after departure is look for a functioning petrol station (sometimes difficult to find due to power failures) – just why they don't fill the tank the night before has always mystified us.

Overnight buses have begun since curfew regulations were relaxed in 1989, but neither passengers nor drivers are especially fond of travelling all night long. Short-distance buses, like service taxis, depart when full (ie jam-packed with people and luggage). They often operate throughout the day, but don't count on anything leaving after about 4 pm.

Don't be too trusting of bus drivers. Most are OK, but others are not. Travellers have had offers from bus drivers to bring them right to the front door of their hotel at no charge. Pulling up to the hotel entrance, the driver then suggests you go in and ask if they have a room. While you're doing this, the bus takes off with your luggage. Your luggage can also be pilfered at toilet stops unless you have a trusted friend watching it or you bring it to the toilet with you. When tied to the rooftop it should be reasonably safe from pilfering, but it will be exposed to constant road dust and sometimes heavy rain. Do not accept drinks from your fellow passengers as you may be drugged and robbed.

Food is a bit of a problem on bus trips. The drivers always stop at the worst restaurants (expensive and lousy food). The driver, of course, gets to eat free of charge and sometimes gets a small commission from the restaurant. The best food is available at truck stops, but as you'll soon observe the truckers and bus drivers always eat at separate restaurants.

---

**Passing Water**

The engines of many older trucks and buses are equipped with an ingenious gravity-powered heat-dissipation system. This supplements the radiator, which cannot cope when these ancient vehicles are heavily overloaded (a frequent occurrence). A drum is attached to the roof of the cab and connected to the engine by a hose routed via the driver's window, where a stopcock is installed to allow him to control the flow. Cold water in the rooftop drum slowly drains into the engine; hot water squirts out the radiator overflow tank. When the drum is empty, the truck stops at any of the numerous water-filling stations that line major highways. ■

## Classes

The appellation 'express' *(toc hanh)* is applied rather loosely in Vietnam. Genuine express buses are considerably faster than local buses, which drop off and pick up locals and their produce at each cluster of houses along the highway. But many express buses are the same decrepit vehicles used on local runs except that they stop less frequently. A good rule of thumb is that local buses average 15 to 25km/h over the course of a journey. Express buses rarely exceed an average speed of 35km/h. However, an average is just that – there are often short stretches of highway where speeds of 100km/h are reached, easily fast enough to get everyone on board killed.

However slow they may be, express buses do offer certain advantages. At ferries, they are usually given priority, which can save an hour or more at each crossing. And since they are marginally more expensive than regular buses, people lugging large parcels around the country to make a few dong reselling something are likely to consider their time and comfort less valuable than the cash.

## Reservations

Buses normally leave early in the morning, so if you don't plan to bargain with the bus driver, show up at the bus station the day before departure and purchase a ticket.

## Costs

Costs are negligible, even though foreigners sometimes pay five times the going rate. Depending on the class of your ticket, figure around US$0.02 per kilometre.

## Open Date Ticket

In backpacker haunts throughout Vietnam, you'll see lots of signs advertising the 'Open Date Ticket' or just 'Open Ticket'. Basically, this is a bus service catering to foreign budget travellers, not to local Vietnamese. The buses run between Saigon and Hanoi and you may enter and exit the bus at any major city along the route. You are not obliged to follow a fixed schedule. Essen-

tially, there are two tickets available: Saigon-Hué for US$32 and Hué-Hanoi for US$22.

Overall, we are not that keen on this deal. Once you've bought the ticket, you're stuck with it. If you're dissatisfied with the service provided by one company, that's too bad. Also, it really isolates you from Vietnam – you should try to have at least some contact with the locals other than the bus driver. Buying minibus tickets all along the way costs essentially the same and you achieve maximum flexibility.

Nevertheless, the Open Tickets are a temptation and many people go for it. If you're buying these, we recommend getting them at one of the following places: Kim Cafe (☎ 835-9859), 270 De Tham St, District 1, Ho Chi Minh City; Dalat Tourist (☎ 822479), 9 Le Dai Hanh St, Dalat; Ha Phuong Tourist, also known as Hanh Cafe (☎ 827814), 5 Tran Hung Dao St, Nha Trang; and Thanh Binh Hotel (☎ 861740), 1 Le Loi St, Hoi An.

## MINIBUS

There are two categories of minibus – public and chartered.

## Public Minibuses

Public minibuses (actually privately owned) cater to the domestic market. They depart when full and will pick up as many passengers as possible along the route. They may also drive around town before departure, hunting for additional customers before actually heading out to the highway. Such minibuses will usually become ridiculously crowded as the journey progresses and are not comfortable by any means. The frequent stops to pick up and discharge passengers (and arrange their luggage and chickens) can make for a slow journey. In other words, public minibuses are really a small-scale version of the large public buses. You'll find these public minibuses congregate in the same general areas as the bus stations, though you can often arrange to have one pick you up at your hotel.

## Chartered Minibuses

The majority of independent travellers in

Vietnam choose this form of transport above all others. Chartered minibuses are just what the name implies. Some cater exclusively to foreigners, but well-heeled Vietnamese also travel this way.

This is the deluxe class – air-conditioning is standard and you can be certain of having enough space to sit comfortably. Such luxury, of course, is something you must pay for – prices will be several times higher than what you'd pay on public buses. Nevertheless, it's still very cheap by any standard.

In places where tourists are numerous, there are bound to be people booking seats on chartered minibuses. Budget hotels and cafes are the best places to inquire about these vehicles. However, there are some unscrupulous cafes which sell you a tourist-priced ticket and then stick you on a malfunctioning local bus.

If the chartered minibuses cannot fill all the seats, they may still pick up some passengers en route. However, any reputable company puts a limit on the number of passengers – they should pick up no more people than they have empty seats and should not pick up anybody with excessive luggage. If you paid top dollar for a chartered minibus and they still pack in a ridiculous number of passengers, then you've been had.

## TRAIN

The 2600km Vietnamese railway system (Duong Sat Viet Nam) runs along the coast between Saigon and Hanoi and links the capital with Haiphong and northern towns. While sometimes even slower than buses, the trains offer a more relaxing way to get around. Large-bodied westerners will find that the trains offer more leg and body room than the jam-packed buses. Dilapidated as the tracks, rolling stock and engines may appear, the trains are safer than the country's kamikaze bus fleet. Furthermore, the railway authorities have been rapidly upgrading the facilities to accommodate foreign tourists – even air-conditioned sleeping berths are now obtainable on the express trains.

One key factor to take into account when deciding whether to go by train or bus is the

hour at which the train gets to where you want to go – trying to find a place to stay at 3 am is likely to be very frustrating.

Even the express trains in Vietnam are slow by developed-country standards, but conditions are improving as the tracks and equipment are being upgraded. The quickest rail journey between Hanoi and Saigon takes 36 hours at an average speed of 48km/h. The slowest express train on this route takes 44 hours, averaging 39km/h for the 1726km trip.

Then there are local trains which do not make the complete journey but only cover part of the route like Saigon to Nha Trang. These local trains at times crawl along at 15km/h. There are several reasons for the excruciating slowness. There is only one track running between Saigon and Hanoi. Trains can pass each other only at those few points where a siding has been constructed. Each time trains go by each other, one of them has to stop on the prearranged sidetrack and wait for the oncoming train to arrive. If one is late, so is the other. Subsequent trains going in both directions may also be delayed.

Petty crime is a problem on Vietnamese trains, especially if you travel in budget class, where your fellow passengers are likely to be desperately poor. While there doesn't seem to be organised pack-napping gangs, as there are in India, the Vietnamese seem convinced that the young men and boys you see hanging out in the stations and on trains have only larceny on their minds. Thieves have become proficient at grabbing packs through the windows as trains pull out of stations. To protect your belongings, always keep your backpack or suitcase near you and lock or tie it to something, especially at night. If you must leave your pack for a moment, ask someone who looks responsible to keep an eye on it.

Another hazard is that children frequently throw rocks at the train. Passengers have been severely injured this way and many conductors will insist that you keep down the metal shield for just this reason. Unfortunately, these shields obstruct the view.

There is supposedly a 20kg limit for

## The Hanoi-Saigon Railway

Construction of the 1726km Hanoi-Saigon railway – the Transindochinois – was begun in 1899 (under Governor-General Paul Doumer) and completed in 1936. In the late 1930s, the trip from Hanoi to Saigon took 40 hours and 20 minutes at an average speed of 43km/h. During WWII, the Japanese made extensive use of the rail system, resulting in Viet Minh sabotage on the ground and US bombing from the air. After the war, efforts were made to repair the Transindochinois, major parts of which were either damaged or overgrown.

During the Franco-Viet Minh War, the Viet Minh engaged in massive sabotage against the rail system. Sometimes they would pry up and carry off several kilometres of track in a single night. In response, the French introduced in 1948 two armoured trains equipped with turret-mounted cannon, anti-aircraft machine guns, grenade launchers and mortars (similar trains are used in Cambodia today on the Phnom Penh-Battambang line). During this period, the Viet Minh managed to put into service 300km of track in an area wholly under their control (between Ninh Hoa and Danang), a fact to which the French responded with sabotage of their own.

In the late 1950s the South, with US funding, reconstructed the track between Saigon and Hué, a distance of 1041km. But between 1961 and 1964 alone, there were 795 Viet Cong attacks on the rail system, forcing the abandonment of large sections of track (including the Dalat spur). A major reconstruction effort was carried out between 1967 and 1969 and three sections of track were put back into operation: one in the immediate vicinity of Saigon, another between Nha Trang and Qui Nhon and a third between Danang and Hué.

By 1960, the North had repaired 1000km of track, mostly between Hanoi and China. During the US air war against the North, the northern rail network was repeatedly bombed. Even now – two decades since the end of US bombing – clusters of bomb craters can be seen around virtually every rail bridge and train station in the north.

After reunification, the government immediately set about re-establishing the Hanoi-Ho Chi Minh City rail link as a symbol of Vietnamese unity. By the time the *Reunification (Thong Nhat) Express* trains were inaugurated on 31 December 1976, 1334 bridges, 27 tunnels, 158 stations and 1370 shunts (switches) had been repaired. ■

luggage carried on Vietnamese trains. Enforcement isn't really strict, but if you have too much stuff you might have to send it in the freight car (hopefully on the same train) and pay a small extra charge. This is a hassle that you'll probably want to avoid. Bicycles can also be sent in the freight car. Just make sure that the train you are on *has* a freight car (most have) or your luggage will arrive later than you do.

Eating is no problem – there are vendors in every railway station who board the train and practically stuff food, drinks, cigarettes and lottery tickets into your pockets. However, the food that is supplied by the railway company (free, as part of the cost of the ticket for some long journeys) could be better. It's not a bad idea to stock up on your favourite munchies before taking a long trip.

### Schedules

Odd-numbered trains travel southward; even-numbered trains travel northward. The fastest service is provided by the *Reunification Express*, which runs between Saigon and Hanoi, making only a few quick stops en route. If you want to stop at some obscure point between the major towns, you'll have to use one of the slower local trains. Aside from the main Saigon-Hanoi run, there are small spur lines which link Hanoi with Haiphong and the Chinese border.

One of the unfortunate things about the train system is that there is not yet a computerised booking system. This is no problem when you are purchasing tickets in Saigon or Hanoi, but becomes a problem when you want to buy a ticket at some other point along the route. For example, many travellers want to board the *Reunification Express* in Nha Trang and take it to Hué, but the staff at Nha Trang railway station aren't always informed about empty seats and thus may not be able to sell you a ticket even when space is available. This is a problem that may be solved eventually.

*Reunification Express* trains depart Saigon station every day at 7.30 am. Trains also depart Saigon on Monday, Wednesday and Saturday at 2.30 pm and on Tuesday, Thursday, Friday and Sunday at 3 pm.

In addition, there are local trains. One train departs Saigon daily at 4.50 pm and arrives in Nha Trang at 5.05 am. There is a local train to Hué departing Saigon every other day at 9.15 am. And there is a local train to Qui Nhon, departing Saigon every other day at 9.50 am.

The train schedule changes so frequently (about every six months) that there's little point in reproducing the whole thing here. The timetables for all trains are posted at major stations and you can copy these down. At one time, free photocopied timetables were also available at some stations but now seem to have vanished – perhaps the railway administration will get smart and start selling these.

It's important to realise that the train schedule is 'bare-bones' during Tet. For example, the *Reunification Express* is suspended for nine days starting four days before Tet and continuing for four days afterwards.

Three rail lines link Hanoi with the other parts of northern Vietnam. One takes you east to the port city of Haiphong. A second heads north-east to Lang Son, crosses the border and continues to Nanning, China. A third goes north-west to Lao Cai and onwards to Kunming, China.

It's *very* important that you hang onto your ticket until you've exited the railway station at your final destination. Some travellers have discarded their tickets while leaving the train only to find that the gatekeepers won't allow them to exit the station without a ticket. In this situation, you could be forced to purchase another ticket at the full price. The purpose of this system is to catch people who have sneaked aboard without paying.

## Classes

There are five classes of train travel in Vietnam: hard seat, soft seat, hard sleeper, soft sleeper (normal) and soft sleeper (air-con). Since it's all that the vast majority of Vietnamese can afford, hard seat is usually packed. Hard seat is tolerable for day travel, but overnight it can be even less comfortable than the bus, where at least you are hemmed in and thus propped upright.

Soft seat carriages have vinyl-covered seats rather than the uncomfortable benches of hard seat.

Hard sleeper has three tiers of beds (six beds per compartment). Because the Vietnamese don't seem to like climbing up, the upper berth is cheapest, followed by the middle berth and finally the lower berth. The best bunk is the one in the middle because the bottom berth is invaded by seatless travellers during the day. There is no door to separate the compartment from the corridor.

Soft sleeper has two tiers (four beds per compartment) and all bunks are priced the same. These compartments have a door. The best trains have two categories of soft sleeper, one with air-con and one without. At the present time, air-con is only available on the very fastest express train.

## Reservations

The supply of train seats is often insufficient to meet demand. Reservations for all trips should be made at least one day in advance. For sleeping berths, you may have to book passage three or more days before the date of travel. Bring your passport and visa when buying train tickets. Though such documents are never checked at bus stations, train personnel may ask to have a look at them.

You do not necessarily need to go to the railway station to get your ticket. Many travel agencies, hotels and cafes have gotten into the business of purchasing train tickets for a small commission.

If you arrive early (7.30 am, for example) at a railway station in central Vietnam, you may be told that all tickets to Hanoi or Saigon are sold out. However, this may simply mean that there are no tickets *at the moment*, but more may become available after 8 pm when Saigon and Hanoi phone through the details of unsold tickets. You do not have to pay a bribe to get these last-minute tickets – just

## Reunification Express, Ho Chi Minh City-Hanoi 44 hours

| Station | Distance from Saigon | Hard seat | Soft seat | Top berth | Middle berth | Bottom berth | Soft sleeper |
|---------|---------------------|-----------|-----------|-----------|--------------|--------------|--------------|
| Muong Man | 175km | US$6 | US$6 | US$8 | US$9 | US$10 | US$10 |
| Thap Cham | 319km | US$10 | US$10 | US$14 | US$16 | US$17 | US$18 |
| Nha Trang | 411km | US$12 | US$13 | US$18 | US$20 | US$22 | US$23 |
| Tuy Hoa | 529km | US$16 | US$16 | US$23 | US$26 | US$28 | US$29 |
| Dieu Tri | 631km | US$18 | US$19 | US$27 | US$31 | US$34 | US$35 |
| Quang Ngai | 798km | US$22 | US$24 | US$34 | US$38 | US$42 | US$44 |
| Danang | 935km | US$26 | US$28 | US$40 | US$45 | US$50 | US$51 |
| Hué | 1038km | US$29 | US$31 | US$45 | US$50 | US$55 | US$57 |
| Dong Ha | 1104km | US$31 | US$33 | US$47 | US$53 | US$58 | US$61 |
| Dong Hoi | 1204km | US$33 | US$36 | US$51 | US$57 | US$64 | US$66 |
| Vinh | 1407km | US$43 | US$45 | US$65 | US$73 | US$81 | US$84 |
| Thanh Hoa | 1551km | US$45 | US$48 | US$69 | US$77 | US$85 | US$88 |
| Ninh Binh | 1612km | US$46 | US$49 | US$70 | US$79 | US$87 | US$90 |
| Nam Dinh | 1639km | US$47 | US$50 | US$72 | US$80 | US$88 | US$92 |
| Hanoi | 1726km | US$48 | US$52 | US$74 | US$82 | US$91 | US$94 |

## Reunification Express, Ho Chi Minh City-Hanoi 36 Hours

| Station | Distance from Saigon | Soft seat | Top berth | Middle berth | Bottom berth | Soft sleeper | A/C Soft sleeper |
|---------|---------------------|-----------|-----------|--------------|--------------|--------------|------------------|
| Nha Trang | 411km | US$16 | US$22 | US$24 | US$26 | US$28 | US$36 |
| Dieu Tri | 631km | US$24 | US$34 | US$37 | US$40 | US$43 | US$55 |
| Danang | 935km | US$36 | US$50 | US$54 | US$59 | US$64 | US$81 |
| Hué | 1038km | US$39 | US$55 | US$60 | US$65 | US$70 | US$90 |
| Hanoi | 1726km | US$65 | US$91 | US$99 | US$108 | US$117 | US$150 |

hang out, be polite and persevere. Again, buying through a travel agency could eliminate this hassle. Of course, not much can be done if all the seats are really sold out.

In any given city, reservations can be made only for travel originating in that city. In Nha Trang, for instance, you can reserve a place to Danang but cannot book passage from Danang to Hué. For this reason – and because train stations are often far from the part of town with the hotels in it – it is a good idea to make reservations for onward travel as soon as you arrive in a city.

If you are travelling with a bicycle (for which there is a small surcharge), it may only be possible to get it out of checked baggage at certain stations.

### Costs

One disadvantage of rail travel is that officially, foreigners are supposed to pay a surcharge of around 400% over and above what Vietnamese pay. It works out to about US$100 for a Saigon-Hanoi ticket in a hard sleeper compartment. This is compared with US$173 to fly the same route.

Some foreigners have managed to pay local prices, but this is almost impossible to do unless you have an Asian face. Even with Asian features, you are supposed to show an ID when the ticket is purchased, though a Vietnamese could buy the ticket for you. The ticket clearly indicates whether you paid foreign or local prices, and the name of the purchaser is also written on the ticket. Most conductors will enforce the rules – if you have blond hair and a big nose, don't think that you're going to fool the conductors into believing you're Vietnamese, even if you do wear a conical hat.

The actual price you pay for a ticket depends on which train you take – the fastest trains are the most expensive. The first price table lists the cost for the *Reunification Express* trains taking 44 hours to make the Saigon-Hanoi run. The second table lists prices for the more expensive train, which takes 36 hours to do this route.

## CAR & MOTORBIKE

The discomfort and unreliability of Vietnam's public transport makes renting a vehicle a popular option. Having your own set of wheels gives you maximum flexibility to visit the backwaters and stop where and when you please. The major considerations are costs, safety, the mechanical condition of the vehicle and the reliability of the rental agency.

Bad road conditions can slow your progress and can be very stressful if you're driving. In general, the major highways are hard surfaced and reasonably well maintained, but flooding can be a seasonal problem. A big typhoon can create potholes the size of bomb craters. In remote backwaters roads are not surfaced and will become a sea of mud if the weather turns bad – such roads are best tackled with a 4WD vehicle or motorbike. Mountain roads are particularly dangerous – landslides, falling rocks and runaway vehicles can add unwelcome excitement to your journey. The occasional roadside cemetery often indicates where a bus plunged over the edge.

The pumps in petrol stations may say 'Regular' or 'Super-Unleaded' or whatever. Basically, this means nothing except that the machinery was purchased from abroad. However, petrol does have an octane rating – 86 would be low and 95 would be top end, but there can be several gradations in between.

Black-market petrol *(xang)* is sold – along with oil *(dau)* – in soft drink bottles at little stalls along major roads and highways. In rural areas, you'll see the bottles stacked by the roadside next to a stall. In Saigon, it's not permitted to stack bottles of petrol by the roadside, so the vendor places a couple of bricks with a rolled-up newspaper stuck between in a vertical direction. In cities, this is the universal sign indicating petrol for

sale. Be forewarned that black-market petrol is often mixed with kerosene (it's cheaper), which will likely cause you to have engine problems – use it in an emergency only. If the vendor claims that bottled petrol costs the same as what you buy in a petrol station, that's a clear warning sign to stay away.

Leaving an unattended vehicle parked out on the street overnight is not wise. If travelling by motorbike you can usually bring it right inside the hotel. If travelling by car, it's necessary to find a hotel with a garage or fenced-in compound (many hotels are so equipped). There are also commercial non-hotel garages.

If you're on a motorbike, serious sunburn is a major risk and something you should take care to prevent. The cooling breeze prevents you from realising how badly burned you are getting until it's too late. Cover up exposed skin or wear sunblock lotion. Bikers also must consider the opposite problem – occasional heavy rains. Especially during the monsoon season, rainsuits and ponchos should be carried. Sunblock is somewhat hard to find in Vietnam, but rain gear is readily available.

### Road Rules

Basically, there aren't any. The biggest vehicle wins, by default. Be particularly careful about children in the road – you'll find kids playing hopscotch in the middle of a major highway. Many young boys seem to enjoy playing a game of 'chicken' – deliberately sticking their arms and legs in front of fast-approaching vehicles and withdrawing them (hopefully) at the last possible moment. Other children entertain themselves by throwing rocks at passing vehicles, particularly in the north. Livestock in the road are also a menace – hit a cow on a motorbike and you'll be hamburger.

In cities, there is a rule that you cannot turn right on a red light. In most countries of the world (where people drive on the right side of the road), turning right on the red is legal. It's easy to run afoul of this law in Vietnam and the police will fine you for this offence.

If you should be involved in an accident,

be aware that calling the police is just about the worst thing you can do. The usual response of the police is to impound both vehicles regardless of who caused the accident. You must pay a substantial sum (around US$100 or more) to get the vehicle back. When Vietnamese have an accident, the usual response is for the two drivers to stand in the street and argue with each other for 30 minutes about whose fault it was. Whoever tires of the argument first hands over some money to pay for damages and it's all settled. As a foreigner, you're at a disadvantage in these negotiations. Perhaps it's best to feign some injury (to gain sympathy) but offer to pay for the other driver's minor damages. If none of this works and you are being asked to pay excessive damages, you could always say you want to call the police. As a foreigner, they might just believe you're crazy enough to do that and therefore the negotiations will likely be concluded quickly.

**Car** Although the police frequently stop drivers and fine them for all sorts of real and imagined offences, we have never seen anybody stopped for speeding. Driving is normally performed Grand Prix style, as if there were some sort of prize for the first car to cross the finish line.

Honking at all pedestrians and bicycles (to warn them of your approach) is considered a basic element of safe driving – larger trucks might as well have a permanent siren attached.

There is no national seat belt law – indeed, the Vietnamese laugh at foreigners who insist on using seat belts. Actually, you'll be hard-pressed to find a vehicle equipped with seat belts or airbags – most Vietnamese drivers remove these 'nuisance' items.

The law says that you are supposed to turn on your headlights at night. That seems elementary enough, but many people drive at night without lights because they believe that this saves petrol (it doesn't).

**Motorbike** The legal definition of a moped is any motor-driven, two-wheeled vehicle 50cc or less, even if it doesn't have bicycle pedals. Motorbikes are two-wheeled vehicles with engines over 50cc. In Vietnam, no driver's licence is needed to drive a moped, while to drive a motorbike you will need an international driver's licence endorsed for motorbike operation. But expats remaining in the country over six months are expected to obtain a Vietnamese driver's licence. The Vietnamese licence will be valid only for the length of your visa! If you extend your visa, you need to extend your driver's licence too.

Technically, the maximum legal size for a motorbike is 125cc. There are indeed larger bikes around – these are classified as 'motorcycles'. To drive a motorcycle, the owner must join a motorcycle association and do voluntary public service work (riding in patriotic parades and sporting events, and so on). There is an awful lot of bureaucracy involved in owning such a vehicle and riders can expect to be stopped by the police frequently to have their papers checked. Most people who own these road hogs are the sons of high-ranking officials – they apparently find loopholes in the regulations. Some foreigners with diplomatic privileges seem to find a way to skirt the rules too.

The major cities have parking lots *(giu xe)* for bicycles and motorbikes – usually just a roped-off section of sidewalk – which charge US$0.20 to guard your vehicle (bike theft is a major problem). When you pull up, a number will be chalked on the seat or stapled to the handlebars and you'll be handed a reclaim chit. Without it, getting your wheels back may be a real hassle, especially if you come back after the workers have changed shifts. Outside of the designated parking lots, some travellers simply ask a stranger to watch their bikes – this may not always be such a good idea. One traveller wrote:

We asked some locals to watch our motorbike while we went to explore a beach in a nearby cove. When we returned, we found that our new 'friends' had removed some vital engine components and we had to buy these back from the very people who stole them.

Locals are required to have liability insurance on their motorbikes, but foreigners are not covered and there is currently no way to arrange this. If you want to insure yourself against injury, disfigurement or death, you'll need some sort of travel insurance with a foreign company (be sure that motorbike accidents are not excluded from your policy!). Travel insurance is something that must be arranged before you come to Vietnam. As for liability insurance, consider burning some incense at a local temple.

The government has been talking about requiring the use of safety helmets. However, most Vietnamese disdain wearing them, in part because of the expense and also because of the tropical heat. You can purchase high-quality safety helmets in Saigon and Hanoi for US$50, or buy a low-quality 'eggshell' helmet for US$15. For the serious biker, bringing a helmet from abroad might be a good idea, but make sure it's something that you can tolerate wearing in hot weather. As a last resort, you might consider purchasing a slightly battered US army helmet from the War Surplus Market – the bullet holes provide ventilation.

The law says that a motorbike can carry only two persons, but we've seen up to seven on one vehicle (and they had luggage). In general, this law is enforced in cities but mostly ignored in rural areas.

### Rental
**Car** Drive-them-yourself rental cars have yet to make their debut in Vietnam, but cars with drivers can be hired from a variety of sources. Given the low cost of labour, renting a vehicle with a driver and guide is a realistic option even if you're a budget traveller. Split between several people, the cost per day can be very reasonable.

Hanoi and Saigon have an especially wide selection of government bodies, state companies and private concerns that hire out vehicles. Vietnam Tourism will hire out new Japanese cars with drivers for US$0.45 per kilometre (with a minimum per-day charge). The same service is offered by various competing agencies, including many provincial tourism authorities and private companies. Bargaining is entirely possible and, when

you've completed negotiations, a contract should be signed to prevent any later disputes.

For sightseeing trips just around the Saigon or Hanoi areas, a car with driver can also be rented by the day or by the hour (renting by the day is cheaper). For definition purposes, a 'day' is eight hours or less with a total distance travelled of less than 100km. Based on this formula, a car costs US$25 per day (or US$4 per hour) for a Russian-built vehicle; US$35 per day (US$5 per hour) for a small Japanese car; US$40 per day (US$6 per hour) for a larger, late-model Japanese car; US$64 per day (US$8 per hour) for a limousine.

Renting a van is worth considering if your group is large. These vehicles can hold approximately eight to 12 passengers, so the cost per person works out to even less than a car. One advantage of vans is that they have high clearance, a consideration on some of the dismal unsurfaced roads.

For the really bad roads of north-west Vietnam, the only reasonably safe vehicle is a jeep. Without 4WD, the muddy mountain roads can be deadly. Jeeps come in different varieties – the cheapest (and least comfortable) are Russian-made, while more cushy vehicles are available from Korea and Japan.

With the exception of Russian-built or really old vehicles, most are equipped with air-conditioning. Since air-conditioned cars often cost more to rent, you might make your preferences known early when negotiating a price. Also, it's been our experience that not having an air-conditioner can be an advantage – Vietnamese drivers usually insist on keeping the air-conditioner at full-blast all day, even if it means wearing a winter coat in the tropical heat.

Many travellers have rented cars from private individuals – some have been satisfied and some have not. Some of these self-proclaimed guides with cars offer very low prices, but they have no insurance and by law are not permitted to transport tourists. Some of the drivers were reckless and the vehicles in lousy mechanical condition, plus you may have trouble with the police. It's often better to find companions and rent a car and driver from a reliable company.

Almost all cars are equipped with a cassette tape player. Bring some music tapes or buy them from the local markets and hope your driver, guide and fellow passengers have the same taste in music as you do!

**Motorbike** Renting a motorbike is now possible from a wide variety of sources – cafes, travel agencies, motorbike shops, hotels etc. If you don't want to drive yourself, many cyclo drivers are also willing to act as your personal motorbike chauffeur and guide for around US$6 per day. However, take care to find someone who you feel is competent and easy to get along with.

How much you pay for a motorbike depends on the engine size. Renting a 50cc moped (the most popular model) is cheap at around US$7 per day, usually with unlimited mileage. Regular motorbikes start from US$10 and there might be a distance charge in addition to the daily fee.

A minor complication is whether or not a deposit or some other security is required. New motorbikes cost about US$2000, so leaving a deposit to cover its value would not be a trivial lump of cash. Some renters may prefer to hold your visa or passport as security until you return the bike. There have not been any huge problems with renters losing or refusing to return these items, though you are placing yourself in their hands. You should definitely sign some sort of agreement (preferably in English or another language you understand) clearly stating what you are renting, how much it costs, the extent of compensation you must pay if the bike is stolen etc. People in the business of renting motorbikes are usually equipped with a standard rental agreement.

Most bikes have their rear-view mirrors removed or turned around so that they don't get broken in the handlebar-to-handlebar traffic. This might make sense in Saigon with its continuous close encounters, but you should have the mirrors properly installed if you're going out on the highway. It's rather important to know when a big truck is bearing down on you from behind.

## Purchase

**Car** Foreigners with resident certificates can purchase a car, but it would be almost madness to do so. Indeed, outside of Hanoi and Saigon, a foreigner driving a car will almost certainly be stopped by the police and the vehicle will be impounded.

Foreign companies can also purchase cars, though companies which do so also usually hire a Vietnamese driver rather than let their foreign employees drive themselves. Special licence plates are affixed to foreign-owned vehicles.

**Motorbike** Except for bona-fide foreign residents, buying a motorbike for touring in Vietnam is illegal. However, some travellers have reported that so far the authorities have turned a blind eye to the practice. Apparently, you buy a bike but register it in the name of a trusted Vietnamese friend. Some shops which sell motorbikes will let you keep the bike registered in the shop's name. This requires that you trust the shopkeepers, but in most cases this seems to work out OK.

The big issue is what to do with the bike when are finished with it. If you return to the city where you originally purchased the bike, you can simply sell it back to the shop you bought it from (at a discount, of course). Another possible solution is to sell it to another foreigner travelling in the opposite direction – notice boards at the cafes in Saigon and Hanoi can be useful in this regard. If you're unlucky, you might have to simply scrap the bike. Given this possibility, it's best not to buy a very expensive motorbike in the first place. But, remember, buying a motorbike is illegal and a crackdown may come at any time.

Japanese-made motorbikes are the best available, but by far the most expensive. The Honda Dream is everyone's favourite – and the most likely to get stolen. A new Dream goes for about US$2700.

Unless you can get an exceptionally good deal on a used Honda, the best alternative is to buy a Russian-made Minsk 125cc, which sells brand-new for around US$550. Its quality is mediocre at best, but at least theft is not a major worry. The two-stroke engine burns oil like mad and the spark plugs frequently become oil fouled, so always carry a spare spark plug and spark plug wrench. The bike consumes too much petrol and, furthermore, you have to manually mix the petrol with oil (be sure you use only 'two-stroke oil'). Despite these hassles, it is a powerful bike and it's very easy to find spare parts and mechanics who can do repairs. The Minsk handles particularly well on muddy roads, a significant point in its favour.

A reasonable compromise is the Taiwanese-made Bonus. This 125cc bike costs US$1900 new and quality is somewhere half way between a Minsk and a Honda Dream. The bike handles well on paved roads, but poorly in the mud – the Minsk is better for mud-slogging.

There are some other bikes from Eastern Europe which are cheap, but basically they are junk and some are illegal to ride because the engine size is over 125cc.

## BICYCLE

A great way to get around Vietnam's towns and cities is to do as the locals do: ride a bicycle. During rush hours, urban thoroughfares approach gridlock as rushing streams of cyclists force their way through intersections without the benefit of traffic lights. Riders are always crashing into each other and getting knocked down, but because bicycle traffic is so heavy, they are rarely going fast enough to be injured. Westerners on bicycles are often greeted enthusiastically by locals who may never have seen a foreigner pedalling around before.

Bicycles are utility vehicles in much of rural Vietnam. To see a bike carrying three pigs or 300kg of vegetables is not unusual. One has to marvel at how they manage to load all these items on the bike and ride it without the whole thing tipping over.

Vietnam is also a possible place for long-distance cycling: much of the country is flat or only moderately hilly, the major roads are of a serviceable standard and the shortage of vehicles makes for relatively light traffic. Bicycles can be transported around the country on the top of buses or in train baggage compartments.

Groups of western cyclists have begun touring Vietnam. The flat lands of the Mekong Delta region are one logical place for long-distance riding. The entire coastal route looks feasible, but the insane traffic makes it unpleasant and dangerous.

Bicycling is probably not a good idea in the winter months north of the DMZ, particularly if you'll be heading from south to north. This is because of the monsoonal wind which blows from north to south – nothing is more depressing than constantly riding into a cold head wind. Doing it from north to south means you'll have the wind to your back, but it will still be cold.

Mountain bikes and 10-speed bikes can be bought at a few speciality shops in Hanoi and Saigon, but you'll probably do better to bring your own if you plan to travel long distance by pedal power. Mountain bikes are definitely preferred – the occasional big pothole or unsealed road can be rough on a set of delicate rims. Basic cycling safety equipment is also not available in Vietnam, so such items as helmets, night lights, front and rear reflectors, leg reflectors and rear-view mirrors should be brought along. For long-distance riding, pack spare parts such as spokes, tubes, a pump, cables and a water bottle. Bring along some tools: a spoke wrench, a chain tool, a multifunction tool and a small bottle of chain lube. A bell is required equipment – the louder the better. Padded gloves ease the shock of rough roads. A pocket-size inner tube repair kit is necessary. Don't forget to deflate your tyres as your bike will likely fly into Vietnam in an unpressurised cabin, which can lead to exploded tubes.

Hotels and some travel agencies are starting to get into the business of renting bicycles. The cost varies but is around US$1 per day or US$0.20 per hour.

There are innumerable roadside bicycle repair stands in every city and town in

Vietnam. Usually, they consist of no more than a pump, an upturned military helmet and a metal ammunition box filled with oily bolts and a few wrenches.

Pumping up a tyre costs US$0.05. Fixing a punctured inner tube should cost about US$0.50 depending on the size of the patch. The common practice is to use 'hot patches', which have to be burned into place – this is more time-consuming than using glue, but it makes for a good seal.

Many travellers buy a cheap bicycle, use it during their visit and, at the end, either sell it or give it to a Vietnamese friend. Locally produced bicycles are available starting at about US$30, but are of truly inferior quality. A decent, one-speed, Chinese-made bicycle costs about US$60 to US$80. A Taiwanese-made mountain bike goes for about US$200 and Japanese-made bikes about US$300. You may occasionally find a European bike, including the German-made Mifa (about US$70), Czech-made Eska (US$120) and French-made Peugeot (US$230).

All Vietnamese-made bicycles have the same mixte (unisex) frame, but the various models are equipped with different accessories. The Vietnamese-made frame is serviceable, but the locally produced moving parts (including brakes, the crank shaft, pedals and gears, as well as tyre inner tubes) should be avoided unless you enjoy frequent visits to bicycle repair shops.

Although you will often see two Vietnamese riding on a single bike, this is generally *not* a good idea, as one traveller discovered:

I rented a bike in Saigon and had the splendid idea to carry my friend on the rear bike rack in order to return to the hotel. However, after only 5m, the rear wheel snapped! Back in the bicycle shop (by cyclo), I pretended an accident had occurred, so they charged me only US$3 extra. Conclusion: these cheap Chinese bikes can carry two local people, but apparently not two westerners.

**Thilo Shönfeld**

## HITCHING

Westerners have reported great success at hitching in Vietnam. In fact, the whole system of passenger transport in Vietnam is premised on people standing along the highways and flagging down buses or trucks. To get a bus, truck or other vehicle to stop, stretch out your arm and gesture towards the ground with your whole hand. Drivers will expect to be paid for picking you up. Some western travellers have had their offers to pay refused, but don't count on this. As long as you look like a foreigner (to many Vietnamese, foreigner = money) you rarely wait for more than a few passenger vehicles to pass before one stops.

One of the advantages of going from Hanoi to Saigon is that most people are doing just the opposite. Many folks pay for car rides heading north, so it's relatively easy to catch an empty car going south. I'd go to larger hotels, meet the driver the night before and make a private deal (not with the driver's boss). I also tried standing by the roadside and flagging cars down. Some drivers knew what was going on and knew exactly how much to charge. But on certain stretches of highway, traffic of passenger vehicles was light indeed. The best advice in such cases is to start out early.

**Ivan Kasimoff**

You can learn a great deal about a vehicle by examining its licence plate. Whether you are in a confusing bus station looking for the right bus or hitchhiking and wishing to avoid accidentally flagging down an army truck, the following information should prove useful.

First, there are the several types of licence plates. Vehicles with white numbers on a green field are owned by the government. Privately-owned vehicles have black numbers on white. Diplomatic cars have the letters NG in red over green numbers on a white field. Other cars owned by foreigners begin with the letters NN and are green-on-white. Military plates have white numerals on red.

The first two numerals on a number plate are the two-digit code assigned to the vehicle's province of origin. Because the vast majority of vehicles in the country are controlled at the provincial level and used to link a given province with other parts of the country, there is usually a 50-50 chance that the vehicle is headed towards its home territory.

## Province Codes

| | |
|---|---|
| 13 | Ha Bac |
| 15 | Greater Haiphong |
| 17 | Thai Binh |
| 18 | Nam Ha & Ninh Binh |
| 20 | Bac Thai |
| 21 | Lao Cai & Yen Bai |
| 28 | Hoa Binh |
| 29 | Greater Hanoi |
| 36 | Thanh Hoa |
| 37 | Nghe An |
| 38 | Ha Tinh |
| 39/40 | Quang Binh, Quang Tri & Thua Thien-Hué |
| 43 | Quang Nam-Danang |
| 44 | Quang Ngai & Binh Dinh |
| 45 | Phu Yen & Khanh Hoa |
| 46 | Kon Tum |
| 47 | Dac Lac |
| 48 | Binh Thuan |
| 49 | Lam Dong |
| 50 | Ho Chi Minh City (government) |
| 51/55 | Ho Chi Minh City (private) |
| 60 | Dong Nai |
| 61 | Song Be |
| 62 | Long An |
| 63 | Tien Giang |
| 64 | Vinh Long |
| 65 | Cantho |
| 66 | Dong Thap |
| 67 | An Giang |
| 69 | Minh Hai |
| 70 | Tay Ninh |
| 71 | Ben Tre |
| 72 | Ba Ria-Vung Tau |

The two-digit number codes for most provinces (listed more or less north to south) are shown in the table above.

## WALKING

You aren't likely to do much long-distance walking in the steamy, tropical lowlands, which are dominated by dense vegetation. However, some spots in the Central Highlands and the far north offer hiking possibilities. The biggest hazard is likely to be the police – you may need permits, especially if you want to spend the night in remote mountain villages where there are no hotels.

One thing to be aware of in the south is that in equatorial regions, there is very little twilight and night comes on suddenly without warning. Therefore, you can't readily judge how many hours of daylight remain unless you have a watch. Pay attention to how long you'll need to get back to civilisation – otherwise, be prepared for an impromptu camping trip.

If you'd rather run, not walk, it's interesting to note that long-distance running has made its debut in Vietnam. At the end of the 80s, someone actually ran from Hanoi to Danang. No wonder the Vietnamese think that foreigners are mad.

## BOAT

Vietnam has an enormous number of rivers that are at least partly navigable, but the most important by far is the multi-branched Mekong River. Scenic day trips by boat are also possible on rivers in Hoi An, Danang, Hué, Tam Coc and even Saigon, but only in the Mekong Delta are boats used as a practical means of transport.

Boat trips are also possible on the sea – a cruise to the islands off the coast of Nha Trang is a particularly popular trip. Boats are a practical means of getting from the Mekong Delta to Phu Quoc Island. If you visit Halong Bay, a cruise to the offshore islands is practically mandatory.

Pay a little attention to the condition of the boats. Small boats with small engines (or no engines) are going to be slow. If the water is rough, small boats will bounce around like a cork. Many people enjoy this, but it's not much fun if you're prone to seasickness. Some of the smaller rivercraft can only accommodate two or three people and you can easily get splashed. Whenever you take such a small boat, it's wise to keep your camera in a plastic bag when not actually in use so as to protect it from being splashed by water.

In some parts of Vietnam (particularly the Mekong Delta), you'll have to make some ferry crossings. This is no big deal, but a few precautions are called for. Passengers are required to get out of their vehicles before these are driven onto the ferries – be sure that your luggage is secure. Don't stand between parked vehicles on the ferry – they can roll and you could wind up as the meat in the sandwich. Be sure you buy a passenger ticket before boarding – at some ferry crossings, you buy the ticket on one side of the river and have to give it to the gatekeeper on the other side. But on some very small ferries (the ones which do not carry cars) you buy the tickets on board – confusing.

## LOCAL TRANSPORT
### Bus

Vietnam has some of the worst local inner-city bus transport in Asia. The bus systems in Hanoi and Saigon have improved in the past few years but are light years behind Hong Kong and, in general, this is not a practical way to get around. Fortunately, there are many other options.

### Taxi

Western-style taxis with meters were introduced to Saigon in 1994 and have spread quickly to other cities.

For details on exactly what is available in each city, see the Getting There & Away and Getting Around sections of each chapter. Hanoi boasts more taxi companies than any other city in Vietnam, having even surpassed Saigon.

### Cyclo

The cyclo (xich lo), or pedicab, short for the French cyclo-pousse, is the best invention since sliced bread. Cyclos offer an easy, cheap and aesthetic way to get around Vietnam's confusing, sprawling cities. Riding in one of these clever contraptions will also give you the moral superiority that comes with knowing you are being kind to the environment – certainly kinder than all those drivers on whining, smoke-spewing motorbikes.

Groups of cyclo drivers always hang out near major hotels and markets, and quite a number of them speak at least broken English (in the south, many of the cyclo drivers are former ARVN soldiers). The ones who speak English charge a little more than the ones who don't, but avoiding the language problem may be worth the minor added expense (we're talking peanuts). To make sure the driver understands where you want to go, it's useful to bring a city map with you, though some drivers cannot read maps either.

All cyclo drivers are male, although they vary in age from around 15 to perhaps 60 years old. Many of the younger ones are transients from the countryside, coming to Saigon and Hanoi to seek their fortune – with no place to live, they may even sleep in their cyclo. Most cyclo drivers rent their vehicles for US$1 per day. The more affluent cyclo drivers buy their own vehicle for US$200, but to do so requires that the owner have a residence permit for the place where the

---

### Urban Orienteering

Urban orienteering is very easy in Vietnam. Vietnamese is written with a Latin-based alphabet. You can at least read the street signs and maps, even if the pronunciation is incomprehensible! In addition, finding out where you are is easy: street signs are plentiful, and almost every shop and restaurant has the street name and number right on its sign. Street names are sometimes abbreviated on street signs with just the initials ('DBP' for 'Dien Bien Phu St' etc). Most street numbering is sequential with odd and even numbers on opposite sides of the street (although there are important exceptions in Ho Chi Minh City and Danang – see Orientation in those sections for details), but unfortunately, number 75 is often three blocks down the street from number 76.

A few tips: many restaurants are named after their street addresses. For instance, 'Nha Hang 51 Nguyen Hue' (nha hang means restaurant) is at number 51 Nguyen Hue St. If you are travelling by bus or car, a good way to get oriented is to look for the post office – the words following Buu Dien (Post Office) on the sign are the name of the district, town or village you're in. ∎

cyclo is to be driven – the transients from the countryside are thus excluded from vehicle ownership. Operating a cyclo is often a family business – a father and son take turns so the vehicle gets used 18 hours a day. But driving a cyclo is no way to get rich – average price charged is around US$0.20 per kilometre. Bargaining is necessary; the drivers know that US$1 or its dong equivalent is nothing to most westerners. If the cyclo drivers waiting outside the hotel want too much, flag down someone else less used to spendthrift tourists. Settle on a fare *before* going anywhere or you're likely to be asked for some outrageous quantity of dong at the trip's end.

Since 1995, the government has been requiring cyclo drivers to obtain a licence. The requirements for this include passing an exam on traffic safety laws.

Have your money counted out and ready before getting on a cyclo. It also pays to have the exact money – drivers will sometimes claim they cannot make change for a 5000d note.

Cyclos are cheaper by time rather than distance. A typical price is US$1 per hour. If this works out well, don't be surprised if the driver comes around your hotel the next morning to see if you want to hire him again.

I had a fingers bargaining session with a cyclo driver, only to discover at the end of the ride that he was bargaining dollars and I was bargaining dong! He got 10,000d not US$10 – much to his disappointment – but I had to be very forceful to get away with it.

**Mike Conrad**

We should point out that these misunderstandings are sometimes sincere, not always attempts to cheat you. We know one traveller who had a vociferous argument when he tried to pay his cyclo driver 1000d rather than US$1. In fact, no one – not even a Vietnamese – can hire a cyclo for 1000d and the price really should have been about US$1. Bargaining with finger-language alone is perhaps not such a good idea – since you cannot possibly hold up 10,000 fingers, the best solution is to write things down.

Recently in Saigon there have been reports of foreigners being mugged by their cyclo drivers. The driver takes a 'shortcut' down a dark alley where some of his accomplices are waiting. This happens almost exclusively at night, so perhaps the lesson is to use cyclos only in the daytime. So far the problem is limited to Saigon, but there is no guarantee that the problem won't spread in the future.

### Honda Om

The *Honda om* is an ordinary motorbike on which you ride seated behind the driver. In other words, it's a motorbike taxi. Don't expect to find one with a meter – negotiate the price beforehand. The fare is a fraction more than a cyclo for short trips and about the same as a cyclo for longer distances. Getting around this way is quite respectable as long as you don't have a lot of luggage.

In places where people congregate – markets, hotels, bus stations – you'll find plenty of Honda om drivers hanging around looking for customers. They make themselves pretty conspicuous so they're not hard to find. However, it can be difficult to find one when you're just walking down a street – there is no set procedure for finding a driver willing to transport you somewhere. Just stand by the roadside and try to flag someone down (most drivers can always use some extra cash) or ask a Vietnamese to find a Honda om for you.

### Xe Lam

Xe Lams are tiny, three-wheeled trucks used for short-haul passenger and freight transport (similar to the Indonesian *bajaj*). They tend to have whining two-stroke 'lawn mower' engines with no mufflers, and emit copious quantities of blue exhaust smoke, but they get the job done.

### Walking

If you don't want to wind up like a bug on a windshield, you need to pay attention to a few pedestrian survival rules, especially in motorbike-crazed Saigon. Foreigners frequently make the mistake of thinking that the best way to cross a busy Vietnamese street is to run quickly across it. Sometimes this works and sometimes it gets you creamed. Most Saigonese cross the street slowly – very slowly – giving the motorbike drivers sufficient time to judge their position so they can pass to either side of you. They will *not* stop or even slow down, but they *will* try to avoid hitting you. Just don't make any sudden moves. Good luck.

## Mekong Delta Special

Two forms of transport used mostly in the Mekong Delta are the *xe dap loi*, a wagon pulled by a bicycle, and the *xe Honda loi*, a wagon pulled by a motorbike.

## ORGANISED TOURS

If you decide to rent a car with driver and guide, you'll have the opportunity to design your own itinerary for what amounts to a private tour for you and your companions. Seeing the country this way is almost like individual travel, except that it's more luxurious, and also offers you the advantage to stop anywhere along the route for that once-in-a-lifetime photo.

The cost varies considerably. On the high end are tours booked through government travel agencies like Saigon Tourist and Vietnam Tourism. A tour booked with these agencies is about US$50 to US$60 a day for one person (and less each for two or more people because transport and lodging costs can be shared). Students receive a 15% discount, which they are more likely to get if they have an official-looking letter from their university registrar to show.

This price includes accommodation at a tourist-class hotel (which costs at least US$25 per night for a single anyway), a guide who will accompany you everywhere, a local guide in each province you visit, a driver and a car. Insist that your guides are fluent in a language you know well – this is often a serious problem with government guides. The cost of the car is computed on a per-kilometre basis, but it varies depending on what type of vehicle you choose.

When you settle on your itinerary, make

sure to get a written copy from the travel agency. If you later find that your guide feels like deviating from what you paid for, that piece of paper is your most effective leverage. If your guide asks for the itinerary, keep the original and give him or her a photocopy, as there have been reports of guides taking tourists' itineraries and then running the tour their way. One traveller wrote:

Our guide was incredibly stubborn and arrogant, always thinking that he knew more than us. Whenever we tried to tell him something, he suddenly developed a hearing problem. But whenever he wasn't sure about something (like the location of a hotel, the name of a temple, etc), he asked to borrow our Lonely Planet book!

A good guide can be your translator and travelling companion and can save you as much money as he or she is costing you (by helping you save money). A bad guide can ruin your trip. Interview your guide thoroughly before starting out – make sure that this is someone you can travel with. Agree on the price before beginning the journey; for a private guide, US$5 to US$7 per day is a typical rate (this might increase in future) and it's proper to throw in a bonus at the end of your trip if your guide proved particularly helpful and saved you money.

A guide hired from a government-owned travel agency will cost you US$20 per day, of which perhaps only US$5 actually goes into the guide's pocket.

With private guides, you are also responsible for their travel expenses – with a guide hired from the government, you need to ask. If you can gather up a small group of travellers, the cost of hiring a guide can be shared among all of you. If you are travelling solo, your guide may be able to drive you around on a motorbike, but you should pay for the petrol and parking fees. If the police stop you, do *not* say that this person is your guide since it is technically illegal for an unlicensed person to work as a guide – this person is 'just a friend'. If your guide gets fined, you should of course reimburse him or her – the cost of the 'fine' can usually be bargained down to US$5 or less.

The best time to look for guides seems to be in the morning – visit the cafes around 7 to 9 am. Otherwise, try the evenings – most of the best guides will be working during daytime hours.

For trips in and around big cities like Saigon and Hanoi, you will often find women working as guides. However, very few women are employed as guides on long-distance trips.

# Ho Chi Minh City

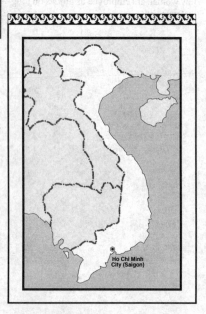

Ho Chi Minh City (Saigon)

In this the largest of Vietnam's cities, you'll see the hustle and bustle everywhere, and there is something invigorating about it all. Images of the exotic and mundane abound. There are the street markets, where bargains are struck and deals are done; the sidewalk cafes, where stereo speakers fill the surrounding streets with a melodious thumping beat; and the sleek new pubs, where tourists chat over beer, pretzels, coffee and croissants. A young female office worker manoeuvres her Honda Dream through rush-hour traffic, long hair flowing, high heels working the brake pedal. The sweating Chinese businessman chats on his cellular phone, cursing his necktie in the tropical heat. A desperate beggar suddenly grabs your arm, rudely reminding you that this is still a Third World city despite the tinsel and trimmings.

The traffic roars. The jackhammers of progress pound the past into pulp to make way for the new. The city churns, ferments, bubbles and fumes. Yet within the teeming metropolis are the timeless traditions and beauty of an ancient culture. There are pagodas where monks pray and incense burns. Artists create their masterpieces on canvas or in carved wood. Puppeteers entertain children in the parks. In the back alleys where tourists seldom venture, acupuncturists poke needles into patients and students learn to play the violin. A seamstress carefully creates an *ao dai*, the graceful Vietnamese costume that could make the fashion designers of Paris envious.

Actually, Ho Chi Minh City is not so much a city as a small province covering an area of 2029 sq km stretching from the South China Sea almost to the Cambodian border. Most of this vast territory is overwhelmingly rural, dotted with villages and groups of houses set amid rice paddies. Rural regions make up about 90% of the land area of Ho Chi Minh City and hold around 25% of the municipality's population. The other 75% of the population is crammed into the remaining 10% that constitutes the urban centre. To put it another way, Ho Chi Minh City differs from a province in name only.

This urban centre is still unofficially called 'Saigon'. But officially, 'Saigon' refers only to District 1, which is only one small piece of the municipal pie. Southerners certainly prefer the name 'Saigon', but northerners tend to toe the official line. Most government officials are from the north and will 'correct' you if you say 'Saigon'. If you have to deal with the bureaucracy, it's best to just bite the bullet and say 'Ho Chi Minh City'.

To the west of the city centre is District 5, the huge Chinese neighbourhood called Cholon, which some people will tell you means 'Chinatown'. In fact, Cholon means 'Big Market', a good indication of the importance the Chinese have traditionally played in

Vietnam's economy. Curiously, its Chinese name (Di An) means 'Embankment'. Whatever it's called, Cholon is decidedly less Chinese than it used to be, largely thanks to the anti-capitalist, anti-Chinese campaign of 1978-79 which caused many ethnic Chinese to flee the country, taking with them their money and entrepreneurial skills. With Vietnam's recent opening to the outside world, many of these refugees are returning (with foreign passports) to explore investment possibilities and Cholon's hotels are once again packed with Chinese-speaking business people.

Officially, greater Ho Chi Minh City claims a population of four million. In reality, perhaps six to seven million is a closer figure. The wide discrepancy is explained by the fact that the government census-takers only count those who have official residence permits, but probably one-third of the population lives here 'illegally'. Many of the illegal residents actually lived in Saigon prior to 1975, but their residence permits were transferred to rural re-education camps after liberation. Not surprisingly, these people (and now their children and grandchildren) have simply sneaked back into the city, though without a residence permit they cannot own property or a business. Furthermore, they are joined by an increasing number of rural peasants who come to Saigon to seek their fortune – many do not find the proverbial 'pot of gold at the end of the rainbow' and wind up sleeping on the pavement.

Still, Saigon accommodates them all. This is the industrial and commercial heart of Vietnam, accounting for 30% of the country's manufacturing output and 25% of its retail trade. Incomes here are three times the national average. It is to Saigon that the vast majority of foreign business people come to invest and trade. It is to Saigon that ambitious young people and bureaucrats – from the north and south – gravitate to make a go of it.

Explosive growth is making its mark in new high-rise buildings, joint-venture hotels and colourful shops. The downside is the sharp increase in traffic, pollution and other urban ills. Yet the past shines through. Saigon's neoclassical and international-style buildings (and nearby sidewalk kiosks selling French rolls and croissants) give certain neighbourhoods a vaguely French atmosphere.

The Americans left their mark on the city too, at least in the form of some heavily fortified apartment blocks and government buildings. The former US embassy is a classic example of tropical, post-modern, mortar-proof architecture. The occasional balcony protected with iron bars or lined with barbed wire and broken glass make you wonder if the war is still on. Of course, there is a war going on, a war against crime. With so much poverty surrounding so much plenty, it's not hard to understand why.

While their rural compatriots are working from dawn to dusk in the country's rice paddies, Saigon's residents are working just as hard at the pursuits of urban people: selling vegetables, buying necessities, cutting business deals and commuting. The city hums and buzzes with commerce. All around you is living evidence of the tenacious will of human beings to survive and improve their lot. There is something reassuring about it and perhaps something frightening too. It is here that the economic changes sweeping Vietnam – and their negative social implications – are most evident.

## History

Saigon was captured by the French in 1859, becoming the capital of the French colony of Cochinchina a few years later. In 1950, Norman Lewis described Saigon as follows: 'its inspiration has been purely commercial and it is therefore without folly, fervour or much ostentation … a pleasant, colourless and characterless French provincial city'. The city served as the capital of the Republic of Vietnam from 1956 until 1975, when it fell to advancing North Vietnamese forces.

Cholon rose to prominence after Chinese merchants began settling there in 1778. Though Cholon still constitutes the largest ethnic-Chinese community in Vietnam, hundreds of thousands of Cholonese have

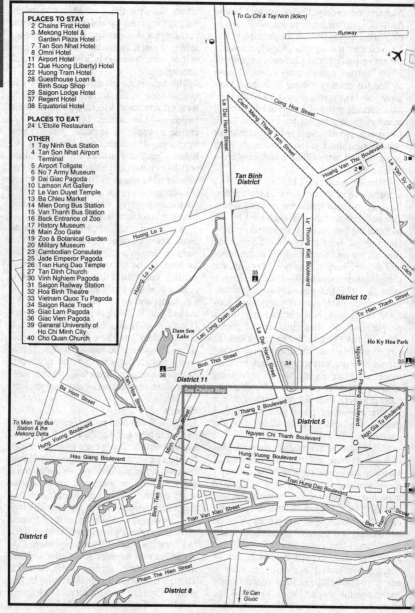

**PLACES TO STAY**
2   Chains First Hotel
3   Mekong Hotel &
     Garden Plaza Hotel
7   Tan Son Nhat Hotel
8   Omni Hotel
11  Airport Hotel
21  Que Huong (Liberty) Hotel
22  Huong Tram Hotel
28  Guesthouse Loan &
     Binh Soup Shop
29  Saigon Lodge Hotel
37  Regent Hotel
38  Equatorial Hotel

**PLACES TO EAT**
24  L'Etoile Restaurant

**OTHER**
1   Tay Ninh Bus Station
4   Tan Son Nhat Airport
     Terminal
5   Airport Tollgate
6   No 7 Army Museum
9   Dai Giac Pagoda
10  Lamson Art Gallery
12  Le Van Duyet Temple
13  Ba Chieu Market
14  Mien Dong Bus Station
15  Van Thanh Bus Station
16  Back Entrance of Zoo
17  History Museum
18  Main Zoo Gate
19  Zoo & Botanical Garden
20  Military Museum
23  Cambodian Consulate
25  Jade Emperor Pagoda
26  Tran Hung Dao Temple
27  Tan Dinh Church
30  Vinh Nghiem Pagoda
31  Saigon Railway Station
32  Hoa Binh Theatre
33  Vietnam Quoc Tu Pagoda
34  Saigon Race Track
35  Giac Lam Pagoda
36  Giac Vien Pagoda
39  General University of
     Ho Chi Minh City
40  Cho Quan Church

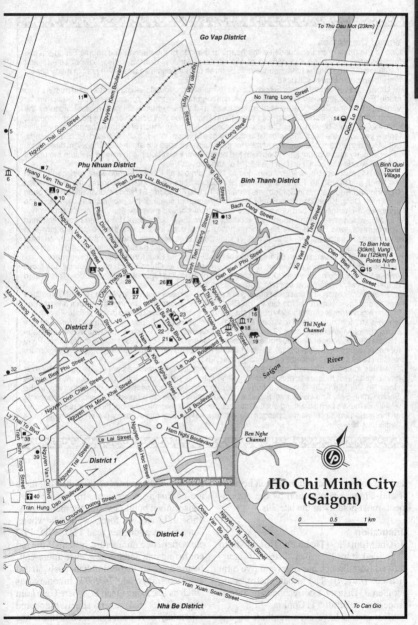

Ho Chi Minh City (Saigon)

0    0.5    1 km

## War of the Names

One of the primary battlegrounds for the hearts and minds of the Vietnamese people during the last four decades has been the naming of Vietnam's provinces, districts, cities, towns, streets and institutions. Some places have been known by three or more names since WWII and, in many cases, more than one name is still used.

Urban locations have borne: French names (often of the generals, administrators and martyrs who made French colonialism possible); names commemorating the historical personages chosen for veneration by the South Vietnamese government; and the alternative set of heroes selected by the Hanoi government. Buddhist pagodas have formal names as well as one or more popular monikers. Chinese pagodas bear various Chinese appellations – most of which also have Vietnamese equivalents – based on the titles and celestial ranks of those to whom they are consecrated. In the highlands, both Montagnard and Vietnamese names for mountains, villages etc are in use. The slight differences in vocabulary and pronunciation between the north, centre and south sometimes result in the use of different words and spellings (such as 'Pleiku' and 'Playcu').

When French control of Vietnam ended in 1954, almost all French names were replaced in both the North and the South. For example, Cap St Jacques became Vung Tau, Tourane was rechristened Danang and Rue Catinat in Saigon was renamed Tu Do (Freedom) St (since reunification it has been known as Dong Khoi (Uprising) St). In 1956, the names of some of the provinces and towns in the south were changed as part of an effort to erase from popular memory the Viet Minh's anti-French exploits, which were often known by the places where they took place. The village-based southern Communists, who by this time had gone underground, continued to use the old designations and boundaries in running their regional, district and village organisations. The peasants quickly adapted to this situation, using one set of names for where they lived when dealing with the Communists and a different set of names when talking to representatives of the South Vietnamese government.

Later, the US soldiers in Vietnam gave nicknames (such as China Beach near Danang) to places whose Vietnamese names they found inconvenient or difficult to remember or pronounce. This helped to make a very foreign land seem to them a bit more familiar.

After reunification, the first order of Saigon's provisional municipal Military Management Committee was to change the name of the city to 'Ho Chi Minh City', a decision confirmed in Hanoi a year later. The new government immediately began changing street names considered inappropriate – a process which is still continuing – and renamed almost all the city's hotels, dropping English and French names in favour of Vietnamese ones. The only French names still in use are those of Albert Calmette (1893-1934; developer of a tuberculosis vaccine), Marie Curie (1867-1934; she won the Nobel Prize for her research into radioactivity), Louis Pasteur (1822-95; chemist and bacteriologist) and Alexandre Yersin (1863-1943; discoverer of the plague bacillus).

All this renaming has had mixed results. Streets, districts and provinces are usually known by their new names. But most residents of Ho Chi Minh City still prefer to call the place Saigon, especially since Ho Chi Minh City is in fact a huge area that stretches from near Cambodia all the way to the South China Sea. And visitors will find that the old names of the city's hotels are making a comeback.

All this makes using anything but the latest street maps a risky proposition, though fortunately most of the important street-name changes were made before any of the maps currently on sale were published. ■

fled the country since reunification because of anti-Chinese persecution by the government, most notably in the late 70s.

## Orientation

Ho Chi Minh City (Thanh Pho Ho Chi Minh) is divided into 17 urban districts (*quan*, derived from French *quartier*) and five rural districts (*huyen*). The urban districts are numbered. District 1 corresponds to Saigon proper and District 5 is Cholon.

Most streets have even numbers on one side and odd numbers on the other, but there are confusing exceptions. In some places, consecutive buildings are numbered 15A, 15B, 15C and so forth, while elsewhere, consecutive addresses read 15D, 17D, 19D etc. Often, two numbering systems – the old confusing one and the new, even-more-confusing one – are in use simultaneously, so that an address may read '1743/697'. In some cases (such as Lac Long Quan St, where Giac Lam Pagoda is located) several streets, numbered separately, have been run together under one name so that as you walk along, the numbers go from one into the hundreds (or thousands) and then start over again.

Another oddity found in Saigon and other Vietnamese cities are streets named after momentous historical dates. For example, 3 Thang 2 Blvd (usually written 3/2 Blvd) refers to 3 February, the anniversary of the founding of the Vietnamese Communist Party.

The Vietnamese post office is comfortable with the English words and abbreviations Street (St), Road (Rd) and Boulevard (Blvd), but of course this is not what you'll see on street signs around Saigon. As in English, the Vietnamese have several words for their streets: Dai Lo (DL), Duong (D) and Pho (P). In Vietnamese, the word 'street' comes before the name, so Le Duan Blvd becomes Dai Lo Le Duan (or abbreviated DL Le Duan).

## Information

**Travel Agencies** Saigon Tourist (Cong Ty Du Lich Thanh Pho Ho Chi Minh) is Ho Chi Minh City's official government-run travel agency. Saigon Tourist owns, or is a joint-venture partner in, over 70 hotels and numerous high-class restaurants around town, plus a car-rental agency and tourist traps like the Vietnam Golf & Country Club, the Chu Chi tunnel site and Binh Quoi Tourist Village, to name a few.

The way Saigon Tourist became so big is simple: the hotels and restaurants were 'liberated' from their former capitalist (mostly ethnic-Chinese) owners after 1975, most of whom subsequently fled the country. The upper-level management of this state company is entirely former Viet Cong (no kidding) and their attitude towards foreigners is still decidedly cool. To be fair, Saigon Tourist has in the past few years been wisely investing much of the profits back into new hotels and restaurants. The company keeps growing bigger – if Vietnam ever establishes a stock market, Saigon Tourist shares will be blue chip.

Vietnam Tourism is the national government's tourist agency and is open from 7.30 to 11.30 am and 1 to 4.30 pm Monday to Saturday. The senior staff of Vietnam Tourism seem to have a slightly better attitude than

that at Saigon Tourist, but both agencies do their best to overcharge for their mediocre service.

There are plenty of other travel agencies in Saigon, virtually all of them joint ventures between government agencies and private companies (it's very difficult for private companies to get a travel agent's licence). These places can provide cars, book air tickets and extend your visa. Some of these places charge the same as Saigon Tourist and Vietnam Tourism, while others are much cheaper. Competition between the private agencies is keen – the price war has turned into a price blood bath and you can often undercut Saigon Tourist's tariffs by 50% if you shop around.

From personal experience, we can recommend several private agencies including Kim Cafe, Ann Tours, Lotus Cafe and Linh's Cafe. Two government-run agencies, Fiditourist and Ben Thanh Tourist (the Pham Ngu Lao branches only), are OK for day trips (Cu Chi, Mytho etc), but not as good for longer trips.

You'll note that enormously successful Sinh Cafe does *not* get a recommendation in this book. The reason is because of the way they treat the staff – employee morale is very bad, which is not surprising since they are forced to work 10 to 16 hours per day, 365 days a year, for stingy pay but plentiful verbal abuse from the management. This place has business because it looks slick and it's cheap. Let your conscience be your guide.

A line-up of some local travel agencies follows. This list is by no means complete nor do we claim that all these agencies are good, so use it as a starting point:

Ann Tours
   58 Ton That Tung St, District 1 (☎ 833-2564; fax 832-3866)
Ben Thanh Tourist
   121 Nguyen Hue Blvd, District 1 (☎ 829-8597; fax 829-6269)
Cholon Tourist
   192-194 Su Van Hanh St, District 5 (☎ 835-9090; fax 835-5375)
Fiditourist
   195 Pham Ngu Lao St, District 1 (☎ 835-3018)
   71-73 Dong Khoi St, District 1 (☎ 829-6264)

Global Holidays
  106 Nguyen Hue Blvd, District 1 (☎ 822-8453; fax 822-8454)
Hung Vi Travel
  110A Nguyen Hue Blvd, District 1 (☎ 822-5111; fax 824-2405)
Kim Cafe, 270-272 De Tham St, District 1 (☎ 835-9859; fax 829-8540)
Linh Cafe, 291 Pham Ngu Lao St, District 1
Lotus Cafe, 197 Pham Ngu Lao St, District 1.
Mai Linh Co
  64 Hai Ba Trung Blvd, District 1 (☎ 825-8888; fax 822-4496)
Saigon Tourist
  49 Le Thanh Ton St, District 1 (☎ 829-8129; fax 822-4987)
Star Tours
  166 Nam Ky Khoi Nghia St, District 3 (☎ 824-4673; fax 824-4675)
Superb Travel
  110A Nguyen Hue Blvd, District 1 (☎ 822-5111; fax 824-2405)
Vietnam Tourism
  69-71 Nam Ky Khoi Nghia St, District 3 (☎ 829-1276; fax 829-0775)
Vyta Tours
  52 Hai Ba Trung Blvd, District 1 (☎ 823-0767; fax 824-3524)
Youth Tourist
  292 Dien Bien Phu St, District 3 (☎ 829-4580)

**Money** There is a bank at the airport which gives the official exchange rate. The only problem is that the staff works to bankers' hours, which means it's closed when at least half of the flights arrive! For this reason, you'd be wise to have sufficient US dollar notes in small denominations to get yourself into the city.

Vietcombank (☎ 829-7245; fax 823-0310), also known as the Bank for Foreign Trade of Vietnam, occupies two adjacent buildings at the intersection of Ben Chuong and Pasteur Sts. The east building is the one that does foreign exchange and it's worth a visit even if you don't change money – the ornate interior is absolutely stunning! It's open from 7 to 11.30 am and 1.30 to 3.30 pm daily except Saturday afternoons and the last day of the month. Besides US dollars, hard currencies which are currently acceptable (but this could change) include Australian dollars, British pounds sterling, Canadian dollars, Deutschmarks, French francs, Hong Kong dollars, Japanese yen, Singapore dollars, Swiss francs and Thai baht. Travellers cheques denominated in US dollars can be changed for US dollars cash for a 2% commission. Especially on Mondays after holidays (like Tet), this bank can be very crowded with long waits.

There is a smaller branch of Vietcombank at 175 Dong Khoi St, opposite the Continental Hotel.

Sacombank at 211 Nguyen Thai Hoc St (the corner with Pham Ngu Lao St) is a popular place to change cash and travellers cheques and to get advances on Visa cards. The bank is right in the centre of the budget travellers' zone.

Fiditourist, a private moneychanger, has a branch in budget travellers' land at 195 Pham Ngu Lao St. It provides cash transactions only – forget travellers cheques. The advantage of changing money here is the long hours – they stay open until 10 pm and work on weekends too.

There are several foreign-owned and joint-venture banks in Saigon, but the catch is that they are compelled by law to charge you higher commissions than Vietnam's state-owned banks. Mostly you'll want to visit these banks only to use their ATMs or do a telegraphic transfer. Some of the more notable foreign banks include:

ANZ Bank
  11 Me Linh Square, District 1 (☎ 829-9319; fax 829-9316)
Bangkok Bank
  117 Nguyen Hue Blvd, District 1 (☎ 822-3416; fax 822-3421)
Bank of America
  1 Phung Khac Khoan St, District 1 (☎ 829-9928, ext 155; fax 829-9942)
Banque Nationale de Paris
  2 Thi Sach St, District 1 (☎ 829-9504; fax 829-9486)
Crédit Lyonnais
  4th floor, 65 Nguyen Du St, District 1 (☎ 829-9226; fax 829-6465)
Deutsche Bank
  174 Nguyen Dinh Chieu St, District 3 (☎ 822-2747; fax 822-2760)
Hongkong Bank
  New World Hotel Annex, 75 Pham Hong Thai St, District 1 (☎ 829-2288; fax 823-0530)

All the major tourist hotels can change money quickly, easily, legally and well after business hours. The catch is that they offer rates around 5% lower than the bank rate.

The men who accost you on the street offering great exchange rates are con artists.

**Post & Communications** Saigon's French-style main post office (Buu Dien Thanh Pho Ho Chi Minh), with its glass canopy and iron frame, is at 2 Cong Xa Paris, right next to Notre Dame Cathedral. The structure was built between 1886 and 1891 and is by far the largest post office in Vietnam. Under the benevolent gaze of Ho Chi Minh, you will be charged exorbitant rates for whatever international telecommunications services you require. The staff at the information desk (☎ 829-6555, 829-9615), which is to the left as you enter the building, speak English. Postal services are available daily from 7.30 am to 7.30 pm. To your right as you enter the building is poste restante, which is curiously labelled 'Delivery of Mail – Mail to be Called For'. Pens, envelopes, aerograms, postcards and stamp collections are on sale at the counter to the right of the entrance and outside the post office along Nguyen Du St.

Faxes can be sent to you at the post office (fax 829-8540, 829-8546) and these will be delivered to your hotel for a small charge. In order for this to work, the fax should clearly indicate your name, hotel phone number and the address of the hotel (including your room number). The cost for receiving a fax is US$0.60.

At the post office don't get tricked into paying more than you should for your local calls. These cost US$0.07 only and not the US$1 the employee behind the desk may tell you (while shielding from view the notice that announces the real price – in Vietnamese only, but the figures are in dollars).

A number of private carriers operate from the post office, including DHL (☎ 823-1525; fax 844-5387), Federal Express (☎ 829-0747; fax 829-0477) and Airborne Express (☎ 829-4310, 829-4315; fax 829-2961). For rates, see the Post & Communications section in the Facts for the Visitor chapter.

Postal, telex, telegram and fax services are available at counters run by the post office at the Caravelle, Majestic, Palace and Rex hotels.

The District 1 post office (☎ 829-9086), which serves downtown Saigon, is on Le Loi Blvd near its intersection with Pasteur St.

**Bookshops** Tiem Sach Bookstore at 20 Ho Huan Nghiep St has a massive selection of mostly used English and French titles. The owner is an elderly ex-journalist. The shop is open daily from 8.30 am to 10 pm and also functions as an ice cream parlour.

Viet My Bookstore (☎ 822-9650) at 41 Dinh Tien Hoang St, District 1, is at the corner of Dinh Tien Hoang St and Le Duan Blvd (see the HCMC map). This place has a number of imported books and magazines published in English, French and Chinese.

Hieu Sach Xuan Thu (☎ 822-4670) at 185 Dong Khoi St, District 1, is the best of the government-run bookstores. You should at least manage to find a good dictionary or some maps here, as well as some more general books in English and French.

The best area to look for general map, book and stationery stuff is along the north side of Le Loi Blvd between the Rex Hotel and Nam Ky Khoi Nghia St (near the Kem Bach Dang ice cream parlours). There are many small privately run shops and one large government bookstore here.

Xunhasaba (☎ 823-0724; fax 824-1321), which is an acronym for State Enterprise for Export & Import of Books & Periodicals, has an outlet at 25B Nguyen Binh Khiem St, District 1.

**Photocopies** There are many photocopy shops around town, but none quite so good as Tao Dan Photocopy (☎ 824-3462) at 55B, 8 Nguyen Thi Minh Khai St, District 1. It's right on the north-western corner of Cong Vien Van Hoa Park. Aside from very low prices and good quality, you can have poster-sized copies made (size A0).

**Libraries** The address of the Municipal Library is 34 Ly Tu Trong St. Nearby at 69 Ly Tu Trong St is the General Sciences Library with a total of 500 seats in its reading rooms.

**Laundry** Almost every hotel does laundry and there is a self-service laundromat (☎ 843-6649) at 221 Tran Quang Khai St, District 1.

**Medical Services** The most advanced general medical facility is the Dien Bien Phu Hospital (☎ 829-9480) at 280 Dien Bien Phu St, District 3.

The Emergency Centre (☎ 829-2071) at 125 Le Loi Blvd, District 1, operates 24 hours. Doctors speak English and French.

The Pasteur Institute (☎ 823-0252) at 167 Pasteur St, District 3, has the best facilities in Vietnam for doing medical tests. However, you need to be referred here first by a doctor.

Cho Ray Hospital (Benh Vien Cho Ray; ☎ 855-4137, 855-4138, 855-8074) with 1000 beds is one of the largest medical facilities in Vietnam. It's at 201B Nguyen Chi Thanh Blvd, District 5 (Cholon), and there is a section for foreigners on the 10th floor. About a third of the 200 doctors speak English and there are 24-hour emergency facilities. The hospital was built in the 1970s before reunification and some of the equipment still dates from that period.

Binh Dan Hospital is said to have belonged to President Thieu during the days when he ruled South Vietnam. This hospital is still one of the best in Vietnam, but it's too far from the centre to be of much use to visitors. It's approximately 13km north-west from the centre in the Tan Binh District.

The Medical Consultancy Service (☎ 844-3441; fax 844-3442) at 243 Hoang Van Thu St, Tan Binh District, provides a 24-hour service seven days a week and has doctors who speak English, German, French, Italian and Dutch.

There is also the OSCAT/AEA International Clinic (☎ 829-8520; 829-8551) at 65 Nguyen Du St, District 1. Aside from general medical practice, this place also offers dental care.

There are several foreign doctors who are resident in Saigon. Dr Philippe Guillaume (☎ 829-4386; fax 824-2862) is a French-speaking doctor at 151 Vo Thi Sau St, District 3. You can contact Dr F Boudey at the Heart Institute (☎ 865-4025), 520 Nguyen Tri Phuong St, District 10.

Asia Emergency Assistance (☎ 829-8520; fax 829-8551), Hannam Office Building, 65 Nguyen Du St, District 1, has a medical services programme for resident expats. The payment of an annual fee buys you regular treatment, emergency medical care and evacuation 24 hours a day. You can also contact International SOS Assistance (☎ 829-4386; fax 824-2862) for information about their health plan and evacuation services.

Dental care in Vietnam is cheap enough (US$20 for a root canal!). The dentists may not have state-of-the-art technology, but most are knowledgeable.

Dr Tran Ngoc Dinh (☎ 832-4598, 839-9463) at 355 Nguyen Trai St, District 1, speaks English; ditto for Dr Do Dinh Hung (☎ 864-0587, 890-4605) at 187 Cach Mang Thang Tam St, Ward 7, Tan Binh District. You can try the Orthodontology Centre (☎ 835-7595) at 263 Tran Hung Dao Blvd, District 1. You'll have to decide yourself what you think of the service at the HCMC Dentistry Academy, 201A Nguyen Chi Thanh Blvd, District 5 (near Cho Ray Hospital).

Pharmacies are everywhere – some good, but many not. One good one is at 678 Nguyen Dinh Chieu St, District 3. The owner there speaks excellent English and French and can even get unusual medicines not normally kept in stock (he makes a phone call and someone delivers the medicines by motorbike within a couple of hours).

**Visa Extensions** For what it's worth, the Immigration Police Office (Phong Quan Ly Nguoi Nuoc Ngoai; ☎ 839-2221) is at 254 Nguyen Trai St. It's open from 8 to 11 am and 1 to 4 pm. Most likely, you will be turned away and told to use the services of a private agency. Hotels, cafes and travel agencies can arrange visa extensions.

**Useful Organisations** The Saigon branch of the Chamber of Commerce & Industry of Vietnam (Chi Nhanh Phong Thuong Mai Va Cng Nghiep, or Vietcochamber (☎ 823-0331, 823-0339; fax 829-4472) is at 171 Vo Thi Sau St, District 3.

IMC (Investment & Management Consulting Corporation; ☎ 829-9062) offers various business services to investors and businesspeople. The External Affairs Office of the Foreign Ministry (So Ngoai Vu; ☎ 822-3032, 822-4311) is at 6 Thai Van Lung St, District 1.

## Places of Worship – Ho Chi Minh City
The following places of worship are on the Ho Chi Minh City (Saigon) map.

**Giac Lam Pagoda** Giac Lam Pagoda dates from 1744 and is believed to be the oldest pagoda in greater Ho Chi Minh City. Because the last reconstruction here was in 1900, the architecture, layout and ornamentation remain almost unaltered by the modernist renovations that have transformed so many other religious structures in Vietnam. Ten monks live at this Vietnamese Buddhist pagoda, which also incorporates aspects of Taoism and Confucianism. It is well worth the trip out here from downtown Saigon.

To the right of the gate to the pagoda compound are the ornate tombs of venerated monks. The *bo de* (bodhi, or pipal) tree in the front garden was the gift of a monk from Sri Lanka. Next to the tree is a regular feature of Vietnamese Buddhist temples, a gleaming white statue of Quan Am (Guanyin in Chinese, the Goddess of Mercy) standing on a lotus blossom – a symbol of purity.

The roof-line of the main building is decorated both inside and outside with unusual blue-and-white porcelain plates. Through the main entrance is a reception hall lined with funeral tablets and photos of the deceased. Roughly in the centre of the hall, near an old French chandelier, is a figure of 18-armed Chuan De, another form of the Goddess of Mercy. Note the carved hardwood columns which bear gilded Vietnam-

ese inscriptions written in *nom* characters, a form of writing in use before the adoption of the Latin-based *quoc ngu* alphabet. The wall to the left is covered with portraits of great monks from previous generations. Monks' names and biographical information are recorded on the vertical red tablets in gold nom characters. A box for donations sits nearby. Shoes should be removed when passing from the rough red floor tiles to the smaller, white-black-grey tiles.

On the other side of the wall from the monks' funeral tablets is the main sanctuary, which is filled with countless gilded figures. On the dais in the centre of the back row sits A Di Da (pronounced 'AH-zee-dah'), the Buddha of the Past (Amitabha). To his right is Kasyape and to his left Anand; both are disciples of the Thich Ca Buddha (the historical Buddha Sakyamuni, whose real name was Siddhartha Gautama). Directly in front of A Di Da is a statue of the Thich Ca Buddha, flanked by two guardians. In front of Thich Ca is the tiny figure of the Thich Ca Buddha as a child. As always, he is clothed in a yellow robe.

The fat laughing fellow, seated with five children climbing all over him, is Ameda. To his left is Ngoc Hoang, the Taoist Jade Emperor, who presides over a world of innumerable supernatural beings. In the front row is a statue of the Thich Ca Buddha with two Bodhisattvas on each side. On the altars along the side walls of the sanctuary are various Bodhisattvas and the Judges of the 10 Regions of Hell. Each of the judges is holding a scroll resembling the handle of a fork.

The red and gold Christmas-tree-shaped object is a wooden altar bearing 49 lamps and 49 miniature statues of Bodhisattvas. People pray for sick relatives or ask for happiness by contributing kerosene for use in the lamps. Petitioners' names and those of ill family members are written on slips of paper which are attached to the branches of the 'tree'.

The frame of the large bronze bell in the corner looks like a university bulletin board because petitioners have attached to it lists

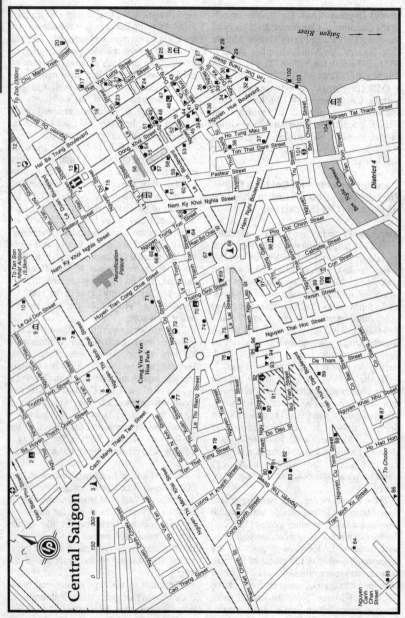

Central Saigon

## PLACES TO STAY
- 5 Saigon Star Hotel
- 6 Bao Yen Hotel
- 7 Sol Chancery Hotel
- 8 International Hotel
- 10 Victory Hotel
- 22 Orchid Hotel
- 30 Riverside Hotel
- 32 Majestic Hotel & Maxim's Restaurant
- 33 Dong Khoi Hotel
- 36 Saigon Prince Hotel
- 39 Palace Hotel
- 42 Saigon Hotel & Cafe Latin
- 44 Bong Sen Hotel & Mondial Hotel
- 45 Century Saigon Hotel
- 48 Caravelle Hotel
- 51 Continental Hotel
- 53 Kimdo Hotel
- 58 Rex Hotel
- 61 Norfolk Hotel
- 64 Tan Loc Hotel
- 65 Embassy Hotel
- 66 Tao Dan Hotel
- 73 Hoang Gia Hotel
- 75 New World Hotel
- 76 Palace Saigon Hotel
- 77 Rang Dong Hotel
- 79 Hoang Yen Mini-Hotel
- 81 My Man Mini-Hotel
- 82 Tuan Anh Hotel
- 83 Guesthouse 127
- 87 Miss Loi's Guesthouse
- 88 Metropole Hotel
- 89 Windsor Saigon Hotel
- 90 Vien Dong Hotel
- 91 Guest Houses
- 95 Giant Dragon Hotel

## PLACES TO EAT
- 15 Annie's Pizza & AEA Clinic
- 16 Bo Tung Xeo Restaurant
- 17 Sapa Bar & Restaurant
- 18 Tex Mex Cantina
- 19 Ashoka Indian Restaurant & Buffalo Blues
- 21 Mogambo's Café
- 24 Kem Bach Dang (ice cream)
- 28 Floating Restaurants
- 31 Palome Café
- 34 Montana Café
- 40 Vietnam House
- 41 Liberty Restaurant
- 47 Indian Restaurant
- 52 Lemon Grass & Augustin
- 59 Kem Bach Dang (ice cream)
- 60 Kem Bach Dang (ice cream)
- 69 Bavaria Restaurant
- 86 Saigon Food Centre
- 93 Kim Café
- 94 Cay Bo De Vegetarian Restaurant
- 97 Tin Nghia Vegetarian Restaurant

## OTHER
- 1 Dien Bien Phu Hospital
- 2 Xa Loi Pagoda
- 3 Thich Quang Duc Memorial
- 4 Tao Dan Photocopy
- 9 War Remnants Museum
- 11 French Consulate
- 12 Former US Embassy (1967-75)
- 13 Main Post Office
- 14 Notre Dame Cathedral
- 20 Chi Chi's Bar
- 23 Gecko Bar
- 25 Apocalypse Now
- 26 Ton Duc Thang Museum & The Landmark
- 27 Me Linh Square & Tran Hung Dao Statue
- 29 Small Boats for Hire
- 35 Tiem Sach Thu Bookstore
- 37 The Old Market
- 38 Huynh Thuc Khang Street Market
- 43 Hien & Bob's Place & Wild West
- 46 Saigon Central Mosque
- 49 Municipal Theatre
- 50 Q Bar
- 54 Saigon Tourist
- 55 Vietnam Airlines
- 56 People's Committee (Hôtel de Ville)
- 57 Phnom Penh Bus Garage
- 62 Revolutionary Museum
- 63 Saigon Intershop & Minimart
- 67 Ben Thanh Market
- 68 Tran Nguyen Hai Statue
- 70 Mariamman Hindu Temple
- 71 Conservatory of Music
- 72 Bus Stop (to Cambodia)
- 74 Bicycle Shops
- 78 Ann Tours
- 80 Thai Binh Market
- 84 Immigration Police Office
- 85 Dr Vannoort's Clinic
- 92 Fiditourist
- 96 Sacombank
- 98 Art Museum
- 99 Dan Sinh Market
- 100 Phung Son Tu Pagoda
- 101 Vietcombank
- 102 Hammock Bar
- 103 Ferries across Saigon River & to Mekong Delta
- 104 Vung Tau Hydrofoil
- 105 Ho Chi Minh Museum

of names: the names of people seeking happiness and the names of the sick and the dead, placed there by their relatives. It is believed that when the bell is rung, the sound will resonate to the heavens above and the underground heavens below, carrying with it the attached supplications.

Prayers here consist of chanting to the accompaniment of drums, bells and gongs and follow a traditional rite seldom performed these days. Prayers are held daily from 4 to 5 am, 11 am to noon, 4 to 5 pm and 7 to 9 pm.

Giac Lam Pagoda is about 3km from Cholon at 118 Lac Long Quan St in Tan Binh District. Beware: the numbering on Lac Long Quan St is extremely confusing, starting over from one several times and at one point jumping to four digits. In many places, odd and even numbers are on the same side of the street.

The best way to get to Giac Lam Pagoda from Cholon is to take Nguyen Chi Thanh Blvd or 3/2 Blvd to Le Dai Hanh St. Go north-westward on Le Dai Hanh St and turn right onto Lac Long Quan St. Walk 100m and the pagoda gate will be on your left. It is open to visitors from 6 am to 9 pm.

**Giac Vien Pagoda** Giac Vien Pagoda is architecturally similar to the Giac Lam Pagoda. Both pagodas share the same atmosphere of scholarly serenity, though Giac Vien, which is right next to Dam Sen Lake in District 11, is in a more rural setting. Giac Vien Pagoda was founded by Hai Tinh Giac Vien about 200 years ago. It is said that the Emperor Gia Long, who died in 1819, used to worship at Giac Vien. Today, 10 monks live at the pagoda.

The pagoda is in a relatively poor part of the city. Because of the impossibly confusing numbering on Lac Long Quan St, the best way to get to Giac Vien Pagoda from Cholon is to take Nguyen Chi Thanh Blvd or 3/2 Blvd to Le Dai Hanh St. Turn left (southwest) off Le Dai Han St on to Binh Thoi St and turn right (north) at Lac Long Quan St. The gate leading to the pagoda is at 247 Lac Long Quan St. From Lac Long Quan St there are signs pointing the way to the pagoda.

Pass through the gate and go several hundred metres down a potholed, dirt road, turning left at the 'tee' and right at the fork. You will pass several impressive tombs of monks on the right before arriving at the pagoda itself. Giac Vien Pagoda is open from 7 am to 7 pm, but come before dark as the electricity is often out.

As you enter the pagoda, the first chamber is lined with funeral tablets. At the back of the second chamber is a statue of the pagoda's founder, Hai Tinh Giac Vien, holding a horse-tail swatch. Nearby portraits are of his disciples and successors as head monk. A donation box sits to the left of the statue. Opposite Hai Tinh Giac Vien is a representation of 18-armed Chuan De, a form of the Goddess of Mercy, who is flanked by two guardians.

The main sanctuary is on the other side of the wall behind Hai Tinh Giac Vien. A Di Da, the Buddha of the Past, is at the back of the dais. Directly in front of him is the Thich Ca Buddha (Sakyamuni), flanked by Thich Ca's disciples Anand (on the left) and Kasyape (on the right). To the right of Kasyape is the Ti Lu Buddha; to the left of Anand is the Nhien Dang Buddha. At the foot of the Thich Ca Buddha is a small figure of Thich Ca (Siddhartha Gautama) as a child. Fat, laughing Ameda is seated with children climbing all over him; far on either side of him are guardians, standing. In the front row of the dais is Thich Ca with two Bodhisattvas on each side.

In front of the dais is a fantastic brass incense basin with fierce dragon heads emerging from each side. On the altar to the left of the dais is Dai The Chi Bo Tat; on the altar to the right is Quan The Am Bo Tat (Avalokiteçvara), the Goddess of Mercy. The Guardian of the Pagoda is against the wall opposite the dais. Nearby is a 'Christmas tree' similar to the one in Giac Lam Pagoda. Lining the side walls are the Judges of the 10 Regions of Hell (holding scrolls) and 18 Bodhisattvas.

Prayers are held daily from 4 to 5 am, 8 to 10 am, 2 to 3 pm, 4 to 5 pm and 7 to 9 pm.

**Jade Emperor Pagoda** The Jade Emperor Pagoda (known in Vietnamese as Phuoc Hai Tu and Chua Ngoc Hoang), built in 1909 by the Cantonese (Quang Dong) congregation, is truly a gem of a Chinese temple. It is one of the most spectacularly colourful pagodas in Saigon, filled with statues of phantasmal divinities and grotesque heroes. The pungent smoke of burning joss sticks fills the air, obscuring exquisite wood carvings decorated with gilded Chinese characters. The roof is covered with elaborate tilework. The statues, which represent characters from both the Buddhist and Taoist traditions, are made of reinforced papier mâché.

The Jade Emperor Pagoda is at 73 Mai Thi Luu St in a part of the city known as Da Kao (or Da Cao). To get there, go to 20 Dien Bien Phu St and walk half a block north-westward (to the left as you head out of Saigon towards Thi Nghe Channel).

As you enter the main doors of the building, Mon Quan, the God of the Gate, stands to the right in an elaborately carved wooden case. Opposite him, in a similar case, is Tho Than (Tho Dia), the God of the Land. Straight on is an altar on which are placed, from left to right, figures of: Phat Mau Chuan De, mother of the five Buddhas of the cardinal directions; Dia Tang Vuong Bo Tat (Ksitigartha), the King of Hell; the Di Lac Buddha (Maitreya), the Buddha of the Future; Quan The Am Bo Tat, the Goddess of Mercy; and a bas-relief portrait of the Thich Ca Buddha (Sakyamuni). Behind the altar, in a glass case, is the Duoc Su Buddha, also known as the Nhu Lai Buddha. The figure is said to be made of sandalwood.

To either side of the altar, against the walls, are two especially fierce and menacing figures. On the right (as you face the altar) is a 4m-high statue of the general who defeated the Green Dragon. He is stepping on the vanquished dragon. On the left is the general who defeated the White Tiger, which is also getting stepped on.

The Taoist Jade Emperor, Ngoc Hoang, presides over the main sanctuary, draped in luxurious robes. He is flanked by the 'Four Big Diamonds' (Tu Dai Kim Cuong), his four guardians, so named because they are said to be as hard as diamonds. In front of the Jade Emperor stand six figures, three to each side. On the left is Bac Dau, the Taoist God of the Northern Polar Star and God of Longevity, flanked by his two guardians; and on the right is Nam Tao, the Taoist God of the Southern Polar Star and God of Happiness, also flanked by two guardians.

In the case to the right of the Jade Emperor is 18-armed Phat Mau Chuan De, mother of the five Buddhas of the north, south, east, west and centre. Two faces, affixed to her head behind each ear, look to either side. On the wall to the right of Phat Mau Chuan De, at a height of about 4m, is Dai Minh Vuong Quang, who was reincarnated as Sakyamuni,

riding on the back of a phoenix. Below are the Tien Nhan, literally the 'god-persons'.

In the case to the left of the Jade Emperor sits Ong Bac De, a reincarnation of the Jade Emperor, holding a sword. One of his feet is resting on a turtle while the other rests on a snake. On the wall to the left of Ong Bac De, about 4m off the ground, is Thien Loi, the God of Lightning, who slays evil people. Below Thien Loi are the military commanders of Ong Bac De (on the lower step) and Thien Loi's guardians (on the upper step). At the top of the two carved pillars that separate the three alcoves are the Goddess of the Moon (on the left) and the God of the Sun (on the right).

Out the door on the left-hand side of the Jade Emperor's chamber is another room. The semi-enclosed area to the right (as you enter) is presided over by Thanh Hoang, the Chief of Hell; to the left is his red horse. Of the six figures lining the walls, the two closest to Thanh Hoang are Am Quan, the God of Yin (on the left), and Duong Quan, the God of Yang (on the right). The other four figures, the Thuong Thien Phat Ac, are gods who dispense punishments for evil acts and rewards for good deeds. Thanh Hoang faces in the direction of the famous Hall of the 10 Hells. The carved wooden panels lining the walls graphically depict the varied torments awaiting evil people in each of the 10 regions of hell. At the top of each panel is one of the Judges of the 10 Regions of Hell examining a book in which the deeds of the deceased are inscribed.

On the wall opposite Thanh Hoang is a bas-relief wood panel depicting Quan Am Thi Kinh, the Guardian Spirit of Mother and Child, standing on a lotus blossom – a symbol of purity. Unjustly turned out of her home by her husband, Quan Am Thi Kinh disguised herself as a monk and went to live in a pagoda, where a young woman accused her of fathering her child. She accepted the blame – and the responsibility that went along with it – and again found herself out on the streets, this time with her 'son'. Much later, about to die, she returned to the monastery to confess her secret. When the emperor of China heard of her story, he declared her the Guardian Spirit of Mother and Child.

It is believed that she has the power to bestow male offspring on those who fervently believe in her. On the panel, Quan Am Thi Kinh is shown holding her 'son'. To her left is Long Nu, a very young Buddha who is her protector. To Quan Am Thi Kinh's right is Thien Tai, her guardian spirit, who knew the real story all along. Above her left shoulder is a bird bearing prayer beads.

To the right of the panel of Quan Am Thi Kinh is a panel depicting Dia Tang Vuong Bo Tat, the King of Hell.

On the other side of the wall is a fascinating little room in which the ceramic figures of 12 women, overrun with children and wearing colourful clothes, sit in two rows of six. Each of the women exemplifies a human characteristic, either good or bad (as in the case of the woman drinking alcohol from a jug). Each figure represents one year in the 12-year Chinese calendar. Presiding over the room is Kim Hoa Thanh Mau, the Chief of All Women.

To the right of the main chamber, stairs lead up to a 2nd floor sanctuary and balcony.

**Dai Giac Pagoda** This Vietnamese Buddhist pagoda is built in a style characteristic of pagodas constructed during the 1960s. In the courtyard, under the unfinished 10-level, red-pink tower inlaid with porcelain shards, is an artificial cave made of volcanic rocks in which there is a gilded statue of the Goddess of Mercy. In the main sanctuary, the 2.5m gilt Buddha has a green neon halo, while below, a smaller white reclining Buddha (in a glass case) has a blue neon halo. Dai Giac Pagoda is at 112 Nguyen Van Troi St, 1.5km towards the city centre from the gate to the airport.

**Vinh Nghiem Pagoda** Vinh Nghiem Pagoda, inaugurated in 1971, is noteworthy for its vast sanctuary and eight-storey tower, each level of which contains a statue of the Buddha. It was built with help from the Japan-Vietnam Friendship Association,

which explains the presence of Japanese elements in its architecture. At the base of the tower (which is open only on holidays) is a store selling Buddhist ritual objects. Behind the sanctuary is a three-storey tower which serves as a repository for carefully labelled ceramic urns containing the ashes of people who have been cremated. The pagoda is just off Nguyen Van Troi St in District 3 and is open from 7.30 to 11.30 am and 2 to 6 pm daily.

**Le Van Duyet Temple** This temple is dedicated to Marshal Le Van Duyet (pronounced 'Zyet'), who is buried here with his wife. The marshal, who lived from 1763 to 1831, was a southern Vietnamese general and viceroy who helped put down the Tay Son Rebellion and reunify Vietnam. When the Nguyen Dynasty came to power in 1802, he was elevated by Emperor Gia Long to the rank of marshal. Le Van Duyet fell into disfavour with Gia Long's successor, Minh Mang, who tried him posthumously and desecrated his grave. Emperor Thieu Tri, who succeeded Minh Mang, restored the tomb, fulfilling a prophesy of its destruction and restoration. Le Van Duyet was considered a great national hero in the South before 1975, but is disliked by the Communists because of his involvement in the expansion of French influence.

Le Van Duyet Temple is 3km from the centre of Saigon in the Gia Dinh area at 131 Dinh Tien Hoang St (near where Phan Dang Luu Blvd becomes Bach Dang St).

The temple itself was renovated in 1937 and has a distinctly modern feel to it. Since 1975, the government has done little to keep it from becoming dilapidated. Among the items on display are a portrait of Le Van Duyet, some of his personal effects (including European-style crystal goblets) and other antiques. There are two wonderful life-size horses on either side of the entrance to the third and last chamber, which is kept locked.

During celebrations of Tet and the 30th day of the 7th lunar month (anniversary of Le Van Duyet's death), the tomb is thronged with pilgrims. Vietnamese used to come here to take oaths of good faith if they could not afford the services of a court of justice. The tropical fish are on sale to visitors. The caged birds are bought by pilgrims and freed to earn merit. The birds are often recaptured (and liberated again).

**Tran Hung Dao Temple** This small temple is dedicated to Tran Hung Dao, a Vietnamese national hero who in 1287 vanquished an invasion force, said to have numbered 300,000 men, which had been dispatched by the Mongol emperor Kublai Khan. The temple is at 36 Vo Thi Sau St, a block northeast of the telecommunications dishes that are between Dien Bien Phu St and Vo Thi Sau St.

The public park between the antenna dishes and Hai Ba Trung Blvd was built in 1983 on the site of the Massiges Cemetery, burial place of French soldiers and settlers. The remains of French military personnel were exhumed and repatriated to France. Another site no longer in existence is the tomb of the 18th-century French missionary and diplomat Pigneau de Béhaine, Bishop of Adran, which was completely destroyed after reunification.

The temple is open every weekday from 6 to 11 am and 2 to 6 pm.

**Cho Quan Church** Cho Quan Church, built by the French about 100 years ago, is one of the largest churches in Saigon. This is the only church we've seen in the city where the figure of Jesus on the altar has a neon halo. The view from the belfry is worth the steep climb. The church is at 133 Tran Binh Trong St (between Tran Hung Dao Blvd and Nguyen Trai St) and is open daily from 4 to 7 am and 3 to 6 pm and Sundays from 4 to 9 am and 1.30 to 6 pm. Sunday masses are held in the morning at 5, 6.30 and 8.30 am, and also in the afternoon at 4.30 and 6 pm.

**Places of Worship – Central Saigon**
The following places are on the Central Saigon map.

**Notre Dame Cathedral** Notre Dame Cathedral, built between 1877 and 1883, is set in the heart of Saigon's government quarter. The cathedral faces down Dong Khoi St. Its neo-Romanesque form and two 40m-high square towers, tipped with iron spires, dominate the city's skyline. In front of the cathedral (in the centre of the square bounded by the main post office) is a statue of the Virgin Mary. If the front gates are locked try the door on the side of the building that faces Reunification Palace.

Unusually, this cathedral has no stained glass windows. The glass was a casualty of fighting during WWII. A number of foreign travellers worship here and the priests are allowed to add a short sermon in French or English to their longer presentations in Vietnamese. The 9.30 am Sunday Mass might be the best one for foreigners to attend.

There are several other interesting French-era churches around Saigon, including one at 289 Hai Ba Trung Blvd.

**Xa Loi Pagoda** Xa Loi Vietnamese Buddhist Pagoda, built in 1956, is famed as the repository of a sacred relic of the Buddha. In August 1963, truckloads of armed men under the command of President Ngo Dinh Diem's brother, Ngo Dinh Nhu, attacked Xa Loi Pagoda, which had become a centre of opposition to the Diem government. The pagoda was ransacked and 400 monks and nuns, including the country's 80-year-old Buddhist patriarch, were arrested. This raid and others elsewhere helped solidify opposition among Buddhists to the Diem regime, a crucial factor in the US decision to support the coup against Diem. This pagoda was also the site of several self-immolations by monks protesting against the Diem regime and the war.

Women enter the main hall of Xa Loi Pagoda by the staircase on the right as you come in the gate; men use the stairs on the left. The walls of the sanctuary are adorned with paintings depicting the Buddha's life.

Xa Loi Pagoda is in District 3 at 89 Ba Huyen Thanh Quan St, near Dien Bien Phu St. It is open daily from 7 to 11 am and from 2 to 5 pm. A monk preaches every Sunday morning from 8 to 10 am. On days of the full

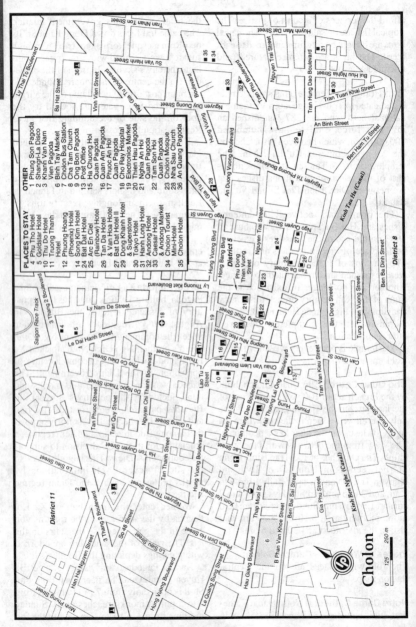

PLACES TO STAY
4    Phu Tho Hotel
5    Goldstar Hotel
10   Thu Do Hotel
11   Truong Thanh Hotel
12   Phuong Hoang (Phoenix) Hotel
14   Song Kim Hotel
24   Bat Dat Hotel
25   Arc En Ciel (Rainbow) Hotel
26   Tan Da Hotel & VT Hotel
27   Bat Dat Hotel II
29   Dong Khanh Hotel & Superstore
30   Tokyo Hotel
31   Hanh Long Hotel
32   Andong Hotel
33   Caesar Hotel
34   & Andong Market Cholon Tourist Mini-Hotel
35   Cholon Hotel

OTHER
1    Phung Son Pagoda
2    Shangri-La Disco
3    Khanh Van Nam Vien Pagoda
6    Binh Tay Market
7    Cholon Bus Station
8    Cha Tam Church
9    Ong Bon Pagoda
13   Post Office
15   Ha Chuong Hoi Quan Pagoda
16   Quan Am Pagoda
17   Phuoc An Hoi Quan Pagoda
18   Cho Ray Hospital
19   Electronics Market
20   Thien Hau Pagoda
21   Nghia An Hoi Quan Pagoda
22   Tam Son Hoi Quan Pagoda
23   Cholon Mosque
35   Nha Sau Church
36   An Quang Pagoda

Cholon

District 11
District 5
District 8

0   125   250 m

**Thich Quang Duc**
Thich Quang Duc was a monk from Hué who travelled to Saigon and publicly burned himself to death in June 1963 to protest the policies of President Ngo Dinh Diem. A famous photograph of his act was printed on the front pages of newspapers around the world. His death soon inspired a number of other self-immolations.

Many westerners were shocked less by the suicides than by the reaction of Tran Le Xuan (Madame Nhu, the president's notorious sister-in-law), who happily proclaimed the self-immolations a 'barbecue party' and said, 'Let them burn and we shall clap our hands'. Her statements greatly added to the already substantial public disgust with Diem's regime; the US press labelled Madame Nhu the 'Iron Butterfly' and 'Dragon Lady'. In November, both President Diem and his brother Ngo Dinh Nhu (Madame Nhu's husband) were assassinated by Diem's own military. Madame Nhu was outside the country at the time.

The Thich Quang Duc Memorial (Dai Ky Niem Thuong Toa Thich Quang Duc) is at the intersection of Nguyen Dinh Chieu and Cach Mang Thang Tam Sts, just around the corner from the Xa Loi Pagoda. ■

moon and new moon, special prayers are held from 7 to 9 am and from 7 to 8 pm.

**Phung Son Tu Pagoda** Phung Son Tu Pagoda, built by the Fujian congregation in the mid-1940s, is more typical of Saigon's Chinese pagodas than is the Jade Emperor Pagoda. The interior is often hung with huge incense spirals that burn for hours. Worshippers include both ethnic-Chinese and ethnic-Vietnamese. Phung Son Tu Pagoda is dedicated to Ong Bon, Guardian Spirit of Happiness and Virtue, whose statue is behind the main altar in the sanctuary. On the right-hand side of the main hall is the multi-armed Buddhist Goddess of Mercy. This pagoda is only 1km from downtown Saigon at 338 Yersin St.

**Mariamman Hindu Temple** Mariamman Hindu Temple, the only Hindu temple still in use in Saigon, is a little piece of southern India in the centre of Saigon. Though there are only 50 to 60 Hindus in Saigon – all of them Tamils – this temple, known in Vietnamese as Chua Ba Mariamman, is also considered sacred by many ethnic-Vietnamese and ethnic-Chinese. Indeed, it is reputed to have miraculous powers. The temple was built at the end of the 19th century and dedicated to the Hindu goddess Mariamman.

The lion to the left of the entrance used to be carried around Saigon in a street procession every autumn. In the shrine in the middle of the temple are Mariamman flanked by her guardians, Maduraiveeran (to her left) and Pechiamman (to her right). In front of the figure of Mariamman are two lingas (phallic symbols). Favourite offerings placed nearby include joss sticks, jasmine flowers, lilies and gladioli. The wooden stairs, on the left as you enter the building, lead to the roof, where you'll find two colourful towers covered with innumerable figures of lions, goddesses and guardians.

After reunification, the government took over the temple and turned part of it into a factory for joss sticks. Another section was occupied by a company producing seafood for export – the seafood was dried in the sun on the roof. The whole temple is to be returned to the local Hindu community.

Mariamman Temple is only three blocks from Ben Thanh Market at 45 Truong Dinh St. It is open from 7 am to 7 pm daily. Take off your shoes before stepping onto the slightly raised platform.

**Saigon Central Mosque** Built by South Indian Muslims in 1935 on the site of an earlier mosque, the Saigon Central Mosque is an immaculately clean and well-kept island of calm in the middle of bustling downtown Saigon. In front of the sparkling white and blue structure at 66 Dong Du St, with its four nonfunctional minarets, is a pool for ritual ablutions (washing) required by Islamic law before prayers. As with any mosque, take off your shoes before entering the sanctuary.

The simplicity of the mosque is in marked contrast to the exuberance of Chinese temple decorations and the rows of figures, facing elaborate ritual objects, in Buddhist pagodas. Islamic law strictly forbids using human or animal figures for decoration.

Only half a dozen Indian Muslims remain in Saigon; most of the community fled in 1975. As a result, prayers – held five times a day – are sparsely attended except on Fridays, when several dozen worshippers (mainly non-Indian Muslims) are present. The mass emigration also deprived the local Muslim community of much of its spiritual leadership; very few Muslims knowledgeable in their tradition and Arabic, the language of the Koran, remain.

There are 12 other mosques serving the 5000 or so Muslims in Saigon.

## Places of Worship – Cholon

The following places are on the Cholon map.

**An Quang Pagoda** The An Quang Pagoda gained some notoriety during the American War as the home of Thich Tri Quang, a politically powerful monk who led protests against the South Vietnamese government in 1963 and 1966. When the war ended, you would have expected the Communists to be grateful. Instead, he was first placed under house arrest and later thrown in solitary confinement for 16 months. Thich Tri Quang was eventually released and is said to still be living at An Quang Pagoda.

The An Quang Pagoda is on Su Van Hanh St, near the intersection with Ba Hat St, in District 10.

**Tam Son Hoi Quan Pagoda** This pagoda, known to the Vietnamese as Chua Ba Chua, was built by the Fujian congregation in the 19th century and retains unmodified most of its original rich ornamentation. The pagoda is dedicated to Me Sanh, the Goddess of Fertility. Both men and women – but more

of the latter – come here to pray for children. Tam Son Hoi Quan Pagoda is at 118 Trieu Quang Phuc St, which is very near 370 Tran Hung Dao Blvd.

To the right of the covered courtyard is the deified general Quan Cong (in Chinese: Guangong) with a long black beard; he is flanked by two guardians, the mandarin general Chau Xuong on the left (holding a weapon) and the administrative mandarin Quan Binh on the right. Next to Chau Xuong is Quan Cong's sacred red horse.

Behind the main altar (directly across the courtyard from the entrance) is Thien Hau, the Goddess of the Sea, who protects fisherfolk and sailors. To the right is an ornate case in which Me Sanh (the Goddess of Fertility; in white) sits surrounded by her daughters. In the case to the left of Thien Hau is Ong Bon, Guardian Spirit of Happiness and Virtue. In front of Thien Hau is Quan The Am Bo Tat (also known as Avalokiteçvara), the Goddess of Mercy, enclosed in glass.

Across the courtyard from Quan Cong is a small room containing ossuary jars (in which the ashes of the deceased are reposited) and memorials in which the dead are represented by their photographs. Next to this chamber is a small room containing the papier mâché head of a dragon of the type used by the Fujian congregation for dragon dancing. There is a photograph of a dragon dance on the wall between Quan Cong's red horse and Me Sanh.

**Thien Hau Pagoda** Thien Hau Pagoda (also known as Ba Mieu, Pho Mieu and Chua Ba) was built by the Cantonese congregation in the early 19th century. Of late it has become something of a showcase for tours operated by Saigon Tourist and Vietnam Tourism, which may explain the recent extensive renovations. This pagoda is one of the most active in Cholon.

The pagoda is dedicated to Thien Hau (also known as Tuc Goi La Ba), the Chinese Goddess of the Sea, who protects fisherfolk, sailors, merchants and anyone else who travels by sea. It is said that Thien Hau can travel over the oceans on a mat and ride the clouds to wherever she pleases. Her mobility allows her to save people in trouble on the high seas.

Thien Hau is very popular in Hong Kong (where she's called Tin Hau) and in Taiwan (where her name is Matsu). This might explain why Thien Hau Pagoda is included on so many tour group agendas (tourists from both these places are known for their free-spending habits).

Though there are guardians to either side of the entrance, it is said that the real protectors of the pagoda are the two land turtles who live here. There are intricate ceramic friezes above the roof-line of the interior courtyard. Near the huge braziers are two miniature wooden structures in which a small figure of Thien Hau is paraded around each year on the 23rd day of the third lunar month. On the main dais are three figures of Thien Hau, one behind the other, all flanked by two servants or guardians. To the left of the dais is a bed for Thien Hau. To the right is a scale-model boat and on the far right is the Goddess Long Mau, Protector of Mothers and Newborns.

Thien Hau Pagoda is at 710 Nguyen Trai St and is open from 6 am to 5.30 pm.

**Nghia An Hoi Quan Pagoda** Nghia An Hoi Quan Pagoda, built by the Chaozhou Chinese congregation, is noteworthy for its gilded woodwork. There is a carved wooden boat over the entrance and, inside to the left of the doorway, is an enormous representation of Quan Cong's red horse with its groom. To the right of the entrance is an elaborate altar in which a bearded Ong Bon, Guardian Spirit of Happiness and Virtue, stands holding a stick. Behind the main altar are three glass cases. In the centre is Quan Cong (Chinese: Kuan Kung) and to either side are his assistants, the general Chau Xuong (on the left) and the administrative mandarin Quan Binh (on the right). To the right of Quan Binh is an especially elaborate case for Thien Hau, Goddess of the Sea.

Nghia An Hoi Quan Pagoda is at 678 Nguyen Trai St (not far from Thien Hau Pagoda) and is open from 4 am to 6 pm.

**Cholon Mosque** The clean lines and lack of ornamentation of the Cholon Mosque are in stark contrast to nearby Chinese and Vietnamese pagodas. In the courtyard is a pool for ritual ablutions. Note the tile *mihrab* (the niche in the wall indicating the direction of prayer, which is towards Mecca). The mosque was built by Tamil Muslims in 1932. Since 1975, the mosque has served the Malaysian and Indonesian Muslim communities.

Cholon Mosque is at 641 Nguyen Trai St and is open all day Friday and at prayer times on other days.

**Quan Am Pagoda** Quan Am Pagoda, at 12 Lao Tu St one block off Chau Van Liem St, was founded in 1816 by the Fujian Congregation. The temple is named for Quan The Am Bo Tat, the Goddess of Mercy.

This is the most active pagoda in Cholon and the Chinese influence is obvious. The roof is decorated with fantastic scenes, rendered in ceramic, from traditional Chinese plays and stories. The tableaux include ships, houses, people and several ferocious dragons. The front doors are decorated with very old, gold and lacquer panels. On the walls of the porch are murals in slight relief picturing scenes of China from the time of Quan Cong. There are elaborate wooden carvings on roof supports above the porch.

Behind the main altar is A Pho, the Holy Mother Celestial Empress, gilded and in rich raiment. In front of her, in a glass case, are three painted statues of Thich Ca Buddha (Sakyamuni), a standing gold Quan The Am Bo Tat (Avalokiteçvara, Goddess of Mercy), a seated laughing Ameda and, to the far left, a gold figure of Dia Tang Vuong Bo Tat (the King of Hell).

In the courtyard behind the main sanctuary, in the pink tile altar, is another figure of A Pho. Quan The Am Bo Tat, dressed in white embroidered robes, stands nearby. To the left of the pink altar is her richly ornamented bed. To the right of the pink altar is Quan Cong flanked by his guardians, the general Chau Xuong (on the left) and the administrative mandarin Quan Binh (on the right). To the far right, in front of another pink altar, is the black-faced judge Bao Cong.

**Phuoc An Hoi Quan Pagoda** Phuoc An Hoi Quan Pagoda, built in 1902 by the Fujian Congregation, is one of the most beautifully ornamented pagodas in Saigon. Of special interest are the many small porcelain figures, the elaborate brass ritual objects and the fine wood carvings on the altars, walls, columns and hanging lanterns. From outside the building you can see the ceramic scenes, each containing innumerable small figurines, which decorate the roof. Phuoc An Hoi Quan Pagoda is at 184 Hung Vuong St (near the intersection of Thuan Kieu St).

To the left of the entrance is a life-size figure of the sacred horse of Quan Cong. Before leaving on a journey, people make offerings to the horse. They then pet the horse's mane before ringing the bell around its neck. Behind the main altar, with its stone and brass incense braziers, is Quan Cong (Chinese: Kuan Kung), to whom the pagoda is dedicated. Behind the altar to the left is Ong Bon, Guardian Spirit of Happiness and Virtue, and two servants. The altar to the right is occupied by representations of Buddhist (rather than Taoist) personages. In the glass case are a plaster Thich Ca Buddha (Sakyamuni) and two figures of the Goddess of Mercy, one made of porcelain and the other cast in brass.

**Ong Bon Pagoda** Ong Bon Pagoda (also known as Chua Ong Bon and Nhi Phu Hoi Quan) was built by the Fujian Congregation and is dedicated to Ong Bon, Guardian Spirit of Happiness and Virtue. The wooden altar is intricately carved and gilded. Ong Bon Pagoda is at 264 Hai Thuong Lai Ong Blvd, which runs parallel to Tran Hung Dao Blvd, and is open from 5 am to 5 pm.

As you enter the pagoda, there is a room to the right of the open-air courtyard. In it, behind the table, is a figure of Quan The Am Bo Tat (Goddess of Mercy) in a glass case. Above the case is the head of a Thich Ca Buddha (Sakyamuni).

Directly across the courtyard from the pagoda entrance, against the wall, is Ong Bon, to whom people come to pray for general happiness and relief from financial difficulties. He faces a fine, carved wooden altar. On the walls of this chamber are rather indistinct murals of five tigers (to the left) and two dragons (to the right).

In the area on the other side of the wall with the mural of the dragons is a furnace for burning paper representations of the wealth people wish to bestow upon deceased family members. Diagonally opposite is Quan Cong flanked by his guardians Chau Xuong (to his right) and Quan Binh (to his left).

**Ha Chuong Hoi Quan Pagoda** Ha Chuong Hoi Quan Pagoda at 802 Nguyen Trai St is a typical Fujian pagoda. It is dedicated to Thien Hau (Goddess of the Sea), who was born in Fujian.

The four carved stone pillars, wrapped in painted dragons, were made in China and brought to Vietnam by boat. There are interesting murals to either side of the main altar. Note the ceramic relief scenes on the roof.

This pagoda becomes extremely active during the Lantern Festival, a Chinese holiday held on the 15th day of the first lunar month (the first full moon of the new lunar year).

**Cha Tam Church** It is in Cha Tam Church that President Ngo Dinh Diem and his brother Ngo Dinh Nhu took refuge on 2 November 1963 after fleeing the Presidential Palace during a coup attempt. When their efforts to contact loyal military officers (of whom there were almost none) failed, Diem and Nhu agreed to surrender unconditionally and revealed where they were hiding.

The coup leaders sent an M-113 armoured personnel carrier to the church to pick them up (Diem seemed disappointed that a limousine befitting his rank had not been dispatched) and the two were taken into custody. But before the vehicle arrived in Saigon, the soldiers in the APC killed Diem and Nhu by shooting them at point-blank range and then repeatedly stabbing their bodies.

When news of the death of the brothers was broadcast on the radio, Saigon exploded into rejoicing. Portraits of the two were torn up and political prisoners, many of whom had been tortured, were set free. The city's nightclubs, closed because of the Ngos' conservative Catholic beliefs, reopened. Three weeks later, US president John F Kennedy was assassinated. As Kennedy's administration supported the coup against Diem, some conspiracy theorists have speculated that Kennedy was killed by Diem's family in retaliation. Then again, there are theories that Kennedy was murdered by the Russians, the Cubans, left-wing radicals, right-wing radicals, the CIA and the Mafia.

Cha Tam Church, built around the turn of the century, is an attractive white and pastel-yellow structure. The statue in the tower is of François Xavier Tam Assou (1855-1934), a Chinese-born vicar apostolic of Saigon. (A vicar apostolic is a delegate of the pope who administers an ecclesiastical district in a missionary region.) Today, the church has a very active congregation of 3000 ethnic-Vietnamese and 2000 ethnic-Chinese.

Vietnamese-language masses are held daily from 5.30 to 6 am and on Sundays from 5.30 to 6.30 am, 8.30 to 9.30 am and 3.45 to 4.45 pm. Chinese-language masses are held from 5.30 to 6 pm every day and from 7 to 8 am and 5 to 6 pm on Sundays. Cha Tam Church is at 25 Hoc Lac St, at the western end of Tran Hung Dao Blvd.

**Khanh Van Nam Vien Pagoda** Built between 1939 and 1942 by the Cantonese, Khanh Van Nam Vien Pagoda is said to be the only Taoist pagoda in all of Vietnam. This statement needs to be qualified since most Chinese practice a mixture of Taoism and Buddhism, rather than one or the other exclusively. The number of 'true' Taoists in Saigon is said to number only 4000, though you can take this figure with a grain of salt since most of the true Taoists are probably Buddhists too.

The pagoda is open from 6.30 am to 5.30

pm every day and prayers are held from 8 to 9 am daily. To get there, turn off Nguyen Thi Nho St (which runs perpendicular to Hung Vuong St) between numbers 269B and 271B; the address is 46/5 Lo Sieu St.

A few metres from the door is a statue of Hoang Linh Quan, chief guardian of the pagoda. There is a Yin and Yang symbol on the platform on which the incense braziers sit. Behind the main altar are four figures: Quan Cong (on the right) and Lu Tung Pan (on the left) represent Taoism; between the two of them is Van Xuong representing Confucianism; and behind Van Xuong is Quan The Am Bo Tat (Avalokiteçvara), the Buddhist Goddess of Mercy.

In front of these figures is a glass case containing seven gods and one goddess, all of which are made of porcelain. In the altars to either side of the four figures are Hoa De (on the left), a famous doctor during the Han Dynasty, and Huynh Dai Tien (on the right), a disciple of the founder of Taoism, Laotse.

Upstairs is a 150cm-high statue of the founder of Taoism, Laotse (Vietnamese: Thai Thuong Lao Quan). Behind his head is a halo consisting of a round mirror with fluorescent lighting around the edge.

To the left of Laotse are two stone plaques with instructions for inhalation and exhalation exercises. A schematic drawing represents the human organs as a scene from rural China. The diaphragm, agent of inhalation, is at the bottom. The stomach is represented by a peasant ploughing with a water buffalo. The kidney is marked by four Yin and Yang symbols, the liver is shown as a grove of trees and the heart is represented by a circle with a peasant standing in it, above which is a constellation. The tall pagoda represents the throat and the broken rainbow is the mouth. At the top are mountains and a seated figure representing the brain and the imagination, respectively. The 80-year-old chief monk says that he has practised these exercises for the past 17 years and hasn't been sick a day.

The pagoda operates a home at 46/14 Lo Sieu St for 30 elderly people who have no families. Each of the old folk, most of whom are women, have their own wood stove made of brick and can cook for themselves. Next door, also run by the pagoda, is a free medical clinic which offers Chinese herbal medicines (which are stored in the wooden drawers) and acupuncture treatments to the community. Before reunification, the pagoda ran (also free of charge) the school across the street.

**Phung Son Pagoda** Phung Son Pagoda (also known as Phung Son Tu and Chua Go) is extremely rich in statuary made of hammered copper, bronze, wood and ceramic. Some are gilded while others, beautifully carved, are painted. This Vietnamese Buddhist pagoda was built between 1802 and 1820 on the site of structures from the Oc-Eo (Funan) period, which was contemporaneous with the early centuries of Christianity. In 1988, a Soviet archaeological team carried out a preliminary excavation and found the foundations of Funanese buildings, but work was stopped pending authorisation for a full-scale dig.

Phung Son Pagoda is in District 11 at 1408 3/2 Blvd, near its intersection with Hung Vuong St. Prayers are held three times a day from 4 to 5 am, 4 to 5 pm and 6 to 7 pm. The main entrances are kept locked most of the time because of problems with theft, but the side entrance (which is to the left as you approach the building) is open from 5 am to 7 pm.

Once upon a time, it was decided that Phung Son Pagoda should be moved to a different site. The pagoda's ritual objects – bells, drums, statues – were loaded onto the back of a white elephant for transport to the new location, but the elephant slipped because of the great weight and all the precious objects fell into a nearby pond. This event was interpreted as an omen that the pagoda should remain at its original location. All the articles were retrieved except for the bell, which locals say was heard ringing whenever there was a full or new moon until about a century ago.

The main dais, with its many levels, is dominated by a gilded A Di Da Buddha, the Buddha of the Past, seated under a canopy

flanked by long mobiles resembling human forms without heads. A Di Da is flanked by Quan The Am Bo Tat, the Goddess of Mercy (on the left), and Dai The Chi Bo Tat (on the right). To the left of the main dais is an altar with a statue of Boddhi Dharma, the founder of Zen Buddhism who brought Buddhism from India to China. The statue, which is made of Chinese ceramic, has a face with Indian features.

As you walk from the main sanctuary to the room with the open-air courtyard in the middle, you come to an altar with four statues on it, including a standing bronze Thich Ca Buddha of Thai origin. To the right is an altar on which there is a glass case containing a statue made of sandalwood. The statue is claimed to be Long Vuong (Dragon King), who brings rain. Around the pagoda building are a number of interesting monks' tombs.

## Museums
**War Remnants Museum** Once known as the 'Museum of Chinese and American War Crimes', the name has been changed so as not to offend the sensibilities of Chinese and American tourists. However, the pamphlet handed out at reception pulls no punches; it's entitled 'Some Pictures of US Imperialists Aggressive War Crimes in Vietnam'.

Whatever the current name, this has become the most popular museum in Saigon with western tourists. Many of the atrocities documented in the museum were well publicised in the west, but it is one thing for US anti-war activists to protest against Pentagon policies and quite another for the victims of these military actions to tell their own story. But no matter what side of the political fence you stand on, the museum is well worth a visit – if for no other reason than to get a sobering reminder that war is anything but glorious.

In the yard of the museum, US armoured vehicles, artillery pieces, bombs and infantry weapons are on display. There is also a guillotine which the French used to deal with Viet Minh 'troublemakers'. Many of the photographs illustrating US atrocities are from US sources, including photos of the famous My Lai massacre. There is a model of the notorious tiger cages used by the South Vietnamese military to house Viet Cong prisoners on Con Son Island. There are also pictures of genetically deformed babies, their birth defects attributed to the widespread spraying of chemical herbicides by the Americans. In an adjacent room are exhibits detailing 'counter-revolutionary war crimes' committed by saboteurs within Vietnam after the 1975 liberation. The counter-revolutionaries are portrayed as being allied with both US and Chinese imperialists.

The main objection to the museum comes from, not surprisingly, American tourists, many of whom complain that the museum is one-sided. There are some unnecessarily crude comments placed under the photos, such as one of an American soldier picking up a horribly mangled body to show the photographer, and a caption saying 'this soldier seems satisfied'. And, of course, there is official amnesia when it comes to the topic of the many thousands of people tortured and murdered by the VC.

Politically neutral war historians will perhaps be more disturbed by the lack of context and completeness of some of the photos and exhibits. It's surprising, for example, that there are no photos of Thich Quang Duc, the monk who burned himself to death to protest the war. Or photos of the Kent State students in the USA who were shot while protesting US policies. Hopefully, the museum will be expanded to include a larger slice of the war's history.

Despite these criticisms, there are few museums in the world which drive home the point so well that modern warfare is horribly brutal and that many of the victims are civilians. Even those who adamantly supported the war will have a difficult time not being horrified by the photos of innocent children mangled by American bombing, napalming and artillery shells. There are also scenes of torture – it takes a strong stomach to look at these. You'll also have a rare chance to see some of the experimental weapons used in the American War which were at one time military secrets, an example being the 'flechette' (an artillery shell filled with thousands of tiny darts).

The War Remnants Museum (☎ 829-0325) is housed in the former US Information Service building at 28 Vo Van Tan St (the intersection with Le Qui Don St). Opening hours are from 8 to 11.30 am and 2 to 5 pm daily. Explanations are written in Vietnamese, English and Chinese.

**Revolutionary Museum** Housed in a white, neoclassical structure built in 1886 and once known as Gia Long Palace, the Revolutionary Museum (Bao Tang Cach Mang; ☎ 829-9741) is a singularly beautiful and amazing building. The museum displays artefacts from the various periods of the Communist struggle for power in Vietnam. The photographs of anti-colonial activists executed by the French appear out of place in the gilded, 19th-century ballrooms, but then again the contrast helps you get a feel for the immense power and self-confident complacency of colonial France. There are photos of Vietnamese peace demonstrators in Saigon demanding that US troops get out, and a dramatic suicidal photo of Thich Quang Duc, the monk who set himself on fire to protest the policies of President Ngo Dinh Diem.

The information plaques are in Vietnamese only, but some of the exhibits include documents in French or English and many others are self-explanatory if you know some basic Vietnamese history. Some of the guides speak English and will often latch on to you in various rooms or on each floor and provide excellent, if unrequested, guided tours. There are donation boxes next to the visitors' books in various parts of the museum where you can leave a tip for the guides (US$1 to US$2 is appropriate). Most of the guides do fine work and get paid nothing for it.

The exhibition begins in the first room on the left (as you enter the building), which covers the period from 1859 to 1940. Upstairs, two more rooms are currently open. In the room to the left is a *ghe* (a long, narrow rowboat) with a false bottom in which arms were smuggled. The weight of the contraband caused the boat to sit as low in the water as would any ordinary ghe. Nearby is a small diorama of the Cu Chi tunnels. The adjoining room has examples of infantry weapons used by the VC and various captured South Vietnamese and American medals, hats and plaques. A map shows Communist advances during the dramatic collapse of South Vietnam in early 1975. There are also photographs of the 'liberation' of Saigon.

Deep underneath the building is a network of reinforced concrete bunkers and fortified corridors. The system, branches of which stretch all the way to Reunification Palace, included living areas, a kitchen and a large meeting hall. In 1963, President Diem and his brother hid here immediately before fleeing to a Cholon church, where they were captured (and, shortly thereafter, murdered). The network is not yet open to the public because most of the tunnels are flooded, but if you bring a torch (flashlight), a museum guard may show you around.

In the garden behind the museum is a Soviet tank, an American Huey UH-1 helicopter and an anti-aircraft gun. In the garden fronting Nam Ky Khoi Nghia St is some more military hardware, including the American-built F-5E jet used by a renegade South Vietnamese air force pilot to bomb the Presidential Palace (now Reunification Palace) on 8 April 1975.

The Revolutionary Museum is at 65 Ly Tu Trong St (corner Nam Ky Khoi Nghia St), which is one block south-east of Reunification Palace. It is open from 8 to 11.30 am and 2 to 4.30 pm Tuesday to Sunday. The museum offices are at 114 Nam Ky Khoi Nghia St. Admission is free.

**History Museum** The History Museum (Vien Bao Tang Lich Su; ☎ 829-8146), built in 1929 by the Société des Études Indochinoises, was once the National Museum of the Republic of Vietnam. It's just inside the main entrance to the zoo on Nguyen Binh Khiem St. Step inside the door and you're immediately confronted by a big statue of guess who? Also, the museum has an excellent collection of artefacts illustrating the evolution of the cultures of Vietnam, from the Bronze Age Dong Son civilisation (13th century BC to 1st century AD) to the Oc-Eo (Funan) civilisation (1st to 6th centuries AD), to the Chams, Khmers and Vietnamese. There are many valuable relics taken from Cambodia's Angkor Wat.

At the back of the building on the 3rd floor is a research library (☎ 829-0268; open Monday to Saturday) with numerous books on Indochina from the French period.

The museum is open from 8 to 11.30 am and 1 to 4 pm, Tuesday to Sunday.

**Ho Chi Minh Museum** This museum (Khu Luu Niem Bac Ho; ☎ 829-1060) is in the old customs house at 1 Nguyen Tat Thanh St just across Ben Nghe Channel from the quayside end of Ham Nghi Blvd. This place was (and still is) nicknamed the 'Dragon House' (Nha Rong) and was built in 1863. The tie between Ho Chi Minh (1890-1969) and the museum building is tenuous: 21-year-old Ho, having signed on as a stoker and galley-boy on a French freighter, left Vietnam from here in 1911, beginning 30 years of exile in France, the Soviet Union, China and elsewhere.

The museum houses many of Ho's personal effects, including some of his clothing (he was a man of informal dress), sandals, his beloved American-made Zenith radio and other memorabilia. The explanatory signs in the museum are in Vietnamese, but if you know much about Ho, you should be able to follow most of the photographs and exhibits.

The museum is open on Tuesday, Wednesday, Thursday and Saturday from 8 to 11.30 am and 2 to 6 pm; on Sundays, it stays open until 8 pm. The museum is closed on Mondays and Fridays.

**Military Museum** The Military Museum is just across Nguyen Binh Khiem St (corner Le Duan Blvd) from the main gate of the zoo. US, Chinese and Soviet war materiel is on display, including a Cessna A-37 of the

South Vietnamese air force and a US-built F-5E Tiger with the 20-mm nose gun still loaded. The tank on display is one of the tanks which broke into the grounds of what is now Reunification Palace on 30 April 1975.

**Art Museum** This classic yellow and white building, with some modest Chinese influence, houses one of the more interesting collections in Vietnam. If you are not interested in the collection, just enter the huge hall with its nice art nouveau windows and floors. The 1st floor seemed to have housed the revolutionary art in former times. Those pieces are either in storage, thrown out or put in some back room close to the toilet. Now what you find on the 1st floor is officially accepted contemporary art. Most of it is kitsch or desperate attempts to master abstract art, but occasionally something brilliant is displayed here. Most of the recent art is for sale and prices are fair.

The 2nd floor displays the old politically correct art. Some of this stuff is pretty crude – pictures of heroic figures waving red flags, children with rifles, a wounded soldier joining the Communist Party, innumerable tanks and weaponry, grotesque Americans and God-like reverence for Ho Chi Minh. Nevertheless, it's worth seeing because Vietnamese artists managed not to be as dull and conformist as their counterparts in eastern Europe. Once you've passed several paintings and sculptures of Uncle Ho, you will see that those artists who studied before 1975 managed to somehow transfer their own aesthetics into the world of proscribed subjects.

Surprisingly, the Vietnamese Communists seem to have only proscribed the subjects, but not the style. Most impressive are some drawings of prison riots in 1973. On the floor are some remarkable abstract paintings. Maybe the most striking fact in these politically correct paintings is that all Vietnamese heroes of great wars look a bit more European than Asian.

The 3rd floor displays a good collection of older art, mainly Funan Oc-Eo sculptures.

Those Oc-Eo pieces strongly resemble the styles from ancient Greece and Egypt. You will also find here the best Cham pieces outside of Danang. Also interesting are the many pieces of Indian art, often an elephant's head. There are some pieces which clearly originated in Angkor culture.

The cafe is in the garden in front of the museum and is a preferred spot for elderly gentlemen to exchange stamp collections and sip iced tea.

The Art Museum (Bao Tang My Thuat; ☎ 822-2577) is at 97A Pho Duc Chinh St in central Saigon. Opening hours are from 7.30 am to 4.30 pm Tuesday to Sunday. Admission is free.

**No 7 Army Museum** Out near the airport and close to the Mekong Hotel is the No 7 Army Museum (Bao Tang Luc Luong Vu Trang Mien Dong Nam Bo) at 247 Hoang Van Thu Blvd, Ward 1, Tan Binh District. We had high hopes for the museum because of its fancy exterior, but inside it proved to be mostly a hollow shell. The main feature is yet another statue of Ho Chi Minh, though there is a small collection of tanks behind the main building. There are a few photos from the French-era Viet Minh battles. Visitors are few and there is no admission fee. The karaoke restaurant upstairs is probably the biggest drawcard.

The museum is open daily except Sunday from 7.30 to 11 am and from 1.30 to 5 pm.

**Ton Duc Thang Museum** This small, rarely visited museum (Bao Tang Ton Duc Thang; ☎ 829-4651) is dedicated to Ton Duc Thang, Ho Chi Minh's successor as president of Vietnam, who was born in Long Xuyen, An Giang Province, in 1888. He died in office in 1980. Photos illustrate his role in the Vietnamese Revolution, including the time he spent imprisoned on Con Dao Island. The explanations are in Vietnamese only.

The museum is along the waterfront at 5 Ton Duc Thang St, half a block north of the Tran Hung Dao statue at the foot of Hai Ba Trung Blvd. It is open Tuesday to Sunday from 8 to 11 am and 2 to 6 pm.

# Life on the Streets

Through the smoke and pollution, groups of battered old men lean against their cyclos. Around the restaurants, hotels, nightclubs and karaoke bars of central Saigon, it's hard to miss these men in their worn clothes and tar-stained sandals, which have been damaged from years of catching their feet in the jagged chains of their cyclos.

Before the war many were doctors, teachers or journalists, but like many of their professional friends were punished for siding with the Americans. After the cease-fire, tens of thousands of them were stripped of their citizenship and sent to re-education camps for seven years or more. Over 20 years later, it is still impossible for them to return to the jobs they are qualified to do and, as most do not have an official residence permit (which means they cannot own property or a business), it's technically illegal for them to be in the city. Many of them have never had families because they could not afford (or were not permitted) a home to live in.

'It's hard to earn one's living. You have to bend in order to pedal and earn a little money', explained Win, a veteran cyclo driver.

The comings and goings at hotels are a constant form of entertainment (and business) for Saigon's cyclo drivers. Nothing misses their sharp eyes. Their courteous propositions hide a desire to find out your first name and establish you as 'their property' while you're in Saigon. 'Miss Juliet', they will cry out from across the street in the hope you will need their services.

*Despite an increasing number of cars, vans and buses on Vietnam's roads, cyclos, motorcycles (especially) and bicycles still predominate.*

TONY WHEELER

*A versatile vehicle, the cyclo can hold up to eight children, but more common cargo would be a family of four, various types of goods, or one or two westerners.*

PHIL WEYMOUTH

They are, however, excellent city guides, as they know every corner of the city and can give you a potted history of the key sites. The front seat of a cyclo really is one of the best ways to see Saigon – but it takes some getting used to. In heavy traffic it's like getting on a roller-coaster at a fairground. The traffic races towards you at startling speeds from every direction and, just when you think you are surely going to die, gaps magically appear in the traffic and your cyclo driver slips into the spaces provided, while you thank the gods that you are still in one piece.

Tourists love to reverse roles and have a go in the saddle, mistakenly thinking that it is easy to spend one's day cycling from place to place, but their opinions quickly change. In most cases they find the cyclos too hard to peddle and, if they advance at all, they do not get very far on the uneven, potholed roads.

The drivers' home is the street corner, which they turn into a colourful and interesting environment using wooden tables and small, multicoloured, plastic footstools which support them only inches off the ground. Their floor is broken up bits of pavement slabs and the 'drivers' drinks cabinet' (a street stall or two) nestles just behind them.

After a day's sightseeing, they might invite you to join them there for either a whisky in a Coke bottle or the local beer Ba, Ba, Ba (pronounce it 'baa-baa-baa' slowly because in Vietnamese it can also sound like you are saying 'three old women'!). An evening with these guys is always worthwhile, but remember it might be opium they are smoking in their wooden pipes.

**Juliet Coombe**

## Parks

**Cong Vien Van Hoa Park** Next to the old Cercle Sportif, an elite sporting club during the French period, the bench-lined walks of Cong Vien Van Hoa Park are shaded with avenues of enormous tropical trees.

This place still has an active sports club, although now you don't have to be French to visit. There are 11 tennis courts, a swimming pool and a club house, which have a grand colonial feel about them. It's worth a look for the pool alone. There are Roman-style baths with a coffee shop overlooking the colonnaded pool.

The tennis courts are available for hire at a reasonable fee. Hourly tickets are on sale for use of the pool and you can even buy a bathing costume on the grounds if you don't have one. The antique dressing rooms are quaint, but there are no lockers! Other facilities include a gymnasium, table tennis, weight lifting, wrestling mats and ballroom dancing classes.

In the morning, you can often see people here practising the art of *thai cuc quyen* or slow motion shadow boxing.

Within the park is a small-scale model of the Cham towers in Nha Trang.

Cong Vien Van Hoa Park is adjacent to Reunification Palace. There are entrances across from 115 Nguyen Du St and on Nguyen Thi Minh Khai St.

**Ho Ky Hoa Park** Ho Ky Hoa Park, whose name means Lake and Gardens, is a children's amusement park in District 10 just off 3/2 Blvd. It is near the Hoa Binh Theatre and behind Vietnam Quoc Tu Pagoda. There are paddleboats, rowboats and sailboats for hire. Fishing is allowed in the lakes and a small swimming pool is open to the public for part of the year. The cafes are open year-round and there are also two arcades of Japanese video games. Within the park boundaries is a rather expensive hotel. Ho Ky Hoa Park is open from 7 am to 9.30 pm daily and is crowded on Sundays.

## Reunification Palace

It was towards this building – then known as Independence Palace or the Presidential Palace – that the first Communist tanks in Saigon rushed on the morning of 30 April 1975. After crashing through the wrought iron gates in a dramatic scene recorded by photojournalists and shown around the world, a soldier ran into the building and up the stairs to unfurl a Viet Cong flag from the 4th floor balcony. In an ornate 2nd floor reception chamber, General Minh, who had become head of state only 43 hours before, waited with his improvised cabinet. 'I have been waiting since early this morning to transfer power to you', Minh said to the VC officer who entered the room. 'There is no question of your transferring power', replied the officer, 'you cannot give up what you do not have'.

Reunification Palace (Hoi Truong Thong Nhat) is one of the most fascinating things to see in Saigon, both because of its striking modern architecture and because of the eerie feeling you get as you walk through the deserted halls, that from here ruled arrogant men wielding immense power who nevertheless became history's losers. The building, once the symbol of the South Vietnamese government, is preserved almost as it was on 30 April 1975, the day that the Republic of Vietnam, which hundreds of thousands of Vietnamese and 58,183 Americans died trying to save, ceased to exist. Some recent additions to the building include a statue of Ho Chi Minh and a video viewing room where you can watch the latest version of Vietnamese history in a variety of languages. The national anthem is played at the end of the tape and you are expected to stand up – it would be rude to refuse to do so.

Reunification Palace is open for visitors from 7.30 to 10 am and 1 to 4 pm daily except when official receptions or meetings are taking place. English and French-speaking guides are on duty during these hours. Each guide is assigned to a particular part of the palace, so you will have numerous guides as you move from room to room. The visitors' office and entrance is at 106 Nguyen Du St (☎ 829-0629). The entrance fee for foreigners is US$4 (free for Vietnamese).

In 1868 a residence for the French governor

## Thai Cuc Quyen

*Thai cuc quyen*, or slow motion shadow boxing, has in recent years become quite trendy in western countries. It has been popular in Vietnam for centuries, but it originated in China, where it is known as *taijiquan*. It is basically a form of exercise, but it's also an art and is a form of martial arts related to Chinese *kung fu*. Kung fu differs from thai cuc quyen in that the former is performed at much higher speed and with the intention of doing bodily harm. Kung fu also often employs weapons. Thai cuc quyen is not a form of self-defence, but the movements are similar to kung fu. There are different styles of thai cuc quyen.

Thai cuc quyen is very popular among old people and also with young women who believe it will help keep their bodies beautiful. The movements are supposed to develop the breathing muscles, promote digestion and improve muscle tone.

A modern innovation is to perform thai cuc quyen movements to the thump of disco music. Westerners find it remarkable to see a large group performing their slow motion movements in the park at the crack of dawn to the steady beat of disco music supplied by a portable cassette tape player.

Thai cuc quyen and all manner of exercises are customarily done just as the sun rises, which means that if you want to see or participate in them, you have to get up early. In Saigon, the best place to see it is at Cong Vien Van Hoa Park, or else the Cholon district because of its large ethnic-Chinese population. In Hanoi, look around Hoan Kiem Lake and at other parks. ■

general of Cochinchina was built on this site. The residence gradually expanded and became known as Norodom Palace. When the French departed, the palace became home for South Vietnamese president Ngo Dinh Diem. So hated was Diem that his own air force bombed the palace in 1962 in an unsuccessful attempt to kill him. Now recognising that he had an image problem, the president ordered a new residence to be built on the same site, but this time with a sizeable bomb shelter in the basement. The new mansion was designed by Paris-trained Vietnamese architect Ngo Viet Thu – work began in 1962 and was completed in 1966. Diem did not get to see his dream house because he was murdered by his own troops in 1963. The new building was named Independence Palace and was home for South Vietnamese president Nguyen Van Thieu until his hasty departure in 1975.

The building, both inside and out, is an outstanding example of 1960s architecture; it is much more interesting up close than you would expect from the street. Reunification Palace has an airy and open atmosphere and its spacious chambers are tastefully decorated with the finest modern Vietnamese art and craft. In its grandeur, the building feels worthy of a head of state.

The ground-floor room with the boat-shaped table was used for conferences. Upstairs, in the Presidential Receiving Room (the one with the red chairs in it, called in Vietnamese Phu Dau Rong, or the Dragon's Head Room), South Vietnam's president used to receive foreign delegations. The president sat behind the desk; the chairs with dragons carved into the arms were used by his assistants. The chair facing the desk was reserved for foreign ambassadors. Next door is a meeting room. The room with gold-coloured chairs and curtains was used by the vice president. For US$1, you can sit in the former president's chair and have your photo taken.

In the back of the structure is the area in which the president lived. Check out the model boats, horse-tails and severed elephants' feet. On the 3rd floor there is a card-playing room with a bar and a movie-screening chamber. The 3rd floor also boasts a terrace with a heliport – there is still a moribund helicopter parked here, but it costs US$1 to walk around on the helipad. The 4th floor has a dance hall and casino.

Perhaps most interesting of all is the basement with its network of tunnels, telecommunications centre and war room (with the best map of Vietnam you'll ever see pasted to the wall). One tunnel stretches all the way to Gia Long Palace, which is now the Revolutionary Museum.

## People's Committee Building

Saigon's gingerbread Hôtel de Ville, one of the city's most prominent landmarks, is now the somewhat incongruous home of the Ho Chi Minh City People's Committee. It was built between 1901 and 1908 after years of the sort of architectural controversy peculiar to the French. Situated at the north-western end of Nguyen Hue Blvd and facing towards the river, the former hotel is notable for its gardens, ornate facade and elegant interior lit with crystal chandeliers. It's easily the most photographed building in Vietnam.

Unfortunately, you'll have to content yourself with admiring the exterior only. The building is not open to the public and requests by tourists to visit the interior are rudely rebuffed.

For gecko fans: at night, the exterior of the building is usually covered with thousands of geckos feasting on insects.

## Zoo & Botanical Garden

The Zoo and Botanical Garden (Thao Cam Vien) are pleasant places for a relaxing stroll under giant tropical trees which thrive amid the lakes, lawns and flower beds. Unfortunately, the zoo facilities are run down and the elephants in particular look like they'd be better off dead (many are close to it now). The other animals – which include crocodiles and big cats – seem to have it somewhat better.

The Botanical Garden, founded in 1864, was one of the first projects undertaken by the French after they established Cochinchina as a colony. It was once one of the finest such gardens in Asia, but this is certainly no longer true. The emphasis now is on the fun fair, with kiddie rides, fun house, miniature train, house of mirrors etc.

A rather gruesome form of amusement exists near the entrance to the zoo. There is a ride here where the animals upon which people sit are real! There are stuffed bears, deer and large cats following each other around the revolving platform. Some of them are looking a little tatty, but this no doubt creates employment for local taxidermists. At least these animals are dead (we hope).

The main gate of the zoo is on Nguyen Binh Khiem St at the intersection of Le Duan Blvd. There is another entrance on Nguyen Thi Minh Khai St near the bridge over Thi Nghe Channel.

The History Museum is next to the main gate. There are occasional water-puppet shows performed on a small island in one of the lakes – a small group can arrange a special showing.

Also just inside the main gate is the Temple of King Hung Vuong. The Hung kings are said to be the first rulers of the Vietnamese nation, having established their rule in the Red River region before being invaded by the Chinese.

Ice cream, fresh French bread and drinks are sold at a few places around the park, but food here is generally expensive and not too good. Just outside the main gate (along Nguyen Binh Khiem St) there are numerous food stalls selling excellent rice dishes, soup and drinks at reasonable prices.

### Whitewashing Nature

Visitors to Ho Chi Minh City have often wondered why the lower half of all the trees are painted white. Theories posited by tourists have included that the paint: 1) protects the trees from termites; 2) protects the trees from Agent Orange; 3) is some government official's idea of art nouveau; or 4) is an ancient Vietnamese tradition. It turns out that the mystery of the white trees has a much simpler explanation – the trees are painted white so people don't bump into them at night. ■

## Binh Soup Shop

It might seem strange to introduce a restaurant in the sightseeing section of this book rather than the Places to Eat section, but there is more to this shop than just the soup. The Binh Soup Shop was the secret headquarters of the Viet Cong in Saigon. It was from here that the VC planned the attack on the US embassy and other places in Saigon during the Tet Offensive of 1968. One has to wonder how many American soldiers must have eaten here, unaware that the waiters, waitresses and cooks were VC infiltrators.

The Binh Soup Shop is at 7 Ly Chinh Thang St, District 3. By the way, the soup isn't bad.

## Binh Quoi Tourist Village

Built on a small peninsula in the Saigon River, the Binh Quoi Tourist Village (Lang Du Lich Binh Quoi; ☎ 899-1831) is a slick tourist trap operated by Saigon Tourist (see the HCMC map). Backpackers are not numerous, but upmarket tourists get brought out here by the busload and some city-weary locals also seem to like it.

The 'village' is essentially a park featuring boat rides, water-puppet shows, a restaurant, a swimming pool, tennis courts, a camping ground, a guesthouse, bungalows and amusements for the kiddies. The park puts in a plug for Vietnam's ethnic minorities by staging traditional-style minority weddings accompanied by music. There are some alligators kept in an enclosure for viewing, but so far no alligator-wrestling shows. River cruises can be fun – the smaller cruise boats have 16 seats and the larger ones have 100 seats.

Next to the water-puppet theatre, you can make bookings for the local nightlife. A sign in English advertises all sorts of fun-filled evening activities, as follows:

Saigon Tourist Brings You: 'Magical Evenings'. Sunset cruise, traditional show, dinner under the stars. Daily: Cruise and dinner show US$20 (5.30 to 9 pm); cultural show alone US$5 (7 to 8 pm).

The *Binh Quoi Bungalows* (☎ 899-1831, 899-1833; 50 rooms) is perhaps one of the better value places to stay. Built on stilts above the water, the bungalows give you a little taste of traditional river life in the Mekong Delta, but with air-conditioning and tennis courts. The price range here is US$20 to US$40.

Binh Quoi Tourist Village is 8km north of central Saigon in the Binh Thanh district. The official address is 1147 Xo Viet Nghe Tinh St. You can get there by cyclo, motorbike or taxi. A much slower alternative is to charter a boat from the Me Linh Square area on the Saigon River.

## Orchid Farm

There are a number of orchid farms (Vuon Cay Kieng) in suburban Ho Chi Minh City, but most are concentrated in the Thu Duc District. These places raise more than orchids. The Artex Saigon Orchid Farm is the largest of all, with 50,000 plants representing 1000 varieties. It is primarily a commercial concern, but visitors are welcome to stop by to relax in the luxurious garden.

The farm, founded in 1970, uses revenues from the sale of orchid flowers for its operating budget, but makes its real profit selling orchid plants, which take six years to mature and are thus very expensive. In addition to varieties imported from overseas, the farm has a collection of orchids native to Vietnam. Ask to see the orange-yellow Cattleya orchid variety called Richard Nixon; they have another variety named for Joseph Stalin. The nurseries are at their most beautiful just before Tet, when demand for all sorts of flowers and house plants reaches its peak. After Tet, the place is bare.

The Artex Saigon Orchid Farm is 15km from Saigon in Thu Duc District, a rural part of Ho Chi Minh City, on the way to Bien Hoa. The official address is 5/81 Xa Lo Vong Dai, but this highway is better known as 'Xa Lo Dai Han', the 'Korean Highway', because it was built during the war by Koreans. At Km 14 on Xa Lo Dai Han there is a two-storey police post. Turn left (if heading out of Saigon towards Bien Hoa), continue 300m and turn left again.

**Pham Ngu Lao St**
And now for something different. The hotel and restaurant centre for budget travellers, Pham Ngu Lao St has nothing of interest for western tourists beyond satisfying basic needs such as eating, drinking, shopping, socialising and sleeping. But it's a different story for the Vietnamese – Pham Ngu Lao is where they go to 'look at the hippies'. Yes it's true – western backpackers have become a tourist attraction, much like the hill tribes of the Central Highlands. If you hang out here, remember to smile for the camera when the tour buses roll by.

Talent scouts from local movie studios even show up occasionally looking to hire westerners as extras. Since movies about the American War are popular, most of the roles are for soldiers (men only). However, there are sometimes roles for hippie war protesters (males and females alike). The pay isn't great, but it could be your big break – even Rambo had to start somewhere.

**Swimming**
Upmarket swimming pools can be found at plush tourist hotels. You needn't stay at these hotels to use the facilities, but you must pay an admission fee of US$5 to US$10 per day. Hotels offering access to their pools include the Embassy (not so good though), Omni, Equatorial, Metropole, Palace and Rex. About the only major hotel which does not offer public access to its pool is the New World.

The International Club at 285B Cach Mang Thang Tam St, District 10, also has an excellent swimming pool.

There are a number of public pools where the Vietnamese go and some of the newer ones are in very good condition. These pools charge by the hour and it works out to be very cheap if you're staying only a short time. One such place is the Olympic-sized Lam Son Pool (☎ 358028), 342 Tran Binh Trong St, District 5 – the weekday charge here is around US$0.50 per hour and rises to US$1 on weekends. For US$1.50 per hour you can visit the pool at the Workers' Club, 55B Nguyen Thi Minh Khai St, District 3.

**Water-Skiing**
Perhaps 'sewage-skiing' would be a more descriptive term. The Saigon River is pretty murky and there is no telling what sort of contagious diseases you might contract by frolicking in the bubbling broth. Nevertheless, some brave or foolish foreigners have on occasion rented a speedboat from Saigon Tourist (or elsewhere) and headed upstream to Bien Hoa where the water is merely brown rather than black. Probably you'd be better off heading down to the Mekong River for this activity, though that will require at least an overnight trip.

**Bowling**
The Saigon Superbowl is near the airport at A43 Truong Son St, Tan Binh District. There are 32 lanes here, though at peak times there can be a two-hour wait for a lane. You can entertain yourself in the meantime at the adjacent video game arcade. Bowling costs US$3, but this increases to US$4 after 5 pm. Shoe rentals are US$0.50.

The Bowling Centre (Trung Tam Bo-ling; ☎ 864-3784) is in the International Club at 285B Cach Mang Thang Tam St, District 10. There are 12 lanes here and 65 video game machines. It's open daily from 10 am until midnight.

**Golf**
The Vietnam Golf & Country Club is another cash cow brought to you by Saigon Tourist. It's actually a joint venture with a Taiwan-based company – the Taiwanese were said to be more interested in the appreciating value of the real estate than the 36-hole golf course. The course was the first in Vietnam to provide night golfing under floodlights. The club (Cau Lac Bo Golf Quoc Te Viet Nam; ☎ 832-2084; fax 832-2083) is at 40-42 Nguyen Trai St, Thu Duc District (Lam Vien Park), about 15km east of central Saigon. Membership ranges from US$5000 to US$60,000, but paying visitors are welcome. It may be worth coming here to use the driving range, which costs US$10, or you can play a full round for US$50. Other

---

**Booby Trap**
The oldest of Saigon's hotels were built early in the century under the French; the newest in the early 1970s to accommodate US military officials, western businesspeople and war correspondents. Some of the latter seem to have learned most of what they knew about Vietnam over drinks at hotel bars.
    When the city surrendered in 1975, North Vietnamese soldiers, fresh from years in the field after having grown up in the spartan North, were billeted in the emptied high-rise hotels. There is an oft-told story about several such soldiers who managed to scrape together enough money to buy fish and produce at the market. To keep their purchases fresh, they put them in the western-style toilet, an appliance completely foreign to them. Then, out of curiosity, one of the soldiers flushed the toilet and the fish and vegetables disappeared. They were outraged by this perfidious, imperialist booby trap and bitterly cursed those responsible. We can't swear that this incident actually took place (or that it happened only once), but we do know that a great deal of damage was done to Saigon's hotels after reunification and that bathroom fixtures were especially targeted. Some of this damage has only recently been repaired. ■

---

facilities on the site include tennis courts and a swimming pool.

Song Be Golf Resort is a slick Singapore-Vietnam joint venture 20km north of Saigon. Unfortunately, this resort is only for members and their guests. This place has it all – tennis courts, a swimming pool, a hotel, a restaurant (surprisingly cheap!), villas, an imported Filipino jeepney (customised jeep) and security guards to keep out curious locals. Oh yes, and there's a golf course too. Memberships are priced from US$7000 to US$75,000. The villas cannot be purchased, but can be leased for 50 years. For further details, you can ring up the resort (☎ 855800; fax 855516) in Song Be Province or visit their office (☎ 823-1218; fax 823-1215) at 254B Nguyen Dinh Chieu St, District 3.

The Rach Chiec Driving Range (☎ 896-0756) is a good place to practice your swing. It's open daily from 6 am to 10 pm. You'll find it in An Phu Village, a 10 minute drive from central Saigon.

Also in the pipeline is a golf course at Gia Dinh Park (Cong Vien Gia Dinh). This is in the northern part of the Phu Nhuan District, close to Tan Son Nhat airport. If/when completed, it will certainly be the closest golf course to central Saigon.

**Hash House Harriers**
This loosely strung organisation meets once

a week for a jogging session followed by a drinking session. The time and meeting place changes, as do the people who do the organising. Look for the latest announcements on the notice board at the Norfolk Hotel, 117 Le Thanh Ton St, District 1. Announcements may also appear in expat pubs around town or in various magazines such as the *Vietnam Economic Times* and *Vietnam Investment Review*. At the time of writing, the current meeting place was the Century Saigon Hotel every Sunday at 3 pm.

**Language Courses**
The vast majority of foreign language students enrol at the General University of Ho Chi Minh City (Truong Dai Hoc Tong Hop) at 12 Dinh Hoang St, District 5. It's near the south-west corner of Nguyen Van Cu Blvd and Tran Phu Blvd (see the HCMC map).

**Organised Tours**
There are surprisingly few day tours available of Saigon itself, though no doubt Saigon Tourist can come up with something in exchange for a hefty fee.

On the other hand, there are heaps of tours to the outlying areas of Cu Chi, Tay Ninh and the Mekong Delta. Some of the tours are day trips and other are overnighters. The cheapest tours by far are available from cafes and agencies in the Pham Ngu Lao area.

## Places to Stay – bottom end

Different categories of travellers have staked out their own turf. Budget travellers tend to congregate around Pham Ngu Lao St on the western end of District 1. Travellers with a little more cash to spare prefer the more upmarket hotels concentrated around Dong Khoi St at the eastern side of District 1. French travellers seems to have an affinity for District 3. Cholon attracts plenty of Hong Kongers and Taiwanese, but western backpackers are rare despite the availability of cheap accommodation here – it seems that the herd instinct is too powerful a force to be resisted.

Touts from private hotels hang around the airport looking for business. Taxi drivers will often shove hotel namecards into your hands. You can be reasonably sure that these places are overpriced – if they weren't paying sizeable commission, the touts wouldn't bother.

If you don't really know where you want to stay, but you're on a budget, it's best to take a taxi to the Pham Ngu Lao area and proceed on foot. It shouldn't take too long to find something.

**District 1** Pham Ngu Lao, De Tham and Bui Vien Sts form half a rectangle which is the heart of budget traveller haven. These streets and the adjoining alleys are bespeckled with a treasure trove of cheap accommodation and cafes catering to the low-end market. Unfortunately, a major construction project will begin soon to redevelop the northern side of Pham Ngu Lao St into a luxury tourist area. The construction is estimated to take about four years and will generate a considerable amount of dust and noise. It's our prediction that the budget hotels and restaurants will quickly retreat from Pham Ngu Lao St one block south to Bui Vien St near the intersection with De Tham St. Indeed, there are already signs of this happening.

An old favourite is the pleasant and friendly *Hotel 211* (☎ 835-2353; fax 836-1883) at 211 Pham Ngu Lao St. Singles/doubles cost US$8/12 with fan or US$12/16 with air-con. All rooms have private bath

with hot water. The hotel has put up a sound-proof glass barricade in front to fend off noise and dust from the street – it's surprisingly effective.

The first place in this neighbourhood to offer dormitory accommodation was *Thanh Thanh 2 Hotel* (☎ 832-4027; fax 825-1550) at 205 Pham Ngu Lao St. Dorm beds start at US$4 and regular rooms cost up to US$12.

Many travellers have had good things to say about the *Quyen Thanh Hotel* (☎ 832-2370; fax 832-4946). Large rooms equipped with everything cost US$20.

At 193 Pham Ngu Lao St is the huge *Prince Hotel* (Khach San Hoang Tu; ☎ 832-2657; 66 rooms). Rooms here range from US$12 to US$40. The cheaper rooms are on the upper floors because there is no lift.

The *Vien Dong Hotel*, 275A Pham Ngu Lao St (☎ 839-3001; fax 833-2812; 139 rooms), has budget rooms on the top floor costing US$20. However, on the lower floors it's considerably pricier at US$35 to US$80. At the time of writing the hotel was undergoing its third renovation since 1990 and, to judge from the past two improvements, these prices will surely rise when it reopens.

The *My Man Mini-Hotel* (☎ 839-6544; 10 rooms) is good, and yes, the name is both English and Vietnamese. Rooms with fan are US$10 to US$14, and with air-con they're US$14 to US$18. The address is officially 373/20 Pham Ngu Lao St, but it's actually down a tiny alley just behind the Thai Binh Market.

In the same vicinity is the friendly *Guesthouse 127* (☎ 833-0761; fax 836-0658) at 127 Cong Quynh St, District 1. Rooms here cost US$10 to US$15. Directly opposite at No 168 is the *Tuan Anh Hotel* (☎ 835-6989; 10 rooms), where rooms cost US$25.

Just one block to the north-west of the Thai Binh Market, at 83A Bui Thi Xuan St, is the *Hoang Yen Mini-Hotel* (☎ 839-1348; fax 829-8540; 10 rooms). The owner speaks French, but not much English. Singles/twins are US$16/21 and the tariff includes breakfast.

South of Pham Ngu Lao is Bui Vien St,

which is rapidly being transformed into a solid string of guesthouses. The price range is about US$8 to US$20, with hot water and air-conditioning pushing the tariff up on the top-end rooms. Places to consider here include:

*Guesthouse 64*, 64 Bui Vien St
*Guesthouse 70* (☎ 833-0569), 70 Bui Vien St
*Guesthouse 72* (☎ 833-0321), 72 Bui Vien St
*Guesthouse 97*, 97 Bui Vien St
*Hai Ha Guesthouse*, 78 Bui Vien St
*Hong Quyen Hotel*, 29-31 Bui Vien St
*Minh Chau Guesthouse*, 75 Bui Vien St
*Tuan Anh Guesthouse*, 103 Bui Vien St
*Van Trang Guesthouse*, 80 Bui Vien St
*Vu Chau Hotel*, 37 Bui Vien St

We've personally found *Guesthouse 64* to be a good one. There have been a lot of complaints against *Huy Hoang Guesthouse* at 18 Bui Vien St – the woman there seems to have numerous quarrels with travellers.

An alternative to the Pham Ngu Lao area is a string of wonderful guesthouses on an alley connecting Co Giang and Co Bac Sts. The first hotel to appear here and probably still the best is *Miss Loi's Guesthouse* (☎ 835-2973), 178/20 Co Giang St. Room prices average US$8 to US$10 for a double. Many of Miss Loi's neighbours are jumping into this business and the area seems destined to develop into another budget travellers' haven.

The *Rang Dong Hotel* (☎ 832-2106; fax 839-3318; 127 rooms) at 81 Cach Mang Thang Tam St is new and nice, and fairly reasonably priced for this standard. Room rates range from US$25 to US$60.

Hidden behind the plush Embassy Hotel is the much cheaper *Tao Dan Hotel* (☎ 823-0299; 94 rooms), 35A Nguyen Trung Truc St. It used to be a favourite with Japanese backpackers, but then 'upgraded' and has since been slowly going downhill. Most of the guests could be described as 'budget business travellers'. Prices are US$20 to US$25 with air-con.

The *Dong Khoi Hotel* (☎ 829-4046, 823-0163; 34 rooms) is at 12 Ngo Duc Ke St (corner with Dong Khoi St). This charming building is notable for its spacious suites with 4.5m-high ceilings and French windows.

**District 5 (Cholon)** The *Phuong Hoang Hotel* (☎ 855-1888; fax 855-2228; 70 rooms) is in an eight-storey building at 411 Tran Hung Dao Blvd. Also known as the *Phoenix Hotel*, this place is just off Chau Van Liem St in the middle of central Cholon. Rooms with fan/air-con cost US$15/25.

Across the street from the Phuong Hoang Hotel, the *Song Kim Hotel* (☎ 855-9773; 33 rooms) is at 84-86 Chau Van Liem St. It's a grungy and somewhat disreputable establishment with twins for US$8 with fan or US$10 with air-con. Reception is up a flight of stairs. You can do better than this for marginally more money.

Just up Chau Van Liem St at 111-117 is the *Truong Thanh Hotel* (☎ 855-6044; 81 rooms). It's definitely a budget place. Rooms with fan are US$8 to US$10, while air-con costs a modest US$18.

Half a block away, at 125 Chau Van Liem St, is the *Thu Do Hotel* (☎ 855-9102; 70 rooms). It looks very much like a dump, a distinction it shares with the neighbouring Truong Thanh Hotel. Rooms cost a modest US$10.

The *Tan Da Hotel* (☎ 855-5711) is at 17-19 Tan Da St, very close to the upmarket Arc En Ciel Hotel. This place is rather tacky and not overly friendly. Rooms with fan/air-con cost US$18/25; with air-con and refrigerator it's US$30.

The five-storey *Dong Khanh Hotel* (☎ 835-2410; 81 rooms) is the pride and joy of Saigon Tourist. At one time a budget hotel, it's been fully renovated into a spiffy pleasure palace. Even if you don't stay here, check out the supermarket next door. The hotel is at 2 Tran Hung Dao Blvd. Singles/doubles are US$55/70 to US$130/160.

The five-storey *Tokyo Hotel* (Khach San Dong Kinh; ☎ 835-7558; fax 835-2505; 96 rooms), 106-108 Tran Tuan Khai St, has all the modern conveniences at nice prices, plus friendly staff. Double rooms with air-con, telephone and refrigerator cost US$25 to

US$45. The hotel boasts a gift shop, restaurant, dance hall and karaoke bar.

The *Bat Dat Hotel II* on Ngo Quyen St is the cheap cousin of the nearby pricey Bat Dat Hotel. At the II you can get twins for US$14 to US$22.

## Places to Stay – middle & top end

The tourist boom at first created a shortage of hotel space, but overbuilding and a slight decline in tourist arrivals has now produced a glut. The famed Saigon Floating Hotel recently shut its doors and there are plans to tow it from its berth in the Saigon River to Palau in the western Pacific. Despite a plentiful supply of international-standard hotel rooms, prices have not really come down, although they remain stable.

**District 1** Stuck between the cheap guesthouses and budget cafes is the *Giant Dragon Hotel* (☎ 835-3268; fax 835-3279) at 173 Pham Ngu Lao St. Although somewhat incongruous in this neighbourhood, the rooms are plush and cost US$30 to US$50.

The *Saigon Hotel* (☎ 829-9734; fax 829-1466; 103 rooms) is at 47 Dong Du St, across the street from the Saigon Central Mosque. Prices are mid-range with twins from US$45 to US$80. The deluxe rooms come equipped with satellite TV.

The *Kimdo Hotel* (☎ 822-5914; fax 822-5915) at 133 Nguyen Hue Blvd is another fancy pleasure-dome brought to you by Saigon Tourist. Rates are US$125 to US$490. It's fair to say you get what you pay for at this place.

The *Bong Sen Hotel* (☎ 829-1516; fax 829-9744; 134 rooms) is affectionately called 'the BS' by travellers. It's at 117-119 Dong Khoi St and offers air-con twins for US$30 to US$200. Formerly called the Miramar Hotel, the Bong Sen is also signposted as the *Lotus Hotel*, which is a translation of its Vietnamese name. There is a restaurant on the 8th floor.

The *Huong Sen Hotel* (☎ 829-1415; fax 829-0916; 50 rooms) is at 70 Dong Khoi St. Once known as the Astor Hotel, it's now an annexe of the nearby Bong Sen Hotel. This place charges US$48 to US$100 for twins. The in-house restaurant is on the 6th floor.

The *Hoang Gia Hotel* (☎ 829-4846; fax 822-5346; 42 rooms) is at 12D Cach Mang Thang Tam St, just near the traffic circle. Recently refurbished, rooms go for US$40 to US$60. Breakfast is included and the hotel has a respectable restaurant.

The *Embassy Hotel* (☎ 823-1981; fax 823-1978; 82 rooms) is a medium-scale place at 35 Nguyen Trung Truc St, not far from Reunification Palace. The hotel has its own restaurant, karaoke bar, live music in the evening and superb air-conditioning. Twins go for US$40 to US$70.

The classiest old hotel in the city is unquestionably the venerable *Continental Hotel* (☎ 829-9201; fax 824-1772; 87 rooms), the setting for much of the action in Graham Greene's novel *The Quiet American*. Just across the street from the Municipal Theatre at 132-134 Dong Khoi St, the hotel dates from the turn of the century but has been renovated more than once since then. The Continental, now run by Saigon Tourist, charges US$105 to US$170 (including breakfast and fruit). During the war, journalists used to sit on the terrace, known as the 'Continental Shelf', and sip beers, but it is now closed.

Another classic hotel in town is the *Rex Hotel* (Khach San Ben Thanh; ☎ 829-6043; fax 829-6536; 207 rooms) at 141 Nguyen Hue Blvd. Its ambience of mellowed kitsch dates from the time it served as a hotel for US military officers. Twins and suites cost US$80 to US$800. The Rex has, among other amenities, a large gift shop, tailor, unisex beauty parlour, photocopy machines, massage service, acupuncture, a swimming pool on the 6th floor, an excellent restaurant on the 5th floor, a coffee shop on the ground floor and a beautiful view from the large 5th-floor veranda, which is decorated with caged birds and potted bushes shaped like animals.

Yet another old favourite is the *Caravelle Hotel* (Khach San Doc Lap; ☎ 829-3704; fax 829-9767; 86 rooms) at 23 Lam Son Square (across the street from the Municipal Theatre).

Once owned by the Catholic Diocese of Saigon, the Caravelle is Saigon's most French hotel. Twins cost US$50 to US$180, but if it helps they throw in a free breakfast and basket of fruit. The hotel features two restaurants, a dance hall, massage services and a sauna.

The *Majestic Hotel* (Khach San Cuu Long; ☎ 829-5514; fax 829-5510; 115 rooms) is located along the Saigon River at 1 Dong Khoi St. It has undergone a recent major renovation and can once again claim its title as one of the city's most majestic hotels. Prices here are US$130 to US$575.

The *Palace Hotel* (Khach San Huu Nghi; ☎ 829-2860; fax 824-4230; 170 rooms) is at 56-64 Nguyen Hue Blvd. This hotel, whose Vietnamese name means 'friendship', offers superb views from the 14th floor restaurant and 15th floor terrace. Twins cost US$60 to US$140 with breakfast included. The Palace has an imported-food shop, a dance hall, the Bamboo Bar and a small swimming pool on the 16th floor.

In the same neighbourhood is the new *Saigon Prince Hotel* (☎ 822-2999; fax 824-1888; 203 rooms) at 63 Nguyen Hue Blvd. Glittering, luxury twins cost US$125 to US$245.

The *New World Hotel* (☎ 822-8888; fax 823-0710; 540 rooms) is a slick luxury tower at 76 Le Lai St. This Hong Kong joint venture is perhaps the most upmarket hotel in Vietnam. The clientele tends to be mainly Chinese-speaking tour groups from Hong Kong and Taiwan, but all with hard currency are welcome. Singles/twins start at US$185/195, while a presidential suite goes for a cool US$850. If it helps, they accept credit cards.

Next door is the *Palace Saigon Hotel* (☎ 833-1353, 835-9421) at 82 Le Lai St. It has doubles for US$25 to US$35.

The *Norfolk Hotel* (☎ 829-5368; fax 829-3415; 109 rooms) is at 117 Le Thanh Ton St. All rooms in this Australian joint-venture hotel boast satellite TV and a minibar. Twins cost US$85 to US$220. The price includes breakfast.

Not far away is the *Tan Loc Hotel* (☎ 823-0028; fax 829-8360) at 177 Le Thanh Ton St.

This place offers twins for US$50 to US$110.

The *Century Saigon Hotel* (☎ 823-1818; fax 829-2732; 109 rooms) at 68A Nguyen Hue Blvd is a Hong Kong joint venture. Rooms go for US$115 to US$200. You can book rooms from Century International offices abroad: Hong Kong (☎ 2598-8888); Australia (☎ (008) 802-1211 or (02) 826-15334); or USA (☎ (808) 895-59718).

The *Riverside Hotel* (☎ 822-4038; fax 825-1417; 75 rooms) is at 18 Ton Duc Thang St, very close to the Saigon River. This old colonial building has been renovated and now features a good restaurant and bar. Twins cost US$90 to US$180.

The *Mondial Hotel* (☎ 829-6291; fax 829-6324; 40 rooms) is at 109 Dong Khoi St, adjacent to the Bong Sen Hotel. Rooms range from US$60 to US$120.

The *Windsor Saigon Hotel* (☎ 835-7848; fax 835-7889; 64 rooms), 193 Tran Hung Dao Blvd, District 1, is a new luxury place with rooms priced from US$99 to US$242.

The *Empress Hotel* (☎ 823-2888; fax 835-8215; 37 rooms), 136 Bui Thi Xuan St, is one of the newest in the city. Twins cost US$80 to US$490.

The *Metropole Hotel* (Khach San Binh Minh; ☎ 832-2021; fax 832-2019; 94 rooms) at 148 Tran Hung Dao Blvd is *not* recommended! There have been too many reports of overcharging and even theft of cameras and luggage from rooms. But if you want to stay, official rates are US$86 to US$150.

**District 3** This district seems to attract a large number of French travellers. Possibly this is because of the local architecture. Whatever the reason, if you speak French you'll have a chance to practice it here.

On the north side of Cong Vien Van Hoa Park at 9 Truong Dinh St is the *Bao Yen Hotel* (☎ 829-9848; 12 rooms). Rooms are a very reasonable US$14 to US$16 and all have air-conditioning.

One place which gets the thumbs up from French travellers is the *Guesthouse Loan* (☎ 844-5313; 30 rooms). This place is also known as the *No 3 Ly Chinh Thang Hotel*, which is also its address (see the HCMC map). Prices are US$20 to US$25 and all rooms have air-con and hot water.

The *Que Huong Hotel* (☎ 829-4227; fax 829-0919; 48 rooms) – also known as the Liberty Hotel – is two blocks from the French consulate at 167 Hai Ba Trung Blvd (see the HCMC map). Singles/twins are priced from US$22/35 to US$32/45.

The *Victory Hotel* (☎ 823-1755; fax 829-9604) at 14 Vo Van Tan St (one block north of Reunification Palace) is in far better shape than the palace itself. Rates are from US$30 to US$60.

The *Saigon Star Hotel* (☎ 823-0260; fax 823-0255; 72 rooms) at 204 Nguyen Thi Minh Khai St is modern and luxurious. The hotel features the Venus Disco from 8 pm until 1 am, plus the Terrace Coffee Shop, a restaurant, a business centre and satellite TV. Room rates are US$99 to US$180.

On the road to the airport is the *Saigon Lodge Hotel* (☎ 823-0112; fax 825-1070; 91 rooms) at 215 Nam Ky Khoi Nghia St (see the HCMC map). This place boasts all the usual hotel amenities, plus satellite TV and halal Muslim food. Twins are US$78 to US$130 or you can rent the 'penthouse' for US$320.

The *International Hotel* (☎ 829-0009; fax 829-0066; 51 rooms) at 19 Vo Van Tan St maintains royal, plush standards and rooms priced from US$85 to US$152.

The *EPCO Hotel* (☎ 825-1125; fax 825-1118; 70 rooms) at 120 Cach Mang Thang Tam St is one of the plushest new hotels in the city. The price range for twins is US$85 to US$260.

Also new is the very sharp-looking *Mercure Hotel* (☎ 824-2525; fax 824-2533 104 rooms) at 79 Tran Hung Dao Blvd. Singles/twins cost US$95/115. Suites are US$189 to US$230.

The *Sol Chancery Hotel* (☎ 829-9152; fax 825-4484; 96 rooms) at 196 Nguyen Thi Minh Khai St is a solid business hotel. Rooms cost US$107 to US$180.

**Tan Binh & Phu Nhuan Districts** This is the area out towards the airport in the northern part of the city (see the HCMC map).

The *Tan Son Nhat Hotel* (☎ 844-0517; fax 844-1324; 25 rooms) at 200 Hoang Van Thu Blvd has some very interesting rooms. This place was built as a guesthouse for top South Vietnamese government officials. In 1975, the North Vietnamese army inherited it along with the nearby headquarters of the South Vietnamese army. A ground-floor room used by South Vietnamese prime minister Tran Thien Khiem has been preserved exactly as it was in 1975, plastic fruit and all. There is a small swimming pool out the back. Room rates are moderate at US$20 to US$50.

Almost within walking distance of the airport is the *Mekong Hotel* (☎ 844-1024; fax 844-4809) at 261 Hoang Van Thu Blvd. Singles/twins in this opulent place are US$40/45, while suites will set you back US$55. It's certainly one of the better deals near the airport.

Just next door to the Mekong is the sparkling, new *Garden Plaza Hotel* (☎ 842-1111; fax 842-4370; 157 rooms) at 309B Nguyen Van Troi St, Tanh Binh District. This Singapore joint venture is Vietnam's first atrium-style hotel. Rates here are US$180 to US$450.

The *Omni Hotel* (☎ 844-9222; fax 844-9200; 248 rooms) at 251 Nguyen Van Troi St is perhaps the most posh accommodation in Saigon. This place has it all, everything from in-room safes to a florist and health club. The price for all this comfort is US$200 to US$800 per night.

The *Chains First Hotel* (☎ 844-1199; fax 844-4282; 132 rooms) at 18 Hoang Viet St boasts a coffee shop, a gift shop, tennis courts, a sauna, massage services, three restaurants, a swimming pool, a business centre and free airport shuttle service. Singles/twins cost US$70/80 to US$140. The management throws in breakfast and a basket of fruit.

Just opposite the Chains First Hotel is the *De Nhat Hotel*, where room rates are US$38 to US$72. From the look of things, it's not worth it.

**District 5 (Cholon)** The *Equatorial Hotel* (☎ 839-0000; fax 839-0011; 334 rooms) at 242 Tran Binh Trong St is one of Cholon's newest and plushest accommodation offerings. The price range at this fine place is US$140 to US$215 (see the HCMC map).

The *Arc En Ciel Hotel* (Khach San Thien Hong; ☎ 855-4435; fax 855-0332; 91 rooms) is also known as the Rainbow Hotel. A prime venue for tour groups from Hong Kong and Taiwan, it boasts everything a tour group would need including the Volvo Disco Karaoke. Single/double rooms cost from US$48/60 to US$58/70. Suites cost US$100. The hotel is at 52-56 Tan Da St (corner Tran Hung Dao Blvd).

A near neighbour to the Arc En Ciel is the *Van Hoa Hotel* (☎ 855-4182; fax 856-3118) at 36 Tan Da St. It looks like a good place and is priced at US$32 to US$50.

The *Bat Dat Hotel* (☎ 855-5817, 855-5843; 117 rooms) at 238-244 Tran Hung Dao Blvd is across from the more well known Arc En Ciel Hotel. This formerly cheap place is now plush and offers twins from US$45 to US$68.

The *Hanh Long Hotel* (☎ 835-0251; fax 835-0742), 1027 Tran Hung Dao Blvd, is a new place. The name means 'happy dragon', but despite this and the location in Chinatown, the staff don't speak Chinese. Room prices range from US$50 to US$110.

The *Regent Hotel* (☎ 835-3548; fax 835-7094), 700 Tran Hung Dao Blvd (see the HCMC map), is also called the *Hotel 700*. The Regent is a joint venture between Vietnam Union and three Thai companies, and facilities are excellent. The price range here is US$45 to US$82.

The *Cholon Hotel* (☎ 835-7058; fax 835-5375; 24 rooms) at 170-174 Su Van Hanh St is superb value and is a major drawcard for Taiwanese travellers. The desk clerks speak both English and Chinese, not to mention Vietnamese. Squeaky-clean singles/twins cost US$25/30 with breakfast part of the package deal.

Right next door is the privately owned *Cholon Tourist Mini-Hotel* (☎ 835-7100; fax 835-5375; 11 rooms) at 192-194 Su Van Hanh St. Like its neighbour, the hotel is of a high standard and caters to the Taiwanese market. Singles/twins cost US$25/30.

The *Andong Hotel* (☎ 835-2001; 45 rooms) is at 9 An Duong Vuong Blvd right at the intersection with Tran Phu Blvd. It's a clean place and all rooms feature hot water, telephone, air-con and refrigerator. Twins cost US$35 to US$45.

Right inside Andong Market is the *Caesar Hotel* (☎ 835-0677; fax 835-0106), a slick, Taiwanese joint-venture operation. The official address is 34-36 An Puong Vuong St, District 5, but just ask taxis or cyclos to bring you to the market. The price range here is a breathtaking US$90 to US$180.

**District 11** About 1km north of central Cholon is the *Phu Tho Hotel* (☎ 855-1309; fax 855-1255) at 527 3/2 Blvd (see the Cholon map). The price range here is US$45 to US$60, with breakfast thrown in. There is a huge restaurant on the lowest three floors with built-in karaoke facilities.

The *Goldstar Hotel* (☎ 855-1646; fax 855-1644) at 174-176 Le Dai Hanh St is a spotlessly clean place where singles/doubles are US$40/50. All rooms have private bath, refrigerator and air-con, and the upper floors give a good view of the race track.

### Rental

There are currently some 15,000 expats living in Saigon and the number is projected to reach 20,000 by the year 2000. Despite the rapid increase, there does not appear to be a shortage of good quality rental accommodation.

Unfortunately, living cheaply is not easy if you don't happen to be Vietnamese. Unless you get married to a Vietnamese national and move in with the family, there isn't much chance of your renting a worker's flat for US$50 per month. The police just will not permit it.

The budget market is served chiefly by the mini-hotels scattered all over town. Discounts can be negotiated for long-term rentals at almost any hotel. If you've got a big budget, but don't need a large space, even the big five-star luxury hotels offer steep discounts to long-termers. The name of the game is negotiation.

Expats with a liberal budget have two basic options – villas and specially constructed luxury flats. The villas seem more popular and Saigon has a large supply. Villas which can be rented by foreigners typically cost from US$2000 to US$5000 a month. The luxury apartments are a new phenomena – some well-known places in this category include the Landmark (☎ 822-2098), Parkland (☎ 898-9000), Riverside (☎ 899-7405), Cityview Apartments, Apartments 27AB (☎ 822-4109), Stamford Court (☎ 899-7405), Saigon Village (☎ 865-0287), Sedona Suites and Regency Chancellor Court (☎ 822-5807).

Real estate agents who cater to the expat market advertise in the *Vietnam Economic Times* and *Vietnam Investment Review*.

## Places to Eat

Both Vietnamese and western food are widely available in Saigon and English menus are becoming more common. Central Saigon is the place to look for fine western and Vietnamese food. Cholon's speciality is Chinese food.

**Food Stalls** Noodle soup is available all day long at street stalls and hole-in-the-wall shops everywhere. A large bowl of delicious beef noodles costs US$0.50 to US$1. Just look for the signs that say 'Pho'.

Sandwiches with a French look and a very Vietnamese taste are sold by street vendors. Fresh French *baguettes* are stuffed with something resembling pâté (don't ask) and cucumbers and seasoned with soy sauce. A sandwich costs between US$0.50 and US$1, depending on what is in it and whether you get overcharged. Sandwiches filled with imported French soft cheese cost a little more.

Markets always have a side selection of food items, often in the ground floor or basement. Clusters of food stalls can be found in the Thai Binh Market, Ben Thanh Market and Andong Market.

The best noodle soup that I had was in the Ben Thanh Market itself. The food stalls inside the market were clean, the food fresh and the soup very tasty. It's also a fun place to eat because you quickly become the centre of attention.

John Lumley-Holmes

**Pham Ngu Lao & De Tham** Pham Ngu Lao and De Tham Sts form the axis of Saigon's budget eatery haven. Western backpackers easily outnumber the Vietnamese here, and indeed the locals have trouble figuring out the menus ('banana muesli' does not translate well into Vietnamese).

As mentioned earlier, a major construction project is starting on the northern side of Pham Ngu Lao St and threatens to drive away tourists. But that remains to be seen.

A long-running hang-out for budget travellers is *Kim Cafe* (☎ 835-9859) at 272 De Tham St. This is a very good place to meet people, arrange tours and get travel information.

The *Lotus Cafe* at 197 Pham Ngu Lao St is possibly the best in the neighbourhood now. The friendly couple who run it prepare excellent Vietnamese and western food at low prices.

The *Saigon Cafe* at 195 Pham Ngu Lao St (corner De Tham St) is also worthy of a plug.

*Linh Cafe* at 291 Pham Ngu Lao St is a great little place run by friendly people.

**Central Area** *Annie's Pizza* (☎ 839-2577) at 57 Nguyen Du St does the best peperoni and mozzarella in town. If you don't feel like trekking over there, then just ring up – they do home deliveries!

*Ashoka Indian Restaurant* (☎ 823-1372) at 17A/10 Le Thanh Ton St, District 1, is the most upmarket Indian restaurant in town (though still moderately priced). For really cheap Indian food, you have to go behind the mosque at 66 Dong Du St (opposite the Saigon Hotel).

The *Givral Restaurant* (☎ 829-2747) at 169 Dong Khoi St (across the street from the Continental Hotel) has an excellent selection of cakes, home-made ice cream and yoghurt. This Japanese joint venture also does Kotobuki-style pastries. Aside from the junk food, there's French, Chinese, Vietnamese and Russian cuisine on the menu.

The *Liberty Restaurant* (☎ 829-9820), 80 Dong Khoi St, is a joint venture with Ben Thanh Tourist (Saigon District 1 government). Despite its government connections, it's a superb place. It's known for very cheap and very good Vietnamese food, plus (more expensive) Chinese and western food. There is live music upstairs in the evening by a Vietnamese band. This place was popular before 1975 when it was known as the *Tu Do Restaurant*.

The *Brodard Cafe* (☎ 822-3966) is an oldie but goodie. Despite ongoing renovations, the decor is still vintage 1960s. This place is known for French food and prices are OK. Brodard is at 131 Dong Khoi St (corner Nguyen Thiep St).

*Bo Tung Xeo Restaurant* at 31 Ly Tu Trong St is perhaps the best Vietnamese restaurant in town. The food is amazingly cheap and amazingly good. The staff speak English and it's a very popular place with expats.

The *Lemon Grass Restaurant* (☎ 822-0496) at 4 Nguyen Thiep St, District 1, is a personal favourite, *the* place for Vietnamese power dining. You'd be hard-pressed to find anything bad on the menu, so if you can't decide what to order just pick something at random. Two women in traditional clothing play musical instruments and serenade while you eat. Aspiring interior designers should come here and check out the bamboo decor.

Just next door to the Lemon Grass is *Augustin* at 10 Nguyen Thiep St. It's an extremely popular spot. Many expats consider it Saigon's best, cheap French restaurant.

If you prefer an expensive French restaurant, *La Cigale* (☎ 844-3930) can accommodate you. The food is fine and it's one of those places where you can dine in little private cubicles. It's at 158 Nguyen Dinh Chin St, Phu Nhuan District, which is on the way to the airport and just opposite the Omni Hotel.

*Le Caprice* (☎ 822-8337) is on the top floor of the Landmark building at 5B Ton Duc Thang St. It's a *very* high class place. The views are stunning and so are the prices.

*L'Etoile* (☎ 829-7939), 180 Hai Ba Trung Blvd, has outstanding French food, but is only recommended for big spenders (see the HCMC map).

*Maxim's Dinner Theatre* (☎ 829-6676) at 15 Dong Khoi St (next to the Majestic Hotel) is very much what the name implies – a restaurant with live musical performances. The menu includes Chinese and French food. If you look western they give you the French menu, but ask for the Chinese menu, which is cheaper and more interesting. The sea slug and duck web has disappointed a few travellers, but the creme caramel and vanilla soufflé should not be missed. There is a very dark nightclub upstairs (free entry) with a live band playing 60s tunes. Maxim's is open from 11 am to 11 pm, but expect it to be empty until around dinnertime. Reservations are recommended on weekends and the place is sometimes closed due to wedding receptions. You can pay in dong or by credit card.

*Vietnam House* (☎ 829-1623) is at 93-95 Dong Khoi St, on the corner of Mac Thi Buoi St. The superb cuisine is Vietnamese-style and you can't complain about the stunning decor. In the 2nd floor dining room, a traditional, four-piece Vietnamese ensemble plays for dinner starting at 7.30 pm. The best part is the bar and lounge on the first floor. There is a young female pianist playing here from 5.30 pm until late at night. It's air-conditioned and beer is served up in a frozen glass with peanuts and shrimp crackers. The restaurant is open from 10 am until midnight.

*Ciao Cafe* (☎ 825-1203) at 72 Nguyen Hue Blvd (near the Palace Hotel) does excellent pizza, spaghetti, sandwiches, cakes, pastries and ice cream.

You can get your fill of snake, turtle, deer antler and other exotic dishes at *Tri Ky Restaurant* (☎ 844-2299) at 478 Nguyen Kiem St, District 3.

The *Paloma Cafe* (☎ 829-5813) at 26 Dong Khoi St is a stylish place with wooden tables, white tablecloths, polished silverware, aggressive air-conditioning and waiters who need to be tipped. Judging from the crowd that packs in every night, they must be doing something right – it's very popular with Vietnamese high society. This place stays open until nearly midnight.

**Dinner Cruises** Wining and dining while floating around the Saigon River is not the worst way to spend an evening. The floating restaurants are all government owned and are docked just opposite the Riverside Hotel. Most of the floating restaurants open at 6 pm, depart the pier at 8 pm and return at 10 pm. Prices vary from US$5 to US$10 for dinner à la carte, though you could spend significantly more if you go heavy on the booze. Tickets for the cruise can be bought at the pier and you can call for information (☎ 822-5401). Most of the boats feature live music and dancing.

Although not exactly a dinner cruise, *Binh Quoi Island* is chock-a-block with waterfront cafes (see the HCMC map). It's popular with both expats and locals and costs are very reasonable.

**Vegetarian** On the first and 15th days of the lunar month, food stalls around the city – especially in the markets – serve vegetarian versions of non-vegetarian Vietnamese dishes.

*Cay Bo De Vegetarian Restaurant* (☎ 839-1545) is in the alley to your right as you face the Giant Dragon Hotel. The official address is 175/6 Pham Ngu Lao St. The food here is excellent and cheap – something like US$0.50 per dish.

The owners of the *Tin Nghia Vegetarian Restaurant* are strict Buddhists. This small, simple little establishment, which is about 200m from Ben Thanh Market at 9 Tran Hung Dao Blvd, serves an assortment of delicious, traditional Vietnamese foods prepared without meat, chicken, fish or egg. Instead, tofu, mushrooms and vegetables are used. It is open from 7 am to 8 pm daily, but closes between 2 and 4 pm so the staff can take a rest. The prices here are incredibly cheap.

**Ice Cream** The best Vietnamese ice cream (kem) in Saigon is served at the three shops called *Kem Bach Dang* (☎ 829-2707). Two

of them are on Le Loi Blvd on either side of Pasteur St (Kem Bach Dang 1 is at 26 Le Loi Blvd and the other is at No 28). The third branch recently opened at 67 Hai Ba Trung Blvd (at Le Loi Blvd, south-east corner). All three are under the same management and serve ice cream, hot and cold drinks and cakes at very reasonable prices. A US$1.50 speciality is ice cream served in a baby coconut with candied fruit on top (kem trai dua).

America's response is *Baskin-Robbins* (☎ 829-5775) at 128A Pasteur St. It will cost you a fair bit to try all 31 flavours, as prices here are not low.

**Self-Catering** Simple meals can easily be assembled from fruits, vegetables, French bread, croissants, cheese and other delectables sold in the city's markets and from street stalls. But avoid the unrefrigerated chocolate bars – they taste like they were left behind by the Americans when they departed in 1975. Apparently, the chocolate gets repeatedly melted by the midday sun, rehardens at night and quickly becomes a ball of rancid mush.

Find yourself daydreaming about Kellogg's Frosties, Pringle's potato chips, Twinings tea or Campbell's soup? If you have an insatiable craving for plastic foods, a good place to satisfy these urges is *Minimart* on the 2nd floor of the Saigon Intershop, which is at 101 Nam Ky Khoi Nghia St (just off of Le Loi Blvd). Prices here are as cheap or cheaper than the street markets. The Minimart is open from 9 am to 6 pm daily.

The *Dong Khanh Department Store* at 850 Tran Hung Dao Blvd has a good supermarket.

The *Saigon Superbowl* near the airport at A43 Truong Son, Tan Binh District, offers western-style mall culture. There is a supermarket here, not to mention a *Donut Magic* and *Jollibee Fast Food*. To pay for it all, there is even a place to cash travellers cheques.

In Cholon, there's *Citimart* (☎ 835-8692) at 235 Nguyen Van Cu Blvd, District 5 (see the HCMC map)– it's one of the largest supermarkets in town. Also in Cholon is the

4

much smaller *Superstore* (☎ 835-7176), 10-20 Tran Hung Dao Blvd, District 5 (next to the Dong Khanh Hotel).

The *Gourmet Shop* (☎ 844-9222) at the Omni Hotel, 251 Nguyen Van Troi St, Phu Nhuan District, is a treasure trove of rare items like cranberry sauce, French cheese, Sri Lankan tea and frozen cherry cheesecake.

*Megamart* (☎ 822-2578), 71 Pasteur St, District 1, is the latest competitor in the imported food business. You can also try *Donamart* (☎ 824-4808), a very large supermarket at 63 Ly Tu Trong St, District 1.

There are at least two places in Saigon calling themselves *7-Eleven*, both of which are imposters. The better of the two is at 16 Nguyen Hue Blvd and carries imported foods (no Slurpies though). There is a real popcorn machine here, possibly the first in Vietnam.

### Entertainment
Wartime Saigon was always known for its riotous nightlife. Liberation in 1975 put a real damper on evening activities, but the pubs and discos have recently staged a comeback. However, periodic 'crack-down, clean-up' campaigns – allegedly to control drugs, prostitution and excessive noise – continue to keep Saigon's nightlife on the decidedly quiet side. Regulations introduced in 1995 require pubs and nightclubs to close by midnight. This doesn't mean that you need to retire to your hotel room by 9 pm for an evening of STAR TV, but if all-night revelry is what you need, consider a visit to Bangkok, Manila or Hong Kong.

**Sunday Night Live** Downtown Saigon is *the* place to be on Sunday and holiday nights. The streets are jam-packed with young Saigonese going *di troi* (cruising) on bicycles and motorbikes. Everyone is dressed in their fashionable best (often with the price tag still attached). The mass of slowly moving humanity is so thick on Dong Khoi St that you may have to wait until dawn to get across the street. It is utter chaos at intersections, where eight, 10 or more lanes of two-wheeled vehicles intersect without the benefit of traffic lights, safety helmets or sanity.

Near the Municipal Theatre, fashionably dressed young people take a break from cruising around to watch the endless procession, lining up along the street next to their cycles. The air is electric with the glances of lovers and animated conversations among friends. Everyone is out to see and be seen – it's a sight you shouldn't miss.

**Pubs** When it comes to nightlife, budget backpacker land (Pham Ngu Lao St) is actually not so good. Still, Pham Ngu Lao has a few hot spots. The *Bar Rolling Stones* at 177 Pham Ngu Lao St is well known for its loud music and party atmosphere. The real budget-minded should try *Nguyen Chat* at 161 Pham Ngu Lao St, a Vietnamese place where you can sample local draft beer (bia hoi) for US$0.40 per litre.

For real nightlife, head down to the central area (around Dong Khoi St). *Apocalypse Now* (☎ 824-1463), 2C Thi Sach St, has long lead the pack. Music is loud and the patrons are apocalyptically rowdy.

The excellent *Sapa Bar & Restaurant* (☎ 829-5754) at 26 Thai Van Lung St is run by a Swiss expat and his Vietnamese wife. You'll find everything here from schnitzel to snake (special order for the latter). Good music, beer and friendly staff all contribute to the pleasant atmosphere.

*Cafe Latin* (☎ 822-6363) at 25 Dong Du St is Vietnam's first, and so far only, tapas bar. There is a superb wine collection and fresh bread baked daily. The attached *Billabong Restaurant* is notable for Aussie food and other international cuisine.

*Chi Chi's Bar* (☎ 822-6585) at 4A Le Thanh Ton St is a long-running place known for billiards, darts and good music on CD.

At 24 Mac Thi Buoi is the legendary *Hard Rock Cafe*. The music here is mellower than the name suggests, but it's certainly a popular spot.

*Buffalo Blues* (☎ 822-2874) at 72A Nguyen Du St is a jazz bar with live music, billiards, darts and backgammon. It boasts the city's longest happy hour (2 pm to 8 pm) and dishes up fine meals. The live music is down in the basement – you might not notice it if you just walk in the front door.

*Bavaria* (☎ 822-2673) at 20 Le Anh Xuan St is a German restaurant and Bavarian-style pub.

*Mogambo's Cafe* (☎ 825-1311) at 20 Thi Sach St is noted for its stunning Polynesian decor. This place is a pub, cafe and guesthouse.

*Montana Cafe* (☎ 829-5067) at 40E Ngo Duc Ke St has a diverse menu, billiards and satellite TV.

The *Tex-Mex Cantina* (☎ 829-5950) at 24 Le Thanh Ton St features Mexican food with a Texan twist. It's also notable for its billiards tables.

*Hien & Bob's Place* (☎ 823-0661) at 43 Hai Ba Trung Blvd (corner of Dong Du St) advertises the coldest beer in town and American-style sandwiches. The interesting thing about this place is that Bob Shibley first came to Vietnam in 1969 as an American soldier. He is the first US veteran to have returned to open up a pub. Hien is his Vietnamese wife. However, now it's just Hien – Bob got deported.

Close to Hien's Place is *Wild West* (☎ 829-5127) at 33 Hai Ba Trung Blvd. The live music here is loud and billiards tables are busy. It's a very lively place in the evenings, even giving Apocalypse Now some competition.

The *Gecko Bar* (☎ 824-2754) at 74/1A Hai Ba Trung Blvd is another expat favourite. There's good food, drinks and satellite TV – and yes, a couple of odd geckos climbing the walls and ceilings.

*Saigon Headlines* (☎ 822-5014) at 7 Lam Son Square is a really cool jazz bar and restaurant at the back of the Saigon Concert Hall. It serves the best Marguerita on the rocks this side of Hong Kong. The atmosphere is relaxed, but chic. There is an excellent band. Open 10 am until 2 am.

Built right into one side of the Municipal Theatre is the *Q Bar* (☎ 829-1299), a trendy place with murals on the walls and tables outside by a little garden. Expats tend to congregate here and swap yarns. This is one of the longest-running bars in Saigon, so they must be doing something right.

The *Press Club* (☎ 829-1948) at 39 Le Duan Blvd (corner Hai Ba Trung Blvd) in District 1 is run by the Ho Chi Minh City Journalists' Association. It appeals to both expats and Vietnamese and you don't need to be a journalist to go there.

The *Hammock Bar* (☎ 829-1468) is the only floating bar in Vietnam. Moored in the Saigon River at Bach Dang Quay (the terminus of Ham Nghi Blvd), the boat can accommodate over 100 people on its two decks. The official address is 1A Ton Duc Thang St.

**Dancing & Discos** *Planet Europe* is the all-new flash place in town. It's in the Saigon Superbowl close to the airport. Happy hour is from 6.30 to 9 pm.

There is dancing with a live band at the *Rex Hotel* (141 Nguyen Hue Blvd) nightly from 7.30 to 11 pm.

*Cheers* (☎ 839-2052) is the disco inside the Vien Dong Hotel at 257 Pham Ngu Lao St. This very popular place was closed for renovation at the time of writing, but should reopen. It's a big unknown if prices will rise, but it was never terribly expensive. In the pre-renovation era, admission was only US$8.

The *VIP Club* (☎ 823-1187) at 32 Nguyen Thi Dieu St is a bar and disco with video game machines and billiards tables. There is also a karaoke room, but despite this the place has been very successful at cashing in on the western expat crowd. The cover charge is US$5.

*Junction 5* (☎ 839-0000) is inside the plush Equatorial Hotel at 242 Tran Binh Trong St, District 5 (see the HCMC map). This place dishes up live music from the in-house band.

The *Starlight Nightclub* is on the 11th floor of the Century Saigon Hotel (☎ 823-1818, ext 46) at 68A Nguyen Hue Blvd, District 1. Here you'll find music of the 60s, 70s and 80s. It's open nightly from 7 pm until 2 am and the cover charge is US$5.

The *Palace Hotel* at 56 Nguyen Hue Blvd, District 1, has a nightclub open from 8 to 11 pm. Ditto for the *Caravelle Hotel* at 19 Lam Son Square, District 1.

The *Venus Club* (☎ 823-0260) is on the 8th floor of the Saigon Star Hotel, 204 Nguyen Thi Minh Khai St, District 3. It's notable for its live music, dancing and karaoke rooms. Cover charge is US$3, but admission is free on Sunday.

The *Queen Bee* (☎ 822-8461) at 104-106 Nguyen Hue Blvd is a very lively place spread over four floors. There is an in-house band and karaoke rooms. Opening hours are 8 pm to 2 am.

The New World Hotel at 76 Le Lai St chips in with *Catwalk* (☎ 824-3760). The disco is particularly big with Hong Kongers. The *Saxophone Bar* (☎ 822-8888) is also here.

It's a bit of a long trek out to *Shangri-La* (☎ 855-6831) at 1196 3 Thang Hai St, District 11 (see the HCMC map). It turns out to be a pretty good discotheque and karaoke. There is also a health club here (gymnasium etc) which will perhaps help you get in shape for the night-time carousing.

By comparison, the *Deelite Disco Club* (☎ 824-4494) at 2B Le Duan Blvd, District 1, is very central.

**Water Puppets** This art really comes from the north, but in recent years has been introduced to the south as it's been a big hit with tourists. The best venue to see water puppets in Saigon is at the War Remnants Museum at 28 Vo Van Tan St. The schedule changes so inquire first.

**Municipal Theatre** The Municipal Theatre (Nha Hat Thanh Pho; ☎ 829-1249, 829-1584) is on Dong Khoi St between the Caravelle Hotel and the Continental Hotel. It was built in 1899 for use as a theatre, but later served as the heavily fortified home of the South Vietnamese National Assembly.

Each week, the theatre offers a different programme, which may be Eastern European-style gymnastics, nightclub music or traditional Vietnamese theatre. There are performances at 8 pm nightly. Refreshments are sold during intermission; public toilets are in the basement.

**Hoa Binh Theatre** The huge Hoa Binh Theatre complex (Nha Hat Hoa Binh, or the Peace Theatre) in District 10 often has several performances taking place simultaneously in its various halls, the largest of which seats 2400 people. The complex is at 14 3/2 Blvd (next to the Vietnam Quoc Tu Pagoda; see the HCMC map). The ticket office (☎ 865-5199) is open from 7.30 am until the end of the evening show.

Evening performances, which begin at 7.30 pm, are usually held once or twice a week. Shows range from traditional and modern Vietnamese plays to western pop music and circus acts. On Sunday mornings there are marionette shows for children at 9 am in the 400-seat hall and well-known Vietnamese pop singers begin performances in the large hall at 8.30 and 11 am.

Films are screened all day, every day, beginning at 8.30 am. Most of the films – from France, Hong Kong and the USA (Disney productions are a favourite) – are live-dubbed (someone reads a translation of the script over the PA system), leaving the original soundtrack at least partly audible. A weekly schedule of screenings is posted outside the building next to the ticket counter.

The disco on the ground floor is open Tuesday to Sunday from 8 to 11 pm. Admission is US$2.

**Conservatory of Music** Both traditional Vietnamese and western classical music are performed publicly at the Conservatory of Music (Nhac Vien Thanh Pho Ho Chi Minh; ☎ 839-6646), which is near Reunification Palace at 112 Nguyen Du St. Concerts are held at 7.30 pm each Monday and Friday evening during the two annual concert seasons, from March to May and from October to December.

Students aged seven to 16 attend the Conservatory, which performs all the functions of a public school in addition to providing instruction in music. The music teachers here were trained in France, Britain and the USA, as well as the former Eastern Bloc. The school is free, but most of the students come from well-off families because only the well-to-do can afford musical instruments. There are two other conservatories of music in Vietnam, one in Hanoi and the other in Hué.

**Cinemas** Many Saigon maps have cinemas (*rap* in Vietnamese) marked with a special symbol. There are several cinemas downtown, including the *Rex Cinema* (☎ 829-2185) at 141 Nguyen Hue Blvd (next door to the Rex Hotel); another on Le Loi Blvd, a block towards Ben Thanh Market from the Rex Hotel; and a third, *Rap Mang Non*, on Dong Khoi St 100m up from the Municipal Theatre. Yet another, *Rap Dong Khoi*, is at 163 Dong Khoi St.

## Spectator Sports

**Saigon Race Track** When South Vietnam was liberated in 1975, one of Hanoi's policies was to ban debauched, capitalistic pastimes such as gambling. Horse race tracks – mostly found in the Saigon area – were shut down. However, the government's need for hard cash has caused a rethink. The Saigon Race Track (Cau Lac Bo TDTT; ☎ 855-1205), which dates back to around 1900, was permitted to reopen in 1989.

Much of the credit for the reopening goes to Philip Chow, a Chinese-Vietnamese businessman who fled to Hong Kong as a youth, but returned to Vietnam in 1987 after the government promised to launch capitalist-style reforms. After getting the race track up and running through his own hard work, Chow was rewarded for his efforts by being sacked from his position. Government officials, sensing the opportunity to line their own pockets, saw no reason to keep an entrepreneur on the payroll.

Ever the optimist, Chow approached the government with a proposal to reopen the Duc Hoa Thung Race Track, 45km from Saigon. Realising that this could draw some of the business away from their own state-run monopoly, government officials have adamantly refused.

Like the state lottery, the race track is extremely lucrative. But grumbling about just where the money is going has been

coupled with widespread allegations about the drugging of horses. The minimum legal age for jockeys is 14 years; most look like they are about 10.

The overwhelming majority of gamblers are Vietnamese though there is no rule prohibiting foreigners. The maximum legal bet is currently US$2. High rollers can win a million dong (about US$90). Races are held Saturday and Sunday afternoons starting at 1 pm. Plans to introduce off-track betting have so far not materialised. However, illegal bookmaking (bets can be placed in gold!) offers one form of competition to the government-owned monopoly.

The Saigon Race Track is in District 11 at 2 Le Dai Hanh St.

**Motorcycle Race Track** It's a little uncertain if you'll be able to see this. Illegal street racing has become a recent fad in Vietnam, with often fatal results. To get the racers off the street, the municipal government has permitted occasional legal races at Phu Tho Race Tracks. In order to keep the fatality rate down, motorbike size has so far been limited to 50cc and 100cc. Some corporate sponsorship has been offered, with the winner receiving a free new Yamaha or Honda.

Unlike the horse races, motorcycle races do not run on any particular schedule. Furthermore, racing is controversial – critics want to ban this decadent practice completely. Make local inquiries to find out what the current situation is.

## Things to Buy

**Arts & Crafts** In the last few years the free market in tourist junk has been booming – you can pick up a useful item like a lacquered turtle with a clock in its stomach or a ceramic Buddha that whistles the national anthem. And even if you're not the sort of person who needs a wind-up mechanical monkey that plays the cymbals, keep looking – Saigon is a good shopping city and there is sure to be something that catches your eye.

Dong Khoi St has a reputation as the centre for handicrafts, but prices here are nothing short of ridiculous. The shopowners

ROBERT STOREY

SIMON ROWE

PHIL WEYMOUTH

BERNARD NAPTHINE

### Ho Chi Minh City

Top: Statuary inside Saigon's Jade Emperor Pagoda.
Middle Left: The former Hotel de Ville, now the home of the People's Committee.
Middle Right: The motorcyle is the dominant form of transport on Saigon's streets.
Bottom: A pho vendor with her mobile kitchen.

BERNARD NAPTHINE

JULIET COOMBE

### Ho Chi Minh City

Top: Burning incense at the entrance to one of Saigon's many pagodas.
Bottom: Flower sellers at the Ben Tanh market in central Saigon.

are rapacious and drive a hard bargain. The Pham Ngu Lao area is better, particularly along Buu Vien St.

Just opposite the Omni Hotel (on the way to the airport) is Lamson Art Gallery (☎ 844-1361) at 106 Nguyen Van Troi St, Phu Nhuan District. This place sells exquisite, but relatively expensive, lacquerware, rattan, ceramics, wood carvings and more. You can watch the artisans create their masterpieces and it's certainly worth stopping by to have a look.

The Ho Chi Minh City Association of Fine Arts (☎ 823-0025), 218 Nguyen Thi Minh Khai, District 1, is where aspiring young artists display their latest works. Typical prices for paintings are in the US$30 to US$50 range, but the artists may ask 10 times that.

**Clothing** At the budget end of the scale, T-shirts are available from vendors along Nguyen Hue Blvd in the centre, or De Tham St in the Pham Ngu Lao area. Expect to pay about US$2 for a printed T-shirt, or US$3 to US$5 for an embroidered one.

Vietsilk (☎ 829-1148) at 21 Dong Khoi St sells ready-made garments, as well as embroidery and drawings on silk.

Women's ao dai, the flowing silk blouse slit up the sides and worn over pantaloons, are tailored at shops in and around Ben Thanh Market or the Saigon Intershop area. Behind Ben Thanh Market you can try a store called Italy, 11 Thu Khoa Huan St.

Thai Fashion at 92H Le Thanh Ton St, District 1, has ready-made women's fashions. You might want to check out nearby Down Under Fashions at 229 Le Thanh Ton St, District 1. Ditto for The He Moi at 87 Pasteur St, District 1.

There are numerous tailors' shops in Cholon and several in downtown Saigon; the Rex and Century Saigon hotels each have in-house tailors.

**Coffee** Vietnamese coffee is prime stuff and is amazingly cheap if you know where to buy it. The best grades are from Buon Ma Thuot and the beans are roasted in butter. Obvi-

ously, price varies according to quality and also with the seasons. You can buy whole beans or have them ground into powder at no extra charge.

The city's major markets are where you can find the best prices and widest selection. We scored some top-grade caffeine from Van Ly Huong at Stall No 905, Zone 3 in the Ben Thanh Market. This market is also the best place to find the peculiar coffee-drippers used by the Vietnamese. Get a stainless steel one rather than aluminium – the latter is cheaper, but a much bigger hassle to use. Also look in the market for a coffee grinder if you're buying whole beans rather than pre-ground ones.

**Eyeglasses** A lot of opticians in Saigon make cheap eyeglasses with very breakable frames and misaligned lenses. One place which offers quality (albeit at a higher price) is Saigon Optic, 46 Pham Ngoc Thach St, District 3. Good things have also been said about Kinh Italy (☎ 823-0483) at 10 Cach Mang Thang Tam St.

**Stamps & Coins** As you enter the main post office, immediately to your right is a counter selling stationery, pens etc, but also has some decent stamp collections. Also as you face the entrance from the outside, to your right are a few stalls which also have stamp collections, as well as other goods such as foreign coins and banknotes. You can even find old stuff from the former South Vietnamese regime. Prices are variable: about US$2 will get you a respectable set of late-model stamps already mounted in a book, but the older and rarer collections cost more.

Many bookshops and antique shops along Dong Khoi St sell overpriced French Indochinese coins and banknotes and packets of Vietnamese stamps.

**Street Markets** The street market which runs along Huynh Thuc Khang and Ton That Dam Sts sells everything. The area used to be known as the Electronics Black Market until early 1989, when it was legalised. It's now generally called the Huynh Thuc Khang

Street Market, although it doesn't have an official name.

You can still buy electronic goods of all sorts – from mosquito zappers to video cassette players – but the market has expanded enormously to include clothing, washing detergent, lacquerware, condoms, pirated cassettes, posters of Ho Chi Minh, posters of Michael Jackson, posters of Mickey Mouse, smuggled bottles of Johnny Walker, Chinese-made 'Swiss' army knives and just about anything else to satisfy your material needs.

**Ben Thanh Market** Saigon has a number of incredibly huge indoor markets selling all manner of goods. They are some of the best places to pick up the conical hats and ao dai for which Vietnam is famous. The most centrally located of these is the Ben Thanh Market (Cho Ben Thanh). The market and surrounding streets is one the city's liveliest, most bustling areas. Everything commonly eaten, worn or used by the average resident of Saigon is available here: vegetables, fruits, meat, spices, biscuits, sweets, tobacco, clothing, hats, household items, hardware and so forth. The legendary slogan of US country stores applies equally well here: 'If we don't have it, you don't need it'. Nearby, food stalls sell inexpensive meals.

Ben Thanh Market is 700m south-west of the Rex Hotel at the intersection of Le Loi Blvd, Ham Nghi Blvd, Tran Hung Dao Blvd and Le Lai St. Known to the French as the Halles Centrales, it was built in 1914 from reinforced concrete and covers an area of 11 sq metres; the central cupola is 28m in diameter. The main entrance, with its belfry and clock, has become a symbol of Saigon.

Opposite the belfry, in the centre of the traffic roundabout, is an equestrian statue of Tran Nguyen Hai, the first person in Vietnam to use carrier pigeons. At the base, on a pillar, is a small white bust of Quach Thi Trang, a Buddhist woman killed during anti-government protests in 1963.

**The Old Market** Despite the name, this is not a place to find antiques. Rather, the Old Market is where you can most easily buy imported (black market?) foods, wines, shaving cream, shampoo etc. However, this is *not* the place to look for electronics or machinery (see the Dan Sinh Market). There is a problem using the Vietnamese name for this market (Cho Cu), because written or pronounced without the tones it means 'penis'. Your cyclo driver will no doubt be much amused if you say that this is what you're looking for. Perhaps directions would be better – the Old Market is on the north side of Ham Nghi Blvd between Ton That Dam and Ho Tung Mau Sts.

**Dan Sinh Market** Also known as the 'War Surplus Market', this is the place to shop for a chic pair of combat boots or rusty dog tags. It's also the best market for electronics and other types of imported machinery – you could easily renovate a whole villa from the goods on sale in this place.

The market is at 104 Yersin St , next to Phung Son Tu Pagoda. The front part of the market is filled with stalls selling automobiles and motorbikes, but directly behind the pagoda building you can find reproductions of what appears to be second-hand military gear.

Stall after stall sells everything from gas masks and field stretchers to rain gear and mosquito nets. You can also find canteens, duffel bags, ponchos and boots. Anyone planning on spending time in Rwanda or New York City should consider picking up a second-hand flak jacket (demand has slumped since the American War ended and the prices are now very competitive). On the other hand, exorbitant overcharging of foreigners looking for a poignant souvenir is common.

**Binh Tay Market** Binh Tay Market (Cho Binh Tay) is Cholon's main marketplace. Actually, it's technically not in Cholon proper, but about one block away in District 6 (Cholon is District 5). Much of the business here is wholesale. Binh Tay Market is on Hau Giang Blvd about 1km south-west of Chau Van Liem St.

**Andong Market** Cholon's other indoor market, Andong, is very close to the intersection of Tran Phu and An Duong Vuong Blvds. This market is four storeys tall and is packed with shops. The 1st floor has heaps of clothing – imported designer jeans from Hong Kong, the latest pumps from Paris, Vietnamese ao dai – and everything else imaginable. The basement is a gourmet's delight of small restaurants – a perfect place to pig out 'on a shoestring'.

**Miscellaneous** No bureaucracy, Communist or otherwise, can exist without the official stamps and seals that provide the *raison d'être* for legions of clerks. This need is catered to by the numerous shops strung out along the street just north of the New World Hotel (opposite side of the street and just west of Ben Thanh Market).

Most Vietnamese also own carved seals bearing their name (an old tradition borrowed from China). You can have one made too, but ask a local to help translate your name into Vietnamese. You might want to get your seal carved in Cholon using Chinese characters, since these are certainly more artistic (though less practical) than the Romanised script now used by the Vietnamese.

### Getting There & Away
**Air** Vietnam Airlines also acts as sales agent for Lao Aviation (Hang Khong Lao) and Cambodia Civil Airlines (Hang Khong Cam Bot). The complete list of airline offices is as follows:

Air France (Hang Khong Phap), 130 Dong Khoi St, District 1 (☎ 829-0891, 829-0982; fax 829-2396)
Asiana Airlines, 141-143 Ham Nghi Blvd, District 1 (☎ 822-2663, 821-2749; fax 822-2710)
Cathay Pacific Airways (Hang Khong Ca-thay Pa-ci-fic), 58 Dong Khoi St, District 1 (☎ 822-3203; fax 825-8276)
China Airlines (Taiwan), 132-134 Dong Khoi St (Continental Hotel), District 1 (☎ 825-1388, 825-1389; fax 825-1390)
China Southern Airlines (Hang Khong Nam Trung Hoa), 52B Pham Hong Thai St, District 1 (☎ 829-1172, 829-8417; fax 829-6800)

Emirates Airlines, The Landmark, 5B Ton Duc Thang St, District 1 (☎ 822-8000; fax 822-8080)
EVA Airways, 32 Ngo Duc Ke St, District 1 (☎ 829-3644, 829-3645; fax 829-3688)
Garuda Indonesia (Hang Khong In-do-ne-xia), 132-134 Dong Khoi St, District 1 (☎ 829-3644, 829-3645; fax 829-3688)
Japan Airlines, 143 Nguyen Van Troi St, District 1 (☎ 842-4462; fax 842-2189)
Korean Air, 65 Le Loi Blvd, District 1 (☎ 824-2869; fax 824-2877)
KLM, 244 Pasteur St, District 3 (☎ 823-1990)
Lauda (book through Lufthansa Airlines)
Lufthansa Airlines (Hang Khong CHLB Duc), 132-134 Dong Khoi St (Continental Hotel), District 1 (☎ 829-8529, 829-8549; fax 829-8537)
Malaysia Airlines (Hang Khong Ma-lay-sia), 55 Le Thanh Ton St, District 1 (☎ 824-2885, 829-2529; fax 824-2884)
Pacific Airlines (Hang Khong Pa-ci-fic), 177 Vo Thi Sau St, District 3 (☎ 820-0978; fax 820-0980)
Philippine Airlines (Hang Khong Phi-lip-pin), 132-134 Dong Khoi St (Continental Hotel), District 1 (☎ 823-0502, 823-0544)
Qantas Airways, Level 3, Administration Building, Tan Son Nhat Airport (☎ 839-3257; fax 829-2218)
Singapore Airlines (Hang Khong Sin-ga-po), 6 Le Loi, District 1 (☎ 823-1583, 823-1586; fax 823-1554)
Thai Airways International (Hang Khong Thai Lan), 65 Nguyen Du St, District 1 (☎ 829-2810, 822-3365; fax 822-3465)
United Airlines, 141 Nguyen Hue Blvd, District 1 (☎ 829-9091; fax 829-9092)
Vasco (☎ 842-2790; fax 844-5224), 114 Bach Dang St, Tan Binh District (just opposite Tan Son Nhat airport)
Vietnam Airlines (Hang Khong Vietnam), 116 Nguyen Hue Blvd, District 1 (☎ 829-2118, 823-0697; fax 823-0273)

It is essential to reconfirm all reservations for flights out of the country. For more information on international air transport to and from Vietnam, see the Getting There & Away chapter.

Domestic flights from Saigon are on both Vietnam Airlines and Pacific Airlines. See the Getting Around chapter for details on air fares, routes and schedules.

Tan Son Nhat airport (it was previously spelled Tan Son Nhut by southerners, but the northerners had the final say) was one of the three busiest airports in the world during the late 1960s. The runways are still lined with lichen-covered, mortar-proof, aircraft revetments (retaining walls) and other military structures. The complex of the US Military Assistance Command (MACV), also known as 'Pentagon East', was blown up by the Americans on 29 April 1975, hours before Saigon surrendered to North Vietnamese troops.

**Bus – Cholon Station** Intercity buses depart from, and arrive at, a variety of stations around Saigon. Cholon station is the most convenient place to get buses to Mytho and other Mekong Delta towns. The Cholon bus station is at the very western end of Tran Hung Dao Blvd in District 5, close to the Binh Tay Market.

**Bus – Mien Tay Station** Less conveniently located than Cholon station, Mien Tay station nevertheless has even more buses to points south of Saigon (basically the Mekong Delta). This enormous station (Ben Xe Mien Tay; ☎ 825-5955) is about 10km west of Saigon in An Lac, a part of Binh Chanh District (Huyen Binh Chanh).

Express buses and minibuses from Mien Tay bus station serve Bac Lieu (six hours), Camau (12 hours), Cantho (3½ hours), Chau Doc (six hours), Long Xuyen (five hours) and Rach Gia (six to seven hours).

Express buses, which receive priority treatment at ferry crossings, all depart twice a day: at 4.30 am and at 3 pm. Tickets are sold from 3.30 am for the early buses and from noon for the afternoon runs.

**Bus – Mien Dong Station** Buses to places north of Saigon leave from Mien Dong bus station (Ben Xe Mien Dong; ☎ 829-4056), which is in Binh Thanh District about 5km from downtown Saigon on National Highway 13 (see the HCMC map). National Highway 13 is the continuation of Xo Viet Nghe Tinh St. The station is just under 2km north of the intersection of Xo Viet Nghe Tinh St and Dien Bien Phu St.

There is express service from Mien Dong bus station to Buon Ma Thuot (15 hours), Danang (26 hours), Haiphong (53 hours), Hanoi (49 hours), Hué (29 hours), Nam Dinh (47 hours), Nha Trang (11 hours), Pleiku (22 hours), Quang Ngai (24 hours), Qui Nhon (17 hours), Tuy Hoa (12 hours) and Vinh (42 hours). All the express buses leave daily between 5 and 5.30 am.

**Bus – Van Thanh Station** Vehicles departing from Van Thanh bus station (Ben Xe Van Thanh; ☎ 829-4839) serve destinations within a few hours of Saigon, mostly in Song Be and Dong Nai provinces. For travellers, most important are probably the buses to Dalat and Vung Tau.

Van Thanh bus station is in Binh Thanh District about 1.5km east of the intersection of Dien Bien Phu St and Xo Viet Nghe Tinh St at 72 Dien Bien Phu St (see the HCMC map). As you head out of Saigon, go past where the numbers on Dien Bien Phu St climb up into the 600s.

An assortment of decrepit US vans, Daihatsu Hijets and Citroën Traction 15s leave Van Thanh bus station for Baria, Cho Lau, Ham Tan, Long Dien, Long Hai, Phu Cuong, Phu Giao, parts of Song Be Province, Vung Tau and Xuan Loc. Xe Lams go to Tay Ninh bus station in Tan Binh District. Vehicles leave when full (and we mean *full*). Van Thanh bus station is open from 6 am to about 6 pm.

**Bus – Tay Ninh Station** Buses to Tay Ninh, Cu Chi and points north-east of Saigon depart from the Tay Ninh bus station (Ben Xe Tay Ninh), which is in Tan Binh District. To get there, head all the way out Cach Mang Thang Tam St. The station is about 1km past where Cach Mang Thang Tam St merges with Le Dai Hanh St.

**Bus – Vung Tau** Just next to the Saigon Hotel and the mosque on Dong Du St is where you catch buses to Vung Tau. This is a bus stop, not an official bus station and so there is always the possibility that the location will be suddenly moved. In other words, inquire first.

**Bus – Cambodia** Details of the bus trip to Cambodia are provided in the general Getting There & Away chapter.

**Train** Saigon railway station (Ga Sai Gon; ☎ 823-0105) is in District 3 at 1 Nguyen Thong St (see the HCMC map). Trains from here serve cities along the coast north of Saigon. The ticket office is open from 7.15 to 11 am and 1 to 3 pm daily. Details of the *Reunification Express* service is provided in the general Getting Around chapter.

**Car** Inquire at almost any tourist cafe or hotel to arrange a car rental. Renting from a licensed agency is safer, albeit more expensive, but you needn't go to the most expensive places like Saigon Tourist. The agencies in the Pham Ngu Lao St area are, needless to say, willing to offer the lowest prices.

**Boat** Passenger and goods ferries to the Mekong Delta depart from a dock (☎ 829-7892) at the river end of Ham Nghi Blvd. There is daily service to the provinces of An Giang and Vinh Long and to the towns of Ben Tre (eight hours), Camau (30 hours; once every four days), Mytho (six hours; departs at 11 am) and Tan Chau. Buy your tickets on the boat. Simple food may be available on board. Be aware that these ancient vessels lack the most elementary safety gear, such as life jackets.

## Getting Around

**The Airport** Tan Son Nhat airport is 7km from central Saigon. In general, metered taxis are your best bet and it works out to around US$7 between the airport and downtown. There are also unmetered taxis, but these are no cheaper. Don't waste your time at the Tan Son Nhat airport Taxi Booking Desk – the minimum fare is US$25 for a standard taxi or US$50 for a limousine.

There is also Skybus, which runs from 7 am to 11 pm between the airport and the Vietnam Airlines office on Nguyen Hue Blvd. The cost is only US$2, but it hasn't proved tremendously popular largely because Vietnam Airlines is in a pricey neighbourhood where few budget travellers want to go. And, of course, upmarket tourists who do stay in that posh neighbourhood would rather take a taxi than the bus. If they would get their act together and stop at Pham Ngu Lao St, the service could be a big hit.

Cyclos (pedicabs) can be hailed outside the gate to the airport, which is a few hundred metres from the terminal building. A ride to central Saigon should cost about US$2. Motorbike 'taxis' hang out near the airport car park and typically ask US$3 to go downtown.

### Your Friendly Taxi Driver

A warning – airport taxis play a little game when it comes to bringing you to your hotel. They want the hotel to pay them a commission. The drivers know which hotels pay commissions and which ones don't – if you want to go to a hotel which does not pay commissions then don't be surprised if the driver claims that place is very dirty, unsafe, expensive or out of business. Many backpackers simply ask the driver to take them to Pham Ngu Lao St, but when you arrive there the driver will normally insist on going inside the hotel first 'to check if there's any rooms'. If the hotel refuses to pay him, then he'll tell you that there are 'no rooms left'. Sometimes the hotels really are full, but to find out the truth you really have to go inside yourself and ask – don't believe what your driver tells you.

Most of the hotels don't like these arrangements, but they are forced to go along with it – otherwise, they lose business. But even nastier is that some of the hotel owners go to the airport to make an agreement with the drivers – if they bring guests to their hotel, then the driver shares 50% of the first night's accommodation fee. With such a strong incentive, it's not surprising that many drivers at the airport try to shove a hotel namecard into your hand and claim it's 'very good'. You can also be assured that it's relatively expensive – in the end it's you who pays the commission.

It's worth knowing that all of the above applies to cyclos, motorbikes and taxis parked at the railway station.

One more problem is the street people who hang around the Pham Ngu Lao area. They watch for tourists and then hurry ahead of them and dive into the hotel to ask for a commission. If they don't get it, they make a big argument causing considerable hassle for the tourists and hotel owners. ■

To get to the airport, you can ring up a taxi (see the Taxi section below for telephone numbers). Some of the cafes in the Pham Ngu Lao budget hotel area also do runs to the airport – these places even have sign-up sheets where you can book share taxis for US$2 per person. This, no doubt, will prove considerably cheaper than the limousine service available at the front desk of the Rex Hotel.

If you take a cyclo or motorbike to Tan Son Nhat, you may have to walk from the airport gate to the terminal. Private cars can bring you into the airport, but must drop you off at the domestic terminal, only a one minute walk from the international terminal.

**Bus** Few foreigners make use of the city buses, though they are safer than cyclos if less aesthetic. Now that Ho Chi Minh City's People's Committee has resolved to phase out cyclos, some money is finally being put into the heretofore badly neglected public transport system.

At present, there are only three bus routes though more undoubtedly will be added. No decent bus map is available and bus stops are mostly unmarked, so it's worth summarising the three bus lines, which are as follows:

*Saigon – Cholon* Buses depart central Saigon from Me Linh Square (by the Saigon River) and continue along Tran Hung Dao Blvd to Binh Tay Market in Cholon, then return along the same route. The bus company running this route is an Australian joint venture – buses have air-conditioning and video movies and the driver is well dressed! All this for US$0.20. Buy your ticket on board from the female attendant (sharply dressed in a blouse and skirt).

*Mien Dong – Mien Tay* Buses depart Mien Dong bus station (north-east Saigon), pass through Cholon and terminate at Mien Tay bus station in the western edge of town. The fare is US$0.40.

*Van Thanh – Mien Tay* Buses depart Van Thanh bus station (eastern Saigon), pass through Cholon and terminate at Mien Tay bus station (western Saigon). The fare is US$0.40.

**Taxi** Metered taxis occasionally cruise the streets, but it's much easier to find one if you ring up their dispatcher. There are currently eight companies in Saigon offering metered taxis and they charge almost exactly the same rates. Flagfall is currently US$0.60 for the first kilometre and US$0.60 thereafter. The eight competitors in this market are: Airport Taxi (☎ 844-6666), Ben Thanh Taxi (☎ 842-2422), Festival Taxi (☎ 845-4545), Mai Linh Taxi (☎ 822-6666), Nguyen Tran Taxi (☎ 835-0350), Saigon Taxi (☎ 842-4242), V Taxi (☎ 820-2020) and Vina Taxi (☎ 842-2888).

**Xe Lam** Xe Lams (tiny three-wheeled vehicles otherwise known as Lambrettas) connect the various bus stations. There is a useful Xe Lam stop on the north-west corner of Pham Ngu Lao and Nguyen Thai Hoc Sts where you can catch a ride to the Mien Tay bus station. This station is where you get buses to the Mekong Delta.

**Car** Travel agencies, hotels and cafes are all into the car rental business. Most of the vehicles are relatively recent Japanese machines – everything from subcompacts to minibuses. However, it's still possible to enjoy a ride in a vintage vehicle from the 50s and 60s. Not long ago, boat-like classic American cars (complete with tail fins and impressive chrome fenders) were popular as 'wedding taxis'. These added considerable charm to Vietnamese weddings, but have fallen out of fashion – prestige these days means a white Toyota. Nevertheless, some of the old vehicles can be hired for excursions in and around Saigon. Aside from American road hogs you'll see the occasional French-built Renaults and Citroëns. The former Soviet Union chips in with vehicles made by Lada, Moskvich and Volga.

**Motorbike** If you're brave, you can rent a motorbike and really earn your 'I Survived Saigon' T-shirt. Many say that this is the fastest and easiest way to get around Saigon and that's probably true as long as you don't crash into anything.

Motorbike rentals are ubiquitous in places where tourists congregate. The Pham Ngu Lao St area is as good as any to satisfy this need. Ask at the cafes or else talk to a cyclo driver for ideas on where to find rentals.

A 50cc motorbike can be rented for US$5 to US$10 per day. Before renting one, make sure it's rideable.

**Cyclo** Cyclos (pedicabs) can be hailed along major thoroughfares almost any time of the day or night. In Saigon, many of the drivers are former South Vietnamese army soldiers and quite a few of them know at least basic English, while others are quite fluent. Each of them has a story of war, 're-education', persecution and poverty to tell.

There are a number of major streets on which cyclos are prohibited to ride. As a result, your driver must often take a circuitous route to avoid these trouble spots since the police will not hesitate to fine them. For the same reason, the driver may not be able to drop you off at the exact address you want though he will bring you to the nearest side street. Many travellers have gotten angry at their cyclo drivers for this, but try to have some sympathy since it is not their fault.

Short hops around the city centre should cost about US$0.50; central Saigon to central Cholon costs about US$1. Overcharging is the norm, so negotiate a price

French and American cars dating from the 50s and 60s are available for hire in Ho Chi Minh City for sightseeing and excursions in and around the city. They are also often used by locals on special occasions, such as weddings.

beforehand and have the exact change ready. Renting a cyclo for US$1 per hour is a fine idea if you will be doing much touring.

Enjoy cyclos while you can – the municipal government intends to phase them out. In an effort to prevent the cyclo population from expanding, the municipal government no longer registers new cyclos. However, enterprising locals have started manufacturing fake licence plates in an effort to thwart the ban on new vehicles. One effect of these 'pirate cyclos' *(xe bo trong)* is that if the driver gives you a bad time and you copy down his licence number to report him to the police, the number may turn out to be a dud.

**Honda Om** A quick (if precarious) way around town is to ride on the back of a motorbike (Honda om). You can either try to flag someone down (most drivers can always use whatever extra cash they can get) or ask a Vietnamese to find a Honda om for you. The accepted rate is comparable to what cyclos charge.

**Bicycle** A bicycle is a good, slow way to get around the city and see things. Bikes can be rented from a number of places – many hotels, cafes and travel agencies can accommodate you.

The best place in Saigon to buy a decent (ie imported) bicycle is at Federal Bike Shop (☎ 833-2899), which has stores at three locations: 139H Nguyen Trai St, 158B Vo Thi Sau St and 156 Pham Hong Thai St. Cheaper deals may be found at some of the shops around 288 Le Thanh Ton St (corner Cach Mang Thang Tam St). You can also buy bike components: Czech and French frames, Chinese derailleurs, headlamps etc. A decent bicycle with foreign components costs about US$100. In Cholon, you might try the bicycle shops on Ngo Gia Tu Blvd just south-west of Ly Thai To Blvd (near An Quang Pagoda). In District 4 there are bicycle parts shops along Nguyen Tat Thanh St just south of the Ho Chi Minh Museum.

For cheap and poorly assembled domestic bicycles and parts, try the ground floor of Cua Hang Bach Hoa, the department store on the corner of Nguyen Hue Blvd and Le Loi Blvd. Vikotrade Company at 35 Le Loi Blvd (across the street from the Rex Hotel) also has locally made components.

For on-the-spot bicycle repairs, look for an upturned army helmet and a hand pump sitting next to the curb. There is a cluster of bicycle repair shops around 23 Phan Dang Luu Blvd (see the HCMC map).

Bicycle parking lots are usually just roped-off sections of a sidewalk. For US$0.10 you can leave your bicycle knowing that it will be there when you get back (bicycle theft is a big problem). When you pull up, your bicycle will have a number written on the seat in chalk or stapled to the handlebars. You will be given a reclaim chit (don't lose it!). If you come back and your bicycle is gone, the parking lot is supposedly required to replace it.

**Boat** To see the city from the Saigon River, you can easily hire a motorised 5m boat. Warning – there have been quite a few unpleasant incidents with bag snatching and pickpocketing at the docks at the base of Ham Nghi Blvd. It's better to go to the nearby area where you see the ships offering dinner cruises. Around that area, you'll always see someone hanging around looking to charter a boat – ask them to bring the boat to you, rather than you go to the boat (they can easily do this).

The price should US$5 per hour for a small boat or US$10 to US$15 for a larger and faster craft. Interesting destinations for short trips include Cholon (along Ben Nghe Channel) and the zoo (along Thi Nghe Channel). Note that both channels are fascinating, but filthy – raw sewage is discharged into the water. Foreigners regard the channels as a major tourist attraction, but the government considers them an eyesore and has already launched a programme to move local residents out. The channels will eventually be filled in and the water will be diverted into underground sewer pipes. At that point, the only possible channel cruises will be by submarine.

For longer trips up the Saigon River, it would be worth chartering a fast speedboat from Saigon Tourist. Although these cost US$20 per hour, you'll save money when you consider that a cheap boat takes at least five times longer for the same journey. Splitting the cost between a small group of travellers makes a lot of economic sense and it's always more fun to travel with others unless you prefer solitude. Although cruising the Saigon River can be interesting, it pales in comparison with the splendour of the canals in the Mekong Delta region (see the Mekong Delta chapter for details). One traveller wrote:

We hired a small boat with driver and female guide for US$5 for an hour for two people and were able to go up the Cholon Channel and see life on the waterfront. The bridges are too low for regular tourist craft. It was extremely interesting to see how these stilthouse dwellers live. We were told that already when the water level is low 'pirate boys' board the boats demanding money, but we had no problems. We were able to take many interesting photographs.

But another traveller had a different attitude:

Boat trips through the Ben Nghe Channel to Cholon are a bit of a rip-off. The pieces of plastic and the water-plants in the very dirty water make the motor stop every two or three minutes. This forces the boat owner to stop and do a cleaning job which takes much time. We spent 35 minutes drifting on 5km of stinking water without any protection from the rain. There are certainly better places in Vietnam to do boat journeys, such as Cantho, Nha Trang, Hoi An and Hué, to name a few.

**Gorrit Goslinga**

Since you hire boats by the hour, some will go particularly slowly because they know the meter is running. You might want to set a time limit from the outset.

Ferries across the Saigon River leave from a dock at the foot of Ham Nghi Blvd. They run every half hour or so from 4.30 am to 10.30 pm. To get on these vessels, you have to run the gauntlet of greedy boat owners and pickpockets.

**Subway** No, Saigon does not yet have a subway, nor is one under construction. However, foreign consultants have been called in and a feasibility study is under way. It's not likely that the subway will be completed within the life span of this book or even during the next edition. Nevertheless, we want to be optimists. When the ribbon-cutting ceremony for the Saigon Metro finally happens, just remember that you read it here first.

# Around Ho Chi Minh City

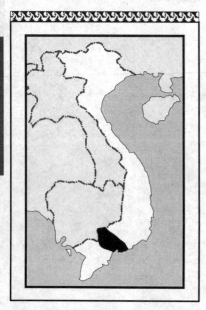

included innumerable trapdoors, specially constructed living areas, storage facilities, weapons factories, field hospitals, command centres and kitchens.

The tunnels made possible communication and coordination between VC-controlled enclaves isolated from each other by South Vietnamese and American land and air operations. They also allowed the guerrillas to mount surprise attacks wherever the tunnels went – even within the perimeters of the US military base at Dong Du – and to disappear into hidden trapdoors without a trace. After ground operations against the tunnels claimed large numbers of casualties and proved ineffective, the Americans resorted to massive firepower, eventually turning Cu Chi's 420 sq km into what Tom Mangold and John Penycate have called 'the most bombed, shelled, gassed, defoliated and generally devastated area in the history of warfare'.

Today, Cu Chi has become a pilgrimage site for Vietnamese school children and Party cadres. Parts of this remarkable tunnel network – enlarged and upgraded versions of the real thing – are open to the public. The unadulterated tunnels, though not actually closed to tourists, are hard to get to and are rarely visited. There are numerous war cemeteries all around Cu Chi, though tour groups don't usually stop at these except on special request.

### History

The tunnels of Cu Chi were built over a period of 25 years beginning in the late 1940s. They were the improvised response of a poorly equipped peasant army to its enemy's high-tech ordnance, helicopters, artillery, bombers and chemical weapons.

The Viet Minh built the first dugouts and tunnels in the hard, red earth of Cu Chi – ideal for the construction of tunnels – during the war against the French. The excavations were used mostly for communication between

## CU CHI TUNNELS

The town of Cu Chi had about 80,000 residents during the American War, but has now become a district of greater Ho Chi Minh City with a population of 200,000. At first glance, there is little evidence here to indicate the heavy fighting, bombing and destruction that went on in Cu Chi during the war. To see what went on, you have to dig deeper – underground.

The tunnel network of Cu Chi became legendary during the 1960s for its role in facilitating Viet Cong control of a large rural area only 30 to 40km from Saigon. At its height, the tunnel system stretched from the South Vietnamese capital to the Cambodian border; in the district of Cu Chi alone, there were over 250km of tunnels. The network, parts of which were several storeys deep,

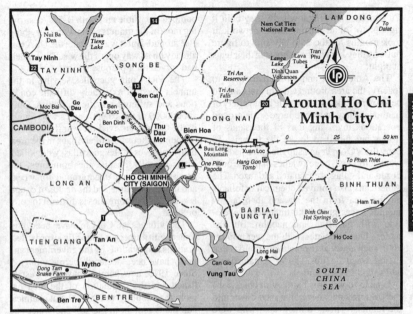

villages and to evade French army sweeps of the area.

When National Liberation Front (Viet Cong) insurgency began in earnest around 1960, the old Viet Minh tunnels were repaired and new extensions excavated. Within a few years the system assumed enormous strategic importance and most of Cu Chi District and nearby areas came under firm Viet Cong control. In addition, Cu Chi was used as a base for infiltrating intelligence agents and sabotage teams into Saigon itself. The stunning attacks in the South Vietnamese capital itself during the 1968 Tet Offensive were planned and launched from Cu Chi.

In early 1963, the Diem government implemented the botched Strategic Hamlets Programme, under which fortified encampments, surrounded by rows of sharp bamboo spikes, were built to house people relocated from Communist-controlled areas. The first 'strategic hamlet' was in Ben Cat District,

next door to Cu Chi. Not only was the programme carried out with incredible incompetence, alienating the peasantry, but the VC launched a major (successful) effort to defeat it – the VC was able to tunnel into the hamlets and control them from within. By the end of 1963, the first showpiece hamlet had been overrun.

The series of setbacks and defeats suffered by the South Vietnamese government forces in the Cu Chi area helped make a complete Viet Cong victory by the end of 1965 seem a distinct possibility. Indeed, in the early months of that year, the guerrillas boldly held a victory parade in the middle of Cu Chi town. VC strength in and around Cu Chi was one of the reasons the Johnson administration decided to involve American combat troops in the war.

To deal with the threat posed by VC control of an area so near the South Vietnamese capital, one of the Americans' first actions was to establish a large base camp in

Cu Chi District. Unknowingly, they built it right on top of an existing tunnel network. It took months for the 25th Division to figure out why they kept getting shot at in their tents at night.

The Americans and Australians tried to 'pacify' the area around Cu Chi that came to be known as the Iron Triangle by a variety of methods. They launched large-scale ground operations involving tens of thousands of troops but failed to locate the tunnels. To deny the VC cover and supplies, rice paddies were defoliated, huge swathes of jungle bulldozed and villages evacuated and razed. The Americans also sprayed chemical defoliants on the area from the air and then, a few months later, ignited the tinder-dry vegetation with gasoline and napalm. But the intense heat interacted with the wet tropical air in such a way as to create cloudbursts that extinguished the fires. The VC remained safe and sound in their tunnels.

Unable to win this battle with chemicals, the US army began sending men down into the tunnels. These 'tunnel rats', who were often involved in underground fire fights, sustained appallingly high casualty rates.

When the Americans began using alsatians trained to use their keen sense of smell to locate trapdoors and guerrillas, the VC put out pepper to distract the dogs. They also began washing with American toilet soap, which gave off a scent the canines identified as friendly. Captured American uniforms, which had the familiar smell of bodies nourished on American-style food, were put out to confuse the dogs further. Most importantly, the dogs were not able to spot booby traps. So many dogs were killed or maimed that their horrified army handlers refused to send them into the tunnels.

The Americans declared Cu Chi a free-strike zone: minimal authorisation was needed to shoot at anything in the area, random artillery was fired into the area at night and pilots were told to drop unused bombs and napalm there before returning to base. But the Viet Cong stayed put. Finally, in the late 1960s, the Americans carpet-bombed the whole area with B-52s, destroying most of the tunnels along with everything else around. But it was too late; the USA was already on its way out of the war. The tunnels had served their purpose.

The Viet Cong guerrillas serving in the tunnels lived in extremely difficult conditions and suffered horrific casualties. Only about 6000 of the 16,000 cadres who fought in the tunnels survived the war. In addition, uncounted thousands of civilians in the area, many relatives of the guerrillas, were killed. Their tenacity despite the bombings, the pressures of living underground for weeks and months at a time and the deaths of countless friends and comrades is difficult to comprehend.

The villages of Cu Chi have been presented with numerous honorific awards, decorations and citations by the government and many have been declared 'heroic villages'. Since 1975, new hamlets have been established and the population of the area has more than doubled to 200,000, but chemical defoliants remain in the soil and water and crop yields are still poor.

For more details, you might want to take a look at *The Tunnels of Cu Chi* by Tom Mangold & John Penycate (Random House, New York, 1985).

## The Tunnels

Over the years the VC, learning by trial and error, developed simple but effective techniques to make their tunnels difficult to detect or disable. Wooden trapdoors were camouflaged with earth and branches; some were booby-trapped. Hidden underwater entrances from rivers were constructed. To cook, they used 'Dien Bien Phu kitchens' which exhausted the smoke through vents many metres away from the cooking site. Trapdoors were installed throughout the network to prevent tear gas, smoke or water from moving from one part of the system to another. Some sections were even equipped with electric lighting.

Presently, two of the tunnel sites are open to visitors. One is near the village of Ben Dinh and the other is at Ben Duoc.

**The Tunnels at Ben Dinh** This small, renovated section of the tunnel system is near the village of Ben Dinh. In one of the classrooms at the visitors' centre, a large map shows the extent of the network (the area shown is in the north-western corner of Greater Ho Chi Minh City). The tunnels are marked in red, Viet Cong bases are shown in light grey and the light blue lines are rivers (the Saigon River is at the top). Fortified villages held by South Vietnamese and American forces are marked in grey, while blue dots represent the American and South Vietnamese military posts that were supposed to ensure the security of nearby villages. The dark blue area in the centre is the base of the American 25th Infantry Division. Most pre-arranged tours do not take you to this former base, but it is not off limits and if you have your own guide and driver you can easily arrange a visit.

To the right of the large map are two cross-section diagrams of the tunnels. The bottom diagram is a reproduction of one used by General William Westmoreland, the commander of American forces in Vietnam from 1964 to 1968. For once, the Americans seemed to have had their intelligence information right (though the tunnels did not pass under rivers nor did the guerrillas wear headgear underground).

The section of the tunnel system presently open to visitors is a few hundred metres south of the visitors' centre. It snakes up and down through various chambers along its 50m length. The unlit tunnels are about 1.2m high and 80cm across. A knocked-out M-48 tank and a bomb crater are near the exit, which is in a reafforested eucalyptus grove.

Entry to the tunnel site, which is now controlled by Saigon Tourist, costs US$3 for foreigners, but is free for Vietnamese nationals.

**The Tunnels at Ben Duoc** These are not the genuine tunnels but a full-fledged reconstruction for the benefit of tourists. The emphasis here is more on the fun fare, and tourists are given the chance to imagine what it was like to be a guerrilla. At this site there is even the opportunity to fire an M-16, AK-47 or Russian carbine rifle. This costs US$1 per bullet but may be the only opportunity you'll ever get. It's recommended that you wear hearing protection.

Admission to the tunnels at Ben Duoc is US$4.

## Cu Chi War History Museum

This museum is not actually at the tunnel sites, but rather just off the main highway in the central area of the town of Cu Chi. Sad to say, the Cu Chi War History Museum (Nha Truyen Thong Huyen Cu Chi) is rather disappointing and gets few visitors.

It's a small museum and almost all explanations are in Vietnamese. Indeed, we only found one English explanation, a placard attached to a canoe which read:

Mr Nguyen Van Tranh's boat. He now is living in hamlet Mui Con, Phuoc Hiep village. During the wars against the French colonialists and the American imperialists, he was using this boat for transporting food and weapons, as well as carrying revolutionary cadres to and fro.

There is a collection of some gruesome photos showing severely wounded or dead civilians after being attacked by American bombs or burned with napalm. A painting on the wall shows American soldiers armed with rifles being attacked by Vietnamese peasants armed only with sticks. A sign near the photos formerly read (in Vietnamese) 'American conquest and crimes', but this was changed in 1995 to read 'Enemy conquest and crimes'. Apparently, some effort is being made to tone down the rhetoric in anticipation of receiving more American visitors.

One wall of the museum contains a long list of names, all Viet Cong guerrillas killed in the Cu Chi area. An adjacent room of the museum displays recent photos of prosperous farms and factories, an effort to show the benefits of Vietnam's economic reforms. There is also an odd collection of pottery and lacquerware with no explanations attached. In the lobby near the entrance is a statue of

Ho Chi Minh with his right arm raised, waving hello.

Admission to the Cu Chi War History Museum is US$1 for foreigners.

### Getting There & Away

Cu Chi is a district which covers a large area, parts of which are as close as 30km to central Saigon. The Cu Chi War History Museum is the closest place to the city, but the actual tunnels that exist now are about 65km from central Saigon by highway. However, there is a backroad which cuts the commute significantly, though it means driving on bumpy dirt roads.

**Bus** Buses from Saigon to Tay Ninh leave from the Tay Ninh bus station (Ben Xe Tay Ninh) in Tan Binh District and Mien Tay bus station in An Lac. All buses to Tay Ninh pass though Cu Chi town, but getting from the town of Cu Chi to the tunnels by public transport is impossible – it's 15km, so you'll have to hire a motorbike.

**Taxi** Hiring a taxi in Saigon and just driving out to Cu Chi is not all that expensive, especially if the cost is split by several people. If you want to visit the 'real' tunnels rather than those open to the public, make this clear to your driver before you cut a deal. A non-English-speaking guide can be hired at the visitors' centre. For details on hiring vehicles in Saigon, see the Getting There & Away and Getting Around sections in the Ho Chi Minh City chapter.

A visit to the Cu Chi tunnel complex can easily be combined with a stop at the headquarters of the Caodai sect in Tay Ninh. A taxi for an all-day excursion to both should cost about US$40.

**Organised Tours** This is the best way to go and not at all expensive. Some of the cafes on Pham Ngu Lao St run combined full-day tours to the Cu Chi tunnels and Caodai Great Temple for as little as US$4. Organised tours run by Saigon Tourist and Vietnam Tourism often visit the Cu Chi tunnels, but these are no bargain.

## TAY NINH

Tay Ninh town, the capital of Tay Ninh Province, serves as the headquarters of one of Vietnam's most interesting indigenous religions, Caodaism. The Caodai Great Temple at the sect's Holy See is one of the most striking structures in all of Asia. Built between 1933 and 1955, it is a rococo extravaganza combining the architectural idiosyncrasies of a French church, a Chinese pagoda, the Tiger Balm Gardens and Madame Tussaud's Wax Museum.

Tay Ninh Province, which is north-west of Saigon, is bordered by Cambodia on three sides. The area's dominant geographic feature is Nui Ba Den (Black Lady Mountain), which towers 850m above the surrounding plains. Tay Ninh Province's eastern border is formed by the Saigon River. The Vam Co River flows from Cambodia through the western part of the province.

Because of the once-vaunted political and military power of the Caodai, this region was the scene of prolonged heavy fighting during the Franco-Viet Minh War. Tay Ninh Province served as a major terminus of the Ho Chi Minh Trail during the American War. In 1969, the VC captured Tay Ninh town and held it for several days.

During the period of tension between Cambodia and Vietnam in the late 1970s, the Khmer Rouge launched a number of cross-border raids into Tay Ninh Province during which atrocities were committed against the civilian population. Several grisly cemeteries around Tay Ninh are stark reminders of these events.

### Information

**Travel Agencies** Tay Ninh Tourist (☎ 822-376) is presently in the Hoa Binh Hotel on 30/4 St. However, the office is supposed to move just across the street when a new building is completed, though no word yet on just when that might be. The staff here have plans to introduce tours to nearby Dau Tieng Reservoir, complete with boat trips and optional water-skiing.

Interestingly, they currently offer tours 17km into Cambodia to the hamlet of Chang

Riet. The destination here is the Southern Central Department Base (Can Cu Trung Uong Cuc Mien Nam), an old VC base 62km north-west of Tay Ninh. It was intentionally located inside Cambodia to avoid attacks by South Vietnamese troops. It served as Communist Party headquarters for the southern command from 1973 to 1975. Unfortunately, these tours are currently only open to domestic tourists. Foreigners may be allowed in the future if certain bureaucratic visa hurdles can be overcome.

### The Caodai Religion

Caodaism (Dai Dao Tam Ky Pho Do) is the product of an attempt to create the ideal religion through the fusion of the secular and religious philosophies of the east and west. The result is a colourful and eclectic potpourri that includes bits and pieces of most of the religious philosophies known in Vietnam during the early 20th century: Buddhism, Confucianism, Taoism, native Vietnamese spiritualism, Christianity and Islam.

The term 'Caodai', which literally means 'high tower or palace', is used to refer to God. The religion is called 'Caodaism' and its adherents are the 'Caodais'. The hierarchy of the sect, whose priesthood is non-professional, is partly based on the structure of the Roman Catholic Church.

**History** Caodaism was founded by the mystic Ngo Minh Chieu (also known as Ngo Van Chieu; born 1878), a civil servant who once served as district chief of Phu Quoc Island. He was widely read in eastern and western religious works and became active in seances, at which his presence was said to greatly improve the quality of communication with the spirits. Around 1919 he began to receive a series of revelations from Caodai in which the tenets of Caodai doctrine were set forth.

Caodaism was officially founded as a religion in a ceremony held in 1926. Within a year, the group had 26,000 followers. Many of the sect's early followers were Vietnamese members of the French colonial administration. By the mid-1950s, one in eight southern

Vietnamese was a Caodai and the sect was famous worldwide for its imaginative garishness. But in 1954, British author Graham Green, who had once considered converting to Caodaism, wrote in *The Times* of London: 'What on my first two visits has seemed gay and bizarre (was) now like a game that had gone on too long'.

By the mid-50s, the Caodai had established a virtually independent feudal state in Tay Ninh Province and they retained enormous influence in the affairs of Tay Ninh Province for the next two decades. They also played a significant political and military role in South Vietnam from 1926 to 1956, when most of the 25,000-strong Caodai army, which had been given support by the Japanese and later the French, was incorporated into the South Vietnamese army. During the Franco-Viet Minh War, Caodai munitions factories specialised in making mortar tubes out of automobile exhaust pipes.

Because they had refused to support the Viet Cong during the American War – and despite the fact that they had been barely tolerated by the Saigon government – the Caodai feared the worst after reunification. Indeed, all Caodai lands were confiscated by the new Communist government and four members of the sect were executed in 1979, but in 1985 the Holy See and some 400 temples were returned to Caodai control.

Caodaism is strongest in Tay Ninh Province and the Mekong Delta, but Caodai temples can be found throughout southern and central Vietnam. Today, there are an estimated three million followers of Caodaism. Vietnamese who fled abroad after the Communists came to power have spread the Caodai religion to western countries, though their numbers are not large.

**Philosophy** Much of Caodai doctrine is drawn from Mahayana Buddhism mixed with Taoist and Confucian elements (Vietnam's 'Triple Religion'). Caodai ethics are based on the Buddhist ideal of 'the good person', but incorporate traditional Vietnamese taboos and sanctions as well.

The ultimate goal of the disciple of Caodaism is to escape the cycle of reincarnation. This can be achieved by the performance of certain human duties, including first and foremost following the prohibitions against killing, lying, luxurious living, sensuality and stealing.

The main tenets of Caodaism include believing in one God, the existence of the soul and the use of mediums to communicate with the spiritual world. Caodai practices include priestly celibacy, vegetarianism, communications with spirits through seances, reverence for the dead, maintenance of the cult of ancestors, fervent proselytising and sessions of meditative self-cultivation.

Following the Chinese duality of Yin and Yang, there are two principal deities, the Mother Goddess, who is female, and God, who is male. There is a debate among the Caodai as to which deity was the primary source of creation.

According to Caodaism, history is divided into three major periods of divine revelation. During the first period, God's truth was revealed to humanity through Laotse and figures associated with Buddhism, Confucianism and Taoism. The human agents of revelation during the second period were Buddha (Sakyamuni), Mohammed, Confucius, Jesus and Moses. The Caodai believe that their messages were corrupted because of the human frailty of the messengers and their disciples. They also believe that these revelations were limited in scope, intended to be applicable only during a specific age to the people of the area in which the messengers lived.

Caodaism sees itself as the product of the 'Third Alliance Between God and Man', the third and final revelation. Disciples believe that Caodaism avoids the failures of the first two periods because it is based on divine truth as communicated through spirits which serve as messengers of salvation and instructors of doctrine. Spirits who have been in touch with the Caodai include deceased Caodai leaders, patriots, heroes, philosophers, poets, political leaders and warriors, as well as ordinary people. Among the contacted spirits who lived as westerners are Joan of Arc, René Descartes, William Shakespeare (who hasn't been heard from since 1935), Victor Hugo, Louis Pasteur and Vladimir Ilyich Lenin. Because of his frequent appearances to Caodai mediums at the Phnom Penh mission, Victor Hugo was posthumously named the chief spirit of foreign missionary works.

Communication with the spirits is carried out in Vietnamese, Chinese, French and English. The methods of receiving messages from the spirits illustrate the influence of both East Asian and western spiritualism on Caodai seance rites. Sometimes, a medium holds a pen or Chinese calligraphy brush. In the 1920s, a 66cm-long wooden staff known as a *corbeille à bec* was used. Mediums held one end while a crayon attached to the other wrote out the spirits' messages. The Caodai also use what is known as *pneumatographie*, in which a blank slip of paper is sealed in an envelope and hung above the altar. When the envelope is taken down, there is a message on the paper.

Most of the sacred literature of Caodaism consists of messages communicated to Caodai leaders during seances held between 1925 and 1929. Since 1927, only the official seances held at Tay Ninh have been considered reliable and divinely ordained by the Caodai hierarchy, though dissident groups continued to hold seances which produced communications contradicting accepted doctrine.

The Caodai consider vegetarianism to be of service to humanity because it does not involve harming fellow beings during the process of their spiritual evolution. They also see vegetarianism as a form of self-purification. There are several different vegetarian regimens followed by Caodai disciples. The least rigorous involves eating vegetarian food six days a month. Priests must be fulltime vegetarians.

The clergy (except at the highest levels) is open to both men and women, though when male and female officials of equal rank are serving in the same area, male clergy are in charge. Female officials wear white robes and are addressed with the title *huong*, which means 'perfume'. Male clergy are addressed as *thanh*, which means 'pure'. Caodai temples are constructed so that male and female disciples enter on opposite sides; women worship on the left, men on the right.

All Caodai temples observe four daily ceremonies, which are held at 6 am, noon, 6 pm and midnight. These rituals, during which dignitaries wear ceremonial dress and hats, include offerings of incense, tea, alcohol, fruit and flowers. All Caodai altars have above them the 'divine eye', which became the religion's official symbol after Ngo Minh Chieu saw it in a vision he had while on Phu Quoc Island.

### Caodai Holy See

The Caodai Holy See, founded in 1926, is 4km east of Tay Ninh in the village of Long Hoa

The complex includes the Caodai Great Temple (Thanh That Cao Dai), administrative offices, residences for officials and adepts, and a hospital of traditional Vietnamese herbal medicine to which people from all over the south travel for treatment. After reunification, the government 'borrowed' parts of the complex for its own use (and perhaps to keep an eye on the sect).

Prayers are conducted four times daily in the Great Temple, though they may be suspended during Tet. It's worth visiting during prayer sessions (the one at noon is most popular with tour groups from Saigon), but take care not to disturb the worshippers. Only a few hundred priests participate in weekday prayers, but on festivals several thousand priests, dressed in special white garments, may attend. The Caodai clergy have no objection to your photographing temple objects, but you cannot photograph people without their permission, which is seldom granted. However, you can photograph the prayer sessions from the upstairs balcony, an apparent concession to the troops of tourists who come here every day.

It is important that guests wear modest and respectful attire (no shorts or sleeveless T-shirts) inside the temple. However, sandals are OK since you have to take them off anyway before you enter.

Above the front portico of the Great Temple is the 'divine eye'. Americans often comment that it looks as if it were copied from the back of a US$1 bill. Lay women enter the Great Temple through a door at the base of the tower on the left. Once inside, they walk around the outside of the colonnaded hall in a clockwise direction. Men enter on the right and walk around the hall in an anti-clockwise direction. Shoes and hats must be removed upon entering the building. The area in the centre of the sanctuary (between the pillars) is reserved for Caodai priests.

A mural in the front entry hall depicts the three signatories of the 'Third Alliance Between God and Man'. The Chinese statesman and revolutionary leader Dr Sun Yatsen (1866-1925) holds an inkstone while Vietnamese poet Nguyen Binh Khiem (1492-1587) and Victor Hugo (1802-85), French poet and author, write 'God and Humanity' and 'Love and Justice' in Chinese and French. Victor Hugo uses a quill pen; Nguyen Binh Khiem writes with a brush. Nearby signs in English, French and German each give a slightly different version of the fundamentals of Caodaism.

The Great Temple is built on nine levels, which represent the nine steps to heaven. Each level is marked by a pair of columns. At the far end of the sanctuary, eight plaster columns entwined with multicoloured dragons support a dome representing – as does the rest of the ceiling – the heavens. Under the dome is a giant star-speckled blue globe with the 'divine eye' on it.

The largest of the seven chairs in front of the globe is reserved for the Caodai pope, a position that has remained unfilled since 1933. The next three chairs are for the three men responsible for the religion's law books. The remaining chairs are for the leaders of the three branches of Caodaism, which are represented by the colours yellow, blue and red.

On both sides of the area between the

## Pagoda or Temple?

Travelling around Vietnam, one continually encounters the terms 'pagoda' and 'temple'. The Vietnamese use these terms somewhat differently from the Chinese and, as a result, there is a bit of confusion (particularly if you've just come from China).

To the Chinese, a pagoda *(bata)* is usually a tall eight-sided tower built to house the ashes of the deceased. A Chinese temple *(miao* or *si)* is an active place of worship.

The Vietnamese regard a pagoda *(chua)* as a place of worship and it's by no means certain that you'll find a tower to store the ashes of the dearly departed. A Vietnamese temple *(den)* is not really a place of worship, but rather a structure built to honour some great historical figure (Confucius, Tran Hung Dao and even Ho Chi Minh). ■

columns are two pulpits similar in design to the *minbars* found in mosques. During festivals, the pulpits are used by officials to address the assembled worshippers. The upstairs balconies are used if there is an overflow crowd downstairs.

Up near the altar are barely discernible portraits of six figures important to Caodaism: Sakyamuni (Siddhartha Guatama, the founder of Buddhism); Ly Thai Bach (Li Taibai, a fairy from Chinese mythology); Khuong Tu Nha (Jiang Taigong, a Chinese saint); Laotse (the founder of Taoism); Quan Cong (Guangong, Chinese God of War); and Quan Am (Guanyin, the Goddess of Mercy).

### Long Hoa Market

Long Hoa Market is several kilometres south of the Caodai Holy See complex. Open every day from 5 am to about 6 pm, this large market sells meat, food staples, clothing and pretty much everything else you would expect to find in a rural marketplace. Before reunification, the Caodai sect had the right to collect taxes from the merchants here.

### Places to Stay

The main place in town accepting foreigners is the *Hoa Binh Hotel* (☎ 822376, 822383; 57 rooms) on 30/4 St. Rooms with fan only are US$8, but most rooms are air-con and are priced from US$12 to US$25. The hotel is 5km from the Caodai Great Temple

The other alternative is the *Anh Dao Hotel* on 30/4 St, 500m west of the Hoa Binh Hotel. There are 14 twin rooms here priced from US$10 to US$22.

### Places to Eat

*Nha Hang Diem Thuy* (☎ 827318) on 30/4 St is a great restaurant with low prices. Giant crayfish *(tom can)* are one of its specialities and, although not cheap, cost only a third of what you'd pay in Saigon.

One kilometre north of the Tay Ninh market near the river is the *Hoang Yen Restaurant*, considered by locals to be the best in town. Right on the river next to the bridge is the government-owned *Festival Restaurant*, which has great ambience, though the food is not spectacular.

### Getting There & Away

**Bus**  Buses from Saigon to Tay Ninh leave from the Tay Ninh bus station (Ben Xe Tay Ninh) in Tan Binh District and Mien Tay bus station in An Lac.

Tay Ninh is 96km from Saigon on National Highway 22 (Quoc Lo 22). The road passes through Trang Bang, where a famous news photo of a severely burned young, naked girl, screaming and running, was taken during an American napalm attack. There are several Caodai temples along National Highway 22, including one, under construction in 1975, that was heavily damaged by the Viet Cong.

**Taxi** An easy way to get to Tay Ninh is by taxi, perhaps on a day trip that includes a stop in Cu Chi. An all-day round trip by taxi should cost about US$40.

## NUI BA DEN

Nui Ba Den (Black Lady Mountain), 15km north-east of Tay Ninh town, rises 850m above the rice paddies of the surrounding countryside. Over the centuries, Nui Ba Den has served as a shrine for various peoples of the area, including the Khmer, Chams, Vietnamese and Chinese. There are several cave-temples on the mountain. The summits of Nui Ba Den are much cooler than the rest of Tay Ninh Province, most of which is only a few dozen metres above sea level.

Nui Ba Den was used as a staging ground by both the Viet Minh and the Viet Cong and was the scene of fierce fighting during the French and American wars. At one time there was a US army firebase and relay station at the summit of the mountain, which was defoliated and heavily bombed by American aircraft.

The name Black Lady Mountain is derived from the legend of Huong, a young woman who married her true love despite the advances of a wealthy mandarin. While her husband was away doing military service, she would visit a magical statue of Buddha at the summit of the mountain. One day, Huong was attacked by kidnappers, but preferring death to dishonour, threw herself off a cliff. She reappeared in the visions of a monk living on the mountain, who told her story.

The hike from the base of the mountain to the main temple complex and back takes about 1½ hours. Although steep in parts, it's not a difficult walk – plenty of old women in sandals make the journey to worship at the temple. At the base of the mountain, you'll have to fend off the usual crowd of very persistent kids selling tourist junk, lottery tickets and chewing gum – they'll pursue you up the mountain, but you can easily outpace them if you wear running shoes and don't carry a heavy bag. Things are much more relaxed around the temple complex, where there are only a few stands selling snacks and drinks and the vendors are not pushy.

If you need more exercise, a walk to the summit of the peak and back takes about six hours.

Visiting during a holiday or festival is a bad idea. Aside from the crowds, at such times the main gate is closed. This forces vehicles to park 2km away from the trailhead, which means you've got another 4km walking added to the return trip. This extra walking eats up a good deal of extra time, making it difficult to complete the trip if you're coming from Saigon and returning the same night.

### Places to Stay
About 500m past the main entrance gate are eight A-frame bungalows where double rooms can be rented for US$8 to US$12.

## ONE PILLAR PAGODA
The official name of this interesting place is Nam Thien Nhat Tru, but everyone calls it the One Pillar Pagoda of Thu Duc (Chua Mot Cot Thu Duc).

The One Pillar Pagoda of Thu Duc is modelled after Hanoi's One Pillar Pagoda, though the two structures do not look identical. Hanoi's original pagoda was built in the 9th century but was destroyed by the French and rebuilt by the Vietnamese in 1954. Saigon's version was constructed in 1958.

When Vietnam was partitioned in 1954, Buddhist monks and Catholic priests wisely fled south so that they could avoid persecution and continue practising their religion. One monk from Hanoi who came south in 1954 was Thich Tri Dung. Shortly after arrival in Saigon, Thich petitioned the South Vietnamese government for permission to construct a replica of Hanoi's famous One Pillar Pagoda. However, President Ngo Dinh Diem was a Catholic with little tolerance for Buddhist clergy and he denied permission.

Nevertheless, Thich and his supporters raised the funds and built the pagoda in defiance of the president's orders. At one point, the government ordered the monks to tear down the temple, but they refused even though they were threatened with imprisonment for not complying. Faced with significant opposition, the government's dispute with the monks reached a stand-off. However, the president's attempts to harass and intimidate the monks in a country that was 90% Buddhist did not go down well and ultimately contributed to Diem's assassination by his own troops in 1963.

In the current politically correct atmosphere, Vietnamese history books say that this pagoda served as a base for Viet Cong guerrillas who disguised themselves as clergy. This is stretching the truth. At this pagoda and others, the VC cadres did pose as poor peasants from the countryside willing to donate their labour to Buddhism. This provided them with a convenient cover so that they could live in Saigon and conduct secret activities (political indoctrination meetings, smuggling weapons, planting bombs etc) at night. While most monks then (and now) were divorced from politics, it's doubtful that they had any idea just to what extent they were being used by the VC.

During the war, the One Pillar Pagoda of Thu Duc was in possession of an extremely valuable plaque said to weigh 612kg. After liberation, the government took it for 'safekeeping' and brought it to Hanoi. However, none of the monks alive today could say just where it is. There is speculation that the government sold it to overseas collectors, but this cannot be confirmed. Certainly, it belongs in a museum.

The One Pillar Pagoda (☎ 896-0780) is in the Thu Duc District, about 15km east of central Saigon. The official address is 1/91 Nguyen Du St. Tours to the pagoda are rare, so most likely you'll have to visit by rented motorbike or car.

## CAN GIO

The only beach within the municipality of Ho Chi Minh City is at Can Gio, a swampy island where the Saigon River meets the sea. The island was created by silt washing downstream, with the result that the beach consists of hard-packed mud rather than the fluffy white sand that sun worshippers crave. Furthermore, the beach sits in an exposed position and is lashed by strong winds. For these reasons, Can Gio gets few visitors and the beach remains entirely undeveloped.

Before you scratch Can Gio off your list of places to visit, it's worth noting that the island does have a wild beauty of its own. Unlike the rest of Ho Chi Minh City, overpopulation is hardly a problem here. The lack of human inhabitants is chiefly because the island lacks a fresh water supply.

The land here is only about 2m above sea level and the island is basically one big mangrove swamp. The salty mud makes most forms of agriculture impossible, but aquaculture is another matter. The most profitable business here is shrimp farming. The hardpacked mud beach also teems with clams and other sea life which island residents dig up to sell or eat themselves. There is also a small salt industry – sea water is diverted into shallow ponds and is left to evaporate until a white layer of salt can be harvested. Can Gio has a small port where fishing boats can dock, but the shallow water prevents any large ships from dropping anchor here.

From about 1945 through 1954, Can Gio was controlled by Bay Vien, a general who also controlled a casino in Cholon. He was something of an independent warlord and gangster, but former President Ngo Dinh Diem persuaded Bay Vien to join forces with the South Vietnamese government. Not long thereafter, Bay Vien was murdered by an unknown assailant.

### Can Gio Market

Can Gio does have a large market, made conspicuous by some rather powerful odours. Seafood and salt are definitely the local specialities. The vegetables, rice and fruit are all imported by boat from Saigon.

### Caodai Temple

Though much smaller than the Caodai Great

Temple at Tay Ninh, Can Gio can boast a Caodai Temple of its own. The temple is near the market and is easy to find. We didn't see anybody around and it seems that you can just walk inside and photograph as you please. Of course, if you encounter any worshippers, be respectful and don't photograph them without asking first.

### War Memorial & Cemetery

Adjacent to the shrimp hatchery is a large and conspicuous cemetery and war memorial (Nghia Trang Liet Si Rung Sac). Like all such sites in Vietnam, the praise for bravery and patriotism goes entirely to the winning side and there is nothing said about the losers. Indeed, all of the former war cemeteries containing remains of South Vietnamese soldiers were bulldozed after liberation – a fact which still causes much bitterness.

The War Memorial & Cemetery is 2km from Can Gio Market.

### Shrimp Hatchery

Coastal Fishery Development Corporation (COFIDEC; Cty Phat Trien Kinh Te Duyen Hai in Vietnamese) is a large company which has sewn up much of the shrimp-breeding industry in Can Gio. This is a joint venture with the Philippines and appears to be very well organised. Two types of shrimp – black tiger and white shrimp – are bred here. One building houses a small plant where the shrimp are cleaned, packed and frozen before being shipped off to Saigon.

COFIDEC has its operational headquarters close to the War Memorial in Can Gio, but the shrimp-breeding ponds stretch out for several kilometres along the beach.

The staff at COFIDEC are friendly and not opposed to your poking around a bit, but please don't interfere with their operations. Foreigners will only continue to be welcomed here if they tread lightly. This is private property and the management could easily put up 'no trespassing' signs if travellers don't behave themselves. Some of the staff speak English and, if you approach them positively, they may be willing to show you around a bit and explain their operation.

### The Beach

The southern side of the island faces the sea, creating a beachfront nearly 10km long. Unfortunately, a good deal of it is inaccessible because it's been fenced off by shrimp farmers and clam diggers. Nevertheless, there is a point about 4km west of the Can Gio Market where a dirt road turns off the main highway to Saigon and leads to the beach. The road can be distinguished by the telephone poles and wires running alongside it. At the beach, you'll find a small collection of buildings belonging to COFIDEC and a forlorn shack selling food and drinks.

The surface of the beach is as hard as concrete and it is possible to ride a motorbike on it. However, this is not recommended as it damages the local ecology. While the beach may seem dead at first glance, it swarms with life just below the surface as the breathing holes in the mud suggest. You can hear the crunch of tiny clam shells as you stroll along the surface. The water here is extremely shallow and you can walk far from shore, but take care – you can be sure that there is a good deal of inhospitable and well-armed sea life in these shallow waters. Stingrays, stone fish and sea urchins are just some of the xenophobic local residents who can and will retaliate if you step on them.

The hills of the Vung Tau Peninsula are easily visible on a clear day. You should also be able to the see offshore oil-drilling platforms which belong to Vietsovpetro.

### Places to Stay

Most visitors do Can Gio as a day trip, and for good reason – the one hotel in town has only four rooms, is overpriced and is a dump. In fact, the *Duyen Hai Hotel* (Khach San Duyen Hai; ☎ 874-0246) is usually full and you need to call ahead for a reservation if you intend to stay. Foreigners are charged US$10 to stay in this shack.

The hotel does have a fresh-water tank, which means you don't have to bathe with sea water. The water is brought in from Saigon by ship, so perhaps this partially justifies the prices charged for this downmarket accommodation. The toilets are a long walk from the main building. In fact, the toilets are built on stilts over a canal, which might just reduce your enthusiasm for eating Can Gio clams.

The hotel is about 4km from the main beach area.

## Places to Eat

There are a few stalls around the market near the fishing port, but one look at the level of sanitation can eliminate your appetite without the need to eat anything at all!

That having been said, Can Gio boasts one remarkably good restaurant with an extensive menu. In fact, it's so good that Saigonese in the know come to Can Gio for no other reason than to eat here. The place you want is the *Duyen Hai Restaurant*, which is a stone's throw from the Duyen Hai Hotel. Unlike the hotel, the restaurant is good value.

There is one solitary food and drink stall next to the beach. Basically, all they have on the menu is Coca-Cola and instant noodles, but it beats starving. It might be prudent to bring some snacks and bottled water with you on the odd chance that this food stall is closed.

## Getting There & Away

**Motorbike** Can Gio is about 60km from central Saigon and the fastest way to make the journey is by motorbike. Travel time is approximately three hours.

Cars can also make the journey, but this is much slower. The reason is that you need to make two ferry crossings. The large ferries which can accommodate cars are infrequent, averaging about one every 1½ hours. By contrast, small boats make these crossings every few minutes, shuttling passengers and motorbikes. These small boats are so cheap that you could even charter one if need be.

The first ferry crossing is 15km from Saigon at Cat Lai, a former US navy base. Small ferry boats cost about US$0.20 for a motorbike and two passengers. Cars must wait for the large ferry, which runs about once every 30 minutes, and there is usually a long queue of vehicles.

The second ferry, which is less frequent, is 35km from Saigon and connects the two tiny villages of Dan Xay (closer to Saigon) with Hao Vo (on Can Gio Island). Motorbike riders can take a small ferry, which costs around US$0.35 and runs about once every 10 to 15 minutes. The car ferry is much less frequent, but there is a posted schedule – departure times are as follows:

| Dan Xay | Hao Vo |
| --- | --- |
| 5.00 am | 5.15 am |
| 7.00 | 7.15 |
| 8.30 | 8.45 |
| 10.00 | 10.15 |
| 11.30 | 11.45 |
| 1.00 pm | 1.15 pm |
| 2.30 | 2.45 |
| 4.00 | 4.15 |
| 5.30 | 5.45 |
| 7.00 | – |

The road is paved up to the first ferry at Cat Lai; after that, it's a dirt surface but gets regular maintenance and is in good nick. Once you get past the first ferry, there is very little traffic and both sides of the road are lined with lush mangrove forests.

**Boat** There is one boat daily between Can Gio and Saigon. From either direction, the boat departs at approximately 5 to 6 am and takes six hours for the journey.

There is also a small boat between Can Gio and Vung Tau. Departures from Can Gio are at 5 am, arriving in Vung Tau at 8 am. The boat departs Vung Tau about noon, arriving in Can Gio three hours later. Occasionally, there is a later boat leaving Can Gio around 2 pm, but you need to inquire because it doesn't run daily.

In Can Gio, you catch boats at the shipyards, which are built on an inlet 2km west of the Can Gio Market. In Saigon, you get the boat at Thu Thiem, the pier on the opposite shore of the Saigon River from the floating hotel. In Vung Tau, you catch the boats from the beachfront market area opposite the Grand Hotel.

## BUU LONG MOUNTAIN

Various tourist pamphlets and even local

residents of Saigon will tell you that Buu Long Mountain is the 'Halong Bay of the south'. Seeing how Halong Bay is northern Vietnam's top scenic drawcard, you might be forgiven for thinking that Buu Long Mountain must be nothing short of stunningly beautiful.

Indubitably, we were stunned when we visited Buu Long Mountain. Mostly, we were stunned that anyone would waste the time and admission fee to visit this place. Residents of Saigon indeed have a vivid imagination to call this another Halong Bay. Residents of Halong Bay ought to consider filing a defamation lawsuit against whoever invented that silly tourist slogan and wrote those pamphlets.

·Nevertheless, if you're bored and want to enjoy some perverse sort of comic relief, it does no harm to visit Buu Long Mountain. The summit towers a big 60m above the car park. During the five-minute walk to the top, you need to fight off a constant parade of beggars and vendors who will follow half a metre behind you the entire way. Your followers might try to steer you off-course to visit the 'English-speaking monk', who will charge you a fee for speaking English to him.

The top of the mountain is marked by a pagoda. From this vantage point, you can look down and clearly see Dragon Lake (Long An). The shoreline is dressed up with a few pavilions and decorative souvenir stands. To reach the lake, you have to descend the mountain and pass through another gate, where you pay an additional admission fee. And for a small extra charge, you can paddle a boat around the slimy green waters in pursuit of the dragon which is said to live at the bottom of the lake. Although we didn't spot the dragon, we did find the boat ride an excellent way to escape the lottery ticket and postcard vendors.

Buu Long Mountain is 32km from central Saigon. It's 2km off the main highway after crossing the bridge that marks the border between Ho Chi Minh City and Dong Nai province. The admission fee is US$0.40, plus there is an extra charge for bringing in a camera. Considering how little there is to see here, you might as well leave the camera at home. There are a few refreshment shops here where you can buy cold drinks and noodles.

## TRI AN FALLS

The Tri An Falls are an 8m-high and 30m-wide cascade on the Be River (Song Be) They are especially awesome in the late fall, when the river's flow is at its greatest. Tri An Falls are in Song Be Province, 36km from Bien Hoa and 68km from Saigon (via Thu Dau Mot).

## TRI AN DAM & RESERVOIR

Further upstream from Tri An Falls is Tri An Reservoir (Ho Tri An). This large artificial lake was created by the Tri An Dam. Completed in the early 1980s with Soviet assistance, the dam and its adjoining hydroelectric station supplies the lion's share of Saigon's electric power.

The reservoir, dam and hydroelectric station are off limits to travellers for security reasons. The area is not much of a tourist attraction anyway because during the dry season the water level drops dramatically leaving an ugly 'bathtub' ring around the reservoir. Probably the main interest this place offers to outsiders could be to foreign investors – the hydroelectric station is severely overtaxed by the surging demand for electricity and the Vietnamese are reportedly looking for foreign partners to provide some sort of solution. Should you happen to be in the electrical engineering business, the Vietnamese would probably like to hear from you.

If you are seriously contemplating a visit to Tri An Dam and Reservoir, be sure that you have official permission.

## VUNG TAU

Vung Tau, known under the French as Cap St Jacques (it was so named by Portuguese mariners in honour of their patron saint), is a beach resort on the South China Sea, 128km south-east of Saigon.

Vung Tau's beaches are easily reached from Saigon and have thus been a favourite of the Saigonese since French colonists first began coming here around 1890. However, these beaches are not Vietnam's nicest by any stretch of the imagination, in large part because the city has cut down most of the palm trees in order to widen the roads.

Seaside areas near Vung Tau are dotted with the villas of the pre-1975 elite, now converted to guesthouses and restaurants for the post-1975 elite. In addition to sunning on the seashore and sipping sodas in nearby cafes, visitors to this city of 100,000 can cycle around, or climb up, the Vung Tau Peninsula's two mountains. There are also a number of interesting religious sites around town, including several pagodas and a huge standing figure of Jesus blessing the South China Sea.

Vung Tau is the headquarters of Vietsovpetro, a joint Soviet-Vietnamese company that operates oil rigs about 60km offshore. There are still some Russian technicians around, though nowhere near the number who lived here in the 1980s.

Vung Tau became briefly famous to the world in 1973, when the last American combat troops in Vietnam departed from here by ship. However, a small contingent of American advisers, diplomats and CIA agents remained in Vietnam for another two years – their moment on the world's centre stage came in 1975 during the rooftop helicopter evacuation from the US embassy in Saigon.

The local fishing fleet is quite active, though many Vietnamese fleeing their homeland by sea set sail from Vung Tau, taking many of the town's fishing trawlers with them. Vietnamese navy boats on patrol offshore ensure that the rest of the fleet comes home each day.

Vung Tau has long competed with Saigon to attract foreign 'sex tours' to Vietnam – massage parlours are ubiquitous. However, the AIDS epidemic has caused some soul searching and there has been a half-hearted crackdown on this most lucrative industry.

Another negative – watch out for kids around the kiosks along Front Beach. Some may try to pick your pockets or snatch a bag.

Vung Tau is heavily commercialised and seems to be getting more so all the time. Despite this and a few other negative points, you'd still have a hard time not enjoying the place – plenty of sand, sun, surf, good food, draft beer and even a few budding discos. It's a party town and – for traffic-weary Saigonese – a welcome change of pace.

### Orientation

The triangular Vung Tau Peninsula juts into the South China Sea near the mouth of the Saigon River. Sewage flowing down the river from Saigon is a considerable source of pollution – Vung Tau's four beaches are none too clean. Pollution from offshore drilling is another factor.

Ben Da fishing village is located in the north-west area of the peninsula. In the north-east is most of Vung Tau's industry and the airport.

### Information

**Money** Vietcombank (Ngan Hang Ngoai Thuong Viet Nam; ☎ 859874) is at 27-29 Tran Hung Dao St.

**Post & Communications** The post office (☎ 852377, 852689, 852141) is at 4 Ha Long St at the southern end of Front Beach.

**Immigration Police** The immigration police operate out of the police station on Truong Cong Dinh St near the intersection with Ly Thuong Kiet St.

### Beaches

**Back Beach** The main bathing area on the peninsula is Back Beach (Bai Sau, also known as Thuy Van Beach), an 8km-long stretch of sun, sand and tourists. Unfortunately, it's also the ugliest stretch of beach in Vung Tau thanks largely to crass commercialisation. The northern section of Back Beach is a little better because the palm trees have been left standing, but even these are now being cut to widen the road. Basically, this is land of concrete, car parks, hotels and cafes. The surf here can be dangerous.

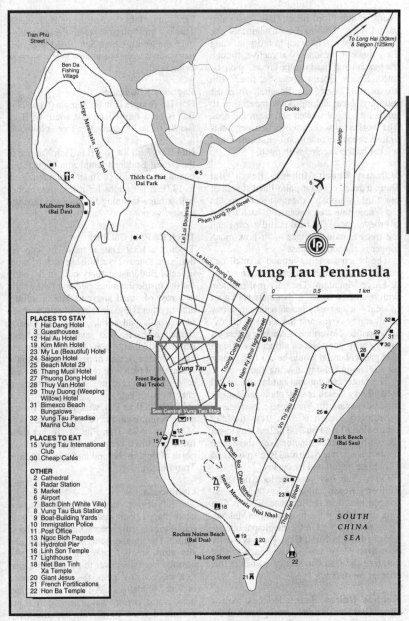

Tran Phu Street

Ben Da Fishing Village

To Long Hai (30km) & Saigon (125km)

Large Mountain (Nui Lon)

Docks

Thich Ca Phat Dai Park

●5

Airstrip

●1

†2

Mulberry Beach (Bai Dau)

■3

●4

6 ✈

Le Loi Boulevard

Pham Hong Thai Street

**Vung Tau Peninsula**

Le Hong Phong Street

0    0.5    1 km

7

Vung Tau

Truong Cong Dinh Street

Nam Ky Khoi Nghia Street

■8

●9

★10

32 ■

29 ■
31 ■
▼30

28 ■

27 ■

Vo Thi Sau Street

Front Beach (Bai Truoc)

See Central Vung Tau Map

11

14
15

12
13

16

26 ■

Back Beach (Bai Sau)

■25

17

Phan Boi Chau Street

Small Mountain (Nui Nho)

24 ■

23 ■

Thuy Van Street

18

Roches Noires Beach (Bai Dua)

■19

20

SOUTH CHINA SEA

Ha Long Street

22

21

**PLACES TO STAY**
1 Hai Dang Hotel
3 Guesthouses
12 Hai Au Hotel
19 Kim Minh Hotel
23 My Le (Beautiful) Hotel
24 Saigon Hotel
25 Beach Motel 29
26 Thang Muoi Hotel
27 Phuong Dong Hotel
28 Thuy Van Hotel
29 Thuy Duong (Weeping Willow) Hotel
31 Bimexco Beach Bungalows
32 Vung Tau Paradise Marina Club

**PLACES TO EAT**
15 Vung Tau International Club
30 Cheap Cafés

**OTHER**
2 Cathedral
4 Radar Station
5 Market
6 Airport
7 Bach Dinh (White Villa)
8 Vung Tau Bus Station
9 Boat-Building Yards
10 Immigration Police
11 Post Office
13 Ngoc Bich Pagoda
14 Hydrofoil Pier
16 Linh Son Temple
17 Lighthouse
18 Niet Ban Tinh Xa Temple
20 Giant Jesus
21 French Fortifications
22 Hon Ba Temple

**Front Beach** Front Beach (Bai Truoc, also called Thuy Duong Beach) borders the centre of town. The trees (a rarity in Vung Tau) make it reasonably attractive, though the beach itself has become eroded and polluted. Shady Quang Trung St, lined with kiosks, runs along Front Beach. Early in the morning, local fishing boats moor here to unload the night's catch and clean the nets. The workers row themselves between boats or to the beach in *thung chai* – gigantic round wicker baskets sealed with pitch.

**Mulberry Beach** Mulberry Beach (Bai Dau), a quiet, coconut-palm-lined stretch of coastline, is probably the most scenic spot in the Vung Tau area because it hasn't been overdeveloped. The road is still narrow and the trees remain in place – for how much longer is anybody's guess.

The beach stretches around a small bay nestled beneath the verdant, western slopes of Large Mountain. The only real problem with Mulberry Beach is that there isn't a lot of sand – it's a rocky beach with only a few small sandy coves and the water is not exactly pristine. Nevertheless, Mulberry Beach's many cheap guesthouses attract low-budget backpackers and it would be our first choice for a relaxing holiday in Vung Tau.

The large and unusual outdoor cathedral at Mulberry Beach is very photogenic and a major drawcard for Vietnamese tourists.

Mulberry Beach is 3km from the city centre along Tran Phu St. The best way to get there is by bicycle or motorbike – there is no public transport and the road is too rough and hilly to be negotiated by cyclos.

On a clear day you can look out from Mulberry Beach and see a low-lying palm-fringed island in the distance. That is Can Gio, an island at the mouth of the Mekong Delta which is within the municipal boundaries of Ho Chi Minh City. There is a daily boat from Vung Tau's Front Beach to Can Gio (see the Can Gio section earlier in this chapter for details).

**Roches Noires Beach** Roches Noires Beach (Bai Dua) is a small, rocky beach about 2km south of the town centre on Ha Long St. This is a great place to watch the sun setting over the South China Sea. Road widening has made it treeless and new hotels are now being built.

### Pagodas & Temples
**Hon Ba Temple** Hon Ba Temple (Chua Hon Ba) is on a tiny island just south of Back Beach. It can be reached on foot at low tide.

**Niet Ban Tinh Xa** Niet Ban Tinh Xa, one of the largest Buddhist temples in Vietnam, is on the western side of Small Mountain. Built in 1971, it is famous for its 5000kg bronze bell, a huge reclining Buddha and intricate mosaic work.

### Thich Ca Phat Dai Park
Thich Ca Phat Dai, a must-see site for domestic tourists, is a hillside park of monumental Buddhist statuary built in the early 1960s. Inside the main gate and to the right is a row of small souvenir kiosks selling, among other things, inexpensive items made of seashells and coral. Above the kiosks, shaded paths lead to several large white cement Buddhas, a giant lotus blossom and many smaller figures of people and animals. A couple of path-side refreshment stalls sell cold drinks. There are several restaurants near the main gate.

Thich Ca Phat Dai, which is open from 6 am to 6 pm, is on the eastern side of Large Mountain at 25 Tran Phu St. To get there from the town centre, take Le Loi Blvd north almost to the end and turn left on to Tran Phu St.

### Lighthouse
The 360-degree view of the entire hammerhead-shaped peninsula from the lighthouse (*hai dang*) is truly spectacular, especially at sunset. The lighthouse was built in 1910 and sits atop Small Mountain. The concrete passage from the tower to the building next to it was constructed by the French because of Viet Minh attacks. A 1939 French guidebook warns visitors that photography is not permitted from here and, unfortunately,

this is still the case half a century and four regimes later.

The narrow paved road up Small Mountain to the lighthouse intersects Ha Long St 150m south-west of the post office. The grade is quite mild and could even be bicycled. There is also a dirt road (which gets muddy during the wet season) to the lighthouse from near Back Beach.

### Giant Jesus
An enormous Rio de Janeiro-style figure of Jesus (Thanh Gioc), with arms outstretched, gazes across the South China Sea from the southern end of Small Mountain.

The 30m-high Giant Jesus was constructed in 1974 on the site of a lighthouse built by the French a century before. The statue can be reached on foot by a path that heads up the hill from a point just south of Back Beach. The path circles around to approach the figure from the back.

Unfortunately, Jesus is literally in a precarious position these days. Small Mountain continues to get smaller – the demand for rock and sand to build new hotels and highways is causing the southern slope of the mountain to be dug up and carted away. The digging has continued almost right up to the base of the statue's feet and there is the real possibility that a bad typhoon could send the whole structure toppling into the sea. Local Christians are reportedly unhappy at the prospect of their statue being made to walk on water and have protested the matter – so far to no avail.

### Bach Dinh
Bach Dinh, the White Villa (Villa Blanche), is a former royal residence set amid frangipanis and bougainvilleas on a lushly forested hillside overlooking the sea. It is an ideal place to sit, relax and contemplate.

Bach Dinh was built in 1909 as a retreat for French governor Paul Doumer. It later became a summer palace for Vietnamese royalty. King Thanh Thai was kept here for a while under house arrest before being shipped off to the French island of Réunion to perform hard prison labour. In the late

1960s to the early 1970s, the building was a part-time playground for South Vietnamese President Thieu.

The mansion itself is emphatically French in its ornamentation, which includes colourful mosaics and Roman-style busts set into the exterior walls. Inside, there is an exhibit of old Chinese (Qing Dynasty) pottery salvaged from an 18th century shipwreck near Con Dao Island. There are also lots of 'new antiques' on sale in the villa's gift shop.

The main entrance to the park surrounding Bach Dinh is just north of Front Beach at 12 Tran Phu St. It is open from 6 am to 9 pm and admission is US$1.20.

### Boat-Building Yards
New wooden fishing craft are built at a location which, oddly enough, is over a kilometre from the nearest water. The boat yards are on Nam Ky Khoi Nghia St, 500m south of Vung Tau bus station.

### Golf Course
The Vung Tau Paradise Marina Club does not have a marina, but it does have an international standard 27-hole golf course. For non-members, green fees are a trifling US$97 per day. Membership costs US$20,000, but then green fees are reduced to just US$12 per day. At these rates, becoming a member will pay off provided you play golf here more than 235 times.

### Small Mountain Circuit
The 6km circuit around Small Mountain (Nui Nho; elevation 197m), known to the French as le tour de la Petite Corniche, begins at the post office and continues on Ha Long St along the rocky coastline. Ha Long St passes Ngoc Bich Pagoda (which is built in the style of Hanoi's famous One Pillar Pagoda), Roches Noires Beach and a number of villas before reaching the tip of the Vung Tau Peninsula. The promontory, reached through a traditional gate, was once guarded by French naval guns whose reinforced concrete emplacements remain, slowly crumbling in the salt air.

Phan Boi Chau St goes from the southern

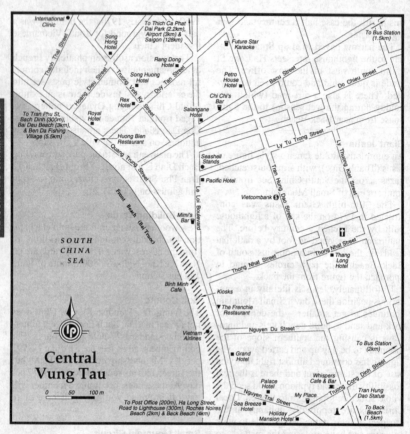

SOUTH
CHINA
SEA

**Central
Vung Tau**

0    50    100 m

end of Back Beach into town along the eastern base of Small Mountain, passing century-old Linh Son Temple, which contains a Buddha of pre-Angkorian Khmer origin.

### Large Mountain Circuit
The 10km circuit around Large Mountain (Nui Lon; elevation 520m) passes seaside villas, Mulberry Beach, the homes of poor families living in old French fortifications and a number of quarries where boulders blown out of the hillside by dynamite are made into gravel by workers using sledgehammers. Blasting sometimes closes the

road for a few hours. At the northern tip of Large Mountain is Ben Da fishing village. The village is notable for its large church and bad roads; from here a road leads up and along the spine of the hill to the old radar installation (rada).

On the eastern side of Large Mountain, which faces tidal marshes and the giant cranes of the Vietsovpetro docks, is Thich Ca Phat Dai statuary park.

### Places to Stay
During holidays, Vung Tau's hotels are usually booked out. Aside from price, the

main consideration is finding a place at the beach you most prefer.

**Back Beach** Cheapest is *Beach Motel 29* (☎ 853481; 12 rooms) at 29 Thuy Van St. Prices on weekdays are US$4 to US$8 with fan only, or US$15 to US$20 with air-conditioning. Prices rise slightly on weekends.

The prettiest budget accommodation is up at the northern end of Back Beach. Here you'll find the *Bimexco Beach Bungalows* (☎ 859916). However, a recent road-widening project is obliterating the trees here, so perhaps only stumps will be left by the time you get there. There are 30 bungalows and each has two rooms. The cheapest rooms with shared bath are US$8. Having a private bath, but no air-con, will cost you US$18. With air-con and cold-water bath it's US$23 and with air-con plus hot water it's US$25.

The *Thuy Duong Hotel* (☎ 852635; nine rooms) is a small but attractive place at the northern end of Thuy Van St. Also known as the *Weeping Willow Hotel*, all rooms have air-con and hot water. The tariff is between US$25 and US$30.

Close to the beach with large spacious grounds is the *Saigon Hotel* (☎ 852317; 120 rooms). There are two large buildings here, but only the old building has sea views. Rooms in the old building are US$13 to US$36; in the new building all rooms are US$27.

*Thang Muoi Hotel* (☎ 852665) at 4-6 Thuy Van St is one of the older places in Back Beach but also boasts an alluring, garden-like environment. Doubles with fan cost US$11 or US$12. With air-con it's US$25 to US$29.

The *Thuy Van Hotel* has 93 rooms with rates of US$18 to US$32.

Everything else in Back Beach is pricey. If you've got the cash, consider the *My Le Hotel* (☎ 852177) on Thuy Van St. It's also known as the *Beautiful Hotel*. Twins are US$35 to US$75.

The *Phuong Dong Hotel* (☎ 852593; 45 rooms) at 2 Thuy Van St is one of the most impressive hotels in Vung Tau. It was built to cater mostly to Hong Kongers, Taiwanese and Singaporeans, as evidenced by the mas-

sive karaoke facilities. Rooms cost US$30 to US$40.

The *Vung Tau Paradise Marina Club* (☎ 859687; fax 859695) was under construction at the time of writing, but should be open soon. Initially, the hotel here will have 524 rooms, but this will eventually expand to 1500 rooms. Facilities include a golf course, a swimming pool and tennis courts. The project is a Taiwanese joint venture. Prices have not been announced yet, but it's fair to say that this won't be for budget travellers.

**Front Beach** The only cheap place in this neighbourhood is the *Thang Long Hotel* (☎ 852175) at 45 Thong Nhat St. Doubles with fan are US$10 to US$20. Air-con will set you back US$15 to US$20.

The *Song Huong Hotel* (☎ 852491; 33 rooms) is at 10 Truong Vinh Ky St. This was once a dormitory for Russian experts, but has seen some recent renovation and steep price increases to match. Twins are US$30 to US$40.

Don't confuse the foregoing with the very similarly named *Song Hong Hotel* (☎ 852137; 39 rooms) at 12 Hoang Dieu St. Twins with air-conditioning and private bath cost US$20 to US$35.

The *Rang Dong Hotel* (☎ 852133; 84 rooms) is at 5 Duy Tan St, just off Le Loi Blvd. This large place was also once a dormitory for Soviet experts, but has been fully renovated. Twins are now US$35.

The *Petro House Hotel* (☎ 852014), 89 Tran Hung Dao St, gets good reviews from travellers. Of course, it should at these prices: twin rooms cost US$53 to US$60, suites US$85 to US$195.

*Salangane Hotel* (☎ 852571), also called *Hai Yen Hotel*, is at 8 Le Loi Blvd. It advertises its restaurant, cafe, dance hall, steam bath and Thai massage. Twins cost US$20 to US$40.

The Czech joint venture *Pacific Hotel* (☎ 852279; 53 rooms) at 4 Le Loi Blvd (corner Ly Tu Trong St) is a clean and modern place. Room rates depend on whether or not you get a sea view. The price range here is US$27 to US$29.

The *Hai Au Hotel* (☎ 852178; 64 rooms) is at 100 Ha Long St on the southern end of Front Beach near the post office (see the Vung Tau Peninsula map). Taiwanese tour groups congregate here. It's a fancy place with tour group amenities, including a swimming pool, private beach, barber shop, post office, disco bar and business centre. Standard rooms cost from US$25 to US$45, but fancier suites are US$60 to US$85.

The *Holiday Mansion Hotel* (☎ 856169; 15 rooms) on Truong Cong Dinh St is a relatively small, but new, place. Twins are US$27 to US$32.

The *Sea Breeze Hotel*, or *Hanh Phoc Hotel* (☎ 852392; fax 859856; 36 rooms), which also serves as an office for express buses to Saigon, is at 11 Nguyen Trai St. There are two categories of rooms, normal (US$40) and special (US$60). The normal rooms look just as nice and seem a much better deal. This hotel is an Australian joint venture.

The *Palace Hotel* (☎ 852265; fax 859878; 105 rooms), also known as the *Hoa Binh Hotel*, is a fancy place owned by the Oil Services Company. The hotel is on Nguyen Trai St, 100m off Quang Trung St. Standard twins cost US$40 to US$55 and suites are US$70 to US$100. The hotel advertises, among other things, 'gentle receptionists'.

The *Grand Hotel* (☎ 856164; fax 859878; 60 rooms) has a grand location at 26 Quang Trung St, just opposite the beach. Owned by the Oil Services Company, the hotel is proud of its souvenir shop, steam bath, disco and Thai massage facilities. Singles with fan and attached cold-water bath are US$15, while twins with air-con are US$20 to US$46.

The *Rex Hotel* (☎ 852135; fax 859862) is a nine-storey high-rise at 1 Duy Tan St. Although the name seems more than coincidental, it's no relation to the very upmarket Rex in Saigon. All rooms have air-con and a terrace and cost US$35 to US$100. Some travellers have complained about the surly staff. The hotel has two restaurants, tennis courts and a night club, but tends to be noisy with echo-chamber hallways.

The *Royal Hotel* (☎ 859852; fax 859851) is at 48 Quang Trung St. The hotel's glossy pamphlet promises that it is 'where the sun-kissed beaches and cool sea breeze bring you into the exciting world of deep crystal blue sea'. The hotel is very classy and very thoroughly air-conditioned and costs US$46 to US$120.

**Mulberry Beach**  There are dozens of guesthouses *(nha nghi)* in former private villas along Mulberry Beach. This is the cheapest neighbourhood in the Vung Tau area, though no longer as dirt-cheap as it once was. This relative cheapness is not because Mulberry Beach is an unattractive place (indeed, the opposite), but because the lack of a white-sand beach and other tourist amusements makes this a relative backwater. If it's a carnival you want, head to Back Beach.

Most of the guesthouses have rooms with fans and communal bathrooms and cost US$15 or less, but several upmarket places have now added air-con and private baths. A few of the guesthouses do meals, but most don't. However, there are plentiful cheap restaurants offering fine sea views.

*Nha Nghi My Tho*, with its rooftop terrace overlooking the beach, is at 47 Tran Phu St. A light, airy room with ceiling fan and beach view will cost you US$8 per person.

*Nha Nghi 128* is at 128 Tran Phu St. Rooms for four cost US$10. It looks rather dilapidated.

*Nha Nghi 29* is right on the seafront. It's a large good-looking place and can be recommended. Rooms with air-con cost US$20.

*Nha Nghi Doan 28* is at 126 Tran Phu St. It's also a large hotel with air-con rooms and private bath. Doubles cost US$25.

*Nha Nghi DK 142* also has relatively high-standard air-con rooms with private bath for US$25.

The *Hai Dang Hotel* (☎ 858536; 17 rooms) at 194 Tran Phu St is one of the larger hotels in Mulberry Beach. Rooms with fan and hot-water bath cost US$30.

*Thuy Tien Hotel* at 96 Tran Phu St is a place to avoid! At US$100, it's so absurdly overpriced that it's hard to imagine it really wants guests at all.

**Roches Noires Beach** This is a new development area – the small guesthouses have been blown away recently and new tourist pleasure palaces are under construction. The first one to open its doors is the sparkling new *Kim Minh Hotel* (☎ 856192; 42 rooms) at 60A Ha Long St. Rooms cost US$45 to US$65 with breakfast thrown in. There is a karaoke and disco.

## Places to Eat
**Back Beach** At the northern end of Back Beach are excellent cheap cafes hidden among the few remaining palm trees. Guests at *Beach Motel 29* can eat breakfast there – it's the only place in Vung Tau with banana pancakes.

**Front Beach** Kiosks lining the beach do cheap noodle dishes. Opposite the kiosks on Front Beach is *The Frenchie Restaurant*, at 26 Quang Trung St, which does fine French food.

For excellent seafood, try *Huong Bien Restaurant* at 47 Quang Trung St. There are several places to eat nearby and quite a few more along Tran Hung Dao St. Hotels with excellent restaurants include the *Palace*, *Pacific* and the *Grand*.

The attractive terrace restaurant at the Palace Hotel does excellent food – better fried rice than we ever had in Hong Kong! The fried eel is highly recommended. A couple of dishes with rice and a few beers cost us US$8. Very limited choice of wine though – expensive white (US$25) or cheap but dodgy looking red with a label all in some Eastern European language we couldn't read. But all in all, a great place to eat.

**Sarah Clifford**

**Mulberry Beach** Mulberry Beach chips in with numerous seaside restaurants. The specialty is, no surprise, seafood.

**Roches Noires Beach** The *Vung Tau International Club* has good food and a sweeping view of the sea (see the Vung Tau Peninsula map).

## Entertainment
Expat bars that get moving in the evening include: *My Place* (☎ 856028) at 14 Nguyen Trai St; *Whispers Cafe & Bar* (☎ 856762) at 438 Truong Cong Dinh St; *Chi Chi's Bar* (☎ 853948) at 236 Bacu St; and Mimi's Bar at Le Loi Blvd.

The *Grand Hotel* has a disco and karaoke lounge which operate from 7 pm until midnight.

The *Future Star Karaoke* (☎ 852805) at 93 Tran Hung Dao St is a Taiwanese joint venture which was once a hotel. Apparently there is more money to be made catering to those aspiring to be a future star.

The *Rex Hotel* (☎ 859559) also operates a karaoke thing on the ground floor.

## Getting There & Away
**Air** There are (sometimes) chartered helicopter flights available from Vung Tau to the Con Dao Islands. The airline to contact is Vasco (☎ 859577; fax 859253) at 4 Le Loi Blvd.

**Bus** The most convenient minibuses to Vung Tau depart from in front of the Saigon Hotel on Dong Du St near the Saigon Central Mosque. Departures are approximately every 15 minutes between 6 am and 6 pm. The 128km trip takes two hours and costs US$4. To return from Vung Tau, you catch these minibuses at the petrol station or the Sea Breeze Hotel.

Large public air-conditioned buses depart from Saigon's Van Thanh bus station.

Vung Tau bus station (Ben Xe Khach Vung Tau) is about 1.5km from the city centre at 52 Nam Ky Khoi Nghia St. There are nonexpress buses from here to Baria, Long Hai, Bien Hoa, Saigon, Long Khanh, Mytho and Tay Ninh.

**Hydrofoil** The best way to reach Vung Tau is by hydrofoil. Tickets cost US$10 and the ride takes 75 to 80 minutes. One hydrofoil can hold 124 passengers.

In Saigon, departures are from the Vina Express office (☎ 822-4621, 825-3888) at 6A Nguyen Tat Thanh St, District 4, which is on the Saigon River just south of the Ben Nghe Channel.

In Vung Tau you board the hydrofoil at Cau Da pier opposite the Hai Au Hotel (Front Beach). Vina Express (☎ 856530) has a Vung Tau office by the pier.

### Getting Around
The best way to get around the Vung Tau Peninsula is by bicycle. These are available for hire from some hotels for around US$1 per day.

There is a place opposite the Rex Hotel that rents motorbikes. A 50cc bike costs only US$5 per day and no driver's licence is required.

Vicaren Taxi (☎ 858485) and Vung Tau Taxi (☎ 856565) are the duopoly suppliers of cabs with meters and air-conditioning.

### CON DAO ISLANDS
The Con Dao Archipelago is a group of 14 islands and islets 180km (97 nautical miles) south of Vung Tau in the South China Sea. The largest island in the group, with a total land area of 20 sq km, is the partly forested Con Son Island, which is ringed with bays, bathing beaches and coral reefs. Con Son

Island is also known by its Europeanised Malay name, Poulo Condore (Pulau Kundur), which means Island of the Squashes. Local products include teak and pine wood, fruits (cashews, grapes, coconuts and mangoes), pearls, sea turtles, lobster and coral.

Occupied at various times by the Khmers, Malays and Vietnamese, Con Son also served as an early base for European commercial ventures in the region. The British East India Company maintained a fortified trading post here from 1702 to 1705 – an experiment which ended when the English on the island were massacred in a revolt by the Macassar soldiers they had recruited on the Indonesian island of Sulawesi.

Under the French, Con Son was used as a prison for opponents of French colonialism, earning a fearsome reputation for the routine mistreatment and torture of prisoners. In 1954, the prison was taken over by the South Vietnamese government, which continued to take advantage of its remoteness to hold opponents of the government (including students) in horrifying conditions. The island's Revolutionary Museum has exhibits on Vietnamese resistance to the French, Communist opposition to the Republic of Vietnam,

### Spratly Spat
The Paracel Islands (Quan Dao Hoang Xa), 300km east of Danang, and the Spratly Islands (Quan Dao Thruong Xa), 475km south-east of Nha Trang, seem likely to be a source of future conflict between all the nations surrounding the South China Sea.

Several of the Paracel Islands, which historically have been only sporadically occupied, were seized by the People's Republic of China in 1951. In the 1960s a few of the islands were occupied by the South Vietnamese, who were driven out by Chinese forces in 1964, an action protested by both the Saigon and Hanoi governments.

The Spratlys, which consist of hundreds of tiny islets, are closer to Borneo than to Vietnam. They are claimed by virtually every country in the vicinity, including the Philippines, Malaysia, Indonesia, China, Taiwan and Vietnam. In 1988, Vietnam lost two ships and 70 sailors in a clash with China over the Spratlys. In mid-1992, Chinese military patrol boats reportedly opened fire on several occasions on Vietnamese cargo vessels leaving Hong Kong, bringing trade between Vietnam and Hong Kong to a near halt. The weak explanation was that China was trying to prevent smuggling.

Both archipelagos have little intrinsic value, but the country that has sovereignty over them can claim huge areas of the South China Sea – reported to hold vast oil reserves – as its territorial waters. China pushed tensions to a new high in 1992 by occupying one of the islets claimed by Vietnam, and by signing contracts with a US company (Crestone Corporation) to explore for oil in the disputed areas. Vietnam returned the favour in 1996 by signing an oil exploration contract with a competing American company, Conoco. In 1996, the Philippine navy destroyed a small Chinese-built radar base on Mischief Reef in the Spratlys. ■

HELEN SAVORY

GLENN BEANLAND

SIMON ROWE

JULIET COOMBE

**Around Ho Chi Minh City**
Top Left: Worshippers at the Caodai Great Temple at Tay Ninh.
Top Right: Sunset at Bai Dua on the Vung Tau peninsula.
Bottom Left: The colourful architecture of the Caodai Great Temple at Tay Ninh.
Bottom Right: A secret entrance to the network of tunnels at Cu Chi.

GREG ALFORD

KAREN O'CONNOR

SARA JANE CLELAND

EMMA MILLER

### Mekong Delta
Top: Plying the waters of the Mekong River at Cantho.
Middle Left: Live chickens and ducks bound for the market.
Middle Right: Vegetable sellers at Cantho's floating markets.
Bottom: Incense maker and her products near Chau Doc.

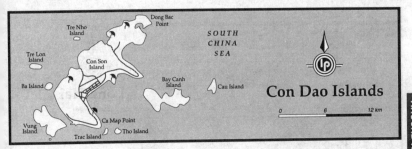

and the treatment of political prisoners held on the island. A ditch in which Communist Party members were dunked in cow's urine is open to the public.

### Places to Stay

Currently, the only place to stay is the *Phi Yen Hotel* (☎ 830168), where twin rooms are US$20 to US$30.

A Vietnamese-Korean joint venture is planning to build a 350-room luxury hotel on Con Son. Facilities will include a golf course, karaoke lounge and floating restaurant. A casino is possible, but the decision on that was still pending at the time of writing. Approval for the US$290 million project has already begin given, but there is no word yet on when it will be completed.

### Getting There & Away

**Air** Vasco Airlines flies approximately once daily from either Saigon or Vung Tau to Con Son Island. The flight is technically a charter, so it won't go if there are insufficient passengers.

**Boat** The 215km route between Vung Tau and Con Dao takes about 12 hours on a ship operated by the Vietnamese navy. Civilians can get permission to do this boat journey provided that there is a reasonably large group making the trip. The place to inquire about this is OSC at 2 Le Loi Blvd in Vung Tau.

When the aforementioned luxury resort hotel complex is completed, the government plans on inaugurating a high-speed hydrofoil service to the island.

### LONG HAI

Commercialised tourism has turned Vung Tau into something of a circus and many travellers crave a less-developed seaside retreat. As a result, backpackers are increasingly heading to Long Hai, 30km north-east of Vung Tau. The western end of the beach is where fishing boats moor and is therefore none too clean. However, the east end is attractive, with a reasonable amount of white sand and palm trees.

There are a couple of drawbacks to staying in Long Hai. Most irritating is the noise. Forget about sitting on your hotel's porch listening to the waves roll in. That sinister plot by hearing-aid manufacturers – karaoke – has taken Long Hai by storm. Your eardrums will be pounded all evening until about 11 pm or so and some of the real enthusiasts fire up their evil noise machines in the morning too. There is no use complaining about this – it comes with the territory. If you're deaf, you should love Long Hai. If you're not, you will be by the time you leave.

Another annoyance are the frequent electric power failures – keep some candles and a torch (flashlight) handy. On the other hand, you may look forward to the power failures as this silences the karaoke machines, albeit temporarily.

### Places to Stay

The best place to stay is the *Huong Bien Hotel* (☎ 868430; 10 rooms). The speciality

AROUND HO CHI MINH CITY

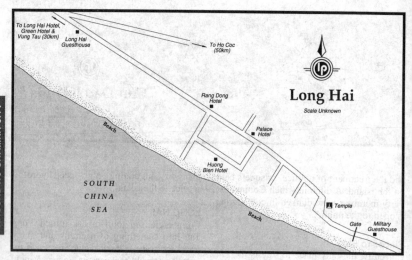

here is the beach bungalows hidden among the palm and pine trees. There are five bungalows with two rooms in each. Most rooms have fan and cold-water bath and cost US$12. With air-con (but still cold water!) it's US$15.

The *Palace Hotel* (☎ 868364; 18 rooms) is an interesting place. It was originally built to accommodate Emperor Bao Dai, who reigned in Vietnam from 1926 to 1945. Bao Dai had a taste for fancy beachside villas and had a chain of them erected in his favourite holiday spots. Bao Dai lost the franchise, but you can rent a room here with fan and cold-water bath for US$15. Air-conditioning (which even Bao Dai didn't have) and hot water will set you back US$20.

The *Military Guesthouse* (Nha Nghi Quan Doi; ☎ 868316; 28 rooms) is also good. The main building has 17 rooms priced from US$8 to US$20. There are also two beach houses (recommended!) where rooms cost only US$7.

The *Rang Dong Hotel* (☎ 868356) is memorable chiefly for the karaoke which cranks up the decibels from about 6 am until midnight. The foul sounds are enhanced by the building's cavernous echo chamber acoustics. Rooms cost US$12 to US$20.

The largest hotel currently on offer is the *Long Hai Hotel* (☎ 868312; 40 rooms). It's difficult to recommend this place – the beach next to the hotel is dirty and the 'massage service' looks rather kinky. Rooms are priced from US$12 to US$25, but they try to push foreigners into the priceyest rooms.

The *Long Hai Guesthouse* (Nha Nghi Long Hai; ☎ 868312) is another alternative. Twins cost US$12 to US$25.

The *Long Hai Green Hotel* (Khach San Xanh Long Hai; ☎ 868337; 13 rooms) is easily forgettable. It's rather far from the best beaches and the staff are not friendly. Rooms with air-con and attached hot-water bath are US$10 to US$12.

### Getting There & Away
There are some Long Hai-Saigon buses, though not many. Getting from Vung Tau to Long Hai is more problematic – you may have to rent a motorbike and drive yourself. Indeed, this is what most travellers do.

Motorbike taxi drivers hang around all the likely tourist spots and will offer you a ride repeatedly whether you want one or not.

### BINH CHAU HOT SPRINGS
About 50km north-east of Long Hai is Binh

Chau Hot Springs (Suoi Nuoc Nong Binh Chau). There is a small resort here, but tacky commercialisation is blessedly absent. The resort is in a compound 6km north of the village of Binh Chau and foreigners have to pay an admission fee of US$0.30.

Massage and acupuncture are on offer. Locals may also offer to take you on a hunting expedition (for a fee) to help exterminate any remaining wildlife in the area. From the looks of things, they've already done a good job – the only wildlife we encountered were the swarms of noisy cicadas buzzing away in the trees.

The resort consists of a hotel and adjoining restaurant. To see the actual hot springs, you have to walk down a wooden path. Be sure that you don't stray from the paths, as the earthen crust is thin here and you could conceivably fall through into an underground pool of scalding water! The hottest spring here reaches 82°C, which is not quite warm enough to boil eggs. However, the Vietnamese all try to boil eggs anyway and, indeed, you'll find a small spring where bamboo baskets have been laid aside for just this purpose. The eggshells and half-boiled eggs lying around here has made quite a mess.

### Places to Stay

If you want to spend the night, the only choice on offer is the *Binh Chau Hotel* (☎ 871131). There is a main hotel building, as well as some bungalows and a *rong* (tree) house. The rong house and bungalows have shared bath only and cost US$10. Rooms in the hotel have attached private baths – with fan only it's US$14 and with air-con you'll pay US$16 to US$22.

### Getting There & Away

Until recently, the road to Binh Chau consisted primarily of mud and potholes. This changed in the early 1990s when the Australian government donated funds to build a new highway. You might question why Binh Chau was so favoured (do Canberra officials have an irresistible urge to visit hot springs?), but you can't complain about the road. Indeed, it's one of the best roads in

Vietnam, but it's a pity that it just sort of dead-ends at Binh Chau and doesn't connect up to National Highway 1. Perhaps some other benevolent government will step in and donate the cash so that the highway can continue all the way up to the massage parlours of Nha Trang.

Good highway or not, there is no public transport. You'll need a motorbike or rented car. If you choose the latter, perhaps you can find some travellers to share the expense. If you drive this highway, be forewarned that there are several crucial intersections where you need to make turns and none of this is signposted.

### HO COC BEACH

About 50km north-east of Long Hai is the remote, but beautiful, Ho Coc Beach. It's still a very undeveloped area, though this will no doubt change. The *Ho Coc Guesthouse* consists of one bungalow with five rooms. Next door is the *Army Guesthouse*, which also has bungalows, but at the time of our visit foreigners were not permitted to stay. If you can't find any satisfactory accommodation here, you may have to stay at nearby Binh Chau Hot Springs.

### Getting There & Away

Public transport can be a little difficult, mainly because there isn't any. Some of the budget cafes on Saigon's Pham Ngu Lao St now offer day trips to Ho Coc. This also makes for a good (but very long) day trip on a motorbike. The 10km road between Ho Coc and Binh Chau Hot Springs is in poor condition.

### HAM TAN

Ham Tan is the new name for this place, but many locals still call it by its former name, Binh Tuy. Basically, it's a pleasantly secluded beach 30km north of Binh Chau Hot Springs. There is a small hotel here, but it's safe to say that visitors of any sort are not frequent.

Unfortunately, Ham Tan is not the easiest place to reach unless you have access to a helicopter. The already-mentioned road which the Aussies so generously built for the residents of Binh Chau peters out immediately after the hot springs resort. If you don't want to visit Ham Tan, you might still want to take a look at the old highway just to praise your good fortune at not having to drive on it. Potholes are the size of bomb craters and you might get to wondering if the Americans didn't build this road from the air using B-52s. A motorbike should be able to make the journey and a few adventurous travellers have even done it on mountain bikes. Any vehicle with four wheels attempting this trip should have four-wheel drive and/or high-clearance. If it's been raining recently, expect a sea of mud.

If you do make it to Ham Tan, it's only another 30km to National Highway 1. However, that road also will give bikers an opportunity to test their motocross skills.

## HANG GON TOMB

Outside the town of Xuan Loc is an ancient tomb which was excavated in the early 1990s. The tomb is about 2000 years old, but the intriguing thing about this place is that nobody knows who built it. The tomb contains ancient script which no one has been able to decipher and does not match the writing of any known ethnic group. UFO theorists and readers of *The X Files* should be enthralled with the place. The bodies of the deceased entombed here were cremated, so there are no remains other than ashes.

### Getting There & Away

There is no public transport available. Xuan Loc is on National Highway 1, and to the south there is an unnamed highway leading to Baria (which is near Vung Tau and Long Hai). From where National Highway 1 intersects with the Baria highway, it's 6km to the south to the turn-off that leads to the tomb, and another 5km on a rough road to the tomb itself.

# Mekong Delta

Pancake flat but lusciously green and beautiful, the Mekong Delta is the southernmost region of Vietnam. It was formed by sediment deposited by the Mekong River, a process which continues today; silt deposits extend the delta's shoreline at the mouth of the river by as much as 79m per year. The river is so large that it has two daily tides – indeed, at low tide in the dry season boats cannot even move through the shallow canals.

The land of the Mekong Delta is renowned for its richness; almost half of the region's total land area is under cultivation. The area is known as Vietnam's 'breadbasket', though 'ricebasket' would be a more appropriate term. The Mekong Delta produces enough rice to feed the entire country with a sizeable surplus left over. When the government introduced collectivised farming to the delta

in 1975, production fell way down and there were food shortages in Saigon. However, farmers in the delta easily grew enough to feed themselves, even if they didn't bother to send it to market. People from Saigon would head down to the delta to buy sacks of black-market rice to take home, but the police set up checkpoints and confiscated rice from anyone carrying more than 10kg to 'prevent profiteering'. All this ended in 1986, and farmers in this region have propelled Vietnam forward to become the world's third largest rice exporter.

Other food products from the delta include coconut, sugar cane, various fruits and fish. Although this area is primarily rural, it is one of the most densely populated regions in Vietnam – nearly every hectare is intensively farmed. An exception is the sparsely inhabited mangrove swamps around Camau in Minh Hai Province, where the land is not very productive.

The Mekong River is one of the world's great rivers, and the delta is one of the world's largest. The Mekong originates high in the Tibetan plateau, flowing 4500km through China, between Myanmar and Laos, through Laos, along the Lao-Thai border, and through Cambodia and Vietnam on its way to the South China Sea. At Phnom Penh, the Mekong splits into two main branches: the Hau Giang (the Lower River, also called the Bassac River), which flows via Chau Doc, Long Xuyen and Cantho to the sea; and the Tien Giang (Upper River), which splits into several branches at Vinh Long and empties into the sea at six points. The numerous branches of the river explains the Vietnamese name for the Mekong, Song Cuu Long (River of Nine Dragons).

The level of the Mekong begins to rise around the end of May and reaches its highest point in September; its flow ranges from 1900 to 38,000 cubic metres per second depending on the season. A tributary of the river which empties into the Mekong at

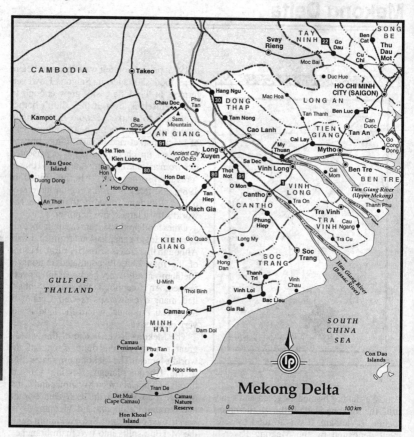

Mekong Delta

CAMBODIA

GULF OF
THAILAND

SOUTH
CHINA
SEA

0     50     100 km

Phnom Penh drains Cambodia's Tonlé Sap Lake. When the Mekong is at flood stage, this tributary reverses its flow and drains *into* Tonlé Sap, thereby somewhat reducing the danger of serious flooding in the Mekong Delta. Unfortunately, deforestation in Cambodia is upsetting the whole delicate balancing act, resulting in more floods in Vietnam's portion of the Mekong River basin.

Living on a flood plain presents some technical challenges. Lacking any high ground to escape flooding, many delta residents build their houses on bamboo stilts to avoid the rising waters. Many roads get submerged or turn to muck during floods – all-weather roads have to be built on raised embankments, but this is expensive. The traditional solution has been to build canals and travel by boat. There are thousands of canals in the Mekong Delta – keeping them properly dredged and navigable is a constant but essential chore.

Estuarine crocodiles are found in the southern parts of the delta rivers, particularly near the Hau Giang (Bassac) River area. These creatures can be dangerous and travellers are advised to keep a healthy distance from them.

The Mekong Delta was once part of the Khmer kingdom, and was the last region of modern-day Vietnam to be annexed and settled by the Vietnamese. The Cambodians, mindful that they controlled the area until the 18th century, still call the delta 'Lower Cambodia'. The Khmer Rouges tried to follow up on this claim by pulling nighttime raids on Vietnamese villages and massacring the inhabitants. This led the Vietnamese army to invade Cambodia in 1979 and oust the Khmer Rouges from power. Most of the current inhabitants of the Mekong Delta are ethnic-Vietnamese, but there are significant populations of ethnic-Chinese and Khmer as well as a few Chams.

Many travellers heading to the delta go by public bus (cheap but rough) or by rented motorbike (good fun, though you can get lost in the maze of roads). The other way is by minibus tour. There are quite a few of these on offer, including many inexpensive ones which can be booked at the budget cafes frequented by travellers on Pham Ngu Lao St. However, before you book anything, do

a little bit of comparative shopping. Cheapest is not always best – the cost largely depends on how far from Saigon the tour goes. This is not to say that you need to book a pricey tour with Saigon Tourist, but sometimes 'rock bottom' means just that and all you will get is a brief glance at the delta region. Obviously, the more days you spend and the more distance travelled, the greater the cost. The standard of accommodation will be another factor.

A major activity in the Mekong Delta is boating. Indeed, the only way you're really going to get a close look at the delta is to rent a boat and tour through the canals. However, it's important to realise that several of the greedy provincial governments in the Mekong Delta have essentially banned private entrepreneurs from renting boats to foreigners. In those places, you are forced to take an organised tour (at very high prices) with the local government-owned monopoly. The police regularly patrol the river in high-powered speedboats and try to catch foreigners who have violated these rules. The

**MEKONG DELTA**

### Search and Destroy

Only one major battle occurred in the Mekong Delta (in 1972 at Cai Lay, 20km from Mytho). Aside from that, all fighting in the delta during the American War was confined to small-scale ambushes. Unfortunately for the Americans, the lush jungles, tall grass and mangrove swamps provided perfect camouflage for the Viet Cong. The high civilian population density made it impossible for the Americans to use indiscriminate bombing, so it was necessary to send in ground-level 'search and destroy missions'. From the air, helicopter gunshops raked the grasslands and jungles with machine gun fire. On the water, US forces used high-speed military boats to patrol the hundreds of canals crisscrossing the delta in an effort to intercept guerillas travelling by canoe to their sanctuaries.

For their part, the VC responded with booby traps, nighttime raids, assassinations of 'uncooperative elements' and mines planted in the canals – essentially, the Communists controlled much of the delta at night. Both the Communists and the ARVN conscripted young men from the delta into their respective armies – it wasn't unusual for brothers to be fighting on opposite sides, often against their will. Desertions from both sides were high.

Caught in the crossfire, local villagers sensibly fled. By 1975, 40% of Saigon's population was from the Mekong Delta region.

Agent Orange was used to clear the mangrove forests of the delta in an effort to deny the guerillas sanctuary. Ironically, spraying the mangroves with defoliants may have backfired on the Americans. Obtaining food and supplies was one of the biggest headaches for the VC. Spraying the mangroves with Agent Orange caused the leaves of the plants to die, fall off and decay, providing a source of nutrition for shrimp which in turn were harvested by the VC. This provided the guerillas with a major short-term gain – the VC ate the shrimp and sold the surplus in the local markets to buy other needed supplies. ∎

situation is particularly bad in Mytho and Vinh Long.

Fortunately, not every provincial government is so restrictive. There are several places in the delta where you can simply rent a boat and go where you like. Probably the most accessible place to do this is Cantho, though it is also possible in Kien Giang Province.

## MYTHO

Mytho, the capital of Tien Giang Province, is a quiet city of 100,000. It's the closest Mekong Delta city to Saigon, and for this reason packaged tourists on a 10-day Vietnam tour come here for day trips. Having spent two hours in Mytho, they can go home and say 'I've seen the Mekong River'.

Being so close to booming Saigon, one would expect Mytho to have profited handsomely from the new economic reforms. Sadly, this is not the case – Mytho is the poorest city in the Mekong Delta, though it has the richest government.

The problem begins and ends with the Tien Giang People's Committee, reputed to be the most corrupt in Vietnam. Most forms of private enterprise are banned. For travellers, this means that tourist facilities are government run, in shoddy condition and overpriced.

Mytho was founded in the 1680s by Chinese refugees fleeing Taiwan for political reasons. The Chinese are virtually all gone now, having been driven out in the late 1970s when all their property was seized by the government. The economy – what's left of it – is based on fishing and the cultivation of rice, coconuts, bananas, mangoes, longans and citrus fruit.

## Orientation

Mytho, which sprawls along the bank of the northernmost branch of the Mekong River, is laid out in a fairly regular grid pattern. The bus station (Ben Xe Khach Tien Giang) is several kilometres west of town. Coming from the bus station, you enter Mytho on Ap Bac St. Ap Bac St turns into Nguyen Trai St, which is oriented west-east.

Paralleling the Mekong River is 30 Thang 4 St, which can also be written as 30/4 St.

## Information

**Travel Agencies** Tien Giang Tourist (Cong Ty Du Lich Tien Giang; ☎ 872154, 872105) is the official tourism authority for Tien Giang Province. The office is near the riverfront on the corner of Rach Gam and Trung Trac Sts.

**People's Committee** You are not permitted to photograph or video the People's Committee building in Mytho. A sign (in Vietnamese) warns you that this activity is prohibited.

## Phoenix Island

Until his imprisonment by the Communists for anti-government activities and the consequent dispersion of his flock, the Coconut Monk (Ong Dao Dua) led a small community on Phoenix Island (Con Phung), a few kilometres from Mytho. In its heyday, the island was dominated by a fantastic open-air sanctuary that looked like a cross between a cheaply built copy of Disneyland and the Tiger Balm Gardens of Singapore. The dragon-enwrapped columns and the multi-platformed tower with its huge metal globe must have once been brightly painted, but these days the whole place is faded, rickety and silent. Nevertheless, it's good kitschy fun – check out the model of the Apollo rocket set among the Buddhist statues! With a bit of imagination though, you can picture how it all must have appeared as the Coconut Monk presided over his congregation, flanked by elephant tusks and seated on a richly ornamented throne.

Considering that there is an admission fee of US$0.50, it would be nice to think that this money is going to maintain the place. Apparently, this is not the case – the island's adornments are falling apart and the place is increasingly becoming a dilapidated tourist trap. As one traveller lamented:

The island is a great disappointment. It has faded almost into nothing. Beware of the cunning old chap claiming to be an ex-monk who drags you around the

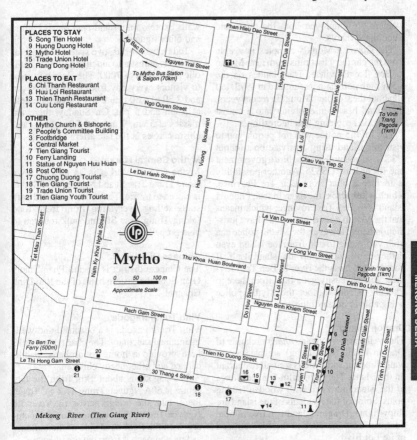

PLACES TO STAY
5 Song Tien Hotel
9 Huong Duong Hotel
12 Mytho Hotel
15 Trade Union Hotel
20 Rang Dong Hotel

PLACES TO EAT
6 Chi Thanh Restaurant
8 Huu Loi Restaurant
13 Thien Thanh Restaurant
14 Cuu Long Restaurant

OTHER
1 Mytho Church & Bishopric
2 People's Committee Building
3 Footbridge
4 Central Market
7 Tien Giang Tourist
10 Ferry Landing
11 Statue of Nguyen Huu Huan
16 Post Office
17 Chuong Duong Tourist
18 Tien Giang Tourist
19 Trade Union Tourist
21 Tien Giang Youth Tourist

Mytho

0    50    100 m
Approximate Scale

MEKONG DELTA

Mekong River (Tien Giang River)

few sights at high speed and then demands you buy him an extortionate beer at the kiosk.

**Sue Grossey**

The Coconut Monk, so named because it is said that he once ate only coconuts for three years, was born Nguyen Thanh Nam (though he later adopted western name order, preferring to be called Nam Nguyen Thanh) in 1909 in what is now Ben Tre Province. He studied chemistry and physics in France at Lyons, Caen and Rouen from 1928 until 1935, when he returned to Vietnam, married and had a daughter.

In 1945 the Coconut Monk left his family to pursue a monastic life. For three years he sat on a stone slab under a flagpole and meditated day and night. He was repeatedly imprisoned by successive South Vietnamese governments, which were infuriated by his philosophy of bringing about the country's reunification through peaceful means. The monk died in 1990.

The Coconut Monk founded a religion, Tinh Do Cu Si, which was a mixture of Buddhism and Christianity. Representations of Jesus and the Buddha appeared together, as did the Virgin Mary and eminent Buddhist women. He employed both the cross and Buddhist symbols.

The Coconut Monk's complex is visible from the car ferry that runs from near Mytho to Ben Tre Province. The plaques on the 3.5m-high porcelain jar (created in 1972) tell all about the Coconut Monk. In recent years, the island has been evolving into a tourist trap and is becoming less interesting.

The Mytho police will not permit you to visit this island using a private boat (about US$3), so you will have to hire a government one for at least US$25. Another possibility is to hire a boat from Ben Tre Province, which is just across the river. In fact, Phoenix Island is in Ben Tre Province, which means that the Mytho police really don't have jurisdiction here. However, the Mytho police can grab you going to and from the island even if they can't come onto the island itself. If you do first cross the river to Ben Tre Province, you can easily get a boat from there to Phoenix Island without the Mytho police being able to do anything.

### Dragon Island

The well-known longan (nhan) orchards of Dragon Island (Con Long) are pleasant to walk through, and there is a small restaurant on the island. The lush, palm-fringed shores of the island are lined with wooden fishing boats. Some of the residents of the island are shipwrights. Dragon Island is a five minute boat trip from the dock at the southern end of Le Loi Blvd.

### Other Islands

The other two islands in the vicinity are Tortoise Island (Con Qui) and Unicorn Island (Con Lan or Thoi Son). For booking a trip to these islands or any others, it's cheapest to arrange a day tour from Saigon. For information on boat tours, see Getting Around later in this section.

### Mytho Church & Bishopric

Mytho Church, a solid pastel-yellow building at 32 Hung Vuong Blvd (corner of Nguyen Trai St), was built about a century ago. The stone plaques set in the church

walls express *merci* and *cam on* to Fatima and other figures.

Today, two priests, two sisters and several assistants minister to much of Mytho's Catholic population of 7000. The church is open to visitors every day from 4.30 to 6.30 am and 2.30 to 6.30 pm. Daily masses are held at 5 am and 5 pm. On Sunday, there are masses at 5 am, 7 am and 5 pm, and catechism classes in the late afternoon.

### Mytho Central Market

Mytho Central Market is an area of town along Trung Trac St and Nguyen Hue St that is closed to traffic. The streets are filled with stalls selling everything from fresh food (along Trung Trac St) and bulk tobacco to boat propellers.

### Chinese District

The Chinese district is around Phan Thanh Gian St on the eastern bank of the Bao Dinh Channel.

### Vinh Trang Pagoda

Vinh Trang Pagoda is a beautiful and well-maintained sanctuary. The charitable monks here provide a home to orphans, handicapped and other needy children.

The pagoda is about 1km from the city centre at 60A Nguyen Trung Truc St. To get there, take the bridge across the river (at Nguyen Trai St). The entrance to the sanctuary is on the right-hand side of the building as you approach it from the ornate gate.

### Places to Stay

Mytho's ever-vigilant People's Committee has placed most of the town's hotels off limits to foreigners. There are currently only four places where you can stay, all of them government owned. The facilities have actually deteriorated in the past few years – many rooms have broken plumbing and non-functioning air-conditioners, so check carefully before you check in.

Most popular with budget travellers is the *Trade Union Hotel* (Khach San Cong Doan; ☎ 874324; 14 rooms) at 61 30/4 St. Good river views are one of the attractions here. A single with fan costs US$8, or you can have a room with air-con and refrigerator for US$20.

The five-storey *Huong Duong Hotel* (☎ 872011; 20 rooms) at 33 Trung Trac St is a neglected dump. Rooms with fan cost US$7. There are air-con rooms for US$10, but the air-conditioners don't work too well.

The eight-storey *Song Tien Hotel* (☎ 872-009; 39 rooms) is the largest in town. Rooms with fan only are US$6, or with air-con US$10 to US$20.

The *Rang Dong Hotel* (☎ 874400; 21 rooms) at 25 30/4 St is one of the best places in town. All rooms have air-con. Rooms with cold-water bath cost US$12, and with hot water US$18 to US$25.

### Places to Eat

Mytho is known for a special vermicelli soup, hu tieu My Tho, which is richly garnished with fresh and dried seafood, pork, chicken and fresh herbs. It is served either with broth or dry (with broth on the side).

There are numerous excellent small and cheap restaurants along Trung Trac St between the statue of Nguyen Huu Huan (a 19th century anti-colonial fighter) on 30/4 St and the Thu Khoa Huan Blvd bridge. The two best ones we've found here are *Chi Thanh Restaurant* and *Huu Loi Restaurant*.

Right on the shore of the Mekong River is the *Cuu Long Restaurant*, which has river views but mediocre food at high prices.

### Getting There & Away

**Bus** Mytho is served by nonexpress buses leaving Saigon from Mien Tay bus station in An Lac.

The Mytho bus station (Ben Xe Khach Tien Giang) is several kilometres west of town; it is open from 4 am to about 5 pm. To get there from the city centre, take Ap Bac St westward and continue on to National Highway 1.

Buses to Saigon leave when full from the early morning until about 5 pm; the trip takes 1½ hours. There is daily bus service to Cantho (five hours; departures at 4 am and 9 pm), Chau Doc (leaves at 4 am), Phu Hoa (departs at 6 pm), Tay Ninh (six hours; departs at 5 am) and Vung Tau (five hours; leaves at 5 am). There are also buses to Ba Beo, Bac My Thuan, Cai Be, Cai Lay, Go Cong Dong, Go Cong Tay, Hau My Bac, Phu My, Tan An and Vinh Kim. There is no express bus service from Mytho.

**Car** By car, the drive from Saigon to Mytho on National Highway 1 (Quoc Lo 1) takes about 1½ hours.

Road distances from Mytho are 16km to

MEKONG DELTA

Water buffaloes remain a common sight around the Mekong Delta, where they contribute to the region's astonishing rice production; every year the region produces enough rice to feed all of Vietnam, with a sizeable surplus to generate much-needed foreign currency.

Ben Tre, 104km to Cantho, 70km to Ho Chi Minh City and 66km to Vinh Long.

**Boat** A little-used passenger ferry to Mytho leaves Saigon daily at 11 am from the dock at the end of Ham Nghi Blvd. The trip should take about six hours if you're lucky. The cost for foreigners is US$6.

The car ferry to Ben Tre Province leaves from a station (Ben Pha Rach Mieu) about a kilometre west of the city centre near 2/10A Le Thi Hong Gam St (Le Thi Hong Gam St is the western continuation of 30/4 St). The ferry operates from 4 am to 10 pm and runs at least once an hour. Ten-person trucks shuttle between the ferry terminal and the bus station.

### Getting Around
**Bicycle** Bicycles can be rented from the Tien Giang Tourist. Yes, even bicycle rentals are a government-run monopoly.

**Boat Tours** Mytho's People's Committee used to have a total monopoly over boat travel, but recent pressure from Hanoi has forced them to permit four travel companies to run boat tours at Mytho. However, all four are government owned. Nevertheless, there is some real competition between them and this has forced prices down somewhat, although you still need to be in a large group to make it economical. If you show up on your own and try to rent a boat, you'll have to pay at least US$25 per hour. If you sign up with a tour group in Saigon, it could work out to as little as US$7 per person for a two-hour tour, including bus transport to/from Saigon to Mytho. When comparing prices, check to see what you are actually getting – the tours can last anywhere from one to four hours (not including the Saigon-Mytho travel time).

Tien Giang Youth Tourist is very expensive if you try to book with it directly; however, it does offer a budget tour through Sinh Cafe in Saigon.

The Trade Union Tourist (☎ 876919, 847324) at 10 30/4 St is much cheaper than Tien Giang Youth Tourist. In Saigon you can

book through its representative, Ben Thanh Tourist, for US$8 per person.

Chuong Duong Tourist (☎ 873379), 12 30/4 St, is the latest agency to set up shop in Mytho. In Saigon you can book a budget tour for US$7 through its representative, Kim Cafe.

Tien Giang Tourist belongs to the People's Committee and has the most expensive tours – we consider this one the least desirable of the lot. In Saigon you can book tours through its representative, Saigon Tourist.

### AROUND MYTHO
**Dong Tam Snake Farm** There is a snake farm at Dong Tam, which is about 10km from Mytho towards Vinh Long. Most of the snakes raised here are pythons and cobras. The snakes are raised for a variety of purposes: for eating; for their skins; and for the purpose of producing snake anti-venoms. The king cobras are raised only for exhibit – they are extremely aggressive and are even capable of spitting poison. Do not get too close to their cages. The regular cobras are kept in an open pit and will generally ignore you if you ignore them, but will strike if provoked. On the other hand, the pythons are docile enough to be taken out of their cages and 'played with' if you dare, but the larger ones are capable of strangling a human.

Dong Tam also has a collection of mutant turtles and fish on exhibit. The cause of their genetic deformities is almost certainly from the spraying of the herbicide Agent Orange during the war, which was particularly intensive in forested parts of the Mekong Delta.

Other creatures kept on exhibit here include sea turtles, deer, monkeys, bears, crocodiles, owls, canaries and various other birds. Unfortunately, all the names and explanations of the creatures are in Vietnamese only.

The Snake Farm is operated by the Vietnamese military for profit. It's definitely open to the public and taking photos is even encouraged. At your request, the staff will drape you with a large python to create that perfect photo for the loved ones back home.

The restaurant at the snake farm does include cobra on the menu. There is also a

## Ecocide

During the American War, the USA employed deliberate destruction of the environment as a military tactic on an enormous scale. In an effort to deny bases of operation to the Viet Cong, 72 million litres of the herbicides known as Agent Orange, Agent White and Agent Blue were sprayed on 16% of South Vietnam's land area (including 10% of the inland forests and 36% of the mangrove forests). It is said that the deforestation caused by spraying these chemicals would have been enough to supply Vietnam's timber harvesters for 30 years. The most seriously affected regions were the provinces of Dong Nai, Song Be and Tay Ninh. Another environmentally disastrous method of defoliation employed by the military involved the use of enormous bulldozers called 'Rome ploughs' to rip up the jungle floor.

The 40 million litres of Agent Orange used contained 170kg of dioxin (2,3,7,8-TCDD). Dioxin is the most toxic chemical known, highly carcinogenic and mutagenic. Today, more than 20 years after the spraying, dioxin is still present in the food chain, though its concentrations are gradually diminishing. Researchers report elevated levels of dioxin in samples of human breast milk collected in affected areas, where about 7.5% of the population of the south now lives. Vietnamese refugees living in the USA who were exposed to Agent Orange have been showing unusually high rates of cancer. Ditto for American soldiers, who filed a class action lawsuit against the US government to seek compensation.

Scientists have yet to conclusively prove a link between the residues of chemicals used by the USA during the war and spontaneous abortions, stillbirths, birth defects and other human health problems. However, the circumstantial evidence is certainly compelling.

Those wishing to pursue this topic further might want to pay a visit to Tu Du Hospital on Nguyen Thi Minh Khai St in Saigon. There are hundreds of dead deformed babies preserved in bottles here, each one marked with the date of birth. The gynaecologists at the hospital speak good English and will tell you all about it if you show genuine interest. Please remember, though, that this is a hospital and not a tourist attraction.

In addition to the spraying, large tracts of forests, agricultural land, villages and even cemeteries were bulldozed, removing both the vegetation and topsoil. Flammable melaleuca forests were ignited with napalm. In mountain areas, landslides were deliberately created by bombing and by spraying acid on limestone hillsides. Elephants, useful for transport, were attacked from the air with bombs and napalm. By war's end, extensive areas had been taken over by tough weeds (known locally as 'American grass'). The government estimates that 20,000 sq km of forest and farmland were lost as a direct result of the American war effort.

Overall, some 13 million tonnes of bombs – equivalent to 450 times the energy of the atomic bomb used on Hiroshima – were dropped on the region. This comes to 265kg for every man, woman and child in Indochina. If the Americans had showered the people of Indochina with the money all those bombs cost (the war cost US$2000 per resident of Indochina), they might have won. ■

shop here where you can stock up on cobra anti-venom.

The Snake Farm was formerly run by a retired Viet Cong colonel named Tu Duoc. He ran the place very efficiently, but, unfortunately, he died in 1990 and the facilities have gone steadily downhill ever since. The cages look dirty, the animals neglected and the employees dispirited. It's certainly a sharp contrast to Bangkok's slick Snake Institute.

Nevertheless, Dong Tam Snake Farm is an interesting place to visit. Admission costs US$1.

## BEN TRE

The picturesque province of Ben Tre is just south of Mytho. The entire province consists of several large islands in the mouth of the Mekong River, but the area gets few visitors because it's off the main highways. The provincial capital is also called Ben Tre, and is a friendly sort of place with a few old buildings near the mighty Mekong River.

### Information
**Travel Agencies** Ben Tre Tourist (☎ 829-618) is on Nguyen Dinh Chieu St.

### Vien Minh Pagoda
Right in the centre of Ben Tre town, this is the head office of the Buddhist Association of Ben Tre Province. Though the history of the pagoda is vague, the local monks say it is over 100 years old. The original structure

**Ben Tre**
Scale Unknown

To Ben Tre Hotel
& Mytho Ferry

Hai Ba Trung Street

Dong Khoi Street

Truc
Giang
Lake

Cach Mang Thang 8 Street

Nguyen Dinh Chieu Street

1 Dong Khoi Hotel
2 Ben Tre Tourism
3 Vien Minh Pagoda
4 Floating Restaurant
5 Boats for Hire
6 Hung Vuong Hotel

Hung Vuong Street

Ben Tre River

was made of wood, but it was torn down to make way for the present building. Reconstruction took place from 1951 to 1958, this time using bricks and concrete.

A feature of this pagoda is a large white statue of Quan The Am Bo Tat (the Goddess of Mercy) in the front courtyard. The Chinese calligraphy which dresses up this pagoda was done by an old monk who has now passed away. None of the current monks can read Chinese, though some of the local worshippers can.

### Truc Giang Lake
Truc Giang Lake, a small but pleasant lake fronting the Dong Khoi Hotel, is a place to play around in paddleboats. The surrounding park is too small for doing much strolling.

### Phoenix Island
The island of the Coconut Monk is actually in Ben Tre Province, and the Ben Tre cops do not care if you hire a small private boat to

visit it (unlike in Mytho, where you must go on an expensive government cruise). Private boats can be hired for US$3 per hour. For more information, see the Mytho section.

### Nguyen Dinh Chieu Temple
This temple is dedicated to Nguyen Dinh Chieu, a local scholar. It's about a one-hour drive from the town of Ben Tre. It's a very charming temple, excellent for photography.

### Bird Sanctuary
The locals make much of the Bird Sanctuary (Vam Ho), which is 36km from Ben Tre town. Storks nest here, but access is difficult enough that most travellers won't bother.

### Places to Stay
There are three hotels in town which can accommodate foreigners. Bottom of the barrel is the *Hung Vuong Hotel* (☎ 822408) at 166 Hung Vuong St. Rooms with fan are US$7 to US$8. Air-con ups the tab to US$18 for a double.

Next in the pecking order is the *Ben Tre Hotel* (☎ 822223) at 226/3 Tran Quoc Tuan St. Rooms with fan only cost US$7, while air-con ranges from US$14 to US$18.

Ben Tre's plushest accommodation can be found at the *Dong Khoi Hotel* (☎ 822240; 35 rooms) at 16 Hai Ba Trung St. All rooms have air-con. Doubles are US$30 to US$35. Even if you don't stay here, take a peak at the hotel's gift shop – the souvenir spoons, chopsticks and ashtrays made of coconut wood may not be the most durable but they certainly are beautiful.

### Places to Eat
The *Dong Khoi Hotel* has the spiffiest restaurant in town. On Saturday night, a band entertains the guests.

The *Floating Restaurant* is anchored on the south side of town near the boat pier. We can't vouch for the food, but you can't beat the atmosphere.

### Getting There & Away
Seeing how this is an island province, crossing the Mekong River is a prerequisite for

reaching Ben Tre. However, this ferry crossing is particularly slow – figure on at least an hour each way.

Slow as it is, the Mytho-Ben Tre crossing is the fastest of the lot. There are other possible ferry crossings farther south that can get you to Ben Tre, but these are so slow and unreliable that you shouldn't count on them. Ferry crossings are quicker if you're travelling by motorcycle (as opposed to a car) since there are numerous small boats which can take you across the river.

### Getting Around
**Boat** Ben Tre Tourist has a high-speed boat for rent, though it's not cheap at US$35 per hour. Like most speedboats, it can hold only five persons. Slower and larger boats can also be rented here, but other bargains can be negotiated at the public pier.

### VINH LONG
Vinh Long, the capital of Vinh Long Province, is a medium-sized town along the banks of the Mekong River about midway between Mytho and Cantho.

### Information
**Travel Agencies** Cuu Long Tourist (☎ 823-616) has four (yes, four!) tour booking offices in town – at least it's optimistic. The sleepy staff have little to do, and they will no doubt be overjoyed if you drop in and help them practice their English.

### Mekong River Islands
What makes a trip to Vinh Long worthwhile is not the town itself but the beautiful small islands in the river. The islands are totally given over to agriculture, especially the raising of tropical fruits, which are shipped to markets in Saigon.

A trip to the islands requires that you charter a boat through the government tourist office. Small boats cost US$25 per person for a three-hour journey. A minimum of three persons is required to get that 'cheap' price. However, you can bargain – the tourist office is desperate for business. The tours include an English or French-speaking Vietnamese guide.

One way to partially bypass the government monopoly is to take the public ferry (US$0.20) to one of the islands and then walk around; however, this is not nearly as interesting as a boat tour.

Some of the more popular islands to visit include Binh Hoa Phuoc and An Binh Island, but there are many others. One of the fascinating things here are the 'monkey bridges' (*cau khi*). These are makeshift footbridges built of uneven logs about 30cm to 80cm wide and from two to 10m above the canals. It's amazing to watch the locals cross these with bicycles and heavy loads balanced between their shoulders on bamboo poles. A fall from one of these bridges could result in serious injury, but the Vietnamese just glide across these things with a smile on their face.

This low-lying region is as much water as land, and houses are generally built on stilts. Bring plenty of film because there are photo opportunities in almost any direction you look.

### Military Museum
It's nothing spectacular, but there is a Military Museum (Bao Tang Quan Su) close to the Cuu Long Hotel. The various military museums in Saigon and Hanoi are significantly better.

### Van Thanh Mieu Temple
A big surprise in Vinh Long is the large and beautiful Van Thanh Meiu Temple by the river. As Vietnamese temples go, it's unusual in a number of respects. To begin with, it's a Confucian temple, and these are very rare in southern Vietnam. Another oddity is that, while the rear hall is dedicated to Confucius, the front hall was built in honour of local hero Phan Thanh Gian.

Van Thanh Mieu Temple is sometimes called Phan Thanh Gian Temple by the locals. A plaque outside the temple entrance briefly tells his story. Phan Thanh Gian led an uprising in 1930 against the French. When it became obvious that his revolt was doomed, Phan killed himself rather than be captured by the colonial army. No one is quite certain

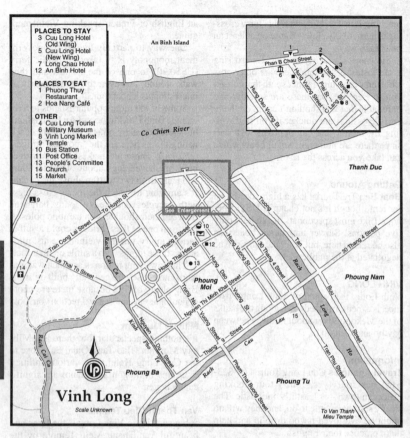

PLACES TO STAY
3 Cuu Long Hotel
  (Old Wing)
5 Cuu Long Hotel
  (New Wing)
7 Long Chau Hotel
12 An Binh Hotel

PLACES TO EAT
1 Phuong Thuy
  Restaurant
2 Hoa Nang Café

OTHER
4 Cuu Long Tourist
6 Military Museum
8 Vinh Long Market
9 Temple
10 Bus Station
11 Post Office
13 People's Committee
14 Church
15 Market

**Vinh Long**
Scale Unknown

when the hall honouring Phan was built, but it seems to have been after 1975.

The rear hall of the large and spacious grounds is dedicated to Confucius, whose portrait hangs above the altar. The building was designed very much in the Confucian style and looks like it was lifted straight out of China. The Confucian Hall was built in 1866.

Van Thanh Mieu Temple is several kilometres south-east of the town centre along Tran Phu St. Don't confuse it with the much smaller Quoc Cong Pagoda on Tran Phu St which you will pass along the way.

## Places to Stay

The *Long Chau Hotel* (☎ 823611; 15 rooms) at 1 1/5 St is a bottom-end hovel that's even worse than it looks. A room with toilet outside is US$6, or you can have a room with attached bath and fan for US$8 to US$10. Air-con rooms are US$12.

The *Cuu Long Hotel* (☎ 822494; fax 823357; 45 rooms) has two branches right on the riverfront. The new wing is at 501 1/5 St. A room with fan costs US$15 or you can have it with air-con for US$35. All air-con rooms have satellite TV.

The *An Binh Hotel* (☎ 823190; 40 rooms)

## A Home Away from Home

A homestay among the people of the Mekong Delta is an unforgettable experience and can give you a unique insight into the day-to-day lives of the local people.

The easiest ways to arrange such a visit are through western travel companies (such as Intrepid Travel), via hotels and cafes in Saigon or through Cuu Long Tourist in Vinh Long. However, independent travellers can make arrangements with freelance agents at the An Binh boat station on arrival in Vinh Long. Rates are typically US$7 to US$10 per night.

Many of the homes that are open to western visitors are on the banks of the Mekong River. When you reach the home of your host family, you should remove your shoes. Most families also prefer women to be well covered up.

The bulk of the local people make their living from growing fruit or cultivating rice, although some of the women work in small buildings making coconut sweets, spending their days boiling large cauldrons of the sticky mixture, before rolling it out and cutting sections off into squares and wrapping them into paper for sale.

The houses are basic. The sleeping area is open plan and has hammocks and wooden beds with mosquito nets hanging overhead (before the last rays of the sun disappear slap on plenty of repellent, as mosquitoes are rampant throughout the area).

A typical supper is the local favourite, elephant-ear fish, served bolt upright on a bed of greens with flourishes of carrots shaped as water flowers. The flesh of the fish is pulled off in chunks with chopsticks and wrapped into a rice paper pancake and dipped into sauce. This is accompanied by crispy spring rolls and is followed by soup and rice (Mekong rice is considered the most flavoursome in Vietnam).

After dinner some families exchange stories and songs over bottles of rice wine long into the night, while others cluster around the television set.

The morning starts as the first lights flicker across the water. Before breakfast everyone takes a bath with the family. Splashing around in the muddy Mekong, fully dressed, can leave you feeling dirtier than when you started! After a hearty breakfast you say your goodbyes and head back to Vinh Long via the floating market.

**Juliet Coombe**

at 3 Hoang Thai Hieu St is nice enough, but not favoured by westerners because it's far from the scenic riverfront. Still, if you're stuck for a place to stay (not likely), you could do worse. Rooms with fan and outside toilet are US$8. Rooms with attached toilet and air-con raises the tariff to US$15 to US$35. Other facilities include tennis courts and massage service.

About 4km from Vinh Long (on the way to the ferry) is the *Truong An Tourist Villas* (☎ 823161). It's an excellent place to stay if you don't mind being away from the town. There are bungalows here for rent costing US$25 to US$30. Whether you stay or not, it's lovely to sit in the cafe by the riverside and enjoy the parklike surroundings.

Cuu Long Tourist can arrange for you to spend the night in the *Farm House* (Ngu Vuon), which is on an island. The house is built on stilts above the river in the traditional Mekong Delta style, but this one was actually designed for tourists. Nevertheless, it's

certainly peaceful and the scant few visitors mostly say they enjoy the place, but you have to be the sort of person who likes isolation. Commuting to town involves a mandatory boat trip. The cost for all this is US$15 to US$20.

### Places to Eat

Opposite the Cuu Long Hotel and right on the riverfront is the *Phuong Thuy Restaurant*. The food isn't bad, but what makes the place is the fine view. Another place for good river views and reasonable meals is the *Hoa Nang Cafe*.

However, if great food at cheap prices is more important than scenery, check out the *Vinh Long Market*. This is also a great place to try some delicious fruit, everything from bananas to mangoes and papayas.

### Getting There & Away

**Bus** Buses to Vinh Long leave Saigon from Cholon bus station in District 5, and from Mien Tay bus station in An Lac. Nonexpress buses take four hours. You can also get there by bus from Mytho. One traveller reported:

In Mytho, I was told that there were no more buses that day to Vinh Long, but *not* that there were plenty of buses to My Thuan. My Thuan is at the ferry head, and from there to Vinh Long is only a ferry hop and a moped ride away.

**Car** Vinh Long is just off National Highway 1, 66km from Mytho, 98km from Cantho and 136km from Ho Chi Minh City. In the year 2000, the government hopes to have a new bridge open across the Mekong River. This will shave about one hour off the travel time between Vinh Long and Ho Chi Minh City.

**Boat** It is possible to go from Vinh Long all the way to Chau Doc, but you should have a Vietnamese guide if you want to attempt this.

## TRA VINH

Bordered by the Tien and Hau rivers (branches of the Mekong), Tra Vinh's location on a peninsula makes it somewhat isolated. Getting there is a straight up and back trip because no car ferries here cross the rivers, but motorbikes can be ferried by small boats. Western tourists are few, though Japanese travellers discovered the place several years ago. There are, in fact, several very worthwhile things to see here.

There are about 300,000 ethnic Khmer people in Tra Vinh Province. At first glance, the Khmers might seem to be an 'invisible minority' – they all speak fluent Vietnamese, and there is nothing outwardly distinguishing about their clothing or lifestyle. However, digging a little deeper quickly reveals that Khmer culture is alive and well in this part of Vietnam. There are over 140 Khmer pagodas in Tra Vinh Province, compared with 50 Vietnamese and five Chinese pagodas. The pagodas have organised schools to teach the Khmer language – most of the locals in Tra Vinh can read and write Khmer at least as well as Vietnamese.

Vietnam's Khmer minority are almost all believers in Theravada Buddhism. If you've visited monasteries in Cambodia, you may have observed that Khmer monks are not involved in growing food and rely on donations from the strictly religious locals. Here in Tra Vinh, Vietnamese guides will proudly point out the rice harvest by the monks as one of the accomplishments of liberation. To the Vietnamese, non-working monks were viewed as 'parasites'. The Khmers don't necessarily see it the same way, and still continue to donate funds to the monasteries surreptitiously.

Between the ages of 15 and 20, most boys set aside a few months or years to live as monks (they decide themselves on the length of service). Khmer monks can eat meat, though they cannot kill animals.

There is also a small but active Chinese community in Tra Vinh, one of the few remaining in the Mekong Delta region. Most of the Overseas Chinese fled this part of Vietnam during the years of persecution in 1978 and 1979. people

### Information
**Travel Agencies** Tra Vinh Tourist (☎ 862-491, 862042; fax 863769) in the Cuu Long Hotel is part of the government-owned monopoly. The staff can book trips to various sites around the province – they seem fond of the pomelo orchards (Vuon Buoi), though the boat trips should prove more interesting.

### Ong Pagoda
The Ong Pagoda (Chua Ong, also known as Chua Tau) is a very ornate, brightly painted building on the corner of Dien Bien Phu and Tran Phu Sts. Unusually for the Mekong Delta region, this is a 100% Chinese pagoda and is still a very active place of worship. The red-faced god on the altar is deified general Quan Cong (in Chinese: Guangong, Guandi or Guanyu). Quan Cong is believed to offer protection against war and is based on an historical figure, a soldier of the 3rd century. You can read more about him in the Chinese classic *The Romance of the Three Kingdoms*.

The Ong Pagoda was founded in 1556 by the Fujian Chinese Congregation, but has been rebuilt a number of times. Recent visitors from Taiwan and Hong Kong have con-

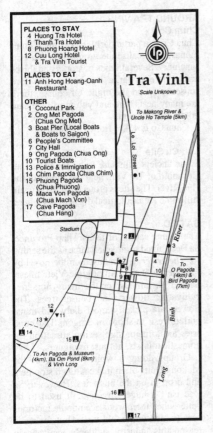

PLACES TO STAY
4 Huong Tra Hotel
5 Thanh Tra Hotel
8 Phuong Hoang Hotel
12 Cuu Long Hotel
& Tra Vinh Tourist

PLACES TO EAT
11 Anh Hong Hoang-Oanh
Restaurant

OTHER
1 Coconut Park
2 Ong Met Pagoda
(Chua Ong Met)
3 Boat Pier (Local Boats
& Boats to Saigon)
6 People's Committee
7 City Hall
9 Ong Pagoda (Chua Ong)
10 Tourist Boats
13 Police & Immigration
14 Chim Pagoda (Chua Chim)
15 Phuong Pagoda
(Chua Phuong)
16 Maca Von Pagoda
(Chua Mach Von)
17 Cave Pagoda
(Chua Hang)

Tra Vinh
Scale Unknown

To Mekong River &
Uncle Ho Temple (5km)

To
O Pagoda
(4km) &
Bird Pagoda
(7km)

To An Pagoda & Museum
(4km), Ba Om Pond (8km)
& Vinh Long

**MEKONG DELTA**

tributed money for the pagoda's restoration, which is why it is currently in such fine shape.

### Ong Met Pagoda

The chief reason for visiting this large Khmer pagoda is that it's the most accessible, being right in the centre of town. Next door is a French-era Catholic church. The monks at Ong Met Pagoda (Chua Ong Met) are friendly and happy to show you the interior.

### Chim Pagoda

An interesting monastery, Chim Pagoda (Chua Chim) sees few visitors because you have to twist and wind your way along dirt roads to find it. It's actually just 1km off the main highway to Vinh Long in the southwest part of town. Having a local take you on a motorbike is probably the best way to get there if you don't have your own wheels.

The friendly monks here claim that the pagoda was originally built 500 years ago, though the present structure is obviously much newer. Unfortunately, all of the monastery's historical records seem to have been destroyed. At the present time, there are 17 monks in residence here.

### Ba Om Pond

Known as Ao Ba Om (Square Lake), this is a spiritual site for the Khmers and a picnic and drinking spot for local Vietnamese. The square-shaped pond is surrounded by tall trees and is pleasant if not spectacular. More interesting is nearby Wat Angkor Icha Borei, a beautiful and venerable Khmer-style pagoda. There is also a new museum on the far side of the lake (away from the highway).

Ba Om Pond is 8km from Tra Vinh along the highway towards Vinh Long.

### Uncle Ho Temple

Sometimes Vietnam throws something at you totally unexpected. Tra Vinh chips in with the Uncle Ho Temple (Den Tho Bac), dedicated of course to late President Ho Chi Minh. Perhaps Tra Vinh's enterprising People's Committee was looking for a way to distinguish their fine town and put it on the tourist circuit. If so, they may have succeeded – although no monks have yet taken up residence, 'worshippers' continue to flock here (Communist Party brass arrive regularly in chauffeur-driven limousines). A locally produced tourist pamphlet calls it the 'Pride of Tra Vinh's inhabitants'. Ho himself would no doubt be horrified.

The Uncle Ho Temple is within the Long Duc commune, 5km from Tra Vinh town.

### An Pagoda & Museum

Four km south-west of Tra Vinh town is the

An Pagoda (Chua An) and Khmer Minority
People's Museum.

### Boat Trips

The narrow Long Binh River meanders southwards from Tra Vinh town for over 10km
before reaching a spillway. The spillway was
built to prevent seawater from intruding at
high tide. Otherwise, the saltwater would
contaminate the river and kill the crops.

It is possible to hire boats from the pier on
the east side of town to take you downstream
to the spillway. Of course, Tra Vinh Tourist
can also book you onto these trips, which
typically take about 1½ hours by speedboat,
more for a slower boat.

Tours can also be arranged to Oyster
Island (Con Ngao), an offshore mud-flat that
supports a small contingent of oyster farmers. Tra Vinh Tourist offers trips for US$100
per boat regardless of group size, though you
should be able to negotiate something
cheaper.

### Places to Stay

The *Huong Tra Hotel* (☎ 862433; 12 rooms),
67 Ly Thuong Kiet St, is Tra Vinh's bottom-
end place. Rooms with shared toilet cost
US$5, but air-con with attached bath goes for
US$12.

Slightly fancier is the *Phuong Hoang Hotel*
(☎ 862270) at 1 Le Thanh Ton St. All rooms
have attached bathroom. Rooms with fan
only are US$5 to US$7, while air-con
doubles are US$13 to US$18.

The *Cuu Long Hotel* (☎ 862615) at 999
Nguyen Thi Minh Khai St offers reasonable
accommodation at US$15 to US$30.

The *Thanh Tra Hotel* (☎ 863621, 863622;
fax 863769), 1 Pham Thai Buong, is where
most of the tour groups put up for the night.
However, there are also some budget rooms
ranging from US$12 to US$35.

### Getting There & Away

Tra Vinh is 68km from Vinh Long and
205km from Ho Chi Minh City. Either Vinh
Long or Cantho would be logical places to
catch buses to Tra Vinh.

## AROUND TRA VINH
### Chua Co

Chua Co is a particularly interesting Khmer
monastery because the grounds form a bird
sanctuary. Several types of storks and ibises
arrive here in large numbers just before
sunset to spend the night. Of course, there
are many nests here and you must take care
not to disturb them.

Chua Co is 45km from Tra Vinh.

### Luu Cu Site

Some ancient ruins are to be found at Luu
Cu, south of Tra Vinh near the shores of the
Hau River. The site is protected and there are
still some archaeological digs going on here.

## SA DEC

The former capital of Dong Thap Province,
Sa Dec gained some small fame as the setting
for *The Lover*, a film based on the novel by
Marguerite Duras. Among the Vietnamese,
Sa Dec is famous for the many nurseries
cultivating flowers and bonsai trees. The
flowers are picked almost daily and transported fresh to shops in Saigon. The nurseries are a major sightseeing attraction for
domestic tourists, not just foreigners.

Groups doing a whirlwind tour of the
Mekong Delta often make a lunch stop here
and drop in on the nurseries. However, Sa
Dec isn't a huge attraction. It used to be
better when there were rice noodle factories
here (which you could visit), but for some
reason this industry suddenly vanished in
1994.

### Hung Tu Pagoda

The Hung Tu Pagoda (Chua Co Hung Tu) is
of classic Chinese design. A bright white
statue of Quan Am (Guanyin in Chinese, the
Goddess of Mercy) standing on a pedestal
adorns the grounds. Don't confuse this place
with the adjacent Buu Quang Pagoda, which
is somewhat less glamorous.

### Nurseries

The nurseries *(vuon hoa)* operate year-
round, though get stripped bare of their
flowers just before Tet. You're welcome to

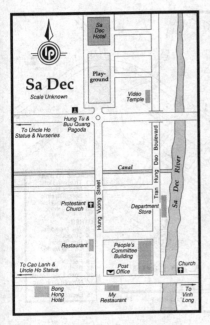

**Sa Dec**

Scale Unknown

You'll need a motorbike to get out there as it's probably too far for cyclos unless you have a lot of time and patience. The statue is along the route to the nurseries, so you can take in both sights on the same journey.

### Places to Stay
Not many foreigners overnight in Sa Dec because nearby Cao Lanh, Long Xuyen and Vinh Long all tend to siphon off the tourists. Still, Sa Dec is a pleasant, if not very exciting, place to spend an evening.

The main tourist accommodation is the *Sa Dec Hotel* (☎ 861430; 38 rooms). All rooms have attached bath. A room with fan costs US$10, and with air-con the range is US$15 to US$25.

The cheapest place to stay is the *Bong Hong Hotel* (☎ 861301; 15 rooms). A room with fan and attached toilet cost US$7.

### Places to Eat
Both hotels do acceptable meals, but the *Bong Hong Hotel* seems to be the better of the two. In the centre of town is the *My Restaurant* (the name means 'American Restaurant'), which has become the hot spot for backpackers.

### Getting There & Away
Sa Dec is in Dong Thap Province, midway between Vinh Long and Long Xuyen.

### CAO LANH
Cao Lanh is a new town carved from the jungles and swamps of the Mekong Delta region. Its up and coming status has much to do with its designation as the provincial capital of Dong Thap Province.

### Information
Dong Thap Tourist (☎ 851343, 851547), 2 Doc Binh Kieu St, deserves kudos for being helpful. This is the best place to inquire about boat tours of the surrounding area.

### War Memorial
The War Memorial (Dai Liet Si) off Highway 30 on the east end of town is Cao Lanh's most prominent landmark. This masterpiece

have a look around, but not to pick any flowers unless you plan on buying them. Photography is certainly permitted – indeed, the flower farmers are very used to it.

The nurseries don't belong to one person. There are many small operators here, each with a different speciality. The most famous garden here is called the Tu Ton Rose Garden (Vuon Hong Tu Ton), which has over 500 different kinds of roses in 50 different shades and colours. The busiest time here is Tet, but that's actually not a good time to visit – the garden is nearly empty then because the roses get shipped off to markets elsewhere.

### Uncle Ho Statue
We're not being facetious – yes, they really call it 'Uncle Ho Statue' (Tuong Bac Ho) in Vietnamese. Ho Chi Minh didn't live in Sa Dec, but his father did. To commemorate this bit of historical consequence, a large statue of Ho Chi Minh (but not his father!?) has been erected a few kilometres west of town.

MEKONG DELTA

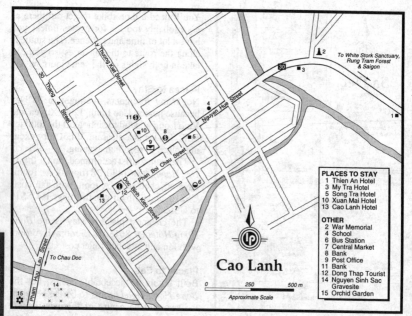

**Cao Lanh**

0      250      500 m

Approximate Scale

**PLACES TO STAY**
1 Thien An Hotel
3 My Tra Hotel
5 Song Tra Hotel
10 Xuan Mai Hotel
13 Cao Lanh Hotel

**OTHER**
2 War Memorial
4 School
6 Bus Station
7 Central Market
8 Bank
9 Post Office
11 Bank
12 Dong Thap Tourist
14 Nguyen Sinh Sac Gravesite
15 Orchid Garden

To White Stork Sanctuary,
Rung Tram Forest
& Saigon

To Chau Doc

MEKONG DELTA

of socialist sculpture boasts a clamshell-shaped building displaying a large Vietnamese star alongside a hammer and sickle. In front of this are several large concrete statues of victorious peasants and soldiers brandishing weapons and upraised fists. The surrounding grounds are decked out with the graves of 3112 fallen comrades who fought for the winning side.

Construction of the War Memorial began in 1977 and finished in 1984. There is no admission fee.

### Nguyen Sinh Sac Gravesite

Aside from the 3112 graves at the War Memorial, another significant tomb is that of Nguyen Sinh Sac (1862-1929). Nguyen's contribution to Vietnamese history was being the father of Ho Chi Minh. His large tomb (Lang Cu Nguyen Sinh Sac) occupies one hectare, about 1km south-west of central Cao Lanh.

Although there are various plaques (in Vietnamese) and tourist pamphlets exhorting Nguyen Sinh Sac as a great revolutionary, there is little evidence to suggest that he was involved in the anti-colonial struggle against the French. Needless to say, the revolutionary credentials of his son are without question.

### Water-Skiing

Enterprising Dong Thap Tourist owns a speedboat and a pair of water-skis which it is willing to rent out at US$25 per hour. Water-skiing on the local canals or even the Mekong River itself should provide an interesting diversion from the standard museum and bird-watching tours.

### Places to Stay

The *Cao Lanh Hotel* (☎ 851061; 16 rooms) is at 72 Nguyen Hue St. This place is considerably older and grottier than the competition and is a definite candidate for renovation work. Until that happens, rooms with fan and cold-water bath cost US$5 to US$6. Air-con rooms with attached hot-water bath are US$9 and US$10.

*Dong Thap Tourist* (☎ 851343) runs a small hotel on the top floor of its office. A nice feature here are the balconies – sit outside in the evening and sip tea while enjoying the pleasant view. Rooms cost US$12.

At 178 Nguyen Hue St is the *Song Tra Hotel* (☎ 852504; fax 852623; 26 rooms). This is the city's most upmarket accommodation, and even features satellite TV. The price range is US$25 to US$35.

The *Xuan Mai Hotel* (☎ 852852; 16 rooms), 2 Cong Ly St, is a new and excellent place behind the post office. All rooms are equipped with air-con, hot water and even bathtubs. Doubles cost US$20 to US$22.

The *Thien An Hotel* (☎ 853041; 26 rooms) is a few hundred metres from the War Memorial in the direction of Saigon. This new place is good value and rooms at the back even have a view of the river. All rooms have air-con and attached hot-water bath, and cost US$10 to US$12.

The *My Tra Hotel* (☎ 851469; 21 rooms) is on the east side of town on Highway 30, opposite the War Memorial. This place is currently under renovation.

### Getting There & Away
Aside from buses direct from Saigon, the easiest bus routes to Cao Lanh are from Mytho, Cantho and Vinh Long. The road between Cao Lanh and Long Xuyen is beautiful, but has few buses – you will probably need to hire your own vehicle to do that route.

### Getting Around
**Boat** Boat tours of the bird sanctuaries and Rung Tram Forest are major attractions in this region. Although you could possibly arrange something privately with boat owners, you'll probably find it easier to deal with Dong Thap Tourist. Fortunately, its rates are reasonable. There are too many different combinations of boat sizes and possible destinations to list them all, but a group of 15 persons would be charged about US$2 per

person for a half-day tour, including all transport. A group of five might pay US$5 each for the same thing. You may not be travelling with 14 companions, but it's not difficult to round up other foreigners at the few hotels in town where everyone stays.

## AROUND CAO LANH
### White Stork Sanctuary
To the north-east of Cao Lanh is a bird sanctuary (Vuon Co Thap Muoi) for white storks. A white stork standing on the back of a water buffalo is the symbol of the Mekong Delta, and you probably have more chance of seeing it here than anywhere else. The sanctuary only covers two hectares, but the birds seem mostly undisturbed by the nearby farmers (who have been sternly warned not to hunt the storks).

The storks are protected from hunting and have grown accustomed to people. As a result, they are fairly easy to spot as they feed in the mangrove and bamboo forests in the area. The storks live in pairs and never migrate with the seasons, so you can see them at any time of the year. The birds live on freshwater crabs and other tidbits that they can catch in the canals.

There are no roads as such to the bird sanctuary, so getting there requires a mandatory boat trip. Dong Thap Tourist can arrange this, though you may be able to arrange it elsewhere. A speedboat costs US$25 per hour, and the ride takes 50 minutes. A slow boat costs US$4 per person, requires 20 persons to get that price and takes a total of three hours to make the return journey. In the dry season, you have to plan your boat trip according to the two daily tides – at low tide the canals can become impassable.

It's usual to include a trip to the White Stork Sanctuary with a visit to the Rung Tram Forest.

### Rung Tram Forest
South-east of Cao Lanh and accessible by boat tour is the 46-hectare Rung Tram Forest near My Long village. The area is one vast swamp with a beautiful thick canopy of tall trees and vines. It's one of the last natural forests left in the Mekong Delta, and by now

MEKONG DELTA

probably would have been turned into a rice paddy were it not for its historical significance. During the American War, the Viet Cong had a base here called Xeo Quit, where top-brass Viet Cong lived in underground bunkers. But don't mistake this for another Cu Chi Tunnel – it's very different.

Only about 10 VC were here at any given time. They were all generals who directed the war from Xeo Quit, just 2km from a US military base. The Americans never realised that the VC generals were living right under their noses. Of course, they were suspicious about that patch of forest, and periodically dropped some bombs on it just to reassure themselves, but the VC remained safe in their underground bunkers.

The location of the base was so secret that the wives of the generals didn't even know its location. The wives did occasionally pay their husbands a conjugal visit, but this had to be arranged at another special bunker.

When the US military departed from Vietnam in 1973, the VC grew bolder and put the base above ground. Attempts by the South Vietnamese military to dislodge the VC were thwarted – while the South was running out of funding and ammunition that the Americans had promised would be forthcoming, the Communists were able to build up their forces in the Mekong Delta and challenge the Saigon regime openly.

Access to the area is by boat, and most visitors combine this with a trip to the White Stork Sanctuary. A speedboat from Cao Lanh to the Rung Tram Forest takes only 10 minutes, but a slow boat will require at least 30 minutes.

Beware of the very mean red ants here – they are huge, fast and exceedingly aggressive. If you are allergic to red-ant bites (many people are), you probably should not visit.

## Tam Nong Nature Reserve

Due north of Cao Lanh is the Tam Nong Nature Reserve (Tram Chim Tam Nong), notable for its large number of cranes. Over 220 species of birds have been identified within the reserve, but ornithologists will be particularly interested in the rare red herons

which nest here from approximately December to June. From July to November, the birds go on holiday to Cambodia, so you've got to schedule your visit to coordinate with the birds' travel itinerary if you want to see them. Also, the birds are early risers – early morning is the best time to see them, though you might get a glimpse when they return home in the evening. During the day, the birds are of course engaged in the important matter of eating.

Seeing these birds requires a fair amount of commitment (time, effort and money), so it's really a special interest tour. Because you'll need to be up at the crack of dawn, staying in Cao Lanh doesn't work out too well – you would have to head out at 4.30 am and travel in the dark over an unlit dirt road. This is not advisable, so you really need to stay at the government guesthouse in Tam Nong, which is much closer to where the birds are.

Tam Nong is a sleepy town 45km from Cao Lanh. The one-way drive takes 1½ hours by car, though in future it may be reduced to one hour when the currently abysmal road gets resurfaced. It is also possible to get there by boat. A speedboat requires only one hour, but costs US$25 per hour to rent. A slow boat which costs US$4 per person can be arranged from Dong Thap Tourist, but this takes four hours for the one-way journey and requires 20 people to make it economically viable. From the guesthouse in Tam Nong, it takes another hour by small boat (at US$15 per hour) to reach the area where the red herons live and another hour to return. To this, add whatever time you spend (perhaps an hour) staring at your feathered friends through binoculars, and then the requisite one to four hours to return to Cao Lanh depending on your mode of transport.

There are actually two guesthouses in Tam Nong, though the one usually open to foreigners is inconveniently far from town (about 2km). The guesthouse has 10 rooms, which cost US$6/10 for fan/air-con doubles. The toilets are outside. We found the guesthouse quite OK except that it was absolutely overrun with thousands of bugs and the staff had no insecticide. Fortunately, we scored a can of bug killer in town (not easy to find!) and proceeded to commit entomological genocide. If you're going to stay here, you may want to stock up on toxic chemicals in Cao Lanh. Go up to the roof of the guesthouse for some great views.

Tam Nong shuts down early – if you want to eat dinner in town, make arrangements before 5 pm. Meals can be served later if you book in advance, but of course you will have to pay extra for the late-night service. There are heaps of mosquitoes here in the evening, so come prepared with insect repellent. If you don't have any, the local pharmacy can sell you the cure-all green oil which works as an acceptable substitute.

## CANTHO
Cantho (population 150,000), capital of Cantho Province, is the political, economic, cultural and transportation centre of the Mekong Delta. Rice-husking mills are a major local industry.

This friendly, bustling city is connected to most other population centres in the Mekong Delta by a system of rivers and canals. These waterways are the major tourist drawcard in Cantho – travellers come here to do economical boat trips. Unlike in Mytho and Vinh Long, Cantho's People's Committee has so far not attempted to monopolise the boat tour business and so prices have remained low.

### Information
**Travel Agencies** Cantho Tourist (Cong Ty Du Lich Can Tho; ☎ 821853, fax 822719) at 20 Hai Ba Trung St is the provincial tourism authority.

**Money** Vietcombank (Ngan Hang Ngoai Thuong Viet Nam; ☎ 820445) is at 7 Hoa Binh Blvd.

**Emergency** The general hospital is on the corner of Chau Van Liem St and Hoa Binh Blvd.

### Munirangsyaram Pagoda
The ornamentation of Munirangsyaram

Pagoda, at 36 Hoa Binh Blvd, is typical of Khmer Hinayana Buddhist pagodas, lacking the multiple Bodhisattvas and Taoist spirits common in Vietnamese Mahayana pagodas. In the upstairs sanctuary, a 1.5m-high representation of Siddhartha Gautama, the historical Buddha, sits under a *potthe* (bodhi) tree. Built in 1946, Munirangsyaram Pagoda serves the Khmer community of Cantho, which numbers about 2000. The two Khmer monks, one in his 70s and the other in his 20s, hold prayers at 5 am and 6 pm every day.

### Cantonese Congregation Pagoda
This small Chinese pagoda (Quan Cong Hoi Quan) was built by the Cantonese Congregation. The original one was constructed on a different site about 70 years ago. The current pagoda was built with funds recently donated by Overseas Chinese. Cantho previously had a large ethnic-Chinese population, but most fled after the anti-Chinese persecutions of 1978-79.

The pagoda occupies a splendid location on Hai Ba Trung St facing the Cantho River.

### Central Market
The Central Market is strung out along Hai Ba Trung St. The main market building is at the intersection of Hai Ba Trung and Nam Ky Khoi Nghia Sts.

### Ho Chi Minh Museum
This is the only museum in the Mekong Delta devoted to Ho Chi Minh, and it's a bit of a mystery why it was built here, as Ho Chi Minh never lived in Cantho. If you are willing to overlook that small sticking point, there is no reason not to visit this large museum, which only opened its doors in 1995. It's near the GPO on Hoa Binh Blvd.

### University of Cantho
Cantho University, founded in 1966, is on 30/4 St.

### Nearby Rural Areas
Rural areas of Cantho Province, renowned for their durian, mangosteen and orange

MEKONG DELTA

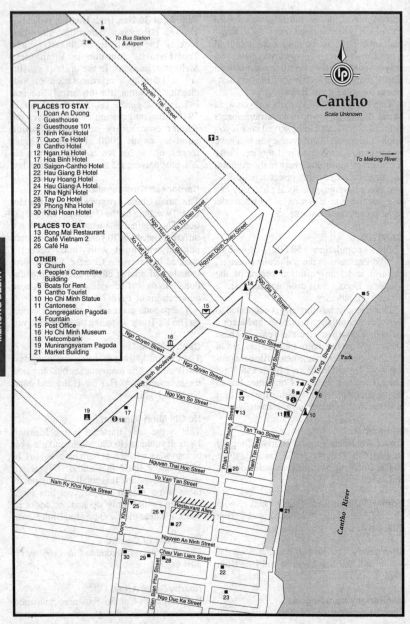

MEKONG DELTA

Cantho

*Scale Unknown*

To Bus Station
& Airport

Nguyen Trai Street

To Mekong River

**PLACES TO STAY**
1 Doan An Duong Guesthouse
2 Guesthouse 101
5 Ninh Kieu Hotel
7 Quoc Te Hotel
8 Cantho Hotel
12 Ngan Ha Hotel
17 Hoa Binh Hotel
20 Saigon-Cantho Hotel
22 Hau Giang B Hotel
23 Huy Hoang Hotel
24 Hau Giang A Hotel
27 Nha Nghi Hotel
28 Tay Do Hotel
29 Phong Nha Hotel
30 Khai Hoan Hotel

**PLACES TO EAT**
13 Bong Mai Restaurant
25 Café Vietnam 2
26 Café Ha

**OTHER**
3 Church
4 People's Committee Building
6 Boats for Rent
9 Cantho Tourist
10 Ho Chi Minh Statue
11 Cantonese Congregation Pagoda
14 Fountain
15 Post Office
16 Ho Chi Minh Museum
18 Vietcombank
19 Munirangsyaram Pagoda
21 Market Building

Vo Thi Sau Street

Ngo Huu Hanh Street

Nguyen Dinh Chieu Street

Xo Viet Nghe Tinh Street

Ngo Gia Tu Street

Tran Quoc Street

Ngo Quyen Street

Ly Thuong Viet Street

Hai Ba Trung Street

Park

Hoa Binh Boulevard

Ngo Quyen Street

Ngo Van So Street

Phan Dinh Phung Street

Tan Trao Street

La Thanh Tri Street

Nguyen Thai Hoc Street

Nam Ky Khoi Nghia Street

Vo Van Tan Street

Dong Khoi Street

Restaurant Alley

Nguyen An Ninh Street

Chau Van Liem Street

Dien Bien Phu Street

Ngo Duc Ke Street

Cantho River

orchards, can easily be reached from Cantho by boat or bicycle.

## Boat Rides

The most interesting thing to do in Cantho is take a boat ride. The cost for this varies but is around US$3 per hour for a small paddle boat which can carry two or three passengers. You won't have to look hard for the boats – they will be looking for you. Just wander by the docks opposite the Quoc Te Hotel and you'll have plenty of offers. Most of the boats are operated by women. Bring your camera, though keep it in a plastic bag when you're not actually shooting because it's easy to get splashed by the wake of motorised boats.

Larger boats with motors can go farther afield, and it's worth considering hiring one to make a tour of the Mekong River itself. The paddleboats only go on the Cantho River, because the current is weaker.

## Places to Stay

Considering how important tourism is to Cantho's economy, it's amazing the local authorities show so little understanding of what little irritations drive tourists mad. The Cantho police have done some damage to the hotel business by insisting that foreigners hand over passports, visas *and* the green entry card. Before you check out of a hotel, make sure that every document is returned and not just two out of three (and check that all three belong to you, and not someone else).

Another real drag is the Voice of Vietnam radio station, broadcasting at eardrum-shattering volume from loudspeakers all over town. The racket starts at 5 am and doesn't end until 9 pm.

If you can put up with the noise and bungling bureaucracy, there are heaps of good accommodation possibilities.

The *Doan An Duong Hotel* (☎ 823623; 56 rooms) on Nguyen Trai St (north end of town) looks great on the outside but is grim on the inside. Rooms are bare dungeons, and it's perhaps interesting to note that the hotel is owned by the army. On the other hand, some of the rooms have balconies with a brilliant view of the river. Rooms with fan/air-con cost US$9/16.

Just across the street is *Guesthouse 101*. Rooms here are arranged around a high-rise courtyard and are pleasant enough. The tariff for fan only with attached cold-water bath is US$10.

The *Huy Hoang Hotel* (☎ 825833) at 35 Ngo Duc Ke St is the most trendy spot for the backpacker crowd. Singles/doubles with fan are US$7/9, or US$10 for air-conditioned comfort.

The *Phong Nha Hotel* (☎ 821615; 20 rooms) at 79 Chau Van Liem St is cheap at US$6 per room, but is on a noisy street with many motorbikes.

Moving downmarket, the *Khai Hoan Hotel* (☎ 835261) at 83 Chau Van Liem St is dirty but dirt-cheap. It doesn't like to take foreigners, but if you're badly dressed then it will accept you. Otherwise, you'll be referred to a 'decent hotel'. Rooms cost US$5.

The *Tay Do Hotel* (☎ 821009; 25 rooms) on Chau Van Liem St is currently closed for renovation.

The *Hoa Binh Hotel* (☎ 820536) at 5 Hoa Binh Blvd will have you believing in miracles – it's a miracle the building doesn't collapse. It really has deteriorated in recent years, and we strongly suspect it will be closed soon and renovated (or torn down). At the moment it's still being held together with tape and glue. Rooms cost US$8.

The *Ninh Kieu Hotel* (☎ 821171; fax 821104; 31 rooms) at 2 Hai Ba Trung St is a very charming place. The hotel is in a spacious compound just north of the Quoc Te Hotel, and boasts a riverside restaurant with superb views. Room prices here are US$25 to US$40.

The *Quoc Te Hotel* (☎ 822079; fax 821-039; 32 rooms) at 12 Hai Ba Trung St is along the Cantho River and is notable for its noisy karaoke bar. The expensive suites have an excellent view of the river, but the low-end rooms are pretty bleak and not really worth the price. The price range here is US$28 to US$55.

On the south side of the Quoc Te Hotel is the *Cantho Hotel* (☎ 822218; 18 rooms) at

14-16 Hai Ba Trung St. It's a fine place overlooking the river and offers rooms from US$10 to US$16.

The *Ngan Ha Hotel* (☎ 822921; fax 823-473; 30 rooms), 39-41 Ngo Quyen St, is a brand-new private hotel. All rooms have air-con and hot-water bath, and cost US$17 to US$30.

The *Nha Nghi Hotel* (☎ 820049; eight rooms) is a sharp-looking place at 1 Dien Bien Phu St. The tariff is US$15 to US$20 for a double with air-con.

The six-storey *Hau Giang A Hotel* (☎ 821851; fax 821806; 32 rooms) at 34 Nam Ky Khoi Nghia St is also very pleasant and attracts many foreigners – even the lobby has air-con. All this luxury costs US$25 to US$40 a night.

The *Hau Giang B Hotel* (☎ 821950; 23 rooms), 27 Chau Van Liem St, is a branch of the foregoing. Rooms with fan and cold-water bath are US$8; rising to US$12 with air-con and cold water, or US$15 with air-con and hot water.

The *Saigon-Cantho Hotel* (☎ 825831; 823288; 46 rooms) at 55 Phan Dinh Phung St is a spanking new luxury pleasure palace. Facilities include massage service, sauna and (horrors) karaoke. Rooms here are equipped with absolutely everything and cost US$58 to US$98.

## Places to Eat

Along the Cantho River waterfront there are several restaurants serving Mekong Delta specialities such as fish, snake, frog and turtle.

The *Quoc Te Hotel* (☎ 822079) operates two restaurants, both with English menus, but the staff speak limited English. The upstairs air-conditioned restaurant is great value – the menu includes deep-fried snake, turtle soup and some of the largest prawns you'll ever see.

*Restaurant Alley* is an appropriate name for Nam Ky Khoi Nghia St between Dien Bien Phu and Phan Dinh Phung Sts. There are about a dozen restaurants lining both sides of the street, all of them good.

## Getting There & Away

**Air** Vietnam Airlines has had on-again off-again flights between Cantho and Saigon. At the time of writing, they were off yet again. Currently, the only way to fly to Cantho is to charter an aircraft from Vasco Airlines in Saigon.

**Bus** Buses to Cantho leave Saigon from Mien Tay bus station in An Lac. Nonexpress buses take five hours; the express bus, which has priority at ferry crossings, takes about 3½ hours.

The main bus station in Cantho is several kilometres out of town at the intersection of Nguyen Trai and Tran Phu Sts. There is another bus depot near the intersection of 30/4 St and Mau Than St.

**Car** By car, the ride from Saigon to Cantho along National Highway 1 usually takes about four hours. There are two ferry crossings between Saigon and Cantho, the first at Vinh Long and the second at Cantho itself. The Cantho ferry runs from 4 am to 2 am. Fruit, soft drinks and other food are sold where vehicles wait for the ferries.

To get from Hoa Binh Blvd in Cantho to the ferry crossing, take Nguyen Trai St to the bus station and turn right onto Tran Phu St.

Road distances from Cantho are as follows:

| | |
|---|---|
| Camau | 179km |
| Chau Doc | 117km |
| Ho Chi Minh City | 168km |
| Long Xuyen | 62km |
| Mytho | 104km |
| Rach Gia | 116km |
| Sa Dec | 51km |
| Soc Trang | 63km |
| Vinh Long | 34km |

## Getting Around

**The Airport** Assuming Vietnam Airlines restarts operations, Cantho airport is 10km from the town centre along the road leading to Rach Gia. Transport by motorbikes will of course be cheaper than by taxi.

**Xe Honda Loi** Unique to the Mekong Delta, these makeshift vehicles are the main form of transport around Cantho. A *xe Honda loi* is essentially a two-wheeled wagon attached to the rear of a motorbike, creating what resembles a motorised cyclo. Of course, it also differs from a cyclo in that there are four wheels touching the ground rather than two. Fares around town should be about US$1, but more for trips to outlying areas.

## AROUND CANTHO
### Cai Rang Floating Market
Just 6km from Cantho in the direction of Soc Trang is Cai Rang Floating Market. There is a bridge here which serves as a great vantage point for photography. Most markets in the Mekong Delta open early to avoid the daytime heat, so try to visit between 6 and 8 am. Some vendors hang out until 11 am, but it's not so interesting by then.

### Phong Dien Floating Market
This is perhaps the best floating market in the Mekong Delta. Like most Mekong Delta markets, it's at its bustling best between 6 and 8 am. Phong Dien is 20km south-west of Cantho.

### Phung Hiep Market
The small town of Phung Hiep is notable for its snake market, though many other things are sold here. Most of the market is on land, but there is a small floating market under the bridge which is also interesting from about 6 to 8 am. Small boats can easily be hired for a tour along the river.

Phung Hiep is right on National Highway 1, 20km from Cantho in the direction of Soc Trang.

## SOC TRANG
The town itself doesn't look like much, but it has a large Khmer population who have built some very impressive temples. Furthermore, there is a very colourful annual festival, and if you're in the vicinity at the right time then it's very much worth your while to catch it.

### Information
**Travel Agencies** Soc Trang Tourist (☎ 821-498, 822015; fax 821993) is at 131 Nguyen Chi Thanh St, adjacent to the Tay Nam Hotel.

### Kh'leng Pagoda
This stunning pagoda (Chua Kh'leng) looks like it's been transported straight out of Cambodia. Originally built from bamboo in 1533, it had a complete rebuild in 1905 (this time using concrete). There are seven religious festivals held here every year (worth seeing!) – people come from all outlying areas of the province and gather here for these events. Even at non-festival times, Khmer people drop in regularly to bring donations and pray.

At the time of writing, 12 monks were residing in the pagoda. This place also serves as Soc Trang's College of Buddhist Education, which at present serves 95 student monks. The monks are friendly and happy to show you around the pagoda and discuss Buddhism.

### Khmer Museum
This museum is dedicated to the history and culture of Vietnam's Khmer minority. Indeed, it serves as a sort of cultural centre, and traditional dance and music shows are periodically staged here. You'll have to make inquiries about performances, because there is no regular schedule; however, there's no doubt that something could be arranged for a group provided a little advance notice is given.

The Khmer Museum is just opposite the Kh'leng Pagoda.

### Dat Set Pagoda
This Chinese pagoda is unusual in that it's made entirely of clay, rather than the brick and concrete which are the currently fashionable building materials in Vietnam. An internal frame keeps the whole thing from cracking and falling apart. Even all the statues inside the pagoda are made of clay.

This pagoda is a very active place of worship, and totally different from the Khmer and Vietnamese Buddhist pagodas found elsewhere in Soc Trang. The pagoda has another name, Buu Son Tu, which means 'Precious Mountain Temple'. It was founded

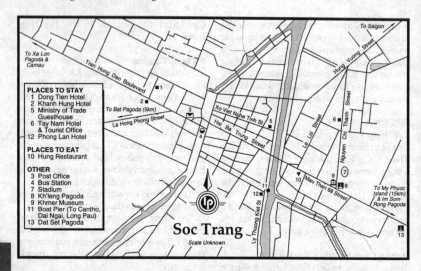

**PLACES TO STAY**
1 Dong Tien Hotel
2 Khanh Hung Hotel
5 Ministry of Trade
   Guesthouse
6 Tay Nam Hotel
   & Tourist Office
12 Phong Lan Hotel

**PLACES TO EAT**
10 Hung Restaurant

**OTHER**
3 Post Office
4 Bus Station
7 Stadium
8 Kh'leng Pagoda
9 Khmer Museum
11 Boat Pier (To Cantho,
   Dai Ngai, Long Pau)
13 Dat Set Pagoda

**Soc Trang**
Scale Unknown

over 200 years ago by a Chinese family named Ngo.

Dat Set Pagoda is on Mau Than 68 St, within walking distance from the town centre.

### Im Som Rong Pagoda

This large, beautiful Khmer pagoda was built in 1961 and is notable for its well-kept gardens. A plaque on the grounds (dedicated in 1996) honours the man who donated the funds to build the pagoda. There are many monks in residence here, and all are very friendly.

Im Som Rong Pagoda is over 1km east of Soc Trang on the road to My Phuoc Island. When you reach the main gate it's another 300m walk inside along a dirt track to the pagoda itself.

### Oc Bom Boc Festival

This is a Khmer name so don't bother trying to look it up in your Vietnamese dictionary. Once a year, the Khmer community turns out for long-boat races on the Soc Trang River, an event which attracts visitors from all over Vietnam and even Cambodia. First prize is

US$1500, so it's not difficult to see why competition is so fierce.

The races are held according to the lunar calendar on the 15th day of the 10th moon, which roughly means December. The races start at noon, but things get jumping in Soc Trang the evening before. Not surprisingly, hotel space is at a premium during the festival, and foreigners without a prepaid hotel reservation will probably have to sleep in a car or minibus.

### Places to Stay

The *Tay Nam Hotel* (☎ 821757; 26 rooms) at 133 Nguyen Chi Thanh St is an OK place to stay, but we were not pleased to find our passports lying on the counter unattended – the staff had gone off to dinner and simply left our valuable documents lying around where anybody could have walked off with them. A double with fan/air-con costs US$10/14.

A bottom-end budget place is the *Ministry of Trade Guesthouse* (☎ 821974), or *Nha Khach So Thuong Mai* in Vietnamese. Rooms with fan/air-con are US$5/8.

The *Phong Lan Hotel* (☎ 821619; 20 rooms) is near the river at 124 Dong Khoi St.

It's pricey by Soc Trang standards – rooms with fan are US$14, while air-con is US$16 with cold-water bath and US$21 with hot water.

The *Dong Tien Hotel* (☎ 821888; 22 rooms) is run by the military and doesn't get many foreign visitors – the sleepy staff were surprised to see us! It's at 2 Duong Trung Tien, down an obscure dirt track where you wouldn't expect to find a hotel. Room rates are reasonable: US$8 for a room with fan and shared bath; US$10 for fan and attached bath; and US$12 with air-con.

The newest and fanciest place by far is the *Khanh Hung Hotel* (☎ 821027; 55 rooms). It's at 15 Tran Hung Dao Blvd and boasts a large cafe with outdoor tables. A room with fan and attached toilet costs US$7. Air-con rooms range from US$12 to US$25.

### Places to Eat

The best place in town is the excellent *Hung Restaurant* (☎ 822268) at 74-76 Mau Tham 68 St. It's open from breakfast time until late into the evening and always seems to be busy.

### AROUND SOC TRANG
### Bat Pagoda

This is one of the Mekong Delta's most unusual sights, and now has become a favourite stopoff for both foreign and domestic tourists. The Bat Pagoda (Chua Doi) is a large monastery compound. You enter through an archway, and almost immediately you can hear the eerie screeching from the large colony of fruit bats which reside here. There are literally thousands of these creatures hanging from the fruit trees. The largest bats weigh about 1kg but have a wing span of about 1.5m.

Fruit bats make plenty of noise – it probably has something to do with their sonar system. The noise in the morning is incredible, and so are the smells. The bats are not toilet trained, so watch out when standing under a tree or bring an umbrella. In the evening, the bats spread their wings and fly out to invade orchards all over the Mekong Delta, much to the consternation of local

farmers. The farmers are known to trap the bats and eat them. Inside the monastery the creatures are protected, and the bats seem to know this, which is why they stay.

Locals tend to show excessive zeal in shaking the trees to make the bats fly around so that foreigners can take photos – it's better to leave the poor things in peace, as you can easily take good photos of the bats hanging off the branches if you have a good telephoto lens.

The monks are very friendly and don't ask for money, though it doesn't hurt to leave a donation. The pagoda is decorated with gilt Buddhas, and murals paid for by Overseas Vietnamese contributors. In one room of the monastery is a life-size statue of the monk who was the former head of the complex.

Behind the pagoda is a bizarre tomb painted with the image of a pig. It was erected in memory of a pig with five toenails. Normal pigs have only four toenails, so this one was unusual indeed. He died in July 1996, but two other rare pigs with five toenails have survived and are being raised by the monks. These pigs are not for eating – they are pets.

Little kids hang out by the front gate and beg from the tourists, but they aren't allowed inside the monastery grounds. We didn't give money but handed over a package of biscuits – the kids devoured them as if they hadn't eaten in over a week. Perhaps they hadn't.

There is a restaurant just opposite the Bat Pagoda, but it does not serve bat meat.

The Bat Pagoda is about 5km west of Soc Trang. Best times for visiting are early morning or at least an hour before sunset, when the bats are most active.

### Xa Lon (Sa Lon) Pagoda

This magnificent, classic Khmer pagoda is 12km from Soc Trang on National Highway 1 in the direction of Camau. The original structure was built over 200 years ago from wooden materials. In 1923 it was completely rebuilt, but proved to be too small. From 1969 to 1985, the present large pagoda was

MEKONG DELTA

slowly built as funds trickled in from donations. The pagoda is particularly stunning because its exterior is composed of beautiful ceramic tiles.

Like at other pagodas, the monks lead an austere life. They eat breakfast at 6 am and beg for contributions until 11 am, when they hold a one-hour worship. They eat again at noon and study in the afternoon – they do not eat dinner.

At present, 27 monks reside here. The pagoda also operates a school for the study of Buddhism and Sanskrit. The reason for studying Sanskrit, as the monks explained, is that all original books about Buddhism were written in this ancient language.

### My Phuoc Island

A 15km journey to the east of Soc Trang brings you to the Hau River (a branch of the Mekong). From there it's a short boat ride to My Phuoc Island. It's an isolated spot, but very suitable for growing fruit. The local government tourist agency likes to bring foreigners here for tours of the orchards. You can do it yourself too, though this is a little complicated since you'll need a motorbike to get yourself to the riverside.

### BAC LIEU

The town has a few elegant but crumbling old French colonial buildings and not much else. Farming is a difficult occupation here because of saltwater intrusion, which means the town has remained fairly poor. Enterprising locals eke out a living from fishing, oyster collection and salt production (obtained from seawater evaporating ponds).

### Places to Stay

Perhaps it's worth visiting Bac Lieu simply to take advantage of the town's cheap accommodation (hotels are notably more expensive than in nearby Camau).

The cheapest place in town is the *Bac Lieu Hotel* (☎ 822621; 26 rooms) at 4 Hoang Van Thu St. A double room with fan and attached bath is US$10, or US$15 to US$20 with air-con.

In case there is a convention in town and the Bac Lieu Hotel is full, you can check out its adjacent neighbour, the *Rang Dong Hotel* (☎ 822437; 34 rooms) at 6 Hoang Van Thu St. Doubles with fan/air-con cost US$13/15.

### AROUND BAC LIEU
### Bac Lieu Bird Sanctuary

Five km from town is the Bac Lieu Bird Sanctuary (Vuon Chim Bac Lieu), notable for its large population of graceful white herons. This is one of the most interesting sights in the Mekong Delta, and is surprisingly popular with Vietnamese tourists. Foreign visitors are rare, probably because Bac Lieu is such an out-of-the-way place.

Whether or not you get to see any birds depends on what time of year you visit. Bird populations are at their peak in the rainy season, which is approximately May through October. The birds hang around to nest until about January, then fly off in search of greener pastures. There are basically no birds from February until the rainy season begins again in May or June.

Because of flooding, most travellers try to avoid the Mekong Delta during the rainy season, so you might want to aim for a December visit.

You'll need to rent a motorbike, jeep or other high-clearance vehicle to reach the bird sanctuary. Although the drive is only 5km, the road is in terrible shape. At the time of writing, a crucial bridge crossing the canal was washed out, so you have to be ferried across the canal in a small boat. That's no problem, but the boat is too small even for motorbikes, so you must walk the last 1.5km to the bird sanctuary. It's likely that a new bridge will be built eventually, which will eliminate the walk (a pity, since it's pleasant enough).

When you reach the entrance of the bird sanctuary itself, there is a small admission fee (US$0.20). You can (and should) hire a guide here – you'll probably get lost without one. Actually, the guides aren't supposed to take any money, so give them a tip (US$2 is enough) discreetly. The guides do not speak English.

The rest of the trek is through a dense jungle. There are *lots* of mosquitoes, so bring plenty of mosquito repellent. There is some mud to slog through – don't wear US$300 Italian shoes and white socks.

Other things you should bring include bottled drinking water, binoculars, film and a camera with a powerful telephoto lens.

### Xiem Can Khmer Pagoda
Following the same road that takes you to the Bac Lieu Bird Sanctuary, you drive 7km from Bac Lieu to reach this pagoda. As Khmer pagodas go, it's OK but you can definitely see better ones in Tra Vinh or Soc Trang (not to mention Cambodia).

### Bac Lieu Beach
The same road to the Bac Lieu Bird Sanctuary and Xiem Can Khmer Pagoda eventually terminates 10km from Bac Lieu at this beach (Bai Bien Bac Lieu). Don't expect white sand – it's basically hard-packed Mekong Delta mud. Quite a few shellfish and other slimy and probably poisonous things crawl around where the muck meets the sea. Tidal pool enthusiasts might be impressed. Locals may be willing to take you for a walk on the mucky tidal flats where they harvest oysters.

### Moi Hoa Binh Pagoda
This Khmer pagoda (Chua Moi Hoa Binh, also called Se Rey Vongsa) is 13km south of Bac Lieu along Highway 1 (look to your left while driving to Camau).

The pagoda is uniquely designed, and chances are good that the monastery's enormous tower will catch your eye even if you're not looking for it. As pagodas in Vietnam go, it's relatively young, having first been built in 1952. The tower was added in 1990 and is used to store bones of the deceased. There is a large and impressive meeting hall in front of the tower.

Most Khmer people in Minh Hai Province head for monastery schools in Soc Trang to receive a Khmer education. Therefore, very few students study at the Moi Hoa Binh Pagoda outside of the small contingent of student monks.

## CAMAU
Built on the swampy shores of the Ganh Hao River, Camau is the capital and largest city in Minh Hai Province, which occupies the southern tip of the Camau Peninsula. The peninsula includes all of Minh Hai Province and parts of Kien Giang and Soc Trang provinces.

Camau lies in the middle of Vietnam's largest swamp. The area is known for mosquitoes the size of hummingbirds – during the rainy season you might need a shotgun to keep them at bay. The mosquitoes come out in force just after dark and some travellers find that they need to sit under their mosquito net just to eat dinner. One traveller reported that his hotel room had the 'mother of all black spider-webs' in one corner.

The population of Camau includes many ethnic-Khmers. Due to the boggy terrain, this area has the lowest population density in southern Vietnam.

Camau has developed rapidly in recent years, but the town itself is rather dull. The main attraction here are the nearby swamps and forests which can be explored by boat. Birdwatchers and aspiring botanists are reportedly most enthralled with the area. Unfortunately, ridiculously high hotel prices, the distance from Saigon and the vampire mosquitoes all conspire to keep the number of foreign tourists to a minimum.

### Information
**Travel Agencies** Camau Tourist (Cong Ty Du Lich Minh Hai; ☎ 831828) is at 17 Nguyen Van Hai St. This seems to be one of the best organised provincial tourism authorities in Vietnam – it even books international air tickets! Other services on offer include foreign currency exchange, boat rentals and visa extensions.

**Money** Vietcombank (☎ 833398) is at 2-3 Ly Bon St.

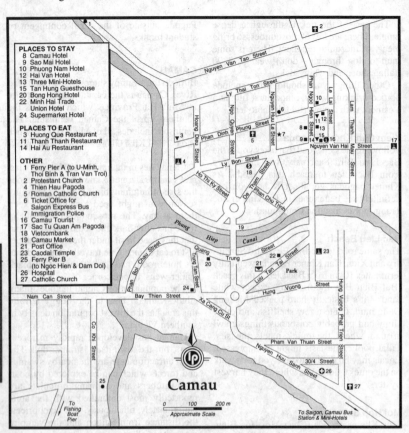

PLACES TO STAY
8 Camau Hotel
9 Sao Mai Hotel
10 Phuong Nam Hotel
12 Hai Van Hotel
13 Three Mini-Hotels
15 Tan Hung Guesthouse
20 Bong Hong Hotel
22 Minh Hai Trade
   Union Hotel
24 Supermarket Hotel

PLACES TO EAT
3 Huong Que Restaurant
11 Thanh Thanh Restaurant
14 Hai Au Restaurant

OTHER
1 Ferry Pier A (to U-Minh,
   Thoi Binh & Tran Van Troi)
2 Protestant Church
4 Thien Hau Pagoda
5 Roman Catholic Church
6 Ticket Office for
   Saigon Express Bus
7 Immigration Police
16 Camau Tourist
17 Sac Tu Quan Am Pagoda
18 Vietcombank
19 Camau Market
21 Post Office
23 Caodai Temple
25 Ferry Pier B
   (to Ngoc Hien & Dam Doi)
26 Hospital
27 Catholic Church

Camau

0    100    200 m
Approximate Scale

To Saigon, Camau Bus
Station & Mini-Hotels

## Zoo

Officially labelled the 19th May Forest Park, Camau's zoo shelters a poorly maintained collection of miserable animals. In the grounds of the zoo, along with a few noisy cafes, is a 'botanic garden', which looks rather like a half-acre patch of weeds. In short, there is nothing particularly inviting to see or do here.

## Fish, Snake & Turtle Market

Try not to get this place confused with the zoo. This is actually a wholesale market,

not a place for housewives to do their shopping. Except for the snakes, the animal life on display here is cleaned, packed into crates, frozen and shipped off to Saigon by truck.

Connoisseurs of snake meat insist that it be served fresh, which means they want to see the creature sacrificed right at the dinner table. Drinking the fresh blood is also part of the ritual, and obviously this doesn't work with frozen blood. All of which explains why the snakes are packed into wire cages and shipped off live to restaurants which specialise in this delicacy.

Even if you're vegetarian, this market is interesting to wander around – it certainly looks different from the supermarkets at home. However, proponents of animal rights will not be pleased.

## Caodai Temple
Though not as large as the one in Tay Ninh, Camau's Caodai Temple is still a charming place staffed by friendly monks. This temple was built in 1966 and seems to be fairly active.

## Places to Stay
By the standards of most other Mekong Delta cities, many of Camau's hotels cost nearly twice what they should.

The *Minh Hai Trade Union Hotel* (Khach San Cong Doan; ☎ 833245; 40 rooms) is a good example. It's at 9 Luu Tan Tai St, almost opposite the Caodai Temple. The rooms with fan only US$17! The air-con rooms are even more outrageous at US$35. Rooms in the centre of the building have all their fresh air blocked by a glass enclosure, a futile attempt to block the noise radiating up from the street.

A bottom-end option is the *Tan Hung Hotel* (☎ 831622; nine rooms) at 11 Nguyen Van Hai St. All rooms have a fan only and you must share the bath, but it's cheap at US$8.

The *Hai Van Hotel* (Nha Tro Hai Van; ☎ 832897; 10 rooms) is another budget option. Rooms with shared bath and fan are US$8.

The *Bong Hong Hotel* at 12 Quang Trung St is truly awful. Rooms with fan/air-con cost US$10/18. It's not recommended.

The *Sao Mai Hotel* (☎ 831035, 834913; 18 rooms), 38-40 Phan Ngoc Hien St, looks better on the outside than the inside. One plus is that all rooms have attached bath and air-con. On the downside, you get to pay US$15 for an air-free windowless box or US$25 if you want a window. The rooms do not smell good. If you still want to stay, then at least take a look at the room before checking in.

Living conditions are much better at the *Camau Hotel* (☎ 831165, 834883; fax 835075; 34 rooms) at 20 Phan Ngoc Hien St. There are just two rooms with fan only, priced at US$18. Rooms with air-con cost US$18 to US$32. All rooms have attached private bath. Breakfast is included.

The *Hai Chau Hotel* (☎ 831255; 15 rooms) on Bay Thien St is a private mini-hotel. A room for US$10 has no bath. Rooms with attached bath are US$15/20.

The *Phuong Nam Hotel* (☎ 831752; fax 834402; 38 rooms) at 91 Phan Dinh Phung St is an excellent place. All rooms have air-con and attached hot-water bath, and are priced from US$18 to US$32. Rooms costing US$22 and up have satellite TV. A free breakfast is included.

The *Supermarket Hotel* (Khach San Sieu Thi; ☎ 832789; fax 836880; 50 rooms) is a large, new upmarket place. The tariff here is US$18 to US$45.

There are a couple of very grotty-looking hotels next to the bus station, 2.5km outside of town in the direction of Saigon. Look for the signs that say 'nha tro' (Vietnamese for 'dormitory'). Prices are the lowest in Camau, but this option is only for the desperate.

## Places to Eat
Shrimp is Camau's speciality, all of which is raised in nearby ponds and mangrove swamps. Camau is also the best place in Vietnam to satisfy any sudden cravings for cobra stew.

The *Thanh Thanh Restaurant* (☎ 831076), 9 Phan Ngoc Hien St, is excellent. The restaurant is owned by Camau Tourist, which also owns the Phuong Nam Hotel just across the street. Like everything else this government-owned company does, it does it well but not cheaply.

There is a cluster of small roadside restaurants on Ly Bon St, at the entrance to the market. They are very cheap and the food is OK.

The friendly outdoor restaurant in the *Minh Hai Trade Union Hotel* is not bad, and certainly more aesthetic than eating in the market.

MEKONG DELTA

# Camau Saves the Ao Dai

MASON FLORENCE

The graceful national dress of Vietnamese women is known as the *ao dai* (pronounced 'ow-zai' in the north and 'ow-yai' in the south). An ao dai consists of a close-fitting blouse with long panels at the front and back that is worn over loose black or white trousers. The outfit was designed for hot weather, and for that reason is much more common in the south, especially in Saigon and the Mekong Delta. Although ao dais are impractical for doing stoop labour in the rice paddies, they are considered appropriate for office workers and female students.

In years past, men also wore ao dais, but these days you are only likely to see this in traditional operas or musical performances. The male ao dai is shorter and looser fitting than the female version. Before the end of dynastic rule, the colours of the brocade and embroidery indicated the rank of the wearer. Gold brocade accompanied by embroidered dragons was reserved for the emperor. High-ranking mandarins wore purple, while lower ranking mandarins had to settle for blue.

Ao dais are even appropriate wear for funerals. Mourners usually wear either white or black ao dais (white is the traditional colour of mourning). More happily, ao dais can be worn to weddings (bright colours with some embroidery on the shirt is fitting for the occasion).

*A resurgence in popularity of ao dais occurred in the mid 80s and they are now a familiar sight, particularly in southern Vietnam.*

MICK ELMORE

MICK ELMORE

The famous 'black pyjamas' of the Viet Cong, immortalised in numerous Hollywood movies, were not ao dais but actually just a common form of rural dress. You will see plenty of people in the countryside wearing 'pyjamas', though not always black.

From 1975 to 1985, ao dais were no longer politically correct. Chic baggy military uniforms were all the rage, and ao dais disappeared everywhere in Vietnam.

Beauty contests – a symbol of bourgeois capitalism – were banned by the Communists but were finally permitted again in Saigon in 1989. Swimsuit competitions were not permitted, but many of the girls did wear their best designer jeans. However, it was the Camau team that stole the show – they wore ao dais. Suddenly, there was a nationwide boom in ao dai production.

Ao dais have been around for a long time, and in the beginning they were anything but revealing. But in the past few years partially see-through ao dais have become all the rage – it's doubtful that even western women would wear something so provocative. The see-through ao dais have even spread to the north.

## Getting There & Away

**Bus** Buses from Saigon to Camau leave from Mien Tay bus station in An Lac. The trip takes 12 hours by regular bus and 10 hours by express bus. The express buses depart at least twice daily, at 5 am and 9 am.

The Camau bus station is 2.5km from the centre of town, along National Highway 1 in the direction of Saigon.

**Car** Camau is the 'end of the line' for National Highway 1, the southernmost point in Vietnam reachable by car and bus. Drivers boldly attempting to drive the 'highway' south of Camau will soon find their vehicles sinking into a quagmire of mud and mangroves.

Camau is 179km from Cantho (three hours by car) and 348km from Ho Chi Minh City (seven hours).

**Boat** Boats run between Camau and Saigon approximately once every four days. The trip takes 30 hours and is certainly not comfortable.

Of more interest to backpackers is the boat from Camau to Rach Gia. This departs at 5.30 am and takes almost 12 hours.

Also popular are the boats to U-Minh Forest. These depart from Ferry Pier A. You'll have to do some negotiation to arrange a tour here. It's also worth asking at the hotels since they may arrange a whole group.

Ferry Pier B is where you catch the speedboats heading south to Ngoc Hien.

## Getting Around

There are plenty of water taxis along the river at the back of the market. For longer trips upriver, larger longboats collect at a cluster of jetties just outside the market area. You can either join the throngs of passengers going downriver or hire the whole boat for about US$5 an hour.

## AROUND CAMAU
### U-Minh Forest

The town of Camau borders the U-Minh Forest, a huge mangrove swamp covering 1000 sq km of Minh Hai and Kien Giang provinces. Local people use certain species of mangrove as a source of timber, charcoal, thatch and tannin. When the mangroves flower, bees feed on the blossoms, providing both honey and wax. The area is an important habitat for waterfowl.

The U-Minh Forest, which is the largest mangrove swamp in the world outside of the Amazon basin, was a favourite hide-out for the Viet Cong during the American War. US patrol boats were frequently ambushed here and the VC regularly planted mines in the canals. The Americans responded with chemical defoliation, which made their enemy more visible but did enormous damage to the forests. Replanting efforts at first failed because the soil was so toxic, but gradually the heavy rainfall has washed the dioxin out to sea (where it no doubt poisons fish) and the forest is returning. Many eucalyptus trees have also been planted here because they have proved relatively resistant to dioxin. Unfortunately, what Agent Orange started, the locals are finishing – the mangrove forests are being further damaged by clearing for shrimp-raising ponds, charcoal making and wood chipping. The government has stepped in and tried to limit these activities, but the conflict between nature and human developers continues. And the conflict will get worse before it gets better, because Vietnam's population is still growing rapidly.

The area is known for its bird life, but these creatures too have taken a beating along with the forest ecology. Nevertheless, ornithologists derive much joy from taking boat trips around Camau; however, don't expect to find the swarms of birds to be nearly as ubiquitous as the swarms of mosquitoes.

Camau Tourist offers all-day tours of the forest by boat. It costs US$135 per boat (maximum 10 persons), though some bargaining is in order. You can also talk to the locals down at Ferry Pier A to see if you can find a better deal. Some of the hotels in town are also interested in getting into this business, so inquire.

### Bird Sanctuary

The Bird Sanctuary (Vuon Chim) is about 45km south-east of Camau. Storks are the largest and most easily seen birds here, though smaller feathered creatures also make their nests in the tall trees. Remember that birds will be birds – they don't particularly like humans to get close to them, and they leave their nests early in the morning in search of food. Thus, your chances of being able to get up close and have them hop onto your finger for a photo session are rather slim.

Camau Tourist offers a full-day tour by boat to the Bird Sanctuary for US$120 (one to 10 persons).

## NGOC HIEN

Except for a minuscule fishing hamlet (Tran De) and an offshore island (Hon Khoai), Ngoc Hien stakes its claim as the southernmost town in Vietnam. Few tourists come to this isolated community, which survives mainly from the shrimp-raising industry.

At the very southern tip of the delta is the Camau Nature Reserve, sometimes referred to as the Ngoc Hien Bird Sanctuary. It's one of the least developed and most protected parts of the Mekong Delta region. In this area, shrimp farming is prohibited. Access is only by boat.

At the southern end of the reserve is the tiny fishing village at Tran De. A public ferry connects Tran De to Ngoc Hien. Tran De can rightly claim to be the southernmost town in Vietnam, at least if you exclude the military base at nearby Hon Khoai Island.

If you really are obsessed with reaching Vietnam's southern tip, you'll have to take a boat from Tran De to Hon Khoai Island. Unfortunately, this is a military base and a travel permit is required to make a visit.

If you're looking to visit another remote spot, you can hire a boat to take you to Dat Mui (Cape Camau), the south-western tip of Vietnam. However, few people find this worthwhile.

### Places to Stay

There is only one hotel in Ngoc Hien, so you'll have little choice unless you plan on camping. The *Nam Can Hotel* (☎ 877039) has rooms costing US$15 to US$40 for foreigners.

### Getting There & Away

A road connecting Camau to Ngoc Hien is shown on most maps of Vietnam, but it's little more than wishful thinking. Basically, it's a muddy track which is underwater most of the time, though some have attempted it by motorbike.

The trip to Ngoc Hien is best done by speedboat. These boats are readily available in Camau and take approximately four hours to do the journey. From Ngoc Hien south to Tran De takes another four hours.

## HON KHOAI ISLAND

This island, 25km south of the southern tip of the Mekong Delta, is the southernmost point in Vietnam. Unlike the delta, which is pancake flat and intensively cultivated, Hon Khoai Island is rocky, hilly and forested. Unfortunately, getting there is fraught with hassles and few people bother. To begin with, the island is a military base, so a travel permit is needed. To get this, apply in Camau at either the police station or through Camau Tourist. More than likely, the police will refuse you anyway and you'll be referred to Camau Tourist, which will of course charge for its services.

From Camau, you need to get yourself to Ngoc Hien, where you change boats for Tran De (the fishing village at the southern tip of the Mekong Delta). And from Tran De you catch a fishing boat to Hon Khoai Island.

The only place to stay in Hon Khoai Island is the military guesthouse.

## LONG XUYEN

Long Xuyen, the capital of An Giang Province, has a population of about 100,000. It was once a stronghold of the Hoa Hao sect, founded in 1939, which emphasises simplicity in worship and does not believe in temples or intermediaries between humans and the Supreme Being. Until 1956 the Hoa

MEKONG DELTA

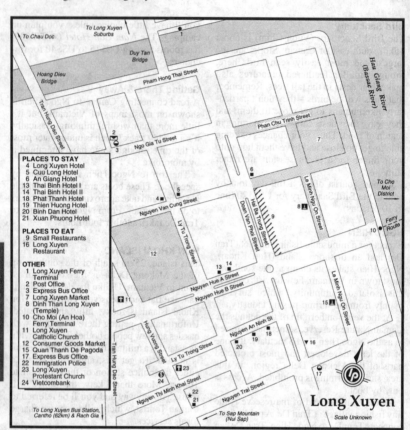

**PLACES TO STAY**
4 Long Xuyen Hotel
5 Cuu Long Hotel
6 An Giang Hotel
13 Thai Binh Hotel I
14 Thai Binh Hotel II
18 Phat Thanh Hotel
19 Thien Huong Hotel
20 Binh Dan Hotel
21 Xuan Phuong Hotel

**PLACES TO EAT**
9 Small Restaurants
16 Long Xuyen Restaurant

**OTHER**
1 Long Xuyen Ferry Terminal
2 Post Office
3 Express Bus Office
7 Long Xuyen Market
8 Dinh Than Long Xuyen (Temple)
10 Cho Moi (An Hoa) Ferry Terminal
11 Long Xuyen Catholic Church
12 Consumer Goods Market
17 Quan Thanh De Pagoda
22 Immigration Police
23 Long Xuyen Protestant Church
24 Vietcombank

**Long Xuyen**

Hao had an army and constituted a major military force in this region.

Today, Long Xuyen is a moderately prosperous town in the Mekong Delta. There are a few sights around town, but for travellers its value is mainly as a transit point, with good food, accommodation and a foreign exchange bank.

### Long Xuyen Catholic Church

Long Xuyen Catholic Church, an impressive modern structure with a 50m-high bell tower, is one of the largest churches in the Mekong Delta. It was constructed between 1966 and 1973, and can seat 1000 worshippers. The church is on the triangular block created by Tran Hung Dao, Hung Vuong and Nguyen Hue A Sts, and is open for visitors from 4 am to 8 pm. Masses are held daily from 4.30 to 5.30 am and 6 to 7 pm; on Sunday, there are masses from 5 to 6.30 am, 3.30 to 5 pm and 6 to 7.30 pm.

### Long Xuyen Protestant Church

Long Xuyen Protestant Church is a small, modern structure at 4 Hung Vuong St. Prayers are held on Sunday from 10 am to noon.

## Cho Moi District
Cho Moi District, across the river from Long Xuyen, is known for its rich groves of banana, durian, guava, jackfruit, longan, mango, mangosteen and plum. The women here are said to be the most beautiful in the Mekong Delta. Cho Moi District can be reached by ferry from the Cho Moi (An Hoa) ferry terminal at the foot of Nguyen Hue St.

## Places to Stay
If cheap is all that matters, there are three adjacent dumps on Nguyen An Ninh St that can accommodate you. First in the line-up is the *Phat Thanh Hotel* (☎ 841708; 20 rooms) at 2 Nguyen An Ninh St. This is the most 'upmarket' of the three dumps. Rooms with fan and private bath are US$4, or US$10 with air-con.

Just next door at No 4 is the *Thien Huong Hotel* (☎ 843152; 12 rooms). Rooms have electric fan only and cost US$3.50 to US$5.50.

Bottom of the barrel is the *Binh Dan Hotel* at No 12. There are 12 rooms here priced from US$3.50 to US$5.

The *Thai Binh Hotel II* (☎ 847078; 16 rooms), 4 Nguyen Hue A St, is a new privately owned place that's very reasonably priced. Rooms with fan and attached cold-water bath cost US$7, or with hot water and air-con it's US$13.

The *Thai Binh Hotel I* (☎ 841184; 27 rooms), 12-14 Nguyen Hue A St, is a state-owned place that was recently renovated and now looks good. Doubles with air-con cost US$16. The hotel is proud of its huge restaurant and karaoke.

The *Xuan Phuong Hotel* (☎ 841041; 12 rooms), 68 Nguyen Trai St, is functional enough. Doubles with air-con and attached cold-water bath cost US$15 to US$20.

The *An Giang Hotel* (☎ 841297; 17 rooms) at 40 Hai Ba Trung St is not bad. Singles/doubles with fan cost US$10/15. Doubles with air-con cost US$16 to US$19.

The *Long Xuyen Hotel* at 17 Nguyen Van Cung St has 39 rooms: with fan and attached bath the tab is US$11; with air-con it's US$13 to US$20.

The *Cuu Long Hotel* (☎ 841365; fax 843176; 20 rooms) is at 15 Nguyen Van Cung St. All rooms have air-con and hot water. Rooms with TV (Vietnamese stations only) cost US$26, or without TV it drops to US$20.

## Places to Eat
The *Long Xuyen Restaurant*, a large place which serves both Chinese and western dishes and specialises in seafood, is near the corner of Nguyen Trai and Hai Ba Trung Sts.

The *Kim Tinh Hotel & Restaurant* serves excellent Vietnamese food and is very cheap. The *Xuan Phuong Hotel* also has a pleasant restaurant. There are restaurants in the hotels *An Giang*, *Cuu Long*, *Long Xuyen* and *Thai Binh*.

## Getting There & Away
**Bus** Buses from Saigon to Long Xuyen leave from the Mien Tay bus station in An Lac.

Long Xuyen bus station (Ben Xe Long Xuyen; ☎ 852125) is at the southern end of town opposite 96/3B Tran Hung Dao St. There are buses from Long Xuyen to Camau, Cantho, Chau Doc, Ha Tien, Saigon and Rach Gia.

**Car** Long Xuyen is 62km from Cantho, 126km from Mytho and 189km from Ho Chi Minh City.

**Boat** To get to the Long Xuyen ferry terminal from Pham Hong Thai St, cross Duy Tan Bridge and turn right. Passenger ferries leave from here to Cho Vam, Dong Tien, Hong Ngu, Kien Luong, Lai Vung, Rach Gia, Sa Dec and Tan Chau.

There may be a ferry service to An Giang Province from Saigon; check at the ferry dock at the river end of Ham Nghi St.

## Getting Around
The best way to get around Long Xuyen is to take a *xe dap loi* (a two-wheeled wagon pulled by a bicycle) or a *xe Honda loi* (a two-wheeled wagon pulled by a motorbike).

Car ferries from Long Xuyen to Cho Moi District (across the river) leave from the Cho Moi (An Hoa) ferry terminal near 17/4

Nguyen Hue B St every half-hour from 4 am to 6.30 pm.

## CHAU DOC

Chau Doc (population 60,000) is a riverine commercial centre not far from the Cambodian border. The city was once known for its pirogue (dugout canoe) races. Chau Doc has sizeable Chinese, Cham and Khmer communities, each of which has built distinctive temples that are worth visiting.

### Chau Phu Temple

Chau Phu Temple (Dinh Than Chau Phu), on the corner of Bao Ho Thoai and Gia Long Sts, was built in 1926 to worship Thoai Ngoc Hau (1761-1829), who is buried at Sam Mountain. The structure is decorated with both Vietnamese and Chinese motifs. Inside are funeral tablets bearing the names of the deceased and biographical information about them.

### Chau Doc Church

This small Catholic church, constructed in 1920, is across the street from 459 Lien Tinh Lo 10 and is not far from Phu Hiep ferry terminal. There are masses every day at 5 am and 5 pm; on Sunday, masses are held at 7 am and 4 pm.

### Mosques

The domed and arched Chau Giang Mosque, which serves the local Cham Muslim community, is in the hamlet of Chau Giang. To get there, take the car ferry from Chau Giang ferry terminal in Chau Doc across the Hau Giang River. From the landing, go away from the river for 30m, turn left and walk 50m.

The Mubarak Mosque (Thanh Duong Hoi Giao) is also on the river bank opposite Chau Doc. In this mosque, children study the Koran in Arabic script. Visitors are permitted, but you should avoid entering during the calls to prayer (five times daily) unless you are a Muslim.

There are other small mosques in the Chau Doc area. These are reachable by boat, but you'll probably need a local guide to find them all.

### Floating Houses

These houses, whose floats consist of empty metal drums, provide both a place to live and a livelihood for their residents. Under each house, fish are raised in suspended metal nets: the fish flourish in their natural river habitat, the family can feed them whatever scraps of biological matter it has handy, and catching the fish does not require all the exertions of fishing. You'll find these houses floating all around the Chau Doc area.

### Places to Stay

*Guesthouse 44* (Nha Khach 44; ☎ 866540; 19 rooms) is a venerable favourite of backpackers, though it's definitely showing its age. Rooms with fan and attached cold-water bath are US$5 to US$8. The hotel is on the corner of Doc Phu Thu and Phan Dinh Phung Sts.

*Hotel 92* (Nha Tro 92) at 92 Nguyen Van Thoai St is a new and good-looking place with only five rooms. All rooms have attached cold-water bath. Doubles with fan are US$7 and with air-con you'll pay US$11.

The *Thai Binh Hotel* (☎ 866221; 16 rooms) at 37 Nguyen Van Thoai St is a real cheapie. Singles/doubles with fan but no bath are US$4/7. A room for four persons with bath outside, but toilet inside, is US$11.

Another bottom-end place is the *Tai Thanh Hotel* (☎ 866147; 22 rooms) at 86 Bach Dang St. All rooms have attached private bath with cold water for US$5 to US$10.

The *Chau Doc Hotel* (☎ 866484; 37 rooms) is a large place at 17 Doc Phu Thu St. There has been some recent renovation work here and it looks quite livable. A room with fan but no bath is US$7. A room with attached cold-water bath and fan/air-con is US$9/15.

The *My Loc Hotel* (☎ 866167; 20 rooms) is at 51 Nguyen Van Thoai St. This popular place has double rooms with ceiling fan and private bath for US$7. Air-con doubles with cold-water bath are US$10. A four-person room costs US$18. Breakfast is included at no charge, but coffee costs extra.

*Thanh Tra Hotel* (☎ 866788; 26 rooms),

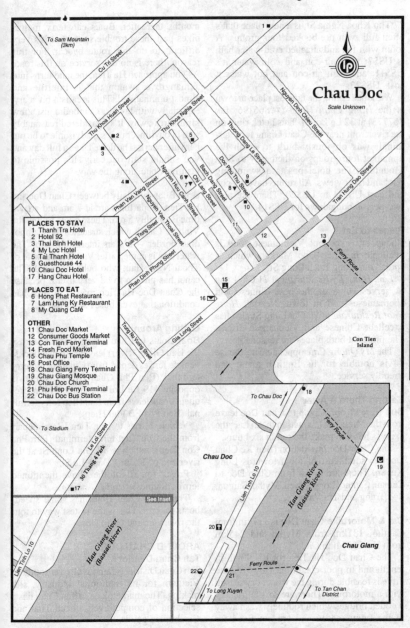

# Chau Doc

Scale Unknown

**PLACES TO STAY**
1 Thanh Tra Hotel
2 Hotel 92
3 Thai Binh Hotel
4 My Loc Hotel
5 Tai Thanh Hotel
9 Guesthouse 44
10 Chau Doc Hotel
17 Hang Chau Hotel

**PLACES TO EAT**
6 Hong Phat Restaurant
7 Lam Hung Ky Restaurant
8 My Quang Café

**OTHER**
11 Chau Doc Market
12 Consumer Goods Market
13 Con Tien Ferry Terminal
14 Fresh Food Market
15 Chau Phu Temple
16 Post Office
18 Chau Giang Ferry Terminal
19 Chau Giang Mosque
20 Chau Doc Church
21 Phu Hiep Ferry Terminal
22 Chau Doc Bus Station

MEKONG DELTA

77 Thu Khoa Nghia St, is a new place that's often full with pre-booked tour groups. A room with fan and attached cold-water bath is US$7; with air-con and cold water it's US$11; and with air-con and hot water it costs US$23.

Without a doubt, the fanciest place in town is the *Hang Chau Hotel* (☎ 866196; fax 867773) at 32 Le Loi St. This hotel, right on the riverfront near the Chau Giang ferry terminal, was obviously built to catch the upmarket tour groups on their way to Sam Mountain. The hotel boasts a swimming pool and river views. All rooms have air-con and cost US$11 to US$20. There are also two-person bungalows for US$14.

### Places to Eat

Cheap but excellent Vietnamese food is available in Chau Doc Market, which is spread out along Bach Dang St.

*Lam Hung Ky Restaurant* at 71 Chi Lang St serves some of the best Chinese and Vietnamese food in town. Nearby, *Hong Phat Restaurant* at 79 Chi Lang St also has excellent Chinese and Vietnamese dishes. The prices at both places are reasonable.

The *My Quang Cafe* opposite Guesthouse 44 is notable for its English menu and friendly service.

### Getting There & Away

**Bus** Buses from Saigon to Chau Doc leave from the Mien Tay bus station in An Lac; the express bus can make the run in six hours.

The Chau Doc bus station (Ben Xe Chau Doc) is south-east of town towards Long Xuyen. There are buses from Chau Doc to Camau, Cantho, Long Xuyen, Mytho, Saigon, Soc Trang and Tra Vinh.

**Car & Motorbike** Chau Doc is 117km from Cantho, 181km from Mytho and 245km from Ho Chi Minh City.

The Chau Doc-Ha Tien road is 90km in length and in poor condition. However, the drive is feasible during the winter dry season with a motorbike. There are several rickety wooden bridges which routinely wash away in the rainy season and are not fixed for

months thereafter. Boats can ferry motorbikes past these trouble spots, but it's very difficult to do this route by car. For this reason, there is no bus service on this road. As you approach Ha Tien, the land turns into a mangrove swamp that is infertile and almost uninhabited. This area is a bit scary, especially with lawless Cambodia just a few kilometres away. It's considered reasonably safe in daytime, but it's inadvisable to be out here after dark. The drive takes a full day and you should start out early. It's possible to visit Ba Chuc along the way.

**Boat** Boats run daily between Chau Doc and Ha Tien. Departures are at 7 am and arrival time is roughly at 5 pm. These boats follow the Vinh Te Canal, which straddles the Cambodian border – it's an interesting trip. The waterway is named after Vinh Te, the wife of Thoai Ngoc Hau, who built the canal. The canal has proven to be very useful because the Chau Doc-Ha Tien road is in such bad condition that even buses don't use it.

### Getting Around

**Boat** Boats to Chau Giang District (across the Hau Giang River) leave from two docks: vehicle ferries depart from Chau Giang ferry terminal (Ben Pha Chau Giang), which is opposite 419 Le Loi St; smaller, more frequent boats leave from Phu Hiep ferry terminal (Ben Pha FB Phu Hiep).

Vehicle ferries to Con Tien Island depart from the Con Tien ferry terminal (Ben Pha Con Tien), which is off Gia Long St at the river end of Thuong Dang Le St.

Prices for all of the above-mentioned ferries doubles at night.

The Hang Chau Hotel has some speedboats for rent. This is the fastest way to tour the rivers around Chau Doc.

## AROUND CHAU DOC
### Tan Chau District

Tan Chau District is famous all over southern Vietnam for its traditional industry, silk making. The marketplace in Tan Chau has a selection of competitively priced Thai and Cambodian goods.

To get to Tan Chau District from Chau Doc, take a boat across the Hau Giang River from the Phu Hiep ferry terminal. Then catch a ride on the back of a *Honda om* for the 18km trip from Chau Giang District to Tan Chau District.

### Sam Mountain

There are dozens of pagodas and temples, many of them set in caves, around Sam Mountain (Nui Sam), which is about 3km south-west of Chau Doc out on Bao Ho Thoai St. The Chinese influence is obvious, and this is a favourite spot for ethnic-Chinese pilgrims from Saigon and ethnic-Chinese tourists from Hong Kong and Taiwan.

Climbing the peak is of course the highlight of a visit to Sam Mountain. The views from the top are spectacular (weather permitting) and you can easily look onto Cambodia. There is a military outpost on the summit, a legacy of the days when the Khmer Rouges made cross-border raids and massacred Vietnamese civilians. The outpost is still functional, but the soldiers are quite used to tourists taking photos now; however, you should ply the soldiers with cigarettes and ask permission before taking photos of them or anything that could be considered militarily sensitive.

Walking down is easier than walking up, so if you want to cheat you can have a motorbike bring you to the summit. The road to the top is on the south-west side of the mountain, so you can walk down along a peaceful, traffic-free trail on the north side which will bring you to the main temple area. The summit road has recently been decorated with amusement park ceramic dinosaurs and the like, perhaps a sign of abominations to come. But there are also some small shrines and pavilions, which add a bit of charm and remind you that this is indeed Vietnam and not Disneyland.

**Tay An Pagoda** Tay An Pagoda (Chua Tay An), on the left as you arrive at Sam Mountain, is renowned for the fine carving of its hundreds of religious figures, most of which are made of wood. Aspects of the building's

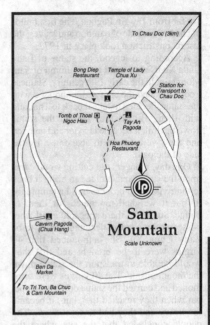

architecture reflect Hindu and Islamic influences. The first chief monk of Tay An Pagoda, which was founded in 1847, came from Giac Lam Pagoda in Saigon. Tay An Pagoda was last rebuilt in 1958.

The main gate is of traditional Vietnamese design. Above the bi-level roof there are figures of lions and two dragons fighting for possession of pearls, chrysanthemums, apricot trees and lotus blossoms. Nearby is a statue of Quan Am Thi Kinh, the Guardian Spirit of Mother and Child (for her legend, see the section on the Jade Emperor Pagoda in the Ho Chi Minh City chapter.

In front of the pagoda are statues of a black elephant with two tusks and a white elephant with six tusks. Around the pagoda there are various monks' tombs.

**Temple of Lady Chua Xu** The Temple of Lady Chua Xu (Mieu Ba Chua Xu), founded in the 1820s, stands facing Sam Mountain not far from Tay An Pagoda. The first building here was made of bamboo and leaves; the last reconstruction took place in 1972.

According to legend, the statue of Lady Chua Xu used to stand at the summit of Sam Mountain. In the early 19th century, Siamese troops invaded the area and, impressed with the statue, decided to take it back to Thailand with them. But as they carried the statue down the hill, it became heavier and heavier, and they were forced to abandon it by the side of the path.

One day, villagers out cutting wood came upon the statue and decided to bring it back to their village in order to build a temple for it; but it weighed too much for them to budge. Suddenly, there appeared a girl who, possessed by a spirit, declared herself to be Lady Chua Xu. She announced that 40 virgins were to be brought and that they would be able to transport the statue down the mountainside. The 40 virgins were summoned and carried the statue down the slope, but when they reached the plain, it became too heavy and they had to set it down. The people concluded that the site where the virgins halted had been selected by Lady Chua Xu for the construction of a temple, and it is at that place that the Temple of Lady Chua Xu stands to this day.

Another story relates that the wife of Thoai Ngoc Hau, builder of the Vinh Te Canal, swore to erect a temple when the canal, whose construction claimed many lives, was completed. She died before being able to carry through on her oath, but Thoai Ngoc Hau implemented her plans by building the Temple of Lady Chua Xu.

The temple's most important festival is held from the 23rd to the 26th day of the fourth lunar month. During this time, pilgrims flock here, sleeping on mats in the large rooms of the two-storey resthouse next to the temple.

**Tomb of Thoai Ngoc Hau** Thoai Ngoc Hau (1761-1829) was a high-ranking official who served the Nguyen lords and, later, the Nguyen Dynasty. In early 1829, Thoai Ngoc Hau ordered that a tomb be constructed for

himself at the foot of Sam Mountain. The site he chose is not far from Tay An Pagoda.

The steps are made of red 'beehive' (da ong) stone brought from the eastern part of southern Vietnam. In the middle of the platform is the tomb of Thoai Ngoc Hau and those of his wives, Chau Thi Te and Truong Thi Miet. Nearby are several dozen other tombs where officials who served under Thoai Ngoc Hau are buried.

**Cavern Pagoda** The Cavern Pagoda (Chua Hang, also known as Phuoc Dien Tu) is about halfway up the western side of Sam Mountain. The lower part of the pagoda includes monks' quarters and two hexagonal tombs in which the founder of the pagoda, a female tailor named Le Thi Tho, and a former head monk, Thich Hue Thien, are buried.

The upper section consists of two parts: the main sanctuary, in which there are statues of A Di Da (the Buddha of the Past) and Thich Ca Buddha (Sakyamuni), and the cavern. At the back of the cave, which is behind the sanctuary building, is a shrine dedicated to Quan The Am Bo Tat (the Goddess of Mercy).

According to legend, Le Thi Tho came from Tay An Pagoda to this site half a century ago to lead a quiet, meditative life. When she arrived, she found two enormous snakes, one white and the other dark green. Le Thi Tho soon converted the snakes, who thereafter led pious lives. Upon her death, the snakes disappeared.

**Places to Eat** For tasty Vietnamese specialities (including cobra and turtle), try *Hoa Phuong Restaurant* between Tay An Pagoda and the Tomb of Thoai Ngoc Hau. This place has a huge garden. *Bong Diep Restaurant* is across from the Tomb of Thoai Ngoc Hau; the selection here is similar to Hoa Phuong Restaurant but the food is not as good.

## BA CHUC

Close to the Cambodian border but just within Vietnam is Ba Chuc, otherwise known as the 'Bone Pagoda'. The pagoda stands as a grisly reminder of the horrors perpetrated by the genocidal Khmer Rouge. Between 1975 and 1978, Khmer Rouge guerillas regularly crossed the border into Vietnam and slaughtered innocent civilians. And this is to say nothing of the million or so Cambodians exterminated by the Khmer Rouge.

Between 12 April and 30 April 1978, the Khmer Rouge murdered 3157 civilians at Ba Chuc. Only two people are known to have survived the massacre. Many of the victims were tortured to death. The Vietnamese might have had other motives for invading Cambodia at the end of 1978, but certainly the outrage at Ba Chuc was a major reason for the invasion.

There are two notable buildings at Ba Chuc, a temple and a 'skull' pagoda. The skull pagoda houses the skulls of the victims. This resembles Cambodia's Choeung Ek killing fields, where thousands of skulls of Khmer Rouge victims are on display. Near the skull collection is a temple which displays gruesome photos taken shortly after the massacre. The display is both fascinating and horrifying – you do need a strong stomach to visit.

Getting to the pagoda will also require a bit of intestinal fortitude because the road from Chau Doc is in dismal condition. A high-clearance van might make it during the dry season, but for much of the year the road turns to muck. A jeep or motorbike are the best vehicles. If the Vietnamese government ever recognises the tourist potential of this place, the road might be improved.

To reach Ba Chuc, follow the unpaved highway that runs from Chau Doc to Ha Tien. You need to turn off this main road onto Highway 3T and follow it for 4km.

## RACH GIA

Rach Gia, the capital of Kien Giang Province, is a booming port-city on the Gulf of Thailand. The population of about 150,000 includes significant numbers of ethnic-Chinese and Khmers.

Kien Giang Province has an enlightened policy towards tourism. Foreigners and Vietnamese are charged the same prices at hotels. Furthermore, there are very few restrictions on where foreigners can stay – in general, any hotel which can accept Vietnamese can also accept foreigners. Travel permits are not needed and the police seem to leave the tourists alone. You can rent boats from private individuals – you are not forced to take government tours. We only wish that the other provinces in the Mekong Delta had the same attitude.

Fishing and agriculture have made the town reasonably prosperous. Access to the sea and closeness to Cambodia and Thailand have also made smuggling a profitable business here. The Rach Gia area was once famous as the source of large feathers used to make ceremonial fans for the Imperial Court, but this is one industry that has little chance of reviving despite the recent economic liberalisation.

Foreigners' main interest in Rach Gia is to use it as an overnight stop on the way to Phu Quoc Island.

### Information

**Travel Agencies** Kien Giang Tourist (Cong Ty Du Lich Kien Giang; ☎ 862081; fax 862111) – the provincial tourism authority – is at 12 Ly Tu Trong St just opposite the Thanh Binh Hotel.

**Money** Rach Gia is the last place you can change money before heading to Ha Tien or Phu Quoc Island. Vietcombank (Ngan Hang Ngoai Thuong Viet Nam; ☎ 863427) is on the corner of 207 and Duy Tan Sts.

### Pagodas & Temples

**Nguyen Trung Truc Temple** This temple is dedicated to Nguyen Trung Truc, a leader of the Vietnamese resistance campaign of the 1860s against the newly arrived French. Among other exploits, he led the raid that resulted in the burning of the French warship *Espérance*. Despite repeated attempts to capture him, Nguyen Trung Truc continued to fight until 1868, when the French took his mother and a number of civilians hostage and threatened to kill them if he did not surrender. Nguyen Trung Truc turned himself in and was executed by the French in the

GULF OF
THAILAND

**Rach Gia**

Scale Unknown

**PLACES TO STAY**
12 Binh Minh Hotel
16 Thanh Binh Hotel
18 To Chau Hotel
20 1 Thang 5 Hotel
22 Palace Hotel

**PLACES TO EAT**
10 Food Stalls
14 Tay Ho Restaurant
21 Dong Ho Restaurant
23 Song Kien Restaurant
24 Rach Gia Restaurant
25 Hoa Bien Restaurant
26 Hai Au Restaurant

**OTHER**
1 Phat Lon Pagoda

2 Bus Station
3 Nguyen Trung Truc Temple
4 Ferry to Phu Quoc Island
5 Post Office
6 Vietcombank
7 Rach Gia Church
8 Mui Voi Ferry Terminal
9 Vinh Than Van Market
11 Rach Gia Market
13 Nguyen Trung Truc Statue
15 Ong Bac De Pagoda
17 Kien Giang Tourist
19 Rach Gia Museum
27 Pho Minh Pagoda
28 Protestant Church
29 Tam Bao Pagoda
30 Cao Dai Temple
31 Rach Gia Bus Station

marketplace of Rach Gia on 27 October 1868.

The first temple structure was a simple building with a thatched roof; over the years it has been enlarged and rebuilt several times. The last reconstruction took place between 1964 and 1970. In the centre of the main hall on an altar is a portrait of Nguyen Trung Truc.

Nguyen Trung Truc Temple is at 18 Nguyen Cong Tru St and is open from 7 am to 6 pm.

**Phat Lon Pagoda** This large Cambodian Hinayana Buddhist pagoda, whose name

means Big Buddha, was founded about two centuries ago. Though all of the three dozen monks who live here are ethnic-Khmers, ethnic-Vietnamese also frequent the pagoda. Prayers are held daily from 4 to 6 am and 5 to 7 pm. The pagoda, off Quang Trung St, is open from 4 am to 5 pm during the seventh, eighth and ninth lunar months (the summer season), but guests are welcome year-round.

Inside the sanctuary *(vihara)*, the figures of Sakyamuni, the historical Buddha, all wear Cambodian and Thai-style pointed hats. Around the exterior of the main hall are eight small altars. The two towers near the main entrance are used to cremate the bodies of deceased monks. Near the pagoda are the tombs of about two dozen monks.

**Ong Bac De Pagoda** Ong Bac De Pagoda, in the centre of town at 14 Nguyen Du St, was built by Rach Gia's Chinese community about a century ago. On the central altar is a statue of Ong Bac De, a reincarnation of the Jade Emperor. To the left is Ong Bon, Guardian Spirit of Happiness and Virtue; to the right is Quan Cong (in Chinese, Kuan Kung).

**Pho Minh Pagoda** Two Buddhist nuns live at Pho Minh Pagoda, which is on the corner of Co Bac and Nguyen Van Cu Sts. This small pagoda was built in 1967 and contains a large Thai-style Thich Ca Buddha (Sakyamuni) donated in 1971 by a Buddhist organisation in Thailand. Nearby is a Vietnamese-style Thich Ca Buddha. The nuns live in a building behind the main hall. The pagoda is open to visitors from 6 am to 10 pm; prayers are held daily from 3.30 to 4.30 am and 6.30 to 7.30 pm.

**Tam Bao Pagoda** Tam Bao Pagoda, which dates from the early 19th century, is near the corner of Thich Thien An and Tran Phu Sts; it was last rebuilt in 1913. The garden contains numerous trees sculpted as dragons, deer and other animals. The pagoda is open from 6 am to 8 pm; prayers are held from 4.30 to 5.30 am and 5.30 to 6.30 pm.

**Caodai Temple** There is a small Caodai Temple, constructed in 1969, at 189 Nguyen Trung Truc St, which is not far from Rach Gia bus station.

**Churches**
**Rach Gia Church** Rach Gia Church (Nha Tho Chanh Toa Rach Gia), a red brick structure built in 1918, is in Vinh Thanh Van subdistrict, across the channel from Vinh Thanh Van Market. Weekday masses are held from 5 to 6 am and 5 to 6 pm; Sunday masses are from 5 to 6 am, 7 to 8 am, 4 to 5 pm and 5 to 6 pm.

**Protestant Church** Services are held every Sunday from 10 am to noon at the Protestant Church, built in 1972. It is at 133 Nguyen Trung Truc St.

**Rach Gia Museum**
The refurbished Rach Gia Museum is at 21 Nguyen Van Troi St.

**Vinh Thanh Van Market**
Vinh Thanh Van Market, Rach Gia's main market area, stretches along Bach Dang, Trinh Hoai Duc and Thu Khoa Nghia Sts east of Tran Phu St.

The luxury goods market is between Hoang Hoa Tham and Pham Hong Thai Sts.

**Places to Stay**
The *Thanh Binh Hotel* (☎ 863053; 15 rooms) at 11 Ly Tu Trong St is an OK place, though nothing to write home about. Rooms with fan cost US$6. Each room has a private cold-water bath shower, but the toilet is down the hall.

Somewhat better is the *Binh Minh Hotel* (☎ 862154; 20 rooms) at 48 Pham Hong Thai St. All rooms have attached private bath. Rooms with fan cost only US$7 to US$8; with air-con the price is US$9 and US$10.

The comfortable *1 Thang 5 Hotel* (☎ 862-103; fax 862111; 18 rooms) is at 38 Nguyen Hung Son St. The name means '1/5' (1 May), which is International Worker's Day (May Day), a worldwide Communist festival which has declined in importance since the break-up of the Soviet Union. The hotel has declined a bit too – it could use a renovation. It is cheap though, with doubles from US$7 to US$14.

The *To Chau Hotel* (☎ 863718; 29 rooms), one of the best in town, is at 4F Le Loi St (next to the Thang Loi Cinema). If you're arriving by rented car, your driver will much appreciate the fact that the hotel has a garage. All rooms have private attached bath; with fan and cold water it's US$8 to US$9; or with hot water it costs US$13 to US$23.

The *Palace Hotel* (☎ 863049; 18 rooms), 41 Tran Phu St, is a new hotel and a good one. Ironically, the cheapest rooms (on the top floor) are the only ones with terraces. Rooms with fan but no bath cost US$9; rooms with hot-water bath and air-con go for US$22 to US$27.

## Places to Eat

Rach Gia is known for its seafood, dried cuttlefish, ca thieu (dried fish slices), nuoc mam (fish sauce) and black pepper.

The restaurant in the *Binh Minh Hotel* is a favourite venue for eating snake. Choose your cobra from a cage and you'll see it massacred before your eyes – then you'll also be presented with a cup of the snake's blood to drink. Can you think of a more interesting way to spend an evening in Rach Gia?

There are also restaurants in the *To Chau* and *1 Thang 5* hotels.

For deer, turtle, cobra, eel, frog and cuttlefish (as well as more conventional fare), try the *Hoa Bien Restaurant*, which is on the water at the western end of Nguyen Hung Son St. There is no sandy beach here, but the restaurant sets up lawn chairs for its customers to admire the view.

The *Tay Ho Restaurant* at 16 Nguyen Du St serves good Chinese and Vietnamese food. The *Dong Ho Restaurant* at 124 Tran Phu St has Chinese, Vietnamese and western dishes.

Other places you might try are the *Rach Gia Restaurant*, on the water at the intersection of Ly Tu Trong and Tran Hung Dao Sts, and the *Song Kien Restaurant*, which is a block away at the intersection of Tran Hung Dao and Hung Vuong Sts. The *Hai Au Restaurant* is on the corner of Nguyen Trung Truc and Nguyen Van Cu Sts.

Cheap, tasty Vietnamese food is sold from stalls along Hung Vuong St between Bach Dang and Le Hong Phong Sts.

## Getting There & Away

**Air** Rach Gia has an airport, but at the time of writing there were no regularly scheduled flights. Vietnam Airlines has contemplated the possibility of chartered flights.

**Bus** Buses from Saigon to Rach Gia leave from the Mien Tay bus station in An Lac; the express bus takes six to seven hours.

The Rach Gia bus station (Ben Xe Kien Giang) is south of the city on Nguyen Trung Truc St (towards Long Xuyen and Cantho). Nonexpress buses link Rach Gia with Cantho, Dong Thap (departs once a day at 7 am), Ha Tien, Long Xuyen and Saigon. There are daily express buses to Saigon (departs 4.30 am) and Ha Tien (departs 2.30 am).

There is an express bus office at 33 30/4 St offering daily express service to Cantho (departs 5 am), Ha Tien (departs 4.30 am) and Saigon (departs 3.45 am). Another express bus to Saigon leaves every morning at 4 am from Trung Tam Du Lich Thanh Nien, which is at 78 Nguyen Trung Truc St.

**Car** Rach Gia is 92km from Ha Tien, 125km from Cantho and 248km from Ho Chi Minh City.

**Boat** In Rach Gia Park at the western end of Nguyen Cong Tru St is where you catch ferries to Phu Quoc Island. There are departures every morning, but the time varies so make local inquiries. The fare is US$5.

Mui Voi ferry terminal *(mui* means nose and *voi* means elephant – so named because of the shape of the island) is at the northeastern end of Bach Dang St. Boats from here make daily trips to Camau (departs 5.30 am), Chau Doc (departs 5.30 pm), Long Xuyen (departs 12.30 pm) and Tan Chau (departs 4.30 pm).

## AROUND RACH GIA
### Ancient City of Oc-Eo

Oc-Eo was a major trading city during the 1st to 6th centuries AD, when this area (along with the rest of southern Vietnam, much of southern Cambodia and the Malay peninsula) was ruled by the Indianised empire of Funan. Much of what is known about Funan, which reached its height in the 5th century AD, comes from contemporary Chinese sources (eg the accounts of Chinese emissaries and travellers) and the archaeological excavations at Oc-Eo, which have uncovered evidence of significant contact between

Oc-Eo and what is now Thailand, Malaysia, Indonesia, Persia and even the Roman Empire.

An elaborate system of canals around Oc-Eo was used for both irrigation and transportation, prompting Chinese travellers of the time to write about 'sailing across Funan' on their way to the Malay peninsula. Most of the buildings of Oc-Eo were built on piles, and pieces of these structures indicate the high degree of refinement achieved by Funanese civilisation. Artefacts found at Oc-Eo are on display in Saigon at the History Museum and the Art Museum and in Hanoi at the History Museum.

The remains of Oc-Eo are not far from Rach Gia. The site itself, a hill 11km inland littered with potsherds and shells, is near Vong The village, which can be reached by jeep from Hue Duc village, a distance of about 8km. Oc-Eo is most easily accessible during the dry season. Special permission may be required to visit; for more information, contact Kien Giang Tourist.

## HA TIEN

Ha Tien (population 80,000) is on the Gulf of Thailand 8km from the Cambodian border. The area, famous for its nearby white-sand beaches and fishing villages, is also known for its production of seafood, black pepper and items made from the shells of sea turtles. All around the area are lovely, towering limestone formations that give this place a very different appearance from the rest of the Mekong Delta region. The rock formations support a network of caves, many of which have been turned into cave temples. Plantations of black-pepper trees cling to the hillsides in places where it's not too steep. On a clear day, Phu Quoc Island is visible across the water to the west.

Ha Tien was a province of Cambodia until 1708 when, in the face of attacks by the Thais, the Khmer-appointed governor, a Chinese immigrant named Mac Cuu, turned to the Vietnamese for protection and assistance. Mac Cuu thereafter governed this area as a fiefdom under the protection of the Nguyen lords. He was succeeded as ruler by his son, Mac Thien Tu. During the 18th century, the area was invaded and pillaged several times by the Thais. Rach Gia and the southern tip of the Mekong Delta came under direct Nguyen rule in 1798.

During the rule of the genocidal Khmer Rouge regime in Cambodia (1975-79), Khmer Rouge forces repeatedly attacked Vietnamese territory and massacred thousands of civilians. The entire populations of Ha Tien and nearby villages – tens of thousands of people – fled their homes. During this period, areas north of Ha Tien (along the Cambodian border) were sown with mines and booby-traps, which have yet to be cleared.

### Warning

Ha Tien itself is considered safe day or night; however, the rural areas north-west of town along the Cambodian border are regarded as dangerous at night. In particular, this includes Mui Nai Beach. Khmer gangsters have slipped across the border at night on occasion to commit robberies or kidnap people for ransom.

### Pagodas & Tombs

**Mac Cuu Family Tombs** The tombs (Lang Mac Cuu) are on a low ridge not far from town. They are known locally simply as Nui Lang, the Hill of the Tombs. Several dozen relatives of Mac Cuu, Chinese émigré and 18th century ruler of this area, are buried here in traditional Chinese tombs decorated with figures of dragons, phoenixes, lions and guardians.

The largest tomb is that of Mac Cuu himself; it was constructed in 1809 on the orders of Emperor Gia Long and is decorated with finely carved figures of Thanh Long (the Green Dragon) and Bach Ho (the White Tiger). The tomb of Mac Cuu's first wife is flanked by dragons and phoenixes. At the bottom of the ridge is a shrine dedicated to the Mac family.

**Tam Bao Pagoda** Tam Bao Pagoda, also known as Sac Tu Tam Bao Tu, was founded by Mac Cuu in 1730. It is now home to several Buddhist nuns. In front of the pagoda is a statue of Quan The Am Bo Tat (the Goddess of Mercy) standing on a lotus blossom in the middle of a pond. Inside the sanctuary, the largest statue on the dais is of A Di Da, the Buddha of the Past. It is made of bronze but has been painted. Outside the building are the tombs of 16 monks.

Near Tam Bao Pagoda is a section of the city wall dating from the early 18th century.

Tam Bao Pagoda is at 328 Phuong Thanh St and is open from 7 am to 9 pm; prayers are held from 8 to 9 am and 2 to 3 pm. From the 15th day of the fourth lunar month to the 15th day of the seventh lunar month (roughly from May to August) prayers are held six times a day.

**Phu Dung Pagoda** Phu Dung Pagoda, also called Phu Cu Am Tu, was founded in the mid-18th century by Mac Cuu's second wife, Nguyen Thi Xuan. It is now home to one monk.

In the middle of the main hall is a peculiar statue of nine dragons embracing newly born Thich Ca Buddha (Sakyamuni, born Siddhartha Gautama). The most interesting statue on the main dais is a bronze Thich Ca Buddha brought from China; it is kept in a glass case. On the hillside behind the main hall are the tombs of Nguyen Thi Xuan and one of her female servants; nearby are four monks' tombs.

Behind the main hall is a small temple, Dien Ngoc Hoang, dedicated to the Taoist jade Emperor. The figures inside are of Ngoc Hoang flanked by Nam Tao, the Taoist God of the Southern Polar Star and the God of Happiness (on the right), and Bac Dao, the Taoist God of the Northern Polar Star and the God of Longevity (on the left). The statues are made of papier mâché moulded over bamboo frames.

Phu Dung Pagoda is open from 6 am to 10 pm; prayers are held from 4 to 5 am and 7 to 8 pm. To get to Phu Dung Pagoda, turn off Phuong Thanh St next to number 374.

**Thach Dong Cave Pagoda** Also known as Chua Thanh Van, this is a subterranean Buddhist temple 3.5km from town.

To the left of the entrance is the Stele of Hatred (Bia Cam Thu) commemorating the massacre of 130 people here by the forces of Khmer Rouge leader Pol Pot on 14 March 1979.

Several chambers of the grotto contain funerary tablets and altars to Ngoc Hoang (the Jade Emperor), Quan The Am Bo Tat (the Goddess of Mercy) and the two Buddhist monks who founded the temples of Thach Dong Cave Pagoda. The wind creates extraordinary sounds as it blows through the grotto's passageways. Openings in several branches of the cave afford views of nearby Cambodia.

### Dong Ho

Dong Ho (*dong* means east; *ho* means lake) is in fact not a lake at all but an inlet of the sea. The 'lake' is just east of Ha Tien, and bound to the east by a chain of granite hills known as the Ngu Ho (Five Tigers) and to the west by hills known as To Chan. Dong Ho is said to be most beautiful on nights when there is a full or almost-full moon. According to legend, it is on such nights that fairies dance here in the moonlight.

### Ha Tien Market

Ha Tien has an excellent market along the To Chau River. It's well worth your while to stop in here – many of the goods are imported (smuggled?) from Thailand and Cambodia, and prices are lower than you can find in Saigon. Cigarette smuggling is a particularly big business.

### Places to Stay

The *To Chau Hotel* on To Chau St is Ha Tien's bottom-end accommodation with seven rooms priced from US$4 to US$5. All of the rooms have an attached shower, but the toilet is outside. You get what you pay for – some of the rooms even lack ceiling fans.

The *Dong Ho Hotel* (☎ 852141; 20 rooms) was recently renovated and is now pretty decent. Rooms with fan are priced at US$5 to US$7, and air-con is available for US$11. The bath is attached, but the toilet is outside the rooms.

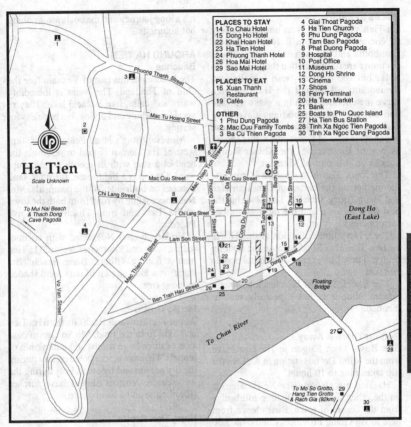

The *Ha Tien Hotel* (10 rooms) is in is a forlorn-looking dump. All rooms have a basic attached washroom, but the toilet is outside. Rooms with fan cost US$4, or you can pay US$9 for air-con.

The *Phuong Thanh Hotel* (☎ 852152; 11 rooms) has rooms with fan for US$5. The toilets are outside.

The *Hoa Mai Hotel* (☎ 852670; four rooms) is a new place. All rooms cost US$13 and have air-con plus cold-water bath. However, the toilets are outside, which makes it not really worth the price.

The *Khai Hoan Hotel* (☎ 852254; 25 rooms), 239 Phuong Thanh St, is a new place and a good one. All rooms come with attached bath and toilet. Prices for rooms with fan/air-con are US$7/14.

The *Sao Mai Hotel* (☎ 852740; 25 rooms) is brand new and very nice. It's south of the floating bridge, about 800m before the bus station. Rooms with fan/air-con are US$7/16. Every room has its own private bath and toilet, a rarity in Ha Tien. The one disadvantage is that all rooms have one large double bed – of course, it's no problem if you're by yourself or don't mind sharing a bed.

## Places to Eat

Ha Tien's speciality is an unusual variety of coconut which can only be found in Cambodia and this part of Vietnam. These coconuts are unique in that they contain no milk, but the delicate flesh is delicious. Restaurants all around the Ha Tien area serve the coconut flesh in a glass with ice and sugar. The Cambodians have long claimed that any place which has these coconuts is part of Cambodia – this served as one of the excuses for Khmer Rouge attacks on this part of Vietnam.

The *Xuan Thanh Restaurant* is opposite the market on the corner of Ben Tran Hau and Tham Tuong Sanh Sts. This place has the best food in town and the most salubrious surroundings.

There is a whole collection of small cafes on Ben Tran Hau St adjacent to the floating bridge. These places can do the usual noodle and rice dishes.

The *Khach San Du Lich* has a basic restaurant but it is not especially recommended.

## Getting There & Away

**Bus** Buses from Saigon to Ha Tien leave from the Mien Tay bus station in An Lac; the trip takes nine to 10 hours.

Ha Tien bus station (Ben Xe Ha Tien) is on the other side of the floating toll bridge from the centre of town. Buses leave from here to An Giang Province, Cantho (at 5.50 am and 9.10 am), Vinh Long Province, Saigon (at 2 am) and Rach Gia (five times a day). The bus trip from Rach Gia to Ha Tien takes about five hours.

**Car** Ha Tien is 92km from Rach Gia, 95km from Chau Doc, 206km from Cantho and 338km from Ho Chi Minh City.

**Boat** Passenger ferries dock at the ferry terminal, which is not far from the To Chau Hotel next to the floating bridge. Daily ferries depart for Chau Doc at 7 am. You can travel by boat all the way from Saigon to Ha Tien with a change of boats in Chau Doc, but

it's a long journey and the boats are anything but luxurious.

## AROUND HA TIEN
### Beaches

The beaches in this part of Vietnam face the Gulf of Thailand. The water is incredibly warm and calm, like a placid lake. They're good for bathing and diving, but hopeless for surfing.

Mui Nai (Stag's Head Peninsula) is 4km west of Ha Tien; it is said to resemble the head of a stag with its mouth pointing upward. On top is a lighthouse; there are sand beaches on both sides of the peninsula. Mui Nai is accessible by road from both the town of Ha Tien and from Thach Dong Cave Pagoda.

No Beach (Bai No), lined with coconut palms, is several kilometres west of Ha Tien near a fishing village. Bang Beach (Bai Bang) is a long stretch of dark sand shaded by *bang* trees.

### Mo So Grotto

About 17km towards Rach Gia from Ha Tien and 3km from the road, Mo So Grotto consists of three large rooms and a labyrinth of tunnels. The cave is accessible on foot during the dry season and by small boat during the wet season. Visitors should have torches (flashlights) and a local guide.

### Hang Tien Grotto

Hang Tien Grotto, 25km towards Rach Gia from Ha Tien, served as a hide-out for Nguyen Anh (later Emperor Gia Long) in 1784, when he was being pursued by the Tay Son Rebels. His fighters found zinc coins buried here, a discovery which gave the cave its name, which means Coin Grotto. Hang Tien Grotto is accessible by boat.

### Hon Giang Island

Hon Giang Island, which is about 15km from Ha Tien and can be reached by small boat, has a lovely, secluded beach. There are numerous other islands off the coast between Rach Gia and the Cambodian border. Some local people make a living gathering precious *salangane*, or swifts' nests (the most important ingredient of that famous Chinese delicacy bird's-nest soup), on the islands' rocky cliffs.

## HON CHONG

This small and secluded beach resort has the most scenic stretch of coastline in the Mekong Delta region. The big attractions here are Chua Hang Grotto, Duong Beach and Nghe Island.

Given the fact that this is the only real beach resort in the entire delta area, you would think that nobody would even consider wrecking it with a horrible industrial development project. Unfortunately, that is exactly what is happening.

A new cement factory was opened in 1995 just 5km from Duong Beach. As if that wasn't bad enough, soon thereafter workers at the cement factory erected ugly huts all along the coastline completely obliterating the view. Only a small section of the beach has been spared, and just wait, they'll get that too.

Yes, we do know that cement production is important to Vietnam's economic development. The great pity is that it would have been little trouble to locate the cement factory close to the older existing one at Kien Luong, thus leaving the rest of the area unspoiled.

At the time of writing, yet a third cement factory was under construction half-way between Duong Beach and Kien Luong.

### Chua Hang Grotto

The grotto is entered through a Buddhist temple set against the base of a hill. The temple is called Hai Son Tu (Sea Mountain Temple). Visitors light joss sticks and offer prayers here before entering the grotto itself, whose entrance is behind the altar. Inside is a plaster statue of Quan The Am Bo Tat (the Goddess of Mercy). The thick stalactites are hollow and resonate like bells when tapped.

### Duong Beach

The beach (Bai Duong) is next to Chua Hang Grotto and is named for its *duong* trees. Although easily the prettiest beach in the Mekong Delta, don't expect powdery white sand. The waters around the delta contain heavy concentrations of silt (and recently cement dust), so the beach tends to be hard packed. Still, the water is reasonably clear here and this is the only beach south of Saigon (excluding those on Phu Quoc Island) that looks appealing for swimming. The beach is known for its spectacular sunsets.

Recently, a lot of new hotels, restaurants and karaoke megaphones have invaded the beach. Don't come here expecting blissful tranquillity.

From the southern end of the beach (near Chua Hang Grotto), you can see Father & Son Isle (Hon Phu Tu) several hundred metres offshore; it is said to be shaped like a father embracing his son. The island, a column of stone, is perched on a 'foot' worn away by the pounding of the waves; the foot is almost fully exposed at low tide.

### Nghe Island

If the cement plant is allowed to open and proves to be the horror that we anticipate, your only real escape will be a boat trip to Nghe Island. This is the most beautiful island in the area, and is a favourite pilgrimage spot for Buddhists. The island contains a cave temple (Chua Hang) next to a large statue of Quan The Am Bo Tat (the Goddess of Mercy), which faces the sea. The area where you'll find the cave temple and statue is called Doc Lau Chuong.

Finding a boat to the island is not too difficult, though it will be much cheaper if you can round up a group to accompany you. Ngha Nhi Hon Tren, one of the hotels at Duong Beach, can arrange a boat trip. This costs US$40 for the full day, and the boat can accommodate 10 persons. The boat ride to the island takes approximately one to two hours.

**Places to Stay** A word of warning: The few hotels all pack out completely when Buddhists go to worship 15 days before Tet and one month after Tet. There is another worship deluge in March and April.

Consider staying at the *Hon Tren Guesthouse* (Nha Nghi Hon Tren; ☎ 854331; 12 rooms). This place is right on the beach and features rooms in a large beach bungalow for US$8. The staff can prepare meals on request, and the manager speaks English.

The *Phuong Thao Hotel* (☎ 854357) is also bungalow style and costs the same as the Hon Tren Guesthouse.

The *An Thuan Hotel* (Nha Tro An Thuan) and *Huong Bien Hotel* (Nha Tro Huong Bien) are both at the beach right near the entrance gate. The cost here is US$7 to US$15.

The *Cong Doan Hotel* (☎ 854332; fax 854338; 34 rooms) is closer to the cement plant, but is a fine place to stay. It's a very quiet place in a large compound surrounded by a wall with gardens inside. All rooms have attached private bath. In the old wing, rooms are really grotty but cheap at US$6 to US$8. Rooms in the new wing are positively luxurious and cost US$16.

**Places to Eat** Aside from special orders prepared at your hotel, there are food stalls just by the entrance of Chua Hang Grotto. For a few dollars, you can point to one of their live chickens, which will be summarily executed and barbecued right on the spot.

This is also a another good place to sample the delicious Ha Tien coconuts, which only grow in this part of Vietnam.

**Getting There & Away** Chua Hang Grotto and Duong Beach are 32km towards Rach Gia from Ha Tien. The access road branches off the Rach Gia-Ha Tien highway at the small town of Ba Hon, which is just west of the cement factory at Kien Luong. Buses can drop you off at Ba Hon, from where you can hire a motorbike.

## PHU QUOC ISLAND

Mountainous and forested Phu Quoc Island (population 55,000) is in the Gulf of Thailand, 45km west of Ha Tien and 15km south of the coast of Cambodia. This tear-shaped island, which is 48km long and has an area of 1320 sq km, is ringed with some of the most incredibly beautiful beaches in Vietnam. There are fantastic views of underwater marine life through the transparent blue-green waters.

Phu Quoc is claimed by Cambodia; its Khmer name is usually rendered Ko Tral. Needless to say, the Vietnamese view it differently, and to this end have built a substantial military base at the southern end of the island. Phu Quoc is governed as a district of Vietnam's Kien Giang Province.

Phu Quoc Island served as a base of operations for the French missionary Pigneau de Behaine from the 1760s to the 1780s. Prince Nguyen Anh, later Emperor Gia Long, was sheltered here by Behaine when he was being hunted by the Tay Son Rebels.

During the American War there was a little fighting here, but Phu Quoc Island was mainly useful to the Americans as a prison for captured Viet Cong.

Phu Quoc is not really part of the Mekong Delta, and doesn't share the delta's extraordinary ability to produce rice. The most valuable crop is black pepper, but the islanders have traditionally earned their living from the sea. Phu Quoc is also famous in Vietnam for its production of high-quality *nuoc mam* (fish sauce).

One other thing the island is known for are the Phu Quoc hunting dogs. The dogs have been a great success – with their help, the islanders have decimated most of the island's wildlife.

Phu Quoc has tremendous tourism potential, so far mostly unrealised. Transport difficulties and lack of hotel space have kept visitors away. A secondary problem is that some of the best beaches are occupied by a military base.

Rather than developing this island for tourism, the national government in Hanoi has announced a half-baked plan to turn Phu Quoc into 'another Singapore'. In other words, skyscrapers, high-tech industries and a container port are envisioned. The government's reasoning is that Singapore and Phu Quoc are both tropical islands and both are about

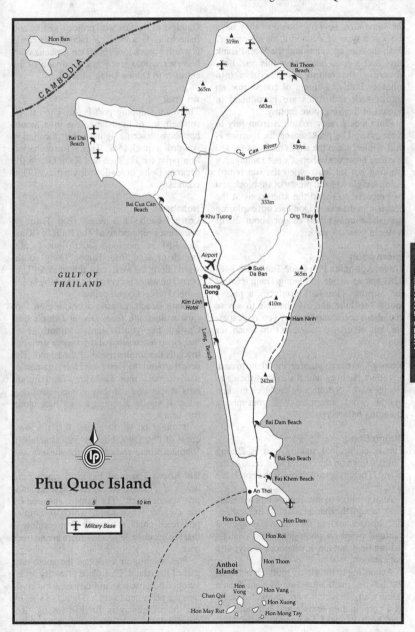

CAMBODIA

Hon Ban

319m

Bai Thom
Beach

365m

683m

Bai Dai
Beach

Cua Can River

539m

Bai Bung

333m

Bai Cua Can
Beach

Khu Tuong

Ong Thay

GULF OF
THAILAND

Airport

Suoi
Da Ban

365m

Duong
Dong

Kim Linh
Hotel

410m

Ham Ninh

Long Beach

242m

Bai Dam Beach

Bai Sao Beach

Bai Khem Beach

An Thoi

Phu Quoc Island

0        5        10 km

✛ Military Base

Hon Dua

Hon Dam

Hon Roi

Hon Thom

Anthoi
Islands

Hon
Vong

Hon Vang

Chan Qui

Hon Xuong

Hon May Rut

Hon Mong Tay

the same size, so why shouldn't they have the same type of economic development? Both the Singaporeans and the World Bank have had a good laugh over this one. Less absurdly, the island could evolve into 'another Bali', assuming of course that no smokestack industries are introduced in pursuit of the Singapore fantasy.

Phu Quoc's rainy season is from July to November. The peak season for tourism is mid-winter, when the sky is blue and the sea is calm; however, when it's not raining, it's stinking hot (at least when the sun is up). Bring sunglasses and plenty of sunblock and be prepared to spend the afternoons at the beach or in the shade. Don't set out exploring the island unless you've got about 2L of water in your daypack.

### Information
**Travel Agencies** Phu Quoc Tourist (☎ 846-028) has an office in Duong Dong, east of the airport. The staff produces a glossy tourist brochure and may be able to advise you about accommodation if you're desperate, but otherwise they can't do much for you.

**Money** There is no place on the island to cash travellers cheques and it's even difficult to change cash US dollars on the black market. In other words, take care of all your money changing before you arrive.

### Duong Dong
The island's chief fishing port is Duong Dong, a town on the central west coast of the island. The airport and most of the hotels are here.

As for things to see, the town is not stunning, though the market is mildly interesting. The bridge next to the market is a good vantage point to photograph the island's fishing fleet, but the tiny harbour is anything but clean.

According to the glossy tourist brochures, the town's main attraction is Cau Castle (Dinh Cau). In fact, it's not so much a castle as a combination temple and lighthouse. It was built in 1937 to honour Thien Hau,

Goddess of the Sea who protects sailors and fisherfolk. As a tourist attraction, the castle is worth a quick look, but it isn't spectacular; however, it does give you a good view of the entrance to Duong Dong's harbour.

### An Thoi
The main shipping port is An Thoi at the southern tip of the island. The town is not blessed with scenic sights, though the market is worth a quick look. This is the embarkation point for Ha Tien and Rach Gia in the Mekong Delta, or for day trips to the An Thoi Islands.

### Beaches
**Long Beach** This beach (Bai Truong), sometimes referred to as Tau Ru Bay (Khoe Tau Ru), is one long (20km) spectacular stretch of sand from Duong Dong southwards along the west coast almost to An Thoi port. The water is crystal clear and the beach is lined with coconut palms.

Long Beach is easily accessible on foot (just walk south from Duong Dong's Cau Castle), but you'll want a motorbike or bicycle to reach some of the remote stretches towards the southern end of the island. The beach around the Kim Linh Hotel is a particularly popular spot. There are a few bamboo huts where you can buy drinks, but bring water if you're planning a long hike along this beach.

It might be worth noting that the west coast of Phu Quoc has the only beaches in Vietnam where you can see the sunset.

**Bai Khem** The most beautiful white sand beach of all is Bai Khem (Bai Kem), meaning 'cream beach'. The name is inspired by the creamy white sand, which resembles powdered chalk. The only shortcoming is that the beach lacks shade – there are no trees here.

The beach is in a cove at the south-east part of the island. This place is totally undeveloped because it's a military area, but civilians are permitted to enter. There is a sign by the main highway in English saying 'Restricted Area – No Trespassing', but you can

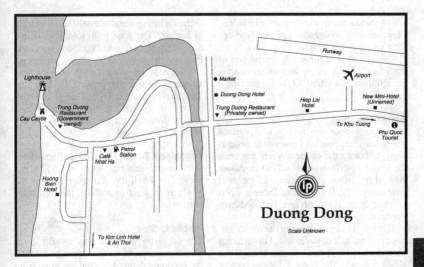

Duong Dong

Scale Unknown

MEKONG DELTA

go in anyway. Follow the dirt track for 1km until you come to a gate – if the gate is open then you can go in. If the gate is closed and a soldier is on duty, this means that the area is currently closed for military exercises and you cannot enter. It's 25km from Duong Dong and 5km from An Thoi, so you'll almost certainly have to go there by motorbike or bicycle. About 100m before the beach is a small stream – it's easy to cross on foot but difficult to get the motorbike across so you may have to park the bike and walk. While walking 100m is no great hardship, you should try to lock the bike securely since you won't be able to watch it; however, bike theft is not a big problem in this remote spot.

The government is considering a foreign joint-venture proposal to build a 150-room luxury tourist resort hotel here. If this comes to pass, it's fair to say the Bai Khem will experience some dramatic changes. It's anticipated that this resort will open by the year 2000, but construction had not even commenced at the time of writing.

**Bai Sao & Bai Dam** Along the south-east part of the island just north of Bai Khem are two other beaches, Bai Sao and Bai Dam.

**Bai Cua Can** This is the most accessible beach in the north-west. Bai Cua Can is 11km from Duong Dong, though it's a rather long dusty trip by motorbike.

**Other Beaches** Bai Dai in the far north-west and Bai Tham on the north-east coast are remote beaches and will require a motorbike ride of at least an hour over very bad roads. You can rest assured that neither beach is crowded.

Unfortunately, both are in military areas. However, the military opens these beaches to civilians on Sunday and you must leave your passport with the military receptionist while you're on the base. This is problematic since most hotels insist on taking your passport until you check out. In any event, do not try to sneak onto the beaches – make local inquiries and obey the rules.

**Suoi Da Ban**
Compared with the water-logged Mekong Delta, Phu Quoc has very little surface moisture; however, there are several springs originating in the hills. The most accessible of these is Suoi Da Ban (Stony Surface Stream). Basically, it's a whitewater creek tumbling

across some attractive large granite boulders. There are deep pools and it's pleasant enough for a swim. Bring mosquito repellent.

The stream is in the south-central part of the island. There is no admission charge, though there is a US$0.30 fee for parking a motorbike.

### Forest Reserves

Phu Quoc's poor soil and lack of surface water has disappointed farmers for generations, although the farmers' grief has been the island's environmental salvation. About 90% of the island is forested, and the trees now enjoy official protection. Indeed, this is the last large stand of forest in southern Vietnam.

The forest is most dense in the mountainous northern half of the island. This area has been declared a Forest Reserve (Khu Rung Nguyen Sinh). You'll need a motorbike or mountain bike to get into the reserve. There are a few primitive dirt roads, but you won't see many vehicles. There are no real hiking trails, and English-speaking guides are nonexistent.

### The An Thoi Islands

Off the southern tip of Phu Quoc are the tiny An Thoi Islands (Quan Dao An Thoi). These 15 islands and islets can be visited by chartered boat, and it's a fine area for sightseeing, fishing, swimming and snorkelling. Hon Thom (Pineapple Island) is about 3km in length and is the largest island in the group. Other islands here include Hon Dua (Coconut Island), Hon Roi (Lamp Island), Hon Vang (Echo Island), Hon May Rut (Cold Cloud Island), Hon Dam (Shadow Island), Chan Qui (Yellow Tortoise) and Hon Mong Tay (Short Gun Island).

The boats all depart from An Thoi, but you can make arrangements through hotels in Duong Dong. One chap at the Kim Linh Hotel was charging US$14 per person, including transport to/from the boat pier.

### Coconut Prison

Being an island and a marginal economic backwater of Vietnam, Phu Quoc was useful to the French colonial administration chiefly as a prison. The Americans took over where the French left off, and Phu Quoc was used to house about 40,000 Viet Cong prisoners.

The island's main penal colony was known as the Coconut Prison (Nha Lao Cay Dua) and is near An Thoi. Though it's considered an historic site, it's still used as a prison. Not too surprisingly, few visitors come to check it out.

**Organised Tours** The Huong Bien Hotel sells pricey minibus tours – US$18 per person for a half-day. Compared with what you can do on a motorbike, this is hardly worth it.

### Places to Stay

The local government was caught completely unprepared for the tourist boom, and the accommodation situation has gone from bad to worse. Although some new hotels are under construction, they are inadequate to meet the sharply rising demand. For the next few years at least, Phu Quoc is likely to suffer from a continuing shortage of hotel rooms during the peak season. To make matters worse, the local government is mostly constructing upmarket hotels, which means budget travellers are not even being considered.

The situation could be greatly alleviated if the government would allow local villagers to rent rooms in their homes to foreigners; however, at present this is not permitted. A suggestion by one visitor that the now-defunct Saigon Floating Hotel be towed to Phu Quoc was simply laughed off by the local tourism authorities.

The *Huong Bien Hotel* (☎ 846050; 75 rooms) is on the west side of Duong Dong right on the beach. The hotel's name means 'fragrant sea', probably a reference to the sewerage discharged from the nearby Duong Dong fishing harbour. Nevertheless, the hotel is the biggest place in town and is the pride and joy of Phu Quoc Tourist (the government-owned travel agency). The 25 rooms in the old building cost US$9 with fan only, or US$15 to US$20 with air-con. The price for the 50 rooms in the new building had not been decided at the time of writing (the building was not yet open but will be shortly). The new annexe is rated three stars, so we would guess around US$30 to US$50 per room.

The *Kim Linh Hotel* (☎ 846611; 13 rooms) is 4km south of Duong Dong. It's a lovely privately owned place right on a palm-studded beach. It remains the favourite of backpackers and is always full, but the management has tried to accommodate the overflow by renting tents and allowing people to sleep on hammocks in the restaurant after it closes. Rooms cost US$11 with fan or US$15 with air-con. There are plans to build some beach bungalows soon, but no word on prices yet. Finding the hotel is a bit of a challenge as there is no sign to mark the turn-off from the highway. Heading south of Duong Dong, look at the numbers on the telephone poles. Between pole Nos 54 and 55 is a path, also identifiable by the two adjacent tombs (one black and one white). Follow this path half a kilometre down to the beach.

The *Hiep Loi Hotel* (☎ 846363; 12 rooms) is a private mini-hotel in Duong Dong about 50m from the airport. Rooms cost US$10.

*Cafe Nhat Ha* (☎ 846281) is indeed a cafe but there are three rooms for rent upstairs at US$8 per room. If you telephone, ask for Miss Kim, as she's the only one who can speak English. The cafe is a short distance to the west of the bridge in central Duong Dong.

The *Duong Dong Hotel* (Khach San Duong Dong) is almost right inside the Duong Dong Market. Rooms are dark boxes, windowless and air-free, but the management is friendly and the location is definitely central. Double rooms have shared bath only and cost US$6.

Although few travellers care to stay in An Thoi (no beach), it's worth considering if you arrive late on the ferry or will be taking the ferry early next morning. The only place in town is the *Thanh Dat Guesthouse* (Nha Khach Thanh Dat; ☎ 844022; seven rooms), though many locals only know its old name

(Nha Khach Phuong Tham). Rooms cost US$6 to US$8 and there is even a dormitory at US$2 per person. Rooms have attached private bath, though only with cold water.

There is another brand-new hotel with no name stuck out in the middle of a swamp about 5km from Duong Dong. There is no beach, no restaurants and no reason why anyone would want to stay here. Since the building is white, we'd like to name it the *White Elephant Hotel*. Despite the hotel shortage, it had no guests. No other information is available – even the staff didn't know the room prices or phone number.

The *Army Hotel* is affectionately known as the 'Hotel from Hell' by backpackers. When everything else is full you might be brought here. It's so bad even the soldiers won't stay here. The beds have no mattresses. The toilets … you don't want to know.

The *Duong To Guesthouse* (Nha Khach Duong To) is a big joke – don't stay! It's 11km south of town and some of the rip-off motorbike drivers try to take you here just to charge you for the long ride. The place is locked and it's doubtful anybody can stay.

## Places to Eat

The restaurant at the *Kim Linh Hotel* wins hands down. There is an English menu, the staff speak both English and French, and the outdoor setting under the palm trees is seductively romantic.

The restaurant at the *Huong Bien Hotel* west of Duong Dong will keep you from starving, but that's about the best we can say for it. Half the dishes on the menu do not exist and the rest are very much geared towards local tastes. There is an English menu, though the staff only speak Vietnamese.

The only classy restaurant in central Duong Dong is the *Trung Duong Restaurant*. The menu is in English (no prices!) and the style of cooking is very Vietnamese. There is another restaurant next to the Cau Castle on the west side of town, but it is government-owned and not so good.

*Cafe Nhat Ha* on the west side of Duong Dong has simple food and not much English spoken, but it is a friendly place to relax.

There are heaps of cheap food stalls all around the centre of Duong Dong.

## Getting There & Away

**Air** Vietnam Airlines offers daily service between Saigon and Duong Dong, Phu Quoc's main town. There is also on-again/off-again air service between Phu Quoc and Rach Gia in the Mekong Delta.

**Boat** All passenger ferries departing and arriving at Phu Quoc use the port of An Thoi on the southern tip of the island.

There are ferries every morning between Rach Gia and Phu Quoc, a 140km trip. Departures are in the morning between 7.30 and 9 am, but it varies somewhat due to the tides. The fare is US$5 and the ride takes up to 10 hours. The boat cannot dock at Rach Gia when the tide is low – passengers and cargo have to be ferried offshore in a small shuttle boat, and this wastes quite a bit of time.

There is another boat every two days connecting Phu Quoc and Ha Tien. This boat only takes four hours (if you're lucky) and the fare is US$3.

Neither boat is very comfortable. Both are too small for comfort and often packed with too many passengers and cargo. Although we haven't heard of any mishaps, neither looks particularly safe.

## Getting Around

**The Airport** Phu Quoc's airport is almost in central Duong Dong. Unless your luggage is heavy, you an easily walk the few hundred metres to the centre of town. However, most of the hotels are somewhat farther, and here is where you must exercise caution. The motorbike drivers at the airport are not particularly honest and some are outright crooks. It's not just that they will overcharge you – they will take you to all the hotels they know are already full. They check beforehand which hotels have empty rooms and carefully avoid those, carting you from hotel to hotel, each time adding more to the fare. So what started out as US$1 is now US$5 or more and you still don't have a hotel room. The airport motorbikes are always more expensive than those you'll find in central Duong Dong, so it may be worth the 300m walk.

**Bus** There is a skeletal bus service between An Thoi and Duong Dong. Buses run perhaps once every hour or two. There is a bus waiting for the ferry at An Thoi to take passengers to Duong Dong, and the fare is US$0.80.

**Motorbike** You'll hardly have to look for the motorbikes – they'll be looking for you. The market area has particularly rich pickings. Some polite bargaining may be necessary. For most short runs within the town itself, US$0.50 should be sufficient. Otherwise, figure around US$0.80 for about 5km. From Duong Dong to An Thoi should cost you about US$3.

Self-drive motorbike rentals are available for US$11 per day. Add about another US$5 if you want a driver. This should be sufficient to get you anywhere on the island. If interested, just ask at your hotel.

There are no paved roads on the island, and after a day of motorbiking you can expect to be covered head to toe with dust.

**Bicycle** If you can ride a bicycle in the tropical heat over these bad roads, more power to you. Bicycle rentals are available through the hotels for about US$1 per day.

# Central Highlands

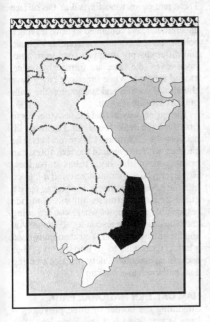

The Central Highlands cover the southern part of the Truong Son Mountain Range (Annamite Cordillera) and include the provinces of Lam Dong, Dak Lak (Dac Lac), Gia Lai and Kon Tum. The region, which is home to many ethno-linguistic minority groups (Montagnards), is renowned for its cool climate, beautiful mountain scenery and innumerable streams, lakes and waterfalls.

Although the population of the Central Highlands is only about two million, the area has always been considered strategically important. During the American War, considerable fighting took place around Buon Ma Thuot, Pleiku and Kon Tum.

With the exception of Lam Dong Province (in which Dalat is located), the Central Highlands was, until 1992, closed to foreigners. Even westerners with legitimate business in the area were arrested and sent back to Saigon. This extreme sensitivity stemmed partly from the limited nature of central government control of remote areas, as well as a concern that secret 're-education camps' (rumoured to be hidden in the region) would be discovered and publicised.

The situation has changed. Most of the Central Highlands is open to foreigners now. However, travel permits are still needed for certain areas.

## Southern Region

### LANGA LAKE
The Saigon-Dalat road (National Highway 20) spans this reservoir, which is crossed by a bridge (see the Around HCMC map). Lots of floating houses can be seen here, all built since 1991. The whole point behind living in a floating house is to harvest the fish underneath. It's a very scenic spot for photography, although the local children have become very pushy beggars because foreigners have been feeding them candy.

Most tourist minibuses on the Saigon-Dalat road make a 10 minute stop at Langa Lake.

### DINH QUAN VOLCANOES
There are volcanic craters near the obscure town of Dinh Quan on Highway 20 (see the Around HCMC map) All three volcanoes are now extinct, but are nonetheless very impressive. The craters date from the late Jurassic period, about 150 million years ago.

You can't see the craters from the highway – you have to do a little walking. One crater is on the left-hand side of the road as you head towards Dalat, at highway marker 112km. On the right-hand side of the road, closer to Dinh Quan at highway marker 118km, is another crater. Guides can be hired cheaply in Dinh Quan.

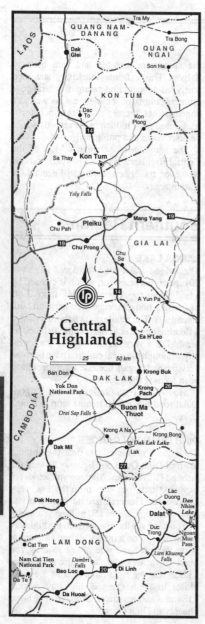

Central Highlands

0    25    50 km

## LAVA TUBES

A little bit beyond the volcanic craters in the direction of Dalat are underground lava tubes. These rare caves were formed as the surface lava cooled and solidified, while the hotter underground lava continued to flow, leaving a hollow space. Lava tubes are rare in Vietnam and differ sharply in appearance from limestone caves (the latter are formed by underground springs). While limestone caves have abundant stalactites and stalagmites, the walls of lava caves are smooth.

The easiest way to find the lava tubes is to first find the teak forest on Highway 20 between the 120km and 124km markers. The children who live around the teak forest can point you to the lava tubes entrances. However, you are strongly advised *not* to go into the tubes by yourself. It's best to have a guide and, furthermore, inform someone responsible who knows where you are going and who can call the rescue squad should you and the guide disappear. You absolutely need a torch (flashlight) to go into the lava tubes and it's an essential safety practice to bring a second torch as a backup.

## NAM CAT TIEN NATIONAL PARK

Straddling the border of three provinces – Lam Dong, Dong Nai and Song Be – this new national park is only 240km from Saigon. Nam Cat Tien was hit hard with defoliants during the American War, but the large old-growth trees survived and the smaller plants have recovered. Just as importantly, the wildlife has made a comeback. The area is said to be the home of the Javan rhino, considered the rarest mammal in existence. Another rare creature found here is a type of wild ox called gaur. The jungles here support a healthy population of monkeys and plentiful birds. On occasion, leopards can be spotted.

Elephants also live in the park, but their presence has caused some controversy. In the early 1990s, the area just outside of Nam Cat Tien was visited by a herd of 10 hungry elephants. In search of food, the creatures fell into an abandoned bomb crater left over from the American War. Local villagers took pity on the elephants and proceeded to dig a ramp to rescue them. For their efforts, 28 villagers have so far been killed by the ungrateful beasts, who have been on a rampage ever since. The problem could have been simply dealt with by shooting the elephants, but the Vietnamese government wasn't willing to risk the wrath of international environmental organisations. However, none of these organisations ever came up with the funds for relocating the elephants and they were finally removed to zoos. In the longer term, such conflicts will likely be repeated – with Vietnam's increasing population, the competition between people and wildlife for the same living space is likely to increase.

### Getting There & Away

Nam Cat Tien National Park is still an undeveloped area and access is difficult. The most common approach is from National Highway 20, which connects Dalat with Saigon. To reach the park, you have to follow a dirt road which branches west from Highway 20. Another approach is to take a boat across Langa Lake and then hike from there. Dalat Tourist has so far ignored the area, which would normally be a blessing except that you do really need a guide if you want to trek in this remote spot.

It's not absolutely necessary to approach the park from the Dalat side. A third entrance to Nam Cat Tien is via Buon Ma Thuot. Unfortunately, this route puts you into Dak Lak Province, where the authorities are a problem. Basically, you will be forced to deal with Dak Lak Tourist, Buon Ma Thuot's government tourist agency. They ask US$200 per day for a jeep, guide and driver (all three required). The guides in Buon Ma Thuot often do not speak English, do not know the area and have a tendency to get totally lost.

---

### FULRO

FULRO (Front Unifié de Lutte des Races Opprimées, or the United Front for the Struggle of the Oppressed Races) was for decades a continuing thorn in the side for the Vietnamese government. FULRO is a band of well-organised guerrillas who were supported by France and later by America, Thailand and China. FULRO's recruits came mainly from Montagnards, who had no love for the Vietnamese majority. Even the old South Vietnamese government suppressed the Montagnards, but the Americans recognised their valuable skills in jungle survival. As fighters, FULRO was far more effective than troops directly under the control of the Saigon government.

Needless to say, when the Communists took over they sought retribution against FULRO rather than attempting to make peace. This may have been a mistake, because FULRO guerrillas did not simply lay down their weapons and submit to 're-education'. They continued their insurrection for years.

When the Communists took over in 1975, FULRO's fighters numbered around 10,000. In just four years, over 8000 were killed or captured. Some were killed by the Khmer Rouge when they crossed into Cambodia. Ironically, when Vietnam invaded Cambodia in 1979 to battle the Khmer Rouge, FULRO benefited – the Khmer Rouge started supplying FULRO with weapons and ammunition which were obtained from China.

By the mid-1980s, FULRO was considered a spent force, with most of its guerrilla bands either dead, captured, living abroad or having given up the fight. However, in 1992, a band of several hundred FULRO adherents was found to be still living in the remote north-eastern corner of Cambodia (Ratanakiri Province) and conducting raids across the border into Vietnam. At the urging of their exiled comrades, the remaining guerrillas surrendered to the Vietnamese government and were flown under UN supervision to the USA.

The insurrection issue would seem to be dead and buried, but the Vietnamese government is still hyper-sensitive about FULRO. Government guides will not answer any questions about the organisation other than to assure travellers that now it's 'perfectly safe' to visit former FULRO areas. Contrary to the far north, where minorities are left alone, the government keeps a very tight grip on the Montagnards of the Central Highlands. Hanoi's policies in this region include: 1) populating the highlands with ethnic-Vietnamese settlers, especially in New Economic Zones; 2) encouraging the replacement of traditional slash-and-burn agriculture with sedentary farming; 3) promoting Vietnamese language and culture (Vietnamisation). ■

Some travel agencies in Saigon have periodically offered customised tours to Nam Cat Tien. However, the tours do not depart on any fixed schedule and good guides are hard to find.

## BAO LOC

The town of Bao Loc (also known as B'Lao; elevation 850m) is a convenient place to break the trip between Saigon and Dalat. Highway 20 is called Tran Phu St as it passes through town. Tea, mulberry leaves (for the silkworm industry) and silk are the major local industries.

For a while after reunification, this area was placed under an 8 pm to dawn curfew because of the FULRO insurgency.

### Bay Tung Falls

The trail to the Bay Tung Falls (Thac Bay Tung, which means Seven Steps) begins 7km towards Saigon from the Bao Loc Hotel along Highway 20 (and 3km from the Dai Lao Bridge over the Dai Binh River). The trailhead is in Ap Dai Lao, a hamlet in the village of Xa Loc Chau, behind a refreshments shop run by Ba Hai. The shop is on the right as you travel towards Saigon.

Suoi Mo (the Stream of Dreaming) is 400m west of Ba Hai's place along a path that passes among wood and thatch houses set amid tea bushes, coffee trees and banana and pineapple plants. The path veers left at the stream and becomes tortuously slippery as it makes its way along the bamboo and fern-lined bank. The first cascade is about 100m straight ahead. Several of the pools along Suoi Mo are swimmable, but the water is of uncertain purity.

### Bao Loc Church

Bao Loc Church is several hundred metres towards Dalat along the highway from the Bao Loc Hotel. There is an old Shell filling station across the road. Masses are held on Sundays.

### Tea Factories

If you've ever wondered how tea is prepared, you might try getting someone to show you around one of Bao Loc's tea-processing plants. The largest is Nha May Che 19/5, which is 2km towards Dalat from the Bao Loc Hotel. The factory, which produces tea for export, is on the top of a low hill next to a modern yellow water tower. The second-largest tea factory is named 28/3. A joint Vietnamese and Soviet concern named Vietso (formerly Bisinée) is another place where you might inquire.

### Places to Stay

The *Bao Loc Hotel* (☎ 864107; fax 828330) is at 795 Tran Phu St. It was built in 1940, but has had a recent (and badly needed) renovation. Twins are US$12 to US$15. About 800m south of the Bao Loc Hotel on the main highway is the *Hong Hoang Mini-Hotel*, which has rooms for US$10 to US$20.

### Getting There & Away

**Bus** The bus station is 2km from the Bao Loc Hotel.

**Car** Bao Loc is 177km north-east of Saigon, 49km west of Di Linh and 131km south-west of Dalat.

## DAMBRI FALLS

This is one of the highest (90m) and most magnificent waterfalls in Vietnam that is easily accessible. The views are positively breathtaking – the walk up the steep path to the top of the falls will almost certainly take your breath away.

Dambri Falls is close to Bao Loc in an area inhabited chiefly by Montagnards. Near Bao Loc, you turn off the main highway and follow a dirt road for 15km. As you're driving this road towards the falls, the high peak off to your right is May Bay Mountain.

Foreigners pay an admission fee of US$1 to visit the falls. By way of compensation, the *Dambri Restaurant*, which adjoins the car park, is cheap and good.

## DI LINH

The town of Di Linh (pronounced 'zeeling'), also known as Djiring, is 1010m above sea level. The area's main product is tea, which is grown on giant plantations founded by the French and now run by the government. The Di Linh Plateau, sometimes compared to the Cameron Highlands of Malaysia, is a great place for day hikes. Only a few decades ago, the region was famous for its tiger hunting.

### Bo Bla Waterfall

The 32m-high Bo Bla Waterfall is 7km west of town.

### Getting There & Away

Di Linh is 226km north-east of Saigon and 82km south-west of Dalat on the main Saigon-Dalat highway. The town is 96km from Phan Thiet by a secondary road.

## WATERFALLS
### Pongour Falls

Pongour Falls, the largest in the Dalat area, is about 55km towards Saigon from Dalat and 7km off the highway. During the rainy season, the falls form a full semicircle.

### Gougah Falls

Gougah Falls is approximately 40km from Dalat towards Saigon. It is only 500m from the highway and is easily accessible.

### Lien Khuong Falls

At Lien Khuong Falls, the Dan Nhim River, 100m wide at this point, drops 15m over an outcrop of volcanic rock. The site, which can be seen from the highway, is 35km towards Saigon from Dalat. Lien Khuong Falls is not far from Lien Khuong airport.

Lien Khuong Falls is not just one, but a number of falls close to the road which are very nice to climb around in. There is a waterfall where you can crawl under the rocky outcrop. The falls are not commercialised – there's not even a sign by the road.
**Per Arenmo**

## DAN NHIM LAKE

Dan Nhim Lake (elevation 1042m) was created by a dam built between 1962 and 1964 by Japan as part of its war reparations.

The huge Dan Nhim hydroelectric project supplies electricity to much of the south.

The lake is often used by Saigon movie studios for filming romantic lakeside scenes. The lake's surface area is 9.3 sq km.

The power station is at the western edge of the coastal plain. Water drawn from Dan Nhim Lake gathers speed as it rushes almost a vertical kilometre down from Ngoan Muc Pass in two enormous pipes.

It is said that the forested hills around Dan Nhim Lake are fine for hiking and that there is good fishing in the area. Unfortunately, the local cops are not likely to allow you to wander around without a permit from Dalat Tourist (see the Dalat section for details about travel permits).

### Places to Stay

There is a hotel in Ninh Son, though currently foreigners cannot use it.

### Getting There & Away

Dan Nhim Lake is about 38km from Dalat in the Don Duong District of Lam Dong Province. As you head towards Phan Rang, the dam is about a kilometre to the left of the Dalat-Phan Rang highway. The power station is at the base of Ngoan Muc Pass near the town of Ninh Son.

## NGOAN MUC PASS

Ngoan Muc Pass (altitude 980m), known to the French as Bellevue Pass, is about 5km towards Phan Rang from Dan Nhim Lake and 64km west of Phan Rang. On a clear day, you can see all the way across the coastal plain to the Pacific Ocean, an aerial distance of 55km. As the highway winds down the mountain in a series of switchbacks, it passes under the two gargantuan water pipes – still guarded by armed troops in concrete fortifications – which link Dan Nhim Lake with the hydroelectric power station. To the south of the road (to the right as you face the ocean) you can see the steep tracks of the *crémaillère* (cog railway) linking Thap Cham with Dalat (see the Dalat section for details).

Sites of interest at the top of Ngoan Muc

Pass include a waterfall next to the highway, pine forests and the old Bellevue railway station.

# Dalat Area

## DALAT

The Disneyland of the Central Highlands, Dalat (elevation 1475m) is situated in a temperate region dotted with lakes, waterfalls, evergreen forests and gardens. The cool climate and the park-like environment make this, in some respects, one of the most delightful cities in all of Vietnam. It was once called Le Petit Paris and to this end a miniature replica of the Eiffel Tower is being built behind the central market place. Dalat is by far Vietnam's most popular honeymoon spot. It's also the favourite haunt of Vietnamese artists and avant-garde types who have made this their permanent home. It's also the final word in Vietnamese kitsch.

Local industries include growing garden vegetables and flowers (especially beautiful hydrangea flowers). The flowers and vegies are sold all over southern Vietnam. But the biggest contribution to the economy of Dalat is tourism (over 300,000 domestic tourists visit every year). The downside is that the locals are trying to create circus-style 'tourist attractions', complete with sailboats, mini-zoos, balloons for the kiddies and Vietnamese dressed as bunny rabbits.

The Dalat area was once famous for its big-game hunting and a 1950s brochure boasted that 'a two-hour drive from the town leads to several game-rich areas abounding in deer, roes, peacocks, pheasants, wild boar, black bear, wild caws, panthers, tigers, gaurs and elephants'. So successful were the hunters that all of the big game is now extinct. However, you will get a whiff of Dalat's former glory by viewing some of the 'souvenirs' about town:

What will stick in my mind most is the appalling stuffed animals they seem so fond of in Dalat. These seem to have spread all over Vietnam, but the

Vietnamese (and the citizens of Dalat in particular) have taken taxidermy to new lows. We had a terrible fit of the giggles as we left the Ho Chi Minh Mausoleum in Hanoi when the thought surfaced of what the Dalat animal stuffers could have done with Ho Chi Minh if the stuffing contract hadn't been given to the Russians.

**Tony Wheeler**

The city's population of 125,000 includes about 5000 members of ethno-linguistic hill tribes, of which there are said to be 33 distinct groups in Lam Dong Province. Members of these 'hill tribes' – who still refer to themselves by the French word *montagnards*, meaning 'highlanders' – can often be seen in the market places wearing their traditional dress. Hill tribe women of this area carry their infants on their backs in a long piece of cloth worn over one shoulder and tied in the front.

There is a New Economic Zone (a planned rural settlement where southern refugees and people from the overcrowded north were semi-forcibly resettled after reunification) 14km from Dalat in Lam Ha District; it has a population of about 10,000.

## History

The site of Dalat was 'discovered' in 1897 by Dr Alexandre Yersin (1863-1943), a protégé of Louis Pasteur who was the first person to identify the plague bacillus. The city itself was established in 1912 and quickly became popular with Europeans as a cool retreat from the sweltering heat of the coastal plains and the Mekong Delta. In the local Lat language, Da Lat means the River of the Lat Tribe.

During the American War Dalat was, by the tacit agreement of all parties concerned, largely spared the ravages of war. Indeed, it seems that while South Vietnamese army officers were being trained at the city's Military Academy and affluent officials of the Saigon regime were relaxing in their villas, Viet Cong cadres were doing the same thing not far away in *their* villas. Dalat fell to North Vietnamese forces without a fight on 3 April 1975. There is no problem with left-over mines and ordnance in the Dalat area.

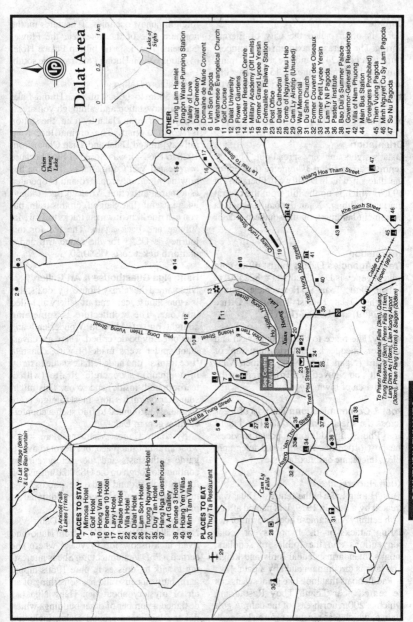

## Dalat Area

0      0.5      1 km

**OTHER**
1  Trung Lam Hamlet
2  Dragon Water-Pumping Station
3  Valley of Love
4  Dalat Cemetery
5  Domaine de Marie Convent
6  Linh Son Pagoda
8  Vietnamese Evangelical Church
11 Golf Course
12 Dalat University
13 Flower Gardens
14 Nuclear Research Centre
15 Military Academy (Off Limits)
18 Former Grand Lycee Yersin
19 Cremaillere Railway Station
23 Post Office
25 Dalat Cathedral
28 Tomb of Nguyen Huu Hao
29 Cam Ly Airstrip (Unused)
30 War Memorial
31 Du Sinh Church
32 Former Couvent des Oiseaux
33 Former Petit Lycee Yersin
34 Lam Ty Ni Pagoda
36 Pasteur Institute
38 Bao Dai's Summer Palace
41 Governor-General's Residence
42 Villa of Nam Phuong
44 Main Bus Station
45 Thien Vuong Pagoda
    (Foreigners Prohibited)
46 Minh Nguyet Cu Sy Lam Pagoda
47 Su Nu Pagoda

**PLACES TO STAY**
7  Mimosa Hotel
9  Golf Hotel
10 Hong Van Hotel
16 Pensee 10 Hotel
17 Lavy Hotel
21 Palace Hotel
22 Villa Hotel
24 Dalat Hotel
26 Lam Son Hotel
27 Truong Nguyen Mini-Hotel
35 Duy Tan Hotel
37 Hang Nga Guesthouse
    & Art Gallery
39 Pensee 3 Hotel
40 Hoang Yen Villas
43 Minh Tam Villas

**PLACES TO EAT**
20 Thuy Ta Restaurant

## Climate

Dalat is often called the City of Eternal Spring. The average maximum daily temperature is a cool 24°C and the average minimum daily temperature is 15°C. The dry season runs from December to March. Even during the rainy season, which lasts more or less from April to November, it is sunny most of the time.

## Orientation

Dalat's sights are very spread out. The city centre is around Rap 3/4 cinema (named for the date on which Dalat was 'liberated' in 1975), which is up the hill from the central market building. Xuan Huong Lake is a prominent landmark on the southern side of town.

## Information

**Travel Agencies** Dalat's tourist office cum travel agency is Dalat Tourist (☎ 822520) at 4 Tran Quoc Toan St. For vehicle rentals, visit the Dalat Tourist Transport Office (☎ 822479) at 9 Le Dai Hanh St.

**Money** The place to change both cash and travellers cheques is the Agriculture Bank of Vietnam (Ngan Hang Nong Nghiep Vietnam). It's on Nguyen Van Troi St right in the central area of town.

**Post & Communications** The post office is across the street from the Dalat Hotel at 14 Tran Phu St. In addition to postal services, the post office has international telegraph, telex, telephone and fax facilities.

## Xuan Huong Lake

Xuan Huong Lake in the centre of Dalat was created by a dam in 1919. It is named after a 17th century Vietnamese poet known for her daring attacks on the hypocrisy of social conventions and the foibles of scholars, monks, mandarins, feudal lords and kings. The lake is circumnavigated by a path.

Paddleboats that look like giant swans can be rented near Thanh Thuy Restaurant, which is 200m north-east of the dam. A golf course, which was recently refurbished with foreign money, occupies 50 hectares on the northern side of the lake near the Flower Gardens. The majestic hilltop Palace Hotel overlooks Xuan Huong Lake from the south.

## Crémaillère Railway

About 500m to the east of Xuan Huong Lake is a railway station and, although you aren't likely to arrive in Dalat by train, the station is worth a visit. The crémaillère (cog railway) linked Dalat and Thap Cham from 1928 to 1964 – it was closed in 1964 because of repeated Viet Cong attacks. The line has now been partially repaired and is operated as a tourist attraction. You can't get to anywhere useful (like Saigon) on this train, but you can ride 8km down the tracks to Trai Mat Village and back again. The fee for this journey is US$3 for the round trip and a platform ticket costs US$0.50.

## Hang Nga Guesthouse & Art Gallery

Nicknamed the 'Crazy House' by locals, this is a guesthouse, cafe and art gallery all rolled into one. The architecture is something straight out of Alice in Wonderland and cannot easily be described. There are caves, giant spider webs made of wire, concrete 'tree trunks', one nude female statue (a rarity in Vietnam), a concrete giraffe (with a tearoom built inside) and so on. This might sound tacky, but it's not – most foreigners are absolutely astounded to find such a counter-cultural gem in Dalat.

By contrast, most Vietnamese are somewhat afraid of the place, but devoted avant-garde enthusiasts and the merely curious continue to cough up the US$0.20 admission fee to look around and take photos. The money gets ploughed back into additional art projects.

The gallery's designer, Mrs Dang Viet Nga (call her 'Hang Nga'), is from Hanoi and lived in Moscow for 14 years, where she earned a PhD in architecture. She is interesting to talk to, dresses in pure 1960s hippie garb, burns incense and has something of an air of mystery about her. Hang Nga has designed a number of other buildings which dot the landscape around Dalat, including

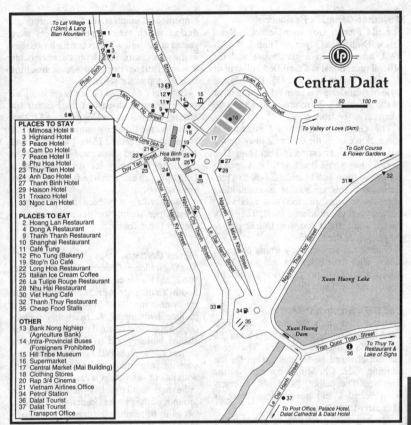

# Central Dalat

**PLACES TO STAY**
1 Mimosa Hotel II
3 Highland Hotel
5 Peace Hotel
6 Cam Do Hotel
7 Peace Hotel II
8 Phu Hoa Hotel
23 Thuy Tien Hotel
24 Anh Dao Hotel
27 Thanh Binh Hotel
29 Haison Hotel
31 Trixaco Hotel
33 Ngoc Lan Hotel

**PLACES TO EAT**
2 Hoang Lan Restaurant
4 Dong A Restaurant
9 Thanh Thanh Restaurant
10 Shanghai Restaurant
11 Café Tung
12 Pho Tung (Bakery)
19 Stop'n Go Café
22 Long Hoa Restaurant
25 Italian Ice Cream Coffee
26 La Tulipe Rouge Restaurant
28 Nhu Hai Restaurant
30 Viet Hung Café
32 Thanh Thuy Restaurant
35 Cheap Food Stalls

**OTHER**
13 Bank Nong Nghiep (Agriculture Bank)
14 Intra-Provincial Buses (Foreigners Prohibited)
15 Hill Tribe Museum
16 Supermarket
17 Central Market (Mai Building)
18 Clothing Stores
20 Rap 3/4 Cinema
21 Vietnam Airlines Office
34 Petrol Station
36 Dalat Tourist
37 Dalat Tourist Transport Office

the Children's Cultural Palace and the Catholic church in Lien Khuong.

The Dalat People's Committee has not always appreciated such innovative designs. An earlier Dalat architectural masterpiece, the 'House with 100 Roofs', was torn down as a 'fire hazard' because the People's Committee thought it looked 'anti-socialist'. However, there is little chance that Hang Nga will have any trouble with the authorities – her father, Truong Chinh, was Ho Chi Minh's successor. He served as Vietnam's second president from 1981 until his death in 1988.

Hang Nga Guesthouse & Art Gallery (☎ 822070) is about 1km south-west of Xuan Huong Lake. The official address 3 Huynh Thuc Khang.

### French District
The area between Rap 3/4 cinema and Phan Dinh Phung St hasn't changed much since the French departed. If, in the year 1934, someone had evacuated a provincial town in France and repopulated it with Vietnamese, this is what it would have looked like 20 years later. This is a delightful area for walking around.

## Governor-General's Residence

The old French Governor-General's Residence (Dinh Toan Quyen, or Dinh 2; ☎ 822-093), now used as a guesthouse and for official receptions, is a dignified building of modernist design built in 1933. The original style of furnishing has been retained in most of the structure's 25 rooms. Shoes must be taken off at the front door.

The Governor-General's Residence is about 2km east of the centre of town up the hill from the intersection of Tran Hung Dao St and Khoi Nghia Bac Son St; it is open to the public from 7 to 11 am and 1.30 to 4 pm. Entrance tickets are sold at an outbuilding (once the servants' quarters) several hundred metres from the residence itself. They may charge you extra if you want to take photographs inside the building.

Guests can stay in the upstairs bedroom suites, with their balconies and huge bathrooms, for US$40 per person per night; for details, contact Dalat Tourist.

## Bao Dai's Summer Palace

Emperor Bao Dai's Summer Palace (Biet Dien Quoc Truong, or Dinh 3) is a tan, 25 room villa constructed in 1933. The decor has not changed in decades except for the addition of Ho Chi Minh's portrait over the fireplace. The palace, filled with artefacts from decades and governments past, is extremely interesting.

The engraved glass map of Vietnam was given to Emperor Bao Dai (born 1913; reigned 1926-45) in 1942 by Vietnamese students in France. In Bao Dai's office, the life-size white bust above the bookcase is of Bao Dai himself; the smaller gold and brown busts are of his father, Emperor Khai Dinh. Note the heavy brass royal seal (on the right) and military seal (on the left). The photographs over the fireplace are of (from left to right) Bao Dai, his eldest son, Bao Long (in uniform), and Empress Nam Phuong, who died in 1963.

Upstairs are the royal living quarters. The room of Bao Long, who now lives in England, is decorated in yellow, the royal colour. The huge semicircular couch was used by the emperor and empress for family meetings, during which their three daughters were seated in the yellow chairs and their two sons in the pink chairs. Check out the ancient tan Rouathermique infra-red sauna machine near the top of the stairs.

Bao Dai's Summer Palace is set in a pine grove 500m south-east of the Pasteur Institute, which is on Le Hong Phong St, 2km south-west of the city centre. The palace is open to the public from 7 to 11 am and 1.30 to 4 pm and shoes must be removed at the door. The entry fee for foreigners is US$1 plus an extra charge for cameras and videos.

Tourists can stay here for US$40 per person per night; for more information, contact Dalat Tourist.

## Flower Gardens

The Dalat Flower Gardens (Vuon Hoa Dalat; ☎ 822151) were established in 1966 by the South Vietnamese Agriculture Service and renovated in 1985. Flowers represented include hydrangeas, fuchsias and orchids *(hoa lan)*. Most of the latter are in special shaded buildings off to the right from the entrance. The orchids are grown in blocks of coconut palm trunk and in terracotta pots with lots of ventilation holes.

Several monkeys live in cages on the grounds of the Flower Gardens – some tourists enjoy tormenting the monkeys by throwing rocks and lit cigarettes, but the monkeys have learned to throw them back.

Near the gate you can buy *cu ly*, reddish-brown animal-shaped pieces of fern stems whose fibres are used to stop bleeding in traditional medicine. One traveller had this to say:

For kitsch, visit the Flower Gardens. I can't describe them, just go there – a marvel!

The Flower Gardens front Xuan Huong Lake at 2 Phu Dong Thien Vuong St, which leads from the lake to Dalat University; they are open from 7.30 am to 4 pm. Ticket sales are suspended for a while around noon.

## Dalat University

Dalat is actually something of an educational centre. The reason for this is the climate – in the era before air-conditioning, Dalat was one of the few places in Vietnam where it was possible to study without working up a sweat. For this reason, a number of educational institutions were located there, with Dalat University the most famous.

Dalat University was founded as a Catholic university in 1957 by Hué Archbishop Ngo Dinh Thuc, older brother of President Ngo Dinh Diem (assassinated in 1963), with the help of Cardinal Spelman of New York. The university was seized from the church in 1975 and closed, but it reopened two years later as a state-run institution. There are presently more than 1200 students from south-central Vietnam studying here, but they all live in off-campus boarding houses. The university library contains 10,000 books, including some in English and other western languages.

Dalat University is at 1 Phu Dong Thien Vuong St (corner Dinh Tien Hoang St). The 38-hectare campus can easily be identified by the red-star-topped triangular tower. The red star is stuck over a cross which was originally erected by the church. The fact that the cross was never actually removed has led some to speculate that the church may some day get the campus returned to it.

Foreign visitors have to pay a fee to enter the campus. The fee is waived, of course, for the several foreign teachers employed here. They teach everything from French and English to accounting and business management.

## Nuclear Research Centre

Dalat's Nuclear Research Centre uses its American-built Triga Mark II reactor for radioactive medicine to train scientists and to analyse samples collected for geological and agricultural research. The centre, financed under the US Atoms for Peace programme, was formally dedicated in 1963 by President Ngo Dinh Diem (who was assassinated four days later) and US ambassador Henry Cabot Lodge. In 1975, as the South

was collapsing, the USA spirited away the reactor's nuclear fuel elements; the centre was reopened in 1984.

Dalat University recently opened a Department of Nuclear Technology and some foreign experts were hired to teach the courses. This has raised a few eyebrows, but no one as yet has accused Vietnam of harbouring ambitions of becoming a nuclear power. However, it does seem like it will be a long time before Vietnam starts building nuclear power stations. The most likely immediate possible peaceful use for nuclear technology would be in medicine.

The Nuclear Research Centre, with its tall, thin chimney, can easily be seen from the Palace Hotel, as well as from the Dragon Water-Pumping Station. It is *not* open to the public.

## Former Petit Lycée Yersin

The former Petit Lycée Yersin at 1 Hoang Van Thu St is now a cultural centre (☎ 822-511) run by the provincial government. Lessons in electric and acoustic guitar, piano, violin, clarinet, saxophone etc are held here, making this a good place to meet local musicians. A new music centre is being established on Tang Bat Ho St.

## Valley of Love

Named the Valley of Peace by Emperor Bao Dai, the Valley of Love (Thung Lung Tinh Yeu, or Vallée d'Amour in French), had its name changed in 1972 (the year Da Thien Lake was created) by romantically minded students from Dalat University.

The place has since taken on a carnival atmosphere; tourist buses line up to regurgitate visitors and boats line up to accommodate them. Paddleboats cost US$0.50 per hour; 15-person canoes cost US$4 an hour; and obnoxious noise-making motorboats cost US$5 for a whirlwind tour of the lake.

This is a good place to see the 'Dalat cowboys' (no relation to the American Dallas Cowboys football team). The 'cowboys' are in fact Vietnamese guides dressed as American cowboys – come back in another year and they'll have the Montagnards dressed up as Indians. We've also seen Vietnamese dressed as bears and we imagine that Mickey Mouse and Donald Duck costumes can't be far behind. The cowboys rent horses to tourists for US$5 (and up) per hour and can take you on a guided tour around the lake. The Dalat cowboys and 'bears' hassle you for cash if you accidentally take their picture – they want about US$0.30 per photo.

Refreshments and local delicacies (jams, candied fruits) are on sale at the lookout near where the buses disgorge tourists.

The Valley of Love is 5km north of Xuan Huong Lake on Phu Dong Thien Vuong St. The entrance fee is US$0.20.

### Cam Ly Falls

Cam Ly Falls, opened as a tourist site in 1911, is one of those must-see spots for domestic visitors. The grassy areas around the 15m-high cascades are the habitat of horses and Dalat cowboys. Many of the cowboys you see around here aren't guides but tourists – for a fee you can get dressed as a cowboy and have your photo taken. The waterfall is between numbers 57 and 59 on Hoang Van Thu St; it is open from 7 am to 6 pm.

### Tomb of Nguyen Huu Hao

Nguyen Huu Hao, who died in 1939, was the father of Nam Phuong, Bao Dai's wife. He was the richest person in Go Cong District of the Mekong Delta. Nguyen Huu Hao's tomb is on a hilltop 400m north-west of Cam Ly Falls.

### Dragon Water-Pumping Station

Guarded by a fanciful cement dragon, the Dragon Water-Pumping Station was built in 1977-78. The statue of the Virgin Mary holding baby Jesus and gazing towards Dalat dates from 1974. Thong Nhat Reservoir is on top of the hill just west of the pumping station.

The Dragon Water-Pumping Station is on top of a low rise 500m west of the entrance to the Valley of Love.

### Pagodas & Churches

**Lam Ty Ni Pagoda** Lam Ty Ni Pagoda, also known as Quan Am Tu, was founded in 1961. The decorative front gate was constructed by the pagoda's one monk, Vien Thuc, an industrious man who learned English, French, Khmer and Thai at Dalat University. During his 27 years here, he has built flower beds and gardens in several different styles, including a miniature Japanese garden complete with a bridge. Nearby are trellis-shaded paths decorated with hanging plants. Signs list the Chinese name of each garden. Vien Thuc also built much of the pagoda's wooden furniture.

Lam Ty Ni Pagoda is about 500m north of the Pasteur Institute at 2 Thien My St. A visit here can easily be combined with a stop at Bao Dai's Summer Palace.

We visited Dalat and went to the Lam Ty Ni Pagoda and met the monk, Vien Thuc. This is an experience not to be missed! Mr Thuc is very warm and friendly and gave us a tour of the pagoda and his living quarters. The gardens are a tad run down as Thuc has been busy painting pictures and writing poetry. We admired some pictures on the wall, mostly abstract black ink on white rice paper and some water colours, all quite striking. He was very pleased and embraced us and took us by the arm into his studio, where he has hundreds of pictures. We asked if we could purchase some and he said we could for only the cost of the materials. We were there for three hours and Mr Thuc never stopped talking or smiling and posed with us for many photos. We ended up taking four or five pictures each and paid about US$3 each, but we met other travellers who gave him less. I admired one of his poems and he whipped out a pot of ink and a bamboo pen and wrote it on my painting. Mr Thuc rolled up our pictures in cardboard and hung them around our necks. There were five of us and we could not stop talking about our visit for weeks.

**Frank Visakay**

**Linh Son Pagoda** Linh Son Pagoda was built in 1938. The giant bell is said to be made of bronze mixed with gold, its great weight making it too heavy for thieves to carry off. Behind the pagoda are coffee and tea plants tended by the 15 monks, who range in age from 20 to 80, and half a dozen novices.

One of the monks here has led a fascinating life, whose peculiar course reflects the vagaries of Vietnam's modern history. Born in 1926 of a Japanese father and a Vietnamese mother, during WWII he was pressed into the service of the Japanese occupation forces as a translator. He got his secondary school degree from a French-language Franciscan convent in 1959 at the age of 35. His interest later turned to American literature, in which he received a master's degree (his thesis was on William Faulkner) from Dalat University in 1975. The monk speaks half a dozen East Asian and European languages with fluent precision.

Linh Son Pagoda is about 1km from the town centre on Phan Dinh Phung St; the street address is 120 Nguyen Van Troi St.

**Dalat Cathedral** Dalat Cathedral, which is on Tran Phu St next to the Dalat Hotel, was built between 1931 and 1942 for use by French residents and vacationers. The cross on the spire is 47m above the ground. Inside, the stained-glass windows bring a hint of medieval Europe to Dalat. The first church built on this site (in the 1920s) is to the left of the cathedral; it has a light-blue arched door.

There are three priests here. Masses are held at 5.30 am and 5.15 pm every day and on Sundays at 5.30 am, 7 am and 4 pm. The parish's three choirs (one for each Sunday mass) practise on Thursdays and Saturdays from 5 to 6 pm.

**Vietnamese Evangelical Church** Dalat's pink Evangelical Church, the main Protestant church in the city, was built in 1940. Until 1975, it was affiliated with the Christian & Missionary Alliance. The minister here was trained at Nha Trang Bible College.

Since reunification, Vietnam's Protestants have been persecuted even more than Catholics, in part because many Protestant clergymen were trained by American missionaries. Although religious activities at this church are still restricted by the government, Sunday is a busy day: there is Bible study from 7 to 8 am, followed by worship from 8 to 10 am; a youth service is held from 1.30 to 3.30 pm.

Most of the 25,000 Protestants in Lam Dong Province, who are served by over 100 churches, are hill tribe people. Dalat's Vietnamese Evangelical Church is one of only six churches in the province whose membership is ethnic-Vietnamese.

The Vietnamese Evangelical Church is 300m from Rap 3/4 at 72 Nguyen Van Troi St.

**Domaine de Marie Convent** The pink tile-roofed structures of the Domaine de Marie Convent (Nha Tho Domaine), constructed between 1940 and 1942, were once home to 300 nuns. Today, the eight remaining nuns support themselves by making ginger candies and by selling the fruit grown in the orchard out the back.

Suzanne Humbert, wife of Admiral Jean Decoux, Vichy-French Governor-General of Indochina from 1940 to 1945, is buried at the base of the outside back wall of the chapel. A benefactress of the chapel, she was killed in a car accident in 1944.

Masses are held in the large chapel every day at 5.30 am and on Sundays at 5.30 am and 4.15 pm.

The Domaine de Marie Convent is on a hilltop at 6 Ngo Quyen St, which is also called Mai Hac De St. The French-speaking nuns are pleased to show visitors around and explain about their important social work for orphans, homeless and handicapped children. A small shop sells handicrafts made by the children and nuns.

**Du Sinh Church** Du Sinh Church was built in 1955 by Catholic refugees from the North. The four-post, Sino-Vietnamese-style steeple was constructed at the insistence of a Hué-born priest of royal lineage. The church is on a hilltop with beautiful views in all directions, making this a great place for a picnic.

To get to Du Sinh Church, go 500m southwest along Huyen Tran Cong Chua St from the former Couvent des Oiseaux, which is now a teachers' training high school.

**Thien Vuong Pagoda** Thien Vuong Pagoda, also known simply as Chua Tau (the Chinese pagoda), is popular with domestic tourists, especially ethnic-Chinese. Set on a hilltop amid pine trees, the pagoda was built by the Chaozhou Chinese Congregation. Tho Da, the monk who initiated the construction of the pagoda in 1958, emigrated to the USA; there are pictures of his 1988 visit on display. The stalls out the front are a good place to buy local candied fruit and preserves.

The pagoda itself consists of three yellow buildings made of wood. In the first building is a gilded, wooden statue of Ho Phap, one of the Buddha's protectors. On the other side of Ho Phap's glass case is a gilded wooden statue of Pho Hien, a helper of A Di Da Buddha (the Buddha of the Past). Shoes should be removed before entering the third building, in which there are three 4m-high standing Buddhas donated by a British Buddhist and brought from Hong Kong in 1960. Made of gilded sandalwood and weighing 1400kg each, the figures – said to be the largest sandalwood statues in Vietnam – represent Thich Ca Buddha (the historical Buddha Sakyamuni; in the centre); Quan The Am Bo Tat (Avalokiteçvara, the Goddess of Mercy; on the right); and Dai The Chi Bo Tat (an assistant of A Di Da; on the left).

Thien Vuong Pagoda is about 5km southeast of the centre of town on Khe Sanh St. A cable car due to open in 1997 will connect it to the new long-distance bus station. This construction project is a Swiss-Vietnamese joint venture.

**Minh Nguyet Cu Sy Lam Pagoda** A second Chinese Buddhist pagoda, Minh Nguyet Cu Sy Lam Pagoda, is reached by a path beginning across the road from the gate of Thien Vuong Pagoda. It was built by the Cantonese Chinese Congregation in 1962. The main sanctuary of the pagoda is a round structure constructed on a platform representing a lotus blossom.

Inside is a painted cement statue of Quan The Am Bo Tat (Avalokiteçvara, the Goddess of Mercy) flanked by two other figures. Shoes should be taken off before entering. Notice the repetition of the lotus motif in the window bars, railings, gateposts etc. There is a giant red gourd-shaped incense oven near the main sanctuary. The pagoda is open all day long.

**Su Nu Pagoda** Su Nu Pagoda, also known as Chua Linh Phong, is a Buddhist nunnery built in 1952. The nuns here – who, according to Buddhist regulations, are bald – wear grey or brown robes except when praying, at which time they don saffron raiment. Men are allowed to visit, but only women live here. The nunnery is open all day, but it is considered impolite to come around lunch time, when the nuns sing their prayers a cappella before eating. Across the driveway from the pagoda's buildings and set among tea plants is the grave-marker of Head Nun Thich Nu Dieu Huong.

Su Nu Pagoda is about 1km south of Le Thai To St at 72 Hoang Hoa Tham St.

### Hiking & Cycling
The best way to enjoy the forests and cultivated countryside around Dalat is either on foot, on horseback or pedalling a bicycle. Some suggested routes include:

* Heading out on 3/4 St, which becomes National Highway 20, to the pine forests of Prenn Pass and Quang Trung Reservoir.
* Going via the Governor-General's Residence and up Khe Sanh St to Thien Vuong Pagoda.
* Taking Phu Dong Thien Vuong St from Dalat University to the Valley of Love.
* Going out to Bao Dai's Summer Palace and from there, after stopping at Lam Ty Ni Pagoda, via Thien My St and Huyen Tran Cong Chua St to Du Sinh Church.

### Golf
The Dalat People's Committee set up a joint venture with a Hong Kong company to renovate the old golf course which was once used by Bao Dai, the last Vietnamese emperor. The renovation has now been completed and the course has been renamed Dalat Pines. Memberships (good for only 20 years) start at US$15,000, but go all the way up to US$60,000 for 'corporate memberships'. Visitors can play here for US$25 to US$35 per day.

## Places to Stay

Due to its popularity with domestic travellers, Dalat has an extensive network of excellent hotels at all different price levels. Unfortunately, only a few of the private hotels are as yet authorised to accept foreign guests.

Demand is particularly heavy on Saturday night. During the high season (June and July) accommodation can be tight. There is another peak season surrounding the Tet holiday (most of February).

Unless you like icy showers, make sure they have hot water before you check in. If there is a power failure, the hot water will be off too, but in that case some hotels will boil water on a gas stove and give it to you in a bucket. No hotels in Dalat have air-conditioning and it's hard to imagine why anyone would want it!

**Places to Stay – bottom end** Cheap hotels currently in vogue with budget travellers include the Cam Do, Highland, Mimosa I and II, Peace I and II and the Phu Hoa.

The *Highland Hotel* (Khach San Cao Nguyen; ☎ 823738) is at 90 Phan Dinh Phung St right in the heart of Dalat. It's a good budget place with singles for US$4 to US$6 and twins priced from US$7 to US$10.

Backpackers have long been fond of the *Peace Hotel* (Khach San Hoa Binh; ☎ 822-787). Twins are US$12 to US$15. The hotel is at 64 Truong Cong Dinh St.

The same place operates the *Peace Hotel II* (Khach San Hoa Binh II; ☎ 822982) at 67 Truong Cong Dinh St. Rooms cost US$8.

The *Mimosa Hotel II* (☎ 822180), also called the *Thanh The Hotel*, is at 118 Phan Dinh Phung St. It offers rooms at the requisite low-end rates: singles are US$4 to US$9 and doubles US$7 to US$15.

The *Thanh Binh Hotel* (☎ 822909; 42 rooms) at 40 Nguyen Thi Minh Khai St is a good budget hotel right across the street from the central market building. Singles are US$8 to US$22 and twins US$12 to US$28.

The *Cam Do Hotel* (☎ 822732) at 81 Phan Dinh Phung St is a standard backpackers' special. It has dormitory beds for US$4 and twins costing US$10 to US$30

The *Phu Hoa Hotel* (☎ 822194) at 16 Tang Bat Ho St is an old, but still reasonably pleasant, place in the centre. Rates for singles are US$7 and doubles are US$10 to US$12.

The *Trixaco Hotel* (☎ 822789) at 7 Nguyen Thai Hoc St is a fine place with views of Xuan Huong Lake. Singles are US$8 and twins US$10 to US$30.

The *Thuy Tien Hotel* (☎ 821731, 822482; eight rooms) is in the heart of the old French section at the corner of Duy Tan and Khoi Nghia Nam Ky Sts. Singles cost US$25 to US$30 and twins US$30 to US$36.

The *Mimosa Hotel* (☎ 822656) at 170 Phan Dinh Phung St (see Dalat Area map) is an old Dalat budget institution. Singles cost US$5 to US$9 and doubles US$8 to US$15.

The *Truong Nguyen Mini-Hotel* (☎ 821-772) at 74 Hai Thuong St is one of the few private hotels which can accept foreign guests. Singles are US$10 and twins US$15 to US$25.

The *Lam Son Hotel* (☎ 822362; 12 rooms) is 500m west of the centre of town in an old French villa at 5 Hai Thuong St. This large, quiet place is good value if you don't mind the 10 minute walk to the town centre. Singles are US$8 to US$10 and twins US$12 to US$14. The management is very friendly and travellers give it favourable comments.

VYC Travel Company is a government-owned company based in Saigon. It's the only company besides Dalat Tourist that is permitted to operate hotels in Dalat. The standards maintained by VYC are somewhat higher than those of Dalat Tourist so you might want to take a look. Unfortunately, all of the VYC hotels are too far to walk from the centre, so you'll need to take a motorbike or rent a taxi from Dalat Tourist.

VYC operates the *Pensee 3 Hotel* (☎ 822-286; nine rooms), 3 Ba Thang Tu St, which is fairly plush and costs US$20 for twins. There is also *Pensee 10* (☎ 822937; six rooms), 10 Phan Chu Trinh St, which costs US$15/20 for singles/doubles, but is a very long way from the centre. And just next to this is the three-star *Lavy Hotel*, (☎ 822507; 40 rooms), also known as the *Lam Vien*

*Hotel*) at 20 Hung Vuong St. It has singles US$8 to US$15 and doubles US$12 to US$20.

**Places to Stay – middle & top end** The *Anh Dao Hotel* (☎ 822384; 27 rooms) at 50 Hoa Binh Square is up the hill from the central market building on Nguyen Chi Thanh St. This hotel has some of the most beautiful rooms in Dalat and can definitely be recommended if it fits your price range. Doubles here are US$29 to US$45 and breakfast is included in the tariff.

The *Ngoc Lan Hotel* (☎ 822136; fax 824032; 33 rooms), a big place overlooking the bus station and the lake, is at 42 Nguyen Chi Thanh St. This old place has been fully renovated. Prices also have been renovated; singles are US$30 to US$42 and doubles US$36 to US$48.

The *Haison Hotel* (☎ 822622; fax 822-623) is a spiffy place at 1 Nguyen Thi Minh Khai St across the roundabout from the central market building. The hotel advertises its 'elegant and cosy dancing hall' and 'urbane service staff'. It is often filled with foreign tour groups. Room rates here are US$25 to US$40.

The *Hang Nga Guesthouse* (☎ 822070) at 3 Huynh Thuc Khang (see the Dalat Area map) is a most amazing place – unique in Vietnam if not the world. This exotic guesthouse is actually an art gallery of sorts and a cafe. Hotel rooms are built inside artificial tree trunks and caves. The owner is the daughter of a former president of Vietnam. Beautiful twin rooms cost US$20 to US$60.

The *Palace Hotel* (☎ 822203; 43 rooms) is a grand old place built between 1916 and 1922. Panoramic views of Xuan Huong Lake can be enjoyed in the hotel's expansive ground-floor public areas, where one can sit in a rattan chair sipping tea or soda while gazing out through a wall of windows. There are tennis courts nearby. A major, three-year renovation has turned this into Dalat's primo luxury accommodation. Twin rooms now cost US$120 to US$350. The hotel's street address is 2 Tran Phu St.

The *Villa Hotel* (☎ 821431) at 8A Ho Tung Mau St is an excellent private hotel just south of Xuan Huong Lake. Twins cost US$25 to US$40.

Another vintage hostelry is the *Dalat Hotel* (☎ 822363; 65 rooms) built in 1907. The building, at 7 Tran Phu St (opposite the driveway of the Palace Hotel), was undergoing renovation at the time of writing and should be open again soon. To judge from the looks of things, it will be close to the standard of the nearby Palace Hotel.

The *Duy Tan Hotel* (☎ 822216; 26 rooms) at 82 3/2 St (corner Hoang Van Thu St) is notable for the fenced-in car park which reassures Americans and Aussies accustomed to motel-style travel. Singles are US$30 to US$42 and twins cost US$36 to US$48.

The *Golf Hotel* (☎ 824082) at 11 Dinh Tien Hoang St is on the edge of the Dalat golf course. It's a lovely place with twins costing US$35 to US$65.

*Minh Tam Villas* (Khu Du Lich Minh Tam; ☎ 822447; 17 rooms) is 3km out of town at 20A Khe Sanh St. There are nice views from here of the surrounding landscape of pine-forested hills and cultivated valleys. The house originally belonged to a French architect who sold it to a well-to-do Vietnamese family in 1954. It underwent several renovations and in 1975 was 'donated' to the victorious Communist government. The A-frame villas were added later. Twin rooms in the main house cost US$50, while smaller (and nicer) villas go for US$45.

You'll find a similar level of accommodation at the nearby *Hoang Yen Villas* (Khu Du Lich Hoang Yen).

Many of Dalat's 2500 chalet-style villas also can be rented. The prime villas are along the ridge south of Tran Hung Dao St and Le Thai To St – these are simply called the *Tran Hung Dao Villas*. There is a whole neighbourhood of villas near the Pasteur Institute (around Le Hong Phong St).

**Places to Eat**
**Local Specialities** Dalat is a paradise for lovers of fresh garden vegetables, which are grown locally and sold all over the south. The abundance of just-picked peas, carrots,

radishes, tomatoes, cucumbers, avocados, green peppers, lettuce, Chinese cabbage, bean sprouts, beets, green beans, potatoes, corn, bamboo shoots, garlic, spinach, squash and yams makes for meals unavailable anywhere else in the country. Persimmons and cherries are in season from November to January. Avocados are eaten for desert with either sugar or salt and pepper. Apples are known here as *bom*, after the French *pomme*. Because of fierce competition in the domestic tourism market, restaurant prices are very reasonable.

The Dalat area is justifiably famous for its strawberry jam, dried blackcurrants and candied plums and peaches, all of which can be purchased from stalls in the market area just west of Xuan Huong Lake. Other local delicacies include avocado ice cream, sweet beans *(mut dao)* and strawberry, blackberry and artichoke extracts (syrups for making drinks). The strawberry extract is great in tea. The region also produces grape, mulberry and strawberry wines. Artichoke tea, another local speciality, is made from the root of the artichoke plant. Most of these products can be purchased at the central market and at stalls in front of Thien Vuong Pagoda.

*Dau hu*, a type of pudding common in China, is also one of Dalat's specialities. Made from soymilk, sugar and a slice of ginger, dau hu is sold by itinerant women vendors who walk around carrying a large bowl of the stuff and a small stand suspended from either end of a bamboo pole.

**Street Market** The stairway down to Nguyen Thi Minh Khai St turns into a big food stall area in the late afternoon and early evening. Women sell all sorts of pre-cooked homemade dishes or prepare them on a portable charcoal stove. Prices are amazingly cheap. Of course, other vendors with more permanent stalls in the marketplace sell similar things, but at higher prices. Most of the people doing business on these stairs are minority people; one thing that should become immediately obvious is how much poorer they are than the Vietnamese. These people sell their goods in early morning or late afternoon because during the day the police chase them away.

**Restaurants** European fare can be had at *La Tulipe Rouge Restaurant* at 1 Nguyen Thi Minh Khai St. *Thanh Thanh Restaurant* at 4 Tang Bat Ho St is an upscale eatery with fine French food. Even more upscale is the pricey *Thuy Ta Restaurant*, at 2 Yersin St, which is built on pilings in Xuan Huong Lake.

The Chinese restaurant in the *Mimosa Hotel* is excellent and cheap. Great spring rolls. And yes, the staff do speak Chinese.

The *Shanghai Restaurant* is on the other side of Rap 3/4 cinema from the central market building; the address is 8 Khu Hoa Binh Square. They serve Chinese, Vietnamese and French food from 8 am to 9.30 pm.

The *Long Hoa Restaurant* on Duy Tan St is also in vogue with travellers and even cheaper than the Shanghai Restaurant. The *Hoang Lan Restaurant* on Phan Dinh Phung St also has excellent food in the budget range.

A good all-round place to eat is the *Dong A Restaurant* (☎ 821033) at 82 Phan Dinh Phung St. This place dishes up Vietnamese, Chinese, western and vegetarian cuisine. The sweet 'n' sour soup is outstanding and can be ordered vegetarian-style or with eel, pork or fish. This restaurant is open from 8 am to 10 pm.

Close to the Shanghai Restaurant is *Pho Tung*, which is not a bad restaurant and has an outstanding bakery. It's hard to resist all those delectable pastries and cakes in the windows – close your eyes as you walk by or else break out some dong and pig out.

**Vegetarian** If it's fresh Vietnamese vegetables you want, the place to find them is the *Nhu Hai Restaurant* on the traffic circle in front of the central market building.

There are also vegetarian food stalls (signposted *'com chay'*, meaning 'vegetarian food') in the market area just west of Xuan Huong Dam. All serve delicious 100% vegetarian food prepared to resemble and taste like traditional Vietnamese meat dishes.

**Cafes** The coffee and cake in Dalat is the

CENTRAL HIGHLANDS

best in Vietnam and a visit to any of the town's finer cafes should make you an instant addict. Other items worth trying are simple meals, breakfast, etc.

*Stop'n Go Cafe* (☎ 821512), Kiosk No 6, Hoa Binh Square, overlooks the market area. This is sort of Dalat's avant-garde hang-out. Mostly drinks are served, but you can also buy 'breakfast' at anytime. Check out the book of poems and the paintings for sale.

The *Cafe Tung* at 6 Khu Hoa Binh Square was a famous hang-out of Saigonese intellectuals during the 1950s. Old-timers swear that the place remains exactly as it was when they were young. As it did then, Cafe Tung serves only tea, coffee, hot cocoa, lemon soda and orange soda to the accompaniment of mellow French music. This is a marvellous place to warm up and unwind on a chilly evening.

The specialities at the *Viet Hung Cafe* (Kem Viet Hung) are ice cream and iced coffee. The cafe has entrances across from 22 Nguyen Chi Thanh St and on Le Dai Hanh St.

## Entertainment

The busy market area just to the west of Xuan Huong Dam provides the main entertainment. This is where you can hang out and drink coffee and chat with the locals.

Hoa Binh Square and the adjacent central market building is the other hot spot. It's one big buy and sell, but this is one of the best places in Vietnam to pick up clothing at a good price.

## Things to Buy

In the past few years, the Dalat tourist kitsch-junk market has really come into its own. Without any effort at all, you'll be able to find that special something for your loved ones at home – perhaps a battery-powered stuffed koala bear that sings 'Waltzing Matilda' or a lacquered alligator with a light bulb in its mouth.

In addition to these useful items, Dalat is known for its *kim mao cau tich*, a kind of fern whose fibres are used to stop bleeding in traditional Chinese medicine. The stuff is also known as *cu ly* (animals) because the fibrous matter is sold attached to branches pruned to resemble reddish-brown hairy animals. The tourists from Taiwan and Hong Kong go crazy for this stuff.

The hill tribes of Lam Dong Province make handicrafts for their own use only – but just wait, Dalat Tourist will get them too. Lat products include dyed rush mats and rice baskets that roll up when empty. The Koho and Chill produce the split-bamboo baskets used by all the Montagnards in this area to carry things on their backs. The Chill also weave cloth, including the dark blue cotton shawls worn by some Montagnard women.

The hill tribe people carry water in a hollow gourd with a corn-cob stopper that is sometimes wrapped in a leaf for a tighter fit. A market for such goods has not yet developed so there are no stores in town selling them. If you are interested in Montagnard handicrafts, you might ask around Lat Village, 12km north of Dalat.

## Getting There & Away

**Air** Vietnam Airlines connects Dalat to Saigon. See the Getting Around chapter for the schedule and pricing information.

Lien Khuong airport is about 30km south of the city. You will need to take a government taxi (about US$20), since foreigners are forbidden to ride in private cars. Another alternative is by motorbike which should cost around US$5.

Cam Ly airstrip, only 3km from the centre of Dalat, is not in use.

The Vietnam Airlines office in Dalat (☎ 822895) is at 5 Truong Cong Dinh St, across the street from Rap 3/4 cinema.

**Bus** Current regulations prohibit foreigners from riding on the public buses. Foreigners are expected to travel by authorised tourist minibus, private car or motorbike.

The regulations could change. To get the latest bus information in Dalat you can talk to the drivers at the Intra-Provincial bus station (Ben Xe Khach Noi Thanh). It's next to the new cable car station, where you get cable cars to Thien Vuong Pagoda. The bus station is about 1km due south of Xuan Huong Lake.

In Saigon, buses to Dalat depart from the Van Thanh bus station, though at the present time these are not an option unless you look Vietnamese.

**Minibus** It's easy enough to book a seat on a tourist minibus. In Saigon, this is most readily accomplished at either Kim Cafe or Dalat Tourist. In Nha Trang, almost any hotel can sell you a minibus ticket to Dalat. To exit Dalat, you can purchase a minibus ticket at most of the hotels which are authorised to accept foreign guests.

**Car & Motorbike** Not all cars are permitted to carry foreign passengers in Dalat. Vietnamese drivers need an official authorisation to carry foreign passengers and not every driver has the required permit.

However, no such rule exists for motorbikes. You may hire a Vietnamese driver to carry you on a motorbike without any official permits. Therefore, if you do come to Dalat by private car, your driver may stop 10km before town and arrange a motorbike to carry you on the last stretch. The same arrangement may be repeated upon departure.

From Saigon, taking the inland route via Bao Loc and Di Linh is faster than the coastal route via Ngoan Muc Pass. Parts of the road between Dalat and Phan Rang are in poor condition, so a high-clearance vehicle is preferred, though not mandatory.

Road distances from Dalat are:

| | |
|---|---|
| Danang | 746km |
| Di Linh | 82km |
| Saigon | 308km |
| Nha Trang | 205km |
| Phan Rang | 101km |
| Phan Thiet | 247km |

A new road connects Dalat to Buon Ma Thuot in the western part of the Central Highlands. However, this road is unsurfaced and only high-clearance 4WD vehicles or motorbikes can get through. The road quickly turns into axle-deep muck after a heavy rain.

## Getting Around
Since private vehicles are forbidden to carry foreigners, you must rent cars or vans from Dalat Tourist.

**Motorbike** Motorbikes can be flagged down along Nguyen Thi Minh Khai St just south of the central market area.

**Cyclo** Dalat is too hilly for cyclos.

## AROUND DALAT
### Lake of Sighs
The Lake of Sighs (Ho Than Tho) is a natural lake enlarged by a French-built dam; the forests in the area are hardly Dalat's finest. There are several small restaurants up the hill from the dam. Horses can be hired near the restaurants for US$4 an hour.

According to legend, Mai Nuong and Hoang Tung met here in 1788 while he was hunting and she was picking mushrooms. They fell in love and sought their parents' permission to marry. But at that time Vietnam was threatened by a Chinese invasion and Hoang Tung, heeding Emperor Quang Trung's call-to-arms, joined the army without waiting to tell Mai Nuong. Unaware that he was off fighting and afraid that his absence meant that he no longer loved her, Mai Nuong sent word for him to meet her at the lake. When he did not come she was overcome with sorrow and, to prove her love, threw herself into the conveniently located lake and drowned. Thereafter, the lake has been known as the Lake of Sighs.

The Lake of Sighs is 6km north-east of the centre of Dalat via Phan Chu Trinh St.

### Prenn Pass
The area along National Highway 20 between Dalat and Datanla Falls is known as Prenn Pass. The hillsides support mature pine forests while the valleys are used to cultivate vegetables. This is a great area for hiking and horseback riding, but make local inquiries before heading out to be sure that there will be no problems with the police.

## Prenn Falls

This is one of the largest and most beautiful falls in the Dalat area, but it is also starting to suffer the effects of commercial exploitation.

Prenn Falls (elevation 1124m) consists of a 15m free fall over a wide rock outcrop. A path goes under the outcrop, affording a view of the pool and surrounding rainforest through the curtain of falling water. An ominous sign of possible kitschy horrors to come is the 'Dalat Tourist Sailboats' now plying the waters of the tiny pool at the waterfall's base.

After a rainstorm the waterfall becomes a raging brown torrent (deforestation and the consequent soil erosion are responsible for the coffee colour). Refreshments are sold at kiosks near the falls. The park around the falls was dedicated by the Queen of Thailand in 1959.

The entrance to Prenn Falls is near the Prenn Restaurant, which is 13km from Dalat towards Phan Rang.

## Quang Trung Reservoir

Quang Trung Reservoir (Tuyen Lam Lake) is an artificial lake created by a dam in 1980. It is named after Emperor Quang Trung (also known as Nguyen Hue), a leader of the Tay Son Rebellion who is considered a great hero for vanquishing a Chinese invasion force in 1789. The area is being developed for tourism; there are several cafes not far from the dam, and paddleboats, rowboats and canoes are for rent nearby. The hillscape around the reservoir is covered with pine trees, most of them newly planted. There is a switchback path up the hill south-west of the water intake tower. Minority farmers live and raise crops in the vicinity of the lake.

To get to Quang Trung Reservoir, head out of Dalat on National highway 20. At a point 5km from town turn right and continue for 2km.

## Datanla Falls

The nice thing about Datanla Falls is the short but pleasant walk to get there. The cascade is 350m from Highway 20 on a path that first passes through a forest of pines and then continues steeply down the hill into a rainforest. The other good thing about this place is the wildlife – lots of squirrels, birds and butterflies. This may have much to do with the fact that hunting is prohibited in the area so the creatures are less scared of humans.

To get to Datanla Falls, turn off Highway 20 about 200m past the turn-off to Quang Trung Reservoir; the entrance fee is US$0.20. There is a second entrance to the falls several hundred metres farther down the road.

## Lat Village

The nine hamlets of Lat Village (population 6000), whose name is pronounced 'lak' by the locals, are about 12km from Dalat at the base of Lang Bian Mountain. The inhabitants of five of the hamlets are of the Lat ethnic group; the residents of the other four are members of the Chill, Ma and Koho tribes, each of which speaks a different dialect.

Traditionally, Lat houses are built on piles with rough plank walls and a thatch roof. The people of Lat Village eke out a living growing rice, coffee, black beans and sweet potatoes. The villages have 300 hectares of land and produce one rice crop per year. Many residents of Lat have been forced by economic circumstances into the business of producing charcoal, a lowly task often performed Montagnards. Before 1975, many men from Lat worked with the Americans, as did Montagnards elsewhere in the Central Highlands.

Classes in the village's primary and secondary schools, successors of the École Franco-Koho established in Dalat in 1948, are conducted in Vietnamese rather than the tribal languages. Lat has one Catholic church and one Protestant church. A Koho-language Bible (Sra Goh) was published by Protestants in 1971; a Lat-language Bible, prepared by Catholics, appeared the following year. Both Montagnard dialects, which are quite similar to each other, are written in a Latin-based script.

There are no restaurants in Lat, just a few food stalls.

To visit the village, you must first go to the immigration police in Dalat to obtain a permit for US$5. If you've booked a day tour, this can be arranged by the tour operator.

To get to Lat from Dalat, head north on Xo Viet Nghe Tinh St. At Tung Lam Hamlet there is a fork in the road marked by a street sign. Continue straight on (that is, northwestward) rather than to the left (which leads to Suoi Vang, the Golden Stream, 14km away). By bicycle, the 12km trip from Dalat to Lat takes about 40 minutes. On foot, it's a two hour walk.

## Lang Bian Mountain

Lang Bian Mountain (also called Lam Vien Mountain) has five volcanic peaks ranging in altitude from 2100m to 2400m. Of the two highest peaks, the eastern one is known to locals by the woman's name K'Lang; the western one bears a man's name, K'Biang. The upper reaches of the mountain are forested. Only half a century ago, the verdant foothills of Lang Bian Mountain, now defoliated, sheltered wild oxen, deer, boars, elephants, rhinoceroses and tigers.

The hike up to the top of Lang Bian Mountain, from where the views are truly spectacular, takes three to four hours from Lat Village. The path begins due north of Lat and is easily recognisable as a red gash in the green mountainside.

As is the case for visiting Lat Village, you need a permit from the Dalat police to visit Lang Bian Mountain.

## Ankroët Falls & Lakes

The two Ankroët Lakes were created as part of a hydroelectric project. The waterfall (Thac Ankroët) is about 15m high. The Ankroët Lakes are 18km north-west of Dalat in an area inhabited by hill tribes.

## Chicken Village

This village has become popular with travellers because it's conveniently situated on the Dalat-Nha Trang highway, 17km from Dalat.

The inhabitants belong to the Koho minority. To a certain extent the Koho have been assimilated into Vietnamese society. For example, they no longer live in stilt houses and they wear Vietnamese-style clothing (although very ragged). Nevertheless, the villagers have a lifestyle all their own and it's certainly worth a stopover if you're heading to Nha Trang anyway.

This place takes its name from a huge concrete statue of a chicken which sits squarely in the centre of the village. We questioned the villagers extensively to learn the history behind this unusual statue and were surprised to find that most had no idea or else refused to discuss when the statue was built or why. It certainly has no religious significance to the villagers. We finally sought out the most educated person in the village (most of the locals here are illiterate) and this was her story:

When a couple gets married here, it's the bride's family who must pay for the engagement ring and wedding party. Her family is also supposed to present the groom's family with a gift. We had a sad case many years ago where the man's family demanded a special gift, a chicken with nine fingers. No one had ever seen such a chicken, but there were rumours that these could be found in the mountains. So the girl went to the mountains to search for one. Unfortunately, her effort was in vain and she died in the wilderness. The villagers were stricken with grief by this senseless tragedy and the girl was made into a hero.

There was fighting in this area during the war and after liberation the government wanted to give the locals some sort of gift. The villagers asked if they could commemorate the brave young girl who died for love. The government officials were touched by this tragic story and complied with the wishes of the villagers. So the concrete chicken was built.

The story does sound a bit farfetched and one local man had a somewhat different tale to tell. He claims that after the Communist victory in 1975, the villagers retreated to the woods and adopted nomadic slash-and-burn agriculture because of attempts to enforce farm collectivisation. Many of the men went into the illegal timber harvesting business, which did quite a bit of damage to the region's forests. The government then granted them several redeeming concessions to entice them to relocate back to their permanent village site. After they returned, the government thought of building some sort of memorial, possibly a statue of Ho Chi Minh. It was finally decided that the concrete chicken would be most appropriate because it would commemorate the hard-working peasants. After all, what better way to symbolise chicken farmers than to build a statue of a chicken?

The residents of Chicken Village are extremely poor, but we were surprised to find no beggars at all. This is particularly remarkable given the large number of tourists who stop here. We'd like to suggest that you do *not* give sweets or money to the children and thus turn them into beggars. If you want to help the villagers, there are a couple of shops where you can buy simple things like drinks, biscuits and such. Some people also have weavings for sale and you can buy these if you like. The weavers are not pushy – in fact, no one is the least bit aggressive in this village – so you can feel free to look around and not be pressured into buying anything. This lack of entrepreneurship and materialism certainly places Chicken Village into sharp contrast with Saigon, or even Dalat. It's a very welcome change and probably the best reason for a visit.

# Western Region

The western region of the Central Highlands along the border with Cambodia and Laos is a vast, fertile plateau with red soil of volcanic origin. The good soil and sparse population has not gone unnoticed – the government has targeted the area for a massive resettlement programme. Most of the new settlers are farmers from the crowded Red River Delta area in the north. The government-financed scheme is mostly successful (the settlers are happy), though it's easy to imagine that the local hill tribes are less than thrilled by the sudden influx of northern Vietnamese. Future development plans call for building a railroad. It's clear that this is Vietnam's last frontier.

The western highlands area has lost most of its natural beauty. There are a few remnant forests remaining, but most of the trees were either destroyed by Agent Orange during the American war or have been stripped off to make way for agriculture. The only thing that really adds a bit of colour to this part of Vietnam are the Montagnards, particularly in the Kon Tum area.

## BUON MA THUOT

Buon Ma Thuot (or Ban Me Thuot; population 70,000; elevation 451m) is the capital of Dak Lak (Dac Lac) Province and the largest town in the western highlands.

The region's main crop is coffee, which is grown on plantations run by German managers who are said to be as imperiously demanding as were their French predecessors. It's the coffee industry which accounts for Buon Ma Thuot's current prosperity. Before WWII, the city was a centre for big-game hunting, but the animals have disappeared along with most of the region's rainforest.

A large percentage of the area's population is made up of Montagnards. The government's policy of assimilation has had its effect in that nearly all the Montagnards now speak Vietnamese quite fluently.

The rainy season around Buon Ma Thuot lasts from April to November, though downpours are usually of short duration. Because of its lower elevation, Buon Ma Thuot is warmer and more humid than Dalat, but it's also very windy.

Buon Ma Thuot is the gateway to Yok Don National Park and even a possible back door to Nam Cat Tien National Park. However, most travellers approach Nam Cat Tien from the Dalat side and Yok Don is something of a bad joke. If you could find a good guide, visiting the coffee plantations and processing plants could be interesting, but good guides are as scarce as snow storms in Buon Ma Thuot. To put it another way, Buon Ma Thuot is basically a wipe-out. There is precious little to hold your interest and, if you come here, you may well find that you're the only foreigner in town.

**Buon Ma Thuot**
*Scale Unknown*

**PLACES TO STAY**
2 White Horse Hotel
4 Cao Nguyen Hotel
5 Tay Nguyen Hotel
7 Hoang Gia Hotel
9 Hong Kong Hotel
10 People's Committee Guesthouse
12 Thang Loi Hotel
19 Bao Dai Villas

**OTHER**
1 Café Asia
3 Thanh Bao Coffee Sales
6 Hardware Stores
8 Buon Ma Thuot Market
11 Catholic Church
13 Victory Monument
14 Post Office
15 Ethnographic Museum
16 Main Post Office
17 Stadium (Elephant Races)
18 Cultural Centre (Minority Dances)
20 Hospital

CENTRAL HIGHLANDS

## Information

**Travel Agencies** Dak Lak Tourist (☎ 852108) – the provincial tourism authority – is in a dilapidated building at 3 Phan Chu Trinh St next to the modern Thang Loi Hotel. Be prepared to pay high prices for guides who may speak only Vietnamese and lose their way while 'guiding' you. This agency knows little about the one and only thing in Buon Ma Thuot that really interests foreigners, the coffee industry.

**Travel Permits** Permits are still required to visit minority villages in the surrounding area, including Yok Don and Nam Cat Tien national parks. See Dak Lak Tourist to get these valuable bits of paper. You do *not* need a travel permit for Buon Ma Thuot itself.

**Money** Vietcombank at 62 Nguyen Chi Thanh St is rather inconveniently located a few kilometres from the centre in the direction of the bus station.

## Ethnographic Museum

There are said to be 31 distinct ethnic groups in Dak Lak Province and the museum is one place to get some understanding of these

## Jugular Vein

Buon Ma Thuot occupies a militarily strategic location in the Central Highlands. The area is like a natural fortress and the coastal plain to the east is but a thin strip. From here, an army could launch an attack and push down to the coastline, cutting off Saigon from Danang. Saigon itself is only some 150km from the southern parts of the Highlands. The strategic significance of this was not lost on American generals, who used to refer to Buon Ma Thuot as South Vietnam's 'jugular vein'. North Vietnamese generals held a similar opinion.

In March 1975, Buon Ma Thuot briefly achieved world fame when North Vietnamese troops (who had been infiltrating via Laos and Cambodia) attacked the city. Just as the Americans had feared, the Communists 'went for the jugular'. In the weeks leading up to the attack, South Vietnamese military intelligence began to detect large numbers of men and equipment moving into the area. Just four days before the North Vietnamese assault came, former vice president and retired air force chief Nguyen Cao Ky warned the military high command that the enemy had probably assembled two divisions (20,000 troops) to strike Buon Ma Thuot. In fact, the North Vietnamese had moved three divisions (30,000 troops, with tanks and artillery) into place almost undetected, a brilliant military achievement. Nonetheless, Ky's advice to reinforce Buon Ma Thuot was not heeded, perhaps because he was a political rival to President Nguyen Van Thieu.

This proved to be the final battle of the war. Communist forces hit Buon Ma Thuot on 10 March and quickly overwhelmed the 2000 or so ARVN defenders in the city. The North Vietnamese had expected a swift counter-attack and fierce fight to the finish, but they could hardly believe what happened next. Rather than engage the enemy, President Thieu ordered a 'strategic withdrawal' from the Central Highlands. As the ARVN troops abandoned their positions without a fight, the North Vietnamese pursued them along Highway 7 to Tuy Hoa, inflicting heavy casualties. The whole withdrawal quickly turned into a rout. By 19 March, the Central Highlands were completely under the control of Communist forces. Broadcasts of the disaster on Vietnamese radio and the Voice of America undermined morale and caused many ARVN troops to desert. NVA troops from the north crossed the DMZ and attacked Hué and Danang, but demoralised ARVN troops put up no significant resistance and instead fled onto ships and aircraft in a desperate attempt to reach Saigon. Danang fell on 29 March and Nha Trang was captured on 4 April. The South Vietnamese military organisation collapsed as high-ranking officials and military officers fled abroad. Some pockets of ARVN forces put up a fierce fight around Saigon (most notably, the 18th ARVN division at Xuan Loc), but by then it was too late.

The ARVN commander with responsibility for defending the Central Highlands, General Pham Van Phu, was arrested in early April on President Thieu's orders. Phu committed suicide on 30 April, the day Saigon fell.

When the North Vietnamese launched their offensive in Buon Ma Thuot, they had expected to fight for at least two years before taking Saigon. Instead, the war came to a conclusion in less than two months. ■

disparate groups. Don't expect too much – there seem to be more minority exhibits in the adjacent souvenir shop than in the museum itself. Displays at the museum feature traditional Montagnard dress, as well as agricultural implements, fishing gear, bows and arrows, weaving looms and musical instruments. There is a photo collection with explanations about the historical contacts between the Montagnards and the majority Vietnamese – some of the history is true, some is pure fiction.

The Ethnographic Museum is also called the Revolutionary Museum. It's at 1 Me Mai St near the Victory Monument.

### Victory Monument

You can hardly miss this place as it domi-nates the central square of town. The victory monument commemorates the events of 10 March 1975, when Viet Cong and North Vietnamese troops 'liberated' the city. It was this battle that triggered the complete collapse of South Vietnam.

### Places to Stay

The *Banme Hotel* (☎ 852415; 52 rooms) is 3km north of the centre, but within walking distance of the bus station. In fact, you should definitely stay here if you arrive by bus late in the evening, because only this hotel has a night porter. This place is designed motel-style, an important consideration if you've arrived by private car and want to park it securely overnight. From the centre, you can catch a motorbike to the hotel for around US$0.40. Rooms with fan and hot water cost US$17. An air-con room is US$30.

The *Hong Kong Hotel* (☎ 852630; 11 rooms) at 30 Hai Ba Trung St has a sign outside in English saying 'Popular'. This grubby place has rooms from US$8 to US$15, but only the most expensive rooms have hot water.

The *Hoang Gia Hotel* (☎ 852161; 14 rooms) is even worse, though all rooms do have hot water. It's an absolute dump and not especially cheap at US$10 to US$12. The hotel is on Le Hong Phong St.

The *White Horse Hotel* (Khach San Bach Ma; ☎ 853963; 22 rooms) is an excellent new private hotel at 61 Hai Ba Trung St. All rooms have attached bath with hot water. With fan/air-con the tariff is US$20/35.

Room rates and standards are good at the *People's Committee Guesthouse* (Nha Khach UBND; ☎ 852407; 33 rooms) at 5 Hai Ba Trung St. The price range here is US$15 to US$30.

Travellers also give reasonably good ratings to the *Bao Dai Villas* (Nha Khach Biet Dien Bao Dai; ☎ 852177) on Doc Lap St. Rooms with air-conditioning cost US$25.

The *Tay Nguyen Hotel* (☎ 851010; 21 rooms) at 106 Ly Thuong Kiet St is adequate if not great. All rooms have hot water and air-con and cost from US$25 to US$30.

One of the two big, classy government-run tourist hotels is the *Thang Loi Hotel* (☎ 857615; fax 857622; 41 rooms) at 3 Phan Chu Trinh St. Thang Loi means Victory, so it's not surprising that the hotel faces the Victory Monument in the centre of town. Rooms here cost US$45 to US$65. The hotel belongs to Dak Lak Tourist, but try not to let that discourage you. You can find most modern amenities here, including satellite TV.

The local People's Committee operates the *Cao Nguyen Hotel* (☎ 851913; fax 851912; 32 rooms) on Phan Chu Trinh St. It's amazingly luxurious, but not too expensive in the top-floor rooms. Prices here are from US$20 to US$50 and all rooms are equipped with satellite TV.

## Places to Eat

*Cafe Diep* at 82 Dinh Tien Hoang St is distinguished less by its food than by its pleasant surroundings. The cafe has a garden of sorts decked out with statues. Local students gather here and many can speak English. The students can often give you some insights into hill tribe culture.

Buon Ma Thuot is justifiably famous for its coffee, which is the best in Vietnam. As usual, the Vietnamese serve it so strong it will make your hair stand on end, and always in a very tiny cup that allows you no room to add water or milk. We tried to teach the staff at *Cafe Asia* how to serve coffee to foreigners – drop in and see if we succeeded. It's at 120 Ly Thuong Kiet St and just next door are two other fine coffee shops. At any coffee shop in Buon Ma Thuot (or almost anywhere else in Vietnam) you may want to avoid visiting after 5 pm, which is when they crank up the karaoke machines. Most coffee shops in Buon Ma Thuot also throw in a free pot of tea (awful stuff) – be sure you don't mistake it for water and use it to dilute your coffee!

## Entertainment

There are occasional minority dances performed at the cultural centre on Doc Lap St. Even rarer are the elephant races, which are held at the stadium during minority festivals.

## Things to Buy

If you like the coffee enough to take home, be sure to pick up a bag at a local grocery store because the price is higher and quality lower in Saigon or Hanoi. There are several good shops around – we stocked up at Thanh Bao Coffee Sales on Hoang Dieu St and were satisfied with what we bought. You can buy whole beans or coffee already ground to a fine powder.

## Getting There & Away

**Air** Vietnam Airlines flies between Buon Ma Thuot and Saigon twice daily. There are direct Danang-Buon Ma Thuot flights daily except Monday. There are Hanoi-Buon Ma Thuot flights (via Danang) three times weekly.

**Bus** There is bus service to Buon Ma Thuot from Danang and Saigon. The Saigon-Buon Ma Thuot buses take 20 hours, so an 8.30 am departure gets you to your destination at 4.30 am. Departures are from Saigon's Mien Dong bus station.

**Car** The road linking the coast with Buon Ma Thuot intersects National Highway 1 at Ninh Hoa (160km from Buon Ma Thuot), which is only 34km north of Nha Trang (see South-Central Coast map). The road is surfaced and in good condition, though a bit steep. Buon Ma Thuot to Pleiku is 197km on an excellent highway.

There is a new road connecting Buon Ma Thuot with Dalat, but it's in horrid condition and you can expect a muddy quagmire if it's been raining. It's only recommended for sturdy motorbikes – even jeeps may have problems.

## AROUND BUON MA THUOT
### Drai Sap Falls
Drai Sap Falls, about 12km from Buon Ma Thuot, is in the middle of a hardwood rainforest.

### Elephant Training Centre
Just outside of Buon Ma Thuot is this centre, which sells and leases trained elephants to the rest of the country for tourism and working purposes. The facilities are interesting to visit, but foreigners are charged an unreasonable US$60 for a four-hour elephant ride through some beautiful forests. You must book these trips through Dak Lak Tourist in Buon Ma Thuot – you cannot simply turn up.

### Tua
The Rhade (or Ede) hamlet of Tua is 13km from Buon Ma Thuot. The people here make a living raising animals and growing manioc (cassava), sweet potatoes and maize. This village has become one of the most heavily Vietnamised in the region, but it has earned a higher standard of living along with the loss of cultural identity.

Rhade society is matrilineal and matrilo-cal (centred on the household of the wife's family). Extended families live in longhouses – each section of which houses a nuclear family. Each longhouse is presided over by a man, often the husband of the senior woman of the family. The property of the extended family is owned and controlled by the oldest woman in the group.

The religion of the Rhade is animistic. In the past century many Rhade have been converted to Catholicism and Protestantism.

### Yok Don National Park
The tourist action centres on the village of Ban Don village in Ea Sup District, 55km north-west of Buon Ma Thuot. There are about 17 ethnic groups here.

The locals are mostly M'nong, a matrilineal tribe in which the family name is passed down through the female line and children are considered members of their mother's family. The M'nong are known for their fiercely belligerent attitude towards other tribes in the area, as well as towards ethnic-Vietnamese.

The M'nong hunt wild elephants using domesticated elephants, dozens of which live in Ban Don. You are *not* permitted to photograph the elephants as it would hurt the local postcard industry.

One traditional activity here in which tourists can partake is drinking wine from a communal jug. Everyone gathers around the wine jug and drinks at the same time through very long straws – it makes for a good photo.

You'll need a jeep or motorbike to reach Ban Don and expect the road to be nearly impassable if it's been raining. There is a 13th century Cham tower 36km north of Ban Don at Ya Liao.

**Places to Stay** For comic relief, try staying at the *Yok Don Guesthouse* (☎ 853110; four rooms). The bath lacks hot water and the beds lack mattresses, but what do you want for US$10? You'd do better to stay in the nearby stilt houses – it may not be cheaper, but at least it's more aesthetic.

## Dak Lak Lake

Dak Lak Lake (Ho Dak Lak) is about 50km south of Buon Ma Thuot. Emperor Bao Dai built a small palace here, but it is now a ruin. Nevertheless, the views over the lake are fantastic and well worth the climb up adjacent hills. The nearby M'nong village is very authentic and a unique experience not to be missed.

## PLEIKU

Pleiku (or Playcu) is the major market town of the western highlands. Roughly 50,000 souls live here now and the population is rapidly growing. The city is 785m above sea level, which makes the climate cool. It's warmer than Dalat, but also windier.

In February 1965, the VC shelled a US compound in Pleiku killing eight Americans. Although the USA already had over 23,000 military advisers in Vietnam, their role was supposed to be non-combatant at that time. The attack on Pleiku was used as a justification by President Johnson to begin a relentless bombing campaign against North Vietnam and the rapid build-up of American troops.

During the war, Pleiku had the largest military base in the Central Highlands. When American troops departed in 1973, the South Vietnamese continued to keep Pleiku as their main combat base in the area. This may have been a mistake as it concentrated their resources far away from more strategic areas further south. Because Pleiku was so heavily fortified, the Communists chose to strike against Buon Ma Thuot and quickly occupied a large part of the Central Highlands. When President Thieu ordered his troops at Pleiku to withdraw, the whole civilian population of Pleiku and nearby Kon Tum fled with them. The stampede to the coastline involved over 100,000 people, but tens of thousands died along the way due to VC attacks and lack of simple necessities such as food and drinking water. Many of the civilians – travelling on foot and bicycle – were also run over by tanks and military trucks during the panicked withdrawal.

The departing soldiers torched Pleiku in an effort to destroy anything that could be of use to the Communists. The city was rebuilt in the 1980s with assistance from the Soviet Union. As a result, the city has a large collection of ugly, Russian-style buildings and lacks much of the colour and quaintness you find elsewhere in Vietnamese towns. Hopefully, the recent inflow of tourist dollars will bring some badly needed improvements to the architecture, as well as the local economy, but for now Pleiku is a pretty monotonous town.

The Jarai minority live in the Pleiku area and have an unusual burial custom. Each deceased gets a portrait carved from wood and for years relatives bring them food. The grave is set up as a miniature village with several people buried in one graveyard. After seven years, the grave is abandoned.

### Information

**Travel Agencies** Gia Lai Tourist (☎ 824271) is at 77 Tran Phu St near the market. However, it's more convenient to go to its Travel Guidance Office (☎ 824891) at the Pleiku Hotel. There are some very good guides working for this company, though it's not certain they are worth the high prices you must pay for them (90% of which goes to the government).

**Travel Permit** While you do not need a permit to stay overnight in Pleiku itself, or to travel the major highways, you do need one to visit hill tribe villages in Gia Lai Province. The permits will cost you money (the exact amount dependent on where you want to go) and you may be forced to hire a guide, car and driver in Pleiku even if you already have your own vehicle. You can figure on all this costing something like US$50 per day, but at least you get much better guides than are available in Buon Ma Thuot. However, the high prices put off many travellers, who usually just skip Pleiku entirely and head for Kon Tum, where the authorities are more hospitable.

If you want a travel permit, you need to visit the already-mentioned Gia Lai Tourist. Do *not* go to the police station – travellers

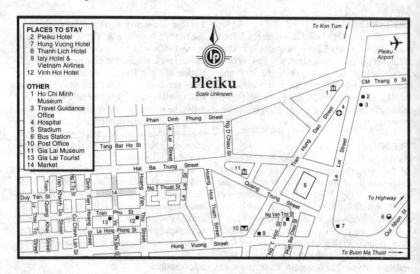

**PLACES TO STAY**
2 Pleiku Hotel
7 Hung Vuong Hotel
8 Thanh Lich Hotel
9 Ialy Hotel &
   Vietnam Airlines
12 Vinh Hoi Hotel

**OTHER**
1 Ho Chi Minh
  Museum
3 Travel Guidance
  Office
4 Hospital
5 Stadium
6 Bus Station
10 Post Office
11 Gia Lai Museum
13 Gia Lai Tourist
14 Market

**Pleiku**
Scale Unknown

who have done so have received a rather rude reception.

### Yaly Falls

Sadly, this place is probably no longer worth visiting. Yaly Falls was once the largest waterfall in the Central Highlands and a hot destination for tourists. However, a new hydroelectric scheme has sucked in most of the water and there is only a trickle left. During a heavy rain it might still look impressive, but otherwise all you are going to see is a damp cliff in the forest.

### Places to Stay

Pleiku currently suffers from a shortage of hotel rooms and if you get in late it can be a hassle finding a place. The government has not helped matters any by putting most private hotels off limits to foreigners.

The place most successful at attracting the backpacker set is *Thanh Lich Hotel* (☎ 824-674) at 86 Nguyen Van Troi St. Rooms here cost a mere US$6.

The *Vinh Hoi Hotel* (☎ 824644; 38 rooms) at 39 Tran Phu St is dirty, but cheap and often full. Rooms with shared bath cost US$5. A

room with attached private bath and hot water is US$10.

The *Ialy Hotel* (☎ 824843; 35 rooms) at 89 Hung Vuong St is a good choice. Rooms with attached bath and hot water cost US$15 to US$35.

The *Movie Star Hotel* (Khach San Dien Anh; ☎ 823855; 20 rooms) at 6 Vo Thi Sau St is Pleiku's most charming accommodation. It's been a big hit with travellers who don't mind spending a little extra for their comforts. There are rooms with fan costing US$12. Rooms with air-con come in three standards costing US$20, US$25 and US$30.

The *Hung Vuong Hotel* (☎ 824270; 20 rooms) at 215 Hung Vuong St is the closest to the bus station. Twin rooms cost US$10 to US$25.

The *Pleiku Hotel* (☎ 824628; 38 rooms) on Le Loi St is a big state-run monolith and the Stalinesque architecture is impressive. It's the only accommodation in town with satellite TV. Rates are US$25 to US$40.

### Getting There & Away

**Air** The booking office of Vietnam Airlines is inside the Ialy Hotel.

There are flights connecting Pleiku to Saigon and Danang. The direct flight between Pleiku and Hanoi has been suspended for years – if you want to fly that way you must transit in Danang.

**Bus** There is a nonexpress bus service to Pleiku from most coastal cities between Nha Trang and Danang.

**Car** Pleiku is linked by road to Buon Ma Thuot, Qui Nhon (via An Khe), Kon Tum and Cambodia's Ratanakiri Province (via Chu Nghe). There is a particularly barren stretch of land on the road from Buon Ma Thuot, probably the result of Agent Orange use and overlogging.

Road distances from Pleiku are 49km to Kon Tum, 197km to Buon Ma Thuot, 550km to Saigon, 424km to Nha Trang and 186km to Qui Nhon.

## KON TUM

Kon Tum (population 35,000; altitude 525m) is in a region inhabited primarily by Montagnards, including the Bahnar, Jarai, Rengao and Sedang.

Many travellers consider Kon Tum to be the garden spot of the Central Highlands. Some may argue that Dalat offers more to see, but Dalat is touristy. So far, Kon Tum remains largely unspoiled and the authorities have remained blessedly invisible.

Like elsewhere in the Central Highlands, Kon Tum saw its share of combat during the war. A major battle between South Vietnamese forces and the North Vietnamese took place in and around Kon Tum in the spring of 1972 – the area was devastated by hundreds of US B-52 raids.

## Information

**Travel Agencies** Kon Tum Tourist (☎ 863-336; fax 862122) is at 168 Ba Trieu St. There is also a branch office inside the Dakbla Hotel.

**Money** There is *no* place to cash travellers cheques in Kon Tum. The nearest place to accomplish this is in Pleiku.

## Montagnard Villages

There are quite a few of these all around the edges of Kon Tum. Montagnard-watching seems to be a favourite sport of travellers looking for the exotic, but please remember to treat the locals with respect. Some travellers seem to think that the hill tribes run around in their costumes for the benefit of photographers – this, of course, is not the case. In general, the local tribes welcome tourists, but only if you are not too intrusive into their lifestyle.

Some of the small villages (or perhaps we should say 'neighbourhoods') are on the periphery of Kon Tum and you can even walk to them from the centre. There are two Bihar villages, simply called Lang Bana in Vietnamese: one is on the east side of town, the other on the west side.

On the east side of Kon Tum is Kon Tum Village (Lang Kon Tum). This is, in fact, the original Kon Tum before it grew up to become a small Vietnamese city.

At the time of writing, the Kon Tum police were allowing foreigners to visit tribal villages without the need for a permit. Let us hope that this enlightened attitude continues.

## Rong House

This isn't much of a tourist attraction, though it might be if you're lucky enough to arrive on an auspicious day. A rong house is a tree house or house built on tall stilts. The original idea of building these things was protection from elephants, tigers and other overly assertive animals. However, nowadays there are few animals left. Kon Tum's rong house is the scene of important local events like meetings, weddings, festivals, prayer sessions and so on. If you stumble upon one of these activities in progress, it could be interesting. Of course, remember that uninvited guests are not always welcome at weddings.

## Nguc Kon Tum

This is an abandoned prison compound on the western side of Kon Tum. The prisoners incarcerated here were Viet Cong and all were freed in 1975 when the war ended.

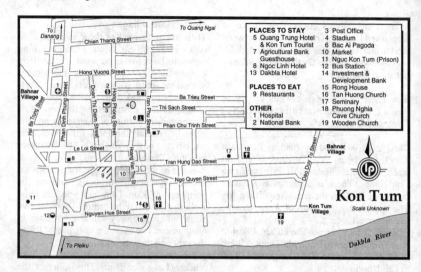

This was one of the more famous prisons run by the South Vietnamese; VC who survived their internment here were made into heroes after liberation. Having a politically correct background was (and still is) very important in post-war Vietnam – many of the high-ranking officers who are *now* in the military were former prisoners at Nguc Kon Tum. ARVN soldiers who were prisoners of the VC have not fared so well.

Nguc Kon Tum is currently open to the public and you can wander inside and have a look. Unfortunately, no effort is being made to preserve the place, nor are there any guides available to explain the historical significance of what you are looking at. Apparently the local tourism authorities have not quite grasped the economic potential of this would-be war museum.

### Dak To & Charlie Hill

This obscure outpost, 42km north of Kon Tum, was a major battlefield during the American War. In 1972, the area was the scene of intense fighting and was one of the last big battles before American troops pulled out and left the Vietnamese to fight their own war.

Dak To has become popular with visiting groups of American veterans, but you probably won't find much of interest if you're not a war buff. More intriguingly, those few Viet Cong veterans with sufficient free time and money also like to come here to stir their memories.

About 5km south of Dak To is Charlie Hill. The hill was a fortified ARVN stronghold before the VC tried to overrun it. The South Vietnamese officer in charge, Colonel Ngoc Minh, decided that he would neither surrender nor retreat and the battle became a fierce fight to the death. Unusually for a guerrilla war, this was a prolonged battle. The VC laid siege to the hill for 1½ months before they managed to kill Colonel Minh and 150 ARVN troops who made their last stand here.

Although largely forgotten in the west, the battle is well known even now in Vietnam. The reason for this is largely because the fight was commemorated by a popular song, 'The People Stayed in Charlie' (Nguoi O Lai Charlie).

Not surprisingly, the hill was heavily mined during the war and is still considered unsafe to climb.

## Places to Stay

It may not be the cheapest place in town, but the *Dakbla Hotel* (☎ 863333; fax 864407; 43 rooms) is so attractive that many backpackers stay here. Rooms cost US$14 to US$30, with the cheapest ones being on the top floor. The hotel is next to the river at 2 Phan Dinh Phung St.

If cheap is all that matters, then the *Ngoc Linh Hotel* (☎ 864560; 17 rooms) is for you. It's on the corner of Phan Dinh Phung and Tran Hung Dao Sts and is not a bad place – it's new and the twin rooms all have air-conditioning and hot water. A twin room with attached bath costs US$16 to US$18. There are dormitory beds for US$6 (four beds in a room with toilet and shower outside).

An interesting local character is 'Tiger', who hangs out at the Ngoc Lin Hotel. He says he has a PhD in economics from Princeton University in the USA, but has never heard of Adam Smith and doesn't really know where Princeton is. Nevertheless, he speaks fine English, is good company and an excellent guide. I'd hire him again.

**Jacque LaPedus**

The *Agricultural Bank Guesthouse* (Ngan Hang Nong Nghiep; ☎ 862853; 20 rooms) is near the bank (surprise) though they don't

change money. Rooms with fan only and cold water cost US$10, or you can have hot water and air-con for US$15. The official address is 90 Tran Phu St.

Another oldie but goodie is the *Quang Trung Hotel* (☎ 862249; fax 862122; 30 rooms) at 168 Ba Trieu St. All rooms have attached bath with hot water. It's US$16 with fan and US$18 with air-con.

## Getting There & Away

**Bus** Buses connect Kon Tum to Danang, Pleiku and Buon Ma Thuot.

**Car** Looking at a map, it might seem feasible to drive between Kon Tum and Danang on Highway 14. Although this is a beautiful drive, the road is in extremely poor condition and only motorbikes or jeeps can get through. The fastest approach to Kon Tum from the coast is on Highway 19 between Qui Nhon and Pleiku. Highway 14 between Kon Tum and Buon Ma Thuot is also in good nick.

Land distances from Kon Tum are 49km to Pleiku, 246km to Buon Ma Thuot, 896km to Saigon, 436km to Nha Trang and 198km to Qui Nhon.

CENTRAL HIGHLANDS

# South-Central Coast

This section covers the littoral provinces of Binh Thuan, Ninh Thuan, Khanh Hoa, Phu Yen, Binh Dinh and Quang Ngai. The cities, towns, beaches and historical sites in this region, most of which are along National Highway 1, which many foreign tourists these days refer to as the 'Ho Chi Minh Trail' (the real one is farther inland), are listed from south to north.

# Binh Thuan Province

### TAKOU MOUNTAIN
What makes this mountain interesting is not its great height, but a white reclining Buddha (Tuong Phat Nam). With a length of 49m, this is the largest reclining Buddha in

Vietnam. There are several monks in residing here.

The pagoda was constructed in 1861 during the Nguyen Dynasty. The reclining Buddha is much more recent, having been built in 1972. The site has become an important pilgrimage centre for Vietnamese Buddhists, many of whom spend the night in the pagoda's dormitory. Unfortunately, foreigners are not allowed to stay overnight without police permission, and this is not easily obtained.

Takou Mountain is just off of National Highway 1, 28km from Phan Thiet (in the direction of Saigon). It's a beautiful two-hour trek from the highway up to the Buddha.

### PHAN THIET
Phan Thiet is best known for its *nuoc mam* (fish sauce) and fishing industry. The population includes descendants of the Chams, who controlled this area until 1692. During the colonial period, the Europeans lived in their own segregated ghetto, which stretched along the north bank of the Phan Thiet River, while the Vietnamese, Chams, Southern Chinese, Malays and Indonesians lived along the river's south bank.

Binh Thuan Province (at least north of Phan Thiet) is one of the most arid regions of Vietnam. The nearby plains, which are dominated by rocky, roundish mountains, support some marginal irrigated rice agriculture. The relative dryness seems to help support a large population of flies – Aussies should feel right at home.

### Orientation
Phan Thiet is built along both banks of the Phan Thiet River, which is also known as the Ca Ti River and the Muong Man River. National Highway 1 runs right through town; south of the river, it is known as Tran Hung Dao St, while north of the river it is called Le Hong Phong St.

**South-Central Coast**

0          50          100 km

## Information

**Travel Agencies** The Hotel 19-4 offers a tour programme – you can book a car and arrange a guide here. This is a new idea for Phan Thiet, so don't be surprised if the other hotels soon follow suit.

## Phan Thiet Beach

To get to Phan Thiet's beachfront, turn east (right if you're heading north) at Victory Monument, an arrow-shaped concrete tower with victorious cement people at the base.

## Fishing Harbour

The river flowing through the centre of town creates a small fishing harbour, which is always chock-a-block with boats. It makes for charming photography.

## Mui Ne Beach

Mui Ne Beach, famous for its enormous sand dunes, is 22km east of Phan Thiet near a fishing village at the tip of Mui Ne Peninsula. There is a stream flowing through the dunes, and it's a beautiful trek to follow it from the sea to its source. You can do the trek barefoot. It might be wise to hire a local guide.

Between 8.30 am and 4 pm, a local bus makes six daily round trips between Phan Thiet bus station and Mui Ne.

There is a small Cham tower called Thap Posaknu about 5km out of Phan Thiet on the way to Mui Ne.

## Golf Course

The Ocean Dunes Golf Course is near the beachfront close to the Mercure Hotel. To drum up business, there is a minibus shuttle service between the golf course and Saigon. Departures are from Saigon's New World Hotel every Saturday at 6.30 am. The minibus leaves Phan Thiet at 2.30 pm on Sunday. The return fare is US$15 for members and guests, or US$20 to US$25 for others. For reservations, ring up Ms Mai in Saigon (☎ 824-3749).

## Places to Stay

The *Phan Thiet Hotel* (☎ 821694; 21 rooms) is at 40 Tran Hung Dao St, right in the centre of town. It was recently remodelled and looks good, though the location is not aesthetic. Doubles cost US$18 to US$25.

The *Hotel 19-4* (☎ 825216; fax 825184; 80 rooms) is an enormous place at 1 Tu Van Tu St on the north side of town. Rooms with fan and hot-water bath are US$16. Adding air-con brings the tab to US$20 or US$25.

Just opposite the Hotel 19-4 is the mini-hotel-style *Thanh Cong Hotel* (☎ 823905; 13 rooms) at 49-51 Tran Hung Dao St. It's the cheapest place in town – a bed in a small dormitory is only US$4. A room with fan and cold-water bath is US$7, but with air-con and hot water it's US$12 to US$15.

The *Mercure Hotel* (Khach San Vinh Thuy; ☎ 822393; fax 825682; 123 rooms) is along the seashore at 1 Ton Tuc Thang St. Doubles with air-con cost US$79 to US$160. To get to the hotel, turn towards the sea (eastward) at the Victory Monument. There are three restaurants in the hotel. Other facilities include a swimming pool, a private beach, tennis courts and a fitness centre. You can rent water scooters and play golf nearby.

The *Hai Duong Resort* (☎ 848401; fax 848403; 25 rooms) is at Coco Beach, 12km from Phan Thiet town. It's a joint venture between a French company and the local People's Committee. The resort is absolutely lovely, with swaying palm trees and white sand. The beach is privately owned, so annoying vendors won't congregate around you. Bungalows cost US$64 and villas are US$124, but add another 15% on weekends. Activities include windsurfing, sailing, water-skiing, sport fishing and snorkelling. There are no water scooters, TV sets or karaoke machines.

The *Phan Thiet Resort* is a very upmarket foreign joint venture at the beach, 7km from Phan Thiet town. It's a beautiful place, and so new that it wasn't open yet at the time of our visit. Since it wasn't open, we can only guess at the price, but it should be roughly similar to what you'd pay at the nearby Hai Duong Resort.

**Places to Eat**
There is a restaurant on the 3rd floor of the

*Phan Thiet Hotel* and another at the *Vinh Thuy Hotel*. The *Hotel 19-4* also has an attached restaurant.

**Getting There & Away**
**Bus** Buses from Saigon to Phan Thiet depart from Mien Dong bus station.

Phan Thiet bus station (Ben Xe Binh Thuan) is on the northern outskirts of town on Tu Van Tu St, which is just past 217 Le Hong Phong St (National Highway 1). The station is open from 5.30 am to 3.30 pm; tickets should be purchased the day before departure. There are nonexpress buses from here to Bien Hoa, Long Khanh, Madagoui, Mui Ne Beach, Phan Rang, Phu Cuong and Saigon, as well as to other destinations within Binh Thuan Province.

**Train** The nearest train station to Phan Thiet is 12km west of the town at Muong Man. The *Reunification Express* train between Hanoi and Saigon stops here. For ticket prices, see the Train section in the Getting Around chapter.

**Car** Phan Thiet is 198km due east of Ho Chi Minh City, 250km from Nha Trang and 247km from Dalat. The road between Phan Thiet and Nha Trang is in very poor condition, though there are plans to repair it.

When driving, be careful of the fish sauce trucks – hit one of these and the odour may be with you for life.

**Getting Around**
Phan Thiet has a few cyclos, some of which always seem to be at the bus station.

**VINH HAO**
Vinh Hao is an obscure town just off National Highway 1 between Phan Thiet and Phan Rang. The town's only claim to fame is its famous mineral waters, which are bottled and sold all over Vietnam. If you spend any length of time in the country, you are almost certain to sip a bottle of Vinh Hao. The Vietnamese claim that Vinh Hao mineral water is exported (but they don't say to where).

GLENN BEANLAND

ROBERT STOREY

BERNARD NAPTHINE

### Central Highlands
Top: Cleaning the carrot harvest at Dalat.
Bottom Left: The spectacular Dambri Falls near Bao Loc.
Bottom Right: Colour and variety at the central market in Dalat.

GLENN BEANLAND

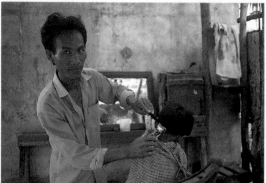
BRENDAN McCARTHY

GLENN BEANLAND

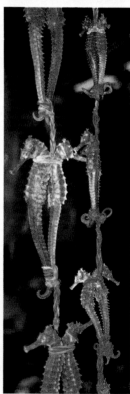
BERNARD NAPTHINE

**South-Central Coast**
Top: The local fishing fleet at anchor in Phan Thiet.
Middle Left: A barber wields the clippers in Nha Trang.
Bottom Left: Spectacular coastal scenery at Ca Na, south of Phan Rang.
Right: Dried seahorses for sale at a market in Nha Trang.

# Ninh Thuan Province

## CA NA
During the 16th century, princes of the Cham royal family would fish and hunt tigers, elephants and rhinoceroses here. Today, Ca Na is better known for its turquoise waters, lined with splendid white-sand beaches dotted with huge granite boulders – it's a beautiful and relaxing spot. The terrain is studded with magnificent prickly pear cacti. Rau Cau Island is visible offshore.

A small **pagoda** on the hillside makes for an interesting, but steep, climb over the boulders.

Farther afield is **Tra Cang Temple**, to the north about midway between Ca Na and Phan Rang. Unfortunately, you have to sidetrack over an abysmal dirt road to reach it. Many ethnic-Chinese from Cholon like to visit the temple.

## Places to Stay
The *Ca Na Hotel* (☎ 861320; 18 rooms) is notable for having five beach bungalows. Rooms in the hotel proper cost US$12 to US$15, while the bungalows are US$17.

The only other place to stay is the nearby *Haison Hotel* (☎ 861318; nine rooms). Rooms with fan and cold-water bath are US$13 to US$15.

## Places to Eat
Both hotels have decent restaurants, and indeed are very popular lunch spots for foreigners on the Saigon-Nha Trang route.

## Getting There & Away
Ca Na is 114km north of Phan Thiet and 32km south of Phan Rang. Many long-haul buses cruising National Highway 1 can drop you here, but there is no train service.

## PHAN RANG & THAP CHAM
The twin cities of Phan Rang and Thap Cham, famous for their production of table grapes, are in a region with a semi-arid climate. The sandy soil supports scrubby vegetation; local flora includes poinciana trees and prickly pear cacti with vicious thorns. Many of the houses on the outskirts of town are decorated with Greek-style grape trellises. The area's best known sight is the group of Cham towers known as Po Klong Garai, from which Thap Cham (Cham Tower) derives its name. You can see Cham towers dotted about the countryside 20km north of Phan Rang.

Ninh Thuan Province is home to tens of thousands of descendants of the Cham people, many of whom live in and around Phan Rang-Thap Cham.

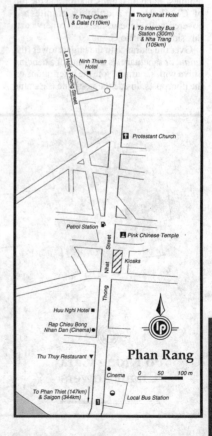

Phan Rang

## Orientation

National Highway 1 is called Thong Nhat St as it runs through Phan Rang. Thong Nhat St is Phan Rang's main commercial street. Thap Cham, about 7km from Phan Rang, is strung out along National Highway 20, which heads west from Phan Rang towards Ninh Son and Dalat.

## Po Klong Garai Cham Towers

Phan Rang-Thap Cham's most famous landmark is Po Klong Garai, four brick towers constructed at the end of the 13th century during the reign of the Cham monarch Jaya Simhavarman III. The towers, built as Hindu temples, stand on a brick platform at the top of Cho'k Hala, a crumbly granite hill covered with some of the most ornery cacti this side of the Rio Grande.

Over the entrance to the largest tower (the *kalan*, or sanctuary) is a carving of a dancing Shiva with six arms. Note the inscriptions on the doorposts. Inside the vestibule is a statue of the bull Nandin, symbol of the agricultural productivity of the countryside. To ensure a good crop, farmers would place an offering of fresh greens in front of Nandin's muzzle. Under the main tower is a *mukha-linga*, a linga (a stylised phallus which symbolises maleness and creative power and which represents the Hindu god Shiva) with a painted human face on it. A wooden pyramid has been constructed above the mukha-linga.

Inside the tower opposite the entrance to the kalan you can get a good look at some of the Cham's sophisticated masonry technology. The structure attached to it was originally the main entrance to the complex.

On a nearby hill is a rock with an inscription from the year 1050 commemorating the erection of a linga by a Cham prince.

On the hill directly south of Cho'k Hala there is a concrete water tank built by the Americans in 1965. It is encircled by French pillboxes, which were built during the Franco-Viet Minh War to protect the nearby

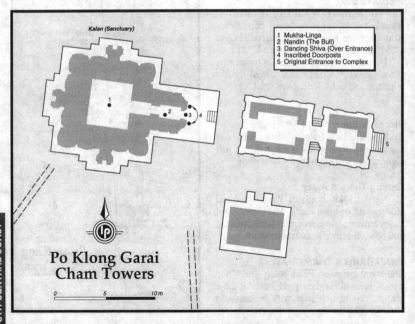

Kalan (Sanctuary)

1 Mukha-Linga
2 Nandin (The Bull)
3 Dancing Shiva (Over Entrance)
4 Inscribed Doorposts
5 Original Entrance to Complex

Po Klong Garai Cham Towers

0    5    10 m

The Cham towers at Po Klong Garai are one of the most enduring sights of southern Vietnam. Built as Hindu temples towards the end of the 13th century by Jaya Simhavarman III, the towers are a testament to the skill of the Cham masons.

rail yards. To the north of Cho'k Hala you can see the concrete revetments of Thanh Son Airbase, used since 1975 by the Soviet-built MiGs of the Vietnamese air force.

Po Klong Garai is several hundred metres north of National Highway 20, at a point 7km towards Dalat from Phan Rang. The towers are on the other side of the tracks from Thap Cham railway station.

### Thap Cham Rail Yards

The Thap Cham Rail Yards are 300m south-east of Po Klong Garai and across the tracks from the Thap Cham railway station. The main function of the yards, which were founded by the French about 80 years ago, is the repair of Vietnamese Railways' ancient one-metre-gauge engines and rolling stock. Spare parts are made either by hand or with antique machine tools and metal presses. Each pair of railroad wheels you see lying about weighs 500kg.

It may be possible to tour the yards, but judging by the small armoury (which includes a 50-calibre machine gun!) kept at the front gate, it seems clear that the area is deemed to have a certain strategic importance. Indeed, the Vietnamese Communists are well aware of how vital railroads are for national security – that's why they used to go to so much trouble to sabotage them during the Franco-Viet Minh War and the American War.

The 86km-long railway from Thap Cham to Dalat operated from 1928 until 1964, when it was closed because of repeated Viet Cong attacks. The line used a *crémaillère* system in which chains were used to pull the trains up the mountainside at a grade of up to 12cm per metre. The steepest sections of track are visible at Ngoan Muc Pass (Belle-vue Pass) on National Highway 20 (which links Phan Rang with Dalat). There are no plans at present to reopen the Thap Cham-Dalat railway. The oldest engine at the Thap Cham Rail Yards is an inoperable steam engine for the crémaillère manufactured by Machinenfabrik Esselingen in 1929.

### Po Ro Me Cham Tower

Po Ro Me Cham Tower (Thap Po Ro Me),

among the newest of Vietnam's Cham towers, is about 15km south of Phan Rang on a rocky hill 5km towards the mountains from National Highway 1. The ruins are very interesting, but unfortunately very difficult to reach. The 'road' is a dirt track that can only be negotiated by motorbike or on foot.

The road to take is between Km 1566 and 1567 from National Highway 1. We did cross small Cham hamlets, which were nice to go through. Following the image of a small distant tower, we took a road that became a path, and then less than that. Even the motorcycle almost did not make it. And after about 2km of the hill, that was it – not even a tiny path to follow. Our poor old bike could not survive the rocks and cactus and died (again!). We finally walked up the hill (great snakes!). That was magic. The feeling of being completely alone on that small hill, with only the distant sound of bells around a cow's neck and nobody around for many kilometres (amazing after weeks in Saigon), was indescribable. At the bottom of the tower are long stairs. The single tower was closed, but still worth the hill climb to get there. It is decorated with beautiful stone statues and there are two Nandin statues just before the entrance. Thank you for at least mentioning its existence, even if we were probably the only foreigners to reach it this year.

**Genevieve Mayers**

The kalan, which is decorated with paintings, has two inscribed doorposts, two stone statues of the bull Nandin, a bas-relief representing a deified king in the form of Shiva and two statues of queens, one of whom has an inscription on her chest. The towers are named after the last ruler of an independent Champa, King Po Ro Me (ruled 1629-51), who died a prisoner of the Vietnamese.

### Tuan Tu Hamlet

There is a minaretless Cham mosque, which is closed to visitors, in the Cham hamlet of Tuan Tu (population 1000). This Muslim community is governed by elected religious leaders (Thay Mun), who can easily be identified by their traditional costume, which includes a white robe and an elaborate white turban with red tassels. In keeping with Islamic precepts governing modesty, Cham women often wear head coverings and skirts. The Chams, like other ethnic minorities in Vietnam, suffer from discrimination and are

even poorer than their ethnic-Vietnamese neighbours.

To get to Tuan Tu Hamlet, head south from town along National Highway 1. Go 250m south of the large bridge to a small bridge. Cross it and turn left (to the south-east) onto a dirt track. At the market (just past the Buddhist pagoda on the right), turn right and follow the road, part of which is lined with hedgerows of cacti, for about 2km, crossing two white concrete footbridges. Ask villagers for directions along the way. Tuan Tu is 3km from National Highway 1.

### Ninh Chu Beach

Ninh Chu Beach (Bai Tam Ninh Chu) is 5km south of Phan Rang.

### Places to Stay

The *Huu Nghi Hotel* (☎ 822606; 21 rooms), 354 Thong Nhat St, is certainly the cheapest and dumpiest hotel in Phan Rang. It's right in the centre of town and therefore noisy, but at least you can't argue with the 'convenient' location (the bus station is within walking distance). Rates are US$10 to US$18. There is air-con available, but no hot water.

The *Ninh Thuan Hotel* (☎ 827100; 24 rooms) at 1 Le Hong Phong St can boast air-con and satellite TV. The hotel is on the north side of town opposite a small park. Rooms here are in the range of US$20 to US$40.

The four-storey *Thong Nhat Hotel* (☎ 825-406; fax 822943; 35 rooms) at 99 Thong Nhat St has been recently renovated and is very cushy. The cushiness costs US$33 to US$40 for a double.

If you have your own set of wheels, you can get away from it all at the *Ninh Tru Hotel* (☎ 873900). This is at Ninh Tru (also spelled Ninh Chu) Beach, 7km from Phan Rang proper. Rooms cost US$20 to US$45.

### Places to Eat

A local delicacy is roasted or baked gecko (ky nhong) served with fresh green mango. If you prefer self-catering and have fast reflexes, you could always try catching your own gecko off the ceiling in your hotel room.

Phan Rang is the grape capital of Vietnam. Stalls alongside National Highway 1 on the south side of town sell fresh grapes, grape juice and dried grapes (too juicy to be called raisins).

The *Thu Thuy Restaurant* is a three-storey eatery on Thong Nhat St.

### Getting There & Away

**Bus** Buses from Saigon to Phan Rang-Thap Cham depart from Mien Dong bus station.

Phan Rang intercity bus station (Ben Xe Phan Rang) is on the northern outskirts of town opposite 64 Thong Nhat St

The local bus station is at the southern end of town across the street from 426 Thong Nhat St.

**Train** The Thap Cham railway station is about 6km west of National Highway 1 within sight of Po Klong Garai Cham towers.

**Car** Phan Rang is 344km from Ho Chi Minh City, 147km from Phan Thiet, 105km from Nha Trang and 110km from Dalat.

# Khanh Hoa Province

### CAM RANH BAY

Cam Ranh Bay is an excellent natural harbour 56km north of Phan Rang-Thap Cham. The Russian fleet of Admiral Rodjestvenski used it in 1905 at the end of the Russo-Japanese War, as did the Japanese during WWII, when the area was still considered an excellent place for tiger hunting. In the mid-1960s, the Americans constructed a vast base here, including an extensive port, ship-repair facilities and an airstrip.

After reunification, the Russians and their fleet came back, enjoying far better facilities than they had found seven decades before. For a while this became the largest Soviet naval installation outside the USSR.

Despite repeated requests from the Russians, the Vietnamese refused to grant them permanent rights to the base. In 1988 Mikhail Gorbachev offered to abandon the installation if the Americans would do the same with their six bases across the South China Sea in the Philippines. The following year, however, the Vietnamese, evidently annoyed with the Soviets, appeared to offer the Americans renewed use of Cam Ranh Bay. The Soviet presence at Cam Ranh Bay was significantly reduced in 1990 as part of the Kremlin's cost-cutting measures. The Cold War ended with the collapse of the Soviet Union in 1991. Furthermore, the USA did close its bases in the Philippines in 1991 (more accurately, the Filipino Senate unceremoniously told the Americans to leave).

Subsequent economic problems have forced the Russians to vastly cut back on their overseas military facilities. However, there are still about 200 to 300 Russians still based here, but only two or three ships at any given time.

Of course, just because the USA and former USSR no longer compete for turf does not mean that there is no need for a military base at Cam Ranh Bay. The Vietnamese are growing increasingly nervous about China's intentions. The Chinese have been rapidly and relentlessly building up their naval facilities in the South China Sea – in 1988 and again in 1992 China seized several islands claimed by Vietnam. In 1995 the Chinese navy seized some more islands claimed by the Philippines. The day may soon come when the Vietnamese will want the facilities at Cam Ranh Bay for their own military use.

The Russian government has informed the Vietnamese of a willingness to permanently withdraw from the bases whenever Vietnam repays its debts. The Vietnamese owe about 30 billion roubles to the former Soviet Union. The Russians are insisting that they should be repaid at the exchange rate in effect at the time of the loans, which was one rouble to one US dollar. The Vietnamese insist that they wish to repay the loan at the present exchange rate of about 4000 roubles to the dollar. The two sides remain far apart on the issue, but until it's resolved, Cam Ranh Bay remains the last hurrah for the Russian navy in Asia.

There are beautiful beaches around Cam Ranh Bay – indeed, Americans stationed here during the war sometimes called it Vietnam's Hawaii. However, as long as this area remains a military base, it isn't likely to develop into a tourist resort. Some American military veterans have managed to tour the facilities at Cam Ranh Bay on organised tours arranged through government-owned travel agencies.

**Places to Eat**

There are some terrific seafood places along National Highway 1 right beside the '63km to Nha Trang' and '41km to Phan Rang' marker. One such place which has become fashionable with foreign travellers is the *Ngoc Suong Seafood Restaurant* (☎ 854603). This is a favourite lunch stop on the Dalat-Nha Trang run.

**NHA TRANG**

Nha Trang (population 200,000), the capital of Khanh Hoa Province, has what is probably the nicest municipal beach in all of Vietnam. Club Med hasn't arrived yet, there are still no Monte Carlo-style casinos and only a couple of neon signs. Nevertheless, this area has the potential to become another flashy resort like Thailand's Pattaya Beach (dread the thought), but that will probably take a few more years.

The turquoise waters around Nha Trang are almost transparent, making for excellent fishing, snorkelling and scuba diving. The service on the beach is incredible – massage, lunch, cold beer, manicure, beauty treatments, you name it. Of late, lots of 'massage' signs have been popping up around town, a sure sign that more visitors are expected.

Nha Trang's dry season, unlike that of Saigon, runs from June to October. The wettest months are October and November, but rain usually falls only at night or in the morning.

The combined fishing fleet of Khanh Hoa Province and neighbouring Phu Yen Province numbers about 10,000 trawlers and junks; they are able to fish during the 250 days of calm seas per year. The area's seafood products include abalone, lobster,

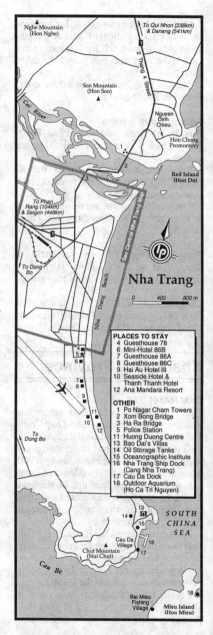

**Nha Trang**

0    400    800 m

**PLACES TO STAY**
4  Guesthouse 78
6  Mini-Hotel 86B
7  Guesthouse 86A
8  Guesthouse 86C
9  Hai Au Hotel III
10  Seaside Hotel &
     Thanh Thanh Hotel
12  Ana Mandara Resort

**OTHER**
1  Po Nagar Cham Towers
2  Xom Bong Bridge
3  Ha Ra Bridge
5  Police Station
11  Huong Duong Centre
13  Bao Dai's Villas
14  Oil Storage Tanks
15  Oceanographic Institute
16  Nha Trang Ship Dock
     (Cang Nha Trang)
17  Cau Da Dock
18  Outdoor Aquarium
     (Ho Ca Tri Nguyen)

prawns, cuttle-fish, mackerel, pomfret, scallops, shrimps, snapper and tuna. Exportable agricultural products from the area include cashew nuts, coconuts, coffee and sesame seeds. Salt production employs 4000 people.

## Orientation

Tran Phu St runs along Nha Trang Beach. The centre of Nha Trang is around the Nha Trang Hotel I on Thong Nhat St.

## Information

**Travel Agencies** Khanh Hoa Tourist (Cong Ty Du Lich Khanh Hoa; ☎ 822753; fax 824206) is the provincial tourism authority. Its office is in the Vien Dong Hotel at 1 Tran Hung Dao St. It's open daily from 7 to 11.30 am and 1.30 to 5 pm.

Right in front of the Nha Trang Sailing Club at 72 Tran Phu St is Hon Tam Tourist (☎ 829100). It's a full-fledged travel agency doing everything from selling boat trips to arranging visa extensions.

**Money** Vietcombank (Ngan Hang Ngoai Thuong; ☎ 822720) is at 17 Quang Trung St. It is open from 7 to 11.30 am and 1 to 5 pm Monday to Saturday, except Thursday afternoon.

**Post & Communications** The GPO is at 2 Tran Phu St, near the northern end of Nha Trang Beach. It is open daily from 6.30 am to 8.30 pm.

## Po Nagar Cham Towers

The Cham towers of Po Nagar, also known as Thap Ba (the Lady of the City), were built between the 7th and 12th centuries. The site was used for Hindu worship as early as the 2nd century AD. Today, both ethnic-Chinese and Vietnamese Buddhists come to Po Nagar to pray and make offerings according to their respective traditions. Out of deference to the continuing religious significance of this site, remove your shoes before entering.

There were once seven or eight towers at Po Nagar, four of which remain. All the temples face east, as did the original entrance to the complex, which is to the right as you ascend the hillock. In centuries past, a person coming to pray passed through the pillared *mandapa* (meditation hall), 10 of whose pillars can still be seen, before proceeding up the staircase to the towers.

The 23m-high North Tower (Thap Chinh), with its terraced pyramidal roof, vaulted interior masonry and vestibule, is a superb example of Cham architecture. It was built in 817 AD by Pangro, a minister of King Harivarman I, 43 years after the temples here were sacked and burned by Malay corsairs, who probably came from Srivijaya on Sumatra. The raiders also carried off a linga made of precious metal. In 918 AD King Indravarman III placed a gold mukha-linga in the North Tower, but it was taken by the Khmers. In 965 AD King Jaya Indravarman I replaced the gold mukha-linga with the stone figure of Uma (a shakti of Shiva), which remains to this day.

Above the entrance to the North Tower, two musicians flank a dancing four-armed Shiva, one of whose feet is on the head of the bull Nandin. The sandstone doorposts are covered with inscriptions, as are parts of the walls of the vestibule. A gong and a drum stand under the pyramid-shaped ceiling of the antechamber. In the 28m-high pyramidal main chamber there is a black stone statue of the goddess Uma (in the shape of Bhagavati) with 10 arms, two of which are hidden under her vest; she is seated leaning back against some sort of monstrous animal.

The Central Tower (Thap Nam) was built partly of recycled bricks in the 12th century on the site of a structure dating from the 7th century. It is less finely constructed than the other towers and has little ornamentation; the pyramidal roof lacks terracing or pilasters. Note the inscription on the left-hand wall of the vestibule. The interior altars were once covered with silver. There is a linga inside the main chamber.

The South Tower (Mieu Dong Nam), at one time dedicated to Sandhaka (Shiva), now shelters a linga.

The richly ornamented North-West Tower (Thap Tay Bac) was originally dedicated to Ganesha. The pyramid-shaped summit of the

Po Nagar
Cham Towers
Scale Unknown

roof of the North-West Tower has disappeared.

The West Tower, of which almost nothing remains, was constructed by King Vikrantavarman during the first half of the 9th century.

Near the North Tower is a small museum with a few mediocre examples of Cham stonework; the explanatory signs are in Vietnamese only. At one time there was a small temple on this site. If you are heading north, be sure to visit the Cham Museum in Danang, which has the finest collection of Cham statuary.

The towers of Po Nagar stand on a granite knoll 2km north of Nha Trang on the left bank of the Cai River. To get there from Nha Trang, take Quang Trung St (which becomes 2 Thang 4 St) north across Ha Ra Bridge and Xom Bong Bridge, which span the mouth of the Cai River.

### Hon Chong Promontory

Hon Chong is a narrow granite promontory that juts out into the turquoise waters of the South China Sea. The views of the mountainous coastline north of Nha Trang and nearby islands are certainly fine. Unfortunately, the place seems to have been taken over by souvenir kiosks which block the view from the promontory.

To the north-west is Nui Co Tien (Fairy Mountain), whose three summits are believed to resemble a reclining female fairy. The peak on the right is her face, which is gazing up towards the sky; the middle peak is her breasts; and the summit on the left (the highest) forms her crossed legs.

To the north-east is Hon Rua (Tortoise Island), which really does resemble a tortoise. The two islands of Hon Yen are off in the distance to the east. About 300m south of Hon Chong (that is, towards Nha Trang) and a few dozen metres from the beach is tiny Hon Do (Red Island), which has a Buddhist temple on top.

There is a gargantuan handprint on the massive boulder balanced at the tip of the promontory. According to local legend, it was made by a drunk male giant fairy when he fell down upon spying a female fairy bathing nude at Bai Tien (Fairy Beach), which is the point of land closest to Hon Rua. Despite the force of his fall, the giant managed to get up and eventually catch the fairy. The two began a life together, but soon the gods intervened and punished the male fairy, sending him off to a 're-education camp' (this is evidently a post-1975 version of the story) for an indefinite sentence.

The love-sick female fairy waited patiently for her husband to come back, but after a very long time, despairing that he might never return, she lay down in sorrow and turned into Nui Co Tien (Fairy Mountain). When the giant male fairy finally returned and saw what had become of his wife, he prostrated himself in grief next to the boulder with his handprint on it. He, too, turned to stone and can be seen to this day.

Hon Chong is 3.5km from central Nha Trang. To get there from Po Nagar, head north on 2 Thang 4 St for 400m. Just before 15, 2 Thang 4 St, turn right onto Nguyen Dinh Chieu St and follow the road for about 700m.

### Beaches

**Nha Trang Beach** Coconut palms provide shelter for both bathers and strollers along most of Nha Trang's 6km of beachfront. Beach chairs are available for rent – you can just sit all day and enjoy the drinks and light food which beach vendors have on offer. About the only time you need to move is to use the toilet or when the tide comes up. The water is remarkably clear.

**Hon Chong Beach** Hon Chong Beach (Bai Tam Hon Chong) is a series of beaches that begin just north of Hon Chong Promontory; fishing families live here among the coconut palms, but their refuse makes the place unsuitable for swimming or sunbathing. Behind the beaches are steep mountains whose lower reaches support crops that include mangoes and bananas.

### Pasteur Institute

Nha Trang's Pasteur Institute was founded in 1895 by Dr Alexandre Yersin (1863-1943), who was – from among the tens of thousands of colonists who spent time in Vietnam – probably the Frenchman most beloved by the Vietnamese. Born in Switzerland of French and Swiss parents, Dr Yersin came to Vietnam in 1889 after working under Louis Pasteur in Paris. He spent the next four years travelling throughout the Central Highlands and recording his observations. During this period he came upon the site of what is now Dalat and recommended to the government that a hill station be established there. In 1894, in Hong Kong, he discovered the rat-borne microbe that causes bubonic plague. Dr Yersin was the first to introduce rubber and quinine-producing trees to Vietnam.

Today, the Pasteur Institute in Nha Trang coordinates vaccination and hygiene programmes for the country's southern coastal region. Despite its minuscule budget and antiquated equipment (the labs look much as they did half a century ago), the Institute produces vaccines (eg rabies, diphtheria, pertussis, typhoid) and tries to carry out research in microbiology, virology and epidemiology. Vietnam's two other Pasteur Institutes are in Saigon and Dalat.

Dr Yersin's library and office are now a museum; items on display include laboratory equipment (such as his astronomical instruments) and some of his personal effects. There is a picture of Dr Yersin above the door to the veranda. The model boat was given to him by local fishers with whom he spent a great deal of time. The Institute library, which is across the landing from the museum, houses many of Dr Yersin's books as well as modern scientific journals. At his request, Dr Yersin is buried near Nha Trang.

To find someone to show you the museum (Vien Bao Tang), ask around in the main building (a mauve-coloured two-storey structure) during working hours (except at lunchtime). The museum is on the 2nd floor of the back wing of the main building. To get there, go up the stairs near the sign that reads Thu Vien (Library).

### Long Son Pagoda

Aside from the beach, the most impressive sight in Nha Trang is Long Son Pagoda (also known as Tinh Hoi Khanh Hoa Pagoda and An Nam Phat Hoc Hoi Pagoda). It's about 500m west of the railway station opposite 15 23/10 St. The pagoda, which has resident monks, was founded in the late 19th century and has been rebuilt several times over the years. The entrance and roofs are decorated with mosaic dragons made of glass and bits of ceramic tile. The main sanctuary is an attractive hall adorned with modern interpretations of traditional motifs. Note the ferocious nose hairs on the colourful dragons which are wrapped around the pillars on either side of the main altar.

At the top of the hill behind the pagoda is the huge white Buddha (Kim Than Phat To), seated on a lotus blossom, which is visible from all over the city. There are great views of Nha Trang and nearby rural areas from the platform around the 14m-high figure, which was built in 1963. As you approach the pagoda from the street, the 152 stone steps up the hill to the Buddha begin to the right of the structure. You should also take some time to explore off to your left, where you'll find an entrance to another impressive hall of the pagoda.

### Nha Trang Cathedral

Nha Trang Cathedral, built in French Gothic style and complete with medieval-looking stained glass windows, stands on a small hill overlooking the railway station. It was constructed of simple cement blocks between 1928 and 1933. Today, the cathedral is the seat of the bishop of Nha Trang. In 1988, a Catholic cemetery not far from the church was disinterred to make room for a new building for the railway station. The ashes were brought to the cathedral and reburied in cavities behind the wall of plaques lining the ramp up the hill.

Masses are held daily at 5 am and 4.30 pm, and on Sunday at 5 and 7 am and 4.30 pm. If the main gate on Thai Nguyen St is closed, go up the ramp opposite 17 Nguyen Trai St to the back of the building.

### Oceanographic Institute

The Oceanographic Institute (Vien Nghiem Cuu Bien; ☎ 822536), founded in 1923, has an aquarium *(ho ca)* and specimen room open to the public; it also has a library. The ground-floor aquarium's 23 tanks are home

to a variety of colourful live specimens of local marine life, including seahorses. It is open daily from 7 to 11.30 am and 1.30 to 5 pm.

Behind the main building and across the volleyball court is a large hall filled with 60,000 dead specimens of sea life, including stuffed sea birds and fish, corals and the corporeal remains of various marine creatures preserved in glass jars.

The Oceanographic Institute is 6km south of Nha Trang's GPO in the port district of Cau Da (also called Cau Be).

As nice as the Oceanographic Institute is, if you really want to see an aquarium you should take a boat across to nearby Mieu Island (see the Around Nha Trang entry later in this section).

### Bao Dai's Villas

Between the mid-50s and 1975, Bao Dai's Villas (Biet Thu Cau Da; ☎ 822449, 821124) were used by high-ranking officials of the South Vietnamese government, including President Thieu. This all changed in 1975, when the villas were taken over for use by high-ranking Communist officials who included Prime Minister Pham Van Dong. Today, low-ranking 'capitalist tourists' can rent a room in the villas (for details, see Places to Stay).

Bao Dai's five villas, built in the 1920s, are set on three hills with brilliant views of the South China Sea, Nha Trang Bay (to the north) and Cau Da dock (to the south). Between the buildings are winding paths lined with tropical bushes and trees. Most of the villas' furnishings have not been changed in decades.

To get to Bao Dai's Villas from Nha Trang, turn left off Tran Phu St just past the white cement oil storage tanks (but before reaching Cau Da village). The villas are several hundred metres north of the Oceanographic Institute.

### Thung Chai Basket Boats

The 2m-wide round baskets used by fishers to transport themselves from the shore to their boats (and between boats) are made of woven bamboo strips covered with pitch.

# Central Nha Trang

To Po Nagar Cham Towers (300m),
Hon Chong Promontory (1.6km),
National Highway 1 Northbound,
Qui Nhon (238km) & Danang (541km)

Xom Bong Bridge

Cai River

Ha Ra Bridge

0        150        300 m

Phuong Sai

Nguyen Hong Son Street

2 Thang 4 Street

Nguyen Cong Tru St

Thai Hoc Street

Quang Trung Street

Tran Qui Cap Street

Thong Nhat Street

Hoang Van Thu Street

Phan Boi Chau Street

Phan Chu Trinh Street

Dinh Phung Street

Le Loi Street

Hai Ba Trung Street

Pasteur Street

Yet Kieu Street

Le Thanh Ton Street

Ly Thanh Ton Street

23 Thang 10 Street

Thai Nguyen Street

To National
Highway 1 Southbound,
Lien Tinh Bus Station,
Phan Rang (104km)
& Saigon (448km)

Le Hong Phong Street

Nha Trang Railway Station

Nguyen Trai Street

Stadium

Yersin Street

Ly Tu Trong St

Nguyen Chanh Street

Hoang Hoa Tham Street

Tran Hung Dao Street

Nguyen Thien Thuat Street

To Hien Thanh Street

Tran Phu Street

Nha Trang Beach

SOUTH
CHINA
SEA

Hung Vuong Street

Nguyen Huu Huan Street

Tran Nguyen Han Street

Phu Dong Street

Nguyen Thi Minh Khai Street

Biet Thu Street

To Airport

To Airport

To Bao Dai's Villas (3km),
Oceanographic Institute,
Cau Da Village & Cau Da Dock

To Bamboo
Island
(Hon Tre)
(2.5km)

To Mieu Island
(4km)

**PLACES TO STAY**
6  Thang Loi Hotel
8  Post Hotel
11  White Sand Hotel
17  Nha Trang Hotel I
18  Nha Trang Hotel II
22  Royal Hotel
25  Thong Nhat Hotel
27  Saigon-Nha Trang Hotel
28  Duy Tan Hotel
29  Hai Au Hotel II
   & Outrigger Hotel
31  Hai Au Hotel I
32  Ha Phuong Hotel
33  Nha Trang Hotel III
35  Thuy Duong Hotel
36  Hung Dao Hotel
37  Vien Dong Hotel
38  Hai Yen Hotel
39  Coconut Grove Resort
   & 4 Seasons Café
41  Nha Trang Lodge
44  Grand Hotel
47  Guesthouse 58
48  Que Huong Hotel
49  Guesthouse 62
50  Khatoco Hotel
51  Vina Hotel

**PLACES TO EAT**
3  Lac Canh Restaurant
   & Hoan Hai Restaurant
4  Vietnam II Restaurant
   & Dua Xanh Restaurant
5  Kinh Do Restaurant
   & Thanh The Restaurant
9  Café des Amis
12  Restaurant 505
14  Ice Cream Shops
15  Restaurant Lys
16  Binh Minh Restaurant
19  Ngoc Lan Restaurant
26  Saiga Bar & Restaurant
34  Hanh Café
40  Hai Yen Café
42  Vinagen Café
45  Sinh Café

**OTHER**
1  Short-Haul Bus Station
2  Dam Market
7  Post Office
10  Pasteur Institute
   & Yersin Museum
13  Vietcombank
20  Giant Seated Buddha
21  Long Son Pagoda
23  Nha Trang Cathedral
24  Bien Vien Tinh (Hospital)
30  Vietnam Airlines
43  War Memorial Obelisk
46  Vietnam Airlines
52  Nha Trang Sailing Club
   & Hon Tam Tourist

They are known in Vietnamese as *thung chai* (*thung* means 'basket', *chai* means 'pitch'). Rowed standing up, a thung chai can carry four or five people.

Nha Trang's fishing fleet operates mostly at night, spending the days in port for rest and equipment repair.

### Activities

For scuba diving, check out the Blue Diving Club (☎ 825390) at the Coconut Cove Resort, on the beach opposite the Hai Yen Hotel.

Hon Tam Tourist (☎ 829100) at 72 Tran Phu St is the place to look for surfboards and snorkelling equipment. Another place to look for water toys is Khanh Hoa Tourist (☎ 822753) inside the Vien Dong Hotel.

Boat trips are the thing to do. For information, see the Around Nha Trang entry later in this section.

### Places to Stay – bottom end

Nha Trang is a trendy place for both domestic and foreign tourists, with the result that accommodation is tight despite the plethora of hotels. The situation may improve as more hotels are built, but for now it can be hard to find a room. This is particularly true if you want to stay near the beach (everybody does) and want something cheap. If you find the beachside hotels to be all full, check out the hotels nearer to the railway station. Also look into the southern area around Bao Dai's Villas because it's relatively far from the centre of things and therefore tends to get fewer visitors.

Another consideration is Nha Trang's climate. Although located well within the tropical zone, Nha Trang has cool evenings and is the first place (outside the highlands) as you head north where you should try to find a hotel with hot water.

The *Huu Nghi Hotel* (☎ 826703; fax 827416; 65 rooms), 3 Tran Hung Dao St, is a time-honoured backpackers' haunt. Doubles cost US$7 to US$23, and quads are US$13 to US$27.

*Guesthouse 58* (Nha Khach 58; ☎ 826304; 45 rooms) is also known as the *Hai Quan Guesthouse* (meaning 'Navy Guesthouse').

As you may have guessed, the address is 58 Tran Phu St. It's a motel-style place, but some of the old colonial rooms with porch are simply marvellous. Rooms cost US$12 to US$20. Reception is buried in the rear building – you may have to search a bit.

*Guesthouse 62* (Nha Khach 62; ☎ 825-095; 38 rooms) at 62 Tran Phu St has an air of dilapidated elegance. Singles with fan and cold-water bath are US$7, but if you add hot water it's US$8. Air-con raises the tariff to US$15.

*Guesthouse 78* (Nha Khach 78; ☎ 826-342; 36 rooms), 78 Tran Phu St, is opposite the beach. This pleasant motel-style place has singles with shared bath for US$6, doubles with cold/hot-water bath for US$8/10, and doubles with air-con and hot water for US$12. There is a luggage storage room, which is a convenience if you're taking a boat trip and will be checking out in the late afternoon.

The *Ha Phuong Hotel* (☎ 829015), 30 Hoang Hoa Tham St, has lots of parking and is a favourite for people arriving with rented vehicles. Doubles are priced at US$12 to US$18.

The *Que Huong Hotel* (☎ 825047; fax 825344), 60 Tran Phu St, positively exudes elegance. Rooms with fan cost US$13, while air-con and satellite TV raises the ante to US$15. It's hard to believe that it will keep the price so low for very long and this could soon move into the 'mid-range' price category.

There's a whole chain of places calling themselves the *Hai Au Hotel*. There's the *Hai Au Hotel I* (☎ 822862) at 3 Nguyen Chanh St; *Hai Au Hotel II* (☎ 823644; 15 rooms) at 4 Nguyen Chanh St; and *Hai Au Hotel III* (☎ 822826; 27 rooms) at 88 Tran Phu St. The price range at all three is around US$10 to US$15 for a room with fan, or US$20 to US$25 for air-con.

*Guesthouse 86A* (☎ 826526; 96 rooms) at 86A Tran Phu St belongs to the army and looks much like a barracks. There are 67 miserable rooms with fan only and shared bath (cold water!) for US$6. Rooms with fan and hot-water bath are US$7, and there are a few air-con rooms for US$15.

*Mini-Hotel 86B*, 86 Tran Phu St, is actually three hotels inside the same building. All three places have air-con, hot water and a sea view. Doubles are US$10.

*Guesthouse 86C* (☎ 824074; 18 rooms), 86C Tran Phu St, is nearby. This place is notable for sea views and the big noisy seafood restaurant on the roof. Rooms with fan and cold-water bath are US$7, while hot water and air-con raises the rate to US$15.

The *Thong Nhat Hotel* (☎ 822966; 80 rooms) at 5 Yersin St is an old place that looks overwhelmed by a massive new hotel construction project just next door (the Saigon-Nha Trang Hotel). Probably all that noise from the construction has driven down room rates, which currently are US$7 to US$20. No one is certain if prices will rise when the jackhammers stop, but the Thong Nhat itself may be a candidate for renovation.

The *Thuy Duong Hotel* (☎ 822534; 14 rooms), 36 Tran Phu St, is a state-run basket-case. The hotel is due for renovation (with price rises to match), but for the moment it's cheap enough. Rooms with attached cold-water bath cost US$6 to US$10. Hot water and air-con will cost you US$12 to US$15.

Both the *Nha Trang Hotel I*, 129 Thong Nhat St, and *Nha Trang Hotel II*, 21 Le Thanh Phuong St, are too far from the beach to be popular with foreigners (many Vietnamese don't care). Consider these two hotels a possibility only if you can't find something closer to the shoreline. Doubles with fan cost US$8, or with air-con it's US$12 to US$25.

The *Royal Hotel* (☎ 822298, 822385; 44 rooms) is at 40 Thai Nguyen St, opposite the railway station. As such, it's far from the beach and therefore not desirable, but will probably be another place that has rooms when the beach area hotels are full. Rooms with fan cost US$6 to US$14. Air-con doubles are US$20.

## Places to Stay – middle

The *White Sand Hotel* (Khach San Cat Trang; ☎ 825861; fax 824204; 20 rooms) at 14 Tran Phu St is a cosy little place near the beach. Doubles are US$18 to US$27. If full, you can book rooms here for the *White Sand*

*Hotel II* (☎ 823732; 25 rooms), which is at 9 Yersin St.

The *Grand Hotel* (Nha Khach 44; ☎ 822-445; 50 rooms) is a large place with a beach view. It looks a bit like a former Communist Party headquarters, but is still not a bad place to stay. Rooms with air-con and hot water cost US$18 to US$63.

The *Thanh Thanh Hotel* (☎ 824657; 823031; 18 rooms), 98A Tran Phu St, is a fine place with balconies overlooking the sea. Rooms are US$10 to US$25 in the low season, and US$15 to US$30 in summer.

Even better is the *Seaside Hotel* just next door. This place was so new during our visit that it didn't have the phones installed yet. The 13 rooms cost US$20 to US$40.

The *Vina Hotel* (☎ 825137; 25 rooms), 66 Tran Phu St, is known for its sea views and massage services. Rates here are US$18 to US$33.

The *Thang Loi Hotel* (☎ 822241; fax 821905; 57 rooms), which resembles a US-style motel, is 100m from the beach at 4 Pasteur St. Aside from being built on a street with a French name, the hotel also has a French nickname (Hotel La Fregate). There are a few bottom-end rooms with fan and cold water for US$7 to US$10, but hot water, air-con and satellite TV will cost you US$16 to US$35.

The *Post Hotel* (Khach San Buu Dien; ☎ 821250; fax 824205; 24 rooms), 2 Le Loi St, is adjacent to the GPO. This fancy place has rooms in the range of US$29 to US$42.

The *Duy Tan Hotel* (☎ 822671; fax 825034; 83 rooms) is a large beachside place at 24 Tran Phu St. This hotel was recently renovated and now looks great. The price range is US$22 to US$50.

The *Outrigger Hotel* is a new place under construction just next to the Duy Tan Hotel. Not much can be said about it except that it's near the beach and should be good.

The *Nha Trang Hotel III* (☎ 823933; five rooms) at 22 Tran Hung Dao St is far superior to Nha Trang Hotels I and II. This one has villas one block from the beach, and everyone who stays here seems to rave about the place. Doubles cost US$30.

The *Vien Dong Hotel* (☎ 821506; fax

821912; 104 rooms), 1 Tran Hung Dao St, has long been a travellers' favourite. The Vien Dong (which means Far East) has a swimming pool, photoprocessing facilities and bicycle rentals. Doubles are US$20 to US$75. According to the Vien Dong's pamphlet, 'weapons and objects with offensive smell should be kept at the reception desk'.

The *Hai Yen Hotel* (☎ 822828; fax 821-902; 120 rooms), whose name means 'sea swift', faces the beach at 40 Tran Phu St. It's notable for its big bright lights at night. The scruffiest rooms with shared bath cost a mere US$5, but these are mostly given to Vietnamese minibus drivers. Foreigners are herded into rooms with air-con and hot water from US$20 to US$100.

*Khatoco Hotel* (☎ 823724; fax 821925; 24 rooms) at 9 Biet Thu St is run by a tobacco company. Anti-smoking activists will perhaps want to stay elsewhere, but others will find this hotel to be fairly plush. The price range is US$30 to US$70. Smoking in bed is not permitted.

Farthest from the town centre are *Bao Dai's Villas* (☎ 881049; fax 821906; 28 rooms), also known as *Cau Da Villas*. These are near Cau Da on the coast 6km south of the railway station. The top-end rooms are spacious with high ceilings and huge bathrooms. This is where Vietnam's ruling elite has rested itself since the days of French rule (including the current elite). Rooms cost US$25 to US$70.

### Places to Stay – top end

The *Nha Trang Lodge* (☎ 810500; fax 828800; 121 rooms), 42 Tran Phu St, has 13 floors, making it Nha Trang's tallest highrise. This glittering luxury tower offers rooms for US$75 to US$145.

The *Ana Mandara Resort* (☎ 829829; fax 829629) is a set of beach villas on the south side of town. We can't tell you too much about it because it was under construction at the time of writing. However, we do know it's a foreign joint venture and promises to be luxurious and expensive.

### Places to Eat

**Beach Area** The *Nha Trang Sailing Club*

(☎ 826528) at 72 Tran Phu St draws in most of the westerners who crave beachside dining.

Up at the northern end of the beach is the *Saiga Bar & Restaurant*. The food isn't memorable, but the sea breeze can't be beat.

Right on the beach opposite the Hai Yen Hotel is the huge *Four Season's Cafe*, which is adjacent to the equally relaxing *Coconut Cove Resort*. Both are outdoor places with a thatched sun roof to offer protection from the weather.

Another notable beachside restaurant is the *Vinagen Cafe*, but it serves Vinagen beer only and blasts continuous karaoke music that often drives western customers away.

*Casa Italia Ristorante* (☎ 823194) is inside the enormous Huong Duong Centre near the southern end of Nha Trang Beach. In the daytime you may want to use the private beach here – vendors are not permitted on the grounds, a restriction you'll come to appreciate with time.

**Central Area** *Hanh Cafe*, 5 Tran Hung Dao St, next to the Huu Nghi Hotel, is the venerable travellers' cafe cum travel agency for backpackers. Another alternative is *Sinh Cafe* at 10 Hung Vuong St.

One of the best restaurants in town is the *Lac Canh Restaurant*, which is a block east of Dam Market at 11 Hang Ca St. Beef, squid, giant shrimps, lobsters and the like are grilled right at your table.

*Hoan Hai Restaurant* at 6 Phan Chu Trinh St is near the Lac Canh and is in some ways better. The menu contains delicious marinated beef, vegetarian dishes and some of the best spring rolls in Vietnam. It has friendly service too.

In the same area is the excellent *Thanh The Restaurant* (☎ 821931) at 3 Phan Chu Trinh St. This place does Vietnamese, Chinese and European-style food.

The *Restaurant Lys* at 117A Hoang Van Thu St is a big, bright and energetic place with an English menu. There's also great seafood at the *Ngoc Lan Restaurant* at 37 Le Thanh Phuong St.

Then, of course, there's *Dam Market* itself, which has a collection of stalls in the

**Dragon Fruit**
Nha Trang is best known for its excellent seafood, but a really exotic treat is green dragon fruit *(thanh long)*. This fruit, which is the size and shape of a small pineapple and has an almost-smooth magenta skin, grows only in the Nha Trang area. Its delicious white meat is speckled with black seeds and tastes a bit like kiwifruit. Green dragon fruit grows on a kind of creeping cactus – said to resemble a green dragon – that climbs up the trunks and branches of trees and flourishes on parched hillsides that get very little water. Thanh long is in season from May to September and can be purchased at Dam Market. It is also exported to Saigon and even abroad (it now fetches a high price in Taiwan), but only in Nha Trang is this fruit cheap and fresh. Locals often make a refreshing drink out of crushed green dragon fruit, ice, sugar and sweetened condensed milk. They also use it to make jam. ■

covered semi-circular food pavilion. Vegetarian food can be found here too.

The *Binh Minh Restaurant*, founded in 1953, is at 64 Hoang Van Thu St (corner Yet Kieu St) in the central area. Its Vietnamese dishes are excellent; however, prices are not cheap.

The *Dua Xanh Restaurant* at 23 Le Loi St is a new spot, with many seafood dishes. The outdoor garden has nine tables, and there are several more indoors. Leave some room for dessert – good cakes, custard and ice cream are served here.

For ice cream, try the shops around 52 Quang Trung St (corner Le Thanh Ton St).

**South Area** The *Cau Da Villas Restaurant* is next to the beach and tennis courts below Bao Dai's Villas. From the reception area in the villas, take the long steps down to the tennis courts. The speciality here is the delicious shrimp and beef barbecued on table-top burners.

### Entertainment
Locals head for karaoke lounges, but foreigners congregate at the *Nha Trang Sailing Club* (☎ 826528) at 72 Tran Phu St right on the beach.

Nearby is the Huong Duong Centre, also known as Paradise Village. Inside you'll find the *Hexagone Disco*, which is open from 8 pm until sunrise.

### Things to Buy
There are a number of shops selling beautiful seashells (and items made from seashells) near the Oceanographic Institute in Cau Da village. As a glossy tourist brochure put it, 'Before leaving Nha Trang, tourists had better call at Cau Da to get some souvenirs of the sea ... for their dears at home'. Inexpensive guitars are on sale at 24 Hai Ba Trung St (corner Phan Chu Trinh St). The Hai Yen Hotel has a small gift shop.

### Getting There & Away
**Air** Vietnam Airlines has flights connecting Nha Trang with Saigon two times daily. There are flights to/from Hanoi once daily. Flights to/from Danang fly four times a week.

Vietnam Airlines' Nha Trang office (☎ 823797) is at 12B Hoang Hoa Tham St.

**Bus** Express and regular buses from Saigon to Nha Trang depart from Mien Dong bus station. By express bus, the trip takes 11 to 12 hours.

Lien Tinh bus station (Ben Xe Lien Tinh; ☎ 822192), Nha Trang's main intercity bus terminal, is on 23/10 St (500m west of the railway station). Nonexpress buses from Lien Tinh bus station go to:

Bao Loc, Bien Hoa (11 hours), Buon Ma Thuot (six hours), Dalat (six hours), Danang (14 hours), Di Linh, Ho Chi Minh City (12 hours), Phan Rang (2½ hours), Pleiku (10 hours), Quang Ngai, Qui Nhon (seven hours).

**Minibus** The preferred way to go, chartered

minibuses are easy to book at most of the places where travellers congregate.

Nha Trang-Saigon costs US$10 and departures are at 6.30 am. Nha Trang-Dalat costs US$8 and departures are at 7 am. Minibuses between Nha Trang and either Hoi An or Danang cost US$15 and depart twice daily at 5 am and 8 pm. Nha Trang-Hué costs US$22 and departures are twice daily at 5.30 am and 8 pm.

**Train** Hotels and travellers' cafes all book train tickets, and it's worth paying the small commission to use these booking services.

The Nha Trang railway station (Ga Nha Trang; ☎ 822113), overlooked by the nearby cathedral, is across the street from 26 Thai Nguyen St; the ticket office is open between 7 am and 2 pm only.

Nha Trang is well served by both express trains connecting Hanoi and Saigon, and a daily local train between Saigon and Nha Trang. For ticket prices, see the Train section in the Getting Around chapter.

**Car** Road distances from Nha Trang are: 205km to Buon Ma Thuot; 541km to Danang; 448km to Ho Chi Minh City; 104km to Phan Rang; 424km to Pleiku; 412km to Quang Ngai; and 238km to Qui Nhon.

A series of roughly parallel roads head inland from near Nha Trang, linking Vietnam's deltas and coastal regions with the Central Highlands.

### Getting Around

**The Airport** The airport is on the southern side of town and so close to many of the hotels that you can actually walk. Even cyclos can get you to the airport for about US$1.

**Taxi** Nha Trang Taxi (☎ 824000) and Khanh Hoa Taxi (☎ 810810) have air-conditioned cars with meters.

**Bicycle** All major hotels have bicycle rentals. The cost is US$1 per day or US$0.20 per hour.

## AROUND NHA TRANG
### The Islands

Khanh Hoa Province's 71 offshore islands are renowned for the remarkably clear water surrounding them. A trip to these islands is one of the main reasons for visiting Nha Trang, so try to schedule at least one day for a boat journey.

Virtually every hotel in town books a standard low-priced island tour, which is in fact operated by Hanh Cafe. This tour is known as the 'TM Brothers Boat Trip', with 'TM' meaning 'trouble makers'. Apparently it was named for the five brothers who starting organising these trips. Each one of the brothers is missing something important (an eye, fingers, an arm etc), and thus collectively acquired the nickname 'trouble'. This boat trip costs US$7 and gets rave reviews. One of the highlights is the lunch, which is an outdoor feast – many say it's the best meal in Nha Trang.

Aside from the TM Brothers, there are other boat trips. You can easily pay more for a less crowded and more luxurious boat which takes you to more islands. Indeed, you'll have to do this if you want to get in much snorkelling.

The place to charter boats is at the Cau Da dock at the southern end of Nha Trang. If you're not with an organised group, you'd better book the day before or go to Cau Da dock early in the morning – by 10 am all the boats are gone.

At some of the fishing villages on the islands, shallow water prevents the boats from reaching shore. In this case, you must walk perhaps several hundred metres across floats, a careful balancing act. The floats were designed for Vietnamese, and overweight westerners might get wet – take care with your camera. Nevertheless, it's all good fun and a visit to these fishing villages is highly recommended.

**Mieu Island** Mieu Island (also called Tri Nguyen Island) is touted in tourist literature as the site of an 'outdoor aquarium' (Ho Ca Tri Nguyen). In fact, the 'aquarium' is an important fish-breeding farm where over 40 species of fish, crustaceans and other marine creatures are raised in three separate compartments. There is a cafe built on stilts over the water. Ask around for canoe rentals.

The main village on Mieu Island is Tri Nguyen. Bai Soai is a gravel beach on the far side of Mieu Island from Cau Da.

Most people will take some sort of boat tour booked through a hotel, cafe or Khanh Hoa Tourist. Impoverished and less hurried travellers might catch one of the regular ferries that go to Tri Nguyen village from Cau Da dock.

**Bamboo Island (Hon Tre)** Several kilometres from the southern part of Nha Trang Beach is Bamboo Island, the largest island by far in the Nha Trang area. Tru Beach (Bai Tru) is at the northern end of the island. All kinds of boats can be hired to take you here.

**Ebony Island (Hon Mun)** This is just southeast of Bamboo Island and is known for its snorkelling. To get here, you'll probably have to hire a boat.

**Hon Tam** This is south-west of Bamboo Island, and is similar to its near neighbour, Ebony Island.

**Hon Mot** This tiny island is sandwiched neatly between Ebony Island and Hon Tam. Again, it's another place for snorkelling.

**Monkey Island (Dao Khi)** The island is named for its large contingent of resident monkeys, and has become a big hit with foreign visitors. Most of the monkeys have grown quite accustomed to receiving handouts from the tourists, so there is little problem getting close enough to take a memorable photo if you bring some food. If you offer it to them, the monkeys will take the food directly from your hand. However, these are wild monkeys, not zoo animals – you should not make any attempt to pet them, shake hands or pick them up. Some travellers have been scratched and bitten when they attempted to embrace their new-found friends.

Aside from being unwilling to cuddle, the monkeys are materialistic. They will grab the sunglasses off your face or snatch a pen from your shirt pocket and run off. So far, we haven't heard of monkeys slitting open travellers' handbags with a razor blade, but you do need to be almost as careful with your valuables here as you do on the streets of Saigon!

Monkey Island is 12km north of Bamboo Island, and one-day boat tours can easily be arranged in Nha Trang. A faster way to get here is to take a motorcycle or car 12km north of Nha Trang – near a pagoda is a place where boats will ferry you to the island for US$1. Bring some corn or beans to feed the monkeys.

**Salangane Island (Hon Yen or Dao Yen)** The name Salangane Island is actually applied to two lump-shaped islands visible in the distance from Nha Trang Beach. Salangane Island and other islands off Khanh Hoa Province are the source of Vietnam's finest *salangane* (swift) nests. The nests are used in bird's-nest soup as well as in traditional medicine, and are considered an aphrodisiac. It is said that Emperor Minh Mang, who ruled Vietnam from 1820 to 1840, derived his extraordinary virility from the consumption of salangane nests.

The nests, which the salanganes build out of their silk-like salivary secretions, are semi-oval and about 5 to 8cm in diameter. They are usually harvested twice a year. Red nests are the most highly prized. Annual production in Khanh Hoa and Phu Yen provinces is about 1000kg. At present, salangane nests fetch US$2000 per kg in the international marketplace!

There is a small, secluded beach at Salangane Island. The 17km trip out to the islands takes three to four hours by small boat.

**Dien Khanh Citadel**
The citadel dates from the 17th century Trinh Dynasty. It was rebuilt by Prince Nguyen Anh (later Emperor Gia Long) in 1793 during his successful offensive against the Tay Son Rebels. Only a few sections of the

walls and gates are extant. Dien Khanh Citadel is 11km west of Nha Trang near the villages of Dien Toan and Dien Thanh.

### Ba Ho Falls
Ba Ho Falls (Suoi Ba Ho), with its three waterfalls and three pools, is in a forested area 17km north of Nha Trang and about 5km west of Phu Huu Village, where you turn off National Highway 1. Ba Ho Falls is near Ninh Ich Xa in Vinh Xuong District.

### Fairy Spring
The enchanting little Fairy Spring (Suoi Tien) seems to pop out of nowhere as you approach it. Like a small oasis, the spring is decorated with its own natural garden of tropical vegetation and smooth boulders.

You'll need to rent a motorbike or car to reach the spring. Driving south on National Highway 1, you come to a spot 17km from Nha Trang where there is an archway to your left (east side of the highway). Turn off the highway here and go through the village. The road twists and winds it's way through the hills until it reaches a valley. Just as the road starts to get bad, you come upon the spring. You will probably see some other vehicles parked here as it's a popular spot with locals.

### DOC LET BEACH
Some call this the most spectacular beach in Vietnam, and it would be hard to argue with them. The beach is long and wide, with chalk-white sand and shallow water. Yet despite its beauty, Doc Let gets few visitors, though this is likely to change. From all appearances, it seems that one earlier attempt was made at tourist development, but this was abandoned and most of the buildings are falling apart. However, there still is one functioning restaurant and guesthouse.

### Places to Stay
The *Doc Let Hotel* is an unimpressive Vietnamese hotel, but there are also six beach bungalows here. Rooms in the hotel cost US$8, while it's only US$6 to rent a whole bungalow. There is no hot water and no air-con.

### Getting There & Away
Doc Let Beach is on a peninsula to the north of Nha Trang. There is no public transport to this spot, so you need to hire a vehicle. To get here, drive 30km north of Nha Trang on National Highway 1. Just north of Ninh Hoa is a petrol station and a fork in the road. You take the right fork (east) and continue for 10km until you reach the beach. A sign in English marks the turn-off. The road is occasionally closed due to flooding.

### DAI LANH BEACH
Semi-circular, casuarina-shaded Dai Lanh Beach is another beautiful spot 83km north of Nha Trang and 153km south of Qui Nhon on National Highway 1. At the southern end of the beach is a vast sand-dune causeway; it connects the mainland to Hon Gom, a mountainous peninsula almost 30km in length. The main village on Hon Gom is Dam Mon (known to the French as Port Dayot), which is on a sheltered bay facing the island of Hon Lon.

At the northern end of Dai Lanh Beach is Dai Lanh Promontory (Mui Dai Lanh), named Cap Varella by the French.

### Places to Stay & Eat
There is a four-storey half-completed tourist hotel just off National Highway 1, a few hundred metres south of town. Apparently, construction has been abandoned and the decaying structure is totally overgrown with weeds – makes an interesting photo. Perhaps a foreign investor will rescue the project, but if so it better happen soon before the whole thing topples over.

Just south of the abandoned hotel shell is the *Dai Lanh Restaurant*, the fanciest place in town. There are also at least a dozen small family-owned restaurants in Dai Lanh.

### Getting There & Away
Dai Lanh Beach runs along National Highway 1, so any vehicle travelling along the coast between Nha Trang and Tuy Hoa (or Qui Nhon) will get you there.

# Phu Yen Province

### TUY HOA

Tuy Hoa, the capital of Phu Yen Province, is a nondescript little town on the coast between Dai Lanh Beach and Qui Nhon. The highway crosses a huge river on the south side of town. The river is navigable and justifies Tuy Hoa's existence – there isn't much else to the place, not even a good beach.

The main interest of Tuy Hoa to travellers is that it has good accommodation, which could be useful if you get a late start heading north or south along National Highway 1.

### Information

**Travel Agencies** Phu Yen Tourist (Cong Ty Du Lich Phu Yen; ☎ 823353) is the provincial tourist office, and can be found at 137 Le Thanh Ton St.

### Places to Stay

The *Huong Sen Hotel* (☎ 823775; fax 823186; 50 rooms) and attached restaurant is a large fancy place near the centre of town. Room rates are US$15 to US$30.

### Getting There & Away

The odd thing about Tuy Hoa is that there is an airport. Vietnam Airlines runs two flights weekly between Tuy Hoa and Saigon.

### SONG CAU

The village of Song Cau is an obscure place that you could easily drive past without ever noticing, but it's worth stopping if you have the time. Near the village is an immense bay, a beautiful rest stop that attracts both foreign and domestic tourists.

Foreigners doing the Nha Trang-Hoi An run often make a stopoff for brunch in Song Cau, and some visitors even spend the night.

The main thing to do here is take a boat trip on the bay, which the hotel-restaurant can organise for US$10. The boat can hold 10 persons.

### Places to Stay & Eat

The *Nha Hang Bai Tien* (☎ 870322; 10 rooms) offers doubles with hot water for US$12. This privately run hotel and restaurant complex is built on stilts over the bay and makes for an attractive setting. The electricity comes from a private generator, which is normally switched on from 6 pm until midnight.

### Getting There & Away

Song Cau is 170km north of Nha Trang and 43km south of Qui Nhon. Highway buses can drop you off and pick you up here (with luck), but most travellers will probably arrive by chartered minibus.

# Binh Dinh Province

### QUI NHON

Qui Nhon (or Quy Nhon; population 200,000) is the capital of Binh Dinh Province and one of Vietnam's more active second-string seaports. The beaches in the immediate vicinity of the city are nothing to write home about, but Qui Nhon is a convenient – though somewhat disappointing – place to break the long journey from Nha Trang to Danang. The town used to be more prosperous a few years ago when smuggling imported goods by sea was the chief industry, but that business has now moved up north to the China border.

There are some Cham towers along National Highway 1 about 10km north of the Qui Nhon turn-off.

During the American War there was considerable South Vietnamese, American, Viet Cong and South Korean military activity in the Qui Nhon area, and refugees dislocated by the fighting and counter-insurgency programmes built whole slums of tin and thatch shacks around the city. During this period, the mayor of Qui Nhon, hoping to cash in on the presence of American troops, turned his official residence into a massage parlour.

### Orientation

Qui Nhon is on the coast 10km east of

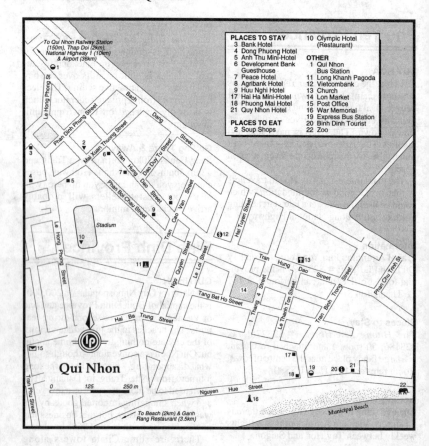

PLACES TO STAY
3 Bank Hotel
4 Dong Phuong Hotel
5 Anh Thu Mini-Hotel
6 Development Bank
  Guesthouse
7 Peace Hotel
8 Agribank Hotel
9 Huu Nghi Hotel
17 Hai Ha Mini-Hotel
18 Phuong Mai Hotel
21 Quy Nhon Hotel

PLACES TO EAT
2 Soup Shops

10 Olympic Hotel
  (Restaurant)

OTHER
1 Qui Nhon
  Bus Station
11 Long Khanh Pagoda
12 Vietcombank
13 Church
14 Lon Market
15 Post Office
16 War Memorial
19 Express Bus Station
20 Binh Dinh Tourist
22 Zoo

To Qui Nhon Railway Station
(150m), Thap Doi (2km),
National Highway 1 (10km)
& Airport (36km)

Stadium

Qui Nhon

0    125    250 m

To Beach (2km) & Ganh
Rang Restaurant (3.5km)

Municipal Beach

National Highway 1. The big highway junction where you turn off to Qui Nhon is called the Ba Di Bridge Crossroad (Nga Ba Cau Ba Di).

Qui Nhon proper is on an east-west oriented peninsula shaped like the nose of an anteater. The tip of the nose (the port area) is closed to the public. The Municipal Beach is on the peninsula's southern coast. The streets around Lon Market constitute Qui Nhon's town centre.

From the Municipal Beach, Cu Lao Xanh Island is visible offshore. Due east of the beach (to the left as you face the water)

you can see, in the distance, an oversize statue of Tran Hung Dao erected on a promontory overlooking the fishing village of Hai Minh.

**Information**

**Money** Vietcombank (☎ 822266), or the Bank of Foreign Trade (Ngan Hang Ngoai Thuong), is at 148 Le Loi St on the corner of Tran Hung Dao St.

**Emergency** There is a large hospital opposite 309 Nguyen Hue St.

### Long Khanh Pagoda

Long Khanh Pagoda, Qui Nhon's main pagoda, is down an alley opposite 62 Tran Cao Van St and next to 143 Tran Cao Van St. Visible from the street is a 17m-high Buddha (built in 1972), which presides over a lily pond strongly defended (against surprise attack?) by barbed wire. To the left of the main building is a low tower sheltering a giant drum; to the right, its twin contains an enormous bell, cast in 1970.

The main sanctuary was completed in 1946, but was damaged during the Franco-Viet Minh War; repairs were completed in 1957. In front of the large copper Thich Ca Buddha (with its multi-coloured neon halo) is a drawing of multi-armed and multi-eyed Chuan De (the Goddess of Mercy; the numerous arms and eyes means she can touch and see all). There is a colourfully painted Buddha at the edge of the raised platform. In the corridor which passes behind the main altar is a bronze bell with Chinese inscriptions; it dates from 1805.

Under the eaves of the left-hand building of the courtyard behind the sanctuary hangs a blow-up of the famous photograph of the monk Thich Quang Duc immolating himself in Saigon in June 1963 to protest the policies of the Diem regime. The 2nd level of the two-storey building behind the courtyard contains memorial plaques for deceased monks (on the middle altar) and lay people.

Long Khanh Pagoda was founded around 1700 by a Chinese merchant Duc Son (1679-1741). The seven monks who live here preside over the religious affairs of Qui Nhon's relatively active Buddhist community. Single-sex religion classes for children are held on Sunday.

### Beaches

Qui Nhon Municipal Beach, which extends along the southern side of the anteater's nose, consists of a few hundred metres of sand shaded by a coconut grove. The nicest section of beach is across from the Quy Nhon Hotel, but it has become increasingly dirty. Farther west, the shore is lined with the boats and shacks of fishing families.

A longer, quieter bathing beach begins about 2km south-west of the Municipal Beach. To get there, follow Nguyen Hue St away from the tip of the peninsula westward. Part of the seafront near here is lined with industrial plants, some of which belong to the military. Ganh Rang Restaurant is at the far end of the beach.

### Binh Dinh-Xiem Riep-Ratanakiri Zoo

This small seaside zoo, whose inhabitants include monkeys, crocodiles, porcupines and bears, is named for the two Cambodian provinces the animals came from. The uncharitable might classify the animals here as war booty (or prisoners of war). The zoo is at 2B Nguyen Hue St.

### Lon Market

Lon Market (Cho Lon), Qui Nhon's central market, is a large modern building enclosing a courtyard in which fruits and vegetables are sold.

### Leper Hospital

This is not a tourist attraction but visitors are welcome, especially if they make a small donation or purchase a few basic items from the locals. As leper hospitals go, this one is highly unusual. Rather than being a depressing place, it's a sort of model village where infected patients live together with their families in well-kept small houses. According to their abilities, the patients work in repair-oriented businesses or small craft shops. The hospital grounds are actually so well maintained that it looks a bit like a resort.

The leper hospital is out on the western end of Nguyen Hue St.

### Places to Stay

The *Bank Hotel* (☎ 823591; fax 821013; 20 rooms) is 300m from the bus station at 257 Le Hong Phong St. This place seems to rake in most of the foreign travellers. Bottom-end rooms with fan and hot-water bath are US$10. Luxuries like air-con pushes the price up to US$15 and US$25.

The modern *Dong Phuong Hotel* (☎ 822-915; 26 rooms) at 39-41 Mai Xuan Thuong

St is best known for its massage service, but the rooms are not bad either. Accommodation costs US$6 to US$16 – the pricier rooms have hot-water bath showers.

The *Anh Thu Mini-Hotel* (☎ 821168; 14 rooms), 25 Mai Xuan Thuong St, is notable for having motorbikes for rent. All rooms have attached bath with hot water. The bottom-end rooms are US$15 (fan only), and with air-con it's US$20 and US$25.

The *Huu Nghi Hotel* (☎ 822152; 20 rooms) at 210 Phan Boi Chau St is a rather grimy state-run place. At least you can't argue with the US$6 price. There is a restaurant on the ground floor which might be OK for a bowl of noodles.

The *Peace Hotel* (☎ 822710; 61 rooms), also known as the *Hoa Binh Hotel*, is at 469 Tran Hung Dao St. The remarkable thing about this place is how much the prices have dropped – it used to be outrageously expensive but is now very reasonable. Rooms with fan and cold water cost US$6 to US$12. Air-con and hot-water bath doubles are US$14.

The *Agribank Hotel* (☎ 822245; fax 821073; 11 rooms) is a gleaming-white place obviously meant to catch the tourist traffic. All rooms have air-con and hot water, and cost US$18 to US$22. The official address is 202 Tran Hung Dao St.

The *Development Bank Guesthouse* (☎ 822012; 11 rooms), 491 Tran Hung Dao St, is hidden down a long, narrow corridor and really looks like a development bank. Cold-water bath rooms with air-con are US$9, while a room with hot water will cost you US$12 to US$15. The hotel does not smell too good.

One block from the city beach is the *Hai Ha Mini-Hotel* at 1A Tran Binh Trong St. There are 10 rooms here and the place is often full. The tariff is US$20 to US$30.

Just facing the beach is the *Phuong Mai Hotel*. Though the rooms look OK and the views from the balcony are not bad, the place seems to be falling apart (especially the plumbing). Nevertheless, there is a certain derelict charm here. All rooms have private bath, though with cold water only. Doubles cost US$10.

The *Quy Nhon Hotel* (☎ 822401; fax 821162; 79 rooms) is at 8 Nguyen Hue St, directly opposite the city beach. Judging from the hotel's brochures, it seems that the management believes the Qui Nhon Municipal Beach and Quy Nhon Hotel are Vietnam's answer to the French Riviera and Club Med. However, shareholders in Club Med are not exactly shaking in their boots. Room rates are US$17 to US$40, which might sound cheap until you look at what you're getting. At least there is plenty of off-street parking inside the spacious compound.

## Places to Eat

There are only a handful of proper restaurants in Qui Nhon. One of the best is the *Olympic Restaurant*, which is on the roof of the Olympic Hotel. The hotel itself does not accept foreigners. The entrance to the Olympic Hotel is from inside the stadium.

The *Dong Phuong Restaurant* at 39-41 Mai Xuan Thuong St is on the ground floor of the Dong Phuong Hotel; it is open from 6 am to 11 pm. It serves reasonably good Vietnamese food and a few western dishes.

The *Ganh Rang Restaurant* is 3.5km west of town along Nguyen Hue St. Built on pylons and set among palms, this privately run restaurant is right on the water at a site said to have been a favourite of Bao Dai's wife.

## Getting There & Away

**Air** Vietnam Airlines flights link Saigon with Qui Nhon five times weekly. There are also flights to/from Danang three times weekly.

Phu Cat airport is 36km north of Qui Nhon. For airline passengers, transport to and from Phu Cat is provided by Vietnam Airlines. Small trucks to Phu Cat depart from the short-haul transport station.

In Qui Nhon, the Vietnam Airlines' booking office (☎ 822953) is near the Thanh Binh Hotel in the building next to 30 Nguyen Thai Hoc St.

**Bus** Qui Nhon bus station (Ben Xe Khach Qui Nhon; ☎ 822246) is opposite 543 Tran Hung Dao St (across from where Le Hong

Phong St hits Tran Hung Dao St). The non-express ticket windows are open from 5 am to 4 pm; the express ticket window (Khach Di Xe Toc Hanh), which is in the fenced-in enclosure next to the nonexpress windows, is open from 4 am to 4 pm. Tickets should be purchased the day before departure.

The express bus station (☎ 822172) is 100m west of the Quy Nhon Tourist Hotel at 14 Nguyen Hue St. There are express buses from here to Buon Ma Thuot, Dalat, Danang, Dong Hoi, Hanoi, Hué, Nha Trang, Ninh Binh, Quang Tri, Saigon, Thanh Hoa and Vinh. All buses depart at 5 am. The ticket window is open from 6.30 to 11 am and 1.30 to 5 pm.

**Train** The nearest the *Reunification Express* trains get to Qui Nhon is Dieu Tri, 10km from the city. Qui Nhon railway station (Ga Qui Nhon; ☎ 822036) is at the end of a 10km spur line off the main north-south track. Only two very slow local trains stop at Qui Nhon railway station and they are not worth bothering with – get yourself to Dieu Tri by taxi or motorbike.

Tickets for trains departing from Dieu Tri can be purchased at the Qui Nhon railway station, though if you arrive in Dieu Tri by train, your best bet is to purchase an onward ticket before leaving the station. For ticket prices on the *Reunification Express* trains, see the Train section in the Getting Around chapter.

**Car** Road distances from Qui Nhon are 677km to Ho Chi Minh City, 238km to Nha Trang, 186km to Pleiku, 198km to Kon Tum, 174km to Quang Ngai and 303km to Danang.

## AROUND QUI NHON
### Thap Doi
The two Cham towers of Thap Doi have curved pyramidal roofs rather than the terracing typical of Cham architecture. The larger tower, whose four granite doorways are oriented towards the cardinal directions, retains some of its ornate brickwork and remnants of the granite statuary that once graced its summit. The dismembered torsos of Garudas can be seen at the corners of the roofs of both structures.

The upper reaches of the small tower are home to several flourishing trees whose creeping tendrilous roots have forced their way between the bricks, enmeshing parts of the structure in the sort of net-like tangle for which the monuments of Angkor are famous. However, the whole place is being restored, and by the time you get there it might look just like new.

Thap Doi is 2km towards National Highway 1 from the Qui Nhon bus station. To get there, head out of town on Tran Hung Dao St and turn right between street numbers 900 and 906 onto Thap Doi St; the towers are about 100m from Tran Hung Dao St.

There are half a dozen or so other groups of Cham structures in the vicinity of Qui Nhon, two of which (Cha Ban and Duong Long) are described below.

### Cha Ban
The ruins of the former Cham capital of Cha Ban (also known at various times as Vijaya and Qui Nhon) are 26km north of Qui Nhon and 5km from Binh Dinh. The city was built within a rectangular wall measuring 1400m by 1100m. Canh Tien Tower (Tower of Brass) stands in the centre of the enclosure. The tomb of General Vu Tinh is nearby.

Cha Ban, which served as the seat of the royal government of Champa from the year 1000 (after the loss of Indrapura, also known as Dong Duong) until 1471, was attacked and plundered repeatedly by the Vietnamese, Khmers and Chinese. In 1044 the Vietnamese prince Phat Ma occupied the city and carried off a great deal of booty as well as the Cham king's wives, harem and female dancers, musicians and singers. Cha Ban was under the control of a Khmer overseer from 1190 to 1220.

In 1377 the Vietnamese were defeated in an attempt to capture Cha Ban and their king was killed. The Vietnamese emperor Le Thanh Ton breached the eastern gate of the city in 1471 and captured the Cham king and 50 members of the royal family. During this, the last great battle fought by the Chams,

60,000 Chams were killed and 30,000 more were taken prisoner by the Vietnamese.

During the Tay Son Rebellion, Cha Ban served as the capital of the region of central Vietnam ruled by the eldest of the three Tay Son brothers. It was attacked in 1793 by the forces of Nguyen Anh (later Emperor Gia Long), but the assault failed. In 1799 the forces of Nguyen Anh, under the command of General Vu Tinh, lay siege to the city and captured it. The Tay Son soon re-occupied the port of Thi Nai (modern-day Qui Nhon) and then lay siege to Cha Ban themselves. The siege continued for over a year, and by June 1801, Vu Tinh's provisions were gone. Food was in short supply; all the horses and elephants had long before been eaten. Refusing to consider the ignominy of surrender, Vu Tinh had an octagonal wood tower constructed. He filled it with gunpowder and, arrayed in his ceremonial robes, went inside and blew himself up. Upon hearing the news of the death of his dedicated general, Nguyen Anh wept.

### Duong Long Cham Towers

The Duong Long Cham towers (Thap Duong Long, the Towers of Ivory) are 8km from Cha Ban. The largest of the three brick towers is embellished with granite ornamentation representing *nagas* (snakes) and elephants. Over the doors are bas-reliefs of women, dancers, standing lions, monsters and various animals. The corners of the structure are formed by enormous dragon heads.

### Hoi Van Hot Springs

The famous hot springs of Hoi Van are north of Qui Nhon in Phu Cat District.

### Quang Trung Museum

The Quang Trung Museum is dedicated to Nguyen Hue, the second-oldest of the three brothers who led the Tay Son Rebellion, who crowned himself Emperor Quang Trung in 1788. In 1789 (a few months before a Parisian mob stormed the Bastille) Quang Trung led the campaign that overwhelmingly defeated a Chinese invasion force of 200,000 troops near Hanoi. This epic battle is still celebrated as one of the greatest triumphs in Vietnamese history. Quang Trung died in 1792 at the age of 40.

During his reign, Quang Trung was something of a social reformer. He encouraged land reform, revised the system of taxation, improved the army and emphasised education, opening numerous schools and encouraging the development of Vietnamese poetry and literature. Indeed, Communist literature often portrays him as the leader of a peasant revolution whose progressive policies were crushed by the reactionary Nguyen Dynasty, which came to power in 1802 and was overthrown by Ho Chi Minh in 1945.

The Quang Trung Museum is known for its demonstrations of *binh dinh vo*, a traditional martial art that is performed with a bamboo stick. To get there take National Highway 19 towards Pleiku. The museum, which is 48km from Qui Nhon, is in Tay Son District 5km off the highway. The Tay Son area produces a wine made of sticky rice.

### Vinh Son Falls

Vinh Son Falls is 18km off National Highway 19, which links Binh Dinh and Pleiku. To get there, you might try taking a Vinh Thanh-bound truck from the short-haul transport station in Qui Nhon and changing vehicles in Vinh Thanh.

# Quang Ngai Province

### SA HUYNH

Sa Huynh is a little seaside town whose beautiful semi-circular beach is bordered by rice paddies and coconut palms. The town is also known for its salt marshes and salt evaporation ponds. In the vicinity of Sa Huynh, archaeologists have unearthed remains of the Dong Son Civilisation dating from the 1st century AD.

### Places to Stay & Eat

There is only one place to stay, the crumbling *Sa Huynh Hotel* (☎ 859208; 16 rooms), which is right on the beach. Doubles cost US$8 to US$15, and triples are from US$12 to US$18. There is only cold water available for bathing, and the local police insist on taking both your passport and visa. The staff are indifferent and the hotel is depressing. In short, other than the beachside setting, there is little to recommend this place.

The state-run restaurant on the hotel grounds is also depressing and the service is poor. Fortunately, there are a number of small roadside cafes on National Highway 1, which do the usual excellent Vietnamese meals. However, there are no English menus to be had in this small town.

### Getting There & Away
**Train** Some nonexpress trains stop at the Sa Huynh railway station (Ga Sa Huynh), but it will be slow going.

**Car** Sa Huynh is on National Highway 1 about 114km north of Qui Nhon and 60km south of Quang Ngai.

### QUANG NGAI
Quang Ngai, the capital of Quang Ngai Province, is something of a backwater. But just how much longer this will remain an undisturbed backwater is a matter of extreme speculation. In late 1994, the Vietnamese government announced plans to build an oil refinery (Vietnam's first) here, along with other industrial projects. So far, the schemes only exist on paper, but foreign financiers are said to be taking an interest. One reason for wanting to develop this region into an industrial base is that so far the area has proved to be of little interest to tourists.

Built on the south bank of the Tra Khuc River (known for its oversized water-wheels), the city is about 15km from the coast, which is lined with beautiful beaches. The city and province of Quang Ngai are also known as Quang Nghia; the name is sometimes abbreviated as Quangai.

### History
Even before WWII, Quang Ngai was an important centre of resistance to the French.

During the Franco-Viet Minh War, the area was a Viet Minh stronghold. In 1962 the South Vietnamese Government introduced its ill-fated Strategic Hamlets Programme to the area. Villagers were forcibly removed from their homes and resettled in fortified hamlets, infuriating and alienating the local population and increasing popular support for the Viet Cong. Some of the bitterest fighting of the American War took place in Quang Ngai Province.

Son My subdistrict, 14km from Quang Ngai, was the scene of the infamous My Lai Massacre of 1968, in which hundreds of civilians were slaughtered by American soldiers. A memorial has been erected on the site of the killings.

As a result of the wars, very few bridges in Quang Ngai Province remain intact. At many river crossings, the rust-streaked concrete pylons of the old French bridges, probably destroyed by the Viet Minh, stand next to the ruins of their replacements, blown up by the VC. As it has for 15 or more years, traffic crosses the river on a third bridge, made of steel girders, of the sort that army engineering corps put up in a pinch.

### Orientation
National Highway 1 is called Quang Trung St as it passes through Quang Ngai. The railway station is 3km west of town on Phan Boi Chau St.

### Information
**Post & Communications** The GPO is 150m west of Quang Trung St on the corner of Phan Boi Chau and Phan Dinh Phung Sts.

### Places to Stay
The *Kim Thanh Hotel* (☎ 823471; 26 rooms) at 19 Phan Boi Chau St seems to be the most attuned to the backpacker market. Doubles cost US$7 to US$20.

The *Hoa Vien Hotel* (☎ 823455; seven rooms) at 12 Phan Chu Trinh St is another good place. Rooms with air-con and hot water are available for US$20.

The *Dung Hung Hotel* at 43 Quang Trung St is on the busy central artery of town – cars

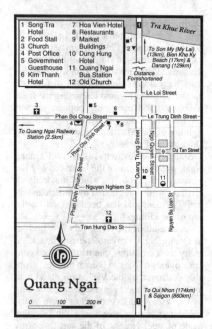

1 Song Tra Hotel
2 Food Stall
3 Church
4 Post Office
5 Government Guesthouse
6 Kim Thanh Hotel
7 Hoa Vien Hotel
8 Restaurants
9 Market Buildings
10 Dung Hung Hotel
11 Quang Ngai Bus Station
12 Old Church

Tra Khuc River

To Son My (My Lai) (13km), Bien Khe Ky Beach (17km) & Danang (129km)

Distance Foreshortened

Le Loi Street

Phan Boi Chau Street

Le Trung Dinh Street

To Quang Ngai Railway Station (2.5km)

Phan Chu Trinh Street

Du Tan Street

Ngo Quyen Street

Quang Trung Street

Nguyen Nghiem St

Phan Dinh Phung Street

Nguyen Ba Loan St

Tran Hung Dao St

Quang Ngai

To Qui Nhon (174km) & Saigon (860km)

0    100    200 m

and buses are not even permitted to stop here to unload passengers, which is a bit of a hassle. Rooms cost US$12.

The *Song Tra Hotel* (☎ 822665; 38 rooms) is a forlorn-looking five-storey structure owned by Quang Ngai Tourist. It's on the northern outskirts of the city next to the bridge, rather far from everything else. More troubling, the staff are aloof to all your needs except collecting the room rent. Prices are US$10 to US$30.

### Getting There & Away

**Minibus** There are now some tourist minibuses between Quang Ngai and Hoi An for US$7. Quang Ngai is 100km from Hoi An and the ride takes about two hours.

**Bus** Quang Ngai bus station (Ben Xe Khach Quang Ngai) is opposite 32 Nguyen Nghiem St, which is about 100m east of Quang Trung St (National Highway 1). Buses from here go to Buon Ma Thuot (and other places in

Dak Lak Province), Dalat, Danang, Hoi An, Kon Tum, Pleiku, Nha Trang, Qui Nhon and Saigon

**Train** The Quang Ngai railway station (Ga Quang Nghia or Ga Quang Ngai) is 3km west of the centre of town. To get there, take Phan Boi Chau St west from Quang Trung St (National Highway 1) and continue going in the same direction after the street name changes to Nguyen Chanh St. At 389 Nguyen Chanh St (which you'll come to as Nguyen Chanh St curves left), continue straight on down a side street. The railway station is at the end of the street.

*Reunification Express* trains stop at Quang Ngai. For ticket prices, see the Train section in the Getting Around chapter.

**Car** Road distances from Quang Ngai are 131km to Danang, 860km to Ho Chi Minh City, 412km to Nha Trang and 174km to Qui Nhon.

## AROUND QUANG NGAI
### Son My (My Lai)

The site of the My Lai Massacre is 14km from Quang Ngai. To get there from town, head north (towards Danang) on Quang Trung St (National Highway 1) and cross the long bridge over the Tra Khuc River. A few metres from the northern end of the bridge you will come to a triangular concrete stele indicating the way to the Son My Memorial. Turn right (eastward, parallel to the river) on the dirt road and continue for 12km. The road to Son My passes through particularly beautiful countryside of rice paddies, manioc patches and vegetable gardens shaded by casuarinas and eucalyptus trees.

The Son My Memorial is set in a park where Xom Lang sub-hamlet once stood. Around it, among the trees and rice paddies, are the graves of some of the victims, buried in family groups. Near the memorial is a museum opened in 1992, for which there is a US$1 admission charge. Inside the museum is a donation box, and it's claimed that the donated money is to help surviving victims and their families; however, local villagers

## My Lai Massacre

Son My subdistrict was the site of the most horrific war crimes committed by American troops during the American War. The My Lai Massacre consisted of a series of atrocities carried out all over Son My subdistrict, which is divided into four hamlets, one of which is named My Lai. The largest mass killing took place in Tu Cung hamlet in Xom Lang sub-hamlet (also known as Thuan Yen sub-hamlet), where the Son My Memorial was later erected.

Son My subdistrict was a known Viet Cong stronghold, and it was widely believed that villagers in the area were providing food and shelter to the VC (if true, the villagers had little choice – the VC was known for taking cruel revenge on those who didn't 'cooperate'). Just whose idea it was to 'teach the villagers a lesson' has never been determined. What is known is that several American soldiers had been killed and wounded in the area in the days preceding the 'search-and-destroy operation' that began on the morning of 16 March 1968.

The operation was carried out by Task Force Barker, which consisted of three companies of US army infantry. At about 7.30 am – after the area around Xom Lang sub-hamlet had been bombarded with artillery and the landing zone raked with rocket and machine-gun fire from helicopter gunships – the three platoons of Charlie Company (commanded by Captain Ernest Medina) were landed by helicopter. They encountered no resistance during the 'combat-assault', nor did they come under fire at any time during the entire operation; but as soon as Charlie Company's sweep eastward began, so did the atrocities.

As the soldiers of Lieutenant William Calley's 1st Platoon moved through Xom Lang, they shot and bayoneted fleeing villagers, threw hand grenades into houses and family bomb shelters, slaughtered livestock and burned dwellings. Somewhere between 75 and 150 unarmed local people were rounded up and herded to a ditch, where they were mowed down by machine-gun fire.

In the next few hours, as command helicopters circled overhead and US navy boats patrolled offshore, the 2nd Platoon (under Lieutenant Stephen Brooks), the 3rd platoon (under Lieutenant Jeffrey La Cross) and the company headquarters group also committed unspeakable crimes. At least half a dozen groups of civilians, including women and children, were assembled and executed. Local people fleeing towards Quang Ngai along the road were machine-gunned, and wounded civilians (including young children) were summarily shot. As these massacres were taking place, at least four girls and women were raped or gang-raped by groups of soldiers. In one case, a rapist from 2nd Company is reported to have shoved the muzzle of his assault rifle into the vagina of his victim and pulled the trigger.

One American soldier is reported to have shot himself in the foot to get himself out of the slaughter; he was the only American casualty that day in the entire operation.

Troops who participated were ordered to keep their mouths shut about the whole incident, but several soldiers who were at Son My disobeyed orders and went public with the story after returning to the USA. When the story broke in the newspapers, it had a devastating effect on the military's morale and fuelled further public protests against the war. Unlike WWII veterans who returned home to parades and glory, American soldiers coming home from Vietnam often found themselves ostracised by their fellow citizens and taunted as 'baby killers'.

Action to cover up the atrocities was undertaken at every level of the US Army command, but eventually there were several investigations. Lieutenant Calley was made chief ogre – he was court-marshalled and found guilty of the murders of 22 unarmed civilians. Calley was sentenced to life imprisonment in 1971. He spent three years under house arrest at Fort Benning, Georgia, while appealing his conviction. Calley was paroled in 1974 after the US Supreme Court refused to hear his case.

Calley's case still causes controversy – many have said that he was made the military's scapegoat because of his low rank, and that officers much higher up ordered the massacres. What is certain is that Calley did not act alone. ■

*Illustration: Lt. William Calley, the only US serviceman to be court-marshalled following the My Lai massacre.*

we've spoken to are adamant that they've never received any of these funds and have no idea where the money goes.

If you don't have a car, the best way to get to Son My District from Quang Ngai is to hire a motorbike *(Honda om)* near the bus station or along Quang Trung St.

### Bien Khe Ky Beach
Bien Khe Ky Beach (Bai Bien Khe Ky) is a

long, secluded beach of fine sand 17km from Quang Ngai and several kilometres past (east of) the Son My Memorial. The beach stretches for many kilometres along a long, thin casuarina-lined spit of sand separated from the mainland by Song Kinh Giang, a body of water about 150m inland from the beach.

# Quang Nam & Danang

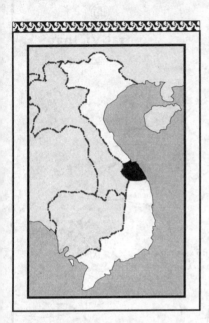

The province of Quang Nam, which surrounds the municipality of Danang, contains Vietnam's most important Cham sites. Major Cham historical sites which have now become the stomping grounds of tourists include My Son and Tra Kieu (Simhapura).

Side trips to places like the Marble Mountains and China Beach continue to draw a steady trickle of travellers. The once-bustling city of Danang is rather quiet these days, but the Cham Museum here is top-notch.

The old port of Faifo (now called Hoi An) has a great deal of rustic charm. It's one of the best spots in Vietnam to relax and imagine what life was like in centuries past.

## CHU LAI

About 30km north of Quang Ngai, the buildings and concrete aircraft revetments of the huge American base at Chu Lai stretch along several kilometres of sand to the east of National Highway 1. Despite the obvious dangers, collecting and selling scrap metal from old ordnance has become a thriving local industry. During the war, there was a huge shantytown made of packing crates and waste tin from canning factories next to the base. The inhabitants of the shantytown supported themselves by providing services to the Americans: doing laundry, selling soft drinks and engaging in prostitution.

### TAM KY

Tam Ky is a nondescript town on the highway between Chu Lai and Danang. Its chief claim to fame is that it's the capital of Quang Nam. However, for travellers the main point of interest is the nearby Cham towers at Chien Dang (Chien Dang Cham).

Three Cham towers, enclosed by a wall, stand at Chien Dang, which is 5km north of Tam Ky, 69km north of Quang Ngai and 62km south of Danang. A broken stele here dates from the 13th century reign of King Harivarman. Many of the Cham statues you can see on display at Chien Dang were collected from other parts of the country after the American War. Many of these statues show signs of war-related damage.

### Places to Stay

The *Tam Ky Hotel* (Khach San Tam Ky) is a decent place next to Highway 1 in the centre of town. This is the only hotel in Tam Ky that accepts foreigners.

# Hoi An

Hoi An is a riverside town 30km south of Danang. Known as Faifo to early western traders, it was one of South-East Asia's major international ports during the 17th, 18th and 19th centuries. In its heyday, Hoi An, a

Central Vietnam

0    25    50 km

contemporary of Macau and Melaka, was an important port of call for Dutch, Portuguese, Chinese, Japanese and other trading vessels. Vietnamese ships and sailors based in Hoi An sailed to Thailand and Indonesia, as well as to all sections of Vietnam. Perhaps more than any other place in Vietnam, Hoi An retains the feel of centuries past, making it the sort of place that grows on you the more you explore it.

### History

Recently excavated ceramic fragments from 2200 years ago constitute the earliest evi-

dence of human habitation in the Hoi An area. They are thought to belong to the late-Iron Age Sa Huynh civilisation, which is related to the Dong Son culture of northern Vietnam.

From the 2nd to the 10th centuries, when this region was the heartland of the Kingdom of Champa – this is when the nearby Cham capital of Simhapura (Tra Kieu) and the temples of Indrapura (Dong Duong) and My Son were built – there was a bustling seaport at Hoi An. Persian and Arab documents from the latter part of the period mention Hoi An as a provisioning stop for trading ships.

Archaeologists have uncovered the foundations of numerous Cham towers in the vicinity of Hoi An (the bricks and stones of the towers themselves were later reused by Vietnamese settlers).

In 1307, the Cham king married the daughter of a Vietnamese monarch of the Tran Dynasty, presenting Quang Nam Province to the Vietnamese as a gift. When the Cham king died, his successor refused to recognise the deal and fighting broke out; for the next century, chaos reigned. By the 15th century, peace had been restored, allowing normal commerce to resume. During the next four centuries, Chinese, Japanese, Dutch, Portuguese, Spanish, Indian, Filipino, Indonesian, Thai, French, English and American ships called at Hoi An to purchase high-grade silk (for which the area is famous), fabrics, paper, porcelain, tea, sugar, molasses, areca nuts, pepper, Chinese medicines, elephant tusks, beeswax, mother-of-pearl, lacquer, sulphur and lead.

The Chinese and Japanese traders sailed south in the spring, driven by winds out of the north-east. They would stay in Hoi An until the summer, when southerly winds would blow them home. During their four-month sojourn in Hoi An, the merchants rented waterfront houses for use as warehouses and living quarters. Some traders began leaving full-time agents in Hoi An to take care of off-season business affairs. This is how the foreigners' colonies got started. The Japanese ceased coming to Hoi An after 1637 when the Japanese government forbade all contact with the outside world.

Hoi An was the first place in Vietnam to be exposed to Christianity. Among the 17th century missionary visitors was the French priest Alexandre de Rhodes, who devised the Latin-based *quoc ngu* script for the Vietnamese language.

Hoi An was almost completely destroyed during the Tay Son Rebellion in the 1770s and 1780s, but was rebuilt and continued to serve as an important port for foreign trade until the late 19th century, when the Thu Bon River (Cai River), which links Hoi An with the sea, silted up and became too shallow for navigation. During this period Danang (Tourane) began to eclipse Hoi An as a port and centre of commerce. In 1916, a rail line linking Danang with Hoi An was destroyed by a terrible storm; it was never rebuilt.

The French chose Hoi An as an administrative centre. During the American war, Hoi An remained almost completely undamaged.

Hoi An was the site of the first Chinese settlement in southern Vietnam. The town's Chinese congregational assembly halls *(hoi quan)* still play a special role among southern Vietnam's ethnic-Chinese, some of whom travel to Hoi An from all over the south to participate in congregation-wide celebrations. Today, 1300 of the Hoi An area's present population of about 60,000 are ethnic-Chinese. Relations between ethnic-Vietnamese and ethnic-Chinese in Hoi An are excellent, in part because the Chinese here, unlike their compatriots elsewhere in the country, have become culturally assimilated to the point that they even speak Vietnamese among themselves.

A number of Hoi An's wooden buildings date from the first part of the 19th century or earlier, giving visitors who have just a bit of imagination the feeling that they have been transported back a couple of centuries to a time when the wharf was crowded with sailing ships, the streets teemed with porters transporting goods to and from warehouses and traders from a dozen countries haggled in a babble of languages.

## Architecture
So far, 844 structures of historical significance have been officially identified in Hoi An. These structures are of nine types:

- Houses & shops
- Wells
- Family chapels for ancestor worship
- Pagodas
- Vietnamese & Chinese temples
- Bridges
- Communal buildings
- Assembly halls of various Chinese congregations
- Tombs (Vietnamese, Chinese & Japanese; no original European tombs survive)

Many of Hoi An's older structures exhibit features of traditional architecture rarely seen today. As they have for centuries, the fronts of some shops (which are open during the day to display the wares) are shuttered at night by inserting horizontal planks into grooves cut into the columns that support the roof. Some roofs are made of thousands of brick-coloured 'Yin & Yang' roof tiles – so called because of the way the alternating rows of concave and convex tiles fit together. During the rainy season, the lichens and mosses that live on the tiles spring to life, turning entire rooftops bright green.

Many of Hoi An's houses have round pieces of wood with a Yin & Yang symbol in the middle surrounded by a spiral design over the doorway. These 'watchful eyes' *(mat cua)* are supposed to protect the residents of the house from harm.

Every year during the rainy season, Hoi An has problems with flooding, especially near the waterfront. The greatest flood Hoi An has ever known took place in 1964, when the water reached all the way up to the roof beams of the houses.

Hoi An's historic structures are gradually being restored and there is a sincere effort being made to preserve the unique character of the city. The local government has put some thought into what is being done – the old houses must be licensed to do restoration work and this must be done in a tasteful manner. The government certifies the historical significance of the buildings – at present, there are four categories of certificates.

Assistance in historical preservation is being provided to local authorities by the Archaeological Institute in Hanoi, the Japan-Vietnam Friendship Association and experts from Europe and Japan. The Old Town section of Hoi An is now closed to motor vehicles – a first in Vietnam.

There is a US$5 ticket which you must buy to get into some of the historical buildings. The ticket entitles you to visit four major sights which you select from a list on the ticket. If you're not satisfied with four sights, you'll have to buy another ticket.

Many of the house owners also charge admission – as much as US$3 for a guided tour of the building – but this is negotiable. The government permits this with the idea that the funds will be used for renovation of the homes rather than towards the purchase of TVs and new motorcycles (but it's a difficult policy to enforce).

### Information

**Money** The Bank of Foreign Trade on Hoang Dieu St can exchange both cash and travellers cheques. However, you cannot get a cash advance on a credit card here – for that, you must go to Danang.

**Post & Communications** The post office is across from 11 Tran Hung Dao St (on the north-west corner of Ngo Gia Tu and Tran Hung Dao Sts).

**Emergency** The hospital is opposite the post office at 10 Tran Hung Dao St.

### Japanese Covered Bridge

The Japanese Covered Bridge (Cau Nhat Ban, or Lai Vien Kieu) connects 155 Tran Phu St with 1 Nguyen Thi Minh Khai St. The first bridge on this site was constructed in 1593 by the Japanese community of Hoi An to link their neighbourhood with the Chinese quarters across the stream. The bridge was provided with a roof so it could be used as a shelter from both the rain and the sun.

The Japanese Covered Bridge is very solidly built, apparently because the original builders were afraid of the earthquakes which are common in Japan. Over the centuries, the ornamentation of the bridge has remained relatively faithful to the original Japanese design, reflecting the Japanese preference for understatement, which contrasts greatly with the Vietnamese and Chinese penchant for wild decoration. The French flattened out the roadway to make it more suitable for their motorcars, but the original arched shape was restored during the major renovation work carried out in 1986.

Built into the northern side of the bridge is a small temple, Chua Cau. Over the door

BERNARD NAPTHINE

SARA JANE CLELAND

GENEVIEVE WEBB

GLENN BEANLAND

### Quang Nam & Danang
Top: An elderly monk at a pagoda in Hoi An.
Middle Left: The Japanese Covered Bridge, which dates from 1593, in Hoi An.
Middle Right: Weathered facades in the historical port city of Hoi An.
Bottom: The rugged coastline at Lang Co near Danang.

MICK ELMORE

BRENDAN McCARTHY

GLENN BEANLAND

BRENDAN McCARTHY

## Hué

Top: Stored at Thien Mu Pagoda is the car captured in the famous photo of the self-immolating monk during the American War. Left: A shy resident of Hué.

Middle Right: Cyclists pass by the 2.5 km-long walls of the Imperial Enclosure.

Bottom Right: The entrance to Nam Giao, the Temple of Heaven.

is written the name given to the bridge in 1719 to replace the name then in use, which meant the Japanese Bridge. The new name, Lai Vien Kieu (Bridge for Passers-by from Afar), never caught on.

According to legend, there once lived an enormous monster called Cu, whose head was in India, its tail in Japan and its body in Vietnam. Whenever the monster moved, terrible disasters, such as floods and earthquakes, befell Vietnam. This bridge was built on the monster's weakest point – its 'Achilles' heel', so to speak – killing it. But the people of Hoi An took pity on the slain monster and built this temple to pray for its soul.

The two entrances to the bridge are guarded by a pair of monkeys on one side and a pair of dogs on the other. According to one story, these animals were popularly revered because many of Japan's emperors were born in years of the dog and monkey. Another tale relates that construction of the bridge was begun in the year of the monkey and finished in the year of the dog.

The stelae listing Vietnamese and Chinese contributors to a subsequent restoration of the bridge are written in Chinese characters (chu nho), the nom script not yet having become popular in these parts.

## Tan Ky House

The Tan Ky House (☎ 861474) was built almost two centuries ago as the home of a well-to-do ethnic-Vietnamese merchant. The house has been lovingly preserved and today it looks almost exactly as it did in the early 19th century.

The design of the Tan Ky House shows evidence of the influence Japanese and Chinese styles had on local architecture. Japanese elements include the crabshell-shaped ceiling (in the section immediately before the courtyard), which is supported by three progressively shorter beams one on top of the other. There are similar beams in the salon. Under the crabshell ceiling are carvings of crossed sabres enwrapped by a ribbon of silk. The sabres symbolise force; the silk represents flexibility.

Chinese poems written in inlaid mother-of-pearl are hung from a number of the columns that hold up the roof. The Chinese characters on these 150-year-old panels are formed entirely out of birds gracefully portrayed in various positions of flight.

The courtyard has four functions: to let in light; to provide ventilation; to bring a glimpse of nature into the home; and to collect rainwater and provide drainage. The stone tiles covering the patio floor were brought from Thanh Hoa Province in north-central Vietnam. The carved, wooden balcony supports around the courtyard are decorated with grape leaves – a European import and further evidence of the unique mingling of cultures that took place in Hoi An.

The back of the house faces the river. In olden times, this section of the building was rented out to foreign merchants.

That the house was a place of commerce, as well as a residence, is indicated by the two pulleys attached to a beam in the storage loft located just inside the front door.

The exterior of the roof is made of tiles; inside, the ceiling consists of wood. This design keeps the house cool in the summer and warm in the winter. The house's floor tiles were brought from near Hanoi.

The Tan Ky House is a private home at 101 Nguyen Thai Hoc St. It is open to visitors for a small fee. The owner, whose family has lived here for seven generations, speaks fluent French and English. The house is open every day from 8 am to noon and from 2 to 4.30 pm.

## Diep Dong Nguyen House

The Diep Dong Nguyen House was built for a Chinese merchant, an ancestor of the present inhabitants, in the late 19th century. The front room on the ground floor was once a dispensary for Chinese medicines (thuoc bac), which were stored in the glass-enclosed cases lining the walls. The owner's private collection of antiques, which includes photographs, porcelain and furniture, is on display upstairs. The objects are not for sale! Two of the chairs were once lent by the family to Emperor Bao Dai.

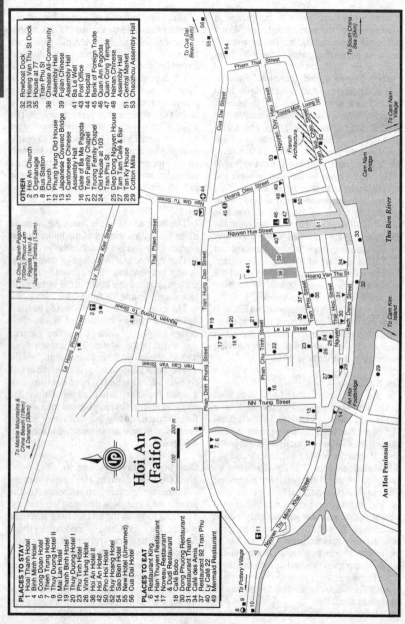

**PLACES TO STAY**
1 Hoai Thanh Hotel
4 Binh Minh Hotel
5 Cong Doan Hotel
7 Thien Trung Hotel
9 Thuy Duong Hotel II
10 Mai Lan Hotel
19 Thanh Binh Hotel
20 Thuy Duong Hotel I
23 Phu Tinh Hotel
26 Vinh Hung Hotel
36 Hoi An Hotel II
42 Hoi An Hotel
50 Huy Hoang Hotel
54 Sao Bien Hotel
55 New Hotel (Unnamed)
56 Cua Dai Hotel

**PLACES TO EAT**
6 Restaurant King
14 Han Thuyen Restaurant
17 Noveau Restaurant & Dudi Restaurant
18 Café Bobo
30 Dong Phuong Restaurant
31 Restaurant Thanh
34 Café des Amis
37 Restaurant 92 Tran Phu
40 Ly Café 22
49 Mermaid Restaurant

**OTHER**
2 Hoi An Church
3 Hrphanaige
8 Bus Station
11 Church
12 Phung Hung Old House
13 Japanese Covered Bridge
15 Cantonese Chinese Assembly Hall
16 Gate of Ba Ma Pagoda
21 Tran Family Chapel
22 Truong Family Chapel
24 Old House at 103 Tran Phu St
25 Diep Dong Nguyen House
28 Tan Ky House
29 Cotton Mills
32 Rowboat Dock
33 Hoang Van Thu St Dock
35 House at 77 Tran Phu St
38 Chinese All-Community
39 Fujian Chinese Assembly Hall
41 Ba Le Well
43 Hospital
44 Post Office
45 Bank of Foreign Trade
46 Quan Am Pagoda
47 Quan Cong Temple
48 Hainan Chinese Assembly Hall
51 Central Market
53 Chaozhou Assembly Hall

The house, which is at 80 Nguyen Thai Hoc St (by the new numbering system) and 58 Nguyen Thai Hoc St (by the old system), is open every day from 8 am to noon and from 2 to 4.30 pm.

## House at 77 Tran Phu St

This private house, which is across the street from the Restaurant 92 Tran Phu, is about three centuries old. There is some especially fine carving on the wooden walls of the rooms around the courtyard, on the roof beams and under the crabshell roof (in the salon next to the courtyard). Note the green ceramic tiles built into the railing around the courtyard balcony. The house is open to visitors for a small fee.

## Assembly Hall of the Cantonese Chinese Congregation

The Assembly Hall of the Cantonese Chinese Congregation, founded in 1786, is at 176 Tran Phu St and is open daily from 6 to 7.30 am and from 1 to 5.30 pm. The main altar is dedicated to Quan Cong (Chinese: Guangong). Note the long-handled brass 'fans' to either side of the altar. The lintel and door posts of the main entrance and a number of the columns supporting the roof are made of single blocks of granite. The other columns were carved out of the durable wood of the jackfruit tree. There are some interesting carvings on the wooden beams that support the roof in front of the main entrance.

## Chinese All-Community Assembly Hall

The Chinese All-Community Assembly Hall (Chua Ba), founded in 1773, was used by all five Chinese congregations in Hoi An: Fujian, Cantonese, Hainan, Chaozhou and Hakka. The pavilions off the main courtyard incorporate 19th century French elements.

The main entrance is on Tran Phu St opposite Hoang Van Thu St, but the only way in these days is around the back at 31 Phan Chu Trinh St.

## Assembly Hall of the Fujian Chinese Congregation

The Assembly Hall of the Fujian Chinese Congregation was founded as a place to hold community meetings. Later, it was transformed into a temple for the worship of Thien Hau, the Goddess of the Sea and Protector of Fishermen and Sailors, who was born in Fujian Province. The triple gate to the complex was built in 1975.

The mural near the entrance to the main hall on the right-hand wall depicts Thien Hau, her way lit by lantern light, crossing a stormy sea to rescue a foundering ship. On the wall opposite is a mural of the heads of the six Fujian families who fled from China to Hoi An in the 17th century following the overthrow of the Ming Dynasty.

The second-to-last chamber contains a statue of Thien Hau. To either side of the entrance stand red-skinned Thuan Phong Nhi, who can hear for great distances, and green-skinned Thien Ly Nhan, who can see for a 1000 miles. When either sees or hears sailors in distress, they inform Thien Hau, who then sets off to effect a rescue. The replica of a Chinese boat along the right-hand wall is in 1:20 scale. The four sets of triple beams which support the roof are typically Japanese.

The central altar in the last chamber contains seated figures of the heads of the six Fujian families. The smaller figures below them represent their successors as clan leaders. In a 30cm-high glass dome is a figurine of Le Huu Trac, a Vietnamese physician renowned in both Vietnam and China for his curative abilities.

Behind the altar on the left is the God of Prosperity. On the right are three fairies and smaller figures representing the 12 'midwives' (ba mu), each of whom teaches newborns a different skill necessary for the first year of life: smiling, sucking, lying on their stomachs and so forth. Childless couples often come here to pray for offspring. The three groups of figures in this chamber represent the elements most central to life: one's ancestors, one's children and economic wellbeing.

The middle altar of the room to the right of the courtyard commemorates deceased leaders of the Fujian congregation. On either side are lists of contributors – women on the left and men on the right. The wall panels represent the four seasons.

The Assembly Hall of the Fujian Chinese Congregation, which is opposite 35 Tran Phu St, is open from 7.30 am to noon and from 2 to 5.30 pm. It is fairly well lit and can be visited after dark. Shoes should be removed upon mounting the platform just past the naves.

### Quan Cong Temple
Quan Cong Temple, also known as Chua Ong, is at 24 Tran Phu St (according to the new numbers) and 168 Tran Phu St (according to the old numbering system). Founded in 1653, this Chinese temple is dedicated to Quan Cong, whose partially gilt statue – made of papier-mâché on a wood frame – is in the central altar at the back of the sanctuary. On the left is a statue of General Chau Xuong, one of Quan Cong's guardians, striking a tough-guy pose. On the right is the rather plump administrative mandarin Quan Binh. The life-size white horse recalls a mount ridden by Quan Cong until he was given a red horse of extraordinary endurance, representations of which are common in Chinese pagodas.

Stone plaques on the walls list contributors to the construction and repair of the temple. Check out the carp-shaped rain spouts on the roof surrounding the courtyard. The carp, a symbol of patience in Chinese mythology, is a popular symbol in Hoi An.

Shoes should be removed when mounting the platform in front of the statue of Quang Cong.

### Assembly Hall of the Hainan Chinese Congregation
The Assembly Hall of the Hainan Chinese Congregation was built in 1883 as a memorial to 108 merchants from Hainan Island in southern China who were mistaken for pirates and killed in Quang Nam Province during the reign of Emperor Tu Duc (ruled 1848-83). The elaborate dais contains plaques in their memory. In front of the central altar is a fine gilded wood carving of Chinese court life.

The Hainan Congregation Hall is on the east end of Tran Phu St, near the corner of Hoang Dieu St.

### Assembly Hall of the Chaozhou Chinese Congregation
The Chaozhou Chinese in Hoi An built their congregational hall in 1776. There is some outstanding woodcarving on the beams, walls and altar. On the doors in front of the altar are carvings of two Chinese girls wearing their hair in the Japanese manner.

The Assembly Hall of the Chaozhou Chinese Congregation is across from 157 Nguyen Duy Hieu St (near the corner of Hoang Dieu St).

### Truong Family Chapel
The Truong Family Chapel (Nha Tho Toc Truong), founded about two centuries ago, is a shrine dedicated to the ancestors of this ethnic-Chinese family. Some of the memorial plaques were presented by the emperors of Vietnam to honour members of the Truong family who served as local officials and as mandarins at the imperial court. To get there, turn into the alley next to 69 Phan Chu Trinh St.

### Tran Family Chapel
At 21 Le Loi St at the intersection with Phan Chu Trinh St (north-east corner) is the Tran Family Chapel. This house for worshipping ancestors was built about 200 years ago with donations from family members. The Tran family traces its origins to China and moved to Vietnam around the year 1700. The architecture of the building reflects the influence of Chinese and Japanese styles. On the altar are wooden boxes containing the ancestors' stone tablets with Chinese characters chiselled in.

### Gate of Ba Mu Pagoda
Though Ba Mu Pagoda, founded in 1628, was demolished by the South Vietnamese government during the 1960s to make room for a three-storey school building, the gate (Phat Tu) remains standing. Enormous representations of pieces of fruit form part of the wall between the two doorways.

The gate of Ba Mu Pagoda is opposite 68 Phan Chu Trinh St.

## Ba Le Well

Water for the preparation of authentic *cao lau* (see Places to Eat) must be drawn from Ba Le Well and no other. The well itself, which is said to date from Cham times, is square in shape. To get there, turn down the alleyway opposite 35 Phan Chu Trinh St and hang a right before reaching number 45/17.

## French Buildings

There is a whole city block of colonnaded French buildings on Phan Boi Chau St between numbers 22 and 73.

## Cotton Weaving

Hoi An is known for its production of cotton cloth. All over the city there are cotton mills with rows of fantastic wooden looms that make a rhythmic 'clackety-clack, clackety-clack' sound as a whirring, cycloidal drive wheel shoots the shuttle back and forth under the watchful eyes of the machine attendant. The elegant technology used in building these domestically produced machines dates from the Industrial Revolution. Indeed, this is what mills in Victorian England must have looked like.

There are cloth mills at numbers 140 and 151 Tran Phu St.

## Caodai Pagoda

Serving Hoi An's Caodai community, many of whom live along the path out to the Japanese tombs, is the small Caodai Pagoda (built in 1952) between numbers 64 and 70 Huynh Thuc Khang St (near the bus station). One priest lives here. Sugar and corn are grown in the front yard to raise some extra cash.

## Hoi An Church

The only tombs of Europeans in Hoi An are in the yard of the Hoi An Church, which is at the corner of Nguyen Truong To and Le Hong Phong Sts. When this modern building was constructed to replace an earlier structure at another site, several 18th century missionaries were reburied here.

## Chuc Thanh Pagoda

Chuc Thanh Pagoda is the oldest pagoda in Hoi An. It was founded in 1454 by Minh Hai, a Buddhist monk from China. Among the antique ritual objects still in use are several bells, a stone gong two centuries old and a carp-shaped wooden gong said to be even older. Today, five elderly monks live here.

In the main sanctuary, gilt Chinese characters inscribed on a red roof beam give details of the pagoda's construction. Under a wooden canopy on the central dais sits an A Di Da Buddha flanked by two Thich Ca Buddhas (Sakyamuni). In front of them is a statue of Thich Ca as a boy flanked by his servants.

To get to Chuc Thanh Pagoda, go all the way to the end of Nguyen Truong To St and turn left. Follow the sandy path for 500m.

## Phuoc Lam Pagoda

Phuoc Lam Pagoda was founded in the mid-17th century. Late in that century, the head monk was An Thiem, a Vietnamese prodigy who became a monk at the age of eight. When he was 18, the king drafted An Thiem's brothers into his army to put down a rebellion. An Thiem volunteered to take the places of the other men in his family and eventually rose to the rank of general. After the war, he returned to the monkhood, but felt guilty about the many people he had slain. To atone for his sins, he volunteered to clean the Hoi An Market for a period of 20 years. When the 20 years were up, he was asked to come to Phuoc Lam Pagoda as head monk.

To get to Phuoc Lam Pagoda, continue past Chuc Thanh Pagoda for 350m. The path passes by an obelisk erected over the tomb of 13 ethnic-Chinese decapitated by the Japanese during WWII for resistance activities.

## Japanese Tombs

The tombstone of the Japanese merchant Yajirobei, who died in 1647, is clearly inscribed with Japanese characters. The stele, which faces north-east towards Japan, is held in place by the tomb's original covering, which is made of an especially hard kind of cement whose ingredients include powdered seashells, the leaves of the *boi loi* tree and cane sugar. Yajirobei may have been a Christian who came to Vietnam to escape persecution in his native land.

To get to Yajirobei's tomb, go north to the end of Nguyen Truong Tu St and follow the sand path around to the left (west) for 40m until you get to a fork. The path that continues straight on leads to Chuc Thanh Pagoda, but you should turn right (northward). Keep going for just over 1km, turning left (to the north) at the first fork and left (to the north-west) at the second fork. When you arrive at the open fields, keep going until you cross the irrigation channel. Just on the other side of the channel turn right (south-east) onto a raised path. After going for 150m, turn left (north-east) into the paddies and walk 100m. The tomb, which is on a platform surrounded by a low stone wall, stands surrounded by rice paddies.

The tombstone of a Japanese named Masai, who died in 1629, is a few hundred metres back towards Hoi An. To get there, turn left (south-east) at a point about 100m towards town from the edge of the rice fields. The tombstone is on the right-hand side of the trail about 30m from the main path.

For help in finding the Japanese tombs, show the locals the following words: 'Ma Nhat' (or 'Mo Nhat'), which means Japanese tombs.

There are other Japanese tombs in Duy Xuyen District, which is across the delta of the Thu Bon River from Hoi An.

### An Hoi Peninsula
Cross the An Hoi footbridge to reach the An Hoi Peninsula, noted for its boat factory and mat weaving factories.

### Cam Nam Village
All those neat fake antiques sold in Hoi An's shops are manufactured in nearby villages. Cross the Cam Nam Bridge to Cam Nam Village, a lovely spot where some of these things are made.

### Places to Stay
Although there are 16 hotels in tiny Hoi An and more under construction, many are full during the peak travel season. Travellers all seem to want to find a room right in the centre, so not surprisingly the most central hotels fill up quickly. Yet the quieter and more spacious hotels tend to be on the outskirts of town. Considering how small Hoi An is and how easily one can walk around, there should be no great compulsion to find a place in the bustling heart of town.

The *Hoi An Hotel* (☎ 861373; 100 rooms) at 6 Tran Hung Dao St is a grand, colonial-style building and one of the largest hotels in Vietnam. There is a wide range of room rates from US$7 to US$63. This is one of the two state-run hotels in town.

The *Hoi An Hotel II* at 92 Tran Phu St is no relation to the mammoth hotel with the almost-same name. Singles with attached bath cost US$8, but this place is usually full.

The *Cong Doan Hotel* (☎ 861899) at 50 Phan Dinh Phung St is Hoi An's only other state-run hotel. The place is not attractive, but it will do if everything else is full. Rooms with fan cost US$10 to US$15 and with air-con US$20.

The *Binh Minh Hotel* (☎ 861943) on Nguyen Truong St has twins for US$10 to US$16. Being a little further out from the centre it's not so often full.

The *Cua Dai Hotel* (☎ 861722) at 18 Cua Dai St is nice in that it's in a rural area, yet still close enough to walk to the centre. Twins cost US$20 to US$35. A new, and as yet unnamed, hotel is under construction nearby.

Up at the northern outskirts of town is the *Hoai Thanh Hotel* (☎ 861242) at 23 Le Hong Phong St. Rooms with a single bed cost US$10 to US$15, while twins are US$25 to US$40.

The *Huy Hoang Hotel* (☎ 861453) at 73 Phan Boi Chau St is by the Cam Nam Bridge. Singles are US$12 and twins cost US$15 to US$30.

The *Pho Hoi Hotel* (☎ 861633), 7/2 Tran Phu St, is rare indeed in offering a dormitory for US$4 per bed. Twins cost US$10 to US$25.

The *Phu Tinh Hotel* (☎ 861297) at 144

Tran Phu St is right on tourist alley. Twins are US$12 to US$25.

The *Sao Bien Hotel* (☎ 861589), or *Sea Star Hotel* in English, is at 15 Cua Dai St. Twins are US$18 and US$28.

The *Thanh Binh Hotel* (☎ 861740) at 1 Le Loi St is close into town and a popular choice. Twins cost US$12 to US$25.

The *Thien Trung Hotel* (☎ 861720) at 63 Phan Dinh Phung St is built motel-style. It's a good place to stay if you're travelling by car as they have ample parking. Rooms cost US$10 to US$15.

*Thuy Duong Hotel I* (☎ 861574) at 11 Le Loi St has rooms with outside toilet for US$8 or with inside toilet for US$10.

The *Thuy Duong Hotel II* (☎ 861394) at 68 Hunh Thuc Khang St is right next to the bus station. Twins cost US$10 to US$14.

The *Mai Lan Hotel* (☎ 861792; fax 862126) at 87 Huynh Thuc Khang St is a new and good-looking place opposite the bus station. Rooms cost US$8 to US$16.

The *Vinh Hung Hotel* on Tran Phu St is a small place on the street closed to cars. Twins cost US$10 with outside bath or US$15 with inside bath.

**Places to Eat**

Hoi An's contribution to Vietnamese cuisine is *cao lau*, which consists of doughy flat noodles mixed with croutons, bean sprouts and greens and topped with pork slices. It is mixed with crumbled, crispy rice paper immediately before eating. Hoi An is the *only* place genuine cao lau can be made because the water used in the preparation of the authentic article must come from the Ba Le Well in town. You'll see cao lau listed on menus all over Hoi An.

Another Hoi An speciality is fried wonton. Again, you can find this in almost any cafe in town.

The market is the cheapest place to eat, even if it does lack aesthetics. The *banh trang* (translucent spring rolls) are particularly nice and cost only US$0.10 each.

There are heaps of restaurants on Nguyen Hue, Tran Phu and Bach Dang Sts where you can enjoy a slow meal or linger over drinks.

Many cooking styles are available, including western (banana pancakes, spaghetti and pizza), Vietnamese, Chinese and vegetarian food for reasonable prices.

*Mermaid Restaurant* (☎ 861527), or *Nhu Y*, is at 2 Tran Phu St. It dishes up great food including late breakfasts.

*Ly Cafe 22* (☎ 861603) at 22 Nguyen Hue St has become a Hoi An institution. If you can't decide what to eat, then try the 'Real Vietnamese Meal or a Little Bit of Everything'. The restaurant opens around 6.30 am, closes when empty and is always crowded.

*Cafe des Amis* (☎ 861360) at 52 Bach Dang St is also along the riverside. This place gets steady rave reviews from satisfied customers. This set-up is unique – there is no menu, just a set meal which changes everyday. Get the price worked out first – you pay by the number of dishes and because the menu varies, the price does too.

Some other popular spots for backpacker cuisine include *Cafe Bobo*, *Noveau Restaurant* and *Dudi Restaurant*, all on Le Loi St.

*Restaurant King* is next to the Thien Trung Hotel at 63 Phan Dinh Phung St. It's a small, unassuming place that specialises in delicious Hué food (try the spring rolls). Aside from the food, it's worth coming here to talk to the owner, who is a gold mine of information on Hoi An. He's also in the process of setting up a book and cassette tape exchange.

*Restaurant 92 Tran Phu* is at – you guessed it – 92 Tran Phu St. Vietnamese food is the house speciality, including the ubiquitous cao lau.

Moving one block south, you hit the riverfront, which is a virtual eating arcade. The *Han Thuyen Restaurant* is also nicknamed the Floating Restaurant, although it doesn't actually float but, rather, is built on stilts over the water. Perhaps it would be better if it did float, seeing how flood-prone this river is.

Also on the riverfront is the *Restaurant Thanh* at 76 Bach Dang St, which does seafood, pizza and vegetarian food. On the same street and also worth trying is the *Dong Phuong Restaurant*.

# Sewing Up a Storm

The historic town of Hoi An must surely be the home of the sewing machine, because you hear them whirring along from dawn until dusk. Hoi An is like a material treasure trove. Fabric of every type can be found all over town – in some places stacked to the ceilings of the various cloth shops.

It's a good experience just spending a morning being pampered in any of the dress-makers' shops in and around the market. Everywhere you look there are rolls of material to choose your new wardrobe from and, for a trifling amount over the cost of the cloth, you can have shirts, trousers, dresses and skirts tailor-made anywhere in the market.

However, the quality of the material and the standard of work is hugely variable. For example, when buying silk it is important to ascertain that the material is real silk and not 'Vietnamese silk' – a term often used to describe polyester and other synthetic fabrics that look and feel like silk.

The only real test for silk is with a cigarette or match (synthetic fibres melt and silk burns), but be careful not to set the shop on fire! Ask for a sample of the material you are thinking of purchasing and go outside to test it if you are concerned about its authenticity.

*Seamstresses abound in the city of Hoi An, where a bit of imagination, an eye for colour and a few hours' measuring and fitting can result in a stylish and economical wardrobe inside two days.*

JULIET COOMBE

*Hoi An's dressmakers stock a vast array of traditional and western-style fabrics in a range of prints and weaves.*

JULIET COOMBE

It is also important to check the seams of the finished garment, as only a single set of stitching along the inside edges will soon cause fraying and, in many cases, great big gaping holes. All well-tailored garments have a second set of stitches (known in the trade as blanket stitching), which binds the edge, oversewing the fabric so fraying is impossible. When having an item of clothing made, ask the person tailoring the outfit to use the same colour cotton as the material – otherwise they will use white cotton throughout. Also, where possible, insist on the clothes being lined, as it helps them move and fall in the right direction.

Many shops also will produce glamorous evening wear – from a pattern or from a photograph in a magazine. They can make anything from a copy of a Lady Di designer ball gown to a top city slicker suit in less than a couple of hours. An evening dress, including the material, starts at around US$15, a summer dress at US$8 and a suit at US$20.

A completely new fitted wardrobe will cost as little as US$100 and, after measuring you from every angle, a few hours later you will have a fitting session to make final adjustments.

Your only problem is whether to carry this new wardrobe around in a backpack or make a dash to the post office to send these creations home.

**Juliet Coombe**

## Entertainment

The only real bar in town is the very excellent *Tam Tam Cafe & Bar* (☎ 862212; fax 862207). Run by an expat Frenchman named Christopher, this place is a most unexpected retreat. There is French wine, a salad bar, French and Vietnamese food, a billiards table, a balcony for summer dining and a collection of over 300 CDs. Breakfast is served from 10 am until noon, but the place really gets lively in the evening. You'll find this place at 110 Nguyen Thai Hoc St (near the Japanese Covered Bridge), just above the Chinese-style Hiep Pho Restaurant.

## Things to Buy

The presence of numerous tourists has turned the fake antique business into Hoi An's major growth industry. Theoretically you could find something here that is really old, but it's hard to believe that all the genuine stuff wasn't scooped up long ago.

On the other hand, there is some really elegant artwork around, even if it was made only yesterday. Wood carvings are a local speciality.

Tailor-made clothing is another of Hoi An's specialities. There are at least 60 shops doing this business.

In the market you can buy saffron cheaply. This spice is very expensive in the west, so if you like it then this is a good place to stock up.

## Getting There & Away

**Bus** The Hoi An bus station is 1km west of the centre of town at 74 Huynh Thuc Khang St. Small truck-buses from here go to Dai Loc (Ai Nghia), Danang, Quang Ngai (once a day departing in the early morning), Que Son, Tam Ky and Tra My. Services to Danang begin at 5 am; the last bus to Danang departs in the late afternoon.

In October, about 30km south of Hoi An, we were delayed at night for six hours by flooding almost a metre deep after heavy rain. Our driver slung up his hammock over the steering wheel and went to sleep. Other more determined (foolish?) drivers proceeded at a walking pace for several kilometres behind two bus boys who waded uncomplainingly through the

water. Their positions marked the edges of the road and the drivers were careful to stay between them. Wherever you looked there was the shimmer of a huge plain of water. In front of us was a line of buses and trucks whose lights sliced in two the black waters all around.

**Gordon Balderston**

**Minibus** Virtually every hotel in Hoi An can sell you a minibus ticket to either Nha Trang or Hué. The Hoi An-Hué minibus goes through Danang and you can be dropped off there if you like. Hoi An-Nha Trang costs US$9, Hoi An-Hué US$5, Hoi An-Danang US$3 and Hoi An-My Lai US$7. Minibuses to Nha Trang depart twice daily at 5 am and 5 pm. The Hué minibus departs twice daily at 8 am and 1 pm. A Hoi An-Danang minibus departs at 5 pm.

**Car** There are two land routes from Danang to Hoi An. The shorter way is to drive to the Marble Mountains (11km from Danang) and continue south for another 19km. Alternatively, you can head south from Danang on Highway 1 and, at a signposted intersection 27km from the city, turn left and head east for 10km.

**Boat** At least a short paddle-boat trip on the Thu Bon River (the Cai River) – the largest in Quang Nam-Danang Province – is recommended. Chartered boats can be found at the Hoang Van Thu Street Dock. A simple boat powered by an oarswoman costs something like US$2 per hour and for most travellers one hour will probably be enough. By motor launch it may be possible to take an all-day boat ride from Hoi An all the way to Tra Kieu (Simhapura) and the My Son area.

Small, motorised ferries leave Hoi An for nearby districts and Cham Island from the Hoang Van Thu Street Dock, which is across from 50 Bach Dang St. The daily boat to Cham Island usually departs between 7 and 8 am. The daily boat to Duy Xuyen leaves at 5 am. There is also frequent service to Cam Kim Island.

## Getting Around

Anywhere within town can be reached on

foot. To go further afield, rent a bicycle for US$1 per day or rent a motorbike for US$5 (without driver) or US$10 (with driver) per day.

# Around Hoi An

## CUA DAI BEACH
The fine sands of Cua Dai Beach (Bai Tam Cua Dai) are usually deserted. When there is a full moon, people come here to hang out until late at night. Changing booths are provided and refreshments are sold in the shaded kiosks.

Cua Dai Beach is 5km east of Hoi An on Cua Dai St, which is the continuation of Tran Hung Dao and Phan Dinh Phung Sts. The road passes shrimp-hatching pools built with Australian assistance. There are plans for a team of Australian submarine archaeologists to excavate sunken ships near here.

## CAM KIM ISLAND
The master woodcarvers, who in previous centuries produced the fine carvings that graced the homes of Hoi An's merchants and the town's public buildings, came from Kim Bong village on Cam Kim Island. These days, most of the wood carvings on sale in Hoi An are produced here. Some of the villagers also build wooden boats.

To reach the island, catch one of the frequent boats from the Hoang Van Thu Street Dock, which is opposite 50 Bach Dang St.

## CHAM ISLAND
Cham Island (Culao Cham) is in the South China Sea 21km from Hoi An; by boat, the trip takes about two hours. The island is famous as a source of swifts' nests, which are exported to Hong Kong, Singapore and elsewhere for use in bird's-nest soup.

A motorised ferry to Cham Island's two fishing villages departs from the Hoang Van Thu Street Dock at about 7 am and takes three hours for the one-way journey. The boat returns in the afternoon.

Scuba diving is one possible form of entertainment here. You can get a permit for fishing.

A hotel was under construction on the island at the time of writing and may be in operation by the time you read this.

The Cham Island festival is kind of like a blessing of the fleet. It marks the start of the fishing season. It's held yearly, though the exact date isn't fixed. When I attended, it was held on 29 March, which is Danang's liberation day, which was also Easter and possibly significant on the lunar calendar too. They had dragon boat races, coracle races (without paddles, the drivers bounce the coracles along), a tug-of-war and a religious part with monks, incense and offerings. Dana Tours organised a tour from Danang for foreigners and it went very well. They had a chartered fishing boat for US$15 each return and accommodation on the beach in two-person tents from about US$15 more, including food. Tourists were allowed to wander freely around the village, go on coracle rides, visit houses etc. Dana Tours now has a boat permanently based at Hoi An to take tourists out to Cham. I'm not sure of the charter costs – best to contact them directly.

**Mark Procter**

## THANH HA
Thanh Ha, which is sometimes called the 'pottery village', is 3km west of Hoi An. In the recent past there were many pottery factories here, but the pottery industry has been in decline. Still, some craftspeople here still do this hot, sweaty work and foreign visitors enjoy watching this. The locals don't mind if you visit their factories, though they'd be happier if you bought something or gave them a tip for showing you around.

## MY SON
One of the most stunning sights in the Hoi An area is My Son, Vietnam's most important Cham site. During the centuries when Tra Kieu (then known as Simhapura) served as the political capital of Champa, My Son was the site of the most important Cham intellectual and religious centre, and also may have served as a burial place for Cham monarchs. My Son is considered to be Champa's counterpart to the grand cities of South-East Asia's other Indian-influenced civilisations: Angkor (Cambodia), Bagan (Myanmar), Ayuthaya (Thailand) and Borobudur (Java).

The monuments are set in a verdant valley

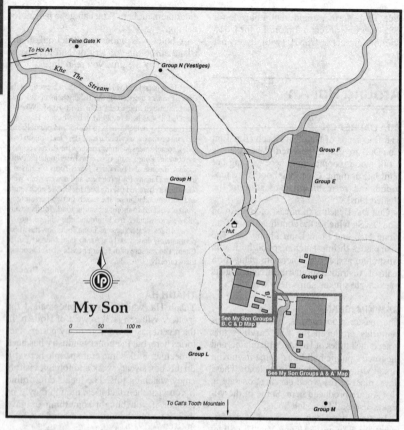

My Son

0    50    100 m

surrounded by hills and overlooked by massive Cat's Tooth Mountain (Hon Quap). Clear brooks (in which visitors can take a dip) run between the structures and past nearby coffee plantations.

My Son became a religious centre under King Bhadravarman in the late 4th century. The site was occupied until the 13th century – the longest period of development of any monument in South-East Asia (by comparison, Angkor's period of development lasted only three centuries, as did that of Bagan). Most of the temples were dedicated to Cham kings associated with divinities, especially

Shiva, who was regarded as the founder and protector of Champa's dynasties.

Champa's contact with Java was extensive. Cham scholars were sent to Java to study and there was a great deal of commerce between the two empires – Cham pottery has been found on Java and, in the 12th century, the Cham king wed a Javanese woman.

Because some of the ornamentation work at My Son was never finished, archaeologists know that the Chams first built their structures and only then carved decorations into the brickwork. Researchers have yet to figure out for certain how the Chams managed to get the baked bricks to stick together. According to one theory, they used a paste prepared with a botanical oil indigenous to central Vietnam. During one period in their history, the summits of some of the towers were covered with a layer of gold.

During the American War, the vicinity of My Son was completely devastated and depopulated in extended bitter fighting. Finding it a convenient staging ground, Viet Cong guerrillas used My Son as a base; in response the Americans bombed the monuments. Of the 68 structures of which traces have been found, 25 survived repeated pillagings in previous centuries by the Chinese, Khmer and Vietnamese. The American bombings spared about 20 of these, some of which sustained damage. Today, Vietnamese authorities are attempting to restore the remaining sites.

Elements of Cham civilisation can still be seen in the life of the people of Quang Nam-Danang and Quang Ngai provinces, whose forebears assimilated many Cham innovations into their daily lives. These include techniques for pottery making, fishing, sugar production, rice farming, irrigation, silk production and construction.

### Warning

During the American War, the hills and valleys around the My Son site were extensively mined. When mine clearing operations were carried out in 1977, six Vietnamese sappers were killed in this vicinity. Today, grazing cows are sometimes blown up, which means that as the years pass and the poor beasts locate the mines one by one, the hills around here are becoming less and less unsafe. Nevertheless, it's recommended that you do *not* stray from marked paths.

### The Site

The monuments of My Son have been divided by archaeologists into 10 main groups, lettered A, A', B, C, D, E, F, G, H and K. Each structure has been given a name consisting of a letter followed by a number.

The first structure you encounter along the trail is the false gate K, which dates from the 11th century. Between K and the other groups is a coffee plantation begun in 1986; peanuts and beans are grown among the coffee bushes.

**Group B** B1, the main sanctuary (*kalan*), was dedicated to Bhadresvara, which is a contraction of the name of King Bhadravarman, who built the first temple at My Son, combined with '-esvara,' which means Shiva. The first building on this site was erected in the 4th century, destroyed in the 6th century and rebuilt in the 7th century. Only the 11th century base, made of large sandstone blocks, remains; the brickwork walls have disappeared. The niches in the wall were used to hold lamps (Cham sanctuaries had no windows). The linga inside was discovered during excavations in 1985 1m beneath where it is now displayed.

B5, built in the 10th century, was used for storing sacred books and precious ritual objects (some made of gold) which were used in ceremonies performed in B1. The boat-shaped roof (the 'bow' and 'stern' have fallen off) shows the influence of Malayo-Polynesian architecture. Unlike the sanctuaries, this building has windows. The fine Cham masonry inside is all original. Over the window on the wall facing B4 is a bas-relief in brick of two elephants under a tree with two birds in it.

The ornamentation on the exterior walls of B4 is an excellent example of a Cham decorative style, typical of the 9th century, said to resemble worms. This style is unlike anything found in other South-East Asian cultures.

B3 has an Indian-influenced pyramidal roof typical of Cham towers. Inside B6 is a bathtub-shaped basin for keeping the sacred water that was poured over the linga in B1; this basin is the only known example of Cham origin.

B2 is a gate. Around the perimeter of Group B (structures B7 through B13) are small temples dedicated to the gods of the directions of the compass (*dikpalaka*).

**Group C** The 8th century sanctuary C1 was

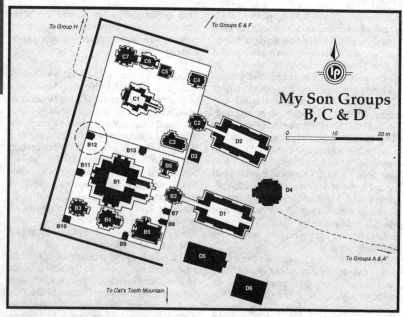

My Son Groups
B, C & D

used to worship Shiva portrayed in human form (rather than in the form of a linga, as in B1). Inside is an altar where a statue of Shiva, now in the Cham Museum in Danang, used to stand. On either side of the stone doorway you can see, bored into the lintel and the floor, the holes in which two wooden doors once swung. Note the motifs, characteristic of the 8th century, carved into the brickwork of the exterior walls.

**Group D** Building D1, once a *mandapa* (meditation hall), is now used as a store-room. It is slated to become a small museum of Cham sculpture. Objects to be displayed include a large panel of Shiva dancing on a platform above the bull Nandin: to Shiva's left is Skanda (under a tree), his son Uma, his wife and a worshipper; to Shiva's right is a dancing saint and two musicians under a tree, one with two drums, the other with a flute. The display will also include a finely carved lion – symbol of the power of the king (the

lion was believed to be an incarnation of Vishnu and the protector of kings) – whose style belies Javanese influence.

**Group A** The path from groups B, C and D to Group A leads eastward from near D4.

Group A was almost completely destroyed by US attacks. According to locals, massive A1, considered the most important monument at My Son, remained impervious to aerial bombing and was finally finished off by a helicopter-borne sapper team. All that remains of A1 today is a pile of collapsed brick walls. After the destruction of A1, Philippe Stern, an expert on Cham art and curator of the Guimet Museum in Paris, wrote a letter of protest to President Nixon, who ordered US forces to continue killing the Viet Cong, but not to do any further damage to Cham monuments.

A1 was the only Cham sanctuary with two doors. One faced the east, direction of the Hindu gods; the other door faced west towards groups B, C and D and the spirits of the ancestor-kings that may have been buried there. Inside A1 is a stone altar pieced together in 1988. Among the ruins, some of the brilliant brickwork, which is of a style typical of the 10th century, is still visible. At the base of A1 on the side facing A10 (which is decorated in 9th century style) is a carving of a worshipping figure, flanked by round columns, with a Javanese *kala-makara* (sea-monster god) above. There may be some connection between the presence of this Javanese motif and the studies in Java of a great 10th century Cham scholar. There are plans to partially restore A1 and A10 as soon as possible.

**Other Groups** Group A', which dates from the 8th century, is at present overgrown and is thus inaccessible. Group E was built during the 8th to 11th centuries, while Group F dates from the 8th century. Group G, which has been damaged by time rather than war, is from the 12th century. There are long-term plans to restore these monuments.

### Places to Stay

Unless you have equipment to camp out at

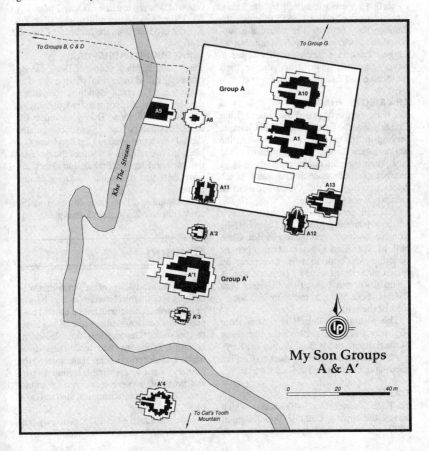

**My Son Groups
A & A'**

0    20    40 m

My Son, the nearest hotels are in Hoi An and Danang.

## Getting There & Away

**Minibus** Numerous hotels in Hoi An book a day trip to My Son that also includes a stop-off at Tra Kieu. At US$6 per person, you could hardly do it cheaper unless you walked. The minibuses depart Hoi An at 8 am and return at 2 pm.

**Honda Om** It's possible to get to My Son by rented motorbike. We have had numerous complaints from travellers that their rented motorbikes were vandalised by the locals, who then asked about US$25 to repair the damage they caused. The police are supposed to have cracked down on this, but we suggest caution nonetheless. It's better to have somebody else drive you on their motorbike and have them wait for you.

## TRA KIEU (SIMHAPURA)

Tra Kieu, formerly called Simhapura (Lion Citadel), was the first capital city of Champa, serving in that capacity from the 4th to the 8th centuries. Today, nothing remains of the city except the rectangular ramparts. A large number of artefacts, including some of the finest carvings in the Cham Museum in Danang, were found here.

You can get a good view of the city's outlines from the Mountain Church (Nha Tho Nui), which is on the top of Buu Chau Hill in Tra Kieu. This modern, open-air structure was built in 1970 to replace an earlier church destroyed by time and war. A Cham tower once stood on this spot. Tra Kieu is about 500m to the south and south-west of the hilltop.

The Mountain Church is 6.5km from Highway 1 and 19.5km from the beginning of the footpath to My Son. Within Tra Kieu, it is 200m from the morning market (Cho Tra Kieu) and 550m from Tra Kieu Church.

### Tra Kieu Church

Tra Kieu Church (Dia So Tra Kieu), which serves the town's Catholic population of 3000, was built a century ago (although the

border of the semicircular patio, which is made of upturned artillery shells, was added later). The priest here was interested in Cham civilisation and amassed a collection of Cham artefacts found by local people.

A 2nd-floor room in the building to the right of the church opened as a museum in 1990. The round ceramic objects with faces on them, which date from the 8th to the 10th century, were affixed to the ends of tile roofs. The face is that of Kala, the God of Time.

Tra Kieu Church is 7km from Highway 1 and 19km from the trail to My Son. It is 150m down an alley opposite the town's clinic of western medicine (Quay Thuoc Tay Y), 350m from the morning market (Cho Tra Kieu) and 550m from the Mountain Church.

## DONG DUONG (INDRAPURA)

The Cham religious centre of Dong Duong (formerly called Indrapura) was the site of an important Mahayana Buddhist monastery, the Monastery of Lakshmindra-Lokeshvara, founded in 875. Dong Duong served as the capital of Champa from 860 to 986, when the capital was transferred to Cha Ban (near Qui Nhon). Tragically, as a result of the devastation wrought by the French and American wars, only part of the gate to Dong Duong remains.

Indrapura is 21km from My Son as the crow flies and 55km from Danang.

# Danang

Back in the heady days of the American War, Danang was often referred to as the 'Saigon of the north'. This cliché held a note of both praise and condemnation – like its big sister to the south, Danang was notable for its booming economy, fine restaurants, busy traffic and glittering shops. 'Entertaining the military' was also a profitable business – bars and prostitution were major service industries. As in Saigon, corruption also ran rampant.

Liberation arrived in 1975, promptly putting a sizeable dent in the nightlife. Even

## Swords into Market Shares

The word is out – it's time to put away the guns and beat the swords into ploughshares. Yes, the war between Vietnam and America is over, but the battle for market share is just beginning. And everyone wants a piece of the action. Joint-venture capitalists from Japan, Korea, Taiwan, France, Germany, England and Australia have been flocking to Vietnam since the beginning of the 1990s.

The most recent arrivals in town have been the Americans and they bring with them several competitive advantages. As with the French, there is this strange nostalgia for doing business with those who were just yesterday Vietnam's enemy. Aside from that, the fact is that the Vietnamese love anything American – be it Mickey Mouse or Michael Jackson. Long prohibited from doing business in Vietnam by a US-imposed embargo (only lifted in 1994), American companies are now beating a path to what they hope will be Asia's newest economic tiger.

The new American warriors don't wear green uniforms or carry M-16s. Rather, they come in pressed suits, carrying Gucci luggage and laptop computers. Their weapons of choice are cola drinks, Hollywood celluloid and compact discs. Their battle cry is 'Stocks, bonds and rock 'n' roll!'.

Consumerism is now rampant in Vietnam, at least among the relatively affluent. Being called a member of the 'upper crust' (once defined as 'a lot of crumbs held together by dough') is no longer an insult. Making money is OK now. And so is spending it. It's this consumer boom that keeps foreign investors awake at night.

American companies have already splashed ashore. Computers sporting the label 'Intel Inside' are on display in newly opened hi-tech electronic shops. Chrysler has formed a joint venture to produce its gas-guzzling Jeep Cherokee in Vietnam. Motorola pagers can be heard beeping in the pockets and handbags of the Vietnamese well-to-do. Pepsi was the first American soft drink vendor to return to Vietnam, but Coke was not far behind.

American fast food should find a ready market among Vietnam's trendy urban elite. McDonald's – when it finally opens a branch in Saigon, Danang or Hanoi – will be an instant hit. That is, of course, if nobody clones the name first. Already, there is a spreading chain of fake 7-Elevens.

The Americans, for their part, are displeased with the lack of protection for intellectual property rights. Trademarks, patents and copyrights are violated with impunity by the Vietnamese. The proliferation of pirated music tapes and fake Rolex watches are potential bones of contention. Nothing is sacred – even downsized copies of the Statue of Liberty have popped up in Vietnam's newest avant-garde cafes. Vietnamese who know their history point out that the original Statue of Liberty was a gift to America from France – 'Why' they ask, 'shouldn't we have one too?' Why not indeed?

On the other hand, the Vietnamese government has so far refused anyone permission to capitalise on Ho Chi Minh's name. A proposal to open an American joint venture called *Uncle Ho's Hamburgers* flew like a lead balloon. Nor were the Vietnamese persuaded when the American business reps pointed out that Ho Chi Minh does vaguely resemble Colonel Sanders. 'No' said the frowning Vietnamese, 'Ho Chi Minh was a general'. ∎

---

today, Danang is still a pretty laid-back city. However, Vietnam's recent economic liberalisation has helped Danang regain some of its former glory.

Danang (population one million) is now Vietnam's fourth-largest city. It's also the northern limits of Vietnam's tropical zone – even nearby Hué is much colder in winter.

While only of marginal interest to travellers, Danang has some very rewarding sights both in town and in the surrounding areas. In the town itself, the highlights are the Cham Museum, Cao Dai Temple, Ho Chi Minh Museum, My Khe Beach and night cruises on the Han River. Points of interest in the outlying areas include the Marble Mountains, China Beach (Bai Non Nuoc), the Cham towers at My Son, Ba Na hill station, Hai Van Pass, Lang Co Island and day cruises on the Thuy Tu River (summer only).

### History

Danang, known under the French as Tourane, succeeded Hoi An as the most important port in central Vietnam during the 19th century.

In late March 1975, Danang, the second-largest city in South Vietnam, was the scene of utter chaos. Saigon government forces were ordered to abandon Hué, while Quang Ngai had fallen to the Communists, cutting South Vietnam in two. Desperate civilians

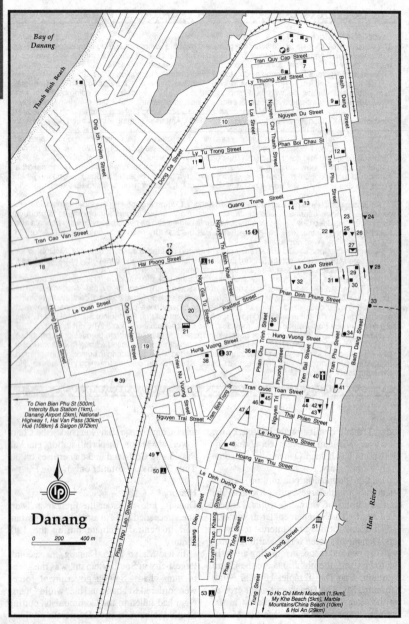

Bay of
Danang

Thanh Binh Beach

Tran Quy Cap Street
Ly Thuong Kiet Street
Nguyen Du Street
Phan Boi Chau St
Bach Dang Street

Le Loi Street
Nguyen Chi Thanh Street

Ong Ich Khiem Street
Dong Da Street

Ly Tu Trong Street

Quang Trung Street

Nguyen Thi Minh Khai Street

Tran Phu Street

Tran Cao Van Street

Hai Phong Street

Le Duan Street

Phan Dinh Phung Street

Ngo Gia Tu Street

Pasteur Street

Hoang Hoa Tham Street

Ong Ich Khiem Street

Hung Vuong Street

Hung Vuong Street

Phan Chu Trinh Street

Phuong Street

Yen Bai Street

Tran Phu Street

Bach Dang Street

Han River

Trieu Nu Vuong Street

Tran Quoc Toan Street

Nguyen Tri

Thai Phien Street

Tran Binh Trong St

Nguyen Trai Street

Le Hong Phong Street

Hoang Van Thu Street

Le Dinh Duong Street

Hoang Dieu Street

Huynh Thuc Khang Street

Phan Chu Trinh Street

Nu Vuong Street

Trung Street

Phan Ngu Lao Street

To Dien Bien Phu St (500m),
Intercity Bus Station (1km),
Danang Airport (2km), National
Highway 1, Hai Van Pass (30km),
Hué (108km) & Saigon (972km)

To Ho Chi Minh Museum (1.5km),
My Khe Beach (5km), Marble
Mountains/China Beach (10km)
& Hoi An (29km)

# Danang

0     200     400 m

| PLACES TO STAY | | 45 | Orient Hotel | 16 | Caodai Temple |
|---|---|---|---|---|---|
| 1 | Thanh Binh | 47 | Pacific Hotel | 17 | Hospital C |
| | Guesthouse | 48 | Minh Tam II Mini-Hotel | 18 | Danang Railway |
| 3 | Huu Nghi Hotel | | | | Station |
| 4 | Danang Hotel | **PLACES TO EAT** | | 19 | Con Market |
| | (Old Wing) | 2 | Café Lien | 20 | Danang Stadium |
| 5 | Danang Hotel | 24 | Hanakim Dinh | 21 | Swimming Pool |
| | (New Wing) | | Restaurant | 25 | Vietnam & Pacific |
| 7 | Peace Hotel | 26 | Thanh Lich | | Airlines Booking |
| 8 | Thu Bon Hotel | | Restaurant | | Office |
| 9 | Elegant Hotel | 28 | Christie's Restaurant | 27 | Post Office |
| 11 | Hai Van Hotel | 32 | Hoang Ngoc | 33 | Ferries Across the |
| 12 | Song Han Hotel | | Restaurant | | Han River |
| 13 | Ami Hotel | 42 | Tiem An Binh Dan | 34 | Danang Market |
| 14 | Royal Hotel | | Restaurant | 35 | Municipal Theatre |
| 22 | Binh Duong Mini-Hotel | 43 | Tu Do Restaurant & | 37 | Dana Tours |
| 23 | Bach Dang Hotel | | Kim Do Restaurant | 39 | Short-Haul Pickup |
| 29 | Riverside Hotel | 49 | Thanh An Vegetarian | | Truck Station |
| 30 | Dong Kinh Hotel | | Restaurant | 40 | Danang Cathedral |
| 31 | Vinapha Hotel | | | 46 | Bookshop |
| 36 | Thanh Thanh Hotel | **OTHER** | | 50 | Phap Lam Pagoda |
| 38 | Thu Do Hotel | 6 | Lao Consulate | 51 | Cham Museum |
| 41 | Hai Au Hotel | 10 | Market | 52 | Tam Bao Pagoda |
| 44 | Dai A Hotel | 15 | Vietcombank | 53 | Pho Da Pagoda |

tried to flee the city as soldiers of the disintegrating South Vietnamese army engaged in an orgy of looting, pillage and rape. On 29 March 1975, two truckloads of Communist guerrillas, more than half of them women, drove into what had been the most heavily defended city in South Vietnam and, without firing a shot, declared Danang 'liberated'.

Almost the only fighting that took place as Danang fell was between South Vietnamese soldiers and civilians battling for space on flights and ships out of the city. On 27 March, the president of World Airways, Ed Daly, ignoring explicit government orders, sent two 727s from Saigon to Danang to evacuate refugees. When the first plane landed, about a thousand desperate and panicked people mobbed the tarmac. Soldiers fired assault rifles at each other and at the plane as they tried to shove their way through the rear door. As the aircraft taxied down the runway trying to take off, people climbed up into the landing-gear wells and someone threw a hand grenade, damaging the right wing.

Those who managed to fight their way aboard, kicking and punching aside anyone in their way, included over 200 soldiers, mostly members of the elite Black Panthers company. The only civilians on board were two women and one baby – and the baby was there only because it had been thrown aboard by its desperate mother, who was left on the tarmac. Several of the stowaways in the wheel wells couldn't hold on and, as the plane flew southward, TV cameras on the second 727 filmed them falling into the South China Sea.

### Orientation

Danang is on the western bank of the Han River. Along the eastern bank, which can be reached via the Nguyen Van Troi Bridge, is a long, thin peninsula at the northern tip of which is Nui Son Tra, known as 'Monkey Mountain' to the Americans. It is now a closed military area. To the south, 11km from the city, are the Marble Mountains. Hai Van Pass overlooks Danang from the north.

### Information

**Travel Agencies** Dana Tours (☎ 822516; fax 824023) at 95 Hung Vuong St is one of Danang's main tour booking agencies. Another place to try is Hoa Binh Tourist (☎ 827183) at 316 Hoang Dieu St.

Everything can be arranged at agencies, including car rentals, boat trips and a trekking journey in nearby Bach Ma National Park.

**Money** Vietcombank is at 104 Le Loi St near the corner of Hai Phong St.

**Emergency** Hospital C (Benh Vien C; ☎ 822480) is at 35 Hai Phong St.

**Consulates** The one particularly useful consulate is for Laos at 12 Tran Quy Cap St. Tran Quy Cap St is at the northern end of town close to the Danang Hotel.

**Visa Amendments & Extensions** If you're going to exit Vietnam overland via the Lao Bao border crossing, you need to get your visa amended to indicate this. The Immigration Police Office, on the corner of Nguyen Thi Minh Khai and Ly Tu Trong Sts, can do this, but you must go through a travel agent rather than directly to the police themselves. Dana Tours and Hoa Binh Tourist are possibilities. You'll also have to go to a travel agent to get your visa extended. The standard cost is US$40.

**Cham Museum**

The best sight in Danang city (and some would say the only sight) is the Cham Museum (Bao Tang Cham). The museum was founded in 1915 by the École Française d'Extrême Orient and has the finest collection of Cham sculpture in the world. Many of the sandstone carvings (altars, lingas, garudas, ganeshas and images of Shiva, Brahma and Vishnu) are absolutely stunning; this is the sort of place you can easily visit again and again. It is well worth getting a knowledgeable guide (a scarce commodity in these parts) to show you around.

The Cham Museum is near the intersection of Nu Vuong and Bach Dang Sts and is open daily from 8 to 11 am and 1 to 5 pm. Admission costs US$2 – make sure you hand over the money to an authorised member of the staff in the ticket booth and not to some entrepreneurial gardener.

A trilingual guidebook to the museum

written by its director, Tran Ky Phuong, Vietnam's most eminent scholar of Cham civilisation, gives excellent background on the art of Champa; it also includes some information on the museum's exhibits. The booklet, entitled *Museum of Cham Sculpture – Danang* and *Bao Tang Dieu Khac Cham Da Nang* (Foreign Languages Publishing House, Hanoi, 1987), is usually on sale where you buy your entrance ticket.

Cham art can be divided into two main periods. Before the 10th century, it was very emotionally expressive, reflecting contact with seafaring cultures from Indonesia. From the 10th to the 14th century, as Champa fell into decline because of unending wars with the Vietnamese, Cham art came under Khmer influence and became more formalistic.

The museum's artefacts, which date from the 7th to 15th centuries, were discovered at Dong Duong (Indrapura), Khuong My, My Son, Tra Kieu (Simhapura), Thap Mam (Binh Dinh) and other sites, mostly in Quang Nam-Danang Province. The rooms in the museum are named after the localities in which the objects displayed in them were discovered.

A recurring image in Cham art is that of Uroja, the 'Mother of the Country', who gave birth to the dynasties that ruled Champa. Uroja, whose name means 'woman's breast' in the Cham language, was worshipped in the form of the nipples one often sees in Cham sculpture. Also common is the linga, phallic symbol of Shiva, which came to prominence after Champa's contact with Hinduism. Cham religious beliefs (and thus Cham architecture and sculpture) were influenced by Mahayana Buddhism as early as the 4th century. In addition to its clear Indian elements, Cham art shows Javanese, Khmer and Dai Viet (Vietnamese) influences.

The four scenes carved around the base of the 7th century Tra Kieu Altar tell part of the *Ramayana* epic in a style influenced by the Amaravati style of South India. Scene A (see diagram), in which 16 characters appear, tells the story of Prince Rama, who broke the sacred bow, Rudra, at the citadel of Videha

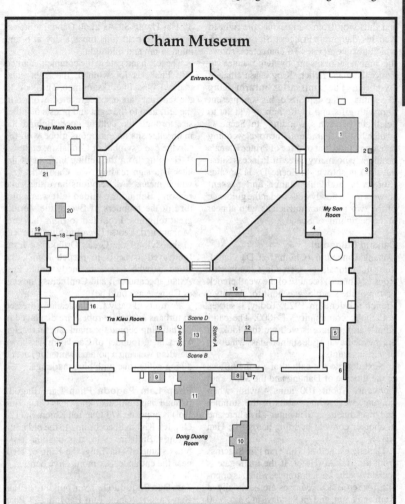

# Cham Museum

*Entrance*

Thap Mam Room

21

20

19

18

My Son Room

1

2

3

4

Tra Kieu Room

16

17

14

*Scene D*

15

13 *Scene C* *Scene A*

12

5

*Scene B*

9

8 7

6

11

Dong Duong Room

10

1　My Son Altar; from My Son, 8th-9th century
2　Ganesha (seated elephant); from My Son, 8th-9th century
3　Birthday of Brahma; from My Son, 8th-9th century
4　Polo players; from Thach An, 7th century
5　Altar ornaments; from Khuong My, 10th century
6　The Goddess Sarasvati; from Chanh Lo, 11th century
7　Vishnu, from Tra Kieu, 10th century
8　A deity; from Dong Duong, 9th-10th century
9　A deity; from Dong Duong, 9th-10th century
10　Dong Duong Altar ornaments; from Dong Duong, 9th-10th century
11　Dong Duong Altar; from Dong Duong, 9th-10th century

12　Linga
13　Tra Kieu Altar; from Tra Kieu, 7th century
14　Dancing Shiva; from Phong Le, 10th century
15　Linga
16　Dancing female apsaras; from Quang Nam-Danang Province, 10th century
17　Altar ornaments; from Binh Dinh, 12th-14th century
18　Lions; from Thap Mam, 12th-14th century
19　Shiva; from Thap Mam, 12th-14th century
20　The elephant-lion Gajasimha; from Thap Mam, 12th-14th century
21　The sea monster Makara; from Thap Mam, 12th-14th century

and thus won from King Janak the right to wed his daughter, Princess Sita. Scene B, which also comprises 16 characters, shows the ambassadors sent by King Janak to Prince Rama's father, King Dasaratha, at Ayodhya. The emissaries inform King Dasaratha of the exploits of his son, present him with gifts and invite him to Videha to celebrate his son's wedding. In Scene C (which has 18 characters), the royal wedding ceremony (and that of three of Prince Rama's brothers, who marry three of Princess Sita's cousins) is shown. In Scene D, 11 apsaras (heavenly maidens) dance and present flowers to the newlyweds under the guidance of the two gandhara musicians who appear at the beginning of Scene A.

### Danang Cathedral
Danang Cathedral (Chinh Toa Da Nang), known to locals as Con Ga Church (the Rooster Church) because of the weathercock on top of the steeple, was built for the city's French residents in 1923. Today, it serves a Catholic community of 4000. The cathedral's architecture is well worth a look, as are the medieval-style stained glass windows of various saints.

Next door to the cathedral are the offices of the diocese of Danang and the Saint Paul Convent. About 100 nuns – who, when praying, wear white habits in the summer and black habits in the winter – live here and at another convent building across the Han River.

Danang Cathedral is on Tran Phu St across from the Hai Au Hotel. If the main gate is locked, try the back entrance, which is opposite 14 Yen Bai St. Masses are held daily at 5 am and 5 pm, and on Sundays at 5 am, 6.30 am and 4.30 pm.

### Pagodas & Temples
**Caodai Temple** The Caodai Temple (Thanh That Cao Dai), built in 1956, is the largest such structure outside of the sect's headquarters in Tay Ninh. There are 50,000 Caodais in Quang Nam-Danang Province – 20,000 in Danang itself. The temple is across the street from Hospital C (Benh Vien C), which is at

35 Hai Phong St. As at all Caodai temples, prayers are held four times a day at 6 am, noon, 6 pm and midnight.

The left-hand gate to the complex, marked 'Nu Phai', is for women; the right gate, marked 'Nam Phai', is for men. The doors to the sanctuary are also segregated: women to the left, men to the right and priests of either sex through the central door. Behind the main altar sits an enormous globe with the 'divine eye', symbol of Caodaism, on it.

Hanging from the ceiling in front of the altar is a sign reading 'Van Giao Nhat Ly', which means 'All religions have the same reason'. Behind the gilded letters is a picture of the founders of five of the world's great religions. From left to right they are: Mohammed; Laotse (wearing blue robes cut in the style of the Greek Orthodox); Jesus (portrayed as he is in French icons); the Buddha (who has a distinctly South-East Asian appearance); and Confucius (looking as Chinese as could be).

Portraits of early Caodai leaders, dressed in turbans and white robes, are displayed in the building behind the main sanctuary. Ngo Van Chieu, founder of Caodaism, is shown standing wearing a pointed white turban and a long white robe with blue markings.

**Phap Lam Pagoda** Phap Lam Pagoda (Chua Phap Lam, also known as Chua Tinh Hoi) is opposite 373 Ong Ich Khiem St (123 Ong Ich Khiem St according to the old numbering). Built in 1936, this pagoda has a brass statue of Dia Tang, the King of Hell, near the entrance. Six monks live here.

**Tam Bao Pagoda** The main building of Tam Bao Pagoda (Chua Tam Bao) at 253 Phan Chu Trinh St is topped with a five-tiered tower. Only four monks live at this large pagoda which was built in 1953.

**Pho Da Pagoda** Pho Da Pagoda (Pho Da Tu), which is across from 293 Phan Chu Trinh St, was built in 1923 in a traditional architectural configuration. Today, about 40 monks, most of them young, live and study here. Local lay people and their children participate actively in the pagoda's lively religious life.

## Ho Chi Minh Museum

The Ho Chi Minh Museum (Bao Tang Ho Chi Minh) has three sections: a museum of military history in front of which American, Soviet and Chinese weaponry are displayed; a replica of Ho Chi Minh's house in Hanoi (complete with a small lake); and, on the other side of the pond from the house, a museum about Uncle Ho.

The museum, which is on Nguyen Van Troi St 250m west of Nui Thanh St (see the Around Danang map), is open Tuesday to Sunday from 7 to 11 am and 1 to 4.30 pm.

## Tombs of Spanish & French Soldiers

Spanish-led Philippine and French troops attacked Danang in August 1858, ostensibly to end the mistreatment of Vietnamese Catholics and Catholic missionaries by the government of Emperor Tu Duc. The city quickly fell, but the invaders soon had to contend with cholera, dysentery, scurvy, typhus and mysterious fevers. By the summer of 1859, 20 times as many of the invaders had died of illness as had been killed in combat. Many of these soldiers are buried in a chapel (Bai Mo Phap Va Ta Ban Nha) about 15km from the city. The names of the dead are written on the walls.

To get there, cross Nguyen Van Troi Bridge and turn left onto Ngo Quyen St (see the Around Danang map). Continue north to Tien Sa Port (Cang Tien Sa). The chapel, a white building, stands on the right on a low hill about half a kilometre past the gate of the port.

## Boat Trips

The Thuy Tu River north of Danang (near Hai Van Pass) has clean water and is good for boating. There are also sandy river beaches here that are fine for swimming. Christie's Restaurant and Dana Tours in Danang organise these trips. The same places also arrange night cruises on the Han River in Danang and trips to Cham Island (see the Around Hoi An section for information on Cham Island).

## Places to Stay – bottom end

Budget travellers usually stay in hotels located at the northern tip of the Danang peninsula. The neighbourhood is not scenic because of an adjacent cargo shipping terminal, but on the other hand it's actually much quieter than the traffic-clogged centre about 2km to the south.

The *Danang Hotel* at 3 Dong Da St is popular with backpackers. The old wing (☎ 821986; 100 rooms) has spartan, but cheap, rooms costing US$6 to US$15. The building was constructed in the late 1960s to house American military personnel and hasn't seen much improvement since then. However, things are different at the adjacent new wing (☎ 821986; fax 823431), which is plush and has rooms priced from US$25 to US$75. Be aware that the hotel could at any time renovate the old wing, which would cause prices to rise significantly.

Next to the Danang Hotel is the *Huu Nghi Hotel* (☎ 821021, 822563; 64 rooms) at 7 Dong Da St. Rooms with fan and icy water cost US$6 to US$12. Rooms with air-con and hot water start at US$10.

A bit further to the south-west is the *Hai Van Hotel* (☎ 821300; fax 823891; 40 rooms) at 2 Nguyen Thi Minh Khai St. It's an old place, but has large rooms, private bath and hot water. All rooms are equipped with both air-con and ceiling fans. The toll is US$12 to US$20.

The *Thu Do Hotel* (☎ 823863; 35 rooms) at 107 Hung Vuong St is relatively close to the railway station and just a few blocks from Con Market (Cho Con). It's cheap enough at US$5 to US$15, but it's getting awfully run down and is not popular.

The *Thanh Thanh Hotel* (☎ 821230; 50 rooms) is a friendly place, but looks dingy. Rooms are priced from US$8 to US$12. The hotel is at 50 Phan Chu Trinh St.

A few blocks south at 63 Hoang Dieu St is the popular *Minh Tam II Mini-Hotel* (☎ 826687; fax 824339; 18 rooms). The price scale here is US$20 to US$35.

The *Pacific Hotel* (Khach San Thai Binh Duong; ☎ 822137) is across the street from the much pricier Orient Hotel. It's an old place, but not bad. Twins cost US$25 to US$40.

*Dai A Hotel* (☎ 827532; fax 825760; 24 rooms) is a relatively new place at 27 Yen Bai St. The range here is US$15 to US$65.

A small, privately run place is the *Dong Kinh Hotel* (☎ 823864) at 83 Tran Phu St, where rooms are US$8. It's very close to Danang Market.

The *Vinapha Hotel* (☎ 825072; 16 rooms) at 80 Tran Phu St seems to be popular with long-term expats and business travellers. This is, in part, due to the very friendly staff. Rooms go for US$18 to US$20.

Many of the more well-heeled backpackers like the *Ami Hotel* (☎ 824494; fax 825532; 16 rooms). It's at 7 Quang Trung St and has rooms for US$18 to US$30.

The *Thanh Binh Guesthouse* (☎ 821239; 120 rooms) at 5 Ong Ich Khiem St is right on Thanh Binh Beach. The beach is known for its crowds and polluted water. This place is reserved for Vietnamese workers on organised union vacations, but they will rent to foreigners for US$10 to US$18. Very few foreigners take them up on the offer.

If you want to stay at a good beach, check out the *My Khe Hotel* (☎ 836125). The bottom-end rooms here cost US$15, but there are more luxurious facilities in the hotel's new wing. To get to the beach from central Danang, you have to take a ferry across the Han River and then a motorbike taxi (see the Around Danang map). Alternatively, just take a motorbike or taxi over the bridge on the south end of town (but this route almost 5km longer).

### Places to Stay – middle & top end

The *Peace Hotel* (Khach San Hoa Binh; ☎ 823984; fax 823161; 25 rooms) at 3 Tran Quy Cap St is relatively new and all rooms have air-con and hot water. Rooms cost US$25 to US$30 and breakfast is part of the package.

Just around the corner is the *Thu Bon Hotel* (☎ 821101; fax 822854; 18 rooms) at 10 Ly Thuong Kiet St. It's not a bad place, but the price range is steep for this standard of accommodation. Rooms cost US$30.

Every time we've checked this place, the management claims that it's 'all full'.

Also in this area is the *Elegant Hotel* (Khach San Thanh Lich; ☎ 892893; fax 835179; 36 rooms). It lives up to its name – it's elegant and then some. Rooms cost US$35 to US$140. The hotel is at 22A Bach Dang St.

The *Song Han Hotel* (☎ 822540; fax 821109; 61 rooms) is along the Han River at 36 Bach Dang St. This recently renovated place has rooms from US$22 to US$80. You can get legitimate massages here.

Close to the top of top-end accommodation in Danang is the *Royal Hotel* (☎ 823295; fax 827279; 28 rooms). This very stylish place is at 17 Quang Trung St. Twins with all the trimmings are priced from US$80 to US$145.

The *Bach Dang Hotel* (☎ 823649; fax 821659; 91 rooms) at 50 Bach Dang St boasts river views. Rooms cost US$38 to US$100.

Also with river views is the new and very elegant *Riverside Hotel* (Khach San Tien Sa; ☎ 832591; fax 832593) at 68 Bach Dang St. Rooms cost US$55 to US$130.

At the bottom end of Danang's mid-range accommodation is the *Binh Duong Mini-Hotel* (☎ 821930; fax 827666; 12 rooms). This hotel dishes up free breakfast and rooms for US$25 to US$35.

The *Hai Au Hotel* (☎ 822722; fax 824165; 29 rooms) opened in 1989 and, for a while, was the best in town, but has since been superseded. The hotel is conveniently located near the centre of town at 177 Tran Phu St, across the road from Danang Cathedral. Single and doubles cost US$40 to US$60. The hotel has a good restaurant.

The *Orient Hotel* (Khach San Phuong Dong; ☎ 821266; fax 822854; 36 rooms) at 93 Phan Chu Trinh St is a classy place with an elegant, wood-panelled lobby. Doubles are US$40 to US$46 and twins cost US$51 to US$57.

Coming soon to Danang's luxury hotel scene will be the 200-room *Furama Hotel* at My Khe Beach (see the Around Danang map). A Hong Kong-Vietnamese joint venture, this place promises to be the poshest accommodation in town when it finally opens. It's been announced that room rates will be from US$140 to US$400 a night.

## Places to Eat

*Cafe Lien* (☎ 820401) at 4 Dong Da St is directly opposite the Danang Hotel. Prices are low and the food is good, plus there is an English menu and friendly staff. The convenient location pulls in all sorts of budget travellers. And this is one place where you never know who you'll meet:

An entertaining local character is Linh, who runs a cafe opposite the Danang Hotel. She can arrange car and motorcycle hire and she will sometimes accompany you on day trips as a guide. A foreign resident with business interests in Danang told me that she was also a police informant and knew everything that was happening in the immediate vicinity of the cafe.

One evening when I was having a beer in the cafe, a blond-haired, blue-eyed and fair-skinned traveller sat down at a nearby table. I judged him to be German or Scandinavian. 'I think you are from Israel', Linh said to him. He was absolutely astonished. 'How do you know that?', he asked her. Linh first gave him a conspiratorial look and then smiled. Finally, she whispered, 'I know everything'.

**Ian McVittie**

*Christie's Restaurant* (☎ 822034) at 9 Bach Dang St is an absolute haven. The restaurant is suspended over the water on pilings so there are nice views of the Han River. Run by an Australian man, this place dishes up continental and Vietnamese food (very nicely presented). There is a bar, book exchange, western newspapers, satellite TV, English-speaking staff and the cleanest toilet in Danang. The restaurant also organises tours such as boat trips to Cham Island. It's a lovely place to watch the light fade on the river at night.

The *Hoang Ngoc Restaurant* is a pleasant place with great service and outstanding food. The lively owner, Mr Hoang, is a gem. You can try his speciality, sea slug, which tastes much better than it sounds. The restaurant is at 106 Nguyen Chi Thanh St, near Phan Dinh Phung St.

The *Thanh Lich Restaurant*, near the post office at 42 Bach Dang St, has an extensive menu in English, French and Vietnamese.

This place has received good reviews from foreign business people.

*Thanh An Vegetarian Restaurant* is a food stall serving vegetable dishes that resemble meat in appearance. The food here is very cheap and the restaurant is open daily from 7 am until 4 pm. This place is half a block from Phap Lam Pagoda and about 1km from the city centre. The street address is 484 Ong Ich Khiem St.

*Tu Do Restaurant* (☎ 821869) at 172 Tran Phu St has an extensive menu, the service is punctilious and the food is in fact quite good, but some of the prices are a lot higher than you'd expect to pay. Next door is the *Kim Do*, a slightly fancier place where the food is excellent, but almost ridiculously expensive. Also nearby at 174 Tran Phu St is the *Tiem An Binh Dan Restaurant*, a modest place with reasonable prices.

Out by My Khe Beach is the place to go for seafood (see the Around Danang map). About 200m north of the My Khe Hotel is a bunch of seafood restaurants with open decks overlooking the ocean. The best of the lot here is the *Loi Restaurant*. Marianne, the boss, speaks good English – she was given her English name by an American soldier when she was a child.

## Things to Buy

Danang Market (Cho Da Nang) is at the intersection of Hung Vuong and Tran Phu Sts. Unusually, this market stays open late and is a fine place to casually shop in the evenings.

The Con Market (Cho Con) is Danang's largest, but functions mostly in the daytime. This huge, colourful market has a selection of just about everything sold in Vietnam: household items, ceramics, fresh vegetables, stationary, cutlery, fruit, flowers, polyester clothes etc.

If you've been on the road for a while and are hard up for reading material, the bookshop next to the Orient Hotel sells *Time* and *Newsweek*.

## Getting There & Away

**Air** During the American War, Danang had

one of the busiest airports in the world. Business declined sharply when the war ended, but Danang now distinguishes itself by having one of Vietnam's three international airports. However, almost all the flights between Danang and other countries go via Saigon, though you can do the immigration and customs formalities in Danang.

Vietnam Airlines has an extensive schedule to/from Danang. For more details, see the Getting Around chapter.

Pacific Airlines flies Danang-Saigon and charges the exact same fare as Vietnam Airlines. More intriguingly, Pacific Airlines also offers Danang's only nonstop international flight, Danang-Macau.

The Danang office of Vietnam Airlines (☎ 822094) is at 35 Tran Phu St. Pacific Airlines (☎ 820990) is right next door at No 37.

**Bus** The Danang intercity bus station (Ben Xe Khach Da Nang) is about 3km from the city centre on the thoroughfare known, at various points along its length, as Hung Vuong St, Ly Thai To St and Dien Bien Phu St (see the Around Danang map). The ticket office for express buses is across the street from 200 Dien Bien Phu St; it is open from 7 to 11 am and 1 to 5 pm.

Express bus services are available to Buon Ma Thuot, Dalat, Gia Lai, Haiphong, Hanoi, Saigon, Hon Gai, Lang Son, Nam Dinh and Nha Trang. Tickets for nonexpress buses to Kon Tum (5 am departure) and Vinh are also sold here. All express buses depart at 5 am.

There are now buses between Danang and Savannakhet in Laos via Dong Ha and the Lao Bao border crossing. Details are provided in the Getting There & Away chapter.

**Minibus** Most travellers prefer to stay in Hoi An rather than Danang, so Hoi An has better minibus services. Nevertheless, it is possible to get a seat on an upmarket minibus in Danang, though your fellow passengers will probably be Vietnamese rather than foreigners. Check at Cafe Lien for information on the minibuses to Hué and Nha Trang.

There is also a daily minibus service between Danang and Hoi An. The bus leaves

at 8 am from Danang and departs Hoi An for Danang at 5 pm. Tickets cost US$3 one way or $5.50 return. In Danang, you can get tickets at Christie's Restaurant. Hotel pickup is available.

**Train** The Danang train station (Ga Da Nang) is about 1.5km from the city centre on Haiphong St at the northern end of Hoang Hoa Tham St. The train ride to Hué is one of the nicest in the country (although driving up and over Hai Van Pass is also spectacular).

Northbound, the quickest ride takes about 3¼ hours to Hué. Local trains take about six hours. Watch your belongings as you pass through the pitch-black tunnels.

Danang is, of course, served by all *Reunification Express* trains. For ticket prices, see the Train section in the Getting Around chapter.

**Car & Motorbike** Unless you're lucky enough to catch the Hué-Hoi An minibus (not so easy because it doesn't usually stop in Danang), the simplest way to get to Hoi An is to hire a car for US$10 or a motorbike for US$8. Look for these vehicles at Cafe Lien or the Danang Hotel. For just slightly more money you can ask the driver to stop off and wait for you while you visit the Marble Mountains and China Beach. You can get to My Son by motorbike (US$12) or car (US$35) and you can be let off in Hoi An on the way back if you don't wish to return to Danang.

Road distances from Danang are as follows:

| | |
|---|---|
| Hanoi | 764km |
| Hoi An | 30km |
| Hué | 108km |
| Lao Bao | 350km |
| Nha Trang | 541km |
| Quang Ngai | 130km |
| Qui Nhon | 303km |
| Saigon | 972km |
| Savannakhet, Laos | 500km |

### Getting Around
**The Airport** Danang's airport is just 2km west of the centre and can even be reached by cyclo in 15 minutes.

**Taxi** Airport Taxi (☎ 825555) and Dana Taxi (☎ 815815) provide modern vehicles with air-con and meters.

**Boat** Ferries across the Han River depart from a dock at the foot of Phan Dinh Phung St.

# Around Danang

## CHINA BEACH

China Beach, made famous in the American TV series of the same name, stretches for many kilometres north and south of the Marble Mountains. During the American War, American soldiers were airlifted here for 'rest-and-relaxation', often including a picnic on the beach. For some, it was their last meal because they were soon returned by helicopter to combat.

Danang locals insist that this isn't the real China Beach at all. The place most popular with American soldiers during the war was My Khe Beach 5km to the north. The motive behind naming the current beach 'China Beach' seems to be to capitalise on the famous name so as to draw foreign tourists to the government-owned China Beach Hotel. Near the hotel, private vendors flog 'China Beach' baseball caps, wooden carvings of Buddha, jade bracelets, new antiques and other tourist paraphernalia.

Perhaps because of its famous name, in December 1992 China Beach was the site of the first international surfing competition to be held in Vietnam.

The swimming season for all of Danang's beaches is from May to July, when the sea is most calm. During other times of the year the water is rough and there are usually no lifeguards on duty. Surfing is best from September to December when there are good breakers.

### Places to Stay & Eat

The *China Beach Hotel* (☎ 836216; fax 836335; 103 rooms), also known as the Non Nuoc Seaside Resort, is right on China Beach. Singles/doubles with fan are US$12/18. Air-

con rooms cost from US$40 to US$50. The hotel has two good restaurants – both charge reasonable prices.

### Getting There & Away

Pickup trucks to China Beach (Bai Tam Non Nuoc) depart when full from the short-haul pickup truck station in Danang.

To get to the China Beach Hotel by car, motorcycle or bicycle, drive to the Marble Mountains (see next entry) and turn left into Non Nuoc hamlet. Follow the road past the largest Marble Mountain and keep going as it curves around to the right (almost parallel to the beach). Before you hit the sand, turn right towards the casuarina grove (and away from the beach) and follow the road around to the left.

## MARBLE MOUNTAINS

The Marble Mountains consist of five stone hillocks, once islands, made of marble. Each is said to represent one of the five elements of the universe and is named accordingly: Thuy Son (Water), Moc Son (Wood), Hoa Son (Fire), Kim So (Metal or Gold) and Tho Son (Earth). The largest and most famous, Thuy Son, has a number of natural caves *(dong)* in which Buddhist sanctuaries have been built over the centuries. When Champa ruled this area, these same caves were used as Hindu shrines. Thuy Son is a popular pilgrimage site, especially on days of the full and sliver moons and during Tet.

A torch (flashlight) is useful inside the caves. Local children have learned that foreign tourists buy souvenirs and leave tips for unsolicited guided tours, so you are not likely to begin your visit alone. The local government adopted a regulation (which they sternly enforce) that the children cannot take tips, but can sell you souvenirs only. This seems counter-productive; most foreigners would rather tip the kids for the guided tours than buy the crappy souvenirs. In general, the kids are good-natured and some of the caves are difficult to find without their assistance. However, many travellers would rather enjoy the caves without pressure to buy souvenirs. One traveller wrote:

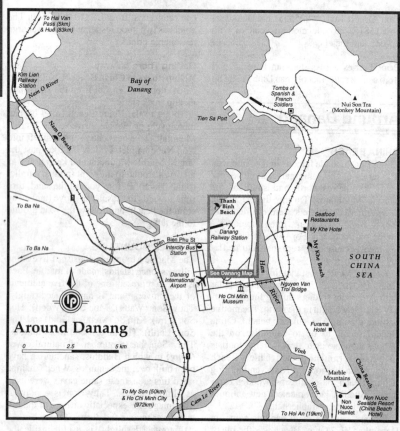

**Around Danang**

0      2.5      5 km

I suggest stronger warnings about the children who sell souvenirs at Marble Mountain. I think that they have outgrown their cuteness and are now quite aggressive and rambunctious. My guide was a girl who could not be more than 11, but claimed to be 16. She was very informative, but obviously not very happy or well treated. I loved the scenery, but found myself depressed by her and wishing very much that she would disappear. Surely something can be done about the way the souvenir shop owners exploit these children.

**Keith L Rakow**

However, someone else said:

Marble Mountain must not be missed. The cave pagodas are the best I've seen in Asia.

Of the two paths leading up Thuy Son, the one closer to the beach (at the end of the village) makes for a better circuit once you get up the top. So unless you want to follow this entry backwards, don't go up the staircase with concrete kiosks and a black cement sign at its base. At either place, there is a very steep admission charge of US$4.

At the top of the staircase (from which Cham Island is visible) is a gate, Ong Chon, which is pockmarked with bullets. Behind Ong Chon is Linh Ong Pagoda. As you enter the sanctuary, you'll see on the left a fantastic figure with a huge tongue. To the right of

Linh Ong are monks' quarters and a small orchid garden.

Behind Linh Ong and to the left, a path leads through two short tunnels to several caverns known as Tang Chon Dong. There are a number of concrete Buddhas and blocks of carved stone of Cham origin in these caves. Near one of the altars there is a flight of steps leading up to another cave, partially open to the sky, with two seated Buddhas in it.

To the left of the small building which is to the left of Linh Ong (ie immediately to the left as you enter Ong Chon gate) is the main path to the rest of Thuy Son. Stairs off the main pathway lead to Vong Hai Da, a viewpoint from which a brilliant panorama of China Beach and the South China Sea is visible.

The stone-paved path continues on to the right and into a canyon. On the left is Van Thong Cave. Opposite the entrance is a cement Buddha, behind which a narrow passage leads up to a natural chimney open to the sky.

After you exit the canyon and pass through a battle-scarred masonry gate, a rocky path to the right goes to Linh Nham, a tall chimney-cave with a small altar inside. Nearby, another path leads to Hoa Nghiem, a shallow cave with a Buddha in it. But if you go down the passageway to the left of the Buddha you come to cathedral-like Huyen Khong Cave, lit by an opening to the sky. The entrance to this spectacular chamber is guarded by two administrative mandarins (to the left of the doorway) and two military mandarins (to the right).

Scattered about the cave are Buddhist and Confucian shrines; note the inscriptions carved into the stone walls. On the right a door leads to two stalactites dripping water that local legend says comes from heaven. Actually, only one stalactite drips; the other one supposedly ran dry when Emperor Tu Duc (ruled 1848-83) touched it. During the American War, this chamber was used by the VC as a field hospital. Inside is a plaque dedicated to the Women's Artillery Group, which destroyed 19 US aircraft as they sat at a base below the mountains in 1972.

Just to the left of the battle-scarred masonry gate is Tam Thai Tu, a pagoda restored by Emperor Minh Mang in 1826. A path heading obliquely to the right goes to the monks' residences, beyond which are two shrines. From there a red dirt path leads to five small pagodas. Before you arrive at the monks' residences, stairs on the left-hand side of the path lead to Vong Giang Dai, which offers a fantastic 180° view of the other Marble Mountains and the surrounding countryside. To get to the stairway down, follow the path straight on from the masonry gate.

### Non Nuoc Hamlet
Non Nuoc Hamlet is on the southern side of Thuy Son and is a few hundred metres west of China Beach. The marble carvings made here by skilled (and not-so-skilled) craftspeople would make great gifts if they didn't weigh so much.

The town has been spruced up for tourism. During the war, the Americans referred to the shantytown near here as 'Dogpatch', named after a derelict town in the comic strip 'Lil Abner'. Most of the residents were refugees fleeing the fighting in the surrounding countryside.

### Getting There & Away
**Short-Haul Pickup Truck** Pickup trucks to the Marble Mountains (Ngu Hanh Son), Non Nuoc Hamlet and nearby China Beach (Bai Tam Non Nuoc) leave when full from the short-haul pickup truck station in Danang. The trip takes about 20 minutes.

**Car** The 11km route from Danang to the Marble Mountains passes by the remains of a 2km-long complex of former American military bases; aircraft revetments are still visible.

The Marble Mountains are 19km north of Hoi An along the 'Korean Highway'.

**Boat** It is possible to get to the Marble Mountains from Danang by chartered boat. The 8.5km trip up the Han River and the Vinh Diem River takes about 1¼ hours.

## OTHER BEACHES

China Beach is Danang's best, but there are several other beaches scattered around the periphery of the city.

### Thanh Binh Beach

Thanh Binh Beach is only a couple of kilometres from the centre of Danang. It is often crowded, notwithstanding the fact that the water is not the cleanest. To get there head all the way to the northern end of Ong Ich Khiem St.

### My Khe Beach

My Khe Beach (Bai Tam My Khe) is about 6km by road from downtown Danang. The beach is said to have a dangerous undertow, especially in winter. However, it is safer than China Beach because it's more protected by the Son Tra (Monkey) Mountains. The best months for swimming here are from March to early September.

Ironically, the dangerous winter surf goes hand-in-hand with large breakers, which are ideal for surfing – assuming that you know what you're doing. The surf can be very good from around mid-September to December, particularly in the morning when wind conditions are right. With this in mind, the Danang Surfers' Club was born in 1992. The club was founded by local Vietnamese; the best place to contact them is at the swimming pool at Danang Stadium (at Hung Vuong and Trieu Nu Vong Sts). Board rentals are available, but you should bring some wax and a ding repair kit since neither can be purchased locally.

My Khe Beach has recently acquired a small fleet of water scooters. This is unfortunate – if you think Vietnamese guys are crazy on motorbikes, you should see them on water scooters! Fortunately, these evil machines seem to spend much of their time being repaired.

Many people insist that My Khe was the real China Beach of wartime fame and that the present China Beach is a fake. For more discussion of this, see the previous China Beach section.

To get there by car, cross Nguyen Van Troi Bridge and continue straight (eastwards) across the big intersection (instead of turning right (southwards) to the Marble Mountains). If you don't have a car, try hopping on a ferry across the Han River from the foot of Phan Dinh Phung St and catching a ride southeastward to Nguyen Cong Tru St.

### Nam O Beach

Nam O Beach is on the Bay of Danang about 15km north of the city. The small community of Nam O has supported itself for years by producing firecrackers. However, these were banned by the government in 1995 and the community has now fallen on hard times. However, the locals have recently gone into making *nuoc mam* instead – it's not as profitable as firecrackers, but better than nothing.

# North of Danang

## HAI VAN PASS

Hai Van (Sea Cloud) Pass crosses over a spur of the Truong Son Mountain Range that juts into the South China Sea. About 30km north of Danang, Highway 1 climbs to an elevation of 496m, passing south of the Ai Van Son peak (1172m). It's an incredibly mountainous stretch of highway with spectacular views. The railway track, with its many tunnels, goes around the peninsula, following the shoreline to avoid the hills. Unfortunately, the buses cannot take this easy route – many break down here.

In the 15th century, Hai Van Pass formed the boundary between Vietnam and the Kingdom of Champa. Until the American War, the pass was heavily forested. At the top of the Hai Van Pass is an old French fort, later used as a bunker by the South Vietnamese army and the Americans.

If you visit in winter, you may find that the pass is almost a visible dividing line between the climate of the north and south. From about November through to March the north side of the pass can be uncomfortably wet and chilly, while just to the south it's warm and dry. Of course, variations in this weather pattern occur and we can't guarantee that you'll be able to observe this phenomenom 100% of the time. But in general, during the winter months when the weather is lousy in Hué, it's good in Danang.

Most buses make a 10 minute rest stop at the top of the pass. You'll have to fight off a rather large crowd of persistent souvenir vendors.

The Vietnamese government has big plans to construct a US$150 million tunnel under Hai Van Pass to facilitate traffic flow. However, many have questioned the wisdom of pouring scarce funds into this low-priority project, so it may come to nought.

## LANG CO ISLAND

Lang Co is a pretty island of palm-shaded sand with a crystal-clear, turquoise blue lagoon on one side and many kilometres of beachfront facing the South China Sea on the other. It's a tranquil spot and lots of travellers make a lunch stop here and some spend the night. However, the local vendors (mostly children) have learned to make pests of themselves. Fortunately, they are not permitted onto the hotel grounds or the beach area, but they hang out by the bus stop and will not leave you alone for five seconds.

There are spectacular views of Lang Co, which is just north of Hai Van Pass, from both Highway 1 and the train linking Danang and Hué.

### Places to Stay & Eat

The *Lang Co Hotel* (☎ 874426; 30 rooms) is the only place in town. Twins cost US$8 to US$20 and air-conditioners are installed in the top-end rooms. The hotel remains open all year round, but it's really only likely to be busy (often full) from May to July. Hotel guests can use the adjacent beach free of charge, but non-guests pay US$0.50 per person.

Food at the hotel's restaurant is amazingly good. So good, in fact, that tour groups often stop here to eat. The speciality is, of course,

seafood. The restaurant remains open from 6 am until 11 pm.

### Getting There & Away

**Train** Lang Co railway station, served by nonexpress trains, is almost 10km from the beach area. It's possible to find someone to bring you from the railway station to the beach by motorbike.

**Car** Lang Co is 35km north of Danang over an extremely mountainous road. A bridge connects the island to Highway 1, so there is no need to take a ferry.

## BA NA HILL STATION

Ba Na, the 'Dalat of Quang Nam-Danang Province', is a hill station along the crest of Mount Ba Na (or Nui Chua) which rises 1467m above the coastal plain. The view in all directions is truly spectacular and the air is fresh and cool: though it may be 36°C on the coast, the temperature is likely to be between 15° and 26°C at Ba Na. Rain often falls at altitudes of 700 to 1200m above sea level, but around the hill station itself the sky is usually clear. Mountain paths in the area lead to a variety of waterfalls and viewpoints.

Ba Na, founded in 1919 for use by French settlers, is not presently in any condition to welcome visitors. As for all those plush colonial-era villas, only a few tattered ruins remain. Nevertheless, the provincial government has high hopes of once again making Ba Na a magnet for tourists.

### Getting There & Away

By road, Ba Na is 48km west of Danang (as the crow flies, the distance is 27km). The road is very steep and in bad condition, so only a jeep or motorbike can make it all the way. If you take a car, you'll have to walk the last 6km. But this is an improvement – until WWII, French vacationers travelled the last 20km by sedan chair!

# Hué

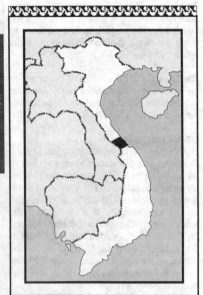

The most historically interesting city in Vietnam, Hué (population 250,000) served as the nation's political capital from 1802 to 1945 under the 13 emperors of the Nguyen Dynasty. Traditionally, the city has been one of Vietnam's cultural, religious and educational centres. Today, Hué's main attractions are the splendid tombs of the Nguyen emperors, several notable pagodas and the remains of the Citadel. As locals will tell you repeatedly, the women of Hué are renowned for their beauty. Most of the city's major sights have an admission charge of US$5 and often an additional charge for video cameras.

Tourism just may have saved Hué's cultural sites from oblivion. Between 1975 and 1990, all the old buildings were regarded as politically incorrect, signs of the 'feudal Nguyen Dynasty'. Everything was left to decay. It was only in 1990 that the local government recognised the tourist potential of the place and declared these sites 'national treasures'. The treasures are now protected, and continuous restoration and preservation work is being done.

### History

The citadel-city of Phu Xuan was originally built in 1687 at Bao Vinh village, 5km northeast of present-day Hué. In 1744, Phu Xuan became the capital of the southern part of Vietnam, which was under the rule of the Nguyen lords. The Tay Son Rebels occupied the city from 1786 until 1802, when it fell to Nguyen Anh. He crowned himself Emperor Gia Long, thus founding the Nguyen Dynasty, which ruled the country – at least in name – until 1945. Immediately upon his accession, Gia Long began the decades-long construction of the Citadel, the Imperial Enclosure and the Forbidden Purple City.

In 1885, when the advisers of 13-year-old Emperor Ham Nghi objected to French activities in Tonkin, French forces encircled the city. Unwisely, the outnumbered Vietnamese forces launched an attack; the French responded mercilessly. According to a contemporary French account, the French forces took three days to burn the imperial library and remove from the palace every object of value, including everything from gold and silver ornaments to mosquito nets and toothpicks. Ham Nghi fled to Laos, but was eventually captured and exiled to Algeria. The French replaced him with the more pliable Dong Khanh, thus ending any pretence of genuine Vietnamese independence.

The city's present name evolved from its former name, Thanh Hoa. The word *hoa* means 'peace' or 'harmony' in Vietnamese. The city has been called Hué for over two centuries now.

Hué was the site of the bloodiest battles of the 1968 Tet Offensive and was the only city in South Vietnam to be held by the Communists for more than a few days. While the American command was concentrating its energies on relieving the Siege of Khe Sanh, North Vietnamese and Viet Cong troops skirted the American stronghold and walked right into Hué, South Vietnam's third-largest city. When the Communists arrived, they hoisted their flag from the Citadel's flag tower, where it flew for the next 25 days; the local South Vietnamese governmental apparatus completely collapsed.

Immediately upon taking Hué, Communist political cadres implemented detailed plans to liquidate Hué's 'uncooperative' elements. Thousands of people were rounded up in extensive house-to-house searches conducted according to lists of names meticulously prepared months in advance. During the 3½ weeks Hué remained under Communist control, approximately 3000 civilians – including merchants, Buddhist monks, Catholic priests, intellectuals and a number of foreigners, as well as people with ties to the South Vietnamese government – were summarily shot, clubbed to death or buried alive. The victims were buried in shallow mass graves, which were discovered around the city over the course of the next few years.

When South Vietnamese army units proved unable to dislodge the North Vietnamese and VC forces, General William Westmoreland ordered US troops to recapture the city. During the next few weeks, whole neighbourhoods were levelled by VC rockets and American bombs. In 10 days of bitter combat, the VC were slowly forced to retreat from the New City. During the next two weeks, most of the area inside the Citadel (where two-thirds of the population lived) was battered by the South Vietnamese air force, US artillery and brutal house-to-house fighting. Approximately 10,000 people died in Hué during the Tet Offensive. Thousands of VC troops, 400 South Vietnamese soldiers and 150 American marines were among the dead, but most of those killed were civilians.

Long after the American War ended, one American veteran is said to have returned to

Hué and, upon meeting a former VC officer, commented that the USA never lost a single major battle during the entire war. 'You are absolutely correct', the former officer agreed, 'but that is irrelevant, is it not?'

## Information
**Emergency** Hué General Hospital (Benh Vien Trung Uong Hué; ☎ 822325) is at 16 Le Loi St close to the Phu Xuan Bridge.

**Immigration Police** Visa extensions can be done at the immigration police office on Ben Nghe St. This office seems to be able to handle such matters in about 15 minutes.

## Citadel
Construction of the moated Citadel (Kinh Thanh), which has a 10km perimeter, was begun in 1804 by Emperor Gia Long (the first Nguyen emperor) on a site chosen by geomancers. The Citadel was originally made of earth, but during the first few decades of the 19th century, tens of thousands of workers laboured to cover the ramparts, built in the style of the French military architect Vauban, with a layer of bricks 2m thick.

The emperor's official functions were carried out in the Imperial Enclosure (Dai Noi, or Hoang Thanh), a citadel-within-a-citadel with 6m-high walls 2.5km in length. The Imperial Enclosure has four gates, the most famous of which is Ngo Mon Gate. Within the Imperial Enclosure is the Forbidden Purple City (Tu Cam Thanh), which was reserved for the private life of the emperor.

Three sides of the Citadel are straight; the fourth is rounded slightly to follow the curve of the river. The ramparts are encircled by a zigzag moat which is 30m across and about 4m deep. In the northern corner of the Citadel is Mang Ca fortress, once known as the French Concession, which is still used as a military base. The Citadel has 10 fortified gates, each of which is reached by a bridge across the moat.

**Flag Tower** The 37m-high Flag Tower (Cot Co), also known as the King's Knight, is

HUÉ

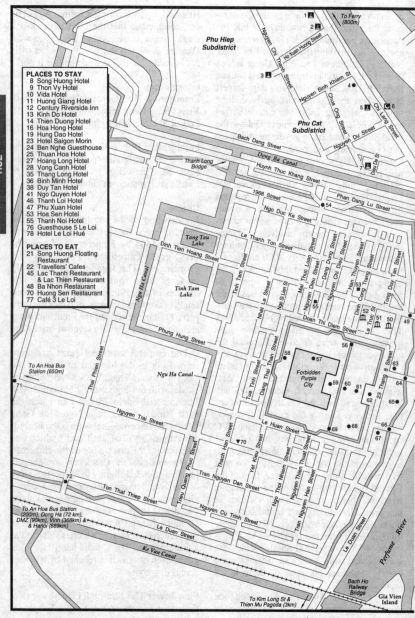

**PLACES TO STAY**
8 Song Huong Hotel
9 Thon Vy Hotel
10 Vida Hotel
11 Huong Giang Hotel
12 Century Riverside Inn
13 Kinh Do Hotel
14 Thien Duong Hotel
16 Hoa Hong Hotel
19 Hung Dao Hotel
23 Hotel Saigon Morin
24 Ben Nghe Guesthouse
25 Thuan Hoa Hotel
27 Hoang Long Hotel
28 Vong Canh Hotel
35 Thang Long Hotel
36 Binh Minh Hotel
38 Duy Tan Hotel
41 Ngo Quyen Hotel
46 Thanh Loi Hotel
47 Phu Xuan Hotel
53 Hoa Sen Hotel
55 Thanh Noi Hotel
76 Guesthouse 5 Le Loi
78 Hotel Le Loi Hué

**PLACES TO EAT**
21 Song Huong Floating
   Restaurant
22 Travellers' Cafes
45 Lac Thanh Restaurant
   & Lac Thien Restaurant
48 Ba Nhon Restaurant
70 Huong Sen Restaurant
77 Café 3 Le Loi

Phu Hiep
Subdistrict

To Ferry
(800m)

Nguyen Chi Thanh Street

Ho Xuan Huong Street

Nguyen Binh Khiem St

Chua Ong Street

Phu Cat
Subdistrict

Chi Lang Street

Nguyen Du Street

Bach Dang Street

Dong Ba Canal

Thanh Long
Bridge

Huynh Thuc Khang Street

Dieu De St

1968 Street

Phan Dang Lu Street

Ngo Duc Ke Street

54

Le Thanh Ton Street

Dinh Tien Hoang Street

Tang Tau
Lake

Mai Thuc Loan Street

Dang Dung Street

Nguyen Chi Dieu Street

Han Thuyen Street

Tong Duy Tan Street

Nga Ha Canal

Tinh Tam
Lake

Tinh Tam Street

Nhat Le Street

Ngo Si Lien St

53

55

Dinh Cong Trang

Le Truc St

Doan Thi Diem Street

50

49

Phung Hung Street

To An Hoa Bus
Station (650m)

71

Ngu Ha Canal

Thai Phien Street

Tue Tinh Street

Dang Thai Than Street

58

57

Forbidden
Purple
City

56

59

60

61

62

63

64

65

23 Thang 8 Street

66

67

Nguyen Trai Street

Le Huan Street

69

68

72

Trieu Quang Phuc Street

Thach Han Street

70

Yet Kieu Street

Ngo Thoi Nhiem Street

Nguyen Thien Thuat Street

Nguyen Tri Phuong Street

Tran Nguyen Dan
Street

Ton That Thiep Street

Tran Nguyen Han Street

Nguyen Cu Trinh
Street

To An Hoa Bus Station
(200m), Dong Ha (72 km),
DMZ (90km), Vinh (368km) &
& Hanoi (689km)

Le Duan Street

Ke Van Canal

Le Loi Street

Bach Ho
Railway
Bridge

To Kim Long St &
Thien Mu Pagoda (3km)

Gia Vien
Island

Perfume River

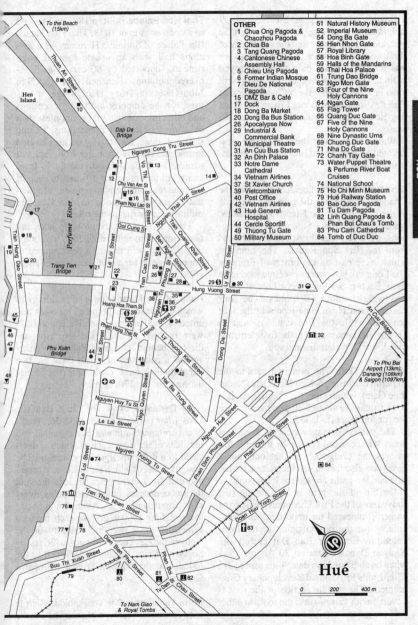

**OTHER**

1 Chua Ong Pagoda & Chaozhou Pagoda
2 Chua Ba
3 Tang Quang Pagoda
4 Cantonese Chinese Assembly Hall
5 Chieu Ung Pagoda
6 Former Indian Mosque
7 Dieu De National Pagoda
15 DMZ Bar & Café
17 Dock
18 Dong Ba Market
19 Dong Ba Bus Station
20 Dong Ba Bus Station
26 Apocalypse Now
29 Industrial & Commercial Bank
30 Municipal Theatre
31 An Cuu Bus Station
32 An Dinh Palace
33 Notre Dame Cathedral
34 Vietnam Airlines
37 St Xavier Church
39 Vietcombank
40 Post Office
42 Vietnam Airlines
43 Hué General Hospital
44 Cercle Sportiff
49 Thuong Tu Gate
50 Military Museum

51 Natural History Museum
52 Imperial Museum
54 Dong Ba Gate
56 Hien Nhon Gate
57 Royal Library
58 Hoa Binh Gate
59 Halls of the Mandarins
60 Thai Hoa Palace
61 Trung Dao Bridge
62 Ngo Mon Gate
63 Four of the Nine Holy Cannons
64 Ngan Gate
65 Flag Tower
66 Quang Duc Gate
67 Five of the Nine Holy Cannons
68 Nine Dynastic Urns
69 Chuong Duc Gate
71 Nha Do Gate
72 Chanh Tay Gate
73 Water Puppet Theatre & Perfume River Boat Cruises
74 National School
75 Ho Chi Minh Museum
79 Hué Railway Station
80 Bao Quoc Pagoda
81 Tu Dam Pagoda
82 Linh Quang Pagoda & Phan Boi Chau's Tomb
83 Phu Cam Cathedral
84 Tomb of Duc Duc

HUÉ

To the Beach (15km)

Thuan An Street

Hen Island

Dap Da Bridge

Nguyen Cong Tru Street

Vo Thi Sau Street

Chu Van An St

Pham Ngu Lao St

Doi Cung St

Ben Nghe Street

Tran Cao Van Street

Nguyen Tran Quang Khai Street

Nguyen Thai Hoc Street

Ly Don Street

Perfume River

Tran Hung Dao Street

Trang Tien Bridge

Phu Xuan Bridge

Le Loi Street

Hanoi Street

Nguyen Tri Phuong Street

Hoang Hoa Tham St

Pham Hong Thai St

Hung Vuong Street

Ly Thuong Kiet Street

Dong Da Street

Hai Ba Trung Street

Nguyen Huy Tu St

Ngo Quyen Street

Le Lai Street

Le Loi Street

Nguyen Truong To Street

Tran Thuc Nhan Street

Buu Thi Xuan Street

Dien Bien Phu Street

Nguyen Hue Street

Phan Dinh Phung Street

Phan Chu Trinh Street

Doan Huu Trinh Street

Pham Bol

Tu Dam St

Chau Street

An Cuu Bridge

To Phu Bai Airport (13km), Danang (108km) & Saigon (1097km)

To Nam Giao & Royal Tombs

Hué

0        200        400 m

Vietnam's tallest flagpole. Erected in 1809 and increased in size in 1831, a terrific typhoon (which devastated the whole city of Hué) knocked it down in 1904. The tower was rebuilt in 1915, only to be destroyed again in 1947. It was re-erected in its present form in 1949. During the VC occupation of Hué in 1968, the National Liberation Front flag flew defiantly from the tower for 3½ weeks.

Wide areas within the Citadel are now devoted to agriculture, a legacy of the destruction of 1968.

**Nine Holy Cannons** Located just inside the Citadel ramparts near the gates to either side of the Flag Tower, the Nine Holy Cannons, symbolic protectors of the palace and kingdom, were cast from brass articles captured from the Tay Son Rebels. The cannons, which were cast on the orders of Emperor Gia Long in 1804, were never intended to be fired. Each is 5m long, has a bore of 23cm and weighs about 10 tonnes. The four cannons near Ngan Gate represent the four seasons, while the five cannons next to Quang Duc Gate represent the five elements: metal, wood, water, fire and soil.

**Ngo Mon Gate** The principal gate to the Imperial Enclosure is Ngo Mon Gate (Noontime Gate), which faces the Flag Tower. It is open from 6.30 am to 5.30 pm; the entrance fee for foreigners is US$5.

The central passageway with its yellow doors was reserved for use by the emperor, as was the bridge across the lotus pond. Everyone else had to use the gates to either side and the paths around the lotus pond.

On top of the gate is Ngu Phung (the Belvedere of the Five Phoenixes), where the emperor appeared on important occasions, notably for the promulgation of the lunar calendar. Emperor Bao Dai ended .the Nguyen Dynasty here on 30 August 1945 when he abdicated to a delegation sent by Ho Chi Minh's Provisional Revolutionary Government. The middle section of the roof is covered with yellow tiles; the roofs to either side are green.

**Thai Hoa Palace** Built in 1803 and moved to its present site in 1833, Thai Hoa Palace (the Palace of Supreme Harmony) is a spacious hall with an ornate roof of huge timbers supported by 80 carved and lacquered columns. Reached from the Ngo Mon Gate via Trung Dao Bridge, it was used for the emperor's official receptions and other important court ceremonies, such as anniversaries and coronations. During state occasions, the king sat on his elevated throne and received homage from ranks of mandarins. Nine stelae divide the bi-level courtyard into areas for officials of each of the nine ranks in the mandarinate; administrative mandarins stood to one side and military mandarins to the other.

There is now a souvenir shop here, but also a music ensemble dressed in traditional outfits. They will put on a performance of imperial music for a small donation of about US$1.

**Halls of the Mandarins** The buildings in which the mandarins prepared for court ceremonies, held in Can Chanh Reception Hall, were restored in 1977. The structures are directly behind Thai Hoa Palace on either side of a courtyard in which there are two gargantuan bronze cauldrons (vac dong) dating from the 17th century.

**Nine Dynastic Urns** The Nine Dynastic Urns (dinh) were cast in 1835-36. Traditional ornamentation was then chiselled into the sides of the urns, each of which is dedicated to a different Nguyen sovereign. The designs, some of which are of Chinese origin and date back 4000 years, include the sun, the moon, meteors, clouds, mountains, rivers and various landscapes. About 2m in height and weighing 1900 to 2600kg each, the urns symbolise the power and stability of the Nguyen throne. The central urn, which is the largest and most ornate, is dedicated to the founder of the Nguyen Dynasty, Emperor Gia Long.

**Forbidden Purple City** The Forbidden Purple City (Tu Cam Thanh) was reserved for the personal use of the emperor. The only servants allowed into the compound were eunuchs, who would have no temptation to molest the royal concubines.

The Forbidden Purple City was almost entirely destroyed during the Tet Offensive. The area is now given over to vegetable plots, between which touch-sensitive mimosa plants flourish. The two-storey Library (Thai Binh Lau) has been partially restored. The foundations of the Royal Theatre (Duyen Thi Duong), begun in 1826 and later home of the National Conservatory of Music, can be seen nearby.

**Imperial Museum** The beautiful hall which houses the Imperial Museum (Bao Tang Co Vat) was built in 1845 and restored when the museum was founded in 1923. The walls are inscribed with poems written in Vietnamese *nom* characters. The most precious artefacts were lost during the war, but the ceramics, furniture and royal clothing that remain are well worth a look.

On the left side of the hall is a royal sedan chair, a gong and a musical instrument consisting of stones hung on a bi-level rack. On the other side of the hall is the equipment for a favourite game of the emperors – the idea of which was to bounce a stick off a wooden platform and into a tall, thin jug.

The building across the street was once a former school for princes and the sons of high-ranking mandarins. Behind the school is the Military Museum, with its usual assortment of American and Soviet-made weapons, including a MiG 17. Nearby is a small natural history exhibit.

The Imperial Museum is at 3 Le Truc St and is open from 6.30 am to 5.30 pm.

**Tinh Tam Lake** In the middle of Tinh Tam Lake, which is 500m north of the Imperial Enclosure, are two islands connected by bridges. The emperors used to come here with their retinues to relax.

**Tang Tau Lake** An island in Tang Tau Lake, which is a few hundred metres from Tinh Tam Lake, was once the site of a royal library. It is now occupied by a small Hinayana pagoda, Ngoc Huong Pagoda.

### Royal Tombs

The tombs *(lang tam)* of the Nguyen Dynasty (1802-1945) are seven to 16km to the south of Hué (see the Hué Area map). They are open from 6.30 am to 5 pm daily and the entrance fee for each tomb is US$5.

Most of the tomb complexes consist of five parts:

- A stele pavilion in which the accomplishments, exploits and virtues of the deceased emperor are engraved on a marble tablet. The testaments were usually written by the dead ruler's successor (though Tu Duc chose to compose his own).
- A temple for the worship of the emperor and empress. In front of each altar, on which the deceased rulers' funerary tablets were placed, is an ornate dais that once held items the emperor used every day: his tea and betelnut trays, cigarette cases etc, most of which have disappeared.
- A sepulchre, usually inside a square or circular enclosure, where the emperor's remains are buried.
- An honour courtyard paved with dark-brown *bat trang* bricks along the sides of which stand stone elephants, horses and civil and military mandarins. The civil mandarins wear square hats and hold the symbol of their authority, an ivory sceptre; the military mandarins wear round hats and hold swords.
- A lotus pond surrounded by frangipani and pine trees. Almost all the tombs, which are in walled compounds, were planned by the Nguyen emperors during their lifetimes. Many of the precious ornaments that once reposited in the tombs disappeared during the war.

**Nam Giao** Nam Giao (Temple of Heaven) was once the most important religious site in all Vietnam. It was here that every three years, the emperor solemnly offered elaborate sacrifices to the All-Highest Emperor of the August Heaven (Thuong De). The topmost esplanade, which represents Heaven, is round; the middle terrace, representing Earth, is square, as is the lowest terrace.

After reunification, the provincial government erected – on the site where the sacrificial altar once stood – an obelisk in memory of soldiers killed in the war against the South

HUÉ

---

**Betelnut**

One thing you'll undoubtedly find for sale at street stalls everywhere is betelnut. This is not a food – swallow it and you'll be sorry! The betelnut is in fact the seed of the betel palm (beautiful trees, by the way) and is meant to be chewed. The seed is usually sold with a slit in it, mixed with lime and wrapped in a leaf. Like tobacco, it's strong stuff that you can barely tolerate at first, but eventually get addicted to. The first time you bite into betelnut, your whole face gets hot – chewers say it gives them a buzz. Like chewing tobacco, betelnut causes excessive salivation – the result is that betel chewers must constantly spit. The disgusting reddish-brown stains you see on sidewalks are not blood, but betel-saliva juice. Years of constant chewing causes the teeth to become stained progressively browner, eventually becoming nearly black. ■

---

Vietnamese government and the Americans. There was strong public sentiment in Hué against the obelisk and the Hué Municipal People's Committee finally tore down the memorial in 1993.

**Tomb of Dong Khanh** Emperor Dong Khanh, nephew and adopted son of Tu Duc, was placed on the throne by the French after they captured his predecessor, Ham Nghi (who had fled after the French sacking of the royal palace in 1885), and exiled him to Algeria. Predictably, Dong Khanh proved docile; he ruled from 1885 until his death three years later.

Dong Khanh's mausoleum, the smallest of the Royal Tombs, was built in 1889. It is about 5km from the city.

**Tomb of Tu Duc** The majestic and serene tomb of Emperor Tu Duc is set amid frangipani trees and a grove of pines. Tu Duc designed the exquisitely harmonious tomb, which was constructed between 1864 and 1867, for use both before and after his death. The enormous expense of the tomb and the forced labour used in its construction spawned a coup plot which was discovered and suppressed in 1866.

It is said that Tu Duc, who ruled from 1848 to 1883 (the longest reign of any Nguyen monarch), lived a life of truly imperial luxury: at every meal, 50 chefs prepared 50 dishes served by 50 servants; and his tea was made of drops of dew that had condensed overnight on the leaves of lotus plants. Though

Tu Duc had 104 wives and countless concubines, he had no offspring. One theory has it that he became sterile after contracting smallpox.

Tu Duc's Tomb, which is surrounded by a solid octagonal wall, is entered from the east via Vu Khiem Gate. A path paved with bat trang tiles leads to Du Khiem Boat Landing, which is on the shore of Luu Khiem Lake. From the boat landing, Tinh Khiem Island, where Tu Duc used to hunt small game, is off to the right. Across the water to the left is Xung Khiem Pavilion, where the emperor would sit among the columns with his concubines composing or reciting poetry. The pavilion, built over the water on piles, was restored in 1986.

Across Khiem Cung Courtyard from Du Khiem Boat Landing are steps leading through a gate to Hoa Khiem Temple, where Emperor Tu Duc and Empress Hoang Le Thien Anh are worshipped. Before his death, Tu Duc used Hoa Khiem Temple as a palace, staying here during his long visits to the complex. The temple contains a number of interesting items, including a mirror used by the emperor's concubines; a clock and other objects given to Tu Duc by the French; the emperor and empress's funerary tablets; and two thrones, the larger of which was for the empress (Tu Duc was only 153cm tall).

Minh Khiem Chamber, to the right behind Hoa Khiem Temple, was built for use as a theatre. Tu Duc's mother, the Queen Mother Tu Du, is worshipped in Luong Khiem Temple, which is directly behind Hoa Khiem Temple.

Back down at the bottom of the stairway, the brick path continues along the shore of the pond to the Honour Courtyard. Across the lake from the courtyard are the tombs of Tu Duc's adopted son, Emperor Kien Phuc (who ruled for only seven months in 1883-84), and Empress Le Thien Anh, Tu Duc's wife.

After walking between the honour guard of elephants, horses and diminutive civil and military mandarins (the stone mandarins were made even shorter than the emperor), you reach the masonry Stele Pavilion, which shelters a massive stone tablet weighing about 20 tonnes. It took four years to transport the stele, the largest in Vietnam, from the area of Thanh Hoa, 500km to the north. Tu Duc drafted the inscriptions on the stele himself in order to clarify certain aspects of his reign. He freely admitted that he had made mistakes and chose to name his tomb Khiem, which means 'modest'. The two nearby towers symbolise the emperor's power.

Tu Duc's sepulchre, enclosed by a wall, is on the other side of a half-moon-shaped lake. In fact, Tu Duc was never actually interred here. The site where his remains were buried (along with great treasure) is not known. Because of the danger of grave-robbers, extreme measures were taken to keep the location secret: every one of the 200 servants who buried the king was beheaded.

Tu Duc's Tomb is about 6km from Hué on Van Nien hill in Duong Xuan Thuong village.

**Tomb of Thieu Tri** Construction of the tomb of Thieu Tri, who ruled from 1841 to 1847, was completed in 1848. It is the only one of the Royal Tombs not enclosed by a wall. Thieu Tri's tomb, which is similar in layout to that of Minh Mang (though smaller), is about 7km from Hué.

**Tomb of Khai Dinh** The gaudy and crumbling tomb of Emperor Khai Dinh, who ruled from 1916 to 1925, is perhaps symptomatic of the decline of Vietnamese culture during the colonial period. Begun in 1920 and com-

pleted in 1931, the grandiose concrete structure is completely unlike that of Hué's other tombs, being a synthesis of Vietnamese and European elements. Even the stone faces of the mandarin honour guards are endowed with a mixture of Vietnamese and European features.

After climbing 36 steps between four dragon banisters, you get to the first courtyard, flanked by two pavilions. The Honour Courtyard, with its rows of elephants, horses and civil and military mandarins, is 26 steps further up the hillside. In the centre of the courtyard is an octagonal Stele Pavilion.

Up three more flights of stairs is the main building, Thien Dinh, which is divided into three halls. The walls and ceiling are decorated with murals of the 'Four Seasons', the 'Eight Precious Objects', the 'Eight Fairies' and other designs made out of colourful bits of broken porcelain and glass embedded in cement. Under a graceless, one-tonne, concrete canopy is a gilt bronze statue of Khai Dinh in royal regalia. Behind the statue is the symbol of the sun. The emperor's remains are interred 18m below the statue. Khai Dinh is worshipped in the last hall.

The Tomb of Khai Dinh is 10km from Hué in Chau Chu village.

**Tomb of Minh Mang** Perhaps the most majestic of the Royal Tombs is that of Minh Mang, who ruled from 1820 to 1840. Known for the harmonious blending of its architecture with the natural surroundings, the tomb was planned during Minh Mang's lifetime and built between 1841 and 1843 by his successor.

The Honour Courtyard is reached via three gates on the eastern side of the wall: Dai Hong Mon (Great Red Gate; in the centre), Ta Hong Mon (Left Red Gate; on the left) and Huu Hong Mon (Right Red Gate; on the right). Three granite staircases lead from the courtyard to the square Stele Pavilion, Dinh Vuong. Nearby there once stood an altar on which buffaloes, horses and pigs were sacrificed.

Sung An Temple, dedicated to Minh Mang and his empress, is reached via three terraces

HUÉ

and Hien Duc Gate. On the other side of the temple, three stone bridges span Trung Minh Ho (Lake of Impeccable Clarity). The central bridge, Cau Trung Dao, constructed of marble, was used only by the emperor. Minh Lau Pavilion stands on the top of three superimposed terraces representing the 'three powers': the heavens, the earth and water. Visible off to the left is the Fresh Air Pavilion; the Angling Pavilion is off to the right.

From a stone bridge across crescent-shaped Tan Nguyet Lake (Lake of the New Moon), a monumental staircase with dragon banisters leads to the sepulchre, which is surrounded by a circular wall symbolising the sun. In the middle of the enclosure, reached through a bronze door, is the emperor's burial place, a mound of earth covered with mature pine trees and dense shrubbery.

The Tomb of Minh Mang, which is on Cam Ke hill in An Bang village, is on the west bank of the Perfume River 12km from Hué. To get there, take a boat across the river from a point about 1.5km west of Khai Dinh's tomb. Visitors have reported gross overcharging by the boat operator. Alternatively, walk along the river a bit to the north and you'll find other smaller boats and people willing to take you across for less.

**Tomb of Gia Long** Emperor Gia Long, who founded the Nguyen Dynasty in 1802 and ruled until 1819, ordered the construction of his tomb in 1814. According to the royal annals, the emperor himself chose the site after scouting the area on elephant-back. The rarely visited tomb, which is presently in a state of ruin, is 14km from Hué on the west bank of the Perfume River.

**Pagodas & Churches**
**Thien Mu Pagoda** Thien Mu Pagoda (also known as Linh Mu Pagoda), built on a hillock overlooking the Perfume River, is one of the most famous structures in all of Vietnam. Its 21m-high octagonal tower, the seven-storey Thap Phuoc Duyen, was built by Emperor Thieu Tri in 1844 and has become the unofficial symbol of Hué. Each of the seven storeys is dedicated to a Buddha

who appeared in human form *(manushi-buddha)*.

Thien Mu Pagoda was founded in 1601 by the Nguyen lord Nguyen Hoang, governor of Thuan Hoa Province. According to legend, a Fairy Woman (Thien Mu) appeared and told the local people that a lord would come to build a pagoda for the country's prosperity. On hearing that, Nguyen Hoang ordered a pagoda to be constructed here. Over the centuries, the pagoda's buildings have been destroyed and rebuilt several times. Five monks and seven novices now live at the pagoda.

The pagoda was a hotbed of anti-government protest during the early 1960s. Surprisingly, it also became a focus of protest in the 1980s when someone was murdered near the pagoda and anti-Communist demonstrators started here, bringing down traffic around Phu Xuan Bridge. Monks were arrested and accused of disturbing the traffic and public order. Things have now calmed down and there are now a few nuns living at the pagoda.

To the right of the tower is a pavilion containing a stele dating from 1715. It is set on the back of a massive marble turtle, a symbol of longevity. To the left of the tower is another six-sided pavilion, this one sheltering an enormous bell, Dai Hong Chung, which is cast in 1710 and weighs 2052kg; it is said to be audible 10km away. In the main sanctuary, in a case behind the bronze laughing Buddha, are three statues: A Di Da, the Buddha of the Past; Thich Ca, the historical Buddha (Sakyamuni); and Di Lac Buddha, the Buddha of the Future.

Behind the main sanctuary is the Austin motorcar which transported the monk Thich Quang Duc to the site in Saigon of his 1963 self-immolation, which was seen around the world in a famous photograph. Around the back are vegetable gardens in which the monks grow their own food.

Thien Mu Pagoda is on the banks of the Perfume River 4km south-west of the Citadel. To get there, head south-west (parallel to the river) on Tran Hung Dao St, which turns into Le Duan St after Phu Xuan Bridge. Cross the railway tracks and keep going on Kim Long St. Thien Mu Pagoda can also be reached by rowing boat.

**Bao Quoc Pagoda** Bao Quoc Pagoda was founded in 1670 by a Buddhist monk from China, Giac Phong. It was given its present name, which means 'Pagoda Which Serves the Country', in 1824 by Emperor Minh Mang, who celebrated his 40th birthday here in 1830. A school for training monks was opened at Bao Quoc Pagoda in 1940. The pagoda was last renovated in 1957.

The orchid-lined courtyard behind the sanctuary is a quiet place where students gather to study.

The central altar in the main sanctuary contains three identical statues, which represent (from left to right) Di Lac, the Buddha of the Future; Thich Ca, the historical Buddha (Sakyamuni); and A Di Da, the Buddha of the Past. Behind the three figures is a memorial room for deceased monks. Around the main building are monks' tombs, including a three-storey, red-and-grey stupa built for the pagoda's founder.

Bao Quoc Pagoda is on Ham Long Hill in Phuong Duc District (see the Hué map). To get there, head south from Le Loi St on Dien Bien Phu St and turn right immediately after crossing the railroad tracks.

**Tu Dam Pagoda** Tu Dam Pagoda, which is about 600m south of Bao Quoc Pagoda at the corner of Dien Bien Phu St and Tu Dam St, is one of Vietnam's best known pagodas. Unfortunately, the present buildings were constructed in 1936 and are of little interest.

Tu Dam Pagoda was founded around 1695 by Minh Hoang Tu Dung, a Chinese monk. It was given its present name by Emperor Thieu Tri in 1841. The Unified Vietnamese Buddhist Association was established at a meeting held here in 1951. During the early 1960s, Tu Dam Pagoda was a major centre of the Buddhist anti-Diem and anti-war movement. In 1968, it was the scene of heavy fighting, scars of which remain.

Today, Tu Dam Pagoda, home to six monks, is the seat of the provincial Buddhist Association. The peculiar bronze Thich Ca Buddha in the sanctuary was cast in Hué in 1966.

Just east of the pagoda down Tu Dam St is Linh Quang Pagoda and the tomb of the scholar and anti-colonialist revolutionary Phan Boi Chau (1867-1940).

**Notre Dame Cathedral** Notre Dame Cathedral (Dong Chua Cuu The) at 80 Nguyen Hue St is an impressive modern building combining the functional aspects of a European cathedral with traditional Vietnamese elements, including a distinctly oriental spire. At present, the huge cathedral, which was constructed between 1959 and 1962, has 1600 members. The two French-speaking priests hold daily masses at 5 am and 5 pm and on Sunday at 5 and 7 am and 5 pm; children's catechism classes are conducted on Sunday mornings. Visitors who find the front gate locked should ring the bell of the yellow building next door.

**Phu Cam Cathedral** Construction of the Phu Cam Cathedral began in 1963 and was halted in 1975 before completion of the bell tower. It is the eighth church built on this site since 1682 and the Hué diocese, which is based here, hopes eventually to complete the structure if funds can be found. Phu Cam Cathedral is at 20 Doan Huu Trinh St, which is at the southern end of Nguyen Truong Tu St. Masses are held daily at 5 am and 6.45 pm and on Sundays at 5 and 7 am and 2 and 7 pm.

**St Xavier Church** This Catholic church was built around 1915. The outside looks derelict, but the inside is well-maintained and has a functioning electric organ. The building at the rear is where you ask to be let in. Some of the caretakers speak French, though not much English.

Realise that this is not a tourist attraction as such, but an active place of worship. There is no admission charge, but you might want to make a small donation to help maintain the place – they could use it.

St Xavier Church is just south of the Binh Minh Hotel on Nguyen Tri Phuong St.

## The National School

The National School (Quoc Hoc) at 10 Le Loi St is one of the most famous secondary schools in Vietnam. It was founded in 1896 and run by Ngo Dinh Kha, the father of South Vietnamese president Ngo Dinh Diem, and many of the school's pupils later rose to prominence in both North and South Vietnam. Numbered among the National School's former students are General Vo Nguyen Giap, strategist of the Viet Minh victory at Dien Bien Phu and North Vietnam's long-serving deputy premier, defence minister and commander-in-chief; Pham Van Dong, North Vietnam's prime minister for over a quarter of a century; Secretary General and former Prime Minister Do Muoi; and Ho Chi Minh himself, who attended the school briefly in 1908.

The school was given a major renovation in 1996 to celebrate its 100th anniversary and a statue of Ho Chi Minh was erected. The National School and the neighbouring Hai Ba Trung Secondary School cannot be visited until after classes finish, which is at about 3 pm. Otherwise, the students would have more interest in the tourists than the teachers.

## Ho Chi Minh Museum

On display at the Ho Chi Minh Museum (Bao Tang Ho Chi Minh) at 9 Le Loi St are photographs, some of Ho's personal effects and documents relating to his life and accomplishments. The museum is down the block and across the street from the National School.

## Phu Cat & Phu Hiep Subdistricts

The island on which Phu Cat and Phu Hiep subdistricts are located can be reached by crossing the Dong Ba Canal near Dong Ba Market. The area is known for its numerous Chinese pagodas and congregational halls, many of which are along Chi Lang St.

**Dieu De National Pagoda** The entrance to Dieu De National Pagoda (Quoc Tu Dieu De), built under Emperor Thieu Tri (ruled 1841-47), is along Dong Ba Canal at 102 Bach Dang St. It is one of the city's three 'national pagodas' (pagodas that were once under the direct patronage of the emperor). Dieu De National Pagoda is famous for its four low towers, one to either side of the gate and two flanking the sanctuary. There are bells in two of the towers; the others contain a drum and a stele dedicated to the pagoda's founder.

During the regime of Ngo Dinh Diem (ruled 1955-63) and through the mid-1960s, Dieu De National Pagoda was a stronghold of Buddhist and student opposition to the South Vietnamese government and the war. In 1966, the pagoda was stormed by the police who arrested many monks, Buddhist lay people and students and confiscated the opposition movement's radio equipment. Today, three monks live at the pagoda.

The pavilions on either side of the entrance to the main sanctuary contain the 18 La Ha, whose rank is just below that of Bodhisattva, and the eight Kim Cang, protectors of Buddha. In the back row of the main dais is Thich Ca Buddha (Sakyamuni) flanked by two assistants, Pho Hien Bo Tat (to his right) and Van Thu Bo Tat (to his left).

**Former Indian Mosque** Hué's Indian Muslim community constructed the mosque at 120 Chi Lang St in 1932. The structure was used as a house of worship until 1975, when the Indian community fled. It is now a private residence.

**Chieu Ung Pagoda** Chieu Ung Pagoda (Chieu Ung Tu), opposite 138 Chi Lang St, was founded by the Hainan Chinese congregation in the mid-19th century and rebuilt in 1908. It was last repaired in 1940. The sanctuary retains its original ornamentation, which is becoming faded but mercifully unaffected by the third-rate modernistic renovations that have marred other such structures. The pagoda was built as a memorial to 108 Hainan merchants who were mistaken for pirates and killed in Vietnam in 1851.

**Hall of the Cantonese Chinese Congregation** Founded almost a century ago, the Hall of the Cantonese Chinese Congregation (Chua Quang Dong) is opposite 154 Chi Lang St. Against the right-hand wall is a small altar holding a statue of Confucius (in Vietnamese: Khong Tu) with a gold beard. On the main altar is red-faced Quan Cong (in Chinese: Guangong) flanked by Trung Phi (on the left) and Luu Bi (on the right). On the altar to the left is Laotse with disciples to either side. On the altar to the right is Phat Ba, a female Buddha.

**Chua Ba** Chua Ba, across the street from 216 Chi Lang St, was founded by the Hainan Chinese Congregation almost a century ago. It was damaged in the 1968 Tet Offensive and was subsequently reconstructed. On the central altar is Thien Hau Thanh Mau, the Goddess of the Sea and Protector of Fishermen and Sailors. To the right is a glass case in which Quan Cong sits flanked by his usual companions, the mandarin general Chau Xuong (to his right) and the administrative mandarin Quang Binh (to his left).

**Chua Ong** Chua Ong, which is opposite 224 Chi Lang St, is a large pagoda founded by the Fujian Chinese Congregation during the reign of Vietnamese emperor Tu Duc (ruled 1848-83). The building was severely damaged during the 1968 Tet Offensive when an ammunition ship blew up nearby. A gold Buddha sits in a glass case opposite the main doors of the sanctuary. The left-hand altar is dedicated to Thien Hau Thanh Mau, the Goddess of the Sea and Protector of Fishermen and Sailors; she is flanked by her two assistants, thousand-eyed Thien Ly Nhan and red-faced Thuan Phong Nhi, who can hear for 1000 miles. On the altar to the right is Quan Cong.

Next door is a pagoda of the Chaozhou Chinese Congregation (Tieu Chau Tu).

**Tang Quang Pagoda** Tang Quang Pagoda (Tang Quang Tu), which is just down the road from 80 Nguyen Chi Thanh St, is the largest of the three Hinayana (Theravada, or Nam Tong) pagodas in Hué. Built in 1957, it owes its distinctive architecture to Hinayana Buddhism's historical links to Sri Lanka and India (rather than China). The pagoda's Pali name, Sangharansyarama (the Light Coming from the Buddha), is inscribed on the front of the building.

### Places to Stay – bottom end

The *Hotel Le Loi Hué* (☎ 822153; fax 824-527; 170 rooms) at 2 Le Loi St is enormous. It's also been enormously successful at attracting backpackers thanks to low prices, good rooms and the fact that it's only a 100m walk from the railway station. Satellite TV is on tap and it's also a good place for booking cars, taxis and tours. Rooms cost US$6 to US$45.

*Ben Nghe Guesthouse* (☎ 823687; 18 rooms) at 4 Ben Nghe St captures a significant slice of the budget traveller market due to its low prices. Twins cost US$8 to US$15 with attached bath and hot water.

The *Thanh Noi* (Forbidden) *Hotel* (☎ 822-478; fax 877211; 12 rooms) at 3 Dang Dung St is deservedly popular. The ideal location on the historic west bank of Hué (near the Forbidden Purple City) is a major drawcard. The quiet, tree-shaded compound has its own restaurant. Rooms cost US$10 to US$25.

Also on the west bank is the popular *Thanh Loi Hotel* (☎ 824803; fax 825344; 21 rooms) at 7 Dinh Tien Hoang St. The location is good and the low prices also help; rooms cost US$10 to US$20.

The *Duy Tan Hotel* (☎ 825001) at 12 Hung Vuong St offers twins from US$10 to US$30. If you're travelling by rented car, this place is good because of the spacious parking facilities.

Nearby is the *Hoang Long Hotel* (☎ 828-235) at 20 Nguyen Tri Phuong St with singles/twins for US$10/15.

The *Thang Long Hotel* (☎ 826462) at 16 Hung Vuong St is fairly new and has twins from US$10 to US$40.

The *Vong Canh Hotel* (☎ 824130; fax 823424) at 25 Hung Vuong St is close to the post office. The private management is very anxious to please. Prices run US$8 to US$12.

The *Ngo Quyen Hotel* (☎ 823278; fax 823502; 70 rooms) at 11 Ngo Quyen St is a large, old, elegant place with that 'seen better days' appearance. A double room with the toilet and bath outside costs US$8 to US$10.

A nice family-run place is the *Binh Minh Hotel* (☎ 825526; 20 rooms) at 12 Nguyen Tri Phuong St. Rates are US$10 to US$40.

The *Song Huong Hotel* (☎ 823675) at 51-66 Thuan An St is up in the north-east part of town across the Dap Da Bridge. It has twins in the old annex for US$10. In the new building rates are US$20 to US$35.

Almost next to the foregoing is the *Thon Vy Hotel* (☎ 825160) at 37 Thuan An St. Doubles with fan are US$8 or US$15 with air-con.

At US$5, the *Hung Dao Hotel* has got to be the cheapest place in town, but you get what you pay for. There are only a few rooms. It's on the west bank on Tran Hung Dao St very close to the Dong Ba Market.

### Places to Stay – middle & top end

The *Phu Xuan Hotel* (☎ 823572; 11 rooms) at 27 Tran Hung Dao St is a new place with rooms for US$25. It's near the Phu Xuan Bridge and is one of the few hotels on the west bank of the Perfume River.

Also on the west bank is the *Hoa Sen Hotel* (☎ 825997) at 33 Dinh Cong Trang St. This place has a very quiet setting among the trees. Rooms cost US$30 to US$50.

The *Vida Hotel* (☎ 826145) at 31 Thuan An St is in the north-east area beyond the Dap Da Bridge. Twins cost US$20 to US$50.

The *Hotel Saigon Morin* (☎ 823526; fax 825155; 60 rooms) at 30 Le Loi St was under renovation at the time of writing. Nobody knows what the new prices will be, but to judge from appearances it should be mid-range. The hotel is on the east bank of the Perfume River very close to the Trang Tien Bridge.

The *Guesthouse 5 Le Loi* (☎ 822155) at 5 Le Loi St has river views and doubles for US$25 to US$60.

The *Dongda Hotel* on Ly Thuong Kiet St was under renovation at the time of writing. Once a well-worn cheapie, don't be surprised if it jumps far upmarket.

The *Thien Duong Hotel* (☎ 825976; fax 828233; 25 rooms) at 33 Nguyen Thai Hoc St gets good reviews. The price range is US$25 to US$45.

The *Kinh Do Hotel* (☎ 823566; fax 823-858; 48 rooms) on Vo Thi Sau St is a large, renovated place with rooms priced from US$25 to US$45.

The *Thuan Hoa Hotel* (☎ 822553; fax 822470; 70 rooms) at 7 Nguyen Tri Phuong St has an intriguing, glossy brochure that reads, 'Come and have a touch with us and you will enjoy life more'. Touching one of their rooms will cost from US$8 to US$75.

Also new and small is the *Hoa Hong Hotel* (☎ 824377; eight rooms) at 1 Pham Ngu Lao St. This place is just opposite the enormous Century Riverside Inn. The tariff here is US$30 to US$90.

The *Ky Lin Hotel* (☎ 826556) at 58 Le Loi St is a medium-sized new place with twins costing US$25 and US$30.

The *Century Riverside Inn* (☎ 823390; fax 823399; 138 rooms) at 49 Le Loi St is a grand place on the shore of the Perfume River. Luxury like this comes at a price – in this case US$65 to US$150.

The *Huong Giang Hotel* (☎ 822122; fax 823102; 102 rooms) at 51 Le Loi St is another huge place on the river near the Dap Da Bridge. Accommodation here is priced from US$50 to US$200 and it's fair to say that you get what you pay for. Don't confuse this hotel with the much smaller *Huong Giang Villa* (☎ 822122) at 3 Hung Vuong St. Twins cost US$25.

### Places to Eat

**West Bank** *Lac Thanh Restaurant* (☎ 824-674) at 6A Dien Tien Hoang St is a fashionable gathering spot for travellers. To order, see the book travellers have written in; the owner, Lac, is deaf and mute so everything is done with sign language. However, his daughter, Lan Anh, has been working hard on improving her English and can now communicate quite well. This is also the best spot in Hué to trade stories and advice with fellow travellers.

The *Lac Thien Restaurant* has sort of cloned Lac Thanh's motif. Six deaf people working here also produce fine food, plus an entertaining atmosphere.

Backpackers on a tight budget should consider eating in the *Dong Ba Market*. Food here is so cheap they might as well give it away. Nevertheless, it's good quality. The only real problem will be finding comfortable chairs (or, for that matter, any chairs) so you can sit down and enjoy your meal.

*Ba Nhon Restaurant* (☎ 823853) at 29 Le Duan St is actually right inside an old bus station. It's great Vietnamese food and low prices, but so far no English menu has appeared. You can stroll into the outdoor kitchen and try pointing at what you like. It's a popular place with many of the bus and truck drivers.

Within the Citadel, the *Huong Sen Restaurant* is at 42 Nguyen Trai St (corner of Thach Han St). This 16-sided pavilion, built on pylons in the middle of a lotus pond, is open from 9 am to midnight. The food is not necessarily the best, but you can't beat the atmosphere.

If you're staying at the *Thanh Loi Hotel* (or even if you're not), the ground floor restaurant is a good place to eat. The food is good, prices are low and you get plenty for your money. It's at 7 Dinh Tien Hoang St.

**East Bank** There is a whole string of nameless budget cafes along the north side of Hung Vuong St near the Trang Tien Bridge. Competition is fierce and the prices low.

*Cafe 2 Le Loi* is within the grounds of the Hotel Le Loi Hué. Unusually for a hotel cafe, it's excellent. The manager speaks English and is full of useful advice.

*Cafe 3 Le Loi* is just across the street from the foregoing. Like its nearby competitor, this place dishes up fine food at cool prices and offers the opportunity to swap travellers' tales. The cafe is open daily from 6 am until midnight.

The *Song Huong Floating Restaurant* is on the bank of the Perfume River just north of the Trang Tien Bridge (near the intersection of Le Loi St and Hung Vuong St). The food here is truly awful and we are not recommending it. The nice atmosphere might make it OK for a drink though (how bad can the coffee be?).

There is a restaurant in the *Cercle Sportif*, which is on Le Loi St next to the Phu Xuan Bridge. The Cercle Sportif has tennis courts and rents paddle boats.

The restaurant on the top floor of the *Huong Giang Hotel* at 51 Le Loi St serves Vietnamese, European and vegetarian dishes. The food is excellent and the prices are surprisingly reasonable; around US$5 to US$10 for a large meal for two people.

**Vegetarian** Vegetarian food, which has a long tradition in Hué, is prepared at pagodas for consumption by the monks. Small groups of visitors might be invited to join the monks for a meal. Stalls in the marketplaces serve vegetarian food on the first and 15th days of the lunar month.

**Entertainment**

*Apocalypse Now* (☎ 820152) at 7 Nguyen Tri Phuong St is the latest addition to what is starting to become a chain store. The music, drink and revelry is as good here as in Saigon.

The *DMZ Bar & Cafe* at 44 Le Loi St is a popular eating and dancing spot for travellers in the evenings.

Hué has borrowed a leaf from Hanoi and now has a water puppet theatre. The show is great and very reasonable at US$2, with no charge for cameras. There are continuous showings from 4 to 8 pm every day. It's at 11 Le Loi St, just next door to where you get a Perfume River boat cruise.

The Municipal Theatre (Nha Van Hoa Trung Tam) is on Huong Vuong St (corner of Ly Quy Don and Dong Da Sts). The entertainment here is really geared mostly towards the locals.

**Things to Buy**

Hué is known for producing the finest conical hats in Vietnam. The city's speciality is 'poem hats', which, when held up to the light, reveal black cut-out scenes sandwiched between the layers of translucent palm leaves.

HUÉ

Hué also has the largest and most beautiful selection of rice paper and silk paintings in Vietnam, but prices asked are about four times the real price. You can often negotiate a 50% discount by just starting to walk away from a souvenir stall.

Dong Ba Market, which is on the west bank of the Perfume River a few hundred metres north of Trang Tien Bridge, is Hué's largest market. It was rebuilt after much of the structure was destroyed by a typhoon in 1986.

## Getting There & Away

**Air** The Vietnam Airlines booking office (☎ 823249) is at 12 Hanoi St and is open Monday to Saturday from 7 to 11 am and 1.30 to 5 pm. There are flights connecting Hué to Saigon and Hanoi.

**Bus** Hué has three main bus stations, one to destinations south (An Cuu bus station), another to destinations north (An Hoa bus station – see the Hué Area map) and a short-haul bus station (Dong Ba bus station). A minor station is Nguyen Hoang bus station, which only has buses to Quang Tri Province, though there is talk of making it into a tourist bus station.

**Minibus** Hué is a major target for tourist minibus companies and most backpackers travel this way. A popular run is the Hué-Hoi An minibus, which also stops in Danang. Departure from either end is twice daily at 8 am and 1 pm and there is usually a scenic, 10-minute stop at Lang Co Island and Hai Van Pass. Hué-Hoi An costs US$5 and Hué-Danang is US$4.

**Train** Hué railway station (Ga Hué; ☎ 822-175) is on the east bank at the south-west end of Le Loi St. The ticket office is open from 7.30 am to 5 pm.

The *Reunification Express* trains stop in Hué. For ticket prices, see the Train section in the Getting Around chapter.

**Car** Ground distances from Hué are as follows:

| | |
|---|---|
| Ben Hai River | 94km |
| Danang | 108km |
| Dong Ha | 72km |
| Dong Hoi | 166km |
| Hanoi | 689km |
| Ho Chi Minh City | 1097km |
| Lao Bao (Lao border) | 152km |
| Quang Tri | 56km |
| Savannakhet, Laos (Thai border) | 400km |
| Vinh | 368km |

## Getting Around

**The Airport** Hué is served by Phu Bai airport, once an important American air base, which is 14km south of the city centre. Taxis are typically US$8. Share taxis at the airport cost as little as US$2 – inquire at hotels to find these vehicles. Vietnam Airlines runs its own minibus from its office to the airport a couple of hours before flight time – these cost US$2 per person.

**Taxi** Co Do Taxi (☎ 830830) has Japanese air-conditioned vehicles with meters.

**Cyclo & Motorbike** A typical scene in Hué is a foreigner walking down the street with two cyclos and a motorbike in hot pursuit, the drivers yelling 'hello cyclo' and 'hello motorbike' and the foreigner yelling 'no, no!'.

Self-drive motorbikes can be hired from some of the hotels. A 70cc to 100cc bike goes for US$7 per day.

**Bicycle** If it's not raining, the most pleasant way to tour the Hué area is by two-wheeled pedal power. Hotel Le Loi Hué at 2 Le Loi St hires out bicycles for US$1 per day or US$0.20 per hour.

**Boat** Boat rides down the Perfume River are highly recommended. Boat tours typically take in the tombs of Tu Duc, Thieu Tri, Minh Mang and the Thien Mu Pagoda. Many restaurants and hotels catering to foreigners arrange these boat tours. Prices vary, but are generally around US$3 per person. The journey takes about six hours and usually runs from 8 am to 2 pm.

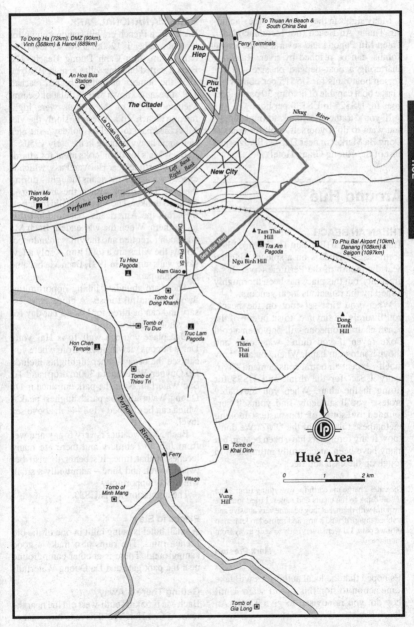

To Dong Ha (72km), DMZ (90km),
Vinh (368km) & Hanoi (689km)

To Thuan An Beach &
South China Sea

Ferry Terminals

An Hoa Bus
Station

Phu
Hiep

Phu
Cat

The Citadel

Nhug   River

Le Duan Street

Left Bank
Right Bank

New City

Thien Mu
Pagoda

Perfume   River

Dien Bien Phu St

See Hué Map

Tam Thai
Hill

Tra Am Pagoda

To Phu Bai Airport (10km),
Danang (108km) &
Saigon (1097km)

Tu Hieu
Pagoda

Nam Giao

Ngu Binh Hill

Dong
Tranh
Hill

Tomb of
Dong Khanh

Tomb of
Tu Duc

Truc Lam
Pagoda

Thien Thai
Hill

Hon Chen
Temple

Tomb of
Thieu Tri

Perfume   River

Tomb of
Khai Dinh

Hué Area

0          1          2 km

Ferry

Village

Tomb of
Minh Mang

Vung
Hill

Tomb of
Gia Long

Many sights in the vicinity of Hué, including Thuan An Beach (not recommended!), Thien Mu Pagoda and several of the Royal Tombs, can be reached by river. Rates for chartering a boat depend on size – a 15-person boat rents for US$15 per hour while a large boat capable of holding 30 passengers goes for US$25 to US$30 per hour.

If you'd rather not book through hotels and want to do it yourself, look for boats at Dong Ba Market or near Dap Da Bridge (just east of the Huong Giang Hotel).

# Around Hué

## THUAN AN BEACH

Thuan An Beach (Bai Tam Thuan An), 13km north-east of Hué, is on a splendid lagoon near the mouth of the Perfume River. It's a great pity, but this place has been thoroughly ruined by the rapacious local vendors.

When you first set foot on the beach, you'll surely be 'invited' to sit in one of the beach chairs. Someone will pop open a cold Coke (even if you didn't want one) and shove it into your hand. When you ask 'how much', expect an outrageous demand – typically US$5 for the drink and US$5 for sitting in the chair. When you inevitably protest, you'll suddenly find yourself surrounded by some of the nastiest-looking Vietnamese this side of the DMZ. We don't know if any foreigners have been beaten, but many have been successfully intimidated to cough up the cash and flee.

The cafes charge the earth for everything from a can of soft drink to the chairs and tables. I tried to argue the point with them, but they became very abusive and grabbed my girlfriend's arm and refused to let her go until we paid. I'd warn everybody to keep away from the place.

**Mark Preston**

It's hoped that the local authorities will take some action to stop this rip-off scam. Until they do, you're advised to give Thuan An Beach a miss.

## BACH MA NATIONAL PARK

Bach Ma, a French-era hill station known for its cool weather, is 1200m above sea level, but only 20km from Canh Duong Beach. The French started building villas here in 1930; by 1937 the number of holiday homes reached 139. It became known as the 'Dalat of Central Vietnam'. Most of the visitors were high-ranking French VIPs. Not surprisingly the Viet Minh tried hard to spoil the holiday – the area saw some heavy fighting in the early 1950s.

Bach Ma's location looks ideal for guarding the coastline near Hai Van Pass, which is exactly what the Americans thought – during the war, US troops turned the area into a fortified bunker. The Viet Cong did their best to harass the Americans, but couldn't dislodge them. When the war ended, Bach Ma was soon forgotten and the villas abandoned. Today, the villas are a total ruin – only a few stone walls remain. In 1991, Bach Ma became a national park.

There are abundant hiking opportunities through beautiful forests. A guide is necessary and can be hired for US$15 per day for the whole group.

One place you can walk to is Hai Vong Dai, a famous viewing point from where you can see the ocean. Other highlights include Do Quyen Waterfall (a 300m drop) and Tri Sao Waterfall. Near the park entrance is Da Duong Waterfall. The park's highest peak – which can be climbed – is 1444 m above sea level.

Bach Ma's weather is very foggy and wet from July to February and there are many leeches at that time. It's better to visit between March and June – admittedly a small window of opportunity.

The admission fee is US$3.

### Places to Stay

A small hotel is being built in one of the old French ruins. The ruins also make a good campground. There is another campground near the park gate and Da Duong Waterfall.

### Getting There & Away

Bach Ma is 55km south-west of Hué near the town of Cau Hai. You'll have to hire a car or motorbike for the last stretch as there is no public transport.

The road into the park is very narrow and steep, but should be accessible without 4WD unless it's been raining heavily recently. The road is gradually being upgraded.

# DMZ & Vicinity

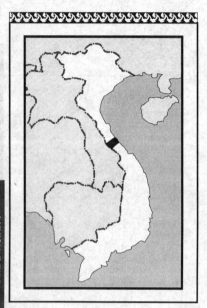

From 1954 to 1975, the Ben Hai River served as the demarcation line between the Republic of Vietnam (South Vietnam) and the Democratic Republic of Vietnam (North Vietnam). The Demilitarised Zone (DMZ) consisted of an area 5km to either side of the demarcation line.

The idea of partitioning Vietnam had its origins in a series of agreements concluded between the USA, UK and the USSR at the Potsdam Conference, which was held in Berlin in July 1945. For logistical and political reasons, the Allies decided that Japanese occupation forces to the south of the 16th parallel would surrender to the British while those to the north would surrender to the Kuomintang (Nationalist) Chinese army led by Chiang Kaishek.

In April 1954 in Geneva, Ho Chi Minh's government and the French agreed to an armistice; among the provisions was the creation of a demilitarised zone at the Ben Hai River. The agreement stated explicitly that the division of Vietnam into two zones was merely a temporary expediency and that the demarcation line did not constitute a political boundary. But when nationwide general elections planned for July 1956 were not held, Vietnam found itself divided into two states with the Ben Hai River, which is almost exactly at the 17th parallel, as their de facto border.

During the American War, the area just south of the DMZ was the scene of some of the bloodiest battles of the conflict. Dong Ha, Quang Tri, Con Thien, Cam Lo, Camp Carroll, the Rockpile, Khe Sanh, Lang Vay, the Ashau Valley, Hamburger Hill – these became almost household names in the USA as, year after year, TV pictures and casualty figures provided Americans with their daily evening dose of the war.

Since 1975, 5000 people have been injured or killed in and around the DMZ by mines and ordnance left over from the war. Despite the risk, impoverished peasants still dig for chunks of left-over metal to sell as scrap, for which they are paid a pittance.

## Orientation

The old DMZ extends from the coast westward to the Lao border; National Highway 9 (Quoc Lo 9) to the south runs more or less parallel to the DMZ. The Ho Chi Minh Trail (Duong Truong Son) – actually a series of roads, trails and paths – ran from North Vietnam southward (perpendicular to Highway 9) through the Truong Son Mountains and western Laos. To prevent infiltration and to interdict the flow of troops and materiel via the Ho Chi Minh Trail, the Americans established a line of bases along Highway 9, including (from east to west) Cua Viet, Gio Linh, Dong Ha, Con Thien, Cam Lo, Camp Carroll, Ca Lu, the Rockpile, Khe Sanh Combat Base and Lang Vay.

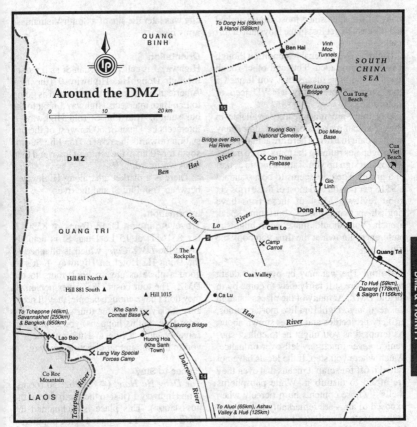

QUANG BINH

To Dong Hoi (66km) & Hanoi (589km)

Ben Hai

Vinh Moc Tunnels

SOUTH CHINA SEA

Hien Luong Bridge

Cua Tung Beach

**Around the DMZ**

0    10    20 km

Truong Son National Cemetery

Doc Mieu Base

Bridge over Ben Hai River

Cua Viet Beach

DMZ

Con Thien Firebase

Ben Hai River

Gio Linh

Cam Lo River

Dong Ha

QUANG TRI

Cam Lo

The Rockpile

Camp Carroll

Quang Tri

Hill 881 North

Cua Valley

To Huế (59km), Danang (178km), & Saigon (1156km)

Hill 881 South

Hill 1015

Ca Lu

To Tchepone (46km), Savannakhet (250km) & Bangkok (950km)

Khe Sanh Combat Base

Dakrong Bridge

Han River

Lao Bao

Huong Hoa (Khe Sanh Town)

Lang Vay Special Forces Camp

Dakrong River

Co Roc Mountain

LAOS

Tchepone River

To Aluoi (65km), Ashau Valley & Hué (125km)

**DMZ & VICINITY**

The old bases along Highway 9 (west of Dong Ha) can be visited as a day trip. The road leading south-east from the Dakrong Bridge goes to the Ashau Valley (site of the infamous Hamburger Hill) and Aluoi. With a 4WD it is possible to drive the 60 rough kilometres from Aluoi to Hué. One traveller described the landscape:

The area is absolutely barren – hardly a few shrubs manage to survive in the burned soil which refuses to recover. The people make a living from scrap metal collecting, selling drinks and food to the few visitors coming here and putting entrance fees into their own pockets. The region is poverty stricken and be pre-

pared to have about a dozen or more people fighting between them to sell you a Coke or some fruit. Here even a 50d note can still be seen! When driving through the DMZ, countless unnamed graves are scattered about, part of Vietnam's 300,000 MIAs (soldiers 'missing in action'). Near the Doc Mieu Base there were signs of recent diggings, part of the search for US MIAs.

## Information

**Guides, Vehicles & Tours** A good guide is required to appreciate the DMZ. After all, this is a historical place and understanding the significance of each site requires some explanation. A guide is also necessary to find many of the sites since most are unmarked and it's easy to get lost in the labyrinth of dirt tracks.

Highway 9 is in terrible condition though it is being upgraded. This and other rough roads in the area means that you'll need a good vehicle, preferably a 4WD jeep or motorbike.

Day tours are most readily available in Hué. You can make bookings at almost any hotel or cafe in town. There are actually only three agencies running the tours, so no matter where you sign up you'll still wind up as part of a group. The cost seems to be a standard US$15 per person and most of these trips get good reviews. Most of these trips have English-speaking guides, but some speak French. You should make your linguistic preferences known at the time you book the trip.

**Warning!** The war may be over, but death and injury are still fairly easy to come by in the old DMZ. At many of the places listed in this section you will find live mortar rounds, artillery projectiles and mines strewn about. As tempted as you might be to collect souvenirs, *never* touch any left-over ordnance. Watch where you step. If the locals have not carted it off for scrap it means that even they are afraid to disturb it. White phosphorus shells – whose contents burn fiercely when exposed to air – are remarkably impervious to the effects of prolonged exposure and are likely to remain extremely dangerous for many more years. If one of these shells happens to explode while you're playing with it, your whole trip will be ruined – and don't expect a refund from Saigon Tourist.

In short, be careful. Don't become a candidate for plastic surgery – or a statistic!

## DONG HA

Dong Ha, the capital of newly reconstituted Quang Tri Province, is at the intersection of National Highway 1 and National Highway 9. Dong Ha served as a US marine command and logistics centre in 1968-69. In the spring of 1968, a division of North Vietnamese troops crossed the DMZ and attacked Dong Ha. The city was later the site of a South Vietnamese army base.

### Orientation

Highway 1 is called Le Duan St as it passes through Dong Ha. Highway 9 (the new American-built branch), signposted as going to Lao Bao, intersects Highway 1 next to the bus station. Tran Phu St (old Highway 9) intersects Le Duan St 600m west of the bus station (towards the river). Tran Phu St runs south for 400m to the centre of town and then turns westward.

There is a market area along Highway 1 between Tran Phu St and the river.

### Information

**Travel Agencies** DMZ Tours (☎ 853047; fax 851617) at 15 Le Duan St is actually inside the *DMZ Cafe*, which is attached to the Dong Ha Hotel on Highway 1. It's as good a place as any to book tours to the DMZ. The tour costs US$15 per person. If they don't have enough people, they'll probably stick you in with a tour group coming from Hué. If this happens, you could conceivably hitch a ride to Hué with them if you're heading in that direction anyway.

### Places to Stay

The *Dong Ha Hotel* (☎ 852262; 30 rooms) is on Highway 1 (just to the north side of the bus station). This place is nicknamed the *DMZ Hotel* and has gained some popularity with travellers largely due to its convenient location. Rooms with hot water cost US$15 to US$18. It's still rather basic and not really worth the money.

A better choice, although further from the centre, is the *Nha Khach Buu Dien Tinh Buu Quang Tri* (☎ 852772; 12 rooms). It's a nice, quiet place with a pleasant courtyard and friendly manager. All rooms have attached bath with hot water and can accommodate four people. There is a security guard on duty at night. The price for foreigners is US$12 to US$20. This hotel is on the south side of town about 1km from the bus station.

*Nha Nghi Du Lich Cong Doan* (☎ 852-744; 18 rooms) is at 4 Le Loi St, about 500m

DMZ & Vicinity – Quang Tri 437

due west of the bus station. Rooms with fan and cold water cost US$10. With air-con and hot water it's US$20.

The *People's Committee Guesthouse* (Nha Khach Uy Ban Tinh; ☎ 852361; 25 rooms) is a pleasant official guesthouse on Tran Phu St. It's just slightly north of Dong Ha Park and 400m to the west. Rooms with shared bath cost US$7 to US$12; a private attached bath raises the tariff to US$20. Hot water is available.

### Getting There & Away
**Bus** Buses from Hué to Dong Ha depart from An Hoa bus station. Citroën Tractions to Dong Ha leave from Dong Ba bus station.

In Dong Ha, the bus station (Ben Xe Khach Dong Ha; ☎ 211) is at the intersection of Highway 1 and Highway 9. Vehicles to Hué depart between 5 am and 5 pm. There are buses to Khe Sanh at 8 and 11 am; to get to Lao Bao, change buses in Khe Sanh. There is service every Monday and Thursday to Hanoi; the bus departs at 5 am, arriving in Vinh at 6 or 7 pm and in Hanoi at 5 am the next day. Buses also link Dong Ha with Danang, Con Thien, Cua, Dien Sanh, Hai Tri and Ho Xa, which is along Highway 1 about 13km west of Vinh Moc.

**Train** Dong Ha railway station (Ga Dong Ha) is a stop for the *Reunification Express* trains. For ticket prices, see the Train section in the Getting Around chapter.

To get to the train station from the bus station, head south-east on Highway 1 for one kilometre. The railway station is 150m across a field to the right (south-west) of the highway.

**Car** Road distances from Dong Ha are:

| | |
|---|---|
| Ben Hai River | 22km |
| Danang | 190km |
| Dong Hoi | 94km |
| Hanoi | 617km |
| Ho Chi Minh City | 1169km |
| Hué | 72km |
| Khe Sanh | 65km |
| Lao Bao (Lao border) | 80km |
| Savannakhet, Laos (Thai border) | 327km |
| Truong Son National Cemetery | 30km |
| Vinh | 294km |
| Vinh Moc | 41km |

## QUANG TRI
The town of Quang Tri, 59km north of Hué and 12.5km south of Dong Ha, was once an important citadel-city. In the spring of 1972, four divisions of North Vietnamese regulars backed by tanks, artillery and rockets poured across the DMZ into Quang Tri Province in what became known as the Eastertide Offensive. They laid siege to Quang Tri City, shelling it heavily before capturing it along with the rest of the province. During the next four months, the city was almost completely obliterated by South Vietnamese artillery and massive carpet-bombing by US fighter-bombers and B-52s. The South Vietnamese army suffered 5000 casualties in the rubble-to-rubble fighting to retake Quang Tri City.

Today, there is little to see in the town of Quang Tri except a memorial and a few remains of the moat, ramparts and gates of the citadel, once a South Vietnamese army headquarters. The Citadel is 1.6km from Highway 1 on Le Duan St (not to be confused with Le Duan St in Dong Ha), which runs perpendicular to the highway. The ruined, two-storey building between the highway and the bus station used to be a Buddhist high school.

Along Highway 1 near the turn-off to Quang Tri is the skeleton of a church – it's definitely worth taking a look inside. It gives you the chills to see the bullet holes and know what took place here – a deadly fight between US forces and the Viet Cong.

Cua Viet Beach, once the site of an important American landing dock, is 16km north-east of Quang Tri. Gia Dang Beach is 13km east of town.

### Getting There & Away
**Bus** The bus station is on Le Duan St (Quang Tri's north-south-oriented main street) 600m from Highway 1. Renault buses to An Hoa bus station in Hué leave at 5.30, 6.30 and 8

## Peace Is Hell

Although the Americans dropped plenty of bombs and artillery shells on the North, the US discarded plans to launch a full-fledged land invasion of North Vietnam. Ironically, the US did make ground incursions into both Laos and Cambodia to strike at enemy soldiers and supply depots, but American soldiers never crossed the DMZ. Not that it wasn't considered – some generals advocated a full-scale military assault on the North, including the use of nuclear weapons. The logic was simple – bringing the war to the North would have taken the military pressure off South Vietnam.

At least on paper, invading North Vietnam looked simple. The American generals were confident that they had sufficient firepower to smash any defences the North could hope to mount. Of course, the French had thought the same thing before they wandered into the quagmire of Dien Bien Phu.

However, the Americans had several reasons for not invading the North, most of which had little to do with the possibility of another Dien Bien Phu. One reason was that the war was becoming increasingly unpopular with the American public, and no doubt an invasion would have been costly in terms of immediate American casualties. Then there was mounting international criticism that the USA was simply engaging in imperialism, trying to subjugate Vietnam as its colony. But the main factor which caused the Americans to pause was the possibility of triggering WWIII.

To this day, military buffs like to debate the issue – would an invasion of the North have changed the outcome of the war? Or would the USA have sunk even further into the morass of never-ending guerrilla combat? And would China and/or Russia have entered the war on North Vietnam's behalf? And if so, would either side have dared to use nuclear weapons? As with all speculative questions, no one can truly answer, but the Americans took the nuclear threat so seriously that they didn't even declare war on North Vietnam. Throughout the entire conflict, America was officially at peace and the entire war was labelled a 'police action'. ∎

---

am and noon. A Citroën Traction to Dong Ba bus station in Hué departs daily at 6.30 am. The daily bus to Khe Sanh leaves at 8 am. There is also service to Ho Xa.

## DOC MIEU BASE

Doc Mieu Base, which is next to Highway 1 on a low rise 8km south of the Ben Hai River, was once part of an elaborate electronic system (McNamara's Wall, named after the US Secretary of Defense 1961-68) intended to prevent infiltration across the DMZ. Today, it is a lunar landscape of bunkers, craters, shrapnel and live mortar rounds. Bits of cloth and decaying military boots are strewn about on the red earth. This devastation was created not by the war, but by scrap-metal hunters, who have found excavations at this site particularly rewarding.

## BEN HAI RIVER

Twenty-two kilometres north of Dong Ha, Highway 1 crosses the Ben Hai River – once the demarcation line between North and South Vietnam – over the decrepit Hien Luong Bridge. Until 1967 (when it was bombed by the Americans), the northern half

of the bridge that stood on this site was painted red while the southern half was yellow. Following the signing of the Paris cease-fire agreements in 1973, the present bridge and the two flag towers were built. A typhoon knocked over the flag pole on the northern bank of the river in 1985.

## CUA TUNG BEACH

Cua Tung Beach – a long, secluded stretch of sand where Vietnam's last emperor, Bao Dai, used to vacation – is just north of the mouth of the Ben Hai River. There are beaches on the southern side of the Ben Hai River as well. Every bit of land in the area not levelled for planting is pockmarked with bomb craters of all sizes. Offshore is Con Co Island, which can be reached by motorised boat; the trip takes about 2½ hours.

### Getting There & Away

There are no buses to Cua Tung Beach, which can be reached by turning right (eastward) off Highway 1 at a point 1.2km north of the Ben Hai River. Cua Tung Beach is about 7km south of Vinh Moc via the dirt road that runs along the coast.

## VINH MOC TUNNELS

The remarkable tunnels of Vinh Moc are yet another monument to the tenacity of the North Vietnamese to persevere and triumph – at all costs and despite incredible sacrifices – in the war against South Vietnam and the USA. A museum has been built on the site. A visit to the tunnels can be combined with bathing at the beautiful beaches which extend for many kilometres north and south of Vinh Moc.

The 2.8km of tunnels here, all of which can be visited, are the real thing and unadulterated for viewing by tourists (unlike the tunnels at Cu Chi). Vinh Moc's underground passageways are larger and taller than the ones at Cu Chi, which makes for an easier (and less creepy) visit.

Local authorities, who prefer not to lose any foreigners in the maze of forks, branches and identical weaving passageways, are adamant that visitors enter the tunnels only if accompanied by a local guide. The tunnels have been chemically treated to keep snakes away.

The entrance fee is US$2 per person or US$1.50 per person if you're with a group. There are lights installed inside the tunnels, but you should bring a torch (flashlight) anyway as the electricity supply has been known to fail unexpectedly.

### History

In 1966, the Americans began a massive aerial and artillery bombardment of North Vietnam. Just north of the DMZ, the villagers of Vinh Moc found themselves living in one of the most heavily bombed and shelled pieces of real estate on the planet. Small family shelters could not withstand this onslaught and the villagers either fled or began tunnelling by hand into the red clay earth.

Of course, the VC found it useful to have a base here and encouraged the villagers to stay. After 18 months of work (during which the excavated earth was camouflaged to prevent its detection from the air), an enormous VC base was established underground. Civilians were employed in the digging and also occupied their new underground homes. Whole families lived here and some babies were even born in the tunnels.

Later, the civilians and VC were joined by North Vietnamese soldiers whose mission was to keep communications and supply lines to nearby Con Co Island open. A total of 11,500 tons of military supplies reached Con Co Island and a further 300 tons were shipped to the south, thanks to the Vinh Moc tunnels.

Other villages north of the DMZ also built tunnel systems, but none were as elaborate as the one at Vinh Moc. The poorly constructed tunnels of Vinh Quang village (at the mouth of the Ben Hai River) were crushed by bombs, killing everyone inside.

The tunnel network at Vinh Moc remains essentially as it looked in 1966, though some of the 12 entrances – seven of which exit onto the palm-lined beach – have been retimbered and others have become overgrown with foliage. The tunnels were built on three levels ranging from 15 to 26m below the crest of the bluff.

The tunnels were repeatedly hit by American bombs, but the only ordnance that posed a real threat was the feared 'drilling bomb'. Only once did such a bomb score a direct hit, but it failed to explode and no one was injured; the inhabitants adapted the hole for use as an air shaft. The mouths of the complex that faced the sea were sometimes hit by naval gunfire.

### Getting There & Away

The turn-off to Vinh Moc from Highway 1 is 6.5km north of the Ben Hai River in the village of Ho Xa. Vinh Moc is 13km from Highway 1.

Offshore is Con Co Island, which during the war was an important supply depot. Today the island, which is ringed by rocky beaches, houses a small military base. The trip from Vinh Moc to Con Co takes 2½ to three hours by motorised fishing boat, but there are few visitors.

## TRUONG SON NATIONAL CEMETERY

Truong Son National Cemetery is a memorial

to tens of thousands of North Vietnamese soldiers from transport, construction and anti-aircraft units who were killed in the Truong Son Mountains (the Annamite Cordillera) along the Ho Chi Minh Trail (Duong Truong Son). Row after row of white tombstones stretch across the hillsides in a scene eerily reminiscent of the endless lines of crosses and Stars of David in US military cemeteries. The cemetery is maintained by disabled war veterans.

The soldiers are buried in five zones according to the part of Vietnam they came from; within each zone, the tombs are arranged by province of origin. The gravestones of five colonels (Trung Ta and Dia Ta) and seven decorated heroes, of whom one is a woman, are in a separate area. Each headstone bears the inscription *'Liet Si'*, which means 'Martyr'. The soldiers whose remains are interred here were originally buried near where they were killed and were brought here after reunification, but many of the graves are empty, bearing the names of a small portion of Vietnam's 300,000 MIAs.

On the hilltop above the sculpture garden is a three-sided stele. On one face are engraved the tributes of high-ranking Vietnamese leaders to the people who worked on the Ho Chi Minh Trail. At the bottom is a poem by the poet To Huu. Another side tells the history of the May 1959 Army Corps (Doang 5.59), which is said to have been founded on Ho Chi Minh's birthday in 1959 with a mission to construct and maintain a supply line to the South. The third side lists the constituent units of the May 1959 Army Corps, which eventually included five divisions. The site where the cemetery now stands was used as a base of the May 1959 Army Corps from 1972 to 1975.

### Getting There & Away
The road to Truong Son National Cemetery intersects Highway 1, 13km north of Dong Ha and 9km south of the Ben Hai River; the distance from the highway to the cemetery is 17km. A rocky cart-path, passable (but just barely) by motorcar, links Cam Lo (on Highway 9) with Truong Son National Cem-

etery. The 18km drive from Cam Lo to the cemetery passes by newly planted rubber plantations and the homes of the Bru (Van Kieu) tribal people, who raise, among other crops, black pepper.

## CON THIEN FIREBASE
In September 1967, North Vietnamese forces, backed by long-range artillery and rockets, crossed the DMZ and besieged the US marine corps base of Con Thien, which had been established to stop infiltrations across the DMZ and as part of McNamara's Wall – an abortive electronic barrier to detect infiltrators.

The Americans responded with 4000 bombing sorties (including 800 by B-52s) during which more than 40,000 tons of bombs were dropped on the North Vietnamese forces around Con Thien, transforming the gently sloping brush-covered hills that surrounded the base into a smoking moonscape of craters and ashes. As a result of the bombing the siege was lifted, but the battle had accomplished its real purpose: to divert US attention from South Vietnam's cities in preparation for the Tet Offensive. The area around the base is still considered too dangerous even for scrap-metal hunters to approach.

### Getting There & Away
Con Thien Firebase is 10km west of Highway 1 and 7km south of Truong Son National Cemetery along the road linking Highway 1 with the cemetery. Concrete bunkers mark the spot a few hundred metres to the south of the road where the base once stood.

Six kilometres towards Highway 1 from Con Thien (and 4km from the highway) is another US base, C-3, the rectangular ramparts of which are still visible just north of the road. It is inaccessible due to mines.

## CAMP CARROLL
Established in 1966, Camp Carroll was named for a US marine corps captain who was killed trying to seize a nearby ridge. The gargantuan 175mm cannons at Camp Carroll were used to shell targets as far away as Khe

Sanh. In 1972, the South Vietnamese commander of Camp Carroll, Lieutenant Colonel Ton That Dinh, surrendered and joined the North Vietnamese army; he is now a high-ranking official in Hué.

These days there is not that much to see at Camp Carroll except a few overgrown trenches and the remains of their timber roofs. Bits of military hardware and lots of rusty shell casings litter the ground. The concrete bunkers were destroyed by local people seeking to extract the steel reinforcing rods to sell as scrap; concrete chunks from the bunkers were hauled off for use in construction. Locals out prospecting for scrap metal can point out what little of the base is left.

The area around Camp Carroll now belongs to the State Pepper Enterprises (Xi Nghiep Ho Tieu Tan Lam). The pepper plants are trained so that they climb up the trunks of jackfruit trees. There are also rubber plantations nearby. The road to Camp Carroll leads on to the fertile Cua Valley, once home to a number of French settlers.

The turn-off to Camp Carroll is 11km west of Cam Lo, 24km south-east of the Dakrong Bridge and 37km east of the Khe Sanh bus station. The base is 3km from Highway 9.

## THE ROCKPILE

The Rockpile was named for what can only be described as a 230m-high pile of rocks. There was a US marine corps lookout on top of the Rockpile and a base for American long-range artillery nearby. The local tribal people, who live in houses built on stilts, engage in slash-and-burn agriculture.

Today there isn't much left of the Rockpile except for souvenir vendors.

The Rockpile is 26km towards Khe Sanh from Dong Ha.

## DAKRONG BRIDGE

The Dakrong Bridge, 3km east of the Khe Sanh bus station, was built in 1975-76 with assistance from the Cubans. The bridge crosses the Dakrong River (also known as the Ta Rin River). Hill tribe people in the area live by slash-and-burn agriculture. Some of

the tribespeople openly carry assault rifles left over from the war; this is against the law, but the government seems unwilling or unable to do anything about it.

The road that heads south-east from the bridge to Aluoi was once a branch of the Ho Chi Minh Trail. Constructed with Cuban help, it passes by the stilted homes of the Brus.

## ALUOI

Aluoi is approximately 65km south-east of the Dakrong Bridge and 60km west of Hué. There are a number of waterfalls and cascades in the area. Tribes living in the mountainous Aluoi area include the Ba Co, Ba Hy, Ca Tu and Taoi. US army Special Forces (Green Beret) bases in Aluoi and Ashau were overrun and abandoned in 1966; the area then became an important transshipment centre for supplies coming down the Ho Chi Minh Trail.

Among the better known military sites in the vicinity of Aluoi are landing zones Cunningham, Erskine and Razor, as well as Hill 1175 (west of the valley) and Hill 521 (in Laos). Further south in the Ashau Valley is 'Hamburger Hill' (Apbia Mountain). In May 1969, American forces on a search-and-destroy operation near the Lao border fought one of the fiercest engagements of the war here, suffering terrible casualties (hence the name). In less than a week of fighting, 241 American soldiers died at Hamburger Hill – a fact well publicised in the American media. A month later, after US forces withdrew from the area to continue operations elsewhere, the hill was reoccupied by the North Vietnamese.

## KHE SANH COMBAT BASE

This is the site of the most famous siege (and one of the most controversial battles) of the American War. Khe Sanh sits silently on a barren plateau surrounded by vegetation-covered hills often obscured by mist and fog. It is hard to imagine as you stand in this peaceful, verdant land – with the neat homes and vegetable plots of local tribespeople and Vietnamese settlers all around – that in this

## Missing in Action (MIA)

An issue which continues to poison relations between the USA and Vietnam is that of US military personnel officially listed as 'missing in action'. More than two decades after US forces were withdrawn from Vietnam, there are still 2265 American soldiers whose bodies have not been found and who are therefore officially 'unaccounted for'.

The families of the missing are generally adamant – many believe that their loved ones are still alive and being held in secret prison camps somewhere in the jungles of Vietnam. POW-MIA groups in the USA continue to lobby Congress to 'do something'. It's a highly emotive issue and one which is often cleverly exploited by some US politicians. 'No compromise', they insist, 'until Vietnam accounts for every one of the MIAs'.

But there are others who think that the POW-MIA groups are flogging a dead horse. The figure of 2265 MIAs is almost certainly too high. About 400 flight personnel were killed when their planes crashed into the sea off the coast of Vietnam – the bodies were never recovered, but they are still listed as MIAs. Many others were killed when their aircraft went down in flames over the jungle and no remains could be recovered. Still others were killed in ground combat, but the tropical jungle quickly reclaims a human corpse. Not much is said about the American MIAs from the Korean War and WWII – it was long ago assumed that all of them are dead. Nor does anyone talk about the 300,000 Vietnamese who are also MIAs – they are difficult to identify because they didn't wear ID tags as the Americans did.

US Senator John Kerry was the chairman of a Senate committee exploring the MIA issue. After visiting Vietnam, he called for a reappraisal of the US body count. During a press conference, he said, 'You have certain instances in which this person was KIA (killed in action) and the body cannot be recovered … this standard has to be reviewed'.

Kerry added that in 1973, when Vietnam returned the last 590 American POWs, there were 37 soldiers believed to have been captured who were not among those released.

Could there still be some American troops being held prisoner in Vietnam? The Vietnamese government adamantly denies it, but the credibility of Vietnam's government officials has to be questioned in view of their poor human rights record. On the other hand, it would make no logical sense for Vietnam to continue holding US POWs.

In the meantime, MIA teams continue to comb the Vietnamese countryside with little success, at a cost to American taxpayers of more than US$100 million. Many Vietnamese labourers are employed in the search teams and 75% of their salaries go to the government. Not surprisingly, the Vietnamese government is in no hurry to see the MIA teams leave, though there is frustration with how the Americans keep raising this bogus issue in diplomatic negotiations. The fact that the MIA teams have been digging through Vietnamese cemeteries looking for American bones has also irritated many locals who would prefer to see their dead rest in peace.

On the other hand, there are plenty of Vietnamese who sense an opportunity in the MIA issue. Vietnamese civilians regularly approach the US government's representatives with fragments of bone which they claim belong to dead American MIAs. Their hope is to get some sort of cash reward or even an immigration visa to the USA. What most do not realise is that the USA does not pay rewards for this information. Even budget travellers have been approached by the bone-pedlars – some Vietnamese believe all western backpackers have great influence with the US government!

Meanwhile, the whole sad saga continues to play itself out. When private POW-MIA groups started circulating photographs showing US soldiers being held prisoner in a Vietnamese camp, there was a flurry of official investigations. The photos proved to be fakes. But POW-MIA groups such as the National League of Families of American Prisoners and Missing in Southeast Asia were very effective at stalling the US government's attempts to forge diplomatic relations with Vietnam. However, the two countries did finally establish diplomatic relations in 1995, a move which the POW-MIA groups vehemently protested. ■

very place in early 1968 the bloodiest battle of the war took place. Approximately 500 Americans (the official figure of 205 American dead was arrived at by statistical sleight-of-hand), some 10,000 North Vietnamese troops and uncounted civilian bystanders died amid the din of machine-guns and the fiery explosions of 1000kg bombs, white phosphorus shells, napalm, mortars and artillery rounds of all sorts.

There's not much left, but little things help you to picture what the history books say happened here. The outline of the airfield remains distinct (to this day nothing will grow on it). In places, the ground is literally carpeted with bullets and rusting shell casings. And all around are little groups of local people digging holes in their relentless search for scrap metal (once, local scavengers say proudly, they unearthed an entire bulldozer!). The US MIA Team, charged with finding the remains of Americans listed as 'missing-in-action', has visited the area countless times to search for the bodies of the Americans who disappeared during the fierce battles in the surrounding hills. Most of the remains they find are Vietnamese.

**History**
Despite opposition from marine corps brass to General William Westmoreland's attrition strategy (they thought it futile), the small US army Special Forces base at Khe Sanh, built to recruit and train local tribespeople, was turned into a marine stronghold in late 1966. In April 1967, there began a series of 'hill fights' between the US forces and the well-dug-in North Vietnamese army infantry who held the surrounding hills. In the period of a few weeks, 155 marines and perhaps thousands of North Vietnamese were killed. The fighting centred on hills 881 South and 881 North, both of which are about 8km northwest of Khe Sanh Combat Base.

In late 1967, American intelligence detected the movement of tens of thousands of North Vietnamese regulars armed with mortars, rockets and artillery into the hills around Khe Sanh. The commander of the US forces in Vietnam, General William Westmoreland, became convinced that the North Vietnamese were planning another Dien Bien Phu (the decisive battle in the Franco-Viet Minh War in 1954). This was an illogical analogy given American firepower and the proximity of Khe Sanh to supply lines and other American bases. President Johnson himself became obsessed by the spectre of Dien Bien Phu: to follow the course of the battle, he had a sand-table model of the Khe Sanh plateau constructed in the White House situation room and he took the unprecedented step of requiring a written guarantee from the Joint Chiefs of Staff that Khe Sanh could be held.

Westmoreland, determined to avoid another Dien Bien Phu at all costs, assembled an armada of 5000 planes and helicopters and increased the number of troops at Khe Sanh to 6000. He even ordered his staff to study the feasibility of using tactical nuclear weapons.

The 75-day Siege of Khe Sanh began on 21 January 1968 with a small-scale assault on the base perimeter. As the marines and the South Vietnamese Rangers braced for a full-scale ground attack, Khe Sanh became the focus of global media attention. It was the cover story for both *Newsweek* and *Life* magazines and appeared on the front pages of countless newspapers around the world. During the next two months, the base was subject to continuous ground attacks and artillery fire. US aircraft dropped 100,000 tons of explosives on the immediate vicinity of Khe Sanh Combat Base. The expected attempt to overrun the base never came and, on 7 April 1968 after heavy fighting, US army troops reopened Highway 9 and linked up with the marines to end the siege.

It now seems clear that the siege of Khe Sanh, in which an estimated 10,000 North Vietnamese died, was merely an enormous diversion intended to draw US forces and the attention of their commanders away from South Vietnam's population centres in preparation for the Tet Offensive, which began a week after the siege started. At the time, however, Westmoreland considered the entire Tet Offensive to be a 'diversionary effort' to distract attention from Khe Sanh!

A few days after Westmoreland's tour of duty in Vietnam ended in July 1968, American forces in the area were redeployed. Policy, it seemed, had been reassessed and holding Khe Sanh, for which so many men had died, was deemed unnecessary. After everything at Khe Sanh was buried, trucked out or blown up – nothing recognisable that could be used in a North Vietnamese propaganda film was to remain – US forces up and left Khe Sanh Combat Base under a curtain of secrecy. The American command had finally realised what a marine officer had expressed long before: 'When you're at Khe

Sanh, you're not really anywhere. You could lose it and you really haven't lost a damn thing'.

## Getting There & Away

To get to Khe Sanh Combat Base, turn northwest at the triangular intersection 600m towards Dong Ha from Khe Sanh bus station. The base is on the right-hand side of the road, 2.5km from the intersection.

## KHE SANH TOWN

Set amid beautiful hills, valleys and fields at an elevation of about 600m, the town of Khe Sanh is a pleasant district capital. The town is known for its coffee plantations, which were originally cultivated by the French.

Many of the inhabitants are Bru tribespeople who have moved here from the surrounding hills. A popular pastime among the hill tribe women is smoking long-stemmed pipes.

The town has now been officially renamed Huong Hoa, but the outside world will forever remember it as Khe Sanh.

## Places to Stay

Currently there are two hotels in town, both of them rather basic. One is the *Mountain Guesthouse* and the other is the *People's Committee Guesthouse*. About the only reason for staying here is if you're planning to hit the road to Laos the next morning.

## Getting There & Away

Khe Sanh bus station (Ben Xe Huong Hoa) is on Highway 9, 600m south-west (towards the Lao frontier) from the triangular intersection where the road to Khe Sanh Combat Base branches off. Buses to Dong Ha depart at 7 am and around noon, while the daily bus to Hué leaves at 7 am. There are two buses a day to Lao Bao; the first leaves at 6 am and the second whenever it is full. The ticket window is open from 6 to 7 am; tickets for later buses are sold on board.

If and when the border with Laos is opened for trade and travel, the public transport situation in the area is likely to improve significantly.

## LANG VAY SPECIAL FORCES CAMP

In February 1968, Lang Vay (Lang Vei) Special Forces Camp, established in 1962, was attacked and overrun by North Vietnamese infantry backed by nine tanks. Of the base's 500 South Vietnamese, Bru and Montagnard defenders, 316 were killed. Ten of the 24 Americans at the base were killed; 11 of the survivors were wounded.

All that remains of dog-bone-shaped Lang Vay base are the overgrown remains of numerous concrete bunkers. Locals can show you around.

## Getting There & Away

The base is on a ridge just south-west of Highway 9 at a point 9.2km towards Laos from the Khe Sanh bus station and 7.3km towards Khe Sanh from Lao Bao.

## LAO BAO

Lao Bao is right on the Tchepone River (Song Xe Pon), which marks the Vietnam-Laos border. Towering above Lao Bao on the Lao side of the border is Co Roc Mountain, once a North Vietnamese artillery stronghold.

Two kilometres from the border post is Lao Bao Market, where Thai goods smug-

---

**Stress**
A growing number of war veterans (mostly Americans, but some Australians) are returning to Vietnam. Many psychologists who deal with the long-term effects of war believe that going back to Vietnam can help groups of veterans confront the root causes of post-traumatic stress disorder (PTSD). It should be added that many Vietnamese suffer from PTSD too, although few of them have the opportunity to consult a psychologist. ■

gled through the bush from Laos to Vietnam are readily available. Merchants accept either Vietnamese dong or Lao kip.

### Getting There & Away

Lao Bao is 18km west of Khe Sanh, 80km from Dong Ha, 152km from Hué, 46km east of Tchepone (Laos), 250km east of Savannakhet, Laos (on the Thai frontier) and 950km from Bangkok (via Ubon Ratchathani). Lao Bao may eventually become an important border crossing for trade and tourism between Thailand and central Vietnam.

# North-Central Vietnam

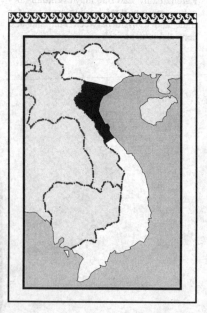

The area north of the DMZ is the former North Vietnam. While the differences between north and south have faded since reunification in 1975, there is still evidence that there were once two different countries with two different political systems.

While the south enjoyed the USA's largesse, which brought wartime prosperity, the north has never been anything but desperately poor – and still is. While the south was the scene of many (mostly small) land battles, it was the north that suffered from bombing – bomb craters and damaged buildings are still a feature in this part of Vietnam.

And there is also a perceptible change in attitudes – southerners see the northerners as provincial. For their part, the northerners think the southerners are money-grubbers. Both sides complain that they have trouble understanding what the other says – the two parts of Vietnam speak a sharply different, though mutually intelligible, dialect.

As a foreigner, you will probably detect some difference in attitudes as you head north of the DMZ – people are more reserved and less friendly. This is not a huge problem by any means, but it is noticeable. Most likely, the economic integration of Vietnam that is now occurring will reduce the differences between north and south, but this will take time.

### DONG HOI

The fishing port of Dong Hoi is the capital of Quang Binh Province. Important archaeological finds from the Neolithic period have been made in the vicinity. During the American War, the city suffered extensive damage from US bombing. When travelling on National Highway 1 north of the DMZ, note the old French bunkers and US bomb craters lining the route; both are especially numerous near road and rail bridges. The Vietnam-Cuba Hospital is 1km north of town.

Usually travellers spend the night in Dong Hoi only if they wish to visit Phong Nha Cave (see that section in this chapter for details). The cave is 55km from Dong Hoi, so it can be visited as a day trip. Some hotels in Dong Hoi book trips to the cave.

### Beaches

Most of Quang Binh Province is lined with sand dunes and beaches. There are dozens of kilometres of beaches and dunes north of town and on a long spit of sand south of town. Nhat Le Beach is at the mouth of the Nhat Le River about 2.5km from central Dong Hoi. Another bathing site in the region is Ly Hoa Beach.

### Nhat Le River

This river flows along the east side of town and boat trips are a pleasant way to pass the time. The Phuong Dong Hotel (see Places to

**North-Central Vietnam**

0        50        100 km

Stay) books boat trips for US$3 per hour per person, but about 10 persons are needed to make this trip economically viable.

### Places to Stay

The most pleasant places to stay are on the west bank of the Nhat Le River, which is just east of National Highway 1.

The largest of the riverside hotels is the *Nhat Le Hotel* (☎ 822180; 45 rooms) at 16 Quach Xuan Ky St. Rooms cost US$10 to US$25.

Just to the north at 20 Quach Xuan Ky St is the *Phuong Dong Hotel* (☎ 822276; fax 822404; 50 rooms). There are several standards of rooms costing between US$10 and US$45. This place books boat trips on the Nhat Le River, and also day trips by car or van to Phong Nha Cave.

Still on Quach Xuan Ky St, but another block to the north, is the *Huu Nghi Hotel* (☎ 822567; 23 rooms). This place has a river view and rooms for US$20 to US$50.

At 5 Ly Thuong Kiet St (actually on National Highway 1) is the *My Ngoc Mini-Hotel* (☎ 822074; 12 rooms). Rooms at this privately run place are US$30, but can be negotiated down to US$15 if you're a 'student'.

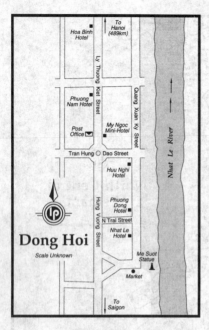

Dong Hoi

Also on Ly Thuong St, the *Hoa Binh Hotel* (☎ 822347; 20 rooms) is a four-storey building, making it a veritable skyscraper by Dong Hoi standards. Unfortunately, it's starting to fall into disrepair, but that hasn't caused the price to come down. Rooms cost US$25.

The *Phuong Nam Hotel* (☎ 823194; 10 rooms) is one block south on Ly Thuong St. It's an old place with some decaying architectural elegance. Rooms cost US$20 to US$30.

### Getting There & Away
**Bus & Car** Dong Hoi is 166km from Hué, 94km from Dong Ha, 197km from Vinh and 489km from Hanoi. Dong Hoi is on National Highway 1 and sees regular bus traffic. Road traffic between Dong Ha and Dong Hoi is light, especially after the early morning.

North of the DMZ, National Highway 1 is being completely rebuilt, which means lots of gravel, dust, mud, potholes and trucks dangerously overloaded with building materials. One irony is that these heavy trucks are breaking up the existing road, even though they will help to build the new one.

There is a ferry crossing at Cua Gianh (also called Song Painh), which is 33km north of Dong Hoi. The ferry is really just a small barge which is pushed and pulled by tugboats, and there is often a long queue of vehicles – it can take an hour or more to get across.

**Train** Dong Hoi is a stop for the *Reunification Express* train. For ticket prices, see the Train section in the Getting Around chapter.

### BO TRACH
Bo Trach (also called Hoan Lao) is a small town that is of no great interest, except as a launchpad to nearby Phong Nha Cave, 35km to the west.

You can, of course, bypass Bo Trach entirely and most travellers do. However, the combination of a beach, hotel and convenient access to the cave has enabled Da Nhay Hotel to carve a niche for itself in the foreign tour-group market. There are no hotels in Bo Trach itself and budget travellers will probably find it more economical to launch their cave explorations from Dong Hoi (20km south of Bo Trach).

### Places to Stay & Eat
For those interested in visiting the cave, it may be worth staying at the *Da Nhay Hotel* (☎ 866041; 20 rooms). It's adjacent to a very good beach 5km north of Bo Trach and just 30km from the cave. The hotel has small but very comfortable rooms costing US$25 to US$30. Unusually for a Vietnamese hotel, the rooms lack TV sets, though there is one in the bar. There are several small restaurants just opposite the hotel entrance.

Inquire at the hotel about booking a vehicle to Phong Nha Cave, but be prepared to bargain because the prices quoted are definitely far higher than they should be. Perhaps some future free-market competition will change all that, but for now this hotel enjoys a local monopoly.

## PHONG NHA CAVE

Phong Nha Cave is in the village of Son Trach, 55km north-west of Dong Hoi. This place is remarkable for its thousands of metres of underground passageways filled with abundant stalactites and stalagmites. It's the largest and most beautiful known cave in Vietnam, and was formed approximately 250 million years ago.

Only recently has anyone made a thorough exploration of the cave. A British caving expedition in 1990 made the first reliable map of Phong Nha's underground (and underwater) passageways. They discovered that the main cavern has a length of nearly 8km. Furthermore, they found many other caves nearby – in total, the British team explored 35km of caves in the vicinity.

Phong Nha means Cave of Teeth & Wind, but, unfortunately, the 'teeth' (or stalagmites) by the entrance no longer remain; however, once you get farther into the cave it's mostly unspoiled.

The Chams utilised the grottoes of Phong Nha Cave as Buddhist sanctuaries in the 9th and 10th centuries; the remains of Cham altars and inscriptions can still be seen. Vietnamese Buddhists continue to venerate these sanctuaries, as they do other Cham religious sites.

In more recent times, the cave was used as a hospital and ammunition depot during the American War. The entrance shows effects of the attack by jet fighters. That US warplanes spent considerable time bombing and strafing the Phong Nha area is not surprising – this was one of the key entrance points to the Ho Chi Minh Trail. Some overgrown remains of the trail are still visible, though you'll need a guide to point them out to you.

### Places to Stay & Eat

A 40-room government-owned hotel was under construction at Son Trach village at the time of our visit. This hotel should be finished before the end of 1998. No one could tell us what the hotel will be named or what the room rates will be.

There is currently only one *restaurant* in Son Trach, and it's not exactly five star. The sign out the front simply says 'Com, Pho' ('Rice, Noodles').

### Getting There & Away

The Phong Nha Reception Department (☎ 823424) in Son Trach village has overall responsibility for tourist access to the cave (a polite way of saying it has a monopoly). At this office you must buy your admission ticket (US$6 per person). You can (and should) rent a generator and lantern here for an additional US$6 (per group), otherwise you won't get to see much. You should still bring a torch (flashlight) just in case the generator fails.

The actual cave entrance is 3km from Son Trach and can only be reached by boat. You book the boat at the same place you buy the admission ticket and rent the generator. The boat can hold about six passengers and the one-way ride takes 30 minutes. Overall, you'll probably spend about two hours for the whole excursion. Unless you have special permission, you are only permitted to explore the first 600m of the cave.

There is no public transport to Son Trach, but hotels and some travel agencies in nearby towns cater to this market.

The Phuong Dong Hotel in Dong Hoi (55km from Son Trach) offers transport for US$50 for 10 persons. (See the earlier Dong Hoi section for details.)

By contrast, the Da Nhay Hotel near Bo Trach (only 30km from Son Trach) is far more expensive, charging US$120 for 12 persons; however, it also has a car which it rents for US$40 that can carry four persons. Not surprisingly, it gets few customers, so there may be latitude here for bargaining. (See the Bo Trach section for details.)

The Hotel Le Loi Hué in Hué (220km from Phong Nha) charges US$90 for a car that carries four persons, or US$10 to US$15 per person for a minibus that can carry nine to 12 passengers.

You can travel by public bus to Bo Trach, where you will find motorcycle taxis at the bus station. You should be able to negotiate a trip to Son Trach for US$5. The drivers will wait for you while you visit the cave.

## DEO NGANG

Deo Ngang (Ngang Pass) is a mountainous coastal area that constitutes the easternmost section of the Hoanh Son Mountains (Transversal Range), which stretches from the Lao border to the sea along the 18th parallel. Until the 11th century, the range formed Vietnam's frontier with the Kingdom of Champa. Later, the French used it as the border between their protectorates of Annam and Tonkin; Annam Gate (Porte d'Annam) is still visible at Ngang Pass from National Highway 1.

The Hoanh Son Mountains now demarcate the border between Quang Binh Province and Ha Tinh Province. There are a number of islands offshore.

This part of Vietnam has traditionally been poor and periodically afflicted by famine. Because vehicles have to slow down when climbing Deo Ngang, the pass has long been a favourite venue for beggars. In 1992 we saw dozens of beggars here lining the highway, many literally throwing themselves in front of moving vehicles to force the drivers to stop. However, returning in 1994 we counted only five beggars and in 1996 just one – we assume that the local economy has seen some recent improvement.

There is a decent hotel just north of the pass right beside the beach. It's certainly not a bad place to stay, though the electricity is supplied by generators and is not too reliable. Rooms cost US$10. There is a restaurant here and the staff are very friendly.

## CAM XUYEN

The town of Cam Xuyen is about 150km north of Dong Hoi and 45km south of Vinh. There is nothing here to see. Cam Xuyen's only significant feature is a grotty guesthouse where you can stay if you're too tired to push on.

The *Nha Khach Cam Xuyen* (☎ 861234; five rooms), on the west side of the road, charges foreigners US$5 for Third World accommodation. It's only for the desperate, so if you're heading north try to make it to Ha Tinh or Vinh.

## HA TINH

Ha Tinh is a nondescript town on the high-

way between Cam Xuyen and Vinh. Most likely the only reason you'd want to stop here is if your car or bus breaks down. Foreigners zipping along National Highway 1 often spend the night here, though Vinh has a wider selection of hotels and cheaper prices.

If you need to change money, there is a branch of Vietcombank (☎ 856775) at 6 Phan Dinh Phung St.

### Places to Stay

Most foreigners travelling National Highway 1 are heading north. If that describes your situation, the first hotel you see on the south side of town (and west side of the highway) is *Nha Khach Cau Phu* (☎ 856-712; 22 rooms). It's a new hotel, the staff speak surprisingly good English and it's probably the second best deal in town. Rooms cost US$20 and US$25.

On the west side of Tran Phu St (National Highway 1) opposite the huge TV tower is the *Binh Minh Hotel* (☎ 856825; 21 rooms). Rooms are OK, but rather pricey at US$30 and US$35.

Ha Tinh's cheapest accommodation (and not bad either) is the *Kieu Hoa Hotel* (☎ 857-025; seven rooms). It's on the west side of Tran Phu St (National Highway 1), slightly north of the TV tower. Rooms cost US$15 and the management tries (not too successfully) to speak English. However, it's a friendly place and has a small restaurant.

The worst deal in town is the *Ha Tinh Relation Hotel* (Khach San Giao Te Ha Tinh; ☎ 855589; 34 rooms), about 1km east of the TV tower. It's very overpriced at US$20 to US$25 for a mediocre room with attached leaking shower and deadly electrical wiring. To make sure you don't oversleep, the hotel blasts military music at 5 am. The hotel is operated by the provincial tourism authority, Ha Tinh Tourist (Cong Ty Du Lich Ha Tinh).

## VINH

The port city of Vinh (population 200,000) is the capital of Nghe An Province. While there is almost nothing of interest in the city itself, there are a few odd sights in the surrounding area. Vinh's economic fortunes

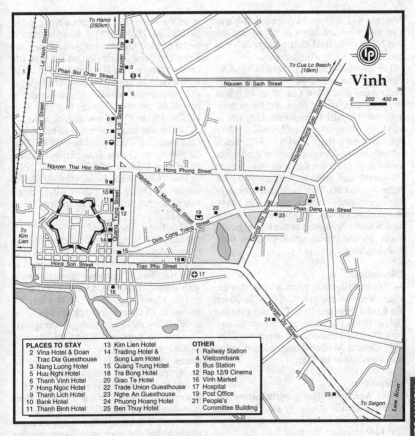

Vinh

0    200   400 m

**PLACES TO STAY**
2  Vina Hotel & Doan
   Trac Dia Guesthouse
3  Nang Luong Hotel
6  Huu Nghi Hotel
7  Thanh Vinh Hotel
9  Thanh Lich Hotel
10 Bank Hotel
11 Thanh Binh Hotel

13 Kim Lien Hotel
14 Trading Hotel &
   Song Lam Hotel
15 Quang Trung Hotel
18 Tra Bong Hotel
20 Giao Te Hotel
22 Trade Union Guesthouse
23 Nghe An Guesthouse
24 Phuong Hoang Hotel
25 Ben Thuy Hotel

**OTHER**
1  Railway Station
4  Vietcombank
8  Bus Station
12 Rap 12/9 Cinema
16 Vinh Market
17 Hospital
19 Post Office
21 People's
   Committee Building

have been greatly improved recently by the sharp increase in traffic on National Highway 1. For travellers, the town is a convenient place to stop for the night if you are going overland between Hué and Hanoi. Vinh is also an essential transit point if you're heading overland to/from Tha Khaek in Laos.

Nghe An and neighbouring Ha Tinh provinces are endowed with poor soil and some of the worst weather in Vietnam. The area frequently suffers from floods and devastating typhoons. The locals say, 'The typhoon was born here and comes back often to visit'. The summers are very hot and dry, while during the winter the cold and rain are made all the more unpleasant by biting winds from the north. The poor climate and many years of half-baked collectivised farming policies have made much of Nghe An and Ha Tinh provinces one of the most destitute regions in Vietnam. The recent economic reforms have greatly improved things, but nobody has yet figured out a way to reform the lousy weather.

### History
Vinh's recent history has not been the happiest. It was a pleasant citadel-city during colonial

days, but was destroyed in the early 1950s as a result of French aerial bombing and the Viet Minh's scorched-earth policy. Vinh was later devastated by a huge fire.

The Ho Chi Minh Trail began in Nghe An Province, and much of the war material transported on the Ho Chi Minh Trail was shipped via the port of Vinh. Not too surprisingly, the US military obliterated the city in hundreds of air attacks and naval artillery bombardments from 1964 to 1972, which left only two buildings intact. The Americans paid a high price for the bombings – more US aircraft and pilots were shot down over Nghe An and Ha Tinh provinces than over any other part of North Vietnam. The heavy loss of planes and pilots was one reason why the USA later brought in battleships to pound North Vietnam with artillery shells fired from offshore.

### Orientation

As National Highway 1 enters Vinh from the south, it crosses the mouth of the Lam River (Ca River), also known as Cua Hoi Estuary. Quang Trung (which runs north-south) and Tran Phu Sts intersect one block north of Vinh Central Market. Street address numbers are not used in Vinh.

### Information

**Travel Agencies** The government-owned Nghe An Tourist (Cong Ty Du Lich Nghe An) is on Quang Trung St just to the north of Rap 12/9 cinema.

**Money** Vietcombank (Ngan Hang Ngoai Thuong Viet Nam) is near the corner of Le Loi and Nguyen Si Sach Sts.

**Post & Communications** The GPO is on Nguyen Thi Minh Khai St, 300m north-west of Dinh Cong Trang St. It is open from 6.30 am to 9 pm.

**Emergency** The general hospital is on the corner of Tran Phu and Le Mao Sts.

### Places to Stay

The *Ben Thuy Hotel* (☎ 855163; 15 rooms)

is on the south side of Vinh on Nguyen Du St (National Highway 1), 1.3km towards the centre of Vinh from the bridge over the Lam River and 2km towards the bridge from the centre of town. This is a very popular place with travellers, largely because it has a large car park where minibuses can be safely parked for the night. Rooms cost US$12 to US$24. The hotel has a small restaurant.

The bottom end of bottom end belongs to the *Doan Trac Dia Guesthouse* (☎ 842784; 10 rooms) on Quang Trung St. A standard hovel costs US$6 to US$10.

The *Thanh Binh Hotel* (☎ 842512; 50 rooms) on Quang Trung St is a large renovated state-run place, with rooms for US$10 to US$25.

The *Bong Sen Hotel* (☎ 844397; 19 rooms) at 20 Quang Trung St is an established cheapie, with doubles from US$7 to US$12.

The *Vina Hotel* (☎ 846990; 20 rooms) at 9 Nguyen Trai St has pretty standard rooms with attached bath for US$10 to US$14.

The *Thanh Lich Hotel* (☎ 844961; 19 rooms) at 28 Quang Trung St appeals more to Vietnamese tastes than to foreigners. There is no satellite TV and the blasting karaoke could raise the dead. Otherwise, rooms are clean and luxurious enough to justify the US$15 to US$25 price tag.

If you don't mind paying a little for the luxury of satellite TV, check out the modern mini-hotel *Hong Ngoc Hotel* (☎ 841314; 19 rooms) at 86B Le Loi St. It's one of those places where staff in crisp uniforms open the door to the air-conditioned lobby and say, 'Good evening, please come in'. Comfortable rooms here will cost you US$25 to US$40.

One of the newest hotels in town is the *Thanh Vinh Hotel* (☎ 847222; 18 rooms) at 9 Le Loi St. Fully equipped rooms with satellite TV cost US$25 to US$40. Breakfast is included.

The *Nang Luong Hotel* (☎ 844788; 50 rooms) is an old but friendly place at 2 Nguyen Trai St. Rooms all have satellite TV and cost US$15 to US$40.

The *Huu Nghi Hotel* (☎ 844633; 74 rooms) on Le Loi St is an aging upmarket place that is no longer worth the money. Rooms cost US$25 to US$90, but only rooms from US$40 and up have satellite TV.

The *Bank Hotel* (Ngan Hang Cong Thuong Nghe An; ☎ 849897; 24 rooms) on Quang Trung St is a recently remodelled building offering rooms from US$8 to US$15.

The *Trading Hotel* (Khach San Thuong Mai; ☎ 830211; fax 830393; 33 rooms) on Quang Trung St gets the nod from business travellers. It's a new place with the requisite satellite TV. Doubles cost US$30 to US$35.

The *Kim Lien Hotel* (☎ 844751; fax 843699; 79 rooms) on Quang Trung St is the largest hotel in Vinh and has everything: air-con, hot water, moneychanger, travel agent, restaurant, satellite TV, massage services, the whole lot. All this luxury will cost you US$25 to US$57.

### Places to Eat

Vinh Market (Cho Vinh) carries the usual plethora of household goods, and there are food stalls around the back. The market is at the end of Cao Thang St, which is the southern continuation of Quang Trung St.

If you poke around town, it won't be long before you notice the peanut candies on sale almost everywhere. There are at least three different kinds, each one outstanding. You'll find plenty of similar-looking candies elsewhere in Vietnam, but the Vinh variety is far and away the best. This stuff is export quality (even though it doesn't get exported) and is highly addictive. If you're on a diet then don't even stop in Vinh.

### Getting There & Away

**Air** The Vietnam Airlines booking office is in the Huu Nghi Hotel.

**Bus** The most exciting news for travellers was the opening of the border with Laos at Keo Nua Pass, 80km from Vinh. For more information about making this border crossing, see the Getting There & Away chapter.

Vinh bus station (Ben Xe Vinh) is on Le Loi St about 1km north of Vinh Market; the ticket office is open from 4.30 am to 5 pm daily. Express buses to Buon Ma Thuot,

Danang, Hanoi and Saigon depart every day at 5 am; express buses to Hanoi leave at other times of the day as well. Nonexpress buses link Vinh with virtually everywhere else.

**Train** Vinh Railway Station (Ga Vinh; ☎ 824-924) is 1km west of the intersection of Le Loi and Phan Boi Chau Sts, which is 1.5km north of Vinh Market. The *Reunification Express* trains stop here. For ticket prices, see the Train section in the Getting Around chapter.

**Car** Road distances from Vinh are as follows:

| | |
|---|---|
| Danang | 468km |
| Dong Hoi | 197km |
| Hanoi | 292km |
| Hué | 363km |
| Lao border | 87km |
| Thanh Hoa | 139km |

### Getting Around

Motorbike taxis charge about US$0.50 to most places in town.

Despite its small size, Vinh has three taxi companies: Phu Nguyen Taxi (☎ 833333), Quynh Ha Taxi (☎ 858585) and Viet Anh Taxi (☎ 843999).

## AROUND VINH
### Cua Lo

This is one of the three major beach resorts in the northern half of the country (which isn't saying much). The other two are at Sam Son and Do Son.

The beach is actually not bad – there's white sand, clean water and a grove of pine trees along the shore which provides some shade and wind break. But as a resort area, Cua Lo is far behind Vung Tau or Nha Trang. Nevertheless, if you're in the area and the weather is suitably warm and dry, Cua Lo could be worth a visit.

**Places to Stay** Hotel rates drop considerably during the winter months – the name of the game is negotiate (but do so politely). During the summer peak season there is little latitude for bargaining.

One place you might want to avoid is the *Hang Khong Guesthouse* (☎ 824421; 15 rooms). The main problem here is there's no hot water! Not that this lowers the price any – doubles cost US$20 to US$30.

The *Hon Ngu Hotel* (☎ 824127; 105 rooms) is a big white high-rise facing the beach. Run by the army with military cleanliness, it's currently the only place in town with satellite TV. Prices range from US$25 to US$60.

The *Pacific Hotel* (Khach San Thai Binh Duong; ☎ 824164; 72 rooms) is another big high-rise near the beach. Doubles are US$20 to US$60.

The *Vien Dieu Duong Hotel* (☎ 824122; 65 rooms) also occupies beachfront real estate. All rooms have hot water and cost US$15 to US$25.

Farther north along the beach is the *Guesthouse of Cua Lo Town* (Nha Khach Thi Cua Lo; ☎ 824541; 18 rooms). Prices in the peak season are US$20 to US$40.

**Getting There & Away** Cua Lo is 16km north-east of Vinh and can be reached easily by motorbike.

### Kim Lien

Just 14km north-west of Vinh is Ho Chi Minh's birthplace. The house in which he was born in 1890 is maintained as a sacred shrine and is a favourite pilgrimage spot for Vietnamese tourists. Ho's childhood home is a simple farmhouse made of bamboo and palm leaves, reflecting his humble background.

Actually there are two houses where Ho's family lived. The first house is in Sen (Lotus) Village, where Ho was born and raised as an infant. In 1895 the family sold this house and moved to Hué so that Ho's father could study. In 1901 the family returned and bought a house in Kim Lien, 2km from Sen Village; however, Ho remained behind in Hué so that he could attend secondary school.

Close to the second house in Kim Lien is a museum. The two houses and museum are open to the public daily, except Monday,

from 6.30 to 11 am and 2 to 5.30 pm. If you want to check on these times, call reception (☎ 825110). Admission to the houses is free, but you are obliged to buy a bouquet of flowers from the reception desk – place the flowers by the altar in Ho's home.

A placard inside the house tells some of the life story of Ho's mother (Hoang Thi Loan) and his father (Nguyen Sinh Sac). Unfortunately, all explanations are in Vietnamese and no English-speaking guides are available.

At the car park by the museum are quite a few vendors plugging the peanut candies for which Vinh is famous. If you haven't bought any yet, this is as good a place as any to stock up.

There is no public transport to Kim Lien, but it's easy enough to hire a motorbike or taxi in Vinh.

## THANH HOA

Thanh Hoa is the capital of Thanh Hoa Province. There is a large and attractive church on the northern outskirts of town.

Thanh Hoa Province was the site of the Lam Son Uprising (1418-28), in which Vietnamese forces led by Le Loi (later Emperor Ly Thai To) expelled the Chinese and re-established the country's independence.

Muong and Red Tai (Thai) hill tribes live in the western part of the province.

### Information

**Travel Agencies** Thanh Hoa Tourist (☎ 852-298, 852517) is the official government tourist authority for Thanh Hoa Province. The office is at 298 Quang Trung St.

### Places to Stay & Eat

The *Thanh Hoa Hotel* (☎ 852517; fax 852104; 50 rooms) has the market sewn up. It's on the west side of National Highway 1 in the centre of town. Rooms cost US$15 to US$50.

Soup shops, tea shops and a few restaurants can be found along National Highway 1, especially near the southern entrance to town.

## Getting There & Away

**Bus & Car** Thanh Hoa city is 502km from Hué, 139km from Vinh and 153km from Hanoi.

**Train** Thanh Hoa is a stop for the *Reunification Express* trains. For ticket prices, see the Train section in the Getting Around chapter.

## SAM SON BEACH

Sam Son is possibly the most popular beach resort in the north. It's too far from Hanoi for day trippers, but during summer the place is chock-a-block with weekenders escaping the oven-hot capital. During the winter, Sam Son is pretty much deserted and only a few hotels bother to stay open.

There are in fact two beaches here, separated by a rocky headland. The mean beach on the north side of the headland is where you'll find all the ugly high-rise hotels. The southern beach is mostly undeveloped, but it can still fill up with picnickers. The headland itself offers some decent hiking and scenic views, though the promontory has a military base and a sign (in English) telling you to keep out. The rest of the headland is a park and is open to the public. The area is notable for its pine forests, enormous granite boulders and sweeping views. Co Tien Pagoda is also in the park.

## Places to Stay

Most of Sam Son's ugly state-run hotels offer luxury-hotel prices without the luxury. Unfortunately, there is not yet much in the way of private accommodation. It's possible to negotiate discounts in winter, though it wouldn't make much point to visit at that time.

One place to avoid is the *Sam Son Guesthouse*. Staff wanted to take our 'ID cards and travel permits' just to answer questions about the room rates. This wasn't necessary and travel permits haven't been required since 1992. A sign on the edge of town (in English) welcomes visitors.

Happily, the staff at all the other hotels in town were courteous to a fault. The mammoth-sized *Huong Bien Hotel* (☎ 821272; 93 rooms) has satellite-TV-equipped rooms for US$20 to US$50. Very similar, though smaller, is the *Hoa Hong Hotel* (☎ 821548; 50 rooms), with rooms from US$20 to US$25.

The *Xay Dung Hotel* (☎ 821372) lacks satellite TV, but costs US$15 to US$45. On par is the *Ke Hoach Guesthouse* (☎ 821358; 48 rooms), with rooms from US$15 to US$38.

## Getting There & Away

Thanh Hoa is the provincial capital and main road and railway junction. It's an unexciting town, but it's only 16km from Sam Son, a short enough trip to do by motorbike.

## NINH BINH

Ninh Binh has evolved into a major travel centre in just the past couple of years. Its sudden transformation from sleepy backwater to tourist resort has little to do with Ninh Binh itself, but rather with its proximity to nearby Tam Coc, 9km away. See the following Around Ninh Binh section for more information on Tam Coc.

Although it is possible to visit Tam Coc as a day trip from Hanoi, many travellers prefer to spend the night in Ninh Binh and thus enjoy the scenery at a more leisurely pace.

## Places to Stay

The Ninh Binh police insist on taking both your passport and visa for registration purposes, and this has no doubt hurt the hotel business.

The *Star Hotel* (Khach San Ngoi Sao; ☎ 871522; fax 871200; eight rooms) is at 267 Tran Hung Dao Blvd. The rooms are fine and cost US$6 to US$28 depending on your need for air-con. The helpful management can book tours or rent motorbikes and give you instructions on where to go and what to see.

The *Thuy Anh Mini-Hotel* (☎ 871602; three rooms) is just across from the Star Hotel on Tran Hung Dao Blvd and is *not* recommended. There have been numerous complaints about the pushy staff who try to book you into tours (which as it turns out are not good value either).

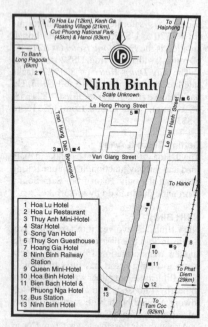

1 Hoa Lu Hotel
2 Hoa Lu Restaurant
3 Thuy Anh Mini-Hotel
4 Star Hotel
5 Song Van Hotel
6 Thuy Son Guesthouse
7 Hoang Gia Hotel
8 Ninh Binh Railway
  Station
9 Queen Mini-Hotel
10 Hoa Binh Hotel
11 Bien Bach Hotel &
   Phuong Nga Hotel
12 Bus Station
13 Ninh Binh Hotel

Kudos go to the *Queen Mini-Hotel* (Khach San Nu Hoang; ☎ 871874; four rooms) for being in the right place with the right facilities. The hotel is just 30m from Ninh Binh railway station, and rooms cost US$12 to US$18. The small restaurant here is also good, and the English-speaking staff helpful at arranging motorbike rentals and tours.

Just around the corner from the railway station on Le Dai Hanh St are three other good mini-hotels. Closest to the corner is *Hoa Binh Hotel* (☎ 873682; seven rooms), which costs US$12; at No 195 is the *Bien Bach Hotel* (☎ 871449; five rooms), which costs US$8 to US$15; and next door at No 197 is the *Phuong Nga Hotel* (☎ 871927), which is almost indistinguishable from its neighbour in terms of price or quality.

At 6 Le Dai Hanh St is the *Hoang Gia Hotel* (☎ 871396; 10 rooms), a busy private mini-hotel, with doubles for US$11.

Right in the centre of town is the *Ninh Binh Hotel* (☎ 871337; 15 rooms) at 2 Tran Hung Dao Blvd. Room rates are US$12 to US$15. Beware of the loud karaoke bar in the evening.

The newish *Thuy Son Guesthouse* (☎ 873-545; 22 rooms) is a state-run place with doubles for US$15 to US$20.

The *Song Van Hotel* (☎ 871975; 21 rooms) is close to the river on Le Hong Phong St. Rooms come in only one standard costing US$15.

The *Hoa Lu Hotel* (☎ 873684; 120 rooms) is by far the largest place in Ninh Binh. It's 300m north of town on Tran Hung Dao Blvd, and has doubles costing US$20 to US$45.

### Getting There & Away
Ninh Binh is a scheduled stop for the *Reunification Express* trains travelling between Hanoi and Saigon. For ticket prices, see the Train section in the Getting Around chapter.

## AROUND NINH BINH
### Tam Coc
Known to travellers as Vietnam's 'Halong Bay without the water', Tam Coc boasts breathtaking scenery. While Halong Bay (see the North-East chapter) has huge rock formation jutting out of the sea, Tam Coc has them jutting out of the rice paddies. There is a striking resemblance here to Guilin and Yangshuo, both major attractions in the People's Republic of China.

Tam Coc means 'three caves'. Hang Ca, the first cave, is 127m long; Hang Giua, the second cave, is 70m in length; and smallest is Hang Cuoi, the third cave, at only 40m.

The way to see Tam Coc is by rowboat on the Ngo Dong River. The boats actually row into the caves, and this is a very peaceful and scenic trip. The boat trip to all three caves takes from two to three hours, including the stops. One boat can seat only two passengers and costs US$3.50. The biggest problem is that the boat owners hassle you almost constantly to buy embroidery – if you don't want it, just say no.

An even more annoying scam are the boat vendors who paddle up alongside your boat and try to sell drinks. If you don't want any, they will 'suggest' (rather strongly) that you buy a Coke for the person rowing your boat. Many travellers do this and then later find that the oarsperson simply sells the Coke back to the drink vendors for half price.

On a sunny day bring sunscreen, a hat or umbrella to protect your skin – there's no shade in the boats. Alternatively, rent an umbrella at the pier for US$0.50.

Bich Dong is another cave with a built-in temple. It's about 2km past Tam Coc and getting there is easy enough. However, many foreigners shun the place because of the very aggressive souvenir vendors (mostly children). Admission to the cave temples is US$1.50.

There are many restaurants at Tam Coc. An excellent one we found is *Anh Dzung Restaurant* (☎ 860230).

In the area behind the restaurant is Van Lan village, known for its embroidery. You can watch the craftspeople make napkins, tablecloths, pillowcases, T-shirts etc. A lot of these items wind up being sold on Hanoi's Hang Gai St, but you can buy them more cheaply here directly from the person who creates them. It's also better to buy embroidery here rather than from the boat owners because you'll find a wider selection in the village and slightly lower prices.

Tam Coc is 9km south-west of Ninh Binh. Follow National Highway 1 south and then west at the Tam Coc turn-off. Many budget cafes in Hanoi book day trips to Tam Coc.

### Hoa Lu

The scenery here resembles nearby Tam Coc, though Hoa Lu has an interesting historical twist. Hoa Lu was the capital of Vietnam under the Dinh Dynasty (ruled 968-80) and the Early Le Dynasty (ruled 980-1009). The site was an attractive place for a capital city because of both its distance from China and the natural protection afforded by the region's bizarre landscape.

The ancient citadel of Hoa Lu, most of which has been destroyed, covered an area of about three sq km. The outer ramparts encompassed temples, shrines and the place where the king held court. The royal family lived in the inner citadel.

Yen Ngua mountain provides a scenic backdrop for Hoa Lu's two remaining temples. The first temple, Dinh Tien Hoang, was restored in the 17th century and is dedicated to the Dinh Dynasty. Out the front is the stone pedestal of a royal throne; inside are bronze bells and a statue of Emperor Dinh Tien Hoang with his three sons. The second temple, Dai Hanh (or Dung Van Nga), commemorates the rulers of the Early Le Dynasty. Inside the main hall are all sorts of drums, gongs, incense burners, candle holders and weapons; to the left of the entrance is a sanctuary dedicated to Confucius.

You must climb about 200 steps to reach the sanctuaries, but you'll be rewarded for your efforts with great views.

There is a US$2 entrance fee to Hoa Lu. There are Vietnamese-speaking guides at the temples who work for free (but you should offer a tip). Or you can hire an English-speaking guide, which costs at an outrageous US$15 per group.

Hoa Lu is 12km north of Ninh Binh. There is no public transport so most travellers get there by bicycle, motorbike or car.

### Banh Long Pagoda

While not spectacular, this Buddhist pagoda is only 6km from Ninh Binh and worth at least a quick look. From National Highway 1 (Tran Hung Dao Blvd in Ninh Binh), turn west on the road between the Hoa Lu Restaurant and the Hoa Lu Hotel.

### Kenh Ga Floating Village

Kenh Ga means 'Chicken Canal'. Chickens may not be a prominent part of the villagers' lives, but the canal certainly is. Everyone here lives on boats floating on the Hoang Long River. About the only other place in Vietnam where you can see anything like this is in the Mekong Delta. On the other hand, nowhere in the Mekong Delta will you find a stunning mountain backdrop as you find at Kenh Ga. Another difference – people in Kenh Ga row boats with their feet.

From what we've seen, this is the best place in northern Vietnam to see river life.

People here seem to spend most of their lives floating on water – children even commute to school by boat.

The village has a hot spring (suoi nuoc nong), where you can take a bath by pouring hot water over yourself with a bucket. There is a US$0.10 fee for entrance to the springs.

From the pier you can hire a rowboat to take you to/from the village for US$5. These boats can only hold three persons. For a more extensive look at the river, you can hire a motor launch – the tour covers about 6km and costs US$7 and the boat can hold 10 persons.

The locals are very friendly. The children gleefully shout 'tay oi' ('westerner') at every tourist they see, even Vietnamese tourists!

Kenh Ga Floating Village is 21km from Ninh Binh. Follow National Highway 1 north for 11km, then it's a 10km drive west to reach the boat pier.

## PHAT DIEM

Phat Diem (Kim Son) is the site of a cathedral remarkable for its vast dimensions and unique Sino-Vietnamese architecture. The vaulted ceiling is supported by massive wood columns almost 1m in diameter and 10m tall. In the lateral naves, there are a number of curious wood and stone sculptures. The main altar is made of a single block of granite. The outside of the church reaches a height of 16m.

During the French era, the cathedral was an important centre of Catholicism in the north and there was a seminary here. The 1954 division of Vietnam caused Catholics to flee to the south en masse and the cathedral was closed. It is now functional again and there are also several dozen other churches in the Phat Diem district. Current estimates are that about 120,000 Catholics live in the area.

The cathedral complex comprises a number of buildings, but the main one was completed in 1891. The whole project was founded by a Vietnamese priest named Six, whose tomb is in the square fronting the cathedral. Behind the main building is a large pile of limestone boulders – Father Six piled them up for a sink test to see if the boggy ground would support his planned empire. Apparently the test was a success.

Opposite the main entrance at the back of the cathedral is the bell tower. At its base lie two enormous stone slabs, one atop the other. Like all the other big carved stones here, these were transported from some 200km away with only primitive gear. What's interesting about these massive stone slabs is that their sole purpose was to provide a perch for the mandarins to sit and observe (no doubt with great amusement) the rituals of the Catholics at mass. Thus did the tradition of Vietnamese 'staring squads' become firmly entrenched!

Atop the cathedral's highest tower is such an enormous bell that Quasimodo's famous chimer at Notre Dame pales in comparison. This bell and all the other heavy metal were pushed and pulled to the cathedral's top via an enormous earth ramp. After construction was completed, the dirt was spread around the church grounds to make the whole site about 1m higher than the surrounding terrain. This has, no doubt, offered important protection against the occasional flood.

Near the main cathedral is a small chapel built of large carved stone blocks, and inside it's as cool as a cave. Also not far from the cathedral is a covered bridge dating from the late 19th century.

Hoards of Vietnamese tourists come to this place, few of whom are Catholic. For reasons we're not sure about, the Vietnamese are extremely curious about churches and Christianity in general. As one reader observed:

Vietnamese staring squads are alive and well. I went to a cathedral for midnight mass on Christmas Eve and found a number of Vietnamese and foreigners huddled on the front pews. Their presence seemed to provide great entertainment for the several thousand Vietnamese onlookers packed into the back of the building. There was a constant buzz of excitement among the rubbernecks, and a massive crush to the middle and even some pillar scaling feats in order to get a better view. The priest interrupted the service several times to try to control the crowd. In between we were able to catch a few lines of the Vietnamese priest delivering his sermon first in Vietnamese, then

French and finally English. Trilingual and very impressive, though his strong French accent made his English difficult to understand. I wasn't surprised to learn that some cathedrals in the south now only permit their congregation members to enter the building for Christmas midnight mass. Apparently, the priests issue members-only passes for the event.

## Getting There & Away

Phat Diem is 121km south of Hanoi and 29km south-east of Ninh Binh. Making the trip by motorbike from Ninh Binh is eminently feasible.

## CUC PHUONG NATIONAL PARK

Cuc Phuong National Park, established in 1962, is one of Vietnam's most important nature preserves. Though wildlife has suffered a precipitous decline in Vietnam in recent decades, the park's 222 sq km of primary tropical forest remain home to an amazing variety of animal and plant life, including 1967 species of flora from 217 families and 749 genera; 1800 species of insects from 30 orders and 200 families; 137 species of birds; 64 species of mammals; and 33 species of reptiles.

Among the extraordinary variety of life forms in the park are several species discovered here, including a tree known as *Bressiaopsis Cucphuongensis* and the endemic red-bellied squirrel *Callosciurus erythrinaceus Cucphuongensis*. The Rhesus macaque *(Macaca mullata)* can sometimes be seen in the forests. Sadly, once-common spotted deer *(Cevus nippon)* now only survive in the park's captive breeding programme.

In Con Moong Cave, one of the park's many grottoes, the stone tools of prehistoric humans have been discovered.

Cuc Phuong National Park, which is 70km from the sea, covers an area about 25km long and 11km wide in the provinces of Ninh Binh, Hoa Binh and Thanh Hoa. The elevation of the highest peak in the park is 648m. At the park's lower elevations, the climate is subtropical.

Ho Chi Minh personally took time off from the war in 1963 to dedicate this national park, Vietnam's first. He offered a short dedication speech:

Forest is gold. If we know how to conserve it well, it will be very precious. Destruction of the forest will lead to serious effects on both life and productivity.

A guide is not mandatory, but it would be foolish and risky to attempt a trek alone through the dense jungle. There are three-day treks to Hmong villages which can be arranged through travel agencies in Hanoi and Ninh Binh. The rangers are very environment-conscious and enthusiastic to protect wildlife from poaching and trees from illegal logging. A few hundred metres from the park's headquarters is a breeding and research centre for spotted deer. There are now attempts being made to reintroduce them into areas from which they were previously annihilated. There is also an experiment to determine if the deer can be bred for commercial meat production.

Poaching and habitat destruction is a constant headache for the rangers. Many native species, such as the black bear, wild cats, various birds and reptiles, have perished in the park due to human impact. In 1993 a ranger was murdered by the Hmong because he tried to stop them from logging in the park. The government responded by moving the villagers to another area farther from the park's boundary. However, the high birth rate among the minorities in this area assures that future conflicts are inevitable.

## Places to Stay

Park headquarters charges US$10 for a few basic rooms in a Muong-style house (shared toilet and cold showers) up to US$35 for upmarket (but sterile) rooms in its guesthouse.

## Getting There & Away

Cuc Phuong National Park is 45km from Ninh Binh. The turn-off is north of Ninh Binh and is the same highway that goes past the Kenh Ga Floating Village. There is no public transport on this route.

## THAI BINH

Rather few foreigners visit Thai Binh because it's not on National Highway 1. You're only likely to come here if you're following the spur route that connects Ninh Binh to Haiphong.

If you miss Thai Binh, you haven't missed much. The only sight of interest around here is nearby Keo Pagoda.

## Keo Pagoda

Keo Pagoda (Chua Keo) was founded in the 12th century to honour the Buddha and the monk Khong Minh Khong, who miraculously cured Emperor Ly Than Ton (ruled 1128-38) of leprosy. The finely carved wooden bell tower is considered a masterpiece of traditional Vietnamese architecture. The nearby dike is a good place to get a general view of the pagoda complex.

Keo Pagoda is in Thai Binh Province, 9.5km from the town of Thai Binh near Thai Bac.

# Hanoi

A city of lakes, shaded boulevards and verdant public parks where beggars fight over a plate of discarded noodles and prosperous shop owners exemplify Vietnam's new economic reforms.

Hanoi (population one million), capital of the Socialist Republic of Vietnam, is different things to different people. Most foreigners on a short visit find Hanoi to be slow paced, pleasant and even charming. Physically, it's a more attractive city than Saigon – there is less traffic, less noise, less pollution, more trees and more open space. Some have called it the Paris of the Orient – Parisians may find that either an insult or a compliment. Hanoi's centre is an architectural museum piece, its blocks of ochre buildings retaining the air of a provincial French town of the 1930s. The people of Hanoi are known for being more reserved – and at the same time more traditionally hospitable – than their southern compatriots.

Hanoi used to be notorious among travellers as a place to avoid. Many western visitors (both backpackers and business people) were routinely harassed by the police, especially at the airport, where officials would arbitrarily detain and fine foreigners as they were trying to leave.

The bad reputation that Hanoi earned by harassing foreigners and resisting economic reform caused most foreign investment to flow into Saigon and other places in the south. Resistance to reform is strongest among ageing officials, but geriatric revolutionaries in the prime of senility are being forcibly retired. The younger generation – with no romantic attachment to the past – is only interested in the side of the bread which is buttered. Attitudes have changed remarkably fast, and the Hanoi of today is dramatically different from what it was just five years ago. The foreigners have returned as tourists, business travellers, students and expatriates. Foreign investors are now looking at Hanoi with the same enthusiasm that only a few years ago was reserved exclusively for Saigon.

The first beneficiaries of the city's recent economic resurgence have been the shop and restaurant owners. No longer is a shopping trip in Hanoi a journey to a large state department store specialising in empty shelves. The colour and liveliness has returned to the streets (and unfortunately, so has the traffic). Buildings are being repaired and foreign companies are now investing in everything from joint-venture hotels to banks and telecommunications. Hanoi, and the rest of the north, has great potential to develop export-oriented manufacturing industries – a potential now only beginning to be realised.

## History
The site where Hanoi now stands has been inhabited since the Neolithic period. Emperor

Ly Thai To moved his capital here in 1010 AD, renaming the site Thang Long (City of the Soaring Dragon). Hanoi served as the capital of the Later Le Dynasty, founded by Le Loi, from its establishment in 1428 until 1788, when it was overthrown by Nguyen Hué, founder of the Tay Son Dynasty. The decision by Emperor Gia Long, founder of the Nguyen Dynasty, to rule from Hué relegated Hanoi to the status of a regional capital.

Over the centuries, Hanoi has borne a variety of names, including Dong Kinh (Eastern Capital), from which the Europeans derived the name they eventually applied to all of northern Vietnam, Tonkin. The city was named Hanoi (The City in a Bend of the River) by Emperor Tu Duc in 1831. From 1902 to 1953, Hanoi served as the capital of French Indochina.

Hanoi was proclaimed the capital of Vietnam after the August Revolution of 1945, but it was not until the Geneva Accords of 1954 that the Viet Minh, driven from the city by the French in 1946, were able to return. During the American War, US bombing destroyed parts of Hanoi and killed many hundreds of civilians; almost all the damage has since been repaired.

Whatever else Ho Chi Minh may have done, he created in Hanoi and much of the north a very effective police state. For four decades, the people of Hanoi and the north have suffered under a regime characterised by the ruthless exercise of police power; anonymous denunciations by a huge network of secret informers; the detention without trial of monks, priests, landowners and anyone else seen as a potential threat to the government; and the blacklisting of dissidents and their children and their children's children. The combined legacy of human-rights violations and economic turmoil produced a steady haemorrhage of refugees, even into China despite that country's less than impressive human-rights record. Ironically, the political and economic situation has turned around so sharply in the 1990s that Vietnamese officials now worry about an invasion of refugees from China.

## Orientation

Hanoi sprawls along the banks of the Red River (Song Hong), which is spanned by two bridges, the old Long Bien Bridge (now used only by non-motorised vehicles and pedestrians) and the new Chuong Duong Bridge.

The attractive centre of Hanoi is built around Hoan Kiem Lake. Just to the north of this lake is the Old Quarter (known to the French as the Cité Indigène). The Old Quarter is characterised by narrow streets whose names change every one or two blocks. Tourists mostly like to base themselves in this part of town.

To the west of the centre is Ho Chi Minh's Mausoleum, and this neighbourhood is where most of the foreign embassies are found. Some new joint-venture hotels have sprung up in the area, including the mammoth Daewoo Hotel (currently Hanoi's largest and most expensive). West Lake (Ho Tay), Hanoi's largest lake, is north of Ho Chi Minh's Mausoleum, and this too is seeing much recent buildup of tourist-oriented facilities.

## Information

**Travel Agencies** There are plenty of travel agencies in Hanoi, both government and private, which can provide cars, book air tickets and extend your visa. Some of these places charge the same as Vietnam Tourism, while others are only half the price. Any of the cafes in the following list should be good for a budget backpacker tour. If you'd like something a little more upmarket, we're willing to give Ann Tours a plug, but the others should be OK too.

New places open all the time, so the following list is not engraved in stone. With that caveat in mind, consider the following:

Ann Tours
   26 Yet Kieu St (☎ 822-0018; fax 832-3866)
Best Service Travel
   72 Ba Trieu St (☎ 826-2386; fax 826-9285)
Darling Cafe
   33 Hang Quat St (☎ 826-9386; fax 825-6562)
ECCO Voyages
   50A Ba Trieu St (☎ 825-4615; fax 826-6519)
Ecomtour
   15 Trang Thi St (☎ 825-4935)

Especen
79E Hang Trong St (☎ 826-6856; fax 826-9612)
Exotissimo Travel
26 Tran Nhat Duat St (☎ 828-2150; 828-2146)
Hanoi Tourism
18 Ly Thuong Kiet St (☎ 826-6714; 825-4209)
Hanoi Youth Tourism
14A Phan Chu Trinh St (☎ 825-4628; fax 824-6463)
Lotus Cafe
42V Ly Thuong Kiet St (☎ 826-8642)
Manfields TOSERCO
102 Hang Trong St (☎ 826-9444; fax 826-9485)
Meeting Cafe
59B Ba Trieu St (☎ 825-8812)
OSC-First Holiday
22 Phan Chu Trinh St (☎ 824-0464; fax 826-9219)
Queen Cafe
65 Hang Bac St (☎ 826-0860)
Red River Cafe
73 Hang Bo St (☎ 826-8427)
Vietnam Tourism
30A Ly Thuong Kiet St (☎ 826-4154; fax 825-7583)

**Visas** The immigration police office is on Hang Bai St. In the majority of cases, however, the police will refuse to grant your visa extension directly and refer you to a travel agency.

**Money** The main branch of Vietcombank is at 47-49 Ly Thai To St. This stately building is one of the most impressive in the city and could be a tourist attraction in itself. There are numerous smaller branches of Vietcombank scattered around town.

Foreign or joint-venture banks with fully functioning branches (as opposed to useless representative offices) can be found, but all are required to impose significantly higher fees than Vietcombank. The current lineup includes:

ANZ Bank
14 Le Thai To St (western shore of Hoan Kiem Lake; ☎ 825-8190; fax 825-8188)
Bank of America
27 Ly Thuong Kiet St (☎ 825-0003; fax 824-9322)
Barclays Bank
33A Pham Ngu Lao St (☎ 825-0907; fax 825-0789)

Chinfon Commercial Bank
55 Quang Trung St (☎ 825-0555; fax 825-0566)
Citibank
17 Ngo Quyen St (☎ 825-1950; fax 824-3960)
Credit Lyonnais
10 Trang Thi St (☎ 825-8102; 826-0080)
Hongkong Bank
8 Tran Hung Dao St (☎ 826-9994; fax 826-9941)
ING Bank
International Centre Building, 17 Ngo Quyen St (☎ 824-6888; 826-9216)
Standard Chartered
27 Ly Thai To St (☎ 825-8970; fax 825-8880)

**Post & Communications** The main post office (Buu Dien Trung Vong; ☎ 825-7036; fax 825-3525), which occupies a full city block facing Hoan Kiem Lake, is at 75 Dinh Tien Hoang St (between Dinh Le and Le Thach Sts). The entrance in the middle of the block leads to the postal services windows where you can send letters, pick up domestic packages and purchase philatelic items; the postal services section is open from 6.30 am to 8 pm.

The same entrance leads to the telex, telegram and domestic telephone office (☎ 825-5918), which is to the left as you enter the building. Telex and domestic telephone services are available from 6.30 am to 8 pm; telegrams can be sent 24 hours a day.

International telephone calls can be made and faxes sent from the office (☎ 825-2030) on the corner of Dinh Tien Hoang and Dinh Le Sts, which is open daily from 7.30 am to 9.30 pm.

Private document and parcel carriers in Hanoi include:

DHL
49 Nguyen Thai Hoc St (☎ 846-7020; fax 823-5698)
Federal Express
6C Dinh Le St (☎ 824-9054; fax 825-2479)
TNT
15 Ly Nam De St (☎ 843-4535; fax 843-4550)
UPS
4C Dinh Le St (☎ 824-6483; fax 824-6464)

**Bookshops** The Hanoi Bookstore (Hieu Sach Hanoi; ☎ 824-1616), 34 Trang Tien St, is the largest bookstore in town; however, most of what it stocks is in Vietnamese. The

# Hanoi

Red River (Song Hong)

West Lake (Ho Tay)

To Ho Tay Villas (5.5km)
& Dog Restaurants (10km)

To Lich River

Buoi Street

Nghi Tam Street

Truc Bach Lake

Trang Thanh Street

Yen Phu Street

Long Bien Bridge

To Gia Lam Bus
Station (2km)
& Gia Lam Airport

To Haiphong (103km)
& Halong Bay (165km)

Chuong
Duong
Bridge

Bach Dang Street

Old Quarter

Hoan
Kiem
Lake

Le Duan Street

Quan Thanh Street

Phan Dinh Phung Street

Hoang Dieu Street

Dien Bien Phu Street

Ton That Dam St

Hung Vuong Street

Quoc Tu Giam Street

Ton Duc Thang Street

Kham Thien Street

Thuy Khue Street

Hoang Hoa Tham Street

Doi Can Le Street

Son Tay St

Nguyen Thai Hoc Street

Cat Linh Street

See North-Central Hanoi Map

Kim Ma Street

Giang Vo Street

La Thanh Street

Giang Vo Lake

7

8

15

14

16

17

Ngoc Khanh Street

Lieu Giai Street

Giang Vo Street

Lang Trung Street

9

12

13

2

3

4

5

6

1

10

11

0    250    500 m

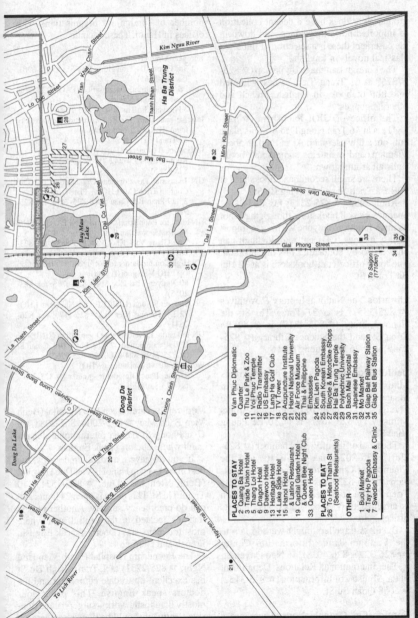

**PLACES TO STAY**
2  Quang Ba Hotel
3  Trade Union Hotel
5  Thang Loi Hotel
6  Dragon Hotel
9  Daewoo Hotel
14  Heritage Hotel
15  Lake Side Hotel
15  Hanoi Hotel
    & Latino Restaurant
19  Capital Garden Hotel
    & Queen Bee Night Club
33  Queen Hotel

**PLACES TO EAT**
26  To Hien Thanh St
    (Seafood Restaurants)

**OTHER**
1  Buoi Market
4  Tay Ho Pagoda
7  Swedish Embassy & Clinic
8  Van Phuc Diplomatic
   Quarter
10  Thu Le Park & Zoo
11  Voi Phuc Temple
12  Radio Transmitter
13  US Embassy
17  Lang Ha Golf Club
18  TV Tower
20  Acupuncture Institute
21  Hanoi National University
22  Air Force Museum
23  Thai & Philippine
    Embassies
24  Kim Lien Pagoda
25  South Korean Embassy
27  Bicycle & Motorbike Shops
28  Hai Ba Trung Statue
29  Polytechnic University
30  Bach Mai Hospital
31  Japanese Embassy
32  Mo Market
34  Giap Bat Railway Station
35  Giap Bat Bus Station

ground floor does have a decent collection of imported news magazines, and down in the basement there is a selection of imported classical novels in English.

The Foreign Language Bookshop (☎ 825-77376) at 61 Trang Tien St has a limited selection of books in English, French and other languages.

The office of GIOI Publishers (☎ 825-3841) is at 46 Tran Hung Dao St. This place puts out a few useful books in English about Vietnam, and maintains some small bookstalls all around town.

There are small secondhand bookshops at 80B Ba Trieu St and 42 Hang Bo St.

Xunhasaba (☎ 825-2313; fax 825-9881) operates a small bookstore, though that's not its main function. Anyone wishing to import books, movies, CDs etc into Vietnam can only do so by contacting this organisation. The main office-cum-bookstore is at 32 Hai Ba Trung St.

**Libraries** The National Library & Archives (☎ 825-3357) is at 31 Trang Thi St; the Hanoi Library (☎ 825-4817) is at 47 Ba Trieu St; and the Science Library (☎ 825-2345) is at 26 Ly Thuong Kiet St.

**Useful Organisations** The Foreign Affairs Ministry Consular Office is at 6 Chu Van An St, near Ho Chi Minh's Mausoleum. The Foreign Press Centre of the Foreign Affairs Ministry (☎ 825-4697) is at 10 Le Phung Hieu St.

The head office of Vietcochamber (☎ 825-2961, 825-3023; fax 825-6446) and the Chamber of Commerce & Industry of Vietnam (☎ 826-6235; fax 825-6446) is at 33 Ba Trieu St. The Trade Service Company, which is attached to Vietcochamber, also has its offices here.

Business travellers might want to talk to the Vietnam Trade Information Centre (☎ 826-3227, 826-4038), 46 Ngo Quyen St.

The International Relations Department of the Ministry of Information (☎ 825-3152) is at 58 Quan Su St.

**Foreign-Aid Organisations** There are a

number of foreign-aid organisations with offices in Hanoi. These include:

European Union (EU)
   3rd Floor, 104 Tran Hung Dao St (☎ 821-6961; fax 821-5361)
Food & Agricultural Organisation (FAO; TC Luong Thuc Va Nong Nghiep)
   3 Nguyen Gia Thieu St (☎ 825-7239)
International Bank for Reconstruction & Development (IBRD – World Bank)
   53 Tran Phu St (☎ 843-2461; fax 843-2471)
International Monetary Fund (IMF)
   Room 308, 12 Trang Thi St (☎ 824-3351; fax 825-1885)
UN Industrial Development Organisation (UNDP; Chuong Trinh Cua LHQ Ve Phat Trien)
   25-29 Phan Boi Chau St (☎ 825-7495; fax 825-9267)
UN Fund for Population Control (UNFPA; Quy LHQ Ve Hoat Dong Dan So)
   Khu Giang Vo – Khoi 3 (☎ 823-6632; fax 823-2822)
UN High Commissioner for Refugees (UNHCR; Cao Uy LHQ Ve Nguoi Ti Nan)
   60 Nguyen Thai Hoc St (☎ 825-6785; fax 823-2055)
UN Children's Fund (UNICEF; Quy Nhi Dong LHQ)
   72 Ly Thuong Kiet St (☎ 826-1170; fax 826-2641)
UN Industrial Development Organisation (UNIDO)
   UNDP compound, 27-29 Phan Boi Chau St (☎ 825-7495, 824-9000; fax 825-9267)
World Health Organisation (WHO)
   2A Van Phuc Diplomatic Quarter (☎ 825-7901; fax 823-3301)

**Medical Services** Bach Mai Hospital (Benh Vien Bach Mai; ☎ 852-2004, 852-2083) on Giai Phong St has an international department where doctors speak English.

If you do have a medical emergency, the best place to go in Hanoi is Viet Duc Hospital (Benh Vien Viet Duc; ☎ 825-3531), 40 Tranh Thi St. This place is open 24 hours and can do emergency surgery. Another plus is that it's located in the central area where most travellers stay. Doctors speak English, French and German.

The Friendship Hospital (Benh Vien Huu Nghi; ☎ 825-2231) at 1 Tran Khanh Du St has excellent up-to-date equipment and the doctors speak English. This place does mostly diagnostic work – surgery and extensive treatment should be done elsewhere.

The Swedish Clinic (☎ 825-2464) is opposite the Swedish embassy in the Van Phuc Diplomatic Quarter. You don't have to be Swedish to come here, but the consultation fee of US$80 will put off many travellers. However, if you have travel insurance, you might be covered. The doctor is on call 24 hours.

The French embassy (☎ 825-2719), 49 Ba Trieu St, operates a 24-hour clinic for French nationals only.

Asia Emergency Assistance (☎ 821-3555; fax 821-3523) has a clinic at 4 Tran Hung Dao St. Resident foreigners can contact it for information about a long-term medical and emergency evacuation plan. A similar plan is offered by International SOS Assistance (☎ 824-2866).

## Lakes, Temples & Pagodas

**One Pillar Pagoda** Hanoi's famous One Pillar Pagoda (Chua Mot Cot) was built by the Emperor Ly Thai Tong, who ruled from 1028 to 1054. According to the annals, the heirless emperor dreamed that he had met Quan The Am Bo Tat (Goddess of Mercy), who, while seated on a lotus flower, handed him a male child. Ly Thai Tong then married a young peasant girl he met by chance and had a son and heir by her. To express his gratitude for this event, he constructed the One Pillar Pagoda in 1049.

The One Pillar Pagoda, built of wood on a single stone pillar 1.25m in diameter, is designed to resemble a lotus blossom, symbol of purity, rising out of a sea of sorrow. One of the last acts of the French before quitting Hanoi in 1954 was to destroy the One Pillar Pagoda; the structure was rebuilt by the new government. The One Pillar Pagoda is on Ong Ich Kiem St near Ho Chi Minh's Mausoleum.

**Dien Huu Pagoda** The entrance to Dien Huu Pagoda is a few metres from the staircase of the One Pillar Pagoda. This small pagoda, which surrounds a garden courtyard, is one of the most delightful in Hanoi. The old wood and ceramic statues on the altar are very different from those common in the south. An elderly monk can often be seen

performing acupuncture on the front porch of the pagoda.

**Temple of Literature** The Temple of Literature (Van Mieu) is a pleasant retreat from the streets of Hanoi. It was founded in 1070 – four years after the Norman invasion of England – by Emperor Ly Thanh Tong, who dedicated it to Confucius (in Vietnamese, Khong Tu) in order to honour scholars and men of literary accomplishment.

The temple constitutes a rare example of well-preserved traditional Vietnamese architecture and is well worth a visit.

Vietnam's first university was established here in 1076 to educate the sons of mandarins. In 1484 Emperor Le Thanh Tong ordered that stelae be erected in the temple premises recording the names, places of birth and achievements of men who received doctorates in each triennial examination, beginning in 1442. Though 116 examinations were held between 1442 and 1778, when the practice was discontinued, only 82 stelae are extant. In 1802 Emperor Gia Long transferred the National University to his new capital, Hué. Major repairs were last carried out here in 1920 and 1956.

The Temple of Literature consists of five courtyards divided by walls. The central pathways and gates between courtyards were reserved for the king. The walkways on one side were for the use of administrative mandarins; those on the other side were for military mandarins.

The main entrance is preceded by a gate on which an inscription requests that visitors dismount their horses before entering. Khue Van Pavilion, which is at the far side of the second courtyard, was constructed in 1802 and is considered a fine example of Vietnamese architecture. The 82 stelae, considered the most precious artefacts in the temple, are arrayed to either side of the third enclosure; each stele sits on a stone tortoise.

The Temple of Literature is 2km west of Hoan Kiem Lake. The complex, which is 350m by 70m, is bounded by Nguyen Thai Hoc, Ton Duc Thang, Quoc Tu Giam and Van Mieu Sts. Enter from Quoc Tu Giam St.

HANOI

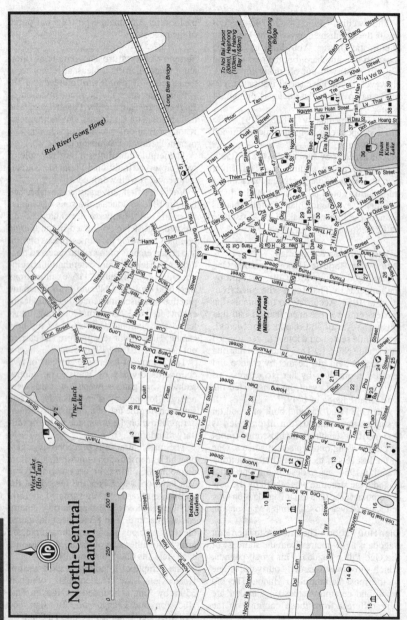

North-Central Hanoi

West Lake (Ho Tay)

Red River (Song Hong)

Trac Bach Lake

Hoan Kiem Lake

Hanoi Citadel (Military Area)

Botanical Gardens

Long Bien Bridge

Chuong Duong Bridge

To Noi Bai Airport (30km), Haiphong (103km) & Halong Bay (165km)

HANOI

0    250    500 m

| PLACES TO STAY | | | |
|---|---|---|---|
| 4 | Planet Hotel & Hang Nga Hotel | 30 | Red River Café |
| 29 | Red River Hotel | 31 | Tin Tin Bar & Café |
| 33 | Hoa Long Hotel & Chinese Restaurant | 32 | Darling Café |
| 35 | Trang An Hotel | 42 | Lonely Planet Café |
| 38 | Energy Hotel & Hanoi Star Mart | 43 | Queen Café |
| 39 | Binh Minh Hotel | | |
| 41 | Royal Hotel | | |
| 45 | Anh Dao Hotel | | |
| 52 | Galaxy Hotel | | |
| 53 | Chains First Eden Hotel | | |
| 54 | Anh Hotel II | | |

| OTHER | |
|---|---|
| 1 | Tran Quoc Pagoda |
| 3 | Quan Thanh Temple |
| 5 | Cua Bac Church |
| 6 | Presidential Palace |
| 7 | Ho Chi Minh's Stilt House |
| 8 | Ho Chi Minh's Mausoleum |
| 9 | Ba Dinh Square |
| 10 | One Pillar Pagoda & Dien Huu Pagoda |
| 11 | Ho Chi Minh Museum |
| 12 | Canadian Embassy |
| 13 | Russian Embassy |
| 14 | Kim Ma Bus Station (City Buses) |
| 15 | Thong Tin Museum |
| 16 | Hanoi Stadium |

| PLACES TO EAT | |
|---|---|
| 2 | Shrimp Cakes Restaurant |
| 25 | Kem Tra My (Ice Cream) |
| 26 | Pastry & Yoghurt Shop |

| | |
|---|---|
| 17 | Temple of Literature |
| 18 | Fine Arts Museum |
| 19 | Chinese Embassy |
| 20 | Flag Tower |
| 21 | Army Museum |
| 22 | Lenin Park |
| 23 | Sunset Pub |
| 24 | German Embassy |
| 27 | St Joseph Cathedral |
| 28 | Hang Da Market |
| 34 | Gold Cock Bar, Polite Pub & Redwoods |
| 36 | Ngoc Son Temple |
| 37 | Water Puppet Theatre |
| 40 | Shoe Market |
| 44 | Royal Palace Night Club |
| 46 | Roxy Bar |
| 47 | 'Chinatown' |
| 48 | Memorial House |
| 49 | Dong Xuan Market |
| 50 | Dai Dong Centropell (Dance Hall) |
| 51 | Long Bien Bus Depot (City Buses) |

It is open Tuesday to Sunday from 8.30 to 11.30 am and 1.30 to 4.30 pm; the entrance fee is US$0.50. There is a small gift shop inside the temple.

**Hoan Kiem Lake** Hoan Kiem Lake is an enchanting body of water right in the heart of Hanoi. Legend has it that in the mid-15th century, Heaven gave Emperor Ly Thai To (Le Loi) a magical sword which he used to drive the Chinese out of Vietnam. One day after the war, while out boating, he came upon a giant golden tortoise swimming on the surface of the water; the creature grabbed the sword and disappeared into the depths of the lake. Since that time, the lake has been known as Ho Hoan Kiem (Lake of the Restored Sword) because the tortoise restored the sword to its divine owners.

The tiny Tortoise Pagoda, topped with a red star, is on an islet in the middle of the lake; it is often used as an emblem of Hanoi. Every morning around 6 am, local residents can be seen around Hoan Kiem Lake doing their traditional morning exercises, jogging and playing badminton.

**Ngoc Son Temple** Ngoc Son (Jade Mountain) Temple, founded in the 18th century, is on an island in the northern part of Hoan Kiem Lake. Surrounded by water and shaded by trees, it is a delightfully quiet place to rest. The temple is dedicated to the scholar Van Xuong, General Tran Hung Dao (who defeated the Mongols in the 13th century) and La To, patron saint of physicians.

Ngoc Son Temple is reached via wooden The Huc (Rising Sun) Bridge, painted red, which was constructed in 1885. To the left of the gate stands an obelisk whose top is shaped like a paintbrush. The temple is open daily from 8 am to 5 pm; the entrance fee is US$0.10.

**West Lake** Two legends explain the origins of West Lake (Ho Tay), also known as the Lake of Mist and the Big Lake. According to one, West Lake was created when the Dragon King drowned an evil nine-tailed fox in his lair, which was in a forest on this site. Another legend relates that in the 11th century, a Vietnamese Buddhist monk, Khong Lo, rendered a great service to the emperor of China, who rewarded him with a vast quantity of bronze from which he cast a huge bell. The sound of the bell could be heard all the way

HANOI

to China, where the Golden Buffalo Calf, mistaking the ringing for its mother's call, ran southward, trampling on the site of Ho Tay and turning it into a lake.

In reality, the lake was created when the Red River overflowed its banks. Indeed, the Red River has changed its course numerous times, alternately flooding some areas and causing silt buildup (which creates new land). The flood problem has been partially controlled by building dikes. The highway along the east side of West Lake is built atop such a dike.

The lake was once ringed with magnificent palaces and pavilions. These were destroyed in the course of various feudal wars. The circumference of West Lake is about 13km.

The **Tran Quoc Pagoda** is on the shore of West Lake just off Thanh Nien St, which divides West Lake from Truc Bach Lake. A stele here dating from 1639 tells the history of this site. The pagoda was rebuilt in the 15th century and in 1842. There are a number of monks' funerary monuments in the garden. This is one of Vietnam's oldest pagodas.

There are already a number of luxurious villas around West Lake, and you can expect more soon. Foreign investors see this as a likely spot for hotel development and are falling over each other to sign joint-venture agreements so the facilities can be completed before the expected floodtide of tourists arrives.

**Truc Bach Lake** Truc Bach (White Silk) Lake is separated from West Lake by Thanh Nien St, which is lined with flame trees. In the 18th century, the Trinh lords built a palace on this site; it was later turned into a reformatory for deviant royal concubines, who were condemned to weave a very fine white silk.

The **Quan Thanh Temple** (Den Quan Thanh) is on the shore of Truc Bach Lake near the intersection of Thanh Nein and Quan Thanh Sts. The temple, shaded by huge trees, was established during the Ly Dynasty (ruled 1010 to 1225) and was dedicated to Tran Vo (God of the North), whose symbols of power are the tortoise and the snake. A bronze statue and bell here date from 1677.

**Tay Ho Pagoda** The Tay Ho Pagoda (Phu Tay Ho) is the most popular spot for worship in Hanoi. Throngs of people come here on the first and 15th day of each lunar month in the hopes of decreasing risk and receiving good fortune.

**Ambassadors' Pagoda** The Ambassadors' Pagoda (Quan Su; ☎ 825-2427) is the official centre of Buddhism in Hanoi, attracting quite a crowd – mostly old women – on holidays. During the 17th century, there was a guesthouse here for the ambassadors of Buddhist countries. Today, there are about a dozen monks and nuns at the Ambassadors' Pagoda. Next to the pagoda is a store selling Buddhist ritual objects.

The Ambassadors' Pagoda is at 73 Quan Su St (between Ly Thuong Kiet and Tran Hung Dao Sts); it is open to the public every day from 7.30 to 11.30 am and 1.30 to 5.30 pm.

**Hai Ba Trung Temple** The Hai Ba Trung Temple, founded in 1142, is 2km south of Hoan Kiem Lake on Tho Lao St. A statue here shows the two Trung sisters (1st century AD) kneeling with their arms raised, as if to address a crowd. Some people say the statue shows the sisters, who had been proclaimed queens of the Vietnamese, about to dive into a river in order to drown themselves, which they are said to have done rather than surrender following their defeat at the hands of the Chinese.

### Ho Chi Minh's Mausoleum

In the tradition of Lenin and Stalin before him and Mao after him, the final resting place of Ho Chi Minh is a glass sarcophagus set deep in the bowels of a monumental edifice that has become a site of pilgrimage. Ho Chi Minh's Mausoleum – built despite the fact that in his will, Ho requested to be cremated – was constructed between 1973 and 1975 of native materials gathered from all over Vietnam; the roof and peristyle are said to evoke either a traditional communal house or a lotus flower – to many tourists it looks like a cold concrete cubicle with columns. While reviewing parades and ceremonies taking place on the grassy expanses of Ba Dinh Square, high-ranking party and government leaders stand in front of the mausoleum.

Ho Chi Minh's Mausoleum is open to the public daily from 8 to 11 am, except Monday and Friday. The mausoleum is closed for three months a year (usually from 5 September to early December) while Ho Chi Minh's embalmed corpse is in Russia for maintenance. Foreigners do not have to queue as the Vietnamese do – go directly to the registration desk.

Photography is permitted outside the building but not inside. All visitors must register and check their bags and cameras at a reception hall on Chua Mot Cot St; if possible, bring your passport for identification. Soundtracks for a 20-minute video about Ho Chi Minh are available in Vietnamese, English, French, Khmer, Lao, Russian and Spanish.

Honour guards will accompany you as you march single-file from near reception to the mausoleum entrance. Inside the building, more guards wearing snowy white bleached military uniforms are stationed at intervals of five paces, giving an eerily authoritarian aspect to the macabre spectacle of the embalmed, helpless body with its wispy white hair. The whole place has a spooky 'sanitised for your protection' atmosphere.

The following rules are strictly applied to all visitors to the mausoleum:

- People wearing shorts, tank-tops etc will not be admitted.
- Nothing (including day packs and cameras) may be taken into the mausoleum.
- A respectful demeanour must be maintained at all times.

- For obvious reasons of decorum, photography is absolutely prohibited inside the mausoleum.
- It is forbidden to put your hands in your pockets.
- Hats must be taken off inside the mausoleum building. Although the rules do not explicitly say so, it is suggested that you don't ask the guards 'Is he dead?'

Many of the visitors are groups of students, and it's interesting to watch their reactions to Ho and to discuss it with them. Most show deep respect and admiration for Ho. Though Vietnamese as a whole are mostly disappointed with Communism, few (at least the younger generation) show any hostility or bitterness towards Ho himself. He is seen as the liberator of the Vietnamese people from colonialism, and Vietnam's subsequent economic and political mismanagement are viewed as the misdoings of Ho's comrades and successors. Of course, this view is reinforced by the educational system which only emphasises Ho's deeds and accomplishments.

If you're lucky, you'll catch the 'Changing of the Guard' outside Ho's Mausoleum – the amount of pomp and ceremony rivals the British equivalent at Buckingham Palace.

### Ho Chi Minh's Stilt House

Behind the Ho Chi Minh's Mausoleum is a stilt house (Nha San Bac Ho) where Ho lived on and off from 1958 to 1969. The house is built on stilts in the style of Vietnam's ethnic minorities, and has been preserved just as Ho left it. It's set in a well-tended garden next to a carp-filled pond. Just how much time Ho actually spent here is questionable – the house would have made a tempting target for US bombers had it been suspected that Ho could be found here.

Near Ho's stilt house is the Presidential Palace, a beautifully restored colonial building constructed in 1906 as the Palace of the Governor General of Indochina. The palace is now used for official receptions.

### Museums

In addition to the usual two-hour lunch break, it's worth knowing that almost all of Hanoi's museums are closed on Monday.

HANOI

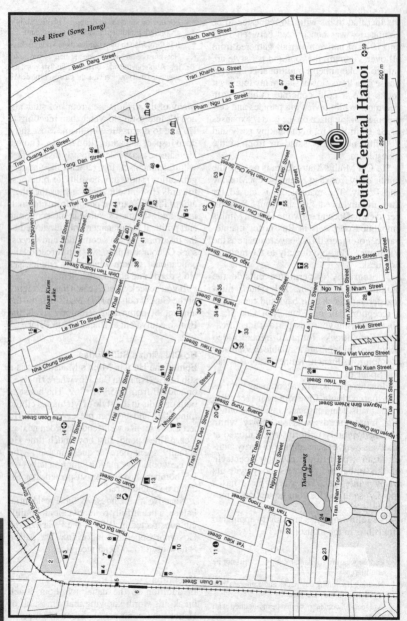

# South-Central Hanoi

Red River (Song Hong)

Bach Dang Street

Bach Dang Street

Tran Khanh Du Street

Pham Ngu Lao Street

Hoan Kiem Lake

Thien Quang Lake

HANOI

| PLACES TO STAY | | 38 | Bodega Café | 30 | Ham Long Church |
|---|---|---|---|---|---|
| 4 | Dong Loi Hotel | 53 | Hué Restaurant | 32 | French Embassy |
| 5 | Mango Hotel | | | 34 | Immigration Police |
| 8 | Saigon Hotel | **OTHER** | | 35 | Thang 8 Cinema |
| 9 | Hotel 30/4 | 2 | Cua Nam Market | 36 | New Zealand |
| 10 | Thu Do Hotel | 3 | Metal Night Club | | Embassy |
| 15 | Especen Hotel | 6 | Hanoi Railway Station | 37 | Women's Museum |
| 18 | Lotus Guesthouse | 7 | Fansland Cinema | 39 | Post Office |
| 26 | Madison Hotel | 11 | Ann Tours | 40 | Hanoi Optic |
| 41 | Trang Tien Hotel | 12 | Australian Embassy | 43 | Hanoi Bookstore |
| 42 | Dan Chu Hotel | 13 | Ambassadors' Pagoda | 45 | Vietcombank |
| 44 | Sofitel Metropole | 14 | Viet Duc Hospital | 47 | Revolutionary |
| | Hotel | 16 | Pacific Airlines & | | Museum |
| 46 | Tong Dan | | National Library | 48 | Municipal Theatre |
| | Guesthouse | 17 | Vietnam Airlines | 49 | History Museum |
| 54 | Army Hotel & | 19 | Pear Tree Pub | 50 | Geology Museum |
| | Jackfruit Tree Pub | 20 | Cambodian Embassy | 51 | The Verandah Bar |
| 55 | De Syloia Hotel | 21 | Lao Embassy | | & Café |
| | | | Consular Section | 52 | UK Embassy |
| **PLACES TO EAT** | | 22 | Lao Embassy | 56 | AEA Clinic |
| 1 | Cam Chi St | 23 | Kim Lien Bus Depot | 57 | Foreign Language |
| | (Restaurant Alley) | | (City Buses) | | College |
| 27 | Mai Hac De St | 24 | Top Disco Club | 58 | Border Guard |
| | (Restaurant Street) | 25 | VIP Club | | Museum |
| 31 | Meeting Café | 28 | Hanoi Star Mart | 59 | Friendship |
| 33 | Orient Café | 29 | Hom Market | | Hospital |

**Ho Chi Minh Museum** The Ho Chi Minh Museum (Bao Tang Ho Chi Minh) is divided into two sections, 'Past' and 'Future'. You start in the past and move to the future by walking in a clockwise direction downwards through the museum, starting at the right-hand side once at the top of the stairs. The displays are very modern and all have a message (eg peace, happiness, freedom).

It's probably worth taking an English-speaking guide since some of the symbolism is hard to figure out (did Ho Chi Minh have a cubist period?). The 1958 Ford Edsel bursting through the wall (a US commercial failure to symbolise the USA's military failure) is a knockout.

The museum is the huge cement structure next to Ho Chi Minh's Mausoleum. Photography is forbidden. Upon entering, all bags and cameras must be left at reception.

The museum is open daily from 8 to 11 am and 1.30 to 4.30 pm.

**Army Museum** The Army Museum (Bao Tang Quan Doi) is on Dien Bien Phu St; it is open daily. Outside, Soviet and Chinese weap-onry supplied to the North are on display alongside French and US-made weapons captured in the Franco-Viet Minh War and the American War. The centrepiece is a Soviet-built MiG-21 jet fighter triumphant amid the wreckage of French aircraft downed at Dien Bien Phu and a US F-111. The displays include scale models of various epic battles from Vietnam's long military history, including Dien Bien Phu and the capture of Saigon.

Next to the Army Museum is the hexagonal **Flag Tower**, which has become one of the symbols of the city.

**History Museum** The History Museum (Bao Tang Lich Su), once the museum of the École Française d'Extrême Orient, is one block east of the Municipal Theatre at 1 Pham Ngu Lao St. The building, constructed of reinforced concrete, was completed in 1930.

Exhibits include artefacts from Vietnam's prehistory (Palaeolithic and Neolithic periods); proto-Vietnamese civilisations (1st and 2nd millennia BC); the Dong Son culture (3rd century BC to 3rd century AD); the Oc-Eo (Funan) culture of the Mekong Delta (1st to 6th century AD); the Indianised kingdom of Champa (2nd to 15th century); the Khmer kingdoms; various Vietnamese dynasties and their resistance to Chinese attempts at domination; the struggle against the French; and the history of the Communist Party.

**Revolutionary Museum** The Revolutionary Museum (Bao Tang Cach Mang) at 25 Tong Dan St presents the history of the Vietnamese Revolution. It's very close to the History Museum.

**Geology Museum** The Geology Museum (Bao Tang Dia Chat) at 6 Pham Ngu Lao St gives the whole story behind the geologic processes that created such beauty spots as Halong Bay; however, most of the explanations are in Vietnamese.

**Border Guard Museum** The Border Guard Museum (Bao Tang Bien Phong) at 2 Tran Hung Dao St is dedicated to those friendly boys in uniform you encountered at the airport.

**Air Force Museum** This is one of the larger museums in Vietnam and, though seldom visited by foreigners, it's very worthwhile.

The Air Force Museum (Bao Tang Khong Quan) has many of its exhibits outdoors. This includes a number of Soviet MiG fighters, reconnaissance planes, helicopters and anti-aircraft equipment. Inside the museum hall are other weapons, including mortars, machine guns and some US-made bombs (hopefully defused). There is a partially truncated MiG with a ladder – you are permitted to climb up into the cockpit and have your photo taken. The museum has other war memorabilia, including paintings of obvious Soviet design and portraits of Ho Chi Minh.

The Air Force Museum is on Truong Chinh St in the Dong Da District (south-west part of the city). From the railway station it's almost 5km, a rather long cyclo ride.

**Fine Arts Museum** The building housing the Fine Arts Museum (Bao Tang My Thuat) served as the Ministry of Information under the French. Here you can see some very intricate sculptures, paintings, lacquerware, ceramics and other traditional Vietnamese fine arts.

Some reproductions of antiques are on sale here, but be sure to ask for a certificate which will clear these goods through customs when you depart Vietnam.

The Fine Arts Museum is at 66 Nguyen Thai Hoc St (corner Cao Ba Quai St), which is across the street from the back wall of the Temple of Literature; it is open Tuesday to Sunday from 8 am until noon and 1.30 to 4.30 pm.

**Women's Museum** The Women's Museum (Bao Tang Phu Nu) at 36 Ly Thuong Kiet St gets good reviews from travellers. There's the inevitable tribute to women soldiers, but, fortunately, there's much more than that. On the 4th floor you can see the different costumes worn by the 54 minority groups in Vietnam. Many of the exhibits have English explanations.

**Memorial House** The Memorial House at 48 Hang Ngang St (north of Hoan Kiem Lake in the Old Quarter), in which Ho Chi Minh drafted Vietnam's Declaration of Independence in 1945, has been preserved as a museum.

### Old Quarter
The Old Quarter is demarcated, roughly speaking, by Hoan Kiem Lake, the Citadel, Dong Xuan Market and the ramparts of the Red River. As they have since the 15th century, the narrow streets of the Old Quarter bear names that reflect the business once conducted there: Silk St, Rice St, Paper St, Chicken St, Bamboo St, Hat St, Comb St and so forth. This interesting area now houses a

variety of small shops. See Hanoi's Living Legacy on page 476-7.

## Hanoi Citadel

Just to the west of the Old Quarter is the Hanoi Citadel, originally constructed by Emperor Gia Long (ruled 1802-1819). Unfortunately, the Citadel is now a military base and also the residence of high-ranking officers and their families – in other words, closed to the public. Also, there is no longer much to see because it was mostly destroyed by French troops in 1894, and US bombing took care of the rest.

## St Joseph Cathedral

Stepping inside neo-Gothic St Joseph Cathedral (inaugurated in 1886) is like being instantly transported to medieval Europe. The cathedral is noteworthy for its square towers, elaborate altar and stained-glass windows. The first Catholic mission in Hanoi was founded in 1679.

The main gate to St Joseph Cathedral is open daily from 5 to 7 am and 5 to 7 pm, the hours when masses are held. At other times of the day guests are welcome, but must enter the cathedral via the compound of the Diocese of Hanoi, the entrance to which is a block away at 40 Nha Chung St. After walking through the gate, go straight and then turn right. When you reach the side door to the cathedral, ring the small bell high up to the right of the door to call the priest to let you in. Across Nha Chung St from the diocese compound is a nunnery where some elderly nuns live.

## Long Bien Bridge

The Long Bien Bridge, which crosses the Red River 600m north of the new Chuong Duong Bridge, is a fantastic hodge-podge of repairs dating from the American War. US aircraft repeatedly bombed the strategic Long Bien Bridge (which at one time was defended by 300 anti-aircraft guns and 84 SAM missiles), yet after each attack the Vietnamese somehow managed to improvise replacement spans and return it to road and rail service. It is said that when US POWs were put to work repairing the bridge, the US military, fearing for their safety, ended the attacks.

The 1682m Long Bien Bridge was opened in 1902. It was once known as the Paul Doumer Bridge after the turn-of-the-century French governor general of Indochina, Paul Doumer (1857-1932), who was assassinated a year after becoming President of France.

## Thu Le Park & Zoo

Thu Le Park & Zoo (Bach Thu Thu Le), with its expanses of shaded grass and ponds, is 6km west of Hoan Kiem Lake. The entrance is on Buoi St a few hundred metres north of Ngoc Khanh St. The zoo is open daily from 6 am to 6 pm.

## Fitness Clubs

A number of international hotels open their exercise centres to the public for a fee. Top of the market is the Clark Hatch Fitness Centre (☎ 826-6919, ext 8881) in the Sofitel Metropole Hotel. Along similar lines is the Daewoo Hotel Fitness Centre (☎ 835-1000). Prices are slightly lower at the Planet Hotel (☎ 843-5888). The Hanoi Club (☎ 823-8115), 76 Yen Phu St, offers a full-service fitness centre. Long-termers can also check out the Hanoi Private Club (☎ 852-8262) at 41 Chua Boc St.

## Golf

King's Valley is a nine-hole golf course 45km west of Hanoi close to the base of Ba Vi Mountain. Membership is US$5000, but the club is open to visitors. This is the only golf course in the northern part of Vietnam.

On the western side of Hanoi, but still within the city limits, is the Lang Ha Golf Club (☎ 835-0908) at 16A Lang Ha St, opposite the TV tower. Basically, this is just a driving range – you'll have to go to King's Valley if you want to pursue a white ball over hills and fields. The driving range is open daily to members and non-members alike from 6 am to 10 pm.

# Hanoi's Living Legacy

JULIET COOMBE

Hanoi's Old Quarter, or 36 Pho Phuong (36 Streets), with its thousand years of history, remains one of Vietnam's most lively and unusual places, where you can buy anything from a gravestone to silk pyjamas.

The commercial quarter evolved from an aquatic trading environment. The Red River, along with the smaller To Lich River, once flowed through the city centre to create an intricate network of canals and riverways teeming with boats.

As these rivers would rise as high as 8m during the monsoon season, dikes were constructed around the city to protect it against the constant flooding. The original dike, now over a thousand years old, can still be seen today along Tran Quang Khai St.

In the 13th century, the city's 36 guilds set up in this area with each of them taking a different street (hence the name '36 Streets'). Some of these divisions remain today. For example, on Hang Bo St you can find bamboo sticks, ladders, baskets and pipes, much as you could six centuries ago. *Hang* in Vietnamese means 'merchandise' and it is followed by the name of the product for sale in that street. Thus, Hang Gai St translates as Silk St, while others translate as Copper St, Paper St, Sugar St, Silver St etc.

Exploring this maze of back streets is fascinating; some streets open up while others narrow into a warren of smaller roads. These back streets are the area of the tunnel, or tube, houses, so called because their narrow frontages hide very long rooms. Since buildings were traditionally taxed by the width of frontage on the street, storage and living space retreated deeper to the rear. By feudal law, houses were limited to two stories and (out of respect to the king) they could not be taller than the Royal Palace, so there are no high-rise buildings to mar the atmosphere.

One interesting spot is on Hang Bac St, where old men and women sit around from dawn to dusk chiselling out gravestones of different shapes and sizes, decorating them with a photo of the deceased.

The 9th century Bach Ma (White Horse) Temple on Hang Buom St is also worth a look. This pagoda, with its red funeral palanquin, is watched over by white-bearded temple guards, who spend their days sipping cups of tea. This

*Hang Thiec St (or Tin St) is the traditional home of vendors of fine lamps, trays, cups and candleholders, but they are increasingly turning to plumbing supplies, boxes and buckets to make their living*

JULIET COOMBE

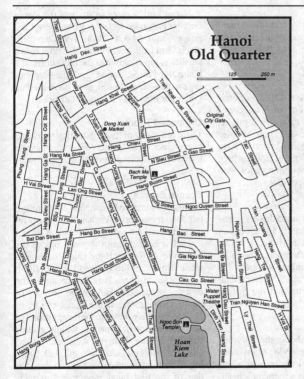

**Old Quarter Street Names**

| | |
|---|---|
| Be | Boat |
| Bac | Silver |
| Bo | Large Basket |
| Bong | Cotton |
| Buom | Sail |
| Can | Weight |
| Chieu | Mat |
| Cot | Basket |
| Da | Leather |
| Dao | Peach |
| Dau | Oil |
| Dieu | Waterpipe |
| Dong | Copper |
| Duong | Sugar |
| Ga | Chicken |
| Gai | Silk/flax |
| Giay | Paper |
| Hom | Coffin |
| Khoai | Sweet Potato |
| Luoc | Comb |
| Manh | Curtain |
| Ngang | Crossway |
| Non | Hat |
| Phen | Alum |
| Thiec | Tin |
| Tre | Bamboo |
| Trong | Drum |
| Vai | Fabric |
| Voi | Lime |

temple has an interesting link to the construction of the city walls in 1749. Legend has it that Ly King, who built the walls, prayed for assistance because they persistently collapsed, no matter how many times he rebuilt them. His prayers were finally answered when a white horse appeared out of the Earth God Temple and guided him to the site where he could safely build his walls. One of the 16 original city gates, Quan Chuong gate, still stands at the end of Hang Chieu St.

On Hang Quat St you will find red candlesticks, funeral boxes, flags and other temple items for sale. For those who prefer something a bit more glamorous, head on to Hang Gai St, where silk, embroidery, lacquerware handicrafts, silk paintings and water puppets can be purchased. This is Hanoi's most popular shopping area – silk sleeping bag linings and elegant Vietnamese dresses are particularly popular among travellers. And don't forget the Dong Xuan market, on Hang Khoi and Dong Xuan Sts, which has been rebuilt following a fire in 1994.

Opportunities to share your wealth with the local people are almost endless. Wander around and you'll find woollen clothes, cosmetics, luxury foods, fake Ray-Ban sunglasses, printed T-shirts, musical instruments, plumbing supplies, herbal medicines, gold and silver jewellery, religious offerings, spices, woven mats and much, much more. (Also see the Things to Buy section on page 489-91)

Alternatively, keep your money in your pocket and just drink in the atmosphere of a part of Vietnam that has retained the essence of life 600 years ago.

**Juliet Coombe**

## Rugby

A part-time amateur rugby team has organised itself for occasional games in Hanoi. For details, ask at the Pear Tree Pub (☎ 825-7812), 78 Tho Nhuom St.

## Swimming

The Sofitel Metropole and Daewoo hotels have swimming pools, but for hotel guests and members only. For the general public, the Ho Tay Villas (☎ 825-8241) out by West Lake has the best deal at US$3 per day. Also by West Lake is the Thang Loi Hotel, which has tennis courts and a swimming pool open to the public for US$10 per day.

## Hash House Harriers

Expats in Hanoi who belong to this organisation get together once weekly for a run, fun and drinking party. Hash House Harriers meets every Saturday afternoon. The location and exact time changes, so check for notices at the Sunset Pub, The Verandah, Jackfruit Tree, Polite Pub and the Sofitel Metropole Hotel.

## Weekend Warriors

This is similar to the Hash, but the activities are more versatile. The WW often does weekend hikes, informal parties and whatever other idea pops into a member's head. The strategy for locating WW is the same as for the Hash – ask around. WW sometimes publishes notice of upcoming events in *Timeout*, the entertainment section of the *Vietnam Investment Review*.

## Language Courses

In the north, Hanoi National University (☎ 858-1468) has the largest market share in Vietnamese language study. The Vietnamese Language Centre is actually inside the Polytechnic University, not at the main campus of Hanoi National University at 90 Nguyen Trai St. There is a dormitory at the Polytechnic University for foreign students (Nha A-2 Bach Khoa) and this is a good place to inquire about tuition. If you enrol, you can stay in this dormitory (rooms cost approximately US$150 to US$250 per month).

Hanoi's other place to study is the Hanoi Foreign Language College, Vietnamese Language Centre (☎ 826-2468). The main campus is 9km from central Hanoi, but there is a smaller campus closer to the city centre at 1 Pham Ngu Lao St. Tuition here varies depending on class size, but should be no more than US$5 per hour for individual tutoring.

## Organised Tours

There are many of these, both day tours and overnighters. The budget cafes (see Places to Eat in this chapter) generally offer the lowest prices.

## Special Events

Tet, the Vietnamese Lunar New Year, falls in late January or early February. In Hanoi, Tet is celebrated in a variety of ways. A flower market is held during the week before the beginning of Tet on Hang Luoc St. A two-week flower exhibition and competition takes place in Lenin Park beginning on the first day of the new year. On the 13th day of the first lunar month in the village of Lim in Ha Bac Province, boys and girl engage in *hat doi*, a traditional game in which groups conduct a sung dialogue with each other; other activities include chess and cock fighting. Wrestling matches are held on the 15th day of the first lunar month at Dong Da Mound, site of the uprising against Chinese invaders led by Emperor Quang Trung (Nguyen Hue) in 1788.

Vietnam's National Day, 2 September, is celebrated at Ba Dinh Square (the expanse of grass in front of Ho Chi Minh's Mausoleum) with a rally and fireworks; boat races are held on Hoan Kiem Lake.

## Places to Stay – bottom end

Compared with Saigon, finding a cheap place to stay in Hanoi is a real hassle. It's not that there is necessarily a lack of budget hotels, it's just that they are not concentrated in any particular area. Furthermore, most of the guesthouses are small, in many cases only three or four rooms. The result is that you can spend a considerable amount of time traipsing from one obscure guesthouse to another in search of a vacancy. Virtually all of the budget guesthouses are in the central area of Hanoi, usually within 1km of Hoan Kiem Lake.

Aside from the places listed below, see the Places to Eat – Travellers' Cafes section later in this chapter. Many of the cafes listed rent cheap rooms or can direct you to some place that does.

*Lotus Guesthouse* (☎ 826-8642; fax 826-8642) at 42V Ly Thuong Kiet St is a very friendly, quiet, clean and cheap place. There are eight rooms costing US$6 to US$12 and some dorm beds for US$4.

The *Bodega Cafe* (☎ 826-7784; 826-7787; 10 rooms) at 57 Trang Tien St has good cheapish rooms, even though the food is so-so. Rooms cost US$20 to US$30.

The *Trang Tien Hotel* (☎ 825-6341; fax 825-1416; 46 rooms), 35 Trang Tien St, seems to have a relationship with the Bodega Cafe. Doubles priced from US$8 to US$45 are excellent value.

The *Tong Dan Guesthouse* (☎ 826-5328; 20 rooms), 17 Tong Dan St, has doubles from US$9 to US$30. It's east of Hoan Kiem Lake, close to the Red River.

The *Hotel 30/4* (Khach San 30/4; ☎ 825-2611; 29 rooms) is named after 30 April 1975, the date when the North Vietnamese entered Saigon. Not surprisingly, it's state-owned. The hotel is at 115 Tran Hung Dao St, conveniently opposite the railway station. Large echo-chamber rooms costing US$8 and US$10 have the bathroom outside, or you can pay US$35 for attached bath. This place is old and run down, but has character and the staff proved friendly.

*Especen Hotel* (☎ 825-8845, 826-6856; fax 826-9612), 79E Hang Trong St, operates nine mini-hotels around the central area of Hanoi. There is no point in listing them all here as its office will give you a map and call ahead to book a room. The hotels all bear creative names such as Especen-1, Especen-2 etc.

The new, but cheap, *Red River Hotel* (☎ 826-1151; fax 8287159) on Hong Bo St is in the Old Quarter. Rooms cost US$8 to US$15. Not far away is the *Anh Dao Hotel*

(☎ 825-0020; fax 825-0020), which costs US$10 to US$35. There are discounts at both these places if you book a tour through the Red River Cafe (☎ 826-8427) at 73 Hang Bo St.

Also near the west side of Hoan Kiem Lake on Hang Trong St is the *Hoa Long Hotel* (☎ 826-9319; fax 825-9228; eight rooms), which has rooms for US$20. This place is easy to spot thanks to the huge Chinese restaurant on the ground floor.

### Places to Stay – middle
**Central Area** The *Anh Hotel II* (843-5141; fax 843-0618; 15 rooms), 43 Nguyen Truong To St, is another small, private mini-hotel in the Old Quarter. Rates here are US$40 to US$60.

The *Army Hotel* (Khach San Quan Doi; ☎ 825-2896), 33C Pham Ngu Lao St, is indeed owned by the army but looks nothing like a barracks. This plush place offers rooms from US$51 to US$121.

*Trang An Hotel* (☎ 826-8982; fax 825-8511; 12 rooms), 58 Hang Gai St, is a good mini-hotel at the north-west corner of Hoan Kiem Lake. Singles/doubles cost US$50/60 and suites are US$100. There is an in-house restaurant and cocktail lounge.

Opposite the railway station at 109 Trang Hung Dao St is the *Thu Do Hotel* (☎ 825-2288; fax 826-1121; 37 rooms), also known as the *Capital Hotel*. A recent renovation here has jacked up prices considerably and rooms now cost US$56 to US$101.

The *Binh Minh Hotel* (☎ 826-6441; fax 825-7725; 43 rooms), 27 Ly Thai To St, is in the same building as the China Southern Airlines office. Doubles cost US$45 to US$50.

The *Energy Hotel* (Khach San Dien Luc; ☎ 825-0457; fax 825-9226; 71 rooms), 30 Ly Thai To St, belongs to the Ministry of Energy. This is the agency responsible for the frequent power blackouts which grip Vietnam. Rooms get progressively cheaper as you go upstairs. Top-floor rooms cost US$30; other rooms are US$40 to US$65.

The old *Dong Loi Hotel* (☎ 825-5721; fax 826-7999; 30 rooms) is at 94 Ly Thuong Kiet

St (very near Hanoi railway station). The door attendants wear crisp-white uniforms and greet you with 'Hello Sir' or 'Good morning Madam.' All this courtesy costs US$60, which is not worth it because – despite the remodelled lobby – the rooms are dingy.

The *Mango Hotel* (☎ 824-3754; fax 824-3966; 60 rooms), 118 Le Duan St, is near the Hanoi railway station. The hotel has spacious grounds and the restaurant seems to have gained a reputation as a good place for Vietnamese wedding banquets. The price range for rooms here is US$35 to US$50.

*Chains First Eden Hotel* (☎ 828-3896; fax 828-4066; 42 rooms), 2 Phung Hung St, is near the Old Quarter at the western end of the Long Bien Bridge. This new and large business hotel has a health club, sauna, business centre, satellite TV and Chinese-Vietnamese restaurant. A night here costs US$60 to US$130.

Very close is the *Galaxy Hotel* (☎ 828-2888; fax 828-2466; 50 rooms), 1 Phan Dinh Phung St. It's a fairly standard business hotel, with business centre, cocktail lounge, restaurant and satellite TV. Rooms here cost US$89 to US$160.

The *Madison Hotel* (☎ 822-8164; 822-5533; 33 rooms), 16 Bui Thi Xuan St, is just to the east of Thien Quang Lake. The management advertises this as Hanoi's first 'boutique hotel' – a flaky description, but it's still a nice place. Perhaps more significant is that this is one of the few hotels in this class that has a lift. Rooms here are US$65 to US$125.

**West Area** Just to the west of Ho Chi Minh's Mausoleum is the *Heritage Hotel* (☎ 834-4727; fax 834-3882; 62 rooms) at 80 Giang Vo St. This very business-oriented Singapore joint-venture hotel has doubles from US$90 to US$140.

**West Lake Area** The *Ho Tay Villas* (Khuy Biet Thu Ho Tay; ☎ 825-8241; fax 823-2126; 40 rooms) is now a tourist hotel, but it previously was the Communist Party Guesthouse. The well-designed, spacious villas,

set amid a beautifully landscaped area on West Lake, were once the exclusive preserve of top party officials; but now visitors bearing US dollars are welcome to avail themselves of the great facilities, excellent food and friendly staff. Even if you don't stay, it's instructive to visit to see how the 'people's representatives' lived in one of Asia's poorest countries. The hotel is 5.5km north of central Hanoi. Rooms are surprisingly cheap at US$35 to US$40.

The Ho Tay Villas are not to be missed. You can even have dinner out on the patio – the waiter put a table out for just us before we'd even asked. Sitting all by ourselves on the patio at night overlooking the vast garden and lake was a weird experience – eating a reasonably good dinner in true KGB style.

**B Bolton**

The *Dragon Hotel* (☎ 829-2954; fax 829-4745; 24 rooms), 9 Tay Ho Rd, is a relatively small place facing the lake. Singles/doubles are US$80/90, and there are also apartments for US$170.

*Quang Ba Hotel* (☎ 829-0053; fax 829-0074; 31 rooms), 27A To Ngoc Van St, is a fairly typical business hotel with rooms from US$50 to US$120. Rooms on the upper floors afford a fine view of West Lake.

**South Area** This is not an area of town that attracts many travellers, but there are some hotels out here. The *Queen Hotel* (☎ 864-1238; fax 864-1237; 32 rooms), 189 Giai Phong St, is near the Giap Bat railway station. All rooms are doubles and cost US$40 to US$80.

**Places to Stay – top end**
A recent trend in Hanoi has been to build completely new hotels, but design them in a French-colonial motif.

**Central Area** A good example of the nouveau French-colonial genre is the charming *Hang Nga Hotel* (☎ 843-7777; fax 843-7779) at 65 Cua Bac St. Rooms on the top floor have a view of West Lake. The price range here is US$75 to US$125.

Just next door to the Hang Nga is the

GENEVIEVE WEBB

MASON FLORENCE

JULIET COOMBE

### Hanoi

Top: Tortoise Pagoda perches on an islet in the tranquil Hoan Kiem Lake.
Middle: Old friends pass the time of day by Hoan Kiem Lake.
Bottom: A vendor at Dong Xuan market in Hanoi's old quarter.

SARA JANE CLELAND

SARA JANE CLELAND

BRENDAN McCARTHY

JULIET COOMBE

## Hanoi

Top Left: An elderly resident of Hanoi's old quarter.
Top Right: The imposing Ho Chi Minh Mausoleum in Ba Dinh Square.
Bottom Left: The old and the new in Hanoi's streets.
Bottom Right: Passing the time in Hanoi's old quarter.

*Planet Hotel* (☎ 843-5188; fax 843-5088; 60 rooms), 120 Quan Thanh St, in the Old Quarter. Like its neighbour, some rooms on the top floor have a view of West Lake. Facilities in this government-owned establishment include a business centre, sauna, massage service and health club. Room rates are US$80 to US$210.

The *De Syloia Hotel* (☎ 824-5346; fax 824-1083; 33 rooms), 17A Tran Hung Dao St, is yet another elegant variation on the French theme. All rooms have an elegant Continental touch and cost US$135 to US$265. There is a fitness centre and sauna here, not to mention the requisite French restaurant.

The *Sofitel Metropole Hotel* (Khach San Thong Nhat; ☎ 826-6919; fax 826-6920; 244 rooms), 15 Ngo Quyen St, is one of Vietnam's great luxury hotels. This place has a French motif that just won't quit – close the curtains and you'll think you're in Paris. The hotel's slogan is 'charms of yesterday ... today'. Facilities include a swimming pool, fitness centre, sauna and beauty parlour, but (blessedly) there is no karaoke. Doubles cost US$219 to US$449. The restaurant is ventilated by some three dozen ceiling fans; if they were all cranked up at once the food would get sucked into the chimney.

The *Saigon Hotel* (☎ 826-8505; fax 826-6631; 44 rooms) at 80 Ly Thuong Kiet St is a well-run upmarket hotel near the Hanoi railway station. The tariff here runs from US$105 to US$165. There is a sauna and massage service, and the roof-top bar is a good hang-out on warm summer nights.

*Royal Hotel* (☎ 824-4230; fax 824-4234; 65 rooms), 20 Hang Tre St, is proud of its Royal Palace nightclub. It's close to the north-east part of Hoan Kiem Lake and offers luxury business facilities. Rooms cost US$145 to US$365.

The *Dan Chu Hotel* (☎ 825-4937; fax 826-6786; 41 rooms) is at 29 Trang Tien St. Once called the Hanoi Hotel, it was built in the late 19th century. Room rates have risen considerably since the 19th century and now range from US$65 to US$129, but breakfast is thrown in free.

**West Area** The *Capital Garden Hotel* (☎ 835-0383; fax 835-0363; 80 rooms), 48A Lang Ha St, is an all new place. It's a good place to work on your swing – it's close to the Lang Ha Golf Club and the hotel offers a 'golf workshop'. There are a few single rooms with queen-sized beds, but otherwise it's doubles from US$160 to US$260.

The second most expensive place to stay in the capital is the *Hanoi Hotel* (☎ 845-2270; fax 845-9209; 224 rooms), D8 Giang Vo St, near Ho Chi Minh's Mausoleum and Giang Vo Lake. Rooms here cost a breathtaking US$148 to US$388, to which you must add 20% in the summer peak season. Facilities cover virtually everything, from karaoke and disco to a beauty parlour and sauna.

The *Lake Side Hotel* (☎ 835-0111; fax 835-0121; 78 rooms), 6A Ngoc Khanh St, is a Taiwanese joint venture also by the shore of Giang Vo Lake. The building is only five-storeys tall and – as the name indicates – most rooms have a lake view. Doubles cost US$160 to US$380. Facilities include a cafe, Chinese restaurant, health club, nightclub and karaoke lounge.

The *Daewoo Hotel* (☎ 831-5000; fax 831-5010; 410 rooms) in the Daeha Centre (west Hanoi) is the city's largest and most expensive hotel. The style at this South Korean joint venture is most definitely *not* French colonial. The hotel is a 15-storey behemoth and offers everything you could want in life, including a swimming pool, nightclub, health club, business centre and three restaurants. Budget rooms are only US$199, but suites go for up to US$899.

**West Lake Area** The *Thang Loi Hotel* (☎ 826-8211; fax 825-2800; 178 rooms) is nicknamed 'the Cuban Hotel' because it was built in the mid-1970s with Cuban assistance. The floor plan of each level is said to have been copied from a one-storey Cuban building, which explains the doors that lead nowhere. Around the main building are bungalows. The hotel is built on pylons over West Lake, and is surrounded by attractive landscaping and a swimming pool. The hotel

HANOI

## Radio Hanoi & Jane Fonda

Hanoi's radio transmitter is nothing to see, but it's worth a historical footnote for the role it played in the war against the USA (the current transmitter is not the original one used during the war).

Those who are old enough to remember the American War will doubtless recall the radio broadcasts from Hanoi made by American film actor Jane Fonda. Fonda was perhaps the most famous anti-war activist of the time. She made only one live broadcast over Radio Hanoi, her famous speech to US pilots. Subsequent broadcasts played over the radio were tape-recorded speeches and conversations made during her stay in North Vietnam.

Jane Fonda went to North Vietnam on 15 July 1972 and returned to the USA on 29 July, travelling via Paris and Beijing. She was not the only US civilian to visit Hanoi during the war, but she was certainly the most famous. In spite of the fact that a war was raging, it was never illegal for US citizens to visit North Vietnam.

That almost changed. As a direct result of Jane Fonda's visit, Representative Ichord, chairman of the House Internal Security Committee, proposed to amend the 1950 Internal Security Act to make it illegal for any US citizen to visit a country at war with the USA. The Ichord Amendment – later known as the 'Jane Fonda Amendment' – never passed.

Her visit continues to stir emotions to this very day. After WWII, an American woman nicknamed 'Tokyo Rose' was convicted for treason (but later pardoned) for making propaganda broadcasts for the Japanese. Another American woman nicknamed 'Axis Sally' was convicted for doing the same for the Nazis. Many veterans who served in Vietnam (and some members of Congress) felt that Jane Fonda's actions were similar, but she was never prosecuted. Not that it wasn't considered – even as late as 1984 the Justice Department under the Reagan administration looked into the matter but decided that Jane Fonda's trip to North Vietnam and her public speeches did not constitute a crime.

Just as Fonda has her critics, she also has her defenders. There are those who say she was simply exercising her right to freedom of speech in speaking out against a war which was morally wrong. It's also fair to mention that she made a sincere effort to visit the captured American pilots at the nearby 'Hanoi Hilton' prison, but her request for the visit was rejected by North Vietnamese authorities. On the other hand, a widely circulated photograph of Jane Fonda sitting behind an anti-aircraft gun wearing a North Vietnamese helmet particularly outraged many Americans, even those who opposed the war.

An act of treason? Or a heartfelt wish to speak out against an unjust war? You be the judge: the following public domain information is a transcript from the US Congress House Committee on Internal Security ('Travel to Hostile Areas', HR 16742, 19-25 September 1972, page 7671 – special thanks to CompuServe Military Veterans Forum):

[Radio Hanoi attributes talk on DRV visit to Jane Fonda; from Hanoi in English to American servicemen involved in the Indochina War, 1 pm GMT, 22 August 1972. Text: Here's Jane Fonda telling her impressions at the end of her visit to the Democratic Republic of Vietnam (follows recorded female voice with American accent)]

This is Jane Fonda. During my two-week visit in the Democratic Republic of Vietnam, I've had the opportunity to visit a great many places and speak to a large number of people from all walks of life –

also boasts tennis courts, a sauna and a massage service. Except for the massage, all this cushy comfort will cost you US$80 to US$163. The hotel is on Yen Phu St, 3.5km from the city centre.

**And More to Come** The building boom continues apace. Major new hotels currently under construction include the *Fortuna*, *Grand Hanoi Lake View*, *Hanoi Central*, *Hanoi Opera*, *Lien West Lake* and the *Sheraton*.

### Rental

As elsewhere in Vietnam, the budget end of the market is served by mini-hotels. Look around for the best deal and don't be afraid to negotiate.

Even well-heeled foreigners with big budgets wind up living in mini-hotels because Hanoi suffers from a serious shortage of rental accommodation. This is despite the fact that only 5000 to 6000 expats live in Hanoi (about three times that many live in Saigon). There are not enough villas and workers, peasants, students, artists and dancers, historians, journalists, film actresses, soldiers, militia girls, members of the women's union, writers.

I visited the (Dam Xuac) agricultural coop, where the silk worms are also raised and thread is made. I visited a textile factory, a kindergarten in Hanoi. The beautiful Temple of Literature was where I saw traditional dances and heard songs of resistance. I also saw an unforgettable ballet about the guerrillas training bees in the south to attack enemy soldiers. The bees were danced by women, and they did their job well.

In the shadow of the Temple of Literature I saw Vietnamese actors and actresses perform the second act of Arthur Miller's play *All My Sons*, and this was very moving to me – the fact that artists here are translating and performing American plays while US imperialists are bombing their country.

I cherish the memory of the blushing militia girls on the roof of their factory, encouraging one of their sisters as she sang a song praising the blue sky of Vietnam – these women, who are so gentle and poetic, whose voices are so beautiful, but who, when American planes are bombing their city, become such good fighters.

I cherish the way a farmer evacuated from Hanoi, without hesitation, offered me, an American, their best individual bomb shelter while US bombs fell near by. The daughter and I, in fact, shared the shelter wrapped in each others arms, cheek against cheek. It was on the road back from Nam Dinh, where I had witnessed the systematic destruction of civilian targets – schools, hospitals, pagodas, the factories, houses, and the dike system.

As I left the United States two weeks ago, Nixon was again telling the American people that he was winding down the war, but in the rubble-strewn streets of Nam Dinh, his words echoed with sinister (words indistinct) of a true killer. And like the young Vietnamese woman I held in my arms clinging to me tightly – and I pressed my cheek against hers – I thought, this is a war against Vietnam perhaps, but the tragedy is America's.

One thing that I have learned beyond the shadow of a doubt since I've been in this country is that Nixon will never be able to break the spirit of these people; he'll never be able to turn Vietnam, north and south, into a neo-colony of the United States by bombing, by invading, by attacking in any way. One has only to go into the countryside and listen to the peasants describe the lives they led before the revolution to understand why every bomb that is dropped only strengthens their determination to resist.

I've spoken to many peasants who talked about the days when their parents had to sell themselves out to landlords as virtually slaves, when there were very few schools and much illiteracy, inadequate medical care, when they were not masters of their own lives.

But now, despite the bombs, despite the crimes being created – being committed against them by Richard Nixon, these people own their own land, build their own schools – the children learning, literacy – illiteracy is being wiped out, there is no more prostitution as there was during the time when this was a French colony. In other words, the people have taken power into their own hands, and they are controlling their own lives.

And after 4000 years of struggling against nature and foreign invaders – and the last 25 years, prior to the revolution, of struggling against French colonialism – I don't think that the people of Vietnam are about to compromise in any way, shape or form about the freedom and independence of their country, and I think Richard Nixon would do well to read Vietnamese history, particularity their poetry, and particularly the poetry written by Ho Chi Minh. [Recording ends] ∎

apartments to meet demand, and what is available commands very high rents. A typical two-bedroom expat flat leases for US$4000 to US$7000 per month. Some new luxury apartments have recently come on line, including Oriental Park (☎ 829-1200), Hanoi Lakes (☎ 821-8051), Golden Lodge (☎ 824-4298), Coco Flower Village (☎ 843-4556), Regency West Lake (☎ 843-0030), Thanh Cong Villas (☎ 835-4875) and the Daeha Centre (☎ 834-9467). Nevertheless, the shortage of expat rental accommodation

is likely to continue until after the turn of the century.

## Places to Eat

**Travellers' Cafes** The budget end of the food business is dominated by a handful of small cafes preparing a variety of Vietnamese and western dishes. Aside from the food, these are good places to look for cheap rooms, meet other travellers and arrange tours.

The *Red River Cafe* (☎ 826-8427) at 73 Hang Bo St deserves a plug – its standard of service is definitely above average. It's a particularly good place for booking tours to such places as Halong Bay and Sapa.

*Tin Tin Bar & Cafe* (☎ 826-0326), 14 Hang Non St, is another backpacker haven. The menu includes juices, crepes, fried rice, pizza, burgers and so on, all at reasonable prices. This place is also quite a good nightlife spot.

Another favourite for backpackers is the *Darling Cafe* (☎ 826-9386; fax 825-6562) at 33 Hang Quat St. There are reasonable Vietnamese dishes and light western food like pancakes and fruit shakes. There are some double rooms here for US$8 and dormitories for US$4.

The *Queen Cafe* (☎ 826-0860) at 65 Hang Bac St is a small place that's been around for a while. Food is light (plenty of baguettes, fried eggs and coffee) and you can book tours here too.

We can assure you that the *Lonely Planet Cafe* (☎ 825-0974) at 33 Hang Be St is in no way affiliated with a certain guidebook company in Melbourne, Australia. However, as Hanoi cafes go, the food is edible and prices reasonable.

The *Meeting Cafe* (☎ 825-8812) at 59B Ba Trieu St is a well-established budget travellers' haven. Here you can find the usual backpacker cuisine (banana pancakes, milkshakes, cakes, coffee and spring rolls) as well as tour booking information.

The *Orient Cafe* (☎ 824-7390), 53 Tran Hung Dao St, is perhaps the latest contender in the tour booking/cheap eats business.

**Speciality Streets** *Cam Chi St* is about half a kilometre north-east of Hanoi railway station. It's a very small street – basically an alley – crammed full of sidewalk stalls. It's really budget-priced, but serves delicious food. Forget about English menus and don't expect comfortable seating. Still, where else can you have a small banquet for US$1 or less?

*Mai Hac De St* is in the south-central area, running in a north-south direction. The northern terminus is Tran Nhan Tong St and

the line-up of restaurants continues for several blocks to the south.

*To Hien Thanh St* runs in an east-west direction, and specialises in small seafood restaurants. It's to the south of the city centre, just east of Bay Mau Lake.

Approximately 10km north of central Hanoi are about 60 *dog meat restaurants* all concentrated in a 1km stretch of Nghi Tam St. This street runs along the embankment between West Lake and the Red River. Even if you have no interest in eating dog meat, it's interesting to cruise this stretch of road in the evening on the last day of the lunar month. Hanoians believe that eating dog meat in the first half of the lunar month will bring bad luck – consequently, the dog meat restaurants are deserted at that time and most of them shut down. Business picks up in the second half of the lunar month and the last day is particularly auspicious – the restaurants are packed! Cruise by in the evening and you'll see thousands of motorbikes parked here. As you drive along, hawkers practically leap out in front of you to extol the virtues of their particular dog meat restaurant.

**Restaurants** There are several restaurants calling themselves *Hué Restaurant*. They are all in a cluster, a big convenience when you want to find these places. Hué food is justifiably famous, and it's worth seeking these places out. The best one we've tried was *Quan Hué Restaurant* (☎ 824-4062), 6 Ly Thuong Kiet St. On the opposite side of the street is *Huu Ngu Binh* (☎ 824-1515) at No 11. The slogan here is 'Our food is more Hué than Hué'.

The *Shrimp Cakes Restaurant* (Nha Hang Banh Tom Hotay; ☎ 825-7839), 1 Thanh Nien St, has a number of great dishes on the menu, including (surprise?) shrimp cakes. Weather permitting, you can sit outside and admire the view of Truc Bach Lake. The food is good and prices are moderate, but this place can be very crowded on weekends and holidays.

The large Chinese restaurant on the ground

floor of the *Hoa Long Hotel* (☎ 826-9319) on Hang Trong St, near the west shore of Hoan Kiem Lake, is well worth checking out.

Fish and chips is the latest rage to hit Hanoi. You can pay a steep premium to sample them at the *Hanoi Hotel*.

There is a Korean restaurant inside the *Lang Ha Golf Club* (☎ 835-0908), 16A Lang Ha St, in the western district.

**Ice Cream & Desserts** The best ice cream bar is inside the *Trang Tien Hotel* at 54 Trang Tien St, but it's down in the basement and is not immediately obvious.

The best ice cream sundaes can be found at *Kem Tra My*, which is on Nguyen Thai Hoc St near Ho Chi Minh's Mausoleum.

For some of the best French pastries and coffee in Vietnam, visit the *Pastry & Yoghurt Shop* (☎ 825-0216) at 252 Hang Bong St near the city centre. The breakfasts are outstanding.

**Pub Grub** The *Sunset Pub* (☎ 823-0173) is at 31 Cao Ba Quat St (a couple blocks south of Ho Chi Minh's Mausoleum). Pizzas and hamburgers are on the menu. There is live jazz on Thursday and Saturday evenings. The pub is run by a Norwegian.

The unforgettably named *Gold Cock Bar* (☎ 825-0499), 5 Bao Khanh St, is an expat favourite. In the same building is the popular *Polite Pub* (☎ 825-0959). On the same street at No 11B is the excellent *Redwoods* (☎ 828-7207), which has billiards and American food. Bao Khanh St is right at the north-west corner of Hoan Kiem Lake.

The *Jackfruit Tree* (☎ 826-5540), 33A Pham Ngu Lao St, is next to the Army Hotel. This is an interesting place on a quiet street with an outdoor setting.

The *Verandah Bar & Cafe* (☎ 825-7220), 9 Nguyen Khac Can St, is an expat hang-out built in a stylish French villa. It's perhaps more cafe than bar, but either way it's a good place, though it closes rather early. It's open daily from 10 am to 10.30 pm, and there are Sunday brunches. The menu includes such things as chicken enchiladas, smoked salmon and quiche. You can sit by the bar or out on the verandah.

The *Pear Tree Pub* (☎ 825-7812), 78 Tho Nhuom St, is just slightly south-east of the Ambassadors' Pagoda.

Just 30m in front of the Hanoi Hotel is the *Latino Pub* (☎ 846-0836) at C8 Giang Vo St. The menu includes Tex-Mex food and other Latin American dishes. The Vietnamese owner lived abroad for a while and speaks fluent Spanish.

The *Met Pub* (☎ 826-6919 ext 8856) is in the new annexe of the Sofitel Metropole Hotel. It's a French pub with fine food, but is very expensive.

**Self-Catering** Many backpackers finally decide that the best way to experience a cheap meal is to pick up a loaf of delicious French bread, some salami, cheese and a Coke or beer, then take it back to their hotel room to enjoy it.

More determined self-caterers can buy fresh vegetables at the *Hom Market* just south of the city centre near the intersection of Hue and Tran Xuan Soan Sts.

Very close to the foregoing is the *Hanoi Star Mart* (☎ 822-5999) at 60 Ngo Thi Nham St. This is probably the best mini-supermarket in town. There is a smaller branch adjacent to the Energy Hotel at 30 Ly Thai To St. You'll also find a *Mini-Market* in the Van Phuc Diplomatic Quarter in the west part of Hanoi.

### Entertainment

**Cinema** *Fanslands Cinema* (☎ 825-7484), 84 Ly Thuong Kiet St, offers the best movies in town. French speakers will also be pleased with what's on offer at *Alliance Française* (☎ 826-6970), 42 Yet Kieu St.

The other place in town with foreign films is the *Thang 8 Cinema* on Hang Bai St (opposite the Immigration Police Office).

Opposite the Daewoo Hotel is a 3-D (*phim noi* in Vietnamese) cinema called *Ngoc Khanh*. Admission is a steep US$5.

# Puppets with a Messiah Complex

PHIL WEYMOUTH

Vietnamese water puppets were invented a thousand years ago by farmers in the Red River Delta region near Hanoi to entertain themselves when the rains flooded their paddy fields.

The puppets were carved from water-resistant fig tree timber (*sung*) in either realistic forms (modelled on the villagers themselves and animals from their daily lives) or more fanciful forms (mythical creatures such as the dragon, phoenix and unicorn). The performances were usually staged in ponds, lakes or flooded paddy fields.

References to water puppetry appear in the ancient scholarly works of Nguyen Cong Bat and Phan Truong Nguyen. Their literature indicates that during the Ly and Tran dynasties (1010-1400) water puppetry had moved from being a simple pastime of villagers to formal courtly entertainment.

Until the 1960s, however, Vietnam's water puppets were virtually unknown outside of northern Vietnam, but the formation of the Municipal Water Puppet Theatre rekindled interest in this ancient art form. The troupe gave its first performance at its theatre on the shores of Hoan Kiem Lake in Hanoi, where it still runs nightly shows.

The puppets themselves are designed and built under the guidance of one of the troupe members, Mr Luong, in a village outside of Hanoi. As each puppet lasts only about three to four months if used continually, puppet production in the village is a full-time industry.

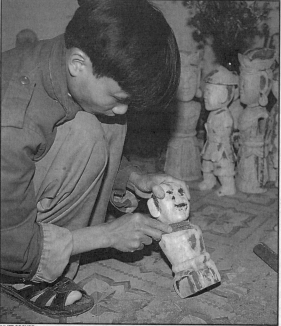

*The resurgence of interest in water puppetry has provided artisans in one village with a full-time industry in puppet production. The puppets are carved and painted by hand and last three to four months.*

JULIET COOMBE

*Suspended from bamboo poles in a darkened auditorium, the puppets sit lightly on the top of the water, creating the illusion of a stable surface.*

JULIET COOMBE

Eleven puppeteers are involved in each performance and each one of them has trained for a minimum of three years. They spend the evening hip-deep in water hidden from the audience by a green bamboo curtain. The puppets are attached to long bamboo poles and are manipulated via strings. In the darkened auditorium it looks as if the puppets are literally walking on water. A group of musicians accompanies the action playing wooden flutes, gongs, cylindrical drums, bamboo xylophones and stringed *dan bau*.

The evening's programme is a combination of 17 stories ranging from scenes of the daily lives of farmers ('Rearing Ducks' and 'Catching Foxes') to historical events ('King Le Loi on Boat Tour'), myths ('Phoenix Dance') and religious rituals ('Harvest Festival').

One of the most spectacular items is 'Dragon Dance'. The lights are dimmed as the orchestra plays the last of three opening songs, when suddenly two dragons dramatically leap out of the still water and attack each other spraying water in every direction (if you are sitting in the first two rows of the theatre, be prepared to get soaked!). The dragons glide across the water flicking their tails in the air and, as quickly as they appeared, they slip silently back beneath the surface. Seconds later they return spouting golden sparks and smoke from their mouths, creating a magical feel to the performance.

**Juliet Coombe**

**Discos & Karaoke** The *Royal Palace Night Club* (☎ 8244226), 20 Hang Tre St, is close to the Chuong Duong Bridge. It's a lively place, with live bands, disco dancing and karaoke rooms. There is a US$5 cover charge. Opening hours are 8 pm to 2 am.

*Metal Night Club* (☎ 824-1975), 57 Cua Nam St, is two blocks north-east of Hanoi railway station. There is a live band every night and expect the music to be *loud*. The cover charge is US$4. Opening hours are 11 am to 2 pm and 7.30 pm to 2 am.

*Dai Dong Centropell*, 46 Hang Ga St, is a combination karaoke and disco. It's in the Old Quarter just east of the Hanoi Citadel. Admission is US$5.

The Hanoi Hotel near Giang Vo Lake is home to the *Volvo Discotheque* (☎ 845-2270). This place is very expensive, so bring your Visa card or a wheelbarrow full of dong. The disco is open from 6 pm to 2 am.

The *Top Disco Club* (☎ 822-6641) at the south-west corner of Thien Quang Lake is another spot catering to the dance market.

If Japanese culture appeals, you can have your own karaoke cubicle and sing songs to yourself at the *VIP Club* (☎ 826-9167) at 60-62 Nguyen Du St. Meals can be delivered to your karaoke cubicle. There is supposed to be a 20% discount from 5 to 8 pm. The VIP Club also has slot machines and a disco with thumping music, strobe lights and large-screen video. The cover charge is US$5 and drinks are priced for VIPs.

The *Queen Bee Nightclub* (☎ 835-2612), 42A Lang Ha St, remains popular with the well-to-do, but it's a long way west of the city centre in the western end of town. Although the disco is lively, there is plenty of emphasis on Japanese-Korean karaoke entertainment. It's open from 2 pm to 2 am.

**Municipal Theatre** The 900-seat Municipal Theatre (☎ 825-4312), which faces eastward up Trang Tien St, was built in 1911 as an opera house. It was from a balcony of this building that a Viet Minh-run committee of citizens announced that it had taken over the city on 16 August 1945. These days, performances are held here in the evenings.

**Circus** One Russian tradition which has survived in Vietnam is the State Circus. Many of the performers (gymnasts, jugglers, animal trainers etc) were originally trained in Eastern Europe, though new recruits can now learn their skills from their Vietnamese elders. The circus performs nightly from 8 to 9.30 pm in a huge tent near the northern entrance to Lenin Park (Cong Vien Le Nin). There is a special show for children on Sunday mornings.

**Water Puppets** This fantastic art form originated in northern Vietnam and Hanoi is the best place to see it. Just on the shore of Hoan Kiem Lake is the Municipal Water Puppet Theatre (Roi Nuoc Thang Long; ☎ 824-9494) at 57B Dinh Tien Hoang St. Performances are given from 8 to 9 pm every night, except Monday. Admission is US$2.

**Massage** The government has severely restricted the number of places licensed to give massages because of concern that naughty 'extra services' might be offered. At the present time, you can get a good *legitimate* massage at the *Hoa Binh Hotel*, *Planet Hotel*, *Dan Chu Hotel* and *Thang Loi Hotel* for US$6 per hour. The *Hanoi Hotel* and *Saigon Hotel* charge US$8 per hour for this service. *Clark Hatch Fitness Centre* in the Sofitel Metropole Hotel also has massage facilities.

There is also the *Eva Club* on the 2nd floor of the Hom Market, on the north-east corner of the intersection where Hue and Tran Xuan Soan Sts meet.

**Bars** *Apocalypse Now* (☎ 824-4302) at 338 Ba Trieu St is known for its loud and raucous music. It opens at 5 pm and closes when the customers trickle away.

The *Roxy Bar* (☎ 824-4094), 8B Ta Hien St, is a very popular place in the Old Quarter. It was built in a converted theatre.

The *Tin Tin Bar & Cafe* (☎ 826-0326) at 14 Hang Non St is a friendly place with western music, drinks and light snacks. It's open from 8 pm until 2 am.

## Things to Buy

Whether or not you wish to buy anything, your first encounter will likely be with the children who sell postcards and maps. Of course, they are found all over the country, but in Hanoi there are many who are orphans and have a special card to prove it, which they will immediately show to foreigners. They are also the most notorious overchargers, asking about triple the going price. Bargaining is called for.

**Markets** The three-storey Dong Xuan Market is 1.3km north of the northern end of Hoan Kiem Lake. The market burned down in 1994, killing five people (all of whom had entered the building after the fire started to either rescue goods or steal them). The market has now been rebuilt and is a tourist attraction in its own right. There are hundreds of stalls here, employing around 3000 people.

Hom Market is on the north-east corner of Hue and Tran Xuan Soan Sts. It's a good general purpose market with lots of imported foods items.

Hang Da Market is relatively small, but good for imported foods, wine, beer and flowers. The 2nd floor is good for fabric and ready-made clothing. The market is very close to St Joseph Cathedral.

Cua Nam Market is a few blocks north of the Hanoi railway station. The market itself is of no great interest (except maybe for the flowers), but Le Duan St between the market and the railway station is a treasure trove of household goods, including electronics, plasticware and the like. It's a particularly

Hanoi's Municipal Theatre holds a special place in Vietnamese history. It was from its balcony in August 1945 that the Viet Minh announced it had taken over the city.

HANOI

good shopping area if you're setting up a residence in Hanoi.

Mo Market is far to the south of the central area on Bach Mai and Minh Khai Sts. It's not a place for tourism, as the main products are fresh meat, fish and vegetables. It is of some interest to expats who prefer to do their own cooking.

Buoi Market out in the far north-west part of town is notable for live animals (chickens, ducks etc), but also features ornamental plants. You can find perhaps better quality ornamental plants for sale at the gardens in front of the Temple of Literature and at the Air Force Museum. You might actually want to visit Buoi Market to *sell* your ornamental plants when departing the country – the vendors are willing to buy back plants and flowerpots if in good condition at about half the original price.

**Shops**  On Trang Tien St you'll find many shops willing to make dirt-cheap eyeglasses in a mere 10 minutes. Unfortunately, quality is mostly abysmal. From personal experience, the one exception we know of is Hanoi Optic (☎ 824-3751), which has modern equipment and skilled English-speaking staff. This is where most expats in Hanoi go to get their eyes examined. It's at 48 Trang Tien St on the 2nd floor (just above another optician shop) – follow the signs that say 'high-class glasses'.

Lots of western customers seem to like the Ho Chi Minh T-shirts. Around Hang Bong/Hang Gai Sts are other T-shirt shops and places selling Viet Cong headgear. T-shirts cost US$2 to US$4 and either printed or embroidered ones are available. However, it might be worth keeping in mind that neither Ho Chi Minh T-shirts nor VC headgear are popular apparel with Vietnamese refugees and certain war veterans living in the west. Wearing such souvenirs while walking down a street in Los Angeles or Melbourne might offend someone, possibly endangering your relationship with the Overseas Vietnamese community, as well as your dental work.

Hang Gai, Hang Khai and Cau Go Sts are

good areas for souvenirs and antiques (real and fake). Hanoi is a good place to have informal clothes custom-tailored. One souvenir item to look for here are Russian-made watches.

Hang Gai St and its continuation, Hang Bong St, are a good place to look for embroidered tablecloths, T-shirts and hangings.

A good shop for silk clothing is Khai Silk (☎ 825-4237), 96 Hang Gai St. The proprietor is fluent in French and English, and the clothes are modern and western in design.

There is an outstanding shoe market along Hang Dau St at the north-east corner of Hoan Kiem Lake; however, it's difficult to find large sizes for big western feet.

Aspiring young artists display their paintings at private art galleries in hopes of attracting a buyer. Prices are in the US$30 to US$50 range after bargaining. Some galleries with English-speaking staff include:

Hoang Ha Art
    149 Le Duan St (☎ 826-9403); open daily from 7.30 am to 10 pm
Thanh Chuong
    89 Ngo Quynh St (☎ 826-1228); open daily from 9 am to 8 pm
Trang An
    15 Hang Buom St (☎ 826-94800; open daily from 9 am to 9 pm

There are also large art exhibitions which come to town periodically, but there is no fixed schedule or location. Since Hanoi (and the rest of Vietnam) lacks any sort of tourist information office, there is no authoritative place to inquire about these events. Most of these exhibits set up at one of the exhibition halls close to Ho Chi Minh's Mausoleum.

There are quite a number of stores in Hanoi offering new and antique Vietnamese handicrafts (lacquerware, mother-of-pearl inlay, ceramics, sandalwood statuettes etc), as well as watercolours, oil paintings, prints and assorted antiques.

North of Hoan Kiem Lake is Hang Buom St, as close as Hanoi gets to having a Chinatown. The goods on sale here differ significantly from what you see elsewhere. It is, for example, the best place to get Chinese chops (seals) carved. If nothing else, it's a picturesque place to stroll.

For philatelic items, try the philatelic counter at the GPO (in the main postal services hall); it is run by the government philatelic corporation, Cotevina (Cong Ty Tem Viet Nam).

## Getting There & Away

**Air** Hanoi has fewer direct international flights than Saigon, but with a change of aircraft in Hong Kong or Bangkok you can get to almost anywhere. As time goes on, more and more air carriers are flying directly into Hanoi. For details on international flights, see the Getting There & Away chapter. A list of Hanoi booking offices for international airlines follows:

Aeroflot
    4 Trang Thi St (☎ 825-6742; fax 824-9411)
Air France
    1 Ba Trieu St (☎ 825-3484, 824-7066; fax 826-6694)
Cathay Pacific Airways
    27 Ly Thuong Kiet St (Hoa Binh Hotel; ☎ 826-7298; fax 826-7709)
China Airlines (Taiwan)
    18 Tran Hung Dao St (☎ 824-2688; fax 824-2588)
China Southern Airlines
    27 Ly Thai To St (Binh Minh Hotel; ☎ 826-9233, 826-9234)
Czech Airlines
    102 A2 Van Phuc Diplomatic Quarter (☎ 845-6512; fax 846-4000)
Japan Airlines
    1 Ba Trieu St (☎ 826-6693; fax 826-6698)
Lao Aviation
    41 Quang Trung St (☎ 826-6538; fax 822-9951)
Malaysia Airlines
    15 Ngo Quyen St (☎ 826-8820, 826-8821; fax 824-2388)
Pacific Airlines
    31B Trang Thi St (☎ 825-2684; fax 825-8905)
Singapore Airlines
    17 Ngo Quyen St (☎ 826-8888; fax 826-8666)
Thai Airways International
    25 Ly Thuong Kiet St (☎ 826-6893; fax 826-7934)
Vasco
    Gia Lam airport (☎ 827-1707; fax 827-2705)
Vietnam Airlines
    1 Quang Trung St (☎ 825-0888, 826-8913; fax 824-8989)

Pacific Airlines is the only company besides Vietnam Airlines to offer domestic flights. Both companies charge the exact same fares on domestic flights, but Pacific Airlines is cheaper on international routes. For details of domestic flights, see the Getting Around chapter.

**Bus** Like Saigon, Hanoi has several main bus terminals and each one serves a particular area.

Gia Lam bus station (Ben Xe Gia Lam) is where you catch buses to points north-east of Hanoi. This includes Halong Bay, Haiphong and Lang Son (near the China border). The bus station is 2km north-east of the centre – you have to cross the Red River to get there. Cyclos won't cross the bridge so you need to get there by motorbike or taxi.

Giap Bat bus station (Ben Xe Giap Bat) serves points south of Hanoi, including Saigon. The station is 7km south of the Hanoi railway station.

Kim Ma bus station (Ben Xe Kim Ma) is opposite 166 Nguyen Thai Hoc St (corner Giang Vo St). This is where you get buses to the north-west part of Vietnam, including Pho Lu and Dien Bien Phu. Tickets should be purchased the day before departure.

**Train** The Hanoi railway station (Ga Ha Noi; ☎ 825-3949) is opposite 115 Le Duan St at the western end of Tran Hung Dao St; the ticket office is open from 7.30 to 11.30 am and 1.30 to 3.30 pm only. There is a special counter where foreigners can purchase tickets. It's often best to buy tickets at least one day before departure to ensure a seat or sleeper.

Where you purchase the ticket is not necessarily where the train departs. Just behind the main station on Le Duan St is a 'B station' (on Tran Qui Cap St) for northbound trains. From the front station entrance to the B station is a two-block walk. Even more complicated is the fact that a few northbound and eastbound trains depart from both the Gia Lam and Long Bien railway stations (both across the bridge on the east side of the Red River). Some of the local southbound trains

**Social Evils**

We were in Vietnam at the height of the social evils campaign on 1996. At the time, we were advised by other tourists that the Vietnamese Department of Cultural Exports had to approve any tourist photographs prior to departure from the country or have the films confiscated at the airport. This rumour was confirmed after contacting the Australian embassy.

After getting five weeks of films developed, we sought out the relevant office on the far side of Hanoi. The films were taken off us and we were told to return immediately with any souvenirs that we had purchased so they could also be assessed. After doing this we were told we should return the next day, as we were flying out that day.

The next day – running out of time – we were interrogated for over an hour about photographs they deemed to reflect Vietnamese culture in a poor light.

The relevant photographs and negatives were confiscated. We were charged for the assessment of the photographs, negatives and souvenirs, and threatened with a hefty fine.

We were advised that a sculpture we had would take three days to assess, and should therefore be left in the country if we wished to leave that day. Finally talking our way out of the office, we proceeded to the airport (with sculpture) only to find that the airport customs officials didn't bother to check our bags, camera or even the documentation we'd been given by the Department of Cultural Exports.

We felt sorry for the guy behind us in Hanoi who had 52 films and a year of souvenirs for these same officials to paw over. This whole scam could have been avoided by going directly to the airport to begin with.

**Nigel & Michelle Gough**

leave from the Giap Bat railway station (about 10km south of Hanoi railway station). Be sure to ask just where you must go to catch your train.

For more information on trains to the Chinese border, see the Land section in the Getting There & Away chapter. For information on trains to Haiphong, see the Haiphong section in the North-East Vietnam chapter.

**Minibus** Tourist-style minibuses can be booked through most hotels and cafes. Popular destinations include Hué and Sapa.

There are frequent minibuses throughout the day to Haiphong from Gia Lam bus station. Service begins around 5 am and the last one leaves Hanoi about 6 pm. These minibuses depart when full (and they really mean 'full'). The cost will typically be around US$3 to US$5 per person. In Haiphong, you catch the minibuses at the Tam Bac bus station.

**Car** To hire a car with a driver, contact a hotel, travellers' cafe or travel agency. The roads in the north-east are generally awful, and in the north-west they are worse than awful. For this reason, you may need a high clearance vehicle or a jeep. Land distances from Hanoi are as follows:

| | |
|---|---|
| Ba Be Lakes | 240km |
| Bac Giang | 51km |
| Bac Ninh | 29km |
| Bach Thong (Bac Can) | 162km |
| Cam Pha | 190km |
| Cao Bang | 272km |
| Da Bac (Cho Bo) | 104km |
| Danang | 763km |
| Dien Bien Phu | 420km |
| Ha Dong | 11km |
| Ha Giang | 343km |
| Hai Duong | 58km |
| Haiphong | 103km |
| Halong City | 165km |
| Hoa Binh | 74km |
| Ho Chi Minh City | 1710km |
| Hué | 658km |
| Lai Chau | 490km |
| Lang Son | 146km |
| Lao Cai | 294km |
| Ninh Binh | 93km |
| Sapa | 324km |
| Son La | 308km |
| Tam Dao | 85km |
| Thai Binh | 109km |
| Thai Nguyen | 73km |
| Thanh Hoa | 175km |
| Tuyen Quang | 165km |
| Viet Tri | 73km |
| Vinh | 319km |
| Yen Bai | 155km |

HANOI

**Motorbike** A long-distance journey from Hanoi into the mountainous hinterland of the north is exciting, though slightly risky in terms of traffic accidents and definitely tiring. You probably wouldn't want to do it during the coldest months (January and February), but in mid-summer you have to contend with occasionally heavy rains. Despite such annoyances, many travellers prefer motorbike travel to all other forms of transport.

Cafes in Hanoi often have motorbike rentals. Quality is extremely variable – some of the bikes on offer are just pure junk. The 125cc Russian-made Minsk is probably the best overall – you will need that kind of power for the mountainous regions.

There are dozens upon dozens of motorbike shops along Hue St, and this is the place to inquire about purchasing a machine. These shops also sell good-quality helmets.

### Getting Around
**The Airport** Hanoi's Noi Bai airport is about 35km north of the city and the journey can take 45 minutes to an hour. The airport freeway is one of the most modern roads in Vietnam, and it's curious to see oxen herded by farmers dressed in rags crossing it. It's also interesting to see how the freeway suddenly terminates in the ghastly suburbs north of Hanoi.

Minibuses from Hanoi to Noi Bai airport depart from the Vietnam Airlines International Booking Office on Quang Trung St, around the corner from Trang Thi/Hang Khai Sts. It's best – though not essential – to book the day before. The schedule follows the departure and arrival times of domestic and international flights. Bus tickets are sold inside the booking office and cost US$4. For US$1 extra, the driver will drop you at your hotel rather than the booking office, though if you're not first in the queue you may get quite a tour of Hanoi's hotels. The minibus service works OK but beware of the usual scams, especially at the airport:

The official airport minibus seems open to fiddling. We got a ticket from the kiosk inside the airport

building, but the driver wanted us to pay him again personally. On the way back, we bought our tickets off the driver, but they didn't look very 'new'.
**B Bolton**

Airport Taxi (☎ 873-3333) charges US$20 for a taxi ride to Noi Bai airport, but only US$15 if going the other way. Furthermore, they do *not* require that you pay for the toll bridge which must be crossed en route. Some other taxi drivers require that you pay the toll, so ask first. A traveller wrote:

There is a toll booth near Hanoi's airport where you have to pay if travelling by taxi. I was travelling with someone I had just met and before we had realised what had happened we both paid US$3 each. We were definitely caught off guard, having only just arrived in Vietnam.

At the airport itself, be careful. The first people to approach you inside the airport ask the highest price for taxis (about US$35). Find the taxi booking desk, where the price is only US$15, but beware of the scam – after buying a ticket you may well be escorted to the minibus (which only costs US$4). Out in the car park, taxis can be negotiated for whatever the market will bear (usually US$15).

In central Hanoi, there is always a collection of taxi drivers just outside the Vietnam Airlines office – it won't take much effort to find one.

**Bus** There are 13 bus lines in Hanoi, though they are numbered one through 14 (route No 13 was axed). Figuring out exactly where the buses go can be a challenge, and service on some of the lines is infrequent. Still, when it comes to economy, only walking is cheaper. Bus fares are typically US$0.10 to US$0.20 depending on the route.

Bus lines were previously shown in red on Hanoi tourist maps, but this is no longer the case as the number of routes has proliferated to the point where it became unmanageable. So far, nobody has published a bus route guide with maps and information on bus stops. Until that happens, we offer the following guide to Hanoi's bus system:

HANOI

1 **Ha Dong – Yen Phu** Nguyen Trai, Nguyen Luong Bang, Kham Thien, Nguyen Thuong Hien, Yet Kieu, Quan Su, Hang Da, Hang Cot, Hang Dau

2 **Ha Dong – Bac Co** Nguyen Trai, Nguyen Luong Bang, Ton Duc Thang, Nguyen Thai Hoc, Hai Ba Trung, Phan Chu Trinh, Bac Co

3 **Giap Bat – Gia Lam bus station** Vong, Kim Lien bus station, Hanoi railway station, Tran Hung Dao, Phan Chu Trinh, Bac Co, Tran Quang Khai, Long Bien bus station, Gia Lam bus station

4 **Long Bien bus station –** Giap Bat railway station Long Bien bus station, Nguyen Huu Huan, Phan Chu Trinh, Lo Duc, Mai Dong, Nguyen Thi Minh Kahi, Mo Market, Truong Dinh, Duoi Ca (Giap Bat railway station)

5 **Nhon – Phan Chu Trinh** Nhon, Cau Dien, Cau Giay, Kim Ma bus station, Nguyen Thai Hoc, Tran Phu, Cua Nam, Hai Ba Trung, Phan Chu Trinh

6 **Long Bien bus station – Ngoc Hoi** Long Bien bus station, Nguyen Huu Huan, Ly Thai To, Co Tan, Phan Chu Trinh, Le Van Huu, Nguyen Du, Le Duan, Kim Lien bus station, Giai Phong, Duoi Ca, Van Dien, Ngoc Hoi

7 **Bo Ho – Cua Nam – Cau Giay** Bo Ho, Hang Gai, Hang Bong, Dien Bien Phu, Le Hong Phong, Doi Can, Buoi, Cau Giay

8 **Long Bien bus station – Mo Market** Long Bien bus station, Hang Dau, Hang Can, Bo Ho, Dinh Tien Hoang, Ba Trieu, Le Dai Hanh, Bach Mai, Mo Market

9 **Long Bien bus station – Cau Bieu**

10 **Bac Co – Yen Vien** Bac Co, Tran Quang Khai, Tran Nhat Duat, Long Bien bus station, Gia Lam bus station, Yen Vien

11 **Kim Lien bus station – Phu Thuy**

12 **Giap Bat – Kim Ma** Kim Lien bus station, Trung Tu, Chua Boc, Thai Ha, Lang Ha, Giang Vo, Kim Ma bus station

14 **Nghia Do – Bo Ho** Nghia Do, Hoang Hoa Tham, Phan Dinh Phung, Hang Cot, Hang Luoc, Luong Van Can, Bo Ho

**Taxi** There are 10 companies in Hanoi offering metered taxis, which is even more than in Saigon! All charge similar rates. Flagfall is US$1.27, which takes you 2km, and then every kilometre thereafter costs between US$0.45 and US$0.60 depending on which company you choose. The competitors in this business include: A Taxi (☎ 832-7327); City Taxi (☎ 822-2222); Five Star Taxi (☎ 855-5555); Hanoi Taxi (☎ 853-3171); Red Taxi (☎ 856-8686); Taxi CP (☎ 824-1999); Taxi PT (☎ 853-3171); Taxi PT2 (☎ 856-5656); Thu Do Taxi (☎ 831-6316); and T Taxi (☎ 821-6262).

There is also a collection of taxis perpetually hanging around the Vietnam Airlines booking office on the corner of Quang Trung and Hang Khai Sts. These drivers of course intend to take you to the airport, but there's no reason why you couldn't pay them to take you elsewhere. There are no meters in these vehicles, so advance negotiation is mandatory.

**Cyclo** The cyclos in Hanoi are wider than the Saigon variety, making it possible for two people to fit in one vehicle and share the fare.

The cyclo drivers in Hanoi are even less likely to speak English than in Saigon, so take a map of the city with you. And finally, some travellers have reported communication problems:

We felt that we were ripped off on more than one occasion in 'misunderstandings' with cyclo drivers. Once we had a really unpleasant time when one young man tried to extort US$15 from us for a 30-minute ride for two.

**Barbara Case**

**Motorbike** You won't have any trouble finding a motorbike rental – just stroll any major street and you'll get an offer every 10 seconds. One rule to watch out for applies only to the circular road around Hoan Kiem Lake – it's illegal to turn left onto this road from any side street. It's an easy rule to unknowingly violate, but the police will happily remind you (the reminder will cost US$5 without receipt, US$25 with).

**Bicycle** The best way to get around Hanoi is by bicycle. Some hotels and cafes offer these for rent. Bike rentals cost about US$1.

If you want to purchase your own set of wheels, Ba Trieu and Hue Sts are the best places to look for bicycle shops.

# Around Hanoi

## BA VI MOUNTAIN
Ba Vi Mountain (Nui Ba Vi) is about 65km west of Hanoi, and is of some interest to Hanoi expats looking for a Sunday escape

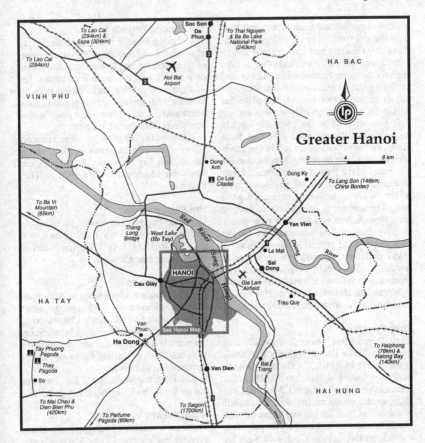

**Greater Hanoi**

0    4    8 km

from the city. The average tourist will probably not be bothered, but anyone who climbs up here will be rewarded with a spectacular view of the Red River valley from the summit (elevation 1287m).

## PAGODAS
### Perfume Pagoda
The Perfume Pagoda (Chua Huong) is about 60km south-west of Hanoi by road. The pagoda is one of the highlights of the Hanoi area and should not be missed. Getting to the pagoda requires a journey first by road and then by river. The boat trip along the scenic

waterways takes about three hours and is good fun.

The Perfume Pagoda itself is a complex of pagodas and Buddhist shrines built into the limestone cliffs of Huong Tich Mountain (Mountain of the Fragrant Traces). Among the better known sites here are Thien·Chu (Pagoda Leading to Heaven); Giai Oan Chu (Purgatorial Pagoda), where the faithful believe deities purify souls, cure sufferings and grant offspring to childless families; and Huong Tich Chu (Pagoda of the Perfumed Vestige).

Great numbers of Buddhist pilgrims come here during a festival that begins in the

HANOI

middle of the second lunar month and lasts until the last week of the third lunar month; these dates usually end up corresponding to March and April. Pilgrims and other visitors spend their time here boating, hiking and exploring the caves. Despite the occasionally large number of visitors, this place has a peaceful and perhaps holy atmosphere.

If you want to do the river trip (highly recommended!), you need to travel from Hanoi by car for two hours to My Duc, then take a small boat rowed by two women for 1½ hours to the foot of the mountain. From where the boat lets you off, you have about a 4km (two hour) walk up to the main pagoda area. The scenery is comparable to Halong Bay, though here you are on a river rather than by the sea. The combined fee for the boat journey and general admission ticket is US$7, and there is no way to bargain around this as the price is set by the government. The return trip to your vehicle is also by rowboat.

Most of the travellers' cafes in Hanoi book inexpensive day trips to the Perfume Pagoda.

## Thay Pagoda

Thay Pagoda (the Master's Pagoda), also known as Thien Phuc (Heavenly Blessing), is dedicated to Thich Ca Buddha (Sakyamuni, the historical Buddha) and 18 *arhats* (monks who have attained Nirvana); the latter appear on the central altar. On the left is a statue of the 12th century monk Tu Dao Hanh, the 'Master' after whom the pagoda is named; on the right is a statue of King Ly Nhan Tong, who is believed to be a reincarnation of Tu Dao Hanh. In front of the pagoda is a small stage built on stilts in the middle of a pond; water puppet shows are staged here during festivals.

The pagoda's annual festival is held from the fifth to the seventh days of the third lunar month. Pilgrims and other visitors enjoy watching water puppet shows, hiking and exploring caves in the area.

Thay Pagoda is about 40km south-west of Hanoi in Ha Tay Province. Some of Hanoi's cafes catering to budget travellers offer combined day tours of the Thay and Tay Phuong (see next entry) pagodas.

## Tay Phuong Pagoda

Tay Phuong Pagoda (Pagoda of the West), also known as Sung Phuc Pagoda, consists of three parallel single-level structures built on a hillock said to resemble a buffalo. The 76 figures carved from jackfruit wood, many from the 18th century, are the pagoda's most celebrated feature. The earliest construction here dates from the 8th century.

Tay Phuong Pagoda is approximately 40km south-west of Hanoi in Tay Phuong hamlet, Ha Tay Province. A visit here can easily be combined with a stop at Thay Pagoda.

## Van Phuc Pagoda

Van Phuc Pagoda, surrounded by hills considered noteworthy for their beauty, was founded in 1037. It is 27km north-east of Hanoi in Ha Bac Province.

## But Thap Pagoda

But Thap Pagoda, also known as Ninh Phuc Pagoda, is known for its four-storey stone stupa dedicated to the monk Chuyet Cong. The pagoda's date of founding is uncertain, but records indicate that it was rebuilt in the 17th and 18th centuries; the layout of the structure is traditional.

But Thap Pagoda is in Ha Bac Province not far from Van Phuc Pagoda.

## HANDICRAFT VILLAGES

There are a number of villages in the Hanoi vicinity which specialise in a particular cottage industry. Visiting these villages can be a rewarding day trip, though you'll need a good guide to make the journey worthwhile.

**Le Mat** is the snake village. The locals raise snakes for the upmarket restaurants in Hanoi. Of course, fresh snake cuisine is available at this village, though it's not really cheap. A large snake can cost US$30 to US$50, but can feed four to six persons. Several upmarket snake restaurants can be found here, including: *Phong Do* (☎ 827-3244), *Phong Do II* (☎ 827-1091) and *Quoc Trieu* (☎ 827-2898). There are also a number of cheaper stalls peddling snake meat and snake elixir. If you haven't stocked up on snake wine yet, this is a good place to do it. On the 23rd day of the third lunar month is the very interesting Le Mat Festival, featuring 'snake dances' and other activities. Le Mat is 7km north-east of central Hanoi.

**So** is a village known for delicate noodles. The village even produces flour from which the noodles are made. The flour is made from yams and cassava (manioc) rather than wheat. So is in Ha Tay Province, about 25km south-west of Hanoi.

**Bat Trang** is known as the ceramic village. You can see artisans create superb ceramic vases and other masterpieces in their kilns. It's hot sweaty work, but the results are superb. Bat Trang is 13km south-east of Hanoi.

**Van Phuc** is the silk village. You can see silk cloth being produced on a loom. Many of the fine silk items you see on sale in Hanoi's Hang Gai St originate here. Van Phuc is 8km south-west of Hanoi in Ha Tay Province.

**Dong Ky** was at one time known as the 'firecracker village'. Prior to 1995 (when the government banned firecrackers) there was always a firecracker festival in Dong Ky. A competition for the loudest firecracker once resulted in the building of a gargantuan firecracker 16m in length!

With the firecracker industry now extinguished, the village survives by producing beautiful traditional furniture inlaid with mother-of-pearl. If you wish, you can have handcrafted furniture custom-made here and exported directly to your address abroad. Arranging the payments may prove a bit tricky if you're leaving Vietnam before the final product is produced and shipped. Dong Ky is 15km north-east of Hanoi.

## CO LOA CITADEL

Co Loa Citadel (Co Loa Thanh), the first fortified citadel recorded in Vietnamese history, dates from the 3rd century BC. Only vestiges of the massive ancient ramparts, which enclosed an area of about five sq km, are extant. Co Loa again became the national capital under Ngo Quyen (reigned 939-44). In the centre of the citadel are temples dedicated to King An Duong Vuong (ruled 257-208 BC), who founded the legendary Thuc Dynasty, and his daughter My Nuong (Mi Chau). When My Nuong showed her father's magic crossbow trigger – which made the Vietnamese king invincible in battle – to her husband (who was the son of a Chinese general), he stole it and gave it to his father. With its help, the Chinese were able to defeat An Duong Vuong and his forces, depriving Vietnam of its independence.

Co Loa Citadel is 16km north of central Hanoi in Dong Anh district.

# North-East Vietnam

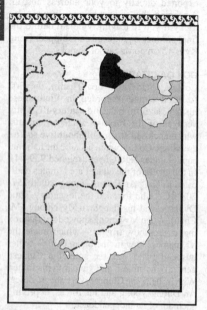

Dominated by the Red River basin and the sea, the fertile north-east is the cradle of Vietnamese civilisation. Much of Vietnamese history was made here, not all of it happy. In particular, Vietnam had less than cordial relations with the Chinese, who invaded in the 2nd century BC and stayed for about 1000 years. Indeed, the last invasion took place only in 1979. And to judge by recent rhetoric, the next invasion might not be far off.

On a more positive note, this part of Vietnam is showing some real economic potential. Much investor interest centres on Haiphong, Vietnam's largest seaport. However, it's scenery – not history, politics and economics – which is the major tourist drawcard here. In particular, the spectacular coastline of Halong Bay, Bai Tu Long Bay and Cat Ba Island offer some of nature's most bizarre geologic displays. Add to that interesting side attractions such as Ba Be Lakes, the mountains around Cao Bang plus easy access to China, and it's not hard to see why Vietnam's north-east is a major magnet for visitors.

## TAM DAO HILL STATION

Tam Dao Hill Station (elevation 930m), known to the French as the Cascade d'Argent (Silver Cascade), was founded by the French in 1907 as a place of escape from the heat of the Red River Delta.

Unfortunately, the grand colonial villas are run-down and many have been replaced by politically correct, Soviet-inspired, concrete box architecture. There is now a belated effort being made to restore the colonial villas.

Hanoi residents sometimes call Tam Dao 'the Dalat of the north'. This has more to do with its high elevation and cool climate. In fact, it bears little resemblance to Dalat.

The big problem with Tam Dao is that it's very small. There just isn't that much to see and do here and most visitors quickly grow bored. However, at least a couple of travellers seemed to enjoy it:

This place is really damp; we had to scrape the mushrooms off our sheets and clothes will stay wet. Perhaps we went at the wrong time of year, but in early April the clouds just drift right in through the open windows into your room … Tam Dao has no nightlife, but for sheer atmosphere you can't beat it. There is a grand stone staircase at the back leading up to a radio transmitter. Over towards the waterfall another path comes out on a wide area of ruins and great balustrades looking over the valley. It's like Babylon or something. The people are very friendly and there are not many tourists … We went to Tam Dao to watch birds, and it is an excellent place to do so.

**Tim Woodward & Phaik Hua Tan**

Our experience was decidedly mixed. We thought the drive to get there was very picturesque, but Tam Dao itself is a bit disappointing because it's small and run-down. If

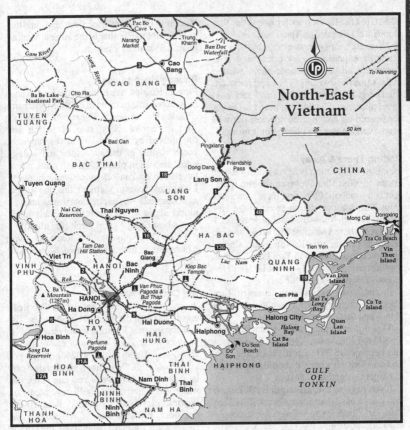

North-East
Vietnam

you're living in Hanoi and would like to find a summer weekend retreat, it might be worth coming up here for the cool weather and a change of pace. In fact, Hanoi expats do occasionally come up here in groups for parties and special events (the Hanoi Weekend Warriors stage an annual Halloween party here). However, travellers with limited time in Vietnam will almost certainly prefer to spend their precious holidays relaxing some place else.

The three summits of Tam Dao Mountain, all about 1400m in height, are visible from the hill station to the north-east. Many hill tribe people live in the Tam Dao region,

though they are largely assimilated. The best times of the year to visit Tam Dao are generally from late May to mid-September and from mid-December to February.

Dampness makes the Tam Dao area particularly rich in flora and fauna. However, logging (both legal and otherwise) has severely affected the environment.

Remember that it is cool up in Tam Dao and that this part of Vietnam has a distinct winter. Don't be caught unprepared.

### Places to Stay & Eat
There are many hotels, mostly charging from

US$10 to US$15. One such place is the *Tam Dao Hotel* (Khach San Tam Dao).

There are heaps of restaurants, but they are generally expensive – ask prices first. The restaurants all have the same menu, written in the same handwriting. The chief items are fried or grilled deer, roast squirrel and roast silver pheasant. The latter delicacy is not yet considered an endangered species, but will soon likely be one, so please don't order it!

### Getting There & Away

Tam Dao Hill Station is 85km north-west of Hanoi in Vinh Phu Province. Public transport is a problem. First, you must take a bus from Kim Ma bus station (west of the city centre) to Vinh Yen – the last one leaves at 1 pm. From there you must hire a motorcycle (about US$2) or taxi for the 24km single-lane track that leads up to Tam Dao. There is a toll for using this road – about US$0.30 for motorbikes or US$1.50 for cars.

Probably the easiest way to reach Tam Dao is to simply rent your own motorbike in Hanoi and drive yourself.

Taxi drivers typically ask something like US$45 to bring you to Tam Dao from Hanoi and perhaps US$30 to come back and pick you up a few days later. It should be possible to bargain something cheaper.

If you're going to Cao Bang or Ba Be Lakes, you could easily arrange a stopoff in Tam Dao for a little extra money. Most people shouldn't bother.

Warning! Beware of the men selling expensive 'compulsory' insurance at the entrance gate to the hill station road. Although you really do get insurance, it isn't compulsory.

### THAI NGUYEN

There isn't a whole lot in Thai Nguyen itself to hold your interest, but there are a couple of lightweight sightseeing attractions in the area that just might be worth visiting if you have time.

### Museum of Northern Vietnam

The only really worthwhile thing to see in the town itself is the Museum of Northern Vietnam (Bao Tang Viet Bac). Despite the nondescript name, this is the largest Montagnard museum in Vietnam.

### Phuong Hoang Cave

Phuong Hoang Cave is one of the largest and most accessible caverns in northern Vietnam (Phuong Hoang means 'Phoenix'). There are four main chambers, two of which are illuminated by the sun when the angle is correct. Most of the stalactites and stalagmites are still in place, although quite a few have been broken off by souvenir hunters. Like many caves in Vietnam, this one served as a 'hospital' – the euphemism for an ammunition depot. If you want to see anything, you'd best bring a good torch (flashlight).

From Thai Nguyen, it's a 40km ride over a bumpy road to reach the cave. Motorbikes can do the trip.

### Nui Coc Reservoir

A now popular scenic spot is Nui Coc Reservoir, 25km to the west of Thai Nguyen. By world standards, it's not a terribly impressive body of water, but it's a major drawcard for city-bound Hanoi residents looking to get away from it all. On summer weekends it can be particularly crowded. You can leave the water-skis at home, but you'll have plenty of opportunities to take a touristy boat trip. A one-hour, circular tour of the lake is *de rigueur* and your cost depends on the size of the boat and number of passengers. Small boats costing US$14 per hour have a maximum capacity of 15 people and a safe capacity of around 10. Larger boats costing US$28 per hour can hold up to 50 people.

You might wish to stay at Nui Coc Reservoir – rooms at the *Nui Coc Hotel* (☎ 825312) cost US$7 to US$22.

The reservoir can be reached by motorbike from Thai Nguyen.

### Getting There

Thai Nguyen is 120km north of Hanoi and the highway is in good nick.

There are buses and minibuses to Thai

Nguyen departing from Hanoi's Gia Lam station.

The Hanoi-Quan Trieu train departs Hanoi at 1.15 pm, stopping at Thai Nguyen en route.

## KIEP BAC TEMPLE

This temple is perhaps of more interest to domestic travellers than foreigners. Indeed, to the Vietnamese it is something of a hallowed shrine.

Kiep Bac Temple (Den Kiep Bac) is dedicated to Tran Hung Dao (1228-1300, born Tran Quoc Tuan). He was an outstanding general of renowned bravery who defeated 300,000 Mongol invaders in the mid-1280s. Second only to Ho Chi Minh, he's one of the most revered Vietnamese folk heroes.

The temple was founded in 1300 and was built on the site where Tran Hung Dao is said to have died. The temple was built not only for the general himself, but also to honour other notable members of his family. For example, there is the general's daughter, Quyen Thanh, who married Tran Nhat Ton, who is credited with founding the Vietnamese sect of Buddhism called Truc Lam.

There is a Tran Hung Dao Festival held at Kiep Bac Temple every year from the 18th to the 20th day of the eighth lunar month. At all times expect to encounter heaps of souvenir vendors at the entrance, though they are not permitted inside the temple itself. One thing you might consider purchasing from them is incense – it's considered proper to burn a few incense sticks in Tran Hung Dao's honour, though foreigners may be excused from this requirement.

Kiep Bac Temple is in Hai Hung Province 61km from Hanoi and 32km from Bac Ninh and can easily be visited on the way to Haiphong or Halong Bay.

## CON SON

This is another place primarily of interest to Vietnamese rather than foreigners. Con Son (in Hai Hung Province) was the home of Nguyen Trai (1380-1442), famed Vietnamese poet, writer and general. Nguyen Trai assisted Le Loi in his successful battle against the Chinese Ming dynasty.

In Con Son there is a temple honouring Nguyen Trai. You'll get some exercise if you want to visit since it's atop a mountain (you have to climb 600 steps to reach it). Or you can take another route which passes by a spring. The mountain is covered with pines and makes for pleasant walking. There's a large lake nearby and, on the opposite side, there's a standard, Communist-inspired war memorial.

At the time of writing, the only place to stay here was the old, but well-maintained, *Con Son Hotel* (☎ 882240; fax 882630; 43 rooms), where twins cost US$30. You can eat at this hotel only if you order meals in advance, or you can go 4km to the town of Sao Do, which has a few restaurants. There was another new hotel being built near the shore of the lake which will probably be open by the time you read this.

## HAIPHONG

By expanding the city limits, Haiphong has become Vietnam's third most populous city (in reality Danang has a higher population). Greater Haiphong has an area of 1515 sq km and 1.3 million inhabitants; Haiphong proper covers 21 sq km and is home to 370,000 souls. Less controversially, this is the north's main industrial centre and one of the country's most important seaports.

The French took possession of Haiphong – then a small market town – in 1874. The city soon became a major port; industrial concerns were established here in part because of its proximity to coal supplies.

One of the immediate causes of the Franco-Viet Minh War was the infamous French bombardment of the 'native quarters' of Haiphong in 1946 in which hundreds of civilians were killed and injured (a contemporary French account estimated civilian deaths at 'no more than 6000').

Haiphong came under American air and naval attacks between 1965 and 1972. In May 1972, President Nixon ordered the mining of Haiphong harbour to cut the flow of Soviet military supplies to northern Vietnam. As part of the Paris cease-fire accords of 1973, the USA agreed to help clear the mines from Haiphong harbour – 10 US navy minesweepers were involved in the effort.

Since the late 1970s, Haiphong has experienced a massive exodus of refugees, including many ethnic-Chinese, who have taken with them much of the city's fishing fleet.

In spite of being a major port and one of Vietnam's largest cities, Haiphong today is a sleepy place with little traffic and many dilapidated buildings. On the other hand, this port city does have the potential to develop rapidly. A Haiphong travel pamphlet has this to say about the city's aspirations for the future:

Nowadays Haiphong is one of the creative and active cities in the socialist construction and in the defence of the socialist country. The people in Haiphong are sparing no effort to build it both into a modern port city with developed industry and agriculture and a centre of import and export, tourism and attendance and at the same time an iron fortress against foreign invasion.

The Haiphong police are intent on maintaining the 'iron fortress against foreign invasion'. They have set up a permanent checkpoint on the northern bank of the Cam River right where the ferry lands and *every* vehicle carrying foreigners will be stopped and fined. We had to pay here and so will you unless you avoid this route. This is the only bus route between Haiphong and Halong Bay. If all you want to see is Halong Bay, you can avoid trouble by driving directly from Hanoi to Halong Bay (there is a more northern route which bypasses Haiphong entirely). All of the travel agencies and cafes in Hanoi which book trips to Halong Bay now avoid Haiphong entirely.

Individual travellers who take the ferry directly from Haiphong to Halong Bay need not fear – the problem currently only exists if you are travelling by car, van or bus. You *probably* will not have trouble if you ride your own motorbike, but we didn't test out that option ourselves in Haiphong.

Beware! By far our most unpleasant experience in Vietnam was at the ferry port in Haiphong. A group of school girls by the pier ostensibly selling postcards and giving 'friendly advice' were suspiciously, but almost convincingly, enthusiastic in trying to persuade us *not* to take the ferry to Hon Gai. They claimed that 'there's no place to stay' in Hon Gai. They almost succeeded in stopping the four of us from having what turned out to be a wonderful experience. They and their 'student' friend (a young man in his early 20s) wanted us to go in a minibus to who-knows-where instead. I'll leave it to the readers to imagine what their purpose might have been, but we all felt ill at ease and our sixth senses told us something was wrong.

**John Holton**

## Information
**Travel Agencies** Vietnam Tourism (☎ 842-957; fax 842974) at 12 Le Dai Hanh St is ready, willing and able to take your money if you'd like to book a trip to Cat Ba or Halong Bay. Don't expect too much in the way of information though.

**Money** Vietcombank (Ngan Hang Ngoai Thuong Viet Nam; ☎ 842658; fax 841117) is at 11 Hoang Dieu St, not far from the post office.

**Post & Communications** The post office is at 3 Nguyen Tri Phuong St (corner Hoang Van Thu St).

**Emergency** If you need medical treatment, you'd do better to get yourself to Hanoi. Otherwise, some places to try include the Traditional Medicine Hospital (Benh Vien Dong Y) on Nguyen Duc Canh St and the Vietnam-Czech Friendship Hospital (Benh Vien Viet-Tiep) on Nha Thuong St.

### Du Hang Pagoda
Du Hang Pagoda, which is at 121 Chua Hang St, was founded three centuries ago. Though it has been rebuilt several times, it remains a good example of traditional Vietnamese architecture and sculpture.

### Hang Kenh Communal House
Hang Kenh Communal House on Hang Kenh St is known for its 500 relief sculptures

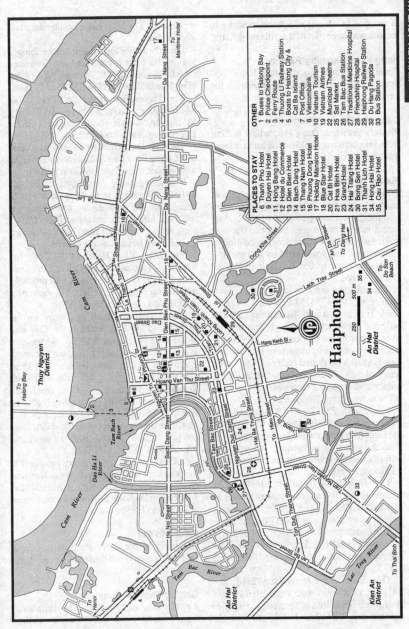

**PLACES TO STAY**

6 Thanh Pho Hotel
9 Duyen Hai Hotel
11 Hong Bang Hotel
12 Hotel du Commerce
13 Dien Bien Hotel
14 Bach Dang Hotel
15 Thang Nam Hotel
16 Phuong Dong Hotel
17 Holiday Mansion Hotel
18 Blue Star Hotel
20 Cat Bi Hotel
21 Hoa Binh Hotel
23 Grand Hotel
24 Hai Trang Hotel
30 Bong Sen Hotel
31 Thanh Lich Hotel
34 Hong Hai Hotel
35 Cau Rao Hotel

**OTHER**

1 Buses to Halong Bay
2 Police Checkpoint
3 Ferry Route
4 Thuong Li Railway Station
5 Boats to Halong City &
   Cat Ba Island
7 Post Office
8 Vietcombank
10 Vietnam Tourism
19 Vietnam Airlines
22 Municipal Theatre
25 Sat Market
26 Tam Bac Bus Station
27 Traditional Medicine Hospital
28 Friendship Hospital
29 Haiphong Railway Station
32 Du Hang Pagoda
33 Bus Station

Haiphong

0    250    500 m

in wood. The area in which the structure is located was once part of the village of Kenh.

## Hang Kenh Tapestry Factory
Founded 65 years ago, the Hang Kenh Tapestry Factory produces wool tapestries for export.

## Dang Hai Flower Village
Flowers grown at Dang Hai, which is 5km from Haiphong, are sold on the international market.

## Places to Stay
While there are some cheap places to stay, at least theoretically, in Haiphong, renovation is rapidly converting the last of the budget hotels into pricey tourist palaces. The best advice we can give about accommodation in Haiphong is that you should try to avoid it – if possible, stay in Cat Ba, Halong Bay or Hanoi instead.

The cheapest place in town is the *Thanh Lich Hotel* (☎ 847361; 18 rooms). It's at 47 Lach Tray St in a park-like compound; the only real drawback of staying here is that it's over 1km from the city centre. Still, you can get there by cyclo or motorbike taxi. Rooms cost US$10 with shared bath or US$15 with attached bath. There is a restaurant inside the compound, though it closes early. Next door is the newer *Bong Sen Hotel*.

The *Thanh Pho Hotel* (☎ 842524; nine rooms) is just opposite the main ferry pier on the Cam River. All rooms for foreigners cost US$25. The staff is friendly and you can amuse or abuse yourself in the evening with a karaoke machine.

The *Hoa Binh Hotel* (☎ 846907; 120 rooms) is across from the railway station at 104 Luong Khanh Thien St. This newly renovated place now costs US$17 to US$35.

The *Cat Bi Hotel* (☎ 846306; fax 845181; 22 rooms) at 30 Tran Phu St is also close to the railway station. Rooms cost US$15 and US$35.

The *Thang Nam Hotel* (☎ 842818; fax 841019; 18 rooms) at 55 Dien Bien Phu St is another place that is theoretically cheap. Rooms cost US$12 to US$25. Still, it's a worth a try. The hotel has a beauty shop and a restaurant.

Directly across the street from the foregoing is the French-era *Hotel du Commerce* (☎ 842706; fax 842560; 35 rooms) at 62 Dien Bien Phu St. The tariff is US$25 to US$40.

The *Duyen Hai Hotel* (☎ 842157; fax 841140; 33 rooms) at 5 Nguyen Tri Phuong St has one single room costing US$25. Everything else costs US$35 to US$40.

The *Bach Dang Hotel* (☎ 842444; 21 rooms) at 42 Dien Bien Phu St has rooms covering a wide price range from US$20 to US$45.

The *Hong Bang Hotel* (☎ 842229; fax 841044; 29 rooms) at 64 Dien Bien Phu St charges US$40 for a double room equipped with bath, refrigerator and colour TV, or US$65 for a deluxe room. The hotel has a restaurant, a steam bath and a massage service.

The *Dien Bien Hotel* (☎ 842264; fax 842977; 20 rooms) is a new place at 67 Dien Bien Phu St. The hotel's name will probably not enthral French travellers, but the rooms are OK and cost US$25 to US$40.

About 2km south of the centre on the highway to Do Son Beach is the *Cau Rao Hotel* (☎ 847021; fax 847586; 60 rooms). It's a quiet and pleasant place, but not much English is spoken. Doubles cost US$15 to US$40. The address is officially 460 Lach Tray St. Just next door is the *Hong Hai Hotel*.

The *Blue Star Hotel* (Khach San Ngoi San Xanh; ☎ 852038) at 34B Da Nang St is a new, five-storey place out in the quiet, eastern part of town. Rooms here are good and priced from US$15 to US$25.

Still farther out on the eastern periphery is the new, large and luxurious *Holiday Mansion Hotel* (Khach San Dau Khi; ☎ 845667; fax 845668) on Da Nang St. The price range here is US$25 to US$50.

## Places to Eat
Haiphong is noted for its excellent fresh seafood, which is available from every hotel restaurant.

## Getting There & Away
**Air** Vietnam Airlines flies the Haiphong-Saigon route twice daily. Pacific Airlines

flies this same route three times weekly. Vietnam Airlines also offers three flights weekly between Haiphong and Danang.

**Bus** Haiphong has several long-distance bus stations. For Bai Chay (in Halong Bay), the station you want is in the Thuy Nguyen District (northern bank of the Cam River). To reach the Thuy Nguyen District, you must take a ferry (see Haiphong map). Bus departures are not frequent (there is only one bus scheduled daily), although minibuses will make the run when demand is sufficient. The scheduled bus departs Haiphong at 9 am for Bai Chay. Departure from Bai Chay is at 12.30 pm. The one-way fare is US$4.

Hanoi-Haiphong buses and minibuses depart from Hanoi's Gia Lam bus station. Departures are approximately from 5 am until 6 pm and the journey takes around 2½ hours. These minibuses depart only when full and generally will be packed to the hilt. In Haiphong, get these buses at the Tam Bac bus station.

**Train** Haiphong is not on the main line between Hanoi and Saigon, but there is a spur line connecting it to Hanoi. There is one express train daily from Hanoi station and another one from Long Bien station (Ga Long Bien, near Hanoi on the eastern side of the Red River).

The train from Hanoi station departs at 5.45 am and arrives in Haiphong at 8.15 am. Going the other way, the train departs Haiphong at 5.55 pm and arrives in Hanoi at 8.10 pm.

The train at Long Bien station departs at 2 pm and arrives in Haiphong at 4.20 pm. For the return, this train departs Haiphong at 10.45 am and arrives in Long Bien station at 1.10 pm.

There are two railway stations within the city limits of Haiphong. The Thuong Li railway station is in the western part of the city, far from the centre. The Haiphong railway station is right in the city centre; this is the last stop for the train coming from Hanoi and this is where you should get off.

**Car** Haiphong is 103km from Hanoi on National Highway 5. The current highway is a mess – allow at least 2½ to three hours for the one-way, Hanoi-Haiphong trip.

This is set to change. A new freeway (Vietnam's first) is being built between the two cities. Travel time should be reduced to just one hour.

**Boat** The two boats of interest to travellers are those going to Cat Ba Island and Hon Gai (Halong Bay). See the Cat Ba and Halong Bay sections for details.

### Getting Around
**Taxi** Haiphong is served by VP Taxi (☎ 828-282), which offers metered, air-conditioned taxis.

## DO SON BEACH
The palm-shaded beach at Do Son, 21km south-east of central Haiphong, is a popular seaside resort and a favourite of Hanoi's expatriate community. The hilly, 4km-long promontory ends with a string of islets. The peninsula's nine hills are known as the Cuu Long Son (Nine Dragons).

The resort is not all it's cracked up to be, or rather it's more cracked up than it used to be. Many of the hotels are looking rather dog-eared. The problem is really that most of the visitors are day-trippers from Hanoi and Haiphong, so the hotels just aren't getting the customers needed to justify extensive renovations. If there was ever any hope that foreign tourists would revive business, it's been quashed by Haiphong's police force.

The town is famous for its ritual buffalo fights which are held annually on the 10th day of the eighth lunar month, the date on which the leader of an 18th century peasant rebellion here was killed.

More recently, the town has become famous for the first casino to open in Vietnam since 1975. This joint venture between the government and a Hong Kong company started operations in October 1994 and it remains to be seen just how successful it will be. Foreigners are permitted to lose their fortunes here, but Vietnamese are barred from entering the casino.

## HALONG BAY

Magnificent Halong Bay, with its 3000-plus islands rising from the clear, emerald waters of the Gulf of Tonkin, is one of the natural marvels of Vietnam. Visitors have compared the area's magical landscape of limestone islets to Guilin in China and Krabi in southern Thailand. These tiny islands are dotted with innumerable beaches and grottoes created by the wind and the waves.

*Ha long* means 'where the dragon descends into the sea'. Legend has it that the islands of Halong Bay were created by a great dragon who lived in the mountains. As it ran towards the coast, its flailing tail gouged out valleys and crevasses; as it plunged into the sea, the areas dug up by the tail became filled with water, leaving only bits of high land visible.

The dragon may be legend, but sailors in the Halong Bay region have often reported sightings of a mysterious marine creature of gargantuan proportions known as the Tarasque. More paranoid elements of the military suspect it's

an imperialist spy submarine, while eccentric foreigners believe they have discovered Vietnam's own version of the Loch Ness monster. Meanwhile, the monster, or whatever it is, continues to haunt Halong Bay, unfettered by the marine police, Vietnam Tourism and the immigration authorities. Enterprising Vietnamese boat owners have made a cottage industry out of the creature, offering cash-laden tourists the chance to rent a junk and pursue the Tarasque before he gets fed up and swims away.

Dragons aside, the biggest threat to the bay may be from souvenir-hunting tourists. Rare corals and seashells are rapidly being stripped from the sea floor, while stalactites and stalagmites are being broken off from the caves. These items get turned into key rings, paperweights and ashtrays which are on sale in the local souvenir shops. You might consider the virtue of not buying these items and spending your cash instead on postcards and silk paintings.

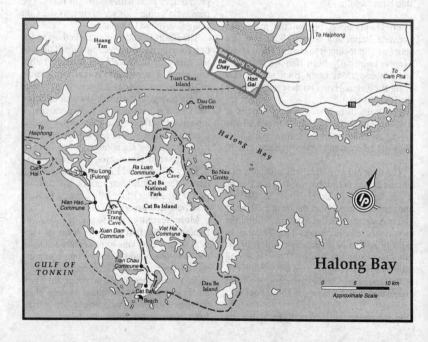

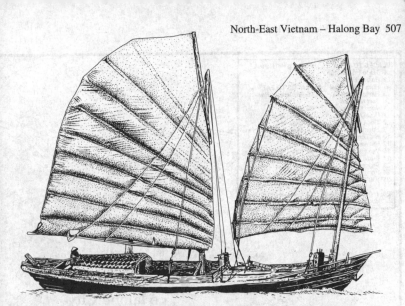

The increasingly rare junks of Halong Bay are slow and creaky, but there are few better ways to discover the tiny, picturesque islands scattered through the emerald waters of the Gulf of Tonkin.

## Orientation

Halong Bay and its numerous islands sprawl out over an area of 1500 sq km.

Food, accommodation and all other life-support systems are to be found in the town of Halong City, the capital of Quang Ninh Province. The town is bisected by a bay – there are five districts on the western side of the bay and 12 districts on the eastern side. For travellers, the most important district on the western side is called Bai Chay. A short ferry ride across the bay takes you to the Hon Gai district (also spelled 'Hong Gai'). The district names are important – most long-distance buses, for example, will be marked 'Bai Chay' or 'Hon Gai' rather than 'Halong City'.

Accommodation can be found on both sides of the bay, but Bai Chay is more scenic, closer to Hanoi and much better endowed with hotels and restaurants. Hon Gai is the main port district and exports coal (a major product of this province), which means this area is dirtier. However, the ferry from Haiphong docks in Hon Gai, so if you arrive late

you may just find it easier to spend the night there before crossing over to Bai Chay the next morning.

## Information

**Travel Agencies** There is an office of Quang Ninh Tourist (Cong Ty Du Lich Quang Ninh; ☎ 846318, 846321) on Bai Chai St in Bai Chay. This agency owns several hotels and can inform you about boat tours and the like.

**Money** Vietcombank has a branch in Hon Gai, which is inconvenient since most of the tourists stay in Bai Chay on the other side of the bay.

## Beach

The 'beach' around Halong City is basically mud and rock – a problem the authorities are trying to 'correct'. A Taiwanese company has a contract to build a beach in Bai Chay with imported sand. It should be interesting to see what they come up with. Officially there are two beaches, creatively named

NORTH-EAST VIETNAM

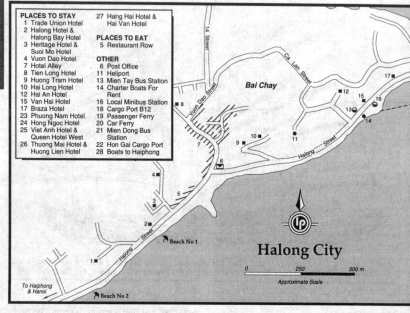

PLACES TO STAY
1   Trade Union Hotel
2   Halong Hotel &
    Halong Bay Hotel
3   Heritage Hotel &
    Suoi Mo Hotel
4   Vuon Dao Hotel
7   Hotel Alley
8   Tien Long Hotel
9   Huong Tram Hotel
10  Hai Long Hotel
12  Hai An Hotel
15  Van Hai Hotel
17  Braza Hotel
23  Phuong Nam Hotel
24  Hong Ngoc Hotel
25  Viet Anh Hotel &
    Queen Hotel West
26  Thuong Mai Hotel &
    Huong Lien Hotel

27  Hang Hai Hotel &
    Hai Van Hotel

PLACES TO EAT
5   Restaurant Row

OTHER
6   Post Office
11  Heliport
13  Mien Tay Bus Station
14  Charter Boats For
    Rent
16  Local Minibus Station
18  Cargo Port B12
19  Passenger Ferry
20  Car Ferry
21  Mien Dong Bus
    Station
22  Hon Gai Cargo Port
28  Boats to Haiphong

Bai Chay

Halong City

0    250    500 m
Approximate Scale

'Beach No 1' (Bai Tam 1) and 'Beach No 2'
(Bai Tam 2).

The current beach is not at all attractive
for swimming. However, it's common practice to take a swim during a boat trip – the
boats can take you to remote coves with clear
water, although only minimal sand. If you do
go swimming, it would be wise to have
someone (hopefully trustworthy) watch your
valuables while you're cavorting in the water.

### Grottoes

Due to the rock type of Halong Bay's islands,
the area is dotted with thousands of caves of
all sizes and shapes.

Hang Dau Go (Grotto of Wooden Stakes),
known to the French as the Grotte des
Merveilles (Cave of Marvels), is a huge cave
consisting of three chambers which you
reach via 90 steps. Among the stalactites of
the first hall, scores of gnomes appear to be
holding a meeting. The walls of the second
chamber sparkle if bright light is shined on

them. The cave derives its Vietnamese name
from the third of the chambers, which is said
to have been used during the 13th century to
store the sharp bamboo stakes which Tran
Hung Dao planted in the bed of the Bach
Dang River to impale Kublai Khan's invasion fleet.

Drum Grotto is so named because when
the wind blows through its many stalactites
and stalagmites, visitors think they hear the
sound of distant drumbeats. Other well-
known caves in Halong Bay include the
Grotto of Bo Nau and 2km-long Hang Hanh
Cave.

### Islands

Some tourist boats stop at Deu (Reu) Island,
which supports an unusual species of monkey
distinguished by their red buttocks. A few
travellers also visit Ngoc Vung Island, which
has a red brick lighthouse.

Tuan Chau Island (5km west of Bai Chay)
is one of the few islands in Halong Bay

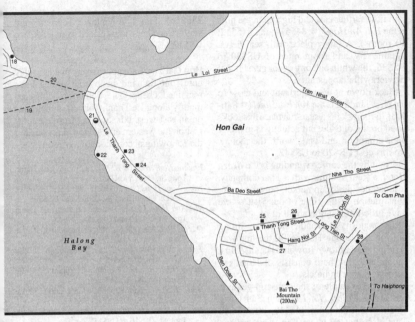

which has seen any development. Ho Chi Minh's former summer residence is here. Currently there are three villas and a restaurant. In early 1997 the government revealed plans to build a US$100 million resort complex here, complete with hotels, villas and a golf course.

### Places to Stay

Some foreigners have reckoned that they could sleep on the boats down by the pier. However, the Halong City police object to this, both to prevent robberies and protect the hotel industry. If you're caught sleeping on a boat, both you and the boat owner can be fined. Most boat owners will not risk the wrath of the police, so you should forget this option.

The majority of travellers prefer to stay in Bai Chay. There are now more than 100 hotels here, with a new one opening up every month or so. Keen competition keeps prices down, though you will probably have to pay more in the peak summer travel season or during Tet.

**Bai Chay**  The hotels are found in several areas. The heaviest concentration is right in the town itself, the so-called 'hotel alley'. This is where you'll find the most mini-hotels, plus very competitive prices. Expect to pay something like US$15 for a double with private bath and air-conditioning.

Up on the hill overlooking hotel alley is the large, state-run *Tien Long Hotel* (☎ 8460-42; 47 rooms). The going rate here is US$20. It's a large spacious place, but has been neglected and is becoming dilapidated.

A couple of mini-hotels on a hill, with good views of the bay, provide a possibly interesting alternative. Two nice places which come to mind are the *Huong Tram Hotel* (☎ 846365; 16 rooms), which only costs US$10, or the better-appointed *Hai Long Hotel* (☎ 846378; 20 rooms), which is priced at US$25.

A little farther east and high up in the hills is the *Hai An Hotel* (☎ 845514; fax 845512; 40 rooms). A fancy place with sea views, satellite TV and room rates of US$30 to US$35, the white balcony decor gives it that 'Riviera villa' appearance.

Back down at the waterfront and close to the ferry landing is the *Van Hai Hotel* (☎ 846-403; 76 rooms). It's a state-run place that looks good on the outside, but actually is in pretty poor condition and isn't worth the money. Rooms cost US$20 to US$42. .

Right by the car ferry landing is the *Braza Hotel*, a joint venture with a Thai company. It looks decidedly upmarket, but was under construction at the time of our visit so we have little information about it.

The majority of the other hotels are strung out for 2km along Halong St, the highway heading west of town (towards Hanoi). Most accommodation here consists of large, expensive, state-run hotels.

A good example of the state-run genre is the *Trade Union Hotel* (Khach San Cong Doan; ☎ 846780; fax 846440; 80 rooms). This place has an interesting, racist pricing policy – Vietnamese pay US$25, members of the Asian race pay US$35 and people with European features are charged US$40. No word yet on what Africans pay.

The *Vuon Dao Hotel* (☎ 846427; 846287) is also a state-run behemoth with rooms priced from US$35 to US$90.

Yet another state-run monstrosity is the *Suoi Mo Hotel* (☎ 846381; fax 846729; 45 rooms), which charges US$30 to US$40.

Almost next door to the Suoi Mo Hotel is the *Heritage Hotel* (☎ 846888; fax 846718) at 88 Halong St. This place is very upmarket with rooms priced from US$105 to US$250. This is a joint venture between a Singaporean and the Vietnamese government.

Nearby is the *Halong Hotel* (☎ 846014). The hotel is divided into four buildings with prices running from US$20 up to US$140. Even the management isn't sure how many rooms they have, but it isn't just a few.

Just to the western side of the Halong Hotel is the all-new *Halong Bay Hotel* (Khach San Vinh Halong; ☎ 845209; fax 846856). This is a Vietnam Tourism joint venture and has rooms priced from US$75 to US$120.

**Hon Gai** There are not so many places to stay here, but demand is low so prices have remained cheap. The hotels are clustered mainly along Le Thanh Tong St, which runs on an east-west axis. Starting from the ferry pier on the western end of Hon Gai, consider the following accommodation offerings:

*Phuong Nam Hotel* (☎ 827242; 12 rooms), Le Thanh Tong St, US$15 to US$30
*Hong Ngoc Hotel* (☎ 826330; fax 826103; 16 rooms), 36A Le Thanh Tong St, US$25 and US$30
*Viet Anh Hotel* (☎ 826243; eight rooms), Le Thanh Tong St, US$10 and US$15
*Queen Hotel West* (☎ 825689; eight rooms), 159 Le Thanh Tong St, US$15
*Thuong Mai Hotel* (☎ 827258; nine rooms), 269 Le Thanh Tong St, US$15
*Huong Lien Hotel* (☎ 826608; six rooms), 283 Le Thanh Tong St, US$15
*Hang Hai Hotel* (☎ 826383; nine rooms), 70 Le Thanh Tong St, US$20 to US$25
*Hai Van Hotel* (☎ 826279; 10 rooms), 78 Le Thanh Tong St, US$10 to US$15

### Places to Eat
Except for mini-hotels, most hotels have restaurants. If you're on a tour, it's likely that meals will be included.

For self-propelled travellers, the area just west of central Bai Chay has a solid row of cheap restaurants, all good. Choices here include the *Binh Minh, Thang Hung, Hai Long, Thanh Lich, Thanh Huong, Phuong Vi* and *Phuong Oanh* restaurants.

### Getting There & Away
For most travellers, it's worth booking a tour at a cafe or hotel in Hanoi. Most of these are very reasonably priced (around US$25 to US$30 per person) and this includes transport, meals, accommodation (two nights) and a boat tour of Halong Bay. You really couldn't do it any cheaper yourself.

Nonetheless, price is not the only consideration – many people prefer independent travel. If this fits your situation, there are buses direct from Hanoi, as well as ferries from Haiphong. On a chartered boat you can also include Halong Bay, along with a trip to Cat Ba Island.

If you book a tour, there is always a small, but real, chance that the boat trip may be cancelled due to bad weather. This may entitle you to a partial refund, but remember that the boat trip is only a small portion of the cost of the journey (it's hotels, food and transport that really add up). Depending on the number of people in your group, you probably won't get back more than US$5 to US$10 if the boats don't sail.

**Bus** Buses for Halong City (Bai Chay) depart from Hanoi's Gia Lam bus station. In Halong City, you catch Hanoi-bound buses from Mien Tay bus station (Ben Xe Mien Tay) in Bai Chay. In either direction, the first bus is at 7.30 am and the last is at 2.30 pm. The fare is US$6.

Buses from Haiphong to Halong City depart Haiphong from a bus station in the Thuy Nguyen District (on the northern bank of the Cam River). The trip takes approximately two hours. The bus station in Halong City is about 1km from the Halong Hotel.

Mien Dong bus station (Ben Xe Mien Dong) in Hon Gai is where you catch buses from Halong City to points north-east (such as Mong Cai on the China border).

**Car** Halong City is 160km from Hanoi, 55km from Haiphong and 45km from Cam Pha. The one-way trip from Hanoi to Halong City by car takes at least three hours.

**Boat** There are two boats connecting Hon Gai to Haiphong, a slow boat and a high-speed hydrofoil.

The slow boat costs US$4 and takes three to four hours. It runs daily, with departures at the following times:

| Haiphong | Hon Gai |
| --- | --- |
| 6 am | 6 am |
| 11 am | 8.30 am |
| 1.30 pm | 11 am |
| 4 pm | 4 pm |

The hydrofoil costs US$7, but takes only 1½ hours to make the journey. It runs only on Monday, Wednesday and Friday and departs Haiphong at 8.30 am. From Hon Gai it leaves at 1.30 pm.

There is a somewhat unreliable Bai Chay-Haiphong boat which runs once daily. It departs Haiphong at 9 am and takes about three hours. If on schedule, it departs Bai Chay for Haiphong at 12.30 pm. The fare is US$4.

**Helicopter** Helijet has a flight every Saturday departing Hanoi at 8 am and returning at 3.30 pm. The US$195 fare includes a four-hour boat trip and lunch. Bookings can be made at the Sofitel Metropole Hotel (☎ 826-6919, ext 8046).

There are also chartered flights from Hanoi to Halong Bay costing US$100 per person one way. This service is offered by Vasco (☎ 827-1707; fax 827-2705), which operates out of Hanoi's Gia Lam airport.

There is yet a third competitor in this business, North SFC (☎ 852-3451; fax 852-1523) at 173 Truong Chinh St in Hanoi.

### Getting Around
**Boat** You won't see much unless you also take a boat to tour the islands and their grottoes. Cruises for a few hours up to a whole day are offered by private boat owners, travel agencies and hotels; competition is fierce. Since the area to be cruised is large, it's advisable to have a fast boat in order to see more. The rare, but romantic, junks are very photogenic (indeed, videogenic) and can be hired as well. However, junks are so slow on a calm day that they hardly seem to be moving at all.

You needn't rent a whole boat for yourself – there are plenty of other foreigners who wouldn't mind getting together a small sightseeing group and it's possible to go with a group of Vietnamese. A small boat can hold six to 12 people and costs around US$6 per hour. Mid-sized boats (the most popular ones) take around 20 passengers and cost US$15 per hour. Larger boats can hold 50 to 100 people and cost US$25 per hour.

In the past there were stories of pirate-style robberies from small boats involving weapons – the foreign passengers lost all their money, passports etc. This has been cracked down upon. Still, be careful with your valuables. Snatch-and-run-style theft is still a possibility, much like the motorbike 'cowboys' in Saigon:

Sometimes a boat approaches and offers fish and crabs, but beware – these people may be robbers! They grabbed the bag of an English guy (with passport, money and cheques) and disappeared. Our tourist boat was slow and couldn't catch that fast boat. Two travellers we met reported that the crew of their boat stole some small things while they were swimming.

**Pat Sanders**

**Helicopter** If you've got the cash to burn, Vasco's helicopters can be chartered for whirlwind tours of the bay. Of course, it's hard to imagine how you're going to get a good look at the grottoes from a helicopter unless the pilots are *really* skilled.

## CAT BA ISLAND
Cat Ba is the largest island in Halong Bay. While the vast majority of Halong Bay's islands are uninhabited, vertical rocks sticking out of the sea, Cat Ba actually has a few tiny fishing villages. The human population is very small – the terrain is too rocky for agriculture and most residents earn their living from the sea. Life has always been hard here and, not surprisingly, many Cat Ba residents joined the exodus of Vietnamese 'boat people' in the 1970s and 1980s. Although the island lost much of its fishing fleet this way, the Overseas Vietnamese have sent back a good deal of money to relatives on the island, thus financing the new hotels and restaurants that you'll see.

There is very little motorised traffic and, indeed, very few roads. Compared with the tourist carnival at Bai Chay, Cat Ba is still very laid back. However, the locals are no fools – they know an opportunity when they see it. Although there is not enough flat land here to build a tourist resort, you can expect a considerable amount of tourism-generated construction in the next few years.

About half of Cat Ba Island (which has a total area of 354 sq km) and 90 sq km of the adjacent inshore waters were declared a national park in 1986 in order to protect the island's diverse ecosystems. These include subtropical evergreen forests on the hills, freshwater swamp forests at the base of the hills, coastal mangrove forests, small freshwater lakes and offshore coral reefs. Most of the coastline consists of rocky cliffs, but there are a few sandy beaches tucked into small coves. The main beaches are Cai Vieng, Hong Xoai Be and Hong Xoai Lon.

There are numerous lakes, waterfalls and grottoes in the spectacular limestone hills, the highest of which rises 331m above sea level. The growth of the vegetation is stunted near the summits because of high winds. The largest permanent body of water on the island is Ech Lake which covers an area of three hectares. Almost all of the surface streams are seasonal; most of the Cat Ba's rainwater flows into caves and follows underground streams to the sea, resulting in a shortage of fresh water during the dry season. Although parts of the interior of the island are below sea level, most of the island is between 50 and 200m in elevation.

The waters off Cat Ba Island are home to 200 species of fish, 500 species of molluscs and 400 species of arthropods. Larger marine animals in the area include seals and three species of dolphins.

Stone tools and bones left by human beings who lived between 6000 and 7000 years ago have been found at 17 sites on the island. The most thoroughly studied site is Cai Beo Cave, discovered by a French archaeologist in 1938, which is 1.5km from Cat Ba village.

Today, the island's human population of 12,000 is concentrated in the southern part of the island, including the fishing village of Cat Ba.

During February, March and April, Cat Ba's weather is often cold and drizzly, although the temperature rarely falls below 10°C. During the summer months, tropical storms are frequent.

JULIET COOMBE

BERNARD NAPTHINE

PETER ROBINSON

DEBORAH SODEN

### North-East Vietnam
Top: The entrance to the Perfume Pagoda at Huong Tich Mountain.
Middle Left: A resident of Lang Son, near the Chinese border.
Middle Right: The picturesque waters and islands of Halong Bay.
Bottom: One of the thousands of watercraft that ply Halong Bay.

SARA JANE CLELAND

MICK ELMORE

MICK ELMORE

### North-West Vietnam
Top: Young Hmong women in the mountains above the town of Sapa.
Bottom Left: A Black Tai woman collecting fish from a drained pond near Dien Bien Phu.
Bottom Right: Breakfast at the market in Sapa.

## Cat Ba National Park

Cat Ba National Park is home to 15 types of mammals – including François monkeys, wild boar, deer, squirrels and hedgehogs – and 21 species of birds have been sighted, including hawks, hornbills and cuckoos. Cat Ba lies on a major migration route for waterfowl (ducks, geese and shorebirds) who feed and roost in the mangrove forests and on the beaches. The 620 species of plants recorded on Cat Ba include 118 timber species and 160 plants with medicinal value.

You pay US$1 admission to the park; the services of a guide cost US$3 regardless of group size. A guide is not mandatory, but is definitely recommended – otherwise, all you are likely to see is a bunch of trees. The guide will take you on a walk through a cave, but bring a torch (flashlight). The guide brings you to a mountain peak, but stops just short of the summit because he's afraid the tourists will fall on the last section of slippery rocks (apparently a foreigner filed a lawsuit after falling). However, the walk is not really difficult, so push on to the summit if you like (but at your own risk) – the views are worth it.

There are two caves in the national park that are open to visitors. One has been preserved in its natural state while the other has historical significance – it served as a secret, bomb-proof hospital during the American War.

To reach the national park headquarters at Trung Trang, take a minibus from one of the hotels in Cat Ba; the one-way trip takes 30 minutes and should cost US$0.50. All of the various restaurants and hotels sell minibus tickets.

There is an 18km (five to six hour) hike through the park that many travellers like to do. You need a guide plus bus transport to the trailhead and a boat to return – all of this can be easily arranged at the hotels in Cat Ba. The cost depends on the size of the group. The hike includes a visit to Viet Hai, a remote minority village. If you're planning on doing this hike, equip yourself with a generous supply of water (two litres in summer) plus some food (bread, eggs, cheese and biscuits should sustain you). There are no opportunities (yet) to buy things en route.

## Places to Stay

There is amazing amount of new construction under way in Cat Ba at the moment and many new hotels are sure to open within six months from the time of writing. Furthermore, at the time of our visit electricity was being supplied to the hotels by private generators (which meant that air-conditioning and TV were not available). But the island will soon be hooked up to the national power grid, which will bring with it such modern amenities as satellite TV, electric hot water heaters and higher prices to match. Keeping this in mind, realise that the following accommodation information is likely to go out of date very quickly.

The island's largest guesthouse is the incredibly scruffy, state-run *Cat Ba Hotel* (☎ 888286; 60 rooms). It might be worth visiting just to get an idea of how things used to be in Vietnam prior to the economic reforms of the 1990s. This place is a real dump and will no doubt be renovated, assuming of course that it doesn't fall down first. Twins cost US$15 in summer or US$6 to US$10 in winter and are not worth it.

The *Van Anh Hotel* (☎ 888201; 14 rooms) is the largest private hotel in town (and currently the most luxurious). Twins cost US$15.

Just next door is the *Quang Duc Family Hotel* (☎ 888231; eight rooms). Twins cost US$10.

The *Hoang Huong Hotel* (☎ 888274; 12 rooms) is near the ferry pier. Twins cost US$7 in winter or US$10 in summer.

The *Lan Ha Hotel* (☎ 888299) is on a quiet (for now) side street. Doubles/twins cost US$6/12. The neighbouring *Ngoc Bich Hotel* is similar.

The *Thuy Linh Hotel* (☎ 888328; four rooms) is a small, dingy place right in the market area (and therefore noisy). Twin rooms in winter/summer cost US$7/14.

One entrepreneur has plans to build beach bungalows within a year, so keep your eyes open for this. The bungalows will be 1km from the town.

A large new hotel was under construction by the entrance gate of the national park at the time of our visit. We can't say much about it yet, but it could be very nice if you don't mind basing yourself far from the town and the beach. Our guess is that it will not prove popular.

**Places to Eat**

The friendly *Huu Dung Restaurant* currently seems to have the best food in town. Almost every hotel also operates a small cafe on the ground floor.

**Getting There & Away**

Cat Ba village is 40km east of Haiphong and 20km south of Bai Chay. A great innovation for getting there is the Russian-built hydrofoil which reduces the Haiphong-Cat Ba journey to around three hours. However, this service is still experimental – it could be axed if it doesn't make a profit. The one-way fare is US$5. The hydrofoil currently runs twice daily in each direction according to the following schedule:

**Haiphong to Cat Ba**

| Haiphong | Cat Hai | Cat Ba |
|----------|---------|--------|
| 6.30 am | 7.30 am | 9 am |
| 12.30 pm | 1.30 pm | 3 pm |

**Cat Ba to Haiphong**

| Cat Ba | Cat Hai | Haiphong |
|--------|---------|----------|
| 6 am | 7.15 am | 9.30 am |
| 1 pm | 2 pm | 4 pm |

There are plenty of slow, chartered tourist boats making the run from Halong Bay to Cat Ba. This takes around five hours. The same cafes and travel agencies in Hanoi which do Halong Bay tours also offer an option to visit Cat Ba. Such trips generally include all transport, accommodation, food and a guide in the quoted price, but ask to make sure.

An alternative (although not recommended) way to reach Cat Ba is via the island of Cat Hai, which is closer to Haiphong. A boat departs Haiphong for Cat Hai, makes a brief stop and continues on to the port of Phu Long on Cat Ba Island.

**Getting Around**

Beware – there is more than one pier on the island. One is in Cat Ba village (which is where most travellers want to go) and the other is at Phu Long some 30km away. At Phu Long there should be a bus waiting to take you to Cat Ba village. The high-speed tourist boat does not stop at Phu Long, but the slow local boats do.

· Motorbike rentals (either with or without driver) are available from most of the hotels. Minibuses (always with driver) are also easily arranged.

You'll have plenty of offers to take a trip around Cat Ba fishing harbour in a rowboat. One enterprising fellow sits in his paddle-boat and calls out to every foreigner the only English sentence he knows: 'Hello how are you I'm fine thank you very much'.

**BAI TU LONG BAY**

There's more to Halong Bay than Halong Bay. The sinking limestone plateau, which gave birth to the bay's spectacular islands, continues all the way to the Chinese border (almost 100km to the north-east of Halong Bay). This area is known as Bai Tu Long Bay.

Bai Tu Long Bay is every bit as beautiful as its famous neighbour. Indeed, you could say it's even more beautiful since it has scarcely seen any tourist development. Visitors of any kind are rare, but this will no doubt change – already some of the tourist cafes in Hanoi have made some pioneering forays into this uncharted region. Hopefully the coming hotel, restaurant and souvenir shop boom will be handled more tastefully than at Halong Bay (don't count on it though). As for the locals, they would certainly welcome any kind of development they can get – the area is dirt poor.

At Halong Bay, you can charter boats to bring you to Bai Tu Long Bay. A boat capable of holding 20 passengers can be had for US$10 per hour; the one-way sailing time is around five hours. Alternatively, you can travel overland to Cai Rong (the main town at Bai Tu Long Bay). At Cai Rong you can travel by public ferry to some of the remote outlying islands, or charter a boat at the usual rates.

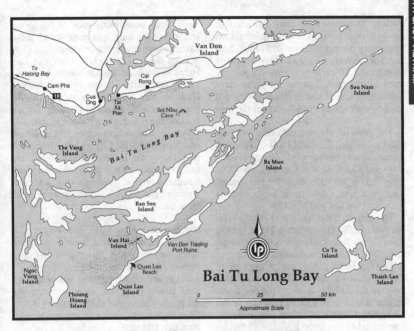

**Bai Tu Long Bay**

At the time of writing there had not yet been any reported incidents of piracy involving foreigners at Bai Tu Long Bay. This is not surprising since there have been scarcely any visitors to rob. However, security could become a problem if many tourists start visiting en masse. A few years ago Halong Bay had a serious problem with piracy until the authorities cracked down with regular police patrol boats. Don't be too surprised if history repeats itself at Bai Tu Long Bay.

### Van Don Island

**Orientation** Also known as Cam Pha, this is the largest and most developed island in the archipelago. The island is about 30km in length and 15km across at the widest point. Cai Rong is the main town on the island.

**Places to Stay** The *Phuc Loc Hotel* (☎ 874-231; 11 rooms) is in the centre almost opposite the market. The rooms aren't bad, but check the plumbing – not all of the ancient

Soviet toilets are in working condition. A twin room costs US$11 with air-con or US$7 without.

It's more pleasant to stay near Cai Rong pier on the south-eastern edge of town. About 100m before the pier is the *Hung Toan Hotel* (☎ 874220; 17 rooms). The three rooms on the top floor are best – they share a huge balcony which affords superb views of Bai Tu Long Bay. Twins cost US$10 to US$13.

As you stand in front of Cai Rong Pier facing out to sea, you'll be able to see a footpath on your left. Follow it a short distance to find the *Thuy Trinh Hotel*, also known as the Mini-4 Hotel. There are eight twin rooms here costing US$7.

**Getting There & Away** Van Don Island is so close to the Vietnamese mainland that some day (when funds are available) a bridge surely will be built. For the moment, the island's inhabitants rely on two rickety old ferries. The passenger ferry (which also carries bikes, motorbikes and chickens) runs once every 30 minutes from 5.30 am to 5.30 pm. The car ferry runs once every two hours (also from 5.30 am to 5.30 pm). The journey takes 30 minutes. The car ferry can carry only six cars, so if you're in car No 7 you'll have to wait another two hours for the next boat.

The town on the mainland side (opposite Van Don Island) is called Cua Ong. There are frequent buses between Hon Gai (in Halong Bay) and Cua Ong; the Cua Ong pier (Cua Ong Pha) is just 1km from the bus station. There are also a few (rare) buses directly between Hon Gai and Van Don.

The pier on Van Don Island is called Tai Xa pier (Tai Xa Pha) which is 7km from Cai Rong. If you didn't take a direct bus, you can pay US$0.50 for a ride on a motorbike.

The Cai Rong pier is just on the edge of Cai Rong town. This is where you catch boats to the outlying islands. You could also charter a boat from here to Hon Gai or Bai Chay for US$10 per hour (the one-way journey takes five hours).

### Quan Lan Island

This is the place with the most potential to develop a beach resort. The main attraction here is a beautiful, white sand beach shaped like a crescent moon. The beach is about 1km in length, the water is clear blue and the waves are even good enough for surfing. The season here for playing in the water is roughly May through October – winter would be too chilly. However, at the present time there are no tourist facilities – no hotels and no restaurants.

Quan Lan Island has a special Rowing Boat Festival (Hoi Cheo Boi) held annually from the 16th to the 18th day of the sixth lunar month. It's the biggest festival in the whole Halong Bay and Bai Tu Long Bay area and thousands of people turn out to see it.

Towards the north-eastern part of the island are some battered ruins of the old Van Don Trading Port. There is little to indicate that this was once part of a major trading route between Vietnam and China. Obvi-

ously, deep water ports such as Haiphong and Hon Gai long ago superseded these islands in economic importance.

Even during the festival, the Quan Lan Island is totally lacking in tourist facilities. There are neither hotels nor restaurants. However, this may change soon as several travel agencies in Hanoi and Halong Bay are considering running tours to the island.

A ferry service between Quan Lan Island and Van Don Island runs daily from each port. Oddly, the ferries both depart at 7 am and cross during the journey, so a trip to the island requires an overnight stay. The one-way fare is US$1.20 and the journey takes three hours.

### Van Hai Island

Ancient Chinese graves have been found here, indicating that this region has seen considerable maritime trade.

There are plenty of good beaches, but a sand mining pit on the island is destroying the place. The sand is used to make glass.

### Ban Sen Island

Also known as Tra Ban Island, it's the closest major island to Van Don Island and for this reason it's easy to visit.

Boats depart Ban Sen daily at 7 am, arriving at Van Don Island between 8 and 8.30 am. Going the other way, boats depart Van Don at 2 pm and arrive in Ban Sen between 3 and 3.30 pm. The one-way fare is US$1.

### Thanh Lan Island

The island is hilly, reaching up to 190m at the highest point. The island's inhabitants manage to grow rice and vegetables in the few flat spots available.

### Co To Island

In the north-east, Co To Island is the furthest inhabited island from the mainland. The highest peak reaches a respectable 170m. There are numerous other hills and a large lighthouse sits atop one of them. Most of the coastline consists of cliffs or large rocks, but there's at least one fine sandy beach. Fishing boats usually anchor just off this beach and you can even walk to the boats during low tide.

Ferries bound for Co To Island depart Van Don Island on Monday, Wednesday and Friday at unspecified times – check the schedule in Cai Rong. The boats return from Co To Island on Tuesday, Thursday and Friday. There are no boats on Sunday. The one-way fare is US$2.25 and the journey takes about five hours (depending on the wind).

## MONG CAI

Mong Cai is on the Chinese border in the extreme north-eastern corner of Vietnam. It's also a free-trade zone and there's plenty of frenetic activity in the city's booming markets.

It wasn't always so. From about 1978 to 1990, the border was virtually sealed. How two former friends became such bitter enemies and now 'friends' again is an interesting story.

China was a good friend of North Vietnam from 1954 (when the French departed) until the late 1970s. But China's relations with Vietnam began to sour shortly after reunification as the Vietnamese government became more and more friendly with the USSR, China's rival. There is good reason to believe that Vietnam was simply playing China and the USSR off against each other, getting aid from both.

In March 1978, the Vietnamese government launched a campaign in the south against 'commercial opportunists', seizing private property in order to complete the country's 'socialist transformation'. The campaign hit the ethnic-Chinese particularly hard. It was widely assumed that behind the Marxist-Leninist rhetoric was the ancient Vietnamese antipathy towards the Chinese.

The anti-capitalist and anti-Chinese campaign caused as many as 500,000 of Vietnam's 1.8 million ethnic-Chinese to flee the country. Those in the north fled overland to China while those in the south left by sea. At least in the south, creating Chinese refugees proved to be a lucrative business for the government – refugees typically had to pay

up to US$5000 each in 'exit fees' to be allowed to leave. In Saigon, Chinese entrepreneurs had that kind of money, but refugees in the north were mostly dirt-poor.

In response, China cut off all aid to Vietnam, cancelled dozens of development projects and withdrew 800 technicians. Vietnam's invasion of Cambodia in late 1978 was the icing on the cake; Beijing was alarmed because the Khmer Rouge were close allies of China. China's leaders – already worried by the huge build-up of Soviet military forces on the Chinese-Soviet border – became convinced that Vietnam had fallen into the Russian camp, which was trying to encircle China with hostile forces.

In February 1979, China invaded northern Vietnam 'to teach the Vietnamese a lesson'. Just what lesson the Vietnamese learned is not clear, but the Chinese learned that Vietnam's troops – hardened by years of fighting the Americans – were no easy pushovers. Although China's forces were withdrawn after 17 days and the operation was officially declared a 'great success', most observers soon realised that China's People's Liberation Army (PLA) had been badly mauled by the Vietnamese. The PLA is believed to have suffered 20,000 casualties in the 2½ weeks of fighting. Ironically, China's aid to Vietnam was partially responsible for China's humiliation by the Vietnamese forces.

Officially, such past 'misunderstandings' are considered ancient history – trade across the Chinese-Vietnamese border is booming and both countries publicly profess to be 'good neighbours'. In practice, China and Vietnam remain highly suspicious of each other's intentions. Continued conflicts over who owns oil-drilling rights in the South China Sea is an especially sore point. China has neither forgiven nor forgotten its humiliation at the hands of the Vietnamese army and has relentlessly been building up its military ever since. Thus, the Chinese-Vietnamese border remains militarily sensitive, though the most likely future battleground is at sea.

If you visit China and discuss this border war, you will almost certainly be told that

NORTH-EAST VIETNAM

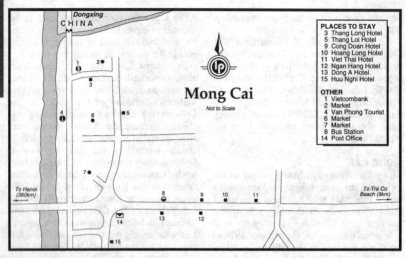

PLACES TO STAY
3   Thang Long Hotel
5   Thang Loi Hotel
9   Cong Doan Hotel
10  Hoang Long Hotel
11  Viet Thai Hotel
12  Ngan Hang Hotel
13  Dong A Hotel
15  Huu Nghi Hotel

OTHER
1   Vietcombank
2   Market
4   Van Phong Tourist
6   Market
7   Market
8   Bus Station
14  Post Office

Mong Cai
Not to Scale

China acted in self-defence because the Vietnamese were launching raids across the border and murdering innocent Chinese villagers. Virtually all western observers, from the CIA to historians, consider China's version of events to be utter nonsense. The Chinese also claim they won this war – nobody outside of China believes that either.

You'd hardly know these tensions exist when you visit Mong Cai. This town appears to be the most popular border crossing for Vietnamese and Chinese nationals, though foreigners almost never come here. Most foreigners prefer to cross the border at Dong Dang or Lao Cai.

One would be hard-pressed to say that Mong Cai is an attractive place, but plenty of tourists (Chinese and Vietnamese) visit. For the Vietnamese the big attraction here is a chance to purchase low-priced (and low-quality) Chinese-made consumer goods. Indeed, even the shops on the Vietnamese side of the border are stocked with mostly Chinese-made products. Chinese tourists find little to buy in Mong Cai, but they seem to enjoy the low-cost Vietnamese food, booze and women.

Lots of cars are exported to China via Mong Cai. This is not because the Vietnamese are

known for producing great cars. It's because many Japanese and Korean companies have set up automobile assembly plants in Vietnam, while they have shunned China (which makes life miserable for foreign car companies).

If you've been learning to speak Chinese, you'll find plenty of opportunity to practice it in Mong Cai. Many of the hotels, restaurants and shops are staffed by Vietnamese who can speak at least basic Chinese. Furthermore, about 70% of the stalls are run by Chinese who come across the border daily to flog their wares. This explains why the market shuts down so early (3 pm) – the Chinese have to head across the border before it closes at 4 pm.

Because so many vendors are Chinese, you won't have any problem spending Chinese yuan if you happen to have any.

Other than the bustling markets (which aren't really all that wonderful), Mong Cai has little of interest to western travellers. Due to unpaved roads, the town is dusty and the buildings are ramshackle. Dongxing (on the Chinese side) is even dirtier.

### Information

Van Phong Tourist (☎ 881195) is a place to

rent cars and hire tour guides. With the requisite visas they can even arrange trips to China.

Vietcombank is close to the China border – travellers cheques can be cashed here.

### Places to Stay

The scruffy *Ngan Hang Hotel* (☎ 881183) is a relative bargain at US$8 if they'll take you at all, which is by no means certain. It's often full, but might be worth a try.

We found the rooms very comfortable at the *Huu Nghi Hotel* (☎ 881408; 881144). Twins with attached bath cost US$15 without air-con, or US$25 with it. Conditions and prices are similar at the nearby *Dong A Hotel* (☎ 881151) and *Thang Loi Hotel*.

Slightly downmarket is the *Hoang Long Hotel* (☎ 881287), where rooms begin at US$12. Even more dilapidated is the neighbouring *Cong Doan Hotel* (☎ 881165) and *Viet Thai Hotel* (☎ 881070).

The *Thang Long Hotel* (☎ 881695; 23 rooms) is opposite Vietcombank. Rooms are reasonable at US$10 to US$15.

### Getting There & Away

Mong Cai is 360km from Hanoi, but on public buses you almost always have to changes buses in Hon Gai (Halong City). Buses on the Hon Gai-Mong Cai run are frequent. The condition of the road varies, but is not too horrible. You'll pass plenty of coal mines en route – your face (and lungs?) will receive a fine coating of black coal dust before the journey is completed. Just pity the folks who live here and have to breathe this crap every day. In Hon Gai you catch the bus at the station just near the Bai Chay ferry – the ride takes about five hours.

There is a customs checkpoint just south of Mong Cai. At times you can encounter lengthy delays here.

Mong Cai-Lang Son is also a five-hour journey. However, buses on this route only leave once or twice a day and only in the early morning. Much of the road is unpaved – expect plenty of dust or mud depending on the weather.

It is possible to charter a boat to take you from Van Don Island to Mong Cai. For this trip, captains in Van Don were asking US$150 one way or US$200 return. The one-way voyage takes six hours.

### AROUND MONG CAI
### Tra Co Beach

Nine km to the south-east of Mong Cai is Tra Co, an oddly shaped peninsula widely touted as a beach resort. Despite a considerable public relations effort, the beach at Tra Co is a disappointment; the sand is dull and hard-packed. Indeed, you can easily drive a car on the beach (and many people do so) – 4WD is not necessary.

The most impressive thing about this beach is its size. At 17km in length, it's one of the longest stretches of sandy beachfront real estate in Vietnam. Another neat feature is that the water is shallow, allowing waders to walk far offshore. It's just a pity that the sand isn't softer and whiter.

There is a large, beautiful, ruined church about 500m back from the beach at Tra Co. Efforts to restore it are now under way.

It's going to be an uphill battle to turn Tra Co into another Nha Trang, but the local People's Committee has lots of ambitious plans to increase tourism. These plans might not be total hogwash – after all, with China just next door, Tra Co does have potential to develop into land of casinos, karaoke lounges and steam bath-massage parlours.

Unfortunately, Tra Co is unlikely to develop until the local police have a change in attitude. At the south-eastern corner of the Tra Co peninsula is Mui Ngoc, a small village with a police station. The chief officer at the time of our visit demanded our passports (which we didn't have because our hotel took them). After making nasty threats, he finally accepted photocopies of our documents, wrote our names down in his police register and then told us to get out of there. We didn't get fined, but he objected to our taking photos. 'Tra Co is near the border' he icily explained – never mind that the only military secret here consists of a beach and some fishing boats. Perhaps the fishing boats are equipped with torpedoes? We weren't so offended by the requirement for a police permit as by the officer's extreme hostility. Most Vietnamese police are polite even when they're fining you. Unfortunately, this individual was about as friendly as a mad dog.

**Places to Stay** The *Tra Co Beach Hotel* (☎ 881264; 26 rooms) is next to the post office. Built like an American-style motel, it's a pleasant enough place to stay, but gets few guests. Twin rooms cost US$13 to US$15, but this drops to US$11 during winter. This place boasts satellite TV – a luxury not yet available at nearby Mong Cai.

Across the street is the less-interesting *Dai Duong Mini-Hotel* (☎ 881140; 18 rooms). At least it's cheap – twins complete with satellite TV are priced from US$7 to US$9.

### Vinh Thuc Island
This large beautiful island is just 8km off the coast of Tra Co. The island is very mountainous and surrounded by lovely white sand beaches. However, our attempts to visit were thwarted by the aforementioned police officer. The villagers at Mui Ngoc were willing to take us to the island for US$12 (return trip) until 'the law' arrived. We were finally told that if we really wanted to visit Vinh Thuc Island, we would need a special permit issued by the police in Hanoi. A later inquiry at the police station in Hanoi produced baffled looks. 'Where the hell', we were asked, 'is Vinh Thuc Island?'

### LANG SON
The capital of mountainous Lang Son Province, Lang Son (elevation 270m) is in an area populated largely by Montagnards (Tho, Nung, Man and Dzao), many of whom continue their traditional way of life. There are also caves 2.5km from Lang Son, near the village of Ky Lua.

However, the real attraction of Lang Son is neither Montagnards nor caves. The town has long served as an important trading post and crossing point into China. However, the border is actually at Dong Dang, 18km to the north.

Lang Son was partially destroyed in February 1979 by invading Chinese forces; the ruins of the town and the devastated frontier village of Dong Dang, 18km to the north, were often shown to foreign journalists as evidence of Chinese aggression. Although the border remains heavily fortified, Sino-Vietnamese trade appears to be in full swing again.

### Orientation
Lang Son is bisected by a river. Most hotels and the post office are on the northern shore, but Vietcombank is on the southern side. On the western side of town are some mountains riddled with attractive caves.

### Things to See & Do
There are two large and beautiful caves just 2.5km from the centre and both are illuminated with lights, which makes exploring easy.

**Tam Thanh Cave** is excellent. A notable feature is a 'bottomless pond'. Its name is Am Ty (Hell) – an indication of just how deep it is. The cave also has a viewing point (a natural 'window') which presents a sweeping view of the surrounding rice fields. There is a place where dripping water is collected in a basin – drinking from this spring is claimed to do wonders for your health.

**Nhi Thanh Cave** has excellent stalactites and stalagmites. The Ngoc Tuyen River flows through the cave, which gives it added charm.

### Places to Stay
The privately owned, friendly, clean and pleasant *Hoang Nguyen Hotel* (☎ 870349; 10 rooms) has twins for US$15. It's at 84 Tran Dang Ninh St.

Just next door at No 92 is the *Hoa Phuong Hotel* (☎ 871233). The standard is similar to its neighbour.

*Ngoc Mai Hotel* (☎ 871837; 14 rooms) at 25 Le Loi St has beautiful rooms and is privately owned. Often full, it's the only place in town that currently offers satellite TV. Twins cost US$16 to US$20.

*Hoa Binh Hotel* (☎ 870807; 12 rooms) at

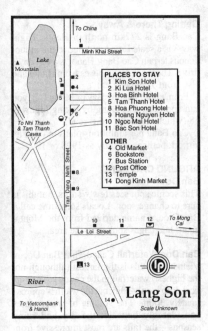

To China

Minh Khai Street

Lake
Mountain

**PLACES TO STAY**
1 Kim Son Hotel
2 Ki Lua Hotel
3 Hoa Binh Hotel
5 Tam Thanh Hotel
8 Hoa Phuong Hotel
9 Hoang Nguyen Hotel
10 Ngoc Mai Hotel
11 Bac Son Hotel

To Nhi Thanh
& Tam Thanh
Caves

**OTHER**
4 Old Market
6 Bookstore
7 Bus Station
12 Post Office
13 Temple
14 Dong Kinh Market

Tran Dang Ninh Street

To Mong
Cai

Le Loi Street

River

To Vietcombank
& Hanoi

**Lang Son**

Scale Unknown

127 Tran Dang Ninh Rd has absolutely beautiful rooms with air-con for US$15. Try to get a room in the back – it's not only quieter, but offers a view of the lake.

*Ki Lua Hotel* (☎ 870020; 13 rooms) at 208 Tran Dang Ninh St offers a depressing cell with shared bath for US$6 or a larger cell with shared bath for US$11. It's state owned.

*Tam Thanh Hotel* (☎ 870979; 18 rooms) at 117 Tran Dang Ninh St is a grotty, state-run place with large dumpy rooms, but it does have some nice views of the lake if you have a room on the top floor. Twins go for US$11 and US$13.

*Kim Son Hotel* (☎ 870378; 34 rooms) at 3 Minh Khai St looks much better on the outside than the inside. A Chinese-Vietnamese joint venture, it will make you feel right at home if you've been travelling in China (leaky plumbing, cigarette-burned carpets, wallpaper peeling off the walls and rude service). Doubles in this dungeon cost US$15 to US$30.

The *Bac Son Hotel* (☎ 871849) on Le Loi

St (near the post office) is in a beautiful, colonial building. Twins cost US$15 and US$25, which includes breakfast. This state-run place is often full.

### Places to Eat
Tran Dang Ninh St and Le Loi St are thick with restaurants. *Pho chua* (a noodle dish) is the budget local specialty of Lang Son. If you'd prefer to eat upmarket, check out the roast duck (*vit quay*) or suckling pig (*lon quay*).

### Things to Buy
The Dong Kinh Market is a four-storey Aladdin's den of cheap goods (that break easily) from China.

### Getting There & Away
**Bus** Buses to Lang Son depart Hanoi's Long Bien bus station at about 6 am. The journey takes roughly five hours.

**Train** There are two trains daily between Hanoi and Dong Dang, stopping at Lang Son en route. For details of this train, please see the Getting There & Away chapter.

### Getting Around
The usual motorbike taxis can be found almost anywhere, but are especially plentiful around the post office and the market.

On Tran Dang Ninh St, you'll see mini-buses looking for passengers heading to the border at Dong Dang.

## CAO BANG
The dusty capital of Cao Bang Province, Cao Bang town is 300m above sea level and has a pleasant climate. The main reason to come here is to make excursions into the surrounding scenic countryside. This is the most beautiful mountain area in the north-east and is worth at least a few days of your time.

About the only thing to do in Cao Bang town itself is to climb the hill leading up the War Memorial. There are great views from the summit.

### Information
Cao Bang Tourist (☎ 852245) is inside the

Phong Lan Hotel and can arrange cars, jeeps and guides for visiting the outlying districts.

At the time of writing there was *no* foreign exchange bank in this town (or indeed the whole province). If you need to change money, do it before you arrive in Cao Bang.

### Places to Stay

The *Phong Lan Hotel* (☎ 852260; 40 rooms) is a somewhat dreary, state-run hotel, but has the cheapest rooms in town. Doubles cost US$8 to US$20.

The *Phuong Dong Guesthouse* has seven rooms priced from US$11 to US$15.

The *Bang Giang Hotel* (☎ 853431; 70 rooms) is an enormous, recently renovated hotel with bright cheery rooms. Rooms on the upper floors in the rear of the building have sweeping views overlooking the river. Twins cost US$20.

The *Duc Trung Mini-Hotel* (☎ 853245; six rooms) is a small, privately-owned place on a quiet street on the edge of town. Twin rooms cost US$20.

The *People's Committee Guesthouse* (☎ 852804; 33 rooms), or Nha Khach UBND, has good rooms priced from US$15 to US$23.

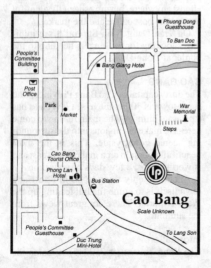

### Getting There & Away

Cao Bang is 272km north of Hanoi. Highway 3 is a sealed road, but due to the mountainous terrain Cao Bang-Hanoi is a full day's drive. There are direct buses from Hanoi and also from Thai Nguyen.

From either Halong Bay or Mong Cai, you can approach Cao Bang by taking highway 48 (which is mostly a dirt road).

Cao Bang has ambitious plans to open an airport, perhaps as early as 1998 or 1999.

### AROUND CAO BANG
### Ban Doc

This scenic spot sees few visitors, but this is sure to change soon. Locals sometime call it Ban Gioc, a name derived from the Montagnard languages spoken in the area.

**Ban Doc Waterfall** Called Thac Ban Doc in Vietnamese, this is the largest (although not the highest) waterfall in the country. The vertical drop is only 53m, but the width is approximately 300m. The volume of water varies considerably between the dry and rainy seasons – the falls are most impressive from May through September. There are three levels to the falls, creating a sort of giant staircase. It's a beautiful sight and should not be missed if you've time to make the journey.

The falls are fed by the Quay Son River, which marks the border with China. There's been a considerable build-up of tourist facilities on the Chinese side of the border in recent years, but virtually nothing yet on the Vietnamese side. The falls are actually in Vietnam and many Chinese sneak across for a better view. There is no official border checkpoint here and the area is only loosely patrolled. Despite this, a police permit is required to visit – you cannot simply rent a motorbike and go on your own. There is talk about eliminating this silly requirement, but at the time of writing a permit was definitely needed. The permit can be organised through travel agencies in Hanoi or Cao Bang, though you actually pick up the permit itself in Trung Khanh (27km before the waterfall).

**Nguom Ngao Cave** The main entrance to

the caves is 2km from the waterfall, just off the road to Cao Bang. Actually, there are two main entrances – it's customary to enter by one and exit by the other. The caves are enormous (about 3km long) and one branch reaches almost all the way to the waterfalls where there is a 'secret' entrance.

To explore the caves you need a guide – fortunately they are readily available. They are paid a pittance and won't accept tips (that will probably change fast), but you might offer them at least cigarettes and a share of your picnic lunch.

Lights have been installed in the caves and the generators are turned on whenever tourists show up. The US$1 entrance fee helps pay the fuel and maintenance cost of the lighting system. Just to be safe, bring a torch (flashlight) – the generator could cut off suddenly without warning. You can always find your way out if you can locate the generator cable.

**Places to Stay & Eat** There are no hotels yet on the Vietnamese side of the border. Unless you want to go camping, you'll have to stay in Trung Khanh, 27km from the falls. The only accommodation here is the *People's Committee Guesthouse* (Nha Khach UBND). Rooms are dormitory-style with four to five beds each and cost US$4 per bed. The facilities are basic and the place is pretty dirty.

There is some limited food available in Trung Khanh, but nothing at all at Ban Doc itself. You'd be wise to prepare at least a picnic lunch for the excursion to the waterfall and caves, and it wouldn't be a bad idea to bring some extra canned goods just in case you're delayed by a vehicle breakdown – otherwise you'll be foraging for nuts and berries.

If the new highway brings in the hoped-for flood of tourists, the food and accommodation situation should improve very rapidly.

**Getting There & Away** Ban Doc is 85km from Cao Banh, but the road is in such bad condition that the journey requires six hours by jeep or sturdy motorbike. However, at the time of writing the road was being rebuilt.

When completed (sometime in 1998) travel time may be reduced to less than three hours. No matter how good the new road, it's never going to be a very fast journey because the route is so mountainous. There is currently no public transport to Ban Doc (it would require a 4WD bus to negotiate the treacherous road), but regular bus transport should become a reality when the new highway is completed.

The scenery along the route is impressive and the last 10km along the Quay Son River is particularly spectacular.

**Thang Hen Lakes**
This is a large lake which can be visited all year round; however, what you get to see varies according to the seasons. During the rainy season (May through September) there are 36 lakes in the area separated by convoluted rock formations.

In the dry season, most of the lakes except for Thang Hen itself become dry. However, it's during this time of year that the lake level drops low enough to reveal a large cave which can be explored by bamboo raft. In the rainy season the cave is submerged.

As yet there are no restaurants or hotels at Thang Hen, nor is there any public transport. To get there you'll need a jeep or motorcycle (though with new road improvements a regular car may be capable of making the trip). From Cao Bang you drive 20km to the top of Ma Phuc Pass. From there it's one more kilometre to where the highway forks – take the left branch and go another 4km. It's close enough to Cao Bang to be visited as a day trip.

At the present time there is no entrance fee to Thang Hen, but that, too, is expected to change.

**Pac Bo Cave**
Pac Bo Cave (Hang Pac Bo) is just 3km from the Chinese border. The cave and the surrounding area is sacred ground for Vietnamese revolutionaries. On 28 January 1941, Ho Chi Minh re-entered Vietnam here after living abroad for 30 years. His purpose in returning to his native land was to lead the revolution that he had long been planning.

## The Legend of the Lakes

A charming setting such as Thang Hen would not be complete without a depressing legend to go along with it. It seems that there was a very handsome and clever young man named Chang Sung. His mother adored him and so decided to plan his whole life for him. Mama deemed that her son should first become a mandarin and then marry a beautiful girl.

Under the old Confucian tradition, the only way to become a mandarin was to pass a competitive examination. This was no mean feat, but Chang Sung was a clever boy – he sat for the exam and passed. He received an official letter bearing the good news and ordering him to report to the royal palace just one week later.

With her son virtually guaranteed admission to mandarinhood, Mama then launched Phase II of her plan. A beautiful girl by the name of Biooc Luong (Yellow Flower) was chosen to marry Chang Sung. A big wedding was hastily arranged.

With everything going so well, Chang Sung couldn't have been happier. In fact, he and Biooc were having such a great time on their honeymoon that he forgot about his crucial appointment at the royal palace next week. Only the night before the deadline did he suddenly remember.

Knowing how disappointed Mama would be if he missed his chance to become a mandarin, Chang Sung decided to summon up dark, magical forces – he would hop in great leaps and bounds to the royal palace. However, he didn't get the aerodynamics right – he leapt 36 times, but couldn't control the direction or velocity and wound up creating 36 craters. His last leap brought him to the top of Ma Phuc Pass, where he died of exhaustion and became a rock. The craters filled up with water during the rainy season and became the 36 lakes of Thang Hen. Mama was no doubt proud of his civil engineering works, but still disappointed that Chang Sung didn't become a mandarin. ■

For almost four years Ho Chi Minh lived in this cave. The reason for remaining so close to China was so that Ho could flee across the border in case the French soldiers discovered his hiding place and tried to arrest him. Ho named the stream in front of his cave Lenin Creek and a nearby mountain Karl Marx Peak. He spent time here writing poetry waiting for WWII to end. In Tay language *pac bo* means 'water wheel' – so called because there's a spring here.

### Narang Market

This is one of the best markets in the provinces. Most of the vendors and customers are local Montagnard groups including the Nung, Tay and Hmong.

### Other Montagnard Markets

In Cao Bang Province, ethnic-Vietnamese (Kinh) are a distinct minority. The largest ethnic group is the Tay (46%) followed by the Nung (32%), Hmong (8%), Dzao (7%), Kinh (5%) and Lolo (1%). Intermarriage, mass education and 'modern' clothing is gradually eroding the tribal and cultural distinctions.

At the time of writing, it could truly be said that most of Cao Bang's Montagnards remain blissfully naive about the ways of the outside world. Cheating in the marketplace, for example, is virtually unknown and even foreigners are charged the same price as locals without any need to bargain. Whether or not this innocence can withstand the onslaught of mass tourism remains to be seen.

The big Montagnard markets in Cao Bang province are held every five days according to lunar calendar dates. They are as follows:

Trung Khanh
> on the 5th, 10th, 15th, 20th, 25th and 30th day of each lunar month

Tra Linh
> on the 4th, 9th, 14th, 19th, 24th and 29th day of each lunar month

Nuoc Hai
> on the 1st, 6th, 11th, 16th, 21st and 26th day of each lunar month

Nagiang
> on the 1st, 6th, 11th, 16th, 21st and 26th day of each lunar month. (This market is held 20km from Pac Bo in the direction of Cau Bang and attracts Tay, Nung and Hmong.)

## BA BE LAKES NATIONAL PARK

This beautiful region boasts waterfalls, rivers, deep valleys, lakes and caves set amid towering peaks. The surrounding area is inhabited by members of the Dai minority who live in homes built on stilts.

The lake region is 145m above sea level and surrounded by steep mountains up to 1754m high. The 1939 Madrolle Guide to Indochina suggests getting around Ba Be Lakes 'in a car, on horseback, or, for ladies, in a chair', meaning, of course, of a sedan chair.

Ba Be (Three Bays) is in fact three linked lakes, which have a total length of 7km and a width of about 400m. It's a tropical rain forest area and the government pays the villagers not to cut the trees. Wildlife in the forest includes bears, monkeys, numerous birds, butterflies and other insects. Hunting is forbidden, but fishing is permitted (for villagers only).

Two of the lakes are separated from one another by a 100m-wide strip of water sandwiched between high walls of chalk rock called Be Kam. The Nang River is navigable for 23km between a point 4km above Cho Ra and the Dau Dang Waterfall (Thac Dau Dang), which consist of a series of spectacular cascades between sheer walls of rock.

An interesting place is Puong Cave (Hang Puong). The cave is about 30m high and 300m long and passes completely through a mountain. A navigable river flows through the cave, making for an interesting boat trip. There are many bats living in the cave, generating some powerful odours.

Dao Dang Falls (or Hua Tang Falls in the Tay language) is in fact a series of rapids spread out over 1km. Just 200m below the rapids is a very small Tay village (only five houses) called Hua Tang Village.

You can also organise boat trips to some nearby tribal villages. Many of the Montagnards are anxious to sell their home-made clothing and handicrafts to travellers.

### Warning

We are not pleased to report that Ba Be Lakes National Park is turning into a rip-off. For this reason, hardly anyone goes there now. Even Vietnamese tourists get ripped off. There is a US$6 entrance fee and the park staff will make you pay even if you only visit Cho Ra town and don't go to the park! Renting a boat costs US$3.50 per hour – and they very often 'go slow' to get more money – plus the mandatory guide costs US$10 per day. It seems that the cash is going into the pockets of the park staff. The provincial government is aware of the situation, but cannot do anything as the national park belongs to the Forestry Ministry in Hanoi.

### Places to Stay & Eat

At the lake, there is a 10-room hotel under construction which will cost US$10 per room (with electricity supplied by a generator). In Cho Ra, 18km from Ba Be Lakes, is the *Ba Be Hotel* (☎ 876115; eight rooms). It charges US$15 per room. There is no air-conditioning, but it has hot water and electricity supplied by generator and it's the only hotel in town. Some small hotels in Cho Ra have food, but there is no food in the national park unless you've specially ordered it (and you'll be charged US$5 per meal). Within the park, if you pay for anything in US dollars rather than dong, then the staff will charge you a 10% commission on each transaction.

On each side of the lake is a village where you can sleep. The main village is Pac Ngoi, a Tay village on the bank of the river leading into the lake. The village is known for its big stilt houses and you can sleep in these, although you won't have much privacy. Hua Tang, the small village below the rapids, is another possible place to stay, but most tourists prefer Pac Ngoi. The national park staff charge you US$7 to stay in a stilt house, but they only give the villagers US$1. The park staff doesn't want you to sleep in the villages, but will allow it if you insist. Food is available in the villages, including fresh fish from the lake. Food prices are reasonable, if not rock bottom, but the Tay people are very honest and at least they won't cheat you, even if the park staff do.

### Getting There & Away

Ba Be Lakes National Park is in Cao Bang Province not far from the borders of Bac Thai

### The Legend of Widow's Island

A tiny islet in the middle of Ba Be Lakes is the source of one local legend. The Tay people believe that what is a lake today was once farmland, and in the middle was a village called Nam Mau.

One day, the Nam Mau residents found a buffalo wandering in the nearby forest. They caught it, butchered it and shared the meat. However, they didn't share any with a certain lonely old widow.

Unfortunately for the villagers, this just wasn't any old buffalo. It belonged to the river ghost. When the buffalo failed to return home, the ghost went to the village disguised as a beggar. He asked the villagers for something to eat, but they refused to share their buffalo buffet and ran the poor beggar off. Only the widow was kind to him and gave him some food and a place to stay for the night.

That night the beggar told the widow to take some rice husks and sprinkle them on the ground around her house. Later in the evening, it started to rain and then a flood came. The villagers all drowned, the flood washed away their homes and farms, thus creating Ba Be Lakes. Only the widow's house remained, which is now the present-day Widow's Island (Po Gia Mai in the Tay language).

One can only hope that the ghost is still around and will soon give the same treatment to the greedy national park staff. ■

Province and Tuyen Quang Province. Ba Be Lakes is 240km from Hanoi, 61km from Bach Thong (Bac Can) and 18km from Cho Ra.

Most visitors to the national park go from Hanoi by chartered vehicle. From Bach Thong onwards, the road gets rough and the last 50km stretch before the park is particularly rough. This should only be attempted with a jeep, very high-clearance vehicle or a powerful motorbike.

Chartering a jeep from Hanoi to the national park should cost about US$200, depending on how long you stay. The one-way driving time from Hanoi to Ba Be Lakes is approximately eight hours; most travellers take three days and two nights for the entire excursion.

Some cafes in Hanoi offer tours to Ba Be Lakes for around US$60, but the high price puts people off and there are few takers. Check the notice boards in Hanoi's cafes to see if anyone is still running these trips. It's a pity that the corrupt national park staff are driving tourists away, thus hurting the whole local economy.

Reaching this national park by public transport is possible, but not easy. The way to do it is to take a bus from Hanoi to Bach Thong (Bac Can) and from there another bus to Cho Ra. In Cho Ra you will have to get a motorbike to do the last 18km stretch of highway unless you are willing to walk (not likely).

# North-West Vietnam

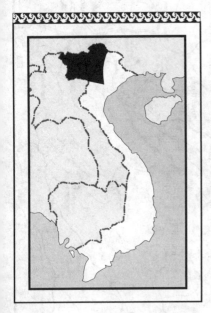

North-west Vietnam includes some of the country's most spectacular scenery. The mountainous areas are home to many distinct hill tribe groups, some of which remain relatively untouched by Vietnamese and western influences.

National Highway 6 winds through beautiful mountains and high plains inhabited by Montagnards (notably the Black Tai and Hmong) who still live as they have for generations. The Tai are most numerous in the lower lands, where they cultivate tea and fruit and live in attractive stilt houses. In the bleaker highlands over 1000m elevation live the hardy Hmong.

Highway 6 is mostly bitumen surface from Hanoi to Tuan Giao, but from there to Dien Bien Phu (where it's called Highway 42) the road is so rough it can jar the fillings out of your teeth. Even more exciting is Highway 32 – the road from Dien Bien Phu to Sapa – a dangerous cliff hanger that is frequently wiped out by landslides.

Of course, you needn't go the entire distance. Many travellers only go as far as Mai Chau, Moc Chau or Son La before turning back. Given the state of the road, this is not surprising. The most interesting (and hair-raising) journey of all is to head for Dien Bien Phu, then north to Lai Chau, Sapa, Lao Cai and back to Hanoi. This loop route requires a jeep or motorbike – a motorbike is safer because the road is so narrow! Furthermore, with a motorbike, locals with small boats can ferry you across the trouble spots. Allow at least a week for this loop trip.

## Warning

In the entire north-west of Vietnam, there is no legal place to cash travellers cheques. Credit cards are of little use either. Only in Sapa can you cash travellers cheques (at some hotels), but this is in fact black market and you will be charged a steep 10% commission. It's somewhat easier to swap US dollars for Vietnamese dong, but you'd be wise to take care of all your money changing transactions in Hanoi. The situation is a bit ridiculous given the number of tourists who pass through here now, but that's the reality.

## HOA BINH

The city of Hoa Binh (Peace), which is the capital of Hoa Binh Province, is 74km south-west of Hanoi. This area is home to many hill tribe people, including Hmong and Tai. Hoa Binh can be visited on an all-day excursion from Hanoi, or as a stop on the long drive to Dien Bien Phu.

Unfortunately, Hoa Binh doesn't have much of a hill tribe atmosphere. The town is on the flatlands just at the base of the mountains and the locals mainly dress in modern Vietnamese garb. However, Montagnard clothing is on sale in the market, even in large sizes specially

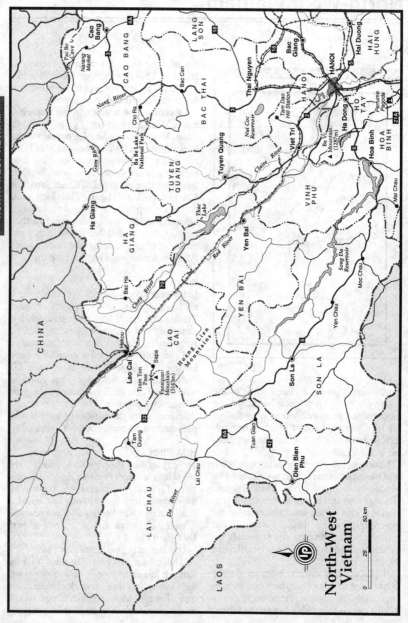

North-West Vietnam

### One for the Road

Based on the latest 1950s technology, Russian jeeps are still being manufactured. There have been absolutely no changes in design for the past 40 years, with the exception of the door handles – the new ones are made of plastic and break more easily than the old metal ones. Obviously intended for the Russian climate, the windows do not even open (a horror in summer). You can get a nice breeze if you put down the vinyl top, but it's quite a complex procedure. By contrast, with a wrench and a screwdriver you could disassemble the whole vehicle – it's a wonder of simplicity. In case you'd like to buy one, a new Russian jeep can be had for US$21,000. They easily exceed the 20kg weight limit imposed by Vietnam Airlines, so you'll have to find another way to get it home. Although the Russian jeeps lack seat belts and roll bars, they are otherwise pretty safe – they negotiate the mud as least as well (or better than) the fancy Japanese-made jeeps. ■

made for tourists. Crossbows, opium pipes and other Montagnard paraphernalia can be purchased in the market or at the souvenir shop in the Hoa Binh Hotel.

### Information

Hoa Binh Provincial Tourist (☎ 854374) is in the Hoa Binh Hotel. Don't confuse this outfit with the very similarly named Hoa Binh Tourist, which is based in Hanoi.

### Places to Stay

The *Hoa Binh Hotel* (☎ 852001; 27 rooms) is built in genuine Montagnard stilt-house style, although a few added amenities like hot water and satellite TV are not exactly traditional. Modern intrusions aside, we must admit it's one of the best hotels in north-west Vietnam. The rooms cost US$30 to US$40.

Just opposite is the *Hoa Binh Hotel II*, which is similar, although not quite as good.

### SONG DA RESERVOIR

Close to Hoa Binh is the site of a large dam on the Da River (Song Da), creating Song Da Reservoir, which is the largest in Vietnam. The flooding of the Da River displaced a large number of farmers upstream for about 200km. The dam is part of a major hydro-electric scheme which generates power for the north. In 1994 a 500 kilovolt power line was extended from this area to the south, freeing Saigon from the seasonal power shortages that often blacked out the city for up to three days at a time.

Though the dam is just 5km from Hoa Binh, it's best to visit the reservoir by taking a spur road that cuts off from Highway 6 at Dong Bang Junction (60km from Hoa Binh). From Dong Bang Junction it's just a short drive to Bai San Pier, where you catch boats to the Ba Khan Islands. The islands are the tops of submerged mountains and the visual effect is like a freshwater version of Halong Bay. A boat to the islands takes three hours for the return trip and costs US$30, but the boats are large and can seat 10 passengers.

Another possible trip is to take a boat to Phuc Nhan village, which is inhabited by members of the Dzao tribe. The return trip costs US$15. The boat actually leaves you at a pier from where it's a steep 4km uphill walk to the village. If you'd like to sleep in the village, take the boat one way for US$10 and get another boat the next day to return to Bai San Pier.

The last possibility is to charter a boat for the 60km trip from Bai San Pier to Hoa Binh. This costs a steep US$120, but again the boat can hold 10 people.

### MAI CHAU

One of the closest places to Hanoi where you can see a real Montagnard village is Mai Chau (elevation 400m). It's a beautiful place and some have called it 'another Sapa' (see the Sapa section in this chapter). Mai Chau itself is very rural with no real downtown – rather, it's a collection of villages, farms and huts spread out over a large area. The people here are ethnic-Tai, though only distantly related to tribes in Thailand.

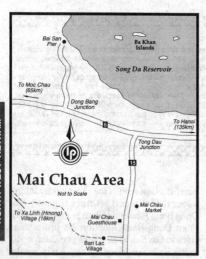

NORTH-WEST VIETNAM

Mai Chau Area

*Not to Scale*

As you enter the town, there is a barricade across the road. All foreigners must stop here and pay an admission fee of US$0.50.

The most interesting thing to do here is trekking. A typical walk is 7km to 8km and a local guide can be hired for US$5.

If you'd like more adventure, there is a popular 18km trek from Mai Chau (Ban Lac village) to a Xa Linh village near a mountain pass (elevation 1000m) on Highway 6. Ban Lac is populated by ethnic-Tai people, while the inhabitants of Xa Linh are Hmong. The trek is too strenuous to be done as a day hike, so you'll have to spend the night in a small village along the way. You'll need a guide, but as part of the deal, a pre-arranged car will pick you up at the mountain pass and bring you back to Mai Chau. Be forewarned that you climb 600m in elevation on this route and that the trail can be dangerously slippery in the rain.

Even longer treks of three to seven days are possible. You can try contacting Hoa Binh Provincial Tourist in the Hoa Binh Hotel to make arrangements.

### Places to Stay & Eat
The only official hotel in town is the *Mai Chau Guesthouse* (☎ 851812, ext 62; 13 rooms), which costs US$15. However, most tours try to arrange an overnight stay in the stilt houses of Ban Lac village, which is far more interesting, as well as being cheaper (about US$3 to US$5).

There are some small restaurants near the market, but you can book a meal at your hotel or house where you're staying. Try to eat the Tai food – it's more interesting than the standard Vietnamese fare.

### Getting There & Away
Mai Chau is 135km from Hanoi and just 5km south of Highway 6 (the Hanoi-Dien Bien Phu route).

You'll be hard-pressed to find any direct public transport to Mai Chau from Hanoi, but buses to nearby Hoa Binh are plentiful. From Hoa Binh you can either get a local bus or hire a motorbike taxi to Mai Chau.

Many cafes and travel agencies in Hanoi run trips to Mai Chau. All transport, food and accommodation is provided for a cost as low as US$30 per person.

### MOC CHAU
This highland town (elevation 1500m) produces some of Vietnam's best tea. Moc Chau also boasts a pioneer dairy industry started in the late 1970s with Australian and, later, UN assistance. It's reassuring to see real cows in Vietnam – the pastoral scenes look like something right out of Holland or New Zealand. The dairy provides Hanoi with such delectable luxuries as fresh milk, sweetened condensed milk and little tooth-rotting sweet bars called 'milk cake' *(banh sua)*.

Not surprisingly, Moc Chau is a good place to sample fresh milk and yoghurt. There are dairy shops all along Highway 6 as it passes through Moc Chau.

Basic accommodation at the *People's Committee Guesthouse* (Nha Khach Uy Ban Nhan Dan Tinh) costs US$5 per person.

Moc Chau is 199km from Hanoi and the journey takes roughly six hours by private car and a little longer by bus. The road is in good condition so there's no need for a jeep.

## YEN CHAU

This small agricultural district is known for its fruits. Apart from bananas, the fruits are seasonal – mango harvesting is done in May and June, longans in July and August and custard apples in August and September.

The mangoes, in particular, are considered to be the best in Vietnam, though foreigners may at first find them disappointing. This is because they are small and green, rather than big, yellow and juicy as they are in the tropical south. However, Vietnamese prefer the somewhat tart taste and aroma of the green ones. The green colour doesn't give a clue as to when the fruit is ripe, so you may need to ask a local 'expert' if the mango you're buying is ripe and ready for eating.

Yen Chau is 260km from Hanoi and driving time is approximately eight hours by car. Yen Chau to Son La is another 60km.

## SON LA

Son La, capital of a province of the same name, makes a good overnight stop for travellers doing the run between Hanoi and Dien Bien Phu. While not one of Vietnam's highlights, the scenery isn't bad and there is certainly enough to see and do to keep you occupied for a day.

The area is populated mainly by Montagnards, including the Black Tai, Meo, Muong and White Tai. Vietnamese influence in the area was minimal until this century; from 1959 to 1980, the region was part of the Tay Bac Autonomous Region (Khu Tay Bac Tu Tri).

### Old French Prison

Son La was once the site of a French penal colony where anti-colonial revolutionaries were held. It was destroyed by the infamous 'off-loading' of unused ammunition by American warplanes returning to base after bombing raids on Hanoi and Haiphong.

The Old French Prison (Nha Tu Cu Cua Phap) has been partially restored in the interests of historical tourism. Rebuilt turrets and watchtowers stand guard over the remains of cells, inner walls and a famous lone surviving peach tree. The tree, which blooms with the traditional Tet flowers, was planted in the compound by To Hieu, one of the former inmates of the 1940s. To Hieu has subsequently been immortalised further – there is a To Hieu St in Son La, a To Hieu Secondary School and other landmarks about town named after him.

The prison tells part of the story, but repression did not end when the French departed. The different Montagnard groups which fought on the colonial side during the Franco-Viet Minh War were afterwards treated as traitors and suffered harsh repression. Surprisingly, the French beret is still worn by many Montagnard men.

From the main highway, a maroon-coloured signpost adorned with large chains marks the entrance to the narrow road leading uphill to the prison. At the end of a road is a People's Committee office – the prison is at the back. The actual entrance to the prison is marked by a faded sign saying 'Penitentaire' above the wrought iron gates.

### Hot Springs

An enjoyable few hours can be spent strolling through some Thai villages south of town and your final reward will be a dip in the hot springs (Suoi Nuoc Nong). The communal pool is free, but you can fork out US$0.10 for a private enclosed bathtub. Although children can frolic nude in the public pool, it's less acceptable for adults. Westerners, in particular, can expect to be the centre of wide-eyed attention. In other words, some sort of bathing costume is recommended.

To get there, from the signpost with the chains (same one which marks the French Prison turnoff), take the road which heads south (opposite direction of the prison). The road leads past the Party headquarters building, after which the pavement ends. From here it's 5km to a couple of small bathing huts right beside the track and a couple of cement pools 50m farther on. A motorbike or high-clearance vehicle can navigate the road, but during the wet season it becomes a mud quagmire.

### Lookout Tower

The tower offers a sweeping overview of Son

NORTH-WEST VIETNAM

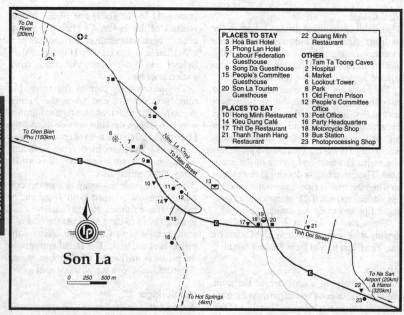

**PLACES TO STAY**
3 Hoa Ban Hotel
5 Phong Lan Hotel
7 Labour Federation Guesthouse
9 Song Da Guesthouse
15 People's Committee Guesthouse
20 Son La Tourism Guesthouse

**PLACES TO EAT**
10 Hong Minh Restaurant
14 Kieu Dung Café
17 Thit De Restaurant
21 Thanh Thanh Hang Restaurant

22 Quang Minh Restaurant

**OTHER**
1 Tam Ta Toong Caves
2 Hospital
4 Market
6 Lookout Tower
8 Park
11 Old French Prison
12 People's Committee Office
13 Post Office
16 Party Headquarters
18 Motorcycle Shop
19 Bus Station
23 Photoprocessing Shop

Son La

0    250    500 m

La and the surrounding area. The climb is steep and will require about 20 minutes, but the view from the top is well worth it. Photography of the scenery is permitted, but the guards will get uptight if you try to photograph the installations, which serve both telecommunications and military purposes.

Immediately to the left of the Labour Federation Guesthouse are the stone steps which lead up to the tower.

**Market**
You can find a small selection of colourful woven shoulder bags, scarves and other Montagnard crafts at Son La's market.

**Tam Ta Toong Caves**
There are many caves in the region, but the Tam Ta Toong Caves are the most accessible from Son La. There are actually two caves here – one dry and one partially flooded. The dry cave is uninteresting, but ironically has an entrance gate and requires permission and

a guide. Both the permission and the guide can be had for a price – inquire at hotels in town if interested.

The flooded cave is adjacent to the dry one, but is more fun and no permit or guide is required. A small adjacent irrigation dam supplies the water which has flooded the cave. The cave goes back about 100m into the hillside. You should find a raft moored at the cave entrance plus an attendant who can take you inside for a negotiable fee. Bring a torch (flashlight).

Tam Ta Toong Caves are a few kilometres north-west of town. Along the highway past the hospital, a bridge crosses a creek just before the pavement ends. Turn left onto a gravel track about 20m before the bridge. Walk along the track by the creek (which is the outflow from the flooded cave) for about 500m, crossing the creek once along the way. An aqueduct crosses the track – turn left and follow the aqueduct to the flooded cave's entrance, which is surrounded by an ugly barbed-wire fence. The dry cave is reached by following the track on the right of the flooded cave up the hill a short distance.

## Places to Stay

Almost all travellers journeying between Hanoi and Dien Bien Phu (or vice versa) spend the night here.

At the budget end is the *Labour Federation Guesthouse* (Nha Khach Du Lich Lien Doan Lao Dong). The bottom-end rooms cost US$8, but twins with hot water are US$12.

The *People's Committee Guesthouse* (Nha Khach Uy Ban Nhan Dan Tinh Son La; ☎ 852-080) is poor value with mediocre rooms for US$12 to US$25.

The *Son La Tourism Guesthouse* (Nha Khach Du Lich Son La) attempts to be one of the town's two 'luxury' hotels. It's almost directly across the road from the long-distance bus station. In the unlikely event that you arrive by air, the airport bus will take you here. Room prices are US$18 to US$35.

The other upmarket establishment is the *Hoa Ban Hotel* (☎ 852395). Prices here are in the range of US$20 to US$30. The hotel is known for its good restaurant and Saturday night disco.

The newest accommodation in town is the *Phong Lan Hotel* (☎ 853516; 20 rooms). Twins are priced from US$12 to US$30 (with breakfast included).

The *Song Da Guesthouse* (Ban Cong Tac Song Da; ☎ 852062) has rooms from US$8 to US$12. There is even a dormitory which can be booked by a small group. This place looked closed to the general public at the time of our last visit and may be permanently full – the hotel was built by the Da River Works Department to house the construction workers for the Ta Bu hydroelectric scheme.

## Places to Eat

*Thit De Restaurant* dishes up Son La's special fare – goat meat. You can try the highly prized local dish *tiet canh*, which is a bowl of goat's blood curd dressed with a sprinkling of peanuts and vegies. Or you can have the more conventional, but tasty, goat-meat steamboat.

*Thanh Thanh Hang Restaurant* does fish, both the freshwater and saltwater varieties. The menu varies by season, but you can find things like king prawns, squid and crab.

*Hong Minh Restaurant* is notable for its house speciality, *thit co lo* ('meat with hole'), which are in fact kebabs (usually called *thit nuong*). Basically, it's delicious meat grilled on a skewer.

*Quang Minh Restaurant* on the eastern edge of town is another good place to eat.

*Kieu Dung Cafe* is a relaxing and comfortable place to enjoy coffee. However, prices are somewhat high, at least by Son La standards.

## Getting There & Away

**Air** Son La's airport is called Na San and is 20km from Son La along the road towards Hanoi. Flights run only once weekly, if they run at all. For the past couple of years the flights have been suspended, but could start up again. There have never been any connecting flights between Son La and Dien Bien Phu.

Assuming flights resume, the former ticket office in Son La was at the Son La Tourism Guesthouse. This was also the place to get the airport bus.

**Bus** Buses take from 12 to 14 hours to travel between Hanoi and Son La, assuming there are no serious breakdowns. From Son La to Dien Bien Phu is another 10 hours.

**Car** Son La is 320km from Hanoi and 150km from Dien Bien Phu. The Hanoi-Son La run typically requires 10 hours. Son La to Dien Bien Phu is another six hours. Car rentals can be arranged in Son La. Drivers ask about US$200 for the round trip to Dien Bien Phu, or US$120 for a Son La-Hanoi round trip.

## TUAN GIAO

This remote town is at the junction of Highway 42 to Dien Bien Phu (80km, three hours) and Highway 6A to Lai Chau (90km, four hours). Most travellers approach from the direction of Son La (75km, three hours) and Hanoi (390km, 13 hours). These driving times assume you are travelling by car or motorbike – for public buses, multiply travel time by at least 1.5.

Not many people spend the night unless they are running behind schedule and can't make it to Dien Bien Phu. The *People's Committee Guesthouse* (Nha Khach Uy Ban Nhan Dan Tinh) can provide basic accommodation.

## DIEN BIEN PHU

Dien Bien Phu was the site of that rarest of military events – a battle that can be called truly decisive. On 6 May 1954, the day before the Geneva Conference on Indochina was set to begin half a world away, Viet Minh forces overran the beleaguered French garrison at Dien Bien Phu after a 57-day siege, shattering French morale and forcing the French government to abandon its attempts to re-establish colonial control of Indochina.

Dien Bien Phu (population 10,000), the capital of Dien Bien District of Lai Chau Province, is in one of the most remote parts of Vietnam. The town is 16km from the Lao border in the flat, heart-shaped Muong Thanh Valley, which is about 20km long and 5km wide and is surrounded by steep, heavily forested hills. The area is inhabited by Montagnard people, most notably the Tai and Hmong. Ethnic-Vietnamese, whom the government has been encouraging to settle in the region, currently comprise about one-third of the Muong Thanh Valley's population of 60,000.

For centuries, Dien Bien Phu was a transit stop on the caravan route from Myanmar and China to northern Vietnam. Dien Bien Phu was established in 1841 by the Nguyen Dynasty to prevent raids on the Red River Delta by bandits.

In early 1954 General Henri Navarre, commander of the French forces in Indochina, sent a force of 12 battalions to occupy the Muong Thanh Valley in order to prevent the Viet Minh from crossing into Laos and threatening the Lao capital of Luang Prabang. The French units, which had about 30% ethnic-Vietnamese members, were soon surrounded by a Viet Minh force under General Vo Nguyen Giap consisting of 33 infantry battalions, six artillery regiments and a regiment of engineers. The Viet Minh force, which outnumbered the French by five to one, was equipped with 105mm artillery pieces and anti-aircraft guns carried by porters through jungles and across rivers in an unbelievable feat of logistics. The guns were emplaced in carefully camouflaged positions dug deep into the hills that overlooked the French positions.

A failed Viet Minh human-wave assault against the French was followed by weeks of intense artillery bombardments. Six battalions of French paratroops were parachuted into Dien Bien Phu as the situation worsened, but bad weather and the Viet Minh artillery, impervious to French air and artillery attacks, prevented sufficient reinforcements and supplies from arriving by air. An elaborate system of trenches and tunnels allowed Viet Minh soldiers to reach French positions without coming under fire. After the idea of employing American conventional bombers was rejected – as was a Pentagon proposal to use tactical atomic bombs – the French trenches and bunkers were overrun. All 13,000 men of the French garrison were either killed or taken prisoner; Viet Minh casualties were estimated at 25,000.

The site of the battle is now marked by the Army Museum (☎ 824971). It's open daily except Monday from 7.30 am to 4.30 pm (with the requisite 1½ hour lunch break). Admission costs US$2.

The headquarters of the French commander, Colonel Christian de Castries, has been re-created and nearby there are old French tanks and artillery pieces. One of the two landing strips used by the French is extant. The old Muong Thanh Bridge is still preserved and closed to motorised traffic. There is a monument to Viet Minh casualties on the site of the former French position known as Eliane, where bitter fighting took place. A memorial to the 3000 French troops buried under the rice paddies was erected in 1984 on the 30th anniversary of the battle. The Dien Bien Phu Cemetery has a remarkably stylish design.

In 1994, the Vietnamese government permitted French veterans of Dien Bien Phu to restage their paratroop drop of four decades earlier.

History is the main attraction here and the scenery – pleasant though it is – is just a sideshow that you can enjoy during arrival and departure overland. Dien Bien Phu seems to hold the same fascination for the French as the DMZ does for the Americans. Not surprisingly, the majority of travellers who come here now are from France.

Tourism is having quite an impact on Dien Bien Phu – most of the buildings you see are very new. Another reason for the construction boom is that Dien Bien Phu was made the capital of Lai Chau Province in 1993. This honour was bestowed upon it mainly because the old capital will be submerged under water in a few years (see the Lai Chau section for details).

**Organised Tours**  Some budget tour operators in Hanoi advertise overland trips for as little as US$60 per person. The actual price will, of course, depend on group size and the standard of accommodation you require.

**Places to Stay**

The *Dien Bien Phu Mini-Hotel* (☎ 824319; 22 rooms) is also known as the *Trade Union Guesthouse II*. This hotel is very dirty and currently is recommended only for the desperate. Twins with attached bath cost US$18, but there are also rooms with shared bath for US$12.

The *People's Committee Guesthouse* (Nha Khach Uy Ban Nhan Dan Tinh; ☎ 825316; 40 rooms) is behind a small lake, 500m (along the same road) from the Dien Bien Phu Mini-Hotel. This massive facility has rooms beginning at US$10.

The *Trade Union Guesthouse I* (☎ 824-841; 20 rooms) is inconveniently located 3km from the town centre. There are only five good rooms here with attached bath costing US$18. The remaining rooms cost only US$6, but have a shared bath with no hot water.

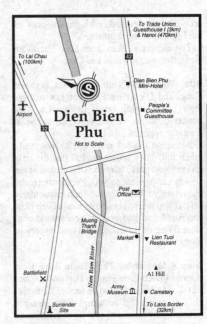

**Places to Eat**

The only good cafe in town is the *Lien Tuoi Restaurant* (☎ 824919), about 500m from the Army Museum. The menu is in both English and French.

**Getting There & Away**

The overland trip to Dien Bien Phu can be more intriguing than the actual battlefield sites for which the town is so famous. Of course, you miss out on most of this if you fly.

The Lao border is only 32km from Dien Bien Phu and there is much speculation about this crossing being opened to foreign tourists. But for now, it's all talk. Nevertheless, keep your ear to the ground – the authorities may just give us a pleasant surprise.

**Air**  Vietnam Airlines runs flights between Dien Bien Phu and Hanoi approximately three times a week. The schedule is varied according to demand, with the majority of the flights during summer.

The airport is 5km from Dien Bien Phu along the road towards Lai Chau.

**Bus** While there's no direct bus between Hanoi and Dien Bien Phu, you can still get there by changing buses in Son La. This almost certainly requires you to spend at least one night in Son La.

Although the bus is cheap, it's not really much fun. They are so packed that the only scenery you get to admire is the armpit of the person sitting next to you. Furthermore, the buses we've seen do not look particularly safe. If you worry about overloaded vehicles, bad roads and bad brakes, you should consider flying or travelling overland by jeep or motorbike.

**Jeep & Motorbike** The 470km drive from Hanoi to Dien Bien Phu on Highways 6 and 42 takes 16 hours (if you're lucky). Conceivably it could be accomplished straight through, but almost everyone overnights in Son La. You certainly wouldn't want to attempt this road in the dark!

In other words, a minimum of five days is required for an overland expedition from Hanoi to Dien Bien Phu return: two days to get there, a day to visit the area and two days to come back. If the road is open and you're feeling brave, it makes more sense to continue on from Dien Bien Phu to Lai Chau, Sapa, Lao Cai and then back to Hanoi – this return journey typically requires six days.

The going rate for renting a Russian jeep to Dien Bien Phu, Lai Chau, Sapa, Lao Cai and back to Hanoi is about US$320. It will cost more for modern Korean and Japanese vehicles. These prices look expensive until you see what is involved – we reckon the drivers are worth every dong of it. Inquire at travel agencies, cafes or your hotel about vehicle rentals.

## LAI CHAU

This small town is nestled in a beautiful valley carved from spectacular mountains by the Da River (Song Da), but beneath Lai Chau's beauty lies a difficult existence for locals. Far from busy trade routes, normal commerce is limited and the town has only been really successful in the harvesting of particularly valuable cash crops. These include opium and timber. Needless to say, opium harvesting does not find favour with the central government. No doubt, some is exported to nearby China, Thailand and possibly even to western countries, but a good portion of it may be supplying junkies in Saigon. The government has been trying to discourage the Montagnards from producing opium poppies.

If the opium business is falling on hard times, the same must be said for the timber industry. In recent years forest cover has been reduced and flooding has increased dramatically. Around 40 people lost their lives in 1991 in a devastating flood on the Da River which swept through the narrow valley. An even worse flood in 1996 killed 100 people and cut all roads into town for two months – four foreigners were stranded here for two weeks until they could be rescued by helicopter.

It seems that floods are about to become a permanent feature of Lai Chau. The government has decided to place a dam in the Ta Bu area (just above the current Song Da Reservoir). When this comes to pass, this will be the largest hydroelectric station in South-East Asia. It also means that in future, the only way to visit Lai Chau will be by submarine.

Recognising that the town was about to go the way of Atlantis, the provincial capital was transferred from Lai Chau to Dien Bien Phu in 1993. However, the actual flooding of the town won't occur until after the year 2000.

Being underwater should at least keep things cooler. Odd as it might seem, in summer Lai Chau is the hottest place in Vietnam. July temperatures can soar to 40°C. It has something to do with the hot summer monsoon blasting in from Thailand and the mountains which prevent the heat from escaping. It's an interesting phenomenon for budding climatologists.

## Places to Stay

The *Lan Anh Hotel* (☎ 852370; 10 rooms) is in the centre of town. It's the better of Lai Chau's two hotels and is therefore often full. Twins cost US$10 to US$15. The restaurant is also recommended.

The *People's Committee Guesthouse* (Nha Khach UBND) is in an old French-style building 2km from town. The place is an absolute dump. There are no showers and the public toilets (there are no private ones) look like they haven't been cleaned since the French colonial era. All this luxury costs US$8 to US$15 – a ridiculous rip-off.

## Getting There & Away

Make local inquiries to find out which roads (if any) are open. The shortest approach is on Highway 6 from Tuan Giao (93km, four hours). Most travellers will arrive from Dien Bien Phu (110km, 4½ hours). The road from Lai Chau to Sapa and Lao Cai (180km, eight hours) is perhaps the most beautiful drive in Vietnam. Remember that all the above-mentioned travel times are hypothetical – one landslide can cause considerable delays.

## TAM DUONG

This is the obscure town between Sapa and Lai Chau. While the town is nothing special, it's the usual lunch stop of travellers making this trip by jeep. When the road gets particularly bad after a heavy rain, the 'lunch stop' may turn into a 'overnight stop' (or even the 'turn-around point').

The local market is worth a visit. The majority here are Montagnards from surrounding villages, although the ethnic-Vietnamese are still the largest single group.

At the *Thanh Binh Hotel*, there are eight rooms priced at US$15. Conditions are slightly poorer at the *Phuong Thanh Hotel*.

The best food in town is found at the *Dzung Restaurant*. The collection of stickers on the refrigerator makes it clear that nearly every travellers' cafe in Hanoi has brought some guests here.

## SAPA

Sapa is an old hill station built in 1922 in a beautiful valley (elevation 1600m) close to the border with China. It's a spectacular area, but getting there from Hanoi has never been particularly easy due to bad roads. Other problems which prevented Sapa from becoming a slick tourist resort included WWII, the guerrilla war against the French, the war with America and the border skirmish with China in 1979, not to mention Vietnam's severe economic decline in the 1980s. The old hotels built by the French were allowed to fall into disrepair and Sapa was pretty much forgotten by nearly everyone (including the Vietnamese themselves).

Suddenly, the place has been discovered. And not only by foreign tourists, but by Vietnamese and even some Chinese who come across the border at Lao Cai.

The tourist boom has caused a sea change in Sapa's fortunes. The bad roads are being upgraded, new hotels are being built, the electricity supply is now pretty reliable and the food has improved immeasurably.

But one inconvenience which will not change quickly is the weather. If you visit off-season, don't forget your winter woollies. Not only is it cold (down to 0°C), but winter brings fog and drizzle. The chilly climate does have a few advantages though – the area boasts temperate-zone fruit trees (peaches, plums, etc) and gardens for raising medicinal herbs. The dry season for Sapa is approximately January through June and afternoon showers in the mountains are frequent.

Sapa would be nothing without the Hmong and Dzao people, the largest and most colourful ethnic groups in the region. They are mostly very poor, but are slowly learning about free enterprise and have gone into the souvenir trinket business. Go a little easy with them when it comes to bargaining – they are not nearly as rapacious as the Vietnamese vendors. Many of the Montagnard people are uneducated (indeed illiterate in Vietnamese) yet they often learn to speak quite good English and French.

## Saturday Market

Montagnards from all the surrounding villages don their most colourful costumes and head

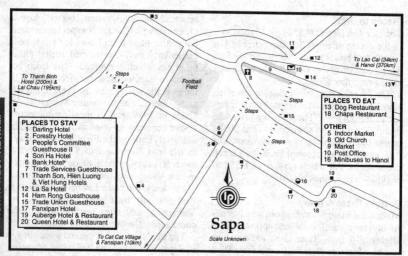

**PLACES TO STAY**
1 Darling Hotel
2 Forestry Hotel
3 People's Committee
 Guesthouse II
4 Son Ha Hotel
6 Bank Hotel*
7 Trade Services Guesthouse
11 Thanh Son, Hien Luong
 & Viet Hung Hotels
12 La Sa Hotel
14 Ham Rong Guesthouse
15 Trade Union Guesthouse
17 Fanxipan Hotel
19 Auberge Hotel & Restaurant
20 Queen Hotel & Restaurant

**PLACES TO EAT**
13 Dog Restaurant
18 Chapa Restaurant

**OTHER**
5 Indoor Market
8 Old Church
9 Market
10 Post Office
16 Minibuses to Hanoi

**Sapa**
Scale Unknown

for the market on Saturday. Or at least they used to – these days there are so many tourists dressed in souvenir Hmong clothing that you have to wonder who is kidding whom.

The market is a magnet for organised tours in Hanoi and many of them plan their visit so that they arrive on Friday night. If you'd rather enjoy Sapa at a more sedate pace, the Saturday market may be something to avoid.

### Fansipan

Surrounding Sapa are the Hoang Lien Mountains, nicknamed the Tonkinese Alps by the French. These mountains include Fansipan, which at 3143m is Vietnam's highest. The summit towers above Sapa, although it is often obscured by clouds and is occasionally dusted by snow. The peak should be accessible year-round to anyone who is in good shape and properly equipped, but don't underestimate its difficulty. It is very wet and usually cold, so you must be prepared. The climbers are about 99% foreigners – the Vietnamese think we are mad.

Fansipan is 9km from Sapa and can only be reached on foot. Despite the short distance, the round-trip takes nearly four days

due to the rough terrain and usually rotten weather. No ropes or technical climbing skills are needed, just endurance. There are no mountain huts or other facilities along the way (yet), so you need to be self-sufficient. This means a sleeping bag, waterproof tent, food, stove, raincoat or poncho, compass and other miscellaneous survival gear. Hiring a reputable guide is essential. Finding porters to carry your gear is difficult at best – you'll almost certainly have to carry everything yourself.

The question arises – can you rent camping equipment in Sapa? Yes, some is available, but it's not good quality and you'll be better off to bring your own gear. The trekking tour business is still very poorly organised in Sapa. However, the local government has already decided to do its part – you are now required to purchase a US$10 permit to climb the mountain.

### Tram Ton Pass

If you travel on the Sapa-Lai Chau road, you will cross this pass, which is on the north side of Fansipan, 15km from Sapa. At 1900m, this is the highest mountain pass in Vietnam. Aside from magnificent views, the bizarre thing about this place is how dramatically the climate changes. On the Sapa side of the mountain you can often expect cold, foggy and generally nasty weather. Drop down a few hundred metres below the pass on the Lai Chau side and it will often be sunny and warm. Ferocious winds come ripping over the pass, which is not surprising given the temperature differences – Sapa is the coldest place in Vietnam and Lai Chau is the warmest. Tram Ton Pass is the dividing line between two great weather fronts – who says you can't see air?

Just alongside the road about 5km back in the Sapa direction is Thac Bac Waterfall. Having a height of 100m, it's a big one, but climbing up alongside it can be dangerous. In the winter dry season it may be reduced to a trickle, but can be magnificent in the rainy season.

You can easily get to Tram Ton Pass by motorbike. Unlike Fansipan, no permits are needed to visit.

## Places to Stay

A big warning is in order concerning the possibility of carbon monoxide poisoning in Sapa. One traveller described her experience:

In Sapa – which is bone-chillingly cold in winter – there are many new private hotels popping up. In order to attract customers, they are advertising and telling people that they have heaters in the rooms. The heaters usually turn out to be a small pot with pieces of burning charcoal. These pots create a deadly smoke that can cause illness or death. With this smoke and the new hotels, which are tightly sealed and not regulated very well by authorities, many travellers have become sick and some have had very close calls.

Two women who were staying in a room across from me had a very scary experience. They fell asleep with this charcoal burner in their room. My roommate and I heard a moaning coming from their room and opened the door to see if they were OK. The women could not move or speak. One woman's body had stiffened so that she couldn't unlock her muscles and joints. She could only move her eyes and moan. After a frightening 30 minutes, a doctor came and rubbed some herbal medicine on some specific points of their bodies. In another 15 minutes, they were able to speak and move a little. They were terribly weak and ill for the rest of the night.

**Chris Conley**

If you're on a tour booked through a cafe or travel agency in Hanoi, then your accommodation presumably will be pre-arranged for you.

However, self-propelled travellers need to exercise caution. Prices fluctuate wildly according to the volume of tourist traffic. On summer weekends there is a shortage of hotel rooms and prices skyrocket. At such times a US$8 room goes for perhaps US$25, if you can find one at all. Needless to say, it's wise to avoid holidays and weekends, especially if you haven't got something pre-booked. In mid-week there should be no problem, especially during the icy winter.

In 1990 there was just one place to stay in Sapa, the very dilapidated *People's Committee Guesthouse*. Now there are roughly 50 guesthouses; trying to list them all would be pointless. The majority of these places are small – maybe just three or four rooms – but some new monster-sized eyesores have recently been built complete with satellite TV and karaoke lounges. Some of the more popular guesthouses are shown on the map in this book, but don't be afraid to wander around and check out the selection yourself. Construction is continuing full bore.

## Places to Eat

There are two places in Sapa which stand head and shoulders above the rest. One is the *Chapa Restaurant*, a true travellers' cafe with the usual banana pancakes and spring rolls. If you peek in the front door the place may appear full, but there are more tables in the room upstairs and also on the balcony.

The other good place is the restaurant inside the *Auberge Hotel*. It's a good place for breakfast and there is also a set vegetarian menu – fine food and good service.

## Entertainment

The foreigners spend their evenings watching satellite TV, while the Vietnamese get into karaoke competitions. But what about the Hmong? The teenagers, it seems, are very romantically minded. The girls get dressed up in their best home-made embroidery, the boys in the latest Viet ration garb, and they all hang out on street corners flirting. It looks like quite a hot pick-up scene, but not one for foreigners to participate in. Saturday night fever, Hmong style.

### Getting There & Away

Sapa's proximity to the border region makes it a possible first stop or last stop for travellers crossing between Vietnam and China.

The gateway to Sapa is Lao Cai, 34km from Sapa. Lao Cai is a border crossing with China. Minibuses do make the trip (two hours), but do not run on any particular schedule. However, the minibuses do wait for the train which arrives from Hanoi. The price for the minibus runs to about US$4 per person depending on how many people they squeeze on board. Some of the 'buses' are also pickup trucks where passengers ride in the back – this is not so great, as the mountain weather is often foul.

Locals are also very willing to drive you up the mountain by motorbike for US$5, but travellers have reported problems with drivers taking them half way and then asking for more money to complete the journey. If you don't cough up the cash, they threaten to leave you stranded.

A new minibus service was setting up in Sapa at the time of writing. The advertised rate for Sapa-Bac Ha is US$12 per person; departures from Sapa are at 6 am and departure from Bac Ha is at 1 pm. For Sapa-Hanoi it's US$20 per person and departure is at 5 am.

Driving a motorbike from Hanoi to Sapa is feasible, but it's a very long trip – start early. The total distance between Hanoi and Sapa is 370km. The last 30km is straight uphill – unless you've been training for the Olympics, it's hell on a bicycle.

Some of the cafes in Hanoi offer four-day bus trips to Sapa for US$50. This is probably the most hassle-free way to do the journey, but most people prefer to do Sapa on their own.

### LAO CAI

Lao Cai is the major town at the north-west end of the rail line and right on the Chinese

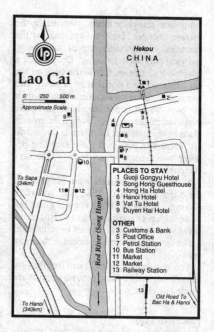

**Lao Cai**

0    250    500 m
Approximate Scale

Hekou
CHINA

Red River (Song Hong)

To Sapa (34km)

To Hanoi (340km)

Old Road To Bac Ha & Hanoi

**PLACES TO STAY**
1 Guoji Gongyu Hotel
2 Song Hong Guesthouse
4 Hong Ha Hotel
6 Hanoi Hotel
8 Vat Tu Hotel
9 Duyen Hai Hotel

**OTHER**
3 Customs & Bank
5 Post Office
7 Petrol Station
10 Bus Station
11 Market
12 Market
13 Railway Station

border. The town was razed in the Chinese invasion of 1979, so all the buildings are new, although to see this dump you'd never guess it.

Needless to say, the border crossing slammed shut during the 1979 war – it reopened in 1993. Nevertheless, the Vietnamese border guards are *still* suspicious of foreigners and every backpacker gets treated like a potential spy. Ironically, Chinese citizens can cross the border easily without the need for a passport or visa and are permitted to stay in Vietnam for 15 days.

Despite the scowling guards and vigorous luggage searches, these days Lao Cai is a major destination for travellers journeying between Hanoi and Kunming (or Sapa and Kunming). But Lao Cai is no place to linger – don't bother spending the night if you don't have to.

The border town on the Chinese side is called Hekou – you'd have to be an enthusiast of Chinese border towns to want to hang out here. It's separated from Vietnam by a river and a bridge – you must pay a small toll to cross.

There is a bank on the Lao Cai side of the river (right near the bridge) that will do foreign exchange, but it's cash transactions only (no travellers cheques or credit cards). Over on the Chinese side you can cash travellers cheques as long as it's not a bank holiday. It's best to have a ready supply of US dollars handy just in case. Be wary of black marketeers, especially on the Chinese side – they frequently short-change tourists. If you do black market dealings, it's best to change only small amounts.

### Places to Stay

In Hekou, on the Chinese side, budget accommodation is available at the old *Hekou Hotel*. Somewhat more pricey is the new, relatively upmarket *Dongfeng Hotel*. Another new place is the *Guoji Gongyu Hotel* just opposite the border gate.

In Lao Cai, closest to the border gate is the *Song Hong Guesthouse* (☎ 830004; 15 rooms). Some rooms have a nice view of the river and China. Twins are US$10 to US$15.

The *Hong Ha Hotel* (☎ 830007; 15 rooms) is a relatively large, but lacklustre, place. Rooms cost US$10 to US$12.

The *Hanoi Hotel* (☎ 832486; eight rooms) is a small but newish place. The restaurant is OK and even has an English menu (but no prices). Rooms cost US$13 to US$17.

The *Vat Tu Hotel* (☎ 831540; 15 rooms) is furthest from the border and offers twin rooms for US$10 to US$15.

The *Post Office Guesthouse* (Nha Khach Buu Dien; ☎ 830006; eight rooms) should stick to selling stamps – the place is a dump. Twins cost US$11 to US$15.

Across the Red River and therefore far from the centre is the *Duyen Hai Hotel* (☎ 822086; 32 rooms). Twins cost US$20 to US$35.

### Getting There & Away

Lao Cai is 340km from Hanoi. Buses make the run, but more travellers prefer to do the journey by train. There are two trains daily in each direction. For details of this train schedule, see the Getting There & Away chapter.

### Getting Around

The border is 3km from Lao Cai railway station. Making this journey is easily accomplished on a motorbike, which costs around US$0.50.

### BAC HA

In the last few years this highlands town has emerged as an alternative to Sapa. Tourism is still in the early stages here and, if you arrive in the middle of the week, the town has a nice, empty feel to it. But things are changing fast – new hotels are opening and restaurants are learning how to make banana pancakes.

One thing slowing down the tourist boom is the loudspeakers on a hill overlooking the town. These broadcast the Voice of Vietnam continuously from 5 am to 9 pm every day. There is a movement under way by some hotel owners to get these turned off. They may succeed – a few years ago, Sapa was similarly bombarded by these 'broadcasts from hell' until the local authorities realised that it was driving away the tourists.

The highlands around Bac Ha are about 900m above sea level, making it somewhat warmer than Sapa. There are 14 Montagnard groups living around Bac Ha – Dzao, Giay, Han, Hoa, Black Hmong, Flower Hmong, Lachi, Lolo, Nhang, Nung, Phula, Tai and Thulao – plus the Kinh (ethnic-Vietnamese).

One of Bac Ha's main industries is the manufacture of alcoholic brews (rice wine, cassava wine and corn liquor). Some of this stuff is so potent that it can ignite (literally). Harvesting opium also used to be a major source of revenue, but the Communists put a stop to that several years ago.

Keep a torch (flashlight) handy if you wander around town in the evening – Bac Ha's electric power supply isn't very stable and sudden blackouts are a common occurrence. One nice thing about the power failures is that this will silence (temporarily) those abominable loudspeakers.

## Plum Blossoms

There are many plum trees around Bac Ha and during the springtime the countryside is white with plum blossoms. The trees bloom in early May. June and July are the best months for eating plums.

## Ban Pho Village

If you want to see what a real Montagnard village looks like, this is your chance. The villagers live simply – don't expect bright lights and loud music. Indeed, don't even expect electricity. What they lack in material possessions, they make up for in their extreme hospitality. The Hmong villagers are some of the kindest people you'll meet in Vietnam. If you visit around noon you may be invited to lunch, though that can be a mixed blessing.

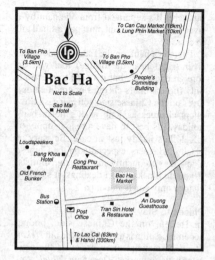

The Montagnard people are not known for good cooking. Hmong cuisine is particularly memorable – they like to flavour their food with raw pig's blood! They also eat something that I could only describe as 'guts soup'. If you want to visit their homes, it's best to do so just after they've all eaten. If you visit during meal times, then you are obligated to eat – no excuses about not being hungry!

Another warning, at least for men – the Hmong are heavy drinkers. If you are toasted, then you must empty your glass. After the market closes, it's not unusual to see a procession of Hmong women heading home, each one leading a horse behind her with her drunken husband slumped over the saddle.

**Vincent Clemente**

Ban Pho is a 7km return trip from Bac Ha. You can take a loop route to get there and back.

## Markets

There are three big markets all within 20km of each other.

**Can Cau Market** This is the best market, but it's only open on Saturday. You'll see plenty of Flower Hmong here – so-called because the women embroider flowers on their skirts. Items on sale include water buffaloes, pigs, horses and chickens.

The market is 18km north of Bac Ha town and 9km south of the Chinese border.

Although you can go right up close to the Chinese border, there is little point in doing so as you cannot cross it.

**Bac Ha Market** This market is in Bac Ha town itself and gets very crowded, but it's lively and interesting. The market mainly operates on Sunday and Thursday.

**Lung Phin Market** This market is between Can Cau market and Bac Ha town, about 10km from the town. It's the least beautiful of the three markets, but it runs on both Saturday and Sunday.

## Places to Stay

Any real estate agent will tell you that three things determine the value of property – location, location and location. In Bac Ha this holds especially true – try to find a place to stay as far away as possible from those infernal loudspeakers. Several new hotels were under construction at the time of writing, but all were near the noisy centre of town. The situation could change quickly, but it's fair to say that for now there is no quiet place to stay in Bac Ha.

The *Sao Mai Hotel* (☎ 880288; 13 rooms) is potentially a great place to stay – the rooms are clean and pleasant, plus the owner is friendly. The hotel has two sections – a concrete building where twin rooms cost US$10 to US$12 and a wooden stilt house where rooms are US$15. The wooden building looks aesthetic, but the walls are thin – you'll find things quieter, if less charming, in the concrete building.

The *Dang Khoa Hotel* (☎ 880290; 14 rooms) in the centre of town provides nondescript accommodation for US$10 to US$15 per room. It's also very close to the loudspeakers.

The *Tran Sin Hotel* (☎ 880240; five rooms) is near the market. Rooms are priced at the Bac Ha 'standard rate' of US$10 to US$15.

The *Anh Duong Guesthouse* (☎ 880329) offers one advantage over the competition – it's currently the furthest hotel from the loudspeakers and would be fairly quiet if the owner would get rid of his vicious, barking dog.

## Places to Eat

Bac Ha is plagued by rather large stray dogs who wander into the restaurants to beg for food. It's often hard to resist the temptation to share your meal with Fido – especially when he weighs 80kg.

If you can defend your dinner from uppity canines, there's plenty of good food to enjoy. The *Cong Phu Restaurant* (☎ 880254) has tasty, low-priced food and an English menu. Ditto for the *Tran Sin Restaurant* on the ground floor of the Tran Sin Hotel.

## Getting There & Away

A bus departs Lao Cai for Bac Ha (63km) daily at 1 pm. Bac Ha is 330km (10 hours) from Hanoi. Locals on motorbikes are also willing to make the Lao Cai-Bac Ha run for about US$10, or even Sapa-Bac Ha (93km) for US$15. Occasional minibuses have also started making the Sapa-Bac Ha run. Some cafes in Hanoi offer four-day bus trips to Bac Ha for around US$60, usually with a visit to Sapa included.

# Glossary

**Agent Orange** – a toxic and carcinogenic chemical herbicide used heavily during the American War

**am & duong** – Vietnamese equivalent of Yin & Yang

**American War** – the Vietnamese name for what most other nations call the 'Vietnam War'

**Annam** – old Chinese name for Vietnam meaning 'Pacified South'

**ao dai** – national dress of Vietnamese women (and men)

**arhat** – monk who has attained nirvana

**ARVN** – Army of the Republic of Vietnam (the former South Vietnamese army)

**bang** – congregation (in the Chinese community)

**bonze** – Vietnamese Buddhist monk

**Buu Dien** – Post Office

**cai luong** – modern theatre

**Caodaism** – indigenous Vietnamese religious sect

**can** – 10-year cycle

**can danh** – brown (literally, 'cockroach wing')

**cay son** – tree from whose resin lacquer is made

**Champa** – Hindu kingdom dating from the late 2nd century AD

**Chams** – the people of Champa

**chu nho** – standard Chinese characters (script)

**chu nom** – also *nom*, Vietnamese script

**Cochinchina** – the southern part of Vietnam during the French colonial era

**crachin** – fine drizzle

**cu ly** – fern stems used to stop bleeding

**cyclo** – pedicab or bicycle rickshaw

**dau** – oil

**dinh** – communal meeting hall

**DMZ** – the misnamed 'Demilitarised Zone', a strip of land which once separated North and South Vietnam

**doi moi** – economic restructuring or reform

**DRV** – Democratic Republic of Vietnam (the old North Vietnam)

**flechette** – experimental American weapon, an artillery shell containing thousands of darts

**fu** – talisman

**Funan** – see *Oc-Eo*

**ghe** – long, narrow rowboat

**giay phep di lai** – internal travel permit

**gom** – ceramics

**hai dang** – lighthouse

**Han Viet** – Sino-Vietnamese literature

**hat boi** – classical theatre in the south

**hat cheo** – popular theatre

**hat tuong** – classical theatre in the north

**ho ca** – aquarium

**Ho Chi Minh Trail** – route used by the NVA and VC to move supplies to guerrillas in the south

**hoi** – 60-year period

**ho khau** – a residence permit needed for everything: to attend school, seek employment, own land, register a vehicle, buy a home, start a business etc

**Honda om** – motorcycle taxi

**huyen** – rural district

**Indochina** – Vietnam, Cambodia and Laos. The name derives from the influence of Indian and Chinese cultures on the region.

**kala-makara** – sea-monster god

**kalan** – sanctuary

**khach san** – hotel

**Khmer** – ethnic-Cambodians

**kich noi** – spoken drama

**Kinh** – Vietnamese language

**Kuomintang** – or KMT, meaning 'Nationalist Party'. The KMT controlled China from around 1925 to 1949 until defeated by the Communists. The KMT still controls Taiwan.

**ky** – 12-year cycle

**lang tam** – tombs

**Liberation** – the 1975 takeover of the South by the North; what most foreigners call 'reunification'

**Lien Xo** – literally 'Soviet Union'; used to call attention to a foreigner

**linga** – stylised phallus which represents the Hindu god Shiva

**mandapa** – meditation hall

**moi** – derogatory word meaning 'savages', mostly used regarding hill tribe people

**naga** – a giant snake, often depicted forming a kind of shelter over the Buddha

**Nam Phai** – For Men

**napalm** – jellied petrol (gasoline) dropped and lit from aircraft, with devastating effect

**nha hang** – restaurant

**nha khach** – hotel or guesthouse

**nha nghi** – guesthouse

**nha tro** – dormitory

**NLF** – National Liberation Front; official name for the Viet Cong

**nom** – see *chu nom*

**Nu Phai** – For Women

**nuoc mam** – fish sauce, added to almost every dish in Vietnam

**nuoc suoi** – mineral water

**nuoc dua** – coconut milk

**NVA** – North Vietnamese Army

**Oc-Eo** – Indianised kingdom (also called Funan) in southern Vietnam between 1st and 6th centuries

**pagoda** – traditionally, an eight-sided Buddhist tower, but in Vietnam the word is commonly used to denote a temple

**Phoenix Programme** – or Operation Phoenix; a controversial programme run by the CIA, aimed at eliminating VC cadres by assassination, capture or defection

**PRG** – Provisional Revolutionary Government, the temporary Communist government set up by the Viet Cong in the South. It existed from 1969 to 1976.

**quan** – urban district

**quoc am** – modern Vietnamese literature

**quoc ngu** – Latin-based phonetic alphabet in which Vietnamese is written

**rap** – cinema

**Revolutionary Youth League** – the first Marxist group in Vietnam and predecessor of the Communist Party; founded in 1925 by Ho Chi Minh in Guangzhou (Canton), China

**roi can** – conventional puppetry

**roi nuoc** – water puppetry

**ruou** – wine

**RVN** – Republic of Vietnam (the old South Vietnam)

**son then** – black

**SRV** – Socialist Republic of Vietnam (Vietnam's current official name)

**Strategic Hamlets Programme** – an unsuccessful programme of the US army and South Vietnamese government in which peasants were forcibly moved into fortified villages to deny the VC bases of support

**Tet** – the Vietnamese Lunar New Year

**thanh long** – dragon fruit

**thung chai** – gigantic round wicket baskets sealed with pitch; used as rowboats.

**toc hanh** – express bus

**Tonkin** – the northern part of Vietnam during the French colonial era; also name of a body of water in the north (Tonkin Gulf)

**truyen khau** – traditional oral literature

**VC** – Viet Cong or Vietnamese Communists; considered a derogatory term until recently

**Viet Kieu** – Overseas Vietnamese

**Viet Minh** – League for the Independence of Vietnam, a nationalistic movement which fought the Japanese and French but later became fully Communist-dominated

**xang** – petrol

**xe dap loi** – wagon pulled by bicycle

**xe Honda loi** – wagon pulled by a motorcycle

**xe Lam** – three-wheeled motorised vehicle, Lambretta

# Index

## MAPS

## TEXT

## Asides & Special Sections

# LONELY PLANET PHRASEBOOKS

Building bridges,
Breaking barriers,
Beyond babble-on

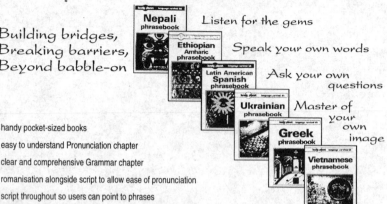

Listen for the gems

Speak your own words

Ask your own
questions

Master of
your
own
image

- handy pocket-sized books
- easy to understand Pronunciation chapter
- clear and comprehensive Grammar chapter
- romanisation alongside script to allow ease of pronunciation
- script throughout so users can point to phrases
- extensive vocabulary sections, words and phrases for every situations
- full of cultural information and tips for the traveller

*'...vital for a real DIY spirit and attitude in language learning'* – Backpacker

*'the phrasebooks have good cultural backgrounders and offer solid advice for challenging situations in remote locations'* – San Francisco Examiner

*'...they are unbeatable for their coverage of the world's more obscure languages'* – The Geographical Magazine

---

Arabic (Egyptian)
Arabic (Moroccan)
Australia
  *Australian English, Aboriginal and Torres Strait languages*
Baltic States
  *Estonian, Latvian, Lithuanian*
Bengali
Burmese
Brazilian
Cantonese
Central Europe
  *Czech, French, German, Hungarian, Italian and Slovak*
Eastern Europe
  *Bulgarian, Czech, Hungarian, Polish, Romanian and Slovak*
Egyptian Arabic
Ethiopian (Amharic)
Fijian
Greek
Hindi/Urdu

Indonesian
Japanese
Korean
Lao
Latin American Spanish
Malay
Mandarin
Mediterranean Europe
  *Albanian, Croatian, Greek, Italian, Macedonian, Maltese, Serbian, Slovene*
Mongolian
Moroccan Arabic
Nepali
Papua New Guinea
Pilipino (Tagalog)
Quechua
Russian
Scandinavian Europe
  *Danish, Finnish, Icelandic, Norwegian and Swedish*

South-East Asia
  *Burmese, Indonesian, Khmer, Lao, Malay, Tagalog (Pilipino), Thai and Vietnamese*
Sri Lanka
Swahili
Thai
Thai Hill Tribes
Tibetan
Turkish
Ukrainian
USA
  *US English, Vernacular Talk, Native American languages and Hawaiian*
Vietnamese
Western Europe
  *Basque, Catalan, Dutch, French, German, Irish, Italian, Portuguese, Scottish Gaelic, Spanish (Castilian) and Welsh*

# LONELY PLANET JOURNEYS

JOURNEYS is a unique collection of travel writing – published by the company that understands travel better than anyone else. It is a series for anyone who has ever experienced – or dreamed of – the magical moment when they encountered a strange culture or saw a place for the first time. They are tales to read while you're planning a trip, while you're on the road or while you're in an armchair, in front of a fire.

JOURNEYS books catch the spirit of a place, illuminate a culture, recount a crazy adventure, or introduce a fascinating way of life. They always entertain, and always enrich the experience of travel.

---

## ISLANDS IN THE CLOUDS
### Travels in the Highlands of New Guinea
### *Isabella Tree*

Isabella Tree's remarkable journey takes us to the heart of the remote and beautiful Highlands of Papua New Guinea and Irian Jaya – one of the most extraordinary and dangerous regions on earth. Funny and tragic by turns, *Islands in the Clouds* is her moving story of the Highland people and the changes transforming their world.

*Isabella Tree*, who lives in England, has worked as a freelance journalist on a variety of newspapers and magazines, including a stint as senior travel correspondent for the *Evening Standard*. A fellow of the Royal Geographical Society, she has also written a biography of the Victorian ornithologist John Gould.

*'One of the most accomplished travel writers to appear on the horizon for many years . . . the dialogue is brilliant'* – Eric Newby

---

## SEAN & DAVID'S LONG DRIVE
### *Sean Condon*

Sean Condon is young, urban and a connoisseur of hair wax. He can't drive, and he doesn't really travel well. So when Sean and his friend David set out to explore Australia in a 1966 Ford Falcon, the result is a decidedly offbeat look at life on the road. Over 14,000 death-defying kilometres, our heroes check out the re-runs on tv, get fabulously drunk, listen to Neil Young cassettes and wonder why they ever left home.

*Sean Condon* lives in Melbourne. He played drums in several mediocre bands until he found his way into advertising and an above-average band called Boilersuit. *Sean & David's Long Drive* is his first book.

*'Funny, pithy, kitsch and surreal . . . This book will do for Australia what Chernobyl did for Kiev, but hey you'll laugh as the stereotypes go boom'*
*– Time Out*

# LONELY PLANET TRAVEL ATLASES

Lonely Planet has long been famous for the number and quality of its guidebook maps. Now we've gone one step further and in conjunction with Steinhart Katzir Publishers produced a handy companion series: Lonely Planet travel atlases – maps of a country produced in book form.

Unlike other maps, which look good but lead travellers astray, our travel atlases have been researched on the road by Lonely Planet's experienced team of writers. All details are carefully checked to ensure the atlas corresponds with the equivalent Lonely Planet guidebook.

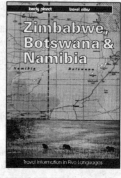

The handy atlas format means no holes, wrinkles, torn sections or constant folding and unfolding. These atlases can survive long periods on the road, unlike cumbersome fold-out maps. The comprehensive index ensures easy reference.

- full-colour throughout
- maps researched and checked by Lonely Planet authors
- place names correspond with Lonely Planet guidebooks
  – no confusing spelling differences
- legend and travelling information in English, French, German, Japanese and Spanish
- size: 230 x 160 mm

*Available now:*
Chile & Easter Island • Egypt • India & Bangladesh • Israel & the Palestinian Territories •Jordan, Syria & Lebanon • Kenya • Laos • Portugal • South Africa, Lesotho & Swaziland • Thailand • Turkey • Vietnam • Zimbabwe, Botswana & Namibia

---

# LONELY PLANET TV SERIES & VIDEOS

Lonely Planet travel guides have been brought to life on television screens around the world. Like our guides, the programmes are based on the joy of independent travel, and look honestly at some of the most exciting, picturesque and frustrating places in the world. Each show is presented by one of three travellers from Australia, England or the USA and combines an innovative mixture of video, Super-8 film, atmospheric soundscapes and original music.

Videos of each episode – containing additional footage not shown on television – are available from good book and video shops, but the availability of individual videos varies with regional screening schedules.

*Video destinations include:* Alaska • American Rockies • Australia – The South-East • Baja California & the Copper Canyon • Brazil • Central Asia • Chile & Easter Island • Corsica, Sicily & Sardinia – The Mediterranean Islands • East Africa (Tanzania & Zanzibar) • Ecuador & the Galapagos Islands • Greenland & Iceland • Indonesia • Israel & the Sinai Desert • Jamaica • Japan • La Ruta Maya • Morocco • New York • North India • Pacific Islands (Fiji, Solomon Islands & Vanuatu) • South India • South West China • Turkey • Vietnam • West Africa • Zimbabwe, Botswana & Namibia

*The Lonely Planet TV series is produced by:*
**Pilot Productions**
The Old Studio
18 Middle Row
London W10 5AT UK

**For video availability and ordering information contact your nearest Lonely Planet office.**

*Music from the TV series is available on CD & cassette.*

# PLANET TALK

## Lonely Planet's FREE quarterly newsletter

We love hearing from you and think you'd like to hear from us.

*When...*is the right time to see reindeer in Finland?
*Where...*can you hear the best palm-wine music in Ghana?
*How...*do you get from Asunción to Areguá by steam train?
*What...*is the best way to see India?

### For the answer to these and many other questions read PLANET TALK.

Every issue is packed with up-to-date travel news and advice including:

* a letter from Lonely Planet co-founders Tony and Maureen Wheeler
* go behind the scenes on the road with a Lonely Planet author
* feature article on an important and topical travel issue
* a selection of recent letters from travellers
* details on forthcoming Lonely Planet promotions
* complete list of Lonely Planet products

*To join our mailing list contact any Lonely Planet office.*

**Also available: Lonely Planet T-shirts. 100% heavyweight cotton.**

---

# LONELY PLANET ONLINE

## Get the latest travel information before you leave or while you're on the road

Whether you've just begun planning your next trip, or you're chasing down specific info on currency regulations or visa requirements, check out Lonely Planet Online for up-to-the minute travel information.

As well as travel profiles of your favourite destinations (including maps and photos), you'll find current reports from our researchers and other travellers, updates on health and visas, travel advisories, and discussion of the ecological and political issues you need to be aware of as you travel.

There's also an online travellers' forum where you can share your experience of life on the road, meet travel companions and ask other travellers for their recommendations and advice. We also have plenty of links to other online sites useful to independent travellers.

And of course we have a complete and up-to-date list of all Lonely Planet travel products including guides, phrasebooks, atlases, Journeys and videos and a simple online ordering facility if you can't find the book you want elsewhere.

**www.lonelyplanet.com**
**or**
**AOL keyword: lp**

# LONELY PLANET PRODUCTS

Lonely Planet is known worldwide for publishing practical, reliable and no-nonsense travel information in our guides and on our web site. The Lonely Planet list covers just about every accessible part of the world. Currently there are eight series: *travel guides, shoestring guides, walking guides, city guides, phrasebooks, audio packs, travel atlases* and *Journeys* – a unique collection of travel writing.

## EUROPE

Amsterdam • Austria • Baltic States phrasebook • Britain • Central Europe on a shoestring • Central Europe phrasebook • Czech & Slovak Republics • Denmark • Dublin • Eastern Europe on a shoestring • Eastern Europe phrasebook • Estonia, Latvia & Lithuania • Finland • France • Greece • Greek phrasebook • Hungary • Iceland, Greenland & the Faroe Islands • Ireland • Italy • Mediterranean Europe on a shoestring • Mediterranean Europe phrasebook • Paris • Poland • Portugal • Portugal travel atlas • Prague • Russia, Ukraine & Belarus • Russian phrasebook • Scandinavian & Baltic Europe on a shoestring • Scandinavian Europe phrasebook • Slovenia • Spain • Spanish phrasebook • St Petersburg • Switzerland • Trekking in Greece • Trekking in Spain • Ukrainian phrasebook • Vienna • Walking in Britain • Walking in Switzerland • Western Europe on a shoestring • Western Europe phrasebook

## NORTH AMERICA

Alaska • Backpacking in Alaska • Baja California • California & Nevada • Canada • Florida • Hawaii • Honolulu • Los Angeles • Mexico • Miami • New England • New Orleans • New York, New Jersey & Pennsylvania • Pacific Northwest USA • Rocky Mountain States • San Francisco • Southwest USA • USA phrasebook • Washington, DC & the Capital Region

## CENTRAL AMERICA & THE CARIBBEAN

Bermuda • Central America on a shoestring • Costa Rica • Cuba • Eastern Caribbean • Guatemala, Belize & Yucatán: La Ruta Maya • Jamaica

## SOUTH AMERICA

Argentina, Uruguay & Paraguay • Bolivia • Brazil • Brazilian phrasebook • Buenos Aires • Chile & Easter Island • Chile & Easter Island travel atlas • Colombia • Ecuador & the Galápagos Islands • Latin American Spanish phrasebook • Peru • Quechua phrasebook • Rio de Janeiro • South America on a shoestring • Trekking in the Patagonian Andes • Venezuela

*Travel Literature:* Full Circle: A South American Journey

## ANTARCTICA

Antarctica

## ISLANDS OF THE INDIAN OCEAN

Madagascar & Comoros • Maldives• Mauritius, Réunion & Seychelles

## AFRICA

Africa on a shoestring • Arabic (Moroccan) phrasebook • • Cape Town • Central Africa • East Africa • Egypt • Egypt travel atlas• Ethiopian (Amharic) phrasebook • Kenya • Kenya travel atlas • Malawi, Mozambique & Zambia • Morocco • North Africa • South Africa, Lesotho & Swaziland • South Africa, Lesotho & Swaziland travel atlas • Swahili phrasebook • Trekking in East Africa • West Africa • Zimbabwe, Botswana & Namibia • Zimbabwe, Botswana & Namibia travel atlas

*Travel Literature:* The Rainbird: A Central African Journey • Songs to an African Sunset: A Zimbabwean Story

# MAIL ORDER

Lonely Planet products are distributed worldwide. They are also available by mail order from Lonely Planet, so if you have difficulty finding a title please write to us. North American and South American residents should write to Embarcadero West, 155 Filbert St, Suite 251, Oakland CA 94607, USA; European and African residents should write to 10 Barley Mow Passage, Chiswick, London W4 4PH; and residents of other countries to PO Box 617, Hawthorn, Victoria 3122, Australia.

## NORTH-EAST ASIA

Beijing • Cantonese phrasebook • China • Hong Kong • Hong Kong, Macau & Guangzhou • Japan • Japanese phrasebook • Japanese audio pack • Korea • Korean phrasebook • Mandarin phrasebook • Mongolia • Mongolian phrasebook • North-East Asia on a shoestring • Seoul • Taiwan • Tibet • Tibet phrasebook • Tokyo

*Travel Literature*: Lost Japan

## MIDDLE EAST & CENTRAL ASIA

Arab Gulf States • Arabic (Egyptian) phrasebook • Central Asia • Iran • Israel & the Palestinian Territories • Israel & the Palestinian Territories travel atlas • Istanbul • Jerusalem • Jordan & Syria • Jordan, Syria & Lebanon travel atlas • Middle East • Turkey • Turkish phrasebook • Turkey travel atlas • Yemen

*Travel Literature:* The Gates of Damascus • Kingdom of the Film Stars: Journey into Jordan

## ALSO AVAILABLE:

Travel with Children • Traveller's Tales

## INDIAN SUBCONTINENT

Bangladesh • Bengali phrasebook • Delhi • Hindi/Urdu phrasebook • India • India & Bangladesh travel atlas • Indian Himalaya • Karakoram Highway • Nepal • Nepali phrasebook • Pakistan • Rajasthan • Sri Lanka • Sri Lanka phrasebook • Trekking in the Indian Himalaya • Trekking in the Karakoram & Hindukush • Trekking in the Nepal Himalaya

*Travel Literature:* In Rajasthan • Shopping for Buddhas

## SOUTH-EAST ASIA

Bali & Lombok • Bangkok • Burmese phrasebook • Cambodia • Ho Chi Minh City • Indonesia • Indonesian phrasebook • Indonesian audio pack • Jakarta • Java • Laos • Lao phrasebook • Laos travel atlas • Malay phrasebook • Malaysia, Singapore & Brunei • Myanmar (Burma) • Philippines • Pilipino phrasebook • Singapore • South-East Asia on a shoestring • South-East Asia phrasebook • Thailand • Thailand travel atlas • Thai phrasebook • Thai audio pack • Thai Hill Tribes phrasebook • Vietnam • Vietnamese phrasebook • Vietnam travel atlas

## AUSTRALIA & THE PACIFIC

Australia • Australian phrasebook • Bushwalking in Australia • Bushwalking in Papua New Guinea • Fiji • Fijian phrasebook • Islands of Australia's Great Barrier Reef • Melbourne • Micronesia • New Caledonia • New South Wales & the ACT • New Zealand • Northern Territory • Outback Australia • Papua New Guinea • Papua New Guinea phrasebook • Queensland • Rarotonga & the Cook Islands • Samoa • Solomon Islands • South Australia • Sydney • Tahiti & French Polynesia • Tasmania • Tonga • Tramping in New Zealand • Vanuatu • Victoria • Western Australia

*Travel Literature:* Islands in the Clouds • Sean & David's Long Drive

# THE LONELY PLANET STORY

Lonely Planet published its first book in 1973 in response to the numerous 'How did you do it?' questions Maureen and Tony Wheeler were asked after driving, bussing, hitching, sailing and railing their way from England to Australia.

Written at a kitchen table and hand collated, trimmed and stapled, *Across Asia on the Cheap* became an instant local bestseller, inspiring thoughts of another book.

Eighteen months in South-East Asia resulted in their second guide, *South-East Asia on a shoestring*, which they put together in a backstreet Chinese hotel in Singapore in 1975. The 'yellow bible', as it quickly became known to backpackers around the world, soon became *the* guide to the region. It has sold well over half a million copies and is now in its 9th edition, still retaining its familiar yellow cover.

Today there are over 240 titles, including travel guides, walking guides, language kits & phrasebooks, travel atlases and travel literature. The company is the largest independent travel publisher in the world. Although Lonely Planet initially specialised in guides to Asia, today there are few corners of the globe that have not been covered.

The emphasis continues to be on travel for independent travellers. Tony and Maureen still travel for several months of each year and play an active part in the writing, updating and quality control of Lonely Planet's guides.

They have been joined by over 70 authors and 170 staff at our offices in Melbourne (Australia), Oakland (USA), London (UK) and Paris (France). Travellers themselves also make a valuable contribution to the guides through the feedback we receive in thousands of letters each year and on our web site.

The people at Lonely Planet strongly believe that travellers can make a positive contribution to the countries they visit, both through their appreciation of the countries' culture, wildlife and natural features, and through the money they spend. In addition, the company makes a direct contribution to the countries and regions it covers. Since 1986 a percentage of the income from each book has been donated to ventures such as famine relief in Africa; aid projects in India; agricultural projects in Central America; Greenpeace's efforts to halt French nuclear testing in the Pacific; and Amnesty International.

*'I hope we send people out with the right attitude about travel. You realise when you travel that there are so many different perspectives about the world, so we hope these books will make people more interested in what they see. Guidebooks can't really guide people. All you can do is point them in the right direction.'*

– Tony Wheeler

# LONELY PLANET PUBLICATIONS

**Australia**
PO Box 617, Hawthorn 3122, Victoria
tel: (03) 9819 1877  fax: (03) 9819 6459
e-mail: talk2us@lonelyplanet.com.au

**USA**
Embarcadero West, 155 Filbert St, Suite 251,
Oakland, CA 94607
tel: (510) 893 8555  TOLL FREE: 800 275-8555
fax: (510) 893 8563
e-mail: info@lonelyplanet.com

**UK**
10 Barley Mow Passage, Chiswick,
London W4 4PH
tel: (0181) 742 3161  fax: (0181) 742 2772
e-mail: 100413.3551@compuserve.com

**France:**
71 bis rue du Cardinal Lemoine, 75005 Paris
tel: 1 44 32 06 20  fax: 1 46 34 72 55
e-mail: 100560.415@compuserve.com

**World Wide Web: http://www.lonelyplanet.com**